EDITED BY

PHILIP BANYARD
GAYLE DILLON
CHRISTINE NORMAN
& BELINDA WINDER

2ND EDITION

ESSENTIAL PSYCHOLOGY

SAGE

Los Angeles | London | New Delhi
Singapore | Washington DC

Los Angeles | London | New Delhi
Singapore | Washington DC

SAGE Publications Ltd
1 Oliver's Yard
55 City Road
London EC1Y 1SP

SAGE Publications Inc.
2455 Teller Road
Thousand Oaks, California 91320

SAGE Publications India Pvt Ltd
B 1/I 1 Mohan Cooperative Industrial Area
Mathura Road
New Delhi 110 044

SAGE Publications Asia-Pacific Pte Ltd
3 Church Street
#10-04 Samsung Hub
Singapore 049483

Editor: Michael Carmichael; Luke Block
Development editor: Christopher Kingston
Assistant editor: Keri Dickens
Production editor: Imogen Roome
Proofreader: Leigh C. Timmins
Indexer: David Rudeforth
Marketing manager: Alison Borg
Cover design: Wendy Scott
Typeset by: C&M Digitals (P) Ltd, Chennai, India
Printed in Great Britain
by Ashford Colour Press Ltd, Gosport, Hants

MIX
Paper from
responsible sources
FSC www.fsc.org   FSC® C011748

Editorial Arrangement © Philip Banyard, Gayle Dillon, Christine Norman and Belinda Winder 2015
Chapter 1 © James Stiller and Philip Banyard 2015
Chapter 2 © Simon Watts and Philip Banyard 2015
Chapter 3 © Garry Young 2015
Chapter 4 © Philip Banyard, Viv Brunsden, David Crundall, Mark Griffiths, Sarah Seymour-Smith and Belinda Winder 2015
Chapter 5 © Thom Baguley, Harriet Smith and Duncan Guest 2015
Chapter 6 © Andrew K. Dunn and Paula C. Stacey 2015
Chapter 7 © Gary Jones, Mark Sergeant and Antonio Castro 2015
Chapter 8 © Thomas Dunn 2015
Chapter 9 © Antonio Castro, Gary Jones and Mark J.T. Sergeant 2015
Chapter 10 © Rachel R. Horsley and Christine Norman 2015
Chapter 11 © Mark J.T. Sergeant, Antonio Castro and Gary Jones 2015
Chapter 12 © Dean Fido and Preethi Premkumar 2015
Chapter 13 © Jens Binder, Mhairi Bowe and Kevin Maguire 2015
Chapter 14 © Mick Gregson, Rowena Hill and Nicholas Blagden 2015
Chapter 15 © Sebastian Teicher, Maria Kontogianni and Alex Meredith 2015
Chapter 16 © Hugh Miller, Patrick Hylton and Jill Arnold 2015
Chapter 17 © Lucy Betts, James Stiller, Rebecca Larkin and Gareth Williams 2015
Chapter 18 © James Stiller, Lucy Betts, Rebecca Larkin and Gareth Williams 2015
Chapter 19 © Gayle Dillon, Janine Coates, Andrew Grayson and Susannah Lamb 2015
Chapter 20 © Emily Coyne, Louise A. Brown and Claire Thompson 2015
Chapter 21 © David J. Wilde and Glenn A. Williams 2015
Chapter 22 © Eva Sundin and Philip Banyard 2015
Chapter 23 © Jill Arnold and Ben Oldfield 2015
Chapter 24 © Claire Thompson, Karen Slade and Laura Hamilton 2015
Chapter 25 © Karen Slade, Laura Hamilton and Claire Thompson 2015
Chapter 26 © Eva Zysk, Eva Sundin, Preethi Premkumar and Philip Banyard 2015
Chapter 27 © Rebecca Lievesley and Helen Elliott 2015

First printed 2010. Reprinted 2013.

Library of Congress Control Number: 2014942690

British Library Cataloguing in Publication data

A catalogue record for this book is available from the British Library

ISBN 9781446274811
ISBN 9781446274828 (pbk)

At SAGE we take sustainability seriously. Most of our products are printed in the UK using FSC papers and boards. When we print overseas we ensure sustainable papers are used as measured by the Egmont grading system. We undertake an annual audit to monitor our sustainability.

CONTENTS

About the Book   v
Acknowledgements   vii
Guided Tour   ix
SAGE edge   xi

Section A – The Foundations of Modern Psychology: What We Know About Human Beings   1

1 Once Upon a Time … The Evolution of Human Behaviour   5
2 How Psychology Became a Science   21
3 Issues and Debates in Psychology   37
4 Doing Psychological Research   49

Section B – Cognitive Psychology: How We Think and Make Sense of the World   69

5 Memory   73
6 An Introduction to Sensation, Perception and Attention   91
7 Thinking and Problem Solving   111
8 Language   129

Section C – Biological Psychology: How Our Brains Affect Our Behaviour   149

9 The Human Nervous System: Functional Anatomy   153
10 Communication within the Brain   175
11 Brain and Behaviour: Sex Differences   193
12 Motivation and Emotion   209

Section D – Social Psychology: How We Interact with Each Other   225

13 Behaviour Within Groups   229
14 Behaviour Between Groups   243
15 Social Judgements and Behaviour   259
16 Critical Social Psychology   277

Section E – Developmental Psychology: How We Grow and Change   293

17 Development during the Early Years   297
18 Development during the School Years   315
19 Atypical Child Development   331
20 Adolescence, Adulthood and Ageing   347

Section F – The Psychology of Individual Differences: How We Know and Measure Our Individuality   363

21 Personality   367
22 Intelligence: Measuring the Mind   385
23 Self   403

Section G – Applied Psychology: How We Use Psychology 421

24	Psychopathology: Theories and Causes	425
25	Psychological Interventions	445
26	Health Psychology	467
27	Forensic Psychology	483

Glossary	503
References	525
Index	573

ABOUT THE BOOK

What is psychology? Everyone seems to have a good idea about what it is, but those ideas often don't match what is studied at university. If you ask someone what a psychologist does then they are most likely to suggest that they:

- read minds
- tell you how to improve your love life
- study body language
- sit you on a couch and talk to you about your mother
- chase serial killers.

Sadly, none of these are true. Take the first one, for example. Psychologists cannot read minds and neither can anyone else. If someone tells you that they can read minds then they are lying, deluded or both. In fact, the complexities of your own mind are so great that you can't even read it that well yourself. We may not be able to read minds, but we can certainly study how the mind works and influences the world around us. The truth is far more exciting than the fiction. Psychology is the scientific study of mind and experience; we leave the myth-making and psychobabble to entertainers.

Psychology, we believe, is an amazing subject. Whether you want to know if a baby smiles because it recognises its mother, or how a driver manages to park their car, psychology offers you a way of exploring these questions. Studying psychology will encourage you to challenge the way you think about yourself and your place in the world.

Our text is aimed at first year undergraduates. We do not assume too much prior knowledge of the subject. Nevertheless, our philosophy in writing the book is that you are introduced to some of the big questions in psychology. These are questions like: Who am I? And why am I here? And why do I feel annoyed when Nottingham Forest loses a game? From big questions to small questions there is so much we don't know about the way that people tick. To be a psychologist is to be an explorer, discovering new information to help those that follow. We invite you to join us on this big adventure.

An example of one of the big questions in psychology concerns the distinction between sensation and perception. Various things hit our senses: for example, light enters our eyes, and changes in air pressure are detected by our ears. We detect these changes in the environment, but the psychological miracle is that our brain processes the information our senses detect, to produce the fantastic images and sounds that we perceive. If you have studied biology at school you'll probably know that we detect light on the flat screen of our retinas at the back of our eyes, but had you wondered how we manage to see in 3D? Our brains turn that flat image into the 3D world we experience. Our brains are sophisticated perceptual detectives. They take in a range of sensory cues to generate a plausible account of the world we experience – the perceived 3D world we are all familiar with.

When you read this book you'll find it full of the information that you might expect in a textbook, but try to keep these bigger questions in mind. The way that we experience the world, interact with people, problem solve and reflect on our own behaviour is a miracle that psychology is only just starting to explore.

THE TEXT

The text is designed around the six areas that make up the core of any undergraduate curriculum in the UK plus an extra section to introduce some applied areas in psychology. We start with the difficult stuff, which comprises the areas commonly referred to as CHIPS by psychologists (conceptual and historical issues in psychology). Our journey begins with an evolutionary explanation to questions about how we came to be as we are, in Chapter 1. This stretches from the cave to the computer and we consider one possible future for human evolution. We go on in Chapters 2 and 3 to look at the history of psychology and the modern ways that we describe what it means to be alive, to be conscious. We have introduced these concepts at the beginning not to put you off or try to impress you, but because we think that these are the ideas that infuse the whole of modern psychology. We finish this section with our own take on methods in which we introduce you to how psychologists study mind and behaviour by looking at some examples of recent research projects.

The following sections discuss cognitive psychology, biological psychology, social psychology, developmental psychology and the psychology of individual differences. In the space available we aim to provide you with enough material to understand and explore the basic concepts in these fields. We also hope to arouse your interest and provide you with enough questions so that you feel the urge to go on to further study in one or more of the areas. The final section looks at examples of how psychology is applied in the areas of crime, health, and mental health.

The text has a number of features that have been chosen to help your understanding of the material and make it interesting to read. These include key studies on particular topics, short biographies of key contemporary researchers, exercises, suggestions for further reading and some lame attempts at humour.

THE AUTHORS

The book has contributions from over 50 academic staff in the Division of Psychology at Nottingham Trent University. It has been edited by four of these staff and we hope that we have created a text that reads as if it has one author rather than many. We were going to include a picture of all the authors but modesty and, frankly, good taste prevailed.

One of the most striking aspects of being an editor is to watch your colleagues adopt the behaviour of students. Much of this is very positive, but some of the negative aspects also crept in. At the university, we have strict deadlines and word limits for student work and it is part of the corridor culture for staff to throw their eyebrows to the ceiling when these basic rules are not met by their students. Lecturers commonly think that it is easy to keep to deadlines and word limits.

Imagine our surprise to find that these same staff used the worst excuses to explain their own lateness. Bargaining for an extension accompanied by the lamest of excuses became a daily event for the editors. Avoidance, denial and emotional blackmail became part of the daily discourse on the corridor. And as for word limits … you'd think it could not get more simple than to ask for 8,500–9,000 words, but only a handful of chapters were submitted around the word limit. The most extreme was 15,000 words, which also included a note to say that they still needed to add another section. Most inexplicable was the 9,500-word chapter that was sent back to the author to reduce it a bit and came back at 10,500 words.

Students, take heart from this. If these authors had been students at this university most of them would have had their work failed for lateness, marked down for being overlength and derided for the poor quality of their excuses. It must be harder being a student than we remember, and that is a key lesson we'll take from this process.

ACKNOWLEDGEMENTS

The editors would like to acknowledge their students at Nottingham Trent University who have put up with our weak attempts at humour over the years and have engaged with us in a positive and productive way. Learning is not something that stops when you get your degree, and our students help us to keep looking at material afresh and keep learning ourselves. In recognition of this, the royalties from this text go into a fund at Nottingham Trent University that is used to enhance the experience of our psychology undergraduates.

The editors would also like to acknowledge the positive and supportive working environment that they enjoy with their colleagues at Nottingham Trent University. This is the second edition of this text which was originally developed by Mark N.O. Davis, who has moved on to work at the University of East London. It was his idea to create a text from within the staff of Nottingham Trent University and his influence can be seen all through the book. We would also like to thank Michael Carmichael and the staff at SAGE who have been very supportive and shown remarkable confidence in, and tolerance of, the editors.

The editors and publishers would like to thank the following academic peer reviewers, and others who chose to remain anonymous, who have provided useful comments at various points throughout the project:

Julie Apps, University of Manchester

Dr Alison Attrill, De Montfort University

Dr Alex Balani, Edge Hill University

Dr Joseph Brooks, University of Kent

Dr Dan Clark, Liverpool Hope University

Dr Stewart Cotterill, University of Winchester

Jonathan Elcock, University of Gloucestershire

Dr Emee Vida Estacio, Keele University

Dr Jennifer Ferrell, University of the West of England

Dr Rachel George, University of East London

Dr Gareth Hall, Aberystwyth University

Dr Simon Hampton, University of East Anglia

Dr Fay Julal, Southampton Solent University

Dr Minna Lyons, University of Liverpool

Professor Linda McGowan, University of Manchester

Professor Chris McVittie, Queen Margaret University

Dr Kirsty Miller, University of Lincoln

Thomas Mitchell, Edge Hill University

Dr Samantha Nabb, University of Hull

Dr Sharon Preston, University of Bolton

Dr Adam Qureshi, Edge Hill University

Dr Diane Stevens, Bath Spa University

Dr Paul Sullivan, University of Bradford

Dr Caroline Wakefield, Liverpool Hope University

Finally, the editors would like to acknowledge the endlessly amusing Christian Adey and namecheck the following, www.resourcd.com, Kitty Fisher, Famille Wardle and The Northerners, Doctor's Orders, Left Lion, His Jumbleship and the full selection of pets and partners (you know who you are). Dr Winder also wants special mentions for the Griffgirlz, Luca, Count Von Chocula, Quincy, Gilly, Pica, Ludo, Stella, Mickey, The Danzigs, Gracie, CJ, Angus, Connor, Morty, Gizmo and Pennie.

And finally, finally, the editing team would like to thank and acknowledge Mick Gregson, Head of Psychology at Nottingham Trent University. Well, we say thank, but we probably mean commiserate. He has around 60 psychologists to manage (keep in order), and many hundreds of students. He cares passionately about what he does, and cares very much about the individuals he feels responsible for. Plus he's a Liverpool fan. Life is hard for some people; but we are very grateful to him for being the person he is.

GUIDED TOUR

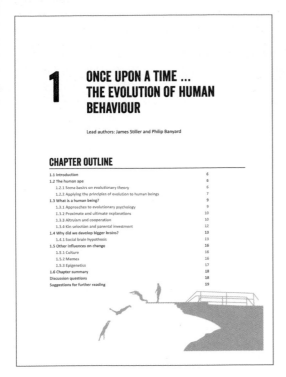

1 ONCE UPON A TIME ...
THE EVOLUTION OF HUMAN
BEHAVIOUR

Lead authors: James Stiller and Philip Banyard

CHAPTER OUTLINE

1.1 Introduction	6
1.2 The human ape	6
1.2.1 Some basics on evolutionary theory	6
1.2.2 Applying the principles of evolution to human beings	7
1.3 What is a human being?	9
1.3.1 Approaches to evolutionary psychology	9
1.3.2 Proximate and ultimate explanations	10
1.3.3 Altruism and cooperation	10
1.3.4 Kin selection and parental investment	12
1.4 Why did we develop bigger brains?	13
1.4.1 Social brain hypothesis	13
1.5 Other influences on change	16
1.5.1 Culture	16
1.5.2 Memes	16
1.5.3 Epigenetics	17
1.6 Chapter summary	18
Discussion questions	18
Suggestions for further reading	19

Chapter Outline: The first page of all chapters includes the list of contents.

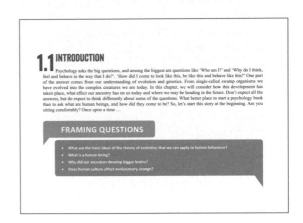

Introduction and Framing Questions: Each chapter begins with an introduction that provides you with the overall framework of the chapter. It gives you a map of the journey you are about to undertake with each topic area, the key ideas, and the contexts in which these ideas developed. The framing questions provide key questions which will emerge in the chapter.

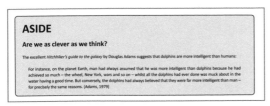

Aside: Not all of the interesting things we want to tell you about fit into the narratives we create in each chapter. We have added some asides which are descriptions of a relevant idea or piece of research. You might like to explore them further once you've read the main body text.

Key Researcher: Every field in psychology has thousands of researchers. We've selected a number of mainly current researchers to highlight their work and also to give a flavour of the range of interests that psychologists have. You may find that you want to follow up their work. If so, then Google them. It's amazing what you can find out.

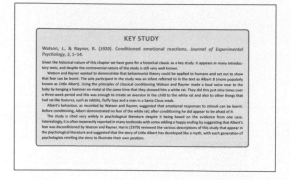

KEY STUDY

Watson, J., & Rayner, R. (1920). Conditioned emotional reactions. *Journal of Experimental Psychology, 3,* 1–14.

Given the historical nature of this chapter we have gone for a historical classic as a key study. It appears in many introductory texts, and despite the controversial nature of the study is still very well known.

Watson and Rayner wanted to demonstrate that behaviourist theory could be applied to humans and set out to show that fear can be learnt. The sole participant in the study was an infant referred to in the text as Albert B (more popularly known as Little Albert). Using the principles of classical conditioning Watson and Rayner made a loud noise near to the baby by banging a hammer on metal at the same time that they showed him a white rat. They did this just nine times over a three-week period and this was enough to create an aversion in the child to the white rat and also to other things that had rat-like features, such as rabbits, fluffy toys and a man in a Santa Claus mask.

Albert's behaviour, as recorded by Watson and Rayner, suggested that emotional responses to stimuli can be learnt. Before conditioning, Albert demonstrated no fear of the white rat; after conditioning he did appear to be afraid of it.

The study is cited very widely in psychological literature despite it being based on the evidence from one case. Interestingly, it is often incorrectly reported in many textbooks with some adding a happy ending by suggesting that Albert's fear was deconditioned by Watson and Rayner. Harris (1979) reviewed the various descriptions of this study that appear in the psychological literature and suggested that the story of Little Albert has developed like a myth, with each generation of psychologists retelling the story to illustrate their own position.

Key Study: Psychology is mainly led by research studies. These are the basic evidence that is at the heart of any theory. To emphasise this we have included outlines of important pieces of research that relate to the topics in the chapter.

EXERCISE: SENSATION AND PERCEPTION

Take a box of matches. Light one of the matches and hold it up in front of a light background. How bright does it look? Try to put a number on your judgement of brightness (your perception). Now light another match in front of a different coloured background. How bright does that look?

The amount of light from the two matches will be the same (sensation) but your judgement might well be different. Try this out with a number of backgrounds and explore the factors that change your perception. By the way, try not to burn down your house during this exercise.

Exercise: We all learn best by doing. With this in mind, we have made some suggestions of things you can do which will clarify or extend your learning. We include group- and individual-based exercises which are designed to provide practical and reflective learning on key issues, concepts and phenomena covered in each chapter.

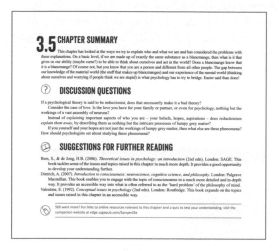

3.5 CHAPTER SUMMARY

This chapter has looked at the ways we try to explain who and what we are and has considered the problems with these explanations. On a basic level, if we are made up of exactly the same substance as a blancmange, then what is it that gives us our ability (maybe curse?) to be able to think about ourselves and act in the world? Does a blancmange know that it is a blancmange? Of course not, but you know that you are a person and different from all other people. The gap between our knowledge of the material world (the stuff that makes up blancmanges) and our experience of the mental world (thinking about ourselves and worrying if people think we are stupid) is what psychology has to try to bridge. Easier said than done!

? DISCUSSION QUESTIONS

If a psychological theory is said to be reductionist, does that necessarily make it a bad theory?

Consider the case of love. Is the love you have for your family or partner, or even for psychology, nothing but the workings of a vast assembly of neurons?

Instead of *explaining* important aspects of who you are – your beliefs, hopes, aspirations – does reductionism *explain them away*, by describing them as nothing but the intricate processes of lumpy grey matter?

If you yourself and your hopes are not just the workings of lumpy grey matter, then what else are these phenomena? How should psychologists set about studying these phenomena?

SUGGESTIONS FOR FURTHER READING

Bem, S., & de Jong, H.B. (2006). *Theoretical issues in psychology: an introduction* (2nd edn). London: SAGE. This book tackles some of the issues and topics raised in this chapter in much more depth. It provides a good opportunity to develop your understanding further.

Dietrich, A. (2007). *Introduction to consciousness: neuroscience, cognitive science, and philosophy.* London: Palgrave Macmillan. This book enables you to engage with the topic of consciousness in a much more detailed and in-depth way. It provides an accessible way into what is often referred to as the 'hard problem' of the philosophy of mind.

Valentine, E. (1992). *Conceptual issues in psychology* (2nd edn). London: Routledge. This book expands on the topics and issues raised in this chapter in an accessible way.

Still want more? For links to online resources relevant to this chapter and a quiz to test your understanding, visit the companion website at edge.sagepub.com/banyard2e

Chapter Summaries: A review of the main concepts and issues covered in the chapter to reinforce the key points. These are followed by **Discussion Questions** to explore with friends on your course or individually and **Suggestions for Further Reading** which point you towards more material to explore relating to the chapter.

edge.sagepub.com/banyard2e

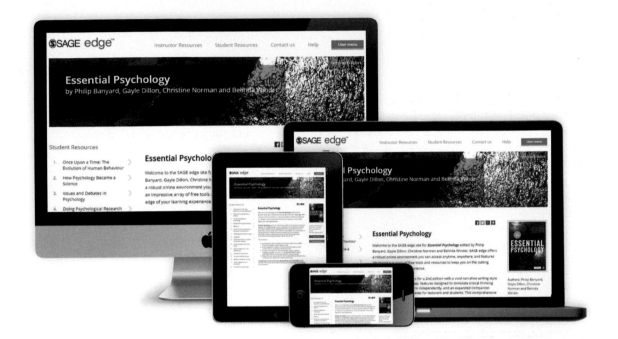

For the cyber-hungry among you, or for those who are more inclined to read in pixels than in print, this textbook comes with SAGE edge (**edge.sagepub.com/banyard2e**), a range of free tools and resources that will enhance the teaching and learning experience.

For Students it provides a personalised approach to help accomplish coursework goals in an easy-to-use learning environment and features:

- Mobile-friendly **eFlashcards** which strengthen understanding of key terms and concepts
- Mobile-friendly **practice quizzes** that allow you to assess your understanding of course material
- Links to **online videos** that offer a new perspective and an alternative learning style
- An **online action plan** which allows you to individualise your learning experience
- **Summaries** and **learning objectives** for each chapter that reinforce the most important material

For Instructors it supports teaching by making it easy to integrate quality content and create a rich learning environment for students. Instructor resources for this book include:

- **Testbanks** including 25 multiple choice and 3 short answer questions per chapter
- **PowerPoint slides** for each chapter that can be edited for use in teaching

SECTION A

THE FOUNDATIONS OF MODERN PSYCHOLOGY: WHAT WE KNOW ABOUT HUMAN BEINGS

If I have seen further it is by standing on the shoulders of Giants.

Isaac Newton, 1676

Human beings are remarkable creatures. Most remarkable is our ability and almost obsession to pass our knowledge on from one generation to another. We have studied our world and recorded the data for thousands of years and from this study we know a lot about the world and also about ourselves.

Modern psychology is commonly dated to the middle of the nineteenth century, but our interest in who and what we are dates back to early civilisations. There are writings from ancient Egypt, China, India and Greece that speculate on what a person is and how we came to be. The way that we think about ourselves today has been developed over generations, and to understand modern psychology, it is important to know about the history of the subject. This is often placed at the end of psychology courses and texts, but we have started our book with this section because we think it presents ideas that will help you understand what follows in later sections.

The distinguishing feature of modern psychology is its position in the sciences, and the key feature of science is the way that it gathers and interprets its evidence. The scientific approach is to be *empirical*, which means that we gather evidence that is open to scrutiny, is preferably replicable (we can repeat the study to check our findings) and is falsifiable. This last point sounds strange at first glance but is actually very important.

Science moves on in small steps. The quote above from Isaac Newton, probably the UK's greatest scientist, shows how even the most eminent scientists are aware of this. The common view of science is that we are able to prove things and discover once and for all how things work. This is not the case, however: we are not able to prove anything, but can only come up with theories that offer the best explanation of the phenomena we observe. If we obtain new information in the future, we might well find that there is a better explanation and so we then discard our original theory.

Knowledge is provisional. This means that we are not uncovering the truth, but inching our way to new understandings. What we 'know' today will be the chip paper of tomorrow. Newton's law of gravity is an example of this. The shock of being hit on the head by an apple (allegedly) helped Newton devise his law, which stood for more than 200 years until a better understanding of the movement of objects in the universe was devised by Einstein in his theory of general relativity. Our psychological theories cannot expect to last as long as Newton's laws.

If we want psychology to progress then we have to accept that what we believe to be true today might well be shown to be not true tomorrow. Our theories therefore have to allow for the possibility of disproof.

The foundation of psychology is based on traditions from philosophy, biology, medicine and literature. It is among a number of new sciences, like economics, that try to analyse and explain the ways that people behave in their world. This section gives the background to the development of this science of behaviour and experience.

KEY ISSUES

One of the key issues for psychologists looking into the history of the subject is to define exactly what the subject is about. The perspective we take to looking at people affects what we see. If we take an evolutionary perspective, then we will see much of human behaviour as being motivated by the drive to reproduce. If we take a physiological perspective, we will see people as biological machines and their actions as largely mechanical responses to changes in their environment. The perspective is important because it will affect not only how we see people, but also how we treat them.

THIS SECTION

In this section we have three chapters looking at the development of psychological ideas and a fourth one looking at how psychology collects its evidence today. We start off (controversially) in Chapter 1 by looking at how Darwin's theory of evolution shapes modern psychology and we speculate about what the next big jump will be in the development of humanity. In Chapter 2, we look at the early psychologists and how they have framed the debate about who we are and what we are, and devised the methods to explore these questions. In Chapter 3, we look at some philosophical issues that have puzzled and continue to puzzle psychologists concerning our consciousness and our identity. Finally, in Chapter 4, we introduce some key ideas in research methods through examples of recent research programmes at our own university. The examples illustrate a spread of techniques and methods used in research, and look at issues around foster parenting, dealing with testicular cancer, investigating sex offenders, problem gambling and driving skills.

ASIDE

Are we as clever as we think?

The excellent *Hitchhiker's guide to the galaxy* by Douglas Adams suggests that dolphins are more intelligent than humans:

> For instance, on the planet Earth, man had always assumed that he was more intelligent than dolphins because he had achieved so much – the wheel, New York, wars and so on – whilst all the dolphins had ever done was muck about in the water having a good time. But conversely, the dolphins had always believed that they were far more intelligent than man – for precisely the same reasons. (Adams, 1979)

1

ONCE UPON A TIME ...
THE EVOLUTION OF HUMAN
BEHAVIOUR

Lead authors: James Stiller and Philip Banyard

CHAPTER OUTLINE

1.1 Introduction	6
1.2 The human ape	6
1.2.1 Some basics on evolutionary theory	6
1.2.2 Applying the principles of evolution to human beings	7
1.3 What is a human being?	9
1.3.1 Approaches to evolutionary psychology	9
1.3.2 Proximate and ultimate explanations	10
1.3.3 Altruism and cooperation	10
1.3.4 Kin selection and parental investment	12
1.4 Why did we develop bigger brains?	13
1.4.1 Social brain hypothesis	13
1.5 Other influences on change	16
1.5.1 Culture	16
1.5.2 Memes	16
1.5.3 Epigenetics	17
1.6 Chapter summary	18
Discussion questions	18
Suggestions for further reading	19

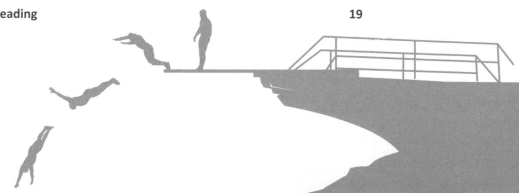

1.1 INTRODUCTION

Psychology asks the big questions, and among the biggest are questions like 'Who am I?' and 'Why do I think, feel and behave in the way that I do?'. 'How did I come to look like this, be like this and behave like this?' One part of the answer comes from our understanding of evolution and genetics. From single-celled swamp organisms we have evolved into the complex creatures we are today. In this chapter, we will consider how this development has taken place, what effect our ancestry has on us today and where we may be heading in the future. Don't expect all the answers, but do expect to think differently about some of the questions. What better place to start a psychology book than to ask what are human beings, and how did they come to be? So, let's start this story at the beginning. Are you sitting comfortably? Once upon a time …

FRAMING QUESTIONS

- What are the basic ideas of the theory of evolution that we can apply to human behaviour?
- What is a human being?
- Why did our ancestors develop bigger brains?
- Does human culture affect evolutionary change?

1.2 THE HUMAN APE

What are we? This has been a question that has stimulated intellectual debate for centuries. In the fifteenth century, the debate was dominated by a view that placed humans at the centre of the universe. Therefore, the philosophers of the day, in line with the European religious doctrine of the time, had the earth at the centre of the universe with all the other planets, including the sun, revolving around the 'seat of man'. This began to change when Copernicus, a Polish astronomer and mathematician, using empirical data, disproved the geocentric theory of the universe. His work, published in *De revolutionibus orbium coelestium* in 1543, challenged the religious thinking of the time by demonstrating that the earth revolved around the sun. The work of Copernicus is seen as the start of the **scientific revolution**.

SCIENTIFIC REVOLUTION In the sixteenth and seventeenth centuries there was a period of rapid change in the intellectual endeavour of making sense of the world that people lived in. Medieval philosophy was replaced by scientific principles of observation, measurement and experimentation. These developments are linked with Bacon (1561–1626), Galileo (1564–1642), Descartes (1596–1650) and Newton (1642–1727).

Growing out of this scientific revolution was a commitment to the scientific ideals of observation, analysis and experimentation (we cover more about the development of science in the next chapter). Over the centuries, science has progressed our understanding (and control) of the world around us. For psychologists, even more significant than the ideas of Copernicus was the contribution in the nineteenth century of **Charles Darwin** (1809–1882), which changed the way we see ourselves in relation to life on earth. From his careful observations on his voyage aboard the *Beagle*, and through his experiments involving selective breeding of domestic animals, such as dogs and cattle, he developed his theory of evolution by natural selection.

1.2.1 SOME BASICS ON EVOLUTIONARY THEORY

Evolution as a concept was not invented by Darwin. Evolution describes a process whereby there is change in the features of some body or system over time. The key question is to find out what are the processes that bring about these changes. In 1859, Charles Darwin published a book entitled *On the origin of species*. A key idea outlined in the book was that human beings share a common ancestor with other contemporary primates, such as chimpanzees and gorillas. Darwin proposed that the way in which organisms changed over time (evolved) was through a process of natural selection. This provided the basis of the explanation of how a common ancestor could evolve into more than one species.

Many people feel they are familiar with the theory of natural selection; however, it is often mistaken as simply being the survival of the fittest, with the term *fittest* being taken to mean the *strongest*. Yet, if we look at Darwin's (1859) and Wallace's (1858) theory of natural selection, we see that the underlying principles of natural selection are far more complex.

There are three key principles that lead to the concept of fitness in Darwinian terms. The first principle is that of *variation*: this suggests that individuals within a species all show variation in their behavioural and physiological traits (the **phenotype** of the individual). If individuals were all the same, then there would be no possibility for change. The second principle is that of *inheritance*, whereby the variations exhibited by individuals are heritable. The third principle is that of *adaptation*. Adaptation refers to an organism's suitability or fit to the environment that it inhabits. That environment contains limited resources (of food, water and safe spaces, for example) and this leads to competition between individuals, groups and species for those resources. Therefore, if an individual has inherited certain variations in behaviour or physical makeup that make them more effective at competing for these resources, then there will be a greater chance that they will produce more offspring and so pass this variation on to the next generation.

These three key principles lead on to the concept of *fitness*, as those individuals that show heritable adaptive traits are likely to leave more offspring. Those offspring that inherit these traits are suggested as having an evolutionary advantage as they are likely to be better adapted to their environment and, as such, natural selection has occurred. This process gives us the rich variation of species on the planet that have each found an environmental niche where they fit. This gives us the neck of the giraffe, the spots of the leopard and the testicles of the chimpanzee (see below).

Since the 1850s, biological science has progressed, and of course when we now refer to natural selection we are also taking into account the genetic makeup of an individual (their **genotype**). The principle of inheritance now refers to how genes that code for specific proteins that can lead to certain behaviours or physiological traits are passed on to future generations. The first person to recognise this process was an Austrian monk called **Gregor Mendel** (1822–1884), who was very observant in his work growing peas. Like any good farmer, he selectively bred his peas to promote certain characteristics, such as flower colour, smoothness of the pea, mushiness, etc. The selective breeding was done systematically and records were carefully maintained so that the lineage of his peas could be clearly specified. Through careful study, Mendel was able to demonstrate that the transmission of the physical characteristics of his peas across generations obeyed certain laws, sometimes referred to as the *basic laws of inheritance*. We now refer to these laws as *Mendelian laws of genetics*. The basic element involved in the transfer was called a **gene** and this has become part of our everyday language. Mendel published his work in 1866 and is seen as the father of genetics. There is no evidence that Darwin was aware of Mendel's work, which was rediscovered at the turn of the century. The gene, however, is the discrete element of inheritance that Darwin attempted to grapple with in his account of the impact of evolution through natural selection.

PHENOTYPE The characteristics of an organism resulting from the interaction between its genetic makeup and the environment. These characteristics can be biological or behavioural.

GENOTYPE Genes that make up the genetic code for an individual are described as the genotype. In humans, the genotype comprises approximately 25,000 genes. Genes mostly come in pairs. Each member of a pair of genes is referred to as an allele.

GENE The basic unit of heredity. It is a segment of DNA that occupies a specific place on a chromosome. Genes act by affecting the synthesis of proteins which in turn influence specific physical traits, such as the shape of a leaf, or the texture of a person's hair. Different forms of genes, called alleles, determine how these traits are expressed in a given individual.

1.2.2 APPLYING THE PRINCIPLES OF EVOLUTION TO HUMAN BEINGS

Building on the work of Darwin and Mendel, we have developed our knowledge of genes and how they affect us. This work is still ongoing and, although we know a lot more than we did 100 years ago, there is long way before we have a full understanding of the processes involved. Indeed, we have to consider whether it might actually be beyond our understanding in the way that cooking is beyond the understanding of a dog.

Richard Dawkins (1976) argued that it is the genes that are the driving force in natural selection and that behaviour and physiology are actually a consequence of genes maximising the chances of their heritability. To put it another way, human beings are just the carriers of genes rather than the main event, and in this case we are like an apple that has developed to ensure that the apple seeds are eaten and planted (think of it as being an apple that is foraged in a forest rather than Sainsburys). The seeds are the main event, not the apple. Such a perspective widens the definition of fitness to the wider gene pool of a species. So, rather than thinking in terms of direct inheritance between parents and offspring, we can now consider inheritance in terms of the contribution to a shared gene pool and the number of genes an individual has in common with others. This leads to the concept of inclusive fitness, whereby not only the genes passed directly to offspring are considered, but also those of close relatives with shared genes.

So how can this be applied to humans? The ever-changing complexity of human behaviour can at first appear to be difficult to break down into simple heritable traits, as we are undoubtedly not genetic automatons. It is perhaps this flexibility in behaviour and the ability to vary our behaviours in response to changing circumstances that is our most important adaptive trait. However, this plasticity in behavioural and physiological traits is still mediated by our evolutionary past and results in characteristic human behaviours.

KEY STUDY: WHY THE CHIMPANZEE HAS BIG TESTICLES: AN EXAMPLE OF THE POWER OF EVOLUTION

Harcourt, A.H. (1977). Sperm competition in primates. *The American Naturalist*, *149(*1), 189–194.

Harcourt, A.H., & Stewart, K.J. (1977). Apes, sex and societies. *New Scientist*, *20*, 160–162.

There are many similarities between chimpanzees and gorillas, as we might expect, but the interesting thing is the differences that exist and how they might have developed. Some of the physical and behavioural differences between the two species are summarised in Table 1.1 (below), and the question to answer is why two similar species develop such striking differences. The key driver for change is often presented as changes in the environment, but in this case the changes are closely linked to the social organisation of the two species.

TABLE 1.1   The differences between chimpanzees and gorillas (from Harcourt & Stewart, 1977)

CHARACTERISTIC	GORILLAS	CHIMPANZEES
Sex differences	Male gorillas are much bigger than the females and also twice the weight	Male and female chimpanzees are nearly the same size as each other
Female sexual swellings	Barely visible	'Enormous' (p. 161)
Size	A male gorilla is about three times the size of a chimpanzee	A chimpanzee's testicles are six times the size of a gorilla's
Male courtship display	Virtually none	Flamboyant and vigorous
Time taken to copulate	Gorillas usually copulate for between two minutes and a quarter of an hour	'... can mount, thrust, ejaculate and dismount, all within the average time of seven seconds' (p. 162)

Chimpanzees live in loose communities with an equal number of males and females. When the males reach adolescence they stay with the group in which they were brought up, which is relatively unusual in mammals, but the females leave the home troop to join a neighbouring one before mating. The males protect the troop and its territory through collective action.

The social organisation of gorillas is very different. Each troop of gorillas is dominated by one large male who tolerates only one or two other males, most likely his offspring, who may well take over the leadership when the old male dies. The other young males leave the troop. The male gorillas do not get together to protect their troop and territory, but challenge each other for control of the small mating groups.

There is a big advantage if you are a male gorilla in being large. Being large means that you can beat off the challenge of other male gorillas and so gain exclusive mating rights with a group of females. Therefore, it is no surprise that the male gorilla has evolved a much larger body, and so is visibly bigger than the female.

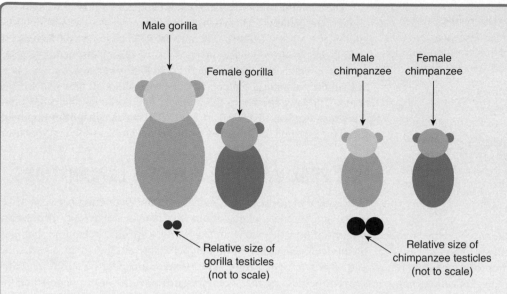

FIGURE 1.1   Graphic to illustrate the differences between chimpanzees and gorillas

The male chimpanzee, on the other hand, gains very little advantage from being large. This is because the female often mates with several males and, if the largest male is fighting off his rivals, then someone else steps in while the fight is going on. So, the male chimpanzee has not developed a more muscular frame because there is no reproductive advantage in it.

So why are chimpanzee's testicles so big and a gorilla's so small? The female chimpanzee might well mate with several males but she develops only one fertilised egg. The male who is most likely to fertilise that egg is the male who mates with her most often or who produces the most sperm. Therefore, the feature of large testicles has been bred into the male line of chimpanzees because larger testicles produce more sperm. The gorilla does not have these competition problems and so has some of the smallest testicles in the animal kingdom.

1.3 WHAT IS A HUMAN BEING?

1.3.1 APPROACHES TO EVOLUTIONARY PSYCHOLOGY

There are a variety of different behaviours that appear to be typically human; these include the use of complex language, cooperation and helping behaviours, complex social networks, and extended childhood to name a few. However, to what extent can these behaviours be considered as evolved behaviours and not simply a consequence of the environment in which we live? An evolutionary approach to the problem allows us to consider what traits are **human universals** and to what extent a behavioural characteristic can be inherited. In order for a trait to have been an evolved adaptation, it has to be passed on to the next generation; this makes studying such areas of psychology particularly tricky given it is difficult to measure and obtain data across multiple generations. However, evolutionary psychologists tackle such obstacles via the use of **comparative studies** with closely related species, **anthropological approaches** that identify human behaviours that appear to be universal traits and by using **experimental and questionnaire studies** to examine the proximate mechanisms that might highlight specific cognitive biases or traits.

A common misconception is that we have evolved from apes and that we can see our ancestors around us on this planet. The error here is to ignore that during the thousands of years of human evolution these apes have also been changing and evolving. Evolution doesn't stand still. The way to think of this is that we have a common ancestor to these apes and so your great great (add a lot more greats here) nan was also the great great etc. nan to the chimpanzees in the zoo. They are your cousins, not your ancestors.

GENUS A class, group or category that possesses common attributes. Our own species exists in the genus *Homo* alongside other species (all of which are now extinct).

SPECIES A group that exists within a genus. Members of a species in the same or in different populations are able to interbreed under natural conditions to produce viable offspring. Species are defined by reproductive isolation. There is one hominid species which we all belong to called *Homo sapiens*.

The evolution of hominids began around 2.5 million years ago. The origin of the **genus** is open to debate, but in general what we see is change in a number of key features. The interesting changes are an increase in overall size, greater emphasis on bipedalism (walking on two legs) and an increase in brain size. From around 1.5 million years ago, our ancestors had similar anatomical features to ourselves, although they had smaller brains. The later **species** in the hominid line portrayed increased brain size. *Homo sapiens* (that's us) are associated with language development, social organisation (culture) and sophisticated problem solving (tool use).

1.3.2 PROXIMATE AND ULTIMATE EXPLANATIONS

One issue that needs to be considered is the distinction between proximate and ultimate explanations for human behaviour. **Proximate** explanations describe the mechanisms involved in terms of how they contribute towards a specific behaviour that may benefit an individual and aid survival. However, **ultimate** explanations for human behaviour examine why a particular behaviour or trait can improve inclusive fitness and why a particular proximate behaviour can be favoured in evolutionary terms. For example, social reasoning, in terms of possessing the necessary cortical functions to understand the viewpoints of others, is a proximate explanation for a behaviour, while social reasoning as an aid towards cooperation and deception in order to maximise inclusive fitness is an ultimate explanation.

There are numerous hurdles that face evolutionary approaches; in particular, the complexity and diversity of human behaviour and whether any one behaviour can be studied in isolation to show that it provides an evolutionary advantage. Therefore, there is not one particular method that is appropriate for all questions that are posed. Comparative methods allow us to look at human behaviour within the context of other species, perhaps where the measurement of fitness outcomes and evolutionary benefits are clearer. For example, Hosken and Ward (2001) demonstrated that when there was increased competition for mates among male yellow dung flies, there was an evolutionary response whereby over subsequent generations there was an increase in testis size in response to sperm competition. Such studies would not be possible on animals with longer lifespans, but, via experiments on flies, they provided some of the first evidence that sperm competition not only has an effect on mating strategies, but can result in traits (testis size) being inherited, increasing the chances of reproductive success.

Comparative methods also allow for comparisons among closely related species – for example, the primates – and allow us to see where in our evolutionary past there might have been a change in behaviour or cognitive ability. However, many approaches tend to focus primarily on the proximate mechanisms and how these might be beneficial to an individual and aid survival. For example, studies of Florida scrub-jays (Woolfenden, 1984) have provided plenty of evidence of the benefits of having close relatives assisting in the rearing of chicks to increase survival; however, there is debate as to whether this behaviour is an evolved trait or a response to environmental pressures.

Anthropological methods allow us to see how different populations have adjusted their behaviour in response to environmental pressures and how culture can provide an adaptive mechanism. Historical data also allow us to examine how certain traits and behaviours might improve inclusive fitness. Voland, Siegelkow and Engel (1991) showed that during the eighteenth and nineteenth centuries, farmers in Krummhörn, Germany, who were subject to limited resources and reduced reproductive opportunities, would invest less in sons, with the youngest son inheriting the farm. This was shown to be a beneficial strategy in that it secured the farming rights and wealth for future generations by delaying inheritance and reducing the potential for multiple heirs, thus improving the inclusive fitness of the family. Anthropological studies also provide a lot of evidence for traits that can be considered as human universals and, as such, might highlight behaviours that could have been considered adaptive in our evolutionary past.

1.3.3 ALTRUISM AND COOPERATION

As a species, humans are experts at cooperation and deception: we are equipped with the necessary cognitive skills to understand the belief and desires of others (see the discussion about Theory of Mind in Chapter 19), think prospectively about possible future outcomes and consequences, and also have the ability to draw upon previous experience to avoid repeating the same mistakes. However, these proximate explanations do not explain why, as a species, we exhibit such complex behaviours and how these traits can be adaptive.

One issue that is of interest to evolutionary psychologists is the problem of altruism (it is also of interest to social psychologists; see Chapter 15). Altruism can be defined as an act that benefits the recipient at a cost to the donor. In evolutionary terms, this can be a bit of an issue as a behaviour that is detrimental to an individual does not immediately appear to be an adaptive trait. However, when we look at such behaviours within the context of an individual's indirect fitness, we see that perhaps there are scenarios where apparent altruism can be an advantageous behaviour. Hamilton (1964) suggested that altruism that preferentially aids individuals that have more genes in common with the donor (i.e. genetic relatives or kin) can ensure that an individual's indirect fitness benefits, even if there is an apparent cost to an individual's direct fitness. Hamilton's rule suggests that if there is a high probability that the donor and recipient have genes in common, then the benefits can outweigh the cost to the donor. So imagine that you are in a life and death scenario – are you more likely to save your siblings or a stranger? In most cases people will favour their relatives and this can be considered as kin selection (Maynard-Smith, 1964).

J.S. Haldane famously said 'I would lay down my life for two brothers or eight cousins' (Connolly & Martlew, 1999, p. 10). This remark refers to the calculation about how many of your genes continue to exist after you have died; as each sibling has 50% of your genes and each nephew has 25% and each first cousin has 12.5%, you can see how your genes can live on.

So what about the flipside of altruism and cooperative behaviour? Does it pay to punish another individual or to allow them to get away with a perceived transgression? One way to study this is to look at how punishing another individual could be detrimental directly or indirectly to an individual's inclusive fitness. The welfare trade-off ratio (WTR) indicates the extent to which an individual or group are willing to trade-off their own welfare against another individual's or group's welfare (Petersen et al., 2010). At a more trivial level, this could involve low-cost actions such as perhaps letting someone go ahead of you in a queue or offering to pick up a neighbour's child from school so that they can work late. However, this model can be applied to more serious scenarios, such as seeking punishments for crime and even when people consider whether it is worth committing a crime.

Factors that need to be considered when looking at welfare trade-off ratios include the formidability, degree of relatedness and the mate value with the other party, as well as the impact an action will have on your own relatives, the resources gained and the social status of the parties involved. Basically, there is a complex interaction between the potential gains and costs that result in either valuing another party or in perceiving a particular action as detrimental and worthy of punishment or reconciliation. Severe punishment would therefore indicate a low WTR as an individual would be placing little value on the other party involved. Of course, this term value does not have to be purely biological-based. It can also refer to the value of cultural traditions between groups, where, for example, insulting another culture's belief system could indicate that one group is not perceived as being as valuable as another group. However, this does raise the issue of group selection and identity in that the cost and benefits to the group have to be considered as well (see Chapter 23 for more about the self and group identity).

EXERCISE: STOP THIEF! (OR NOT)

Consider the following scenario: you are in a restaurant having a meal and you have caught someone stealing a significant amount of money from your wallet (which will mean you cannot pay your bill). You have two choices: first, you could call the police and have them arrested; second, you could let the criminal go free. What decision would you make for the following criminals?

1. Your sibling (brother or sister)
2. A stranger
3. A very attractive member of the opposite sex
4. A known member of a violent crime syndicate that will retaliate (i.e. a Berserker)
5. A homeless person who is likely to starve to death without the money

Arguably, your decisions might be influenced by your current financial status, how others see you, your marital status, whether you are seeking a mate, how aggressive the criminal or the degree of relatedness you have with the perpetrator. As such, you would be making a series of complex trade-offs between the costs and benefits of punitive action.

Although many historical documents and fiction might not necessarily present an accurate interpretation of human behaviour, they can provide clear examples of how evolutionary principles can be attributed to specific behaviours or, at the very least, an example of how individuals construct their mental worlds. Indeed, if we look at the concept of murder and revenge, on the surface a maladaptive trait, we can see how in terms of inclusive fitness such behaviours could be tolerated. For example, the Icelandic Viking sagas highlight the impact of cost and kinship in relation to Viking Berserkers. Berserkers were fearsome individuals who were renowned for their ruthlessness on the battlefield. Within the Viking sagas, if a relative was murdered, the victim's family were entitled to either blood money or a revenge killing. However, if the murderer was a known to have a Berserker in the family, there was a reduced chance of a revenge killing, therefore lessening the likelihood of further revenge killings (from an exceptionally brutal adversary). Similarly, murder could be a response to a multitude of issues, including trivial disagreements at a feast or in relation to the acquisition of land or resources. Vikings were also less likely to murder close kin over trivial disagreements and would only contemplate this if there were significant gains to be had (e.g. gaining land and resources). However, among non-relatives there was no such distinction (Dunbar et al., 1995). In many respects, the Viking sagas demonstrate a clear understanding of welfare trade-off ratios and how low WTRs can exist between certain groups based on formidableness, relatedness, social status and potential gains.

1.3.4 KIN SELECTION AND PARENTAL INVESTMENT

Parental investment is necessary to rear offspring successfully, especially if an individual is to pass on the genes to subsequent generations. Several factors can influence the amount of parental investment that is provided. This can include paternity certainty, culture and environmental pressures. Frequency-dependent selection would suggest that parental investment might be preferentially attributed towards either sons or daughters, dependent on the balance of the sexes within the overall population, so if there was a lack of males in the population (perhaps due to war), then it would be expected that there might be a shift in the normal 50:50 sex ratio in humans, with preferential investment of sons over daughters in the subsequent generation. Similarly, with cultural influences where there is a societal structure whereby it is advantageous to marry daughters up the social hierarchy, then it would pay to invest more in the eldest daughter, perhaps at the expense of the sons and the younger daughters. These examples illustrate how the amount of parental investment can aid the prospect of future generations.

Paternity uncertainty can play a significant role in the amount of parental investment provided by fathers. Unlike mothers, there is no 100% guarantee (without a DNA test) that your father really is your father. This uncertainty is reflected in the amount of parental investment. With mothers giving birth and breast-feeding, there is little doubt about this genetic bond; however, the fathers are not so certain. This lack of certainty can be seen in a variety of different areas. For example, a study in 1996 by Euler and Weitzel showed that, among a German sample, the maternal grandmother and grandfather provided more care for their grandchildren than the paternal grandmother and grandfather. Taking into

KEY RESEARCHER Robin Dunbar

Professor Robin Dunbar is currently the director of the Social and Evolutionary Neuroscience Research Group at Oxford University. He has previously held chairs in Anthropology at University College London (1987–1994), and in Psychology and Biology at University of Liverpool (1994–2007). He is probably best known for his research into the cognitive limitations on human group size and, in particular, Dunbar's number (see main text). He has also researched social evolution in a range of mammals, including feral goats on the Isle of Rum and Gelada baboons in Ethiopia, and has been a prolific writer of popular science books. He was also co-director on the 'Lucy to Language: The Archaeology of the Social Brain' Centenary research project awarded by the British Academy.

FIGURE 1.2   Robin Dunbar

account the genetic distance in terms of kin, combined with paternity uncertainty, it makes sense to allow the maternal side to contribute more to the rearing of grandchildren.

The role of the grandparent in childrearing has been shown to be particularly important in childrearing in the Gambia where, commonly, the grandmother from the maternal side provides extensive childrearing support (Sear, Mace, & McGregor, 2000). This improves the inclusive fitness of the grandmother by ensuring that her grandchildren get the best start in life. Also, it allows for the transmission of social knowledge and survival strategies to the grandchildren. If we look at the human lifespan in more detail, we notice that there is perhaps a good reason for this investment in grandchildren. Women, unlike men, undergo a menopause whereby they stop producing eggs and are then considered in biological terms as having low reproductive value. The human menopause is early compared to other species. For example, chimpanzees continue to have offspring for most of their natural life, and this suggests that it might have an evolutionary advantage in improving inclusive fitness. By living longer than their reproductive period, women are available to invest more in their children and their grandchildren. Within the environment of evolutionary adaptation, this would have enabled grandmothers to pass on vital knowledge for survival, help with the childcare and thus enable their offspring to have healthier and potentially more offspring.

So far this section has focused on positive aspects of childcare. However, Daly and Wilson (1988) showed that when looking at family homicide, the degree of relatedness is also an important factor as to whether a family member is killed. Their data suggest that step-parents are more likely to kill their step-children than their biological children. This picks up on the issue of kin selection and the fact that the cost of murdering one's own offspring is detrimental to the individual's inclusive fitness. Similarly, romantic partners are more at risk of violence than genetic relatives. Arguably, such violence can be considered as being related to paternity certainty and mate guarding. In terms of a welfare trade-off ratio, we have all the key elements in place as the violence tends to be towards a physically weaker individual, not close relatives, and the consequences have little impact on the perpetrator's inclusive fitness. Of course, the extent of this crime is severe enough to be maladaptive in that the perpetrator will likely be punished by the social group, and have reduced chances of reproductive success or aiding in the inclusive fitness of relatives.

1.4 WHY DID WE DEVELOP BIGGER BRAINS?

Compared to our closest living primate relatives, the chimpanzee, with whom we share approximately 97% of our genes, humans have significantly larger brains in proportion to our body size. If we look at changes in our brain size compared with ancestral humans (since *Homo erectus*, who would have lived between 1.8 million and 140,000 years ago), we see that the size of the brain has increased from approximately 900 cubic centimetres in *Homo erectus* to 1,350 cubic centimetres in modern humans. In particular, the areas associated with the frontal lobe (see Chapter 9 for more information about brain structure) show an increase in volume. These brain areas are associated with problem solving and reasoning.

So why is it humans have evolved larger brains? The benefits of larger brains are that we are able to use more complex tools to solve problems, we have a greater ability to plan future actions, we can make indirect links between events (e.g. if we saw a footprint, we could make the link between it being caused by another animal and even the direction the animal was walking). All of these are undoubtedly advantageous but do not answer why this change has occurred. In our ancestral past, there was an environmental pressure that must have favoured larger brains and made this an evolutionary advantageous trait. One key argument as to why we have evolved these larger brains is that they have enabled us to deal with increasingly complex social lives.

1.4.1 SOCIAL BRAIN HYPOTHESIS

Why do humans have language? Undoubtedly, the ability to talk is an evolved trait, but to what extent does possessing a complex language system actually aid our survival and inclusive fitness? Imagine you are a macaque and do not possess the complex vocalisations that are capable of expressing emotions (such as love and friendship) – how would you try to show another macaque that you care? Or that you would like to be friends with them? The chances are you would have to groom them (see Figure 1.3). Many primate species reinforce their social bonds by grooming each other; this is a very time-consuming activity as only one primate can be groomed at a time, but it can help to maintain strong social bonds within the group. Now consider the benefits of language: you can talk to more than one person at a time, thereby maintaining social bonds, and in far less time than it takes to groom each other's fur (if you have fur).

FIGURE 1.3 Macaques maintaining close contact through grooming

© Acon Cheng/Shutterstock.com

SOCIAL GROOMING OR ALLOGROOMING

A behaviour seen in many social species, including our own. It involves an individual or individuals assisting others to keep clean and in good condition. In addition to the obvious health benefits, the behaviour has also taken on a significant social function.

If you consider the use of vocalisations in other primate species, it is limited to a few key characteristic vocalisations that indicate food sources, submissive or dominance status, and predator detection. Despite a somewhat limited vocabulary, primates are capable of some complex signals. For example, Seyfarth and Cheney (1990) identified that Vervet monkeys use a variety of different signals as alarm calls, depending on the type of predator and response required. Vervet monkeys have characteristic alarm calls for leopards, snakes and birds of prey; each signal requires a different response, such as 'climb a tree' for ground predators or 'seek shelter' for aerial predators. One of the interesting aspects of this varied communication is that it is not in the individual's interest to make itself more conspicuous to danger, but is actually a form of social communication to others (close kin and fellow group members). Zuberbühler (2002) and colleagues also noted that this sharing of social information is not species-specific; some species of primates that live in mixed species social groups will behave similarly to the Vervet monkeys when faced with a threat.

How does this link in with humans? If we consider how human language is used, it is not only for indicating food sources, danger, social status or mate selection. Language is essential in forming strong long-lasting bonds with other people. A study of the topic of conversation in a university refectory showed that the main topics of conversation were what could be termed gossip, that is, the topic of conversation was not to do with imminent survival or work, but was related to more trivial topics such as who did what last night in the pub. So what are the benefits of

ASIDE

Wearing the monkey suit

FIGURE 1.4 When we look at primates do we see a person in a monkey suit?

©iStock.com/CWellsPhoto

When we look at an ape, are we misinterpreting what we see? Do we see an animal or do we treat them as if they are a human in a hairy suit?

Anthropomorphism is the attribution of human characteristics to inanimate objects, animals, forces of nature, and others. When we say dogs are loyal or foxes are cunning, we are treating the animals as if they think and behave like humans. We often take this a step further and attribute human qualities to machines; for example, talking to your computer as if it is deliberately messing you about.

When we are anthropomorphic, we are assuming that the animals or machines have a theory of mind, that they know what they are doing, and they are also responding to us. There is usually a simpler explanation for their behaviour and they are not thinking or feeling in ways that we do. Sorry about that. (*This is a lie, they are! – Ed.*).

trivial conversation? One benefit is that it allows individuals to identify with other group members and form strong emotional bonds. It also allows for the detection of social cheats, it allows the development of cultural identity and it allows for indirect learning. Language becomes an essential tool in maintaining direct and indirect social bonds between group members, and in policing social groups. In order to process such complex social information, the human brain has to possess the appropriate hardware for the job. This is where the relative size of the neocortex (the outer layer of the brain associated with higher cognitive functions) in comparison to the rest of the brain (neocortex ratio) becomes an important factor.

Comparative studies of the neocortex ratio between primate species suggest that there is an association between neocortex ratio and social group size (Dunbar, 1998). This suggests that, as the average group size for a particular species increases, so does the associated neocortex ratio. By extrapolating the data from non-human primate species, and based on the human neocortex ratio, it can be predicted that the average human social group size should be approximately 150 individuals. This 150 has since become known as *Dunbar's number*, and subsequent analysis of human social networks suggest that this is a commonly occurring number in human social networks – for example, church congregations, Christmas card lists and hunter-gatherer communities.

This theory allowed for the extrapolation of the findings to predict the social group sizes of early hominid species such as *Homo neanderthalis*, *Homo erectus*, *Homo habilis* and *Australopithecines*, based upon their estimated neocortex size (which can be obtained from fossil skulls). Again, using a comparative approach, Dunbar and colleagues looked at the amount of time that would be required for social grooming, be that via language or physical grooming. The results suggest that *Australopithecines*, an ancient hominid that lived approximately 3 million years ago, would have had a required grooming time below the limits of current living primates and monkeys. This indicates that these ancient hominids were probably relying on more direct approaches to grooming. It was not until the appearance of modern humans, approximately 500,000 years ago, that the grooming time required exceeded that of other living primates and therefore language became an essential grooming tool. This could suggest that it was not until the arrival of *Homo sapiens* that complex language was required to deal with the cognitive demands of larger societies and this in turn accelerated the need for a larger neocortex.

The social brain hypothesis (outlined above) is a compelling account of how brain size and social complexity evolved alongside each other. **Consciousness** (awareness of self and others) gives us the

> **CONSCIOUSNESS** Often used in everyday speech to describe being awake or aware, in contrast to being asleep or in a coma. In psychology, the term has a more precise meaning concerning the way in which humans are mentally aware so that they distinguish clearly between themselves and all other things and events.

KEY STUDY

Gonçalves, B., Perra, N., & Vespignani, A. (2011). Modeling users' activity on Twitter networks: validation of Dunbar's number. *PLOS One*. DOI: 10.1371/journal.pone.0022656.

A challenge to Dunbar's calculations about human group size is posed by the social networks that people create online. For example, many people will have a list of friends in the thousands on facilities such as Facebook. These facilities allow us to be connected with an ever-increasing number of individuals, and a question arises about whether digital technologies are changing our social behaviour and our social environment.

It can be argued that microblogging facilities, such as Twitter, enhance the way we deal with social interactions and that this creates a new social environment in an online world, where the limits on human social interaction are changed and where Dunbar's number becomes obsolete. An opposing view is that these microblogging facilities merely speed up the interaction but do not change the structure. If this is the case, the basic limits to social interactions will not be any different in the digital world.

In this paper, the authors analysed over 380 million tweets from which they were able to extract 25 million conversations. They used this data to create a pattern of social networks involving 1.7 million users. They argue that their data supports Dunbar's number in that users commonly have a maximum of between 100 and 200 stable relationships on Twitter.

ability to place our actions in a social and historical context. It is seen as assisting an individual in identifying group members, their motives and how best to operate within the social world of the group. In terms of human psychology, there is considerable interest in the nature of consciousness, particularly when applied to children or other individuals who demonstrate conscious states different from our own. This begins to lead us towards **theory of mind,** which explores how we develop an idea of another person's thoughts and feelings (see Chapter 17, and also Chapter 19 for a discussion about theory of mind hypotheses and autism).

1.5 OTHER INFLUENCES ON CHANGE

1.5.1 CULTURE

A criticism that is often used against evolutionary approaches in psychology is the issue of culture, and to what extent it can be explained in terms of our cognitive hardware (brains) and genetic factors. There is little doubt that humans are a cultural species and, as such, any attempt to examine human behaviour would be incomplete without acknowledging this. Despite this, it can be a difficult topic to study given that culture is a term that is used frequently in a wide range of contexts and with different meanings. There are three key questions that need to be considered prior to discussing culture from an evolutionary perspective.

1 What is the working definition of culture?
2 What are the units of culture, how are these transmitted and how do they evolve?
3 What is the relationship between biological evolution (genes) and cultural evolution?

The term *culture* can have many different connotations depending on the context within which it is studied. For many, culture is something aspirational and demonstrates a sophisticated level of understanding, mortality and appreciation of the world. For others, it is a shared set of values and beliefs within a society, or it could be considered as a behavioural variation that is passed down across generations via social learning. In terms of an evolutionary approach to studying culture, a good definition would be that 'culture is information that is acquired from other individuals via social transmission mechanisms such as imitation, teaching or language' (Mesoudi, 2011: 2–3). This definition highlights the social aspect of culture and distinguishes it from simply being an extension of our phenotype (i.e. a typical behaviour), acknowledging that culture is very much a social construct. One characteristic of culture is that it changes during transmission and these changes can be very rapid and viral in nature.

1.5.2 MEMES

Dawkins (1989) proposed that culture can be examined in terms of selection pressures by adopting the term *meme* to describe units of thought or culture that are then replicated in the brain. If culture is considered in terms of memes, then these units can be replicated; there can be variation and mutations in this memetic information, and more memes will exist than can successfully replicate as a consequence of environmental and competing social pressures. So what exactly is a meme? A meme can be anything from a single idea/thought to a specific ritual or way of preparing food. As such, a meme is a very flexible cultural unit in terms of what it actually encompasses. However, unlike genes, cultural transmission is not exclusively from parent to offspring, but also occurs horizontally via peers and social groups.

Susan Blackmore (1999) suggests that, in our evolutionary past, the increase in human brain size (neocortex ratio) can be accounted for by memetics. So, for example, once our ancestors had started to imitate behaviours, memes could be transmitted between individuals, and those individuals who were able to adopt specific memes that aided survival (perhaps the meme for fashioning stone tools from flint) would have had a greater chance of survival and greater reproductive success. Therefore, having the associated cognitive hardware to replicate memes and imitate behaviour would have been advantageous and provided behavioural flexibility, making those individuals thrive.

Similar to Dunbar's (1998) social brain hypothesis, the human cognitive system has evolved to deal with complex social information, but it is the ability to imitate cultural elements (which arguably could require gossip as a key transmission mechanism) that is driving reproductive success and therefore creating a strong meme–gene interaction.

So, although the actual meme might not be an evolved trait, the ability to propagate culture and imitate can be seen as an adaptive trait. However, as Dawkins (1989) points out, it is important to note that some memes can actually be detrimental to an individual's fitness, for example, some religious practices that involve chastity or abstinence. However, the benefits of the associated hardware (big brains) outweigh the costs of these anomalies in terms of the overall inclusive fitness of the gene pool at large.

Although the memetic approach to culture can provide a mechanism for understanding how the brain acts as a meme replication machine, allowing for cultural transmission, Boyd and Richerson (2005) provide a useful framework for examining how biologically-based mechanisms and the cultural ideas can both be seen as adaptive traits. According to the dual-inheritance model, culture is inherited in parallel with genetic inheritance. This frees up the concept that human evolution is solely the product of genetic change. In this model, there is an evolved social learning mechanism that will have developed as a result of natural selection, whereby it is beneficial to use a low-cost learning strategy such as imitation (rather than learning by individual trial and error).

There is also the cultural evolution process which is not genetic-based but follows the methods of transmission outlined earlier (horizontal and vertical). However, we now have to consider what affects the replication of specific behaviours. Two key biases are conformist bias and prestige bias, both of which provide a simple low-cost heuristic (rule of thumb) for adopting specific cultural traits. *Conformist bias*, whereby the most common behaviour within a group is imitated, results in the adoption of a particular behaviour or cultural trait based on the heuristic that an action can be perceived as advantageous if the majority of people use it. *Prestige bias* shifts the focus away from conforming with the group towards the characteristics of a particular person carrying out the behaviour, whereby if an individual appears to be successful (e.g. they might be wealthy, have many mates), then the way these individuals are acting could contribute to their perceived prestige.

So far, the relationship between genetics and culture has been unidirectional, in that the cognitive hardware is selected and this allows for the epiphenomenon of culture to evolve. However, when looking at the adaptive properties of cultural activities, it is clear that culture can influence our genetic evolution too. So many cultural practices, such as cooking, using tools and wearing clothes, can be seen as practices that, once adopted by the group, can change our environment or the extent to which the environment impacts upon our lives. This in turn is changing our resource requirements and the environmental pressures that natural selection acts upon, and therefore can impact on our phenotype.

Henrich and McElreath (2009) provide a nice example that summarises this. At some point in our ancestral past, the practice of cooking meat would have spread by social learning. This trait in itself is adaptive as it makes food easier to chew, easier to digest and kills harmful parasites. Over subsequent generations, the requirements for large teeth and large intestines to break down the food are no longer needed or favoured by natural selection, freeing up energy that can be used to develop larger brains. In this way, a cultural practice has modified the biology of the organism, and therefore the cultural evolution and natural selection are working reflexively with each other in changing the human phenotype.

Finally, it is important to note that not all cultural traits are adaptive. Examples of maladaptive cultural practices abound, and again many of these maladaptive traits can be acquired via inappropriate adoption of a conformist or prestige bias.

1.5.3 EPIGENETICS

Over the past few decades, there has been a wealth of studies looking at identical twins and to what extent certain traits (ranging from depression to vulnerability to diseases) are inherited due to shared genes. However, more recently it has been acknowledged that the old-fashioned view of one gene coding for one protein is actually wrong. One gene can account for several proteins and as such it becomes increasingly difficult to suggest that there are specific genes for specific traits. However, perhaps due to selective reporting, there has been an emphasis on the similarities between identical twins in terms of behaviour, personality and psychiatric disorders. What is often neglected is why in identical twins, who by definition should have identical sets of genes, there are so many differences. One argument is that this is due to the environment and that not all traits are inherited; some are acquired via experience. However, this does not explain why certain traits then appear to be inherited in later generations. Traditional gene-behaviour arguments would suggest that life experience cannot be inherited. Another argument is that some of these differences are **epigenetic**.

> **EPIGENETICS** The study of heritable changes in gene expression that occur without changes to the genotype (DNA). So traits (these can be physical and/or behavioural) that are inherited via epigenetics are not due to changes in the gene combinations, but are due to changes in whether a gene is actively expressed or not.

EXERCISE: WHAT INFLUENCES YOUR ADOPTION OF CULTURAL PRACTICES?

Consider the following cultural traits and decide whether your adoption of these traits is due to a conformist bias or prestige bias and whether or not they are adaptive or maladaptive (or perhaps neither adaptive nor maladaptive). Just to make you feel better, we will give you an example of a prestige bias in the 1970s, when there was a trend for wearing ridiculously high platform boots. Many celebrities and pop acts of the time wore them and, as such, there was prestige associated with them, with many people consequently adopting the trend (including one of the editors, ahem, PB), despite this being a maladaptive trait – as wearing these skyscraper heels increased the risk of falling over, vertigo and hitting your head on low doors.

So, looking at the list below, are you showing a conformist or a prestige bias when you make the following decisions?

1. Your choice of clothes to wear in the morning
2. Whether you choose to drink alcohol or not
3. Your choice of food in the evening
4. The music you listen to
5. Your religious beliefs

The epigenetic argument suggests that genes can be effectively switched off by a process called methylation. So, for example, let us say there is a set of identical twins where both individuals share a gene that is associated with happiness, yet only one of the twins actually exhibits the trait (i.e. is happy). The relevant gene in one of the twins could have been 'switched off' so they do not show the happy trait. This could be the result of methylation of the associated gene due to some life experience (e.g. a traumatic childhood accident).

What is interesting is that for a few generations this trait might be passed on in its shut-down form to offspring. Therefore, the happy twin will have happy children and the traumatised twin will have less happy children. If we revisit the yellow dung fly from the earlier example, it could be argued that perhaps the increase in testes size across the generations is an epigenetic response. In other words, the environment has had an effect on gene expression that is inherited. This does not mean the fly has lost the gene for normal-sized testes, but simply that it has been switched off in response to environmental pressures.

In evolutionary terms, epigenetic traits are of particular interest as they highlight how some traits can be temporarily passed on without an actual change in genes. Therefore, there has not been an evolutionary change in response to the environment as there is no mutation or change in genetic material across the generations, but instead some genes might not be expressed.

1.6 CHAPTER SUMMARY

We have seen how the development of science enabled people to explain the world around them, drawing upon empirical data. This allowed them to challenge superstitious beliefs with evidence gained from the natural sciences. Psychology has, at its heart, a commitment to empiricism. It also draws significantly from the sister biological disciplines of palaeoanthropology, neo-Darwinian evolutionary theory and behavioural genetics. The story of human evolution is the story of how our brain and our psychology have evolved alongside each other. Communication, problem-solving and tool-making are key abilities within our species. Evolutionary psychology can provide a framework for understanding why certain human behaviours have become widespread, and how our cognitive hardware has evolved in response to our physical environment, limited resources and social environment.

DISCUSSION QUESTIONS

Can you think of examples of our own, contemporary behaviour that may be explained from an evolutionary point of view? To help, think of what men tend to look for in their partners if they are attracted to the opposite sex, and contrast this with the signals women use to select men. To what extent do both sexes rate features in the same way? If not much, is this a case of different natural selection pressures applying to the sexes in making a mate choice?

 # SUGGESTIONS FOR FURTHER READING

Buss, D. (2008). *Evolutionary psychology: the new science of the mind* (3rd edn). Harlow: Pearson Higher Education. David Buss is one of the key people in the field of evolutionary psychology. The book is written in a style that engages you to consider the argument as an active reader. You are not told what to think but are invited to apply what you are reading to a range of questions that arise from the work he covers.

Dawkins, R. (1989). *The selfish gene* (3rd edn). Oxford: Oxford University Press. The modern evolutionary approach continues to have a significant impact on how behavioural scientists, including psychologists, think about the function and maintenance of behaviour. This is a classic and very readable text that helped promote the importance of neo-Darwinian thinking in relation to behaviour.

www.apa.org/science/genetics/. If you are interested in exploring further the relationship between genetics and behaviour, we recommend you visit the very helpful website hosted by the American Psychological Association.

 Still want more? For links to online resources relevant to this chapter and a quiz to test your understanding, visit the companion website at edge.sagepub.com/banyard2e

2

HOW PSYCHOLOGY BECAME A SCIENCE

Lead authors: Simon Watts and Philip Banyard

CHAPTER OUTLINE

2.1 Introduction — 22

2.2 Key moments in the emergence of modern psychology — 22

    2.2.1 Determinism — 22

    2.2.2 The riddle of our selves — 23

    2.2.3 An important decision for psychology — 24

2.3 Psychology as a study of the conscious mind: Helmholtz, Fechner, Wundt and a 'natural science of the mental' — 26

    2.3.1 Quantification — 26

    2.3.2 The introspective method — 28

2.4 Two alternative ways of founding psychology: Sigmund Freud and the unconscious, William James and functionalism — 29

    2.4.1 And in the USA . . . — 30

2.5 Conditioning: Watson, Pavlov, Skinner and the study of behaviour — 32

    2.5.1 Man and brute — 32

2.6 Modern psychology: cognitive science, humanism and the return of the social sciences — 34

2.7 Conclusion — 35

2.8 Chapter summary — 35

Discussion questions — 35

Suggestions for further reading — 36

2.1 INTRODUCTION

The history of psychology is not a straightforward tale. In fact, history is by no means an exact science: this means that the important stuff is inevitably a matter for interpretation and debate. What follows, therefore, is not *the* history of psychology, but *a* history. It's a history of psychology designed especially to introduce you to the main issues, concepts, people and debates that have helped to shape and define a fascinating and multifaceted discipline. Chapter 1 was about how we came to be human and we now move this on to look at how we came to develop theories of ourselves and our behaviour. It's a work in progress because there is so much to understand. Psychology has become an important part of the story of science and we will concentrate on that in this chapter.

FRAMING QUESTIONS

- How has the discipline of psychology developed? What have been the main stages in its development?
- To what extent has psychology developed as a natural science and to what extent as a social science?
- How have questions about what *type* of discipline psychology is affected what type of behaviour of experience we choose to study?

2.2 KEY MOMENTS IN THE EMERGENCE OF MODERN PSYCHOLOGY

The beginnings of modern psychology are usually traced to the year 1879. That's when **Wilhelm Wundt** (1832–1920) established the first dedicated psychological laboratory at Leipzig. The selection of this date is somewhat arbitrary. Wundt himself had, for example, highlighted the possibility of a distinct psychological discipline as early as 1862 (in his book *Contributions to the theory of sensory perception*). Yet the key events which led Wundt and others to this distinct discipline occurred even earlier.

Such events lie at the very heart of modern science, in the work of such great scientists as **Isaac Newton** (1642–1727) and **Charles Darwin** (1809–1882). Newton's work in physics had a profound influence on psychology. First, he developed a scientific 'method' consisting of observation, the formulation of hypotheses designed to predict events and outcomes, and the subsequent testing of these hypotheses through further observation. In this way, the scientific method worked towards the revelation of ever more general explanatory laws (Cushing, 1998). Such principles remain central to the scientific method that is used in psychology.

Second, and crucially, Newton had great success in applying these methods. He was able to offer an explanation of the entire physical universe based upon a limited number of basic laws (describing a limited number of basic 'forces'), each of which was expressed in a purely mathematical or quantitative form. In principle, it was thought that if you knew where all the physical bodies in the universe were at time *A*, Newton's laws would allow you to predict their future movements and hence to know (in advance) their respective locations at time *B*. Though this is a simplification, the basic point is that the behaviour of all physical bodies was shown to be lawful and knowledge of the laws appeared to make the subsequent trajectories and relative positions of these bodies entirely predictable. According to this theory, everything behaved in a mechanistic or machine-like fashion because the behaviour of everything was determined by the impact of the same set of basic forces.

2.2.1 DETERMINISM

This theory of mechanical **determinism** has been a strong influence on psychology. Newton's ideas also impacted on people in general. The pre-Newtonian worldview was characterised by its **anthropocentrism**. That is, people considered themselves to have a central and fundamental place in the universe. Newton's work brought this anthropocentrism into question. The universe was mechanical and its behaviour predetermined: it was 'as it was', regardless of our existence. Far from being central, people and their opinions and viewpoints appeared superfluous. The sense of alienation that resulted from this view was the key that opened the door to psychology. Alexandre Koyré captures this nicely:

> modern science . . . united and unified the universe. . . . But . . . it did this by substituting for our world of quality and sense perception, the world in which we live, and love, and die, another world . . . the world of quantity . . . a world in which though there is a place for everything, there is no place for man. Thus the world of science – the real world – became estranged and utterly divorced from the world of life. (Cited in Prigogine & Stengers, 1984: 35–36)

DETERMINISM The idea that every event, including human thought and behaviour, is causally determined by an unbroken chain of prior events. According to this idea, there are no mysterious miracles and no random events.

ANTHROPOCENTRISM OR **ANTHROCENTRISM** The belief that people (*anthro*) are the most important thing in the universe rather than the very small, here-today-gone-tomorrow little creatures that we are.

The point here is that Newton and his scientific methods – the modern mind at its best – solved the riddle of the universe, but in so doing produced a dramatic (and tragic) side-effect. They appeared to separate us from the universe. Serious questions followed about 'mind' itself, about where humans, and the qualities and perceptions of the everyday human world, fitted in. Our place in the bigger scheme of things was under threat. And, vitally for psychology, this threat made 'us' the next scientific riddle to be solved.

2.2.2 THE RIDDLE OF OUR SELVES

The 'riddle of our selves' became even more pressing following the publication of Darwin's *On the origin of species* in 1859. As we have seen, Newton had 'decentred' us and lessened our apparent importance. However, at least the principles of mechanical determinism remained and these were widely held to be 'consonant with the generally accepted theological belief in an omnipresent, omniscient God' (Cushing, 1998: 168). Newton himself stayed true to the belief that 'the mechanical universe required the active intervention of God, not just to create and order it, but also to maintain it' (1998: 168).

Darwin's theory of evolution by natural selection (see Chapter 1), on the other hand, sat far less comfortably with conventional religious ideas. In fact, it directly challenged them. Human beings, which Christian religion saw as the 'closest thing to God', became the 'nearest thing to apes' in the blink of a scientific eye (Figure 2.1). This was a bitter pill to swallow and one which **Sigmund Freud** (1856–1939) called 'the second great blow to the human ego' (following the Newtonian blow described earlier). Darwin's theory reignited debates about humans' fundamental nature. It was in the midst of this debate that Wundt's psychological laboratory was founded, just eight years after Darwin's publication of *The descent of man, and selection in relation to sex* (in 1871). It was a good time to be a psychologist.

FIGURE 2.1 AND FIGURE 2.2 The riddle of our selves. On the ceiling of the Sistine Chapel in Rome is a picture that shows one view of where people come from: God reaches out and creates the first man – Adam. Darwin's version would have Adam reaching back to touch his past – a monkey.

© Jim Zuckerman/Corbis and Frans Lanting/Corbis

2.2.3 AN IMPORTANT DECISION FOR PSYCHOLOGY

The previous section suggests that psychology emerged in order to solve the 'riddle of our selves'. Thanks to Newton, the discipline also appeared at a time when its most immediate subject matter (the human world of life, quality and sense perception) had been 'estranged and utterly divorced' from the *real* world that Newtonian science had begun to reveal. Our scientific approach has given us answers to many questions about how things work. We know something about how the planets move (the theory of gravity) and we know something about how our senses work (see Chapter 6). What is much more puzzling, however, is our own existence on this world and how we make sense of it. The contrasts in what we know and what we are still puzzling over is shown in Table 2.1.

The word *psychology* means 'a science of mind or soul', and the psychological world (psychology's most immediate subject matter) appears on the right of Table 2.1. It is worth remembering both these points as we proceed. For the moment, however, psychologists had to decide how best to study this subject matter. Two basic models presented themselves. On the one hand, there was Newton's natural science model, which employed **quantitative** research methods and pursued nomothetic knowledge as a priority (i.e. objective and lawful knowledge which is considered to be generally applicable). This system had triumphed in the physical world.

> **QUANTITATIVE DATA** Focus on numbers and frequencies rather than on meaning or experience.
>
> **QUALITATIVE DATA** Describe meaning and experience rather than providing numerical values for behaviour, such as frequency counts.

On the other hand, a social science model was also a possibility. This approach predominated in the humanities and was embodied by the German word *Geisteswissenschaft* (which means 'science of the spirit'). Under this model, the aim was to study humans, human life and human events by re-creating their meaning for the actors involved, in order to find out their *reasons* for doing what they were doing. To achieve this goal, **qualitative** research methods were generally employed and idiographic knowledge was pursued as a priority (i.e. subjective and specific knowledge of a person, event or situation which reveals that person, event or situation in its uniqueness).

This distinction (between the social and natural sciences) was popularised by the historian **Wilhelm Dilthey** (1833–1911). Dilthey offered clear advice to psychology. First, he acknowledged that humans and human events both possess important physical properties. As an example, your brain is a physical object and its physical properties are going to be pretty important if you want to think. I'm sure you'd realised that (see 'Aside'). This simple observation nonetheless creates a serious complication for psychology, because it means that our status as physical and material 'objects' has a massive effect on our capacity to be psychological. In other words, in order to fully grasp the psychological world (captured on the right of Table 2.1), the discipline of psychology must also engage with aspects of the physical world (captured on the left of Table 2.1). This latter task demands a natural scientific

TABLE 2.1 The big riddles. The universe that Newtonian science dealt with is on the left. The universe it missed out is on the right. Consider the opposing categories carefully. The dualism they represent has been fundamental to psychology and to Western thought and culture more generally

THE RIDDLE OF THE UNIVERSE	THE RIDDLE OF OUR SELVES
The world of *science*	The world of *life*
The *real* world	The *perceived* world
The *objective* world	The *subjective* world
The world of *quantity*	The world of *quality*
The *physical* world	The *psychological* world
The *somatic* world	The *semantic* world
The world *as it is*	The world *as it is experienced!*
A science of *matter*	A science of *mind [and of things that matter!]*

ASIDE

Thinking about thinking

Had you realised that 'thinking' (biologically speaking) involves the passage of electrical impulses through the nerve cells of the brain and the chemical transmission of those impulses across lots of tiny 'gaps' between the nerve cells called **synapses**? If you were to start counting the synapses now, at a rate of one per second, you would finish in approximately *30 million* years time. The brain is extraordinary. The number of possible pathways available to the brain's electrical impulses (and hence the possibilities for thought) are *greater than the number of atoms in the known universe*.

And to go a step further, when we describe these electrical impulses we are using an entirely different language from the language we use to describe thinking. Will it ever be possible to match up these two descriptions of the same event and connect the internal experience with the external observation?

approach. But while psychology cannot avoid our physical or somatic properties (the latter means 'of the body'), Dilthey also warned that:

> explaining human actions is fundamentally different from explaining physical events. A woman shooting a man is a physical event. However, understanding the event in human terms involves more than tracing the path of the bullet and showing how the bullet caused the man's death. We need to know *why* she shot the man, not just *how* she did so. (Leahey, 2004: 248)

'Why' questions are central to psychology. The brain, for example, is a good way of explaining *how* we think but not *why* we do it. It doesn't cause us to think, any more than having legs causes us to run. In the same way, any rigorous psychological explanation of running would require that we understand *why* the running is taking place and not just *how* it is taking place (the latter presumably involving a series of neuronal signals leading to a more or less rapid movement of the legs).

Dilthey wanted psychology to remember that its primary subject matter was the subjective or psychological world itself, not just the physical properties that made this world possible. Dilthey suggested that if we want to find out 'why', priority must be given to the psychological world – the ways that people make sense of their experience and the meanings they attach to them. In other words, to understand why I am running, you will first need to understand my experience of the current situation and the meanings I assign to it, because only in this way can you find out my motives and reasons for acting. This task demands a social scientific approach.

So what should psychology do? If the psychological world was its proper subject matter, then surely psychology was a humanitarian discipline? For this reason, Dilthey felt a social scientific approach was preferable. But the psychological world can only exist through the physical world. If I don't have a physical body I can't see or hear, for example. Psychology couldn't ignore this either. It needed to study the physical world as well and the natural scientific model dominated in this domain.

This double-edged nature of psychology was (and remains) both a challenge and an opportunity. Psychology had the chance to bridge the divide between the natural and social sciences and it could do so by retaining a foot in both camps (Danziger, 1990). **Nomothetic** and **idiographic** knowledge, quantitative and qualitative methods, could all be embraced. It needed to study its subject matter from both perspectives. Wilhelm Wundt tried to support this vision (as did other early psychologists), but it was not a vision that psychology would ultimately sustain. As we're about to see, psychology was intent on becoming a natural science.

NOMOTHETIC AND IDIOGRAPHIC MEASURES
Nomothetic approaches look for laws of behaviour and collect measures that can be observed and verified and quantified. They are concerned with averages and norms. By contrast, idiographic approaches look for unique and individual experiences.

'NOMOTHETIC FALLACY' The common belief that if you can name a problem then you have solved it. For example, if you feel very upset and someone says you have post-traumatic stress, you still feel upset.

2.3 PSYCHOLOGY AS A STUDY OF THE CONSCIOUS MIND: HELMHOLTZ, FECHNER, WUNDT AND A 'NATURAL SCIENCE OF THE MENTAL'

All things being equal, psychology in the late nineteenth century is probably best categorised as one of the humanities (Windelband, 1894/1998). And the subject matter left to it by the natural sciences – the psychological and inherently subjective world of perception, quality and experience – probably required the application of methods traditionally associated with the social sciences. But all things were not equal. The unprecedented success of the natural science model had a big influence on the emergence of psychology. It also established the view that natural scientific methods were 'the only reliable methods for securing useful and reliable knowledge about anything' (Danziger, 1990: 41). In order to flourish, psychology *had* to align itself with the methods of the natural sciences.

This conclusion was nonetheless complicated by a long-standing philosophical belief that subjective, mental phenomena were not amenable to natural scientific analysis. **Immanuel Kant** (1724–1804), for example, had rejected the possibility of a 'science of mind' on the grounds that mental phenomena (1) had no spatial dimension, (2) were too transient to observe, and (3) could not be experimentally manipulated in a controlled fashion. Overall, Kant concluded that mental phenomena couldn't be mathematically analysed or described (Fancher, 1996). Such phenomena, he felt, could only ever support a qualitative and philosophical analysis.

> **REDUCTIONISM** Curt describes reductionism as 'the attempt to reduce or "boil down" any complex phenomenon into the simple elements which are thought to constitute it or cause it' (1994: 241).
>
> **MATERIALISM** Philosophically speaking, materialism encapsulates the view that the world/universe is entirely constituted of matter. This view leaves little room for the psychological world. Materialism is sometimes also known as 'physicalism'.

To overcome this barrier, psychology exploited the fact that our psychological world is connected to our physical properties. Earlier, we suggested (as a means of explaining Dilthey's arguments) that the brain does not cause us to think. But if the brain doesn't cause us to think, then what does? So psychology went along with the idea that all mental phenomena could, in fact, be explained in terms of physiological causes. This double whammy of **reductionism** and **materialism** reduced the psychological world to a by-product of the physiological properties which produced it. It also neatly sidestepped Kant's objections. As a by-product, subjective mental phenomena were no longer psychology's primary subject matter; physiology was. And natural scientific methods operated very comfortably in this physical domain. As Leahey puts it:

> by insisting that the nervous system is the basis of all mentality, and by defining psychology as the investigation of the physiological conditions of conscious events, the new field . . . could establish itself as a [natural] science. (Leahey, 2004: 235)

But defining psychology in this way was not enough. Establishing psychology as a natural science also demanded that psychological experimentation be carried out in the same way as the natural sciences, and this in turn demanded that psychological phenomena be mathematically measured and described. This was now to involve the 'investigation of the physiological conditions of conscious events' (rather than the events themselves), yet those conditions would still have to be counted and measured.

2.3.1 QUANTIFICATION

The first attempts at counting and measuring in psychology, otherwise known as quantification, were developed by a number of people in a number of different ways. In 1850 **Hermann von Helmholtz** (1821–1894), an eminent natural scientist, demonstrated that nerve impulses travelled at finite speeds which could be measured in terms of *reaction times*. He did this by passing electric currents through the severed leg of a frog. He also established the psychological principle that human perception (by which he implied the psychological reality we experience) was not a simple replication of the physical reality captured by our senses. Helmholtz proposed instead that sensations were *transformed* into perceptions in a mechanical and lawful fashion by the physiological machinery of our minds.

F.C. Donders (1818–1889) built upon Helmholtz's reaction-time work. Donders realised that the time between the presentation of a stimulus and a person's response to it could be used as a quantifiable measure of the speed of physiological and mental processes (processes which could not otherwise be observed). It was even possible, by making a person choose between two stimuli, to ascertain the exact duration of a mental judgement. This act of quantification (which became known as *mental chronometry*) was exactly what psychology needed if it was to distinguish itself as a natural science.

Gustav Fechner (1801–1887) quantified psychological phenomena in a different way. Like Helmholtz, Fechner had noticed that the information gathered by our senses was processed and transformed *before* it reached conscious awareness. In particular, he observed that the *perceived* intensity of a physical stimulus did not perfectly reflect its *physical* intensity. A lighted match would, for example, appear to be brighter when it was placed against a dark background. If, Fechner surmised, we could somehow measure the physical *and* the perceived intensity of the stimulus, it might become possible to mathematically determine their relationship (and hence to mathematically connect the psychological and physical worlds).

But how could we measure the perceived intensity? Fechner realised that you couldn't quantify it directly or as an absolute value. What you could do, however, was quantify the smallest *perceptual discrimination* people are capable of making, and you could do this as a function of changes in the physical intensity itself. Let's say, for example, that I put a weight in your right hand and its physical intensity is 100 grams. What is its perceived intensity? There is of course no pure mathematical answer. So suppose I start putting weights into your left hand, one by one – 101 grams, 102, 103, and so on. The question becomes, 'At what weight can you perceive a difference (or discriminate) between the two weights?'. And, thanks to Fechner, we know the answer. On average it's when the weight in your left hand is 1/30th (or 3.33%) heavier or lighter than the weight in your right (or, in our example, when the weight in your left hand is 103.33 grams or more). Fechner called this perceived change in intensity a 'just noticeable difference' (or JND) and it constituted a quantitative measure of perceived intensity.

Fechner was able to measure the JND across a range of sensory functions and to graphically represent the relationship between physical and perceived stimulus intensities in each case. He also demonstrated that the relationship between physical and perceived intensity could *always* be expressed via a single mathematical formula. In truth, this law was anything but perfect. Nonetheless, Fechner's psychophysical experiments had clearly shown that: (1) the content of the psychological world could be manipulated by controlling the stimuli presented to it; (2) while such content might actually represent a subjective 'distortion' of the physical world, such distortion was nevertheless carried out (by our physiology) in a mechanical and lawful fashion; and (3) as a result, the content of the psychological world could be shown to have a lawful and quantifiable relationship with the content of the physical world.

Other important work on counting and measuring psychological qualities was occurring at roughly the same time. Perhaps the most notable was the development of mental and intelligence testing procedures, via the work of **Francis Galton** (1822–1911) in Britain (see key researcher box and also Chapter 22), **Alfred Binet** (1857–1911) in France (see Chapter 22) and America, and latterly **William Stern** (1871–1938) in Germany. The truth is, then, that the new discipline's desire to become a 'natural science of the mental' was already well established before Wundt's laboratory ever appeared.

Wundt had indeed called his first taught course in psychology 'Psychology as a natural science' (in 1862), and both mental chronometry and Fechner-like experiments quickly characterised the work of Wundt's laboratory at Leipzig. Yet, in common with most German academics, Wundt remained a strong advocate of the distinction between the *Natur-* and *Geisteswissenschaften* (natural and social sciences), and his general approach recognised that psychology stood at the point of transition between the two. This is not surprising because Wundt had been employed at Leipzig to teach philosophy and to teach psychology as a part of that humanitarian discipline (Leahey, 2004). His methodological

EXERCISE: SENSATION AND PERCEPTION

Take a box of matches. Light one of the matches and hold it up in front of a light background. How bright does it look? Try to put a number on your judgement of brightness (your perception). Now light another match in front of a different coloured background. How bright does that look?

The amount of light from the two matches will be the same (sensation) but your judgement might well be different. Try this out with a number of backgrounds and explore the factors that change your perception. By the way, try not to burn down your house during this exercise.

KEY RESEARCHER Francis Galton (1822–1911)

FIGURE 2.3   Francis Galton

© Bettmann/CORBIS

Elsewhere in this text we have highlighted the work of contemporary psychologists, but in this chapter about the history of the subject we have chosen to look at an historical figure. Galton was a cousin of Charles Darwin and shared his interest in science. He contributed to a wide range of scientific areas and we mention him here because of the range of techniques and concepts that he developed (see Fancher, 1996), including:

- *Self-report questionnaires*: in 1873 Galton wrote to all the Fellows of the Royal Society (eminent scientists) with a lengthy questionnaire to discover the common features of people who are successful in science.
- *Twin studies*: he devised the first of these, as well as carrying out the first comparison of the resemblance of natural and adopted children to their parents.
- *Eugenics*: the term describing the attempt to breed a superior group of people was also invented by Galton.
- *Scatterplots*: Galton wanted to find ways to present his data on family resemblances and he devised the scatterplot.
- *Statistics*: Galton developed his scatterplots and also developed regression lines and the correlation co-efficient.

The above is a phenomenal list, but it is only a selection of his output and you can add *word association* to it. Galton devised a word association technique and the paper he wrote on this was read by Freud and contributed to the development of one of the major techniques of psychoanalysis. Oh, and he also produced the first weather map. We'll consider more of Galton's influence when we look at the heritability of intelligence in Chapter 22.

In 1884 Galton created a mental testing laboratory in the Natural History Museum (in Kensington) where he collected anthropometric measures such as visual acuity, strength of grip, colour vision, hearing acuity, hand preference etc., from the visitors to the exhibition who, incidentally, paid Galton for the privilege. He hoped to use these measures to estimate people's hereditary intelligence. Before Galton, psychology had been looking for general principles of experience. By contrast, Galton's anthropometric laboratory looked for individual differences. Although we would not recognise Galton's tests and measures of mental abilities today, they do mark the beginning of mental testing.

approach duly combined the new methods of quantification described above with a more traditional method called *introspection*, which had been employed by the 'old-fashioned philosophical psychology … to reveal the contents and workings of the mind' (2004: 237).

2.3.2 THE INTROSPECTIVE METHOD

In 1873, Wundt's *Principles of physiological psychology* described the emerging discipline of psychology. It combined physiology, which 'informs us about those life phenomena that we perceive by our external senses', with a psychological and introspective approach in which 'the person looks upon himself from within' (1873: 157). The introspective method, which relied on a process of self-report about the 'goings-on' in one's psychological world, had previously been dismissed by scientists and philosophers alike because of its unreliability and inherent subjectivity. Wundt himself doubted its effectiveness. He had responded, however, by trying to transform this unreliable act of internal perception into something akin to scientific observation (Danziger, 1990).

To do this, Wundt restricted his so-called physiological psychology to the study of processes that were simultaneously accessible to both internal and external acts of observation. In practice, a stimulus was presented to a participant and quantified response measures were gathered at the same time as subjective reports of the conscious content elicited by the stimulus (Figure 2.4). In this way, the introspective data always appeared alongside the more important objective measures. In order to control the style of the introspective reports they were only collected from trained researchers. This move was clever in as much as it gave introspection a new status as a special skill. Only a trained scientist could carry out these scientific observations with sufficient reliability. Despite this, the qualitative data introspection produced were still not accepted as a basis for knowledge claims. Only quantitative data could do that.

These many restrictions limited Wundt to the study of psychological processes on the edge of conscious experience: basically, sensation, perception and motor responses. But this did not concern Wundt, for he considered these to be the only processes properly accessible to natural scientific analysis and the only ones directly and mechanistically caused by physiological processes. Higher-order mental processes (complex thought, memory, voluntary effort, creativity, etc.) were, for Wundt, part of a distinct psychic causality, and they were caused not by physiology, but by an underlying layer of unconscious psychological mechanisms. These mechanisms were said to be qualitative in nature and for this reason Wundt

FIGURE 2.4 Wundt (right) in his laboratory in Leipzig: the team are shown taking part in a joke-telling experiment

felt they would always resist experimental or natural scientific analysis. Non-experimental approaches would also be required.

Wundt spent the last 20 years of his life developing his *Völkerpsychologie*, that is a kind of historical and comparative psychology which looked at people as part of a collective and which tried to understand them within their social, cultural and communal context. Wundt believed these historical, qualitative and distinctly social scientific analyses were a very necessary addition to experimental studies of individual people in the laboratory. He felt strongly that the 'experimental method plus *Völkerpsychologie* would furnish a complete, albeit not completely natural-scientific, psychology' (Leahey, 2004: 239).

Few agreed: Wundt's desire for psychology to retain links with the humanities was at odds with the prevailing vision. Psychology wanted to be a natural science completely. **Hermann Ebbinghaus** (1850–1909) had already demonstrated (in 1879) that the higher-order mental process of memory could potentially be made accessible to experiment (Fancher, 1996) and Wundt's influence was waning. He died in 1920 along with many of his ideas.

Introspection, meanwhile, was to flourish in the work of two of Wundt's students, **Oswald Külpe** (1862–1915) and **Edward Titchener** (1867–1927). Both the Würzburg School of systematic introspection established by Külpe and Titchener's 'structural psychology' relieved introspection of its restrictions. Memory, thinking and complex feelings became legitimate topics for introspective analysis and the resulting qualitative data took centre stage. Titchener described these changes in 1912:

> The experimenter of the early nineties trusted, first of all, in his instruments . . . [which were] of more importance than the observer. . . . There were still vast reaches of mental life which experiment had not touched. . . . Now . . . we have changed all that. The movement towards qualitative analysis has culminated in what is called . . . the method of 'systematic experimental introspection'. (Cited in Danziger, 1990: 43)

Yet this was ultimately a backward step. Simply calling introspection 'systematic' and 'experimental' could not hide the fact that psychology's subject matter had once again drawn the discipline away from the natural sciences and back towards the humanities. As Titchener's experimental psychology explored the 'vast reaches of mental life', so a qualitative analysis along the lines of the old philosophical psychology had reappeared. The first attempts to establish a natural science of the mental had reached a dead end. Alternatives were required.

2.4 TWO ALTERNATIVE WAYS OF FOUNDING PSYCHOLOGY: SIGMUND FREUD AND THE UNCONSCIOUS, WILLIAM JAMES AND FUNCTIONALISM

In truth, the work of Sigmund Freud is something of a distraction in a chapter about psychological science. Had Freud's work developed differently, this might not have been the case: when in 1894/1895 Freud was writing his *Project for a*

ASIDE

Hysteria

Hysteria is a condition in which physical symptoms appear in the absence of any obvious physical cause.

Today, hysteria might well be called a dissociative disorder. In Freud's time, only women were thought to be hysterical. Nice. This is a prime example of the masculine bias which has long afflicted psychology.

In fact, Freud initially proposed (*very* controversially) that all hysterics had suffered sexual abuse in childhood. He later retracted this 'seduction theory' of hysteria. He nonetheless retained the belief that many of the hysteric's 'potentially damaging' ideas and desires were of a sexual nature and that much of *everybody's* behaviour was driven by the repression of such sexual desires.

scientific psychology he 'defined his Newtonian "intention … to furnish a psychology that shall be a natural science: that is, to represent psychical processes as quantitatively determinate states of specifiable material particles"' (cited in Leahey, 2004: 267). This statement, early in Freud's work, was reminiscent of Wundt's view. Yet Freud was to depart dramatically from these intentions.

Freud's work in psychology began with an interest in **hysteria**, a complaint in which physical symptoms appeared in the absence of any obvious physical cause, and his psychoanalytic approach emerged as a therapy to deal with this problem. He believed the physical symptoms were caused by unconscious (and potentially damaging) psychological memories, needs or desires, as they made themselves manifest in the hysteric's behaviour. Psychoanalysis itself was a 'talking cure' in which patients voiced their problems and feelings under the guidance of a therapist, with the aim of bringing the hitherto unconscious desires into conscious awareness.

On the basis of just six case studies of psychoanalytic therapy (of which only two were claimed as successes) and a process of self-analysis, Freud came to the conclusion that all human behaviour was caused by psychological drives and events occurring in the unconscious mind (and were of a primarily sexual and pleasure-seeking nature). In non-hysterics, Freud saw dreams as the primary means of uncovering and interpreting this unconscious content (and he regarded his 1900 publication *The interpretation of dreams* as his master work).

Freud undoubtedly wanted psychoanalysis to be a science. Yet most of his claims about the nature and influence of the unconscious mind have never been substantiated by scientific evidence. He did not try 'to create an experimental psychology of the unconscious, nor did he welcome attempts to scientifically verify his ideas' (Leahey, 2004: 265). As a result, Freud's ideas have generally been vilified by a psychological discipline intent on emulating the natural sciences (Eysenck, 2004).

It is nonetheless important to acknowledge the huge popularity of psychoanalysis. Freud's ideas and concepts have also greatly influenced 'contemporary ways of thinking about human feelings and conduct' (Gay, 1989: xii). It may not be science, but Freud's conceptual scheme clearly remains a compelling means of reading and interpreting human behaviour. Psychology was also affected by Freud in two further ways. First, his ideas led the way into abnormal psychology (and studies of mental health); and second, they showed that psychology was not just an academic discipline, but also an *applied* and therapeutic one. The psychologist could be a scientist and/or the practitioner.

2.4.1 AND IN THE USA . . .

This tension between academic and applied psychology was first noted by **William James** (1842–1910). James was to American psychology what Wundt had been in Europe: a founding father for the new discipline. He was initially impressed by the work of Wundt and the German physiological psychologists. The mechanical, causal explanations they offered and the idea that psychology might be based upon natural scientific principles excited him intellectually. On the other hand, he found its implications quite distressing from a spiritual perspective. And you can see his point. Are we really so mechanical and predictable? Are we really so controlled by our physiology? For James, such explanations left little room for the expression of human choice, creativity and free will.

EXERCISE: DO YOU HAVE FREE WILL?

The free will versus determinism debate remains a key argument for psychologists. Is our behaviour determined by physiology, unconscious forces or even environmental influences? Or are we free to act according to our own free will? It's a tricky one, but in everyday life we tend to fall down on the free will side of the debate.

Try this one out on family and friends. Try using determinist arguments to get yourself out of tricky situations like crashing your mum's car. For example, try saying 'I couldn't help myself, I was born that way', or 'I was just responding to the flux of neurochemicals washing around my brain'. If you get a response that is anything other than a two-word sentence where the second word is 'off', then let us know. That's how much people don't believe in determinism.

James's resolution of this personal conflict is ultimately central to understanding his later work. He decided that it was useful to accept mechanistic explanations in a scientific context. He even accepted that psychology had little choice but to progress in this direction. But this didn't mean he had to think and behave in a predictable and determined fashion. In this personal context, he would live creatively and with free will. This course of action, which rested on the principle that an idea may be true or have utility only in a specific context, was to become a central feature of James's later career in philosophy.

This personal accent on free will and his ultimate preference for philosophy also hint at James's subsequent attitude to psychology. In his much acclaimed *Principles of psychology* (1890), James strongly criticised the experimental and structural approach to psychology he associated with Wundt and Titchener. This approach was, for James, both very reductive and a bore! Its pursuit of basic mental structures or elements involved a wholly artificial and barbaric dissection of mental life. In contrast, James emphasised the continuous, indivisible and ever-changing nature of mental life via his concept of the stream of consciousness. He saw consciousness as both selective and functional. It was selective in so far as it evolved in order to help people choose (between various courses of action) and it was functional in as much as these choices were vital in helping the individual adapt to their environment.

European psychology had founded itself on the principles of Newtonian science and this allegiance created a focus on mental structures and underlying explanatory mechanisms. James's emphasis on the functional and adaptive significance of consciousness demonstrates the alternative but 'powerful influence of Darwin on early U.S. scientific psychology' (Hergenhahn, 2005: 313). From around 1900, American psychology steadily moved away 'from the traditional psychology of conscious content … toward a psychology of mental adjustment inspired by evolutionary theory' (Leahey, 2004: 341–342).

This movement inspired important changes in the view of psychology and its subject matter. First, the conscious mind came to be understood as just another biological adaptation. It existed because it served an evolutionary function, and that function was to enable people to adapt their behaviour in relation to their current circumstances. Given this association of mind with biology, it is not surprising to find that mind and body, and particularly mind and behaviour, were increasingly viewed as inseparable and synonymous entities. Mind was an 'outgrowth of conduct, a superior and more direct means of adjusting the organism to the environment' (Bolton, 1902, cited in Leahey, 2004: 343). In a very real sense, mind *became* action.

This theoretical shift initially showed itself in renewed attempts by psychologists to make psychology useful in an applied and therapeutic way. Psychology, it was felt, had to have a practical *function*. And it could achieve this by bringing about improvements in education and learning, by intervening in matters of abnormal psychology (now increasingly defined as maladaptive behaviour), and by bringing about human and societal betterment through these interventions. If mind involved mental adjustment, psychology could help us adjust more profitably. The Great War (1914–1918), so damaging in so many ways, actually gave applied psychology a tremendous boost. The mental testing procedures of Galton and Binet, exploited most famously in America by **James McKeen Cattell** (1860–1944), thrived in this sort of applied environment. And they have done so ever since. These methods have formed the basis of an individual differences tradition in psychology. Section F in this text will tell you all you need to know.

But this applied success, while welcome, still failed to satisfy the natural scientific and experimental ideal that the academic discipline held so dear. This needed to be remedied. If mind *is* action, the argument went, then a person's psychological world was freely observable and accessible in the physical world by simple reference to what they do. Experimental psychology was about to start a new life, most 'satisfactorily defined as the science of human behaviour' (Pillsbury, 1911: 1).

THE FOUNDATIONS OF MODERN PSYCHOLOGY

2.5 CONDITIONING: WATSON, PAVLOV, SKINNER AND THE STUDY OF BEHAVIOUR

In 1913, **John B. Watson** (1878–1958) laid out an aggressive manifesto for this science of human behaviour in a paper entitled 'Psychology as the behaviorist views it':

> Psychology as the behaviorist views it is a purely objective branch of natural science. Its . . . goal is the prediction and control of behavior. Introspection forms no essential part of its methods, nor is the scientific value of its data dependent on the readiness with which they lend themselves to interpretation in terms of consciousness. The behaviorist . . . recognizes no dividing line between man and brute. (Watson, 1913: 158)

FUNCTIONALISM In the philosophy of mind, functionalism refers to the idea that mental states can be defined by their causes and effects.

BEHAVIOURISM A school of thought which holds that the observation and description of overt behaviour is all that is needed to comprehend the human being, and that manipulation of stimulus–response contingencies is all that is needed to change human behaviour.

This all seems quite straightforward. Introspection had reached a scientific impasse and the functionalists had begun to see mind as synonymous with behaviour. As one might predict, therefore, Watson's rejection of introspection caused little argument. Watson's technology of behaviour also set out to ignore the facts of consciousness, and for this reason even Titchener (the undisputed champion of introspection) did not see it as competition. It just wasn't psychology. Yet most psychologists trained in the ways of **functionalism** were quite happy to accept a form of methodological **behaviourism** which allowed them to acknowledge the presence of conscious experience, but also to ignore it as something hopelessly unsuited to scientific analyses.

The use of mentalistic terminology such as 'the mind' or 'consciousness' did indeed become more and more problematic for psychologists over the next decade or so. For the strict behaviourist, consciousness had no place in the discipline or in human life more generally. Behavioural adaptation was not a function of consciousness; it was instead a function of our capacity to learn.

This principle had already been demonstrated by **Edward Thorndike** (1874–1949) and perhaps more famously by **Ivan Pavlov** (1849–1936). Pavlov received a Nobel Prize for work which exploited the (delightful) fact that dogs salivate at the merest expectation of food. Pavlov demonstrated, by repeatedly pairing a particular stimulus (the food) with a sound (famously a bell, but more probably a metronome), that his dogs would eventually salivate in response to the sound alone. They had, in other words, learned to connect the food (known as the unconditioned stimulus) with the sound (or conditioned stimulus). This form of learning, in which new stimulus–response connections were created, became known as classical conditioning. Thorndike, on the other hand, showed through a series of clever 'puzzle box' experiments that animals could be trained to produce a specific behavioural response more frequently if that response elicited a tangible reward. This form of learning, which could be used to strengthen (or weaken) pre-existing response tendencies, became known as operant conditioning.

2.5.1 MAN AND BRUTE

These animal studies nonetheless became directly applicable to psychology only when Watson, in true Darwinian style, forcefully pointed out that 'man and brute' were no longer seen as divided. Watson argued that, because we are animals, so the study of other, simpler, animals could shed light on the way humans function. Following this emphasis on learning, Watson was also able to argue that 'instinct' was another concept that psychology could do without. We began life as a blank slate (with no personality, no intelligence – just a mental blank canvas) and everything we subsequently did, all our knowledge and skills, was the result of processes of learning or deliberate training. And the latter, the training and ultimate control of behaviour, was now the central aim of the psychologist. As Watson (1930) put it, we 'can build any man, starting at birth, into any kind of social or a-social being upon order' (cited in Leahey, 2004: 377).

KEY STUDY

Watson, J., & Rayner, R. (1920). Conditioned emotional reactions. *Journal of Experimental Psychology, 3*, 1–14.

Given the historical nature of this chapter we have gone for a historical classic as a key study. It appears in many introductory texts, and despite the controversial nature of the study is still very well known.

Watson and Rayner wanted to demonstrate that behaviourist theory could be applied to humans and set out to show that fear can be learnt. The sole participant in the study was an infant referred to in the text as Albert B (more popularly known as Little Albert). Using the principles of classical conditioning Watson and Rayner made a loud noise near to the baby by banging a hammer on metal at the same time that they showed him a white rat. They did this just nine times over a three-week period and this was enough to create an aversion in the child to the white rat and also to other things that had rat-like features, such as rabbits, fluffy toys and a man in a Santa Claus mask.

Albert's behaviour, as recorded by Watson and Rayner, suggested that emotional responses to stimuli can be learnt. Before conditioning, Albert demonstrated no fear of the white rat; after conditioning he did appear to be afraid of it.

The study is cited very widely in psychological literature despite it being based on the evidence from one case. Interestingly, it is often incorrectly reported in many textbooks with some adding a happy ending by suggesting that Albert's fear was deconditioned by Watson and Rayner. Harris (1979) reviewed the various descriptions of this study that appear in the psychological literature and suggested that the story of Little Albert has developed like a myth, with each generation of psychologists retelling the story to illustrate their own position.

Behaviourism reached its height between 1930 and 1950 and is now most prominently associated with the work of **B.F. Skinner** (1904–1990). Skinner developed Thorndike's ideas into a fuller theory of operant aka instrumental conditioning. Using similar apparatus, he focused on *contingencies of reinforcement*: in other words, the nature and specific patterns of reward-giving through which spontaneously emitted and random behaviours (or operants) could best be 'shaped' into direct, learned (or conditioned) responses. Theoretically, Skinner shared Watson's radical behaviourism: he stressed the determining influence of environmental influences on behaviour, while excluding all reference to mental states (Hergenhahn, 2005).

In two philosophical publications (*Walden two*, published in 1948, and *Beyond freedom and dignity*, in 1971), Skinner also explored the ultimate behaviourist vision of a utopian society in which people 'were conditioned into socially admirable ways of acting' (Harré, 2006: 18). In this brave new world, people would be rewarded for good behaviour and the society would be ordered, productive and calm. Crime would be low and happiness would be everywhere. It's easy to mock this ambition, but if we could create a better and happier world by engineering the rewards that people got for their behaviour, then at first glance this might appear to be a good idea. Further reflection, however, reveals a serious flaw with this ambition in that someone has to decide what constitutes a 'better' or 'happier' world and also what behaviours are worthy of reward. We could end up with a Ministry of Happiness run by psychologists in a world with no dissent and no challenge to authority.

Skinner and behaviourism were both enormously important. Skinner was voted the most influential psychologist of the twentieth century by other psychologists (Dittman, 2002). The methodological approach associated with behaviourism, which promoted 'a causal metaphysics, an experimental methodology based upon independent and dependent

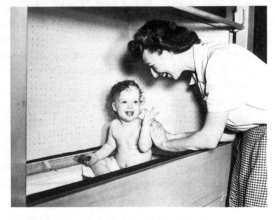

FIGURE 2.5   The human Skinner box. Skinner applied his science to designing a living box for babies. Called the 'air crib', it provided a temperature- and humidity-controlled environment that was relatively dust free. It captured the public imagination because it looked like an attempt to mechanise child care but nothing could have been further from the truth, as confirmed by his daughter Deborah as an adult (see her article in *The Guardian*, Skinner-Buzan, 2004)

© Bettmann/CORBIS

GESTALT PSYCHOLOGY A school of psychology that began in Germany in the first half of the twentieth century. It proposed that an experience or behaviour can only be understood as a whole, not by understanding the individual constituent parts.

variables applied to a population and the use of statistics as the main analytical tool', is still used by the discipline as *the* benchmark for 'what a scientific psychology should be' (Harré, 2006: 8). The classes in research methods that you attend will no doubt confirm that this methodology is still very much alive and well in psychology.

Eventually, however, the influence of behaviourism itself began to give way. In Europe in particular, work in a more traditional psychological vein (with a focus on active mental processes) had continued throughout the period of behaviourist domination. **Frederic Bartlett's** (1886–1969) work on *Remembering* (1932) and **Jean Piaget's** (1896–1980) approach to cognitive development are good examples, as is the work of the **Gestalt psychologists**. Even in the midst of American behaviourism, influential theorists like **Edward Chace Tolman** (1886–1959) and **Clark Leonard Hull** (1884–1952) also promoted the idea that mental processes played a fundamental role in the determination of behaviour. Both acknowledged these processes as 'intervening variables' (so called because they intervened between the stimulus and response) in their respective behaviourist theories.

In the end, the demise of behaviourism was almost inevitable. It had always been problematic to draw conclusions about humans on the basis of animal studies. Animals often behaved in an apparently mindless fashion, but this needn't mean that humans were similarly without minds. The image of humans as pawns in the environment also seemed unnecessarily negative. It is a depressing view of humanity if we think of ourselves as being puppets that are manipulated by changes in our environment.

The most damning indictment of behaviourism was nonetheless painfully straightforward: it wasn't psychology. Psychology, after all, means the study of mind, so abandoning that concept really did create a problem and limit the areas that psychology could investigate. We have seen throughout this chapter that psychology has tended (for mainly methodological reasons) to sidestep what may be its key subject matter: the subjective world of mental phenomena. But behaviourism took this avoidance to its logical conclusion. In the final section we will briefly consider modern attempts to put this right.

2.6 MODERN PSYCHOLOGY: COGNITIVE SCIENCE, HUMANISM AND THE RETURN OF THE SOCIAL SCIENCES

In the middle of the last century behaviourism ran out of steam, and it became obvious that we needed to look at the thought processes that intervene between stimulus and response. It was no longer enough to see us as puppets just responding to whatever stimulus came our way. Cognitive science (the study of mental processes) took over from behaviourism as the dominant paradigm in psychology around 1960 and it remains dominant to this day. A benefit of this is that cognitive science's tendency to exploit the behaviourist experimental model, combined with a focus on information processing, has made psychology look like a 'natural science of the mental' once again. It has made a significant contribution to the discipline's progress in recent years (the cognitive approach is dealt with in Section B).

On the downside, many psychologists would argue that cognitive science has again avoided the psychological world of subjective, mental phenomena in order to study a whole host of supposedly more permanent mental and causal structures which are said to lie beneath. These structures have various names – traits, attitudes, schemas, personalities, and so on: the list is very long. And unlike the subjective, mental phenomena themselves, these entities are hypothesised to have an enduring existence, to be experimentally manipulable in a controlled fashion, and hence to possess a substance which allows mathematical analysis and description. The problem is that nobody has ever proved their existence. Harré launches a critique along precisely these lines:

> People, for the purposes of psychology, are not internally complex. They have no parts. . . . There are no mental states other than the private thoughts and feelings people are aware of from time to time. There are no mental mechanisms by which a person's powers and skills are implemented, except the occasional private rehearsals for action in which we sometimes engage. The whole top heavy apparatus of . . . cognitive psychology is at worst a fantasy and at best a metaphor. (Harré, 1998: 15)

A related critique focuses on methods. Clearly, natural science has progressed a long way since Newton; yet despite its long-held desire to emulate these disciplines, psychology has not moved with it (Harré, 1999). The experimental methodology based upon independent and dependent variables we described earlier is, in truth, an invention of psychology (Harré, 2006) which is not properly reflective of any natural science model.

Psychologists are nonetheless resourceful creatures and two distinct responses to this situation are now discernible. The experimental and quantitative tradition in psychology has, for example, developed a number of statistics and techniques which are closely related to modern developments in physics and chemistry (Gelman & Hill, 2007). Huge advances in both structural and functional brain scanning technology have also allowed *cognitive neuroscience* to link subjective mental phenomena to brain function (and physiology) in ways that would have amazed Wundt and James (Frith, 2007).

A second response has involved the re-emergence of more 'humanitarian' values and methods within psychology. This began with the humanist movement in the 1960s, which offered itself as a 'third force' in psychology. It aimed to provide an antidote to the negativity which seemed to characterise behaviourism and Freudian psychoanalysis. Most associated with **Abraham Maslow** (1908–1970) and **Carl Rogers** (1902–1987), humanism suggested that the subjective mental phenomena (or 'reality') which psychology had so often ignored were actually the primary guide for human behaviour. Behaviour was not *caused*; rather, it was motivated by each individual's desire to *self-actualise* and reach their full potential. Humanism stalled, however, primarily because it failed to come up with a method of collecting data about people and ultimately because its uncritical and positive assessment of humans felt more like a form of wishful thinking than a serious scientific endeavour.

In the last 30 years, the social scientific model has nonetheless returned to psychology in a more rigorous fashion. To a large extent, this movement continues to be inspired by suspicions that natural science may be inappropriate as a model for psychology. There is a renewed belief that the subjective world of meaningful human experience (look at Table 2.1 again!) really *is* psychology's rightful subject matter. A proliferation of qualitative research methods has duly emerged to interrogate particular aspects of this extraordinarily diverse, and very human, world of life (see Willig & Stainton Rogers, 2007).

2.7 CONCLUSION

This is an exciting time to be studying psychology. As we've just discussed, the natural and social scientific models are showing marked signs of convergence. Psychologists are connecting human meaning-making and creativity to brain function in ever greater detail (Edelman, 2006). Psychology is now armed with a range of quantitative and qualitative methods, as well as some very advanced technologies, which all satisfy the scientific ideal (in a range of different ways). Research which deliberately 'mixes' methods traditionally associated with the natural and social sciences has also become very fashionable (Creswell & Plano Clark, 2007). Psychology finally seems to be accepting its position at the divide between the natural and social sciences, and acknowledging that to take full advantage of this position it really *has to* retain a foot in both these (increasingly connected) camps. Now comes your chance to contribute …

2.8 CHAPTER SUMMARY

Modern psychology traces its immediate origins to the late nineteenth century, when Wilhelm Wundt created his laboratory in Leipzig. Since that time, the discipline has moved to and fro between conceptions of psychology as (1) a natural science and (2) a social science. Much has hinged on the question of focus: to what extent should psychology study the mind and our experiences of the world, and to what extent should it focus on what is externally observable and measurable? Over the past 150 years psychology has developed a range of methods, approaches and measures, yet the central questions remain.

(?) DISCUSSION QUESTIONS

As we have seen, psychology has developed through debate between those who believe the discipline should be modelled on natural science and those who believe it should be modelled on social science. What arguments can you see for and against each of these positions? Where do you stand yourself on this debate?

What are the implications of the two views above for (1) what topics or phenomena should be studied, and (2) the methods that should be used?

SUGGESTIONS FOR FURTHER READING

Benjamin, L.T. (1996). *A history of psychology*. New York: McGraw-Hill. If you want a comprehensive account, there are a number of large texts designed for US courses on the history of psychology of which this is one.

Fancher, R.E. (1996). *Pioneers of psychology* (3rd edn). New York: W.W. Norton. One of the best texts to pick up to explore the beginnings of psychology. This book looks at key ideas and key people chapter by chapter, and provides very useful background to several other chapters in this text.

Miller, G. (1966). *Psychology: the science of mental life*. London: Penguin. Another text that has stood the test of time, this also covers the pioneers of psychology with some interesting insights into their lives and ideas.

Richards, G. (2010). *Putting psychology in its place: critical historical perspectives* (3rd edn). Hove: Routledge.

Tyson, P., Jones, D., & Elcock, J. (2011). *Psychology in social context: issues and debates*. London: BPS Blackwell. A readable text written for the UK market.

 Still want more? For links to online resources relevant to this chapter and a quiz to test your understanding, visit the companion website at edge.sagepub.com/banyard2e

3

ISSUES AND DEBATES IN PSYCHOLOGY

Lead author: Garry Young

CHAPTER OUTLINE

3.1 Introduction	38
3.2 The mind–body problem	38
3.2.1 Cartesian dualism	39
3.2.2 An explanatory problem: How does the mind interact with the body?	40
3.2.3 Mind–brain identity theory: removing the need for interaction	42
3.2.4 Problems with identity theory	44
3.2.5 How to capture rational relations: introducing folk psychology	44
3.3 Reductionism	45
3.3.1 Problems with reduction in psychology	46
3.3.2 Moving away from reductionism	46
3.4 Conclusion	47
3.4.1 Folk psychology versus scientific psychology	47
3.4.2 A note of caution	48
3.5 Chapter summary	48
Discussion questions	48
Suggestions for further reading	48

3.1 INTRODUCTION

Who am I? What am I doing? What's it all for? Why are we here? These are the questions that come up when we have time to ponder the wonder of our existence. Staring at the night sky on a summer evening, we can only wonder at it all. Such questions also tend to come up at weak moments as we struggle through the events of daily life: for example, when we confront our own mortality or when we lose someone close to us or even when things just seem to be going against us. Alternatively, these questions can be induced by alcohol or by dropping your choc-ice.

In this chapter, we are going to consider some of the thinking around the above questions. We will examine ideas about consciousness and the mind–body problem. We will also explore some of the tensions in psychological thinking that arise from the clash between two approaches to psychology, namely (1) reductionism and (2) folk psychology. Though these terms may not be familiar to you yet, they will be explained below.

In developing our thinking on these questions, we will explore some areas where two disciplines – namely, psychology and philosophy – frequently overlap or interact with each other.

FRAMING QUESTIONS

- What is consciousness?
- What, if any, is the distinction between my mind and my body?
- Is it possible to explain everything by reducing phenomena to their constituent parts?
- How do our everyday explanations of what we do and why we do it compare to what science tells us about human behaviour and experience?
- To what extent is psychology a natural science?

3.2 THE MIND–BODY PROBLEM

Imagine that you are having a confidential conversation with a friend, who says to you, 'I may look happy, but inside I am crying'. This statement is not difficult to understand. A straightforward interpretation might be that your friend is hiding the fact that he or she is feeling sad. The statement refers both to what we might call an overt behavioural expression (looking happy) and an emotional state (feeling sad) – and the two clearly do not correspond.

Typically, we don't expect these statements to be literally true (e.g. we don't take the word 'crying' to mean that tears are literally welling up inside the person). The use of 'inside' here is metaphorical. This metaphor is revealing: it indicates that there is both a private and a public component to our being.

Note that when we use the word 'private' here, we don't mean simply that there are some things we would prefer to keep to ourselves (because they are personal, might be embarrassing, and so on). Instead, in this context, we are using the word 'private' to mean that there are some things we *cannot* make public. Each person has direct access only to his or her *own* experiential content: only *you* can directly access the inner world of *your* own thoughts and feelings. In this sense, when we say 'You don't know how I feel', we are being 100% accurate.

If we accept that as humans we have both a private (experiential) and a public (behavioural and physiological) component to our being, we can ask how this affects the way we explain our existence and how we investigate it. It is useful here to introduce two contrasting terms, namely, 'mental states' and 'brain states'. In everyday usage, talk of thoughts and feelings, or of **mental states**, is often assumed to refer to the mind. Mental states are private in the sense already mentioned. Brain states, on the other hand, are public. That is to say, while they are not typically on display or observed, they are nevertheless directly observable in principle, and in a way that mental states are not. We can, for example, monitor brain activity by using scanning devices such as positron emission tomography (PET) or functional magnetic resonance imaging (fMRI; see Chapter 9), or even by employing more invasive techniques such as direct electrode stimulation. This latter technique was famously employed by Wilder Penfield.

Penfield (1958, 1975) stimulated regions of the exposed brain of a conscious patient who then reported what he experienced. During this research, Penfield stood perhaps as close as anyone could do to what is regarded by most as the vessel that 'houses' the mind – the living brain. The brain was clearly observable; the mind was not. When Penfield stimulated the brain, the effect this had on the individual – in terms of what that person *experienced* – could only be recorded indirectly. To illustrate, when Penfield stimulated one particular region of the patient's brain, the patient's arm moved and he began to clench his fist. The patient was unable to resist performing this action. However, when asked to move his arm voluntarily, what the patient experienced was different. The movement stimulated by Penfield lacked the latter's accompanying sense of **volition**. What Penfield was unable to observe directly was the presence or absence of this *sense* of volition (the experience of willing the movement to occur).

We can summarise this point by saying that the patient has first-person access to the content of their own mind, whereas Penfield (and anyone else) must be satisfied with third-person access only. This third-person access is gained indirectly, through observation of the patient's behaviour, through measures of their (neuro) physiological states, and, of course, what they tell us about their experience.

There is, then, a discrepancy between how I gain knowledge of my own mental states (acquired through first-person access) and how I gain knowledge of someone else's (acquired through third-person access); or even a discrepancy between how I come to know states of my own mind (first person) and states of my brain (third person). As we will see, this discrepancy has direct bearing on the study of psychology.

MENTAL STATES In the philosophy of mind, a mental state is unique to thinking and feeling beings, and forms part of our cognitive processes. These processes include our beliefs and attitudes as well as our perceptions and sensations, such as the taste of wine or the pain of a headache.

VOLITION The act of deciding to do something. It is also referred to as 'will' (e.g. I am reading this chapter of my own volition, and not because someone has put a gun to my head).

ASIDE

Epistemology

The study of what we know and how we know it is called epistemology. It is one of those topics, like 'thinking about thinking', that most people find mentally extremely taxing. Elsewhere in this book we consider similar issues: for example, Jean Piaget (see Chapter 18) examined how children develop their thinking and come to know the world they live in. In this text, we have tried to deal with these issues as fully as we can while using accessible language.

3.2.1 CARTESIAN DUALISM

Does this difference between *how* I come to know my mental states and *how* I come to know my brain states mean that these states come from two different things, my mind and my brain?

Someone who drew precisely this conclusion (that the mind and the brain are different things) was the philosopher René Descartes (1596–1650). Descartes established a way of thinking about the mind and the body that has become known as **Cartesian dualism**. This is the view that the mind is **immaterial** (i.e. not made up of material things), and therefore distinct and independent from the **material** body (including the brain). In other words, we are made up of a mind (which we can't see) and a body (which we can). You can also think of this model in terms of 'a ghost in the machine'.

Descartes famously arrived at this idea after thinking about the problem using his 'method of doubt'. This was a method of argument that involved doubting anything he could not prove to be true. Descartes argued that, though he could doubt that his body actually existed, he could not doubt that he himself existed. His argument was that the very

CARTESIAN DUALISM The idea that we are made up of two parts, a mind and a body. The body is like all other material objects and can be examined using the material sciences, whereas the mind is not physical and cannot be measured.

MATERIAL AND IMMATERIAL If something is material, it is made up of the atoms and molecules that are building blocks of our world, whereas if it is immaterial it is not made up of these things. We cannot measure or see immaterial things such as 'mind', which challenges their existence. The existence of immaterial things is a matter of belief rather than evidence.

fact that he was able to doubt something showed that he must exist: if he didn't, he would not be able to doubt or to think at all. Descartes summarised this argument using the Latin phrase *cogito, ergo sum* ('I think, therefore I am').

In short, Descartes attempted to draw a conclusion about the nature of his being from the discrepancy that exists between how he came to know his body and how he came to know his mind. He also employed what is known as Leibniz's law in support of this distinction. This law relates to what it means when two things are exactly the same (sometimes referred to as the *indiscernibility of identical*). The law states that for A and B to be identical, all properties of A must be identical to all properties of B, and vice versa. Applying Leibniz's law, Descartes concluded that A (the mind) and B (the body) cannot be identical because they have different properties. The body can be doubted and so has the property of doubtability. The mind cannot be doubted and so does not have this property. To reiterate, if the mind and body have different properties, they cannot be the same.

Despite concluding that he was his mind (and thus distinct from his body), Descartes did recognise (because he experienced it as such) that he was intimately related to *his* body like no other. This ambiguity – that I (as a mind) am distinct from the physical body, yet intimately related to one body in particular, which I call mine – can be seen in the English language. For example, think about the statement 'I hate my body'. Here, the 'I' doing the hating appears distinct from the body which is hated. There does, however, appear to be a relationship between them: one of ownership (the body somehow belongs to the 'I'). But this still indicates a difference. If they were the same – that is, referring to the same thing – then you should be able to turn this around. Yet it does not seem to make sense to say 'My body hates I' or even 'My body hates my body.' There is clearly some ambiguity here – an ambiguity made all the more apparent in the two examples that follow.

Consider here the statements: 'I hate my body' and 'I hate myself'. Are they equivalent? If so, in what way? If not, why not? What extra ingredient is contained within the reference to my *self* that is absent in the case of my body? Next, consider this example: 'I am envious of my body.' While it makes sense (so to speak) to be envious of someone else's body, it makes no sense to be envious of one's own. Here the 'I' and 'my body' seem to be too closely related for the statement to be meaningful. It could be argued that these examples simply reflect a limitation in the English language. Perhaps. Nonetheless, they do illustrate a dualism in our expression of self.

ASIDE

Hope for students

René Descartes was a frail individual, and he usually spent most of his mornings in bed, where he did most of his thinking, fresh from dreams in which he often had his revelations. In his later years, Descartes moved to Sweden to give Queen Christina lessons in philosophy. Unfortunately for Descartes, the Queen was an early riser who wanted her lessons at 5.00 in the morning. This new schedule did no favours to Descartes's fragile health, and he contracted pneumonia, from which he died on 11 February 1650 at the age of 54. There is a lesson here for all of us: get up later!

3.2.2 AN EXPLANATORY PROBLEM: HOW DOES THE MIND INTERACT WITH THE BODY?

There are many problems with Cartesian dualism (too many for us to discuss all of them here). Perhaps the most damning is the problem of explaining how the ghost can work the machine (Figure 3.1). This is known as the problem of interaction. To explain: if, as Descartes maintains, the mind and the body are distinct – one being immaterial and the other material – then how do such utterly different and incompatible substances interact? In other words, how can the mind have an effect on the body (or how can the ghost work the machine)?

Descartes's solution, incidentally, was to claim that the interaction occurred at the pineal gland within the brain. Even if this were true, which it is not, and the pineal gland were indeed the seat of mind–body interaction, there is a problem: knowing *where* something occurs is not an explanation of *how* it occurs. When pushed on this matter, Descartes' response was to claim that the interaction is *sui generis* (unique). This is possible, of course, but unlikely; and, philosophically, it is a weak position to adopt. He might as well have said 'It's magic'.

What is appealing about Descartes' dualism, however, is the causal role it gives to the mind. It seems intuitively the case that my thoughts cause my actions, at least some of the time. So according to Descartes, the mind can be the cause of some behaviours and experiences and this prevents it from being regarded as having no effect on the body. Under Descartes, then, the mind is found at the centre of explanations of human action.

Despite its intuitive appeal, the Cartesian 'problem of interaction' remains a major challenge to overcome when attempting to explain the causal connection between mind and body. To illustrate: suppose I claim that with the power of my (Cartesian) mind alone I can move a small physical object on the table in front of me – a pen, say. Would you bet against me? Jedi mind tricks aside, would you believe that it is something I could do? If I did manage to do this, I suspect you would be very impressed. However, consider how totally unimpressed you would be if I claimed, instead, that with the power of my mind alone I could raise my arm in the air! Why is it that this latter feat is so underwhelming? The raising of arms in the air is, I suppose, something that is often witnessed, whereas the movement of a pen by the power of one's mind is not.

Yet, according to Cartesian dualism, the same interaction of immaterial mind with material object, necessary to move the pen, is required every time we engage in deliberate behaviour, even when it is as mundane as raising one's arm in the air. Therefore, no matter how detailed the description, and no matter how complete our understanding of the underlying neurophysiology of the behaviour, if the desire to move the arm is generated by a Cartesian self, then this desire must ultimately have stemmed from an immaterial mind. Consequently, at some point, our detailed explanation of the action, which includes a description of the neurophysiology involved in raising a hand in the air, must also explain how the mind, and the desire it generates, caused this change in neurophysiology to occur.

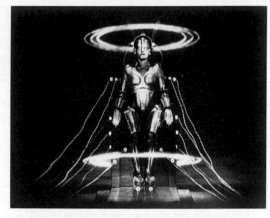

FIGURE 3.1 The mind–body problem is the key idea behind many science fiction films. One of the first was the silent classic *Metropolis* by Fritz Lang (1927). The female robot is used by the callous factory owner to take the place of the saintly Maria and create chaos among the workers. The key question concerns how we can distinguish between the machine and the person (the machine with a soul).

© Bettmann/Corbis

EXERCISE: GET YOUR MIND AND BODY TO INTERACT

Carry out a small test to show that your mind and body can interact.

First, let's demonstrate that your mind can affect your body. You can do this by using your mind to think about the person you most dislike in all the world. Keep thinking about them and imagine that they win the lottery. This will probably make you feel angry and you will notice changes in your body and even your behaviour brought about by these thoughts. You can create different changes in your body by thinking about the person you most fancy in the world. Leave that for later.

Now see how your body can affect your thoughts. Take in a small amount of a psychoactive food – something you are used to drinking (e.g. a pint of lager, an energy drink or a cup of coffee) and observe how your thoughts can change as a result. The use of alcohol is the most obvious example: it is common for people who have drunk a lot of alcohol to have 'beer goggles' and think about the world and people in a very different way, and to change their assessment of risk (and attraction).

KEY STUDY

Hofstadter, R.D., & Dennett, D.C. (1981). *The mind's I: fantasies and reflections on self and soul.* **Brighton: Harvester.**

The study of the relationship between mind and body doesn't offer much opportunity for traditional experiments in psychology. One of the techniques that has been developed to test out ideas is the *Gedankenexperiment* (thought experiment). The fabulous advantage of this technique is that you can do a *Gedankenexperiment* while sitting in your chair with a cup of hot chocolate on the table. The disadvantage is that you have to think very hard and very long.

One of the most entertaining thought experiments was devised by Dennett (Hofstadter & Dennett, 1981), and is particularly applicable to section 3.2.3. Imagine having your brain removed by keyhole surgery, keeping it alive in a glass container and replacing all the severed nerve connections with nanotechnology radio transmitters. This is the stuff of nightmares and many science fiction films. You have now separated your brain from your body. Imagine your body moving to the other side of the room and looking at your brain (which it can still see because your eyes have been reconnected via the radio transmitters). Now ask yourself the question, 'Where am I?'. Are you over there, or over here, and who, in any case, is doing the asking?

Go one step further and watch the body carry out a murder (Don't try this at home! Ed.). Now which bit of you should be locked up, your body or your brain?

The example in the key study illustrates the difficulty faced by Cartesian dualism. For although it is true that within our everyday language we often distinguish mind from body, it seems there is a limit to how far this distinction can be taken. In turning the mind and the body (and therefore the mind and the *brain*) into two distinct substances, Descartes' theory therefore entails the problem of interaction.

Cartesian dualism also raises an important methodological question, namely: what role would there be for scientific psychology in the study of an entity (the mind) that exists outside the realm of the physical sciences? If we are our minds and scientific psychology's role is to help solve the 'riddle of our selves', then scientific psychology faces a problem, namely: how can the material sciences and therefore scientific psychology study an immaterial, non-physical mind?

3.2.3 MIND–BRAIN IDENTITY THEORY: REMOVING THE NEED FOR INTERACTION

Perhaps the solution is to alter the status of the mind, and with it its relation to the body (including, of course, the brain). Mind–brain identity theory (hereafter, identity theory) (Lewis, 1966; Place, 1956; Smart, 1959), in contrast to Descartes, holds that the mind and the brain are one; or, more specifically, that a particular mental state (call it M_1) is identical to a particular neurological state (call it N_1). There is no interaction between the mind and the brain, nor does there need to be, for they are one and the same thing.

Mind–brain identity theory is based on the idea that there is nothing above or beyond the physical. It reduces mental states to the level of neurological states. It does not deny that mental states exist, but rather argues that they are identical to brain states. Identity theory therefore employs a **reductionist** explanation (see section 3.3) when accounting for how mental states cause human action. Such actions and interactions are explained using the same language as the natural sciences. The cause of an action is described in terms of the neurophysiological state of the person: a descriptive state that can be explained at (and therefore reduced to) the level of physics.

Identity theory also uses a reductive methodology. The relationship between mind and brain can only be discovered through observation. This means that knowledge about which mental state is identical to which brain state can only be discovered through the use of brain scanning techniques, or other more intrusive methods used to record localised brain activity, or through the study of corresponding

REDUCTIONISM The idea that a complex system is nothing more than the sum of its parts, and that a description of a system can be reduced to descriptions of the individual components.

PARSIMONY The idea that 'less is better' and, in particular, that a complicated explanation is not needed when a simple one is sufficient.

KEY RESEARCHER Susan Blackmore

Susan Blackmore is a freelance writer, lecturer and broadcaster, and a Visiting Professor at the University of Plymouth. She has a degree in psychology and physiology from Oxford University (1973) and a PhD in parapsychology from the University of Surrey (1980). Her research interests include memes, evolutionary theory, consciousness and meditation. She practises Zen and campaigns for drug legalisation.

She writes for several magazines and newspapers, blogs for *The Guardian* newspaper and *Psychology Today*, and is a frequent contributor and presenter on radio and television. She is author of over 60 academic articles, about 50 book contributions, and many book reviews. Her books include *Dying to live* (on near-death experiences, 1993), *The meme machine* (1999, now translated into 13 other languages), *Consciousness: an introduction* (a textbook, 2003), *Conversations on consciousness* (2005) and *Ten Zen questions* (2009).

FIGURE 3.2 Susan Blackmore (photograph by Adam Hart-Davis)

behaviour or reported subjective experience. In short, in order to explain changes in a person's mental states we give explanations involving changes in brain states.

There is one further important idea to consider here. According to identity theory, the changes or damage to states of the brain do not *cause* changes in the person's mental states, in the sense of A causing B. Instead, any change to a given brain state *equates* to differences in the subject's experience (because the mind and brain are one and the same thing). Therefore, understanding what caused differences in a person's mental states requires us to understand what caused differences in the same person's neural states: to understand one is to understand the other. When we give an explanation of a person's action in terms of mental states, such as beliefs and desires, then, according to identity theory, we are actually explaining that behaviour in terms of the changes in the person's neurophysiology. Why? Because mental states and brain states are one and the same.

Identity theory has a number of points in its favour. As a theory of mind–body relations, it is certainly **parsimonious**. For some, it may even appear intuitively sound. Certainly it is compatible with evidence introduced as a result of advances in brain imaging equipment. Functional magnetic resonance imaging (fMRI) scans, for example, allow the anatomical structure and function of a living brain to be studied. With such equipment we can observe and record those areas of the brain that exhibit increased (or even decreased) activity when an individual performs a particular mental task. We can even examine patients suffering injury or disease in order to identify which parts of the brain, when damaged, correspond to deficits in mental function and/or experiential content. Francis Crick, one of the co-discoverers of the structure of DNA, once famously remarked that our joys and sorrows, our memories and ambitions, are nothing more than a vast assembly of nerves cells and molecules (Crick, 1994).

Identity theory, with its idea that mind and brain are one and the same, is able to sidestep the problem of how the mind interacts with the brain. The mind can bring about changes in the brain, but as the mind is the brain there is no problem of interaction to explain. Talk of thoughts causing behaviour is, then, nothing but talk of neurological states causing behaviour. In reality, the mind has no causal power independent of the brain because it is not independent of the brain. As a result, explanations of why we do things do not need to use the language of the psychological or the mental. (We will return to this point below.)

3.2.4 PROBLEMS WITH IDENTITY THEORY

There are a number of difficulties with identity theory, some of which we will discuss here. First, although the claim made by identity theory that the mind and brain are identical is compatible with the evidence provided by brain imagery, being compatible is not the same as being able to fully support the identity relation in a manner identity theorists would like. Crudely speaking, brain scans measure brain activity, and often these are taken in conjunction with patient behaviour and reported mental activity: that I am thinking about animals which begin with the letter A, for example. But this does not necessarily establish that the mental event 'thinking about animals beginning with the letter A' is identical to brain activation (the excitation of certain neurons). What it actually shows is the co-occurrence of thinking (based on the patient's report) and brain activity. The co-occurrence of two things – even if one is a reliable indicator of the other – does not necessarily make them identical, and so is not proof of the strict identity relation being proposed here.

Second, although identity theory allows that the mind (mental states) is the cause of certain behaviours (in virtue of being identical to brain states), given that it is really the brain doing the work (so to speak), when proposing a causal explanation of such behaviour, there seems little explanatory worth in referring to mental states; one may as well use the language of the (neuro)physiological and talk about particular brain states causing behaviour – in which case, the language of mental events, which includes terms such as beliefs, desires, hopes and aspirations, should be replaced by neurological terminology because it more accurately describes the underlying cause of behaviour. Given this, imagine receiving a Valentine's card from an eliminative material. While the following inscription may be accurate (so to speak) – 'Every time I see you I enter neurological state N501'– it lacks a certain romance.

Other than wishing to champion romance, is there a stronger argument for retaining the language of the mental events? To remove reference to mental states such as beliefs or desires from our explanations of actions is to ignore an important component: the rational nature of reasons. We make sense of our lives through our beliefs and desires. In fact, we explain our behaviour in these terms, so to ignore them and just describe behaviour in terms of chemical changes in the brain or neuronal excitation fails to capture in an important way why we do what we do and what we hope to achieve. Without these important mental states we cannot hope to provide a full picture of human behaviour.

3.2.5 HOW TO CAPTURE RATIONAL RELATIONS: INTRODUCING FOLK PSYCHOLOGY

Suppose you know (from some previous conversation) that I do not enjoy spending time in crowded places and that I try to avoid them whenever possible. Suppose further that one day you see me enter a café you know to be crowded, and then, seconds later, leave. You might conclude that because I have a desire to avoid crowded places (whenever possible), and because the café is crowded (and I have come to the belief that the café is crowded after entering the premises), I decide to leave.

If this is your conclusion, then it amounts to what is sometimes referred to as a **folk psychology** account of my actions (Stitch & Ravenscroft, 1994). Put simply, you explain my actions in terms of the beliefs and desires you have attributed to me: that I have a desire to avoid crowded places and a belief that the café is crowded. Part of this explanation is your assumption that my beliefs and desires *caused* my behaviour (see Chapter 15 for more about making attributions about our own, and others' behaviour).

This simple folk psychology explanation is clearly intended to be a causal explanation (explaining why it happened). Now, this in itself is not a problem for identity theory because what is really being stated here is that a neural state (identical to my desire to avoid crowded places) and another neural state (identical to my belief that the café was crowded) caused me to leave the café. However, folk psychology here provides not only a causal explanation, but also a reason-giving explanation. The reason I left the café was because I have a desire to avoid crowded places, and the café was crowded. As well as citing the cause of my behaviour, then, this explanation shows my behaviour to be rational, or at least reasonable under the circumstances, based as it is on my beliefs and desires.

Beliefs and desires, generally speaking, are connected to each other. They form a network of interrelated structures that express themselves through behaviour deemed reasonable within a given context. Such rational relations seem appropriate when talking about beliefs and desires. What is less clear is how appropriate it is to talk about neurological states being connected rationally to each other.

FOLK PSYCHOLOGY Ways of thinking about the mind that are implicit in how we make everyday attributions of mental states to ourselves and others.

What the crowded café example illustrates is that there are essentially two types of explanation, one causal and the other reason-giving. Folk psychology explanations are explicitly reason-giving and implicitly causal: we imply that the reasons given for our actions are at the same time the cause of our actions. In contrast, neurological explanations are predominantly causal, and no attempt to capture reason-giving explanations at the level of electrochemical excitation and inhibition of neurons seems possible. If identity theory is to provide a valid explanation of the relationship between mind and brain, then it must be able to capture at the level of neuronal interaction the rational connections that so clearly exist at the psychological level. The reductionist approach to understanding human behaviour is not solely the domain of identity theory (which reduces the mental to the physical), but can be seen in a number of guises in psychology, as we shall see in the next section.

3.3 REDUCTIONISM

In scientific psychology, reductionism is the view that any complex phenomenon is simply the sum of the components that make it up. So feeling happy, for example, is best described as a series of physical changes (such as smiling) and chemical changes in the brain that create a sensation we call happiness (Figure 3.3). Thus, according to reductionism, psychological phenomena are nothing but physical phenomena which can be explained using physical facts and studied using methods appropriate to measuring this more fundamental level of reality.

We have already seen this viewpoint expressed in the context of identity theory. In the rest of this chapter, we will look more closely at reductionism in general within scientific psychology, and at the challenges that arise when trying to reduce psychological states to states of the brain themselves.

Reductionism has been successfully applied to physics, and to the other natural sciences of chemistry and biology. After Newton (1642–1727), and later Darwin (1809–1882), our view of our place in the universe changed: instead of seeing ourselves as the centre of the universe and the reason the universe exists, humans began to see

FIGURE 3.3 Reductionism: Wallace and Gromitt (shown here with creator Nick Park) appear to be alive when we watch them on film but we know that their actions are created step by step by animators moving bits of plasticine. The reductionist argument is that when we learn more about people we will be able to see that our actions can be explained in a very similar way. For example, a behaviourist might see our behaviour as being a series of small steps that are caused by rewards and punishments.

© Louis Quail/Corbis

themselves as part of a continuum of organic life. According to the fundamental laws of physics, it would seem that organic life itself forms part of a continuum with the inorganic. For though, at this fundamental level, organic life differs from inorganic material in terms of its complexity, it does not do so in terms of its substance. It would seem we are all fundamentally made of the same stuff (ashes to ashes and dust to dust: we start as particles of dust and we end up the same way).

EXERCISE: REDUCTIONISM

Reductionism is a useful method for answering some problems but not others. For example, if we want to find out the cause of an illness, then it is a good idea to study each variable individually and eliminate the ones that have no effect. Eventually we might find a single cause for the illness and be able to treat it, though it is fair to say that this approach does not work for every illness. On the other hand, if we want to find out what an emotion like love is, then it is more difficult to see how we can reduce it to its component parts, though you can have a try if you like.

Make two lists of ideas in psychology, one list of ideas that can be examined with a reductionist approach and one list of ideas that require a more holistic approach. It's not as easy as it sounds and you might like to come back to this as you discover more about the subject (the psychoactive food you tried earlier in the chapter might also help).

If, however, we are all made of the same stuff, and if the same laws of physics that apply to the inorganic likewise apply to us, it would seem to be logical that the same principles used to study and explain the inorganic should be used to study and explain us. This is certainly an argument proposed in support of reductionism. However, an important objection to this idea is that we differ from objects in one important aspect: our minds.

Once again, the problem of explaining the mind within a physical universe needs to be dealt with. To argue, much as Descartes did, that the mind is distinct is to reject reductionism as an exhaustive approach and to claim that what exists is more than just the physical. Few psychologists support this position, preferring instead to champion *substance monism* – the view that there is only one substance, which is physical.

3.3.1 PROBLEMS WITH REDUCTION IN PSYCHOLOGY

Yet there is dissatisfaction with reductionism in psychology. Let us consider some of the reasons. According to Burwood et al. (1999), when we use a reductionist analysis we must be able to explain all the phenomena in the higher property by the lower property we are reducing it to, so that there is no distinct role for the higher property to be playing independently of the lower-level ones. In our example of happiness, we must be able to explain all the features we experience in happiness by the physical and chemical changes in our body. When it comes to psychological phenomena like this, we have already identified a potential problem for reductionist explanations, namely how to capture the reason-giving explanations that exist between psychological states at the more fundamental neurological level. With happiness, sometimes we feel happy because we think of happy thoughts, and so our higher processes have created the physical changes that we associate with happiness.

Neurological explanations do have a role to play in explaining human action, however, and can be seen as *compatible* with higher-level psychology. Importantly, what they are not capable of doing is capturing the nature of the relation that exists between psychological phenomena. A useful way to illustrate this is by demonstrating the difference between a *movement* and an *action*.

What is the difference between your signature and a squiggle? To the unknowing eye they may look the same, but one of them means something and the other one does not. If you think about the processes in your brain that created the squiggle and the signature, what would be the difference between them? Even if they originated in two different regions of the brain, it seems reasonable to ask why that should be. What is it about them that makes one originate in one area and the other in a different one? Similarly, when tracing the neural route through the body – from brain to muscles in the arm and hand – what would be the difference between the two actions? There may be slight variations in muscle movement, but these variations would be there when comparing the movement involved in the same person writing their signature on two separate occasions (no two signatures are ever exactly the same).

A signature on a document, for example, is likely to mean that I am authorising something – possibly a transaction. A squiggle, by comparison, is fairly meaningless, though it might suggest I was bored and doodling. The neurological explanation provides a detailed account of the movement in each case (it explains *how* the behaviour occurred), but each movement is only differentiated at the level of action ('What sort of action is it?', 'What does it mean?'), and this is a psychological differentiation that cannot be captured at the lower level.

To appreciate the value of a psychological level of explanation, think about life and death. At the biological level, you can clearly distinguish between life and death. At this level, you might even draw a distinction between a natural death and a non-natural, intentional act of killing (by observing that a foreign object had entered the system – a bullet or poison, say – or even that the organism's head had been removed from its body; see Chapter 27 section 27.4.1 on violent offending and murder for more on this). However, at *purely* the biological level, you cannot distinguish between killing and murder: that is, between legal execution and unauthorised death. It is only possible to make this distinction by incorporating into your thinking differences that occur only at the *psychological* level: for it is only at this level that you are able to differentiate between killing that is judged to be legal and that deemed illegal. Even if you were to argue that all intentional killing is murder, such an argument is only meaningful *as an argument* at the psychological level.

3.3.2 MOVING AWAY FROM REDUCTIONISM

Those who oppose a reductionist approach to psychology argue that a methodology that tries to give explanations of human behaviour at the neurological level alone is impoverished. This is because such a methodology is capable of supporting explanations only of movement, and critically, as humans, we do not engage in movement *per se*. Rather, our *movements* form the basis for our *actions* and, as the signature and killing examples illustrate, an action is something more than just a movement; it is something that cannot be explained fully at the level of interconnecting neurons. For a fuller explanation of behaviour, we also need to draw on higher-level psychological terms, such as beliefs and desires, or to incorporate the symbolic nature of the movement into the explanation (murder or sanctioned execution). Psychological explanation transforms the movement into a meaningful act within a social context.

> **EXPLANATORY PLURALISM** That different levels of description, like the psychological and the neurophysiological, can coevolve, and mutually influence each other, without the higher-level theory being replaced by, or reduced to, the lower-level one.

Reductionism is not without its problems, as the signature and killing examples help to illustrate, but, for Hull and Van Regenmortel (2002), reductionism is not to be despised. Rather, it must be placed in its proper context. As an alternative, **explanatory pluralism** holds that different levels of description, like the psychological and the neurophysiological, can coevolve, and mutually influence each other, without the higher-level theory being replaced by, or reduced to, the lower-level one (Bem, 2001; Looren de Jong, 2001). The properties of the higher-level explanation are often described in terms of their function – in terms of what it is the function of the lower level to do. Importantly, though, the higher-level, functional property cannot be reduced to this lower level.

3.4 CONCLUSION

3.4.1 FOLK PSYCHOLOGY VERSUS SCIENTIFIC PSYCHOLOGY

The purpose of this chapter has been to outline some of the challenges involved in trying to answer the fundamental questions (e.g. 'Who am I?') that make up the 'riddle of our selves'. These challenges arise from differences that are said to exist between a scientific approach to the study of our selves and the qualities that make up our experience of being alive: in particular, the way we can reflect on our selves and our very existence. This reflective experience lies at the heart of everyday folk psychology accounts of *why* we do what we do.

As we have seen, folk psychology explanations provide a reason-giving role to psychological states such as beliefs, or desires, or hopes, and see them as the *cause* of our actions. I left the crowded café *because* I wanted to avoid crowds and believed the café to be crowded. The word 'because' in that last sentence indicates that the *want* and the *belief* are the cause of the subsequent action because they are rationally related to each other and to the behaviour that follows. It makes sense, given the person's belief and wants, that he should exit the café within moments of entering it.

The challenge faced by scientific psychology is twofold. First, it must be capable of providing a scientific explanation of behaviour that captures the rational relations that exist between our psychological states and our subsequent behaviour, as well as the phenomenal quality of our experiential content which helps us to explain why we do what we do: the reason pain causes me to cry out is because it hurts! Second, it must do this without violating the principles of physicalism, otherwise we would become Cartesian dualists.

An immediate objection to this challenge might be to claim that scientific psychology should replace, rather than respect, folk psychology explanations. The question here is what we could replace folk psychology with. As we have seen, scientific attempts to reduce psychological explanation to questions of neurophysiology encounter difficulties. A scientific psychology that reduces the psychological to the level of neuronal interactions thus seems self-defeating. In short, if we were to reduce the rational relations characteristic of psychological states to the neuronal level, psychology would become nothing more than a science of the brain. How, then, could we differentiate psychology from, say, neurobiology?

This chapter has illustrated the challenges that reductionist accounts face when trying to capture the psychological at the level of neuronal interactions. A promising, though by no means problem-free, approach has been to recognise the irreducible nature of psychological states and their interdependent rational relations.

Such an approach maintains the spirit of folk psychology explanations, but also tries to adopt the rigours of science, at least when trying to provide an account of how the lower-level states of the brain work. Within such an account of mind–brain relations, the discipline of psychology is able to maintain its independence from a pure *science of the brain*. It does, however, raise a fresh question for you to consider: If psychology gains its independence as a discipline through focusing on the study of states and properties that are not reducible to lower-level explanations, can it still rightly be called a science?

3.4.2 A NOTE OF CAUTION

We will end this chapter on a cautionary note. While folk psychology is not itself infallible as a means of explaining human action – we can, after all, be mistaken about the reasons we attribute to a given action (as research on attribution theory shows: see Chapter 15) – it does nevertheless remind us about a fundamental component of our behaviour: its meaningfulness. If, therefore, we adopt the view that such behaviour *can* and *should* be studied using the natural scientific methods, then we must resolve the problem of mind. However, if we rely on a model of mind that is reducible to the natural sciences, this is likely to result in the reduction of psychology itself to the natural sciences. Psychology therefore risks becoming a science of the brain. If, on the other hand, the explanation of mind adopted by psychology cannot be reduced to the natural sciences, then, although its independent status may be preserved, its recognition as a science may be challenged. It may be that psychology is guilty of *scientism*: 'the borrowing of methods and a characteristic vocabulary from the natural sciences in order to discover causal mechanisms that explain psychological phenomena' (Van Langenhove, 1995: 14).

A psychology that at its heart embraces the philosophy and methodology of the natural sciences while maintaining its independence as a distinct discipline must face the challenge of bridging the explanatory gap that exists between mind and brain, between the reducible and the irreducible. The problem, then, is one of accommodation: how to accommodate the mental within the physical, and psychology within the natural sciences.

3.5 CHAPTER SUMMARY

This chapter has looked at the ways we try to explain who and what we are and has considered the problems with these explanations. On a basic level, if we are made up of exactly the same substance as a blancmange, then what is it that gives us our ability (maybe curse?) to be able to think about ourselves and act in the world? Does a blancmange know that it is a blancmange? Of course not, but you know that you are a person and different from all other people. The gap between our knowledge of the material world (the stuff that makes up blancmanges) and our experience of the mental world (thinking about ourselves and worrying if people think we are stupid) is what psychology has to try to bridge. Easier said than done!

 DISCUSSION QUESTIONS

If a psychological theory is said to be reductionist, does that necessarily make it a bad theory?

Consider the case of love. Is the love you have for your family or partner, or even for psychology, nothing but the workings of a vast assembly of neurons?

Instead of *explaining* important aspects of who you are – your beliefs, hopes, aspirations – does reductionism *explain them away*, by describing them as nothing but the intricate processes of lumpy grey matter?

If you yourself and your hopes are not just the workings of lumpy grey matter, then what else are these phenomena? How should psychologists set about studying these phenomena?

SUGGESTIONS FOR FURTHER READING

Bem, S., & de Jong, H.B. (2006). *Theoretical issues in psychology: an introduction* (2nd edn). London: SAGE. This book tackles some of the issues and topics raised in this chapter in much more depth. It provides a good opportunity to develop your understanding further.

Dietrich, A. (2007). *Introduction to consciousness: neuroscience, cognitive science, and philosophy*. London: Palgrave Macmillan. This book enables you to engage with the topic of consciousness in a much more detailed and in-depth way. It provides an accessible way into what is often referred to as the 'hard problem' of the philosophy of mind.

Valentine, E. (1992). *Conceptual issues in psychology* (2nd edn). London: Routledge. This book expands on the topics and issues raised in this chapter in an accessible way.

 Still want more? For links to online resources relevant to this chapter and a quiz to test your understanding, visit the companion website at edge.sagepub.com/banyard2e

4 DOING PSYCHOLOGICAL RESEARCH

Lead authors: Philip Banyard, Viv Brunsden, David Crundall, Mark Griffiths, Sarah Seymour-Smith and Belinda Winder

CHAPTER OUTLINE

4.1 Introduction	**51**
4.2 Researching psychology	**51**
4.2.1 Data and data analysis	51
4.2.2 Design	53
4.2.3 Quality control	53
4.2.4 Ethics	55
4.3 Example One: Using visual methods to explore the experience of foster care	**55**
4.3.1 The aim and the method	56
4.3.2 The analysis	56
4.3.3 Evaluating the method	57
4.4 Example Two: Using discursive methods to explore how people deal with testicular implants	**57**
4.4.1 Analysing gendered mechanisms of support in online interactions about testicular implants	57
4.4.2 Data and analysis	58
4.5 Example Three: Using mixed methods to investigate individuals who have been convicted of sexual offences	**59**
4.5.1 Mixed methods	59
4.5.2 Evaluation of the use of anti-libidinal medication with sexually preoccupied sex offenders	60

4.6 Example Four: Using behavioural tracking to investigate online gambling   61

4.7 Example Five: Using experimental methods to investigate driving behaviour   62

    4.7.1 The study   63

    4.7.2 The findings   63

    4.7.3 A reflection on the use of eye-tracking measures   64

4.8 Why psychology?   64

    4.8.1 Issues with applied research   65

    4.8.2 Giving psychology away   66

4.9 Chapter summary   67

Discussion questions   67

Suggestions for further reading   67

4.1 INTRODUCTION

This chapter is about the methods which psychology researchers use to collect data, and the ways in which they set about using their data to answer research questions. We will do this by looking in detail at five examples of recent research, and the difficulties and delights of doing research studies. These examples have been chosen to illustrate a spread of techniques and methods used in research, and to look at issues around foster parenting, dealing with testicular cancer, investigating sex offenders, problem gambling and driving skills. The chapter will cover the basic themes of psychological research and explore some key techniques. It will try to get beyond the dry accounts of research methods textbooks and behind the scenes of a published research paper. The aim of the chapter is to present an honest review of how research is developed in a psychology department in the UK and to inspire you, the reader, to want to be part of that collective activity.

FRAMING QUESTIONS

- How do psychologists acquire their evidence?
- What are the relative merits of the various methods in psychology?
- How is psychological research conducted?
- What is the value to our society of psychological research?

4.2 RESEARCHING PSYCHOLOGY

Psychology is grounded on empirical inquiry and evidence. Empirical inquiry is any kind of research which involves collecting data. Generally speaking, psychologists will not accept something to be the case unless they are able to point to empirical evidence in the literature. This reliance on evidence is what makes psychology a science.

Psychologists love evidence and they love their methods. Over the years, we have been responsible for developing numerous statistical tests, as well as numerous techniques for analysing qualitative data (see below). We write very precise Methods sections in our papers and we scrutinise the work of others in the finest detail. Some would argue that we love our methods too much and end up fetishising them above the content of our studies. As a result, we are in danger of producing methodologically brilliant, but pointless studies, or 'impeccable trivia' (Reicher & Haslam, 2006).

We will present the positive side of research in this chapter and try to convince you that the work presented here is both relevant and important, as well as being high quality scientific evidence.

In the first section we will look at three core aspect of the research process, namely (1) data and data analysis; (2) design; and (3) quality control. Each of these aspects is worth a book in itself, so we are providing signposts to further study rather than trying to provide a detailed account. We then go on to look at how these principles of research are applied in five examples of recent research.

4.2.1 DATA AND DATA ANALYSIS

A starting point for looking at data is to consider the distinction between qualitative and quantitative data. Qualitative data are about 'qualities' of things. They are descriptions, words, meanings, pictures, texts, and so forth. They are about what something is like, or how something is experienced, for example, the experience of foster care, or the way that men 'do' support in the context of decisions about whether or not to have a testicular implant (see below). Quantitative data are about 'quantities' of things. They are numbers, raw scores, percentages, means, standard deviations, and so forth. They are measurements of things, telling us how much of something there is.

The default in psychology has been to collect quantitative data (notwithstanding many instances of observational data in the work of pioneers like Piaget, or indeed the use of case studies in psychodynamic theory), but in the past 30 years there has been significant growth in the use of qualitative data and a development of techniques and methods to allow the robust analysis of what can be extremely rich and complex data sets. A marker in this change was the paper by Henwood and Pidgeon (1992) in the *British Journal of Psychology*, which argued that qualitative research is an ideal way to generate theory that is contextually sensitive, persuasive and relevant. With this growth has come increasing acceptance of the value of this work, such that it has moved from 'the margins to the mainstream in psychology in the UK' (Willig & Stainton Rogers, 2008: 8).

The growth of qualitative research has been controversial and has been resisted in some parts of psychology. As a result, the division between qualitative and quantitative is sometimes presented as being a confrontational battle between mutually exclusive opposites. Although we acknowledge the tensions and the disputes, we do not recognise the two approaches as being either opposites or mutually exclusive. Far from it. And in this chapter we present research on sex offenders and online gamblers that use both qualitative and quantitative data.

If you are a research junky, like most academic staff in psychology departments, then the thing that you most crave is data. And when you get this data, you can satisfy your craving by analysing it. How you analyse it depends on the type of data you have acquired and what sort of questions you want to ask of it.

At the straightforward end of data analysis there are strategies that simply involve collation and summarisation. For quantitative data, this might involve the use of simple descriptive statistics, such as measures of central tendency and percentages. Descriptive statistics do just what they say they do: they describe the data. They tell us things like the mean score of participants, the range of scores, the proportion of participants who achieved a certain score, and so forth. If we saw all of the data, then it would look like a jumble of information. Essentially, descriptive statistics help us to see patterns and relationships in the data. Straightforward analytic strategies for qualitative data include sorting units of textual information into categories.

More complex forms of qualitative analysis include discourse analysis; an example of this is described below in the work by Seymour-Smith (2013) on testicular implants. Discursive psychology is grounded in conversation analytic principles, and involves the systematic data analysis of naturalistic data, focusing on participants' orientations through an analysis of their 'turn-taking' in conversations. This is not about how polite people are when having a conversation, but about what people 'take' from another person's remark, and how they then position themselves. The job of a discursive analyst is to describe these practices. This involves a detailed analysis of (sometimes) small amounts of transcribed text as a means of reasoning through a complex set of propositions about our social world. One criticism of qualitative data is that it uses only 'small' numbers of participants. Although this is not always true (e.g. grounded theory may utilise as many participants as you would find in an experiment), it should also be remembered that the actual data are far more detailed and complex than one would normally find in quantitative research. Moreover, while the number of participants in some qualitative methods may be more modest (e.g. 5–15 participants in IPA – Interpretative Phenomenological Analysis), the qualitative researcher will continue to collect data until a 'saturation' point is reached (i.e. where the researcher judges they are not gaining any novel information from additional interviews or data extracts). Of course, the latter is somewhat subjective, as the closer you look at rich qualitative data, the more emerges, so it will depend on the skill of the researcher in determining a sufficient sample for their analysis.

EXERCISE: CHOOSING YOUR METHOD

Look at the research questions below and think about how you might get evidence to best answer the questions. We come back to all these questions later in the chapter so try this exercise now before you read on. Then you can compare your suggestions to ours, while bearing in mind that there is more than one answer to each of these problems.

1. What are the emotional experiences of foster carers?
2. How do men deal with and adapt to having testicular implants?
3. What is the effect of anti-libidinal medication on sex offenders?
4. Can we identify distinct patterns of behaviour in problem gamblers?
5. How do car drivers perceive hazards?

In relation to quantitative data, if researchers have studied a genuinely representative sample of a specified population, then they are allowed to infer that the patterns they see in the data from the sample also apply to the population from which the sample was drawn.

4.2.2 DESIGN

Probably the most widely used method in psychological research is the **experiment**. An experiment is basically a structured observation involving the systematic manipulation of one or more independent variables and the measurement of the effect of the manipulation on a dependent variable. It is held that experiments enable us to pick apart causality. In other words, experiments enable us to find out about the causes of things. One common mistake in the early stages of finding out about psychological research is carelessly to refer to every research study as 'an experiment'. This is wrong. Experiments are one kind of research method, which have a particular structure and logic to them (see section 5.2.1, 'The anatomy of the memory experiment' in Chapter 5).

> **EXPERIMENT** A form of research in which variables are manipulated in order to discover cause and effect.

The starting point for an experiment is an hypothesis. An hypothesis is a prediction about what will happen in the experiment. In the example below on eyetracking research, one of the predictions is that if you prime drivers to expect hazards, then it will affect the way they scan a road scene. The hypothesis is worded in such a way that a well-designed experiment will show the prediction to be either right or wrong. The hypothesis is formulated on the basis of a theory. If the prediction is found to be right (if the hypothesis is supported by the data), then this lends support to the theory. If the prediction is found to be wrong (if the hypothesis is not supported by the data), then this puts a question mark against some aspect of the theory. Of course, one experiment is never enough either to support or refute an entire theory.

> **INFERENTIAL STATISTICS** A way of using statistics to enable us to make inferences from data about relationships among variables, particularly with reference to cause and effect. This involves going beyond the data, hence the term 'inferential'. A contrast can be made with descriptive statistics.

> **PSYCHOMETRIC TESTS** Instruments which have been developed for measuring mental characteristics. Psychological tests have been developed to measure a wide range of things, including creativity, job attitudes, brain damage and, of course, 'intelligence'.

There are a wide range of **inferential statistical tests** that can be used to estimate the probability that differences in scores across experimental conditions could have occurred by chance. The choice of tests depends on the design of the study and the types of data that have been collected. If you want to explore these issues in greater depth, we recommend that you pick up one of the many texts on behavioural statistics, although if you start to enjoy it, we recommend you seek professional help (see Chapter 25 for a full range of psychological interventions that might help you).

Experiments and observational studies typically provide us with a third-party analysis of behaviour, one which is constructed completely from the 'outsider' perspective of the researcher. This is only likely to give us one part of the picture as far as human psychology is concerned, given that a crucial feature of the human condition is our ability to reflect on our own behaviour and experience. So psychology researchers also use methods which set out to explore participants' own perspectives on things. Sometimes these methods genuinely try to take as their starting point the perspective of the participant, as is usually the case in semi-structured interviewing, and in collaborative, humanist style research. For example, the studies on fostering and on sex offenders described below both use Interpretative Phenomenological Analysis to try to understand the meanings that people make of their own lives. In such a case, the design of appropriate interview schedules is crucial to facilitate the collection of rich data on how people feel or experience a particular phenomenon. More frequently, these methods are about getting participants' responses to researcher-defined items and questions. All these approaches we have lumped together under the generic heading self-report methods, though note that getting participants' responses to things like questionnaire items is frequently a component of observational and experimental studies. We discuss psychometric methods in Chapters 21 and 22.

4.2.3 QUALITY CONTROL

It is all very well collecting data, but how confident can we be of our findings? Measurement can never be completely accurate and we have to accept that 'all measurement is befuddled by error' (McNemar, 1946: 294). Psychologists try

RELIABILITY The reliability of a psychological measuring device (such as a test or a scale) is the extent to which it gives consistent measurements. The greater the consistency of measurement, the greater the tool's reliability.

VALIDITY The question of whether a psychometric test or psychological measure is really measuring what it is supposed to measure.

to make their measures as accurate and error-free as possible and they consider a number of issues when they do this. Some of the error is outside the control of the researcher, but some of it can come from the design of the study and the biases of the researchers.

The starting point for quality control is **reliability**. This refers to how consistent our measures are, so if we measure someone on Monday morning will we get the same result when we measure them on Friday afternoon. And, if not, why not? Psychologists have developed a range of techniques for assessing reliability, such as test-retest reliability where we take measures on two occasions and compare the results, and inter-rater reliability where we get more than one person to observe the same event and compare their observations.

The concept of replication is associated with reliability and it is a tenet of science that findings of empirical work should not be trusted unless they can be replicated. This means that an independent researcher should be able to copy the procedure of a given research study, and obtain the same pattern of results. The issue here is that replication studies are not often published in major journals and so there is no incentive for psychologists to carry out these replications.

The second major aspect to quality control in relation to measurement is **validity**. A measurement technique is said to be valid if it measures what it claims to measure. Note that this is related to, but not the same as, the notion of reliability. For a measure to be valid, it must first be reliable (it cannot be valid if it gives inconsistent measurements of the same thing), but it must also have other properties. For a start, it is possible to have a perfectly consistent (reliable) measure which is perfectly consistently rubbish. For example, we might develop a measure of intelligence which involves measuring the circumference of a person's head (see Chapter 22), and then converting the resulting measurement into an IQ score. This would give high levels of test-retest reliability and inter-observer reliability but it would not, validly, measure intelligence.

The conventional procedures for assessing reliability and validity in research which uses quantitative data are relatively well rehearsed in research methods textbooks. Researchers who deal with qualitative data are under no less of an obligation to demonstrate that their findings are trustworthy, but do not have recourse to the traditional statistical procedures for doing this. Indeed, they may prefer to use different terms, such as credibility (whether the findings are believable) and transferability (whether the results can be applied to other contexts) (Guba & Lincoln, 1994). Regardless, qualitative researchers are just as concerned with the robustness of their analysis, but the methods that are used to demonstrate this may vary from one research tradition to another, and the story is too involved to be tackled here. Suffice it to say that the secrets of doing good research, whatever tradition you are working in, is to be aware of the range of quality control procedures that are used within that tradition, and to be prepared to face the legitimate question of the sceptic, which is, in essence, 'Why should I believe your findings?'.

Another aspect of quality control is sampling. Your choice of participants will affect the data that you get. If, for example, you want to collect data from prisoners, you will need to get agreement of the prison authorities and also the prisoners themselves. This means that you will have a selective sample of those you are allowed access to and those who are willing to talk to you and this will restrict your ability to make generalisations about the prison populations as a whole. This does not

ASIDE

Journalogy

When we say that something is very common or popular among scientists, how do we know? Or how do we know that a scientific method or discovery is important? We might say that a lot of our friends use it, but that might be because we hang out with weird friends. The reason we know is because of citations. When a journal article includes a reference to a paper or a book, this means (usually) that the authors of that paper have read it and thought it was worth repeating. So every time your paper appears in the references of another article you notch up another citation. Citations are how we know that our published research is appreciated by other researchers. They are the academic equivalent of 'likes'.

invalidate the research, but it does require researchers to consider what biases are introduced into their data by their resultant sample.

Other sources of error include demand characteristics, experimenter effects and reactivity. **Demand characteristics** refer to the natural tendency for participants to try to guess the aim of the study and provide answers that fit that guess. **Experimenter effects** refer to the bias in the observer to see what they expect to see. Ideally, we reduce experimenter effects by creating studies where the participant is not aware of the hypothesis and neither is the person who is carrying out the research. This is referred to as a **double-blind** design. **Reactivity** refers to the changes in participant behaviour that occur when they are aware that they are part of the study. Just think about what you do when you see someone pointing a camera at you. You can't help but react to it.

As you can see, there is a lot to quality control in psychological inquiries and we have only been able to scratch the surface of it here. As we go on through the examples of research studies, we will return to these points.

4.2.4 ETHICS

Ethics are often presented as a checklist of things to do and not to do, but it is a more thoughtful process than that. It all starts with *morals*, which are rules to guide our behaviour. They are based on a number of socially agreed principles which are used to develop clear and logical guidelines to direct behaviour. They also contain ideas about what is good and what is desirable in human behaviour. *Ethics* are a moral framework that is applied to a narrow group of people, such as doctors or maybe a particular religion or even psychologists.

The British Psychological Society (BPS) has published a set of ethical principles with guidance for how psychologists should interpret these, and the most recent revision was published in 2009. The Code is based on four ethical principles, *respect*, *competence*, *responsibility* and *integrity*. You can access these guidelines and associated notes via the BPS website.

At our university, like most other universities in the UK, we have an Ethics Committee and all our work has to be scrutinised by them. This scrutiny includes all practical work carried out by our students who have to make individual submissions to the Committee of their final year project proposals. This is not a straightforward process and each year the research work of our students and researchers poses new problems to address. For example, we are very concerned to gain informed consent from people for the use of their data, but what if that data appears in the public domain on the websites of support groups? We can anonymise that data by giving the person a new name, but if we use an extract from their comments it would not be difficult to Google that quote and track them down. And what about copyright issues? Our research projects with prisoners, including sex offenders (see below), raise a lot of issues about confidentiality and consent, and on top of these we also have to ensure the safety and wellbeing of our colleagues (and their participants), both physically and emotionally.

There is a further moral question concerning the value of our research and the uses to which the data are put. We'll come back to that at the end of the chapter after we have looked at examples of the different research designs and techniques.

DEMAND CHARACTERISTICS Those aspects of a psychological study (or other artificial situation) which exert an implicit pressure on people to act in ways that are expected of them.

EXPERIMENTER EFFECTS Unwanted influences in a psychological study which are produced, consciously or unconsciously, by the person carrying out the study.

DOUBLE-BLIND CONTROL A form of experimental control which aims to avoid self-fulfilling prophecies by ensuring that neither the participants nor the experimenter who carries out the study are aware of the experimental hypothesis.

REACTIVITY A term used to describe the way in which the behaviour of research participants can be affected by some aspect of the research procedure. Most commonly it is used to describe the way in which the behaviour of someone who is being observed is affected by the knowledge that they are being observed.

4.3 EXAMPLE ONE: USING VISUAL METHODS TO EXPLORE THE EXPERIENCE OF FOSTER CARE

Viv Brunsden

This first example of research collected qualitative data on the experiences of foster parents. It used the unusual but potentially very rich method of photo-elicitation to draw out the data. This data was then explored using Interpretive Phenomenological Analysis (IPA), a method that is also used in a later example in this chapter of people convicted of sex offences.

4.3.1 THE AIM AND THE METHOD

The aim of this work was to explore the experiences of foster carers, particularly in relation to their emotional experiences. There are a wide variety of ways in which data around emotional experiences can be captured. Here it was decided to use Photovoice (Wang & Burris, 1997). This is a form of photo-elicitation whereby photographs are analysed as data in their own right, but are also used as a stimulus for discussions. The resultant talk then also forms part of the holistic data set alongside the photographs.

The Photovoice technique was originally developed for use within the discipline of sociology as a method of recording and documenting a community's concerns. Participants from that community were given cameras, took photographs that captured and reflected their everyday lives and would then be gathered together to discuss the photographs. Both the photographs and extracts from the discussions could then be presented back to the participating communities in the form of an exhibition delivered within that community and with an intention of influencing policy makers. This did not quite fit with our needs, or the concerns of psychology more generally, but a framework has been established for adapting Photovoice for psychological research (Brunsden & Goatcher, 2007) and this is what we followed here.

In effect, Photovoice is a data collection technique. It does not advocate any particular form of analysis and there are many techniques that can be applied to a data set consisting of both visual and verbal data. We decided to use Interpretive Phenomenological Analysis (IPA). We chose this because IPA is concerned with understanding the meaning that participants make of their own lives, synthesised with the interpretative meaning the analyst brings to the data. This emphasis on meaning and sense-making fitted very well with the research questions' focus on experience and on emotions. While usually IPA is applied to verbal data, it can also be used very well on visual images.

4.3.2 THE ANALYSIS

Five superordinate (overarching) themes emerged during the analysis. Each of these contained a number of sub-themes (see Figure 4.1).

FIGURE 4.1   The structure of superordinate and subordinate themes arising from the analysis

We found that the participants came to the interviews relaxed and ready to talk freely because they had already thought so much about their experiences in order to craft their photographs. They knew why they had taken each particular image and what it represented for them. The talk flowed naturally and, because many of the photos were metaphorical rather than literal, they were able to use these as an entry route into talking about some difficult issues that could have been tricky to articulate, or sensitive issues that they may otherwise have been reluctant to discuss. For example, one participant presented a photo of a continuously running tap to express the perpetual physical and emotional draining she felt (see Figure 4.2), while another deliberately shook the camera to create a blurred image to represent the ambiguity and confusion in her position of foster parent with its conflicted emotions, as distinct from the emotional clarity she felt towards her own 'real' child (see Figure 4.3).

FIGURE 4.2   Photovoice example 1

FIGURE 4.3   Photovoice example 2

4.3.3 EVALUATING THE METHOD

A key benefit of using this method was that we had forms of data to draw upon, each facilitating the production of the other. Hardly any questions had to be asked, meaning that the participants led the interview into the areas they truly wanted to discuss rather than it following any forced agenda predetermined by the researcher. Instead, questions became reactive, acting to clarify participants' talk, rather than directing and driving it. The talk also facilitated understanding of the images as their meanings could have been misconstrued without the interview to clarify. For example, the blurred image could have been seen as a mistake and that data ignored if the interview had not clarified its intended meaning.

The creative process that participants engaged in made the research process fun. Interviews can sometimes seem intimidating or daunting for participants and it can take time to build rapport between the researcher and interviewee. Here, however, participants were enthusiastic about how much they had enjoyed the photo-taking, which in turn set up the interview as an enjoyable experience. During the interviews, which still sometimes touched on some very sensitive topics, the physical act of holding an object, the photograph, seemed to relax participants, who used it physically at times, pointing at it when words failed them, incorporating it in gestures.

There is also a benefit in dissemination as the photographs can be used in the reporting alongside extracts from the talk. This can make for a more engaging piece of writing, but it also opens up new possibilities for dissemination, such as exhibitions of the photos alongside research posters offering the academic interpretations.

4.4 EXAMPLE TWO: USING DISCURSIVE METHODS TO EXPLORE HOW PEOPLE DEAL WITH TESTICULAR IMPLANTS

Sarah Seymour-Smith

This research collected qualitative data in the form of posts from online forums to examine how men dealt with the loss of a testicle and its replacement with an implant. The data was explored using discourse analysis.

4.4.1 ANALYSING GENDERED MECHANISMS OF SUPPORT IN ONLINE INTERACTIONS ABOUT TESTICULAR IMPLANTS

The loss of a testicle, as a result of having testicular cancer, may lead to feelings of inadequacy in men (Carpentier & Fortenberry, 2010). For those men who are concerned about their post-surgery body, the insertion of a testicular implant is a possibility. However, surgeons prefer to perform the orchiectomy (the nice way of saying removing a testicle) and insertion of a prosthesis (implant) within 24 hours of diagnosis, effectively limiting decisions about choice. One place where men can explore the possibility of whether or not to have a testicular implant is through interactions on internet support groups. It is typically argued that men search for medical information, whereas women tend to seek social and emotional support (Seale, Ziebland, & Charteris-Black, 2006: 2577) and Seale et al. (2006: 2588) argued that women enact greater emotional expressivity. I was interested in exploring gendered differences in communication in an online forum for testicular cancer (Seymour-Smith, 2013).

Studies of gendered communication have often used **content analysis**, but this approach loses the interactive features of communication (Seale et al., 2006). Furthermore, Gooden and Winefield (2007) found that both men and women engaged in emotional talk, yet the language used to express emotion varied. They demonstrated the importance of analysing talk that, at first glance, might not employ emotion words yet still had an emotional content. What was needed was a method of analysing interaction which placed more emphasis on the context in which accounts were produced. Discursive psychology (Edwards & Potter, 2001) is a method which examines, in detail, how individuals perform social action. The consideration is about what is actually being 'done' with the messages in the settings in which they are produced (Potter,

> **CONTENT ANALYSIS** A quantitative technique that involves the formal categorisation and the counting of frequencies of things in texts (particular words, phrases, ideas and so forth). It can be used with any medium that can be recorded and reviewed.

1996). Rather than treating language as a transparent medium and tool to access what people really think, discursive approaches treat language as social action (Edwards & Potter, 2001). The argument is that language is constructive, and the focus of analysis switches to how social realities and identities are built up by individuals for specific purposes.

The four longest threads about prostheses, taken from four separate testicular cancer online support forums, were analysed in this study. During the coding process, attention was paid to the rhetorical organisation of the posts in order to examine how people manage issues of their stake and interest (Potter, 1996) in their descriptions. The discursive features of 'support' and 'emotive talk' were considered over courses of interaction where such instances took place within the threads, in order to shed light on how participants 'did support' and communicated 'emotion'. The analytic principle of the next-turn proof-procedure (illustrated below) was applied to the analysis of sequential posts. By examining a response to a post, it is possible to elicit how the initial post was understood, grounding the analysis in the interpretations of the members of the support group.

4.4.2 DATA AND ANALYSIS

In order to demonstrate the analysis we will look at two annotated posts.

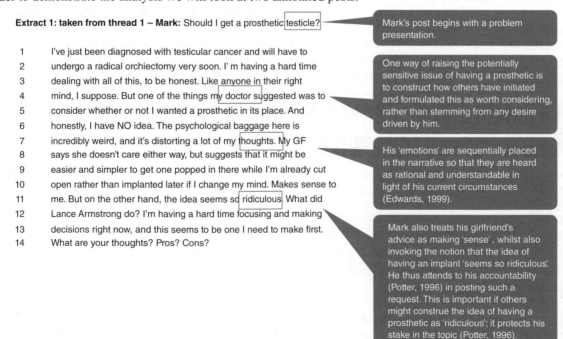

Extract 1: taken from thread 1 – Mark: Should I get a prosthetic testicle?

Mark's post begins with a problem presentation.

1   I've just been diagnosed with testicular cancer and will have to
2   undergo a radical orchiectomy very soon. I'm having a hard time
3   dealing with all of this, to be honest. Like anyone in their right
4   mind, I suppose. But one of the things my doctor suggested was to
5   consider whether or not I wanted a prosthetic in its place. And
6   honestly, I have NO idea. The psychological baggage here is
7   incredibly weird, and it's distorting a lot of my thoughts. My GF
8   says she doesn't care either way, but suggests that it might be
9   easier and simpler to get one popped in there while I'm already cut
10 open rather than implanted later if I change my mind. Makes sense to
11 me. But on the other hand, the idea seems so ridiculous. What did
12 Lance Armstrong do? I'm having a hard time focusing and making
13 decisions right now, and this seems to be one I need to make first.
14 What are your thoughts? Pros? Cons?

One way of raising the potentially sensitive issue of having a prosthetic is to construct how others have initiated and formulated this as worth considering, rather than stemming from any desire driven by him.

His 'emotions' are sequentially placed in the narrative so that they are heard as rational and understandable in light of his current circumstances (Edwards, 1999).

Mark also treats his girlfriend's advice as making 'sense', whilst also invoking the notion that the idea of having an implant 'seems so ridiculous'. He thus attends to his accountability (Potter, 1996) in posting such a request. This is important if others might construe the idea of having a prosthetic as 'ridiculous'; it protects his stake in the topic (Potter, 1996).

While it is possible to see that Mark frames his request carefully in a way that protects his stake and identity (Potter, 1996), elements of his post could be classed by content researchers as an 'emotive' account. Previous research then might indicate that men would not take up the 'emotive' tone, but let's follow the thread and see how this plays out.

Extract 2 – taken from thread 1 – Craig

1   As a guy who's been there, and opted not to get a prosthesis;
2   1) My doc said they actually would do the operation to remove the
3   cancerous testicle, let that heal, then do the implant in a separate
4   procedure. That might depend on the doc. Ask yours about it; this
5   gives you a chance to test out what it's like having only one.
6   2) Does your insurance cover the prosthesis? They might not. This may
7   influence your decision.
8   3) You know how sometimes you sit down and get your balls jammed
9   between your legs or otherwise crammed into a painful and awkward
10   position, and have to adjust yourself? That has never happened to me
11   since the operation.
12   4) Other than 3, it doesn't really feel awkward. It's little weired
13   having less of a handful down there sometimes, mostly due to lack of
14   symmetry, but honestly, it's not a showstopper
15   Believe me, I know what you mean about emotional baggage – I had less
16   than 48 hours between diagnosis and surgery. Not much time to make
17   decisions. So, ask your doc if he'll do the implant after you're
18   healed up. That way you don't have to decide now.

> Second stories are designed to align with a previous initial story and function to display an understanding and stance towards the initial story (Arminen, 2004).

> In providing an alternative, Craig 'does support' through offering information which is argued to be empowering (Bartlett and Coulson, 2011).

> Craig also employs humour in detailing the downside of having two testicles in contrast to his current situation.

> Craig acknowledges the 'emotional baggage' as being a consequence of the lack of time for this decision to be made. In doing so, Craig attends to Mark's concerns about presenting a rational response by aligning himself as also subject to such pressure.

Second stories are designed to align with a previous initial story, and function to display an understanding and stance towards the initial story (Arminen, 2004). Studies of empathy and sympathy (Pudlinski, 2005; Staske, 1998) have considered how the employment of such 'me too' responses (Staske, 1998: 71) normalise problematic feelings and attend to these experiences as reasonable and expectable. By categorising himself as similarly experiencing 'emotional baggage', Craig aligns himself with Mark in a manner that sanctions this way of talking.

The benefits of a discursive approach in this study are that it allowed the examination of the support mechanisms that men employed in practice in an everyday setting. A sequential analysis demonstrated how members 'did support' by attending to concerns raised in initial posts, something that might be missed in analyses that do not focus on the interactive nature of such groups. The mechanics of support are displayed through the collective practices of these men. It was possible to consider how masculine identities were invoked, and how members payed close attention to such nuances and designed their responses accordingly. Others have urged that strategies must be found to help men express 'emotions' (Lieberman, 2008). However, the findings of this study indicate that it is possible that concerns about men's emotional presentations are not as problematic as once were thought.

4.5 EXAMPLE THREE: USING MIXED METHODS TO INVESTIGATE INDIVIDUALS WHO HAVE BEEN CONVICTED OF SEXUAL OFFENCES

Belinda Winder, Rebecca Lievesley, Helen Elliott and Nicholas Blagden

This example is part of a programme of research conducted by the Sexual Offences, Crime and Misconduct Research Unit (SOCAMRU) at Nottingham Trent University. The unit was set up in 2007 to build upon the collaborative relationship between forensic researchers in the Psychology Division at NTU and HMP Whatton (the largest sex offender prison in Europe, holding approximately 840 convicted male sex offenders). The research presented here describes a mixed methods approach (using qualitative and quantitative data) to study the potential effectiveness of anti-libidinal drugs to reduce sexual preoccupation (thinking about sex all the time) and hypersexuality in convicted sex offenders.

4.5.1 MIXED METHODS

In a mixed methods study, researchers often triangulate data by directly comparing and contrasting quantitative statistical results with qualitative findings for corroboration and validation purposes (Cresswell & Plano Clark, 2007) and to gain a 'fuller' understanding of the research problem (Morse, 1991). The integration of two methodologies (qualitative, perhaps in the form of thematic analysis or IPA, and quantitative) can significantly enhance research findings and the overall contribution of the research study to the evidence base that is so vital in forensic psychology. Thus, in one mixed methods study, we examined the rehabilitative climate of a sex offender prison. We interviewed prisoners to ask them how they felt about living as a sex offender in a sex offender prison and used quantitative measures to examine similar phenomena, for example institutional climate, attitudes towards sex offenders and beliefs that sex offenders can change. The research concluded that prisons which foster therapeutic and rehabilitative climates can provide an environment which is more conducive to sex offender rehabilitation, and this was 'seen' through the results of the quantitative psychometric study, and 'heard' through the voices of the sex offenders interviewed about their experiences of living in a sex offender prison (see Blagden, Winder, & Hames, 2014).

4.5.2 EVALUATION OF THE USE OF ANTI-LIBIDINAL MEDICATION WITH SEXUALLY PREOCCUPIED SEX OFFENDERS

Sexual preoccupation has been defined as 'an abnormally intense interest in sex that dominates psychological functioning' (Mann, Hanson, & Thornton, 2010: 198), potentially resulting in a high number of sexual behaviours and hypersexuality (e.g. masturbating 20 times a day, every day). Sexual preoccupation is a significant predictor for sexual, violent and general reoffending (Hanson et al., 2007), which is why we are interested in it. Not surprisingly, it is found to be common in individuals convicted of sexual offences. In order to reduce the likelihood of sex offenders reoffending, **anti-libidinal medication** has been offered to prisoners at a UK sex offender prison for over four years, to reduce levels of preoccupation. Our research has been concerned with understanding whether this medication is effective at reducing levels of sexual preoccupation and hypersexuality in prisoners – and consequently, we hope, in reducing sexual reoffending (see Lievesley, Winder et al., 2012).

ANTI-LIBIDINAL MEDICATION Drugs that reduce testosterone levels to those found in pre-pubescent boys, with the aim of decreasing sexual interest and arousal. Anti-libidinal medication (in the form of anti-androgens) are associated with a range of side-effects, including the risk of liver damage, breast growth, hot flushes, depression and a decrease in bone density.

The main study we designed was quantitative and it examined whether there was a relationship between individuals taking anti-libidinal medication and their levels of sexual preoccupation and hypersexuality, as assessed by clinical questionnaires (Winder, Lievesley, Kaul et al., 2014). The participants were 60+ prisoners convicted of sexual offences (primarily offences against children). Data about their medication and levels of *sexual preoccupation* and *hypersexuality* (number of times masturbating per week) were collected. The findings (analysed through mixed factor repeated measures ANOVAS) showed that anti-libidinal medication significantly reduced both sexual preoccupation and hypersexuality. This quantitative analysis showed us that the medication was effective, but we wanted to understand more about the experiences and feelings of offenders taking the medication.

Consequently, qualitative research studies were conducted to understand the experiences of the individuals receiving anti-libidinal treatment (Lievesley et al., 2014). Thirteen offenders were interviewed (for between one and seven hours each) and thematic analysis was used to analyse the rich data set. A number of salient findings emerged: notably, that offenders reported that the medication gave them 'a clearer way of thinking: from sexually preoccupied to "human"', offenders confirmed the findings of the quantitative analysis, that the medication reduced their sexual preoccupation and hypersexuality, but also reported that it helped them to manage negative emotions generally in their lives, particularly anger. The analysis also showed there were a number of barriers to offenders continuing to take their medication regularly, with side-effects and the desire to 'recover' their sex drive interfering with patient compliance at times.

These findings fed back into the main evaluation and the process of referring individuals and prescribing medication, as well as helping us to understand more clearly the benefits of the medication for individuals (i.e. they had more headspace which previously they filled with sexual thoughts, they became less angry in general, and they no longer needed to find times and places to masturbate throughout the day).

4.6 EXAMPLE FOUR: USING BEHAVIOURAL TRACKING TO INVESTIGATE ONLINE GAMBLING

Mark Griffiths

Mark Griffiths is Director of the International Gaming Research Unit (IGRU). The IGRU has a primary research focus on the psychosocial factors related to various forms of gambling, gaming and cyberpsychology. The research of the unit collects and analyses all manner of qualitative and quantitative data. The example presented here looks at the behaviour of gamblers online by tracking the bets of 5,000 gamblers.

Online gambling is a psychological and sociological phenomenon that is becoming a focus of interest for an increasing number of researchers in the social sciences. As the internet offers a new venue for gambling, the risks for engaging in pathological behaviours are potentially increased (Griffiths, 2003). This has resulted in a large increase of empirical research into online gambling. Over the past decade, researchers in the gambling studies field have started to use online methods to gather their data, rather than traditional offline research approaches (Griffiths, 2010, 2014; Griffiths & Whitty, 2010; Wood & Griffiths, 2007).

There are a number of reasons why the online medium is a good place to conduct research with online gamblers. For instance, Griffiths (2014) notes the internet (1) is usually accessible to these gamblers, and they are usually proficient in using it; (2) allows for studies to be administered to potentially large-scale samples quickly and efficiently; (3) can facilitate automated data inputting allowing large-scale samples to be administered at a fraction of the cost and time of 'pen and paper' equivalents; (4) has a disinhibiting effect on users and reduces social desirability, leading to increased levels of honesty (and therefore higher validity in the case of self-report); (5) has a potentially global pool of participants, therefore researchers are able to study extreme and uncommon behaviours as well as make cross-cultural comparisons; (6) provides access to 'socially unskilled' individuals who may not have taken part in the research if it was offline; (7) can aid participant recruitment through advertising on various bulletin boards and websites; and (8) can aid researchers because they do not have to be in the same geographical location as either the participants or fellow research colleagues.

There have been a number of different approaches to collecting data from and about gamblers. This has traditionally included self-report methods (surveys, focus groups, interviews, etc.), experiments (in the laboratory or in gambling venues) and participant and/or non-participant observation. Very recently (i.e. since around 2005), a number of researchers in the gambling studies field have been given direct access to gambling data collected by gaming companies from their commercial online gambling sites. These types of data (i.e. behavioural tracking data) are providing insights into gamblers' behaviour that is helping to better understand how such people act and behave online and over long periods of time.

Over the past few years, innovative social responsibility tools that track player behaviour with the aim of preventing problem gambling have been developed, including *PlayScan* (developed by the Swedish gaming company Svenska Spel), *Observer* (developed by Israeli gaming company 888.com) and *mentor* (developed by neccton Ltd) (Griffiths, Wood, & Parke, 2009; Griffiths et al., 2007). These new tools are providing insights about problematic gambling behaviour that in turn may lead to new avenues for future research in the area. The companies who have developed these tools claim that they can detect problematic gambling behaviour through analysis of behavioural tracking data (Griffiths et al., 2009).

Behavioural tracking tools generally use a combination of behavioural science, psychology, mathematics and artificial intelligence. Some tools (such as *PlayScan*) claim to detect players at risk of developing gambling problems, and offer the gamblers ways to help change their behaviour (e.g. tools that help gamblers set time and money limits on what they are prepared to lose over predetermined time periods). Unlike the conventional purpose of customer databases (i.e. to increase sales), the objective of these new tools is the opposite. They are designed to detect and help those who would benefit from playing less. Such tools have been compared to a safety belt (i.e. something you use without intending to actually make use of). The use of these systems is voluntary, but the gaming operator strongly recommends its customers to use it (Griffiths et al., 2009). These tools use many parameters from the player's behaviour from the preceding year that is then matched against a model based on behavioural characteristics for problem players. If it predicts players' behaviour as risky, they get an advance warning together with advice on how they can change their patterns in order to avoid future unhealthy and/or risky gambling. Behavioural tracking data can also be used to evaluate whether the tools and advice given to gamblers can actually change (i.e. reduce) potentially problematic behaviour.

For instance, a study by Auer and Griffiths (2013) used behavioural tracking data to evaluate whether the setting of voluntary time and money limits helped players who gambled the most. Data were collected from a representative random sample of 100,000 online players who gambled on the *win2day* gambling website during a three-month test period. This sample comprised 5,000 registered gamblers who chose to set themselves limits while playing on the *win2day* website. During the registration process, there is a mandatory requirement for all players to set time and cash-in limits. For instance, the player can limit the daily, weekly and/or monthly cash-in amount and the playing duration. The latter can be limited per playing session and/or per day. In the three-month test period, all voluntary limit-setting behaviour by online gamblers was tracked and recorded for subsequent data analysis. Changes in gambling behaviour were analysed overall and separately for casino, lottery and poker gambling.

The results of this study clearly showed that voluntary limit setting had a specific and statistically significant effect on high-intensity gamblers (i.e. voluntary limit setting had the largest effect on the most gaming-intense players). More specifically, the analysis showed that (in general) gaming-intense players specifically changed their behaviour in a positive way after they limited themselves with respect to both time and money spent. Voluntary spending limits had the highest significant effect on subsequent monetary spending among casino and lottery gamblers. Monetary spending among poker players significantly decreased after setting a voluntary time limit. Studies such as this highlight the advantageous way in which behavioural tracking methodologies can be used to provide results and insights that would be highly difficult to show using other more traditional methodologies.

This study highlights that when it comes to studying online gambling behaviour, behavioural tracking methodologies offer a number of advantages for researchers. The main advantages are that behavioural tracking data (1) provide a totally objective record of an individual's gambling behaviour on a particular online gambling website (whereas gamblers in self-report studies may be prone to social desirability factors, unreliable memory, etc.), (2) overcome the problem of finding suitable online gambling participants as it provides an immediate data set (if access is granted by the gaming company), (3) provide a record of events and can be revisited after the event itself has finished (whereas in general self-report studies cannot), and (4) usually comprise very large sample sizes (e.g. studies by Auer and Griffiths [2013, 2014] have used databases of over 100,000 online gamblers). Some types of study, such as the evaluation of whether social responsibility tools actually have an effect on subsequent player behaviour, demonstrate that behavioural tracking methodologies appear to be the only reliable way of collecting data to show that specific interventions have a direct effect on player behaviour.

4.7 EXAMPLE FIVE: USING EXPERIMENTAL METHODS TO INVESTIGATE DRIVING BEHAVIOUR

David Crundall

David Crundall was Co-Director of the Accident Research Unit and Director of the Nottingham Integrated Transport and Environmental Simulation facility (NITES) at the University of Nottingham before moving accross town to Nottingham Trent University. The research highlighted here uses the technique of eyetracking to experimentally explore the factors that influence how drivers perceive hazards.

Why do drivers crash? Most collisions are due to human error, and many of these errors are based in lapses of attention. In other words, drivers often fail to look in the right place at the right time, and will occasionally suffer the consequences (Lee, 2008; Underwood, 2007). For this reason, researchers in the field of driver safety have been recording the eye movements of drivers for over 40 years in an effort to understand why these collisions occur.

As early as 1596, the eyes have been considered as the 'windowes of the mind' (Du Laurens, cited by Van Gompel et al., 2007: 3), and the notion of eye gaze direction providing important cues to current thought processes has persisted.

Just and Carpenter (1980) termed this the eye–mind assumption, which suggests the brain only processes what the eye is looking at, and the eye will remain fixated on an object until processing is completed. Unfortunately, things are not quite so simple. Have you ever read a sentence in a book and then realised that you haven't taken in any of the information? Have you ever pulled away from a traffic light when it changes to green, without actually looking directly at the traffic light? Both of these examples (fixating without awareness, and awareness without fixating) invalidate the eye–mind hypothesis. While it is safe to say that what we are currently looking at is *usually* also the focus of mental processing, these exceptions to the rule mean that we have to be very careful when interpreting eye movement measures during driving (Crundall & Underwood, 2011). Let us look at an example study (taken from Crundall, van Loon, & Underwood, 2006) which shows the usefulness of eye-tracking methodology, but also the need to be cautious in interpreting the results.

4.7.1 THE STUDY

The study was sponsored by a company selling roadside advertising space who owned poster boards that were mounted on roadside poles three metres off the ground. The sponsor believed that their advertisements would be looked at more often than bus shelter advertisements of the same size (their main competitor) primarily because the pole-mounted signs were more visible against the uncluttered backdrop of the sky. Unfortunately, there is plenty of existing evidence to suggest that the majority of driver's external visual search is dedicated primarily to the focus of expansion, and then to a horizontal hazard window around the focus of expansion (this is the area in which most driving hazards will occur; see Figure 4.4).

FIGURE 4.4 A representation of the typical locations that a car driver will look at most predominantly while driving, with red, yellow and green colours representing decreasing dwell time in these areas. Most external fixations tend to fall in this horizontal inspection window.

On this basis, you might imagine that a bus shelter advertisement will be fixated more frequently as it is more likely to fall within the horizontal inspection window than the pole-mounted adverts. Would the saliency of the pole-mounted adverts be sufficient to attract attention away from the horizontal window? Would this even be desirable in terms of driver safety? While the question held practical ramifications for the sponsor in terms of pricing their advertising space, it also had great theoretical interest for us as driving psychologists interested in road safety.

Eye-tracking measures were the obvious choice to investigate whether drivers looked at pole-mounted advertisements more than bus shelter advertisements. These measures allowed us to calculate how frequently drivers looked at these adverts and for how long. According to the eye–mind assumption, a greater number of fixations or longer fixation durations would suggest that the advert is being processed to a greater extent.

Eye movements can be tracked in the laboratory or in the field (using head-mounted or dashboard-mounted eye trackers). As the focus of this research was concerned with how advertisements potentially attract (or distract) attention away from the driving task, we made the decision to do the study in the laboratory using a series of video clips of real roads filmed from a moving car as it drove past these advertisements. Eye movements are very sensitive to the salience of objects. Thus we tried to ensure that the pole-mounted adverts were exactly the same as those in the bus shelters wherever possible.

Finally, we knew that the horizontal inspection window becomes especially restrictive when drivers are concerned about hazards. All drivers were told to rate each clip for hazardousness. However, while one group were specifically primed for lots of potential hazards (let us call these the 'hazard anxious' drivers), a second group was also told that they should feel free to look wherever they wanted to, with the concomitant suggestion that the clips wouldn't actually be that dangerous ('hazard relaxed' drivers). This latter condition provided the best opportunity for drivers to make fixations outside the typical horizontal window.

4.7.2 THE FINDINGS

Initial analysis of the general eye-movement measures produced a clear pattern. Overall, bus shelter advertisements were fixated more often than pole-mounted signs, and were fixated sooner. The duration of these glances to the bus

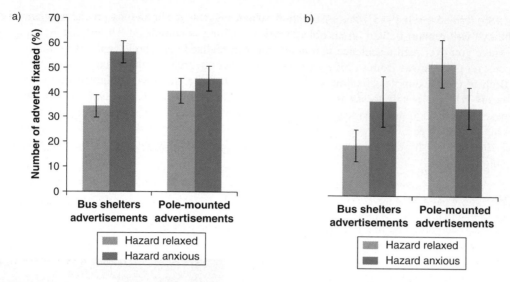

FIGURE 4.5 The percentage of bus shelter and pole-mounted signs that were (a) fixated, and (b) correctly identified in a four-item forced-choice memory task (with standard error bars)

shelters was also much longer than those to the pole-mounted advertisements. The eye–mind assumption would therefore suggest that the bus shelter advertisements are the most successful in attracting attention.

When the results were broken down across the two driver groups, however, a different pattern emerged. The bus shelters only received greater attention from the hazard anxious group, and actually received the least number of glances from drivers who were more relaxed about the hazards, and felt free to look wherever they wanted (Figure 4.5a). The longest fixation durations on bus shelter advertisements were also produced by the hazard anxious group. The greater frequency and duration of fixations on bus shelter advertisements did not, however, translate to performance accuracy on a subsequent memory test (Figure 4.5b). In fact the pole-mounted adverts were the most accurately recalled when participants were relaxed about the hazards.

We concluded that bus shelter advertisements do indeed receive more attention than the pole-mounted adverts, though this occurs when the participants are primarily engaged in a search for hazards. Thus we labelled the increased attention to bus shelters as *distraction* from the driving task. This presumably unwanted capture of attention while searching for hazards may have a negative impact on safety, and also fails to benefit the advertiser, as the long fixations do not translate into memory for the adverts. In contrast, there was a tendency for participants to fixate the pole-mounted adverts more than bus shelters, when they felt able to do so (i.e. when they were relaxed about the hazards), and these fixations did translate to improved memory accuracy. Thus the pole-mounted adverts appeared to *attract* attention when drivers felt it was safe to give it.

4.7.3 A REFLECTION ON THE USE OF EYE-TRACKING MEASURES

Without monitoring the eye movements of drivers in this study we would not be able to say for sure which type of adverts received the most fixations, which is crucial in this type of study. However, blindly adhering to the eye–mind assumption runs the risk of misinterpreting your data. In this case, the manipulation of hazard anxiety provided a useful interaction to help interpret the longer, more frequent fixations on bus shelters. Furthermore, the use of the memory test provided converging evidence from a different response measure.

4.8 WHY PSYCHOLOGY?

The above examples of research at this university on foster care, people convicted of sexual offences, testicular cancer, online gambling and driving skills illustrate both the range of research interests in one psychology department and the focus on applied research in this department. As well as these research projects the department carries out research into areas such as the emergency services, autism, reading, commuting, social networks, bees, bullying, ageing, digital technologies, drug abuse and many more.

4.8.1 ISSUES WITH APPLIED RESEARCH

This focus on applied research means that we are making a contribution to knowledge that we hope will directly benefit individuals and groups in our community. This applied focus comes at a price, though, which is that when you conduct applied research you often can't put the same level of control into the research as you would wish, and you are also working to the agenda of other groups who are stakeholders in the research.

One example of where controls are difficult can be seen in the anti-libidinal research described above. In our summary of methods above, we mention the need to have double-blind designs in order to remove expectation effects. If the participant is aware that they are being given a drug, for example, they might well experience a **placebo effect**, and if the experimenters know which participants have been given the active drug, then they will be prone to creating experimenter effects. It has not been possible to create either single or double-blinded trials for the anti-libidinal studies. In fact, this is often the case with medical and psychological treatments. The studies are often carried out by the people who are trying to show that the treatment works and it is often impracticable to create a placebo condition. This clearly puts a limitation on the conclusions we can draw from the study, but research cannot be perfect and we have to collect the best evidence we can.

PLACEBO EFFECT An inactive substance or fake treatment that produces a response in patients.

The issue of how much we can make generalisations from our findings is often raised with qualitative research. The examples above about the experience of foster care and how men 'do' testicular implants collected evidence from a small number of people. The researchers argue that they are providing rich insights from their sample and that generalisation is not a necessary feature of the work. Indeed, while the findings may not be *generalisable*, they may be *transferable*, and help understand others in the same situation, without the claim that ALL people in this situation will feel the same.

An even more complex issue arises about the effects we have on people's lives. If we think about research into gambling, we might discover a feature of a particular game that hooks people into playing it more. This is valuable information and tells us something about the nature of gambling addictions, but who will benefit most from this information? The person with the behavioural addiction is unlikely to benefit from this even if they become aware of it. The providers of games, on the other hand, might take a keen interest and incorporate this into new versions of their games.

EXERCISE: CONTRACT RESEARCH

The following quote about research is attributed to British Prime Minister, Winston Churchill:

> . . . when I call for statistics about the rate of infant mortality, what I want is proof that fewer babies died when I was Prime Minister than when anyone else was Prime Minister. That is a political statistic.

Think of some psychology research questions that have the potential to be leaned on to become political statistics.

Applied research is often funded by organisations who have a clear outcome in mind. Research at this university into the impact of technology in education (see the key researcher box on Jean Underwood) received several grants from government organisations who had an interest in showing that digital technologies boost educational performance. Research carried out over a 10-year programme of work sought initially to measure the impact of digital technologies on performance in schools (Underwood et al., 2007; Underwood et al., 2009). Although the research was able to show that practices of teaching and approaches to learning were changing, we were unable to connect these innovations to improved academic performance. One explanation for this lack of a measurable effect centres on the measurement tools that are selected for the purpose. Traditional testing of academic performance is still largely based on techniques and types of learning that are independent of the new technologies. As a consequence, they are not able to capture the impact of these technologies and so a lot of learning remains unassessed and unreported (Banyard, 2010). Findings such as these are uncomfortable for the organisations funding the research and can create tensions.

KEY RESEARCHER Jean Underwood

Jean Underwood was appointed as the first Professor of Psychology at Nottingham Trent University in 1998. Since then she has led research teams on a wide range of projects, most notably looking at the impact of technology in schools, and she also led the development of research in the department. She has a research focus on the cognitive development of the learner and the impact of digital technologies on learning and on behaviour in general. She has been working in these areas since the 1980s, is recognised internationally as a leading expert in the field, and has advised the government on issues such as internet safety and online bullying. Her outputs include 75 refereed research articles, 23 contract reports and numerous books and book chapters. She has been the editor of *Computers and Education* since 1997 and on the editorial board of several other journals. She has also been the recipient of numerous research grants in her career to date, bringing in millions of pounds to Nottingham Trent University.

The above information is what commonly appears in a (very good) academic CV, but research leadership goes way beyond these simple metrics. Underwood's contribution has been vital in building the research activity of the department from a handful of researchers when she arrived, to one of the largest research units in the University today, with a good reputation for the quality of its outputs. The development of a research department requires a lot of unseen and unreported activity, such as mentoring and team building and grant writing. The work of key researchers like Underwood goes beyond the academic papers and grants and makes a major contribution to the development of a vibrant research culture.

One final issue concerns the focus of psychological research on the individual rather than the groups that we inhabit. There are a lot of benefits in this approach but it is sometimes important to also take a wider perspective. For example, David Wilson (2009) argues that murder is not as individual an event as you might imagine it, but a societal event. The people who are commonly murdered by serial killers come from low status and vulnerable groups in our society, such as sex workers or the elderly. It's almost as if society is choosing the people it doesn't value and the serial killers respond to that. With regard to the studies on sex offenders described above, we focus on the offenders and their treatment, but a wider perspective would also consider the relentless sexualisation of children in our society (Lumby & Albury, 2010; Papadopoulos, 2010) that creates a climate where we are encouraged to see children in a sexual light. Our vilification of paedophiles is only matched by our consumption of media representations of children in an adult (and hence sexualised) way.

4.8.2 GIVING PSYCHOLOGY AWAY

Research rarely sets out its aims as being to make the world a better place but, ultimately, that is the goal. Even this apparently clear and worthy ambition has a difficult side to it. We might believe that the world would be a better place if there was, for example, more order, less crime, less waste and less anger. We might be able to achieve these through behavioural, medical or even surgical interventions, but in so doing we might well cut across individual rights in the pursuit of the greater good for the community.

So, what are the values that frame psychological research? George Miller (1969) in his presidential address to the American Psychological Association (APA) reminded his audience that the stated aim of the APA is to promote human welfare. He went on to consider what he meant by this phrase because it can be interpreted in different ways. Miller's argument was not to improve life by controlling people, but to suggest that psychology can contribute to quality of life by encouraging a better understanding of ourselves so that we can be more aware of 'what is humanly possible and humanly desirable'.

In his view, we are all psychologists. Every day we make judgements about our own behaviour and the behaviour of others. Just to engage in a casual conversation with you I have to make a mental model of what you are thinking and feeling and then match my words accordingly. Some psychology acknowledges this, but some psychology seeks to create an expert status for psychologists as people who know lots more about life and behaviour than ordinary people can ever hope to know. Miller does not buy into this and suggests: 'Our responsibility is less to assume the role of experts and try to apply psychology ourselves than to give it away to the people who really need it …'.

Whatever view you take on the 'psychologist as expert' issue, you might well think that it is important for psychological research to make a useful contribution either to our knowledge or to the application of the subject. You might well suggest that there should be an additional ethical principle of *usefulness*, and that psychological research is required to demonstrate that it is making a contribution to improve the world we live in (see Chapter 16 for discussion about why psychologists should think more about what they do and the impact their work has on the world).

In this brief look at the principles of research and some examples of how it is done, we believe that we have presented an honest account of what it means to do psychological research in the UK at the start of the twenty-first century. We also believe that our focus on applied areas illustrates how psychologists can get their hands dirty with real-life issues and move their work away from the 'impeccable trivia' of research for its own sake to the research that has a positive impact on the lives of people in our community.

4.9 CHAPTER SUMMARY

In this chapter we have looked at the key components of psychological research. In so doing we saw the importance of data and data analysis, research design and also quality control. Psychology is exceptional for engaging with the widest range of methods, and this quest for data has led psychology to be in the forefront of the development of new methods and analytical techniques. We presented examples of applied research from our own department that looked at the experience of foster care, how men 'do' testicular implants, research into people convicted of sexual offences, research into online gambling behaviour and experimental studies of driving behaviour. These applied studies show the breadth of work within a psychology department and also the shared ambition to have an impact on our community through our work.

 # DISCUSSION QUESTIONS

A topic that generates a lot of heat is the relative value of qualitative and quantitative data. It is worth considering, however, whether this is a phony distinction and whether either tradition can exist without the other. So, the discussion is to consider how far you can get with just one approach on its own.

In the text we have presented a range of applied research examples and argued that this style of research can make a valuable contribution to our community. There are many research projects, however, in UK psychology that would be regarded as 'pure' science. That is, they are exploring theoretical rather than practical ideas. Can you make a case for them as well as the applied research?

If we consider our applied research example, what do think should be the priorities of the researchers? How important are the concerns and interests of the organisation who fund the research?

 # SUGGESTIONS FOR FURTHER READING

The bookshelves groan with the weight of methods books in psychology. There are many excellent texts but you could start by trying:

Field, A.P. (2013). *Discovering statistics using IBM SPSS Statistics: and sex and drugs and rock 'n' roll* (4th edn). London: SAGE. This is the industry standard text for quantitative data analysis and the best seller.

For qualitative methods you could try:

Forrester, M.A. (Ed.) (2010). *Doing qualitative research in psychology: a practical guide*. London: SAGE.

 Still want more? For links to online resources relevant to this chapter and a quiz to test your understanding, visit the companion website at edge.sagepub.com/banyard2e

SECTION B

COGNITIVE PSYCHOLOGY: HOW WE THINK AND MAKE SENSE OF THE WORLD

Our senses are bombarded with information and we do something very special with it: we use it to create our perceptions of the world. There is a big gap between what we sense and what we perceive and that gap is what cognitive psychology is most interested in. We study how we see the world, how we store and recall information, how we communicate and how we think.

It is commonly reported that the first psychology laboratory was set up by Wilhelm Wundt (1832–1920) in Leipzig, Germany in 1879. Wundt's view was that psychology is the study of immediate experience – which does not include any issues of culture or social interaction. About half the work in the laboratory dealt with the topics of sensory processes and perception, though they also looked at reaction time, learning, attention and emotion. During the first half of the twentieth century, cognitive psychology was not as prominent as it is today, but we still draw on work from psychologists in that time, for example, Jean Piaget and Frederic Bartlett.

THE COGNITIVE REVOLUTION

Cognitive psychology became prominent in psychology in the middle of the twentieth century. George Miller hosted a seminar in the USA in 1956 where Newell and Simon presented a paper on computer logic, Noam Chomsky presented a paper on language, and Miller presented his famous paper on 'The magical number seven, plus or minus two'. Each of these presentations defined their field, and modern cognitive psychology was born.

The models of cognitive psychology reflect the technology of the time. So the early models of human information processing (e.g. Broadbent, 1958) were based on the way that a telephone exchange works. As technology has developed, the models of cognitive psychology have developed with it. The models are now based on computer processes. This brings up a question about whether cognitive psychology is studying the cognitive processes of people or the cognitive processes of computers. It also brings up a much deeper question about what it means to be human and be alive. Can a computer think? Can it be aware of itself? Can it have a theory of mind? These are questions that the material discussed in this section of the book and also in Section A will enable you to think about.

Artificial intelligence (AI) is one of the key strands of modern cognitive psychology. This is the science of making intelligent machines, especially intelligent computer programs. The origins of AI can be seen in the work of British scientist Alan Turing in the 1950s on intelligent machines. Turing believed that eventually computers will be programmed to acquire abilities that rival human intelligence. He created an 'imitation game', in which a human being and a computer can be questioned under conditions where the questioner would not know which was which. This is possible if the communication is entirely by written messages. Turing argued that if the questioner cannot distinguish them, then we should see the computer as being intelligent. Turing's 'imitation game' is now usually called 'the Turing test'. An argument against is outlined in Searle's (1980) 'Chinese room' thought experiment, which is described in Chapter 7.

Most recently, cognitive psychology has expanded into cognitive neuroscience which looks at the biological connections to cognition. This is by no means as straightforward as it sounds, because the two areas use different languages in that neuroscience talks about observations of physical changes in the brain and cognitive psychology uses evidence from individual experiences. How to match my experience of perception to the changes that can be observed in the brain is one of the great puzzles in science.

FIGURE B.1 Science fiction films often have robot characters that appear human and make us think about what is the difference between people and machines

© Ociacia/Shutterstock.com7

KEY ISSUES

One of the key issues for cognitive psychologists concerns the mechanical models it uses. On the plus side, these models have told us a lot more about how the brain processes information and also the limitations of that processing. On the down side, the focus on thought has sometimes neglected the emotional side of our life. It has also concentrated on logical thinking (the way a computer works) rather than intuitive thinking (the way people often work).

THIS SECTION

In this section we have four chapters looking at various aspects of cognition. Chapter 5 looks at memory: Are there different types of memory? How does memory work? And how can we apply such knowledge in practice, for example in exam revision? Chapter 6 looks at how information from the outside world gets to our brains (via our senses), how we attend to that information and how we interpret it. Chapter 7 looks at how we solve problems and to what extent we think logically when drawing conclusions about events. Finally, Chapter 8 looks at the wonder of language and how we understand the sounds and rhythms we call speech.

5 MEMORY

Lead authors: Thom Baguley, Harriet Smith and Duncan Guest

CHAPTER OUTLINE

5.1 Introduction	**74**
5.2 Theoretical foundations	**74**
5.2.1 The anatomy of a memory experiment	74
5.2.2 Short-term and long-term memory	76
5.2.3 From encoding processes to retrieval processes	80
5.2.4 Forgetting	82
5.2.5 Memory as a reconstructive process	84
5.3 Memory in action	**85**
5.3.1 Eyewitness memory	85
5.3.2 Flashbulb memories	88
5.3.3 Revising for an exam	88
5.4 Chapter summary	**89**
Discussion questions: forgetting	**90**
Suggestions for further reading	**90**

5.1 INTRODUCTION

We tend to think about our memory only when it lets us down (when we fail to remember something) or when it surprises us by giving us an obscure answer to a quiz question, but our memories are central to what makes us human. Without memories we wouldn't know where we are, what we are or even who we are. This is the wonder of memory, and psychologists have studied it for over 150 years. This chapter looks at some of that research.

One obvious characteristic of humans, both individually and collectively, is that they collect information. This information allows us to become skilled, for example, in essential areas, such as sailing, farming and tool use. When we use our memory and expertise in particular circumstances we find new learning opportunities *in those circumstances*: the more you know, the more you learn about what you know. This crudely explains why individuals develop highly specialised skills and why we hear of extraordinary individuals with great knowledge in areas as diverse as chess, European train timetables or 1980s pop trivia. Coupled with language skills, and another basic characteristic – that humans live in communities as social animals – this accumulation of knowledge has been transmitted across society and generations to sum to what we might call civilisation.

What follows from this is a vastness of human knowledge. Most of us get to learn and need to remember a great deal of information to get by. Memory is key to everyday behaviour and experience and we are only just starting to find out how it works.

FRAMING QUESTIONS

- Why do people forget?
- If memory is so central to human functioning and survival, why is so much information apparently discarded?
- Why is recent information better remembered than information from the distant past?
- Why does wanting or needing to remember something have so little impact on subsequent memory?

5.2 THEORETICAL FOUNDATIONS

A first step is to understand some of the core principles of memory that psychological research has revealed or, perhaps more accurately, begun to reveal. In this section we set out some of the theoretical foundations of research on human memory. The section will begin, however, with an overview of the 'anatomy' of a memory experiment.

Like much of psychology, memory research has a lot of technical terms ('jargon') that, although useful for experts, can be an obstacle for newcomers. Understanding the technical terms may also help you see how some theoretical research relates very directly to applied research.

5.2.1 THE ANATOMY OF A MEMORY EXPERIMENT

Let's begin with the 'bare bones' of an experiment on human memory. All memory experiments start with a simple distinction between **presentation** and **test**:

presentation → test

At *presentation* the experimenter will expose participants to the to-be-remembered material (e.g. a list of words, a set of faces or odours). At *test* the experimenter will attempt to measure participants' memory for the material that was presented.

From this simple beginning there are many ways to manipulate the structure of the experiment. A good researcher will not pick these manipulations at random, but will usually be guided by their knowledge of memory theory in general, and often by a particular theory. This usually leads to one or more hypotheses about what will happen. We can get a richer appreciation of how this is done by considering a very basic general theory of memory. Such a simple view might break down memory processing into three stages: **encoding**, **storage** and **retrieval**. In this account, encoding occurs at presentation, retrieval occurs at test and storage occurs between presentation and test.

> **ENCODING** The stage of memory involving interpreting and transforming incoming information in order to 'lay down' memories.
>
> **STORAGE** The stage of memory between encoding and retrieval.
>
> **RETRIEVAL** The stage of memory where information is brought back into mind to be used or reported.

ENCODING

It follows that a researcher can learn about encoding by manipulating the conditions under which presentation occurs. They can manipulate the quantity, duration, order or timing of presentations to influence encoding (not to mention manipulating the to-be-remembered material itself). A very common manipulation is whether or not to tell participants that they will be tested. If participants are not told they are to be tested, this is referred to as **incidental** learning or memory. If participants are told they are going to be tested, it is an **intentional** learning or memory experiment. Often, incidental memory is markedly worse than intentional memory, but this is not always the case, and this is an interesting puzzle for memory research. Hyde and Jenkins (1969) found that asking participants to rate the pleasantness of words produced levels of incidental memory that were as good as or better than intentional learning of words. This is a striking example of the phenomenon that merely having the intention or desire to remember something won't necessarily result in good memory (Anderson & Schooler, 2000).

STORAGE

Manipulating how encoded material might be stored is less straightforward. These manipulations tend to be indirect. It is possible to manipulate the duration of storage by increasing the **retention interval** (the gap between presentation and test). Researchers can investigate what factors might be important for storage (and hence subsequent forgetting) by manipulating the activities that take place prior to testing (e.g. sleeping versus staying awake; Jenkins & Dallenbach, 1924).

RETRIEVAL

Retrieval processes can be investigated by manipulating the way memory is tested. One of the most important decisions to consider in testing memory is how to measure it; a key distinction is between **recognition** and **recall**.

EXERCISE: THE ROYAL WEDDING, PART 1: HOW WELL DO YOU THINK YOU CAN REMEMBER EVENTS?

Psychologists have studied how accurately people remember key events. Can you remember the Royal Wedding in 2011? This news excerpt might help to jog your memory.

The Royal Wedding

On a warm summery day in 2011 Prince William married Kate Middleton at Westminster Abbey. The Abbey was decorated with trees and colourful flowers and was packed with 1,900 guests including foreign dignitaries, diplomats, members of the UK government and the couple's family and friends. Kate wore a beautiful lace wedding gown by British designer, Sarah Burton. William, who was in the Royal Air Force at the time, wore a traditional military uniform. After the service, 650 of the guests attended a reception at Buckingham Palace. Prince William then drove his new bride to Clarence House in his father's old Aston Martin. Close friends and family were invited for dinner at Buckingham Palace in the evening.

We will return to the Royal Wedding later in the chapter.

RECOGNITION

Recognition involves re-presenting the original material and asking participants to determine whether it occurred in the experiment. Although recognition appears to be a very simple procedure, it is surprisingly complex. For example, in an **old–new recognition test** only one item is presented at a time and a 'new' (unrecognised) or an 'old' (recognised) response is required. In a **two-alternative forced-choice recognition test** the 'new' and 'old' items are presented together and the recognised item is selected. Researchers often manipulate other factors, such as the proportion of 'new' and 'old' items or their similarity to those originally presented.

RECALL

Recall involves prompting participants to remember material that was originally presented. Here the main options are **free recall**, where the prompt is general and retrieval undirected (e.g. 'remember as many words as you can from the list'), and **cued recall**, where specific prompts or cues are used to direct or constrain recall (e.g. 'try to recall the first word on the list'). A good example of cued recall is paired-associate learning (PAL). In PAL, participants are presented with **word pairs** such as 'Dentist–Smug'. At test they are given one half of the word pair (e.g. 'Smug') as a cue to retrieve the other. All sorts of things can act as recall cues: indeed, applied memory research often looks to reproduce the kinds of memory cues that occur in everyday life (e.g. someone's face acts as a cue to retrieve their name).

Most memory research uses what are known as **explicit memory tests** where the participant is told that they are being tested. However, it is also possible to have an **implicit memory test**. An implicit test involves performing an activity apparently unrelated to memory at test (e.g. asking people to complete the word stem 'BA____' with the first word that comes to mind). Participants' responses are then examined to determine whether material presented earlier has influenced the implicit memory task (e.g. a participant who encoded BATTLE might respond with that word more often than a control participant exposed to the word CATTLE). It is tempting to conclude from these studies that implicit memory tests tap into unconscious memory processes while explicit memory tests tap into conscious processing, but the issue of whether there is a separate, unconscious 'implicit' memory system is controversial. What if only part of the stimulus was encoded? Such a fragment might make it more likely that a word stem was completed with the original item, yet might not be sufficient to produce explicit recall (Whittlesea & Dorken, 1993). Furthermore, it seems unlikely that any measure of memory is purely explicit or implicit (e.g. participants are probably aware that some of their responses on the word stem completion task were also on the earlier word list). The implicit–explicit dichotomy is one of many proposed distinctions in memory.

5.2.2 SHORT-TERM AND LONG-TERM MEMORY

EXERCISE: MEMORY FOR FILMS, PART 1

Take a blank sheet of paper and a pen. Give yourself three minutes. Think about films you have seen at the cinema and write down the names of as many of the films as you can.

We will return to this exercise later in order to reflect on it.

One of the best known of such distinctions is between **short-term memory** and **long-term memory**. These are terms that we use in everyday speech and they seem to fit with our experience. Some things can be remembered from years ago, but at the same time you will be unable to recall some of the things you wanted when you set off to the Co-op just five minutes ago. Researchers tend to use short-term or immediate memory to describe experiments where tests closely follow presentation, and long-term memory where there is a delay between presentation and test (Neath & Suprenant, 2003).

ASIDE

Is the magical number 1, 4 or 7?

One of the best known works in experimental psychology is George Miller's 1956 paper *The magical number seven, plus or minus two: some limits on our capacity for processing information*. This is one of the most widely cited (and mostly widely misunderstood) journal articles in psychology. In it Miller quips that he has been 'persecuted by an integer' after finding that performance in a range of different tasks seems to be limited to around seven items. In the end, he concludes that the number 7 +/−2 is not special.

One of the phenomena he addresses is the capacity limit in short-term memory tasks in which people can typically repeat back about seven 'chunks'. A chunk (in this context) is a coherent unit of information in long-term memory (e.g. a word, number or name). Miller's paper spurred a great deal of important work on short-term and long-term memory (e.g. on how people use chunks in long-term memory to increase short-term memory capacity). However, it also led to the widespread claim that psychologists have established that short-term memory has a capacity of seven items or so.

Both before and since Miller (1956), psychologists have debated not only what the capacity of short-term memory is, but also whether there is a capacity limit (or indeed whether there are separate short-term and long-term stores). For instance, the great British psychologist Donald Broadbent argued that the limit was around three or four items – the level of errorless performance in immediate recall (Broadbent, 1975).

Cowan (2001) reviewed the literature on capacity limits in short-term memory and argued that there is a limit, but that it falls around four items. The fundamental problem in establishing any limit is trying to eliminate tricks (such as chunking) that people routinely use to extend short-term memory. Experiments that eliminate these tricks (e.g. by using meaningless materials that can't easily be associated as a single chunk or looking at indirect effects of the capacity limit) find that young adults recall around three to five items or 4 +/−1 (Cowan, 2001, 2010).

Ultimately, the question of a capacity limit is interesting because it requires a model about the relationship between short-term memory, long-term memory and attention. For instance, Oberauer (2002) proposed a model that distinguishes between the focus of attention (one item), a capacity-limited region of direct access and the set of active items in long-term memory. In this model the short-term store is an emergent property of attention and long-term memory.

So, what is the correct answer? Given present understanding, the answers 1, 4 and 7 are all reasonable answers to slightly different questions. There appear to be some situations in which we can only attend to one item at a time, but young adults can typically hold around four items of information without resorting to strategies such as chunking. If given the opportunity to extend capacity through chunking or other mechanisms, people can recall more than four chunks – and 7 (+/−) is a reasonable estimate for many common situations.

It turns out that there are important differences in short-term and long-term memory experiments. For instance, Postman and Phillips (1965) looked at free recall for 10-, 20- or 30-word lists with either no delay between presentation and test or a short delay of 15 or 30 seconds. They looked at what happens as the serial position (order of presentation) of an item changes. The results for the 20-word list are shown in Figure 5.1 in the form of a **serial position curve**. With immediate testing, recall shows a characteristic bow-shaped serial position effect, with good recall for both the first few items – the **primacy effect** – and the last few items – the **recency effect**. Recall for the middle serial positions is poor. The primacy effect is unaffected by delay. In contrast, the recency effect is dramatically reduced by the 15-second delay, and after 30 seconds disappears altogether. These and other findings led to an intuitively appealing explanation: that of separate short-term and long-term memory stores.

According to this view, participants rehearse (e.g. by repeating them silently or out loud) the items in the order they are presented. If we assume, as most psychologists do, that **primary memory** has a limited capacity, then the first few items will rapidly exceed this capacity. As more items are presented, participants abandon rehearsal of the early items and switch to rehearsing middle and later items. On balance, however, early items benefit from more rehearsal than later items. Assuming that rehearsal increases the chance of an item entering a **long-term store** (LTS), then this accounts for the primacy effect. A separate **short-term store** (STS) can account for the recency effect: immediate testing allows a participant to output the contents of the STS first. However, even a short delay involving a cognitively demanding activity (e.g. Postman and Phillips' counting task) seems to eliminate these items from the STS and disrupts the recency effect. Consistent with this, Waugh (1970) showed that recalls from later serial positions (recent items) are faster than those for earlier ones.

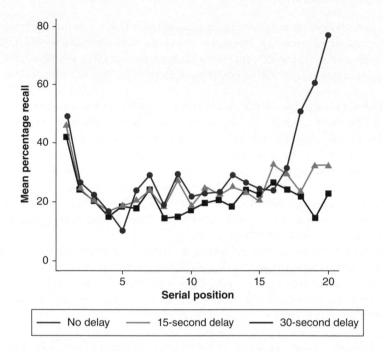

FIGURE 5.1   Serial position curves plotting percentage recall against order of presentation for 20-word lists with no delay, 15-second filled delay or 30-second filled delay (adapted from Postman & Phillips, 1965). For the delay conditions the retention interval is filled with a counting task to prevent rehearsal

The concept of separate long-term and short-term stores was incorporated into a number of models of short-term memory in the 1960s and 1970s (e.g. Atkinson & Shiffrin, 1968; Waugh & Norman, 1965). The best known of these, Atkinson and Shiffrin (1968), has become known as the **modal model** of short-term memory. This model is set out in Figure 5.2. In this simple version of the model (which does not include sensory memory, added in later versions), items enter the short-term store as a consequence of attention to environmental input. The STS has a limited capacity and items in the store **decay** rapidly or are displaced by new input unless maintained by rehearsal. The longer an item

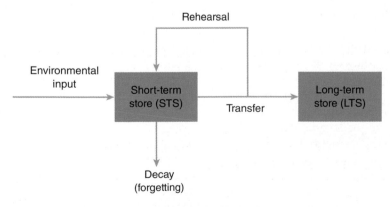

FIGURE 5.2   The Atkinson and Shiffrin (1968) modal model of short-term memory

spends in the STS, the more likely it is to enter the LTS, which has unlimited capacity. Rundus (1971) tested the model by asking participants to rehearse out loud. The number of times an item was rehearsed predicted recall, except for the most recent items – just as predicted by the modal model.

Despite its intuitive appeal, the modal model rapidly became untenable as an account of short-term memory. Studies of brain-damaged patients (originally taken as support for separate STS and LTS) suggested that impaired short-term memory did not disrupt long-term memory (Shallice & Warrington, 1970) as it should do if items only enter the LTS via the STS. Studies by Bjork and Whitten (1974) and Tzeng (1973) showed that engaging in an activity such as arithmetic for a short period after presenting a list of word pairs eliminated the recency effect, but not if the activity took place after each word pair. This makes no sense in the modal model because in neither case should participants be able to access recent words from the STS. More generally, **long-term recency** effects have also been found. For example, Baddeley and Hitch (1977) found that rugby players showed recency effects for the last few matches they had played.

KEY STUDY

Bjork, R.A., & Whitten, W.B. (1974). Recency-sensitive retrieval processes in long-term free recall. *Cognitive Psychology, 6*, 173–189.

This influential study challenged the account of the recency effect in the modal model. According to the modal model account, recent items are recalled better than items in the middle of the list because they are still in the STS if recall is tested immediately after presentation of the list. Consistent with this, Glanzer and Cunitz (1966) showed distractor activity immediately after the list (e.g. 30 seconds of mental arithmetic) almost completely eliminates the recency effect – presumably because it prevents rehearsal. Bjork and Whitten (1974) took this idea a step further and looked so see what happened if 12 seconds of distractor activity was added after each item in the list (and 20 seconds after the final item) in what is known as a continual distractor task. According to the prevailing theories of the time, Bjork and Whitten expected to find recency completely abolished. To their initial surprise, adding distractor activity after each item reinstated the recency effect. Given the surprising nature of their initial finding, Bjork and Whitten (1974) report two further experiments that replicate this long-term recency effect. Since then there have been numerous replications of the study and several other examples of long-term recency effects (e.g. such as memory for songs).

Bjork and Whitten (1974: 189) argued that 'the customary two-process theoretical account of immediate free recall is certainly incomplete, if not wrong'. This is a clear attack on the modal model and the two separate processes it invokes to explain primacy and recency effects. They proposed instead that both short-term and long-term recency effects depend on the ease of discriminating memories of different ages, which depends on the ratio of their temporal separation. Thus a one-second-old and a three-second-old memory are easy to discriminate (a ratio of 1:3), but a 31-second-old and a 33-second-old memory are hard to discriminate (ratio 31:33). In a continual distractor task, however, all the items have greater temporal separation. Therefore, the most recent items are relatively easy to discriminate from the older items because the ratio between them is lower (e.g. a ratio of 21:35 for the final two items) than if there was no continual distractor task (e.g. a ratio of 21:23 if items are presented every two seconds).

Baddeley and Hitch (1974) responded to the shortcomings of the modal model by proposing a multiple component **working memory model**. This model dominated short-term memory research in the 1980s and 1990s and is still very influential. The model recognised the importance of the STS in coordinating and monitoring numerous processes that feed into the activities we are currently working at (e.g. sitting at a desk typing a book chapter), hence working memory. As we have seen, however, STS seems to have a very limited capacity, so how can it possibly coordinate all these processes? Baddeley and Hitch's answer was that STS is built up of a number of sub-components and although each is limited in capacity, they draw upon different resources. To work out what these subsystems were, working memory researchers used a dual task procedure. This involved asking participants to complete two or more tasks that both require short-term storage at the same time (e.g. reading a word list while tapping a rhythm). If these two tasks draw on the same memory resources, then performance should suffer greatly when performing both together compared to when performing them individually. Building on experiments using this procedure, the original working memory model proposed that the STS is composed of three subsystems. The first subsystem, the central executive, is the control system. It is responsible for directing attention between tasks and coordinating the two other components: the phonological loop and the visuo-spatial sketchpad. The phonological loop is a temporary store which holds acoustic and verbal information. Verbal information can be maintained in the loop through articulatory rehearsal (mentally repeating the words, phrases or sounds). The sketchpad is the visual equivalent; a temporary store of visual and spatial information. According to the working memory model, tapping a rhythm should not interfere with reading a word list because it does not draw upon the resources of the phonological loop. In contrast, articulatory suppression (repeatedly saying 'the, the, the') would interfere with reading a word list because it would compete for the limited resources of the phonological loop.

As with any theory, the working memory model proposed by Baddeley and Hitch in 1974 has undergone significant development (e.g. Baddeley, 2000) and Baddeley (2012) provides a good review of this. As with any theory, there have also been alternative conceptualisations of working memory (e.g. Cowan, 2005), but it is beyond this chapter to provide a full discussion of these. The important point is that whether we consider the STS as a single system or try to break it down into sub-components, being able to store information for short periods of time is vital to everyday tasks such as reading, mental arithmetic or understanding a conversation.

So far, we have focused on the distinctions between the STS and LTS. But is it necessary to propose distinct STS and LTS at all? An increasingly popular view is that there may only be a single memory system. Is it possible to explain long-term recency and short-term recency effects with the same mechanism? The most likely candidate is *temporal distinctiveness* (Bjork & Whitten, 1974; Glenberg & Swanson, 1986). This suggests that what makes memories easier to retrieve is their recency in time. According to this explanation, remembering involves discriminating between various competing memory traces. This discrimination is a perceptual process and, just as it is easier to detect a large item among a set of small objects, so it should be easier to detect a recent memory among a set of old memories. Research on perception suggests that such discrimination depends on the ratio of the time interval between the encoding and retrieval of items (not on the absolute difference in times). Retrieving something presented five seconds ago is much easier than something presented 10 seconds ago (a ratio of 1:2). But there will not be much difference in the ease of retrieving items presented 105 and 110 seconds ago (a ratio of 21:22).

EXERCISE: MEMORY FOR FILMS, PART 2

Now look back at the list of films you made in the previous exercise.
Are the last three or four films you have seen on the list? Is there any evidence of a long-term recency effect?
Are more recent films recalled earlier or later in the list?

5.2.3 FROM ENCODING PROCESSES TO RETRIEVAL PROCESSES

Although a lot of research on memory has focused on the distinction between memory structures such as the STS and the LTS, this can distract from a more fundamental issue: How does memory operate? The beginnings of the answer to this question lie in considering the processing that occurs when items are encoded and retrieved.

The way we process material at encoding influences whether it will be retrieved. Craik and Lockhart (1972) proposed that how well we remember material was determined by the extent to which we extract meaning from it (which they term 'depth'). Their **levels of processing theory** argues that shallow, **perceptual processing** leads to worse retention than deep, **semantic processing**. Many studies have found that perceptual tasks (e.g. counting the number of times the letter 'E' appears in a word) result in poorer memory than tasks that involve the semantics of a word (e.g. deciding whether it completes a sentence).

PERCEPTUAL PROCESSING Processing of material to extract superficial sensory characteristics such as shape or colour.

SEMANTIC PROCESSING Processing of material that extracts meaning from it.

Levels of processing theory sparked enormous interest in the way processing influences later memory performance. There is evidence that the quantity of processing (Johnson-Laird, Gibbs, & de Mowbray, 1978), the distinctiveness of processing (Eysenck, 1979) and the extent to which processing elaborates or links items (Anderson & Reder, 1979; Marschark & Surian, 1989) all influence memory performance.

Levels of processing theory have had mixed fortunes. Many researchers (e.g. Baddeley, 1978) were unhappy with the focus on depth rather than other aspects of processing. A critical problem is the difficulty of determining depth independently of later memory performance: it is tempting to explain poor performance as resulting from 'shallow' processing because it is difficult to determine precisely how much meaning participants have extracted during encoding. Last, but not least, it neglects the role of retrieval processes.

KEY STUDY

Morris, C.D., Bransford, J.D., & Franks, J.J. (1977). Levels of processing versus transfer appropriate processing. *Journal of Verbal Learning and Verbal Behaviour, 16,* 519–533.

This important study contrasted perceptual and semantic processing. For the former, a participant might hear the sentence 'BLANK rhymes with legal' followed by the word 'Eagle' or 'Train'. For the latter, they might hear 'The BLANK had a silver engine' followed by the word 'Eagle' or 'Train'. In each case they had to make a 'Yes' or 'No' decision about whether the target word filled the BLANK.

The big difference between this and levels of processing experiments is the inclusion of a rhyme recognition test. In this test participants were presented with a list of words such as 'Regal' or 'Plane' and were asked to decide whether the word rhymed with a word that had previously been presented.

Using a standard recognition test, a depth of processing effect was observed: semantic processing produced better memory than perceptual processing. This effect was reversed with the rhyme recognition test: words learned with the perceptual (rhyming) task were recognised better than words learned with the semantic (sentence completion) task.

Morris et al. (1977) interpreted this in terms of **transfer-appropriate processing**. What matters is the overlap in processing between encoding and retrieval, rather than just encoding processes. Processing the sound of the word when it is encoded (which must happen if you have to decide whether it rhymes with another word) makes it possible to associate the sound of the word with aspects of the *context* at encoding. If you are subsequently prompted with those sounds at test, this cues the retrieval of the associated context.

The importance of the relationship between encoding and retrieval is captured by what Tulving and Thomson termed the **encoding specificity principle**:

> Specific encoding operations . . . determine what is stored, and what is stored determines what retrieval cues are effective. (Tulving & Thomson, 1973: 369)

Our memories can be triggered by all manner of things. Sometimes we remember a childhood event when we hear a song that was playing at the time. This song is an example of a **retrieval cue**, but it could just as easily be something that you see, smell or touch. Retrieval cues are effective because they are part of what was encoded. The principle is important because it helps remind us of the interrelationship of encoding

RETRIEVAL CUE Any stimulus that helps us recall information, for example, a picture, an odour or a sound.

and retrieval, but it is not very useful as a theoretical statement. After all, in its most general form it does not predict what cues are effective: it only implies that, once found, an effective cue must overlap with what was encoded. Nevertheless, encoding specificity is useful in understanding a number of well-known and sometimes puzzling effects in the literature. For instance, a number of studies have shown that reinstating at test the original context in which something was presented improves memory. One striking demonstration of this **context-dependent memory** is Godden and Baddeley (1975), who showed that if a word list is learned under water, it is better remembered if testing also takes place under water (rather than on dry land). Of course, you might ask what possible use there is to learning a list of words under water, and the answer is something to do with counting fish (and you probably do not want to know any more than that).

5.2.4 FORGETTING

Studying forgetting turns out to be especially tricky. We can measure what is remembered in different ways (e.g. recognition or recall) and we can influence what is retrieved by the effectiveness of the cues used at test. Even so, there are two particular issues in forgetting that have been widely debated in the literature and which are worth exploring here. These are the form of the **forgetting function**, and the question of what causes us to forget.

> **FORGETTING FUNCTION** The mathematical equation that determines the precise rate of forgetting as a function of time.

It is important in research on forgetting to be sure that the material was ever in memory at all. Otherwise it cannot be forgotten. This is usually achieved by ensuring items are learned to criterion (e.g. repeating items until accuracy on an immediate test is 100%). A famous example is from Ebbinghaus (1885/1913), who used the percentage savings – the reduction in repetitions required to relearn a set of items (see Figure 5.3).

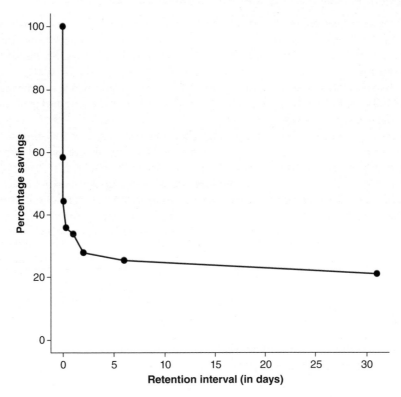

FIGURE 5.3 The Ebbinghaus forgetting function depicting the percentage savings on relearning lists of nonsense syllables as a function of the time elapsed since learning

We also need to consider that just because material has not been retrieved it does not mean that it has been permanently lost. As Tulving and Pearlstone note: 'it is useful to draw a distinction between what information or what traces are *available* in [memory] and what are *accessible*' (1966: 381–382). Any time memory is tested, the relationship between retrieval cues and what was encoded means that only a subset of what is potentially accessible is available. One explanation of the loss of information between presentation and test is therefore *cue-dependent forgetting*. Cue-dependent forgetting is undoubtedly a major source of everyday forgetting. However, it is incomplete as an explanation of forgetting because it fails to address the fundamental observation that memory performance declines over time.

An explanation of forgetting therefore requires us to consider the deceptively simple problem of why memory gets worse over time. The two main rival explanations of time-based forgetting are **decay** and **interference**. Decay can be considered the 'deterioration of the organic correlate' of learning (McGeoch, 1942: 455). That physical damage of brain tissue (e.g. via brain injury) can result in memory loss is indisputable. Thus, if we suppose that brain tissue suffers 'wear and tear' over time, then decay is a plausible explanation of forgetting. However, McGeoch (1932, 1942) is widely regarded as having killed off decay as a popular explanation of forgetting in long-term memory, his crucial argument being:

> that forgetting is found to vary with the character of the events which fill a constant interval and with the conditions obtaining at the time of measuring retention. (McGeoch, 1942: 455)

McGeoch's account is supported by Jenkins and Dallenbach (1924). In their study two participants learned word lists and were tested at delays of one, two, four or eight hours. Each participant was tested twice: once after sleeping, and once after staying awake during the retention interval. At test they recalled fewer words if they had stayed awake than if they had slept. An obvious explanation of this, favoured by McGeoch, is that during sleep the participants were not exposed to material that might interfere with what they had learned.

McGeoch's explanation appeals to what is now termed **retroactive inhibition** (RI). In RI, learning new material during the retention interval interferes with older learning (e.g. learning dog–bone would interfere with an earlier dog–cat association). Experiments have also shown that **proactive inhibition** (PI) can occur (e.g. a prior dog–cat association makes it harder to learn dog–bone). Much of the subsequent research on interference has focused on PI. PI is relatively easy to demonstrate in laboratory experiments (e.g. Underwood, 1957), whereas psychologists have struggled to show consistent evidence of RI in the laboratory.

> **DECAY** An explanation of forgetting that suggests memories fade or deteriorate over time.
>
> **INTERFERENCE** An explanation of forgetting in which other learning (old or new) can disrupt or prevent retrieval.

Wixted (2004a) has argued that research in experimental psychology (wrongly) focused on PI as a source of forgetting and largely rejected the leading account of RI: **consolidation theory**. This was the idea that memories are fragile and easily disrupted immediately after encoding and require time to consolidate before storage in long-term memory. Wixted also notes that most laboratory experiments that suggest PI causes forgetting used massed learning: several lists presented in a short space of time. Indeed, Underwood (1957) excluded studies without massed learning from his analysis. In contrast, everyday memory usually involves learning information spread out over long periods of time. This point is vital because PI pretty much disappears if learning is spread over a longer period (Underwood & Ekstrand, 1967).

A more plausible account of the results of laboratory and everyday experiments on forgetting, which was anticipated by Keppel (1968), is that forgetting is caused by non-specific RI. In other words, prior learning may interfere with new learning only when items are similar (PI), but new learning interferes with all old learning (RI). Wixted (2004a, 2005) argues that formation of new memories interferes with old memories – possibly because of some processing bottleneck (e.g. because consolidation and encoding share processing resources). If so, RI did not occur in studies using massed learning because participants were learning new information at a high rate throughout the study (and therefore RI is more or less constant). Wixted's account of forgetting is rather elegant and has also been proposed as an explanation of the mathematical form of the forgetting curve: in particular, a phenomenon known as *Jost's law of forgetting* (Wixted, 2004b).

According to Jost's law, if two memories are equally likely to be recalled at some point in time, the younger of the two memories will be forgotten more quickly (see Figure 5.4). Wixted suggests that this is because of consolidation: the older memory is less vulnerable to RI than the younger memory.

This work has coincided with (and probably sparked) a renewed interest in theoretical analysis of the causes of forgetting. Lansdale and Baguley (2008) proposed an alternative explanation of forgetting that can also account for the mathematical form of the forgetting function (and hence also Jost's law). Their explanation, known as the *population dilution model*, starts with the simple idea that remembering can be considered as a process of sampling a memory trace from a population of traces (rather like drawing cards at random from a deck). This population contains correct traces (ones that contain relevant details of whatever a person is trying to remember), null traces (memories that are not relevant and produce no recall) and errors. The probability of a correct response in a memory experiment therefore depends on the proportion of correct traces in the total population (e.g. if there are 100 traces, and 82 of them are correct, the probability of a correct response is 82%). In this model it is possible to explain forgetting simply by assuming that the overall population of traces is diluted (by null traces) at a steady rate over time.

Lansdale and Baguley suggest that this dilution occurs because the original event becomes less temporally distinctive. This is potentially intriguing because it links long-term forgetting to mechanisms introduced to explain recency

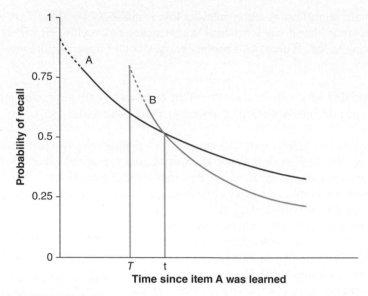

FIGURE 5.4   An illustration of Jost's (1897) law of forgetting. Item A receives more learning than item B, but is learned earlier than time *T*. According to Jost's law, the probability of recalling the more recent item (B) decreases faster than the older item (A) and therefore the two forgetting curves meet at time *t*

effects in both long- and short-term memory (Bjork & Whitten, 1974; Glenberg & Swanson, 1986). Brown, Neath and Chater (2007) have also argued that forgetting in both the long and the short term may be accounted for by common mechanisms such as temporal distinctiveness, though they doubt that a single explanation for the form of the forgetting function exists. One source of support for this conclusion comes from the observation that the form of the function for measures such as savings differs from that typically observed for recognition or recall (Lansdale & Baguley, 2008).

EXERCISE: THE ROYAL WEDDING, PART 2: TEST YOUR MEMORY

Test your memory of the Royal Wedding. Do not look back at the news excerpt at the start of the chapter – try to rely on your memory.

What time of year did Kate and William get married?

Spring / Summer / Autumn / Winter

What time of day was the wedding?

Late morning / Early afternoon / Late afternoon

What colour were the flowers decorating the Abbey?

White / Blue / Red / Yellow

What colour was William's jacket?

What vehicle did William and Kate travel in after leaving Westminster Abbey?

You can check your answers later in the chapter

5.2.5 MEMORY AS A RECONSTRUCTIVE PROCESS

Most experimental research on memory has focused on memory for 'impoverished' material such as word lists. Everyday memory typically involves richer, structured material, such as conversations, pictures or events. Research with such 'real-world' material suggests that memory works in a constructive or reconstructive way. The best known example is Bartlett's

(1932) 'War of the ghosts' study. Bartlett gave participants stories, including the American Indian folk tale 'War of the ghosts', and asked them to reproduce them after a 15-minute retention interval and again one or more times at retention intervals of weeks, months or years (six years being the longest interval).

Bartlett found that the reproductions often contained rationalisations of parts of the story participants did not understand, as well as intrusions or distortions (adding or changing details of the stories). Participants tended to reconstruct a story that made sense to them, filling in missing elements that made sense to them even if it meant including details that were not in

> **SCHEMA** A mental representation of some aspect of the world built from experience and into which new experiences are fitted.

the original. A particular emphasis of Bartlett's work is that social and cultural factors will influence recall: the rationalisations and errors in memory are not random, and inaccurate recall is rather more common than some might suppose. Bartlett's findings are usually explained in terms of **schema** theory – the key ideas of which are found in Bartlett's (1932) own theory of remembering.

There are a number of striking demonstrations of schematic effects in the memory literature. Anderson and Pichert (1978) have shown that schemata can operate both at encoding and at retrieval. They asked participants to read a description of a house while adopting one of two perspectives: that of a home buyer or that of a burglar. At test they asked people either to adopt the same perspective or to switch perspective. Participants tended to remember details appropriate to the perspective they adopted (e.g. valuable items for the burglar), and switching perspective after an initial attempt to recall allowed people to retrieve information that had not previously been reported.

Although schema theory was a popular account of how memory is influenced by prior knowledge, it has somewhat fallen out of favour. There are probably two main reasons for this. While many of the phenomena predicted by schema theory can be demonstrated in laboratory and real-world settings, the concept of a schema is not necessary to account for them (Hintzman, 1986).

A second reason is that some of the phenomena reported by Bartlett, notably rationalisation and distortions, do not occur as extensively as in his original studies (e.g. Gauld & Stephenson, 1967). Only relatively recently have Bartlett's repeated reproduction studies been fully replicated (Bergman & Roediger, 1999). Bergman and Roediger suggest that the spacing of tests (including the 15-minute delay for the first tests) and the subsequent retests are probably important contributors to Bartlett's original findings and conclusions. An immediate test may protect against some of the distortions and rationalisations. This is relatively easy to understand in terms of a multiple trace memory model. Any errors from earlier tests are part of the population of traces to be recalled in later tests, while omissions create gaps that encourage or require rationalisations from the participants. Successful correct recall increases the population of correct traces and makes subsequent retests more accurate, as well as leaving fewer opportunities for rationalisation or distortion. Indeed, it is well known that successful retrieval improves later accuracy and reduces forgetting (e.g. Ballard, 1913; Roediger & Karpicke, 2006).

5.3 MEMORY IN ACTION

This section considers how some of the theoretical work discussed above has practical consequences. Our particular focus will be on three domains – eyewitness memory, flashbulb memories and exam revision – which are likely to be relevant for many readers.

5.3.1 EYEWITNESS MEMORY

As we have seen in this chapter, human memory is fallible. This has important implications when considering the reliability of eyewitness testimony. After a crime has taken place, police officers interview witnesses about what they remember and sometimes witnesses might be asked to try to identify the perpetrator from a line-up. Information from witnesses can therefore be crucial in securing a conviction. However, we know that memory is not like a video camera, and its intricacies and fallibilities can make it difficult for the police to accurately reconstruct the events of a crime. Much psychological research has therefore investigated variables that affect accurate recall and recognition in order that juries and legal professionals can better understand the way that witness memory operates.

In many real-world cases of eyewitness memory, people don't know that they will later be interrogated about an event. Eyewitness laboratory studies therefore use the test of **incidental learning**, as discussed earlier in section 5.2.1.

Let us look at recall and recognition in turn.

RECALL

Cast your mind back to a situation in which you and a close friend or a sibling have been reminiscing about a past event. Did you remember the event the same way, or were there differences? One of the issues with eyewitness memory is that, in trying to reconstruct memory of an event, a witness might be exposed to different information about an event when discussing an event with other witnesses or the police. Sometimes, this information might simply be in the way in which a question is asked. Psychological research has examined how this might distort witness memory.

Research by Loftus and colleagues has focused on reconstructive processes in memory. In a famous study by Loftus, Miller and Burns (1978) participants were shown a series of slides depicting a red Datsun car making a turn at an intersection and hitting a pedestrian. Half the participants were shown slides depicting a 'stop' sign at the intersection and half were shown a 'yield' sign. Participants were later asked a series of questions, one of which took the form: 'Did another car pass the red Datsun while it was stopped at the _____ sign?' They were asked which of the two photographs corresponded to what they had originally seen. For half the participants the blank was filled with a word consistent with what they'd seen, and for half it was inconsistent (e.g. 'stop' if they had seen a slide with a yield sign). For the consistent group the accuracy was around 75%, while for the inconsistent group it was only about 40%.

KEY RESEARCHER Elizabeth Loftus

FIGURE 5.5   Elizabeth Loftus

Professor Elizabeth Loftus is a hugely influential figure in memory research. A 2002 list in the *Review of General Psychology* ranked Loftus 58th on the list of the 100 most eminent psychologists of the twentieth century (the highest-placed woman on the list). As well as making major theoretical contributions to the study of human memory, she is also widely recognised as a leading pioneer of applied memory research and eyewitness memory in particular.

Her major contributions have included research into false memories and the accuracy of memory in real-world settings. Her work on the misinformation effect (see text) has shown how people can 'remember' specific details about events (when in reality the detail did not occur) simply by being given misleading or suggestive information. Her work on the potential unreliability of eyewitness testimonies has also been hugely influential in the field, and she has acted as an expert witness in a number of high-profile criminal trials (Haggbloom et al., 2002).

Many subsequent experiments have confirmed that this kind of post-event information can distort people's eyewitness testimony (e.g. Wright & Loftus, 2008). This is especially true when memory is weak, or when misleading post-event information is applied to a peripheral, rather than central, feature of the event (Luna & Migueles, 2009). Exactly what is going on in these studies is still a matter of some debate (and there may be more than one factor contributing to this misinformation effect). One relatively simple explanation is again in terms of a multiple trace model of memory. Traces for both the original event and the post-event information may compete for recall. Factors such as recency, or the similarity of the testing context with the context in which the post-event information was presented, may explain why the post-event information rather than the correct information is retrieved.

What would help improve recall? So far we've considered factors that might influence eyewitness memory prior to retrieval. It is also possible to manipulate conditions at test to influence memory. Geiselman et al. (1986) did exactly this when they developed the cognitive interview to enhance the accuracy of eyewitness memory. This involves a number of different components, but one of the most important seems to be context reinstatement: witnesses are asked to imagine themselves back in the original context prior to recall (this draws on ideas such as transfer-appropriate processing, discussed earlier). The effects of the cognitive interview can be quite striking, with several studies showing 40–50% increases in the quantity of the information recalled.

Often there is a relatively long gap between witnessing a crime and being interviewed as a witness. A long retention interval between encoding and test can undermine the quality of eyewitness recall (Ebbesen & Rienick, 1998). It also increases the likelihood of exposure to misinformation. In order to minimise this problem, researchers in the UK have been working on a Self-Administered Interview (Hope, Gabbert, & Fisher, 2011). This form, using principles of the Cognitive Interview, can be filled in by witnesses at the scene of the crime, drastically reducing the retention interval between encoding and test.

RECOGNITION

Mistaken identification can lead to false convictions. The Innocence Project in the USA showed through DNA testing that 75% of false convictions were due to eyewitness misidentification. In psychology, typical eyewitness identification experiments use target-present line-ups (featuring the perpetrator), and target-absent line-ups (consisting of distractor faces) to investigate how witnesses might perform when either a guilty or innocent suspect has been apprehended.

Using this paradigm, numerous variables have been shown to affect identification accuracy. For example, a perpetrator with a distinctive face is more likely to be correctly identified at line-up (Carlson & Gronlund, 2011). Exposure time is also a key factor, with a recent meta-analysis confirming that longer exposure times lead to greater line-up accuracy (Bornstein et al., 2012). Another important consideration is what to show in a line-up. For example, for suspects with a distinctive facial feature (e.g. a birth mark) you do not want witnesses to select someone based on that feature alone, so you have to choose whether to alter the other people in the line-up to include a facial feature or to conceal the feature from the suspect. It turns out that replicating the feature yields better identification of the suspect, as this amplifies the difference in how familiar the suspect and the other faces in the line-up feel (Zarkadi, Wade, & Stewart, 2009).

Witness age also influences accuracy because older adults and children are believed to be less efficient at encoding and storing information. The balance of evidence suggests that compared to young adults, both children (Pozzulo & Lindsay, 1998) and older adults (Searcy, Bartlett, & Memon, 1999) are more likely to incorrectly select someone from a target-absent line-up. However, these studies suggest that performance differences across age groups are less likely on target-present line-ups.

So what might help improve recognition? Various line-up procedures are thought to improve identification performance, most commonly by reducing false alarm rates (incorrectly saying that the perpetrator is in the line-up when they are not). Warning witnesses that the perpetrator may or may not be present (Malpass & Devine, 1981) significantly reduces false alarm rates on target-absent line-ups (Steblay, 1997). Research has also addressed how to reduce false alarm rates for child witnesses. Havard and Memon (2013) included a man's silhouette with a superimposed question mark in the line-up. They told children as young as five that if they did not recognise anyone on the line-up they should select the silhouette. This successfully reduced false alarm rates.

EXERCISE: THE ROYAL WEDDING, PART 3: HOW ACCURATE WAS YOUR MEMORY?

The 'news excerpt' we gave you about the Royal Wedding was designed to be suggestive and to influence your memory for some of the answers to the questions shown later. See how well you did – here are the answers:

1. Spring. They got married on 29 April. The excerpt said a summer-like day; did this make you more likely to think it was summer?
2. Late morning. The wedding took place at 11.00 am. Perhaps calling it a summer-like day made it sound more like the wedding was in the afternoon?
3. Most of the flowers decorating the Abbey were white. The excerpt said colourful flowers, did this make you more likely to choose a non-white colour?
4. William wore a red jacket and a blue sash. The excerpt mentioned William was in the RAF, and traditional RAF colours are blue. Did this make you more likely to remember him as wearing a blue jacket?
5. William and Kate travelled in an open-top, horse-drawn carriage from Westminster Abbey to Buckingham Palace. The excerpt mentioned them travelling in an Aston Martin later on in the day. Did this interfere with your memory?

As has been shown, research into the way that memory operates is not only important from a theoretical point of view, but it can have important implications for real-world problems. Misunderstanding the way that memory works could even change the outcome of a criminal trial.

5.3.2 FLASHBULB MEMORIES

When a shocking or dramatic event takes place, such as the two planes crashing into the World Trade Center on 11 September 2001, people often experience detailed and vivid memories of the time that they heard the news. Flashbulb memories often include six characteristic pieces of information: people remember who told them the news, where they were told, what was happening at the time, how they felt, how those around them felt, and how the event affected them personally (Brown & Kulik, 1977).

Brown and Kulik (1977) proposed that the shock associated with these kinds of events triggers a special mechanism, making flashbulb memories more accurate and long-lasting than other types of autobiographical memory. Indeed, recent evidence suggests that people are more likely to develop flashbulb memories if the shocking event personally affected them. Berntsen and Thomsen (2005) investigated memories of significant events in Denmark during the Second World War. They compared wartime flashbulb experiences of people involved in the Danish resistance, and of people who were less involved. Members of the resistance were more likely to have flashbulb memories.

One issue with flashbulb memories is that it can be quite difficult for psychologists to test them. One needs both an extremely shocking event and a way of measuring the accuracy of the information participants are recalling. Research therefore often uses prominent public events for which details are known. However, by their very nature, these are rare events. Also, to best examine the accuracy of flashbulb memory, the initial memory test must take place soon after the event with subsequent memory tests being compared for consistency to the results of the initial test. All these considerations make it difficult, but not impossible, to investigate flashbulb memories.

One claim about flashbulb memories is that they are more consistent, and therefore more accurate, than other memories. In a British study focusing on the abrupt resignation of Margaret Thatcher in 1990, Conway et al. (1994) found that flashbulb memories were still accurate after as long as 26 months. However, studies that have tested memory at longer retention intervals find flashbulb memories to be vulnerable to distortion. In 1994–1995, O.J. Simpson, a well-known American celebrity, was tried for the murder of his ex-wife and her friend. This widely publicised trial was referred to in the US as the 'Trial of the Century'. Schmolck, Buffalo and Squire (2000) studied how people's memories of the O.J. Simpson murder trial verdict changed over 32 months. Participants were tested three days after the verdict was announced, then 15 months or 32 months subsequently. Although participants tested after 15 months were still quite accurate, those tested after 32 months demonstrated memory inaccuracy. Participants produced detailed recollections they were very confident in, but almost 40% of these recollections were totally incorrect. Schmolck et al. (2000) conclude that flashbulb memories are not 'special'; they are just as susceptible to forgetting as ordinary autobiographical memories.

In order to adequately test this assumption it is necessary to directly compare the accuracy of flashbulb memories to those of 'ordinary' everyday memories. Talarico and Rubin (2003) did just this, finding no difference in the consistency between people's memories of a recent 'ordinary' event and the events surrounding them hearing the news about the terrorist attacks on 11 September. Participants were tested on 12 September 2001, then either a week later, six weeks later, or 32 weeks later. The only differences were that participants rated their flashbulb memories as more vivid, and were consistently more confident in their accuracy than they were in the accuracy of the everyday memory. However, accuracy declined similarly over this period for both types of memory.

Research into flashbulb memories highlights that people are relatively unaware of how their own memories work. A flashbulb memory can be very vivid, and although people are often convinced they are accurate, the evidence suggests that flashbulb memories are just as likely to be inaccurate as memories of other events.

5.3.3 REVISING FOR AN EXAM

While, with any luck, most people will only very rarely be witnesses of a crime, we can apply an understanding of memory theory in at least one far more common situation: revising for an exam or a test. Much of what we have covered in this chapter can be used to design an effective revision strategy. While there are lots of factors to consider, there are also many constraints imposed by what someone is learning and how they will be tested. In a traditional examination, the material to be learned, the environmental context at retrieval and the time of testing are likely to be fixed. On the other hand, the way material is presented, the environment in which learning takes place and the time course of presentation are usually easy to manipulate. Organising a study environment so it is similar to the testing environment (e.g. sitting at a desk in a quiet room) is probably a good starting point. If this isn't possible, imagining the context in which you learned (i.e. context reinstatement) when you to try to retrieve information may help. However, there are far simpler revision strategies that are known to have a very powerful effect on learning.

Ample research has shown that what people do with the material they are trying to learn has an enormous impact on what is remembered (e.g. Craik & Lockhart, 1972; Hyde & Jenkins, 1969). It also matters what you are trying to learn. If you are trying to understand the content of a text (as opposed to remembering the exact wording), it is a good idea to write a summary of it (Schmalhofer & Glavanov, 1986). Given that many (but not all) exams involve understanding the meaning of material, both depth of processing and transfer-appropriate processing would suggest that extracting meaning from the material to be learned is a good idea. In addition, it will be easier to retrieve material that is more distinctive or has more links to other material. One of the best ways to learn material is therefore to structure or organise it in some way. Mandler (1967) asked one group of participants to learn a set of words and one group simply to sort them into semantic categories (without instructions to learn them). The categorisation group learned as well as the intentional learning group. Organisation provides a structure that can be used to deliberately cue memory, to reconstruct the original material, as well as to make links that increase the opportunities for spontaneous cueing to occur. These principles can be recruited to construct **mnemonics** (e.g. the colours of the rainbow are often remembered as 'Richard Of York Gave Battle In Vain', representing the colours red, orange, yellow, green, blue, indigo and violet). Stories and rhymes (or even songs!) also make excellent recall structures.

MNEMONICS Strategies for helping people to remember information, usually involving cues such as rhyme or imagery.

Two further principles are particularly important in planning a revision strategy. The first is that spaced learning is very much more efficient and more durable than massed learning (this is sometimes termed the *distributed practice effect*). So, four hours of revision spread out over four days is more effective than if it is crammed into one afternoon. This may seem counter-intuitive. 'Cramming' just before a test can be effective – but such material is forgotten rapidly (Cepeda et al., 2006; Neath & Suprenant, 2003). Furthermore, if you have a lot to learn, the material encoded at the start of your cramming session may experience interference from the most recently learned material (Wixted, 2005). Spaced learning is a particularly good strategy for university students because the learned material is more resistant to forgetting; this is essential if what you learn early on is important for your later studies. Retrieving information from memory is itself an excellent way to learn material. Roediger and Karpicke (2006) have shown that this testing effect is not simply because tests offer opportunities for relearning, and other researchers (e.g. Lansdale & Baguley, 2008) have suggested that testing memory for an item has a bigger impact than re-presenting an item.

Although revising for an exam involves many other factors (e.g. motivation, anxiety, fatigue), a good understanding of memory can help someone design a revision strategy that will be both effective and relatively painless to implement.

5.4 CHAPTER SUMMARY

Early theorists divided memory into short- and long-term stores (Atkinson & Shiffrin, 1968) based on evidence of seemingly different properties. For example, short-term memory was theorised to be affected by recency and long-term memory by primacy effects. Later models refined this modal model to produce a working memory model (Baddeley & Hitch, 1974), although more recent theories favour a single memory system.

Although lots of research has focused on the distinction between memory structures such as STS and LTS, the more fundamental issue is how memory operates. Several factors at encoding have been proposed to influence whether material will be retrieved. The levels of processing model suggests that it is the depth of processing (in particular processing meaning) that influences how well material is remembered. The phenomenon of context-dependent memory demonstrates that the cues available at encoding aid retrieval; it is thought this is because they are stored along with the material being encoded.

What causes us to forget has been examined, and there is relatively little evidence that memory is discarded *per se*. Although decay may occur and memory loss may result from what McGeoch called 'deterioration of the organic correlate', we can explain most (possibly all) of forgetting in terms of the effects of interference or the matching of retrieval cues to what was originally encoded. If memories compete for recall – the essence of most interference theories – then learning new information inevitably carries a cost. Forgetting thus occurs because it is necessary to keep memory efficient (e.g. see Anderson & Schooler, 2000).

Memory is unreliable. It is a reconstructive process in which we interpret what has been experienced in light of our expectations, which in turn are based on existing mental representations (schemata) about the world. Memory has also been demonstrated to be influenced by later events that interfere with earlier memory traces. Psychological investigation of such misinformation effects has been influential in our understanding of the accuracy of memory and has made a significant contribution to real-world issues like eyewitness testimony and the phenomenon of false memory.

Anderson and Schooler (2000) suggest that it is puzzling, in evolutionary terms, why intention to learn has so little effect on what we remember. But this finding is less puzzling if we think of memory in terms of transfer-appropriate processing. People are probably only rarely aware that they'll need to know something in future (or what retrieval cues will be available when they try to remember it). A logical consequence of transfer-appropriate processing is that it is probably unwise to think of memory as separate from other aspects of cognition. The processing involved in interacting with and thinking about the world, from perception through to reasoning or problem solving, probably produces memory as a by-product (e.g. Crowder, 1993; Lansdale, 2005; Payne & Baguley, 2006). Of course, it is somewhat ironic to end a chapter on memory by noting that memory shouldn't just be considered in isolation from the rest of cognition – or indeed the rest of psychology.

 # DISCUSSION QUESTIONS: FORGETTING

Recent work on forgetting suggests that forgetting is largely (or possibly entirely) an issue of trace discrimination. Does this mean that once something is learned it is never truly lost from memory?

In this chapter we focused strongly on forgetting in long-term memory. What account of forgetting is most strongly supported for short-term memory? What does this tell us (if anything) about the difference between short-term and long-term memory?

 # SUGGESTIONS FOR FURTHER READING

Cohen, G., & Conway, M.A. (2008). *Memory in the real world* (3rd edn). Hove: Psychology Press. This text provides an excellent overview of research on everyday memory (both inside and outside the laboratory).

Gluck, M.A., Mercado, E., & Myers, C.E. (2008). *Learning and memory: from brain to behavior*. Basingstoke: Palgrave Macmillan. This provides an overview of learning and memory from a neuroscience perspective, looking at findings in both animals and humans.

Kelley, M.R. (Ed.) (2009). *Applied memory*. Hauppauge, NY: Nova Science. This is an interesting edited volume showing how research grounded in theories of memory can be applied in a surprising range of domains.

Neath, I., & Suprenant, A.M. (2003). *Human memory: an introduction to research, data, and theory* (2nd edn). Belmont, CA: Wadsworth. This gives an excellent review of the history of memory research with particular emphasis on major models and theories of memory.

 Still want more? For links to online resources relevant to this chapter and a quiz to test your understanding, visit the companion website at edge.sagepub.com/banyard2e

6 AN INTRODUCTION TO SENSATION, PERCEPTION AND ATTENTION

Lead authors Andrew K. Dunn and Paula C. Stacey

CHAPTER OUTLINE

6.1 Introduction	93
6.2 Sensation, perception and attention	93
6.3 The senses	94
6.3.1 Vision (seeing)	94
6.3.2 The eye	94
6.3.3 Eye to brain	95
6.3.4 Audition (hearing)	96
6.3.5 The ear	96
6.3.6 Ear to brain	97
6.4 Perceiving the world	98
6.4.1 Top-down versus bottom-up processing	98
6.4.2 Bottom-up approaches	99
6.4.3 Top-down approaches	100
6.4.4 Perceptual organisation	102
6.4.5 Multisensory integration	103
6.4.6 Summary	104

6.5 Attention   **104**

    6.5.1 Auditory attention   104

    6.5.2 Visual attention   107

6.6 Are we aware of everything?   **108**

    6.6.1 Change blindness, inattentional blindness and visual neglect   108

    6.6.2 So what does it all mean?   109

6.7 Chapter summary   **109**

Discussion questions   **110**

Suggestions for further reading   **110**

6.1 INTRODUCTION

Perception is one of the wonders of being alive. We tend to take it for granted, but a little thought reveals just how remarkable it is. William James, in his *Principles of psychology*, written in 1890, described the perceptual world of the newborn baby as 'one great blooming, buzzing confusion' (1890: 488). The wonder is how we manage to organise that blooming, buzzing confusion into the meaningful sounds and shapes that we experience every day when we wake. These perceptual experiences are at the very core of human experience, but how exactly do we use them to make sense of the world? How do we encode and represent what we see, hear, smell, taste or touch?

In this chapter we will first explain how we deal with incoming sensory information and then consider how our brain decodes this information in order to perceive the world around us. We will go on to examine a phenomenon known as attentional processing. What we 'pay attention' to determines, to a large extent, what aspects of the environment we perceive in the first place and which sensory inputs get further processing.

Finally, we will consider some of the problems that occur when our perceptual and attentional systems go wrong. But first we will begin by outlining what we mean by sensation, perception and attention, and provide some idea of the issues involved.

FRAMING QUESTIONS

- How do we encode and represent what we see and hear?
- How do we make sense of our perceptions? From the bottom up or from the top down?
- At what point in the process of attention is auditory information filtered?
- Is our attention to visual scenes object-based or space-based?

6.2 SENSATION, PERCEPTION AND ATTENTION

Psychologists often use everyday language, but in more precise ways. A good example is 'sensation'. For psychologists, **sensation** is the initial stimulation of our sensory systems (sight, hearing, touch, taste and smell); it is the sequence of physiological events that causes our nervous system to send electrical impulses to our brain. The stimulation of our senses is the first step on the road to our mental representation of the external world, and is in some respects the first step on the road to mental life.

Perception is the apparently holistic experience of the external world. That is, perception seems to provide us with experience of a reality that is integrated and complete when, for example, we look around us, watch television, talk or eat. Yet, intriguingly, perception does not produce an exact copy of the physical world: rather, perception involves a mental re-creation. It is not an *accurate* representation of our environment but an *adequate* one. **Perception** is, in effect, a best guess, derived from an endless stream of external information (such as light and sound), and influenced by our arousal states (e.g. whether we are alert, distracted or sleepy) and past experience (e.g. we may interpret situations differently according to whether they are novel or familiar to us). Sensing and perceiving the world around us is a monumentally complex task that we do not fully understand, and yet somehow we do it, for the most part, effortlessly.

Attention plays a critical role in making sense of our sensations. The world is a complex place, and at any one time there are multiple sources of information that we could process. Since we do not have limitless cognitive resources, we limit what we process by focusing on what is important (*selective attention*), but this is only one aspect of attention. Attention is a multifaceted phenomenon that is difficult to define. Perhaps the best way to define it is to ask not what it consists of, but rather what it is *for* and what it *does*. Ultimately, attention directs, filters and controls how we process the vast amount of external information bombarding our senses and produce internal responses to it.

Sensing, perceiving and attending to the world around us are complex. The aim of this chapter is to introduce you to these interrelated processes in more detail. Here we will focus our discussion on the primary senses of vision and audition in particular. We begin with sensation.

6.3 THE SENSES

6.3.1 VISION (SEEING)

Vision dominates the human experience and we rely heavily upon it in our day-to-day interactions. It is thought that vision evolved to support motor action (Milner & Goodale, 1995) and, for typically developing humans, vision is the most immediate and commanding sense. It is commonly reported that over 80% of all information about our external world comes through vision and about 50% of the cortex is given over to visual processing alone – as compared with about 10% for audition (Snowden, Thompson, & Troscianko, 2006).

6.3.2 THE EYE

The eye has an amazingly complex anatomical structure (Figure 6.1) specialised for detecting light energy. Vision begins when light enters the eye through the **cornea**, a transparent protective layer on the surface of the eye. It then passes through to the **pupil** and is focused onto the back of the eye (the **retina**) by the **lens**. The retina contains a number of different types of cell that convert light energy into electrochemical signals, so that they can be transmitted to and interpreted by the brain. Of prime concern here are the **photoreceptor cells**. Put simply, their chemical structure changes when they encounter light energy. Human photoreceptor cells come in two types, **rods** and **cones**, so called because of their shape.

There are approximately 125 million rods and 6 million cones in the human eye. The cones are mostly concentrated in a tiny area (approximately 0.3 mm) in the centre of the retina called the **fovea**. The fovea is responsible for most of what we think of as vision: fine detailed information (often referred to as high visual acuity) and colour vision. The rods are distributed throughout the rest of the retina, except in the **blind spot** where the **optic nerve** (which carries information to the brain) is formed. Rods are extremely sensitive to movement but not to colour, and they do not carry fine detailed information (they have poor visual acuity).

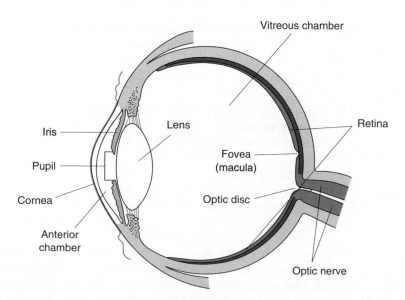

FIGURE 6.1   The structure of the eye (Andrew Dunn)

EXERCISE: FIND YOUR BLIND SPOT

+   O

Close your left eye and stare at the cross. Now move your head towards the page and the circle will at some point disappear. This is the point at which it enters the blind spot on the retina. Keep moving closer and it will magically reappear.

Chemical changes in the rods and cones are detected by the **bipolar cells**, which respond by either depolarising or hyperpolarising (see Chapter 10 for a description of how neuronal cells conduct information) in response to changes in the rods and cones. Such changes in the bipolar cells trigger action potentials in the **retinal ganglion cells**. There are approximately 1 million retinal ganglion cells, some of which condense information from the rods (ratio 120:1), while others receive more or less uncondensed information from the cones (ratio between 1:1 and 6:1).

6.3.3 EYE TO BRAIN

The axons of the retinal ganglion cells form the optic nerve which carries information to the brain. There are two significant visual pathways to the brain: the *primary visual pathway* and the evolutionarily older *retino-tectal pathway*. In normal visual processing these pathways work in parallel.

The primary visual pathway (Figure 6.2) goes from the eye, via the optic nerve, across the optic chiasm (where there is a partial crossover of axons projecting from each eye) to the dorsal part of the **lateral geniculate nucleus (LGN)**. The precise function of the LGN is poorly understood, but it seems to play an important role in regulating information flow (Blake & Sekular, 2006). From here, information is projected along the optic radiations to the primary visual cortex in the occipital lobe.

The visual cortex is the primary site for processing visual information in the brain. It comprises five main areas, V1–V5. Each area has a specialised function and is characterised by different connections to other parts of the brain. Beyond here, information travels along two large cortical pathways: a ventral stream that terminates in the temporal lobes, and a dorsal stream that terminates in the parietal lobes. Goodale and Milner (1992) argue that the ventral stream is specialised for processing visual information for perceptual purposes ('what' processing) while the dorsal

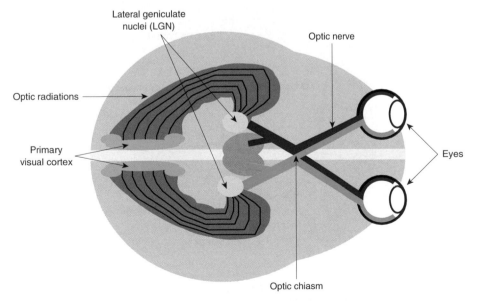

FIGURE 6.2   The primary visual pathway (Andrew Dunn)

stream processes visual information for visual motor purposes ('how' processing). However, it should be stressed that while these two streams perform functionally different tasks, in normal everyday processing they are complementary, working together such that one informs the other.

6.3.4 AUDITION (HEARING)

Although hearing is sometimes described as our second most important sense, it is clear that our ears provide us with an abundant source of information. Human communication systems rely heavily on the ability to hear, and adults who lose their hearing often suffer from social isolation. Hearing is by no means a minor sense.

6.3.5 THE EAR

The ears are specialised for detecting **sound waves**. Sounds differ along three key dimensions: amplitude, frequency and complexity. These dimensions correspond to people's perception of sound, which can be characterised according to loudness, pitch and timbre.

We can divide the auditory sensory apparatus (the ear) into three interdependent portions (Figure 6.3):

1 The **outer ear**: comprising the **pinna** (the bendy bit on the side of your head), the **auditory canal** and the **tympanic membrane** (the ear drum).
2 The **middle ear**: comprising the **ossicles** – made up from three connected bones called the malleus (hammer), the incus (anvil) and the stapes (stirrup) – and the **Eustachian tube** (which helps regulate air pressure).
3 The **inner ear**: comprising the **cochlea**.

The process of audition begins when sound waves enter the ear and travel down the auditory canal, causing the oval-shaped tympanic membrane to vibrate. The tympanic membrane (surface area 68 mm^2 in humans) is exquisitely sensitive and works with remarkable efficiency even when perforated. It is sensitive to vibrations that displace the membrane by only 1/100,000,000 of a centimetre – the width of a single hydrogen atom.

Tympanic vibrations are transmitted through the air-filled middle ear by the three tiny bones of the ossicles. Vibration passes to the inner ear when the stapes makes contact with the oval window – a covered opening in the bony wall of the fluid-filled cochlea.

The cochlea (meaning snail) is a spiral-shaped structure about the size of a child's marble, and is divided into three chambers (**vestibular canal, tympanic canal** and **cochlear duct**) by two flexible membranes called the **basilar membrane** and **Reissner's membrane**. When the stapes makes contact with the oval window, vibrations are sent down the length

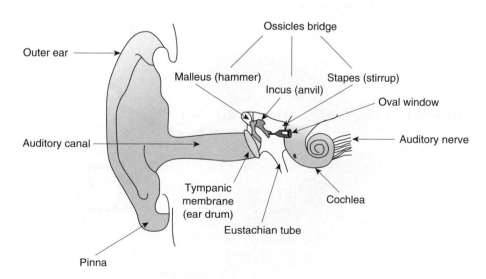

FIGURE 6.3 Peripheral auditory system (Andrew Dunn)

of the basilar membrane, much like the cracking of a whip. The basilar membrane is **tonotopic**, that is, the tones are ordered spatially adjacent to each other according to similarity in frequency, with high tones at one end through to low tones at the other (Figure 6.4). The frequency that gives maximum response at a particular place on the basilar membrane is known as the characteristic frequency of that place.

> **TONOTOPIC** The spatial organisation of responses to different sound frequencies, with low-frequency sounds being represented at one location and high frequencies at another.

Just above the basilar membrane in the cochlear duct is the **organ of Corti**. It is responsible for converting the movement of the basilar membrane into electrical brain activity. Movement of the basilar membrane in relation to the **tectorial membrane** disturbs the **inner hair cells**, causing electrical signals to be sent towards the brain.

6.3.6 EAR TO BRAIN

Signals from the ear are sent to the auditory cortex of the brain via the auditory nerve along the **ascending auditory pathway**. There are between 10 and 20 auditory nerve fibres connected to each inner hair cell, which means the response of each nerve fibre is determined by a very small section of the basilar membrane (Moore, 2003). As the hair cells are selective for particular sound frequencies, the responses in the auditory nerve fibres are highly *frequency selective*.

Auditory signals reaching the brain are subject to increasingly complex processing in different brain regions. Following processing by the brain stem, mid brain and thalamus, signals reach the **primary auditory cortex**, situated in the temporal lobes. The primary auditory cortex is tonotopic: low-frequency sounds are positioned at the front (anterior) portion and high-frequency sounds at the rear (posterior).

Beyond the primary auditory cortex is the highly interconnected auditory association area. The cells here respond to complex features of the incoming auditory signals (such as location, object identity and speech). Projecting from here are two important cortical streams (see Clarke et al., 2002; Rauschecker & Tian, 2000): an auditory ventral stream that terminates in the orbitofrontal cortex, and an auditory dorsal stream that terminates in the dorsolateral prefrontal cortex (both in the frontal lobes). The ventral stream has been labelled the 'what' pathway of audition, since damage to this stream leads to deficits in identifying different sounds (*auditory agnosia*) but leaves sound location processing intact. The dorsal

> **DOUBLE DISSOCIATION** A term used in brain sciences to indicate that two cognitive processes are distinct, such that damage to a particular brain region affects one of those processes but not the other. For example, damage to Broca's area of the brain means a patient cannot speak but can still understand speech, whereas damage to Wernicke's area means a patient cannot understand speech but can still speak.

stream has been labelled the auditory 'where' pathway, since damage to this stream leads to deficits in locating sounds (*auditory neglect*) but leaves sound differentiation processing intact. A similar sort of **double dissociation** (complementary deficits) has been identified in vision (Goodale & Milner, 1992).

ASIDE

Restoring hearing with a cochlear implant

Since the mid-1990s, people with profound hearing loss have been able to have their hearing (partially) restored by **cochlear implants**. A cochlear implant is an electronic device which consists of the following components:

- a **microphone** which picks up sound from the environment;
- a **speech processor** which codes the incoming sounds and divides the speech into different frequency channels;
- a **transmitter** sends these sounds to a **receiver** which has been placed in the bone under the skin;
- an **electrode array** which has been surgically inserted into the cochlea.

(Continued)

(Continued)

A cochlear implant takes advantage of the tonotopic organisation of the cochlea. Signals which are low in frequency are directed towards electrodes that are placed in the apical end of the cochlea, and signals which are higher in frequency are sent to electrodes that are located at the basal end of the cochlea (Figure 6.4).

Cochlear implantation has proved to be a highly successful intervention and is now routinely offered to people whose hearing loss is too extreme for them to benefit from hearing aids. Children as young as six months of age can now receive cochlear implants. Follow this link for a neat demonstration of a baby hearing for the first time through their implant: www.youtube.com/watch?v=HTzTt1VnHRM

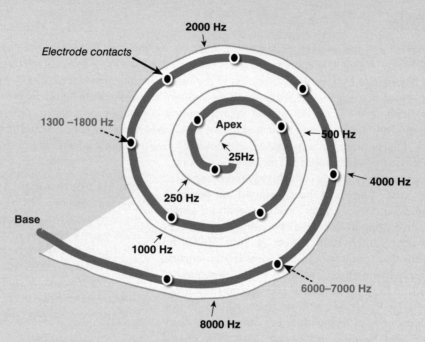

FIGURE 6.4 Tonotopic organisation of the cochlea, with an electrode array inserted. The blue numbers correspond to the characteristic frequencies of different places on the basilar membrane, and the green numbers show the frequencies of sounds being delivered by the electrode array of the cochlear implant

6.4 PERCEIVING THE WORLD

So far we have focused on how our perceptual systems encode and transform incoming sensory information. However, perception is more than this: it is about making sense of the incoming information. With perception we are able to turn a series of changes in air pressure into the glory of music and enjoy 'These Arms of Mine' by Otis Reading (clearly the greatest song ever written). Also with perception we can turn a series of electrical changes in our eyes into an image that can bring tears to those eyes. So how might we do this?

6.4.1 TOP-DOWN VERSUS BOTTOM-UP PROCESSING

There is no single theory of perception. However, a key question for perceptual scientists concerns the extent to which **bottom-up** and **top-down** processes contribute to our perceptual experiences. People who place more importance on bottom-up processing (e.g. Gibson, 1950, 1966) argue that low-level sensory information is the most important determinant of what we perceive. In contrast, top-down theorists such as Gregory (1970, 1997) posit that higher-level cognitive processes are the important determinants of perception. The truth, as usual, is somewhere in between.

6.4.2 BOTTOM-UP APPROACHES

The best-known theory emphasising the importance of bottom-up processing was proposed by J.J. Gibson (1966), and is known as a theory of *direct perception*. Gibson argued that what we perceive is directly determined by the information in the visual scene, and that no higher-level cognitive processing is necessary. He proposed that movement through the environment is crucial for generating information, and that *action* is key to perceiving the world around us. Accordingly, the distribution of light energy in the environment, the so-called *optic array*, provides a rich and immediate source of information. Movement in the environment causes the information in the optic array to change and we directly perceive this change through our eyes (what he terms the *ecological optics*). The perception of visual change is influenced by *invariants* – sources of information in the visual field which remain constant. A comparison of the changing (variant) versus unchanging (invariant) aspects of the visual scene provides direct information about the visual environment. For example, when you are driving down an open road the horizon remains constant. However, as you speed towards your destination, there is variance in the rate at which cars pass you (this movement of objects is called **optic flow**) and in the apparent size of the cars in front of you (of course, real size is invariant). Thus you can gauge the relative speed at which you and others are travelling from changes in the rate of optic flow, or from the increase/decrease in apparent car size.

> **BOTTOM-UP PROCESSING** A cognitive process that starts with simple (low-level) processes and builds up to the more complex higher levels. It doesn't depend on prior knowledge.
>
> **TOP-DOWN PROCESSING** A way of explaining a cognitive process in which higher-level processes, such as prior knowledge, influence the processing of lower-level input.

Another important aspect in Gibson's theory is the notion of **affordances**. According to Gibson, the purpose of objects can be directly perceived, without any prior knowledge. For example, the function of a chair (to be sat upon) is directly perceived because it *affords* sitting upon. Likewise, the function of a ladder can be directly ascertained because the structure of the object affords climbing.

Gibson's theory has been highly influential, particularly since it encourages visual scientists to think about perception in the real world rather than in an artificial lab-based environment where natural sources of visual information are stripped away. Gibson's work shows that natural visual scenes are information rich, that the visual scene is dynamic not static, and that to underestimate these factors is to limit our understanding of perception. He also highlights the importance of action and movement in perception, something which had (has) been largely overlooked in other theories.

The theory is problematic, however, and has been subject to quite harsh criticisms. In particular, critics raise concern with the apparently contrived notion of affordances. Is it really plausible that we can always directly perceive the function of an object, even if we have no prior knowledge of that object? For example, how would we know that an apple was for eating and not for playing cricket if we had no prior experience of apples?

FIGURE 6.5 An example of direct perception using invariant cues of object size and distance scaling (small far away: big close up)

6.4.3 TOP-DOWN APPROACHES

Top-down theories assume that higher-level processes, such as knowledge and memory, have important influences on perception. Theorists such as Richard Gregory (1970, 1997) have provided **constructivist** accounts. These are accounts based on the idea that our perceptual experiences are constructed from the imposition of high-level processing on sensory perceptions. Such theories have been around for a long time. And while there is no one unifying theory, all constructivist accounts have three things in common (Eysenck & Keane, 2005). They all take perception to be:

1 not just sensation, but an active and constructive process;
2 a direct by-product of sensations and hypotheses about the world and how it works;
3 influenced by individual differences and personal experiences.

Accordingly, Gregory (1970, 1997) argues, in contrast to Gibson, that sensory input is impoverished, and that we have to interpret the information provided by our senses in order to make sense of what is going on. The existence of **perceptual constancies** (cognitive assumptions about the world) and the effects of visual **illusions** provide support for a constructivist approach.

As we navigate our way around the world, the image falling on the retina is constantly changing. Thus, if the image falling on our retina were the sole determinant of what we perceived, then visual objects would appear to change shape and size as our position changed. But because of perceptual constancies, perceptual experience remains stable. In the earlier example, the size of the image of a car on the retina changes as we move nearer to it. However, rather than perceiving the object as changing in actual size, we perceive a change in viewing distance (*size constancy*: see Figure 6.6). This is because the brain applies *constancy scaling* and scales up or down the mental image of the car to take into account our relative movement.

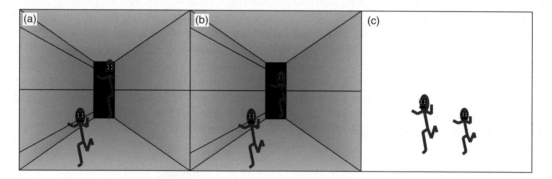

FIGURE 6.6   An example of size constancy. (a) The stick person in the front appears to be smaller than the stick person at the back. In fact they are the same size. (b) The stick people appear to be the same size but in fact the one at the back is smaller. (c) When the background is removed from (b) the difference is more obvious (Andrew Dunn)

Likewise, the image of the shape of a door changes on the retina (or in a photograph) depending on whether it is open or closed, but we easily recognise that these differently shaped images are the same object (Figure 6.7). This is because the brain applies constancy scaling.

Visual illusions illustrate that perception is an active, interpretive process. They work because we are trying to make sense of the visual information, even though the specific cause is different from one illusion to another and there may be more than one mechanism at play. The Müller–Lyer illusion (see Figure 6.8) is a classic example. Here the line with the outward-facing fins appears to be longer than the line with the inward-facing fins. Gregory (1963, 1997) proposed that this is because the fins imply depth. The inward-facing fins imply the front of an object that recedes from us (e.g. the front corner of two walls), and the outward fins imply the far inside corner of an object that advances towards us (e.g. the far corner of a room). Gregory calls this *misapplied scaling constancy*, and similar processes are thought to underlie some other visual illusions.

The constructivist approach is important in showing that knowledge and memory *can* and *do* influence perception. However, critics (e.g. Gibson, 1950; Morgan & Casco, 1990) argue that too much emphasis is placed on the importance of visual illusions, which are frequently artificial two-dimensional stimuli. After all, how could you possibly hope to understand how a machine works if you only consider what it is doing wrong or what happens when it is broken? Nevertheless, the constructivists' basic point remains: top-down processes influence perception.

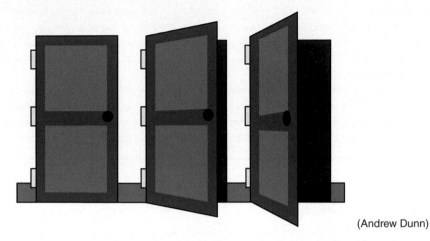

(Andrew Dunn)

FIGURE 6.7 Constancy scaling. Although the shape and dimensions of the door change on the retina (right edge of the door increases in size as the width decreases), the door does not appear to change in physical size. Rather, it is scaled in a manner consistent with a door opening towards the viewer (Andrew Dunn)

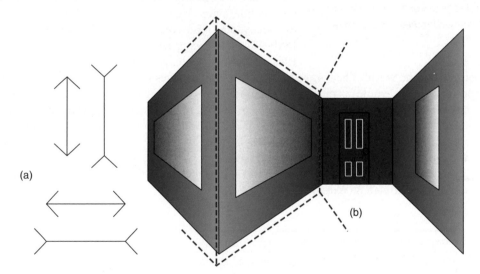

(a)

(b)

FIGURE 6.8 The Müller–Lyer illusion. (a) The line above appears to be shorter than the line below. (b) An example of how receding or advancing objects have the shapes seen in the Müller–Lyer illusion (in this case, rotated through 90°) (Andrew Dunn)

KEY STUDY

Kozlowski, L.T., & Cutting, J.E. (1977). Recognizing the sex of a walk from a dynamic point-light display. *Perception and Psychophysics, 21,* **575–580.**

Humans are especially good at extracting important information (e.g. sex, emotional state, identity) from another person, just from the way they walk and move (biological motion). Early work by Kozlowski and Cutting (1977), explored just how much information we can extract from biological motion, using simple point-light displays. In their experiments, they had observers watch

(Continued)

(Continued)

film footage of moving fluorescent dots that had been placed on the joints (e.g. the elbows, knees, ankles, wrists, shoulders) of three male and three female walkers. They also had them look at still photographs made from the film footage. For each viewing, participants had to identify whether the dots were of a man or a woman. They found that when the dots were moving the participants were accurate 63% of the time (higher when one female walker was removed). But, when dots were still, performance was very poor (below chance level of 50%). They also showed that as long as the dots were moving, you didn't need all of them to see that it was a person or to identify their sex.

What this and other studies tell us is that you need very little information (a few dots) to identify both the form of a moving person and their sex. It's also very easy to identify what the person (the dots) might be doing (e.g. walking, dancing, kicking a ball). However, if the dots are not moving, or if they are not moving in a way that a person would move, we can tell virtually nothing from the point-light displays. Visit 'Motion lab!' for some examples at www.biomotionlab.ca.

6.4.4 PERCEPTUAL ORGANISATION

GESTALT PSYCHOLOGY A school of psychology that began in Germany in the first half of the twentieth century. It proposed that an experience or behaviour can only be understood as a whole, not by understanding the individual constituent parts.

You've probably never really thought about it, but we tend to perceive our environment as a whole (albeit containing distinct objects) as opposed to lots of different parts. This is surprising given that the sensory systems break down the incoming sensory information into basic constituents (e.g. wavelength, spatial frequency, etc). The **Gestalt psychologists** (e.g. Max Wertheimer, 1880–1943, Wolfgang Kohler, 1887–1967 and Kurt Koffka, 1886–1941) sought to understand how we organise and piece together perceptual experience of the world. They argued that perception involves much more than the incoming signal and that what is experienced (the whole) is much more than the parts it comprises. They sought to identify principles (*Gestalt laws*) that explained how elements in a scene are put together perceptually. Some of the laws, along with visual examples (these principles *do not only* apply to vision), are shown in Figure 6.9. For example, in the closure example (Figure 6.9d) we perceive a whole white triangle, even though it does not exist. We do this because our brains interpret the cut-out sections of the black circles as the corners of a triangle. Although here we have listed these principles independently, in the real world they can work independently or together and sometimes they may interfere with each other (Quinlan & Wilton, 1998).

Law/Principle	Explanation
Similarity	Items that are similar in type (e.g. colour or shape) tend to be grouped together
Proximity	Items that are close together tend to be grouped together
Continuity	We tend to perceive lines as continuing in their established direction (e.g. in (c) we tend to perceive a truck)
Closure	The mind tends to 'complete' 'objects' in order to perceive regular figures

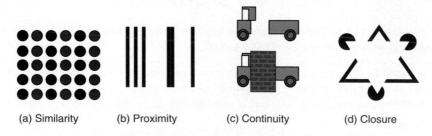

(a) Similarity (b) Proximity (c) Continuity (d) Closure

FIGURE 6.9 Gestalt laws and explanations (Andrew Dunn)

6.4.5 MULTISENSORY INTEGRATION

Up until now, we have considered the senses in isolation. However, our brains need to combine information from vision, audition, touch, etc. in order to form a holistic representation of our world. The way in which information from different sensory modalities interact with one another is of great interest to psychologists. In this section, we will first describe the **McGurk effect** to illustrate how vision and audition combine for speech perception, and then consider the phenomenon of **synaesthesia**, which demonstrates what can happen when the brain combines information from different senses.

MCGURK EFFECT

It has long been known that seeing the face of a talker helps people understand speech, particularly in noisy environments when speech is difficult to hear. The McGurk effect (McGurk & MacDonald, 1976) illustrates nicely how we integrate information from vision and audition to understand speech. In this illusion, people are presented with the auditory component of one sound (e.g. /ba/), they see the facial movements that correspond to another sound (e.g. /ga/), and the resulting perception is that of a novel sound (e.g. people hear /da/). Essentially, the brain integrates the information from the auditory and visual streams and fuses them together to perceive an entirely novel sound. Follow this link to watch a YouTube video of the effect: www.youtube.com/watch?v=jtsfidRq2tw

SYNAETHESIA

Synaethesia is a condition in which the stimulation of one sensory system (e.g. audition) also triggers an experience in another sensory modality (e.g. vision). For example, one form of synaesthesia is between sound and colour, and some musicians report perceiving different colours when listening to different musical notes or instruments. Other people with synaesthesia may perceive letters as inherently coloured (e.g. a 'p' is red, a 'b' is green), associate different words with taste, or associate the days of the week with different spatial locations. Synaesthesia is interesting because it demonstrates the remarkable level to which different brain regions interact with one another, and neuroimaging studies have demonstrated that the brains of people with synaesthesia display increased connections between different sensory areas (Sperling et al., 2006). Recently, researchers have identified multiple areas of the genome that appear to be associated with the condition (Asher et al., 2009), and it is thought that people with the genetic propensity for synaesthesia experience increased myelinisation during childhood, making them more likely to form connections between different sensory systems. Have a look at website of Professor Sean Day, a scientist who has synaesthesia, at: www.daysyn.com/index.html. As the video by Richard Cytowic observes, 'cross-talk in the brain is the rule, not the exception'.

KEY RESEARCHER Peter Thompson

FIGURE 6.10 Peter Thompson

Visual scientist Peter Thompson is a Senior Lecturer at the University of York, where he teaches and researches in visual perception. Peter graduated from the University of Reading with a BSc in Psychology (1972) and a PGCE (1973). He then studied for his PhD at the University of Cambridge (1976). He is the Executive Editor of the journal *Perception* and the co-creator of Viperlib (http:/viperlib.york.ac.uk), an online resource for visual perception. Peter has worked in the USA and spent six months at NASA's Ames Research Center in California (1990). He is a Royal Society and British Association Millennium Fellow and received an HEA National Teaching Fellowship in 2006. He also happens to be the creator of the solar system. No, seriously: look it up at www. solar.york.ac.uk.

(Continued)

(Continued)

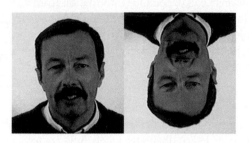

FIGURE 6.11   The Thatcher illusion

Peter's primary research interest is in movement perception (e.g. Thompson, 1982), though he has broader interests in visual sciences and has published a wide range of articles in this area. He is perhaps best known (at least outside academic circles) for the Thompson illusion (also called the Thatcher illusion) (Thompson, 1980). Faces convey all manner of social, emotional and personality information, and they are a special kind of visual object for humans. We are especially sensitive to the eyes and mouth, but only when the face is the right way up. The Thompson illusion illustrates this beautifully. Look at the images in Figure 6.11. They appear to be perfectly normal. Now turn the page round – urgk! Interestingly, newborns do not show this effect, which suggests that the effect is learnt (we usually see faces upright, but newborns have never seen a face). A dynamic illustration of the illusion can be found at OUP Thatcher illusion on YouTube: www.youtube.com/watch?v=jdADSx8JpfI.

6.4.6 SUMMARY

At present there is no single general theory of perception. Matlin and Foley (1992) argue that perception works because (1) the sensory world is rich in information (there's lots of information out there), (2) human sensory systems are good at gathering information and (3) high-level concepts shape (impose constraints on and determine) what we experience. Ultimately, the brain and the rest of the nervous system have evolved to create a system that is best suited to extracting and filtering out what it needs to sense and perceive what is in the stimulus-rich world around us.

6.5 ATTENTION

Attention plays an important role in sensation and perception, though these are by no means the only aspects of cognition in which it operates (e.g. memory, learning, planning). It's probably easier to think about attention in terms of what it does, rather than what it is. Nevertheless, psychologists often talk about different kinds of attention. For example, selective attention: attending to one thing while ignoring everything else (e.g. reading this page while ignoring the television); divided attention: processing several inputs simultaneously (reading this page while also watching television); sustained attention: maintaining our attention for long periods of time (e.g. getting to the end of this chapter); conflict resolution: inhibiting automatic responses (e.g. falling asleep while reading this chapter). As you might expect, given all the jobs attention is involved in, there is no one single mechanism at work, but many (Allport, 1993).

Attention is involved in both choice and awareness, and operates both explicitly (overtly and intentionally) and implicitly (covertly and without intent). So, when choosing to read this chapter, you stop overtly attending to the music playing behind you or the chair you are sitting on, though you *know* they are both there (did you suddenly feel your chair?). But if the music stopped or the chair broke you would be immediately aware, so you must be attending to them at some level (covertly). Chalmers (1996) has suggested that conscious attention allows us to process objects for action (e.g. open the book to read) and that unconscious attention sustains automatic reactions (e.g. reaching out to stop or cushion your fall when the chair breaks). Attention is operating all the time, though you may not be aware of everything.

In due course we will see intriguing examples of what happens when attention is faulty (*neglect*), how attention does not work the way you might think it should (*change blindness* and *inattentional blindness*), and what all this says about attentional processing. But first we will look at the development of attention research, beginning with auditory attention.

6.5.1 AUDITORY ATTENTION

Interest in auditory attention was sparked following Cherry's (1953) research into the *cocktail party effect*. This is the problem of how we can follow what one person is saying when there are several people speaking in the same room. Indeed, it is quite remarkable how, in the busy room soundscape, we are able to focus on one conversation and ignore the rest of the noise, and then just as easily switch to another conversation across the room just because it's more interesting. To investigate this phenomenon experimentally, Cherry devised the *shadowing (dichotic listening) task* (see Figure 6.12). In this task, different messages were presented to the left and right ears, and participants were asked to 'shadow' (repeat out loud) the message presented to one of the ears. Cherry found that people had very little memory for the meaning of the *unattended message* in the non-shadowed ear. Listeners even failed to notice when the unattended message was in a foreign language, or in reversed speech. Participants in such experiments have even failed to notice when words in the unattended message were repeated 35 times (Moray, 1959). However, physical characteristics of the unattended message, such as the sex of the speaker, could almost always be remembered.

FIGURE 6.12   The dichotic listening task to test divided auditory attention

Various theories of auditory attention have been proposed to explain these and subsequent findings. Of particular concern here is the seminal work of Broadbent (1958), his student's later work (Treisman, 1964) and an alternative theory by Deutsch and Deutsch (1963). Common to all these accounts is the notion of a *bottleneck*, which acts as an information **filter** that affects what is and isn't attended to. The key difference between them is where this filter lies. For both Broadbent (1958) and Treisman (1964) the filter appears early, and in Treisman's scheme it is more flexible. For Deutsch and Deutsch (1963) the filter occurs much later. A summary of all three models can be seen in Figure 6.13.

FILTER   In the context of attentional processing, a filter serves the purpose of allowing some sensations of stimuli through to be processed while screening out others. This is based on the theoretical approach that we can only cope with a limited amount of information and so select which stimuli to process.

BROADBENT'S EARLY FILTER THEORY

Broadbent's (1958) work on attention paved the way for much of what we know today and remains hugely important. According to him, information first enters a *sensory buffer* where it is held for a very short time. The selective filter then identifies one of the messages on the basis of its physical properties (e.g. location, intensity, sex of speaker). Only one message can get through this filter; the unattended message receives no further processing, while the attended message receives semantic analysis by a *limited capacity processor*. Capacity limitation is a key aspect of Broadbent's theory. He assumed that our cognitive resources are finite. Since we cannot process everything at the same time there must be some constraints on what is or isn't processed.

Broadbent was able to explain Cherry's main findings. However, more of the unshadowed message is processed than Broadbent had predicted. Thus his model does not explain why, for example, one-third of participants could hear their own name if it was presented in the unattended message (Moray, 1959). This is because Broadbent took little account of message context or message meaningfulness (he used strings of meaningless numbers). Taking these into account, Gray and Wedderburn (1960) demonstrated that when a meaningful message is split across the two streams of sound (part of the message is delivered to one ear, e.g. '7, fire, 1', and the other part is simultaneously delivered to the other ear, e.g. 'red, 1, engine') listeners report the meaningful message (i.e. 'red fire engine') but ignore the meaningless material. People also automatically switch between messages: on about 6% of trials people automatically switched ears and began to repeat the previously unshadowed message if it was contextually relevant (Treisman, 1960). Thus listeners are not constrained by the physical properties of the stimulus, but are able to switch and divide their attention using meaning and context. Treisman's (1964) model provides an explanation of why.

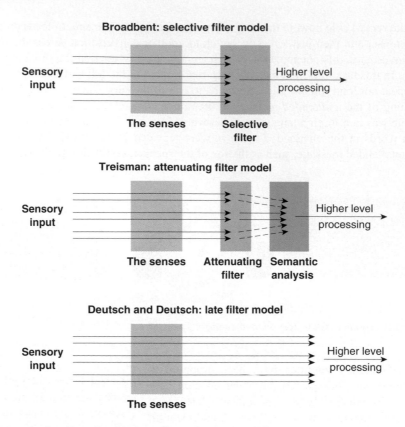

FIGURE 6.13   The three main theories of auditory attention (Andrew Dunn)

TREISMAN'S ATTENUATOR MODEL

Treisman's (1964) work built on Broadbent's earlier model, and she has been highly influential in attention research. There are similarities between her model and Broadbent's. The key difference between them lies in the location of the filter. Specifically, Treisman replaced Broadbent's selective filter with an **attenuator**, which acts to turn down the processing of the incoming unattended message. Treisman (1964) argued that the processing of unattended messages is not halted completely. Unattended messages are processed, but to a lesser degree because there is reduced capacity in the unattended channel. Accordingly, processing auditory information proceeds in a hierarchy, beginning with physical cues and ending with semantic analysis. In essence, the early bottleneck becomes more flexible. Usually there are only sufficient resources for the physical properties of unattended stimuli to be extracted. However, some stimuli (e.g. names and context-relevant messages like 'FIRE!') have a *low threshold* for identification (they are easy to identify and take priority), especially if they are primed on the basis of information in the attended channel ('matches, petrol, flame'). Thus Treisman was able to explain why physical properties of a message are almost always remembered, and why some information is able to 'break through' from the unattended message. Triesman's work has remained hugely influential. However, the concept of the attenuator is poorly specified. How does it actually work, and how can there be attenuated processing of meaning?

DEUTSCH AND DEUTSCH'S LATE SELECTION MODEL

Deutsch and Deutsch's (1963) model of attention is somewhat different from other earlier models. According to them, all incoming stimuli are *fully* analysed, but it is only the most important or relevant stimulus that determines how we respond. Thus, their filter occurs at the response stage rather than at the analysis stage. This notion is highly counter-intuitive, and for a long time Deutsch and Deutsch's work seemed at odds with what appears to be happening with attention.

Like Treisman, Deutsch and Deutsch can explain why the physical properties of messages can be reliably reported, why 'breakthrough' occurs, and how meaning can be extracted from unattended messages. In fact, distinguishing between Deutsch and Deutsch's and Treisman's theories is difficult since both make very similar predictions experimentally. However, two sources of evidence suggest that Treisman's account might be more accurate than Deutsch and Deutsch's. First, the rate of message 'breakthrough' is low; if both messages were fully analysed, the rate of breakthrough should be much higher. Second, neuropsychological evidence indicates that there are differences between attended and unattended messages much earlier on in processing than would be predicted by Deutsch and Deutsch (e.g. Woldorff et al., 1993). This suggests that attention modulates the early parts of our sensory systems (Umiltà, 2001). However, it is clear that attention can also operate at a much higher level before the object of concern becomes consciously reported (see Lamme, 2003). One mediating factor is *perceptual load*: essentially, how much there is to perceive and how busy perception is (Lavie, 1995). When perceptual load is high, the processing resources are allocated to the main task and selection occurs early. When perceptual load is lower, we have more cognitive resources available and late selection tends to occur (Lavie, 1995).

In summary, auditory attention operates with a filter or an attenuator that extracts the attended message using both physical properties of the message and/or meaning. Attention may operate early, using the physical properties of the message, or late, depending upon context, the importance of the message and demands on cognitive resources.

Although these principles are generally true, particularly limitations on available resources, this does not necessarily mean that attention operates in the same way in other sensory modalities (e.g. vision). Our next section will consider visual attention.

6.5.2 VISUAL ATTENTION

Theories of selective visual attention fall within two main categories: *space-based* and *object-based* theories. Space-based (attentional spotlight and zoom lens) theories assume that we direct our attention to discrete regions of space within the visual field. Object-based theories assume that we direct our attention to the object, rather than its location *per se*.

SPACE-BASED ATTENTION: SPOTLIGHT AND ZOOM LENS THEORY

Early accounts of visual attention (e.g. Eriksen & Eriksen, 1974) used a *spotlight* analogy. They assumed that everything within a small region of space – within the radius of the attentional spotlight – enters conscious awareness, while everything else receives only a cursory degree of processing. Indeed, decision response times about a target are relatively faster or slower if attention is directed towards (valid cue) or away from (invalid cue) the target location before it appears (Posner, 1980). This is because in the valid-cue condition, attention is already at the location when the target arrives, which saves processing time. But in the invalid-cue condition, attention must move to the true target location, which costs processing time.

Zoom lens models (e.g. Eriksen & Yeh, 1985) also assume that people attend to a particular area of space. However, unlike spotlight theory, the zoom lens model assumes that the area of focus can be increased or decreased according to task demands. Take the example of talking on the phone while driving. Normally, while driving we are able to distribute our attention widely across the visual scene and effectively process important information. However, it has been shown (Strayer & Johnson, 2001) that if we use a phone while driving we are much more likely to fail to notice red lights, and Patten et al. (2004) showed that drivers were less able to detect lights in the periphery when they were conversing on a mobile phone. Hold this in mind, as it relates to change blindness and inattention which will be discussed later.

OBJECT-BASED ATTENTION

Attention does not have to be space based. First, the focus of attention can be split over multiple locations (e.g. Awh & Pashler, 2000; Castiello & Umiltà, 1992). For example, we could be attending to more than one member of One Direction at once. Second, we can pay attention to visual (Rock & Gutman, 1981; Watson & Kramer, 1999) or auditory (Dyson & Ishfaq, 2008) objects as well as the space they occupy (e.g. Harry's voice as well as the beautiful space he and Zayn occupy). Memory for unattended objects in the same spatial location can be very poor – 'Liam, where?' (Rock & Gutman, 1981), and reaction times to properties of one object (e.g. shape or colour) can be faster than responses to the same properties in another object that occupies the same spatial location (Dyson & Ishfaq, 2008; Watson & Kramer, 1999), for example the curl of Harry's hair as opposed to Liam's beautiful smile.

So which account – space-based or object-based – is correct? The answer is 'Both!': object-based attention appears to operate *within* the attended spatial region (*spatial spotlight*). Certainly, participants are better at spotting two object properties if both properties appear on the same object, but if participants only attend to a small region of space, then the object bias disappears (Lavie & Driver, 1996).

EXERCISE: FIND THE BLUE DIAMOND IN EACH OF THESE PANELS

You will have found that task was much easier for the left panel. According to Treisman and Gelade's (1980) feature-integration theory of attention, single features of objects are processed preattentively (automatically before attentional processing) and in parallel across the visual field. However, when features need to be combined, participants need to selectively attend to each of the objects in the search array. So on the left, the attribute 'blue' pops out in a background of pink shapes, making the search very quick. However, on the right we need to bind together the attributes 'blue' and 'diamond', requiring an attentive visual search of all of the possibilities.

6.6 ARE WE AWARE OF EVERYTHING?

It feels to us that we are aware of everything around us, and yet object-based attention illustrates that under normal operating conditions we do not in fact attend to everything we thought we were attending to. Our brain has incredibly powerful processing capacity, but it is a finite resource and failures of attention are a commonplace occurrence (*change blindness* and *inattentional blindness*). However, damage to our brain can also lead to failures of attention (*visual neglect/hemispatial inattention*).

6.6.1 CHANGE BLINDNESS, INATTENTION BLINDNESS AND VISUAL NEGLECT

Change blindness (CB) refers to when people fail to perceive (big or small) changes in the very thing they are attending to. A simple (static) illustration of this can be found in traditional 'spot the difference' games. However, CB also occurs in dynamic scenes (e.g. change in object colour, or features being added or taken away) as they are being attended to. Take a look at the key study for a remarkable illustration of change blindness.

In *inattentional blindness* (IB) observers miss changes or events in the visual scene while they are attending to something else. These changes may be quite small (e.g. a briefly presented shape or word) but they can also be quite dramatic. For example, Simons and Chabris (1999) showed naive participants a video event in which two teams were playing a game of basketball. The viewers were asked to concentrate on just one of the teams and to count the number of passes they made. During this event (and unexpected by the viewers), either a woman holding an umbrella or a man in a gorilla suit walked fairly slowly in front of the game. Unbelievably, high numbers of people did not see the unexpected event: in one condition only 8% saw the gorilla! The video shown to participants can be found at http://viscog.beckman.illinois.edu/flashmovie/15.php.

KEY STUDY

Simons, D.J., & Levin, D.T. (1998). Failure to detect changes to people during a real-world interaction. *Psychonomic Bulletin and Review, 5,* **644–649.**

How much do we notice in our day-to-day interactions? Surprisingly little, it seems. Simons and Levin first demonstrated this in their now famous change blindness studies. In the first of these they had an experimenter dressed as a workman (in hard hat and tool belt) stop and ask passers-by for directions. During the conversation two other workmen (who were actually fellow experimenters) walked straight between the two people, carrying a large door that obscured the passer-by's view of the person asking for directions. At the same time, the workman asking for directions swapped places with one of the two men carrying the door, who then continued the conversation about directions. Remarkably, 8 out of the 12 passers-by reported noticing no change and carried on giving directions, even though the change was quite dramatic (i.e. the workmen wore different coloured clothes and generally looked and sounded nothing like each other). Three passers-by retrospectively claimed to have noticed. Even if these are taken into account, this still leaves almost half not noticing at all. It seems incredible but it's absolutely true.

Simon's research group has repeated this basic experiment in many different forms. You can see one of Simon's experiments in action at www.youtube.com/watch?v=mAn Kvo-fPs0.

Visual neglect (VN) or *hemispatial inattention* refers to an absence of awareness on one side of visual space. Typically, this occurs in the left visual field (left side of visual space) after damage (e.g. a stroke) to the right parietal portion (along the top side, near the back) of your brain. As a consequence, VN patients might miss or ignore food on the left side of their plate (until you turn the plate round so it's on their right), bump into objects that are on their left, or even fail to shave the left side of their face. The patient's visual system is perfectly intact (and they are implicitly aware of the objects they cannot explicitly see); the problem is with visual-spatial attention rather than being able to perceive (see) the ignored area. Indeed, VN can also occur within visual objects, leaving visual space around the object unaffected (e.g. they might read a word as '**puter**' rather than '**com**puter', or they might only see half of a clock but see the wall around it. Depending upon the extent of the damage, the effects of VN can be short-lived. However, they often have a permanent effect and, without support, are debilitating and even life-threatening. Two useful sources of further information about this condition can be found at: www.hemianopsia.net/visual-neglect/ and www.scholarpedia.org/article/Hemineglect.

6.6.2 SO WHAT DOES IT ALL MEAN?

Clearly, we do not attend to everything we think we do, and most examples of these absences go unnoticed in our day-to-day interactions. Focused attention results in the generation of a specific representation relating to the task being engaged in. But it is not a complete, general-purpose representation of the attended scene (Rensink, 2002). The examples of CB and IB are intriguing and amusing, but it should be remembered that these are phenomena which occur as part of the way attention works when it is doing its job properly! Consequently, everyday acts involving focused attention, like driving, operating machines or flying aeroplanes, are potentially fraught with danger. Imagine just how much more dangerous things become when we are dividing our attention across tasks, like using a mobile phone or talking with your friends while driving. You have been warned.

6.7 CHAPTER SUMMARY

This chapter's aim was to introduce themes and issues in sensation, perception and attention. In doing so we have discussed how we manage to detect, process and manage information from the noisy, information-rich environment in which we live. We have shown how we construct a representation of the world through a combination of bottom-up and top-down processes, and highlighted the role of experience and context. Our sensory, perceptual and attention systems are powerful tools that work together, but our resources are finite. It feels as though we experience and represent everything. In fact we do not do this. Instead we have evolved systems that extract what is necessary to interact with our world, and at best our representation of the world is adequate, even if it is not accurate. Human perception is not perfect and we do not fully understand it, but it works just fine . . . well, most of the time!

 # DISCUSSION QUESTIONS

Why might our representation of the world not be entirely accurate?

Now that you have seen evidence that what we perceive of the world does not equate with what is 'out there' and that perception requires us to construct and interpret the world, how trustworthy would you say our perceptions are?

How might the matters we have discussed in this chapter relate to such phenomena as delusions and hallucinations? To what extent is the above account adequate for explaining them?

 # SUGGESTIONS FOR FURTHER READING

Mather, G. (2009). *Perception*. Hove, UK: Psychology Press. For more on sensation and perception, this is a useful and accessible text.

Snowden, R., Thompson, P., & Tronscianko, T. (2006). *Basic vision: an introduction to visual perception*. Oxford: Oxford University Press. This is a good starting point for those primarily interested in visual sensation and perception. It is engaging, colourful and often funny.

Styles, E. (2006). *The psychology of attention*. Hove, UK: Psychology Press. For pure attention-related material, this book is hard to beat. It's comprehensive, informative and readable.

Johnson, A., & Proctor, I.W. (2004). *Attention: theory and practice*. Thousand Oaks, CA: SAGE. This book is very readable and has some nice practical applications.

Quinlan, P., & Dyson, B. (2008). *Cognitive psychology*. Harlow, UK: Prentice Hall. A general cognitive psychology text, but relevant chapters here are 5, 6, 8, 9 and 13. A punchy, colourful, humorous but informative text.

 Still want more? For links to online resources relevant to this chapter and a quiz to test your understanding, visit the companion website at edge.sagepub.com/banyard2e

7 THINKING AND PROBLEM SOLVING

Lead authors: Gary Jones, Mark Sergeant and Antonio Castro

CHAPTER OUTLINE

7.1 Introduction	112
7.2 Problem solving	112
7.2.1 Theories of problem solving	114
7.2.2 Insight problem solving	117
7.3 Reasoning	121
7.3.1 Probabilistic reasoning	121
7.3.2 Deductive reasoning	123
7.3.3 Inductive reasoning	124
7.4 Chapter summary	125
Discussion questions: confirmatory bias	125
Suggestions for further reading	126
Answers to problems	126

7.1 INTRODUCTION

Two children were sitting in front of me on the bus the other day. It was a cold and rainy day and the two boys noticed that the inside windows of the bus were full of condensation. One boy said to the other, 'These windows are wet because it's wet outside'. The other, noticing that blowing on the window caused further condensation, said, 'No, it's because my breath is wet!' (while quickly drawing a smiley face in the condensation, naturally). In a sense, both of them were correct: condensation in this instance is caused because our breath contains water vapour, which on contact with a cold surface (the windows of the bus on a cold day) causes condensation.

This simple example shows our thought processes at work: the two boys were wondering why there was condensation on the windows and their thoughts produced two possible solutions to their question. Because we use thought in everyday situations, there is a danger that we take it for granted. However, thought is a crucial attribute that humans possess. Without it, we would not be able to reason about the world. In this chapter we examine this broad area, discovering that, although we may be inclined to take it for granted, thought is actually rather difficult to explain. We will examine two important areas in the process of thinking: problem solving and reasoning.

FRAMING QUESTIONS

- Do humans solve problems in the same way as computers?
- Are there different ways to solve problems?
- What is reasoning?
- How logical are we in our thinking?
- What is insight, and can I have some?

7.2 PROBLEM SOLVING

A problem occurs when we are faced with a particular state of the world that we want to change or to explain but there is no obvious way to accomplish this. Problems may take many different forms: for example, needing to discover how to find the quickest route by car from Nottingham to London, how sunlight creates a rainbow, or how to change your profile on a website.

Problem solving is interlinked to many other domains in cognitive psychology. For example, to solve a problem we may need to memorise certain things, or use our visual capabilities to examine the characteristics of a problem. In this case, a theory of problem solving cannot consider only the processes governing the actual problem solving, because some of these processes may well lie outside problem solving *per se*. For example, if the problem we are facing is performing an arithmetic sum in our heads, then part of the constraint on how well we can solve the problem is how long we can keep numbers in memory when we are doing the arithmetic sum. This should be borne in mind when examining theories of problem solving. This section will mainly cover Newell and Simon's (1972) theory of problem solving because, as we will see, most subsequent theories of problem solving and related areas are derived from it.

Let us first consider the common elements that are involved in basic problem solving. A problem must have an initial *starting state*, a given *goal (or desired) state*, and some *constraints*. For example, in finding a route, the initial starting state may be, say, Nottingham, the given goal (i.e. the destination) may be London, and the constraint may be the need to find the quickest route. There may also be states other than the starting state or the goal state, as we manipulate the problem and work towards the solution (e.g. being on the M1 heading south towards London). Let us use a well-known problem-solving scenario, the Tower of London problem, to illustrate these concepts.

The Tower of London problem (Shallice, 1982) consists of a number of coloured balls placed on pegs. The goal is to arrange the balls on the pegs in a specific way. Our example scenario (shown in Figure 7.1) has three coloured balls (red, blue and green) and three pegs, and the goal is to have all three balls on the first peg in the order red, blue, green, from bottom to top. Therefore we have an initial state where the green and red balls are on the first peg (green at the bottom) and the blue ball is on the second peg, and we have a desired state where the red, blue and green balls are all on the first peg, in that order from the bottom. Two constraints are specified in the Tower of London problem: balls can only be moved one at a time; and any move must place a ball on a peg (i.e. balls can't be set aside).

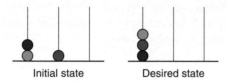

Initial state   Desired state

FIGURE 7.1   Example of initial and desired states for the Tower of London problem

If we were mindless problem solvers who did not know anything about the problem domain, then the simplest way of trying to solve it would be by **trial-and-error**. Trial-and-error means trying every possible move until – if we're lucky – we finally reach the desired (goal) state. This would mean continually moving balls and comparing the ncw state of the problem (i.e. the current state of balls on pegs) to the desired state to see if it matched. A diagram of all the possible moves could be produced, and this would illustrate every state that could be created (i.e. all possible configurations of balls on pegs). Such a diagram might look a little like that in Figure 7.2. At the top is the initial state and below this are all the possible states that arise from applying all the possible first moves to the initial state. Below each of these new states are all the possible moves that can be made (excluding the move that was made to get to the state in the first place!), and so on.

In problem solving, this type of diagram is called the **search space** or problem space, and it represents all the possible states that can be achieved in a given problem. This is important because it means that by necessity the search

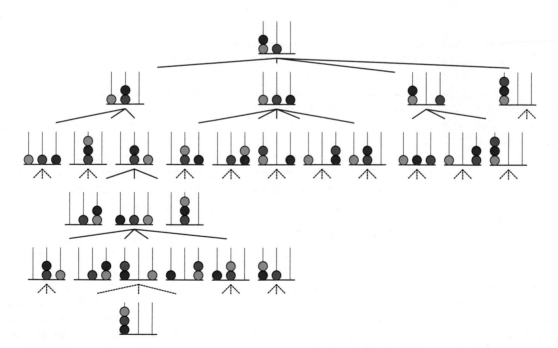

FIGURE 7.2   States that could be reached in the Tower of London problem by applying all possible moves to the initial starting state (note that due to space limitations not all moves are shown)

space must contain the desired (goal) state. Even a mindless problem solver could therefore work their way through this search space by continually moving balls onto pegs (in this example, a move from one state to the next is achieved by moving a ball from one peg to another) until they reach a state that matches the desired state.

Obviously, the search space for all the possible states that can be visited in the problem will be huge. However, with a little bit of memory, the search space can be cut down a great deal (e.g. by never making a move that would result in a state that had been encountered before). There are also other things that can be done to cut down the search space: for example, the problem solver could impose some kind of structure to their problem solving. Let's think what we would do when trying to solve this problem. One possibility is that we might try to break the problem down into smaller, more achievable goals: for example, setting a goal of moving the green ball from the bottom of the first peg. Applying structure to our problem solving helps cut down the amount of search that we are likely to have to do. All these things should be borne in mind when we look at Newell and Simon's (1972) theory of problem solving, for they consider and explain many of them.

7.2.1 THEORIES OF PROBLEM SOLVING

Newell and Simon's (1972) theory of problem solving derives from their earlier work (e.g. Newell, Shaw, & Simon, 1958). Their belief is that a theory of problem solving can be implemented as a computer program, although they stress that this should not be seen as analogous to the way the human brain accomplishes problem solving. What they argue is that the necessary mechanisms and processes can be implemented as a program, but this is not absolutely necessary because the processes and mechanisms can be described and worked through using paper and pencil; it is simply that a computer program can work through them more quickly.

KEY RESEARCHER Herbert Alexander Simon (1916–2001)

FIGURE 7.3 Herbert Simon

Simon was a US social scientist who carried out research across a range of disciplines including cognitive psychology and computer science. He is regarded as one of the founding fathers of modern scientific areas such as artificial intelligence and decision making in economics. He is described as a uniquely innovative thinker and his achievements are evidenced by the number of awards he received during his life, most notably the Nobel Prize for Economics in 1978 for 'pioneering research into the decision-making process within economic organizations'; the US National Medal of Science in 1986; and an American Psychological Association Award for Outstanding Lifetime Contributions to Psychology in 1993.

A notable quotation from Simon is:

What information consumes is rather obvious: it consumes the attention of its recipients. *Hence a wealth of information creates a poverty of attention*, and a need to allocate that attention efficiently among the overabundance of information sources that might consume it. (Simon, 1971, pp. 4–41, italics added)

MEANS–ENDS ANALYSIS Setting a goal and then breaking it down to produce subgoals which need to be achieved.

The basic idea of the theory is that, as with all problems, there is an initial state and a desired state. A goal is set to transform the initial state into the desired state (i.e. to solve the problem). This goal is then broken down into further subgoals, which need to be achieved in order to accomplish the main goal. The whole process of breaking down a problem into subgoals and further subgoals is termed **means–ends analysis**, and is short for 'accomplishing a means to an end'. It really just means setting subgoals (and further subgoals, or sub-subgoals if you like) that help to achieve the overall goal.

Providing some structure to the problem by the use of means–ends analysis obviously means that the search space is narrowed down so that only the most relevant states are likely to be visited. In the Tower of London example in Figure 7.1, the first subgoal might be to remove the green ball from the leftmost peg, so that the red ball can be the lowest on that peg. This would immediately rule out initial moves that did not involve removal of the green ball in the search space that was outlined above (e.g. initial moves involving the blue ball).

DESIRED STATE The ultimate state, that is, when the problem is solved.

GOAL STATE A desired state for a subgoal of the problem-solving process.

In order to work out what aspects of the problem the goals and subgoals should involve, Newell and Simon suggest the problem solver compares problem states to see what the differences between states are, and then sets goals and subgoals to remove those differences. For example, in the Tower of London problem, the initial state is the green and red balls on the left peg and the blue ball on the middle peg; the **desired state** is the red ball, then blue ball, then green ball on the left peg. Newell and Simon suggest that these two states will be compared, and some difference will be found to set a subgoal to attain. For example, it may be noticed that the green ball is the first ball on the left peg; a subgoal will thus be set to move the green ball to another peg (say the right peg).

The combination of means–ends analysis and comparing the differences between the current state of the problem and the desired state means that a problem can be structured somewhat so that problem solving does not progress by simple trial-and-error. Note that with each subgoal, there is a slightly different desired state from the initial one: for example, the desired state for moving the green ball to the right peg is a state whereby the green ball is actually on the right peg. For this reason, the desired states for subgoals are often called **goal states**, so as not to confuse them with the overall desired state, which is the ultimate goal of the problem.

Further to means–ends analysis, Newell and Simon also put forward the idea that a problem is constrained by operators – the mechanisms and processes that can act upon the initial state (and each subsequent state) in order to attempt to change it to the desired state. In the Tower of London example, there was really only one operator: moving a ball from one peg to another. Other problems may have many possible operators though. For example, given the starting equation $2x = 6$ (the initial state) with a desired state to find x, a goal state can be set to have x by itself on one side of the equation. The set of operators for this problem would be the set of mathematical processes which can change the current state of the problem. For example, an operator could be based around knowledge such as the fact that adding the same number to both sides of an equation (i.e. to both sides of the equal sign) keeps the equation equal. These operators can continually be applied to change the state of the problem and thus try to solve subgoals or goals. So in the example, the problem solver would eventually divide both sides of the equation by 2 in order to get x by itself on one side, leading to the solution $x = 3$, as follows:

$$2x = 6$$

$$2x/2 = 6/2$$

$$x = 3$$

One type of problem examined in detail by Newell and Simon was that of **cryptarithmetic**. This is where a sum is made from letters of the alphabet, with a goal of finding the numeric values of all of the letters so as to make the sum correct. Take the problem shown in Figure 7.4. Each letter is assigned a number from 0 through 9, with no number being assigned to more than one letter. A head start has been given by informing the problem solver that $D = 5$.

GENERAL PROBLEM SOLVER (GPS) A computer program created in 1957 by Herbert Simon and Allen Newell to build a universal problem-solving machine.

Remember that Newell and Simon implemented their theory as a computer program – which they called the **general problem solver** (GPS). The GPS began with four basic operators for cryptarithmetic: (1) to process a column in order to infer something about it; (2) to generate possible values of a letter; (3) to assign a value to a letter; and (4) to test whether a letter could take a specified value.

```
   D O N A L D      D = 5
 + G E R A L D
 -------------
   R O B E R T
```

FIGURE 7.4 An example of a cryptarithmetic problem (the answer is at the end of the chapter)

KEY STUDY

Newell, A., & Simon, H.A. (1972). *Human problem solving*. Englewood Cliffs, NJ: Prentice Hall.

Not a study as such, but a whole set of studies related to problem solving. This is *the* book on problem solving, and to give an impression on how important it is, it has been cited over 13,000 times to date. Newell and Simon detail a suite of studies (several of which are outlined in this chapter) and also outline their theory of problem solving, of which a simplified version is given in this chapter. It is a must-read for anyone learning about problem solving.

Using these operators together with means–ends analysis as a method for breaking down the problem into goals and subgoals, in conjunction with comparing the current state of the problem with the desired state (the identification of all of the letters in terms of what numerical values they are assigned), the GPS is able to solve the problem.

The way in which the GPS solved cryptarithmetic problems compared favourably to verbal protocols of people solving problems. A verbal protocol is the transcript produced when someone 'thinks aloud' when they are performing something. Newell and Simon analysed the verbal protocols from problem solvers in order to identify the types of goal, subgoal and operator that they were trying to apply in different situations in a problem. This would then give them some idea as to whether their theory carried out problem solving in a similar way to humans. In general, they found that there was a great deal of overlap between how the GPS solved cryptarithmetic problems and how human participants solved them.

However, although the theory does predict some human problem-solving behaviour, it does not predict all. For example, novice problem solvers may solve problems like the GPS does (using means–ends analysis) but experts do not. For example, Larkin (1983) studied physics problems using students and professional physicists. The students, who had little knowledge of physics, would solve the problems in a similar fashion to the GPS. The professional physicists, however, would solve the problem in a completely different way: they would classify the problem as being similar to a set of problems they knew already, and then apply the methods and processes that would be used for this class of problem – a process called analogy. Other researchers have also shown how individual differences can influence problem-solving behaviour in ways that are not captured by the GPS (Handley et al., 2002). Furthermore, solution attempts of the GPS did not always correspond to those of participants for problems that would be expected to require means–ends analysis. For example, discrepancies have been seen for problems such as the missionaries and cannibals problem.

It should also be noted that there are arguments against depicting the human brain as analogous to a computer program. Searle (1980) famously described his 'Chinese room', whereby someone who knows only English can sit in a room and follow instructions for how to manipulate strings of Chinese characters such that to people outside the room there is the appearance that the person within the room can speak Chinese. That is, in the same way that the English person in the room does not know Chinese yet appears to, a computer program may perform similarly to people in certain problems yet might achieve this performance in a way that is completely different from people. Nevertheless, Newell and Simon's theory of problem solving has provided a basis for many of the more contemporary theories of problem solving.

EXERCISE: ZOMBIES AND PSYCHOLOGISTS PROBLEM

(This is often referred to as the missionaries and cannibals problem but we thought that was offensive so have devised our own version) Three zombies and three psychologists are on one bank of a river. They all need to cross the river but there are three constraints: (1) there is only one boat which holds a maximum of two people; (2) the number of psychologists on each river bank must at least equal the number of zombies, otherwise the zombies will eat the psychologists; (3) the boat must be occupied by at least one person whenever it crosses the river. Devise a sequence of river crossings that enable all six to cross the river while keeping within the constraints outlined.

Answer at the end of the chapter.

More recent theories of problem solving have retained several elements of Newell and Simon's theory, particularly the goal-oriented aspects and the idea of representing the theory as a computer program. The main current theory is adaptive character of thought–rational (ACT–R) (Anderson, 1993, 2007). ACT–R is intended as a general theory of human intelligence, of which problem solving is only a part. ACT–R is implemented in the form of a production system. Rather than covering ACT–R in detail here, we will briefly cover production systems so that you have some idea of how contemporary ideas of problem solving are implemented.

Production systems hold two types of knowledge: factual knowledge and **procedural knowledge**. Factual knowledge is statements about what we know: for example, I like football. Procedural knowledge is represented by the rules of the game. A rule is an *if . . . then* construct. For example, *if* I like football, and I know a football match is on the television, *then* I stay in and watch the football. **Declarative knowledge** is used to see if any of the *if* parts of rules can be matched, and if this is the case, then that rule is put forward as a possible rule to be used.

> **PRODUCTION SYSTEM** A system that uses facts and rules about those facts to govern its behaviour. The term arises because rules are also known as productions.

Take the following pieces of declarative knowledge: I like football, I like rugby, I want to play football, I want to play rugby. Now take the following rules: *if* I like football, and I want to play football, *then* I go outside and play football; *if* I like rugby, and I want to play rugby, *then* I go outside and play rugby. If all of this knowledge was in the production system, then both rules could be used (the first would suggest playing football and the second would suggest playing rugby). How would we select which rule should be used at a given moment in time?

When more than one rule can be used at any given time, the system is said to be in conflict, in which case **conflict resolution** will be utilised to decide which rule should be used. There are a variety of methods for resolving conflict: in the example above, the most obvious method is to place weightings on the rules, so that (for example) a preference for playing football over rugby could be reflected by that rule having a higher weighting. There are also alternative ways of resolving conflict: the rule that was used most recently could be selected, or the rule which uses the most recently added knowledge to declarative memory.

Behaviour in production systems proceeds in the manner of selecting which rules can be used for the given set of declarative knowledge, selecting a rule from this set using conflict resolution, and then applying the rule. Note that the *then* part of the rule can change declarative knowledge, which would mean that the next time the system examined which rules can be used, a completely different set of rules might appear. For example, given the rule 'if I like Jessie J's new single *then* buy it as a download', together with a liking for Jessie J's new single, the fact that we want to buy it as a download is placed in declarative knowledge. Other rules would then act upon this knowledge (e.g. going onto the internet etc.). More detailed explanations of production systems can be found in Anderson (1993, 2000, 2007).

Using production systems as a basis for intelligent behaviour, ACT–R has simulated problem-solving behaviour in the **Tower of Hanoi** problem, transfer problems, and geometry problem solving. ACT–R also provides a timing estimate of how long a rule takes to be executed. Comparisons with human data have been very favourable, illustrating how ACT–R compares well to human problem solving in terms of not only timing data but also general problem-solving behaviour.

> **TOWER OF HANOI** A problem-solving puzzle similar to the Tower of London problem but using size of disk for correct ordering instead of colour. It consists of three rods on which are placed a number of disks of various sizes (placed in order of size from large to small). The aim is to move all disks onto another rod in the correct order of size. The constraints are that only one disk can be removed at a time and may not be placed on top of a smaller disk. It must also be placed on a peg, that is, it cannot be put to one side. The aim is to use the smallest number of moves to achieve the goal. You can see it in action on YouTube at: www.youtube.com/watch?v=5Wn4EboLrMM

7.2.2 INSIGHT PROBLEM SOLVING

Not all of human problem solving fits neatly into the idea that we apply rules based on certain facts about the world, however. Have you ever given up on a problem only for its solution to suddenly appear out of the blue in what can be described as a 'flash of **insight**'? These are the types of problem we discuss in this section.

> **INSIGHT** This is when we reach a dead end in problem solving until suddenly – 'aha!' – we realise the solution. A rare phenomenon.

Consider the anecdote of King Hiero asking Archimedes to prove that the amount of gold in his newly made crown equalled the amount of gold given to the goldsmiths. Archimedes considers the problem for some time and becomes stuck in an **impasse**: he simply cannot see a solution. Some days later when taking a bath, he notices that his body displaces the water in the bath tub. Immediately, he has his flash of insight and runs naked through the streets, crying out 'Eureka! I have found it!' (Gruber, 1995). This is the essence of insight – a situation where the solution to a problem seems impossible until suddenly it appears as if from nowhere. The **Gestalt psychologists** were the first to illustrate insight in the early 1900s, though relatively recently insight has had a resurgence of interest, with two theories being proposed as to why insight occurs.

The Gestalt psychologists (e.g. Köhler, 1925; Scheerer, 1963) argued that insight was a process of restructuring: the problem solver needs to restructure the problem in a different way from that originally considered. One of the first studies of insight actually involved chimpanzees. Köhler (1925) set up a problem situation where a banana was hanging out of reach in a chimpanzee's cage. On the floor was a set of crates. The idea was that the chimpanzee should stack the crates in such a way as to create a set of steps leading to the banana. Köhler found that this solution came to the chimpanzees quite suddenly, and was normally preceded by a period of intense thought.

This confirmed the two states we have met: *impasse* (where the problem solver becomes stuck on the problem and either keeps repeating problem-solving moves or stops and thinks about the problem for a while), and *insight* (where the solution to the problem suddenly appears). Of course, just being in an impasse does not necessarily mean insight will subsequently follow. If only it did!

Taking Köhler's lead, Maier (1931) examined insight in humans, setting up a room where two pieces of string hung from the ceiling, each out of arm's reach from the other (an example of the room is given in Figure 7.5). The goal was to tie the two pieces together. Various implements (e.g. scissors) were given to help. The correct solution was to tie one of the implements to one of the pieces of string and set it in a pendulum motion so that both pieces could then be held. Participants in this problem had great difficulty in solving it, often needing a hint (the experimenter 'accidentally' brushing against one of the pieces of string and setting it into motion). Previously, the implements were seen in terms of their function, a concept the Gestalt psychologists called **functional fixedness** – an early recognition that insight problems might be difficult because of prior experience. After the hint, for example, the scissors might be seen not in terms of their usual function (cutting things), but rather in terms of what else they could be used for (a pendulum weight). Today we might refer to this as 'thinking outside the box', where we try to come up with new solutions to a problem. In this case we look for new uses for all the objects at our disposal and see that the scissors can help create a pendulum.

FIGURE 7.5   Maier's (1931) two-string problem

One recent theory of insight uses these Gestalt ideas. The representational change theory (Knoblich et al., 1999; Knoblich, Ohlsson & Raney, 2001; Ohlsson, 1992; Öllinger et al., 2012; Öllinger, Jones & Knoblich, 2014) suggests that, because of prior experience, the problem solver begins with a representation of the problem that is incorrect for its solution. Only by changing this representation can the problem be solved. This is done in one of two ways: constraint relaxation and/or chunk decomposition. **Constraint relaxation** involves relaxing constraints that the problem solver unnecessarily imposes on the problem (e.g. thinking of the function of scissors as being only to cut things). **Chunk decomposition** involves realising that certain components of the problem can be broken down further (e.g. the Roman numeral for 4, IV, can be broken down into an I and a V).

Knoblich and colleagues used a Roman numeral matchstick arithmetic domain to illustrate the theory. In Roman numeral matchstick arithmetic, an incorrect equation is written out in Roman numerals using matchsticks, with the goal being to move one, and only one, matchstick to make the equation correct. Figure 7.6 shows an example problem.

The problem outlined in Figure 7.6 requires the relaxation of the constraint that numerical values in equations cannot be arbitrarily changed without some corresponding change to the other side of the equation (i.e. you would not normally change a 4 into a 6 on one side of the equation without also adding 2 to the other side of the equation). The problem also requires decomposing the chunk IV into the components I and V (i.e. thinking of the I as a matchstick that can be moved and not thinking of it as having to be part of the IV).

> **GESTALT PSYCHOLOGY** A school of psychology that began in Germany in the first half of the twentieth century. It proposed that an experience or behaviour can only be understood as a whole, not by understanding the individual constituent parts.

FIGURE 7.6 An example matchstick problem (the solution can be found at the end of this chapter)

Sets of matchstick problems were created and predictions were made by the theory as to the difficulty of each problem, based on what constraints needed to be relaxed and what chunks needed to be decomposed. The predictions of the theory were borne out, with participants quickly solving arithmetic equations that the theory predicted should be easy, and taking a long time to solve equations that the theory predicted to be hard.

There is an alternative theory of insight, however, the constraint for satisfactory progress theory (MacGregor, Ormerod, & Chronicle, 2001), which is based on Newell and Simon's problem-solving theory. If we think of an insight problem in terms of a search space, where all possible moves to be made in the problem are outlined, then it seems strange that people struggle to solve insight problems, because surely they should just search this space of possible states in the problem to find the solution. MacGregor and colleagues suggest that this is in fact what people do, but their search space does not contain *all* of the possible moves. Only when people have tried all of the available (but fruitless) moves will they realise that the problem space requires expanding.

Ormerod, MacGregor and Chronicle (2002) examined the theory using the eight-coin problem. In this problem, a set of eight coins is laid on a table; the task is to move two coins so that each coin touches three, and only three, others. Two initial configurations of coins were given (see Figure 7.7). The idea was that if people searched their space of possible moves, a configuration that offered plenty of initial moves in which a coin would touch three others would lead to people

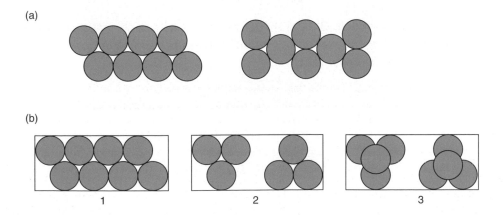

FIGURE 7.7 **The eight-coin problem** (a) Two initial configurations for the eight-coin problem. (b) The solution is to stack coins. Using the left side configuration as an example (1), a solution would be to move the upper coin in the third column (2) on top of the triangle of coins in columns one and two (3), and to move the lower coin in the second column on top of the triangle of coins in columns four and five (3), as illustrated

taking a long time to reach a solution: they would feel they were satisfying subgoals of moving a coin to touch three others. On the other hand, a configuration where there are no obvious initial moves for a coin to touch three others should result in insight being achieved more quickly. This is exactly what the researchers found, with the configuration on the left side of Figure 7.7 being solved more often and more quickly than the configuration on the right side.

The two theories of insight have both been shown to be effective, but in the context of different insight problems. It has therefore been suggested that perhaps the best explanation of insight is a theory that encompasses elements of both theories (Jones, 2003; Öllinger et al., 2014).

EXERCISE: THE NINE-DOT PROBLEM

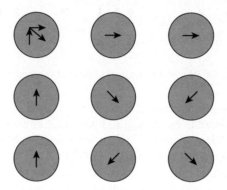

FIGURE 7.8   The nine-dot problem

Figure 7.8 shows nine dots. Your task is to connect the 9 dots with four straight lines. In doing so, you are not allowed to lift your pen from the paper or retrace a line. [Hint: The arrows that you can see within the dots are not usually given – you can use them to help you solve the problem; without the arrows, solution rates to this problem are extremely low.]

KEY STUDY

Öllinger, M., Jones, G., & Knoblich, G. (2013). The dynamics of search, impasse, and representational change provide a coherent explanation of difficulty in the nine-dot problem. *Psychological Research*. [Published online 25 May 2013]

The nine-dot problem that is given as one of the chapter exercises is the archetypal insight problem. It is easily the most studied because people find the problem extremely difficult. Many people fail to solve it even after 100 solution attempts and after being told that the solution must go beyond the perceived 3 × 3 square (see solution at end of chapter). Öllinger, Jones and Knoblich explained the reasons why the nine-dot puzzle was so difficult, by combining the representational change theory with that of Newell and Simon's problem space search theory. When beginning the problem, people perceive a 3 × 3 square and therefore place an unnecessary 'boundary constraint' on the problem – that is, they only consider lines that stay within the perceived square. However, when the constraint is relaxed, lines can extend to almost any location on the piece of paper. So, when the boundary constraint is imposed, the problem space is *too small* because it doesn't include the solution; but when the boundary constraint is relaxed, the problem space is *too large* to be searched within a reasonable time frame. Öllinger and colleagues provided hints like the arrows seen in Figure 7.8 to enable the problem solver to reduce the search space after they had relaxed the boundary constraint, resulting in significant increases in solution rates and providing an effective explanation for difficulty in the problem.

ASIDE

Thinking about thinking

Insights are remarkable things. We sometimes have lightbulb moments when a solution to a problem suddenly appears. Fortunately most of us don't decide to suddenly run down the street naked like Archimedes (see text), as this would create a whole set of new problems to solve. When we look back at where the answer came from, it can sometimes appear almost mystical. Suddenly it all became clear and we got a sense that we understood the puzzle we were thinking about. Sometimes the puzzle can be like those described here, and sometimes they can be human problems like why your partner dumped you. Something happens in our thinking and we dramatically restructure our thoughts and see the world in a different way. Most remarkably, this restructuring often happens when we are not thinking about the problem. A famous example of this is the discovery of the benzene ring by German chemist Friedrich Kekulé in 1890 after a dream about a snake eating its own tail.

7.3 REASONING

Reasoning is the process of drawing conclusions through logical thinking. It tends to be considered part of problem solving but also part of thinking in general. There are a variety of forms of reasoning, such as **probabilistic reasoning**, **inductive reasoning** and **deductive reasoning**, all of which will be briefly covered here.

7.3.1 PROBABILISTIC REASONING

Probabilistic reasoning is how we reason under varying degrees of uncertainty. This has links with everyday reasoning, because often problems and situations may involve a variety of factors which are uncertain, for example, when you leave your house to go to the shops, you may consider how likely it is to rain so that you can determine whether or not to take a coat with you. The weakness of this sort of reasoning can be seen in the observation that it usually rains when you leave your coat at home and is very sunny when you wrap up against the weather.

Uncertainty is usually represented by a probability measure, which is a number between 0 and 1 (0 being no chance of something happening, 1 being certainty that something will happen, and 0.5 representing a 50/50 chance that something will happen). Probability can be influenced by frequency (how often something has happened in the past) and belief (your own belief in whether something will happen).

EXERCISE: LOGICAL FALLACIES

Before you read on, try to solve this problem.

A taxi-cab was involved in a hit and run accident one night. Two cab companies, Green and Blue, operate in the city. You are given the following information:

1 In the study, 85% of the cabs are Green, 15% are Blue.
2 In a court, a witness identified the cab as being Blue.

The witness's ability to identify the colours of cabs was tested, and it was shown that the witness was able to correctly identify the colour of a cab 80% of the time and was wrong 20% of the time.

What is the probability that the cab involved in the accident was Blue rather than Green?

There is a way of calculating probability taking into account frequency and belief – **Bayes' theorem**. We won't explain how Bayes' theorem works (it's a quite complicated mathematical formula!) but it basically outlines how frequency information can be used when calculating probability. If people always used Bayes' theorem, their probabilistic reasoning would be error-free. However, in reality, people are relatively poor at working with probabilities. This is partly because people do not use theorems like the one outlined by Bayes, but partly for various other reasons. Tversky and Kahneman have played a major role in identifying those reasons (e.g. Kahneman & Tversky, 1972; Tversky & Kahneman, 1974, 1980, 1983). This section therefore focuses on the work of Tversky and Kahneman since they have been instrumental in shaping how we think about probabilistic reasoning.

One reason that we often get it wrong in calculating probability is due to the **base rate fallacy**. This is where people fail to take into account the base rate when calculating the probability of an event occurring. The base rate is the prior probability of a certain event occurring when the data related to the event are *not* taken into account (this is $p(H)$ in Bayes' theorem). Take the example shown in the cab exercise (from Tversky & Kahneman, 1980). Most individuals state that the probability of the taxi being Blue is 80%; however, this answer completely ignores the base rate of a taxi being Blue, which is only 15%. Bayes' theorem can be used to compute the correct probabilities, and would actually show that the chances of the cab being Blue are 0.41 (41%), meaning that there is in fact more chance of the taxi being Green.

Another reason for our poor probability calculations is the *availability heuristic*. This applies where more emphasis is placed on information that is readily available to us. For example, Tversky and Kahneman (1974) asked questions of the form:

> If a word of three letters or more is chosen at random from a dictionary, is there more chance of it beginning with a K or more chance that the third letter is a K?

The majority of participants get this question wrong. People are likely to say there is more chance of the word beginning with a K, when in fact there is more chance of a K being the third letter. The reason they do this is that we can quickly think of words that begin with K, and it is more difficult to think of words which have a K as their third letter; that is, words beginning with a K are more *available*. This type of fallacy occurs for many things, such as people thinking certain causes of death (e.g. murder) are more common than other less publicised causes (e.g. suicide) (Lichtenstein et al., 1978).

> **HEURISTIC** A mental shortcut (or rule of thumb) that represents a 'best guess', allowing people to make solution attempts or make decisions quickly and efficiently (though not always correctly).

The *representativeness heuristic* applies where people often become misled by instances that they believe to be representative of a category. It's easier to think of such representative instances (e.g. that people studying English would go on to become journalists) than instances which tend not to be representative of a category (e.g. that people who study English would go on to be footballers) (Tversky & Kahneman, 1983).

The *gambler's fallacy* is where people become completely misled in their belief of what is likely to happen by chance. For example, when tossing a coin six times, people believe a sequence of heads and tails of THHTHT to be much more likely to happen than a sequence of TTTHHH, even though both are equally as likely (Kahneman & Tversky, 1972). See also the TV programme *Deal or No Deal*, where people believe that there is a strategy in their actions to guess which box has the most money.

Anchoring and adjustment refers to instances where people's judgements are misled by the first piece of evidence that they see. For example, when given very short times to estimate sums, people will give lower estimates for $1 \times 2 \times 3 \times 4 \times 5 \times 6 \times 7 \times 8$ than they do for the same sum in reverse ($8 \times 7 \times 6 \times 5 \times 4 \times 3 \times 2 \times 1$) simply because the former begins with lower numbers than the latter.

Optimism bias is a belief that a person has less chance of experiencing a negative event than other people of equal footing, for example, a smoker believing they are less likely to contract lung cancer than other people who smoke a similar amount.

Conjunction fallacy illustrates a belief that two events happening have a larger probability than either one or the other event. Consider the classic example from Tversky and Kahneman (1980): 'Linda is 31 years old, single, outspoken, and very bright. She majored in philosophy. As a student, she was deeply concerned with issues of discrimination and social justice, and also participated in anti-nuclear demonstrations.' When asked which has the greater chance of being correct – Linda is a bank manager or Linda is a bank manager who is active in the feminist movement – significantly more people selected the latter. This cannot be true under laws of probability (i.e. if the probability of Linda being a bank manager were 0.5 [or 50%] and the probability of her being in the feminist movement were also 0.5, then the probability of Linda being a bank manager and in the feminist movement are 0.5 * 0.5 = 0.25).

Loss aversion describes the situation where, when faced with opportunities relating to losses and gains, people prefer to limit losses and to seek gains. For example, when given the choice of a certain loss of £1 or a one in three chance of losing £3, people will select to lose £1; however, if the same choice is framed as a gain, people would take the one in three chance of gaining £3.

7.3.2 DEDUCTIVE REASONING

Another type of reasoning is deductive reasoning. This is reasoning which involves deducing a conclusion from a set of given premises. Take the example shown in Figure 7.9.

```
All S are M.
All M are P.

Therefore:

A   All S are P.
B   All S are not P.
C   Some S are P.
D   Some S are not P.
E   None of the above.
```

FIGURE 7.9   Example of deductive reasoning

Deductive reasoning is usually examined in the form given in Figure 7.9 – that is, using **syllogisms**. A syllogism has two *premises* (e.g. all S are M; all M are P) and a *conclusion* (therefore, all S are P). As we will see, people tend to find deductive reasoning difficult, particularly when the premises and conclusion involve items or things that are unfamiliar to them or contradict their real-world beliefs. Take the following two syllogisms:

War times are prosperous times, and prosperity is highly desirable; therefore, wars are much to be desired.

Philosophers are all human, and all human beings are fallible; therefore, all philosophers are fallible, too.

Both of the conclusions to these statements are true based on the premises. However, people are much happier to accept the second as true, and less happy to accept the first as true. This illustrates how our prior knowledge can affect our deductive reasoning (see also, for example, De Neys, Schaeken, & d'Ydewalle, 2005), something which is called *belief bias* (e.g. Evans, Barston, & Pollard, 1983; Klauer, Musch, & Naumer, 2000), where believable conclusions are much easier to accept than unbelievable ones.

SYLLOGISMS A form of deductive reasoning consisting of a major premise, a minor premise and a conclusion. For example, all Liverpool players are divers; Steven Gerrard is a Liverpool player; therefore Steven Gerrard is a diver.

There are other factors that also affect our ability to interpret syllogisms. For example, the way in which the premises and conclusions are ordered (called the *figure* of the syllogism) can hamper the reasoning process, as illustrated in the following statements:

Some people eat cake, and some cake eaters believe in ghosts; therefore, some people believe in ghosts.

Some cake eaters are people, and some people who believe in ghosts eat cake; therefore, some people believe in ghosts.

The two statements are exactly the same, but they are ordered differently. In the first, the standard format is used, whereby the first statement begins with people and specifies a relationship to cake eaters, and then the second begins with cake eaters and specifies a relationship to believers in ghosts. This is called an A–B, B–C format, and it is the easier format for people to interpret. In the example, the A represents people, the B cake eaters, and the C believers in ghosts. The second has an order of B–A, C–B, because the first part begins with cake eaters and specifies their relationship to people, and the second part begins with believers in ghosts and specifies their relationship to cake eaters. People tend to find the first version much easier to interpret than the second (e.g. Dickstein, 1978).

Finally, the *mood* of the syllogism can also affect performance (e.g. Evans, Newstead, & Byrne, 1993). The mood describes the terms used to illustrate the relationships in the syllogism, e.g. *some, all, some . . . are not*. For example, the inclusion of 'not' in the first syllogism below seems to make the interpretation of the syllogism more difficult than the second one:

Some artists are not painters, and some painters are rich; therefore, some artists are not rich.

Some artists are painters, and some painters are rich; therefore, some artists are rich.

Belief bias, mood and figure combine to affect our reasoning. For example, people find A–B, B–C premises easier, *but* find them harder for unbelievable conclusions (Newstead et al., 1992). For example, the first syllogism below is easier to interpret than the second even though it does not follow the A–B, B–C format, because the second one contains information that contradicts prior beliefs:

Some animals are not cats, and milk drinkers are cats; therefore, some animals drink milk.

Some canaries are not birds, and some birds drink coffee; therefore, some canaries drink coffee.

What we see from deductive reasoning is that interpreting syllogisms is based on a variety of factors that combine to make the syllogism either easy or hard to interpret. There are some explanations of deductive reasoning, in particular mental models (e.g. Johnson-Laird, 2004; Johnson-Laird & Byrne, 1991). We do not have space to go into this theory, but you should be aware of its existence – and if you want to read about it further, you should seek out Johnson-Laird (1983, 1999, 2004).

7.3.3 INDUCTIVE REASONING

Inductive reasoning involves working from the specific to the general (as opposed to deductive reasoning where we apply general rules to specific instances). What we mean by this is that in inductive reasoning we form a general conclusion based on certain instances or facts. For example, if it has rained for the last three Wednesdays, then it will rain the following Wednesday. That is, based on evidence (it has rained for the last three Wednesdays), a hypothesis has been derived (it rains on Wednesdays). Of course, in this simple example we know from prior experience that the hypothesis is unlikely to be true; even though the weather is bad in the UK, it never usually rains every single Wednesday! Nevertheless, inductive reasoning is a key process, particularly in science, where hypotheses are often derived from sets of factual evidence.

However, much of our inductive reasoning is based on evidence that confirms our hypothesis: for example, we derived the hypothesis that it rains on Wednesdays based on evidence that confirmed this hypothesis (that it had rained the last three Wednesdays). Popper (1968) argued that it is not enough to conclude hypotheses based on confirmatory evidence alone; one must also seek to find any evidence that disconfirms the hypotheses (and therefore the hypotheses are no longer valid). If no disconfirming evidence can be found, then this indicates a high likelihood that the hypotheses are true.

Unfortunately, people tend to show a confirmation bias: that is, they derive hypotheses from supporting facts and don't often look for disconfirming evidence. This is illustrated in a classic study by Peter Wason – the 2–4–6 task. Wason's (1960) 2–4–6 task was created with the intention of investigating the significance of Popper's claims regarding falsification. The outline of the task is as follows:

I have a rule in mind that specifies how a sequence of three numbers (triples) can be ordered. Your task is to discover what my rule is. To start you off, I can tell you that '2-4-6' is a triple that fits my rule. In order to discover the rule, you should produce number triples, and I will tell you whether your number triple fits my rule or not. You can try as many or as few triples as you wish, and once you feel you have discovered the rule, then you can state it aloud to me.

Wason was interested in the types of triples that people would generate. His idea was that people would hypothesise a rule and would then test this rule using triples. His main interest was in seeing whether people would produce triples to confirm their hypothesised rule, and/or whether they would produce triples that attempted to disconfirm their hypothesised rule. The correct answer is 'any ascending sequence', but people rarely manage to derive this rule (only around 20% of people arrive at this answer). The vast majority of people produce an overly restrictive rule, such as 'numbers increasing by two'.

Wason found that people who solved the task produced not only more triples, but triples with more variation. Non-solvers of the task tended to produce fewer triples, and their triples did not vary as much in terms of what they tested. For example, they might suggest triples of 12–14–16 and 20–22–24 if they hypothesised a rule along the lines of 'ascending numbers increasing by two'. If they tried a triple of (for example) 8–21–52 they would find that such a triple also received positive feedback, but they would be less likely to try it because it would invalidate their hypothesised rule. The majority of people seek to confirm their hypotheses and fail to look for evidence that might disconfirm their hypotheses, thereby showing 'confirmation bias'.

Confirmation bias is very strong and has been found in a variety of research related to the 2–4–6 task (e.g. Mynatt, Doherty, & Tweney, 1977). Even when participants are given explicit instructions to use a non-confirmatory strategy to test their rules, performance does not seem to improve (Tweney et al., 1980). However, it seems that the confirmation bias can be removed, in the 2–4–6 task at least, by altering the instructions. In the final study of Tweney et al. (1980), participants were given a 'dual-goal' task – being asked to discover two rules rather than one. The first rule was called the Dax rule and was the same as that in the Wason task (triples containing an ascending sequence of numbers) and the second rule was called the Med rule (all other triples). They were given an example of a triple that fitted the Dax rule (2–4–6). Even though this task was much the same as that of Wason (1960), success rates rose dramatically. Why should this be the case? Various reasons have been put forward, but this is a question that is arguably still unanswered in the reasoning literature. Nevertheless, these studies show that under normal circumstances people do not seek to disconfirm their hypotheses, yet they can do when circumstances are presented that encourage them to do so.

7.4 CHAPTER SUMMARY

We have now covered a variety of perspectives on thought. In the problem-solving section we looked at Newell and Simon's (1972) influential theory of problem solving and then saw how this theory has influenced subsequent ones, not only the ACT–R theory (e.g. Anderson, 2007), but also contemporary theories of insight problem solving. We also looked at different types of reasoning (probabilistic, deductive, inductive) and illustrated how and why we can find reasoning about the world difficult. You have been provided with many fundamental areas of thought, and knowledge of these areas will be invaluable to you, not only for comprehending the basics, but also if you now seek to explore further information in these areas.

(?) DISCUSSION QUESTIONS: CONFIRMATORY BIAS

If we have a bias towards confirming our hunches and beliefs, this bias might well affect the ways that people carry out their work.

Consider the way you study. See whether you can identify examples of where you have unwittingly been influenced by the confirmatory bias.

Consider also one or more of the following: (1) how doctors make a diagnosis; (2) the way police investigate crime; and (3) the way psychologists collect evidence. How do you think confirmatory bias might affect these practices? How could confirmatory bias be challenged or prevented?

SUGGESTIONS FOR FURTHER READING

Anderson, J.R. (2009). *Cognitive psychology and its implications* (6th edn). New York: Worth. A good cognitive psychology text that has chapters on problem solving and reasoning.

Eysenck, M.W., & Keane, M.T. (2010). *Cognitive psychology: a student's handbook* (6th edn). Hove: Psychology Press. Comprehensive text on cognitive psychology that includes problem solving and reasoning. A good source of material for the beginner wishing to learn more about cognitive psychology.

Mayer, R.E. (2005). *Thinking, problem solving, cognition* (3rd edn). New York: Freeman. A comprehensive review of the literature that covers most of the topics in this chapter in great depth plus related areas such as analogical problem solving.

Quinlan, P., & Dyson, B. (2008). *Cognitive psychology*. Harlow: Prentice Hall. An easy-to-read book that covers all of the fundamental areas of cognitive psychology, including problem solving and reasoning.

Robertson, S.I. (2001). *Problem solving*. Hove: Psychology Press. An in-depth examination of problem solving, covering search spaces, heuristics, insight and much more.

ANSWERS TO PROBLEMS

CRYPTARITHMETIC

G = 1, O = 2, B = 3, A = 4, D = 5, N = 6, R = 7, L = 8, E = 9, T = 0

MATCHSTICK ALGEBRA

VI = III + III

EIGHT-COIN PUZZLE

FIGURE 7.10   Answer to the eight coin puzzle

DEDUCTIVE REASONING

The correct conclusion from the premises is option A.

ZOMBIES AND PSYCHOLOGISTS PROBLEM

RIVER BANK 1	BOAT	RIVER BANK 2
PPPZZZ		
PPPZ	ZZ ->	
PPPZ		ZZ
PPPZ	<- Z	Z
PPPZZ		Z
PPP	ZZ ->	Z
PPP		ZZZ

PPP	<- Z	ZZ
PPPZ		ZZ
PZ	PP ->	ZZ
PZ		PPZZ
PZ	<- PZ	PZ
PPZZ		PZ
ZZ	PP ->	PZ
ZZ		PPPZ
ZZ	<- Z	PPP
ZZZ		PPP
Z	ZZ ->	PPP
Z		PPPZZ
Z	<- Z	PPPZ
ZZ		PPPZ
	ZZ ->	PPPZ
		PPPZZZ

FIGURE 7.11 The solution to the zombies and psychologists problem

NINE-DOT PROBLEM

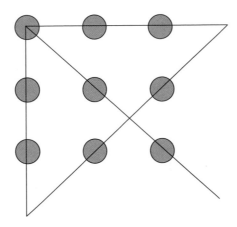

FIGURE 7.12 The solution to the nine-dot problem

 Still want more? For links to online resources relevant to this chapter and a quiz to test your understanding, visit the companion website at edge.sagepub.com/banyard2e

8 LANGUAGE

Lead author: Thomas Dunn

CHAPTER OUTLINE

8.1 Introduction	**131**
8.2 Function and origins of language	**131**
8.2.1 The big brain theory	131
8.2.2 The gesture development theory	131
8.3 Language and cognition	**133**
8.3.1 A cognitive approach to understanding language	133
8.3.2 Language and thought	133
8.4 From thought to language: How do we produce language?	**135**
8.4.1 Speech errors	135
8.5 Cognitive models of speech production	**136**
8.5.1 Bock and Levelt's (1994) model of speech processing	136
8.5.2 Dell's (1986) connectionist model of speech production	138
8.5.3 Serial versus parallel models of speech production	139
8.6 From language to thought: How do we comprehend language?	**140**
8.6.1 Auditory language comprehension	140
8.7 Cognitive models of speech perception	**140**
8.7.1 Motor theory of speech perception	141
8.7.2 Direction perception theory	141
8.7.3 Fuzzy logic theory (FLT) of perception	141
8.8 Eye movements and language processing	**142**

8.9 Cognitive models of word identification   **143**

8.9.1 Interactive activation model   144

8.9.2 The logogen model   144

8.9.3 The cohort model of lexical processing   145

8.10 A cognitive model of writing   **146**

8.10.1 Flower and Hayes' (1981) model of writing processes   146

8.11 Chapter summary   **147**

Discussion questions   **147**

Suggestions for further reading   **147**

8.1 INTRODUCTION

Language is one of the phenomena that separate humans as a species. Evolving over many years, the human capacity and desire to communicate is no better reflected in contemporary culture than with the development of sophisticated communication networks and systems such as mobile phones, social networking and electronic mail (or 'email' as it is now called!). Language is an interpersonal and intrapersonal phenomenon. It exists within ourselves as well as within the interactions that we have with others. To answer the question of 'What is language?' is perhaps best approached by asking 'What is the function of language?'. According to evolutionary theory, language must have developed because it offered benefit to us in terms of communication. Such communication is the foundation of humans as social animals. This chapter focuses on the cognitive mechanisms behind language production and language comprehension. These skills can arguably be considered responsible for the unparalleled advancement of humans over all other species.

FRAMING QUESTIONS

- What is the relationship between thoughts and language?
- What is the cognitive approach to understanding language?
- What models aim to explain how we produce language (written and auditory)?
- What models aim to explain how we comprehend language (written and auditory)?

8.2 FUNCTION AND ORIGINS OF LANGUAGE

Although the benefits of language for humans are apparent, just how language came about is not entirely understood. There are two broad theories which aim to explain the creation of language. These are the *big brain theory* (Gould & Lewontin, 1979) and *gesture development theory* (Atchison, 1996).

8.2.1 THE BIG BRAIN THEORY

The big brain theory (Gould & Lewontin, 1979) proposes that owing to evolutionary forces, humans developed large brains, and therefore processing capacities, which allowed for language to become attainable. Given some of the obvious benefits to survival of being efficient at communicating information, such as the location of foods or to provide warnings as to predators' whereabouts, it is not surprising that those who possessed brain capacities which afforded effective communication survived and passed on the genetic material responsible for brain growth and development. Some authors argue that a big brain and language developed in a reciprocal manner (Deacon, 1997), in the sense that as language expanded it required more brain power and as brain power increased it likewise allowed for more complex forms of language communication. The answer to the question of why language became important to survival can perhaps be related back to population growth, where groups became larger and therefore social interactions became more frequent and thus important.

8.2.2 THE GESTURE DEVELOPMENT THEORY

The gesture development theory argues that language was a natural progression from the use of gestures to communicate. That is, we began by employing basic gestures (i.e. pointing) in order to communicate and we then internalised these gestures to form early mental representations that could be considered language. However, recent evidence suggests that it was more likely that language and gestures developed in parallel (Atchison, 1996). Concurrent development of gesture and language is also in line with big brain theory in that a big brain may have developed as a consequence of a growing demand for gestural and verbal communication.

Although, the big brain theory and gesture development theory contribute to our understanding of the development of language, neither can wholly offer a concrete solution. In fact, it is clear that there is likely much interaction among environmental, cultural and biological mechanisms that have driven the evolution of language. Christiansen and Kirby (2003) put forward a model that takes into consideration the general recent consensus in the field. The model aims to set out how culture, biology and the individual may have interacted during the evolution of language (see Figure 8.1).

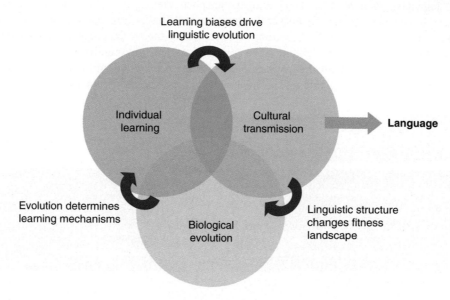

FIGURE 8.1   Christiansen and Kirby (2003) model of language evolution

EXERCISE: THE BOUBA–KIKI EFFECT

Take a second to assign one of the words either 'Bouba' or 'Kiki' to each of the objects below.

FIGURE 8.2   The Bouba–Kiki effect

In this exercise (originally conducted as a research study by Ramachandran & Hubbard, 2001), the majority of individuals assign Kiki to the left-hand image and Bouba to the right-hand image. Did you? Let's see why.

Another important and interesting question regarding the development of language is how we internally assigned symbols or sounds to external objects. A predominant and interesting proposition has emerged when attempting to answer this question. Before we discuss this let's try it out on ourselves.

Widely known as the Bouba–Kiki effect (Ramachandran & Hubbard, 2001), this effect helps to explain how objects may have originally been assigned sounds which allowed them to be universally recognised by a collection of individuals and become useful. In essence, the Bouba–Kiki effect stems from a series of experiments that suggest that the sounds which are assigned to represent an object are reflective of the physical structure of that object. In the example above, the sound 'kiki' is considered by most people to be a sharp sound and 'bouba' a softer, rounder sound.

8.3 LANGUAGE AND COGNITION

8.3.1 A COGNITIVE APPROACH TO UNDERSTANDING LANGUAGE

Owing to the close relationship between thought (a component of cognition) and language, is it easy to see why language is an important area for cognitive psychologists. Cognitive psychology takes the approach of computer processing to explain how the brain might deal with sensory information in a way that allows for perception. Language is no exception to this approach and is considered under the general umbrella of cognitive psychology as a form of information processing that results in what we experience as language. Language also falls under the remit of cognitive psychology because of its connection with other central cognitive capacities, such as memory and perception.

8.3.2 LANGUAGE AND THOUGHT

An extremely important component of language and one that naturally brings psychology as a discipline into the study of language is the connection between thoughts and language. Through the process of introspection our thoughts are experienced consciously in the form of language. The language that our thoughts comprise stems from the particular language that, over the course of our development, we have acquired. Research shows that the complexity of language often relates to the complexity of our thinking. As Ludwig Wittgenstein once wrote, 'The limits of my language means the limits of my world' (cited in Malcolm, 1995: 103). At present, there are four hypotheses that offer different views on the relationship between thought and language (Kellogg, 2003). The first is the idea that thought and language are one and the same (known as the *identity hypothesis*), the second is that language may stem from thought (known as the *general resources hypothesis*), the third proposes thought may stem from language (known as the *linguistic relativity hypothesis* [or the *Sapir-Whorf hypothesis*]), and the fourth is an hypothesis which states that language is a distinct and isolated process which is independent of thought (known as the *modularity hypothesis*).

Although there is evidence in support of one or more of the above hypotheses, there remains nothing conclusive or overly persuasive for any particular one. However, via a rather intriguing method, research has managed to discount the identity hypothesis. The identity hypothesis (proposed initially by Watson, 1924) states that muscular actions involved in speech (known as subvocal speech) are responsible for thought. This hypothesis was put to bed in 1947 by Smith et al. when Smith agreed to have his body temporarily paralysed to see if he was still capable of thought after paralysis had set in. As it turns out, once Smith had been paralysed, preventing any possibility of subvocal speech (movements of the vocal tract), his capacity to think remained intact (I wonder what Smith was thinking about Watson?).

Owing much to the work of Fyodor in the 1980s and 1990s revitalising earlier arguments by linguists such as Chomsky, the modularity hypothesis states that language is independent of other cognitive processes. The primary evidence which supports such an idea comes from individuals who have severe cognitive impairment but retain normal or close to normal language abilities. The argument here is that if language relies extensively on general cognitive capacities, then disruption to those capacities should result similarly in disruptions of any mechanisms which might utilise those capacities, such as language. A good example of this comes from a developmental disorder known as Specific Language Impairment (SLI) (Dąbrowska, 2004). Children who suffer with SLI usually retain cognitive abilities in all other domains but have specific difficulties with language. A counter-argument to this comes from

APHASIA Literally speaking, an absence of speech, but is commonly taken to mean an impairment of language, affecting the production or comprehension of speech and the ability to read or write.

evidence of people suffering with dementia and **aphasia** (discussed in more detail later) (Kellogg, 2003). These individuals have deficits to cognitive systems such as memory and attention which, according to the modularity hypothesis, should not impact upon language ability. However, with dementia and aphasic patients language is nearly always affected when memory and attention capacities are impaired. This suggests that at least some general cognitive abilities, such as memory and attention, are involved in language.

The general resource hypothesis proposes that in fact language *is* dependent on other more general cognitive abilities. Piaget (see Chapters 17 and 18) was the first to propose this idea. He showed that language ability tends to build upon previously acquired cognitive skills, such as basic reasoning and gesturing. In essence, this suggests that language progresses from early remanence of thought. However, after language has been acquired, whether it goes on to rely on other cognitive processes, in the same way, is debatable.

In contrast to the general resource hypothesis, the linguistic relativity hypothesis (also known as the Sapir–Whorf hypothesis after its two founding proponents) argues that thought is in fact heavily influenced by language. The hypothesis states that individuals who employ different forms of language for communication may behave differently based on how language impacts their thoughts. For example, Boroditsky, Schmidt and Phillips (2003) provide some interesting evidence for linguistic relativity. They found stark perceptual differences for the same object (e.g. a key) between two languages which assign different genders to that object. For example, when comparing the descriptive words produced when shown the object of a key, they found that Germans would describe the object with words that pertained to the arbitrarily assigned masculine gender of that object (e.g. *der Schüssel* – hard, heavy, jagged, metal, serrated and useful) whereas Spanish people would describe it using more feminine words, in line with the female gender assigned to that object in Spanish (e.g. *la tecla* – golden, intricate, little, lovely, shiny and tiny). This suggests that the way we structure language may impact the way we think about certain things.

The general resource hypothesis and the Sapir–Whorf hypothesis, although putting forward opposing ideas of what came first, language or thought, both go on to emphasise the possibility of interactive processes between thought and language. Whether thought initially stems from language or language from thought, the evidence for an interactive process is perhaps the most convincing argument as it currently stands. The most widely accepted hypothesis for the

ASIDE

Reading to yourself

There is some contention as to when, as humans, we developed the capability of reading silently. Some propose that it is a relatively recent activity in the development of human kind. Proponents of this idea note that in the latter part of the fourth century St Augustine writes concerning his surprise of his contemporary, Ambrose: 'When [Ambrose] read, his eyes scanned the page and his heart sought out the meaning, but his voice was silent and his tongue was still.'

This, and this alone, has been the sole and staple evidence that has been used to suggest that the ancients could not read silently (you may have even heard something like this yourself). It has been the *communis opinio* (generally accepted view) of some of the greatest intellectuals over the past centuries (e.g. Nietzsche). However, Burnyeat (1997), Gavrilov (1997) and Johnson (2000) provide us with a much more grounded view of the ancients' capacity to read silently. Namely, they offer evidence from ancient texts of individuals reading silently. In Euripides's play *Hippolytus*, which dates to 428 BC (nearly 800 years prior to St Augustine's writings), it is noted that the King 'silently reads the letter'. Not only that, but Gavrilov relies on cognitive models of reading to argue that silent reading is a component of reading out loud and therefore is accessible to anyone who can read out loud. Specifically, Gavrilov relies on something known as the *eye–voice span*. This is essentially how far the eyes are ahead in the text from what is actually being said. Gavrilov argues that owing to the fact all people reading aloud must have the capacity to inwardly read text before it is voiced, ancient orators more than likely read silently just as they did out loud.

connection between language and thought is a compromise between the general resource hypothesis and the Sapir–Whorf hypothesis. This is known as the *weak* Sapir–Whorf hypothesis and acknowledges that language and thought may be interactive processes influencing each other.

8.4 FROM THOUGHT TO LANGUAGE: HOW DO WE PRODUCE LANGUAGE?

At this point we will turn to the cognitive processes involved in language production. Humans are capable of producing up to seven words per second (usually when they are really excited). But where do these words come from? Cognitive psychologists often refer to a

> **MENTAL LEXICON** The mental store of words that can be drawn upon in thought or speech.

bank or store of linguistic information as a **mental lexicon**. Seeing as words cannot be represented physically in the mind, they are thought to be represented by the mental lexicon. 'Lexicon', coming from the Greek for 'of words' and 'book', literally means a book of words. Although the mental lexicon can change and evolve over time, with words being added and lost, it is estimated that on average the mental lexicon contains 45,000 word representations (Bock & Garnsey, 1998). Considering sentences of 20 words or less, this would offer nearly limitless combinations of words to form sentences. In fact, the number of combinations is around 10^{30} (Kellogg, 2003), which is more than all of the stars in the known universe.

8.4.1 SPEECH ERRORS

The next question is how we might retrieve this information from such a store and use it in a manner which allows us to produce words (verbally or graphically). Owing to the idiosyncratic linguistic responses usually produced by individuals, it is quite a challenge to examine language production (Bock, 1996). One way to get around this problem has been to rely on speech errors to provide insight into how normal speech functions. Awareness of errors in speech has long been reported. Freud is famous for his 'Freudian slips', where one word is said to be replaced with another word representative of a subconscious desire. For example, when introducing a person called Maria Mahon, a friend of ours said '*and this is Maria Moron*'. The Freudian analysis would suggest that our friend did not think very highly of the woman and her true opinion had leaked out. By coincidence, that is exactly what our friend thought of Ms Mahon but did not mean to say it out loud.

Although this might seem a little tenuous, Freud was more pragmatic when it came to the insights speech errors may provide. For example, upon analysis of a patient presenting with common speech errors, Freud asked 'whether the mechanisms of this disturbance cannot also suggest the probable laws of the foundation of speech' (Freud, 1924: 71). This is certainly more in line with the view taken in modern-day cognitive psychology, where speech errors are seen as malfunctions in normal cognition.

The following is a list of the most common speech errors. See if you can remember making one (or more!) of these errors:

1 *Anticipation* – this occurs when a speaker prematurely anticipates a **phoneme** (usually a consonant), which results in that particular phoneme being brought forward to an incorrect position in the sentence or phrase. This often comes out as

> **PHONEME** The smallest distinguishing unit in spoken language.

alliteration. For example, the phrase 'I'm reading a book' becomes 'I'm beading a book' – the /b/ sound is anticipated too early and attached to the prior word 'leading' to form 'beading'.

2 *Preservation* – this is essentially the reverse of anticipation where a prior section replaces a later section. In other words, the section is preserved and carries over to a word where it does not belong. For example, the phase 'I want to tell you' becomes 'I want to well you', where /w/ has been preserved into the later word 'tell'. Other examples include middle section preservation. For example, 'leave no stone unturned' becomes 'leave no stone unstoned', where /sto/ replaces /tur/.

3   *Deletion* – this occurs when a consonant is simply deleted from a word. This can occur at the beginning, end or middle of a word. For example, 'speech error' may become 'peach error' when the /s/ from speech is omitted, or 'cucumber' may become 'coocumber' when the /y/ from 'yoo' is omitted to form 'oo'.

4   *Substitution* – this is when one word is replaced for another. For example, 'give me a spoon' becomes 'give me a fork', or perhaps a more infamous substitution when George H.W. Bush, talking about Ronald Regan, said 'we've had some sex' instead of 'we've had some setbacks' (I would highly recommend looking this one up on YouTube).

5   *Transposition* – this occurs when two language sections are switched. These are also known as spoonerisms, named after Reverend William Archibald Spooner (1844–1930), a regular sufferer of transposition errors. Examples of transpositions include 'is the bean dizzy?' instead of 'is the dean busy?', or 'guess whose mind came to name' instead of 'guess whose name came to mind'. This leads to some people naming their pet cat Cooking Fat.

6   *Blending* – this is where two meaningful words become one and form a new meaningless word. An example is 'you have a very nice garden/lawn' which becomes 'you have a very nice larden/gawn'.

7   *Cognitive intrusions* – these are particularly interesting ones as they offer insight as to how our thoughts and feelings at a particular moment can influence or intrude on our speech. If a person is hungry, instead of saying 'get out of the car' they may say 'eat out of the car', or if someone is looking at a particularly nice tree they may say 'don't you have a lovely tree' instead of 'don't you have a lovely house'. Some researchers point out that speech errors such as cognitive intrusions may also highlight the difference between the language we employ to express our thoughts and the language we employ in the form of inner speech (i.e. thoughts) (Fodor, 1975). For example, cognitive intrusions suggest that our inner thoughts may generally be quite disorganised as a consequence of the bombardment from many and varied types of sensory information. It is on the occasions where inhibition of stimuli intrusions into actual language fail that speech errors occur.

8.5 COGNITIVE MODELS OF SPEECH PRODUCTION

In order to try to explain some of the interesting insights from language errors a number of cognitive models have been proposed over the years. These models can broadly be categorised into two camps. The first assumes the idea that speech production is a serial process. That is, the mechanisms that underlie speech production occur one after the other and only once one process has been completed can a different process be initiated. The second group of models takes the approach that the processes involved in speech production can occur in parallel. That is, more than one process can occur concurrently. Like any proposition, time tends to decide the fate of their usefulness. A few models have stood the test of time better than others and will be discussed in this section.

8.5.1 BOCK AND LEVELT'S (1994) MODEL OF SPEECH PROCESSING

Bock and Levelt (1994) developed a model aimed at explaining sentence formation. The model contains a number of stages through which processing must pass in order to produce a sentence. The stages go from selection of linguistic material from the mental lexicon, assembly of material into a sentence, through to the output of the constructed sentence. These stages are described as the message stage –> functional processing stage –> positional processing stage –> phonological encoding stage –> output stage (see Figure 8.3).

The *message stage* is essentially the intended or desired idea waiting to be prepared for production. For example, this might be to inform someone that a bird is sitting on a tree. The next stage is *functional processing*. Functional processing must perform two tasks. First, it must select the correct words from the **lexicon** (known as lexical selection). Second, it must assign a **grammatical** function to the word which determines where it should be located in the sentence (functional assignment stage). The grammatical representation of a word is stored in the lexicon as a **lemma**. Lemmas specify the **semantic** and grammatical features of a word.

The next stage is known as *positional processing*. This stage places the words in order (constituent assembly) and adds any necessary inflections (inflection stage) such as making nouns plural or verbs in past tense. All grammatical

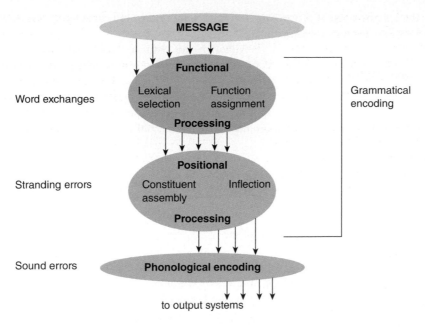

FIGURE 8.3 Bock and Levelt's (1994) model of speech processing

encoding (word selection, function assignment, ordering and adding inflections) must occur before any *phonological encoding* can commence. Phonological encoding involves assigning sounds and intonations to each word in the sentence. The phonological representation of words in the lexicon is known as a **lexeme**.

Although, according to the model, some information can be passed to the next stage before all information is processed, it remains a serial processing model because it does not allow for different processes to occur concurrently. Blackmer and Mitton (1991) provide some evidence to support the idea that speech production is a serial process. They argue that all stages of production are monitored for errors. Such monitoring is evidenced by the fact that a large proportion of speech errors are corrected immediately at the point of error. They argue that if parallel processing was occurring (i.e. all processes happened at the same time), then monitoring of an error as and when it occurred would happen. In other words, it would not be possible to monitor specific speech production errors because by the time the errors had occurred, all other processes would have completed.

Additional evidence for a serial model of speech production comes from the kinds of speech errors that we make and how these speech errors can be mapped onto the various stages of Bock and Levelt's model. For example, substitution errors (see definition above) occur during the **lexical** selection stage where semantically similar words are selected by accident (e.g. 'pass me a fork' becomes 'pass me a spoon'). Syntactical errors occur at the function assignment stage where the syntactical function of a word is incorrectly assigned (e.g. 'I like football' becomes 'I like*s* football'). The tip of the tongue (TOT) phenomenon is also thought to provide evidence for the independence of lemmas and lexemes. This is in line with Bock and Levelt's model where lemma selection occurs during functional processing, whereas lexeme assignment occurs later during positional processing. This is thought to reflect those situations when an individual knows the word they want to say but they just cannot quite access it (i.e. it's said to be on the tip of their tongue). It is proposed that the correct lemma has been selected but an error

GRAMMATICAL Relating to grammar, which is the structure of language.

LEMMA An abstract concept that specifies the meaning of what is to be said but does not map directly onto any specific sounds.

LEXICON A language's inventory of lexemes (a basic unit of meaning regardless of the number of inflections or words).

LEXEME A basic unit of meaning regardless of the number of inflections or words.

LEXICAL Relating to the words or vocabulary of a language.

SEMANTIC Relating to the meaning of a word.

has occurred during the lexeme stage of processing, leaving the individual the capacity to 'see' the word but failing to produce the sounds for it (i.e. lexeme assignment has failed).

> **SYNTAX** The rules that govern sentence structure.

Although the evidence for Bock and Levelt's model is quite compelling, another interesting model has been proposed which has also stood the test of time and in fact can account for some aspects of speech production which serial processing models of language struggle to. The second model is in contrast to Bock and Levelt's model because it does not assume serial processing of information incrementally, but rather argues for a parallel processing model of speech production.

8.5.2 DELL'S (1986) CONNECTIONIST MODEL OF SPEECH PRODUCTION

In Dell's (1986) model of speech production there are three separate levels of speech production. These include a conceptual level, which contains semantic features of the words; the word level, which contains the physical features of the word (lexical nodes); and the sound level, which contains all stored sounds that comprise a word (phonological segments). As can been seen from Figure 8.4, words can share features on a semantic level or on a phonological level. For example, the words 'cat' and 'dog' are close in terms of semantics but share little in the way of sounds used to produce those words. This would lead 'cat' and 'dog' to share semantic nodes but no phonological nodes. Information passes across the nodes via a process of spreading activation. Spreading activation is a search method that allows information to be organised and to pass from one organised area (i.e. node) to another. When a word is selected from the mental lexicon, all nodes (i.e. all semantic/phonological components) are activated.

Owing to the fact that words can share common nodes (i.e. they are similar in meaning or pronunciation), this means that sometimes incorrect words are selected based on cross-activation of common nodes. The incorrectly activated word may be similar in meaning but not quite the right word (e.g. substitution error) or they may be completely distinct in terms of meaning but share similar sounds (e.g. transposition error). This is the premise of how Dell's model can account for multiple speech errors.

A worked example of how a speech error may occur can be seen in Figure 8.5. Here a person may incorrectly produce the sentence 'don't forget to put your feet on' instead of 'don't forget to put your boots on'. On this occasion it can be seen how 'boot' and 'feet' are related via semantic association links. The error really occurs when the activation for feet is greater than the activation for boot. Why this occurs has not been hugely researched, but some authors think it is probably linked to neuronal activity and a misfiring of an over-zealous neuron. Relating back to the information processing approach taken in cognitive psychology, errors can occur in the cognitive system in much the same way as they do in the computing system, for many different reasons!

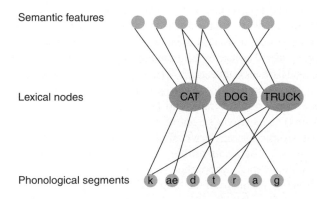

FIGURE 8.4 An example of nodes in Dell's (1986) connectionist model of speech production

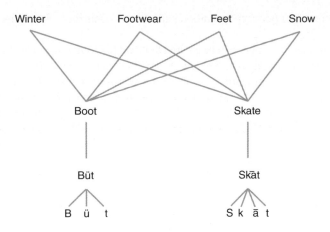

FIGURE 8.5   A worked example of a speech error according to Dell's (1986) connectionist model

KEY STUDY

Baars, B.J., Michael, T.M., & Donald G.M. (1975). Output editing for lexical status in artificially elicited slips of the tongue. *Journal of Verbal Learning and Verbal Behavior*, 14(4), 382–391.

Baars, Michael and Donald (1975) provided one of the first experiments that actually allowed for the systematic investigation of speech errors and therefore the underlying rules of speech production. Naturally occurring speech errors are rare, which makes them difficult to study, so prior to this study, the majority of research, although it had been ongoing for 50 years, was anecdotal. The particular type of speech error that Baar et al. induced was a spoonerism (see section 8.4.1 on types of speech errors).

The primary concern of the study was to test any differences in output editing of word versus non-word pairs. In essence, the general hypothesis was that the frequency of speech errors (i.e. spoonerisms) will change as a function of the lexical status of the pair, that is, word versus non-word pairing. For example, a non-word pair (e.g. darn–bore) will become a word pair (e.g. barn–door) more frequently than a word pair (e.g. dart–board) will become a non-word pair (e.g., bart–doard). Participants were primed with word pairs before being given either a non-word combination (darn–bore) or a real-word combination (barn–door) to say. Of the total amount of speech errors (i.e. spoonerisms), 76.2% were produced when the lexical output could be a word pair (e.g. darn bore–barn door), whereas only 23.8% came about when the lexical output was a non-word pair (e.g. dart board–bart doard).

Baars et al. argued that the difference in frequency of errors was a consequence of some kind of editing or monitoring process. They suggest that it is more efficient to have a system which tries to 'avoid talking nonsense in our everyday life than it is to avoid talking sense in a nonsense situation' (Baars et al., 1975: 389). The effect that Baar et al. highlighted later became known as the 'lexical bias effect'. Besides being an interesting methodological study, this research became a key piece of evidence relating to models of language production (see section 8.5.3 for how).

8.5.3 SERIAL VERSUS PARALLEL MODELS OF SPEECH PRODUCTION

Dell's model allows for simultaneous processing of information by way of concurrent node activation. This concurrent activation helps to explain a number of speech errors which are more difficult to explain with serial processing models such as Bock and Levelt's. For example, speech errors such as word or phrase blends and cognitive intrusions occur when the error is either semantically of phonetically similar to the target word. Owing to the fact that errors are only sometimes observed, it suggests that competition between activation pathways is occurring. For competition to occur, both must be activated simultaneously.

There is also another phenomenon which is in line with Dell's model, but which is difficult to explain when applying Bock and Levelt's model. This phenomenon is known as the 'the lexical bias effect'. The lexical bias effect is the disproportionate occurrence of making real word errors from non-words as opposed to making non-word errors from real words. A classic experiment by Baars et al. (1975), providing evidence for this effect, is described in the key study above.

The lexical bias effect can be explained by Dell's model through 'backwards activation of nodes'. Backwards activation can produce a bias in favour of real word combination because they contain a real morpheme structure in comparison to non-words, which do not. Therefore, the activation of a real word combination will be greater than a non-word combination. In contrast to this finding, the serial processing foundation of Bock and Levelt's model assumes no interaction between grammatical and phonological encoding (as they are considered separate units). Owing to the fact that words are produced more than non-words (i.e. they have the correct grammatical structure but are incorrect in terms of the sounds [phonological structure]), this indicates that in fact grammatical and phonological features must interact and are therefore not likely to be discrete independent units of processing.

Seeing as both models explain different types of speech error that we make, it suggests that no one model can account for speech production. However, it does show how each have their advantages and can help to explain how the cognitive system might go about producing speech.

8.6 FROM LANGUAGE TO THOUGHT: HOW DO WE COMPREHEND LANGUAGE?

The next three sections look at how we process information communicated to us and decode it to allow us to comprehend it for the purpose of producing an appropriate response (i.e. the previous section!). These sections tackle language comprehension by way of breaking it down into two distinct components: auditory language comprehension (i.e. auditory signals predominantly speech) and visual language comprehension (i.e. visual signals predominantly written language).

8.6.1 AUDITORY LANGUAGE COMPREHENSION

One important feature of the auditory signal of language is that it is a continuous sound. Many people assume that because language is separated into words and sentences the auditory signal accompanying this must also be separate. However, speech in fact produces a continuous signal. Try introducing minutiae pauses between words to see how unnatural speech sounds become. Thus, we must have the capacity to discriminate between these continuous sounds. Moore and Glasberg (1986) describe this capacity as frequency discrimination, which allows the detection of changes in frequency of sound waves.

Although auditory distinction is important, individuals must also be able to integrate auditory information to form complete words. Take, for example, the sounds (i.e. phonemes) \r\, \u\ and \n\. These sounds must be considered together for the listener to comprehend the word 'run'. Auditory signals can arrive in two distinct frequencies. These have been categorised as vowel sounds (A, E, I, O, U) and consonants (all the others!). Such a categorisation is by no means arbitrary. Vowel and consonant sounds tend to be on different areas of the sound wave spectrum, which helps us to more easily discriminate the sounds which make up words and which separate words from each other. For example, Jenkins, Strange and Edman (1983) showed that the perception of vowel sounds is reliant on the transition in and out of the vowel sound (Payne & Wenger, 1998).

8.7 COGNITIVE MODELS OF SPEECH PERCEPTION

There are a number of theories as to the processes behind how we perceive speech. These include motor theory, direct perception theory and fuzzy logic theory.

8.7.1 MOTOR THEORY OF SPEECH PERCEPTION

Highlighted above is the role of processing auditory signals directly through the auditory system (i.e. ears). However, one interesting theory in psychology suggests that when we hear a spoken word we do not in fact encode the auditory signal *per se*, but rather the implied motor actions that are associated with the sound. In other words, when we hear the sounds \r\, \u\ and \n\ to form 'run' we are actually converting the sounds to movements that would have been produced by our vocal tract in order to produce those sounds.

8.7.2 DIRECTION PERCEPTION THEORY

Direct perception theory suggests that unlike motor theory, where an auditory signal is identified and then that signal is decoded to understand the motor action behind the signal, the auditory signal is not processed but rather the motor actions behind it are perceived directly from the source. In other words, it differs from motor theory because it suggests that there is no need to decode auditory signals. Instead, humans are able to directly perceive the motor tract action from the auditory signal (i.e. the auditory signal *is* a motor tract signal).

8.7.3 FUZZY LOGIC THEORY (FLT) OF PERCEPTION

Motor perception and motor theory both concentrate on localised features of spoken language to help explain how individuals can comprehend language. In contrast to these ideas are information processing models. These models apply an understanding of general cognitive mechanisms to the problem of speech processing. They suggest that the way in which information is stored, organised, integrated and transformed by the cognitive system allows us to comprehend language. When speech is produced, multiple sources of information are available to the perceiver. The perceiver has access to information regarding sound, gestures, lip movements and context. This means that we must rely on numerous mechanisms, such as visual perception, working memory and prior knowledge, to process multiple sources of information. Massaro (1987) applied a model known as fuzzy logic, which allows for the idea that speech processes must to some degree involve the processing of multiple sources of information.

The basis of fuzzy logic is that there is a probabilistic value assigned to the likelihood of a speech sound belonging to a specific speech category. This means that when a speech sound occurs, additional influences can help the perceiver to define the most likely use for that sound. Fuzzy logic helps to immediately narrow down possibilities of where a speech sound belongs. A probability can be deduced from prior knowledge of speech sounds. Such prior knowledge would have been obtained during the long period it takes to understand speech as a human. Thus, as we develop our 'internal' fuzzy logic, models of speech perception become more refined.

An example of fuzzy logic could come from a situation where sound is ambiguous, like on a busy street. Say you are with a friend and you have been supplied with prior knowledge that your friend is hungry. Fuzzy logic theory proposes that you can pick up multiple fragments of information from your friend and you can process this in a way that enables you to make the most likely correct response given the situation. For example, due to the overwhelming sound of traffic noise all you can hear from your friend is '....ized/....izg/'. A second source of information comes in the form of visual cues. In this case it is your friends lip movements. From your friend's lip movements you receive additional information in the form of '/h/....d/....'. With the integration of both sources of information you have: '/h/....ized/....izg/'. Given your prior knowledge (i.e. memory), you know that your friend is hungry. You look around and see a street vendor selling hotdogs. Thus, you might conclude that the most likely words your friend is saying are 'hot dog'.

In summary, according to Massaro's (1987) model, three processes occur during language comprehension: (1) evaluation of the input, (2) integration of the results of that evaluation and (3) a decision based on the results of the integration. This highlights that each stage involved in language comprehension is dependent (or builds) on the prior stage. It was also suggested in Massaro's model that language comprehension involves the integration of multiple sources of information, one of which is visual information. Much research has focused on the role of the visual system, and in particular eye movements, when it comes to comprehending written language.

8.8 EYE MOVEMENTS AND LANGUAGE PROCESSING

Written language was first used for the purpose of completing business transactions. This was observed in the Persian Empire around 5,000 years ago (Gelb, 1963). Later, around 2,000 years ago, this developed into more modern styles of written communication, namely those reliant on the Greek alphabet as well as Aramaic and Hebrew scripts. Unlike auditory signals, visual signals arrive at the perceiver from the written word via one modality, the eye. This is why some researchers have focused purely on what the eye does when a person is faced with the task of encoding a series of graphical symbols that comprise letters, words and sentences. When examining eye movements, there are a limited number of important actions in which researchers are interested. These include **saccades**, **backwards saccades** (also known as regressions) and **fixations**.

A saccade is a small jump in eye movement as you read along a sentence. Saccades were first discovered in the nineteenth century by Emile Javal. Javal had participants read a short text silently and used a mirror located on the opposite page to observe their eye movements. He found that eye movements were far from fluid, but rather were discontinuous and appeared to move in a rapid, jerky motion. In between saccades the eye pauses briefly and brings the content of the stimuli into focus; this is known as a fixation. During a fixation the majority of reading occurs. That is, the eye has stopped long enough to encode the information it has settled on. In terms of the span of information that

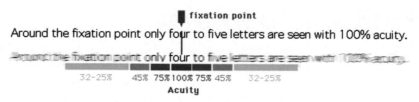

FIGURE 8.6   Level of visual acuity from a single fixation

Source: Hans-Werner34/Wikimedia Commons

KEY STUDY

Hardyck, C.D., & Petrinovich, L.F. (1970). Subvocal speech and comprehension level as a function of the difficulty level of reading material. *Journal of Verbal Learning & Verbal Behavior*, *9*, 647–652.

Previous research had shown that learning text material was dependent on the degree of vocalisation of the text. Specifically, it was shown that learning progresses faster if individuals are able to whisper the material as opposed to being completely silent. Additionally, if individuals were allowed to read aloud learning progressed even further still. Hardyck and Petrinovich's research focuses on subvocal speech. Subvocal speech is said to occur if you intend to speak a word but don't actually say it. In this instance, the same neurological signal is sent to the voice box in exactly the same way as if you had said the word, but instead resulting in no overt vocal sound.

Hardyck and Petrinovich pointed out that no subvocal (i.e. speech muscle) activity had been considered when individuals were instructed to be silent in much previous research. They therefore set out to investigate how subvocal speech relates to the difficulty level of the material to be read as well as how well the material has been comprehended. Using an electromyogram (measuring electrical activity of the vocal muscles) to precisely detect subvocal speech, Hardyck and Petrinovich showed that as the difficulty of reading material increased, so too did the level of subvocal speech activity. They also showed that if you can suppress the level of laryngeal activity (i.e. reducing the possibility of subvocal speech), the level of comprehension of reading material is significantly reduced.

This study is important as it provided future research with ideas of the links between visual and auditory cues and their interaction with memory process (namely, working memory) during language processing. Interestingly, by employing technology (electrodes on the throat and computer processing software), it is possible to decode what someone is saying without them moving their lips or making a sound, simply through analysing their subvocal activity!

can be encoded during a fixation, it is approximately up to 15 characters either side of the fixation point. However, of these 15 characters only four to five can be seen with 100% acuity (see Figure 8.6).

After a fixation, the eyes are off again on another saccade. The distance travelled for each saccade varies between one and 20 characters, although on average the eye jumps between seven and nine characters at a time (Rayner & Pollatsek, 1989). Saccades, once initiated cannot stop halfway, but rather they have to complete their initial trajectory before they can begin another jump. The direction of saccades is generally determined by the reading direction of the language. For example, an English reader's saccades will generally travel from left to right. However, saccades can also move backwards. This movement is known as a backward saccade or a regression. For every four to five saccades the reader will make one backward saccade. Backward saccades have been implicated in the monitoring and reviewing of what has been read previously. Owing to the fact that reading is a relatively fast action, eye movements are therefore equally fast. Saccades take around 20–40 milliseconds (Rayner et al., 2001) and fixations, needing a little longer, allowing for the **fovea** to come into focus, take around 200–250 ms (Sereno & Rayner, 2003).

By examining as and when these actions occur, researchers have been able to make a number of interesting observations as to where we look, and hence infer where our attention is directed, while we read. First, reading is a word-by-word process and, unlike speech, it is non-continuous. Research found that individuals tend to fixate on a word and then rapidly move to fixate on the next word (Carpenter & Just, 1983). Of these fixations, 80% accounted for content words (e.g. nouns, verbs, adjectives) and 20% for function words (prepositions, articles, pronouns) (Rayner & Duffy, 1986). Second, there is a relationship between the frequency of the word (i.e. how often we might use or come across it) and the length of the fixation. Typically, the more frequent the word the shorter the fixation time (this evidence has been used to support various models on word identification, which is discussed later). Also, the predictability of the word in the text can determine the length of the fixation, with more predictable words requiring less fixation time (Rayner & Well, 1996).

8.9 COGNITIVE MODELS OF WORD IDENTIFICATION

Another important process that has been heavily researched in cognitive psychology is how individuals go about identifying a word. There are three dominant models when it comes to explaining the process of identifying words. These are the interactive-activation model, the logogen model and the cohort model.

EXERCISE: DOES READING OUT LOUD SPEED UP LEARNING?

As we saw from the key study on subvocalisation, there is evidence that we learn faster if we vocalise what we are reading. Does that mean you should revise for exams by reciting material out loud? Try learning one of these sentences by reading it aloud and the other by silent reading. Time how long it is before you can say each without fault.

Sentence 1: I went to market and I bought a prize, a guitar, a dove, a hook, morning coffee, ink, a ladder, a ghost, a picture, a mask, some masking tape and a daisy.

Sentence 2: I went to market and I bought a taxi, some evil, a T-shirt, a desk, a perch, a flag, a mouse, some pepper, a cruise ship, a cartridge, a radiator and an arm.

Which method was quicker? Although this was a rough test (we didn't control properly for factors such as complexity, distinctiveness and familiarity of words), this may mean you can't revise in the library anymore without annoying the people around you!

8.9.1 INTERACTIVE ACTIVATION MODEL

The first word identification model to be considered is the interactive activation model by McClelland and Rumelhart (1986). This model proposes an hierarchical structure to word identification. The hierarchy can be thought of to start at the lowest level with discrete physical property processing (e.g. vertical lines), which leads to higher-level processing often involving combination or integration of components from a previous stage or level. For example, the first level deals with features of words (known as the feature level). These typically involve the processing of the minutiae patterns contained within visual information, such as the vertical, horizontal and diagonal lines used to form letters. The next level of activation is the letter level and, based on prior activation at the feature level, begins to activate whole letters. This level also organises letters in terms of order. This then leads to the highest level of activation, which is the word level. This is the point where entire words in the lexicon become activated. McClelland and Rumelhart in their model distinguish between excitatory and inhibitory activation. Excitatory activation aims to increase the likelihood of activation whereas inhibitory activation aims to limit or restrict activation. This aspect of the model is derived from a biological interactive-activation system in the human body, which possesses similar excitatory and inhibitory networks – the nervous system. Hence, this model attempts to map cognitive processes directly to biological building blocks.

8.9.2 THE LOGOGEN MODEL

The word 'logogen' comes from the Greek words *logos*, meaning word, and *genus*, meaning birth. The logogen model was original conceptualised by Morton (1970) with subsequent additions to the model later by Marslen-Wilson and Welsh (1978) and Harris and Coltheart (1986). The logogen model proposes that special units called **logogens** are employed to help comprehend both spoken and written language. Logogens are thought to be made up of a combination of word-related characteristics such as the sound, meaning and look of the word. Logogens are really discrete markers for the information that is needed to recognise a word. They do not contain the words themselves, but rather information pertaining to components of a word (i.e. its sound, meaning or appearance).

LOGOGENS An array of specialised recognition units, each able to recognise one particular word.

This is how the model works. First, a word is presented to the cognitive system for processing (via either a visual or auditory pathway). Then a matching process occurs whereby the components of the input word are compared to all

KEY RESEARCHER Professor William Marslen-Wilson

Dr William Marslen-Wilson is an Honorary Professor of Language and Cognition. His main research interests are in the cognitive science and neuroscience of language. Dr Marslen-Wilson studies the comprehension of spoken language in terms of cognitions and underlying brain functioning. He applies interdisciplinary techniques with the aim to categorise the neuronal firings that allow us to comprehend spoken utterances.

Dr Marslen-Wilson has conducted ground-breaking research for the past three decades. He has been cited over 16,000 times by other researchers and his most cited article is entitled 'Functional parallelism in spoken word-recognition', published in 1987. Dr Marslen-Wilson's most seminal contribution to the field has come in the form of his cohort model of lexical retrieval (see section 8.9.3). His current research brings together behavioural, neuropsychological and neuroimaging data from a wide variety of languages (including Arabic, Polish and English) with the principal aim of identifying common underlying cognitive and biological structures to language.

FIGURE 8.7 William Marslen-Wilson

previously stored logogens. If a match occurs between the input and a logogen, then this logogen is said to become activated. According to the model, there is a certain threshold of activation that is required for the logogen to be employed for the purpose of comprehension. If more than one logogen is activated (i.e. passes the threshold), then the one with the greatest level of activation is given priority.

A concise example of this process is as follows. Imagine you have a lexicon (storage of words) of a limited three words. These words are 'house', 'mouse' and 'television'. You are presented with the word 'house'. Due to matching occurring with both 'house' and 'mouse' (because they share similar features) they both pass the activation threshold. However, due to 'house' matching more components than 'mouse', it is the 'house' logogen that is involved in the word identification response. According to the logogen model, higher frequency words would require less cognitive effort to be selected from the lexicon and should therefore be recognised faster than less common words. This is indeed the case and is evidenced with the word frequency effect, where higher frequency words (those used more often) are activated (i.e. have a lower threshold) more easily than lower frequency words.

8.9.3 THE COHORT MODEL OF LEXICAL PROCESSING

The last model, known as the cohort model, was proposed by William Marslen-Wilson in the 1980s. This model proposes that word identification is an interactive process employing both bottom-up and top-down processes in parallel. The cohort model, based on evidence from a series of experiments, suggests that we start whittling down word possibilities from the very first instances of the word (either visual or auditory) (the bottom-up component). Specifically, the model suggest that neurons in the brain are activated the instant some kind of input is detected. If we assume we are hearing a word, then we begin to 'work out' what the word might be from the first or second **phoneme** of that word. For example, if the spoken word was 'candle', the process would look something like Figure 8.8, where as more phonemes become available the number of correct possibilities within the lexicon reduces.

As can also be seen from Figure 8.8, the point of recognition need not always be when the last and final phoneme has been processed. In fact, the more unusual the word, and hence the fewer possible conflicts with other words, the more likely it will be that we will recognise a word at an early stage of phoneme processing (e.g. a unique word, such as 'spaghetti', will be recognised relatively early on). Evidence for such bottom-up processing comes from experiments showing that it takes individuals longer to recognise whether a word is a word or non-word dependent on the recognition point of the word, not the word length. For example, Taft and Hambly (1986) showed that individuals were faster at recognising 'crocodile' as a word in comparison to 'dial', even though it is a longer word and therefore should take longer to process. This is due to the recognition point of the word 'crocodile' (the letter 'd') coming sooner (in terms of phonemes) than the recognition point in 'dial' (the letter 'l').

Importantly, the cohort model also considers the impact of top-down processes when it comes to word recognition. Under the cohort model, the context encompassing a word is thought to bear some impact upon the recognition of that word. For example, read the following two sentences and see how context can filter the chosen word:

'Yes, I know Chris he lives just down the str . . .'

'I have had a very busy day and feel somewhat str . . .'

Phoneme processing as a word is heard	C	CA	*Time* CAN	CAND	CANDL	CANDLE
Word possibilities within a lexicon	Canada	Canada	Canada	~~Canada~~	~~Canada~~	~~Canada~~
	Computer	~~Computer~~	~~Computer~~	~~Computer~~	~~Computer~~	~~Computer~~
	Candle	Candle	Candle	Candle	Candle	Candle
	Cat	Cat	~~Cat~~	~~Cat~~	~~Cat~~	~~Cat~~
	Candy	Candy	Candy	Candy	~~Candy~~	~~Candy~~
	Court	~~Court~~	~~Court~~	~~Court~~	~~Court~~	~~Court~~

FIGURE 8.8   Table illustrating the processing of auditory linguistic information according to the cohort model

Hopefully, you will have filtered words by context and phonemes and selected 'street' and 'stressed'. The main advantage of the cohort model over the logogen model is that it allows for word recognition before the word has been entirely processed. The logogen model, on the other hand, does not consider whether other words are possible or not, which means activation may not occur until long after no other words are possible.

8.10 A COGNITIVE MODEL OF WRITING

8.10.1 FLOWER AND HAYES' (1981) MODEL OF WRITING PROCESSES

Often forgotten when it comes to language production is the act of producing language through writing. Although there has not been as much focus on writing, a number of models have been proposed which aim to account for the cognitive mechanisms that are involved with producing language in the written form. Based on a series of experiments which involved participants speaking aloud their thoughts while they wrote, Flower and Hayes (1981) proposed a model of writing. They highlight four key processes that emerged from their research:

1 **Planning stage:** First, a writer tackles the composition or planning of what is to be written. During the planning stage ideas are created and organised and goals set.
2 **Translating stage:** The next stage involves converting ideas to words. Flower and Hayes suggest that during this stage a writer forms an internal representation of the sentence which is guided by thought and knowledge of linguistic structures, such as grammar.
3 **Reviewing stage:** Once composition has begun and words have been translated into text, the text itself then feeds back into the model. The process by which this feeds back is via a reviewing module.
4 **Monitor stage:** The fourth major component of the model allows for communication across all prior stages. This module emphasises the role of feedback across all stages of the writing process as an important component to progression.

The major contribution of the Flower and Hayes model is the idea of writing as a process of evolution driven by goals which then change and drive subsequent goals. They also propose that goals are hierarchically organised and

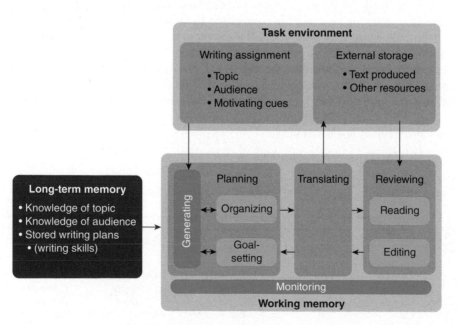

FIGURE 8.9   Flower and Hayes' (1981) model of writing

Source: Aaron J. Newman/Wikimedia Commons

that the quality of connection between the levels in the hierarchy is a factor which determines writing ability. For example, they argue that a writer who sets achievable low-middle-high goals will be successful in their writing aims, whereas a writer who sets unrealistic goals, which leaves huge disparities between low and middle goals, results in poorer writing ability.

As can be seen from the model, there is an input from long-term memory during the writing process. Memory in fact plays a vital role in all cognitive models. Both Bock and Levelt (1994) and Dell (1986) also include a long-term memory component in their models. After all, all models must retrieve information from somewhere to interact with current input information, to create new information (e.g. a new sentence). Recently, there has also been a lot of interest in the demands on working memory when writing. Traxler and Gernsbacher (1992) highlight that in order to produce written language multiple processes must often occur concurrently. To give an idea of just how much mental effort is involved in writing, Kellogg (1994) observed that it roughly equates to the level of mental effort required of an expert during the mid-stages (typically the most effortful stage) of a chess game!

8.11 CHAPTER SUMMARY

This chapter has highlighted some important aspects of language and, in particular, how the cognitive sciences have sought to apply computational and informational approaches to help us to understand the complex processes that underlie language. Research adhering to this philosophy has shown an intricate relationship between language and thought. In particular, it shows that the way we think can influence the way we speak, and vice versa. Much research in the field has focused on the errors that we often make when producing or comprehending language. Based on this research, numerous cognitive models have been proposed which aim to account for the way in which we might process information that can lead to us making linguistic errors. A number of these models have attempted to map cognitive and biological processes onto language processes, such as word detection. It is clear that linguistic abilities, which we all carry out with ease every day, are extremely complex and multifaceted, which is reflected in the models highlighted above. Although this chapter (and typically the research field as well) has been separated out into language comprehension and language production, these two aspects of language are inextricably linked. It is clear that an overarching model of linguistic information processing must include the biological substrates of language and, until more advanced methods of investigation are available, a focus on language errors is crucial. This continuance in the development of testable models of language is vital in advancing our understanding of the mechanisms that afford us the ability to communicate with such effectiveness.

 ## DISCUSSION QUESTIONS

How far does the cognitive approach take us in explaining language?

Can humans really be conceptualised as nothing more than a powerful computer?

How do you think cognitive models of language can be applied to the real world?

Can you think of any other chapters in the book that might be helpful in explaining language?

 ## SUGGESTIONS FOR FURTHER READING

Eysenk, M., & Keane, T.M. (2010). *Cognitive psychology: a student's handbook* (6th edn). Hove: Psychology Press. This book has an in-depth section on language, specifically taking a cognitive approach.

Pulvermuller, F. (2002). *The neuroscience of language: on brain circuits of words and serial order*. Cambridge: Cambridge University Press. We haven't had time to cover the neuroscience of language here but it relates well to the cognitive aspects discussed. Chapters 3 and 4 in this book are very good overviews of the neuroscience of language. An added advantage of this book is that is can be downloaded online for free at: http://assets.cambridge.org/97805217/90260/frontmatter/9780521790260_frontmatter.pdf.

Whitney, P. (1993). *The psychology of language*. Pacific Grove, CA: Wadsworth. This book covers lots of the same areas as the current chapter but in a greater detail and from perspectives other than cognitive psychology.

 Still want more? For links to online resources relevant to this chapter and a quiz to test your understanding, visit the companion website at edge.sagepub.com/banyard2e

---

SECTION C

BIOLOGICAL PSYCHOLOGY: HOW OUR BRAINS AFFECT OUR BEHAVIOUR

'My brain ... that's my second favourite organ!' says Woody Allen (in *Sleeper*, 1973), and who can disagree with him? What a fantastic thing the brain is. It creates for us an amazing array of sounds, smells and tastes. It thinks, it remembers, it feels and it communicates. The more you think about it, the more remarkable it becomes. Roger Sperry, who was awarded a Nobel Prize for his work on brains, commented:

> Prior to the advent of brain, there was no color and no sound in the universe, nor was there any flavor or aroma and probably rather little sense and no feeling or emotion. Before brains the universe was also free of pain and anxiety. (Sperry, 1964: 2)

This is a remarkable quote, and one that is quite hard to digest. One of the things he is saying is that there is no such thing as sound. What happens is that there are changes in air pressure caused by movement. Over the course of evolution we have developed a sense to detect very small changes in air pressure. This is useful because the creatures that can detect movement are the ones that are most likely to be able to run away from bigger and hungrier creatures. We detect these changes through our ears, and our brains have transformed changes in air pressure into the phenomenon we call sound. You might think that Conchita Wurst (Eurovision winner, though probably long forgotten before this book hits the shelves) is making the music, but really she is just creating changes in air pressure and your brain is doing most of the work converting it into sound.

The discovery that the brain is the main controller of behaviour and experience was relatively recent. It is commonly dated to Franz Josef Gall (1758–1828), who was a pioneer in the field. Unfortunately he blotted his copybook and these days is remembered more for inventing the bogus pseudoscience of phrenology (studying bumps on the head). After Gall, it was clear that the brain could control our movements and our bodily functions. The next breakthrough for our understanding came with the work of Paul Broca (1824–1880), who was able to show that a small area of the brain is responsible for the production of speech. Damage to this area renders a person speechless even though they can still understand the spoken word. This area is still referred to as Broca's area. The striking discovery here is that the brain is also clearly important in cognitive functions such as thought and language, which seems obvious to us now but was a major breakthrough at the time.

Since then the brain has been enthusiastically studied and we can now connect a number of cognitive processes to specific parts of the brain. However, some of the work has been surprisingly disappointing: for example, the attempt by Karl Lashley (1890–1959) to look for the part of the brain responsible for memory. Despite decades of work with rats, in which he systematically removed parts of their brains to observe the effects on their memory, he was unable to find a specific site. He eventually proposed the law of mass action, which states that the decline in performance of the animal is related to the amount of brain tissue that is removed rather than which bit is removed. This shows that although we talk about having a memory, there is no evidence that such a thing exists in the brain. We have found parts of the brain that affect our ability to recall faces or events or maps, but we have not been able to find a part of the brain that would correspond to a computer hard drive. In other words, we remember things but we don't have a part of the brain that we can identify as the memory store.

The past hundred years has seen an explosion in brain research and we now know a lot more about how the brain is wired and how it influences our behaviour. Most recently, the development of a range of scanning techniques has allowed us to observe the brain while it is actually working. Despite all this research, the big questions still remain unanswered. In particular, what makes the collection of chemicals and cells in the brain become the reflective, thinking, feeling organism that is aware of itself and able to act and make choices? We have discovered many remarkable things about our brains – and this itself is one of the most remarkable phenomena. When we study the brain, who and what is studying who and what? At one level we might suggest that the brain is studying the brain. This is very puzzling, and we recommend you don't spend too long thinking about it.

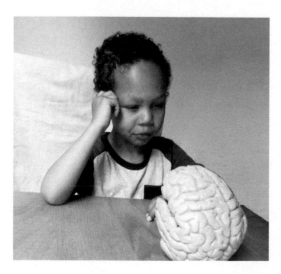

FIGURE C.1 A brain looking at a brain

© mickythemartian

KEY ISSUES

Biological psychology has an underlying assumption that people are biological machines. These biological machines are made up of chemicals and cells which control our thoughts, feelings and behaviour. This assumption allows us to research the brain and develop models of the effect it has on our behaviour and experience. The main problem with the model is that it does not match our experience of being alive. We might say 'I love you' to someone, but never 'my attachment neurons fire more strongly when I see you'.

The machine model leads us to some strange contradictions. Look at the following quote from physiological psychologist Peter Milner:

> I am interested in organisms as pieces of machinery, and I would like to know much the same about them as I once wanted to know about the gadgets I saw around me: first, what happens when the controls or inputs are manipulated and, a little later, how it happens. (Milner, 1970: 1)

If I went to my doctor and said, 'I feel like a machine. I am a gadget. One of my bits is going wrong, could you fix it please', the doctor might regard this statement as a sign of my mental instability and immediately send for the straitjacket. If, on the other hand, I make this statement to a conference of psychologists, and make it not about myself but about 'people', then I can be hailed as a scientific genius.

THIS SECTION

In this section we have four chapters looking at the biology of the brain. Chapter 9 presents an overview of how the human brain is organised in terms of its different structures and their various functions. Chapter 10 describes how information is processed within the brain to enable it to function. Chapter 11 discusses how the brain interacts with behaviour, using sex as an example. Finally, Chapter 12 explores what emotion and motivation are, how they influence each other, how they are researched within psychology, and why they are important for our social wellbeing.

9 THE HUMAN NERVOUS SYSTEM: FUNCTIONAL ANATOMY

Lead authors: Antonio Castro, Gary Jones and Mark J.T. Sergeant

CHAPTER OUTLINE

9.1 Introduction	**155**
9.2 Overview of the nervous system	**155**
9.2.1 General divisions within the nervous system	155
9.2.2 Neuroanatomical directions and planes	156
9.3 Central nervous system	**159**
9.3.1 The brain	159
9.3.2 Telencephalon (division 1)	160
9.3.3 Diencephalon (division 2)	164
9.3.4 Midbrain (division 3)	165
9.3.5 Metencephalon (division 4)	165
9.3.6 Myelencephalon (division 5)	166
9.3.7 Spinal cord	166
9.3.8 Protection of the central nervous system	167
9.4 Peripheral nervous system	**168**
9.4.1 Somatic nervous system	168
9.4.2 Autonomic nervous system	169
9.5 Neuroanatomical and neurofunctional methods	**169**

9.5.1 Structural imaging techniques 169

9.5.2 Functional imaging techniques 170

9.6 Chapter summary 172

Discussion questions 173

Suggestions for further reading 173

Answer to question 173

9.1 INTRODUCTION

The remarkable organ at the top of our necks is responsible for giving us the rich experience that we call consciousness. This sense of consciousness involves thoughts, feelings, memories and perceptions. Some of these experiences of the world come from direct contact with the environment. For example, if someone stands on your toe, a message is passed from your toe to your brain and you have a sensation of pain.

The way the message is passed to your brain, and the way that you process that message and respond to it, are of interest to biological psychologists. Not all processes in the brain involve contact with the environment: for example, we can happily sit with our eyes closed creating a visual scene from our imagination and having a strong emotional response to it. The organ that allows us to do this is the brain. The brain also sorts out the complicated stuff of staying alive without us having to worry about it: we are able to breathe, maintain our heart rate, get about in the world and eat, for example, without having to be taught how to do it or think much about it.

The more you think about the brain and its processes, the more remarkable it appears. All these processes require some biological basis for them to exist and this is what biological psychologists study. The structure of the nervous system has evolved over millions of years and it has developed some remarkable specialisations. What started out as a collection of cells in a simple creature has evolved into the complex human brain made up of 100 billion neurones, each connected to hundreds of other cells, as well as trillions of support cells. The part of the nervous system that processes information and takes decisions is anatomically quite different from the part that interacts with the outside world.

This chapter covers the basics of biological psychology and focuses in particular on the physical layout of neuroanatomical structures as well as on their functions. To help you achieve an understanding of the biological bases of behaviour, the next section provides an overview outlining the general layout of the nervous system and some key neuroanatomical terms, which are particularly useful in describing the location of various structures within the nervous system.

Equipped with this knowledge, it will be easier for you to gain an insight into the five major divisions of the brain and an appreciation for the spinal cord. You will also learn about the four ways in which the central nervous system is protected from hazard. And the chapter will end with an account of the somatic and autonomic divisions of the peripheral nervous system with which we regulate the functioning of internal organs and interrelate with the external environment.

FRAMING QUESTIONS

- How can you find your way around the nervous system?
- Which brain regions control which behaviours?
- How well protected is the central nervous system?
- What systems allow the brain to interact with the environment?
- How do we measure brain structures and function in a living brain?

9.2 OVERVIEW OF THE NERVOUS SYSTEM

9.2.1 GENERAL DIVISIONS WITHIN THE NERVOUS SYSTEM

The human nervous system is largely considered to be a system of twos as it is composed of two divisions: the central nervous system (CNS) and the peripheral nervous system (PNS) (Figure 9.1). The central nervous system itself can be subdivided into the brain and spinal cord. The peripheral nervous system, which conveys messages to and from

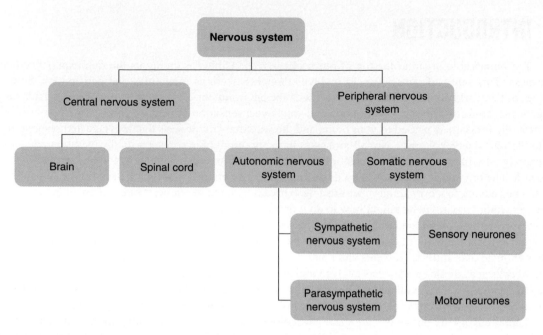

FIGURE 9.1   The hierarchical structure of the nervous system: a system of 'twos'

the central nervous system, has two parts as well: the somatic division and the autonomic division. Furthermore, the somatic nervous system consists of cranial nerves and spinal nerves that can be either sensory or motor, and the autonomic nervous system has sympathetic nerves and parasympathetic nerves.

The brain is the part of the central nervous system located within the skull. It processes information received by the spinal cord and cranial nerves, thinks, takes decisions and is capable of experiencing emotions. It also sends action commands to the peripheral nervous system which may or may not travel through the spinal cord.

The spinal cord is the part of the central nervous system located within the spinal or vertebral column. It passes on the motor commands received from the brain to the muscles, transmits sensory information received from receptors to the brain, and is also capable of responding directly to sensory stimuli by means of spinal reflexes.

The peripheral nervous system is the means by which human beings are able to interact with the world. Thanks to the somatic nervous system we can act on and be influenced by the external environment, and thanks to the autonomic nervous system we are able to regulate the internal environment (i.e. glandular activity and internal organ functioning).

9.2.2 NEUROANATOMICAL DIRECTIONS AND PLANES

Neuroanatomy is much easier to understand when you know some basic terminology used to describe the position of areas, structures, nuclei and nerves in the nervous system. These terms are as useful as the terminology that would allow you to find the student union in your university campus or the location of the main post office in the nearest city to your home. Hence, learning neuroanatomy is much like finding your way when you are out and about. Once you become familiar with these terms, you will find it easier to understand and remember how the nervous system is arranged.

When describing the location of a particular area of the brain, we will be using the terminology described in Table 9.1. All these terms are used in a relative sense. For example, the brain structure called the hypothalamus is said to be ventral to the thalamus but dorsal to the pituitary gland. Now see whether you can work out where these three structures are in relation to each other (answer at end of this chapter).

The direction in which the information flows is also important in neuroanatomy as it gives you an idea about the sort of information that is being carried and the type of nerve that is being used. Nerves or tracts that carry messages towards a given structure are said to be *afferent*; those that carry messages away from the structure are said to be *efferent*; and if the structure is not mentioned, you should assume that the statement is made in reference to the central nervous system. For example, afferent projections or neurons carry information to the central nervous system, so these

TABLE 9.1   Terms for anatomical directions and locations

TERM	MEANING
Dorsal	Towards the top or above for brain
	Back for brain stem and spinal cord
Ventral	Towards the bottom or below for brain
	Front for brain stem and spinal cord
Medial	Towards the middle
Lateral	Towards one side
Ipsilateral	Towards the same side
Contralateral	Towards the opposite side
Bilateral	On both sides
Proximal	Close together
Distal	Far apart
Anterior	Towards front
Posterior	Towards back

ASIDE

Making sense of terms, or, why do I have to learn all this?

As perhaps you are discovering, there is a good deal of specialist terminology in biological psychology. To enable scientists of all nationalities to communicate there needs to be a common set of terms. It just so happens that the terminology was developed in the days when Greek and Latin dominated the language of science. The names for brain areas were often simple descriptions of their appearance: for example, the brain region called the **hippocampus** was so named because it resembles a seahorse in appearance (from *hippo*, the Greek for 'horse' and *kampus*, the Greek for 'sea monster'). Without these common terms there would be little communication possible. For example, two students observing slices of rat brains under a microscope were overheard. One was suggesting that they start their investigation at the 'pepperami' and stop at the 'dickie bow'. These terms may have provided an accurate pictorial description of the areas being examined, but it is unlikely that if these students had written down their method using these terms, everyone would understand them.

It is difficult for students not familiar with ancient Greek or Latin to learn these terms because we don't know the references that would have originally made sense. There is no easy way around this; you just have to learn them. For some words, you can take an educated guess. For example, 'subcortical' means below the cortex in the same way that 'submarine' means under the sea and 'subway' means under the road. You can guess where the hypothalamus is because 'hypo' also means below, so it is below the thalamus, in the way that 'hypodermic' means below the skin.

are potentially sensory nerves; and efferent projections or neurons carry information from the central nervous system, which makes them potentially motor nerves. We can have sensory neurons and motor neurons in the same nerve and this would make it a mixed nerve.

When it comes to observing particular brain structures it is common practice, in order to keep matters simple, for most neuroanatomists to convert three-dimensional parts of the nervous system (the dimensions being height, width

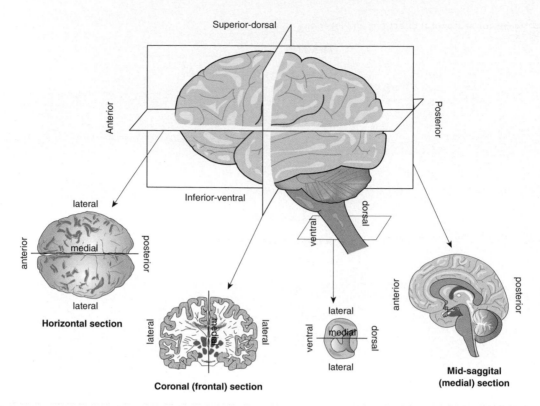

Superior-dorsal

Anterior

Posterior

Inferior-ventral

dorsal

ventral

lateral

anterior | posterior

medial

lateral

Horizontal section

lateral | lateral

medial

Coronal (frontal) section

ventral | dorsal

lateral

medial

lateral

anterior | posterior

Mid-saggital (medial) section

FIGURE 9.2 Neuroanatomical directions and planes (adapted from http://homepage.smc.edu/russell_richard/Psych2/ Graphics/2013_Brain_Orientation_pictures.pdf)

(Dr Worm)

CEREBRAL HEMISPHERES The right and left halves of the most anterior part of the brain. They play a primary role in most of our mental abilities, such as language, attention and perception. This is another example of the nervous system being a system of twos.

and depth) into two-dimensional images (e.g. just height and width). This seems like a sensible thing to do if you want to make something more practically manageable. In effect, this practice provides us with an anatomical map: that is, a limited, two-dimensional representation of a three-dimensional world. Anatomical planes can be as useful as geographical maps when you are trying to find your way around. The neuroanatomical planes are illustrated in Figure 9.2.

Different neuroanatomical planes denote different orientations or perspectives of the nervous system, and there are three main planes: the sagittal plane, the coronal plane and the horizontal plane. A sagittal plane cuts the brain vertically, perpendicularly to the long axis of the body, and divides it into left and right parts. Using this type of plane, it is possible to see anterior and posterior areas as well as dorsal and ventral areas, but it is not feasible to see both **cerebral hemispheres** of the brain at once. All but one of the sagittal sections are actually parasagittal sections; they cut through just one hemisphere. The sagittal section that severs the brain between the two hemispheres is called a midsagittal section. Hence, to see and compare both hemispheres, one would have to look at more than one sagittal image or apply one of the other two main planes.

Choosing which plane to look at depends on the structure you want to see. For example, a coronal plane cuts the nervous system vertically, perpendicularly to the sagittal plane, and produces an anterior or a posterior section. Using a coronal plane it is possible to see dorsal and ventral areas as well as medial and lateral areas, but it is not possible to see anterior and posterior areas of the brain in the same coronal section. To view anterior and posterior areas, it would be necessary to look at a succession of coronal sections or choose one of the other two main planes.

Finally, a horizontal plane cuts the brain at a right angle to the spinal cord and produces an upper and lower part. Using this type of plane it is possible to see anterior and posterior areas as well as medial and lateral areas, but not dorsal (top) and ventral (bottom) areas. To see these areas of the brain, one would have to look at more than one horizontal image or apply one of the other two main planes. You cannot lose a dimension and expect no drawbacks; simplicity has its price and its advantages.

9.3 CENTRAL NERVOUS SYSTEM

9.3.1 THE BRAIN

To understand how the brain is divided into five divisions, it helps to look at brain development from conception. In the fourth week after conception, the neural tube which will later become the human brain develops three swellings (also known as vesicles). These primary swellings are the **forebrain**, **midbrain** and **hindbrain** (Figure 9.3). A week later, week five of gestation, two of these divisions subdivide into two other subdivisions. The forebrain gives rise to the telencephalon and diencephalon, the midbrain remains undivided, and the hindbrain gives rise to the metencephalon and myelencephalon – resulting in five divisions altogether. This section will outline these five divisions and their functions.

It is worth noting that the higher in the brain a structure is positioned in terms of brain divisions, the more complex is its function. The more complex brain processes are often referred to as higher-order functions (such as problem solving, planning and using language) as opposed to basic functions (such as breathing or moving).

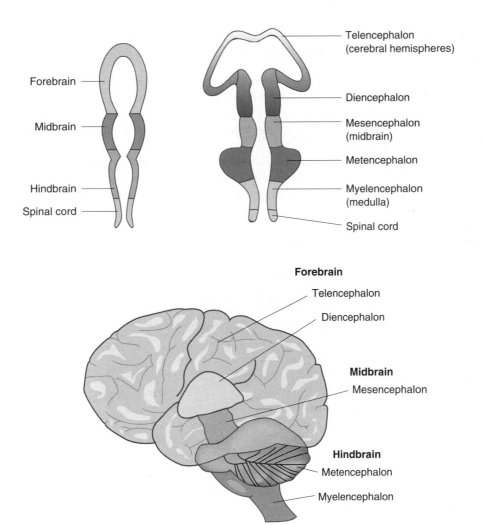

FIGURE 9.3   Divisions within the brain

(Dr Worm)

9.3.2 TELENCEPHALON (DIVISION 1)

The telencephalon is the most anterior (furthest forward) of the five divisions within the brain and one of the two divisions of the forebrain. It includes the cerebral cortex, the limbic system and the basal ganglia.

CEREBRAL CORTEX

The **cerebral cortex** surrounds the telencephalon and is deeply convoluted or wrinkled. These convolutions considerably enlarge the surface area of the cortex, which is approximately 2500 cm². However, it is these very wrinkles that are responsible for higher mental processes. In this context, deep clefts or grooves are called fissures and shallower clefts are known as *sulci* (singular 'sulcus'). Ridges or bulges between grooves are called *gyri* (singular 'gyrus'). One of the most prominent fissures in the cerebral cortex, the longitudinal fissure, separates the left hemisphere from the right hemisphere. The two hemispheres are nearly, but not completely, symmetrical. They are connected by axons and these neuronal axons are grouped into bundles called *commissures*.

The largest commissure in the brain is the **corpus callosum**, connecting the two hemispheres (Figure 9.4). This makes it possible for each of the hemispheres to know what the other hemisphere is up to and for the two hemispheres to cooperate with each other. However, some functions are located primarily in one side of the brain (and this is referred to as functional laterality). For example, in most people the left hemisphere specialises in language functions and the right hemisphere is better in visual-spatial functions. Because cell bodies predominate in the cerebral cortex, the outer surface of both hemispheres has a greyish appearance: hence the term 'grey matter'. Beneath the cerebral cortex, it is a quite different story. There, fast-conducting myelinated axons with their characteristic opaque white appearance outnumber cell bodies: hence the term 'white matter'.

The two hemispheres are each described as having four lobes: the frontal lobe, the parietal lobe, the temporal lobe and the occipital lobe. They are named after the bones of the skull that cover them. The frontal lobe is separated from the parietal lobe by the central sulcus. The temporal lobe is also clearly separated from the frontal and parietal lobes by the lateral fissure. However, the anatomical boundary between the occipital lobe and the parietal and temporal lobes is not as clearly defined.

The frontal is the largest of the four lobes and is mostly involved in planning and movement. Just anterior to the central sulcus is the precentral gyrus, which is occupied mainly by the primary motor cortex. The primary motor cortex is somatotopically organised and is involved in the initiation of voluntary movements. The fact that it is

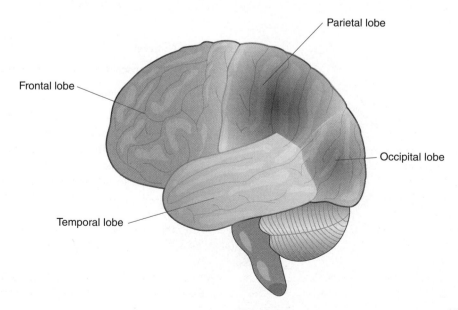

FIGURE 9.4 Lobes of the cerebral cortex

(Dr Worm)

somatotopically organised was described beautifully by Penfield and Jasper in 1954 from their experiments during brain surgery. Patients who required surgery for medical reasons gave permission for areas of the cortex to be electrically stimulated and the resulting sensations recorded. From these experiments Penfield produced his homunculus: a cartoon representation of the localisation of areas of cortex to body parts, in which the drawn size of body part represents the amount of cortex dedicated to it rather than its physical size.

> **SOMATOTOPICAL ORGANISATION** The arrangement of brain structures whereby regions of the brain represent particular parts of the body. For example, when the hand area in the primary motor cortex is activated, the hand moves.

The primary motor cortex is also contralaterally organised (or cross-wired) so that we are able to move the right side of the body voluntarily thanks to the left primary motor cortex, and vice versa. In addition, those parts of the body with which we can conduct fine movements, such as with our fingers, are overrepresented in the primary motor cortex. The premotor area and the supplementary motor area, known as secondary motor areas and also located in the frontal lobe, are functionally related to the programming of specific patterns of movements.

The frontal lobe is also where Broca's area is located. This area is implicated in the production of written and spoken language. Finally, the prefrontal cortex of the frontal lobe is involved with personality and formulating plans and strategies. These functions and a change in personality were precisely those impaired in the case of a famous patient called Phineas Gage, who had his prefrontal cortex seriously damaged as a result of sustaining a penetrating brain injury caused by a tamping rod in the course of a job-related accident (Damasio et al., 1994). Medical reports at the time described a change of personality from a respectable, hardworking and energetic businessman to a profane, disrespecting, capricious and impulsive type (Harlow, 1894, in Neylan, 1999).

The parietal lobe is posterior to the central sulcus and anterior to the occipital lobe (Figure 9.4). The postcentral gyrus in this lobe corresponds to the primary somatosensory cortex, which is where information about touch, pain, pressure, temperature and body position is initially processed in the cortex. In a similar way to the primary motor cortex, the primary somatosensory cortex is also organised somatotopically, and parts of the body where we have a very fine sense of touch, such as the hands and the mouth, are overrepresented. The parietal lobe, usually that of the left hemisphere, is also concerned with language comprehension. In addition, the posterior area of this lobe receives projections from the occipital lobe carrying visual information and is involved in spatial orientation and perception.

KEY STUDY

Bryden, M.P., & MacRae, L. (1989). Dichotic laterality effects obtained with emotional words. *Neuropsychiatry, Neuropsychology, and Behavioral Neurology, 1*(3), 171–176.

Bryden and MacRae in 1989 published a neat research study that illustrates a body of research that has investigated the hemispheric lateralisation of language and emotion in the normal human brain. The authors used a behavioural technique known as the dichotic listening task, which involves presenting different stimuli (such as words) simultaneously to each ear via headphones. In this case the experimental stimuli consisted of four similar sounding words (power, bower, dower and tower), each spoken in four different emotional tones (happy, sad, angry and neutral). For example, the word 'power' spoken in a happy voice was presented to the left ear while the word 'bower' spoken in a sad voice was presented to the right ear. Participants were asked to detect either a specific word or a specific emotion.

Results revealed that when words were the target, there was a significantly greater level of accuracy if the word in question was presented to the right ear (i.e. right ear advantage for words), whereas when emotions were the target, they were more accurately detected in the left ear (i.e. left ear advantage for emotions).

Given that the auditory system is anatomically crossed, although not as completely crossed as the visual system, these results confirm that the left hemisphere is dominant for language, whereas the right hemisphere is dominant or superior for emotional material.

The research also shows that the idea of functional specialisation by our cerebral hemispheres is something that, with ingenuity on the part of the researcher, can be studied in the general population using relatively inexpensive means. You may like to consider how you could explore this topic further through your studies.

ASIDE

Phineas Gage

Given what we know about the functions of the prefrontal cortex today, the attribution of a change in the personality of Phineas Gage to brain damage seems a sensible conclusion to draw. However, we should remember that there is only anecdotal evidence of the character of Gage prior to his injury (i.e. no reliable baseline measure) for comparison. Also, who knows what effect a near-death experience might have on one's motivation to work hard and be a productive member of society!

The temporal lobe is where the primary auditory cortex is located. This area receives auditory information from a subcortical structure, the thalamus, which will be explained later in the chapter, and it is in the primary auditory cortex that auditory information is processed for the first time in the cerebral cortex. Destruction of this area of the temporal lobe leads to cortical deafness, an inability to recognise sound despite an intact auditory system within the ear.

The posterior portion of the superior temporal gyrus, usually in the left hemisphere, is where Wernicke's area is located. This area is known to play a fundamental role in the comprehension of language. The medial part of the temporal lobe is concerned with intricate aspects of learning and memory. The ventral surface of the temporal lobe is a visual association area implicated in higher-order processing of optical information.

The main function of the occipital lobe is the analysis of visual information. The primary visual cortex, located in this lobe, receives visual information from the thalamus and is where visual information is processed for the first time in the cerebral cortex. Damage to the primary visual cortex or brain regions that project to it causes 'blindsight' – that is, an ability to see some features of the visual environment but unconsciously. Patients with blindsight will report being unable to see visual stimuli in the area of the visual field that is damaged, and yet if asked to make a guess where a stimulus is they can accurately pinpoint it 99% of the time (Weiskrantz et al., 1974). This is because the more primitive visual area responsible for location (the superior colliculus in the brain stem) remains intact.

It is a pity that Weiskrantz et al. made their discoveries too late to save the injured soldiers who, during the First World War (1914–1918), reported blindness but were 'found out' by neurosurgeons (and subsequently shot) because they caught a ball that was thrown towards them. It is likely that many of these poor individuals were genuinely suffering from blindsight as a result of brain injury.

The rest of the occipital lobe is referred to as the visual association cortex and is concerned with more complex analysis of visual information.

LIMBIC SYSTEM

The **limbic system** is also part of the first brain division (the telencephalon) and plays a major role in emotions and memory. It includes the hippocampus, the amygdala and the cingulate gyrus. The hippocampus, a long and curved structure (the seahorse, remember), and the **amygdala**, a much smaller and rounded structure, are located at the base of a large cerebral cavity in the temporal lobe of both hemispheres; the amygdala is anterior to the hippocampus. The cingulate gyrus can be found at the medial edge of the cerebral hemispheres, surrounding the corpus callosum dorsally.

The amygdala is concerned with emotional memories and emotional feelings, such as fear or anger. For example, in post-traumatic stress disorder, where following trauma fear arousal is easily triggered, there is evidence of increased reactivity of the amygdala (van der Kolk & Fisler, 1995). The hippocampus plays a major role in learning and memory, particularly spatial memory. Most famously, a study by Maguire et al. (2000) showed that London taxi drivers, who have to study for years to learn 'The Knowledge' of the London street plan, have enlarged areas of their hippocampus compared to other drivers. The cingulate gyrus, which has an important role in attention, is also involved in the experience of emotions.

KEY RESEARCHER Vilayanur S. Ramachandran

FIGURE 9.5 Vilayanur S. Ramachandran

Ramachandran is Director of the Centre for Brain and Cognition and Professor in the Psychology Department and Neurosciences Programme at the University of California, San Diego in the United States. He studied for an MD at Stanley Medical College in India, where he was born, and subsequently moved to England where he obtained a PhD from Trinity College at the University of Cambridge. Before becoming Professor at the University of California, he also spent some time as a postdoctoral fellow at Oxford University.

Most of his academic life has been dedicated to the study of visual perception and neurological syndromes such as phantom limbs, synesthesia and autism. For example, in the area of phantom limbs he is credited with introducing the use of visual feedback as a treatment for the pain that is often associated with this condition. The way in which he went about doing this was theoretically well informed and quite ingenious.

Ramachandran hypothesised that the paralysis experienced by patients with phantom limbs is due to visual and proprioception feedback received by the brain when trying to move the phantom limb. Basically, the brain gives repeated orders to move but the phantom limb refuses. To resolve this learned paralysis, he invented a mirror box (yes, just a box with a mirror inside) and asked patients to move their able arm in front of the mirror. Of course patients did so without any difficulty, and the interesting thing is that by looking at the reflection produced by the mirror box they saw and felt as if their phantom limb was back alive. The even more striking thing was that by being able to experience the imaginary limb move many of these patients stopped feeling phantom pain.

The results of this line of research and many of his other research projects have been published in over 180 scientific papers, several of them in high-impact journals such as *Nature* and *Science*. He also wrote *Phantoms in the brain* (1998) with Sandra Blakeslee and is the editor of the *Encyclopaedia of the human brain*. In 2003 he gave the BBC Reith Lectures, entitled 'The Emerging Mind' (www.bbc.co.uk/radio4/reith2003/), and in 2007 was conferred with the title of Padma Bhushan by the President of India. It is no surprise then that he has been called 'the Marco Polo of neuroscience' by Richard Dawkins and 'the modern Paul Broca' by Eric Kandel.

If you want to follow Ramachadran's blog, it can be found at http://cbc.ucsd.edu/blog/blog.php. You can also find more about him by searching for his Facebook website. Do you think he is a researcher role model?

BASAL GANGLIA

The **basal ganglia** consist of three large hemispheric nuclei located beneath the anterior regions of the cerebral cortex. They are the caudate nucleus, the putamen and the globus pallidus. Together, the caudate nucleus and the putamen form the dorsal striatum, but the putamen and the globus pallidus form the lenticular nucleus. No, the caudate nucleus and the globus pallidus do not form any other nucleus (there is no need to complicate matters unnecessarily!), but all three nuclei form a circuit with the cortex and another brain section, the midbrain. This provides an example of how a structure can form part of more than one brain system. It demonstrates that we have imposed an order onto brain structures that suits our understanding, often based on function. Functionally, the basal ganglia are involved in the control of movement and in habit learning. They play a crucial role in the sequencing of movements and in maintaining posture and muscle tone. Degeneration of neurons in the basal ganglia is seen in Huntington's disease (Walker, 2007), a hereditary disorder of motor and intellectual function that eventually becomes terminal.

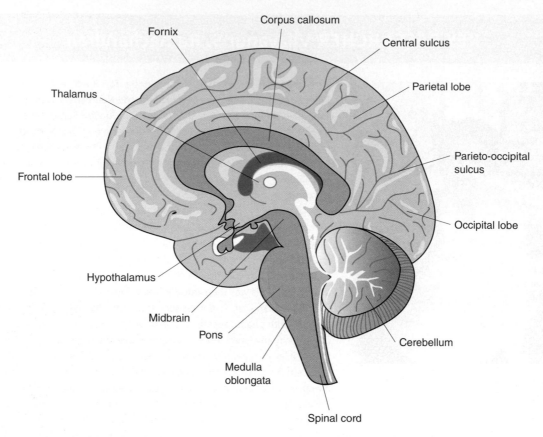

FIGURE 9.6 Sagittal section of the brain

(Dr Worm)

9.3.3 DIENCEPHALON (DIVISION 2)

> **ENDOCRINE SYSTEM** A series of small organs responsible for producing hormones that regulate a variety of processes, including growth and development, metabolism and puberty.

The second division of the forebrain is the **diencephalon**, which is located between the telencephalon and the midbrain. It includes two main structures: the thalamus, a subcortical relay station, and the **hypothalamus**, a collection of nuclei that regulate the **endocrine system** and control many aspects of behaviour (Figure 9.6).

THALAMUS

The **thalamus** is an oval structure in the diencephalon that is composed of many nuclei. There is one thalamus in each cerebral hemisphere, and they tend to be fused in many, but not all, human brains by the interthalamic adhesion or massa intermedia. As neuroanatomists do not yet know or cannot agree on what purpose this adhesion serves (it is absent in some brains), the first reader to discover its advantageous or disadvantageous function gets a prize! The nuclei of the thalamus relay sensory and motor information to different parts of the cerebral cortex. All sensory information except olfactory (smell) information reaches the cerebral cortex through the thalamus. The thalamus also relays information between cortical areas.

HYPOTHALAMUS

The hypothalamus is a relatively small structure that lies under the thalamus, forming the ventral part of the diencephalon. Despite its small size, its activity has far-reaching implications across the body. The hypothalamus is involved in regulating the functioning of internal organs and takes part in many crucial aspects of motivated behaviour, such as eating, drinking, sleeping and having sex. It is also involved in temperature regulation and emotional behaviour. It controls the production of hormones produced by a gland that sits just beneath it, the **pituitary gland**, and thanks to this direct influence it is able to regulate the endocrine system.

KEY STUDY

Nijboer, F., Sellers, E.W., Mellinger, J., Jordan, M.A., Matuz, T., Furdea, A., Halder, S., Mochty, U., Krusienski, D.J., Vaughan, T.M., Wolpaw, J.R., Birbaumer, N., & Kübler, A. (2008). A P300-based brain–computer interface for people with amyotrophic lateral sclerosis. *Clinical Neurophysiology*, *119*(8), 1909–1916.

Would it not be wonderful if we could communicate directly with computers without having to type or talk to them? This means of communication would bypass the need for muscular activity and could be particularly useful for patients suffering from severe neuromuscular disorders such as amyotrophic lateral sclerosis. Well, this is what this study was about.

Patients were presented with a grid of letters on a computer screen where rows and columns flashed randomly. They had to pay attention and count the number of times a letter they were interested in came up – one letter at a time – until a whole message was complete. While this was going on, their brain electrical activity was recorded by having small sensors attached to the top of their heads. The key here is that every time a relevant letter flashed, a switch would be turned on in the brain. This switch is called P300, cunningly named because it is a positive wave that occurs about 300 milliseconds after a relevant event. The mean number of selections per minute using this device ranged from 1.5 to 4.1 and only a small number of them were mistakes.

This research demonstrated that computers can read our minds, albeit imperfectly and with a bit of help from us, and that in so doing they can be used as an alternative means of communication. Thinking back, this may remind you of bicycles; yes, a means of transportation that can be used without our feet having to touch the ground. The very first bicycles – those with a giant front wheel and a tiny back wheel – were rather slow and unstable. Though they were a great invention, we have come a long way from them to the carbon-fibre beauties available nowadays. So, given the levels of accuracy and communication speed referred to above, we could ask ourselves if a 'front wheel' is at all needed in the next brain–computer interface and if it is, how to make it smaller.

9.3.4 MIDBRAIN (DIVISION 3)

The midbrain (sometimes called **mesencephalon**) consists of two main divisions: the **tectum** and the **tegmentum**. The tectum is situated in the dorsal part of the midbrain and contains the **superior** and **inferior colliculi**. The superior colliculi, of which there are two, are part of the visual system and are primarily involved in visual reflexes, such as blinking. The inferior colliculi, of which nature has also produced two, are part of the auditory system and mediate hearing-related behaviours.

Ventral to (below) the tectum is the tegmentum, the second division of the midbrain. This division is larger than the tectum and it also contains a greater number of structures (too numerous to mention here), but is involved in basic behaviours such as pain perception, voluntary movement and postural adjustments. One important structure within the tegmentum is the **reticular formation**, a diffuse and interconnected network of neurons which extends beyond the tegmentum into posterior parts of the brain. Functionally, it maintains consciousness and is involved in sleep, attention and arousal.

9.3.5 METENCEPHALON (DIVISION 4)

The **metencephalon** is the most anterior division of the hindbrain. It consists of the **cerebellum** and the **pons**. The cerebellum is the dorsal part of the metencephalon and looks like a cauliflower. It has two hemispheres, which although much smaller than the cerebral hemispheres also present a somewhat convoluted cortex and subcortical nuclei; it is this appearance of a small cerebrum that gives it its name (cerebellum).

Functionally, the cerebellum is involved in equilibrium, postural control and muscle tone as well as coordination, learning and planning of movements. It may even play a part in cognitive tasks, such as attention. However, one of its main functions is the adjustment of ongoing movements. It does this by comparing the visual, auditory, vestibular and somatosensory information it receives from sense organs about movements that are being conducted with information about movements that are being intended, allowing it to make appropriate changes in real time. Damage to the cerebellum is known to result in postural defects, impaired walking and poor coordination of movements (Konczak & Timmann, 2007).

Next to the cerebellum is the pons, the second part of the metencephalon. This large bulge contains a section of the reticular formation and relays information from the cerebral cortex to the cerebellum. Many neural messages from cranial nerves and the spinal cord also pass through this hindbrain structure.

9.3.6 MYELENCEPHALON (DIVISION 5)

BRAIN STEM The part of the brain that regulates vital reflexes such as heart rate and respiration; it consists of the midbrain, the pons and the medulla. It is activity or the lack of it in this region that is used by medics to establish whether a patient is 'brain dead'.

Finally, the most posterior part of the hindbrain, and hence also the most posterior part of the brain, is the myelencephalon. This is where the **brain stem** and the reticular formation end and the spinal cord begins. The myelencephalon, often called **medulla oblongata** or just medulla, is involved in fundamental functions that are essential for life: for example, respiration and the regulation of the cardiovascular system. The medulla also intervenes in reflexive responses such as coughing, salivating and vomiting, and relays sensory information received from some of the cranial nerves. It also acts as a passageway and synaptic area for some neural tracts carrying afferent information toward the brain and efferent information toward the spinal cord.

EXERCISE: HOW SENSITIVE ARE YOU?

Skin contains many sensory receptors, such as pain, touch, pressure and heat receptors. They convey sensation via peripheral sensory nerves to the cortex to enable behavioural response to environmental stimuli. These sensory receptors are present in varying concentrations: for example, areas such as hands and face have far more touch receptors per square centimetre than areas such as arms or legs. This is of course related to the function of body areas (e.g. we explore fine detail with our fingertips, not elbows).

You can demonstrate this using a two-point discrimination test on a friend. Bend a paperclip into the shape of a U with the tips about 2 cm apart and level with each other. Get your participant to close their eyes (or blindfold them if you don't trust them not to peep). *Lightly* touch the two ends of the paper clip to the back of their hand, making sure both tips touch the skin at the same time. Ask how many points they can feel.

If they report feeling two points, then gradually decrease the distance between the points until they report one point. Record this distance. Conversely if the participant could only feel one point at 2 cm apart, then widen the points and repeat the touch test until they can feel two. Comparing various areas of skin, you can work out which areas are most sensitive and therefore have most touch receptors.

9.3.7 SPINAL CORD

The **spinal cord** is the most posterior part of the central nervous system. In adult human beings, it is about 42 to 45 cm long and about 1 cm in diameter. It consists of 31 segments systematically related to areas of skin and muscles. Sensory information from receptors enters these segments through the dorsal roots, whereas motor information destined for muscles leaves them through the ventral roots. This is known as the Bell–Magendie law.

The main function of the spinal cord is to carry sensory information to brain structures such as the thalamus, the cerebellum and the brain stem, and to carry motor information from the cerebral cortex and various brain stem nuclei towards the periphery. It may help here to think of the spinal cord as the central nervous system's motorway. However, the spinal cord is also capable of acting without the involvement of the brain. It achieves this degree of autonomy thanks to spinal reflexes such as the patellar reflex or knee-jerk reflex. These stereotyped responses to sensory input allow quick reactions without conscious analysis, leaving the brain free to concentrate on other tasks.

> **TETRAPLEGIA** Paralysis characterised by inability to move and/or feel the lower part and most of the upper part of the body, secondary to damage in the cervical segments of the spinal cord.
>
> **PARAPLEGIA** Paralysis characterised by failure to move and/or feel the lower part of the body due to damage in the thoracic, lumbar or sacral segments of the spinal cord.

The ascending and descending myelinated tracts (see Chapter 8) form the spinal cord's white matter. The neuronal cell bodies and short, unmyelinated axons form the spinal cord's grey matter. So the spinal cord, as the brain, has grey and white matter. However, whereas the grey matter is on the outer part and the white matter is on the inner part of the brain, in the spinal cord the white matter is on the outer side and the grey matter is in the inner side. This grey matter looks like a butterfly in a cross-section of the spinal cord.

Damage to this part of the central nervous system can cause tetraplegia or paraplegia depending on where in the spinal cord the lesion is located (Castro, Díaz, & van Boxtel, 2007). If the lesion is localised in any of the eight cervical segments, the diagnosis will be that of **tetraplegia**; if it is localised in any of the thoracic, lumbar or sacral segments, it will be a case of **paraplegia**. The damage to the spinal cord can also be complete (when no sensory or motor signals cross the injured area) or incomplete (when some neural signals are able to pass through). The degree of functional impairment is greater in cases where the damage is complete and located in any of the eight cervical segments.

9.3.8 PROTECTION OF THE CENTRAL NERVOUS SYSTEM

Owing to their crucial importance for normal life, the brain and spinal cord are the most preciously protected divisions of the nervous system. They are encased in bone, surrounded by three membranes and washed in **cerebrospinal fluid**; the brain is further protected by the **blood–brain barrier**. These means, which defend the central nervous system from injury and infection, are explained below in greater detail.

The brain is protected from injury by the skull or cranium, a bony structure resulting from the fusion of a number of bones. The spinal cord is enclosed in the spinal column or backbone. This protective and long formation consists of 24 interlocking bones called vertebrae as well as the fused bones of the sacral and coccygeal areas.

Between the skull and the brain, and between the spinal column and the spinal cord, there are three layers of connective tissue which offer a second level of protection to the central nervous system. These protective sheaths or membranes are called **meninges**. The outermost meninx is the dura matter, which is thick, tough and flexible but non-stretchable; it encloses the central nervous system in a somewhat loose sack. The middle meninx, soft and spongy, is the arachnoid. And between the arachnoid and the pia mater, which is the innermost meninx, lies the **subarachnoid space**, which is filled with cerebrospinal fluid. The pia mater, thin and delicate, is the membrane that adheres closely to the surface of the brain and spinal cord.

The inflammation or infection of any or all of these meninges is called meningitis. This condition is caused by bacteria, viruses, fungi or parasites and may include symptoms such as severe headache, stiff neck, fever and intense sensitivity to light (Chávez-Bueno & McCracken, 2005). It can be life threatening if not treated promptly with appropriate medication.

An additional level of protection in the central nervous system is provided by the ventricular system and cerebrospinal fluid. The ventricular system consists of four **ventricles**, which are a series of interconnected chambers within the brain. All four ventricles are filled with cerebrospinal fluid. This fluid is a colourless solution extracted from the blood that resembles blood plasma in its composition. It is produced continuously by the choroid plexus of each ventricle and flows through the ventricular system, the subarachnoid space and the central canal of the spinal cord until it is finally reabsorbed by the blood supply.

From a functional point of view, the cerebrospinal fluid plays a mechanically supportive role and acts as a shock absorber. It may also constitute a medium for the exchange of materials, such as nutrients and metabolic waste, between blood vessels and the brain, and for neuroactive hormones to flow within the nervous system.

Finally, blood vessel walls in the brain are much more tightly packed than in the rest of the body. Additionally, a type of glial cell called an astrocyte sends out fatty protrusions that wrap around the capillaries and neurones, preventing substances from diffusing across the cell membrane. This is what is known as the blood–brain barrier. This barrier mechanism prevents the passage of many molecules from the blood into the brain and hence protects the brain from many chemical substances, some of which would be toxic to the brain. Because of the fatty composition of the glial protrusions, lipid soluble molecules, such as nicotine and caffeine, are able to pass through the barrier relatively easily, whereas water-soluble molecules such as sodium and potassium ions find it much more difficult.

9.4 PERIPHERAL NERVOUS SYSTEM

The second major division of the nervous system is the peripheral nervous system, through which human beings interact with the environment by conveying messages to and from the central nervous system. It consists of the somatic nervous system and the autonomic nervous system.

9.4.1 SOMATIC NERVOUS SYSTEM

The **somatic nervous system** receives input in the form of sensory information from receptors and sends output in the form of motor commands to skeletal muscles; it comprises cranial nerves and spinal nerves.

CRANIAL NERVES

Twelve pairs of nerves enter or leave the human brain through small openings in the skull or cranium and can be found on the ventral surface of the brain; they are the **cranial nerves**. All but the vagus nerve (or cranial nerve X as it is sometimes mysteriously called) serve sensory and/or motor functions of the head and neck. The vagus nerve, instead, wanders around the body and carries information to and from thoracic and abdominal organs, including the heart, liver and intestines.

SPINAL NERVES

As described earlier in the chapter, dorsal and ventral roots emerge from spinal cord segments. The ventral roots are formed by axons of neurons whose cell bodies are contained within the grey matter of the spinal cord, whereas the dorsal roots are formed by axons of neurons whose cell bodies are grouped outside the spinal cord, in the dorsal root

EXERCISE: DO YOU HAVE A LATERAL PREFERENCE?

Some people (i.e. right-handed or dextral) prefer to use their right hand, some (i.e. left-handed or sinistral) their left and yet others (i.e. ambidextrous) don't really have a first choice as they would use both hands with equal ability. But, is that all there is when it comes to lateral preference? Let's find out.

Take a piece of paper, make it into a small ball and then throw it in front of you. Roll another piece of paper into a telescope and look through it using just one eye (no cheating!) to see the ball you have just thrown in front of you. Take the paper ball back, put it on the floor, closer to you, and give it a kick. Finally, pretend that the stack of paper you have been depleting for the purpose of this demo is a radio you want to listen to, but the volume is so low that you can hardly hear it so you decide to bend forward until one of your ears touches the loudspeaker.

As you may have realised, lateral preference refers not only to our hands but also to our feet, eyes and ears. Most people, but not all of us, are congruent across our side-preferences. That is, most people who prefer to throw an object with their right hand, for example, also prefer to use their right foot, eye and ear when only one of them is required. We also tend to be more skilled and do better when using the side of the body we prefer. That is it; you now know what your lateral preference profile is and I hope you are still left with some stationery on your desk!

ganglia. It is the merger of these dorsal and ventral roots that gives rise to the 31 pairs of **spinal nerves** present in the human body. Each one of these pairs leaves the vertebral column at regularly spaced intervals through the intervertebral foramen of the spinal column, with one of the members destined for the right side of the body and the other destined for the left side of the body. Afferent axons bundled in them carry information to the brain from sensory receptors found in areas of the body covered by strips of skin called dermatomes, whereas efferent axons carry information from the brain, innervating muscles and glands, also in a systematic way.

9.4.2 AUTONOMIC NERVOUS SYSTEM

The **autonomic nervous system** regulates glandular activity and the functioning of internal organs. It consists of a **parasympathetic division** and a **sympathetic division**.

PARASYMPATHETIC NERVOUS SYSTEM

The parasympathetic division of the autonomic nervous system is generally involved in activities of rest or recovery that preserve or increase energy levels in the body. These activities include salivation, gastric and intestinal motility, decreased cardiac output and blood pressure, as well as constriction of the pupils and bladder contraction.

SYMPATHETIC NERVOUS SYSTEM

Sympathetic nerves are more widely distributed than parasympathetic nerves and generally (but not exclusively) have the opposite function, in that the sympathetic nervous system is involved in activities that require expenditure of energy. These activities can be triggered by conditions that promote arousal and many of them prepare the organism to respond to situations perceived as dangerous – what is often called the 'fight or flight' response. For example, when you are in actual or perceived danger, your sympathetic nervous system will generate an increase in heart rate and respiration, dilate your pupils and divert blood from the skin and gut to skeletal muscles (so that you can leg it or fight if necessary). The sympathetic nervous system is involved in all kinds of arousal, not just fear, and so you may recognise many of these symptoms, for example when you are physically attracted to someone.

9.5 NEUROANATOMICAL AND NEUROFUNCTIONAL METHODS

The neuroanatomical structures discussed above can be studied in the living brain through a range of methods. Some of these methods can be used to assess the brain anatomically or in a static fashion, while others are useful in assessing its activity or physiology. What is common about all of them and yet quite extraordinary is that the very high detail of analysis that they produce is provided without the need for any surgery.

9.5.1 STRUCTURAL IMAGING TECHNIQUES

COMPUTERISED TOMOGRAPHY

Computerised (axial) tomography (CAT or CT) produces anatomical images of the brain by radiating it with x-ray energy at various angles and measuring the amount of radiation not absorbed. The quantity of non-absorbed energy will depend on how dense the material is. Fluids with low density, like cerebrospinal fluid, absorb little energy and therefore appear black in the output images, whereas dense mate-

> **COMPUTERISED (AXIAL) TOMOGRAPHY** A method of imaging that uses x-rays to form cross sectional or three-dimensional images of structure.

rials, like the skull, absorb much more energy and this makes them appear white. Neuronal-tissue absorption is situated between these two extremes, appearing grey. The images are generated by a computer connected to a cylinder-shaped scanner, which is where the individual would lay down while the procedure takes place. This technology has proven very useful in detecting haemorrhages, strokes, tumours and cortical atrophy. However, its greatest disadvantage is that it involves the use of ionising radiation.

MAGNETIC RESONANCE IMAGING

There is no need for x-rays (i.e. ionising radiation) in **magnetic resonance imaging (MRI)**. The non-toxicity of this method is clearly a plus. Instead, the way MRI works is by placing the individual into a scanner that contains a very large tube-shaped magnet. Subjecting the brain to a very strong magnetic field causes protons (hydrogen nuclei, present, of course, in water) to line up. Once lined up, a radio wave is used to knock them over. When this pulse stops, protons relax back to their original state, emitting radio frequency energy. As the concentration of hydrogen varies along the brain so does the amount of radio frequency energy that is emitted. MRI uses this energy to create very detailed images of the brain.

The magnetic field used to produce these images is so powerful that it can pull a pen into the scanner at more than 100 miles per hour. It can also erase credit card codes in a split of a second (but not your credit card debt!). I guess this is why it is best to leave any ferromagnetic and electromagnetic materials outside the scanner room. Unfortunately, this means, for example, that individuals with pacemakers cannot undergo MRI scanning. MRI also provides clearer images than CT. This better **spatial resolution** can be useful in detecting subtle changes in the brain, such as the local loss of myelin that is characteristic of multiple sclerosis.

> **SPATIAL RESOLUTION** In imaging, the precision with which minute adjacent points or details of an object can be distinguished.

In fact, MRI has the best spatial resolution of current imaging techniques. See Figure 9.7 for an example of an MRI image of the brain of one of the editors (but be polite enough not to mention the lack of frontal lobe tissue!)

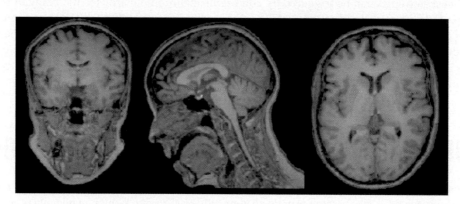

FIGURE 9.7   An MRI image of the brain of one of the editors

9.5.2 FUNCTIONAL IMAGING TECHNIQUES

POSITRON EMISSION TOMOGRAPHY

Positron emission tomography (PET) is used to infer neuronal activity – *not* neuronal anatomy – by measuring metabolic activity or blood flow in the nervous system. Similar to CT, PET involves the use of ionising radiation. However, in this case the radioactivity is emitted by a substance injected into a blood vessel, inhaled as a gas or swallowed in the form of a tablet or capsule.

A common PET technique employs a radioactive form of glucose, which is the primary metabolic fuel of the brain; a type that mimics glucose by travelling to parts of the brain where energy is needed. During its short life, the radioactive substance releases positrons, which are tiny, positively charged radioactive particles. The positrons then break down, emitting gamma waves that are detected by the PET scanner and used to obtain colour-coded images of the brain's activity.

To find out what areas become relatively more or less active as the individual engages in a particular task, the activity recorded during a neutral or rest condition is subtracted from an active condition. This data can be averaged from various trials or participants to highlight areas of genuine activity by reducing background noise. Cognitive functions that can be studied this way include, for example, visual processing, selective attention or spatial memory. For an example and explanation of how PET is used to measure the neurotransmitter (brain chemical) dopamine, see Chapter 10, section 10.5.3. Also the key study by Howes and Kapur (2009) in that chapter shows an example of how PET is used to provide evidence of the role of dopamine in schizophrenia.

FUNCTIONAL MAGNETIC RESONANCE IMAGING

In **functional magnetic resonance imaging (fMRI)** the basic technology is the same as in MRI, but it is employed differently to produce images to represent brain activity. Magnetic fields are used to detect changes in brain metabolism, particularly oxygen use, while the subject is engaged in a particular task. A key assumption in fMRI is that the more active neurons are, the more oxygenated blood they will use. Thus, despite being classed as a neuroimaging technique, fMRI (similar to PET) does not actually measure neuronal activity. It only measures neuronal activity

> **TEMPORAL RESOLUTION** The precision with which an event can be measured in time.

indirectly through the nervous system's need for oxygen. The signal that it records is known as the blood-oxygen-level-dependent (BOLD) signal.

This method is both non-invasive and non-toxic, and similar exclusion criteria apply to those in MRI regarding ferromagnetic and electromagnetic materials. Regarding its **temporal resolution**, it takes seconds to obtain an fMRI

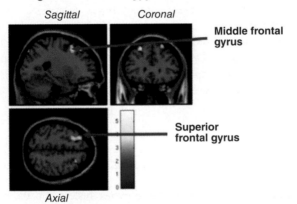

Greater activation during criticism than neutral comments in high and low schizotypy individuals

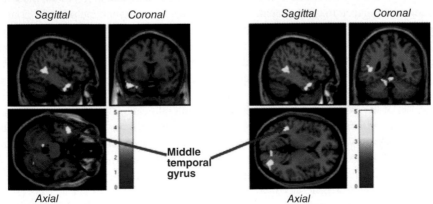

Lesser activation during criticism than neutral comments in high and low schizotypy individuals

FIGURE 9.8   An example of fMRI

image and neuronal responses occur in the order of milliseconds, thus restricting its use in the study of psychological processes. It is faster than PET but slower compared to electroencephalography.

ELECTROENCEPHALOGRAPHY

Brain electrical activity is usually recorded non-invasively from electrodes placed on the scalp in human electroencephalography. The record of this spontaneous activity is referred to as an **electroencephalogram (EEG)**. It results mainly from the sum of **post-synaptic potentials** (see Chapter 10, section 10.3.4 for an explanation of what these are) generated in the underlying cortex and synchronise into what you might think of as brainwaves. These are characterised into four types of wave or rhythm – alpha, beta, theta and delta – each of which has been associated with particular states of consciousness. For example, the alpha rhythm, with a frequency of 8–12 Hz, is predominant in relaxed wakefulness. Beta, with a frequency of 13–30 Hz, is associated with alert wakefulness. The EEG has been particularly useful in the study of sleep and epilepsy.

FIGURE 9.9   An EEG cap with electrodes attached

Recordings of electroencephalographic activity that are not spontaneous but related to a stimulus or response are called **event-related potentials (ERPs)**. They are very difficult, if not impossible, to identify directly in the background EEG because of their relatively tiny size. Fortunately, averaging can be used to try to extract them from the larger background noise that spontaneous EEG is in ERP studies. This process requires the recording of brain electrical activity while the same event is presented many times. Averaging will cancel out or at least attenuate the weight of the random and unrelated electrical activity, leaving in the activity that is actually related to the event. One of the most studied ERPs using this method is P300; a positive brain wave that occurs at about 300 milliseconds from the presentation of a relevant stimulus and has been related to attention and the updating of memory. In general, ERPs (similar to EEG) provide a very high temporal resolution, in the order of milliseconds, but poor spatial resolution because the recording from the scalp means that it is quite difficult to identify their neural generators within the brain.

9.6 CHAPTER SUMMARY

The two divisions of the human nervous system are the central nervous system and the peripheral nervous system. The central nervous system consists of the brain and spinal cord. The brain enables us to think, take decisions, experience emotions and move voluntarily. It consists of the telencephalon, which includes the cerebral cortex, the limbic system and the basal ganglia; the diencephalon, which comprises the thalamus and hypothalamus; the midbrain or mesencephalon, which contains the tectum and tegmentum; the metencephalon, which includes the pons and the cerebellum; and the myelencephalon. The spinal cord, which is divided into segments each representing an area of skin (dermatome), conveys motor commands from the brain to the muscles and transmits sensory information from receptors to the brain.

The brain and spinal cord are the most protected divisions of the nervous system. They are encased in the skull and the spinal column, are covered by three membranes called meninges and are washed in cerebrospinal fluid. The brain is further protected by the blood–brain barrier.

The second division of the human nervous system, the peripheral nervous system, conveys messages to and from the central nervous system. It consists of the somatic nervous system via which we interact with the external environment, and the autonomic nervous system with which we regulate the functioning of internal organs. The somatic nervous system consists of 12 pairs of cranial nerves and 31 pairs of spinal nerves, whereas the autonomic nervous system has a parasympathetic division, which is largely involved in building up energy levels and preserving energy, and a sympathetic division, which is generally involved in expending energy.

Several methods can be used to study the living nervous system, particularly the brain. When the interest lays in assessing the brain structurally, CT or MRI are two of the available options to consider. Alternatively, when what we want is to be able to conduct a functional analysis to find out how the brain is working, PET, fMRI, EEG or ERPs might prove useful. There is no perfect method so the decision on which one to use depends on the questions that need answering.

DISCUSSION QUESTIONS

During this chapter we have examined the structure and function of various brain systems: for example, the limbic system is involved in emotion. How far do you think that knowledge takes us in understanding our behaviour and emotions? What other information would we need to consider? When you feel happy, for example, at one level that could be described as activity in regions of the brain involved in reward, but what other levels of explanation might come into play?

SUGGESTIONS FOR FURTHER READING

Carlson, N.R. (2007). *Physiology of behavior.* Boston, MA: Pearson. Chapter 3. This text uses easily accessible language and explanations.

Haines, D.E. (1991). *Neuroanatomy: an atlas of structures, sections and systems* (3rd edn). Baltimore, MD: Urban & Schwarzenberg. This atlas contains illustrations of brain structures and pictures of brain scans in full colour.

Kolb, B., & Whishaw, I.Q. (2003). *Fundamentals of human neuropsychology.* New York: Worth. Chapter 3. This text is more detailed than most of the introductory biological psychology texts.

Nolte, J. (1999). *The human brain: an introduction to its functional anatomy.* St Louis, MO: Mosby. This whole book is devoted to anatomy and so is far more detailed than the general texts.

Pinel, J.P.J. (2006). *Biopsychology.* Boston, MA: Pearson. Chapter 3. Of the introductory biological psychology texts, this one is particularly good on anatomy.

Rosenzweig, M.R., Breedlove, S.M., & Watson, N.V. (2005). *Biological psychology: an introduction to behavioral and cognitive neuroscience.* Sunderland, MA: Sinauer. Chapter 2. This text is rich on detail.

Witelson, S.F., Kigar, D.L., & Harvey, T. (1999). The exceptional brain of Albert Einstein. *Lancet, 353,* 2149–2153. An interesting article on the great man.

ANSWER TO QUESTION

The hypothalamus is below the thalamus and above the pituitary gland, that is, it is between the two.

Still want more? For links to online resources relevant to this chapter and a quiz to test your understanding, visit the companion website at edge.sagepub.com/banyard2e

10 COMMUNICATION WITHIN THE BRAIN

Lead authors: Rachel R. Horsley and Christine Norman

CHAPTER OUTLINE

10.1 Introduction	176
10.2 Cells in the nervous system	176
10.2.1 Neuronal cells	176
10.2.2 Glial cells	178
10.3 Communication within the neurone	178
10.3.1 Anatomy of the neurone membrane	179
10.3.2 Membrane potentials	179
10.3.3 Action potentials	180
10.3.4 Post-synaptic potentials	182
10.4 Communication between neurones	182
10.4.1 The chemical synapse and pre-synaptic events	183
10.4.2 Receptor activation and post-synaptic events	183
10.4.3 Termination of the signal	184
10.5 Neurotransmitters and drugs	184
10.5.1 Neurotransmitters	184
10.5.2 Drugs and the brain	186
10.5.3 How do we measure neurotransmitter function in the brain?	189
10.6 Chapter summary	190
Discussion questions	191
Suggestions for further reading	191

10.1 INTRODUCTION

When you are awake, your brain generates 25 watts of power – which is enough to power a light bulb. That energy comes from all the activity of sending and receiving messages between the 100 billion cells that make up your brain and there are at least 10 trillion connections between those cells (this is starting to sound like a show presented by Brian Cox!). If you started to count them at one every second it would take you over 300,000 years to get them all. In the previous chapter we took a brief tour of the main structures of the nervous system. Now it is time to examine how information is transported around those systems in order to achieve the various functions.

At its most basic, the brain's purpose is to monitor and respond to the environment. It receives information from its surroundings, processes it and signals the body to respond, but how does the nervous system communicate this information? In this chapter we will find out by examining the processes of communication of information within and between neurones (brain cells). In addition, we will outline the major neurotransmitter (brain chemical) systems and examples of how drugs can produce their effects by acting on the processes involved in these systems.

FRAMING QUESTIONS

- What types of cells make up the nervous system?
- How is information handled within and between cells in the nervous system?
- How do drugs interact with the natural chemistry of the brain?
- How do we measure neurotransmitters in the brain?
- Will you be the same person after reading this chapter?

10.2 CELLS IN THE NERVOUS SYSTEM

The mature brain is composed of approximately 100 billion individual neurones (specialised brain cells). The function of the neurone is to transmit information, in the form of electrochemical signals, around the brain. It receives the signal at one end, conducts the signal along its length and transmits it to the next neurone from the other end. These processes will be described in detail, but first it is helpful to look at the anatomical and functional characteristics of two different types of cell found in the brain: neurones and glial cells.

10.2.1 NEURONAL CELLS

All **neurones** follow the same basic design (see Figure 10.1). The five gross components of a typical neurone are dendrites, soma, axon, axonal branches and synaptic buttons. Here we will consider each of these in turn.

The **soma** is the factory of the neurone and is filled with a potassium-rich salty fluid called **cytoplasm** which contains little structures called **organelles** (little 'organs'). Each type of organelle has a specialised role, but together they provide energy, manufacture parts and form a production line to assemble the parts into completed products.

Overseeing and controlling these processes is the **nucleus**. Within the nucleus are genes consisting of **deoxyribonucleic acid (DNA)**. Their function is to hold the cell history and the basic information to manufacture all the proteins characteristic of that cell. Such proteins are necessary for the formation and maintenance of dendrites, axons, etc.

Dendrites form a major receiving part of neurones: they can be thought of as extensions of the soma (cell body) because the soma itself is also capable of receiving input from other neurones. Dendrites most likely evolved to

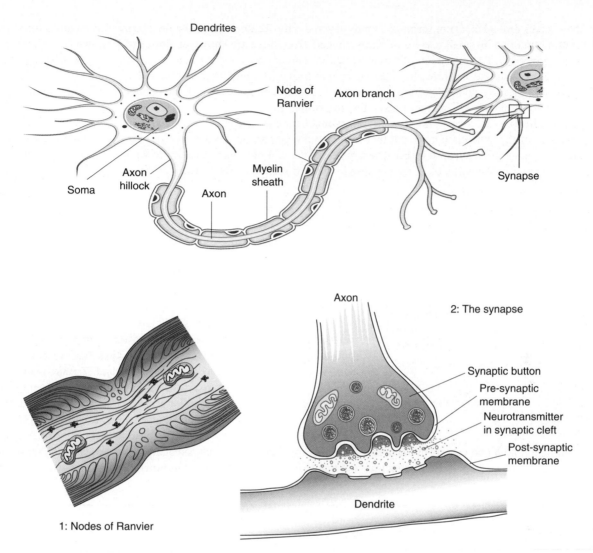

FIGURE 10.1 The neurone. Dendrites are branch-like structures that emanate from the soma (cell body). Their role is to receive information from other neurones in the form of chemical messages, convert these chemical messages into electrical impulses and convey them towards the soma. The axon then conveys electrical information away from the soma towards the axonal branches and synaptic buttons. When the electrical information reaches these, it triggers the release of chemical messages (neurotransmitters) to be received by dendrites on other neurones. Inset 1: Nodes of Ranvier: unmyelinated sections of myelinated axons. Action potentials happen only at these nodes. Inset 2: The synapse: consists of the pre-synaptic membrane, the synaptic cleft and the post-synaptic membrane

(Dr Worm)

increase the receptive surface of the soma, so neurones can receive many more synaptic inputs from other neurones than they could receive to the soma alone. In this way, a given neurone is able to integrate information from many different sources.

The **axon** conducts information in the form of an electrical impulse (**action potential**) that flows away from the soma towards the synaptic buttons. Axons can be very long (in some cases over a metre in length) and can carry impulses at a speed of up to 100 metres per second or more. The greater the diameter of the axon, the faster the electrical impulses will travel along it.

Another very important factor determines the speed with which axons are able to conduct impulses, namely **myelin**. Myelin is insulation around the axon deposited by specific glial cells known as **oligodendrocytes** (in the peripheral nervous system (PNS) the same job is done by **Schwann cells**). Oligodendrocytes send out flat, paddle-like processes which wrap themselves around an axon, forming a many-layered fatty sheath as an insulator. The myelin sheath is interrupted every millimetre or so by small regions of unmyelinated axon: these are known as **nodes of Ranvier** (see Figure 10.1, node of Ravier inset). The insulation of axons has three consequences: saving time, energy and space. It speeds up the conduction of nerve impulses, through a mechanism that does not require large amounts of additional space or energy. A non-myelinated axon would need to have a diameter of several centimetres in order to conduct nerve impulses as rapidly as a myelinated fibre with a diameter of just a few **micrometres**.

Synaptic buttons are located at the end of the **axonal branches** and are the terminal points of the neurone. Together, the membrane of the synaptic button and that of the receiving part on the dendrite or soma of the next cell form the **synapse** (see Figure 10.1, synapse inset). The synapse is the unit of communication from one neurone to the next, but that's jumping ahead. We will look at the synapse in the next section on the transfer of information between neurones.

10.2.2 GLIAL CELLS

Glia means 'glue', and for many years scientists thought that **glial cells** performed the humble task of holding the brain together. However, they are a lot more interesting than that! Over time, it has emerged that they perform a wide variety of vital tasks in the central nervous system (CNS), having roles in providing nutrients, in managing waste, in the formation and maintenance of synapses and even in the transmission of electrical signals.

BLOOD–BRAIN BARRIER Protective barrier between the brain and blood vessels, providing a mechanism by which certain substances are prevented from entering the brain.

PHAGOCYTES Cells which are able to 'swallow' and break down unwanted materials such as pathogens and cell debris.

There are three main types of glial cell in the CNS. You recall oligodendrocytes that provide the myelin for neurons in the CNS. In addition, there are **astrocytes** (so called because they are star shaped). One role of astrocytes is to provide a physical support matrix – so they are the glue – but astrocytes also have a very important role in protecting the brain from toxic substances that can be found in the blood. They achieve this by the formation of the **blood–brain barrier**. Astrocytes send out processes known as glial feet to form a fatty layer of insulation around blood vessels in the brain. This fatty layer means that only substances that are fat soluble can cross into the brain. Some astrocytes are **phagocytes** and maintain the extracellular environment by clearing away debris.

ASIDE

(Bad) Biopsychology joke

How do you know when a glial cell is happy?
When its myelin!

Astrocytes also support neurons in other important ways, such as supplying them with nutrients and enhancing transmission of the signal from one neurone to another by surrounding and isolating synapses so that they work more effectively. **Microglia** are the in-house immune system for the CNS; for example, they cause an inflammatory response when the brain is injured. Like astrocytes, they can also be phagocytes.

10.3 COMMUNICATION WITHIN THE NEURONE

Here we consider how information is handled within individual neurones. The transmission of information along the neurone results from the specialised nature of its structure, and so the anatomy of the neuronal membrane and the physical forces acting upon it will be described. This will show how the electrical state of the neurone membrane is maintained when it is at rest and then what happens when the resting electrical state of the neurone is disturbed. It is this disturbance in electrical state that leads to transmission of a signal by producing an action potential.

All neurones are bounded by a membrane known as the **neurone membrane** (the external boundary to the cell, or 'skin' if you like). This is a crucial structure in determining the electrical state of the neurone. All neurones carry an electrical charge called a membrane potential. Essentially, we are interested in three types of membrane potential in neurones: the resting potential, post-synaptic potentials and the action potential. To understand how the neurone membrane is involved in these potentials it is necessary to look at the anatomy of the membrane itself.

10.3.1 ANATOMY OF THE NEURONE MEMBRANE

The neurone membrane contains tiny pores known as **ion channels**. Three **ions** are central to producing resting and action potentials: two positively charged ions, **sodium** and **potassium**, and one negatively charged ion, **chloride**. Each ion has its own specialised channels, that is, potassium passes through potassium channels, chloride through

> **ION CHANNELS** Pores (formed by proteins) found in cell membranes that allow or restrict the passage of ions in and out of the cell.

chloride channels, and so on. However, sodium is small enough to leak through potassium channels, the consequences of which we shall see later. Ion channels can be in one of two states: open or closed. The resting potential of the neurone membrane is largely determined by ions passing freely in and out of the neurone through permanently open channels. However, other ion channels are gated, that is, they can open and close depending on the state of the neurone membrane.

10.3.2 MEMBRANE POTENTIALS

First, we will examine the processes involved in maintaining the resting **membrane potential** (electrical charge). In a neurone at rest, the inside of the cell is −70 **millivolts (mV)** compared to the outside. This difference in voltage is what constitutes the membrane potential. The inside of the cell is more negative than the outside because the neurone contains protein molecules that are negatively charged and are too large to pass out of the cell. However, the resting potential is also dependent on the passage of ions such as sodium and potassium, in and out of the cell via the ion channels.

> **DYNAMIC EQUILIBRIUM** When two opposing processes operate at equivalent rates.

This movement is constant and results in a **dynamic equilibrium** between positively and negatively charged elements produced by the forces of **diffusion** and **electrostatic pressure** acting on the cell. To understand the processes involved in maintaining resting potentials and in the production of action potentials, we must first understand these physical forces.

Diffusion involves the natural movement of molecules. Here the laws of physics determine that molecules are redistributed from areas of high concentration to areas of low concentration. For example, if there were a lot of sodium ions outside the neurone, and few sodium ions inside the neurone, diffusional forces would move sodium ions into the neurone. Electrostatic pressure is the second force that moves ions around; in this case it is the electrical charge of the ion that is important. All ions have an electrical charge, either positive or negative. Positive and negative (opposite) charges are attracted to each other, whereas the same charge repels. This means that a balance of positive and negative charges will be present inside and outside the neurone. For example, if too many ions with a positive charge are present inside the neurone compared to outside, electrostatic pressure will result in some of the positively charged ions leaving the neurone or some negatively charged ions entering. Figure 10.2 shows how diffusion and electrostatic pressure act on the neurone membrane to maintain the resting potential at −70 mV.

As we saw above, potassium, sodium and chloride ions play a role in maintaining the resting potential at −70 mV. This is because potassium cannot pass entirely freely as some of the ion channels are closed by gates (chloride can cross only half as freely, and sodium 1/20th as freely, but both of these ions play only a small role in determining the resting potential). At the same time as electrostatic pressure is attracting potassium into the cell (because of its positive charge), diffusion is acting in opposition; diffusion demands that potassium be evenly distributed and pulls potassium back out of the cell. Restrictions on free movement result in more potassium inside the cell and more chloride outside, producing the potential difference of −70 mV. The potential difference of −70 mV will remain constant providing ion concentrations remain steady. However, ion concentrations do not remain steady.

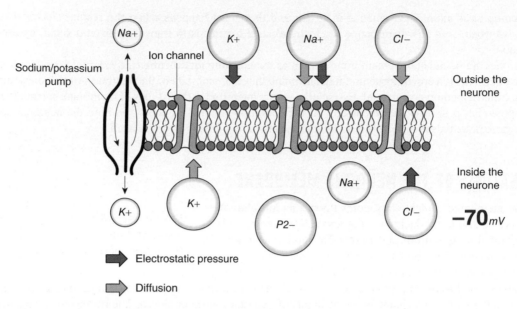

FIGURE 10.2 Physical forces acting on the membrane of the neurone

(Dr Worm)

Remember that we said earlier that sodium is small enough to pass through potassium ion channels? Sodium slowly leaks into the cell due to strong diffusional and electrostatic pressure and forces potassium back out of the cell to compensate. This leads to an imbalance in ion concentrations. In order to deal with this there is a *sodium/potassium pump* in the membrane to pump sodium out of the cell and potassium back in to restore ion concentrations.

10.3.3 ACTION POTENTIALS

The neurone conducts information along its length in the form of a rapid, transient change in voltage. These changes in voltage or potential are a result of the ability of positively and negatively charged ions to move in and out of the neurone quickly. Thus an **action potential** is a discrete region of voltage change that is conducted along the axon from soma to synaptic buttons like a bead sliding down a wire.

> **VOLTAGE-GATED CHANNELS** Ion channels that are sensitive to voltage and open to allow the passage of ions once a certain voltage is reached. For example, potassium channels are voltage-gated, only opening when the voltage inside the membrane becomes positive.

The action potential is originally triggered at the **axon hillock**, located at the point at which the axon leaves the soma (Figure 10.1). Charge builds up here as a result of input from other cells via dendrites and soma. An action potential develops when the input from other cells results in a build-up of charge such that the threshold of excitation is exceeded; this is when the membrane changes from its resting −70 mV to approximately −60 mV.

When the threshold of excitation is reached, it causes sodium channels to open, allowing sodium to enter the cell by diffusion and electrostatic pressure, until the voltage reaches +50 mV. The voltage does not exceed this as it has reached its **equilibrium potential**. Shortly after sodium channels open, so do voltage-gated potassium channels. The voltage at this stage, due to the influx of sodium, is positive and so potassium begins to move out, resulting in restoration of the resting potential. However, potassium ion channels are slow to close, resulting in an 'overshoot' beyond −70 mV. In terms of ion distribution, there is by this stage more potassium outside the neurone and more sodium inside the neurone than in the resting state, so a specialised sodium/potassium pump in the cell membrane helps to restore levels by moving potassium and sodium out of the neurone. This transporting pump expels three sodium ions and takes two potassium ions into the cell, thus gradually increasing the negative voltage inside the cell (as both potassium and sodium ions are positively charged). It is this 'reset' process that results in the action potential only ever travelling in one direction, that is, from axon hillock to synaptic buttons. In principle, action potentials could travel either way on an axon, but the time taken to 'reset' the voltage level within the neurone to −70 mV (the *refractory period*) prevents this. The processes involved in an action potential are summarised in Figure 10.3.

The above account describes the events that underpin the action potential at any given point on the axon. Now we will examine how the action potential moves along an unmyelinated axon. Once the action potential is triggered, sodium moves into the axon at the site of the action potential and the adjacent axon membrane **depolarises** (becomes less negative than −70 mV). The influx of sodium depolarises the membrane because positive charge builds up on the interior of the membrane near open gates and does so until the charge reaches the threshold (−60 mV) for adjacent sodium channels to open. Sodium enters, an action potential occurs there, and so the cycle repeats itself, propagating the action potential along the length of the axon. In other words, the axon potential is regenerated at every point along the entire length of the unmyelinated axon.

In myelinated axons, things are a little different. Recall that the myelin sheaths enveloping axons are interrupted by small regions of axon that are unmyelinated: nodes of Ranvier. Myelin is an insulator, so charge cannot cross the membrane anywhere else on the axon other than at these unmyelinated nodes. Fortunately the **axoplasm** (fluid inside the axon) is a good conductor, so current can be conducted quite rapidly along the interior of the axon between nodes. Positive charge accumulates at a node until the threshold for sodium gates to open is reached and the action potential is regenerated at that node. This provides sufficient charge to be conducted down the interior of the axon to the next node. Thus in myelinated axons, the action potential is regenerated at the nodes of Ranvier.

> **EQUILIBRIUM POTENTIAL** Each type of ion has its own equilibrium potential, which is the voltage at which the net effect of the passage of a given ion in and out of the cell is zero.
>
> **DEPOLARISATION** Movement of the membrane potential towards zero. In the case of the neurone, depolarising from the negative resting potential towards a positive value.

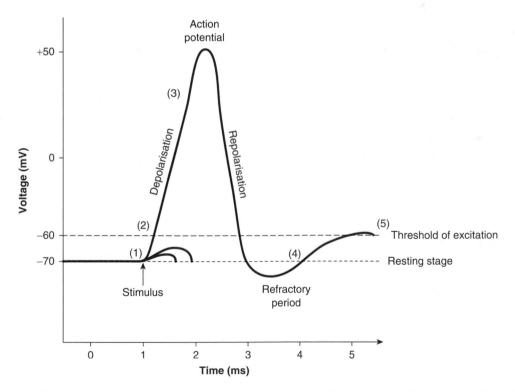

FIGURE 10.3 The five stages of an action potential: (1) electrical charge builds at the axon hillock; (2) threshold of excitation is reached; (3) depolarisation of the membrane occurs (action potential); (4) equilibrium returns with the restoration of the original electrical charge (membrane potential); (5) the message (this change in membrane potential) is triggered in the next section of axon; and so on.

(Dr Worm)

This method is termed *saltatory conduction* and is faster than in unmyelinated axons because the charge does not need to be regenerated at every point; this kind of conduction saves time, energy and space. In that case, why not myelinate the entire length of the axon and do away with nodes of Ranvier altogether? Although axoplasm is a good conductor, the strength of the action potential diminishes with distance; thus nodes are necessary in order that the action potential can regenerate and not 'die out' as it travels along the axon.

Ultimately, the action potential, once it has passed down the axon and along the axonal branches, arrives at the synaptic buttons. Here it triggers the release of a chemical transmitter that diffuses across the gap to affect the next neurone. We will discuss this important process in detail in section 10.4. For now, it is enough to know that when the chemical transmitters reach the next neurone, they produce changes in the electrical state of that neurone known as post-synaptic potentials. It is also useful at this point to introduce some terminology: the neurone sending information (from the synaptic buttons) is the **pre-synaptic neurone** and the one receiving that information is the **post-synaptic neurone**.

10.3.4 POST-SYNAPTIC POTENTIALS

The processes involved in producing an action potential follow the laws of axonal conduction. An action potential either happens or not, depending on whether the threshold of excitation has been reached: there are no half measures. This is the **all-or-none law**. Regeneration of the signal at the nodes of Ranvier also means that action potentials are always the same strength, no matter how long or branching the axon is. This has consequences for indicating the strength of a signal as it cannot rely on differing strengths of the action potential. Instead, it depends on the rate at which action potentials are fired (**rate law**). In the CNS, a single input from a single synapse is not usually sufficient to trigger an action potential in a post-synaptic neurone; instead, the frequency of inputs is added up. This is known as *temporal summation* (number of inputs over time). Additionally, inputs from several pre-synaptic neurones are typically needed and these are also summed. As these come in from various locations, this is known as *spatial summation*. Therefore both frequency and location of inputs determine the size of the signal received by the post-synaptic neurone.

To further complicate matters (hang on in here), inputs from pre-synaptic neurones can have excitatory or inhibitory effects, respectively increasing or decreasing the likelihood that the post-synaptic cell will produce an action potential. These inputs are called **post-synaptic potentials** and congregate at the axon hillock. **Excitatory post-synaptic potentials** (EPSPs) make an action potential more likely because they depolarise the membrane, opening potassium and sodium channels and triggering the axon potential. Importantly, this means that EPSPs (unlike action potentials themselves) are graded: that is, the more excitatory synapses activated, the bigger the total EPSP will be and the more likely it is that an action potential will develop. In principle, **inhibitory post-synaptic potentials** (IPSPs) work in a similar fashion to EPSPs, except that they open chloride and potassium ion channels, not sodium channels. The influx of chloride into the neurone and the efflux of potassium make the neurone more negative (hyperpolarised) than usual and so less likely to fire an action potential, as a greater number and/or rate of excitatory inputs is needed to reach the threshold of excitation.

In summary, what determines whether an action potential will fire is the net activity produced by both excitatory and inhibitory inputs summed over space and time.

10.4 COMMUNICATION BETWEEN NEURONES

So far we have looked at how information travels along a neurone. This section will focus on how information is conveyed from one neurone to another. Charles Sherrington (1897) was the first to introduce the synapse as the mechanism that accounted for communication between individual nerve cells. There are at least 10 trillion synapses (connections) between neurones in the brain, and a given neurone might have several thousand synaptic connections with other neurones. Thus synaptic transmission of information is the critical event that underpins all the 'doings' of the nervous system, from blinking to ballet and beyond.

Until the 1930s it was not known whether communication between neurones in the CNS was electrical or chemical. However, we now know that there are both chemical and electrical synapses distributed throughout the brain (Furshpan

& Potter, 1959). Here we will concentrate on the dominant method of communication between neurones: chemical transmission. However, if you would like to find out more about **electrical synapses**, please see the suggestions for further reading at the end of this chapter.

> **NEUROTRANSMITTERS** Chemical substances released from neurone terminals into the synaptic cleft that can affect the activation of another adjacent neurone.

To understand how information is communicated between neurones with **chemical synapses** we will need to look in greater detail at **pre-synaptic events**, that is, how the chemicals (called **neurotransmitters**) are released, at how the pre-synaptic neurone forms a synapse with a post-synaptic neurone at receptors, and at **post-synaptic events**, that is, how neurotransmitters affect the post-synaptic neurone.

10.4.1 THE CHEMICAL SYNAPSE AND PRE-SYNAPTIC EVENTS

Synapses are junctions between neurones that involve parts of two different neurones being in very close proximity to one another (see Figure 10.1). Usually this involves the synaptic button of a pre-synaptic neurone (the *sending* neurone) synapsing onto a dendrite or soma of the post-synaptic (receiving) neurone. Where two neurones synapse, they do not actually touch; rather, the **pre-synaptic membrane** and **post-synaptic membrane** are separated by a tiny 20-nanometer gap (the **synaptic cleft**). Communication occurs when a chemical (neurotransmitter) is released from the synaptic button of the pre-synaptic neurone into the synaptic cleft, where it diffuses across and activates receptors on the post-synaptic neurone.

The process of neurotransmission is straightforward: the action potential travels down the axon of a neurone to the synaptic button. In the same way that there are sodium and potassium ion channels in the axon membrane, there are voltage-dependent calcium ion channels in the membrane of the synaptic button. As the action potential reaches them, the change in voltage causes voltage-gated calcium ion channels to open. Consequently, calcium rushes into the cell, attracted in by diffusional forces because there is a higher calcium concentration outside the cell than inside. Within the synaptic button, **vesicles** containing neurotransmitter congregate around the release zone and some are already docked onto the membrane via protein bonds. The arrival of calcium into the synaptic button causes the vesicles to open, releasing neurotransmitter into the synaptic cleft by a process called **exocytosis** (see Figure 10.1, synapse insert). During exocytosis, calcium binds with the protein bonds that join the vesicle to the membrane. This binding causes the vesicle membrane to fuse with and so become part of the pre-synaptic button membrane. This results in the vesicle contents (neurotransmitter molecules) being released into the synaptic cleft (Almers, 1990).

10.4.2 RECEPTOR ACTIVATION AND POST-SYNAPTIC EVENTS

Neurones can do one of two things to influence another cell: they can make the other cell more excitable or less excitable (remember excitatory and inhibitory post-synaptic potentials). Using the fast excitatory neurotransmitter **acetylcholine** (ACh) as an example, unsurprisingly the action is to excite the post-synaptic cell. Here, ACh diffuses across the synaptic cleft and attaches to **receptors** (protein molecules: see Figure 10.1, synapse insert) on the post-synaptic membrane. In turn, this causes sodium channels to open in the post-synaptic cell. Note that the sodium ion channels in the post-synaptic membrane are chemically

> **RECEPTORS** Proteins embedded in cell membranes that respond to ligands (specific chemical substances, e.g. neurotransmitters).

gated (opened by ACh rather than a change in membrane potential, as is the case with **voltage-gated channels** involved in the action potential). Sodium enters (due to diffusional and electrostatic pressure) and the post-synaptic cell becomes slightly depolarised. The entrance of sodium produces an EPSP that is then conducted towards the axon hillock, making an action potential *more* likely to be triggered in the post-synaptic cell than before because the cell's electrical charge has become more positive.

Neurotransmitters and receptors are somewhat specific to each other; usually only one type of neurotransmitter can dock onto a given type of receptor (although this is perhaps not always the case). The molecular structure of the neurotransmitter fits into the receptor like a lock and key (Fischer, 1894). As we shall see later, it is the ability of some drugs to 'mimic' the structure of a neurotransmitter in this way that allows them to have psychoactive effects.

Additionally, there are subtypes of each receptor. These all bind the neurotransmitter concerned but are structurally different, resulting in differing effects of binding. When we get on to specific neurotransmitters and drugs you will see that these subtypes are important.

10.4.3 TERMINATION OF THE SIGNAL

A neurotransmitter released into the synaptic cleft will continue to affect the post-synaptic neurone as long as it is present. How then does the process of neurotransmission stop? Excess neurotransmitters must be removed from the synaptic cleft. For most neurotransmitters the signal is terminated by reuptake of the neurotransmitter into the pre-synaptic button it was released from by **reuptake** transporters. These are proteins in the pre-synaptic membrane specific to the neurotransmitter and actively carry molecules of neurotransmitter back into the cell. This process is discrete, controllable and rapid but requires lots of energy. A less common method of termination of the signal is by **enzymatic degradation**. Neurotransmitters are complex chemicals made up of simpler components. Proteins known as enzymes are involved in the processes of both building them from simple proteins (amino acids) and breaking them down again. For ACh, for example, an enzyme known as **acetylcholineresterase** (AChE) cleaves to ACh and breaks it down into its two constituent parts, choline and acetate, rendering it inactive at the receptors.

Once a neurotransmitter has been taken back into the synaptic button it is not wasted, but is recycled into vesicles ready to be used again. Recall that the release of a neurotransmitter from the pre-synaptic membrane involves the membrane of the vesicle becoming part of the pre-synaptic membrane (Figure 10.1, synaptic insert). As a result, the pre-synaptic membrane gets bigger and would continue to do so if it were not for this recycling process. Sections of membrane are pinched off into vesicles within the synaptic button and repackaged with neurotransmitter. This process is conducted by organelles called **cisternae** (Heuser & Reese, 1973).

EXERCISE: VIRTUAL NEUROPHYSIOLOGY

This exercise involves using the Howard Hughes Virtual Neurophysiology Lab. Access this resource at: www.hhmi.org/biointeractive/vlabs/neurophysiology/index.html.

Investigate the nervous system of the leech using the virtual dissection of the leech followed by use of fluorescent dyes to visualise the anatomy of different sensory neurones. Record electrical activities of individual neurones when they are stimulated. Identify the neurones based on their morphology and their response to different mechanical stimuli.

10.5 NEUROTRANSMITTERS AND DRUGS

Neurotransmitters work in circuits or systems and these interact to produce cognition, experience and behaviour. A given neurotransmitter or neurotransmitter circuit may be involved in producing many different psychological and behavioural phenomena. Rather than look here at all of the many, many neurotransmitters in the brain, we will focus on a few examples to equip you with basic knowledge. This will enable you to do further reading on other neurotransmitters. We will then look at examples of how drugs that are active in the brain (*psychoactive*) exert their effects.

10.5.1 NEUROTRANSMITTERS

There are many neurotransmitters in the brain and they are grouped into classes based on their structure. There are four major neurotransmitters in the CNS that are important to know about: acetylcholine (ACh), dopamine (DA), norepinephrine (NE) and serotonin (5-HT). For a brief overview of their roles see Table 10.1 below.

Neurotransmitters are complex chemicals built up from simple proteins by the action of **enzymes**. The basic building blocks that make up neurotransmitters are called **precursors** and are obtained from our diet in the form of essential amino acids. For example, the neurotransmitter serotonin is made from the precursor tryptophan, an amino acid found in bananas, among other foods (which is why bananas allegedly help recovery from a hangover by aiding the replacement of depleted serotonin). These precursors are acted upon by particular enzymes in the body, which lead to addition and/or subtraction of molecular components in a step-by-step fashion. For example, the neurotransmitters dopamine and norepinephrine are built from the amino acid tyrosine (obtained from food) that is converted to L-DOPA by an enzyme called tyrosine hydroxylase. This L-DOPA is converted to dopamine by the enzyme DOPA decarboxylase. Dopamine is a neurotransmitter in its own right, but if it is in the presence of an enzyme called dopamine β-hydroxylase it can be converted into norepinephrine.

> **LIPIDS** Substances that are fat soluble.

> **PRECURSOR** In biochemistry, a substance from which more complex compounds are made.

Neurotransmitters work in systems made up of a collection of neurones (although some neurones contain more than one neurotransmitter). Typically, the cell bodies congregate together into what are called nuclei. These are often situated in a lower part the brain, from where the axons project forward (in a bundle) to terminate onto other structures they connect with (synapse onto).

Again, let's look at the neurotransmitter dopamine as an example of this. There are four dopaminergic systems with differing functions, but we will look at one of them, the nigro-striatal system, to illustrate how neurotransmitter systems are organised (see Figure 10.4). The nigro-striatal system starts with the nuclei of cell bodies in an area of the brain called the substantia nigra (in the midbrain). The bundle of axons project forward as part of a structure made up of many axons called the medial forebrain bundle and synapse onto the dorsal striatum (made up of two brain regions, the caudate and putamen). So when action potentials are activated in the substantia nigra the signal passes down the axons to the dorsal striatum, where dopamine is released and activates the dorsal striatum.

This particular dopaminergic system is involved in the control of movement. If it is damaged, too little dopamine gets through to the dorsal striatum and movement is impaired. This is what happens in the disease known as *Parkinson's disease*, resulting in muscular rigidity, tremors, and problems with balance and with the initiation of

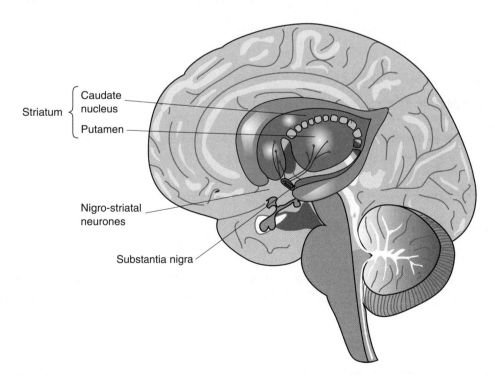

FIGURE 10.4   The anatomy of the nigro-striatal system

(Dr Worm)

KEY RESEARCHER Arvid Carlsson

FIGURE 10.5   Arvid Carlsson

Professor Arvid Carlsson (born 1923) has had an extensive and illustrious career in biological science, and in particular in the field of pharmacology, for which he is most well known. Carlsson (with Paul Greengard and Eric Kandel) received the Nobel Prize in Physiology or Medicine in 2000 for ground-breaking work on signal transduction in the nervous system.

Carlsson's famous discovery was that dopamine is an active neurotransmitter substance in its own right; it had been thought that dopamine was a precursor (building block) for another neurotransmitter, norepinephrine. He then went on to discover the role of dopamine in movement. Reducing dopamine in animals disrupted motor control, and when Carlsson restored dopamine levels by administering a dopamine precursor, control of movement returned.

Carlsson's findings have had far-reaching implications for our understanding of certain neuropsychiatric disorders. The discovery that dopamine plays a key role in movement led to the development already discussed of L-DOPA as a treatment for Parkinson's disease. The startling effects of dopamine depletion and reinstatement, as discovered by Carlsson in animals, are dramatically illustrated in humans in the book *Awakenings* by Oliver Sacks (1973). This is an account of his treatment of survivors of a disease called encephalitic lethargica who 'awake' from their catatonic state when treated with L-DOPA. It was later made into a film of the same name, starring Robin Williams as Sachs and Robert De Niro as one of his patients – well worth a watch but be warned about the sad ending.

ASIDE

Neurotransmitters that 'walk through walls'

Soluble gases are one of the most unusual transmitter substances because they can 'walk through walls'. Rather than travelling across synapses in the regular way, they pass from one cell to another as soon as they are produced, activate an enzyme for a second messenger, then degrade immediately.

movement. Interestingly, Parkinson's disease has been a focus of research using *stem cells* (undifferentiated cells that are special because they have the potential to develop into any type of cell depending on the environment that they are in). Parkinson's disease is an ideal candidate for stem cell therapy because the deficiency is specific (dopaminergic cells are lost) and discrete (in a small area, the substantia nigra) compared to the complex and widespread loss in most other brain diseases. Stem cells have been implanted into the substantia nigra of Parkinsonian patients in an attempt to regenerate dopaminergic cells and so restore normal function, but to date with limited success.

10.5.2 DRUGS AND THE BRAIN

Until now we have looked only at the process of synaptic transmission involving naturally occurring substances originating within the body (**endogenous** substances), like neurotransmitters. Now we will look at how substances from outside the body (**exogenous** substances), such as **drugs**, affect the nervous system.

Any substance which binds to a receptor is a **ligand**. Ligands therefore include both endogenous neurotransmitters and exogenous drugs that 'mimic' the structure of a certain neurotransmitter. Drugs can have functionally **agonist** effects (facilitating the effects of neu-

> **LIGAND** Any substance (e.g. neurotransmitter or drug) with the capacity to bind to a receptor.

rotransmitters on the post-synaptic neurone) or can have functionally **antagonist** effects (inhibiting the effects of neurotransmitters on the post-synaptic neurone). There are many ways that agonist and antagonist effects can be produced by drugs. Recall the processes involved in synaptic transmission (Figure 10.1, synapse insert); drugs can affect any of the steps involved. Table 10.1 has some examples of how drugs exert their effects.

A drug could prevent or facilitate the synthesis of neurotransmitters, causing more or less to be produced. For example, a drug that has an agonist effect at this stage is L-DOPA, a treatment for Parkinson's disease. You recall that Parkinson's disease is a result of depleted dopamine. L-DOPA improves the condition because it is a precursor (building block) of dopamine. Its presence facilitates the production of dopamine and so treats the symptoms. Interestingly, if you have high levels of dopamine (in a brain system called the mesolimbic system) this has been found to be related to psychiatric conditions such as schizophrenia (see below and the key study). The antipsychotic drugs used to reduce the symptoms of these conditions block the transmission of dopamine and sometimes create the symptoms of Parkinson's disease.

Neurotransmitter release itself might be affected by a drug. Remember, an action potential is necessary to trigger neurotransmitter release, so a drug could interfere with the action potential directly, for example, by affecting ions like sodium. The infamous Japanese delicacy, pufferfish, contains a poison that does exactly that. The flesh itself is safe to eat, but within the liver is a compound called tetrodotoxin that binds to the sodium channels on neurones in muscles. This prevents the channels from opening and so prevents action potentials, resulting in paralysis of muscles – to deadly effect as respiratory muscles are affected. No wonder chefs need a licence to prepare pufferfish!

Alternatively, drugs could affect neurotransmitter release by helping or hindering the release of neurotransmitters (exocytosis). For example, *botox* (botulinum toxin), the compound well loved by Hollywood stars for its ability to immobilise facial muscles (although expressing that delight is difficult for them), works by preventing vesicular

TABLE 10.1 Major neurotransmitters, their function in the brain and examples of drug effects

| NEUROTRANSMITTER | | | EXAMPLES OF DRUGS | | |
NEUROTRANSMITTER	FUNCTION	DRUG	MECHANISM	EFFECT
Acetylcholine (ACh)	Role in REM sleep, attention, learning and memory	Curare	Post-synaptic receptor blocker (of nicotinic type of ACh receptor)	Antagonist
		Black widow venom	Stimulates release of ACh	Agonist
Dopamine (DA)	Role in movement, memory, planning, problem solving, emotion, attention, reinforcement and motivation	Chlorpromazine (antipsychotic) Amphetamine	Post-synaptic receptor blocker (of D2 type of receptor) Reverses action of reuptake transporter	Antagonist Agonist
Serotonin (5-HT)	Role in sleep, mood, sex, anxiety, feeding, pain	Ritanserin (antipsychotic, but also used for insomnia)	Post-synaptic receptor blocker (of 5-HT 2 type of receptor)	Antagonist
		Fluoxetine (Prozac)	Reuptake transporter blocker	Agonist
Norepinephrine (NE)	Role in attentional focus, mood, arousal and sexual behaviour	Clonidine (used to treat Tourette syndrome)	Stimulates pre-synaptic autoreceptor resulting in feedback to slow down NE production	Antagonist
		Venlafaxine (antidepressant)	Reuptake transporter blocker	Agonist

KEY STUDY: HENRI LABORIT AND THE DISCOVERY OF ANTIPSYCHOTICS

Pena Trevino, R. (1955). Introduction of Dr Henri Laborit from France at the meeting of the Academy on 8 March 1955. *Cirugia y Cirujanos*, *23*(4), 181–182.

Schizophrenia, characterised by disordered thought, emotions and perception, is treated largely by the use of antipsychotic drugs. These drugs exert their effect predominantly by decreasing dopamine transmission in a dopaminergic system known as the mesolimbic system. The drugs were first discovered by surgeon Henri Laborit in 1952, who noted that a drug he used to reduce anxiety prior to surgery produced what he described as indifference and relaxation but without loss of consciousness. Laborit's suggestion that it might be useful for psychiatric disorders was revolutionary at the time and not well received, but persistence paid off. Eventually the drug, chlorpromazine, was tried out on any and all psychiatric disorders (in the days before ethics committees). It had little effect on most disorders but a profound effect on symptoms of schizophrenia. So effective was this drug that many other similar compounds followed; antipsychotics became the most common treatment for schizophrenia, and remain so today.

Antipsychotics have been through several generations of drug type. The most recent third generation includes exciting 'smart' drugs that can alter the level of dopamine turnover either up or down depending on the basal level and so reduce side-effects to a minimum.

Whatever the controversies around drug treatments for psychiatric disorders (now there's a fascinating discussion), there is no doubt that this discovery revolutionised (for good or ill) the way that people with schizophrenia were treated from then on, resulting in many people being allowed out of psychiatric institutes and having a far-reaching influence on the field of psychiatry.

release of ACh from the pre-synaptic button. Remember that ACh signals contraction of skeletal muscles and so prevention of release will result in inability to move muscles.

Another stage of neurotransmission that could be affected by drugs relates to events that take place within the synaptic cleft. Drugs binding to receptors on the post-synaptic membrane can agonise or antagonise. An agonist here binds to the post-synaptic receptor if its structure is close enough to that of the neurotransmitter to 'fool' the receptor (remember the lock and key analogy) and activate it as the neurotransmitter itself would. Alternatively, an antagonist might fit the receptor but not activate it, thus blocking up the receptor to prevent the neurotransmitter from binding and so from activating it. To further the key analogy, it's like having a key that fits into the lock but won't turn. An example of this is antipsychotic drugs used to treat **schizophrenia** (see the key study by Howes and Kapur later in this chapter). Almost without exception, antipsychotics are dopamine antagonists that block the D2 receptor (a specific type of dopamine receptor), thus preventing naturally produced dopamine from binding to these sites and reducing dopamine transmission.

The final stage of neurotransmission that drugs could affect is the termination of the signal. Here the processes of reuptake or enzymatic degradation could be facilitated or inhibited. If reuptake of excess neurotransmitters was prevented (e.g. because a drug was blocking reuptake transporters), the neurotransmitter would remain in the synaptic cleft and continue to affect the post-synaptic neurone. This would be an agonist effect. Prozac, the well-known treatment for depression, works in this way by blocking serotonin reuptake transporters (hence it is known as a selective

EXERCISE: MOUSE PARTY

Click on the link to go to a cartoon world where mice are taking drugs. There select a mouse and its drug of choice and observe how the drug is interacting at the synapse to produce its effects.

http://learn.genetics.utah.edu/content/addiction/drugs/mouse.html

serotonin reuptake inhibitor, or SSRI). Interestingly, amphetamines put the reuptake transporters into reverse, moving dopamine back out of the synaptic button via the reuptake transporters and so having an agonistic effect. It should be noted that many drugs have effects at more than one of these stages or on more than one neurotransmitter at once.

10.5.3 HOW DO WE MEASURE NEUROTRANSMITTER FUNCTION IN THE BRAIN?

Measuring neurotransmitters in the brain of humans is a difficult task because we don't have imaging techniques that can pick up most neurotransmitters. The most commonly used imaging technique, functional magnetic resonance imaging (fMRI, see Chapter 9, section 9.5 for a reminder), will tell us which brain regions are active but not which neurotransmitter is involved. PET (again, see section 9.5 for an explanation of the technique) can be used to track some neurotransmitters but not all, and so its use is limited. PET can be used to look at dopamine transmission by using radio-labelled L-DOPA. As already discussed, L-DOPA is one of the building blocks that the brain uses to make dopamine. If radioactive L-DOPA is used to make dopamine, it results in radio-labelled dopamine, enabling dopamine activity to be seen and measured by PET. There are technical problems that limit its usefulness, for example, differences between some dopamine receptor types cannot be distinguished (e.g. D2 and D3) and some radio labels pick up serotonin as well as dopamine. However, PET has been used successfully to look at dopamine transmission (see the key study by Howes & Kapur, 2009).

In animals there is a technique to measure neurotransmitters that is much more versatile and reliable, called **microdialysis**. This involves a very fine probe (a few millimeters wide) being implanted into the brain area of interest. The probe has an outer **semi permeable membrane**, that is one that only allows certain-sized molecules to pass in and out of it. It has an inlet tube and an outlet tube so that an artificial version of cerebrospinal fluid (aCSF) can be pumped through and collected at the other end. As the aCSF passes slowly through the probe, molecules of neurotransmitters in the CSF of the brain region being measured pass through the semi permeable membrane into the aCSF and this fluid is collected. Some of the neurotransmitter released in synapses makes its way to the extracellular CSF and so can be collected and measured in this way. The fluid collected is analysed using a chemical technique called high-performance liquid chromatography (HPLC) that measures the amount of neurotransmitter in the fluid. Microdialysis with HPLC can be used to measure most neurotransmitters and is specific to very small areas of the brain, so it is a very useful technique. For example, the amount of dopamine released into the ventral striatum can be compared in rats given amphetamine versus those given a saline (control) injection. Amphetamine increases dopamine release as much as 150–300 fold (Wise, 2004).

KEY STUDY: THE DOPAMINE THEORY OF SCHIZOPHRENIA

Howes, O.D., & Kapur, S. (2009). The dopamine hypothesis of schizophrenia: version III – the final common pathway. *Schizophrenia Bulletin*, *35*(3), 549–562.

The dominant theory of the biological underpinnings of schizophrenia has been the dopamine hypothesis, proposing (in its simplest form) too much dopamine activity in a neural circuit called the mesolimbic system. Based primarily of the effectiveness of antipsychotic drugs (which you will remember are dopamine antagonists) in reducing the strength of some symptoms of schizophrenia, such as hallucinations and delusions, it has had several incarnations over the last 50 or so years. Beginning with a simple idea of 'too much dopamine' (van Rossum, 1966), it was later developed to specify the dysfunction as too much dopamine activity in mesolimbic areas but too little in the prefrontal cortex (Davies, 1991). For many years the dopamine hypothesis was out of fashion, being challenged by competing neurotransmitter theories, such as serotonin or glutamate dysfunction, fuelled by evidence that the second generation of antipsychotic drugs affected more neurotransmitters than just dopamine. However, one of its champions, Shitij Kapur, has recently proposed a refined version of the dopamine hypothesis, backed by recent convincing evidence that has given the dopamine hypothesis renewed strength.

(Continued)

(Continued)

In this paper outlining the theory, Kapur and colleagues have drawn together the various theories of the causes (etiology) of schizophrenia, such as genetic predisposition, drug abuse and physical or psychological trauma, which they term 'hits' (you have to have your own terms if you want to have your own theory). The theory states that one or a combination of these 'hits' produces too much dopamine activity in the mesolimbic system, initially as a result of too many post-synaptic receptors (see Figure 10.1 for a reminder of the synapse), and then later as a result of too much dopamine production within the synaptic button itself, which results in increased dopamine release. The paper provides strong support for this aspect of the theory in the form of positron emission tomography (PET) imaging evidence. PET scanning (described in Chapter 9, section 9.5.2) can be used to radio label dopamine so that its activity shows up on a scan of the brain. Howes and Kapur showed that in seven of the nine studies that have been conducted on people with schizophrenia there was an increased amount of dopamine activity. Importantly for this theory, the response to a dose of amphetamine was higher in those with schizophrenia compared to the control group. This is good evidence of an increase of pre-synaptic dopamine levels because, if you remember from the earlier discussion (section 10.5.2), amphetamine reverses the dopamine transporters on the (pre-synaptic) membrane of the synaptic button causing dopamine to be released into the synapse. The more dopamine present in the synaptic button, the more will be available to be released after taking amphetamine.

Howes and Kapur are specific in the scope of the theory in that they propose that this increase in dopamine transmission produces the positive symptoms of schizophrenia (hallucinations, delusions etc.) rather than all the symptoms. Perhaps the most unique aspect of their version of the dopamine hypothesis is that it proposes that this increase in dopamine results in something called 'aberrant salience'. Mesolimbic dopamine is known to play a role in signalling the salience (relevance) of stimuli in the environment. Stimuli are usually salient if they themselves are useful for survival (food, warmth etc.) or if they predict these, for example in conditioning where a clicker predicts food reward. According to the aberrant salience theory, overactivity of this dopamine system means that it is signalling stimuli as salient when they are not, resulting in associations being made between stimuli that are not usually connected together. This is in fact a well recognised symptom of schizophrenia and is usually called 'loosening of associations'.

The theory suggests that when stimuli that aren't usually salient become so, the person has to make sense of why the stimuli are particularly attention-grabbing and this may lead to them creating 'stories' to make sense of it. These might lead to delusions, for example a delusion of reference where an individual begins to see everything as signalling to them (e.g. someone touching their nose on the other side of the street is actually signalling to them). This might develop into a delusion that they are being monitored or are part of a secret group. As regards hallucinations, the aberrant salience theory suggests that if one's own voice during thinking has increased salience, maybe it seems more powerful and less like one's own thoughts. This might eventually lead to it being thought of as a different voice. The increased salience attributed to that voice might mean it becomes very intrusive and difficult to ignore. This aspect of the hypothesis is difficult to evidence. There is evidence of aberrant salience in schizophrenia in cognitive tests, for example during conditioning (Gray, 1995), but it is difficult, if not impossible, to demonstrate that this can produce hallucinations and delusions. So at present this aspect remains an interesting theory. However, the other aspects of this theory, based on recent evidence, give the dopamine hypothesis a strength it has previously lacked.

10.6 CHAPTER SUMMARY

Neurones have three basic functions: sending sensory information to the brain, sending motor commands from the brain, and shuttling information around the brain itself. Information is handled *within* the neurone as electrical charges triggered by neurotransmitters received from other (pre-synaptic) neurones. Any resulting action potential (a small region of voltage change that exists as a result of the rapid movement of ions in and out of the neurone) travels down the axon to the synaptic buttons, where it triggers the release of neurotransmitters which in turn produce changes in electrical charge on the post-synaptic neurone.

Communication *between* neurones occurs when a neurotransmitter is released from the synaptic button of the pre-synaptic neurone into the synaptic cleft, where it diffuses across and binds to receptors on the post-synaptic neurone. The signal, for most neurotransmitters, is terminated by reuptake of the neurotransmitter into the pre-synaptic neurone.

Neurotransmitters work in circuits or systems and these interact to produce cognition, experience and behaviour. Drugs can affect the functioning of neurones by 'mimicking' the structure of neurotransmitters, and can have agonist or antagonist effects at any of the various stages of synaptic transmission to produce change.

DISCUSSION QUESTIONS

Are you the same person after reading this chapter? Neurones undergo changes as a consequence of being activated by our experiences; synaptic connections can be formed or 'die away', or receptor numbers can increase or decrease. This enables our brains to remain 'plastic' (basically, the capacity of the nervous system to change in response to events). This ability to change raises an interesting philosophical debate. In his inspiring book *Into the silent lands*, Paul Broks (2004) retells the story of a philosophical debate that centres on the nature of identity. In the story it is possible to teleport, which is achieved by reassembling an exact copy of the person at their desired location out of locally available materials, while simultaneously destroying the 'original'. There is a law against duplicates, so destruction of one duplicate must happen. Broks tells the tale of a man whose 'original' is not destroyed due to a malfunction in the teleportation device. The question is, which duplicate should be destroyed: the 'copy' or the 'original'? Moreover, at what point do the experiences (and consequent structure and function of their brains) of the two duplicates diverge such that they are no longer copies of one another and are essentially different people?

Antipsychotic drugs are the predominant treatment for those with a diagnosis of schizophrenia. As we have read, they affect the symptoms of schizophrenia by changing dopamine levels within the meso cortico limbic system of the brain. Does this suggest, then, that schizophrenia is a biological disorder? A brain disease?

SUGGESTIONS FOR FURTHER READING

Breedlove, S.M., & Watson, N.V. (2013). *Biological psychology: an introduction to behavioral, cognitive, and clinical neuroscience.* Sunderland, MA: Sinauer. This text is strong in detail on communication within the neurone.

Carlson, N.R. (2013). *Physiology of behaviour.* Boston, MA: Pearson. A basic biological psychology text written in a very accessible style. This text is strong in detail on neurotransmitters and drugs.

Grilly, D.M., & Salamone, J. (2012). *Drugs, brain and behavior.* Boston, MA: Pearson. This text offers more depth on drug action than the general biological psychology texts and is particularly good for detail on psychiatric drugs.

McKim, W.A., & Hancock, S.D. (2012). *Drugs and behavior: an introduction to behavioral pharmacology.* London: Prentice Hall. This text provides more depth than the general biological psychology texts and has some good introductory chapters on the basics.

Shepherd, G.M. (1991). *Foundations of the neuronal doctrine.* Oxford: Oxford University Press. An interesting text providing the history of the discovery of the anatomy and function of neurones. It offers insight into the scientific process and describes electrical synaptic transmission (alluded to in this chapter).

Still want more? For links to online resources relevant to this chapter and a quiz to test your understanding, visit the companion website at edge.sagepub.com/banyard2e

11 BRAIN AND BEHAVIOUR: SEX DIFFERENCES

Lead authors: Mark J.T. Sergeant, Antonio Castro and Gary Jones

CHAPTER OUTLINE

11.1 Introduction	194
11.2 The process of sexual differentiation	195
11.2.1 Genetic sexual differentiation	195
11.2.2 Organisational hormones	195
11.2.3 Atypicality during sexual differentiation	197
11.3 Sex differences	200
11.3.1 Sex differences in the brain	200
11.3.2 Puberty	201
11.3.3 Cognitive and behavioural sex differences	201
11.4 Sexual orientation	202
11.4.1 The search for gay genes	202
11.4.2 The role of organisational hormones	203
11.4.3 Sexual orientation and the brain	204
11.4.4 Sexual orientation and behaviour	205
11.5 Chapter summary	206
Discussion questions	206
Suggestions for further reading	207

11.1 INTRODUCTION

When describing another person, one of the first things likely to be mentioned is whether they are male or female. This is not only because males and females tend to look different, but also because we tend to make a number of assumptions about an individual's temperament and behaviour based on their sex. As our perception of what it means to be male and female has varied over time, and varies enormously between cultures, some have assumed that any differences between the sexes are socially created rather than **innate**. There are some obvious exceptions to this however, such as the ability of females to become pregnant and bear children.

Yet what do we mean by the term *sex*? What are the differences between males and females? And what is the difference between sex and *gender*? This chapter will examine these questions, looking in particular at how differences between males and females begin at the genetic level, at the process of sexual differentiation in the womb, and at sex differences in the brain and behaviour. In doing so, the chapter builds on the base of the biological knowledge established in the previous two chapters. We will also examine what happens when individuals undergo an atypical process of sexual differentiation and provide an overview of research into the biological basis for an individual's sexual orientation.

FRAMING QUESTIONS

- What makes someone male or female?
- What is the difference between sex and gender?
- Are males really better than females at maths?
- What are intersex conditions?
- Is there a biological basis to homosexuality?
- What are the implications of any biological basis to homosexuality?

ASIDE

Sex or gender?

The terms 'sex' and 'gender' are not interchangeable. 'Sex' refers to the biological characteristics used to differentiate individuals and identify them as either male or female. Sex can be measured by examining an individual's chromosomes (whether they possess XY or XX sex chromosomes), gonads (whether they possess testes or ovaries) and external reproductive organs (whether they possess a penis and testes or a vagina).

'Gender' refers to the sociocultural characteristics that are associated with a biological sex. The concept of gender is frequently subdivided into (1) gender identity and (2) gender role. Gender identity refers to an individual's own perception of whether they are male or female. Usually this is concordant with an individual's sex chromosomes and reproductive organs, but transsexual individuals, for example, feel that their sense of gender identity is incompatible with their biological sex. Gender role refers to the behaviours that society deems are appropriate or acceptable to be expressed by a particular sex, for example mowing the lawn versus changing nappies (no prizes for guessing which role is attached to which gender).

With sex, we refer to individuals as being male or female, whereas with gender, we talk about people being masculine or feminine.

11.2 THE PROCESS OF SEXUAL DIFFERENTIATION

11.2.1 GENETIC SEXUAL DIFFERENTIATION

Human cells contain 46 **chromosomes** arranged into 23 pairs. Twenty-two of these pairs of chromosomes are autosomes (non-sex chromosomes), and do not differ between males and females. They are not significantly involved in the process of sexual differentiation, which is the process by which an individual begins to develop into either a male or a female.

The final pair of chromosomes, known as sex chromosomes, differs between males and females. The sperm (male reproductive cell) and the egg (female reproductive cell) both only contain one copy of the 23 chromosome pairs common to humans. Once the sperm reaches the nucleus of the egg they fuse together to form a complete set of 23 chromosomal pairs (fertilisation).

In humans, eggs always contain an X sex chromosome while sperm can potentially carry either an X or a Y sex chromosome. If the sperm contains an X sex chromosome the embryo will eventually develop into a female, as two X chromosomes (XX) are present. If the sperm contains a Y sex chromosome the embryo will develop into a male, as X and Y chromosomes (XY) are present.

> **HORMONES** From the Greek *horman*, 'to excite' or 'impetus'. Hormones are chemical messengers, released by the endocrine system, that are carried to other areas of the body through the bloodstream. Once they have reached a specific area of the body, they bind to certain receptor sites within tissues or organs and induce physiological change. Hormones have powerful effects on physiology and behaviour.

11.2.2 ORGANISATIONAL HORMONES

After the two sex chromosomes have combined during fertilisation, the process of prenatal sexual differentiation begins (see Figure 11.1). Following this, the egg begins to divide, first becoming a two-celled organism, then a four-celled organism, then an eight-celled organism, and so on. After 28 days, the embryo has divided numerous times and reached a length of approximately 1 cm.

Twins occur either when a fertilised egg divides into two identical copies (identical or *monozygotic twins*, who share 100% of their genes) or when two different eggs are fertilised by two different sperm (fraternal or *dizygotic twins*, who share 50% of their genes).

For up to 28 days after conception, there is no discernible difference between a male and a female foetus: the foetus remains in an undifferentiated state. By the seventh week after conception, some basic structures have emerged in the foetus, which are the precursors to either the male or the female reproductive systems. The foetus possesses gonads and undeveloped external genitalia (the urethral fold, the genital swelling and the genital tubercle). At this time both male and female foetuses also possess two sets of ducts – the Müllerian ducts and the Wolffian ducts.

In females, the gonads develop into the ovaries and the Müllerian ducts develop into parts of the female reproductive system (the uterus, inner vagina and fallopian tubes, specifically). The urethral fold develops into the inner labia, the genital swellings develop into the outer labia and the genital tubercle develops into the clitoris. In females, the Wolffian ducts do not develop and are reabsorbed into the foetus.

Among males, this development is different. The short arm of the Y chromosome contains the **SRY gene**. If the foetus possesses a Y chromosome, the undifferentiated gonads do not develop into ovaries but instead begin to produce the SRY protein, causing the gonads to develop into testes. The testes then begin to secrete the anti-Müllerian hormone that causes the Müllerian ducts to cease development and be reabsorbed into the body (Vainio et al., 1999). The testes also begin to produce

> **SRY GENE** The 'sex determining region of the Y chromosome' (Haqq et al., 1994). This is part of a group of genes referred to as testes determining factor (TDF).

testosterone, which masculinises the foetus, and the Wolffian ducts begin to develop into parts of the male reproductive system (the ejaculatory duct, vas deferens and epididymis). Testosterone also causes the tissue around the urethra to form into the prostate gland. **Dihydrotestosterone** causes the external genitals to develop; the urethral fold develops into the shaft of the penis, the genital swellings develop into the scrotum and the genital tubercle develops into the glans of the penis.

In many instances, male and female reproductive organs are homologous, which means that they develop from the same embryonic tissue. The timing of this development, however, differs between males and females. The

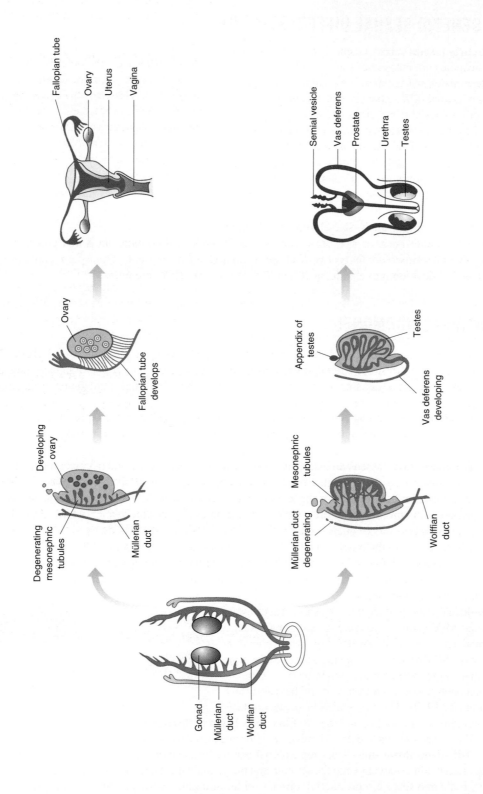

FIGURE 11.1 Development of the male and female reproductive organs (adapted from www.medscape.com)

(Dr Worm)

undifferentiated gonads develop into testes around seven weeks after conception, while the ovaries develop slightly later, around week 13 or 14. Approximately 16 weeks after conception, the external genitals of the foetus clearly indicate its sex.

At this point it is worth highlighting that two kinds of hormones are discussed in this chapter. The first kind, involved in foetal development (such as testosterone and dihydrotestosterone), are referred to as **organisational hormones**. These hormones affect the structure of the developing foetal brain and their effects are set in place for life. The other types of hormone are referred to as **activational hormones**. These hormones can vary enormously over the course of an individual's lifespan and are linked to a variety of behaviours. For example, the physiological changes that individuals go through at puberty have been linked to a sudden surge in activational hormone levels (see section 11.3.2).

TESTOSTERONE The primary type of androgen, involved in the development of male characteristics and sexual functioning.

DIHYDROTESTOSTERONE An androgen converted from testosterone by the actions of the enzyme 5-alpha reductase.

ANDROGEN A class of male sex hormones responsible for the maintenance and development of male characteristics.

11.2.3 ATYPICALITY DURING SEXUAL DIFFERENTIATION

Although the process of sexual differentiation *usually* causes the development of either male-typical or female-typical characteristics, for some individuals this process is not so straightforward. Individuals who are born with both male and female sexual characteristics have historically been labelled **hermaphrodites**. They have both ovarian and testicular tissue. Such individuals are extremely uncommon (Blackless et al., 2000). However, much more common, occurring in approximately one in 2,000 births, are individuals known as **pseudo-hermaphrodites** (Colapinto, 2000). These individuals have gonads that are consistent with their sex chromosomes (ovaries in females and testes in males) but have ambiguous internal and external genitalia.

HERMAPHRODITE A term derived from Hermaphroditus, a Greek deity believed to possess both male and female attributes. Such individuals possess both testicular and ovarian tissue.

PSEUDOHERMAPHRODITES These individuals have gonads that are consistent with their sex chromosomes (ovaries in females and testes in males) but have ambiguous internal and external genitalia.

The term 'hermaphrodite' has fallen out of favour in recent years, and is being replaced by a newer term **intersex**, which refers to an individual who has undergone atypical sexual differentiation and has external genitalia that appear to be between those of a typical female and a typical male (Morris, Jordan, & Breedlove, 2004). Intersex conditions can result from either atypicality in the combination of sex chromosomes an individual receives, or from some form of atypicality in the effects of organisational hormones. We will look at these in turn. By studying the atypical development of intersex individuals we gain greater insight into how the process of sexual differentiation functions.

EXERCISE: BEYOND MALE AND FEMALE

From 2013 onwards, children born in Germany with intersex conditions will no longer have to be registered as male or female. Instead, their parents can leave the category of sex blank on their birth certificates, indicating an 'indeterminate sex'. Do some investigating to identify which other countries also allow individuals to be recognised as being of an 'indeterminate sex' or a 'third sex' and why these changes came about. Will such changes be of benefit for the children in question? What could be the implications for them in later life?

SEX CHROMOSOME ATYPICALITY

More than 70 atypical conditions resulting from sex chromosomes have been documented. Detailed below are four of the most well-known conditions: Klinefelter's syndrome, Turner's syndrome, XYY syndrome and XXX syndrome.

Males typically receive X and Y chromosomes during conception, but individuals with **Klinefelter's syndrome** have XXY sex chromosomes. As a result of the additional X chromosome, male-typical development is altered, resulting in the emergence of an undersized penis and abnormal testes that are incapable of producing sperm (Winter & Couch, 1995). This condition occurs in approximately one in 500 to one in 1,000 live male births. Although there is considerable variation in expression, males with Klinefelter's syndrome also tend to be more feminine, having a more rounded body shape, narrower shoulders, less body hair and possibly breasts. Individuals with Klinefelter's syndrome also tend to express reduced, and sometimes absent, sexual **motivation** and tend to be tall in stature. Treatment with testosterone can aid in the development of male-typical secondary sexual characteristics and sexual motivation.

Although females typically inherit two X chromosomes, individuals with **Turner's syndrome** only inherit a single X chromosome (signified as XO). This syndrome is rare, occurring in around one in 2,000 live female births (Blackless et al., 2000). Such females have underdeveloped or absent ovaries although, as no SRY gene is present, they develop as females. Due to their underdeveloped or absent ovaries, females with Turner's syndrome do not menstruate, are unable to become pregnant, do not develop breasts during puberty and are generally short in stature (Gravholt et al., 1998). However, females with Turner's syndrome do not differ from typical females in terms of their behaviour and interests (Kagan-Krieger, 1998).

Human males can sometimes receive an additional Y sex chromosome during sexual differentiation, referred to as **XYY syndrome**. Given the overwhelming function of the Y chromosome in the development of testes, possessing an additional Y chromosome is not necessarily debilitating. Such individuals are virtually indistinguishable from typical (XY) males, though XYY males tend to be slightly taller in stature and have larger canine teeth. Most XYY males also experience male-typical sexual development and are able to father children. There is some evidence, however, that such individuals have an increased risk of learning difficulties and delayed language skills. This is not an inherited condition, but instead usually occurs as an error during sperm production. This syndrome is quite rare, occurring in around one in 1,000 live male births.

Also known as X trisomy or super X syndrome, **XXX syndrome** occurs when a female inherits an additional X chromosome during sexual differentiation. Ordinarily only one X chromosome is needed for normal function in a woman (one X chromosome is active and the other dormant). As a result, XXX females simply carry two inactive X chromosomes rather than the one inactive chromosome typical of XX females. XXX females do not have any distinguishing features and are virtually impossible to tell apart from typical XX females, though they tend to be taller in stature and more at risk of developing learning difficulties. Such individuals go through female-typical sexual development, though they may begin menstruation prematurely, and are able to conceive without problems. As with XYY syndrome, this is not an inherited condition, but is instead caused by an error during the formation of either sperm or eggs. This syndrome is quite rare, occurring in around one in 1,000 live female births.

ORGANISATIONAL HORMONE ATYPICALITY

In addition to possible atypicality resulting from sex chromosomes, a variety of conditions have been linked to the actions of organisational hormones. Three such conditions are described below. The first two of these affect individuals who are genetically male: androgen insensitivity syndrome and 5-alpha reductase syndrome. Both conditions are associated with a decreased sensitivity to the masculinising effects of organisational hormones. The third condition, congenital adrenal hyperplasia, affects individuals who are genetically female, and is the consequence of female foetuses being exposed to an excess of **androgens**, or androgen-like substances, in the womb.

Although individuals with XY sex chromosomes develop as males, the process of sexual differentiation is dependent upon the masculinising effects of androgens in the womb. With complete **androgen insensitivity syndrome**, a male produces typical levels of androgens in the womb but is unresponsive to their masculinising effects; the individual does not produce androgen receptors for the androgens to bind to. This syndrome develops due to a mutation in the gene responsible for creating androgen receptors, located on the X chromosome. As a result, individuals who are genetically male and born with two testes (due to the presence of the SRY gene) are also born with the external genitalia of females. With no obvious sign of atypicality, such individuals are typically raised as girls and fully adopt a feminine gender identity. However, as these individuals possess testes rather than ovaries they do not menstruate and are incapable of becoming pregnant. Individuals with androgen insensitivity syndrome also tend to have fair complexions and well-developed breasts.

Individuals with **5-alpha reductase syndrome** are genetically male (they possess XY sex chromosomes) but they appear to be female at birth. They possess a small penis, approximately the same size as the clitoris, and a vaginal pouch in place of a scrotum. The syndrome is caused by a rare recessive genetic mutation that reduces the production of 5-alpha reductase. Given their female appearance, such individuals are typically raised as girls and adopt a feminine gender identity. However, during puberty, when testosterone production accelerates (see section 11.3.2), their penises fully develop and their body develops a muscular build and narrow hips. Such individuals are known as guevodoces (meaning 'eggs [testes] at 12 [years]'). Interestingly, there is evidence that this change in external genitalia is accompanied by a change in gender identity. Among the 18 documented cases of guevodoces reported by Imperato-McGinley et al. (1979), 17 expressed a male gender identity, with the majority of these individuals forming romantic relationships with females.

KEY STUDY

Money, J. (1975). Ablatio penis: normal male infant sex-assigned as a girl. *Archives of Sexual Behavior*, 4, 65–71.

FIGURE 11.2 David Reimer

Many parents of children born with ambiguous genitalia decide their child should undergo sex reassignment surgery. In the majority of cases, this involves surgically altering babies with more masculinised ambiguous genitalia into boys and more feminised ambiguous genitalia into girls, regardless of what sex they actually are. John Money argued that this process was successful and that children could be brought up to be comfortable in whatever gender was chosen for them. This view was challenged by, among others, Milton Diamond (Diamond, 1997; Diamond & Sigmundson, 1997).

Around the time of this academic debate, six-month-old twin boys were taken into hospital to have circumcision operations. Unfortunately, one boy, David Reimer, had his penis severed beyond repair. Some months later the family saw John Money on television describing his theory and made contact with him. He advised them to reassign the boy into a girl. This provided a perfect test of his theory as the boy had a twin to compare with as they grew up. The decision was made at 17 months of age to raise David as a girl. His testes were removed and surgery was soon performed to make his features more typical of a female. Oestrogen treatment was used to encourage the development of female-typical characteristics.

The psychologist John Money advised David's parents that their son would adopt a female gender identity later in life following his surgery. In numerous follow-up studies, Money reported that Brenda (the new name given by his parents) was successfully developing as a female and was interested in a number of sex-typical activities (Money, 1975).

Money, however, did not allow access to the case files or the family and the full story did not emerge for over 20 years. Diamond finally made contact with the family and spoke to the boy who had been brought up as a girl. He was by this time living as a man and was unaware of the celebrity of his story. His childhood had been one of continual struggle with his identity and he had been unable to live successfully as a girl. The story is recorded in brief in the reports by Diamond (Diamond, 1997; Diamond & Sigmundson, 1997) and more fully in a text by a US journalist (Colapinto, 2000).

Congenital adrenal hyperplasia can affect individuals who are genetically female (they possess XX sex chromosomes) and possess ovaries which have developed in a sex-typical fashion. During development, however, the adrenal glands do not produce corticosteroids (a type of hormone) as normal, but instead begin to produce large amounts of androgens. The cause of this atypicality is a recessive genetic condition. Due to the excess of androgens present during prenatal sexual differentiation, a number of characteristics do not develop in a female-typical fashion. The clitoris is enlarged and often resembles a penis, while the labia often fuse together so there is no vaginal opening. Some parents choose for their daughter to have reconstructive surgery to give the external genitals a more feminine appearance, increasing the size of the vaginal opening and reducing the size of the clitoris. Corticosteroids are prescribed to reduce the levels of circulating androgens that are still being produced.

It is possible that the degree of masculinisation may be more pronounced, however, and in such cases the parents may decide to enhance the masculine appearance of the external genitals by fully closing the fused labia to create a scrotum and inserting artificial testes. In such instances the child is raised as a boy (the ethics of this type of surgery are discussed below). Females with congenital adrenal hyperplasia demonstrate elevated levels of masculine behaviour during childhood play, and several studies have also documented elevated levels of homosexuality among these individuals.

11.3 SEX DIFFERENCES

11.3.1 SEX DIFFERENCES IN THE BRAIN

In addition to influencing the development of genitals, organisational hormones also affect the brain of the developing foetus, possibly resulting in sex differences in the structure and function of the brain. As equipment designed to measure brain development in the foetus has not yet been developed, much of what we know about this process comes from the study of non-human animals (Morris et al., 2004). The study of differences in brain function between the sexes has, as I am sure you can imagine, been extremely controversial over the years. Only a few centuries ago it was thought that a woman's brain would overheat if she attempted to do anything as complex as read!!

The simplest way to compare the brains of adult males and females is to look at the overall size and volume of the brain. Human males have an overall brain size approximately 15% larger than human females (Gibbons, 1991). Based on this size difference, some people have concluded that males are usually more intelligent than females, working on the assumption that bigger brain equals more intelligence. Such an approach is too simplistic. Instead, what should be considered is the overall ratio between brain and body size, which is comparable in both males and females (remember, human females are on average smaller than human males). Note that we do not use the entire brain for every action we perform. Parts of the brain are specialised to perform specific tasks (see below), so if we are interested in looking at how males and females may differ on these tasks, it is important to study the specific brain area in question.

Although several areas of the brain appear to differ in size, one of the most widely studied structures is the hypothalamus. This structure controls the actions of the pituitary gland and, as such, controls hormone production in the human body (see Chapter 9 for more information on its whereabouts and function). Among many other functions, the hypothalamus has been linked to sexual behaviour: for example, human males have shown increased activation in the hypothalamus when sexually aroused (Arnow et al., 2002).

As discussed above, the actions of organisational hormones are dependent upon receptor sites. If testosterone is present in the womb, then specialised receptor cells in the hypothalamus do not respond to oestrogen (as in males). Alternatively, if oestrogen is present, the receptor cells become sensitive to oestrogen later on (as in females). A specific region of the hypothalamus showing differences between males and females is the preoptic area (Swaab, Gooren, & Hoffman, 1995), a part of the brain involved in regulating body temperature. One tiny portion of the hypothalamus, the bed nucleus of the stria terminalis (believed to be linked to stress and anxiety responses), also shows a difference between males and females, with a posterior section of this area being approximately twice as large in males (Allen & Gorski, 1990). However, it has been argued that this difference may emerge due to the behaviour of males and females differing over the course of the lifespan rather than being **innate**.

A recent study by Ingalhalikar et al. (2014) has examined not just a specific area of the brain, but has also looked for sex differences in the connections of neural networks within the entire brain (known as the *connectome*). Based on a large-scale study of 949 youths, Ingalhalikar et al. (2014) report that male brains are organised for intrahemispheric communication (communication within separate hemispheres), whereas female brains are more organised for interhemispheric communication (communication between the separate hemispheres). This is a new area of research, and as such is best viewed cautiously, but is supported by previous research documenting a sex difference in the size of the corpus callosum, the structure that connects the two hemispheres of the brain, reported to be larger in females (Allen et al., 1991).

11.3.2 PUBERTY

The second important time for the development of sex differences, after the prenatal one, is **puberty**, the physiological process resulting in sexual maturity. The precise mechanisms behind puberty are not completely understood, but it appears that between 8 and 14 years of age large amounts of gonadotropins (a type of hormone) are released into the body. In males, the gonadotropins cause the testes to produce large amounts of testosterone, while in females they cause the ovaries to begin producing large amounts of oestrogen. This process is marked in males by the onset of sperm production (spermarche), while in females it triggers the onset of the menstrual cycle (menarche), approximately two years after which ovulation begins. The specific age at which menarche occurs has been falling since the start of the twentieth century (Anderson, Dallal, & Must, 2003) and is linked to a variety of factors such as general health, the percentage of body fat a girl has and even altitude. Psychologically, the most important event associated with puberty is often the first menstruation for females and the first ejaculation for males.

There are notable sex differences in the timing that puberty begins, as well as there being substantial individual variability in the onset and length of puberty. In Western countries, boys typically begin puberty between the ages of 10 and 14, while for girls this process occurs roughly two years before. Similarly, while boys often do not reach their full height until the age of 18, or even later, girls normally reach their full height by the age of 16.

During puberty, secondary sexual characteristics also develop. These are characteristics other than sperm and egg production that indicate sexual maturity. For example, males get facial hair and a deepening of their voice (due to changes in the larynx); females experience the development of their breasts and hips; and both sexes experience the development of pubic and underarm hair as well as sebaceous gland development (linked to the onset of acne). External genitalia also develop further, with the penis and testes increasing in size among males, and the labia and clitoris increasing in size among females. After puberty, males are statistically larger than females, with greater bone mass and less body fat.

As with prenatal sexual differentiation, atypicality can also occur during pubertal development. Sexual maturity has been previously documented in young children, some less than one year of age. Such development (referred to as precocious puberty) can be the result of disease or abnormal hormone exposure, or may simply reflect variation in normal development. While the effects of such a precocious puberty are not dangerous in themselves, sexual maturity at such a young age can profoundly affect development and may make the child a target for unwanted sexual advances. Alternatively, puberty can also be delayed for several years after the usual age of onset as a result of poor nutrition, stress, ill-health and a variety of medical complaints such as glandular tumours. If the child in question is otherwise healthy, medical intervention is usually unnecessary; it is simply a case of waiting for pubertal development. However, hormone treatment (with testosterone for males and estradiol and progesterone for females) can help to speed up the process.

11.3.3 COGNITIVE AND BEHAVIOURAL SEX DIFFERENCES

Given that there are certain differences between male and female brains, researchers have been curious about how behaviour differs between the sexes. In a review of over 2,000 studies, Maccoby and Jacklin (1974) concluded that there are four robust sex differences: males are more aggressive than females; males perform better on visual-spatial tasks; males demonstrate greater mathematical abilities; and females have superior verbal skills. Many popular beliefs of the time, such as the belief that males were superior at higher-level cognitive functions and girls were better at simpler cognitive tasks, were not supported.

Before we examine these findings in more detail, as well as more recent research, it is important to consider the nature of these sex differences. Are observed sex differences based on an innate difference between males and females, or do they result from a process of socialisation? Adults often treat boys and girls very differently based on societal gender roles, usually encouraging boys to express more masculine traits and girls to express more feminine traits. It is possible that this type of socialisation could alter the expression of behaviour over time, and explain any adult sex differences that are observed. For example, although Maccoby and Jacklin (1974) reported that males show greater mathematical ability than females, this difference has decreased noticeably in recent years (Else-Quest, Hyde, & Linn, 2010). Indeed, some feminist authors have suggested that sex differences are used as a means of maintaining established gender norms and inequality between the sexes (e.g. Fausto-Sterling, 2000).

A number of feminist authors, however, acknowledge and celebrate the innate differences between males and females, believing that a possible sex difference in characteristics such as mathematical ability or emotional reasoning does not make one sex 'better' or 'worse' than the other (e.g. Fisher, 1999).

Hyde (2005) has conducted a review of 46 meta-analyses on research investigating possible sex differences. A total of six categories of possible differences were examined: cognitive variables (such as mathematical ability), motor behaviour (such as throwing velocity), social or personality variables (such as aggression), verbal or non-verbal communication, psychological wellbeing (such as self-esteem) and miscellaneous behaviour (such as moral reasoning).

Of all the characteristics considered, 78% showed little or no difference between males and females, suggesting that the sexes are more similar than different in many regards. However, large sex differences were noted for certain motor behaviours, such as throwing velocity (particularly after puberty when males generally have greater muscle mass than females), levels of physical aggression, and certain aspects of sexual behavior, such as an interest in uncommitted sex. For each of these characteristics, males scored, on average, higher than females.

When considering reported differences between males and females, we should remember that we are dealing here only with averages and that there can be considerable overlap between the sexes. For example, female boxers are likely to be more aggressive than the average male person. In addition, it is important always to be very specific about the nature of the characteristic being discussed. For example, although the evidence strongly suggests that males show more physical aggression than females, the differences for other types of aggression (such as verbal aggression) can be virtually non-existent (Archer, 2004). Similarly, when considering sex differences in verbal abilities, females tend to score significantly higher than males for tasks of verbal fluency, but not for specific abilities such as reading comprehension or vocabulary (Eagly, 1995).

EXERCISE: MEN ARE BETTER AT MAP READING: FACT OR FICTION?

Make a list of abilities that show a difference between men and women. Do a quick survey of family or friends to include their views in the list. What do you think are the implications of such sex differences for the way society sees men and women? Also, do you think it matters whether these differences are real or perceived?

11.4 SEXUAL ORIENTATION

Sexual orientation refers to the attractions, both sexual and romantic, that individuals experience towards members of the opposite sex (*heterosexuality*) or the same sex (*homosexuality*) (see the discussion question at the end of this chapter for consideration of *bisexuality* and *asexuality*). Working out the frequency of homosexuality among the population is complicated for a number of reasons (including what question you use to ask participants!), but the rough consensus is that 2.5% to 5% of males are exclusively homosexual and between 0.5% and 1% of women are exclusively homosexual (Wilson & Rahman, 2008).

Psychosocial theories typically see an individual's sexual orientation as the result of various environmental factors or 'life incidents', such as the child-rearing strategies employed by an individual's parents. Such theories tend to produce rather vague predictions about how homosexuality actually develops and generally lack substantial empirical support (see LeVay, 2011). An alternative approach is to examine the possible biological underpinnings of an individual's sexual orientation, focusing on genetic factors and the influence of organisational hormones.

11.4.1 THE SEARCH FOR GAY GENES

The first real indication that an individual's sexual orientation may have a heritable component came from a series of twin studies. Twin studies indicate the relative contribution of genetic factors to the formation of specific characteristics. This is calculated by comparing the similarities found in identical or monozygotic (MZ) twins to those found in fraternal or dizygotic (DZ) twins. Since MZ twins share 100% and DZ twins only 50% genetics in common, yet both types of twin are likely to share the same environment during early development, any trait which MZ twins share more frequently than DZ twins implies a greater influence of genetic factors.

Bailey and Pillard (1991) recruited a large sample of homosexual individuals who had a twin. Fifty-two per cent of male MZ twins and 48% of female MZ twins had the same sexual orientation, compared to 22% of male DZ twins and 16% of female DZ twins. Although precise rates of homosexuality differ between the studies that have followed, and some methodological criticisms have been made of earlier studies in this area, a number of researchers have reported significantly higher similarity for sexual orientation among MZ compared to DZ twins (e.g. Bailey, Dunne, & Martin, 2000; Kendler et al., 2000). This strongly suggests a genetic influence on both male and female homosexuality. Although initial work to identify genes linked to the development of homosexuality in males has begun (see below), there has been no substantial work on the specific genes involved in female homosexuality.

Researchers have also studied rates of homosexuality within close family groups, following the logic that a potentially heritable trait, such as homosexuality, would tend to be more common in families where at least one member was homosexual. In an analysis of 7,321 individuals, Blanchard (1997) revealed that adult homosexuality in males was specifically associated with having a large number of older brothers (known as the **fraternal birth order effect**, FBOE). There was no significant relationship between having a homosexual orientation and the number of older sisters, younger brothers and younger sisters, or the mother's age. To date, there is no evidence for such a birth order effect among homosexual females, suggesting this is a phenomenon unique to male homosexuality. Cantor et al. (2002) estimated that each male foetus a mother has after the first raises the chance of homosexuality by 33%, equating to a 2% chance of homosexuality among first-born sons, rising to 6% among fifth-born sons. The influence of the fraternal birth order effect is not mediated by a male growing up with older stepbrothers, but is influenced by them having biological brothers (who share the same mother) regardless of whether they are raised together or apart (Bogaert, 2006). Blanchard and Bogaert (1996) proposed that this prenatal origin of the FBOE was specifically due to the mother's immune system reacting to certain antigens that are only carried by male foetuses.

Hamer et al. (1993) reported that homosexual males had a larger number of homosexual relatives on their mother's side, particularly maternal uncles and cousins. As mothers pass on an X chromosome to their sons, the high rates of homosexuality among maternal relatives was an indication that genes associated with homosexuality may be present on the X chromosome. Hamer et al. (1993) looked at the X chromosome in 40 pairs of homosexual male brothers and found that 33 of the pairs (82% of the sample) had co-inherited the same region of the X chromosome, labelled Xq28. Although this was the first attempt to identify a so-called 'gay gene', the results were far from conclusive: 18% of the sample did not co-inherit the same region of the X chromosome, and subsequent research on Xq28 and homosexuality has been contradictory (e.g. Rice et al., 1999).

A comprehensive study of the genes contributing to male homosexuality was conducted by Mustanski et al. (2005) and involved a full genome scan of 456 homosexual males from 146 families. Three regions of interest emerged: 7q36 on the seventh chromosome, 8p12 on the eighth chromosome and 10q26 on the tenth chromosome. Although the precise function of each of these genes is yet to be determined, it is interesting that 7q36 contains two genes that potentially relate to the development of the supra-chiasmatic nucleus, an area that is enlarged in homosexual males (see later), while 8p12 contains genes involved in the creation, regulation and release of certain hormones.

11.4.2 THE ROLE OF ORGANISATIONAL HORMONES

As described above, organisational hormones are crucial to the process of sexual differentiation and have marked effects on the sex-typical development of an individual's brain and body. Given that homosexual individuals are attracted to sex-atypical romantic partners (i.e. members of the same sex), researchers have questioned whether organisational hormones may be involved in the formation of a homosexual orientation. The key principle of Ellis and Ames's (1987) prenatal androgen theory is that male homosexuality results from underexposure to prenatal androgens during sexual differentiation, compared to male-typical levels. Female homosexuality is seen to result from exposure to an excess of androgens during this period. Such thinking was based in part on a number of studies demonstrating a connection between organisational and activational hormones on sex-atypical mating behaviour in non-human animals (e.g. Phoenix et al., 1959).

Empirically testing Ellis and Ames's (1987) theory is problematic. It would be highly unethical to conduct experiments where we directly manipulate the levels of organisational hormones that a foetus is exposed to in order to see the resulting effects on their adult sexual orientation. However, there are other ways of evaluating this theory. The first is to examine the sexual orientation of individuals who were exposed to unusually high or low levels of organisational hormones. One such group is females with congenital adrenal hyperplasia (see earlier). In addition to elevated levels of masculine behaviour during childhood play, a number of studies have reported significantly elevated levels of homosexual preference among females with congenital adrenal hyperplasia (reviewed in Meyer-Bahlburg et al., 2008).

A second means of evaluating the effects of organisational hormones on sexual orientation is to look at certain proxy markers – physical characteristics believed to reflect the hormone levels a foetus was exposed to. One such characteristic is the length of certain bones in the arms and hands. Among adults, these bones tend to be longer in heterosexual males compared to heterosexual females. Research by Martin and Nguyen (2004) suggests that heterosexual males and homosexual females experience greater bone growth, consistent with exposure to higher levels of organisational androgens, than both homosexual males and heterosexual females.

The findings for these proxy markers are often not unidirectional, however: that is, homosexual males do not always display feminised traits, while homosexual females do not always display masculinised ones. For example, Bogaert and Hershberger (1999) report penis size, which covaries with organisational hormone levels, to be larger (i.e. more masculinised) among homosexual males than heterosexual males. It may therefore be more accurate to say that homosexual individuals possess a mosaic of masculinised, feminised and sex-typical traits (reviewed in Wilson & Rahman, 2005).

11.4.3 SEXUAL ORIENTATION AND THE BRAIN

Researchers have attempted to identify areas of the brain that may differ between heterosexual and homosexual individuals. Given the sex atypicality that homosexual individuals often show, most of the initial studies on the brain have

---

KEY STUDY

LeVay, S. (1991). A difference in hypothalamic structure between heterosexual and homosexual men. *Science*, *253*, 1034–1037.

Perhaps the best known report of a difference between the brains of heterosexual and homosexual males concerns an area of the hypothalamus called INAH-3 (the third interstitial nucleus of the anterior hypothalamus, to give it its full title!). This is an area of the brain that is significantly larger in heterosexual males compared to heterosexual females (Allen et al., 1989) and in non-human animals it plays a role in sexual behaviour.

In 1991, Simon LeVay published an article in the leading academic journal *Science* which examined the relative size of INAH-3, and other nearby nuclei (INAH-1, INAH-2 and INAH-4) among cadavers of heterosexual males, heterosexual females and homosexual men. LeVay not only reported that the size of INAH-3 differed between his heterosexual male and heterosexual female participants, but also reported that INAH-3 was significantly smaller in homosexual males compared to heterosexual males. This finding suggested that the size of INAH-3 was comparable in the brains of heterosexual females and homosexual males.

Some researchers, however, questioned this finding due to the participants used; the research was an autopsy study where all of the homosexual males, but only around half of the heterosexual males, had died from complications associated with AIDS. It was suggested that the differences observed in INAH-3 among homosexual males could possibly have been the result of the development of AIDS rather than a difference attributable directly to their sexual orientation. However, LeVay counters this assertion by pointing out that there were no obvious pathologies in the autopsy specimens he examined and that there were no differences in the size of INAH-3 between heterosexual males in his study who had died of AIDS and those who died of other causes.

In more recent research on INAH-3, Byne et al. (2000) confirmed a significant difference in this area of the brain between heterosexual males and females, and also supported the assertion that this area did not differ in size between individuals who had died of AIDS and those who had not. However, this study only recorded a non-significant trend for INAH-3 to be smaller among homosexual males. Although this study does not refute the findings from LeVay's 1991 study, neither do they offer definitive support. It can be concluded that sexual orientation in males does *appear* to relate to the size of INAH-3, but that further research is needed to substantiate the strength of this relationship.

focused on areas showing sex differences, particularly the hypothalamus (see earlier). One of the first differences documented between the brains of homosexual and heterosexual males was the size of the supra-chiasmatic nucleus, an area of hypothalamus involved in the regulation of circadian rhythms. Compared to heterosexual males, this area of the brain was found to be significantly larger and elongated in homosexual males, a pattern consistent with the brains of heterosexual females (Swaab & Hofman, 1990).

Two final differences have been observed between heterosexual and homosexual males in areas of the brain connecting the two cerebral hemispheres. Allen and Gorski (1992) report that one of these areas, the anterior commissure, was larger in homosexual males and heterosexual females compared to heterosexual males. However, a replication of this study by Lasco et al. (2002) did not find any significant differences based on either sex or sexual orientation. Witelson et al. (2008) recently reported that right-handed homosexual males also show a larger isthmus of the corpus callosum, a bundle of fibres that carry information between the two hemispheres of the brain, than heterosexual males.

11.4.4 SEXUAL ORIENTATION AND BEHAVIOUR

Based on the differences in both neuroanatomy and other physical characteristics between heterosexual and homosexual individuals, a number of researchers have questioned whether there are also behavioural differences between these groups. Many of these studies have focused on characteristics and abilities that usually show marked sex differences (see earlier). Given the sex atypicality that homosexual individuals often show, homosexual males are usually predicted to respond or score in a way more characteristic of heterosexual females, while homosexual females would score or respond in a way more characteristic of heterosexual males. There is certainly some evidence to support this, with homosexual males as a group performing worse on mental rotation tasks and better on verbal fluency tasks compared to heterosexual males (e.g. McCormick & Witelson, 1991; Rahman, Andersson, & Govier, 2005; Sanders & Wright, 1997). This is a pattern consistent with findings for heterosexual females. The trend for homosexual females is not as consistent (e.g. Rahman, Abrahams, & Wilson, 2003), but does indicate that for some tasks homosexual females perform in a heterosexual male-typical direction (e.g. Rahman, Wilson, & Abrahams, 2003).

KEY RESEARCHER Qazi Rahman

FIGURE 11.3 Qazi Rahman

Qazi Rahman is currently a senior lecturer in cognitive biology at the Institute of Psychiatry (King's College, London). Dr Rahman obtained his BSc (Hons) in Psychology at the University of Staffordshire and his PhD at the Institute of Psychiatry (King's College, London), where he examined the neurodevelopmental, sensorimotor and neurocognitive basis of human sexual orientation. He has held lectureships at the University of East London, the Institute of Psychiatry and Guy's, King's and St Thomas's Schools (King's College, London).

Rahman's research focuses on the psychobiology of human sexual orientation and sex differences in cognition. His projects include the investigation of:

- sexual-orientation-related differences in basic spatial abilities (such as the manipulation of spatial relations)
- spatial memory (involving navigating and finding important objects in the environment)
- linguistic ability
- social or emotional cognition (e.g. 'reading' emotions in another person's face or eyes)
- the genetic basis of sexual orientation using twin modelling and molecular genetics
- the role of sexual orientation in human mating tactics and partner preferences
- the utility of proxy somatic markers (e.g. finger length ratios, handedness, and hair whorl patterning) as windows on the prenatal development of sexual orientation.

According to Hyde's (2005) meta-analysis (see earlier), two of the largest sex differences were noted for certain motor behaviours, such as throwing velocity and levels of physical aggression. How, then, are these characteristics expressed in homosexual individuals? With regard to throwing *accuracy*, the pattern of findings is remarkably consistent. Hall and Kimura (1995) report heterosexual males have significantly greater throwing accuracy than heterosexual females. Furthermore, homosexual males were not as accurate as heterosexual males and in fact tended to perform in a similar fashion to heterosexual females. Homosexual females were more accurate than heterosexual females and tended to perform in a similar fashion to heterosexual males. With regard to physical aggression, the findings are not so consistent. Homosexual males have been reported to show lower levels of physical aggression than heterosexual males (Gladue & Bailey, 1995; Sergeant et al., 2006), a pattern that is consistent with heterosexual females. The findings for homosexual females, however, are more inconsistent, with some studies suggesting *lower* levels of physical aggression than heterosexual females (Gladue, 1991), contrary to the predicted pattern, while other studies find no difference between these two groups (Gladue & Bailey, 1995).

11.5 CHAPTER SUMMARY

Sex describes the biological characteristics used to identify individuals as either male or female, and can be measured by examining an individual's sex chromosomes, gonads and external reproductive organs. Gender refers to the sociocultural characteristics associated with being either male or female, and is frequently divided into gender identity and gender role.

The sex chromosomes that an individual possesses (usually XX among females and XY among males) begin the process of sexual differentiation. Among females, the Müllerian duct system develops into the female reproductive system, whereas in males the presence of the SRY gene causes the development of the Wolffian duct system, which in turn develops into the male reproductive system. Organisational hormones in the womb influence the developing foetal brain and body, usually causing the foetus to develop in a male-typical or female-typical fashion.

The process of sexual differentiation does not always proceed in a typical manner. A number of conditions can arise due to sex chromosome atypicality, such as Klinefelter's syndrome or Turner's syndrome. Alternatively, a variety of atypical conditions, such as 5-alpha reductase syndrome or congenital adrenal hyperplasia, can arise due to the action of organisational hormones. The appropriate course of treatment for many individuals born with such conditions is contentious.

The second important time for the development of sex differences, after the prenatal one, is puberty. During this time an individual sexually matures and secondary sexual characteristics develop. Although many people believe there are large-scale behavioural and psychological differences between the sexes, current research suggests that only a limited number of these differences, such as levels of physical aggression, are significant in magnitude.

The current research suggests there is a biological basis to homosexuality. A number of studies have identified a heritable component to both male and female homosexuality, and research is currently under way to identify so-called 'gay genes'. Organisational hormones also appear to play a prominent role in the development of homosexuality. Research has identified areas of the brain and certain cognitive and behavioural tasks that appear to vary based on an individual's sexual orientation, particularly among males.

(?) DISCUSSION QUESTIONS

- **Sex testing at the Olympics:** Most humans can be classified as male or female, with their sex chromosomes, gonads and external genitalia all developing in either male-typical or female-typical fashion. However, for some individuals, one or more of these components may be inconsistent with the others, leading to difficulty in establishing an individual's biological sex.

  Problems with sex typing at international sporting events are recurrent in the twentieth century. In the 1936 Olympic Games, Helen Stephens was accused of being a man in disguise after winning the women's 100 metre race. Following a number of controversial articles about her in the press, Stephens took a sex test to clear her name and it confirmed her status as a female. The process of determining an athlete's sex by examination of their sex chromosomes was initiated by the International Olympic Committee (IOC) in 1968. Such a move was motivated by fears that male athletes were disguising themselves and entering competitions established for female athletes.

One recent case of note is that of Casta Semenya, a female South African runner who was required by the International Association of Athletics Federations (IAAF) to take a sex test before she was allowed to run (and subsequently win) the women's 800 metre race at the World championships in Berlin in August 2009. It was reported that she had an intersex condition, having internal testicles and no ovaries or uterus. In 2009, it was announced that Casta Semenya would be allowed to keep her gold medal and in 2010 she was cleared by the IAAF to return to international competition, although the results of Casta's sex testing were not revealed to the press due to privacy issues. In 2012, she carried the South African flag during the opening ceremony of the 2012 Olympic Games, and went on to win a silver medal in the women's 800 metres.

Sex chromosome testing is largely discontinued by the IOC but has been used recently by the IAAF. How far do you agree with these decisions and on what grounds? From your research beyond this chapter, what alternative methods would you say are available?

- **Sexism:** Some people assume that discussing possible differences between men and women is sexist. How do you think that 'sex differences' and 'sexism' relate to each other? How do you think these concepts relate to our concept of gender and gender studies?
- **Sexual orientation:** So far we have only discussed two types of sexual orientation – heterosexuality and homosexuality. Do you think that everyone's sexual orientation fits into these two discrete groups, or do you think that it is expressed on a continuum, with numerous intermediate stages (i.e. varying degrees of bisexuality)? Do you think this is the same for both males and females? Why do you think researchers tend to focus on heterosexual and homosexual, rather than on bisexual, participants? Some researchers also accept *asexuality*, a lack of romantic or sexual attraction to others, as a fourth sexual orientation. What do you think about this concept as an additional sexual orientation?

SUGGESTIONS FOR FURTHER READING

Archer, J., & Lloyd, B. (2002). *Sex and gender* (2nd edn). Cambridge: Cambridge University Press. A very good book discussing research into sex differences and highlighting the distinction between sex and gender.

Crooks, R., & Baur, K. (2011). *Our sexuality* (11th edn). Belmont, CA: Wadsworth. An easily accessible textbook, aimed at undergraduate students, which provides further information on a variety of biological and social topics connected with sex and sexuality.

LeVay, S. (2011). *Gay, straight and the reason why*. Oxford: Oxford University Press. An excellent book providing a comprehensive and insightful review of research into the psychobiology of homosexuality.

Pinel, J.P.J. (2014). *Biopsychology* (8th edn). Harlow, UK: Pearson Education. A classic biological psychology textbook. Chapter 13 provides additional material on the process of sexual differentiation in human and non-human species as well as introductory material on human genetics.

Still want more? For links to online resources relevant to this chapter and a quiz to test your understanding, visit the companion website at edge.sagepub.com/banyard2e

12 MOTIVATION AND EMOTION

Lead authors: Dean Fido and Preethi Premkumar

CHAPTER OUTLINE

12.1 Introduction	210
12.2 Basics of emotion	210
12.2.1 Theory of emotion	211
12.2.2 Classification of emotions	211
12.3 Biological underpinnings of emotion	212
12.3.1 Event-related potentials in emotion processing	213
12.3.2 Expressing and regulating emotion	214
12.4 Biases in emotion processing	215
12.5 What is motivation and how is it researched?	216
12.5.1 Motivation as personality: reward sensitivity theory	217
12.5.2 A neurobiological theory of motivation	218
12.6 Expressed emotion and psychiatric disorder	219
12.7 Forensic implications of dysfunctional emotion procession	220
12.7.1 Alterations in brain anatomy leading to psychopathic tendencies	221
12.7.2 Brain functional changes during emotion processing due to psychopathic behaviour	221
12.8 Chapter summary	223
Discussion questions: How aware are we of our emotions and motivations?	223
Suggestions for further reading	223

12.1 INTRODUCTION

What are emotions and why do we often find that the behaviours of our normally rational selves are suddenly taken over when we feel angry or sad? What motivates us to behave as we do? What factors decide what plan of action we follow? This chapter will introduce you to a discussion about what emotion and motivation are, how they influence each other, how they are researched within psychology, and why they are important for our social wellbeing. We will explore the commonly considered 'basic emotions', along with what happens within the brain when we encounter them in others and express them ourselves. Furthermore, we will explore how such emotions may motivate physical and verbal behaviours, before discussing possible implications of dysfunction to these systems within populations characterised by poor emotion processing.

EMOTION A temporary feeling deriving from a mood or an affective state.

MOOD A prevailing state of feeling.

The terms 'emotion', 'mood' and 'affect' are often, and understandably, used interchangeably within the literature, yet for the sake of accurate comparison, this should not be the case. To be specific, **emotion** reflects the feeling, appraisal and expression of a *short-lived* experience whereas **mood** should be considered as a more intense state over a longer duration, ranging from minutes to months (Ekkekakis, 2013). **Core affect**, on the other hand, is an overarching concept, present to some degree at all times, manifesting in emotion and mood accordingly.

Emotion acts to drive motivation via the anticipation of existing associations with reward and punishment. Imagine for a moment that you had no emotions at all. Why would you bother to do anything? Without anticipation of pleasure, pain or any other emotion you would probably find it hard to motivate yourself to even get out of bed (as may be the case in clinical depression). Understanding the neural systems that process reward and punishment has increased our understanding of addictive behaviours, such as gambling and drug use. It raises issues of whether we are conditioned to automatically perform these behaviours or whether we carefully evaluate their effects before we engage in them. These are questions that will be addressed in this chapter.

FRAMING QUESTIONS

- What are the basic emotion types?
- What roles do the limbic and frontal regions of the brain play during emotion processing?
- What are some of the disorders which can result from dysfunctional emotion processing and how are they related to emotion?
- What are some of the social effects resulting from atypical emotion processing?

12.2 BASICS OF EMOTION

Being able to recognise emotions in other people's facial expression can tell us about their frame of mind. We have a natural ability to understand what emotions are being conveyed when people make certain facial expressions. As social animals, this allows us to predict how others will respond to us (e.g. are they about to shout at you or greet you warmly?). In turn, being able to categorise facial emotions accurately can reveal vital information about our own mental state. This ability has been extensively researched in people who have a diagnosis of psychiatric disorder, such as **schizophrenia** (Premkumar, Cooke et al., 2008), as well as in people who have a diagnosis of personality disorder, such as **psychopathy** (Blair et al., 2001). Individuals with these diagnoses are more likely to erroneously attribute certain emotions, such as sadness and threat, to other emotions. Such a poor ability to correctly attribute basic facial expressions to certain emotions could in turn indicate difficulty in understanding the underlying mental states of others.

12.2.1 THEORY OF EMOTION

One of the earliest accounts of the nature of emotions is contained in the James–Lange theory in the late nineteenth century. William James and Carl Lange (1894/1922) argued that emotion was essentially a physiological response that arose from the **peripheral autonomic nervous system** and the **cardiovascular system** that in turn produced behavioural changes. Emotions were seen as feelings derived through internal feedback received about these behaviours and physiological responses (Fehr & Stern, 1970). So, for example, you might see an angry dog running towards you and have the physical response of a racing heart and trembling first, then you may experience that physical response as fear second. However, Wundt criticised this theory heavily as being **reductionist** (see Chapter 3 for more on reductionism) and science's attempt to find explanations for conscious experiences in the physical state (Lang, 1994). Cannon also criticised this view of emotion as being secondary to bodily states by noting that: (a) the length of time needed for visceral (physical) changes is too long to account for the immediacy of emotional behavior; (b) artificial induction of visceral changes does not necessarily produce emotion; (c) the viscera are 'insensitive structures'; (d) visceral changes are the same in many emotions; and (e) interruption of afferent feedback from the periphery does not influence emotional behavior (Fehr & Stern, 1970). Instead, Cannon argued for a fight-and-flight arousal system whereby the body prepares for action upon anticipation of threat (Lang, 1994).

12.2.2 CLASSIFICATION OF EMOTIONS

Broadly, emotions can be categorised as positive and negative, such as happy and sad. Emotions can also be classified into several discrete internal states, for example happiness, sadness, anger, fear, surprise. The classification of emotion has been studied systematically in terms of primary (basic) and secondary (complex) emotions. Ekman (1999) put forward six categories of basic emotion that can be recognised across all cultures: happiness, anger, fear, sadness, disgust and surprise. He suggested that these emotions have a universal quality in that they can be recognised by people across different cultures. Indeed, there was a surprising level of agreement among people from 21 different countries in being able to correctly recognise these types of facial emotions, suggesting that these emotions are universal. Emotions were then seen as lying on a continuum around these basic emotions. Ekman (1993) argues that emotions can be clustered into meaningful categories, such as amusement, pleasure and pride (seen as positive emotion). By morphing certain features of facial expressions, it was possible to create a continuous array of facial emotional expressions, now generically referred to as 'Ekman faces'. The idea conveyed in these studies is that emotion is transient and can be taken as a snapshot of one's internal mood.

A challenge to this understanding of emotion is that no information is given about the context in which the emotional expression occurs, for example, the events preceding the facial expression that would help a person to make an informed decision in judging a facial emotion (Ekman, 1993). Therefore the real-world value of research into recognising discrete facial emotions may be questioned (Izzard, 2007) because it could be argued that emotions are emergent and conveyed over prolonged social interaction. An effort to distinguish between the transient and the emergent quality of emotion is captured in Izzard's (2007) exposition on the concepts 'basic emotion' and 'emotion schemas'. According to Izzard, basic emotions have evolutionarily old neurobiological substrates, where the feelings and capacity for expression have an evolutionary origin. Emotion schemas are the processes involved in the dynamic interplay of emotion, appraisals and higher-order cognition. They have a cognitive content not found in basic emotions. Advances in emotion research have meant that emotion is seen as a phenomenon that (1) has neural systems dedicated at least in part to emotion processes; (2) elicits physical and behavioural responses; and (3) motivates cognition and action (Izzard, 2007).

We will now consider some of the factors that affect the recognition of emotions. One of the factors that allows us to recognise an emotion is the use of the spoken language to classify emotions into categories. When we say we recognise a facial expression as denoting a certain emotion, we have a set of verbal expressions to describe it. In fact, Johnson-Laird and Oatley (1989) set out to systematically classify words into different emotional categories. They argued that the reason we experience an emotion is because it allows us to communicate our feelings to others. It is possible that certain emotions can be given a verbal meaning without any hesitation. Such emotions can be seen as being part of our in-built or automatic ability to provide a behavioural response in certain situations, such as smiling when you feel happy. Johnson-Laird and Oatley (1989) identified 560 words that had such emotional properties (e.g. cheerful, irritable and panicky). They then classified these words into happiness, sadness, anger, fear, disgust. The words that were derived from these basic emotions cannot be interpreted further because the emotions they refer to are primitive and cannot be broken down into simpler internal experiences. In contrast, complex emotions are experienced as a result of self-evaluation, such as regret, embarrassment and shame.

More recently, it has been suggested that emotions can be experienced without using words to experience them. These emotions can be imagined visually rather than verbally. Holmes et al. (2008) studied the use of mental imagery to process emotional scenes. They tested the use of imagery and verbal information to see whether emotion processing was facilitated by either imagery or verbal encoding. For example, a picture of a rock climber appeared with a caption that had a negative consequence, for example 'slip', or a benign consequence, 'stable'. Participants viewed 20 picture–word combinations designed to elicit emotionally negative representations. They were instructed to integrate the picture and word using either a descriptive sentence or a mental image. Instructions to form mental images to integrate the picture and word caption led to greater changes in self-reported mood than did verbal processing instructions. They argued that images may be linked with emotion because basic emotion systems in the brain evolved early, before language.

12.3 BIOLOGICAL UNDERPINNINGS OF EMOTION

The study of emotion taps into fundamental aspects of our everyday life. Emotional events may occur unexpectedly and change quickly. We often find ourselves switching from one state of emotion to another. In order to help us to understand why individuals feel and behave the way they do, emotion could be studied from a variety of psychological approaches, asking questions such as how it affects our cognition or behavioural performance or what the biological underpinnings are of how we perceive, feel and express emotion. In addition to informing us about everyday behaviours, looking at the biology could aid development of treatment programmes for atypical behaviours. To study this, a combination of brain imaging techniques is often used (**fMRI**, **EEG**, etc.; see Chapter 9, section 9.5.2 for an explanation of these techniques).

FUNCTIONAL MAGNETIC RESONANCE IMAGING (fMRI) A spatially accurate brain imaging technique that is based on the nuclear properties of protons (e.g. hydrogen) in the blood.

ELECTROENCEPHALOGRAPHY (EEG) A temporally accurate brain imaging technique that is based on the electrical discharge to the surface of the brain due to neuronal firing.

In 1872, Charles Darwin's seminal writings on *The expression of the emotions in man and animals* distinguished fear from other emotions by both the extreme responses projected during fear expression and the rapid processing which takes place on encountering fear-inducing stimuli. This innate ability for responding rapidly to threatening stimuli and assessing others' distress is of high importance for our wellbeing. It allows us to quickly assess our risk from others and avoid anyone who could be potentially dangerous. It also allows us to judge how our actions may be harming or threatening to others (and hopefully cease such behaviour).

So how do we react to fearful situations? Let us propose that on entering your dark bedroom late at night, you turn on your bedside lamp. As the bulb flicks on, you notice a large spider at the base of the lamp. What do you do? Do you run out of the room screaming or do you stop and remember that your little brother was playing with a toy spider in your room earlier that day? Irrespective of the behaviour you choose, two parallel neural pathways are evoked within the brain, facilitating these possible behaviours. There are great benefits to quickly responding to threatening situations, such as protecting one's personal safety and one's belongings, although, as this example shows, this isn't always practical and may leave us over-reacting to situations not warranting such aversive responses.

The first neural pathway involves stimulus input. Information about the stimulus (the spider) is sent to the thalamus, a relay centre for visual, auditory and olfactory sensory input (Figure 12.1). From here, the amygdala, a region highly involved in emotional processing, particularly fear, interprets this stimulus as a threat. A fight-or-flight response (run out of the room; squash the spider) is initiated within the hypothalamus (Blair, 2001). This pathway is very fast-acting but very coarse, taking the stimulus as-is and failing to incorporate historic or contextual information.

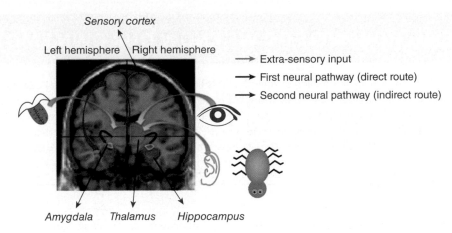

Sensory cortex

Left hemisphere \ Right hemisphere

→ Extra-sensory input

→ First neural pathway (direct route)

→ Second neural pathway (indirect route)

Amygdala   Thalamus   Hippocampus

FIGURE 12.1 Schematic representation of the emotion circuit as seen through a coronal section of the brain. Information flows from sensory organs to the thalamus and then to the limbic system either directly (first pathway) or indirectly (second pathway) through the frontal cortex

The second pathway serves to incorporate this information, but at a time cost. Here, the input (the spider) is transmitted from the thalamus to the sensory cortex to interpret the information at a higher cognitive level, before memory information from the hippocampus is incorporated (Have I seen this spider before? Isn't it a little too big to be a real spider?). After realising that this toy poses no danger to you, the pre-initiated amygdala response is mediated, and any fight-or-flight behaviour is abolished.

12.3.1 EVENT-RELATED POTENTIALS IN EMOTION PROCESSING

When individuals encounter emotional faces, they don't instantly recognise their emotions, nor do they even recognise the stimuli as a face. Due to this processing stage occurring rapidly, it is commonly measured using the brain imaging method of EEG as this method more than others has good **temporal resolution**; that is, it is very precise in measuring the time at which an event occurs (see Chapter 9, section 9.5.2 for a description of EEG and how it works). Approximately 170 milliseconds after face presentation, a brainwave peak (also described as an **event-related potential**; ERP) known as the N170 occurs. Larger peaks indicate greater brain resources being used at that time. This peak is thought to represent the categorical encoding of faces, that is, is it a face or an ordinary object? (Chai et al., 2012). Larger peaks at this time are commonly associated with facial stimuli compared to other objects. At this stage, the specific facial elements, such as eyes, mouth, etc., are not processed; rather, just is it a face or not? (Eimer, 2000)

Some literature suggests that the type of emotion may affect the N170 marker, though there is ambiguity as to whether greater activation is evoked to fearful and negative stimuli (Batty & Taylor, 2003) or by positive stimuli (Pfabigan et al., 2012). Other research fails to find any emotional effect on this early facial processing stage in a group of students scoring highly for callous (disregard for others) and uncaring traits (Fido et al., in prep.).

The specific brain regions creating the N170 can be identified using fMRI. Two brain regions in the temporal lobe have been suggested during this facial processing stage. First, the posterior fusiform gyrus, a region highly involved in face and body recognition (Rossion et al., 2003), and second, the superior temporal sulcus (STS) (Itier & Taylor, 2004). The STS showed greater activation during facial processing, compared to objects, and when viewing inverted compared to upright faces. Greater STS activation suggests a possible need for greater recruitment during difficult facial processing experiences.

EEG measurement shows that emotional faces might be distinguishable from neutral stimuli at 200 ms. A peak at this time (the P200) is thought to indicate attention directed to processing emotional visual or auditory stimuli. After visual input, the P200 is thought to represent activation of brain regions within the visual (bilateral occipital lobes) and auditory (temporal lobes) cortices (Liu, Perfetti, & Hart, 2003). Being able to attend to emotional stimuli allows us to process this information quickly.

EXERCISE: HOW WELL DO WE KNOW OUR OWN EMOTIONS?

We often don't reflect on how we are feeling or the effect it is having on our behaviour and thoughts. When we do, we find that sometimes our emotions are straightforward to recognise but at other times they can be more subtle and complex. Over the last week, reflect on a couple of specific situations you have encountered and the emotions that you felt. How was the experience of emotion obvious to you? What factors helped you to recognise the emotion? Was it the response of others or your own reflections? How did the emotion affect your thinking and behaviour in that situation?

Slight discrepancy exists about how emotions affect this processing stage. Whereas early research suggests negative stimuli may result in greater brain responses than positive stimuli (Carretié et al., 2001), recent literature has begun to question if it is as simple as that. For example, Paulmann, Bleichner and Kotz (2013) found that spoken sentences of anger, happiness and surprise resulted in increased neuronal responses when compared with disgust, fear and sadness. We are yet to see how this effect is transferred to visual stimuli.

12.3.2 EXPRESSING AND REGULATING EMOTION

So far, this section has given a brief overview of some of the earlier neurological processes occurring during emotion processing, and in the case of fear, the underlying neurological mechanisms that simultaneously interact to respond to perceived threat. However, it is not just the attention to and perception of emotion that interests us. Expression and regulation of emotion is vital for everyday social interactions, so it is these aspects that we turn to next.

The emotion circuit highlighted in Figure 12.1 is mostly centred on the **amygdala**, a core structure within the **limbic system**, responsible for primal expressions of emotion, most notably aggression. Aggression, alongside fear, tends to be the focus of emotion expression from an evolutionary perspective, encompassing behaviours utilised to hunt for food, attract mates and defend social hierarchy. However, in most situations, such behaviour is not socially acceptable. Reacting in an aggressive manner can cause detriment to social and professional bonds, and therefore, on a daily basis, we need to recruit the ability to modulate responses to negative affect. Here we will examine the brain circuits that allow that appraisal and modulation of response to emotion.

TOP-DOWN PROCESSING A way of explaining a cognitive process in which higher-level processes, such as prior knowledge, influence the processing of lower-level input, often involving voluntary control and regulation.

As already alluded to earlier, the amygdala is activated during emotional arousal, particularly in response to negative stimuli, such as an angry face. Consensus within the literature indicates that the control of these initial emotional responses emerges from **top-down** inhibitory mechanisms within the **prefrontal cortex** (PFC). The dorsolateral PFC and anterior cingulate cortex (ACC) are both activated when attention is paid to the negative emotions of others, and when these emotions are experienced (Banks et al., 2007). When participants were asked to alter their negative emotions, this was best achieved when an area of the prefrontal cortex called the **orbitofrontal cortex** (OFC) and the amygdala had good connectivity. One of the OFC's roles is to incorporate previously experienced behavioural consequences with emotional responses to produce top-down inhibitory responses. For example, in the case of anger relating to fighting, the OFC might register that previous punishments arose from specific behaviours (I got banned from the Mothers' Union for punching someone for being rude about my Victoria sponge cake) and so provide a top-down inhibition to discourage further behaviour.

This and other evidence suggests that where top-down inhibition fails, for example when expressions of anger and uninhibited aggression are demonstrated as a response to fear or anger, they may arise from a combination of an oversensitive amygdala response and a lack of inhibition that would usually come from the prefrontal cortex due to poor connectivity between the two.

12.4 BIASES IN EMOTION PROCESSING

As we touched on earlier, recognition of emotion involves interpretation of context and therefore has a cognitive element. Cognitive biases in the processing of emotions, such as fear, can have pathological effects. For example, in helping to understand patients with anxiety disorders, fear is thought to involve 'excessive response elements and resistance to modification' (Foa & Kozak, 1986). Emotion processing theory is used to describe experiences of post-traumatic stress disorder and other anxiety disorders. Fear structures of trauma survivors with **post-traumatic stress disorder** (PTSD) include two basic dysfunctional cognitions that underlie the development: (1) the world is completely dangerous (e.g. it is dangerous to be alone); and (2) one is totally incompetent (e.g. I can't handle any stress, my PTSD symptoms mean that I am going crazy). Understanding of such a cognitive model of fear evaluation can aid clients' awareness of their biased thinking styles and helps to reduce their level of anxiety as well as retrain their thinking and behaviour (see Chapter 25 for more about working with fears and anxieties using cognitive therapy).

POST-TRAUMATIC STRESS DISORDER An anxiety disorder characterised by recurrent episodes of extreme anxiety in the form of panic, flashbacks, sleep-disturbances, etc., following exposure to one or repeated serious traumatic events, such as death, injury or sexual violence.

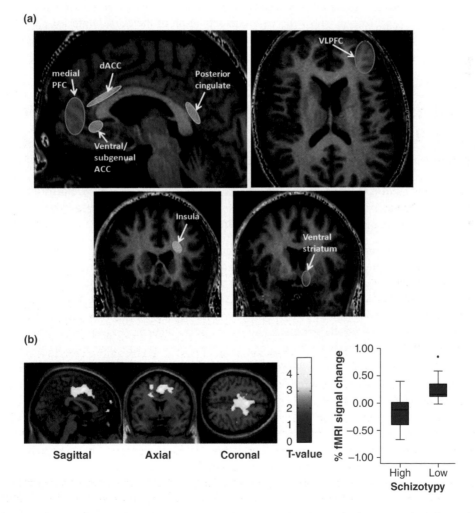

FIGURE 12.2 (a) Regions of interest implicated in experiencing rejection (in yellow) and emotion regulation (in red) during rejection tasks. (b) Lower dorsal anterior cingulate activation during rejection in high compared to low schizotypy individuals

SCHIZOTYPY The presence of certain stable features or personality characteristics in the typical population that when high may suggest an increased risk for schizophrenia. These include a tendency for (what many may consider) odd beliefs, such as belief in special, almost magical powers, or having the ability to read others' minds; they also include unusual perceptions, lack of enjoyment from social sources and reckless behaviour.

SCHIZOPHRENIA A psychiatric disorder characterised by the presence of hallucinations and delusions, loss of affect (e.g. social avoidance and emotional withdrawal), and poor social functioning.

Another type of emotion processing bias is a fear of being rejected that relates to difficulty understanding emotional expressions in social situations. Rejection sensitivity is the heightened tendency to perceive or anxiously expect disengagement from others during social interaction. In such situations, the person seeks reassurance, feels vulnerable about their relationships, and/or shows retaliation and aggression (Langens & Schuler, 2005; Lemay & Clark, 2008; Sinclair, Ladny, & Lyndon, 2011). Rejection sensitivity is on a continuum with a need for affiliation, wherein there is a general expectation of positive reinforcement (need for affiliation) or negative expectation (rejection sensitivity) from others (Mehrabian & Ksionsky, 1970). Being high in rejection sensitivity produces a cognitive bias in emotional processing meaning that interactions are more likely to be interpreted as indicating rejection.

As regards the brain circuits recruited in feeling rejected, there are two aspects to consider. First, the network of frontal brain regions associated with experiencing social pain, namely dorsal anterior cingulate cortex, and second, the down-regulation of the intensity of distress due to rejection, namely medial PFC and ventrolateral PFC (Premkumar et al., 2012; and Figure 12.2a). Interestingly, there is evidence that rejection sensitivity is related to **schizotypy**. For example, when processing scenes depicting social rejection, individuals high in schizotypy show increased de-activation of the dorsal anterior cingulate during rejection scenes that suggests increased self-distancing to avoid pain (Premkumar et al., 2013 and Figure 12.2b).

KEY STUDY: DEVELOPMENTAL INFLUENCES ON THE NEURAL BASES OF RESPONSES TO SOCIAL REJECTION: IMPLICATIONS OF SOCIAL NEUROSCIENCE FOR EDUCATION

Sebastian, C.L., Tan, G.C., Roiser, J.P., Viding, E., Dumontheil, I., & Blakemore, S.J. (2011). Developmental influences on the neural bases of responses to social rejection: implications of social neuroscience for education. *NeuroImage*, *57*(3), 686–694.

Peer relationships among adolescents are characterised by a need for affiliation and acceptance by peers. If we have doubts about whether peers will be approving of an adolescent's desire for friendship, this can lead to a fear of rejection. Sebastian et al. (2011) studied the neural response in a group of female adolescents and adults during a virtual ball-tossing game, 'Cyberball'. Here, participants (adolescents, *n* = 19, mean age = 15.44 years; and adults, *n* = 16, mean age = 28.7 years) played with two virtual players. However, participants were made to believe that the players they were playing with were real. After a few trials, the female participant was quietly excluded from the game by the other players (explicit social exclusion condition). Adolescents reported being more distressed and excluded during the social exclusion, than social inclusion, condition. The study found that the right subgenual anterior cingulate cortex and left ventro-lateral prefrontal cortex were activated more during exclusion than inclusion. Specifically, the right ventro-lateral prefrontal cortex was activated more during exclusion than inclusion in adults, but weaker during exclusion than inclusion in adolescents. These findings demonstrate that there are important neurodevelopmental differences between adults and adolescents when experiencing social exclusion.

12.5 WHAT IS MOTIVATION AND HOW IS IT RESEARCHED?

Motivation is the drive, incentive or interest to initiate, perform or maintain a behaviour. **Motivation** often arises from cognitive and emotional processes. I may, for example, be motivated to exercise based on an emotional

ASIDE

Effect of mindfulness on emotion

Sometimes we let our emotions get the better of us. While our emotions vary day to day, hour to hour, some people find themselves in situations where negative emotions, particularly poor self-beliefs, are fairly constant. It may be possible to regulate these emotions using mindfulness-based stress reduction (MBSR) techniques such as breath- and attention-focused paradigms, making one aware of their bodily responses at the present moment. Goldin and Gross (2010) identified 16 patients suffering from social anxiety disorder, commonly known as SAD, who underwent functional MRI scanning while reacting to negative self-beliefs, and while attempting to regulate resulting negative emotions using two types of MBSR. The use of MBSR led to (a) a decreased negative emotion experience (social anxiety, perceived depression, poor self-esteem), (b) reduced amygdala activity (a region highly involved in the perception and expression of emotion – see text), and (c) increased activity in brain regions implicated in attention deployment.

For more on what mindfulness is about take a look at this link: http://bemindful.co.uk/mbsr/experience-mbsr/

and cognitive response to not being able to fit into my favourite jeans anymore. Of course, whether that translates into actually engaging in exercise will depend on more than just motivation; it may require access to resources, time, money, etc. Therefore, motivation may be seen as the preparatory phase before this action is executed. It is important because the success of behavioural therapies, such as smoking cessation, depends on motivation to engage based on the client's perceived benefit of changing his/her behaviour. One aspect of motivation to partake in therapy may be perception of the amount of reward or punishment one expects the therapeutic behaviours to yield (see Chapter 25 for more about therapeutic interventions). This characteristic of motivation has raised a lot of interest in understanding how we continue to engage in excessive or appetitive behaviours (behaviours that indicate pleasure-seeking), such as addiction to smoking, drugs and gambling (see Chapter 4, section 4.6, for more about gambling), and has led to extensive research.

> **MOTIVATION** An internal state or desire that initiates or maintains behaviour.

12.5.1 MOTIVATION AS PERSONALITY: REWARD SENSITIVITY THEORY

Personality can be used as a way to understand motivation. A personality reflects a stable pattern of responding to any given situation (see Chapter 21 for a whole chapter devoted to personality). According to reward sensitivity theory (Gray, 1972), there are two personality types, those that tend towards approaching stimuli and those that tend towards avoiding them. These two styles are represented by the behavioural activation system (BAS) and the behavioural inhibition system (BIS) and each is based on a specific biological substrate. Those of us for which BAS dominates have a tendency to approach or be attracted to appetitive stimuli. It is a positive feedback system that responds to and is sensitive to reward. The behavioural inhibition system (BIS) dominates in those who tend to withdraw from or avoid aversive stimuli. It is a negative feedback system that responds to and is sensitive to punishment. These preferences or tendencies are seen as personality traits that motivate or drive behaviours.

Evaluation of reward (gain) and punishment (loss) is fundamental to learning and plays a key role in a preference for approach or avoidance behaviour (Corr & McNaughton, 2012). In 1972, Jeffrey Gray proposed the original reinforcement sensitivity theory (RST) of personality that impulsive individuals are most sensitive to signals of reward, while anxious individuals are most sensitive to signals of punishment (Corr, 2004). The revised RST (Gray & McNaughton, 2000) identified three systems: (1) the fight-flight-freeze system which mediates reactions to all aversive stimuli; (2) the BAS which mediates reactions to appetitive stimuli; and (3) the BIS which detects goal conflict between reward and punishment. Essentially, the BIS inhibits behaviours that have the potential to cause conflict between the perceived goals of each behaviour. For example, the BIS can stimulate memory of the risks associated with each behaviour in order to resolve the conflict.

The conflict between reward and punishment has been studied using cognitive tests (Bechara, Damasio, & Damasio, 2000; Bechara et al., 1994). The Iowa Gambling Task is a computerised task where participants select cards from four decks of cards (A, B, C and D) in order to win money (Figure 12.3). Occasionally, these monetary gains are accompanied by monetary losses. The goal of the task is to win as much money as possible. While players can switch between decks at any time, some decks are associated with more monetary loss than others and so should be avoided. The task ends once 100 deck choices are made. The pattern of choice of decks tells us what type of motivational style is being followed. Three factors decide how an individual chooses cards from the decks (Busemeyer & Stout, 2002; Yechiam et al., 2007):

(1) *Attention to reward*: High values on this factor indicate a strategy that is based solely on gains or losses received during the task, whereby greater attention is paid to gains rather than losses. Consequently, there is a greater motivation towards reward relating to the BAS aspect of personality.

(2) *Memory for past, relative to recent, outcomes*: This factor describes the degree to which card choices are influenced by past experiences with particular decks. High values of this factor indicate strong recency effects such that the most recent trials are more influential in determining choices, whereas outcomes from past trials are discounted. High scorers on this parameter make future choices that are based on the most recent outcome of a deck selection.

(3) *Choice consistency*: This parameter evaluates how reliable the player is when making the card selection. High values of this parameter indicate that the deck with maximum expectancy to yield a reward will almost certainly be chosen on each trial and therefore lead to less impulsivity. This factor relates to the BIS aspect of personality, where low values reflect an inconsistent, random and impulsive choice behaviour.

FIGURE 12.3   The Iowa Gambling Task

Individuals with orbitofrontal cortex damage show impaired Iowa Gambling Task performance (Bechara, 2004) because their performance is motivated by reward value and they are oblivious to the losses. In addition to patients with orbitofrontal cortex lesions, altered motivational styles are seen in other psychiatric disorders. People with a diagnosis of schizophrenia show a style of performance that is similar to that of orbitofrontal cortex lesion patients (Nakamura et al., 2008), most likely because of poor memory for past relative to recent outcomes on the Iowa Gambling Task (Premkumar, Fannon et al., 2008). Neuroimaging research has even indicated a brain structural basis for the abnormality, wherein the association between greater orbitofrontal cortex grey matter volume and better Iowa Gambling Task performance that is present in healthy participants is lost in schizophrenia patients (Nakamura et al., 2008; Premkumar, Fannon et al., 2008), thus indicating that orbitofrontal cortex abnormality can influence motivational behaviour.

12.5.2 A NEUROBIOLOGICAL THEORY OF MOTIVATION

A dominant biological and psychological theory of reward and motivation is the incentive sensitization theory (Robinson & Berridge, 2003, 2008), which was specifically developed to explain addictive behaviour but in turn tells us something about typical motivation. According to the theory, repeated drug use leads to persistent neuroadaptations of the dopaminergic neurones responsible for motivation (Robinson & Berridge, 1993), producing pathological levels of motivation for drugs and any associated stimuli which become 'motivational magnets'. Thus addiction is characterised as the overwhelming motivation to obtain and take a drug irrespective of whether it is 'liked' or not. Motivation to obtain an appetitive stimulus is psychologically and physiologically different from enjoyment of it. For many years, research into the brain reward pathways conflated the two together. This is likely because the research was mostly conducted in animals and reward was measured by how willing a rat was to press a lever to obtain something enjoyable such as sucrose. This kind of measure cannot distinguish between 'wanting' and 'liking' the sucrose. The incentive sensitization theory (Berridge & Robinson, 1998) considers these two behaviours to be separate psychological components of reward with separate neural pathways. It proposes that the neurotransmitter dopamine mediates 'wanting' (motivation), whereas neurotransmitters called opiates mediate 'liking' (pleasure).

This goes against the more traditional view that dopamine is about hedonia (pleasure) and is still opposed by some (Wise, 2004).

Robinson and Berridge evidence this role for dopamine by using measures that separate wanting and liking, 'liking' being measured by facial reactivity to pleasure (in rats this consists of lateral and rhythmic tongue protrusions and paw licks) and 'wanting' by specific types of conditioning that pinpoint changes in motivation only (e.g. the Pavlovian to instrumental transfer test; Wyvell & Berridge, 2000). They found that, in the nucleus accumbens (part of the mesolimbic system that is known to be involved in the brain reward circuit), increasing dopamine levels by injecting amphetamine did not increase facial reactivity and therefore did not manipulate liking. On the other hand, depletion of dopamine in the nucleus accumbens by destroying dopamine neurones did not prevent such liking responses in response to sucrose, suggesting that removal of dopamine does not remove the neural pathway for registering liking. Robinson and Berridge argue that opioid, endocannabinoid and GABA-benzodiazepine neurotransmitter systems are linked to 'liking' behaviour and regarded as 'hedonic hotspots' (Berridge, Robinson, & Aldridge, 2009). It should be noted, though, that there are those who continue to argue a role for dopamine in liking (Wise, 2004).

KEY RESEARCHER Barry Everitt

FIGURE 12.4   Barry Everitt

Professor Barry Everitt is a distinguished neuroscientist who has contributed to understanding of the neural and psychological basis of addictive behaviour by studying the interactions between Pavlovian and instrumental learning mechanisms in drug seeking, drug taking and relapse. He has demonstrated how initial, voluntary drug seeking and drug taking ultimately becomes established as the compulsive habit that is the hallmark of drug addiction. Neurally, he has shown how ventral striatal structures that mediate the reinforcing effects of drugs and underlie goal-directed actions eventually become subordinate to dorsal striatal control of habitual drug seeking. The emergence of compulsive behaviour is associated with the loss of top-down inhibitory control by the prefrontal cortex, and his research has shown that individuals with an impulsive behavioural trait are those that become compulsive drug takers after a prolonged history of drug taking.

He is a Professor of Behavioural Neuroscience at the University of Cambridge. He is a Fellow of the Royal Society (FRS), a Fellow of the Academy of Medical Sciences (FMedSci), and has been awarded Honorary DSc degrees by Hull University and Birmingham University, where he completed his Bachelors in Zoology and Psychology and his PhD, respectively. He has been included on a list of the 100 most cited neuroscientists by the Institute for Scientific Information. He received the American Psychological Association 'Distinguished Scientific Contribution' Award and the European Behavioural Pharmacology Society 'Distinguished Achievement Award' in 2011 and, in 2012, the Federation of European Neuroscience Societies European Journal of Neuroscience (FENS-EJN) Award and the British Association of Psychopharmacology Lifetime Achievement Award.

12.6 EXPRESSED EMOTION AND PSYCHIATRIC DISORDER

Poor social interaction among family members in patients with psychiatric illness contributes to the poorer mental health outcome of patients. Here we will look at an example of this in the form of the effects of expressed emotion by caregivers on those with a psychiatric illness. Expressed emotion is measured as (a) expressed criticism towards the patient about their symptoms, personal habits and day-to-day household activities; (b) dissatisfaction with who the patient is as a whole; and/or (c) self-sacrificing behaviour, over-protectiveness, warmth and too much concern about the patient's wellbeing. Having a carer with high expressed emotion increases the likelihood of patients experiencing illness symptoms more frequently and spending more time in hospital (Bebbington & Kuipers, 1994; Butzlaff & Hooley, 1998). Brown and colleagues (1962, 1966, 1972) pioneered this field of research. They conducted a series of studies of the family members of patients with schizophrenia. Different family members were interviewed on several occasions about their adjustment to the patient's symptoms in patients who had recently been discharged from hospital and at nine months follow-up. A high degree of emotion expressed by relatives at the time of discharge was found to be strongly associated with symptomatic relapse during the nine months following discharge. Studies have found that having a carer with high expressed emotion is related to patients with a diagnosis of psychosis being hospitalised longer (Marom et al., 2005) and having more depression and anxiety (Docherty et al., 2011).

There are several ways in which carer expressed emotion can be measured, the most accepted form being the Camberwell Family Interview (Brown, Birley, & Wing, 1972; Brown & Rutter, 1966; Vaughn & Leff, 1976). The Camberwell Family Interview is a one- to two-hour structured interview of a carer (defined as a person who spends 10 or more hours a week in contact with the patient) about the patient's psychiatric symptoms, quality of life and the general home environment over the last three months. Another measure of expressed emotion is the Five Minute Speech Sample Test (Magana et al., 1986) where the relative is invited to talk continuously for five minutes about their adjustment to the patient's illness. The Perceived Criticism Scale is a single-item scale asking the patient to rate 'How critical is your spouse/relative of you?' on a 10-point Likert scale (Hooley & Teasdale, 1989). In patients with psychosis, greater patient perceived criticism has been associated with more expressed emotion as criticism (Docherty et al., 2011; Onwumere et al., 2009). High carer expressed emotion during the Camberwell Family Interview translates to more emotional communication styles during face-to-face interaction between the patient and the carer (Miklowitz, 1989).

Research is beginning to uncover the neural processes that are involved when individuals vulnerable to psychiatric disorder are sensitive to expressed emotion as criticism. While studies of the effect of carer expressed emotion suggest a deleterious effect of high carer expressed emotion on the mental state of patients with psychiatric disorder, the emotional and cognitive processes in patients that lead to this outcome are less understood. Neuroimaging research offers valuable insight into the emotional and cognitive processes that operate when people attend to criticism. In patients with schizophrenia, the lateral middle frontal gyrus and anterior cingulate are activated when listening to carer criticism compared to criticism from a stranger (Rylands et al., 2011). These areas have been implicated in emotion regulation. In individuals high in the schizotypal personality trait of unusual experiences, the left middle and superior frontal gyri are more active when listening to a close relative's criticism than neutral comments (i.e. effects are present across groups) (Premkumar et al., 2013). Similarly, in individuals from the general population, greater neuroticism (which indicates more anxious mood and emotional reactivity) was associated with greater connectivity between the superior and middle frontal gyri when listening to standardised criticism (Servaas et al., 2013). Again, these findings indicate that patients with schizophrenia and also individuals in the general community with high schizotypy or neuroticism have greater level of regulation of emotion and top-down processing when listening to criticism from a close relative.

Understanding the neural responses to these interpersonal situations in patients who already have a history of mental disorder and in individuals who are at risk for psychiatric disorder may inform theoretical models of how family interventions operate and help to improve the prognosis and social functioning of at-risk individuals. Family intervention as an adjunctive therapy to standard care is found to be more effective than standard care alone in reducing risk of relapse and hospital admission and improving social functioning (National Institute of Clinical Excellence, 2014).

12.7 FORENSIC IMPLICATIONS OF DYSFUNCTIONAL EMOTION PROCESSING

Thus far in this chapter, we have observed fundamental processes occurring during the perception, processing and expression of emotion. Healthy-functioning individuals may, from time to time, express deviant behaviours as a result of affective states. But how does this differ from anti-social and aggressive behaviour in populations known to have poor emotion processing and behaviour regulation? This section will observe how healthy-functioning individuals differ from aggressive offenders and psychopaths.

What makes a violent person want to get into a fight with an innocent victim? During a social confrontation, we assess emotional states of others, empathise with them, and guide our social behaviour according to what is acceptable within our society. Problems occur when facial expressions are inaccurately processed. Marsh and Blair (2008) highlight that anti-social populations have deficits for recognising distress (fear and sadness) in others, but a large group of 145 males, imprisoned for committing a variety of crimes, suggests a general facial-processing deficit rather than just for fear and sadness (Hastings, Tangney, & Stuewig, 2008). The worst deficits were associated with greater ratings for psychopathy.

> **PSYCHOPATHY** A personality type characterised by anti-social behaviour, callousness and the ability to charm and manipulate others

> **EMPATHY** The ability to feel or share another's experiences or emotions.

There is evidence that some violent offenders may misinterpret emotional expressions. Violent offenders have been found to perceive ambiguous and neutral faces as threatening. Pardini and Phillips (2010) used fMRI to show that the amygdala in chronically violent offenders (those having a history of violence from childhood to adulthood) activated similarly to neutral and threatening facial expressions. This attribution of threat to a neutral expression could perhaps result in an unjustified aggressive outburst.

In addition to misinterpretation of emotional expression, violent and aggressive behaviour has been associated with low **empathic** responses (ability to understand others emotions) to the suffering of others (Blair, 2005). It is an empathic response to feel the distress or pain of others that is thought to explain why people might stop behaving aggressively if their victim shows signs of distress (the violence inhibition mechanism (VIM) (Blair, 1995; Blair et al., 1999). Typically, distressing facial expressions draw attention and evoke an empathic response. By realising the suffering of others, this prompts individuals to cease behaviour causing this distress. Literature on psychopaths and children with psychopathic traits shows deficits in detecting and empathically responding to facial and vocal distress (Stevens, Charman, & Blair, 2001) and may explain the callousness and aggression seen in this group.

12.7.1 ALTERATIONS IN BRAIN ANATOMY LEADING TO PSYCHOPATHIC TENDENCIES

Within individuals characterised for their inability to processes and regulate emotional responses, two main brain systems show dysfunction: the limbic system and the PFC (see Chapter 9 for a reminder of their structure and function). Comprised of structures including the hippocampal formation, amygdala, hypothalamus and nucleus accumbens (Siegel & Victoroff, 2009), the limbic system is the core region within the animal and human brain dedicated to perceiving and expressing emotion (Papez, 1937).

The hippocampus incorporates memory processes and emotional events. It assists in controlling emotional responses such as aggression. The hippocampus is reduced in patients with borderline personality disorder (BPD), a disorder associated with aggressive traits, compared to healthy controls (Soloff et al., 2008), although this may only relate to male rather than female patients (Rüsch et al., 2003). Low hippocampal blood flow, indicating reduced activation, has been observed in violent offenders compared to non-violent controls (Soderstrom et al., 2000). No comparison has of yet been made to a non-violent offender sample which could tease this association apart further.

A population that has been demonstrated to have reduced amygdala volume is that of the psychopath (Yang et al., 2009). Given the role of the amygdala in emotion, this finding may represent psychopaths' reduced ability for emotional learning and facial recognition of emotion (Blair, 2003). In other populations exhibiting aggressive behaviours, such as BPD, reduced amygdala volume has been found in both sexes (Gopal, 2013; Rüsch et al., 2003), although not consistently (Zetzsche et al., 2006). The amygdala also shows increased activation to threat in boys with conduct disorder (Jones et al., 2009). This may indicate that aggressive individuals have a greater reaction to perceived threat, which, if not inhibited, may result in an aggressive act. (See Chapter 27, for more about aggressive acts, including murder and robbery.)

12.7.2 BRAIN FUNCTIONAL CHANGES DURING EMOTION PROCESSING DUE TO PSYCHOPATHIC BEHAVIOUR

There is a wealth of literature within the clinical and forensic fields utilising a variety of scanning techniques (MRI, SPECT, PET) to associate frontal lobe deficits with aggressive behaviour (Bufkin & Luttrell, 2005). Building on the description of the neural substrates involved in fear response to a spider (section 12.3) we will expand on the role of the frontal cortex. Frontal brain systems regulate affective and behavioural responses and so a deficit means a lack of inhibition of these behaviours. The limbic system, as we have already seen, responds to emotionally salient stimuli, for example, someone shouting or looking angry. If uninhibited, this limbic signalling may result in extreme expressions of emotion (attacking the individual or running away). However, within the frontal lobes, the prefrontal cortex (PFC) controls limbic activity in a top-down manner. The PFC deficits play a strong role in aggression by failing to inhibit, or stop, such behaviour (Moffitt, 1993).

The anterior cingulate cortex (ACC), particularly the ventral section (Etkin et al., 2006), shares anatomical connections with the amygdala (Aggleton, 1985), forming an emotion generation–regulation circuit that is implicated in attention to threat and interpretation of emotional stimuli (Ghashghaei, Hilgetag, & Barbas, 2007). Furthermore, the orbitofrontal cortex (OFC) may modulate behaviour by taking into account the expected outcomes of a behaviour that emotionally salient stimuli might prompt (Saddoris, Gallagher, & Schoenbaum, 2005). To unpick this, contextual information (shouting at a football game rather than directly at me, for example) may be recruited to explain perceived emotion, mediating the outward response (Davidson et al., 2000; Izquierdo, Suda, & Murray, 2005). OFC impairment may lead to a misunderstanding of how aggressive behaviours fit in with socially acceptable norms. Unconstrained aggression may be chosen to resolve a conflict.

It has long been acknowledged that in both individuals historically demonstrating repetitive and purposeful violent behaviour (Volkow et al., 1995) and murderers (Raine et al., 1998), blood flow is reduced within frontal lobes. Raine et al. (1998) suggests this effect is likely to be dependent on one's ability to regulate emotion with a cross-comparison of individuals convicted of predatory murder (indicative of an ability to mediate strong emotional responses). Although these findings discuss the frontal lobe as a whole, fMRI indicates reduced OFC activity coupled with increased amygdala activity in intermittent explosive disorder patients, in response to provocation (Coccaro et al., 2007). A failure to recruit frontal systems may result in aggressive behaviour outweighing any given provocation.

KEY STUDY: SEPARATING CONDUCT DISORDER, ANTI-SOCIAL PERSONALITY DISORDER AND PSYCHOPATHY

Blair, R.J.R. (2001). Neurocognitive models of aggression, the antisocial personality disorder, and psychopathy. *Journal of Neurological and Neurosurgical Psychiatry, 71,* 727–731.

In 2001, Blair published a paper delineating the related constructs of conduct disorder, anti-social personality disorder and psychopathy. Although these disorders are related to characteristics of delinquency and aggression, they are conceptually different in the behaviours they evoke. Blair argues a difference between reactive, hot-blooded aggression and goal-orientated, instrumental aggression (see Chapter 27, section 27.3.2 for more about these types of aggression), each having different underlying neurological substrates.

Reactive aggression (in response to provocation), emerging through poor inhibition, is explained through two models. The somatic marker model attributes orbitofrontal cortex dysfunction, a region acting as a knowledge repository used during behaviour adaptation whereby bad ideas and their consequences are rejected. Second, the social response reversal model proposes inhibition resulting from others' angry expressions.

On the other side of the coin, empathy may aid animals through instrumental control (purposeful goal-directed). Submissive cues (distress) may halt an attacker by increasing arousal, attention and brain stem activation, resulting in freezing behaviours.

Blair's investigation allows appreciation of the underpinnings of our seemingly related, yet conceptually different, behaviour. Furthermore, we can see how emotions may modulate behaviour and how disruption to emotional circuitry may impact our everyday socialisation.

12.8 CHAPTER SUMMARY

Our emotions, and the way in which we process, regulate and express them, are fundamental to us as humans. Emotion processing is a vital skill that our brains become specialised in from an early age, and this helps guide our lives within the social environment we encounter every day. Across the basic emotions (anger, happiness, sadness, fear, surprise and disgust), this act of processing differs not only among emotions, but as a function of underlying neuronal functioning, social input and motivational exposure. Different emotions recruit a wide range of networks within the brain, with others recruited during the controlling of our behaviours manifesting from these emotional events.

Motivational systems are intricately linked to our emotions and determine how we process reward. Dysfunctional reward systems lead to aberrant behaviours such as addiction and compulsive behaviours, while dysfunction to core emotional processing and inhibitory systems may result in anti-social and aggressive behaviours. This has been evidenced in both clinical and forensic populations.

DISCUSSION QUESTIONS: HOW AWARE ARE WE OF OUR EMOTIONS AND MOTIVATIONS?

The study of emotions has long provoked the interest of man and we have come a long way since James and Lange's seminal theory of emotion. Nevertheless, it is difficult to reach a definitive understanding of emotion. This is partly because it is not easy to identify discrete emotions. One important question remains: Do our thoughts influence our emotions or vice versa? Even if we are aware of our emotions, how easy is it to modify them?

It is also evident that changes in our brain's structure and function increase the likelihood of the persistence of certain emotions. Signature neural circuits comprise the limbic system, anterior cingulate cortex and prefrontal cortex. Are there, then, specific neural substrates for identifying and expressing specific emotions, and can the same neural substrates be associated with emotion recognition and expression?

The study of emotion has been dominated by the study of negative emotions, such as fear, anger and sadness, whereas the study of positive emotions, such as happiness, has received much less attention. Why do you think this is?

Finally, motivation is intricately linked with emotion, since the desire for reward and aversion of punishment can influence our moods. Are addictive behaviours simply a response to craving for the 'highs' associated with certain substances or actions or a personality that tries to minimise the conflict between craving and abstinence?

SUGGESTIONS FOR FURTHER READING

Blair, J., Mitchell, D., & Blair, K. (2005). *The psychopath: emotion and the brain.* Malden, MA: Blackwell. Psychopathy is always an interesting topic and this book is a good read. It covers the whole range of evidence about psychopathy but emphasises neurocognitive accounts.

Carlson, N.R. (2007). Emotion. In N.R. Carlson (Ed.), *Physiology of behaviour* (9th edn, Chapter 11). Boston, MA: Pearson Education. This is a good basic text to get you started on the biology and cognition of emotion.

Corr, P.J. (2006). Personality: emotion and motivation. In P.J. Corr (Ed.), *Understanding biological psychology*. Malden, MA: Blackwell. A similar text to that of Carlson but this chapter (Chapter 17) includes motivation as well as emotion.

Ekkekakis, P. (2013). *The measurement of affect, mood, and emotion: a guide for health-behavioral research.* New York: Cambridge University Press. As the title suggests, this text is an in-depth look at how to measure such complex phenomena as emotions.

Still want more? For links to online resources relevant to this chapter and a quiz to test your understanding, visit the companion website at edge.sagepub.com/banyard2e

SECTION D

SOCIAL PSYCHOLOGY: HOW WE INTERACT WITH EACH OTHER

Social psychology is about the phenomena of social behaviour. It attracts a lot of attention because it is about the events and processes that make up our daily lives. It looks at our feelings, our thoughts and our behaviour, and tries to describe and explain aspects of the human condition, such as love and hate, happiness and sadness, pride and prejudice, comedy and tragedy. More than any other field of psychology, it is directly about me and you.

We live in a world that is awash with psychological analysis. We are looking to explain why someone is a good contestant on *I'm a Celebrity*... or a good prime minister, and we commonly look to their character and their relationships with other people. This analysis is carried out with varying degrees of scientific rigour and, to be fair, it rarely rises above the level of speculation and gossip. The field of scientific social psychology, however, has over 100 years of research findings to inform our understanding of social behaviour.

The start of social psychology is sometimes dated to 1897 and the experimental work of Norman Triplett into the effects of cooperation and competition on performance. Triplett observed that racing cyclists achieved better times on a circuit when they had someone pacing them. In a ride of 25 miles, the average times per mile were 20% quicker when using a pacemaker on practice runs and even quicker in real competition. He went on to observe this improved performance in other tasks and found, for example, that children wound fishing reels faster when there were other children also winding fishing reels in the same room.

The main concerns of social psychology commonly reflect the concerns of the time. For example, at the end of the nineteenth century there were social concerns about the behaviour of crowds. In particular, there was increasing unrest on the part of working people against repressive social conditions, and the emergence of strategies of collective political action, such as mass strikes and demonstrations. These demonstrations frequently led to violence as police and army forces attempted to suppress them. It was during this time that Le Bon (1895/1995) carried out his research and proposed that the source of this violence lay in a kind of 'mob psychology'. When people were in a crowd, their individual conscience and autonomy were suppressed, and they reverted to what Le Bon described as a primeval, animalistic state in which they would commit acts of aggression which were unthinkable to the same people when acting as individuals. These ideas have been challenged and developed by modern psychologists and we cover some of them in this section.

During the middle of the twentieth century, social psychologists carried out some of the great studies that have defined the field for generations of students. The Milgram study on obedience, the Seligman study of cult membership and the Sherif study on prejudice are just some of the many investigations that had a wide scope and have challenged the ways that we think about ourselves. For many years following these studies, social psychology largely withdrew to the laboratory and carried out clever but very narrow research. More recently, the field has been looking outwards again and dealing directly with real-life behaviour, and sometimes carrying out large-scale studies (e.g. Reicher & Haslam, 2006). There is also a strong focus on applied work looking at health behaviours and crime, for example.

The revolution in social communication over the last 20 years has been a new focus for social psychology. Research has looked at social networking and online behaviours that cause concern, such as bullying. One question concerns whether these digital technologies are providing opportunities for new behaviours or whether we are carrying out the same behaviours we always did but in a new environment. Discuss.

FIGURE D.1 Triplett showed that cyclists achieve better times when cycling with someone rather than alone

© Hulton-Deutsch Collection/Corbis

KEY ISSUES

One of the key issues for social psychology concerns the way it carries out its studies. If we carry out a study in chemistry, for example, we look at some chemicals in a flask and do stuff to them. We are in control of most of what is happening. This is not the case in psychology because the things we are studying (i.e. people) are thinking about what is going on and changing their behaviour accordingly. Every social psychology experiment is a social situation, and the objects of the experiment (the people) are responding to the demands of that situation. So we can never be sure whether their behaviour is due to the variables we are investigating in the study or the social situation of the experiment itself.

THIS SECTION

In this section, we have four chapters looking at the work of social psychologists. In Chapter 13, we explore how being in a group can affect an individual's behaviour and decision making. Commonly, these influences are positive and are part of daily social interaction, but sometimes the group can lead us into poor decisions. In Chapter 14, we look at how groups behave towards each other and how we categorise and respond to people from various groups. One of the issues here concerns the nature of prejudice and racism. In Chapter 15, we explore how we make judgements about other people and how we try to explain their behaviour, focusing on attributions and attitudes. Finally, in Chapter 16, we look at critical social psychology, which broadens the context of our discussions about social behaviours to look at them in a moral and political framework.

13 BEHAVIOUR WITHIN GROUPS

Lead authors: Jens Binder, Mhairi Bowe and Kevin Maguire

CHAPTER OUTLINE

13.1 Introduction	230
13.2 Different types of group and different types of group behaviour	230
13.3 Small-scale groups	231
13.3.1 Norm formation in small groups	231
13.3.2 Group decision making	232
13.3.3 Work performance	233
13.3.4 Are (small-scale) groups good or bad?	233
13.4 Large-scale groups	234
13.4.1 Early accounts of the crowd	235
13.4.2 Deindividuation and the crowd	235
13.4.3 Social identity accounts of crowd behaviour	237
13.5 Environmental factors and applied settings	238
13.5.1 Groups for a purpose?	238
13.5.2 Just a group?	239
13.5.3 What happens in work groups	240
13.6 Chapter summary	241
Discussion questions	242
Suggestions for further reading	242

13.1 INTRODUCTION

The focus of psychology, almost by definition, is on the individual, and most research traditions have tended to regard humans as systems in isolation, without a clear notion of the environment or context in which humans exist. Ironically, evidence from early on (e.g. Triplett, 1898) suggested strongly that our social environment, and group contexts in particular, will have a strong influence on our thoughts, feelings and actions. But even within social psychology, groups were given a hard time for decades. Allport (1924) once famously remarked that no one had ever tripped over a group, thereby questioning their status of existence. Therefore, the starting point for this chapter will be to consider what we typically mean when we talk of groups.

FRAMING QUESTIONS

- Why are groups relevant to social psychology and to psychology at large?
- How is the behaviour of individuals, together with underlying cognitive and motivational processes, changed in a group context?
- What are the benefits and downsides of groups?

13.2 DIFFERENT TYPES OF GROUP AND DIFFERENT TYPES OF GROUP BEHAVIOUR

A group is not a group is not a group. Two examples may serve to illustrate this. First, consider a highly motivated student working in a team with others on an assignment. As the work progresses, it becomes increasingly clear that some

(a) Groups as networks

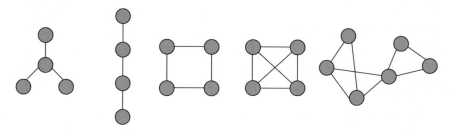

(b) Groups as categories

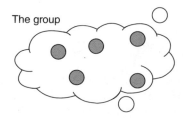

The group

FIGURE 13.1   Two different approaches to the concept of groups with circles representing individuals

team members are simply waiting for others to do the job. In turn, the student finds it hard to stay motivated. Second, consider an immigrant belonging to a highly visible ethnic minority. After a series of news reports on discrimination and police abuse, the immigrant becomes more and more wary of the authorities and socialises exclusively with other minority members. These examples point to two different concepts of groups: (1) groups as small, interacting aggregates of individuals with clear boundaries (teams, work groups) and (2) groups as social categories that may apply to huge numbers of humans (gender, ethnicity, organisational affiliation). In the following, we will consider both types of groups. This is further illustrated in Figure 13.1.

Regardless of group type, the general take on group behaviour in psychology has also been two-fold. On the one hand, many researchers have been concerned with an overall trend towards convergence within groups. Groups are generators of consensus through processes such as norm formation (Sherif, 1936), social comparison (Festinger, 1954) and social identification (Turner, 1991). On the other hand, groups carry the potential of radicalisation, namely when the group as a whole moves towards a more extreme position. This has been widely discussed for group decision making and crowd behaviour, which will both be discussed in this chapter. As will also become clear in this chapter, the switch from positive to negative group effects often does not become clear unless wider environmental factors are taken into account.

13.3 SMALL-SCALE GROUPS

The approach to small-scale groups builds on the notion of lots of pair-wise interactions going on within a limited set of actors. Small groups, at least in principle, can be dissolved into individuals doing things together. We can imagine such groups as not too complex networks of people. Some classical studies (Bavelas, 1950; Mullen, Johnson, & Salas, 1991; Shaw, 1964) have shown that

> **INTERDEPENDENCE** The basic principle that the actual results of individuals' actions are dependent on other individuals' actions.

it matters a lot to group members where they are precisely located in these networks. Central and well-connected group members are typically more satisfied with being in the group than those who are pushed to the periphery with fewer connections to others. The network concept implies that all members actually or potentially depend on each other, or, in other words, that such groups are high in **interdependence** (Kelley et al., 2001).

Small-scale groups come and go. Work teams form to carry out specific projects and disband afterwards. We join hobby groups to pursue particular free-time activities, but turn to other things after a while. Even where groups take on a more formal and stable character (think of an association or a club), their composition will be subject to strong fluctuation as new members join the group and others leave. The life cycle of such groups often follows stages, for example in the well-known model by Tuckman (1965): forming (group members meet for the first time), storming (initial conflict and hostility as members adjust to the group setting), norming (resolution of conflict and establishment of standards), performing (namely, the group tasks) and adjourning (after tasks have been completed) follow one another. Interestingly, the group membership of individuals has also been described by stage models! According to Moreland and Levine (1982), our career as a group member progresses fairly orderly, in line with our commitment to the group, and it is only as a full group member that we will show highest levels of commitment to group needs and goals.

Switching perspectives again, it seems that such member behaviour is strongly expected by the group as a whole. Full membership and commitment to group goals are supposed to go together. This is best illustrated by research on group deviance (Levine, 1989). Members who do not abide by group norms and who show open disagreement with the rest of the group are subject to social pressure in the form of frowns and ridicule. Pressure keeps mounting until the target falls in line with the group again – or until the target is given up as a hopeless case, with marginalisation within the group following suit.

13.3.1 NORM FORMATION IN SMALL GROUPS

The dynamics introduced so far ultimately secure the ongoing existence of small-scale groups, or at least an orderly beginning and end. Group dynamics suggest processes that channel individual behaviour and synchronise individuals' actions to achieve a particular outcome. One of these outcomes is the establishment of norms, as described for the case of deviant group members above. Sometimes a group simply provides much needed orientation to individuals. Observing

INFORMATIONAL INFLUENCE Social influence due to others providing factual information and help with verifying or correcting such information.

NORMATIVE INFLUENCE Social influence due to others serving as models to demonstrate what counts as desirable behaviour.

a dot of light in a pitch-dark room, a group will soon reach consensus about the distances that the light dot is moving about, and individual members will use this consensus as a basis for subsequent estimates that they give on their own – even when, in reality, the light dot is not moving at all (Sherif, 1936). Adding to this **informational influence** in groups is **normative influence** (Deutsch & Gerard, 1955). When faced with the opinions of an overpowering and unwavering majority in a group, people will often fall in line when it comes to voicing their own opinion in public (Asch, 1951). Even though such majority influence can bring about startling effects, such as subscribing to demonstrably wrong judgements, it usually does not lead to any real changes in opinion. In fact, as Moscovici (1980) has argued so convincingly, dedicated minorities are the drivers of deeper changes in groups. Presenting study participants with a confident and unwavering minority leads to less conformity, but the effects go beyond public statements and extend to private opinions. This has been demonstrated in simple colour perception tasks (Moscovici & Zavalloni, 1969) as well as hotly disputed discussion topics (Maass & Clark, 1983).

The discussion so far seems to imply that groups will in the end arrive at something like an averaged position. However, under some circumstances, there is no guarantee that group consensus will reflect anything we would call moderate! Group discussions of opinions and attitudes in settings where members already tend to move away from a middle position typically lead to a consensus that is more extreme than the average of members' initial positions. Groups can drive members actively away from moderation, an effect that has been called group polarisation (Isenberg, 1986). Various explanations have been offered for this effect. For example, social comparison may drive members to compete over more extreme positions. Likewise, once in a group, members start to negotiate a prototypical, and more extreme, group norm because they want to be seen as distinct from others (Turner, 1991).

EXERCISE: WHAT DO I WANT TO DO? WHAT DO YOU WANT TO DO?

Our own opinions are constantly checked with our social environment. Try it out yourself. Find a not-so-easy question you have to decide on (say, what to do on one of the coming weekends). Write down the main options you have, three to five maybe. For each option, note how attractive this would seem to you. Use a scale from 1 to 7, if you want numbers. Now discuss your options with a friend, or two. Check whether the attractiveness of options has changed for you after the discussion. Has it gone up or down?

13.3.2 GROUP DECISION MAKING

Leaving aside issues of social influence for the moment, seemingly neutral information processing in groups is also subject to general group dynamics, often with quite detrimental consequences. In fact, groups have been depicted as being fairly bad at reaching good decisions. In a set of influential case studies, Janis (1972) described group-think as a specific syndrome that can be found when groups are under external and internal pressure to reach a decision on a complex topic. Groupthink is characterised by collective closed-mindedness that prevents members from discussing and assessing all of the available options. A classic example is the decision by the CIA and the US Government to give support to an ill-fated attempt at invading Cuba in 1961. Even though instances of groupthink have been documented time and again (e.g. Moorhead, Ference, & Neck, 1991), there is also a simple way of safe-guarding against this syndrome (see Figure 13.2). Accepting the role of a devil's advocate into a group helps to raise the quality of decisions (Schweiger, Sandberg, & Rechner, 1989) by avoiding close mindedness.

Sometimes, however, group members simply fail to detect good decisions, even though the necessary information is readily available. In so-called hidden profile tasks (Stasser & Titus, 1985), each group member starts a discussion with different pieces of knowledge, some of them known to all members, some of them unique. If all information gets shared, a group should have little difficulty making a good choice (out of a set of job candidates, for example). Yet a standard finding of such studies is that the sharing of information is strongly impaired in groups (Stasser & Titus, 2003). Interestingly, similar to groupthink, one way out of this trap is to introduce more conflict to the discussion, for example in the form of minority dissent (Schulz-Hardt et al., 2006).

13.3.3 WORK PERFORMANCE

Going beyond information processing and decision making, a major focus in small-group psychology has been on group productivity. Contributing once more to a questionable image of small groups, research has mostly demonstrated negative effects of group dynamics. Early studies on manual labour in teams (Ringelmann, 1913) have charted increasing performance losses with growing group size. Comparing groups with sets of individuals ('pseudo groups'), both of the same size, routinely shows the superiority of individual work. This loss cannot be fully attributed to coordination among members (Ingham et al., 1974), but is also due to a generally reduced motivation when working in groups (Latané, Williams, & Harkins, 1979). Indeed, the most influential framework of team performance, proposed by Steiner (1972), leaves little room for high group productivity and emphasises solely losses: **process losses** (i.e. due to coordination) and **motivation losses**. Various answers have been given to the question of why we are less motivated to give our best when in groups: general laziness and propensity to loafing (Latané et al., 1979), lack of clear performance standards (Harkins & Szymanski, 1988), lack of individual feedback (Jackson & Harkins, 1985) and observing others not 'pulling their weight' (Kerr & Bruun, 1983). Studies in which these obstacles were removed have shown increased group output.

Moving from manual labour to less physical activities, a lot of attention has been given to creativity and idea generation in groups. Inspired by Osborn's (1957) brainstorming method, several studies came to the conclusion that real groups are actually strongly underperforming in comparison to pseudo groups (Diehl & Stroebe, 1991; Taylor, Berry, & Block, 1958). The main reason for this is the turn-taking that becomes necessary in group discussions, which results in **production blocking** (Diehl & Stroebe, 1991). Listening to others prevents us from generating own ideas. Interestingly, an internal debate stirred up by deviating minorities can lead groups to become more creative (Nemeth, 1986). As before, moderate conflict in teams can lead to better outcomes in the end (De Dreu & West, 2001).

FIGURE 13.2 Tony Blair visiting British troops in Iraq when he was the British Prime Minister. The Butler report into the decision to invade Iraq in 2003 suggested that the UK intelligence service had developed a groupthink about the issues. This analysis has also been applied to the way that Tony Blair looked for advice and took the final decision to go to war

© Corbis

PROCESS LOSSES Losses in group performance that occur when individuals' inputs are combined due to coordination difficulties – assuming that individuals do not adjust their performance levels.

MOTIVATION LOSSES Losses in group performance that occur independent of coordination difficulties – due to individuals adjusting their performance levels in the presence of others.

PRODUCTION BLOCKING The simple fact that some task setups require group members to act in sequence rather than at the same time. Such a setup, by definition, is less productive than a setup in which members do not block each other.

13.3.4 ARE (SMALL-SCALE) GROUPS GOOD OR BAD?

What, then, are groups good at? The conclusion so far looks like this: groups tend to bully members into stating wrong judgements, they can push general opinion off to extremes, they are disastrous when it comes to making important decisions, they fail at something as simple as pooling information together from members, they show reduced performance when compared to individuals, and they do not even provide a stimulating environment for generating novel ideas!

There are several ways to respond to this negative perspective which has dominated psychology for decades. For one thing, echoing Allport's (1924) original scepticism, it is not the group that is acting (or feeling or thinking), but the group members, the individuals. Being in a group is one of the basic conditions of life, and it is a state that is often beneficial and desirable for us as the social animals that we are. Second, laboratory research has also been criticised for setting up groups to fail and for systematically neglecting factors that would portray groups in a more favourable light. As discussed above, studies have also shown that simple changes to the situation – for example, having minority dissent in a group – can markedly affect group dynamics and outcomes. A few researchers actually set out to demonstrate that groups can perform better than individuals. Hertel, Kerr and Messé (2000) were successful in this through a revival of the almost-forgotten 'Köhler effect'. Köhler (1927) first documented that work teams with a slightly uneven distribution of individual performance levels provided an environment that stimulated weaker individuals to increase their input compared to working alone. Seeing others just ahead of you in this case provides an incentive to make more of an effort. These stimulating impulses coming from a group setting are at present vastly underrepresented in psychology.

KEY STUDY

Hertel, G., Kerr, N.L., & Messé, L.A. (2000). Motivation gains in performance groups: paradigmatic and theoretical developments on the Köhler effect. *Journal of Personality and Social Psychology,* *79*, 580–601.

When does working together really motivate us? Hertel, Kerr and Messé went through a lot of effort to pursue this question. Following a number of pioneers in the field of group research, they decided to create their own ingenious device for measuring performance. Participants had to hold a metal bar in one hand (up to three metres long in one condition), with arms stretched out. If they lowered the arm more than 25 cm, they touched a trip rod. This boundary in turn was connected to two electrical switches that set red flashlights going. The experimenters measured how long the metal bar could be held above the trip rod. Participants did this either alone or together in pairs. In the latter condition, both held on to the metal bar, which was twice as long (and heavy) as in the individual condition. A motivating setup was provided in the form of a 'battle of the sexes': participants were led to believe that the performance of male and female teams would be compared in the study. Under these conditions, the researchers found that pairs showed better performance levels than the individual performances taken together – in direct contradiction to the accepted wisdom on team performance. Maybe it is all about proper motivation, after all?

13.4 LARGE-SCALE GROUPS

As well as belonging to small-scale groups, such as work colleagues or peers, individuals can also belong to large-scale groups. Indeed, **social identity approaches** like **self-categorisation theory** (Turner et al., 1987) emphasise how important large-scale groups are for our sense of self and how strongly they can affect our emotions, cognitions and behaviours. Just as with smaller groups and experimentally created groups, individuals categorise themselves as members of large groups by a similar process of self-stereotyping and social identification, even though they might not have actually met each member of that group. For example, individuals might categorise themselves as members of their national group, and their national identity might then provide them with a sense of self-esteem and belonging, just as smaller groups, such as the family, can. Therefore, even though this group might be more symbolic than interactional in nature, it still shapes our understandings of who we are and how we act in the social world (Reicher & Hopkins, 2001). Much of the social psychology of large-scale groups

SOCIAL IDENTITY APPROACH First developed as social identity theory by H. Tajfel and J.C. Turner (1979), these approaches follow the notion that group memberships are central to our self-concept and self-evaluation, thus linking groups and individuals.

SELF-CATEGORISATION THEORY Building directly on social identity theory, Turner et al. (1987) focused on the social-cognitive effects that arise from putting oneself into a group, for example, the adoption of group norms derived from the concept of a prototypical group member.

has been concerned with how psychological processes affect behaviour *between* groups (or *intergroup* processes; more on this in Chapter 14), but behaviour *within* groups (or *intragroup* processes) has also received considerable attention. This section will be concerned with exploring large-scale within-group behaviours in one of the most controversial and widely analysed contexts: the crowd.

13.4.1. EARLY ACCOUNTS OF THE CROWD

The crowd is a collective phenomenon that has been speculated about for centuries. It seems at first to push our understanding of what constitutes a group to the extreme: a loosely structured, disorganised aggregate of individuals. And yet, like other, more clearly defined groups, the crowd provides a social context that systematically shapes individuals' behaviours. This shaping has often been thought to be a negative one. Even in ancient times, Plato speculated that, as part of the crowd, individuals became uncivilised and subject to a collective 'mob' consciousness. His observations reflect two key characteristics of early accounts of the crowd: (1) they tended to view crowds as negative; and (2) they tended to focus on what happens to individuals as they are taken over by a 'group mind'. Within psychology, the individualistic scepticism discussed above in relation to small groups was also applied to crowds when Allport (1924) suggested that groups, like crowds, and concepts like group mind, should not be studied due to their unscientific nature. He suggested that crowd behaviour was reducible to the sum of individual actions and was a result of the collection of individual dispositions of crowd members (a different perspective on the reductionism approach explored in Chapter 3). However, the notion of a collective consciousness also influenced accounts given by early psychologists such as Sigmund Freud and William McDougall. Much of this influence can be laid at the feet of the nineteenth-century writer Gustave Le Bon.

Le Bon (1895) wrote extensively on his observations of the crowds involved in the political uprisings at the time of the French Revolution. He argued that, in a crowd, previously civilised individuals became primitive, barbaric and were ruled by animalistic instincts instead of reason. In this situation, he believed individuals became submerged in the crowd, thus losing their sense of self. This meant they lacked any self-control and made rapid, disinhibited and irrational decisions due to this inferior thinking. Moreover, he suggested this irrationality and animalism spread through the crowd by a process of 'social contagion', ultimately affecting all members of the crowd. Of course, it is hard to ignore the fact that Le Bon must have been influenced by his political views and bourgeois position in French society at the time, but this observation does not often feature in accounts of his theories. This failure to acknowledge the context of crowd behaviour is something we will revisit later.

13.4.2 DEINDIVIDUATION AND THE CROWD

One of the key features of LeBon's ideas about crowds was the suggestion that crowds give people a sense of anonymity. This anonymity means crowd members' behaviour is unregulated and unrestrained by the usual social norms because it is not monitored by others, or themselves. In the latter half of the twentieth century, psychologists took the idea of anonymity on board and linked it with a loss of accountability and moral restraint in crowd situations when they developed accounts of *deindividuation*. The deindividuation process was believed to lead to anti-social behaviour because people could deviate from their usual social behaviour (Festinger, Pepitone, & Newcomb, 1950; Zimbardo, 1969). Diener (1980) further developed deindividuation theory, suggesting that the process involved a loss of self-awareness. Empirical evidence seemed to support the idea that deindividuation could lead to unusual negative behaviour. For example, Singer, Brush and Lublin (1965) showed people were more likely to use obscene language in the darkness or when concealed by large overcoats. Diener et al., (1976) also famously showed that children who trick-or-treated with masks to conceal their identity were more inclined to take excessive amounts of sweets from residents they visited. Many studies of this nature followed and added weight to claims that feelings of anonymity and loss of self-awareness might lead to aggressive or anti-normative behaviour.

Although influential, the link between deindividuation and negative behaviour was later drawn into question. In a reanalysis of Zimbardo's (1969) study that showed participants' increased willingness to administer electric shocks to stooge participants when deindividuated by large hoods, Johnson and Downing (1979) found that when their participants were dressed as nurses they administered *less* shocks. This showed that deindividuation did not necessarily lead to anti-social or aggressive behaviour. One possible explanation for this study is that during

SIDE (SOCIAL IDENTITY MODEL OF DEINDIVIDUATION EFFECTS) This model postulates that deindividuation involves a switch from personal to collective identity, rather than a loss of identity and the automatic adoption of negative behaviours.

deindividuation participants' behaviour might be influenced by the activation of particular types of collective identity (and the social norms associated with them) rather than by a loss of identity. This idea is central to the more recent **social identity model of deindividuation effects (SIDE)** (Lea & Spears, 1991; Reicher, Spears, & Postmes, 1995).

Traditional accounts of deindividuation were nonetheless applied to crowd psychology, despite suffering from some obvious limitations. For example, they could not account for why some crowd members did not seem affected by the anonymity of being in a crowd or why spectators of crowds were not also affected. As an alternative, the idea that crowd behaviour might be governed by norms gained popularity after Turner and Killian (1972) published their account of crowd behaviour. They viewed norms as *emergent* in crowd situations and suggested that the behaviour of the crowd was influenced by identifiable crowd members displaying distinctive behaviours, which were copied by other group members and became norms governing the whole crowd's behaviour. This approach was useful because it challenged notions that crowd behaviour is always irrational and non-normative. The assumption that crowds are irrational can be seen to be problematic by observing crowds in

KEY RESEARCHER Steve Reicher

Steve Reicher is Professor of Social Psychology at the University of St Andrews. He has worked closely with the two authors of social identity theory, Henri Tajfel and John Turner, and has been involved in the formulation and subsequent developments of self-categorisation theory. Through his social identity approach to crowd behaviour, he has challenged long-standing notions of the irrationality of groups. This work has had implications on many levels: it has changed our perspective on the relationship between individuals and groups; it has given an edge to academic and political debates on protests and collective actions settings; and it has informed recommendations for policing. Steve has pursued this interest in collective action looking, for example, at nationalism and national identity. Together with Alex Haslam, Steve Reicher has revisited our understanding of obedience and conformity to investigate if the early findings are seen today. As such, he has revisited Milgram's classic obedience studies and was a researcher and advisor for the BBC Prison Study, which featured in the television programme *The Experiment*. This study was designed as a re-examination of the famous Zimbardo Stanford Prison experiment. This research suggests that in our current society individuals may still conform – not necessarily to authority, but rather based on group identity.

FIGURE 13.3   Steve Reicher

emergency situations. For example, Drury, Cocking and Reicher (2009) showed that during the 7 July bombings in London in 2005, victims of the bombing operated together in an organised series of collective actions to facilitate helping and escape from dangerous areas although they were crowded together. However, despite this useful move towards a more rule-governed account of crowd behaviour, many social psychologists were unsatisfied with the emergent norms account, primarily because it failed to explain the exact processes by which norms would emerge and why they should influence all people in the crowd.

13.4.3 SOCIAL IDENTITY ACCOUNTS OF CROWD BEHAVIOUR

One approach that appeared to answer these questions was offered by Reicher (1982, 1987), who put forward a social identity approach to understanding crowd behaviour. He suggested that crowd behaviour is social behaviour like any other, and as such it does not occur in a normative vacuum. What he meant by this is that crowds can have their own history and reasons for coming together before collective action takes place. He suggested that instead of losing a sense of identity in crowds, there is a shift from personal to social identity. This idea was supported by his observations of crowd behaviour during the 1980 St Paul's riots in Bristol (Reicher, 1984). This disturbance occurred after police raided a café in an area of Bristol and performed an unjustified search of a black customer. Significant levels of community destruction and crowd violence occurred in response to this, but two key features of this crowd behaviour were noted: (1) the violence and destruction were rationally targeted at symbols of the police and establishment, and

---

EXERCISE: CROWD BEHAVIOUR

Think of a contemporary example of crowd behaviour and to try to interpret its cause. Can your chosen crowd be thought of as a group? Does that group have existing norms or did they only emerge when the crowd came together? Try to write an account of the events that took place from both deindividuation and social identity perspectives, and decide whether social context is relevant, or whether people in crowds truly are irrational and animalistic.

---

avoided local residents and their property; and (2) the riots occurred in a context of pre-existing racial tension, deprivation and poor relations between community members and the police. It was also found that, despite these events, community cohesion actually increased following the riots and this led social identity theorists to link crowd events with the expression of group sentiments and meaningful collective action (Reicher, 2001).

The social identity approach therefore shows that social context is essential for understanding crowd behaviour. It has also highlighted that there are often two groups involved in crowd situations and led to an intergroup approach to crowd behaviour. This approach explored how police views of the crowd as pathological and dangerous could influence policing strategies and lead to conflict in relation to riots (e.g. the 1990 poll tax riot) and at events such as football matches (Stott & Reicher, 1998a, 1998b). Stott, Hutchison and Drury (2001) studied the behaviour of football crowds in the 1998 World Cup, revealing that an illegitimate view of English fans as 'hooligans' by the police led to escalated conflict during their matches, whereas conflict was greatly reduced during Scotland's matches because Scottish fans were viewed as generally friendly and so were treated fairly by the police during their interactions. This acknowledgement of the role of dynamic social contexts, legitimate actions and intergroup behaviours in crowd psychology led to a new elaborated social identity model (ESIM) of crowd behaviour (Drury & Reicher, 2000).

The idea of anonymity, aggression and lack of restraint still influence popular understandings of crowd events in today's society. However, the above social psychological inquiries have shown these might massively misrepresent crowd behaviours by ignoring the importance of identity, and in particular social identity. As a result, social psychologists have offered up alternative perspectives on many contemporary large-group events, such as the August 2011 riots in London and beyond (see Reicher & Stott, 2012). These accounts offer a perspective where crowd behaviour can be viewed as group-based and rational. In doing so, they provide another way of seeing groups as good for us because they facilitate meaningful social expression and action. They also show just how relevant groups are for social psychology and psychology at large because they can help us understand social movements and political actions such as protests, demonstrations and even riots.

KEY STUDY

Drury, J., Cocking, C., Beale, J., Hanson, C., & Rapley, F. (2005). The phenomenology of empowerment in collective action. *British Journal of Social Psychology*, *44*, 309–328.

Being able to do something about a perceived injustice typically makes us feel better, in particular together with others. But what exactly is the link between collective action, in the form of activism, and a subsequent sense of empowerment and other positive emotional responses? Following a social identity approach, the authors of this study argue that collective self-objectification (CSO) plays a key role, that is, action taken to assert an ingroup's social identity against an overpowering and dominant outgroup. Taking detailed interviews with 37 activists, in pursuit of political, environmental and moral issues, the researchers were able to show that CSO featured prominently in interviewees' past experiences and was among the most cited factors associated with a sense of empowerment. Further, more instances of CSO were related to more positive emotions, and CSO turned out to be the best predictor of positive emotions among a range of other factors, such as feelings of unity or support. In other words, there is something in the process of jointly resisting dominance which makes us feel good.

ASIDE

The social cure

In recent years, a small group of social identity researchers have been interested in providing one particular response to the question of whether groups are good for us by looking at the impact of groups on mental and physical health. Jetten, Haslam and Haslam (2012) argue that groups can be considered as a 'social cure' for all kinds of ills, such as stress, trauma, depression and recovery from serious illness and injury. By showing how processes of collective identification are linked with psychological processes like investment in the group, a sense of belonging and meaning, and the availability of social support, they argue that valued social groups are essential for good health in residential, clinical, social and organisational contexts.

13.5 ENVIRONMENTAL FACTORS AND APPLIED SETTINGS

13.5.1 GROUPS FOR A PURPOSE?

So far, groups have been shown as small aggregates engaged in decision making or simple motor tasks. Groups themselves have also been shown as powerful social environments, as crowds developing a social identity and bringing forth collective action. In this last part of the chapter, the importance of environmental factors that lie outside the group will be considered. Workplace settings and organisational contexts are good examples of complex environments in which every actor (e.g. a worker) comes with a whole range of needs and goals and has to interact with other actors. Such settings first of all question the idea that groups always come with a clearly defined task and always serve one particular purpose. We might initially think that work groups in particular are there for a purpose, but that purpose is not always obvious. Tajfel et al. (1971) revealed how a randomly constructed group can give a sense of identity and Bion's work (see later) reveals much about the emotional roles of groups. The (in)famous Hawthorne studies (again see later) also illuminate the complexity of group needs and performance in an organisational setting, showing that task orientation in itself is not enough.

While a purpose or aim might be explicit for a group (especially for working methods), context and environment are often more influential in group achievement and behaviour. Such a clash can be seen where a culture exists within a milieu of contingent influences, something especially evident in times of changes. We cannot explore all the theories of organisational culture but will focus on the influential grid and group theory of the anthropologist Mary Douglas (1992). A crude, but useful, reduction of this sees cultures as one of four types: bureaucratic, egalitarian, individualistic and isolationist, each cultural form having its own set of values, ideas and ways of behaving. Using Douglas's categories, we can explain earlier descriptions of the problems of trying to get an egalitarian culture to accept a bureaucratic way of working: it was not successful (Gouldner, 1954). A culture, for Douglas, maintains the strong group bonds by a 'policing' of activity which she calls the *forensic use of culture*: a process whereby all harms (e.g. accidents at work) are blamed on behaviours deviant to the cultural values and ways. For example, in a bureaucratic culture (which she describes as ancestor-worshipping and rule-bound), an industrial injury would be blamed on someone not following precedent and not abiding by the rules drawn up by the *experts*.

Cultures, however, are not invincible: contingent forces will often change them. For example, great changes in technology and an altered socio-economic environment, nearly 50 years after Gouldner, have successfully increased the bureaucracy of mine working. Contingency theory, as developed in the early 1950s and 1960s (e.g. Woodward, 1958), at first focused on the shaping of the environment by means of technologies that act as the dictator of group form and activity. Later versions of contingency theory (Donaldson, 2001) talked about a fit between organisational form and its working environment with optimum fit resulting in optimum performance. Of course, one set of cultural forces can become a contingency to another culture. The clash between a culture and the group contingencies, however, is never fully won by one side, as revealed by Kamoche and Maguire (2011) who found older egalitarian cultures still surviving (and being relied upon!) within UK coal mining.

As a general rule, competing forces are abundant in complex organisations. Within the working group, aims might conflict not only within a small group but among constituent groups within a larger group. Thus optimal performance in one group might result in sub-optimal performance in the larger group or organisation. This is particularly a problem where each group has a different set of unifying values and behaviours (i.e. differ culturally), as written about by, among others, Perrow (1970, 1972). Similarly, individual group members might also have their own aspirations; these too might compete and, again, become contingent forces (Perrow, 1970, 1972). As an example, think of the effect of a supplies department in a factory that optimises its own performance by reducing its budget through lower stock levels and restricted opening times, measures that are likely to be perceived negatively by other departments.

13.5.2 JUST A GROUP?

The (in)famous **Hawthorne studies** in the 1940s were seen as a breakthrough in theorising and managing people in groups. While the previous management approach had been a Taylorian scientific management one (see Braverman, 1974), such an approach had been unsuccessful in raising productivity at the Hawthorne Works of Western Electric in the USA (Haslam, 2001). In consequence, Mayo and his team, as a result of other work, were called in. They demonstrated (and 'gave birth to') the human relations approach to management when, '[r]egardless of the conditions, whether there were more or fewer rest periods, longer or shorter workdays . . . the women worked harder and more efficiently' (Freedman et al., 1981, cited in Levitt & List, 2011: 225). Mayo's work revealed that group dynamics and relations between workers were *at least* as important in designing work for human machinery. Interestingly, Bramel and Friend (2003) considered that 'The distortions presented [in the contemporary reporting of the studies] … were probably important in preserving a view of workers as irrational and unintelligent' (Bramel & Friend, 2003: 97), a point also made by Braverman (1974).

> **HAWTHORNE STUDIES AND THE HAWTHORNE EFFECT** Workers in the Hawthorne Works, having been found to work more productively as a result of someone showing an interest in them (rather than just being seen as an adjunct to production), led to the expression 'Hawthorne effect', which is taken to mean that people (whether in industry or in the psychological laboratory) always perform better when being observed – even if the only alteration of conditions is that they are observed.

Despite the importance of relations within the group being demonstrated so long ago, there remains a conflict between approaching groups from a task-oriented and relations-oriented point of view, particularly in managing them. Marrying the two and understanding how people work with a task is one of group theory's goals. One such attempt has been using systems approaches based on the cybernetics of the 1950s. Here the organisation is treated as one kind of system that exists within a particular environment (see Figure 13.4). The system has inputs from that environment and sends outputs to it. In between is the transformational function. Envisaging the system and the permeability of

TAVISTOCK INSTITUTE A UK-based charitable group founded in 1947 to study and promote human relations in various social settings, including industry, commerce and healthcare. Their 'hallmark' is their use of psychoanalytic and open systems approaches to groups and organisations and, in the spirit of action-research, feeding back findings to that group or organisation as part of their intervention.

the boundary separating it from the environment becomes important. Such an approach can be used to reframe contingency theory and is a key to the development of the **Tavistock's socio-technical systems approach** (see later) to groups.

Particularly in work settings, the boundary of the group is not such an easy thing to define, something in Bittner's (1974) asking 'What is an organisation?' and Perrow's (1972) analysis of *Complex organisations*. We can see that 'no group is an island', with subdivisions within an explicitly identified group not always working together and 'separate' groups (sometimes from different organisations) effectively working as a single group. For example, a marketing group within a company is often found to be in conflict with the production group, and,

on the other hand, a very large company like the Ford Motor Company organises its sub-contractors to the point that they are an extension of themselves (Perrow, 1970).

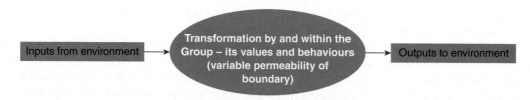

FIGURE 13.4 A systemic framework for modelling the dynamics of a group culture within an environment

SOCIO-TECHNICAL SYSTEMS From identifying the social interactions between people in a work group or organisation (along with their needs), and identifying the more traditional cybernetic system of the work task, a socio-technical system is one which combines the two into a single larger and more complex system. Workers are not expected to contort themselves in order to serve inhuman and inflexible work demands. Rather, the technical requirements of the larger system are worked out in tandem with the social needs of the working group. The aim is improved sustainable working patterns resulting in better organisational output.

Socio-technical systems theory was originally developed to understand why new equipment and working methods for coal mining in post-war Britain's nationalised coal production were not producing the expected increases in productivity (Trist, Susman, & Brown, 1977). Investigations found that the organisation required to operate the new equipment was not in harmony with the working methods developed in the Durham coal fields (where this work was done). Rather, they noticed that 'any work site contains two interdependent systems, a technical system and a social system' (Trist, Susman, & Brown, 1977: 207). Once again, we see the clash between task and group, between scientific management and human relations. The Tavistock group's solution was for both social systems and technical systems to work together as a larger system, hence the name. In order to achieve this, they developed semi-autonomous work groups (a little like the pre-war butty system – see Goffee, 1981) where group identity was strong: in systems theory parlance, this was the transformational part of the system.

13.5.3 WHAT HAPPENS IN WORK GROUPS

It may come as a surprise, but one approach for researchers to tackle the challenge of explaining complex dynamics in work settings has come out of further developments of psychoanalysis. Interestingly, these theories have introduced alternative ways of accounting for the switch between positive and negative group outcomes. Of particular relevance to this tradition is Wilfred Bion's (1961) psychoanalytic theory of groups. Growing out of his early experiences as an army officer, his training as a psychiatrist and his further analytic training under Melanie Klein, Bion developed a theoretical approach to people in groups. For Bion, groups are either in a *working group* state or a *basic assumptions group* state, and a group will switch between the two.

When there was a 'good group spirit' (*working group*) he noticed the following qualities: common purpose; common recognition of group boundaries; flexibility (the capacity to absorb new members and to accept members leaving without the group falling to pieces); an absence of subgroups with rigid boundaries; a valuing of all group members and an acceptance of their free movement; the capacity to face discontent and a means of coping with it (Bion, 1961: 25–26). Groups, however, do not always work with harmony and purpose – or rather with stated purpose. Dysfunctional groups are said to be in the *basic assumption* state when Bion postulates the existence of a *group mentality* which aims to stop the group and its members progressing. He was quite clear that there was individual mental functioning; this was not a matter of herd instinct. The mental functioning he considered to be similar to the infant trying to understand and operate in a world with contradictions (similar to Klein's classic description of the developing infant's reactions to the breast).

The basic assumptions group might be in one of three phases: *dependency*, *flight-flight* or *pairing*. In a dependency group (baD), members look to the leader and want everyone to behave in what they think of as the proper role. They hang on to the leader's every word. Yet when the leader performs out of expected role, members are quick to castigate the leader and to elevate another upon whom they can depend. In the flight-fight group (baF) members move between attacking someone in the group and 'running away' from ideas raised or suggested. In the pairing group (baP), two group members take on special significance and are paired by the group (in what Bion saw as a sexual bonding). Whatever the actual phase of the basic assumptions group, there is an avoidance of the 'real work'. Rather, as group members become aware of their anxieties generated by 'the complexities of life in a group the adult resorts, in what may be a massive regression to mechanisms described by Klein' (Bion, 1955: 141), that is, they try to avoid them with the same primitive strategies they learnt for dealing with their complex contradictory universe that they began to meet as a small child. The group thus becomes both the place in which anxieties are generated and the resource used to avoid those same anxieties.

More on the idea that particular group dynamics are best seen as a way of dealing with anxiety comes out of the work of Isobel Menzies in her study of nurses. A large teaching hospital in London approached the Tavistock Institute of Human Relations: organisational demands for 'nursing labour' were taking precedence to the detriment of the training needs of nurses, leading to 'acute stress . . . [and] a danger of complete breakdown in the system of allocation' (Menzies, 1960: 96). Menzies and her team treated this as the 'presenting problem', and diagnosis of the 'real problem' began with interviews of 70 nurses plus senior staff along with observations and 'many informal contacts' (1960: 97). They noted 'high levels of tension, distress, and anxiety', which were intolerable, leading to 'withdrawal from duty', including a third of student nurses leaving before completing their training, senior staff frequently changing jobs and seeking post-graduate training, and high rates of sickness absence. The causes of the anxiety were understandable:

> constant contact with people who are physically ill . . . recovery is not certain . . . [or] complete . . . Nurses are confronted with the threat and the reality of suffering and death as few lay people are. . . . [They] carry out tasks which are, by ordinary standards, distasteful, disgusting, and frightening. Intimate physical contact with patients arouses strong libidinal and erotic wishes and impulses. . . . [Their work arouses] pity, compassion, and love; guilt and anxiety; hatred and resentment of the patients who arouse these strong feelings; envy of the care given the patient. The list goes on. No wonder there is 'withdrawal from duty'. (Menzies, 1960: 97–98)

As a psychoanalytically oriented practitioner, Menzies considered that the anxieties in nurses arose because the 'everyday' features of their work stimulated anew 'the phantasy situations that exist in the individual in the deepest and most primitive levels of the mind' (1960: 98), theorising the work in terms of Klein (1948) at an individual level and Bion (1955, 1961) at a group level. Although it can be questioned whether Menzies' psychoanalytical approach provides the best explanation of what is happening with the nurses, it raises awareness of the fact that individuals can face deep-running difficulties when thrown into groups and that groups can easily become dysfunctional in a work setting under pressure.

13.6 CHAPTER SUMMARY

Being a group member is an integral part of our everyday lives. Groups may take on any form, from small teams to crowds, to mere labels for social categories, and the influence of a group context on the individual is manifold and far-reaching. This is reflected in the variety of theories that researchers have used to explain behaviour in groups. These theories quite often reflect an underlying evaluation of groups, from mindless and evil to focused and task-oriented. They also reflect the complexities of the setting under scrutiny as in the investigation of organisational systems.

Most approaches to the study of groups have to come to terms with complex dynamics within those groups and, at the same time, with complex interactions between a group and its environment. In the end, our own impression of groups and group membership will always influence our preferences for particular models and explanations.

 # DISCUSSION QUESTIONS

Can being in a group change the way we think and behave? Think about how we behave and feel when we are alone. Can groups affect us even when we are alone and the 'group' is not physically present?

Are groups good for us? What are the benefits of identifying with a group? Think through the different groups you belong to and what the benefits are to you.

Are we humans made to live in groups? Could we live without groups?

One of the ideas this chapter has presented is that groups can be difficult to define or conceptualise. Are groups real? Do they only exist in our heads?

 # SUGGESTIONS FOR FURTHER READING

Diamond, M., & Allcorn, S. (2003). The cornerstone of psychoanalytic organizational analysis: psychological reality, transference and counter-transference in the workplace. *Human Relations*, *56*(4), 491–514. This article gives a good overview of the application of psychoanalysis to organisational settings, as introduced in section 13.5 of this chapter.

Drury, J., & Reicher, S. (1999). The intergroup dynamics of collective empowerment: substantiating the social identity model of crowd behavior. *Group Processes & Intergroup Relations*, *2*(4), 381–402. This is a further elaboration of Reicher's initial account of crowd behaviour and shows theoretical developments on this topic over the course of a decade.

Kerr, N.L., & Tindale, R.S. (2004). Group performance and decision making. *Annual Review of Psychology*, *55*, 623–655. This overview can be seen, in many ways, as an update to McGrath's book, 20 years later. It does highlight, among other things, the move towards a more balanced view on group performance that is not as negative as it used to be.

McGrath, J.E. (1984). *Groups: interaction and performance*. Englewood Cliffs, NJ: Prentice Hall. A modern classic in small-group research that covers, in a pioneering way, lots of aspects in section 13.3 of this chapter.

Reicher, S.D. (1987). Crowd behaviour as social action. In J.C. Turner, M. Hogg, P. Oakes, S. Reicher, & M. Wetherell (Eds), *Rediscovering the social group: a self-categorization theory*. Oxford: Blackwell. A central and seminal piece on the new take on crowd behaviour, as outlined in section 13.4 of the chapter.

 Still want more? For links to online resources relevant to this chapter and a quiz to test your understanding, visit the companion website at edge.sagepub.com/banyard2e

14 BEHAVIOUR BETWEEN GROUPS

Lead authors: Mick Gregson, Rowena Hill and Nicholas Blagden

CHAPTER OUTLINE

14.1 Introduction	**244**
14.2 Fundamental concepts	**244**
14.2.1 Interpersonal versus intergroup behaviour	244
14.2.2 Social categorisation and stereotyping	245
14.2.3 Prejudice, discrimination and ethnocentrism	248
14.3 Explaining prejudice and discrimination	**249**
14.3.1 Frustrated and prejudiced individuals	249
14.3.2 Frustration and aggression	249
14.3.3 Personality and prejudice	250
14.3.4 Realistic conflict theory	251
14.3.5 Social categorisation to social change: social identity theory	252
14.3.6 Social psychology, racism and prejudice	254
14.4 Reducing intergroup conflict	**255**
14.4.1 Contact	255
14.4.2 Superordinate goals	257
14.4.3 Crossed category membership	257
14.5 Chapter summary	**258**
Discussion questions	**258**
Suggestions for further reading	**258**

14.1 INTRODUCTION

Barack Obama's inauguration in January 2009 as the first black President of the USA was witnessed by veterans of the US Civil Rights movement who 40 years earlier fought for basic rights denied to black people in some parts of the USA. In his inaugural speech, President Obama emphasised the USA's diversity as 'a nation of Christians and Muslims, Jews and Hindus, and nonbelievers … shaped by every language and culture'. Nearly five years later President Obama was one of very many heads of state and dignitaries from all over the world who attended the memorial service in South Africa following the death of Nelson Mandela, who had played such a significant role in ending the apartheid system and gone on to be that country's first black president.

These events are remarkable partly because of the prejudice and discrimination against black people that have over centuries contributed to social inequality. Conflict between groups is very much a feature of human societies. You'll be aware of some current conflicts as they appear in the news, but even armed conflict is not always deemed newsworthy. A glance at the website www.warsintheworld.com reveals the extent and number of disputes around the world. While conflict is not the only characteristic of behaviour between groups, it is one of the most important and the most studied by psychologists interested in intergroup behaviour, and it is the aspect that we will concentrate on in this chapter. Even the most fortunate among us will have some direct relevant experience of conflict between groups. Before reading on, consider the following. While still at school, you may have witnessed, or even taken part in, verbal or physical conflict between pupils from different areas or different schools. Pupils with a 'different' appearance and lifestyle may have been targets of rumour and gossip, verbal abuse, physical threats or even violence. What similarities can you see between this kind of conflict and the kind of political and social divisions that may lead, in the most extreme cases, to genocide – or are they completely different?

FRAMING QUESTIONS

- How have social psychologists explained behaviour between groups?
- To what extent are prejudice and discrimination inevitable?
- How have psychological approaches been influenced by the social context?
- How can conflict between groups be reduced?

14.2 FUNDAMENTAL CONCEPTS

14.2.1 INTERPERSONAL VERSUS INTERGROUP BEHAVIOUR

Intergroup relations can only exist when we have groups. In everyday life we have no problem in using the word 'group' and knowing what we mean by this, so it should be straightforward to discuss intergroup relations. A classic definition, provided by Sherif (1966), suggests that this is the case:

> whenever individuals belonging to one group interact, collectively or individually, with another group or its members in terms of their group identifications we have an instance of intergroup behaviour. (Sherif, 1966: 12)

Though this seems clear, defining the meaning of 'group' more precisely is problematic (as highlighted in Chapter 13). Different criteria have been employed by different psychologists at different times. Psychologists interested in behaviour in small groups focus on factors such as face-to-face interaction, group norms and interdependence (e.g. Johnson & Johnson, 1987). The behaviour of very large groups may differ so that here we would be interested in looking not so much at individual, face-to-face interactions, but rather at interactions on the group level, and the 'us versus them' scenarios that arise as groups confront each other.

To encompass large-scale social conflict and to avoid some of the problems associated with defining groups in more specific ways, Tajfel (1978) proposed that a group is essentially a set of people who feel that they are a group. This can be applied to anything from a small 'gang' of friends to very broad groupings such as a religious grouping or a nation. According to Tajfel, the salience of a group membership for us will depend on the context. For example, many people become more conscious of their nationality at times of conflict or major sporting competition.

Tajfel proposed that there is a continuum of behaviour between acting purely in terms of self and acting purely in terms of group. These extremes are 'ideal' in the sense that we can never act completely independently of our group memberships or of our own personal characteristics and relationships. Rather, we may be acting more or less in terms of self or group, and this will vary according to changes in the context. Changes from the interpersonal to the intergroup may occur quite suddenly.

EXERCISE: ARE YOU TALKING ABOUT ME?

Imagine two students, new to university, who have just met. They find each other attractive and both seem to be enjoying chatting away happily on quite a personal level. They begin talking about the different parts of the country where they come from, and then one makes a sarcastic comment about people from the other's region based on a well-known stereotype.

Consider a spectrum of behaviour running from 'acting in terms of self' at one end to 'acting in terms of group' at the other. Analyse the above example in terms of this spectrum. At different stages of the interaction, where would you place the behaviour of the two students on this continuum? Would you expect any change to follow from the sarcastic comment? What would this depend on?

Now reflect on how you imagined the scenario. For example, did you imagine the two students to be of the same or different sex; of similar or different ages or ethnic backgrounds? What difference would it have made if you'd imagined them differently?

14.2.2 SOCIAL CATEGORISATION AND STEREOTYPING

In everyday life, we can categorise objects as being similar to some other objects (e.g. cars and vans are similar) and different from others (e.g. pedestrians are 'different' from cars). Similarly for intergroup behaviour, we can distinguish between members of one group (e.g. fellow students) and another (e.g. lecturers). A failure to perceive group similarities and differences can lead to social embarrassment and could even put us in danger. Without this process of social categorisation, intergroup behaviour cannot occur.

Social categorisation is partly a *cognitive* process, and early approaches rested on a view that prejudice results from inflexible and faulty cognitive processing (Allport, 1954). Central to this is the concept of **stereotyping**. The term was popularised by Lippmann, who claimed that 'stereotypes ... preconceptions ... mark out certain

> **STEREOTYPE** An oversimplified, generalised impression of a group and its members.

objects as familiar or strange, emphasising the difference, so that the slightly familiar is seen as very familiar, and the somewhat strange as sharply alien' (Lippmann, 1922: 59).

This accentuation of difference between categories (e.g. the familiar and the strange) may result from categorisation itself (Tajfel & Wilkes, 1963). Corneille et al. (2002) asked Belgian and American participants to make judgements of the lengths of eight lines. Half the participants had a ready-made means of categorising the lines as the lines were labelled in a systematic way (the four shortest were labelled 'A' and the four longest labelled 'B'). Those viewing the labelled lines accentuated the difference in length between the four shortest and the four longest lines, compared with

FIGURE 14.1 Stereotyping. Political parties can boost support by appealing to people's fears of other groups of people.

© Richard Baker/In Pictures/Corbis

PREJUDICE An unreasonable or unfair dislike of something or, more usually, of someone, typically because they belong to a specific race, religion or group.

DISCRIMINATION The consideration or treatment of others based on general factors (e.g. their race, religion or some other grouping), rather than on individual merit.

those who viewed unlabelled lines. This difference was increased under conditions of greater uncertainty resulting from the use of unfamiliar measures (i.e. when the Americans gave estimates in centimetres and the Belgians gave estimates in inches). Tajfel (1981) argued that *social* categorisation can similarly lead to overestimation of intergroup differences, just as Lippmann had argued concerning stereotypes.

You can probably easily generate a list of well-known and widely-used stereotypes. For example, try to complete some of these sentences: 'politicians are…'; 'car salesmen are…'; 'football players are…'; 'sex offenders are…'. The potential disadvantages of such stereotyping (i.e. crude oversimplifications and overgeneralisations) do not seem to stop people making use of stereotypes. One reason for this is that they act as 'mental shortcuts', simplifying our environment for us and allowing us to make sense of the world without too much effort (Hamilton & Crump, 2004). Another is that important stereotypes are not developed by isolated individuals but are *shared* with other group members and thus serve a function for the group (Oakes, Haslam, & Turner, 1994; Snyder & Miene, 1994; Stangor & Schaller, 1996). Stereotypes of a minority group may allow a powerful majority to blame them for societal problems or to justify acting in an exploitative way towards them (see Figure 14.1).

These examples take us from a simple focus on stereotyped *beliefs* about other groups to matters of **prejudice** and **discrimination**. Stereotypes matter because they have *effects*. Lyons and Kashima (2001) showed that, when accounts are passed on from one person to another, information that does not conform to stereotyped expectations tends gradually to be dropped. In their research, they showed that in later versions of a story about Australian Rules football players, the story tended to retain information about their beer drinking (stereotypical behaviour) but lose information about their listening to classical music (non-stereotypical behaviour). Lyons and Kashima (2003) showed that the emphasis on stereotypical information was strongest when the story teller and their audience shared the same stereotypes. Communication processes thus help maintain stereotypes of other groups as people may just omit, deny or ignore information which does not 'fit' a stereotype. This can have important consequences: for example, stereotypical images of sexual offenders as 'dirty old men with thick glasses' conceal the fact that sex offenders are from all works of life and from all social areas and are often skilled at leading 'double lives' (Blagden, 2012; Salter, 2001). Such stereotypical thinking may lead to victim blaming, with people reluctant to believe that a doctor, neighbour, police officer, lawyer, father or brother are capable of such actions (Blagden et al., 2011).

In an important account of these processes, Pettigrew (1979) refers to 'the ultimate attribution error'. This is the tendency for individuals to explain (a) negative behaviours of outgroup members as resulting from the dispositional characteristics of members of that group (e.g. their genes) while blaming ill fortune or other situational factors for the same behaviour of in-group members, and (b) positive outgroup behaviours as exceptional and more likely due to situational factors such as luck or accident (Chapter 15 has a discussion of similar attributional errors).

Memories also reflect stereotypes (e.g. Belleza & Bower, 1981; McRae, Hewstone & Griffiths, 1993). Fiske (1998) concludes that the tendency for memories to match stereotyped expectations is greatest in complex social

KEY STUDY

Burt, M.R. (1980). Cultural myths and supports for rape. *Journal of Personality and Social Psychology, 38*(2), 217–230.

In 1980, Martha Burt published what became a very influential paper on how **rape myths** served to justify rape. She defined rape myths as 'prejudicial, stereotyped, or false beliefs about rape, rape victims, and rapists' (1980: 217). Such myths include the beliefs that 'only bad girls get raped' and 'women ask for it', as well as common myths and stereotypes about rapists as 'sex starved' or 'insane' (or both).

Burt devised a rape myth acceptance (RMA) scale incorporating 19 rape myths, and was the first to operationalise the concept of rape myths. Items on the scale included: 'If a woman gets drunk at a party and has intercourse with a man she's just met there, she should be considered "fair game" to other males at the party who want to have sex with her, whether she wants to or not.'

She demonstrated that many people in the USA do subscribe to rape myths and that such beliefs are related to sex role stereotyping, a belief that sexual relationships are fundamentally exploitative, distrust of the opposite sex, an acceptance of interpersonal violence, and a relative lack of education. Rape myth acceptance can be seen as a way of justifying and legitimising the rapist's behaviour while shifting blame onto the victim. This has significant implications for the criminal justice system and wider society as it is notoriously difficult to secure a conviction for rape (Thomas, 2005). Finch and Munro (2005) found that jurors frequently held views about the attribution of blame and responsibility that were inconsistent with the application of the law. Jurors were found to consider many extra-legal factors when reaching a decision and these often included rape myths.

environments, in which stereotypes are strong and where people do not, because of time pressure or for some other reason, have the mental resources to focus on information which is not in line with the stereotype. The bias for remembering in line with expectations can have important practical consequences in eyewitness testimony (Boon & Davies, 1987; Loftus, 1996).

What effects does stereotyping have on those who are stereotyped? In an important development, Steele (1997; Steele, Spencer, & Aronson, 2002) introduced the concept of **stereotype threat**. Steele argues that when an individual is aware that they could be the target of a negative or demeaning stereotype, their performance may be impaired on tasks relevant to that stereotype. Yeung and von Hippel (2008) examined this in relation to driving. Female participants took part in a realistic driving simulation during which pedestrians unexpectedly appeared in the road. Among participants reminded beforehand of the stereotype that women are poor drivers, 59% struck the pedestrians, compared with 25% of participants who were not reminded.

> **STEREOTYPE THREAT** A situation in which an individual may find themselves confirming a negative stereotype of a social group they belong to.

Steele argues that the 'threat in the air' of low expectations of black students' abilities in terms of academic performance can lead to distracting thoughts and anxiety in test situations. Steele and Aronson (1995) compared the performance of black and white undergraduates at Stanford University (one of the top universities in the USA) on a very difficult standardised verbal ability test. Before taking it, the students were all told that the task was very difficult and either that the test measured intellectual ability or that it was simply a laboratory task to examine how people solve problems. The prediction was that black students told they were taking a test of intellectual ability would experience stereotype threat and would thus perform less well. The results confirmed this finding. There were no differences between the performance of black and white students when they had not been told the test was a measure of ability, but the black students performed significantly worse than the white students when they thought the test was measuring intellectual ability. Similar findings have been obtained in other studies involving a range of different groups in different situations (Kassin, Fein, & Markus, 2008).

ASIDE

Is it just a joke?

Q: How many psychologists does it take to change a lightbulb?

A: Only one, but the lightbulb really has to want to change!

There are thousands of lightbulb jokes, and most of them exemplify the pervasiveness of intergroup relations. Our example is slightly different from the norm, but the general form of the joke is:

Q: How many [of some group] does it take to change a lightbulb?

A: *N* [any number] . . . [followed by some derogatory comment about the group in question].

Thus:

Q: How many students does it take to change a lightbulb?

A: Two: one to hold the bulb, and the other to drink until the room spins!

As a student, you may or may not find that joke amusing. You may enjoy or be offended by the stereotype of students on which it is based. It doesn't take much imagination, or web searching, to find variants of the joke which are very unlikely to be amusing to the targets of the joke, who may be accused of being stupid (*A*: Five: one to hold the bulb and four others to turn the ladder); criminally violent (*A*: Two: one to take the bulb out and another to glass a random stranger's face with it); or lazy and exploitive of others (*A*: None, they expect us to do it for them). From an intergroup relations perspective, then, jokes are not simply a laughing matter, even when they are funny, because many of them rely on the expression of negative stereotypes of other groups and may further serve a function of making other expressions of prejudice more acceptable. See Ford et al. (2008) and Billig (2001) for two very different studies of the importance of humour in the maintenance of **sexism** and racism respectively.

14.2.3 PREJUDICE, DISCRIMINATION AND ETHNOCENTRISM

In the previous section we focused on stereotyped beliefs about groups and their members. Stereotyped beliefs may be associated with negative or prejudiced attitudes or feelings about another group and with discriminatory behaviour towards them. Prejudice is typically defined as having a biased (usually negative) *attitude* towards another group and its members, while discrimination refers to unfair or unequal *behaviour* towards others on the basis of their group membership (Dion, 2003). Prejudice from this perspective involves both negative thoughts and feelings about another group, which may or may not be expressed as discriminatory behaviour. This will depend on the circumstances and other factors governing social behaviour. For example, fear of legal consequences may constrain even the most prejudiced individual from acting completely in line with their hatred of another group.

> **ETHNOCENTRISM** A stance in which an individual believes that their own ethnic group (or aspects of it, e.g. its culture) is superior to other groups.

> **OUTGROUP** Social group of which an individual believes they are not a member.

> **INGROUP** A group of which a person believes they are a member.

Ethnocentrism is a concept introduced by Sumner (1906) in relation to cultural identity and intercultural relations. As well as encompassing people's attitudes and behaviours towards groups to which they do not belong (i.e. **outgroups**), it emphasises the importance of their attachment and identification with the group to which they do belong (i.e. the **ingroup**) and has underpinned much thinking on intergroup behaviour ever since (Brewer, 1999). Sumner argued that 'one's own group is at the centre of everything' (Sumner, 1906: 13), while Brewer, writing about Sumner's concept of ethnocentrism, declared that ethnocentrism engenders 'positive sentiments toward the ingroup: pride, loyalty, and perceived superiority. However, Sumner also believed that these positive sentiments towards the ingroup were directly correlated with contempt, hatred and hostility toward outgroups' (Brewer, 1999: 430).

Brewer (1999) questions whether strong positive feelings about one's own group are necessarily accompanied by hostility and strong negative feelings about other groups but, as she points out, Sumner's proposal has been reflected in the social psychological literature. Several approaches associate over-idealisation of the ingroup with strong prejudice against outgroups, and key historical examples include the Nazi idealisation of the pure Aryan type and their dehumanisation and genocide of Jews, homosexuals, occultists, people with learning difficulties or mental health problems, and other minority groups.

14.3 EXPLAINING PREJUDICE AND DISCRIMINATION

Here we describe some theories of prejudice and discrimination chosen for their importance in psychology's attempts to confront these issues and because they illustrate different kinds of explanation. Prejudice, discrimination and intergroup relations have been at the heart of social psychology for many decades (Duckitt, 1992). Any brief account of the theory and research developed in that time must be selective. For a more comprehensive view, see the further reading at the end of this chapter.

14.3.1 FRUSTRATED AND PREJUDICED INDIVIDUALS

The idea that we may 'take out' our frustrations on someone or something innocent is commonplace in everyday life. A refereeing decision may cause an angry football manager to kick out at whatever inanimate object happens to be nearby, or the TV commentator may refer (metaphorically) to the manager's cat 'getting a kicking tonight'. For some reason, it seems acceptable in the UK to refer to kicking cats, but there would be more concern if the commentator referred to the manager's dog instead; and any commentator foolish enough to confuse family members and cats would be looking for a new job in the morning! Some expressions of annoyance are more socially acceptable than others, and the restraint required to meet norms of social acceptability in relation to aggression is a basis of theories derived from Freud's ideas.

14.3.2 FRUSTRATION AND AGGRESSION

The **frustration-aggression hypothesis** (FAH) was developed by Dollard et al. (1939). The basic propositions of the original FAH were that individuals frustrated (or thwarted) in their pursuit of a goal will become aggressive and that all acts of aggression are preceded by such frustration. The small child who screams and hits its parent who has just stopped it having a sweet would be a straightforward example of this.

But just as our angry football manager did not run on to the pitch and attack the referee, the cause of his frustration, then so children learn that hitting their parents is neither acceptable nor likely to be successful. They learn to suppress their immediate urge to be aggressive. However, in line with Freudian thinking, the FAH proposes that an unreleased urge to aggress causes an unpleasant build-up of psychic energy which needs to be released in some way, a process known as **catharsis**. If aggression cannot be expressed against the source of the frustration (the parent in our example), then it needs to be released in some other way (e.g. through sport) or *displaced* onto another target against which it is safer or more acceptable to aggress. The child may hit another child or a doll rather than its parents.

What has this got to do with intergroup relations and discrimination? The argument is that widely experienced frustrations resulting from social, economic or political factors may not be expressed against those responsible (governments, elites, the military, etc.), who may be too powerful. Instead, minority groups may be **scapegoated**. For example, Hovland and Sears (1940) investigated whether the number of lynchings of black people in the

> **CATHARSIS** The release of built-up emotional energy. The term is generally used to typify a healthy and restorative outpouring of such energy.
>
> **SCAPEGOAT** Someone who is (often unfairly) made to take the blame for something.

FIGURE 14.2 Two men are lynched in Indiana, USA, in 1930. After being accused of murdering a man and assaulting his girlfriend, two young African-American men are taken from the Grand County Jail and lynched in the public square. It was an event for the crowds. So although economic events will affect the rate of lynching, the context for this activity was the deeply racist and brutal culture that tolerated the systematic abuse and murder of some of its citizens

© Bettmann/CORBIS

southern states of the USA over a 50-year period up to 1930 was related to economic conditions. They found a negative correlation between the number of lynchings and the price of cotton (a key crop in those states); thus, as the price of cotton went up, the number of lynchings went down. Hovland and Sears claimed that the lynchings (killings) were a consequence of displaced aggression resulting from the frustrations associated with economic hardship (see Figure 14.2).

The above explanation cannot be the complete one (it says nothing, for example, about the form of aggression), and later work (Green, Glaser, & Rich, 1998) casts doubt on the relationship between economic conditions and collective violence. The FAH has been modified considerably, with frustration now recognised as only one possible instigator of aggression (along with pain, discomfort, etc.), and aggression being just one possible response to frustration (Berkowitz, 1993a, 1993b). Bandura (1977), in his influential social learning theory, convincingly argued that the expression of aggression, rather than being cathartic, may increase the likelihood of future aggressive acts. Nevertheless, the notion that frustration lies behind some aggression and that collective violence is a response to economic conditions remains very influential, and Staub (2000) includes it as an important instigator of 'ethnic cleansing' and genocide.

14.3.3 PERSONALITY AND PREJUDICE

Published just after the Second World War (1939–1945), *The authoritarian personality* (Adorno et al., 1950) was a major attempt to understand the psychological dynamics involved in the anti-Semitism and wider ethnocentrism of the pre-war and war years. Carried out in the USA, the research involved a 'widening circle of covariation' (Brown, 1965). The researchers started by developing a scale to measure the extent to which individuals agreed with anti-Semitic statements (e.g. 'I can hardly imagine myself marrying a Jew') and then gradually broadened out the work to include other attitudes, beliefs and personality characteristics which were shown to covary (i.e. cluster together). As well as questionnaires, the research used projective tests and in-depth clinical interviews, reflecting the psychoanalytic basis of the theory that the authors developed.

The first stages of the work showed that anti-Semitism among those sampled (mostly white, non-Jewish and middle-class individuals) was associated with a more general ethnocentrism in which various outgroups other than the Jews were also disparaged and in which the 'American Way' of life and family was viewed very positively. Ethnocentrism (E) was then shown to be related to political and economic conservatism (PEC) or the extent to which the person 'liked things as they are'. Clinical interviews and projective test results with a group who scored highly on the E-scale led the researchers to believe that a personality syndrome lay beneath this cluster of prejudiced and conservative attitudes. People with this kind of personality were seen to be potentially fascist. The F-scale (potential for Fascism scale) was developed as a measure of this personality syndrome. It was designed to measure nine aspects of what came to be known as authoritarianism.

Any approach that focuses on individuals may underestimate the power of situations and social and political circumstances, and people may do things that they would be unlikely to do without this added pressure (e.g. Milgram, 1974). Conforming to society's norms may lead people to act in discriminatory ways irrespective of their personality. While authoritarianism may be associated with individual differences in prejudice *within* a society or group, differences *between* groups result more from social norms (Pettigrew, 1958). Changes in attitudes to particular groups occurring in response to world events may happen too quickly to be explicable in terms of changes in child-rearing practices (Brown, 1995).

Nevertheless, the concept of authoritarianism remains an important one. Better measuring instruments have been devised, including Altemeyer's (1998) Right Wing Authoritarianism (RWA) scale, leading to a renewed interest in this field. Some research indicates that authoritarian values and behaviour may increase as a response to external threats, for example after terrorist attacks (Perrin, 2005), or to changes in the social context such as increased unemployment (Doty, Peterson, & Winter, 1991), rather than resulting from upbringing.

14.3.4 REALISTIC CONFLICT THEORY

Sherif (1966) advocated a completely different group-level approach to intergroup conflict. He argued that discrimination and psychological constructs like prejudice and negative stereotyping of outgroups have their basis in competition for scarce resources. In his view, psychological processes followed from 'material relations' and thus the psychological relations between groups follow from their objective relations. For example, in a time of increased competition for jobs, 'immigrants' may be blamed by more established groups for taking away 'our jobs'.

Sherif and his co-workers carried out three famous studies between 1949 and 1954 to test out his ideas. Unlike many studies in social psychology, these did not take place in controlled laboratory conditions. Instead, they were field experiments, each carried out over several weeks. The participants in the studies were 11- to 12-year-old boys attending a camp for the summer holiday. They were unaware that they were there for the purpose of research. The researchers played various roles in running the camp (and thus perhaps had to work a lot harder than many psychologists do when collecting data). Great care was taken in selecting the boys attending the camps to ensure they were similar in terms of factors such as religion (they were all from Protestant families) and family background. None of the boys knew each other before they arrived at the camp. The reason for all of these checks was to try to ensure that the behaviour of the boys could not be explained in terms of prior friendships or problems in the family.

Of the three studies, the first two sought to test Sherif's ideas about the development of intergroup conflict. The third study, known as the 'robber's cave' study, was slightly different in that an additional goal was to test ideas on the resolution of intergroup conflict. We discuss this famous study further below. The experiments were each carried out in three stages. The first two studies contained the following stages, while the final study omitted the first stage:

1 *Friendship development*: The boys arrived at the camp and spent a few days getting to know each other, taking part in the camp's activities and forming friendships.
2 *Group formation*: Two groups were formed. Boys who had become friends during the first stage were split up and put in separate groups as far as possible. The groups were kept isolated from each other, living in separate areas and taking part in different activities.
3 *Intergroup competition*: After a week of being observed separately, the groups were brought together to compete against each other for prizes in a tournament or series of sports and games.

During the second stage the groups developed group structures with leaders, norms of behaviour, group names and insignias. Friendships were now with the members of their own groups. Once the competitions started, the initial good sportsmanship disappeared quite quickly, to be replaced by intergroup hostility. Name calling, fights and insults became common and 'raids' on the other group's camp took place. As well as hostility towards the outgroup, ingroup solidarity increased during this stage. When the boys were asked to estimate performance in games, the performance of ingroup members tended to be overestimated, while that of the other group's members was underestimated.

What Sherif and his colleagues had demonstrated was that the introduction of real conflict of interest between the groups had led to manifestations of ethnocentrism, including negative stereotypes of the outgroup, prejudice, discrimination, aggression and greater valuing of the ingroup. The effect was so strong that the first two studies ended with the two groups still exhibiting animosity to each other. However, as you'll see below in the section on conflict reduction, there was a happy ending to the third summer camp study.

Blake and Mouton (1961) showed that it is not just young boys who behave in this way. They studied business executives on management training courses and also examined established management and union relations in industry. They found that intergroup competition affected ingroup relations (groups becoming more cohesive), perceptions of the outgroup (stereotypes) and relations between the groups when it came to negotiating solutions to problems. For example, in the training context, group representatives strongly tended to see their own group's solutions to problems as superior to those of the competing group, even when, in the eyes of objective judges, one group had produced a clearly

> **REALISTIC CONFLICT THEORY** A theory explaining how conflict and hostility between groups arises as a result of conflicting goals and access to resources.

better solution than the other. Studies in other contexts and other cultures have also provided support for **realistic conflict theory** (RCT) (Jackson, 1993). If you watch the TV programme *The Apprentice*, you may find it interesting to analyse it in terms of group and intergroup processes.

14.3.5 SOCIAL CATEGORISATION TO SOCIAL CHANGE: SOCIAL IDENTITY THEORY

One key question asked about RCT is whether competition is necessary for group conflict to occur. In Sherif's work, there were indications that skirmishes between the groups took place before the stage of competition was introduced, and other studies (e.g. Ferguson & Kelley, 1964) showed that groups may adopt a competitive approach to each other even when there is no objective reason for them to do so. These observations led to the development by Tajfel and his colleagues of a series of experiments designed to explore the minimum conditions under which intergroup discrimination would take place.

> **MINIMAL INTERGROUP STUDIES** A way of exploring the minimal conditions necessary for discrimination to occur.

In the first of these **minimal intergroup studies**, Tajfel et al. (1971) attempted to set up an experiment in which, apart from the social categorisation between one group and another (ingroup and outgroup), there were none of the usual factors influencing group behaviour, that is, there was no previous hostility between the groups, no interaction and no explicit competition, and all actions were anonymous. The participants were schoolboys who were told they were taking part in a study of decision making. Each participant was randomly assigned to one of two groups (although they were told that this was based on preference for paintings by either Klee or Kandinsky) and their task was to assign points (which were worth money) to other participants in the study.

The task involved the participants making a series of choices, in each of which they allocated points to two other boys who were identified only in terms of a code number and the group they belonged to (e.g. 'member 52, Klee group'). The choice 'matrices' were carefully constructed to examine the strategies used by the boys in making their decisions (see Figure 14.3 for examples of the kinds of matrices used). The participants would indicate their choice by circling one of the columns.

In-group	19	18	17	16	15	14	13	12	11	10	9	8	7
Out-group	1	3	5	7	9	11	13	15	17	19	21	23	25

MIP MD   Fair   MJP

In-group	7	8	9	10	11	12	13	14	15	16	17	18	19
Out-group	1	3	5	7	9	11	13	15	17	19	21	23	25

MIP MD   Fair   MJP

MD = maximise difference in favour of in-group
MIP = maximise in-group profit
MJP = maximise joint profit

FIGURE 14.3 Examples of payoff matrices used by Tajfel et al. (1971)

Several strategies were available to them, including:

1   *Maximise joint profit (MJP)*: To give away as many points as possible irrespective of whom they were giving them to. In the matrices in Figure 14.3, this would be done by choosing one of the columns to the right of the matrix.
2   *Fair*: To allocate points as equally as possible. In the examples given, this would be done by choosing an option near the centre of the matrix.
3   *Maximise ingroup profit (MIP)*: To give as much money as possible to the member of the ingroup. In the first matrix this would be done by choosing a column to the left, and in the second matrix by choosing one to the right.
4   *Maximise difference (MD)*: To maximise the difference in favour of the ingroup. In both matrices shown, the column at the left end would be the favoured choice if using this strategy. Note that in the second matrix, if this approach was adopted the ingroup member would actually receive less money than with any other choice.

The unexpected finding was that, while fairness did play a part in determining the allocations made, the preferred strategy was one which favoured ingroup members over outgroup members. In other words, the preferred strategy was to discriminate in favour of the ingroup. Given the 'emptiness' of the situation, this raises many questions about why discrimination was taking place. One possibility is that the boys thought that their friends would probably share their views on painting and thus thought that they were in the ingroup. However, Billig and Tajfel (1973) found the same effect even when the participants were explicitly told they had been randomly allocated to groups.

This finding of 'intergroup discrimination in minimal group settings has proved to be a remarkably robust phenomenon' (Brown, 1995: 47) and has been replicated many times. If you now think back to the distinction between 'acting as self' and 'acting as part of a group', it seems that, in these studies, a simple and arbitrary social categorisation leads the participants to act in terms of group. Does this mean that ethnocentrism is an inevitable consequence of social categorisation? Turner (1975) showed that if participants could 'act in terms of self' and allocate money to themselves, then group membership did not influence allocations to others unless group membership was made more salient to the participants. Grieve and Hogg (1999) showed that 'subjective uncertainty' influenced allocations: participants given more confidence in the use of the matrices displayed less intergroup bias. Thus it seems that social categorisation may be necessary for intergroup discrimination, but may not be sufficient.

Although it is perhaps surprising that one of the most influential of intergroup theories should have its roots in these simple experiments, social identity theory (Tajfel, 1978; Tajfel & Turner, 1979) has 'perhaps become the pre-eminent contemporary social psychological analysis of … intergroup relations' (Hogg & Vaughan, 2008: 407). The theory rests on the distinction made earlier between acting in terms of self and acting in terms of the group, and on the idea that we have multiple and shifting social identities related to our various group memberships. The theory proposes that people want to belong to groups about which they feel positive and which provide them with a positive social identity. This happens when group members feel their group is positively distinct from other relevant groups in terms of some valued characteristics. For example, inhabitants of a rural region may feel proud of the relative friendliness and generosity they believe people from their region display, compared to people from a nearby city. The city dwellers in turn may look down on what they see as a lack of sophistication in the rural population. In this case, both groups can be said to have a positive social identity, as each values the characteristics in which they see themselves as having superiority.

Having a positive social identity, then, involves a process of social comparison with another group or groups from which the ingroup is seen as positively distinct. What if a group's members do not have a positive social identity? There are several possibilities, including:

1   In some cases, individual group members may simply try to exit the group and develop other social identities. This kind of social mobility may not be possible. In many situations, passing from one group to another is very difficult to achieve.
2   Alternatively, they may 'accept' their inadequate social identity because there is a belief within the group that the differences between them and other groups are legitimate or that there are no achievable alternatives to the existing situation. Group members may focus instead on within-group social comparison.

3   When potential alternatives are seen to be appropriate and achievable, a group may act to try to achieve social change through collective action. This may involve:

   (a) attempts to directly challenge other groups and engage in social conflict; or
   (b) more creative approaches such as adopting new positive characteristics or redefining existing negative group characteristics so that they come to be seen as positive.

For example, parents of young children may be proud of the school their children attend and have a positive social identity as a consequence. If this is not the case, though, and there are few constraints on changing schools, they may just leave. If changing schools is not an option and they see few possibilities for change at the current school, parents may simply focus on getting the best for their own individual child. Alternatively, they may seek to change the school's image by making a virtue out of its existing characteristics or by helping the school to develop new valued characteristics (perhaps a summer camp for all the children?). Finally, if they believe the school to be unfairly under-resourced compared to other schools and they see the possibility for changing this, they may take collective action to lobby the local authority for a reallocation of funds.

The theory is an ambitious attempt to combine social psychological processes and societal factors to account for social change, and some writers (Hogg, 2006; Reicher, 2004; Rubin & Hewstone, 2004) argue that its scope and complexity have been underestimated by critics. These writers argue that, although there are problems with, and large gaps in, the research that has been conducted on social identity theory, the theory is sound in most respects. While this is not the point they are making, it is useful to consider to what extent the kinds of laboratory experiments done can illuminate real-life attempts at social change.

14.3.6 SOCIAL PSYCHOLOGY, RACISM AND PREJUDICE

Duckitt's (1992) historical overview of the psychological study of prejudice analyses the changes in the explanations put forward by psychologists over the last 100 years or so. At different times, theories have focused on individual psychopathology, situational forces or socio-cultural factors. Some of these changes may be seen as attempts to remedy inadequacies or limitations in older approaches, but Duckitt argues that this is not the complete story. Older approaches are not usually replaced; rather, there are shifts in the nature of the questions being asked or the issues being addressed. This may partly be a response to topical events, but Duckitt argues that historical circumstances affect not just topic choice but also the questions that are asked which, in turn, influence the kinds of theories and research methods that are developed.

> **IMPLICIT ASSOCIATION TEST** An indirect measure of psychological constructs which are typically sensitive or subject to social desirability.

In terms of racism, Duckitt argues that conceiving of prejudice as a problem requiring psychological study did not occur in the USA until the 1920s. Before then, the white majority simply assumed that they were superior, and thus the work of psychologists in this area was in mapping the different characteristics and abilities of 'inferior peoples'. This is an approach which continued through the 1930s and 1940s, especially in Nazi Germany (Billig, 1978), and which re-emerges periodically. In mainstream psychology in the USA, a number of social changes during the 1920s led to the beginnings of questioning the inferior status of minority groups and their level of deprivation relative to white people. This was the initial period of research on racial prejudice. Duckitt outlines seven stages (up to the early 1990s) in the 'historical evolution' of psychology's understanding of prejudice. The key points here are as follows:

1   Psychology as a discipline does not stand outside the wider social context in which inequalities between social groups exist. Social and political events may change the questions that psychologists ask, the methods that they adopt and the answers that they provide.

2   There has been a tendency for Western psychologists to assume that the processes they have identified are 'universal' (i.e. they apply across cultures). This belief may not be warranted. Henrich, Heine and Norenzayen (2010) argue that too much psychology rests on the study of unusual or 'WEIRD' people who are unrepresentative of most people on Earth. You might be able to work out what the acronym stands for … it refers to people from Western, Educated, Industrialised, Rich and Democratic societies.

3   The uses to which psychological research is put may result from political or other forces. Psychology has been used to justify exploitation as well as to combat it (Billig, 1978).

4   Psychology is only one of a number of disciplines being applied to these issues. A full understanding requires a multidisciplinary approach.

EXERCISE: DO YOU HAVE HIDDEN BIASES?

One of the disadvantages of many measures of prejudice is that they rely on self-report and thus are open to social desirability effects where people concerned about how they may be seen if they provide true responses try to disguise their feelings about other groups when answering questions about these groups. The **implicit association test** (IAT) purports to measure unconscious bias and thus reduce social desirability effects. You can try versions of the IAT at the following sites: https://implicit.harvard.edu/implicit/ www.understandingprejudice.org/iat/index2.htm.

Try these out before reading up on the IAT. What do you think? Does this approach reveal something different from self-reports? Is it less prone to social desirability? Now read some reports of research which have used the technique. What do you think now?

14.4 REDUCING INTERGROUP CONFLICT

Up to this point, the research that we have discussed has provided little that could be deemed positive. However, we will now consider whether and how conflicts between groups can be resolved through psychological intervention.

14.4.1 CONTACT

The contact hypothesis proposes that if contact between groups is encouraged (under appropriate conditions), then prejudice between groups will reduce. The initial hypothesis (Allport, 1954) suggested that contact between groups should be encouraged if four conditions are satisfied. First, social conditions, like education, housing and law, should be equal for both groups. Second, the groups should share common goals that, third, they cooperate to achieve. Fourth, the officials and authorities of those groups must support the contact. Subsequently, there have been a number of additions to those conditions. These include the need for contact to be rewarding (Amir, 1969), close and for a sustained period of time (Cook, 1978). These two additions allow potential for friendship to grow between members of the different groups. Friendships between individuals from different groups can improve intergroup relations directly (Pettigrew, 1997) and also indirectly, as other group members come to know of these friendships (Wright et al., 1977).

Thus contact has the potential to reduce intergroup conflict, but providing the required conditions is very difficult. For example, people from different cultures may live in the same area but have little contact and, when they do, it may not be on either an equal or a personal footing. This limited contact could simply provide opportunities for expressing rather than reducing prejudice (Hogg & Vaughan, 2013). However, Pettigrew and Tropp's (2006) meta-analysis of over 500 relevant studies showed that, while meeting Allport's conditions enhances the prejudice-reducing impact of contact, contact may also be effective in the absence of these conditions. Yet, the positive effects of contact are greater for members of majority groups than of minorities (Tropp & Pettigrew, 2005) and thus 'it remains a challenge for contact as an intervention to prove equally effective for (majority and disadvantaged) groups' (Hewstone & Swart, 2011: 375).

If you think about your own contact with members of other groups, much of it will be through what you have heard from other people or through media such as television or the internet. Allport was referring to the effects of *direct* contact between groups and it is only relatively recently that indirect contact has become a greater focus of research. Amichai-Hamburger and McKenna (2006) argue that positive contact between conflicting groups can be more easily achieved through internet communication, partly for practical reasons to do with, for example, distance,

KEY RESEARCHER Rhiannon Turner

FIGURE 14.4 Rhiannon Turner

Rhiannon Turner is a Professor of Social Psychology at Queens University Belfast whose work focuses on prejudice reduction in particular, and intergroup contact, recategorisation, and intergroup relations more generally. Although her work has considered several forms of contact between groups, she is perhaps best known for her work with Richard Crisp and others on the role that imagined intergroup contact can have in reducing prejudice. This has given a new dimension to research on the contact hypothesis since her first major publication on the topic in 2007 and has a number of implications for interventions designed to reduce prejudice between groups. The quality and significance of Rhiannon's work has been reflected in the awards she has received, which include the BPS Award for Outstanding Doctoral Research Contributions to Psychology (2007), the Society for Personality and Social Psychology's Robert B. Cialdini Award for excellence in field research (2008), and the Gordon Allport Intergroup Relations Prize (2011). One of her colleagues and co-authors, Keon West, has a YouTube channel which includes several videos outlining some of the research on imagined contact (and intergroup relations more generally). We would recommend that you have a look at his channel at www.youtube.com/user/keonwestpsychology, and especially the video on Imagined Contact (which one of us was excited to discover includes an excerpt from a well-known film featuring a giant flying dog).

KEY STUDY

Binder, J., Zagefka, H., Brown, R., Funke, F., Kessler, T., Mummendey, A., Maquil, A., Demoulin, S., & Leyens, J.P. (2009). Does contact reduce prejudice or does prejudice reduce contact? A longitudinal test of the contact hypothesis among majority and minority groups in three European countries. *Journal of Personality and Social Psychology, 96*(4), 843–856.

One key question about the relationship between contact and lower levels of prejudice concerns the causal relationship between the two: thus, assuming that there is a causal relationship between these two variables, does contact reduce prejudice as Allport (1954) proposed or is the relationship simply a result of prejudiced people avoiding contact with those they are prejudiced against? While Pettigrew and Tropp (2006) do provide evidence that contact reduces prejudice, most of the studies they reviewed were cross-sectional in design. Longitudinal studies are more difficult to carry out, and are thus much rarer, but are better able to assess the direction of causality. Binder et al. (2009) predicted that causality works in both directions, with prejudiced people seeking less contact with other groups but with greater contact serving to reduce prejudice. To test this they carried out a survey of school students in Germany, Belgium and England. The participants completed questionnaires about their friendships, contact with, anxiety about and prejudice against members of other groups. They did this twice, with an interval of about six months between each testing, and found that both hypotheses were supported, although, as found by Tropp and Pettigrew (2005), the contact was more effective in reducing prejudice among majority group members than in ethnic minorities.

but also because it may give participants a greater feeling of control and reduce their anxiety when compared with face-to-face contact.

Going a step further, Rhiannon Turner and her colleagues (e.g. Turner & Crisp, 2010; Turner, Crisp, & Lambert, 2007) have shown that just *imagining* positive contact with a member of another group can have effects in reducing bias and that this can be seen whether explicit measures of prejudice (i.e. self-reports) or implicit measures are used.

The idea behind implicit measures is that they are meant to tap into something beyond the individual's conscious control so that he or she cannot disguise their prejudice. For example, Turner and Crisp (2010), in their first experiment, asked their student participants in the imagined contact condition to spend two minutes imagining themselves meeting an elderly stranger and discovering some 'interesting and unexpected things about the person' (2010: 134) which they then had to list. Compared to a control group, the imagined contact showed more positive explicit attitudes towards elderly people as measured by attitude scales, and less implicit bias as measured by the implicit association test (IAT) (see Nosek, Greenwald, & Banaji, 2007, for a review).

14.4.2 SUPERORDINATE GOALS

The concept of superordinate goals derives from realistic conflict theory. Remember that the third summer camp study run by Sherif had a final stage in which attempts were made to reduce conflict. After some failed attempts at contact (e.g. eating together just produced 'garbage wars' in which the groups threw food at each other), some 'superordinate' goals were introduced. These are goals which the groups shared but which they could only achieve through cooperation. The reasoning was that, if conflict arises from competition, reduced conflict should follow from cooperation in contexts in which the groups are dependent on each other for achieving their goals. Therefore, the staff engineered a series of 'problems', such as the water supply failing or the bus breaking down, which could only be solved by the groups working together. This was successful, and at the end of the camp the groups, rather than being on hostile terms, chose to go home together in the same bus (we told you it had a happy ending).

It helped that the two groups in Sherif's study were not actually very different or well established, thus facilitating their *recategorisation* as one large group rather than two separate groups (Gaertner & Dovidio, 2000). They also succeeded in their cooperative task. Worchel (1979) has shown that failure on such a task may lead one group to blame the other for the failure. Nevertheless, this simple idea has had a great deal of influence. It is the root of 'jigsaw classrooms'. These consist of small desegregated groups of children who have to rely on each other to learn material and succeed in class, as each pupil has key elements of information necessary to complete a task. Aronson (2008) claims success in improving self-esteem and performance in minority group children using this technique.

14.4.3 CROSSED CATEGORY MEMBERSHIP

Social identity theory argues that we each have many social identities depending on the groups we belong to. Which of these social identities is salient at any one time will depend on the context. At one moment you may be talking to a lecturer and your identity as a student may be most salient, but if you discover a shared interest in the music of a particular band, then the social identity of 'fan' may become more relevant. In conflict situations, this fluency of identity may be decreased and simple 'us–them' distinctions may predominate, leading to ethnocentrism.

This suggests, then, that making people more aware of their multiple group memberships could play a part in reducing conflict. However, this is only likely to work if the various group memberships are cross-cutting rather than simply overlapping (Deschamps & Doise, 1978). If you and your friends are prejudiced against engineering students but rather like rugby players, then an encounter with the engineering department's rugby team might be less problematic than with a group of non-rugby-playing engineers. Of course, if you are also prejudiced against rugby players, this might not be the start of a wonderful evening!

There is considerable evidence that cross-cutting group memberships reduces intergroup conflict (Brewer & Brown, 1998). For example, Crisp, Hewstone and Rubin (2001) researched students' prejudice against other students at different universities (such rivalries between universities are sometimes fierce). After asking the students to think of as many ways as possible in which they could describe the other students, rather than simply thinking they attended a different university, intergroup bias was reduced. In many contexts, however, one dimension of group difference may outweigh all others in importance. Hewstone, Islam and Judd (1993), in a study in Bangladesh, found that religion (Muslim or Hindu) greatly outweighed nationality (Bangladeshi or Indian) in importance, and thus the effect of cross-cutting categorisations was reduced. Nevertheless, after reviewing some of the evidence, Crisp concludes: 'Our multiple identities may ultimately prove critical in addressing some of the most pressing social issues that we face' (Crisp, 2008: 209).

14.5 CHAPTER SUMMARY

In this chapter we have looked at the effect that group membership can have on our behaviour. It is easy to slip into supporting your group, and often this has positive effects, but not always. Supporting each other is what makes a community strong, and can make life simpler and better for the individual members. The problems arise for people who are either rejected by the group or not in the group. This can create conflict at an individual level and also at a group or even national level. The puzzle for us is to balance the benefits of group cohesion with the obvious downsides of ethnocentrism.

DISCUSSION QUESTIONS

Social psychologists often assume that the same processes occur both in 'big' political and historical events and in small-scale everyday actions. Are they right?

Can social psychology study illuminate major real-world issues while still adhering to appropriate ethical principles? Think about this in relation to Zimbardo's Stanford Prison experiment.

What effect has the internet and social media had on intergroup relations? To what extent are the theories discussed in this chapter relevant to the kinds of interactions you have seen or heard about on social media sites such as Facebook, Twitter or Google+?

Is there too much emphasis on reducing prejudice? Does this run the risk of leaving unchallenged, or even of helping to maintain, the kinds of social injustice which need to be confronted through collective action?

SUGGESTIONS FOR FURTHER READING

Brewer, M.B. (2003). *Intergroup relations* (2nd edn). Buckingham: Open University Press. Written by one of the major figures in the area, this comprehensive but readable review is now a little dated but covers most facets of intergroup relations from basic cognitive processes to international relations and war.

Hogg, M.A., & Abrams, D. (2001). *Intergroup relations: essential readings*. Philadelphia, PA: Psychology Press. Provides an easily accessible opportunity to read the original classic papers of writers such as Sherif and Tajfel alongside later authors whose research has built on these foundations.

Hogg, M.A., & Vaughan, G.M. (2013). *Social psychology* (7th edn). Harlow: Prentice Hall. With more emphasis on European research than most American textbooks, this provides a comprehensive overview of mainstream social psychology and shows how intergroup relations connects with other topics in social psychology.

Schmid, K., & Hewstone, M. (2010). Combined effects of intergroup contact and multiple categorization: consequences for intergroup attitudes in diverse social contexts. In R. Crisp (Ed.), *The psychology of social and cultural diversity* (pp. 297–321). Chichester: Wiley-Blackwell. An interesting review relating two approaches to reducing intergroup conflict.

Still want more? For links to online resources relevant to this chapter and a quiz to test your understanding, visit the companion website at edge.sagepub.com/banyard2e

15 SOCIAL JUDGEMENTS AND BEHAVIOUR

Lead authors: Sebastian Teicher, Maria Kontogianni and Alex Meredith

CHAPTER OUTLINE

15.1 Introduction	**261**
15.2 Attributions	**261**
15.2.1 Theories and models of attribution	261
15.2.2 Correspondent inference theory	262
15.2.3 Covariation model	263
15.2.4 Shortcomings	263
15.3 Attribution errors	**263**
15.3.1 Fundamental attribution error	263
15.3.2 Group attribution error	264
15.3.3 Ultimate attribution error	265
15.3.4 Actor–observer effect	265
15.3.5 False consensus effect	266
15.3.6 Self-serving bias	266
15.4 Practical application of attribution research	**267**
15.5 Attitudes	**268**
15.5.1 Attitude research	268
15.5.2 Attitudes and behaviour	269
15.5.3 Theory of planned behaviour	269

15.6 Prosocial behaviour **270**

 15.6.1 Evolution and helping behaviours 270

 15.6.2 Social theories, social factors and helping behaviours 271

 15.6.3 Online prosocial behaviour 272

 15.6.4 Bystander effect (online and offline considerations) 272

 15.6.5 Practical applications of prosocial behaviour research 274

15.7 Chapter summary **274**

Discussion questions **275**

Suggestions for further reading **275**

15.1 INTRODUCTION

The Dutch philosopher Baruch Spinoza (1632–1677) observed that men 'are scarcely able to lead a solitary life, so that the definition of man as a social animal has met with general assent; in fact, men do derive from social life much more convenience than injury' (de Spinoza, 1997). Humans might not get along all the time, but the majority of our lives are spent with others as we are social creatures by nature. The way we relate to, and interact with, each other is determined by our perceptions of each other. In this chapter we will consider three different facets of social interaction: **attributions**, **attitudes** and **prosocial behaviour**.

ATTRIBUTION The process of giving reasons for why things happen.

ATTITUDES The preferences and opinions you have about other things, people and concepts in the world.

PROSOCIAL BEHAVIOUR The act of helping out another person, whether as a helping behaviour or as an act of altruism.

In the section on attributions, we will look at the decisions you make when deciding why things have happened and the errors that might affect your judgement. We will then discuss attitudes – what they are and how they relate to behaviour. Finally, we will examine the nature of prosocial behaviours – when and why do people help each other? Each section will introduce you to some of the classical key studies in the area, but fear not! The practical application sections will show you that this area of social psychology is very much alive and finds application in all sorts of ways.

FRAMING QUESTIONS

- How do people explain their own and other people's behaviour in social situations?
- Think about your attitudes towards others. Where do you think these attitudes came from?
- Do you always act in accordance with your attitudes, or are there other factors that influence your behaviour?
- Think about a situation where you helped somebody. Why did you do it? Were there any benefits to you?

15.2 ATTRIBUTIONS

Imagine the following: You are watching a football game and one side is taking a free kick. The ball sails through the air across the heads of the defenders and, after 35 metres, lands in the back of the net. How would you explain this impressive feat? Would you put it down to luck or ability? And what if you knew the teams were local amateurs? Or if they were Premier League teams with international superstars? How would that affect your decision?

What you are trying to do is attribute the cause of the goal to a disposition (an internal factor, such as a personality trait or, in this case, individual skill), or the situation (external or circumstantial factors, in this case, luck). Most people would attribute such an impressive goal to a player's disposition (skill) if it was a Premiership club, and to the situation (luck) if it was an amateur player. But why is that? We will look at a number of theories that try to explain the attribution process.

15.2.1 THEORIES AND MODELS OF ATTRIBUTION

The pioneer of attribution theory, Fritz Heider (1958), suggested that when we try to explain everyday events we rarely do so by random guesswork. Instead, we act like **naive scientists** and rationally examine possible dispositional and situational explanations. For instance, when considering the football example, we would think about the intention and ability of the player, as well as anything in the environment that would have made the task easier or more difficult (maybe none of the defenders were paying attention and the goal keeper had left his post). But despite our rational analysis, Heider suggested that we prefer stable explanations and are therefore more likely to make dispositional attributions (i.e. explain events in terms of the individual involved rather than the situation). This was the starting point for the study of causal attribution, and we will now look at a number of theories that followed on from this.

15.2.2 CORRESPONDENT INFERENCE THEORY

One of the first theories that followed from Heider's assertions was developed by Jones and Davis (1965). They suggested that, when observing people's behaviour, we make assumptions about their intentions and traits. Indeed, picture the following scene:

> An elderly lady gets on a crowded bus. After a short while, a young man stands up and offers her his seat. Why did he do that? Is it because he is a very polite and kind person or because he thought that everybody around him expected him to get up?

Correspondent inference theory (CIT) proposes a number of factors that determine the extent to which we attribute observed actions to a disposition (the man is very polite) or the situation (the man gave in to social pressure). These factors are outlined below:

- **Free choice:** To make a dispositional attribution, we need to know that the person chose freely to act in the way they did, rather than being influenced by an external factor.
- **Desirability:** When an action results in an effect that is universally or socially desirable, it tells us very little about an individual's disposition (after all, everybody would do the same), and we attribute the behaviour to the situation. However, the more we think that effects are *negative* for the individual, the more likely we are to attribute the behaviour to the individual's disposition.
- **Unusual:** The more a person acts differently from what most people would do, the more we would attribute it to their disposition.
- **Hedonic relevance:** If the results of an action are beneficial to us, or in line with our own particular values, we tend to make positive inferences about an individual's disposition. Conversely, if the results are negative, or go against our values, we are more likely to make negative inferences. For example, some people might describe a person taking trapeze lessons as reckless and irresponsible, while others would see them as daring and carefree, depending on their own level of sensation-seeking (and also if the individual was still alive after the trapeze lesson!). Heider (1958) called this the 'general balance principle': bad things are done by bad people, good things are done by good people.
- **Personalism:** When an action affects us, we ask ourselves to what extent this was intended by the individual. The more convinced we are that the action was deliberate, the more confident we are at making inferences, and a person doing something beneficial to *us* (or in line with our values) will be seen more positively than the person showing the same behaviour to others.

HEURISTIC A mental shortcut (or rule of thumb) that represents a 'best guess', allowing people to make solution attempts or make decisions quickly and efficiently (though not always correctly).

While CIT provides a good starting point for understanding behavioural attribution, it does not address the consequences of unintentional behaviour. Furthermore, what observers think of as the most desirable (and therefore intended) behavioural consequence may only be based on our own interpretation and **heuristics** (see Chapter 7, section 7.3.1 for more about heuristics) – the individual themselves may have been trying to do something completely different. Our interpretations of others' intentions are influenced by cultural differences and social stereotypes, and thus we will move on to a model that is a development of CIT.

15.2.3 COVARIATION MODEL

In his covariation model, Harold Kelley (1967, 1973) suggests that when we observe an effect, we attribute it to the cause with which it co-occurs over time – an interaction between actor (disposition), entity (an external cause) and time (the particular circumstance). To determine which of these factors is the cause, we make attributions along the three dimensions of **distinctiveness** (how unique the observed behaviour is to the situation), **consensus** (whether other people behave in a similar way) and **consistency** (whether the actor shows similar behaviour over time).

Imagine Ebenezer Scrooge exclaiming 'Bah, humbug!' at Christmas time. If we know that Scrooge has a general dislike for all festivities (low distinctiveness), that other people think Christmas is a jolly good thing (low consensus) and that Scrooge has shown the same behaviour over many years (high consistency), we would make a dispositional attribution and conclude that Scrooge is an uncaring miser. Alternatively, if Scrooge usually enjoys all festivities apart from Christmas (high distinctiveness), other people share his dislike for Christmas (high consensus) and this is not the first time (high consistency), we would conclude that there is something about Christmas (the entity) that causes people to be miserable. Lastly, imagine that we know Scrooge has always enjoyed Christmas (low distinctiveness), other people have enjoyed it (high consensus), but this is the first time he expresses his misgiving (low consistency); then we would think that something specific must have happened that day to Scrooge that made him so miserable (circumstances).

Now think about yourself. Is this the way you make attributions? We will now have brief look at some more general shortcomings of attribution theories.

15.2.4 SHORTCOMINGS

Apart from being influenced by cultural and personal stereotypes and individual interpretation, the assumption that people act like naive scientists and either thoroughly consider all possible intended effects (CIT) or conduct multiple observations before making an attribution (covariance model) is somewhat on the idealised side. As Kelley (1973) admits, people lack time and motivation to conduct a thorough systematic analysis. Instead, people make inferences based on single observations and rely on heuristics to make decisions and save mental resources – a concept that has been described as the 'cognitive miser' model (Taylor, 1981). Researchers appear now to have come to the conclusion that people can be best described as 'motivated tacticians' (Fiske, 1993; Fiske & Taylor, 1991; Molden & Higgins, 2012) who use a variety of resource-intense and cost-saving strategies, depending on the intended goal.

15.3 ATTRIBUTION ERRORS

We have already seen that making attributions is not an exact science, that we tend to take cognitive shortcuts, and that interpretations of behaviour are easily influenced by factors such as our cultural background. We will now take a look at a number of other factors that may bias the attribution process.

15.3.1 FUNDAMENTAL ATTRIBUTION ERROR

The term fundamental attribution error (FAE) was coined by Jones (1977), and refers to our tendency to attribute behaviour to dispositional rather than situational factors. It originates from a study by Jones and Harris (1967), who explored the influence of free choice on attribution within the context of CIT. Participants were asked to rate the true attitude of a person based on an opinion statement that person had given. They were provided with a short student essay that was either in favour of or against the former Cuban leader Fidel Castro (there was a fierce anti-communist stance in the USA at the time). Participants had been

FIGURE 15.1 The fundamental attribution error. You wait for someone and they turn up late. They say 'the bus was late' (situational explanation). You say 'you didn't leave enough time and anyway you are always late' (dispositional explanation). Many domestic disputes start (and continue) like this

© Peter Gudella/Shutterstock.com

informed either that the writer had been assigned to a pro/contra essay or that they were given a choice on how to write the essay (pro or contra). Surprisingly, the results showed that even when participants knew that the person had been assigned to a side with no choice whatsoever, they still thought that the expressed opinion was to some degree reflective of the person's true attitude.

There is a generally held view that collectivist cultures such as China or Japan are much less likely to show the FAE as they place much more emphasis on the situational context of behaviour (e.g. Choi et al., 1999; Miller, 1984; Norenzayan & Nisbett, 2000). However, some studies have found little cultural influence (e.g. Krull et al., 1999), and it is possible that the previously identified differences were due to the student samples used in those studies, as the general public is far less prone to the FAE (Bauman & Skitka, 2010).

15.3.2 GROUP ATTRIBUTION ERROR

The group attribution error (GAE) actually refers to two types of misattribution. The first concerns our tendency to generalise from an individual group member's characteristics to the rest of the group. Hamill et al. (1980) were the first to examine this error in a study where participants read the description of an irresponsible unemployed woman who had been receiving benefits for a number of years. The length of time she had been receiving benefits was described as either typical or atypical in relation to other unemployed people. Although the latter (atypical scenario) suggested that the woman was an extreme and unrepresentative case, when asked about their opinion of unemployed people in general, participants in both conditions expressed similar negative views. So the next time you read something in the tabloid press about benefit cheats or evil asylum seekers, beware of the GAE!

The second GAE, first described by Allison and Messick (1985), concerns our tendency to assume that group decisions reflect the attitudes of individual group members even when information is available that suggests otherwise. Don't believe it? Read on. In their experiment, participants read a short vignette describing the enactment of a city law that had been decided either by an *appointed* city representative, by an *elected* representative, by a *majority vote* of 54% of the citizens or a near *unanimous vote* of 92%. When participants were asked to rate the extent to which the decision taken reflected the attitude of the typical citizen it was no surprise that the highest correspondence occurred in the 92% condition. However, the ratings between the remaining scenarios were virtually identical, and indeed very close to the

KEY RESEARCHER Mark Levine

Professor Mark Levine is a UK researcher at the University of Exeter who conducts some interesting research on the behaviour of bystanders in criminal incidents and emergencies, using both experimental and observational methods. The football shirt study summarised elsewhere in this chapter is an example of one of his experiments. He also analyses real-life CCTV footage of violent incidents to understand the behavioural dynamics of the perpetrators, victims and bystanders. For instance, one study shows that bystander intervention plays an important role in the de-escalation of aggressive confrontations, in particular when multiple bystanders take appeasing actions (e.g. making open-hand gestures or holding people back). Another study showed that men find it difficult to intervene in female-on-female violence as they think their physical intervention might be seen as inappropriate by others.

More recently, he has used virtual reality environments to study the behaviour of bystanders in simulated violent confrontations. Participants who are wearing virtual reality headsets and headphones experience the incidents in an immersive simulation that allows the study of actual bystander behaviour (from physical reactions such as gaze to

FIGURE 15.2   Mark Levine

interventions) in an ethical and controlled manner. For example, one study that used the football shirt ingroup and outgroup method in a virtual bar found that bystanders thought that an ingroup victim was looking more often in their direction than an outgroup victim, resulting in more frequent bystander intervention. However, both ingroup and outgroup victims were programmed to look at the participants for the same amount of time. This demonstrates nicely how our beliefs influence our perception and impact on our behaviour.

The work on bystander behaviour has also led to studies on social relations in public, for example, the way that surveillance technology such as CCTV and public drinking legislation are understood and shape our behaviour. Another area of work concerns interactions in the night-time economy, such as the relationship between police, door staff and the public.

92% condition. In other words, even when the decision was made by an unelected representative it was assumed that this was representative of the citizens' attitudes. So when the next general election comes around, remember that the rest of the world will hold you responsible for whoever comes into power, whether you like it or not.

15.3.3 ULTIMATE ATTRIBUTION ERROR

The ultimate attribution error (UAE) (Pettigrew, 1979) outlines how we maintain prejudice and explain away positive behaviour by an outgroup we dislike. We do so by attributing negative behaviour to a dispositional cause ('that's them all over') and positive behaviour to a situational cause ('it's not like them to help but circumstances meant they couldn't do anything different').

> **INGROUP** A group of which a person believes they are a member.
>
> **OUTGROUP** Social group of which an individual believes they are not a member.

In his review of 19 studies, Hewstone (1990) found that, although the UAE did not always occur (and that the effect was more pronounced in prejudiced individuals), overall there was some support for Pettigrew's predictions: people tended to attribute positive outgroup actions to situational influences and negative actions to dispositional factors.

15.3.4 ACTOR–OBSERVER EFFECT

The actor–observer effect (Jones & Nisbett, 1972) occurs in situations where an actor can be blamed for negative behaviour (e.g. while walking past people waiting for a bus you stumble and fall flat on your face – embarrassing, isn't it?). The actor will blame the situation for their behaviour (why can't the council fix the road surface?),

> **META-ANALYSIS** A literature review that summarises and contrasts findings by calculating effect sizes.

whereas an observer will make a dispositional attribution (you are a clumsy person and/or are too busy fiddling with your iphone). A possible explanation is that the actor evaluates themself in light of the situation (you stumble as a reaction to poor road conditions), whereas an observer only sees the action (you stumbling). Furthermore, you would know that normally you are perfectly capable of walking on the road, so this behaviour is not the norm. An observer, however, only sees this one incident.

The actor–observer hypothesis has been a key concept in attribution theory. However, a meta-analysis of 173 studies by Malle (2006) showed that overall there was little support for the effect. As a result, Malle (2011) presented an alternative theory for explaining intended behaviour: the folk conceptual theory of action explanation.

Malle (2011) suggests that rather than looking at cause and effect, we try to understand an actor's reason for the behaviour and the degree of its intentionality. In most situations, we rely on past experiences and heuristics to make a snap judgement. However, if there is some ambiguity or it is important to be certain, we go through more systematic thought processes based on one of three modes of explanation:

- **Reason explanations:** These can be based on desires or beliefs. Desire reasons refer to the actor's goal or preferred outcome and can be strongly influenced by culture and context. Belief reasons relate to an actor's knowledge, feelings and assessments about the action as well as its outcome and their causal relation – they are 'the map by which we steer' (Dretske, 1988). However, beliefs are much more difficult to infer than desires, and one desire or goal can be based on many beliefs. For instance, people donating to the same charity all share a common goal, but might do so because of different beliefs.

- **Causal history of reason (CHR) explanations:** These relate to the background of the reasons, such as the actor's personality, upbringing and culture. They consider the basis on which a reason is formed and narrow down the possible choices. For example, when we say that 'John is cooking dinner for his new housemates because he is friendly', we do not infer that this is what John was thinking, but that his friendly personality was a subconscious influence on his reasoning.
- **Enabling factor explanations:** These are factors that offer no direct explanation for intentions but attempt to clarify how it was possible that the action was successfully performed (e.g. a person's skill, effort or circumstances). If we say that 'Angela rushed off because she thought she was late for the cinema', we identify her lateness as the factor that led to her action (the inferred intention is that she wants to be on time for the start of the film).

Malle's (2011) findings suggest that the actor–observer effect occurs because it is much easier for actors to provide a *reason explanation*. After all, they were the ones who decided to act for a certain reason. Observers, on the other hand, have to resort more often to *causal history of reason* (CHR) explanations.

15.3.5 FALSE CONSENSUS EFFECT

The false consensus effect (FCE) (Ross, Greene, & House, 1977) refers to our tendency to see our own behavioural choices and judgements as relatively common ('everybody would do the same in my place'), while viewing alternative responses as a deviation from the norm. This was first demonstrated by Ross, Greene and House (1977) when they asked participants to indicate whether they would wear a sandwich board saying 'Eat at Joe's' or 'Repent' around campus, and to estimate how many of their peers would choose to wear the sandwich board. Participants were also asked to rate the personality traits of the kind of person who would or wouldn't wear it. Roughly half of all students indicated they would wear the board, while the other half declined. Interestingly, the former group (those who would wear the board) thought that around 62% of their peers would make the same choice as they had, while the latter group (would NOT wear the board) thought that 67% would agree with them. It was also found that ratings of personality traits were much more exaggerated for the kind of people who would act differently from the participants' own view. Thus it seems we draw strong inferences about a person's characteristics if their behaviour does not conform to our perceived consensus view.

A possible explanation for the FCE is that it helps us to justify our choices as appropriate and rational, particularly in ambiguous situations. There is also the issue of selective exposure and availability: we tend to associate with people who share similar interests. These people might also act in a similar way to us, thus creating an illusion of consensus that is not representative of the rest of the population (just look around your close circle of friends and ask yourself how different they are from you). The effect is quite robust and has been demonstrated across numerous studies (Mullen et al., 1985; Mullen & Hu, 1988).

15.3.6 SELF-SERVING BIAS

EXERCISE: SELF-ANALYSIS

Think about the last time you got a good grade or achieved something. Why did you get the grade? What contributed to your achievement? Write down a few key factors.

Now think about the last time you received an unexpectedly low grade, or think of something that you tried to do but failed to achieve. Again, ask yourself why did you get that grade? Why was your attempt unsuccessful? Write down some key factors.

Now read on.

The self-serving bias (SSB) relates to our tendency to attribute success to our own abilities and blame failure on external factors. This concept was originally put forward by Heider, who noted that attributions in ambiguous situations are influenced by 'a person's own needs or wishes' (Heider, 1958: 118), or, as the saying goes, a bad workman always blames his tools. A possible explanation for this relates to our cognition (Miller & Ross, 1975). Assuming that we have put in some effort, we usually expect to succeed in tasks, so when the outcome matches our expectation we take that as confirmation of our abilities (although, as every psychology student knows, correlation never equals causality).

15.4 PRACTICAL APPLICATION OF ATTRIBUTION RESEARCH

So far in this chapter we have mainly looked at historical studies that paved the way for attribution research, so you would be forgiven for thinking that this branch of social psychology is an old and outdated field. But even though the theories and errors are a few decades old, they are still valid and help us not only to understand how people make attributions in various situations in real life, but also to give us a powerful set of tools when trying to communicate information and affect change.

For example, a topic that receives continuous debate is climate change. Does it exist? And, if so, are we responsible for it? Although there is considerable evidence to suggest that yes, it is real, and yes, we are (at least partially) responsible, there remains a lot of scepticism towards it. Jang (2013) showed that Americans who were provided with information that blamed the USA as a major contributor to climate change tended to attribute climate change to a natural rather than human cause. Furthermore, they also expressed less concern about climate change in general and were less supportive of policies to combat climate change. In contrast, Americans who received climate change information that held another nation accountable not only thought that humans were mostly responsible, but were also more concerned about the problem and more supportive of the policies. This is a good demonstration of our tendency to automatically protect our ingroup from criticism by blaming a negative effect on an external factor, and relates to the ultimate attribution error. It also has implications for how we should communicate important issues if we want to effect a behavioural change.

The false consensus effect can have very useful applications in real life. For example, it can help us to understand the process of radicalisation of extreme political views. Wojcieszak (2011) studied the activity of neo-Nazis in online discussion boards in relation to their perception of public support for their cause. Those who were most active on the board exhibited the greatest false consensus effect by substantially overestimating the extent to which the general public shared their ideology. Interestingly, the fact that offline the neo-Nazis were mostly interacting with people who did not share their views did not diminish their false perception of consensus. This demonstrates that the false consensus

KEY STUDY

Perkins, J.M., Perkins, H.W., & Craig, D.W. (2014). Misperception of peer weight norms and its association with overweight and underweight status among adolescents. *Prevention Science*. DOI: 10.1007/s11121-014-0458-2.

Rising levels of obesity and eating disorders are a real concern for health campaigners. A recent study demonstrated the importance of the false consensus effect in the perception of weight norms and its effect on weight. Surveying a large number of US secondary schools, Perkins et al. (2014) found that, in their sample of over 40,000 students, 26% of males and 20% of females overestimated the weight of their peers by more than 5%. A further 38% of males and females underestimated their peers' weight by the same margin. More importantly, they found that students who overestimated peer weight were more likely to be overweight themselves, and those who underestimated weight norms were also more likely to be underweight. This shows how our biased perception of what is normal can affect our behaviour, and the need for health campaigns to address the false consensus around weight norms in order to tackle obesity and eating disorders. Oh, and if you think that such a thing is unique to the USA, think again. An earlier study by the same authors with over 2,000 secondary school students in London yielded similar results (Perkins, Perkins, & Craig, 2010).

effect even occurs in virtual communities, and has important implications for counter-terrorism agencies who are trying to prevent the radicalisation of political extremists. The false consensus effect has also been used to explain the errors of financial analysts responsible for forecasting companies' performance (Williams, 2013) – clearly a worrying thing in times of economic instability. These are just a few examples to illustrate how attribution research is used to understand real-life issues. We will now turn our attention to another aspect of social psychology: attitudes.

ASIDE

Words of wisdom

'A positive attitude will not solve all your problems, but it will annoy enough people to make it worth the effort.' (Attributed (no pun intended) to Herm Albright, obscure German painter)

15.5 ATTITUDES

Imagine the following scenario. You are sitting on your sofa watching TV and relaxing. The latest reality show follows the journey of several adults who are trying to lose weight. One of the characters in the programme is attempting to lose the excess weight by taking weight loss pills and other diet aids. Another character is opting for bariatric surgery. 'Hmm, I am not sure this is the answer to their problems!' you exclaim. 'Surely, overweight people should just exercise, eat a healthy and balanced diet and get off their sofa and start moving. I do not agree with all the pill-taking and going under the knife mumbo-jumbo!'

> **ATTITUDES** '[A] psychological tendency that is expressed by evaluating a particular entity with some degree of favour or disfavour' (Eagly & Chaiken, 1993: 1).

You just expressed your view on this matter and have taken a clear position on an issue which seems to be affecting humans in most of the Westernised world. When asked to express their view on a matter, people tend to find it relatively easy to respond. People's views on global warming, immigration, obesity, train ticket prices or indeed hairless cats are very important aspects of the social world and psychologists have been studying them for decades. These views and stances on critical or mundane topics have been called '**attitudes**' by researchers.

You probably possess myriad attitudes on a wide variety of topics. In this section, we will examine attitude research and whether attitudes can predict behaviour. Going back to the example used above, if your attitude towards overweight people is negative (i.e. they simply need to exercise and eat less), what is your behaviour on this issue? Are your actions congruent or incongruent with your attitude?

15.5.1 ATTITUDE RESEARCH

Attitudes were initially seen as a central concept in social psychology, the study of which could potentially lead to greater understanding of social behaviour. Early theorists, such as Thomas and Znaniecki (1918), argued that social psychology is the scientific study of attitudes. This was later reinforced by Allport, who argued that 'the concept of attitudes is probably the most distinctive and indispensable concept in Social Psychology' (Allport, 1935: 798). Attitudinal research received great attention during the 1920s and the 1930s, with a focus on whether attitudes can predict behaviour.

A famous example from this era was the LaPiere study, which investigated the link between prejudiced views towards a Chinese couple and any discriminatory behaviour towards them. LaPiere and the Chinese couple travelled across the United States, staying at 66 hotels, motels and caravan sites and dining at 184 restaurants. Public views towards Chinese people in the USA in the 1930s were fairly negative and discriminatory, so LaPiere expected to see this reflected in people's behaviour, through refusals of service in the restaurants and accommodation establishments. Every time they arrived at an establishment, LaPierre would stay back and let the Chinese couple deal with the proprietors on their own, noting down details such as how the couple were received and whether smiles were exchanged. Contrary to expectations, the Chinese couple was served in every single place bar one. After returning home, LaPierre allowed six months to go by and then sent letters with questionnaires to all the establishments they had visited. The letters included the question: 'Will you accept members of the Chinese race as guests in your establishment?' Replies were received by 81 restaurants and 47 hotels, and an overwhelming 92% of restaurants and 91% of hotels responded with a resounding 'no'. The rest of the proprietors responded with 'maybe' or with 'it depends on circumstances'. One caravan park owner responded with a 'yes' and included a handwritten note describing the wonderful Chinese couple who visited her camp during the summer. LaPiere's study was far from perfect in methodological terms but it raised a very important question: Can attitudes predict behaviour?

15.5.2 ATTITUDES AND BEHAVIOUR

LaPiere's study brought attention to the fact that people may say one thing and do another. Attitudinal research during the 1950s and 1960s focused on investigating the link between attitudes and behaviour. A pessimistic view at the time was that attitudes cannot predict behaviour and that an attitude, as a concept, is pointless because it cannot be accurately measured (Abelson, 1972). LaPiere's study was criticised by Fishbein and Ajzen (1975) for failing to examine a 'specific attitude'. For example, the question LaPiere asked referred to 'members of the Chinese race' and not the specific two individuals who visited the hotels and the restaurants. LaPiere reported that the Chinese gentleman and his wife were very good at 'smiling' and being courteous. One wonders if the results would have been different if LaPiere had asked the proprietors to respond to a question that referred directly to this specific Chinese couple. In fact, research conducted more recently indicates that the strength of the attitude–behaviour link depends on certain conditions. People's behaviour is influenced by their immediate environment and by all the cultural trends that surround them. Social norms cannot be ignored when attempting to understand individual actions and reactions. Similarly, the formation of attitudes is influenced by previous experiences, personality traits, values and beliefs, family and friends and the media (Fazio & Zanna, 1981).

FIGURE 15.3 Recycling. My attitude to recycling is that it is a good thing because global warming is reality (cognition) and I worry about the poor penguins that don't have any ice to stand on (affect). However, the bottle bank is at least 400 metres from my house and I end up throwing my glass in the general rubbish. Another example of attitudes not matching behaviour (oh don't judge me!)

© koh sze kiat/Shutterstock.com

15.5.3 THEORY OF PLANNED BEHAVIOUR

Ajzen (1991) wanted to explore the attitude–behaviour link in conjunction with peripheral determinants that may affect whether attitudes predict behaviour. He argued that there are processes which affect whether an individual will decide to act in a certain way as a result of their overall attitude towards a target concept or person. His *theory of planned behaviour* (TPB) suggests that behavioural intentions can be determined by examining three interrelating factors: *attitudes towards the behaviour*, *subjective norms* and *perceived control*. The process always starts with the attitudes, which are informed by an individual's values, beliefs and previous experiences. People tend to know in an instant whether their attitude towards something or someone is positive or negative. They have a clear stance which is supported by their own estimations of the likely consequences should they choose to behave in accordance with that attitude. The process continues with a calculation of the perceived expectations of important others, usually close family and friends. The individual considers what others might think or feel if he or she acts in a certain way. An important element at this stage is the individual's willingness and motivation to conform to significant others' expectations. The final factor relates to the individual's sense of control over the situation. A belief that the behaviour can be performed and controlled easily is seen as a key predictor in the process. If they believe that they possess a high sense of control over the behaviour, then they are more likely to intend to do it.

Imagine that you want to improve your health by losing the excess weight you are carrying. Let's see how the TPB may help you calculate the likelihood of achieving your goal. There are three factors you need to consider: the attitudes element (I want to lose weight), the subjective norms element (my friends and family agree that I should lose weight) and the perceived control element (I can/cannot do it). All three elements affect the strength of the behavioural intention, which in turn affects whether you are going to perform the behaviour you set out to perform. In other words, what you need to achieve your goal of losing weight is a positive attitude, which is in agreement with your significant others' expectations and a high sense of perceived control, which can strengthen your resolve (behavioural intention) and help you behave in the appropriate manner (some form of self-imposed health regime of eating healthily and exercising). 'Brilliant!' you might think, 'Now I have the template I need to turn all my positive attitudes to positive behaviours and live happily ever after.'

Unfortunately, it is not that simple. The TPB makes the assumption that people carefully calculate the strength of their values and beliefs to work out how strongly they intend to act in a certain way. This assumption implies that people go through a logical and complex process before acting. Using the weight loss regime as an example, consider whether you logically and rationally analyse the situation when faced with a simple decision 'to eat cake or not to eat cake'. What is more likely to influence your intention to act in this scenario? There is evidence to suggest that your emotions, impulsive tendencies and biases affect your behaviour on a daily basis. Wansik and Sobal (2007) argued that people engage in 'mindless eating' on a daily basis. They calculated that, on average, a person makes over 200 food-related decisions per day and that approximately 59 of them are related to what type of food to eat. Their study indicates that individuals may not be such rational and strategic thinkers after all, and that behaviour may not be based on a careful cost–benefit analysis of the available options.

On the note of cost–benefit analysis, we will now turn our attention to what motivates people to help each other.

15.6 PROSOCIAL BEHAVIOUR

In our day-to-day life we encounter numerous examples of people helping each other – from donating money to charity, to a Royal Marine throwing himself on top of a grenade to protect his comrades (Lance Corporal Matthew Croucher survived with barely a scratch and was awarded a George Cross for his bravery in 2008 for doing just this). In this section, we will have a closer look at so-called prosocial behaviour. We generally differentiate between 'normal' helping behaviour (that includes the possibility of you expecting something in return) and altruism (where you act selflessly, sometimes even at a cost to yourself, and expect nothing in return). We will now consider a number of explanations for prosocial behaviour.

> **PROSOCIAL BEHAVIOUR** '[A]ny voluntary behaviour intended to benefit another' (Eisenberg et al., 2006: 646).

15.6.1 EVOLUTION AND HELPING BEHAVIOURS

Unless you were keen and skipped ahead, you have already encountered evolutionary theories in Chapter 1. In the context of helping, evolutionary psychology would suggest that prosocial behaviour is a trait that we are born with. Indeed, it might surprise you to learn that there is substantial evidence of animals displaying prosocial and even altruistic behaviour. From chimpanzees sharing food with one another (de Waal & Suchak, 2010) to vampire bats (yes, they drink blood) regurgitating food to share it with other starving bats (Carter & Wilkinson, 2013), the animal kingdom is full of examples of evolutionary-related prosocial behaviour. Stevens, Cushman and Hauser (2005) reviewed four models that attempt to explain the reasons behind cooperation in an evolutionary context:

- **Mutualism:** Helping each other out is beneficial to everyone involved, and anybody who fails to cooperate will be worse off.
- **Kin selection:** As discussed in more detail in Chapter 1, an individual can promote their genetic future by making sacrifices on behalf of others who are genetically related. The closer the relationship the more the individual is willing to sacrifice.

- **Reciprocity:** One helps somebody else in the hope of future cooperation and repayment ('I'll scratch your back if you scratch mine').
- **Sanctioning:** By punishing an individual for past behaviour, the punisher hopes to gain a future reward. Alternatively, an individual could be harassed during present behaviour with the harasser hoping for an immediate reward.

There is also some evidence for an evolutionary explanation of helping behaviour when studying humans. For instance, when presented with a hypothetical life-or-death situation, people chose more frequently to help close relatives and teenage children rather than strangers and the very young/old (Burnstein, Crandall, & Kitayama, 1994). Moreover, altruistic behaviour has also been observed in infants as young as 14–18 months (Warneken & Tomasello, 2009), further supporting the idea that altruistic tendencies are part of our natural behaviour. However, as the evolutionary perspective doesn't quite explain why we help strangers or why some people help where others don't, we need to consider other factors, including social influences on behaviour.

15.6.2 SOCIAL THEORIES, SOCIAL FACTORS AND HELPING BEHAVIOURS

A key theory in explaining prosocial behaviour is Bandura's (1977) social learning theory. Throughout our lifespan, we learn by observing others and through our own experiences that good behaviour reaps rewards and bad behaviour gets punished. As most people would prefer reward over punishment, we learn to behave in a way that yields the most rewards, and so we act prosocially. More specifically, Cialdini et al. (1981) proposed a three-stage developmental model of prosocial behaviour. Very young children at the presocialisation stage learn to act prosocially only through material rewards and punishments. When they get to primary school age, they become more aware of **social norms** and desirable behaviour, while still also motivated by social rewards and punishments. In teenage years, individuals will have internalised the social norms, maintaining their orientation to rewards and avoiding punishment, but now also experience internal gratification as a reward; thus, the more we help, the better we may feel about ourselves.

Other factors that determine prosocial behaviour are societal norms. If we adhere to these (sometimes unwritten) rules, we get rewards (in the form of integration and societal approval), while violations are punished (perhaps by social isolation or even imprisonment). There are two specific norms that could explain prosocial behaviour. The first norm of **reciprocity** (Gouldner, 1960) has already been mentioned in relation to evolutionary theories, but there are social processes that dictate the extent of our help. For example, Simpsons and Willer (2008) found that egotistic people are much more likely to engage in prosocial behaviour when their reputation is threatened and, overall, there is substantial evidence that people do comply with the norm of reciprocity (Wilke & Lanzetta, 1970, 1982).

The second norm of **social responsibility** suggests that we should help those who depend on us when they are in need, without expecting something in return (Berkowitz, 1972). In practice, however, the rule is much more complex (Darley & Latané, 1970), and linked to causal attribution. So if we think that a person is responsible for their miserable situation (e.g. they gambled their money away), we are less likely to help than when there is an external explanation (e.g. they are the victims of an earthquake). It is also related to whether we believe that 'everybody gets what they deserve': the **just-world hypothesis** (Lerner, 1965). If people believe strongly in a 'just-world', they are less likely to help someone if they can be blamed for their own misfortune (Kogut, 2011). However, if a person is considered blameless, then just-world believers are much more likely to help (DePalma et al., 1999) as they need to realign their view of the world as a fair place.

The extent to which we believe we are in control of a situation also influences our helping behaviour. Bierhoff, Klein and Kramp (1991) examined witnesses of car accidents and compared those who gave first aid with those who did not. They found that as well as scoring higher on just-world beliefs, those who gave first aid had a stronger internal locus of control than those who did not intervene.

LOCUS OF CONTROL The extent to which people believe they are in control of the events that affect them. People with an internal locus of control think that situations around them are the direct result of their own actions and can therefore influence them. In contrast, people with an external locus of control believe that the events are due to circumstantial factors that are completely outside their control.

JUST-WORLD HYPOTHESIS The belief that people have a need to believe that we live in a world where people generally get what they deserve and deserve what they get.

As demonstrated in a classic study by Benson, Karabenick and Lerner (1976), we are also much more likely to help those who are similar to us. Benson and colleagues left addressed and stamped envelopes containing university applications in public phone boxes (the things people used before the invention of mobile phones), and observed what people who found them did. In one variation of the study, the application form contained a photo of the applicant (half of the applicants were white Americans and the other half black Americans). It was found that the participants (who were all white) were much more likely to post the letters of the white applicants.

This preference for our ingroup is an important factor when it comes to helping behaviour, and a 'sense of we-ness … leads to more positive behaviors such as helping' (Dovidio et al., 1997: 404). This was also demonstrated by Levine et al. (2005), who arranged an encounter between participants and a jogger who seemingly slipped and injured his ankle. All of their participants were Manchester United fans and the jogger wore either a Manchester United shirt or one of their bitter rivals', Liverpool FC. When the jogger appeared to be a fellow fan (ingroup), people were much more likely to offer help than when he was wearing the rival shirt (outgroup). However, in a second study, Levine and colleagues (Levine et al., 2005) also showed how easy it is to alter the ingroup boundaries. Prior to encountering the jogger, the Manchester United fans were told that the aim of the study was to find out what fans in general get out of their love for football. After being primed to consider themselves as part of the larger ingroup of football fans in general, participants helped the jogger regardless of which shirt he wore.

The majority of prosocial research discussed so far has been focusing on face-to-face interactions. However, the widespread use of the internet and the popularisation of social networking sites has led some researchers to wonder whether people engage in prosocial behaviour online as they do offline.

15.6.3 ONLINE PROSOCIAL BEHAVIOUR

One of the first studies to examine online prosocial behaviour was carried out by Wang and Wang (2008), who wanted to investigate whether online gamers who score high in altruism would be more likely to help other players in the game. The results revealed that altruistic online gamers offered more help to other players and answered more questions than their less altruistic counterparts. This early study indicated that helping behaviours are transferable online and that individuals who are good Samaritans on the streets are likely to continue with their good deeds in virtual environments too. You might want to argue that helping behaviour as part of an online game is probably simply the result of having common goals, such as advancing to a new level or acquiring special equipment. One has to wonder whether this type of prosocial behaviour is artificial or instrumental.

To examine this further, Wright and Li (2011) investigated online prosocial behaviours as they are found in social networking sites (SNS), chat rooms, text messages and emails. They found positive correlations between face-to-face and online prosocial behaviours, indicating that people who are likely to help others offline also help others in online spaces. This finding is supported by looking at the opposite side of the spectrum, aggression research, where a link between offline and online aggression has been established (Calvete et al., 2010).

Young adults who behave aggressively in face-to-face situations are likely to extend their aggression to the cyber world by engaging in cyberaggression. In a similar manner, a person who has the tendency to help others offline is likely to continue to behave in prosocial ways when they log in. SNS and online chat spaces are seen by some as nothing more than a microcosm of society. In society, in the offline world, one can witness an abundance of behaviours, both 'good' and 'bad', and the story is no different in the cyberworld where the good, the bad and the ugly seem to occupy common territory. The 'good' could be acts of kindness, the 'bad' could be the cyber version of bystander apathy, also known as the bystander effect and the 'ugly' incidents of cyberbullying and cyberaggression.

15.6.4 BYSTANDER EFFECT (ONLINE AND OFFLINE CONSIDERATIONS)

After all this prosocial behaviour, you are probably thinking that you would do the 'right thing' and help another person if that person was distressed, attacked or having a medical emergency. Some psychologists in the 1960s would probably predict that you are wrong in your estimation and that you would be more likely to suffer from a phenomenon called **bystander apathy**. This phenomenon received great attention following the murder of a young woman in New York in 1964. Initial media reports of the murder spoke of an alleged 39 witnesses who did nothing to help the young woman. Latané and Darley (1969) wrote a series of research articles on the bystander effect in an attempt to explain why some people remain apathetic to the misfortune of others instead of taking responsible action to help them. As it transpired much later, the event which triggered this research was more fiction than fact (Manning, Levine, & Collins, 2007). The newspaper articles omitted some information (i.e. that one bystander shouted at the attacker) and fabricated some of the witness reports. Nevertheless, the case led to a number of research studies, most of which concentrated their efforts on trying to work out under which circumstances people are most likely to help.

EXERCISE: ONLINE BYSTANDER EFFECT

Do you think that the bystander effect can be seen in online interactions? Next time you use a social networking site or online newspaper, take a look at the comments people leave. What can you observe? If you look closely, you will see cyberaggression incidents between people who know each other, but also between strangers. Is anyone stepping in to help individuals who are seemingly being targeted? What are the psychological processes involved?

Latané and Darley's (1969) model was created in order to explain the decision-making processes involved in an emergency situation. The model has five stages:

(1) Noticing (that something is wrong)

In a fast-paced and cognitively demanding environment, you simply might not notice that something is happening. If you are stressed, preoccupied or anxious, you might not notice that someone is experiencing difficulty.

(2) Interpreting (understanding what is going on)

Maybe you have noticed the incident but you don't understand what is going on. Uncertainty about the event will prevent you from deciding that you should act.

(3) Deciding-responsibility (whether it is your responsibility to act)

You have interpreted what is going on and you know it is an emergency. But you are not sure it is your responsibility to do something about it. You are unlikely to take the lead if there is someone else there who looks more qualified than you (a first aider, a uniformed official, a teacher).

(4) Deciding skills

You want to help but you do not know if you have the right skills. Uncertainty about your ability to provide effective help may hold you back.

(5) Final decision and help

You reached the final stage in the process but you still have inhibitions. You may be thinking about any negative consequences of your actions. This final stage is crucial in the process. Your brain is calculating the pros and cons and weighing up positive and negative effects.

These five stages outline the complexities a bystander is facing when presented with an incident. As you can see, and contrary to popular belief, bystander apathy is a phenomenon that may affect pretty much everyone.

KEY STUDY

Parks, M.J., Osgood, D.W., Felson, R.B., Wells, S., & Graham, K. (2013). Third party involvement in barroom conflicts. *Aggressive Behavior*, *39*(4), 257–268.

Imagine the following scenario: you are at your local pub enjoying a non-alcoholic beverage with a good friend when a fight erupts at the table next to you. The fight is getting worse and you are concerned that it is getting out of hand. What do you do? You quickly weigh up the pros and cons in order to decide whether to intervene or not. Are you more likely to intervene if the people involved in the fight are drunken men or when the fight is between a man and a woman? What do you think?

Parks et al. (2013) conducted a study to examine the situational factors which influence third-party intervention in a pub fight. They sent out observers across 503 nights in 87 large clubs and bars in Toronto, and encountered a total of 860 aggressive incidents (interestingly, the most frequent type involved a man making unwanted advances towards a female). Most people will have a very clear template for situations such as a fight in a bar, thanks to their popular depiction in films. 'Stay out of it!', you can hear your brain screaming at you. 'Oh, unless there is a lone victim involved, in which case go, step in and help them out.' This is logical and agrees with social schemas; however, it is not what Park et al. found in their study. Third-party intervention was more likely when two males were involved and least likely when there was a confrontation between a man and a woman. What is more, if the fighting parties were visibly intoxicated, the likelihood of third-party involvement went up. Parker and colleagues suggest that this is because bystanders assess the dangerousness of the situation and are more likely to intervene if the potential to escalate is high (man versus man incidents are likely to result in physical violence; man versus woman less likely so).

15.6.5 PRACTICAL APPLICATIONS OF PROSOCIAL BEHAVIOUR RESEARCH

Have you ever wondered what processes lie behind prosocial behaviours such as volunteering in the community, donating blood, giving money to charity or becoming an organ donor? Prosocial behaviour research contributes to society by providing evidence and offering tangible and practical solutions for a wide variety of societal issues. One example is a study by Guéguen and Lamy (2011), who investigated whether different types of words increased the amount of money people donated to charity. The researchers placed charity collection boxes in different bakeries in France. They wanted to see if adding the word 'love' on the label would have any effect on the money collected. There were three types of collection box, all of which had a standard message printed on the label: 'Female business students organising humanitarian action in Togo. We are relying on your support.' In addition to the standard message, the boxes displayed two different labels positioned directly under the money slot. One had the words 'Donating = Loving', and the other had the words 'Donating = Helping'. The third type of box had no additional message. The researchers wanted to see if there was any difference in the amount of money collected in each type of box. The results revealed that, although the boxes with the 'helping' label on them did not yield a bigger amount, the ones with the word 'loving' on the label did. In fact, the money collected in the 'Donating = Loving' boxes was almost double that of the control boxes. The researchers argued that using love as a primer probably enhanced people's altruistic sentiment by reminding them of other related terms, such as compassion, support and solidarity.

15.7 CHAPTER SUMMARY

As we have seen in this chapter, the causal attribution of behaviour is a surprisingly complex affair, and we are far from perfect in our judgements. Partially, this is due to us not having the time or cognitive resources to conduct in-depth analyses. Instead, we are motivated tacticians who rely on heuristics to take mental shortcuts. In the process of doing so, we make ourselves vulnerable to committing a variety of errors, such as the fundamental attribution error. We have also seen how attribution models, theories and errors find practical application in modern real-life research, helping us to understand important societal concerns, such as radicalisation processes in a counter-terrorism context, or how to tackle attitudes to climate change.

We also learned that predicting behaviours by attitudes alone can be challenging. The classic study by LaPierre provides a clear illustration of how attitudes towards minority groups did not predict how people behaved towards them. The theory of planned behaviour was put forward as a way to better predict behaviour. This model considers subjective norms, the consequences of engaging in the behaviour, and the extent to which the person believes they are capable of engaging in the behaviour.

Finally, we looked at prosocial behaviour. Several theories have been offered to explain why individuals engage in helping behaviours. Evolutionary theories suggest that prosocial behaviour is in the interest of species survival, while social theories emphasise the importance of social learning and social norms in encouraging us to act altruistically. We have also seen how prosocial behaviour plays out in the online world.

DISCUSSION QUESTIONS

This section has been all about why people do or do not help others. Bearing in mind what we have just covered in this chapter, can you remember a situation in the recent past where someone needed help? If so, try using the following questions to help you reflect on the situation:

- Did you help them? Or did you decide not to?
- What were the reasons for your choice?
- Can you think of any particular factors in the situation, about the person or about yourself, which made a difference?
- In the future, in what situations do you think you might help?
- What might make a difference when you next encounter someone who needs help?

SUGGESTIONS FOR FURTHER READING

Hedegaard, T.F. (2014). Stereotypes and welfare attitudes: a panel survey of how 'Poor Carina' and 'Lazy Robert' affected attitudes towards social assistance in Denmark. Available at SSRN 2376779. A very current and applied study examining a public debate on welfare recipients in Denmark.

Padilla-Walker, L.M., & Carlo, G. (Eds). (2014). *Prosocial development: a multidimensional approach*. Oxford: Oxford University Press. If you want to know more about prosocial behaviour, this book covers everything in great depth. A bit heavy at times but certainly current and comprehensive.

Raihani, N.J. (2014). Hidden altruism in a real-world setting. *Biology Letters*, *10*(1), *20130884*. A very short and accessible study on altruism and the violation of norms when donating on fundraising websites.

Have a look on YouTube for various field experiments on the bystander effect, for example: www.youtube.com/watch?v=cgE5q5rDlaA

Still want more? For links to online resources relevant to this chapter and a quiz to test your understanding, visit the companion website at edge.sagepub.com/banyard2e

16 CRITICAL SOCIAL PSYCHOLOGY

Lead authors: Hugh Miller, Patrick Hylton and Jill Arnold

CHAPTER OUTLINE

16.1 Introduction   278

16.2 What are 'critical psychology' and 'critical social psychology'?   278

16.3 Methodology   281

16.4 Power   283

    16.4.1 Research   283

    16.4.2 The discipline of psychology   283

    16.4.3 The world outside the discipline   284

16.5 Ideology   285

16.6 Individualist versus collectivist approaches: the critique of individualism   287

    16.6.1 Intersubjectivity   288

    16.6.2 Blaming the individual   288

16.7 The relationship between academic psychology and everyday life   289

16.8 Chapter summary   291

Discussion questions   292

Suggestions for further reading   292

16.1 INTRODUCTION

Surely, all psychology has a critical component, so why put the word 'critical' in the title? The difference here is the context of the criticism. Instead of looking at research in the context of previous studies and also in the context of the methods that have been used, the critical psychology approach broadens that to look at questions such as why we are choosing to do this research in the first place. This chapter will address five separate, but related, issues in social psychology. They all examine the science of psychology in a political and moral framework.

METHODOLOGY   and the critique which developed from the 1970s 'crisis in social psychology'. An examination of the underlying assumptions of research and the full context of when, where and by whom the research was done, and who paid for it.

POWER   and those imbalances that distort psychological practices and affect the usefulness and impact of its outcomes.

IDEOLOGY   and those systems of beliefs that affect people's social behaviour and also the psychological practices of researchers and theorists.

INDIVIDUALIST VERSUS COLLECTIVIST   approaches and how the predominance of individualism in Western psychology has affected the debate as to whether psychology ought to be about objectively described behaviour or subjectively lived experience.

ACADEMIC PSYCHOLOGY AND ITS RELATIONSHIP TO EVERYDAY LIFE   and how people use psychology to understand themselves.

FRAMING QUESTIONS

- What does it mean to be critical in psychology?
- Do we need to be critical in psychology as a social science in a way which is different from being critical in the physical sciences?
- How does the academic practice of psychology affect people in their ordinary lives?
- How do external social pressures and processes affect the process of academic psychology?
- Can psychology ever be a 'value-free' science or is it bound to reflect the culture of the society that produces it?

16.2 WHAT ARE 'CRITICAL PSYCHOLOGY' AND 'CRITICAL SOCIAL PSYCHOLOGY'?

It is important for scientists, and scholars in general, to be critical of their subjects. The quality of evidence should be questioned, the logic of explanations examined and the frame of reference of research should be clarified. Indeed, students of psychology are expected to adopt such a critical approach in their studies and previous chapters in this book will have encouraged that kind of evaluative approach (see, e.g. Chapter 4). So why is there a separate chapter with 'critical' in the title?

We are suggesting a different level of criticality here: criticality of the enterprise of psychology as a whole, and of the social situations in which academic psychology is practised. We do not see psychology as a value-free science conducted in a social and moral vacuum, but as a social activity carried out by particular people with particular backgrounds and ways of understanding the world derived from the society in which they live. Psychology is also an industry that is dependent on certain sources of finance, with career structures for its workers, and is required to produce culturally acceptable products to justify the investment made in it. Critical Psychology (CP), as a movement, takes the view that psychology cannot be fully understood without considering these factors, and as the findings of psychology can have far-reaching social and political consequences, its worth must be considered in terms of its social impact and relevance, not just its academic scientific validity.

The kind of criticality described here can, and we would argue *should*, be applied in all areas of psychology, and in order to understand the practice of psychology as a whole, wider social and political implications need to be examined. For example, there were non-scientific reasons for the rise in importance of cognitive psychology in the late twentieth century and, more recently, the dominance of physiological and evolutionary 'explanations' in all areas of psychology have become part of significant *social* movements. However, CP has mainly focused on the social aspects of psychology, hence the title of this chapter: Critical Social Psychology (CSP). There are three specific reasons for this focus.

The first is that social psychology needs to be concerned about the social practices of the discipline and the social implications of that practice. This is because psychology's pronouncements on things like conformity and leadership can have more *real world impact* than findings on the phonological loop or the structure of the primary visual cortex. The second reason, as argued most strikingly by Kenneth Gergen (1973), is that social psychology is *qualitatively* different from other areas of psychology in that human social nature is *historically changeable*, and that since we are thinking, intentional beings, our awareness of the findings of social psychology (e.g. in media accounts and through applications in education and health policies) actually *changes* our psychology.

EXPERIMENTER EFFECTS Unwanted influences in a psychological study which are produced, consciously or unconsciously, by the person carrying out the study.

DEMAND CHARACTERISTICS Those aspects of a psychological study (or other artificial situation) which exert an implicit pressure on people to act in ways that are expected of them.

SOCIAL PROCESSES Those ways in which individuals or groups interact and how relationships and social understandings about what is happening affects decision making and behaviour.

NORMATIVE INFLUENCE The process by which the normal or ideal is defined and, by implication, set up as a standard which people should aim for.

So social psychology is both reflexive and dependent on the historical time and cultural circumstances in which it take place, which Gergen characterises as 'history', rather than 'science'. These criticisms, of course, also apply in other areas of psychology, most obviously developmental psychology (e.g. parenting practices and what 'influences' children), but the general point is that social psychology is not a timeless scientific project. The third reason is historical. After the Second World War (1939–1945), social psychology, especially in the USA, prospered as a laboratory subject. In the urgent need to explain the psychology of the actions of people during and after great political upheavals, many classic, objective, well-controlled studies of conformity, obedience, cooperation, persuasion and leadership were conducted and found their way into introductory texts.

In the 1960s and 1970s, there was growing disquiet about the relevance and usefulness of this research, supported by Rosenthal and Jacobson's (1968) study on **experimenter effects** and Orne's (1962) on **demand characteristics**. It seemed that the artificial, and often absurd, world of the laboratory was producing artificial and absurd behaviour which bore little relation to **social processes** in the outside world. Further, by restricting social psychology to questions which could be operationalised and studied experimentally, much of the *point* of social life was being missed. There was also concern about the **normative influence** of psychology: it was being used to define how people *should* behave, and the research was driven by culturally-bound (and often restricted) assumptions of what was right and *normal* behaviour.

This concern was characterised as 'the crisis in social psychology' (Elms, 1975). Elms suggested that 'Relief [from the crisis] may come from acceptance of theoretical and methodological pluralism, from re-evaluation of research expectations and ethical stances, and from the development of realistic responses to societal demands' (Elms, 1975: 967). These are the issues that CP took up and the 'crisis' became the natural focus for the development of much critical *social* psychology.

KEY RESEARCHER Kenneth J. Gergen

FIGURE 16.1   Kenneth J. Gergen

When Kenneth Gergen graduated from Yale University in 1957, experimental social psychology was rapidly developing many of the famous theories that were to have a huge impact within psychology and beyond as explanations of social life. Ten years later, when Gergen was appointed as Professor of Psychology at Swarthmore College, he had begun to critically challenge prevailing research methods and the conclusions being drawn from them. His first major contribution to critical social psychology was the publication in 1973 of his paper 'Social psychology as history', which became one of the most cited papers in psychology. In that article, he argued that the search for *universal* 'laws' of social interaction was futile (whether based on laboratory experimentation or gathered as 'truths from out-there'), as patterns of social life were in continuous transformation, and the attempt to study and document these patterns could potentially function so as to change these patterns. Because scientific descriptions of human behaviour carried implicit values and were ideologically saturated, so would exposure to social psychological research influence people's actions. Thus, the very attempt to study human behaviour would undermine the 'truths' it sought to establish.

This meta-psychology had repercussions! First, its impact contributed to the 'crisis' in social psychology, a general sense that the course of the discipline was misdirected. It also functioned as a critique of the experimental testing of hypotheses. Ultimately, it formed the basis of the social constructionist movement in psychology, and the broad concern with how people *socially and actively construct* their realities, rationalities and moralities, along with their life stories, their identities and their social institutions. Further, Gergen's work contributed to critical ideas that see psychology as a moral and political enterprise that can change society for good or ill, and therefore should take responsibility to ensure research is undertaken, disseminated and presented in terms which make sense to those being studied and which do not perpetuate a concept of value-free or unprejudiced knowledge.

Ken Gergen has received major awards for his community, therapeutic and educational work, often done in collaboration with others, including his wife Mary Gergen, and his recent work includes 'performative' social science, positive ageing and the global dimensions of qualitative inquiry, along with developing the work of the Taos Institute, which he co-founded with others who believed that social constructionist ideas have powerful and positive implications for human life and well-being. References to his work can be found at the end of the chapter and at the following websites:

www.swarthmore.edu/academics/kenneth-j-gergen.xml

www.taosinstitute.net/kenneth-j-gergen-phd

IDEOLOGY A set of ideas, beliefs and perspectives from which to interpret social and political realities and so inform actions. When used pejoratively it means how hidden aims and interests are achieved by distorting (or ignoring) social, political realities. For example, Karl Marx described how the ideology of the ruling class (in order to serve their class interests) promoted a 'false consciousness' in other classes that their ideas were universal truths.

LAISSEZ-FAIRE CAPITALISM An economic system where transactions between private parties are free from government regulations (such as restrictions, tariffs and subsidies) except for rights to protect property.

Being critical of the practice of psychology involves challenging psychology's mainstream methodologies, and the **ideologies** of Western psychology and its practitioners. Being critical of the social situation within which psychology is practised can involve a wholesale challenge to individualistic, **laissez-faire capitalism**, or a more localised critique of the academic world which prioritises the publication of frequently-cited research papers over any consideration of the usefulness or relevance of psychology as it is practised. 'Critical Psychology' doesn't necessarily have to involve all areas of criticism: if you read articles by writers cited in this chapter, you will come across a wide range of focuses of criticality and political positions. It is important to realise that this chapter is an argument about the practice of psychology. Readers should feel free to accept or reject this argument. The chapter is not presenting 'the facts' about a certain area of psychology. We would argue, though, that the psychological 'facts' presented elsewhere are actually socially mediated constructions and interpretations of scientific practice, and should be read accordingly.

16.3 METHODOLOGY

The choice that psychology made in the nineteenth century (and then again in the second half of the twentieth century) was to establish itself as a reputable, academic, and above all scientific discipline, and those of us who chose to become psychologists all signed up to that while getting our qualifications. Critical psychologists have, however, taken the philosophical and **epistemological** view that as

> **EPISTEMOLOGY** How we come to know things. If we question what knowledge is, we need to critically consider how it has been acquired.

'science is largely a by-product of the Western cultural tradition at a particular time in its historical development' (Gergen et al., 1996: 497), the nature of science, research methods and practices, and the construction of knowledge in traditional psychology, need to be challenged.

One question for students, academics or researchers that arises is whether the reverence psychology has for experimentation is justified, and just what do we think we are trying to do? Is it to understand and generate theories *of* people or something adequate *for* people? For most critical social psychologists, the response would be to try to understand people, but also to help them understand and articulate their views, and to work with people to develop situations that are beneficial to them. But how is this to be achieved, given the reverence for a science equated with experimentation, and as noted in Koch's (1959) observation that 'from the earliest days of the experimental pioneers, man's stipulation that psychology be adequate to science outweighed his commitment that it be adequate to man' (Koch, 1959: 783, cited in Howard, 1985: 259)? Given the cultural times we live in, psychology therefore has had to justify its 'scientific credentials' (Richards, 1996: 2) and the dominance of quantitative and experimental practices. As Winston and Blais state: 'the remarkable social consensus on the definition and role of *experiments* as *the* investigative practice of psychology' (1996: 599, italics in original) helped to legitimate this claim.

Experimentalism is of course an approach that, if performed correctly, guarantees objectively reliable data uncontaminated by biases. It allows valid claims. Wilson (2005: 186), for example, states that 'experiments are what separate us [psychologists] from related disciplines' and are the reason why social psychology has so much to offer compared with other social disciplines. But, wherever there is assumed 'consensus' and practices are taken for granted and a dominant view exists, critical psychologists would want to look closer. For example, the embracing of the American model of experimentation in which individuals are the focus of attention ('individualism') needs to be critically evaluated. A second issue is 'scientism': 'that when it comes to facts, and explanations of facts, science is the only game in town' (Byrnes, 2006, quoting Daniel Dennett).

CSP also proposes a move from traditional experimental social psychology for three, more practical, reasons. The first is that, following the crisis in social psychology, people lost faith in the ability to simulate real social processes in the laboratory, and as this problem seems at its greatest in social psychology, there was a general call for 'increased ecological validity' in psychology research. Also, there is a recognition that a methodology based on using techniques like analysis of variance to look for simple causal main effects may not be appropriate for social processes.

The second reason comes from a desire to change the relationship between the researcher and the researched. CSP maintains that the 'experimenter–subject' relationship can be exploitative, especially when the power imbalance involved means that what is 'discovered' is what the dominant party is looking for, which answers *their* question, rather than any questions the people studied would like addressed. We should use methodologies which give power to people and which allow them to communicate what social processes are relevant, which gives the possibility of doing research that will benefit the subjects (not objects) of the research, rather than mining them for information to justify their oppression.

The third reason is less high-minded. People know when they are being experimented on, can probably work out what the hypothesis is, and are almost bound to modify their responses because of that understanding, whether it is to help things come out right or to resist unwelcome manipulation. Moreover, if, as Gergen (1973) points out, psychological knowledge changes people's social lives, social psychology cannot be a static knowledge-based inquiry. Once it is recognised that the psychological experiment is a set of *social* practices that have been institutionalised as the right way to work, it becomes clear that alternative approaches can also be legitimate practices. Social psychology is a reflexive, negotiated subject, and it needs a methodology that reflects this.

So is there an alternative to psychology's experimental obsession? Critical approaches would argue there is, and rather than using only **quantitative** methods concerned only with measures of behaviour, *qualitative* methods, which are concerned with what people say about their understandings and intentions, in real-life contexts, can

ACTION RESEARCH tries to solve immediate problems by working as part of community practice. Such research leads to social action based on reflexive planning, action and fact-finding, either as participatory action in an organisation to change things as the research is being conducted or when an organisation is guided by professional researchers to improve practices, etc.

address the three points raised. Further, participants in qualitative research are assumed to be active socially cognitive persons and should be allowed to discuss the issues being researched as active collaborators.

So qualitative methodologies that use language as their data rather than numbers, and have an interpretative, naturalistic approach (e.g. **action research**, critical discourse analysis, focus groups, narrative, phenomenological methods, visual research methods, etc.; see Biggerstaff, 2012), are seen as appropriate means to investigate *social* psychological phenomena (Harré, 2004a). For Harré, qualitative methodology can stake a claim to be most suited for psychology because 'Psychology is the study of meaning making and management, and the skills necessary to accomplish it' (2004a: 4) and so the *intentions* of people can be identified and understood.

Critical psychologists would say, as Harré points out, that whatever humans are aware of will have two properties – material and intentional. A good example to explain this difference is to consider sound. It has a material quality that can be measured (decibels, frequency) and fits into the natural science methodological approach – quantitative, experimentation, etc. But in the human world a sound can have an intention – the sound made by a rock band is done for a purpose and this is psychological and needs interpretation. Measuring its loudness would fail to recognise the human experience of people at the concert. It's not about which band is the loudest, but which type of music you prefer and why you prefer it. There's classic rock on the left versus Latino-punk on the right – take your pick (find them on Facebook/YouTube).

FIGURE 16.2 Who Cares Anyway? and The Zeroes. Hear them and decide which you prefer at: https://soundcloud.com/duncanlovell/sets/the-zeroes (pictures courtesy of Rob Winder and Sharon Cooper Photography)

Since every culture has ways to report thoughts and social processes, qualitative methodologies fit with the natural occurrences of psychological phenomena. Qualitative methods focus on language and therefore move away from individualism, for language depends on how people construct meaning *together*.

In most psychology degrees, methods are taught as something independent, free-standing from psychology topics. The uncritical use of *any* methodological approach may of course narrow the understanding of the phenomenon being studied. 'Methodolatry' is giving special status to a particular method that 'works to prevent us looking at the assumptions behind our research' (Chamberlain, 2000: 293), and while experimentation's primary position in psychology can be seen as an element of this, Chamberlain points out that qualitative research also has 'methods police' (2000: 287) who are overly concerned with 'how to do it' rather than understanding the phenomenon studied. If there is a priority in critical psychology, it must be to use whatever resources are available to advance the interest of the group or individual of interest. For CSP, being critical of methods ensures that psychological practices are reflexive and respectful to fellow members of society.

16.4 POWER

CSP concerns itself with power, or more specifically imbalances of power, at several levels. Imbalances of power distort the practice of psychology and undermine its potential usefulness. These imbalances have an effect within research, in the discipline of psychology more widely, and in the world outside the discipline.

16.4.1 RESEARCH

Traditionally, the psychologist researcher instructs or observes people, who usually, as volunteers, agree to follow the instructions they are given. It is generally accepted that to call research participants 'subjects' is demeaning, and more acceptable terms like 'participant' or 'respondent' are encouraged, but it is still the case that these people are required to do what is asked, and their function is to provide the researcher with information and insights in return, perhaps, for student credits or a small payment. There is a long-standing criticism (Nobles, 1976) that by mining them for 'knowledge', the objects of such research are exploited and the published scientific results, while building the researcher's career, will leave them no wiser, and worse, at risk that the results will not necessarily be used in their best interests.

In contrast, a critical approach requires that all parties should have rights in the process of research, and all should potentially benefit from it. One way to achieve this is to follow a process of action research where one aim is to help those being researched, who are also encouraged to become co-researchers, helping in decisions about the form and direction of the research and about its interpretation and application.

It is over-optimistic to think that parity of power can ever be achieved, however. It is generally the researcher who decides what or who to study in the first place, and has power to make assumptions or hypotheses about likely outcomes. They also generally reserve the right to interpret (or re-interpret) the data, including, in qualitative work, people's utterances and understandings. In early discourse analysis research, for example, Wetherell and Potter (1992), in a study in New Zealand of discourses about race, showed how people's 'I'm not racist, but …' discourses were used to justify discrimination and disguise racism. They then presented an account which was critical of that disguised racism without questioning their power as psychologists to do so.

16.4.2 THE DISCIPLINE OF PSYCHOLOGY

Academic psychology is also an industry, and researchers and teachers are workers within that industry, required to produce saleable products and conform to the industry's working practices. The products are research publications and students. As in any industry, workers who do not contribute products in appropriate quantity and quality will not do well and may lose their job. The powers that decide what is appropriate are universities, professional organisations and journals. CSP (Parker, 1992) aims to question the motives and operations of these organisations and break down their control, as such power limits and distorts the best practice of psychology.

For those of us raised and trained in the mainstream and imbued with the dominant ideology, it can be difficult to see hidden abuses of power, misleading theories and ideological control, which is one reason why many powerful initiatives in CSP have come from those outside the dominant **hegemony**: women, people of colour, LGBTs. Sometimes it is easier to see the issues in historical retrospect, for instance how the American Psychological Association ignored Kenneth and Mamie Clarke in the 1950s, whose research on black schoolchildren was very important in the movement to abolish racially segregated schooling in the USA, where it steadfastly refused to give any recognition to these black psychologists, however distinguished, and however closely they were involved in momentous social changes (Benjamin & Crouse, 2002).

> **HEGEMONY** The situation where the interests of the powerful can marginalise and counter the claims of other groups. Where there is such dominance, some ideas will therefore be subordinated so, for example, the views of less powerful groups will be denigrated and thought to be of less value.

KEY STUDY

Lazar, M.M. (2007). Feminist critical discourse analysis: articulating a feminist discourse praxis. *Critical Discourse Studies, 4*(2), 141–164. Also available at: http://dx.doi.org/10.1080/17405900701464816.

Feminist approaches have made a significant contribution to debates, theories and practical action in critical social psychology, especially about how gender, traditionally treated as the causal outcome of biological sex differences, is socially complex and varies across cultures; the effects of asymmetry of social power; and how gender identity interacts with other social factors.

This paper takes a critical feminist perspective to show how ideas about gender are discussed within and outside psychology. You can read more about the methods of critical discourse and conversation analysis in Chapter 23 (Self) and in Chapter 4 (Methods), but here is both a useful example of discourse analysis from a critical feminist perspective and also a comprehensive meta-discussion of why it is necessary to be critical of how gender is understood in mainstream social psychology, how it matters who is doing the research, how that research is conducted, and how much power those who are paying for it have to present women and men that negatively discriminate supposed differences. You can ask yourself how the points raised by Lazar illustrate and explain important issues in critical social psychology:

- Is gender an ideological matter?
- What are the key principles identified by critical feminist psychology that would affect how and in what way we do social psychology?
- Do analysing such cultural discourses reveal the depth and hidden inequality of gender relations in Western society?
- Do you agree that dominant discourses perpetuate gender discrimination?
- If we critically address *who* does social psychology, *how* we do social psychology and *who has the power to decide what it all means* or interpret studies, how will this bring about increased social justice?

16.4.3 THE WORLD OUTSIDE THE DISCIPLINE

It is important to challenge oppression outside the discipline as well as within it, and CSP supports research that highlights oppression of class, gender, sexual orientation or minority ethnicity. Part of that is to enable people, of whatever grouping, to own their psychology, but also to document how oppression and discrimination have psychological effects, how these might support a vicious cycle of disadvantage, and how psychological understanding can support people in overcoming discrimination.

Gergen and Gergen (1988) describe how the dominant cultural discourses provide us with understandings about who and what we can be in our social groups: 'One is not free simply to have any form of history he or she wishes' (Gergen & Gergen, 1988: 29). Critical and feminist social perspectives argue that one is of the sources of power that contributes to prejudiced ideas about people is the dominance of those patriarchal institutions that control, produce and edit all media. This includes the outputs of psychology itself. Critical psychologists (e.g. Carter & Steiner, 2003; Kagan et al., 2011) show how those who 'have a voice' and can use visual representations in newspapers, magazines, TV shows, together with politicians in the news, the news process itself, adverts and psychology publications provide **dominant discourses** to dictate what it means to be a certain category of person (age, gender, class, status, etc). These ideas are then reflected in how *we* judge others and ourselves. These categories, and how people intersect them, are rarely discussed with any sophistication outside CSP. Further, traditional psychology rarely recognises how such power is used for political or ideological reasons to embed sexism, racism, ageism, xenophobia, etc. in our judgements.

DOMINANT DISCOURSES This is a way of speaking or behaving on any given topic that appears most prevalent in a particular social group or society. Such speech and writing will reflect the ideologies of those who have the most power in the society or have authority to control, for example, the media or knowledge. A dominant discourse about a certain subject will affect how people adopt the beliefs and actions of those in power, which can eventually become the social norm. If it does this, then few people will challenge the ideas, or even if they want to, they may lack power to get their message across.

KEY STUDY

Seligman, M., & Fowler, R. (2011). Comprehensive soldier fitness and the future of psychology. *American Psychologist, 66*(1), 82–86.

Martin Seligman is an important figure in the early twenty-first century development of the Positive Psychology movement, having used his 1998 presidential address to the American Psychological Association (available at www.ppc.sas.upenn.edu/aparep98.htm) to call for 'what I call "positive psychology," that is, a reoriented science that emphasises the understanding and building of the most positive qualities of an individual: optimism, courage, work ethic, future-mindedness, interpersonal skill, the capacity for pleasure and insight, and social responsibility' (Seligman, 1999: 559). Much recent positive psychology research takes an individualistic approach (how can individuals take action to improve their wellbeing or happiness?) and uses experimental methods (Seligman, 2002). If you've followed this chapter so far, you will realise that a CSP approach will have theoretical criticisms of this research, both for its methodology and for locating problems and solutions within the individual.

This article describes an initiative that raises the other kind of criticism: What should psychology be used for? It describes a large-scale ($100+ million, $43 million to Seligman's team) cooperation between the University of Pennsylvania Resiliency Project team and the US military to respond to the need of 'unprecedented levels of posttraumatic stress disorder, depression, suicide, and anxiety along with a need for a resilient Army capable of meeting the persistent warfare of the foreseeable future' (Seligman & Fowler, 2011: 82). From the critical psychology viewpoint of making clear the assumptions/ideology behind research, it is striking that the account explicitly assumes 'the persistent warfare of the foreseeable future' and sees this programme as significant for the 'future of psychology'.

The project has a website at http://csf2.army.mil/index.html and there is related material at the University of Pennsylvania Positive Psychology Centre: www.ppc.sas.upenn.edu/index.html. Here, large amounts of government funding (remember the discussions on power earlier in the chapter, and how economic power is very important in directing the practice of psychology) are being used to support a programme to help soldiers to recover from the experience of active service and also to become more resilient in the face of 'persistent warfare'. Not surprisingly, other psychologists have raised issues about whether this is the kind of work psychology should be doing and whether and how this programme could be evaluated. The whole of the January 2011 issue of *American Psychologist* (volume 66, issue 1) is given over to articles on this topic, and there are follow-up comments in later issues that year (e.g. Eidelson, Pilisuk, & Soldz, 2011; Krueger, 2011; Phipps, 2011 and others in the October issue of *American Psychologist*: there's also a reply here from Seligman, 2011).

There isn't space to set out the arguments here; your task is to look at some of these articles and websites and decide not just whether this is a good, worthwhile and justified programme or not, but whether issues of morality, social impact – and even value for money – are important criteria to consider in evaluating what psychologists do.

The effect of all this is that the norms and values of what it means to be an old woman, a consumer, a working-class man, a young person not-in-employment-education-or-training, a single mother, a black youth, etc. is uncritically accepted. The power of political and cultural discourse is that it is how people make sense of others through social rules, policies, laws and self-monitoring. Critical social psychology has therefore to consider how social interactions work rather than how individuals are induced to act collectively in mindless, or at least not-thought-through, ways. Such different perspectives are not traditionally taken into account when using quantitative methods to study social interaction.

16.5 IDEOLOGY

'Ideology' refers to a system of beliefs held by a group, nation or society. This makes the point that ideologies are local, not universal. There are two aspects of ideology: one is a set of values and principles which can guide action, the other is a way of ordering the world so that it makes sense to us. The first aspect of ideology is conscious and explicit. The second might be something of which we are completely unaware: it's just the belief system we are immersed in, and no more of our conscious experience than water is to fish or air is to us. Examples of the more conscious everyday ideologies are political or religious beliefs, which are good examples of the ways differences in ideology can lead different people to experience and understand the same objective occurrence in totally different ways. CSP engages with both aspects of the ideology of current academic psychology.

ASIDE

As time goes by

Our experience of time is an example of a less conscious ideology. We *know* that time continues at a steady, regular pace, and will continue for ever more. However, the everyday regularity of clock time is a historical development, following the development of precise timekeeping as an aid to international navigation in the eighteenth century, and the necessity of following strict timetables as a way of preventing railway accidents in the nineteenth century. Actually, experience shows that time varies greatly in its subjective speed of passing, as writers have commented for centuries and anyone who has had to wait for a download on a poor broadband connection knows, but we accept that as not the *real* nature of time (though it's certainly our experiential reality) because of the scientific ideology we live by – without really considering or questioning it. Certainly, there's no way we can travel in time. . . . Similarly, although the End of Time features in several belief systems, most people don't believe that will happen tomorrow, if ever – because that's the way things are, isn't it? Generally, anyone who challenges this kind of deep ideology is seen as crazy, rather than intellectually adventurous. However, it is possible to examine the experiential nature of time, both experimentally (Ornstein, 1975) and culturally (Bluedor, 2002).

What's that got to do with psychology? The explicit ideology of modern psychology is scientific: it must be rational, objective, demonstrable and replicable. In the last 20 years, after a generation of being mainly cognitive, psychology has become increasingly physiological: people are explained in terms of brain structure and activity, and most newspaper articles about psychological discoveries are supported by a colourful brain-scan picture. That physiological ideology is still optional for psychologists, but the basic scientistic approach is less so, and someone like Kenneth Gergen, who thinks that psychology is better considered as a history of experience, rather than a science of behaviour, is not sympathetically received by the psychological mainstream.

Also, mainstream psychologists are concerned with the behaviour and experience of individuals, or maybe face-to-face groups, otherwise they might be sociologists, or economists, living by different assumptions and value systems. As you have seen previously in this chapter, CSP challenges this scientistic ideology. That's a matter for conscious argument, but CSP also points out some of the less obvious aspects of mainstream psychological ideology that can be invidious. The most general one is individualism, which we'll discuss later in this chapter.

Another mainstream ideology is the universality of psychological principles and laws. There are two aspects to this: one is the currently held ideological position that all people are equal, exemplified by psychology's resistance to racism (and sexism etc.). The other aspect is an assumption that white Westerners (usually fairly well-off, young, male), the small minority of humanity (Arnett, 2008) used in much twentieth-century psychological research, could be considered as 'standard' people and taken as a model for the whole of humankind. The equally ethnocentric ideology of 'cross-cultural' psychology, which compares other cultures with the Western established 'norm', fails to address the problem. Calls for a psychology which starts from, say, African principles, rather than from mainly North American ones (Baldwin, 1986; Jones, 1991; Nobles, 1976), have mainly gone unheeded.

The recent perspectives of positive psychology (Seligman & Csikszentmihalyi, 2000), which attempt to develop a science about the brighter side of human psychology, focusing on happiness, human flourishing and emphasising the strengths of individuals, can also be seen as an attempt to shift mainstream ideology. However, Christopher and Hickinbottom (2008) argue that positive psychology is also heavily ethnocentric and based on an individualistic framework. They point out that it assumes an innate motivation for emotional satisfaction derived purely from feelings about the self, and that this emotional satisfaction is strongly correlated with the person's sense of their individuality. In contrast, members of collective cultures are more likely to consult social norms and seek the evaluation of others in order to gain a sense of emotional satisfaction. For Christopher and Hickinbottom (2008), the entire structure of positive psychology is founded on individualistic Western assumptions that are thought to lead to a better life.

There is also an ideological issue with psychology's account of sexual orientation. Psychology's blithe assumption that some forms of sexuality are more interesting and problematic than the 'norm' was nicely pointed out by Wilkinson and Kitzinger (1993). They set out to ask those who had identified themselves as heterosexual the same kind of question routinely asked of those with other orientations: 'When did you first realise you were heterosexual?'; 'Have you come out to your parents as heterosexual?'; 'Has your heterosexuality caused you problems in your life?' Such questions might seem ridiculous, inappropriate and provocative to ask of 'normal' people, but, if you stop and think, they're perfectly reasonable for those of any sexual orientation. Certainly, the authors know many heterosexuals for whom their orientation has caused problems! Wilkinson and Kitzinger's aim was provocative: to provoke other gender and sexuality researchers to examine the ideology that some sexual preferences need to be examined and accounted for more than others.

EXERCISE: REVEALING IDEOLOGY

Implicit, taken-for-granted claims – ideology – can be seen in Kilby, Horowitz and Hylton's (2013) analysis of an article by Goodhart that was published in liberal/left-thinking outlets: *Prospect* (Goodhart, 2004a), reprinted in *The Guardian* (Goodhart, 2004b). Goodhart claims that two cherished left-wing values oppose each other: solidarity/social cohesion versus multiculturalism/diversity. For Goodhart, the diversity created by multiculturalism is a threat to the solidarity/social cohesion necessary for a welfare state because people only want to support others who are like them. Kilby et al. (2013) highlighted strategies that Goodhart's paper uses to convey a liberal perspective, but under closer inspection an ideology opposite to such a stance is endorsed. Read Goodhart's paper (available online at www.theguardian.com/politics/2004/feb/24/race.eu) and ask yourself whether you were convinced and/or unsettled by its arguments. Now look at Kilby, Horowitz and Hylton's response and see if it changes how you originally felt about the article.

16.6 INDIVIDUALIST VERSUS COLLECTIVIST APPROACHES: THE CRITIQUE OF INDIVIDUALISM

One of the problems that CSP highlights is the focus on psychological phenomena having 'their origins or solutions beneath the skin' (Nightingale & Cromby, 2001: 122). This focus on the psychology of the individual, the notion of 'the self-contained person … who does not require or desire others for his or her completion' (Sampson, 1977: 770) has directed us to a misleading view of our nature. Traditional social psychological theories of interaction more often than not speculate about processes inside an individual, for example, cognitive dissonance, attribution, social categorisation, social identity theory, etc. How are these speculations of internal cognitive processes supposed to capture the flow of our social interaction with each other? Traditional psychology's focus on describing social life in terms of hypothetical models of individual decision making has only been effectively challenged by critical social constructionist theories (Gergen, 1994, 2001, 2009; Gergen & Gergen, 2003, 2004). (See also Chapter 23 on Self, which discusses how our sense of individuality arises out of social interactions.)

However, focusing on the individual remains the dominant methodological practice of traditional social psychology (indeed, of psychology generally) where 'subjects' are isolated in booths and given tests, inventories, questionnaires or experiments, etc. to do, and instructed not to speak to anyone. The social world is excluded. Even when studies and experiments are undertaken 'in the field', the person is often expected to act as a discrete and isolated figure whose actions do not take account of any background, context, culture, history or zeitgeist. This reinforces the notion of a 'possessive individualism' (Shotter, 1989) in which people see themselves as 'having' capacities, traits and qualities that are not due to any contribution from society. Such a stance is useful in a capitalist society because it supports the notion of humans as being rationally calculating costs-and-benefits actors with narrowly self-interested goals, when they are not being swayed by the crowd into mindless behaviour.

CARTESIAN PHILOSOPHY The philosophy of René Descartes (1596–1650), who emphasised reason, thinking and logical analysis to ascertain the truth about the world. Descartes was uncertain about how we could 'know' the world (and his body) and the only certainty was that he knew he existed because as an *individual* he could think (cogito ergo sum). The problem of how the mind and the body are related was thereafter seen as a problem for philosophers and psychologists.

This detached, self-contained entity is very much a Western ideology which can be traced to, among other things, **Cartesian philosophy** (Shotter, 1990) and notions of independence and self-knowledge. However, in contrast to this Eurocentric notion, people in other cultures understand themselves in other ways. For example, many African cultures emphasise the collective 'we' rather than 'I', as in the maxim 'I am because We are, and because We are therefore I am' (Mbiti, 1970, cited in Nobles, 1991: 300). Christopher and Hickinbottom (2008) claim that the Western notion of individualism is only endorsed by 30% of the world: the majority of peoples of the world think of themselves in a collective way. Thus critical psychologists 'would want to take issue with the traditional … starting point for psychological research which locates everything in the "I" of the individual … [and instead] would highlight cultural rather than universal character, and replace it with thinking in terms of the practical social processes going on "between" people' (Shotter, 1989: 135).

16.6.1 INTERSUBJECTIVITY

The central idea of this individualistic ideology is based on the seemingly undeniable experience we have of our psychological phenomena – thoughts, feelings, sensations – and having a sense of an 'I' that exists somewhere 'inside' us, and the sense that no one else can know these. While no critical social psychology would deny these experiences, we can ask how you come to know what these experiences and sensations are. We would point out that we use language to think and understand the world, as discussed in Chapter 23 (Self), and our sense of identity is a social matter.

The critical argument is that we do not come to know this or that experience, sensation or feeling from subjecting our inner worlds to internal self-contained analysis. Rather, the first stage in coming to have an inner world is by the process of **intersubjectivity**, whereby through interacting with people we develop a subjectivity that can be known by others. An important contribution to this understanding is found in the work of Lev Vygotsky (1896–1934), who argued that higher cognitive processes were social in their origins.

INTERSUBJECTIVITY The process of psychological exchange or shared cognitions between people that affect our social behaviour. We may agree about the meaning of a particular social event, but often agreement *is assumed* – psychologists included. Many 'common-sense' ideas are constructed by people from the same social background and used as an everyday way to interpret the meaning of social and cultural life. If people share 'common sense', then they share an intersubjective understanding of social situations.

His theory that human development is the result of the interactions between people and their social environment includes people's interactions with cultural artefacts, of which language (spoken, written, number systems, various signs and symbols, etc.) is the most important. From this view, all psychology's practices need to take a step back to understand the nature of our psychology and to look at, first, principles in our interaction and joint activities with each other and the importance of language. Language is a social tool and the most significant means by which we interact with each other, and when children practise and internalise dialogues with others (Vygotsky, 1978) cognitive functions of mind are structured through the skills language provides. In CSP, it is clear that the focus of psychology should be on the use of language, for this is the essential means by which we construct our experience and understanding.

16.6.2 BLAMING THE INDIVIDUAL

It is worth highlighting that the main significance for taking intersubjectivity seriously for a critical approach to *social* psychology is the awareness that our subjective experience is constructed by social interaction with our outer world. The implication is that, rather than our thinking and mental processes determining what we do, it is what we do and our social practices that dictate our thinking, feeling and experience! This reversal of traditional psychological thinking makes CSP critical like no other approach in psychology. Sustaining a certain social practice maintains a certain thinking; critical social psychology recognises that to make changes means addressing these social practices. The individualism of psychology is blind to this because it seeks to change or 'mend' the individual while leaving the (social, political) practices in place. This stance supports society's ideology. For example, the world recession starting in 2008 is commonly blamed on 'greedy bankers', but blaming individuals allows the present practices in the banking system to continue largely untouched.

Psychology has had a long preoccupation with explaining social problems in terms of internal mechanisms. For example, Caplan and Nelson (1973) revealed that in articles interpreting social problems related to black Americans, 82% could be classed as viewing these difficulties in terms of individuals' shortcomings. This 'person-centred' approach logically encourages initiatives to change individuals, and is useful because 'person-blame interpretations are in everyone's interest *except* those subjected to analysis' (Caplan & Nelson, 1973: 210, italics in original). The critical challenge to such individualism recognises that it acts as an apology for certain institutional and social policies by displacing blame from them, reinforces social myths about one's degree of control over one's fate, and amounts to 'blaming the victim'.

For critical social psychologists, psychology should act to challenge taken-for-granted assumptions and such victim blaming. For example, Mani et al. (2013) showed how conditions of poverty can impose a mental burden equivalent to losing 13 IQ points when low-income people who were primed to think about financial problems performed poorly on a series of cognition tests. As the authors put it:

> Being poor means coping not just with a shortfall of money, but also with a concurrent shortfall of cognitive resources. The poor, in this view, are less capable not because of inherent traits, but because the very context of poverty imposes load and impedes cognitive capacity. The findings, in other words, are not about poor people, but about any people who find themselves poor. (Mani et al., 2013: 980)

CSP's attitude to this research and analysis is one that wants to help individuals by recognising them in a social matrix, rather than what occurs in social psychologising presently, which merely acts to individualise people.

16.7 THE RELATIONSHIP BETWEEN ACADEMIC PSYCHOLOGY AND EVERYDAY LIFE

> The very fact that psychologists do not question or think about the status quo can be considered an ideological victory for those interested in perpetuating the predominant social system. (Prilleltensky, 1994: 25)

At the beginning of this chapter, we argued that the critical approach to psychology was that it should be thought of as a moral science rather than a natural science. With the natural sciences (e.g. in physics), there is no right or wrong or correct way for atoms to interact with other atoms, they just do. Harré (2005), however, asserts that psychology does not exist as an impartial science, but always occupies a position of social, moral and political standing:

> It incorporates at its very heart a distinction between what is the sane, balanced, and ordinary thing to do and what it is not proper or correct to do. There are right and wrong versions of all the human activities that have been listed as parts of the broad field of the subject matters of psychology. There are wrong ways to tackle problems, inadequate attempts to make friends, inappropriate emotions, and so on. (Harré, 2005: 29)

So psychology has an important impact on everyday life and people's views of who they are. The very subject matter of psychology is about people's thinking, feeling and behaviour, and it therefore informs people about how to understand themselves. It can provide, emphasise or de-emphasise a vocabulary for understanding their experience. For instance, the psychodynamic language of repression, regression, projection, introjection or displacement gives a way to understand other people's actions (see Chapter 25 for explanations of these terms). But psychological accounts also use the language that already exists about psychological processes, and necessarily need to do so to make psychological sense.

This overlooked aspect of traditional psychology is partly due to psychologists clinging on to the view of a 'value-neutral psychology'. Such a stance serves two functions (Prilleltensky, 1994): it portrays psychology as depoliticised and objective, so portraying psychological claims to be merely descriptive rather than prescriptive assertions; and it predisposes the public to accept psychology's claims unquestioningly, regarding them as true rather than social-historical conditional statements. For instance, Winch (2013) reported research by Vaillancourt (2013) that suggests that women are naturally 'indirectly competitive'.

This notion 'entails actions such as getting others to dislike a person, excluding peers from the group, giving some-one the "silent treatment", purposefully divulging secrets to others, and the use of derisive body and facial gestures to make another feel self-conscious' (Vaillancourt, 2013: 1). As Winch claims, this kind of evolutionary psychology can be seen to condone misogyny, and that 'This is another way of saying that women are naturally two-faced: women can't help but bitch'. Winch sees Vaillancourt's paper as providing so-called scientific credence to the notion that all women biologically desire to be thin and states 'To turn the desire for skinniness into a biological imperative – through questionable scientific experiments – has a political motive. It denies a position from which to critique the industries that are profiting from women's insecurities and body hatred' (Winch, 2013).

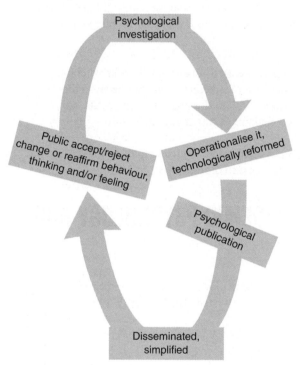

FIGURE 16.3 The looping effect between psychological discipline and society

The relation between published psychology and social life can be described as the 'looping effect' (Brinkmann, 2005; Hacking, 1995), whereby a feedback or 'loop' exists between psychology and the phenomena it is concerned with (see Figure 16.3). There is no loop between natural sciences and nature, as minerals are unaffected by the study of their chemistry and cannot intentionally change in ways that then affect how science accounts for them. This looping between the discipline of psychology and the psychologies of those outside the discipline world has an influence on people. It not only acts on people outside psychology, but also on the psychologists themselves, re-making and constraining what is and is not possible and permissible, for 'When new descriptions become available, when they come into circulation, or even when they become the sorts of things that it is alright to say, to think, they are new things to choose to do. I live in a world of opportunities' (Hacking, 1995: 236). In many respects, this is what Gergen means when he says 'social science can fruitfully be viewed as a protracted communications system' (Gargen, 1973: 310) in which the psychologist describes the psychology of the other and communicates it back to the public through mass-media channels.

The 'looping effect' can also work at the individual level where psychologists are engaged in a process of 'making up people' (Hacking, 2006) and people actively react to psychological knowledge, for instance, the self-fulfilling prophecy (e.g. Rubie-Davies, Hattie, & Hamilton, 2006). By 'making up people', Hacking is pointing out that naming and labelling is an act of production in which we construct an understanding that there are certain kinds of people with certain properties. For instance, Hacking states that 'the homosexual and the heterosexual as kinds of persons (as ways to be persons, or as conditions of personhood) came into being only toward the end of the nineteenth century. There has been plenty of same-sex activity in all ages, but not … same-sex people and different-sex people' (Hacking, 1998: 161). Being made into a kind of people, in many respects, turns people into objects that can be classified (e.g. Gamers), diagnosed (e.g. ADHD), controlled (e.g. Psychotic), helped (Depressed), or admired and ever more emulated (Gifted and Talented).

In this critique of traditional psychology, no claim is being made that psychologists consciously mislead the public (Prilleltensky, 1994). Rather, the claim is that the relationship between psychology and society in which psychologists have undergone a very efficient socialisation has taught them not to question the existing social system, and hence made them complicit in maintaining society's status quo.

Psychology as a discipline has a privileged position in society in influencing practices in areas such as education, business, the military, the judicial system, government, prison, etc. According to Danziger (1990), such a position was secured when North American elites were seeking remedies to social problems in the 1900s. From this moment, the society and psychology link was made concrete, and society was 'psychologised' (Prilleltensky, 1994). At government level, an example is the Behavioural Insights Team set up by the UK Government. This unit employs Nudge Theory (Thaler & Sunstein, 2008), the psychological principle that claims features of a person's setting can be modified so as to 'nudge' them to behave in a predictable way. This unit aims to use 'levers of state' to 'improve' segments of society's behaviour (McSmith, 2010). This assumes that someone's social context can be arranged so as to increase the likelihood that they make personal choices that are more 'responsible' or 'paternal'.

If psychology is seen as a moral science in that its assertions are prescriptions of what is acceptable and normal, and that such descriptions 'make up people', then clearly any group that dominates the discipline will be privileging a certain notion of reality over another. Prilleltensky (1994) reminds us that most social scientists belong to a social class whose political and economic interests are usually in accordance with those of the dominant sector. Moreover, the theories of psychology come from a particular geographical location. The ideas exposed by psychology are Western psychology and predominantly those of white middle-class men. In an analysis of the representations of people of the world in seven prestigious APA journals, Arnett (2008) concluded that the theories generated by psychology are predominantly based on North Americans, who only make up 5% of the world's population. In what is surely a passage that would encourage us to reflect on what we are doing in psychology, Arnett states:

> … no other science proceeds with such a narrow range of study. It is difficult to imagine that biologists, for example, would study a highly unusual 5% of the world's crocodile population and assume the features of that 5% to be universal. It is even more difficult to imagine that such biologists would be aware that the other 95% of the world's crocodile population was vastly different from the 5% under study, and highly diverse in habitat, eating habits, mating practices, and everyday behaviour, yet show little or no interest in studying that 95% and continue to study the 5% exhaustively while making universal claims. An outside observer would regard such a science as incomplete, to say the least, and would wonder why there was such intense focus on that unusual 5% while the other 95% was neglected. Yet in studying human beings, whose environmental, economic, and cultural differences make them more diverse than any other animal species, this is what American psychologists do. (Arnett, 2008: 608)

16.8 CHAPTER SUMMARY

Critical social psychology recognises that our psychological claims about ourselves have a history and a socio-political and cultural context which advocates one particular stance while simultaneously obscuring another possible position, which is that psychology is what people do, say and feel in their everyday mundane happenings. The task of the psychologist is to place these accounts in the spotlight and to consider with our participants what alternative might be better suited to fit their agenda while recognising our responsibilities to others. For psychology students, lecturers and researchers the questions that might be asked are these: Did you come into psychology to understand theories of people? Or did you come into psychology to understand people? For a critical social psychology, most of psychology is about the former question. If the latter is what we are seeking, then the whole context of the person needs to be considered. For example, Hylton and Miller's (2004) article about 'black identity' attempted to do this by recognising that our understanding is a story we can tell about ourselves because of the available ideas (academic and popular literature, artwork, music, novels, etc.) that circulate in society. Drawing on these resources, they argued that 'black identity' can be understood as the articulation of different dominant stories whereby certain available 'ideas' about identity animate people in different eras, and that in order to understand the present, recognition of the past and the socio-political context of the present is needed. They then went on to propose what might be another way of understanding black identity, taking the critical step in challenging the present for what they might see as an alternative, and possibly better, future. With our unique position as psychologists – or 'professional human beings' – the moral and social consequences of our account of human nature necessitates us offering a vision, being open about where we stand, and having that account subjected to moral and political evaluation, not just empirical assessment. To hide behind the idea of objectivity and science is to adopt the position of washing our hands of responsibility for our discipline, for psychology as a discipline does more than merely describe – it prescribes a reality.

This chapter has presented critical social psychology as an alternative to mainstream social psychology, but we would like to suggest that it would be useful to import this kind of criticality into all of psychology as an aspect of how psychologists see their practice. Referring back to Koch's quote from the methodology section: 'from the earliest days of the experimental pioneers, man's stipulation that psychology be adequate to science outweighed his commitment that it be adequate to man' (Koch, 1959: 783, cited in Howard, 1985: 259), a psychology which is critical of its fundamental principles and approaches is most likely to be 'adequate' to man (and woman and child too, of course).

 # DISCUSSION QUESTIONS

Does psychology always have to have a position? Isn't it enough that psychologists create practical solutions to every-day problems? You might like to look at Chapters 26 and 27 on health and forensic psychology to see this more pragmatic approach.

Most of psychology, and also the world beyond psychology, does not follow this critical style. Why do you think this is? Is it too challenging or is it not useful?

Many people are excluded from the pages of psychology texts and journals. What can be done to include people from a range of backgrounds and lifestyles into the general discussions about psychology?

 # SUGGESTIONS FOR FURTHER READING

Fox, D., Prilleltensky, I., & Austin, S. (Eds) (2009). *Critical psychology: an introduction* (2nd edn). London: SAGE. A wide-ranging review, with chapters from authors with different perspectives.

Gough, B., & McFadden, M. (2001). *Critical social psychology: an introduction*. Basingstoke: Palgrave. A clear and straightforward introduction, with a minimum of fancy terms, which gives a critical perspective on classic social psychology topics like self, sexuality, aggression and prejudice.

Gergen, K. (2000). *The saturated self: dilemmas of identity in contemporary life.* New York: Basic Books. An account of postmodern ideas of the self in a world of changing technologies (which have changed even more since 1991, but in a direction which fits Gergen's argument). An example of critical social psychology in practice.

Millerpsych: a not-entirely serious blog by one of the authors – which does touch on serious topics: http://millerpsych. wordpress.com.

 Still want more? For links to online resources relevant to this chapter and a quiz to test your understanding, visit the companion website at edge.sagepub.com/banyard2e

SECTION E

DEVELOPMENTAL PSYCHOLOGY: HOW WE GROW AND CHANGE

The transformation from gurgling and gurning baby to thinking and feeling adult is something that never ceases to amaze. Watch a baby and you can't help but wonder how we change from the unknowing, wriggling infant to being aware of our surroundings and ourselves. Developmental psychology looks at the changes that individuals go through during their lives. It is often thought of as child psychology because much of the research has focused on children, but this view would be misleading because psychologists are actually interested in how we develop 'from the cradle to the grave'. In fact, modern scientific techniques mean that we can track development even before the cradle and so we should really say 'from conception to the grave'. Having said this, the research we cover in this section reflects the traditional preoccupation with children.

Modern developmental psychology is often dated back to William Preyer's book *The mind of the child*, which was published in 1882. Like many of the developmental psychologists that followed him, he based his work on observations of his own child. In fact, this use of psychologists' own children is one of the very cute/deeply irritating (delete to taste) aspects of the subject. What distinguished Preyer's work and what set the pattern for developmental psychology was the use of scientific procedures, in particular accurate and thorough recording of behaviour and the identification of patterns of change in that behaviour.

Over the following 130 years psychologists have focused on various areas of development, especially the development of cognition (e.g. the work of Jean Piaget, and more recently, the research into autism), emotion (e.g. the work of Sigmund Freud and later Mary Ainsworth) and behaviour (e.g. the work of the behaviourist John Watson and later Albert Bandura). In this section we will look at all these areas and see what current research can tell us about how we change from babies to hoodies. We also go on to explore some of the changes that occur during adult life.

KEY ISSUES

There are two key issues for developmental psychologists. One is the nature–nurture question (see Chapter 17), which explores how much of a behaviour is the product of genetically determined factors (nature) and how much of experience (nurture). We are born with some remarkable behaviours: for example, babies under six months old have a diving reflex, so if they go under water they automatically hold their breath and make swimming-like movements. Also, we clearly share some characteristics with our parents, but how much of that is due to being brought up by them and how much to sharing their genetic structure?

The second key issue is about the timing and plasticity of development. Some behaviours develop at specific times in our lives: for example, the diving reflex mentioned above fades by the age of one. The concept of plasticity refers to the amount that a behaviour can change and adapt or how rigid it will be once it has developed. Some psychologists see the changes as developing steadily and progressively, and some describe the changes as going through a series of stages. The interest for all developmental psychologists is in the things that bring about these changes.

EXERCISE: WHAT IS A CHILD?

The answer to the question 'What is a child?' is not as obvious as you'd think. Different cultures and different times in history clearly have a range of views about what it means to be a child. For example, have a look at the painting shown here of a child from the Middle Ages. There is something very strange about it. You will notice that it looks not like a child but like a scaled-down adult. The head is too small and the face too grown-up. Does this mean that the people of this time saw children in this way?

Your task is to make a list of the similarities and differences between children and adults and, more problematically, consider at what age a child takes on the characteristics of an adult.

THIS SECTION

In this section we have three chapters looking at how children develop and one looking at adults. Chapter 17 looks at the early years from before birth up till about four years of age. It looks at some of the innovative methods that psychologists have created to study children and explores the issues identified above. It also looks at how infants make sense of the world, moving from early mental representations of the world to early language development, and finally it examines how the environment can assist in the development of later social interactions. Chapter 18 looks at how children develop through the school years, focusing on language and social reasoning. It goes on to consider how the social world of children changes as they enter school and how this is reflected in the importance of peer relationships, friendships and experiences of bullying. In Chapter 19 we look at atypical development and how we can understand and respond to the unique needs of each individual child. Finally, in Chapter 20 we look at developments in adult life, starting with adolescence and working our way through to old age.

FIGURE E.1 Example of medieval art showing the adult features of the child

© Arte & Immagini srl/Corbis

17 DEVELOPMENT DURING THE EARLY YEARS

Lead authors: Lucy Betts, James Stiller, Rebecca Larkin and Gareth Williams

CHAPTER OUTLINE

17.1 Introduction	**299**
17.2 Influences on infant development	**299**
17.3 Making sense of the social world: infancy and beyond	**300**
17.3.1 Methods of studying infant behaviour	300
17.3.2 Face perception and imitation	301
17.3.3 Object and category perception	301
17.3.4 Implications for the development of mental representations	302
17.4 Early language development	**303**
17.4.1 Discriminating between speech sounds	303
17.4.2 Early language production	304
17.4.3 Imitation and reinforcement	305
17.4.4 Child-directed speech	305
17.5 Later language development	**305**
17.5.1 Pidgins and creoles	305
17.5.2 Syntactic development and grammatical understanding	306
17.6 Early social development in infancy	**306**
17.6.1 The importance of early relationships	306
17.6.2 Importance of attachment and relationships	307

17.6.3 Development of self-awareness 310

17.6.4 Development of theory of mind 310

17.6.5 Development of gender roles 312

17.7 Chapter summary 312

Discussion questions 312

Suggestions for further reading 313

17.1 INTRODUCTION

What goes on inside the mind of an infant? Remarkably, we can never really know the answer to this despite the fact that we were all infants once ourselves. This chapter introduces you to the topic of developmental psychology during the early years, focusing on the cognitive and social skills developed through early infancy. The chapter explores some of the factors that influence an infant's early cognitive and social development. For the purpose of this chapter, we have defined the 'early years' from prenatal through to the age of four. The chapter explores whether we are born with innate capabilities or whether the skills we acquire are learnt from interactions with the environment. Additionally, we evaluate some of the methods used to examine development during the early years and consider whether the data generated from these can be interpreted in a way that clearly illustrates innate abilities in infants. We also discuss how infants make sense of the world, from early mental representations of the world to early language development, and also how the environment can assist in the development of social interactions.

FRAMING QUESTIONS

- What methods can psychologists use to examine development?
- How do infants make sense of their social world?
- How do infants use language?
- What is the basis for infants' social development?

17.2 INFLUENCES ON INFANT DEVELOPMENT

One of the most contentious issues within developmental psychology is whether or not our development is driven by nature (i.e. genetics) or nurture (environment). The first part of this chapter explores the evidence for both sides of this argument.

There is growing evidence that our genes, in conjunction with other prenatal influences, shape who we are. For example, exposure to some maternal hormones before birth can influence the development of borderline personality disorders in later life (Evardone, Alexander, & Morey, 2008). Also, factors such as high maternal stress during pregnancy have been linked to emotional development: infants who are exposed to higher maternal stress are more likely to have lower levels of emotional response at the age of four months (Mohler et al., 2006). Recent research has also reported that stress and anxiety during pregnancy have longer consequences: 10- to 11-year-olds who experienced greater prenatal stress experienced greater emotional and behavioural difficulties (Leis et al., 2014). Some researchers report that 50% of internalising problems (e.g. anxiety) can be accounted for by genetics (Saudino et al., 2008).

Although there is evidence that our genetic composition is important for our development, the studies conducted so far fail to provide evidence that the link between our genetics and our development is a complete match. Therefore, this implicates the importance of other factors for development. According to the nurture side of the debate, the environment is more influential. Returning to prenatal development, environment influences can impact on the developing child. During pregnancy, there are a number of critical periods when certain environmental factors can cause substantial changes to organ development in the unborn infant (Thornton, 2008). The timing of these critical periods differs for each organ. For example, for the nervous system the most sensitive period is three to six weeks post-conception, whereas for the heart it is four to seven weeks. However, outside these times the developing infant is still at risk from environmental influences.

One of the most likely causes of disruption to the developing child during the critical period is teratogens. Common examples of potential **teratogens** are alcohol and nicotine. Consuming alcohol during pregnancy can lead to foetal

TERATOGENS Substances or environmental influences that affect development of the foetus resulting in physical abnormalities.

FOETAL ALCOHOL SYNDROME Foetal abnormalities caused by alcohol consumption during pregnancy.

alcohol syndrome. **Foetal alcohol syndrome** affects one per 1,000 births, and symptoms include changes in brain structure, cognitive impairment and behavioural problems that become more pronounced during adolescence (Kodituwakku, 2007; Niccols, 2007). Smoking during pregnancy has been linked to attentional problems, hyperactivity and conduct problems (Button, Maughan, & McGuffin, 2007), bipolar disorder (Talati et al., 2013) and borderline personality disorder (Schwarze et al., 2013).

The transactional model seeks to explain possible links between genes and the environment (Sameroff & Chandler, 1975). According to this approach, a child's development should be regarded as a complex interaction between the child, the child's social context and the child's immediate environment. This makes intuitive sense: while our genetic composition may predispose development, the environment is fundamental to acting as a trigger. Consequently, it seems that it is the combination of these factors that shapes an individual's development (Thornton, 2008).

17.3 MAKING SENSE OF THE SOCIAL WORLD: INFANCY AND BEYOND

In the remainder of this chapter we explore aspects of infant development and consider innate and environmental influences in the development of cognitive, language and social skills. First, however, let's consider how researchers study infant behaviour.

17.3.1 METHODS OF STUDYING INFANT BEHAVIOUR

Early studies into infant visual perception were primarily based upon observations of how infants interact with the visual environment around them. However, these studies did not allow researchers to examine experimentally what properties of a visual stimulus, or what environmental conditions, the infant was responding to. The primary difficulty in conducting such experimental research is that infants do not necessarily understand complex instructions and they cannot provide complex verbal feedback on their thinking or understanding. Similarly, preverbal infants become easily distracted and can be rather unpredictable participants. Nevertheless, psychologists have devised several innovative methods to examine early infant cognition:

1 Preferential looking technique builds on the idea that young infants have an innate predisposition to respond to novel stimuli in their visual environment. So, when presented with two objects, infants would gaze at the object that was of greater interest or was unfamiliar to them. The time spent looking at each stimulus indicates the infant's ability to discriminate between novel and familiar stimuli. If an infant spends longer observing one of the stimuli, this demonstrates an ability to discriminate between the two objects.

2 Habituation tasks are a refinement of Fantz's (1963) original preferential looking tasks (see Figure 17.1). They take advantage of an infant's uncanny ability to become bored very quickly. In the initial stages of the habituation paradigm the infant is familiarised with a stimulus until they pay little or no attention to it. The infant can then be presented with another stimulus alongside the habituated one, and the preferential looking task can be reapplied. If the infant focuses their attention on the new stimulus, it can be assumed that the new stimulus has captured their attention.

3 Preferential sucking technique allows for a range of different non-visual stimuli to be tested (such as recognition of familiar sounds or voices). If a novel stimulus attracts the infant's attention, there is a subsequent reduction in the rate of their sucking behaviour.

It is clear that such techniques provide an insight into infants' interactions in their environment and their underlying cognition. However, the techniques depend on the experimenters' interpretation, so they may not have measured preferences in the infant. Nevertheless, in the following sections we illustrate the importance of using such methods to examine the underlying cognitive skills in infancy, from facial recognition to early categorisation of objects. All the evidence suggests that although young infants are born with some strong innate predisposition to understand their world, such understanding requires active involvement in their environment and social interactions with others.

17.3.2 FACE PERCEPTION AND IMITATION

A big question regarding infant processing of facial stimuli is whether or not this is an innate behaviour. So, it asks whether infants are predisposed to recognise human faces or particular pattern types, or whether visual processing of facial stimuli is the result of learnt expertise. One of the earliest and most influential experimental studies into infant face perception used the preferential looking task. Fantz (1963) demonstrated that two-month-old infants show a preference for patterned stimuli and, in particular, for face-like stimuli over jumbled face-like stimuli or patterned stimuli with facial configurations (see Figure 17.1). However, more recent studies have shown that, straight after birth, infants prefer to look at face-like patterns and images over scrambled faces or non-face-like stimuli, including toys (DeNicola et al., 2013; Goren, Sarty, & Wu, 1975; Johnson & Morton, 1991; Valenza et al., 1996). This ability to differentiate between face and non-face stimuli has led some researchers to suggest that infants are born with an innate inbuilt ability to recognise faces.

On one level, being able to recognise faces is an important step in early infancy. However, infants need to be able to do more than simply recognise faces. Faces convey a large amount of information, for example emotion or directing gaze. Infants imitate their caregivers, and imitating facial expressions is thought to help infants make sense of this information. Meltzoff and Moore (1977, 1983) showed that 12- to 21-day-old infants are capable of imitating facial gestures and body movements. Again, this could be explained in terms of novelty because newborn infants have an innate preference for things that change. However, imitation of facial gestures, and body movements, suggests that infants are born with an innate ability to respond to the actions of people and that infants possess an innate representation of their own bodies. Nevertheless, such imitative behaviours could be considered innate reflexes or responses rather than specifically guided imitation of human facial expressions.

FIGURE 17.1   The jumbled faces task devised by Fantz was used to show that very young children can tell the difference between a face and another interesting pattern

© mickythemartian

17.3.3 OBJECT AND CATEGORY PERCEPTION

The human infant is aware of his/her surroundings and can differentiate between novel and habituated stimuli. However, this does not provide any evidence to suggest that the infant is capable of understanding what characteristics define a particular object or stimuli. Some physical properties of the infant's visual environment appear to be innate. One example is depth perception. This was shown by the 'visual cliff' experiment in which Walk and Gibson (1961) demonstrated that most infants, moving towards a precipice across a piece of Plexiglass, would stop at the point where the floor beneath them appears to drop off. This suggests that infants have an understanding of depth and perspective.

Recently, Quinn, Westerlund and Nelson (2006) showed that six-month-old infants can categorise objects. Infants were familiarised with images of cats, and the event-related potentials associated with the presentation of

EVENT-RELATED POTENTIALS A characteristic electrophysiological response by the brain to a stimulus, usually recorded using EEG (electroencephalography).

the images were recorded. Once the infant was familiarised with the cat stimulus, they were then presented with novel cat images interspersed with dog images. The **event-related potentials** recorded for the cat and dog stimuli were significantly different, suggesting that we have the relevant neural architecture in place for object categorisation within the first six months of life. This experiment also suggests that the habituation task itself might reflect object categorisation via a preference for novelty in young infants. Further studies suggest that between 14 and 18 months old, infants can start to understand categories and attribute objects to categories (Booth & Waxman, 2002).

17.3.4 IMPLICATIONS FOR THE DEVELOPMENT OF MENTAL REPRESENTATIONS

Having established that infants are capable of recognising faces and objects from a relatively early age, we can ask questions concerning whether infants develop mental representations of objects. Similarly, questions can be raised concerning the underlying cognitive structures that are developing as infants interact with their social environment.

EGOCENTRIC THINKING When an individual has little regard for the views or interests of others, which may involve individuals memorising objects in relation to themselves.

MENTAL REPRESENTATIONS An internal cognitive map of stimuli.

Piaget's description of the sensorimotor stage of development (between birth and two years) pioneered discoveries in children's thinking in early infancy. During the sensorimotor stage, Piaget argued, infants are essentially limited in their thinking and show a primitive understanding of objects in their environment. They are learning to match up what they experience (their senses) with what they do (their actions or motor activity) – hence this is known as the sensorimotor stage. Further, infants are essentially **egocentric** in their thinking, and before nine months cannot form **mental representations** of the objects in their environment or recognise that when an object is out of view it continues to exist.

To test these theories, Piaget (1952) devised a simple retrieval task to examine the mental representations of six- to nine-month-old infants for everyday objects. During the task, a toy and a cloth were placed in front of the infant and, once the infant was interested in the toy, the toy was either partially or completely hidden under the cloth. The infant's ability to retrieve the object was then observed. At around six to seven months, infants failed to retrieve the object even when it was partially hidden, but by eight to nine months, infants would retrieve the hidden object, suggesting that they had developed a mental representation of the object even when it was out of sight.

In subsequent studies, with nine- to 12-month-old infants, Piaget (1952) used two cloths in front of the infant with a toy hidden under one of the cloths. In this situation, nine-month-olds retrieved the toy on most trials. After several trials of hiding the toy under one of the cloths, the toy was then moved under a different cloth in full view of the infant. However, nine- to 12-month-olds failed to retrieve the toy once it had changed location, with the majority of infants looking under the original cloth. Piaget used these findings as evidence that infants are largely egocentric in their thinking, failing to make a distinction between objects in the world and their own actions.

ALLOCENTRIC The skill of memorising the position of an object in relation to other objects.

There are, nevertheless, alternative explanations to Piaget's interpretations of these results. Harris (1973) suggested that Piaget's results indicate the fragility in infants' short-term memory. However, Butterworth (1977) argued that the results were evidence of the infant's inherent difficulty in coding or memorising positions of objects with their location. He suggested that nine- to 12-month-olds were not using **allocentric** forms of coding the location of the object, but were instead using egocentric forms of coding.

In summary, it is clear that infants between nine and 12 months do develop some form of mental representations of objects they see within their immediate environment, allowing them to search for objects even when they are completely out of sight. However, while Piaget's findings have been replicated, the interpretations of these findings have been challenged (for further information on Piaget, see Chapter 18). What remains clear is that young infants continue to demonstrate an understanding of the social world and continue to interact with the agents in it. Because of this interaction they are continually developing internal mental representations of objects, whether these objects are shapes, toys or human beings.

17.4 EARLY LANGUAGE DEVELOPMENT

Language is arguably what makes humans special, as no other species has mastered communication at such a complex level. How humans develop language skills is therefore a key area of study in developmental psychology, and has been subject to much debate. In this section we consider early language development. It is worth avoiding falling into the traditional assumption that newborn infants lack any language skills. In fact, similar to their perceptual capabilities, even from the early days of life, newborns are inbuilt with facilities to make sense of people's speech as language rather than as general sounds.

17.4.1 DISCRIMINATING BETWEEN SPEECH SOUNDS

Infants show considerable skills in discriminating between sounds even before birth, and complex learning of sound discrimination develops during infancy. There is considerable evidence that an infant's interaction with their environment is fundamental in their learning of language. DeCasper and Fifer (1980) examined infants' ability to discriminate between different voices from birth to three days old and the preferential sucking technique. Infants showed a preference for their mother's voice compared to a stranger's voice. This evidence suggests that young infants are perhaps pretuned to recognise, and respond to, their mother's voice from birth.

Nevertheless, it could be argued that, at two to three days old, these infants had been exposed to language and therefore DeCasper and Fifer's (1980) findings could be the direct results of learning. While this is a reasonable interpretation, there is evidence that young infants are capable of learning even before birth, with studies providing evidence of prenatal speech learning. A study by Lecanuet (1998) revealed that two-day-old infants could demonstrate a preference for melodies that had been repeatedly played during pregnancy compared to unfamiliar melodies. Moon, Pannenton-Cooper and Fifer (1993) also illustrated young infants' ability to demonstrate a preference for their own native language (English) over non-native languages (such as Spanish) at two to three days after birth.

A key limitation, however, is that researchers can only infer the occurrence of prenatal speech learning: they cannot test this directly. There is one exception (DeCasper et al., 1994), which is described in the key study below. Clearly, this evidence suggests that infants are capable of learning about language from an early age. Even within the womb, we are actively learning about the outside environment and developing skills to discriminate between different speech sounds. Therefore, language development begins well before birth.

There is also evidence that newborn infants are highly attuned to attend, and respond, to spoken language. Infants can notice elements of speech when it is played forwards but not backwards, suggesting there is something unique to speech over other sounds (Ramus et al., 2000). Also, infants can spot changes in syllables of spoken speech (Bijeljac-Babic, Bertoncini, & Mehler, 1993) and when pre-recorded sounds change from 'ba' to 'da'. These processes are, to some degree, available to other animals as well. For example, tamarin monkeys (Ramus et al., 2000) and macaques (Kuhl & Padden, 1982) can also discriminate between changes in human speech patterns. However, it is from these

EXERCISE: CLARITY OF SPEECH

If infants are learning about language at least partly through exposure, then the quality of adult speech becomes of great interest. Our everyday speech production is often very unclear, which in turn makes infant language development all the more astounding. To appreciate this lack of clarity, record yourself and a friend or family member (with their permission of course) having a one-minute conversation about an everyday event, such what you will be having for tea, and then transcribe the conversation. First, note down all the places where there is a significant pause in speech, say longer than a second. Do these pauses seem to occur in logical places? Do these pauses reflect word boundaries? Second, circle all the words that are not fully articulated or which seem to 'run into' surrounding words. Now consider why child-directed speech has been found to have a positive effect on language learning.

KEY STUDY

DeCasper, A.J., Lecanuet, J.P., Busnel, M.C., Granier-Deferre, C., & Maugeais, R. (1994). Fetal reactions to recurrent maternal speech. *Infant Behavior and Development, 17,* 159–164.

By the seventh month of gestation, the auditory apparatus of the human foetus is fully functioning. However, as the foetus is snugly encased within the womb, speech sounds have to travel through membranes, muscle and fluid. By the time the sound waves finally reach the foetus, the high-frequency sounds have been filtered out and what remains is the rhythm, stress and intonation of speech, otherwise known as the prosody.

Starting at the 33rd week of gestation, DeCasper et al. asked pregnant women to repeat a short children's rhyme three times a day over a four-week period. During the testing phase of the study, two rhymes were spoken by an unfamiliar adult and played to the foetus: the rhyme which had been repeated by the mother and an unfamiliar control rhyme. While this was happening, the pregnant women wore headphones, to ensure they did not react to the rhymes being played and thus confound the experiment. The heart rates of the foetuses were recorded while the rhymes were played to measure their reaction. It was found that the foetuses' heart rates reduced when they heard the familiar rhyme, indicating that they recognised the sequence of speech sounds.

The study by DeCasper et al. is extremely important because it demonstrates that humans are able to recognise familiar speech patterns while they are still in the womb. Furthermore, this study shows that this recognition is not limited to the voice of the foetus's mother. The foetus can in fact distinguish between a familiar and unfamiliar story being read by a complete stranger.

basic processes that newborn humans begin to sample the world around them and begin to acquire the language of their environment. Picking up where words begin and end, and the main features of the language, allows infants to start to piece together the vocabulary of the world around them. Acquisition of language generally needs two things: vocabulary development and, much later, grammar acquisition. In the main, much of what is acquired initially comprises words to describe things.

Language acquisition therefore clearly involves a complex interaction between the infant and the world around him/her, especially in the early years of development (see section 17.4.4 on child-directed speech).

17.4.2 EARLY LANGUAGE PRODUCTION

Language production is an area of rapid progression for an infant, moving in a set of noticeable stages from cooing to short sentences by around two years of age. A newborn has cooing and crying (and more crying) at their disposal initially when it comes to language communication, representing the first noticeable type of language production. One of the main problems with crying is that parents often need to resort to either trial-and-error or context to work out what the crying is about (Thompson et al., 2007).

> **BABBLING** A child appears to be experimenting with making the sounds of language, but is not yet producing any recognisable words.

Crying generally gives way to babbling at around seven months of age, which is considered a universal step in typical language development (Harley, 2001). At this stage, whole ranges of consonant and vowel combinations are spoken and these tend to be strung together in repetitive utterances. Some months later, infants tend to only babble those consonant–vowel combinations that occur in the language around them. Hearing infants of deaf parents, where speech is not present in the surroundings, tend to stop **babbling** at this stage. However, recent research has shown that these babies do continue to babble, but with hand signals instead (Petitto et al., 2004). Generally, both babbling and the reduction in consonant–vowel combinations suggest that the process needs a mixture of sampling from the environment and inner processes of development for speech to progress.

At around 12 months, infants start to make single-word utterances. These are not always clear words but are the beginnings of intelligible speech. Often a word is used to represent a range of objects: for example, 'car' may be used for four-wheeled objects like cars and trucks but not for other things in the infant's environment (Boelens et al., 2007). Learning what words go with which objects might have much to do with what interests the infant at the time the word is spoken (Pruden et al., 2006). From only a few words at 12 months, spoken vocabulary and naming tend to expand quite rapidly between 18 months and two years of age, with around 200 words available by the end of this period (Fenson et al., 1994). Further, around this age infants are starting to put words together to make two-word sentences. Clearly, this vocabulary spurt provides an adequate basis for later (and more sophisticated) language development.

17.4.3 IMITATION AND REINFORCEMENT

Early theories of language development suggested that children learn through imitation of adults around them. This theory emphasises the importance of the environment for language learning, and coincides with research demonstrating that children from families with limited education know fewer words than children from less deprived backgrounds (Snow, 1999). However, children's spoken language is often quite different from that of adults, which causes a problem for the theory. The best illustration of this is when young children aged three to four years overgeneralise regular verb endings to irregular verbs (e.g. a child might say 'I falled over' instead of 'I fell over'). Adults do not produce such errors, so how can children have learned to do this through imitation?

Skinner (1957) built on the idea of imitation and suggested that children learn language through reinforcement from adults. In this way, vocabulary, grammar and syntax can be gradually shaped, expanded and improved. Yet Skinner has been criticised for failing to appreciate that adults rarely correct children's grammar, but rather tend to be interested in the content of children's utterances.

17.4.4 CHILD-DIRECTED SPEECH

If you have had any contact with small children in the past, think for a moment about how you spoke to them. You may recall that you spoke more slowly than usual, used simple grammar and concrete vocabulary, and exaggerated the pitch and intonation of your speech. This adaptation of speech when talking to small children used to be called **motherese**, but is now more sensibly called child-directed speech.

Another notable feature of child-directed speech is the repetition of key words and phrases. Research shows that infants prefer to listen to child-directed speech compared to normal speech (Cooper & Aslin, 1990) and this may help explain infants' rapid language development. However, this argument is limited because child-directed speech is not present in all cultures (Pye, 1986), yet nearly all children develop impressive language skills within the first two years of life. When interacting with infants with hearing impairments, adults use **motionese**, such that they slow down the pace of their gesturing to infants and make their gestures more exaggerated and simple (Dunst, Gorman, & Hamby, 2012).

Therefore, while child-directed speech is known to facilitate language learning, it is not needed for children to develop a complex understanding of grammar and a wide vocabulary. This brings us back to the argument for an innate predisposition towards learning language, which may set humans apart from other species.

> **CHILD-DIRECTED SPEECH (MOTHERESE)** The act of using a sing-song voice, speaking slowly or using simple language when talking to an infant.
>
> **MOTIONESE** The act of slowing down the pace of gestures, exaggerating and simplifying gestures when interacting with an infant.

17.5 LATER LANGUAGE DEVELOPMENT

At around 24 months, children are producing two-word sentences, which are still very basic. However, children's development of language beyond this telegraphic phase has been questioned (Smith, Cowie, & Blades, 2011). This section will consider the development of more complex forms of language, namely the understanding of grammar and later syntactical development.

17.5.1 PIDGINS AND CREOLES

Children are actively constructing their own understanding of language through interactions with the environment. Spoken communication tends to develop between people irrespective of differing language backgrounds.

PIDGIN AND CREOLE A shared language developed when two communities with different languages join together.

Pidgin and creole languages are examples of this and suggest that we may have innate language ability. These types of languages occur where people with different languages are displaced by wider social factors and come together as a community. Aspects of different languages become mixed together and what emerges is a 'good enough' language for daily use. Pidgin languages are typically only oral languages and tend to be uncomplicated in structure (Baptista, 2005).

Later-generation speakers of pidgin languages tend to formalise the language to follow particular grammar rules and include or exclude certain vocabulary. Languages where this has occurred tend to be called creoles. Creoles might arise from a pidgin language but they can also appear without it (Kam & Newport, 2005). One possible theory is that children of pidgin speakers tend to turn the language into a more regular structure using innate principles for things like grammar and the structure of languages (Bickerton, 1984). But this self-organising process in communication, where languages appear to emerge from interaction irrespective of original languages, has led some to argue that this is evidence of strong innate drives to the structures found in languages (Pinker, 1995).

17.5.2 SYNTACTIC DEVELOPMENT AND GRAMMATICAL UNDERSTANDING

Around two years of age, infants develop a more sophisticated understanding of language and have already started to make simple one- or two-word sentences and progress through the telegraphic stage of language. Two-word sentences have been the focus of a number of studies. Early research suggested that children use a particular set of grammar rules (Brown, 1973), possibly providing evidence of a primitive prototype language. On the other hand, these two-word utterances might simply reflect limitations of the child's cognitive system, with children applying the words that are most available for a given situation to achieve a certain goal (Tomasello, 2000).

The progression of grammar rules actually occurs by three to four years of age, and while vocabulary still develops as children grow older, much of the focus moves to picking up the rules needed to put words in the right order to make sentences. By the time that children reach school they have gone from crying and cooing to babbling, to limited one-word speech, to being able to produce complex sentences.

17.6 EARLY SOCIAL DEVELOPMENT IN INFANCY

We now turn our attention to children's social development. The most immediate consideration is the family structure. However, as children grow up, socialisation occurs outside the immediate family and they start becoming integrated into more and more social networks, including wider family, friends, religious groups or cultural groups. These social networks provide a reference point for the children's knowledge and opportunities for the acquisition of the behaviours and norms that govern social interactions (Lewis, 2005). This section considers the implications of the early interactions for social and emotional development.

17.6.1 THE IMPORTANCE OF EARLY RELATIONSHIPS

As we have seen, infants are tuned into their environment, show a readiness to relate to faces, voices and social beings,

MESHING How an adult's and an infant's behaviours fit together.

PROTOCONVERSATIONS Early turn-taking behaviour between adults and infants whereby adults tend to vocalise when the infants are not vocalising.

and are biologically predisposed to interact with others. The nature of an infant's first relationship is particularly crucial to understand because the mother–infant dyad is important to securing early social relationships (Winnicott, 1964). One way of understanding this early relationship is to look at the concepts of **meshing** and **protoconversations**.

Observations of protoconversations are important in showing how well the baby's and mother's behaviours are meshed during their early interactions (see Oates, 2005). This form of meshing can occur through both non-verbal behaviour and verbal interactions, such as speech and turn-taking. Turn-taking in conversations is an important aspect of establishing social relationships (Kaye & Fogel, 1980). Over time the type and frequency of infants' face-to-face greetings change from earlier reactive types of interaction (responding solely to interactions) to more proactive types of interaction (such as sustaining or initiating the interaction). Therefore, adults initiate more interactions than infants, especially in the first few months. However, aside from face-to-face actions, turn-taking also occurs through a variety of other non-verbal interactions, such as feeding. Kaye and Brazelton (1971) showed the importance of turn-taking through feeding in terms of jiggling infants on the knee. Remarkably, infants show a reduction in feeding behaviour during this jiggling but resume feeding when it stops. In fact, synchronising this behaviour establishes a 'conversation-like' interaction.

We have already seen the importance of imitation for examining infants' representations of facial features earlier in this chapter. However, imitation can also be seen as an important precursor to social development. While previous work has acknowledged the extent to which infants can imitate their mothers' facial features, such as tongue protrusion or widening of the mouth (Meltzoff & Moore, 1977), in reality it is not the infant that is engaging with imitation. Work has shown that it is the mother (or caregiver) that imitates their baby's facial features more frequently as a way of securing a bond and establishing communication with their infant (Pawlby, 1977). Therefore, infants produce behaviours, but it is the caregivers that actually use these behaviours to frame interaction sequences accordingly (Pawlby, 1977). This imitation of infants' behaviours decreases in both frequency and duration over the first year of the infant's life as the dyadic (two-person) relationship between caregiver and infant becomes more secure (Kaye & Marcus, 1981). In some ways, this ability to frame interactions and imitate infants' behaviours can be seen as methods for scaffolding social interactions (e.g. Bruner, 1975).

17.6.2 IMPORTANCE OF ATTACHMENT AND RELATIONSHIPS

Perhaps the most influential relationship of all is that which the child forms with their primary caregiver during infancy. John Bowlby was one of the first, through his attachment theory, to highlight the importance of the relationship we have with our primary caregiver. While working during the 1930s with boys experiencing adjustment problems, he began to formulate his ideas that disruption to the maternal bond during early childhood is detrimental to later adjustment in the form of psychopathology (Bretherton, 1991).

Bowlby's (1969) deprivation theory states that any interruption to the attachment process will result in problems associated with attachment quality (Thornton, 2008). Four phases of attachment are outlined:

Phase 1: Pre-attachment (birth to two months) in which the infant interacts socially with everyone and does not show a specific preference for a particular caregiver.

Phase 2: Early attachment (two to seven months) in which the infant begins to discriminate between caregivers and develops a strong preference for the primary caregiver. As the strength of the preference for the primary caregiver increases, the child moves to phase 3.

Phase 3: Attachment (seven months to two or three years) where the child exhibits separation anxiety if they are not in contact with their primary caregiver. Also the child shows stranger anxiety, which means that they are fearful of people they do not know. As the child gets older, the attachment figure becomes a resource and this is marked by entry to phase 4.

Phase 4: Partnership (from two or three years). Bowlby also proposed that our interactions with our primary caregiver lead to the development of internal working models – subconscious processes that guide the development of relationships.

Although Bowlby outlined the importance of attachment, Mary Ainsworth and her colleagues were instrumental in current thinking on attachment through the development of the 'strange situation' studies. Ainsworth et al. (1978) developed the strange situation as a method of assessing children's attachment to their primary caregiver. Specifically, through a series of observations where the primary caregiver and infant (1) interact, (2) are separated and (3) are reunited, it is possible to classify the attachment relationship between the individuals. The central premise is that the infant uses the primary caregiver as a secure base while exploring the world around them.

TABLE 17.1 The four attachment categories

ATTACHMENT CATEGORY	CHARACTERISTIC BEHAVIOUR
Insecure avoidant	Child subtly avoids the primary caregiver
Secure	Child uses the caregiver as a base to explore the situation and environment
Ambivalent/resistant	Child clings to primary caregiver and may also be ambivalent
Disorganised	Child displays behaviour that does not fit into the other categories

Through these studies, Ainsworth initially developed three attachment classifications: insecure avoidant; securely attached; and ambivalent/resistant (see Table 17.1). Later, a fourth category – disorganised – was added by Main and Solomon (1990).

An important factor associated with attachment styles is how mothers respond to their infants. Displaying high levels of maternal sensitivity and responsiveness to six-month-old infants was associated with greater levels of attachment security at 12- and 18-months (Raby et al., 2012) and during adolescence (Beijersbergen et al., 2012). Therefore, how 'tuned in' a mother is to the needs of her infant influences the quality of the attachment relationship that develops.

KEY RESEARCHER Mary Ainsworth

Mary Ainsworth (1913–1999) obtained her PhD in developmental psychology in 1939 and then joined the Canadian army. After the Second World War, Ainsworth held academic positions at various institutions, including the Tavistock Clinic in London and the University of Virginia. In 1985 she received an Award for Distinguished Contributions to Child Development; in 1989 she received a Distinguished Scientific Contribution Award from the American Psychological Association (APA); and in 1998 she received a Gold Medal Award for Life Achievement in the Science of Psychology from the APA.

Her research focused on early social development, including the effects of maternal separation on personality development. Although she is most famous for the strange situation paradigm, she also wrote a number of books and articles exploring aspects of infant development. In particular, she conducted a longitudinal study examining the infant–mother attachment processes in Uganda.

The importance of developing a secure attachment cannot be underestimated. Some researchers argue that a secure attachment is crucial because it helps to protect the child from stress, provides emotional security (Slater, 2007) and promotes positive psychosocial adjustment (Balbernie, 2013; Bridges, 2003; Thompson, 2000). Children who develop an insecure attachment or those maltreated by their primary caregiver are more likely to develop emotional disorders (Morton & Browne, 1998). Due to the importance of developing a secure attachment, a number of policy changes have been implemented across the world. In the UK, these include changes to the provision of nursery care, decisions made by the courts in response to custody proceedings, hospital care for children, practices implemented by social services, and the Sure Start initiative (Slater, 2007).

Although many researchers have advocated the importance of secure attachments for children's development, attachment theories are not without their critics. For example, attachment theories have been wrongly used as a tool to pressure mothers to stay at home and to 'blame' mothers for their actions if they return to work and use day care (Slater, 2007). However, there is evidence that children can develop resilience in response to poor attachments (Lewis, 2005). So, despite their poor attachment qualities, these children are still well adjusted. Also, attachment theories are limited in their consideration of the father's role and the role of the wider family (Lewis, 2005). Therefore, traditional attachment theories may fail to fully take into consideration the range of social relationships in which infants engage.

The role of the father has, to some extent, been overlooked, especially in the early attachment research, which focused almost exclusively on mothers as primary caregivers. More recently, researchers have reported that the nature of the father–child relationship is different from the mother–child relationship. While fathers are more likely to engage in physical rough-and-tumble play activities, mothers are more likely to engage in play with toys and conversation with their children (Schoppe-Sullivan et al., 2013).

Some have used attachment theory to argue that children placed into day care are at risk of being disadvantaged. So, are there implications for children if they attend day care? It is argued that day care is a protective influence for some children and can actively promote the development of a strong parent–child attachment (Ahnert, Pinquart, & Lamb, 2006). Day care can be particularly effective when there are low child-to-carer ratios, and the child is cared for in small groups (Ahnert et al., 2006). Another important fact is that day care can be one environment where children interact with their peers, and during this time children acquire a range of social skills.

ASIDE

FIGURE 17.2 Not all childhoods are the same. Thousands of children around the world end up in armies and militias

© Maurizio Gambarini/dpa/Corbis

Not all childhoods are the same

Most of the studies on child development are carried out on Western children in wealthy countries. Around the rest of the world, children have very different experiences, and some of them are very hostile. For example, it is estimated that there are 300,000 child soldiers worldwide (UNICEF website) in at least 18 countries. Although the term 'child soldier' commonly brings up a picture of gun-waving teenage boys, the reality is a little different. A number of child soldiers are girls, maybe as many as 40% in some countries, and many of the soldiers are as young as seven or eight. Not all of these children carry weapons, but their roles as support to weapons units puts their lives in danger (Figure 17.2).

Some children take up arms to deal with poverty, abuse or discrimination. Some are seeking revenge for violence against themselves or their families. Sometimes they are abducted and forced to join armed groups, and sometimes they become separated from their families and the armies are their only source of food and shelter. The subsequent recruitment and mobilisation of child soldiers are made possible by the widespread availability of small arms (some 638 million are currently in circulation). Many weapons are so light and portable that a 10-year-old can easily carry, strip and load them.

Other family members also shape children's development. Around 80% of children in Europe and the USA have a sibling (Dunn, 2002). Sibling relationships have a number of unique characteristics, including providing a source of emotional support for the stressful situations a child encounters within the family unit (Brody, 1998), facilitating social skill understanding (Stormshak, Bellanti, & Bierman, 1996) and higher levels of disclosure (Howe et al., 2001). However, some research has suggested that the relative position or birth-order in which a child finds themselves within the family can result in distinct experiences. Research suggests that first-born children tend to be more adult-oriented, helpful and self-controlled, whereas later born children tend to be less fearful and anxious (Sulloway, 2001). On the other hand, only children tend to be less anxious and have higher levels of personal control than children with siblings (Mancillas, 2006). Although these results suggest birth-order influences subsequent development, it is important to note that the effect sizes for this type of research are often very small.

Grandparents also influence children's development, and many grandparents now fulfil many aspects of the parental role because of the costs of child care and changing family dynamics. Grandparents may also act as a source of emotional support to both children and their parents when stress occurs within the family (Dunifon, 2013), and can facilitate the transmission of family tradition (Smith, 2005). However, other forms of intergenerational transmission have also been reported, such as aggressive and anti-social behaviour (Smith & Farrington, 2004).

As well as being influenced by the relationship that infants develop with their primary caregiver and other family members from very early on in life, children are influenced by their peers. Specifically, newborn babies are believed to influence the propensity with which other babies cry, with one crying infant triggering crying in others (Hay, Nash, & Pedersen, 1981). This social interaction and preference for similar-age mates continues as the infant develops, and by the time that infants are six months old they show preferences for other similar-aged infants through reaching out to touch them and also through smiling (Hay, Nash, & Pedersen, 1983). During the first year of life, children's relationships with their peers are characterised by prosocial behaviour, but as infants approach their first birthday they also begin to engage in aggressive behaviour (Hay, Payne, & Chadwick, 2004). From approximately 18 months old, children develop preferences for specific playmates, and by the time a child reaches their third birthday they have developed strong preferences for particular playmates (Hay et al., 2004). Other preferences continue to be established, such as an increasing preference to play with same-gender peers during early childhood (Maccoby, 1988, 1990).

FIGURE 17.3   A two-year-old demonstrating self-awareness using the rouge test

17.6.3 DEVELOPMENT OF SELF-AWARENESS

During the first year of life, infants begin to develop a sense of self-awareness. This involves the development of the subjective self and the objective self. The subjective self is the recognition that the individual is separate from others, whereas the objective self is the recognition that the self is an object with properties (Bee & Boyd, 2005). Self-awareness has been assessed using the rouge test, in which an infant is positioned in front of a mirror, a dot is placed on their head, or nose, and then their reaction is measured (Bertenthal & Fischer, 1978; Lewis & Brooks-Gunn, 1979). If the infant tries to remove the mark, they are showing a sense of self-awareness. As a child's self-awareness increases, they begin to insist on doing things for themselves, show a possessive attitude towards their toys and eventually begin to develop an awareness of their own competencies (Harter, 1982, 1987).

17.6.4 DEVELOPMENT OF THEORY OF MIND

If you are going to interact with other people effectively, you need to understand that they are likely to have different thoughts, beliefs and views of the world from yourself. This understanding will be based on the possession on your part of what is known as a **theory of mind** (or ToM) (Premack & Woodruff, 1978). The ability to attribute a theory of mind to another person seems to be a very easy thing to do for most adults, but just a brief thought about what we are doing to achieve this shows that it is a task that requires a lot of skill. Studies of child development suggest that the ability to take the viewpoint of others is not so straightforward, and studies have shown that young children below the age of four often have problems taking the viewpoint of other individuals (e.g. Piaget's three-mountain task) and often fail at solving simple false belief tasks.

The **false belief** task described below is based upon the assumption that in order to understand if someone has been deceived (or possesses a false belief about a situation), an individual needs to understand that others have their own individual viewpoint.

THEORY OF MIND The ability to attribute mental states such as beliefs, intentions and desires to yourself and others, and to understand that other people have beliefs, desires and intentions that are different from your own.

FALSE BELIEF This is when an individual incorrectly believes a statement or scenario to be true when it is not. This is the basis of the false belief tasks used in the theory of mind experiments.

One widely recognised test of theory of mind is the Sally–Anne task (Baron-Cohen, Leslie, & Frith, 1985). This examines false beliefs by using two dolls, Sally and Anne. Sally has a basket and Anne has a box. Sally also has a marble and places this in her basket before disappearing out of sight. Anne quickly moves the marble from the basket into her box. The child is then asked, '*When Sally returns, where will she look for her marble?*'. Baron-Cohen et al. found that three-year-old children tend to say with confidence that Sally will look in the box. This is because the child knows the marble is in the box and is unable to appreciate that Sally has a different view of the world (a false belief). In contrast, four-year-old children are usually able to understand that Sally thinks the marble is still in her basket, thus demonstrating a theory of mind.

KEY STUDY

Lohmann, H., Carpenter, M., & Call, J. (2005). Guessing versus choosing – and seeing versus believing – in false belief tasks. *British Journal of Developmental Psychology*, *23*, 451–469.

Between three-and-a-half and four years old, children's performance on the traditional false belief task (Baron-Cohen et al., 1985; Wimmer & Perner, 1983) has been shown to result in a 50:50 chance of getting the correct answer.

In the traditional false belief task, a main protagonist places an object in a box and then leaves the room; a second protagonist enters and, unseen by the main protagonist, moves the item to a new location. When the main protagonist returns they are unaware a switch has occurred. Lohmann et al. (2005) decided to investigate whether or not children were just guessing or whether they were certain in their beliefs, and whether the children were relying solely on the visual cues present in the traditional task. So, in addition to this false belief scenario, Lohmann et al. introduced three other conditions: a first condition where the main protagonist knew the location of the item; a second condition where the main protagonist is lied to about the position of the item (a verbal version of the false belief task); and a third scenario where the main protagonist would have to guess the location of the object.

In the condition where the main protagonist knew the item's location – by witnessing the switch, by being told about the switch, or by knowing that the object was not moved – the children consistently performed better in the 'no switch' scenario, which entails low processing demands compared with the verbal and visual equivalents. In the guess condition, the main protagonist is not present when the second protagonist hides the object in a box. The scenario is then obscured, providing no indication to the child or main protagonist as to the object's location. The children performed at chance on this condition.

Over half the children in the sample failed the false belief task, replicating the findings of Wellman, Cross and Watson (2001). However, in terms of uncertainty, the children showed less uncertainty in the false belief task (regardless of whether it was the verbal lie condition or the traditional visual scenario) than in the guessing task, and these levels of certainty did not significantly vary between the children who passed and failed the tasks. This suggests that the children in this age range are not simply guessing answers to the false belief task, but do have a certain belief about the outcome of the task.

Lohmann et al. (2005) next examined the individual differences in children's performance and showed that children who had higher vocabulary and grammar scores were more likely to pass the traditional false belief task and the lie condition. In conclusion, the children are not guessing but relying on their own knowledge and performance, and this is largely governed by the child's linguistic abilities.

These techniques of assessing theory of mind have recently come under some criticism, however, as they are subject to the 'curse of knowledge'. This refers to having too much information and then focusing on the wrong bit. The curse of knowledge suggests that a child (or even an adult) can fail a false belief task as the additional information they are provided with in the scene they observe, together with personal experience, can influence their decision, resulting in a wrong conclusion (Birch & Bloom, 2007). For example, a childs standing in a room with three different coloured boxes (one red, one blue, one purple) and decides to put her favourite toy in the blue box. She then leaves the room and her friend decides to move the toy to the red box and then shuffles the boxes around. The child might not only look in the blue box where she left the toy (traditional false belief scenario) but she might choose to look in whatever box is in the same location as the original box instead. This shows how previous knowledge might influence an individual's decision in such a false belief scenario.

Even when these false belief tasks are more realistic and relevant to the participant, the child may still fail. For example, Perner, Leekam and Wimmer (1987) developed the Smarties task, where a child is shown a Smarties tube and asked what is inside. The child (normally) responds with 'Smarties' or 'sweets'. The experimenter then shows the child, to their surprise, that the tube is actually full of not very tasty pencils. The child is then asked what their friend, not present during the experiment, will think is in the tube. Again, children below the age of four tend to falsely rely on their current world-state knowledge and suggest that their friend will think there are pencils in the Smarties tube, rather than the correct belief-state assumption that their friend will make the same conclusions that they originally made, that is, there are sweets in the tube.

There is evidence that children may fail these theory of mind tasks before the age of four years. False belief tasks require considerable mentalising on the part of the child. It has been suggested that the ability to perform tasks that require the mental rotation of different people's viewpoints are strongly associated with a child's verbal ability (Hughes et al., 2005) and the child's general language ability (Ruffman et al., 2003). This strong association with language could suggest that by improving the quality of social interaction and communication, a child can better develop their understanding of others' belief states (see the key study above).

17.6.5 DEVELOPMENT OF GENDER ROLES

Alongside the development of a sense of self, children also begin to develop an awareness of their gender. For a child to apply the gender categorisation to themselves they must move through the processes of gender identity, gender stability and gender consistency. Gender identity involves the infant being able to correctly label other people according to their gender. By the age of around three, when shown photographs, children begin to correctly identify which of the people in the photographs is the same gender as themselves (Ruble & Martin, 1998). Gender stability is the recognition that people remain the same gender throughout their life (Bee & Boyd, 2005) and is a skill children develop around the age of four. The final stage is gender consistency, which is the notion that people's biological sex remains the same even though their appearance can change.

During the development of children's gender roles, children also begin to show an awareness of gender role stereotypes. For example, three- to four-year-olds can apply stereotype knowledge to jobs, with children able to say which job is stereotypically performed by adults of each gender (Ruble & Martin, 1998). Children also show a preference to play with gender-stereotyped toys from about the age of 18 months (O'Brien, 1992), and from the age of three children prefer to interact with same-gender peers (Maccoby, 1988, 1990). Theories draw on biological factors, social learning theory, cognitive-developmental approaches and social-cognitive approaches to explain the process of sex-appropriate behaviour (see Smith et al., 2011).

17.7 CHAPTER SUMMARY

In this chapter we have looked at the development of cognitive, language and social skills in relation to development during the early years. We have also evaluated the methods used to examine development, especially in young infants. Hopefully, you should now be able to reflect on the appropriateness of these different methodologies and to question the types of conclusion drawn from studies using these methods.

One of the main questions we have discussed is the validity of researchers' interpretations of research evidence concerning infants' early mental and cognitive capabilities. As we have illustrated, though results from experiments may often be replicated, interpretations of these results may vary according to the nature of the study.

Finally, we have illustrated how the interaction between genes and the environment should be seen as a complex relationship. Through this interaction infants can begin to develop a better sense of the social world, through the development of mental representations, language skills and social relationships.

DISCUSSION QUESTIONS

Can we accurately measure perception in infants? What implications does this have for the conclusions drawn from research with regard to innate predispositions?

Can the nature–nurture debate ever be settled with regard to development in the early years?

What evidence can you find in support of the view that young infants develop a relatively early understanding of language?

What methods are used to study cognitive skills in young infants?

To what extent do day care settings encourage the development of attachment in young infants? How important is attachment in the understanding of infants' early emotional development?

SUGGESTIONS FOR FURTHER READING

Bremner, G., & Fogel, A. (2004). *The Blackwell handbook of infant development*. Oxford: Wiley Blackwell. This book provides answers to the key questions that are pertinent to infants' development. The book brings together theory and research across a range of key areas.

Oates, J., & Grayson, A. (2004). *Cognitive and language development in children*. Oxford: Blackwell. This book provides an overview of how children's language and thinking skills develop and also outlines the links between these two topics. Chapters 2 and 4 provide a particularly helpful overview of children's first words and how children develop an understanding of grammar.

Smith, P.K., & Hart, C.H. (2010). *Wiley-Blackwell handbook of childhood social development* (2nd edn). Oxford: Blackwell. This book provides an overview of children's social development from preschool to adolescence. The text also includes details of a range of theories and research pertinent to the area as well as providing details of the historical background to the area.

Still want more? For links to online resources relevant to this chapter and a quiz to test your understanding, visit the companion website at edge.sagepub.com/banyard2e

18 DEVELOPMENT DURING THE SCHOOL YEARS

Lead authors: James Stiller, Lucy Betts, Rebecca Larkin and Gareth Williams

CHAPTER OUTLINE

18.1 Introduction	316
18.2 Cognitive development	316
18.2.1 Piaget's stage account of learning and development	316
18.2.2 Challenges to Piaget's work	318
18.2.3 Vygotsky: linking social and cognitive development	319
18.3 Later language development	320
18.3.1 Language acquisition device (LAD)	320
18.3.2 Grammatical awareness	320
18.4 School-led development and instruction	321
18.4.1 Development of reading skills	321
18.4.2 Importance of phonological awareness	321
18.4.3 Reading instruction	322
18.4.4 Development of mathematical skills	323
18.4.5 Development of counting principles	323
18.4.6 Mathematical concepts and procedures	324
18.5 Changing dynamics in a social world	325
18.5.1 School adjustment and social development	325
18.5.2 Importance of peers and friends	325
18.5.3 Bullying and socialisation	327
18.5.4 Moral development	327
18.6 Chapter summary	329
Discussion questions	329
Suggestions for further reading	330

18.1 INTRODUCTION

How do children develop their abilities and become adults? This chapter will consider the role of child development during the school years. We will focus on the development of cognitive, language and social skills. We begin by discussing factors that influence children's development within the school environment and how the environment plays a fundamental role in refining our understanding of how children continue to develop throughout their school years. Following on from Chapter 17, we will discuss theories of cognitive development, including the work of Piaget and Vygotsky, and the implications of these theoretical approaches for children's learning and their schooling. The chapter will then consider children's language development and changes that occur in children's theory of mind and social reasoning, all of which are important for the development of social skills in later years. We will also discuss the skills that children learn while they are at school and the processes that underlie the development of language and reading ability. Finally, in this chapter we will consider how the social world of children changes as they enter school and how this is reflected in the importance of peer relationships, friendships and experiences of bullying.

FRAMING QUESTIONS

- How can the theories of (1) Piaget and (2) Vygotsky be applied to education and schooling?
- How important are cultural tools in children's development?
- What is theory of mind and how does it help us understand the world?
- What are the important skills in learning to read?
- How important is social adjustment to children's schooling?
- What are the functions of peers and friends during the school years?

18.2 COGNITIVE DEVELOPMENT

As outlined in Chapter 17, it is clear that we are born with a range of cognitive abilities. In this chapter, we begin by discussing how children's cognitive abilities develop during the school years. We look at some of the implications for children's development within the school context and classroom instruction, with a particular emphasis on the relative importance of **cultural tools** and teaching. It is argued that a child's interaction with their immediate environment is important to enable them to develop and learn new skills. However, to understand children's development in the later years it is important to appreciate the role of social context and to recognise how children develop skills with the assistance of others through scaffolding and peer collaboration.

CULTURAL TOOLS Tools that help us to understand the world more fully by solving problems, measuring the environment, making calculations and storing information (e.g. books, number systems language, computers and calculators).

18.2.1 PIAGET'S STAGE ACCOUNT OF LEARNING AND DEVELOPMENT

Jean Piaget (1896–1980) challenged the way in which psychologists understood how a child's mind develops, and he is arguably the most influential theorist of cognitive development. Piaget considered a child to be like a small scientist, actively discovering the world around them, rather than a passive sponge that absorbs knowledge passed down by adults. Many of Piaget's conclusions have been challenged by more recent research. However, Piaget's work has been hugely influential in terms of developing our understanding of how children think and, importantly, how children's thought processes differ from those of adults.

Piaget (1952) proposed a theory of cognitive development that he considered to be universal, regardless of a child's background or culture. This theory is a 'stage theory', because it consists of a set of qualitatively distinct stages through which each child progresses during childhood and adolescence. Piaget also argued that all children must complete the stages in the same order, although some children will progress through them at a faster rate than others.

Piaget's theory centres on children developing **cognitive schemas**. Simply put, these schemas are cognitive structures that represent the world around the child. As children encounter new experiences in the world, their schemas need to be adjusted to take into account this new and revised understanding. Piaget used the term **assimilation** to refer to how children try to fit new information from the world into an existing schema. For example, a child who has never seen a cat before but has plenty of experience of dogs might see a cat for the first time and fit it under the schema of 'dog'. After all, it has four legs, a tail and is furry. However, the child might then notice that this new 'dog' has very pointy ears and whiskers and makes a strange 'miaow' sound. This information no longer fits in with the existing schema for 'dog', so the child is forced to adjust their view of the world and make a new place within this schema for the cat. This process, by which children adjust existing schema to take account of new information, is **accommodation**. In order for a child to be comfortable with and understand the world around them, a balance between the processes of assimilation and accommodation is needed. Piaget used the term **equilibration** to refer to this balance between these two processes.

Table 18.1 outlines the four main stages highlighted in Piaget's theory. The ages given alongside each stage are only approximations; this is because Piaget was aware that children develop at slightly different rates. Some of the key characteristics of each stage are also included in Table 18.1 and these will be discussed in more detail below.

Piaget's first stage occurs before school age. Between birth and two years infants gradually develop an awareness of the world around them, accumulating the ability to develop more sophisticated coordinated reflex actions, and this interaction with the environment allows them to develop a better understanding and greater use of language (**symbolic thought**). One of the hallmarks of this stage is the infant's ability to understand that just because they cannot see something it does not necessarily mean that the object no longer exists (**object permanency**). Piaget argued that towards the end of the sensorimotor stage infants are able to understand that out of sight does not have to mean out of mind. For example, an infant who has acquired object permanency will actively search for a toy that has suddenly been removed from view (and will probably be very surprised that the object was moved in the first place!).

By the time the child enters the preoperational stage, they have acquired an awareness of the world around them, and are rapidly developing their language skills. As part of this process, children tend to engage in pretend play, often attributing human characteristics to

---

COGNITIVE SCHEMAS Mental representations and plans used to enact behaviours.

ASSIMILATION The incorporation of new experiences into pre-existing cognitive schemas.

ACCOMMODATION The modification and expansion of pre-existing cognitive schemas in order to adapt to new experiences.

EQUILIBRATION This is when a child's set of schemas are balanced and not disturbed by conflict.

SYMBOLIC THOUGHT The representation of reality through the use of abstract concepts such as words, gestures and numbers.

OBJECT PERMANENCY This is the ability to understand that an object still exists even if it is no longer visible.

ANIMISM The attribution of life-like qualities to inanimate objects (for example, toys).

TABLE 18.1 An illustration of the four stages of development in Piaget's theory (adapted from Smith, Cowie, & Blades, 2011)

STAGE	APPROXIMATE AGES	KEY CHARACTERISTICS
Sensorimotor	1–2 years	Symbolic thought develops, object permanency (egocentrism)
Preoperational	2–7 years	Egocentrism, animism, centration
Concrete operational	7–12 years	Able to conserve, able to think logically
Formal operational	12 + years	Able to carry out abstract and hypothetical reasoning

CENTRATION The focusing of attention on one aspect of a situation while excluding the rest of the scenario.

CONSERVATION The understanding that certain properties of objects remain the same under transformation. These properties include quantity, weight and volume.

inanimate objects (**animism**). Children in this stage will also tend to be rather egocentric, which means that they seem preoccupied with their own thoughts and ideas rather than paying attention to other people's. You may have noticed that when young children play together they often seem to be involved in quite different aspects of the game, and pay little attention to what another child says or does.

Centration is also an important characteristic of the preoperational stage, whereby children tend to be able to concentrate on only one aspect of a problem at any one time. The classic tasks Piaget used to assess this were based around the idea of **conservation**. This refers to the understanding that something remains the same even if superficial characteristics are changed (Figure 18.1).

In one famous conservation task, children were presented with two rows of counters. There were equal numbers of counters in each row, and the tester would initially arrange them so the two rows were identically spaced out. The child would be asked whether the number of counters was the same in each row, to which most children would reply 'yes'. The tester would then increase the spaces between the counters in one of the rows so that it looked longer. Again, the child would be asked whether the number of counters was the same in the two rows, to which children in the preoperational stage tended to reply 'no'. Piaget argued that this error occurs because the children are only able to focus on one aspect of the problem, in this case the difference in length between the two rows.

In the concrete operational stage, children are able to carry out conservation tasks successfully. Children are also able to carry out problem-solving tasks in a logical manner. There are limits to this logic, however, and they struggle with abstract ideas such as algebra. Finally, in the formal operational stage, children are able to carry out hypothetical and abstract reasoning, and this continues to develop later into adulthood (in line with the transition into secondary school and beyond). With this type of thinking they approach a problem in a methodical way, exploring all the possibilities in the way that we like to think that science is done.

18.2.2 CHALLENGES TO PIAGET'S WORK

Piaget's theory has been challenged on several points. Perhaps the most general criticism is that he overlooked the importance of social influences on children's development. He concentrated on the ways that individual children solve problems and make sense of the world by themselves. However, it should be noted that while Piaget emphasised that children learn by discovery, he did not argue that this should occur in isolation.

Researchers such as Margaret Donaldson have also argued that Piaget's tasks were often too difficult for children to understand, leading to an underestimation of young children's cognitive abilities. For example, think back to Piaget's conservation task with the rows of counters. Children were asked the same question twice (i.e. 'Are the number of counters the same in the two rows?'). In a classroom situation, teachers only tend to ask the same question twice if the first answer was wrong. Therefore, many children may change their initial answer for this reason, and not because they do not understand how to conserve number. Accepting Piaget's theory also relies on us being happy to think of development occurring in discrete, qualitatively distinct stages. Is this what really happens in the context of everyday learning?

FIGURE 18.1   Five-year-old Christian is thinking about a Piaget conservation task. The reward of Smarties is helping to focus his attention

© mickythemartian

Despite the many criticisms of Piaget's work, researchers (referred to as neo-Piagetians) have continued to develop his ideas over the past 40 years. Like Piaget, these researchers argue that children develop their own knowledge through exploration and discovery. Neo-Piagetians also agree that children progress through a series of discrete stages. Their work has shown us more about the ways in which children process information and make decisions (see Morra et al., 2007).

ASIDE

Piaget's stages of development

Piaget suggested that his four stages of development were universal and characterised key changes in children's thinking and reasoning throughout development. However, how reliable are these four distinct stages? Consider how valid these stages are in the light of the following:

- changes in cultural norms and values
- children with distinct learning difficulties
- children without access to formal schooling
- delay in language development.

Clearly, there are environmental factors that may not allow children to meet these distinct stages in line with other children, which would lead us to question the validity of using these developmental milestones as fixed.

18.2.3 VYGOTSKY: LINKING SOCIAL AND COGNITIVE DEVELOPMENT

Unlike Piaget, Lev Vygotsky (1896–1934) did not produce a detailed model of how children's internal mental representations or cognitive skills develop. Instead, Vygotsky emphasised the broad link between cognitive and social development. While Piaget considered the child to be a discoverer of the world around them, Vygotsky argued that children learn most from interaction with other children and adults.

Vygotsky used the term *cultural tools* to refer to the tools with which children can develop the appropriate psychological skills, and the values passed on to children by older generations. These tools may provide one path for children's intellectual adaptation through computers or teaching methods. Language can be considered the most important cultural tool, and Vygotsky believed that use of language underpinned the development of reflective thought. Children's development of language begins with the social environment (social speech – talking to others) and then over time this becomes internalised (private speech – talking to yourself) to guide and develop thought.

Vygotsky's (1978) emphasis on social interactions to guide children's learning and cognitive development is clearly demonstrated in the following quotation:

> Every function in the child's cultural development appears twice: first, on the social level, and later, on the individual level; first, between people (interpsychological) and then inside the child (intrapsychological). This applies equally to voluntary attention, to logical memory, and to the formation of concepts. All the higher functions originate as actual relationships between individuals. (Vygotsky, 1978: 57)

However, we can still ask how the environment provides children with appropriate skills for development. Vygotsky and his **social constructivist** account do not deal with fixed stages of development, but describe 'leading activities' typical of certain age periods, around which intellectual development is organised. It is through such leading activities that children interact with their environment and develop

SOCIAL CONSTRUCTIVISM A theoretical approach that emphasises the role of culture and context in children's understanding and development.

ZONE OF PROXIMAL DEVELOPMENT (ZPD) This is the gap between what a child can do by themselves and what they can achieve under adult guidance or collaboration.

SCAFFOLDING This occurs when adults guide the learning of a child by simplifying the structure of the child's learning environment.

appropriate skills in learning and thinking. The emphasis is clearly on guiding children's development across a range of different activities and this, according to Vygotsky, governs children's intellectual development and rate of learning.

As a way of explaining the importance of guiding children's learning, Vygotsky developed the idea of the **zone of proximal development**, based on his argument that children can only achieve a limited amount on their own. With assistance from adults or more developed peers, children can achieve considerably more. **Scaffolding** refers to how a child can be helped to achieve their goal with structured support from an adult or an older child. As the child becomes more competent at the task, the support (or scaffold) is gradually removed. Having a dynamic, flexible scaffold – or framework – therefore assists the child in mastering new skills or obtaining new information. Ultimately, this can be seen as a tool to aid development. The idea of scaffolding was later developed to refer to other leading activities, such as guided participation, which involves the use of adult or peer collaboration to guide children to the next level of understanding through leading activities (Rogoff, 1990).

18.3 LATER LANGUAGE DEVELOPMENT

As suggested in Chapter 17, the process of language development is rather complex. Although infants are born with some ability to recognise familiar sounds or their mother's voice from an early age, this process does not end in infancy. In fact, language skills are still developing when children enter the later years, especially during school. The development of later language skills will be examined in this section, with a particular focus on syntactic development and an understanding of grammar.

Many early theories of language development emphasise imitation or learning with reinforcement as processes that drive language learning in early years. Yet there are a number of problems with this as an explanation. The main one is that languages are complex and dynamic, and users of languages tend to be very creative in how they communicate. Few utterances are ever the same, and so it is unlikely that someone could learn a language only from imitating others. We are predisposed to explore and use language from an early age and this goes beyond what would be expected from simple learning and reinforcement from others.

18.3.1 LANGUAGE ACQUISITION DEVICE (LAD)

LANGUAGE ACQUISITION DEVICE (LAD) A system proposed by Chomsky that young infants have. It helps them navigate the grammar of language, which in turn helps language development.

In the 1960s Noam Chomsky developed an influential theory to explain how children are able to develop language skills so quickly and to such a high degree of complexity. They argued that all children are born with an innate **language acquisition device (LAD)**, and that there is an area (or a module) in the brain that is preprogrammed to learn language. When a child is exposed to language in their environment, their LAD will gradually be switched to the relevant settings for their native tongue. Chomsky referred to this as setting the parameters of the LAD. Therefore, while all children are born with the capacity to adapt to any language, their environment will quickly determine which language(s) they actually develop. Lenneberg (1967) added to this theory by suggesting that there is a critical period for language learning which occurs before children reach puberty. Learning language outside this critical period is thought to be very difficult and may explain why older children and adults have difficulties in learning other languages.

18.3.2 GRAMMATICAL AWARENESS

How do children develop their awareness of grammar? Some ideas have come from the mistakes that young children make while learning to apply grammatical rules. This applies especially to the overgeneralising of rules which have regular grammatical forms to those which are less regular. Evidence for the LAD was largely based on the finding that children produce over-regularisation errors that they could not have learned from imitation. Therefore, this aspect of spoken language would seem to have come from inside the child, rather than from the external environment. However, these types of error are actually very rarely produced by children (Thornton, 2008). Therefore, they provide limited support for Chomsky's universal theory that children's grammar is being driven by an innate language module.

Let's consider some examples. When you talk about things that happened in the past, you might say that you have *closed* doors or *cleaned* cars, but you won't have *teached* history or *eated* an apple. For word plurals, you can have *cats*, *dogs* and *lions* but only *sheep*. To take the example of past tense, there are two routes to apply past tenses in grammar (Pinker & Prince, 1988). One route is for common grammar forms, and in the case of past tense we follow the rule: apply 'ed' *to the end of the word*. A second route stores information about irregular past tenses: that is, when the word needs to be modified in other ways (e.g. *eat* becomes *eaten* and *teach* becomes *taught*). When the tense of a word needs to be applied, the route with the irregular forms is looked up; if there is no irregular form for the word, then 'ed' is added to the end of the word. Over time more irregular past tenses are stored, and so these will be applied in place of simply adding 'ed' to the end of the word. A similar process would take place for applying plurals to words.

In summary, we may have a general preset guide that is sensitive to the idea that rules are needed to take individual words and use them for communication. Then a child's interaction with the world around them and the feedback that they receive help them to navigate the subtleties of the language in their environment.

18.4 SCHOOL-LED DEVELOPMENT AND INSTRUCTION

As we have already seen, the social environment plays a key role in the context of children's learning – especially in the provision of appropriate opportunities for children to learn. Vygotsky emphasised the role of scaffolding and collaborative learning and how these processes are guided by a more skilled individual who scaffolds the child's progress (Wood, Bruner, & Ross, 1976). As the child develops on certain tasks, the level of scaffolding or support should change to allow autonomy over their own learning. As a result, there is a strong emphasis on the use of cultural tools and receiving tuition to help develop skills across schooling, especially with regard to children's language and literacy development. This section considers children's reading development and how instruction plays a fundamental role in developing literacy skills.

18.4.1 DEVELOPMENT OF READING SKILLS

Learning to read is a fairly complex task which involves the combination of a variety of cognitive skills, including the development of spoken language. Although the link between early language skills and reading seems fairly obvious, in some ways children do need to show some competency in their own native language before acquiring skills in reading. However, reading itself is not an automatic process. It requires formal instruction. In fact, reading is a linguistic skill that is learned only after children have acquired considerable proficiency in using oral language.

It is clear that many children develop linguistic awareness through everyday communicative activities, but learning to read is not solely determined through the development of such language skills. In fact, reading is an artificial activity that requires explicit teaching.

18.4.2 IMPORTANCE OF PHONOLOGICAL AWARENESS

The most important set of linguistic abilities that a child requires in order to read is knowledge of sounds – often referred to as 'phonological awareness'. Phonological awareness is defined as the ability to perceive and manipulate the sounds of spoken words. Three important levels of phonological awareness have been distinguished within the reading literature: syllables, **rimes** and **phonemes** (Goswami & Bryant, 1990). Phonological awareness is unique for learning to read an alphabetic language. The importance of different levels of phonological awareness through syllables, rimes and phonemes, and the link between these levels of phonological awareness and reading development, are now fairly well established (Goswami & Bryant, 1990).

The awareness of syllables, onsets and rimes appears to emerge around three to four years of age, before the child enters formal schooling. The awareness of phonemes, by contrast, appears to emerge around the age of five to six years, when children in the UK are taught to read formally (see Carroll et al., 2003). Primarily, the reason for phoneme awareness developing at a later age is that phonemic judgements are often difficult for young children to grasp without any prior reading experience. This often occurs as they begin to learn about the alphabet, combining written letters with spoken sounds. The question therefore remains as to which aspect of phonological awareness contributes the greatest to developing proficiency in learning to read.

RIME The vowel sound of a word followed by the subsequent consonants, for example, the rime of 'ham' is 'am'. When two words share the same rime unit, they can be said to rhyme.

PHONEMES The smallest unit of sound that is able to carry some meaning in language.

RHYME This is where one word sounds the same as another word, for example 'stair' and 'pear'. They do not necessarily contain the same rime unit (consonants and vowel sequence).

There is evidence for **rhyme** awareness and links to later reading development. It has been shown that children as young as three years can solve rhyme oddity tasks, that is, identifying the odd word out from a selection (e.g. *cat*, *hat* and *pin*; Bradley & Bryant, 1983), and this ability is linked to the progress they make in learning to read. There is also strong support for the relationship between an early sensitivity to rhyme (nursery rhymes) and later reading development (see Bradley & Bryant, 1983). The question we need to ask is how this early awareness of rhyme contributes to the development of early word reading. Goswami's (1986, 1988) early work has shown that many young children (even before learning to read) can use existing knowledge of words from memory (e.g. *look*) to aid their attempt at identifying other unknown printed words that share similar rime units (e.g. *took*, *cook*). This use of analogies has since been shown to be extremely useful in teaching words, even to pre-readers and those in the first year of receiving formal instruction.

Although rhyme is important, there is strong evidence to show that a child's understanding of phonemes (the smallest phonological unit) is also an important aspect of early reading development (Hulme et al., 2002). Studies have found that phoneme skills are strong predictors of children's reading success even two to three years later (Duncan, Seymour, & Hill, 1997). In fact, several of these studies directly compared the contribution of rhyme and phoneme skills to children's later reading within the same study and found that phoneme skills were the best predictor after the contribution of rhyme skills was controlled (Hulme et al., 2002). Therefore, despite some studies finding that when rhyme and phoneme skills are measured in the same way, such as using similar tasks, both contribute well to reading. However, there does seem to be a greater emphasis on phoneme awareness as a predictor of early word reading in children.

18.4.3 READING INSTRUCTION

Given the importance of these phonological skills, how should they be taught in schools? One answer that is fashionable at the moment is to promote reading skills in young children through phonics teaching. There is a distinction to be made here between two approaches, namely (1) synthetic phonics and (2) analytic phonics. They emphasise different phonological units as a way of promoting reading discovery. However, in analytic phonics, the predominant method in the UK, letter sounds are taught after reading has already begun; children begin using a whole word approach to identify text, usually initially learning to read words by sight, often in the context of meaningful text. There is a strong focus on the recognition and identification of spelling patterns. For instance, analytic phonics emphasises the importance of onset-rime units, especially how the rimes of words can be used to help children read and spell by analogy.

Synthetic phonics, by comparison, is a much more accelerated form of phonics that focuses primarily on phoneme skills and letter-sound knowledge. After the first few of these have been taught, children are then taught series of different phonemes (the smallest units of sound) and their related graphemes (the written symbols for the phoneme) and they are shown how these sounds can be blended together to build up words. But which approach is more efficient in accelerating children's early reading skills? There is evidence that receiving synthetic phonics training leads to better reading, spelling and phonemic awareness than an analytic phonics approach (Johnston & Watson, 2004)

Researchers have argued that synthetic phonics has a major and long-lasting effect on children's reading and spelling attainment and even accelerates the reading and spelling skills in children who have English as a second language (Stuart, 1999). Indeed, explicit phoneme-based training seems to be a good intervention for young children at potential risk of developing reading difficulties, such as dyslexia (Hatcher, Hulme, & Snowling, 2004). Nevertheless, irrespective of our approach to reading instruction, the conclusion is that a focus on teaching children phonological skills generally is crucial to supporting their later reading development. However, when evaluating different methods for teaching reading skills, it is important to be aware of how reading skills may develop in different ways across different languages (see Goswami et al., 2003).

This section has examined how children learn to use language and to read. However, while acquiring a knowledge of language and reading during their early education, children also undergo mathematical instruction, which is looked at in more detail in the next section.

KEY RESEARCHER Usha Goswami

Usha Goswami is Professor of Education at the University of Cambridge and a Fellow of St John's College, Cambridge. In 2005 she became Director of the new Centre for Neuroscience in Education at the faculty. She received her DPhil from Oxford University in 1987. Her research topic was reading and spelling by analogy. Her current research examines relations between phonology and reading, with special reference to rhyme and analogy in reading acquisition, and rhyme processing in dyslexic and deaf children's reading.

A major focus of the research is cross-linguistic, and current projects include cross-language studies of the impact of deficits in auditory temporal processing on reading development and developmental dyslexia; neuroimaging studies of the neural networks underpinning reading in good and poor deaf adult readers; and precursors of reading development in deaf children with cochlear implants.

FIGURE 18.2 Usha Goswami

Usha Goswami has made a significant contribution to our knowledge regarding the role of phonological representations and auditory processing in children with dyslexia. She remains one of the most prominent UK figures in developmental psychology with regard to her work in children's reading development.

18.4.4 DEVELOPMENT OF MATHEMATICAL SKILLS

Mathematics can be considered a universal language, but most of it is explicitly taught. However, it is suggested that some aspects of mathematical knowledge could be innate and present from birth, for example, the ability to discern between different quantities (i.e. large versus small), while understanding of the relationships and associations between numbers are predominantly learnt. Although mathematics can be considered a universal language, there are distinct language and cultural differences in how counting systems are used. For example, in English, words like 'eleven' and 'twelve' do not directly reflect the values that they stand for, 10 + 1 and 10 + 2. In French, the word for 90, *quatre-vingt-dix*, literally translates as four-twenty-ten, again a relatively unclear method of representing numbers. However, in Chinese, the number system is very logical, with words that directly reflect the values that are used. For example, the number 20 in Chinese, *ershí*, literally translates as 'two-ten'. But it is not only the linguistic representation of numbers that differs; the counting systems used also differ. Although the decimal system predominates today, other counting systems, for example the base 20 system in Mayan culture or the old British currency, do exist.

Cultural differences, and the extent of schooling, can have an extensive effect on the development of advanced arithmetic skills. Carraher, Carraher and Schliemann (1985) reported that adult Brazilian street vendors with no formal schooling were able to perform successfully on additive tasks using coins and had a clear understanding of equivalence based upon sets of coins with different numerations. The conclusion was that an understanding of numeration can be obtained orally and not through formal schooling or knowledge of writing numbers.

18.4.5 DEVELOPMENT OF COUNTING PRINCIPLES

Gelman and Gallistel (1978) identified five principles that constrain how children learn to count. The first principle is that of a *one-to-one correspondence* between objects in an array and number. Gelman and Gallistel suggest that children as young as two-and-a-half years old will assign one, and only one, tag to each item in the set. This allows the child to make a direct, one-to-one comparison of quantity between two sets. Children using this principle do not have to be able to assign a specific tag to the quantity, but simply to understand that one item is equivalent to one item in another array. The second principle suggested by Gelman and Gallistel is that of *stable ordering*, whereby the child tags each item with a unique label and follows regular counting constraints. Even if the tags do not match the numbers, for example 1, 2, 5 and 7, stable ordering can be said to be occurring as long as the tags are used in a consistent counting manner and one tag is attributed to each item.

The third principle is that of *property indifference*, in that there is no restriction to what can be counted, for example not only physical objects that share the same properties, but also sounds and actions. The fourth principle is that of *order indifference*, whereby there is understanding that it does not matter where counting starts within an array and that the order in which the items in an array are counted will not affect the counting outcome. Baroody and Gannon (1984) suggest that an ability to understand order indifference is a prerequisite for understanding complex mathematical strategies such as commutativity, in that the order in which items in an array are counted does not affect the final value attributed to the array. As children's instruction in mathematical procedures progress, they show a greater understanding of more conceptual knowledge of the principle of commutativity (e.g. $2 + 4 = 4 + 2$) where children understand that one representation of a problem set $(2 + 4)$ is equivalent to another $(4 + 2)$. Canobi (2004) showed that six- to eight-year-old children had a good understanding of additive commutativity. However, the sample did not fare so well when trying to use such conceptual knowledge to solve subtraction tasks (e.g. $5 - 2 = 3: 5 - 3 = 2$).

Gelman and Gallistel's fifth principle is that of *cardinality*. The principle of cardinality suggests that children can attribute a cardinal value to a set, ascribing the final count item as the value of the set. Wynn (1990) demonstrated a clear distinction between the abilities of two-year-olds and three-year-olds in attributing a cardinal value to a set. When asked to count an array of objects the two-year-olds do not repeat the final value of the set being counted, for example 1, 2, 3, 4, 5, while the three-year-olds will repeat the final label attributing a cardinal value to the set, for instance 1, 2, 3, 4, 5…5. In another of Wynn's experiments, children were required to give a puppet between one and six toys from a pile of soft toy animals. Again, it was only the children aged over three who were able to exhibit counting behaviour and count out the correct number of toys to give to the puppet. The children aged two years old only exhibited grabbing behaviour and no actual selection/counting behaviour. This has been suggested as another example of the development of cardinality in young pre-school children.

EXERCISE: HOW DO YOU SOLVE THIS?

To what extent do children really learn via developmental stages? Siegler (1988) suggests that when solving mathematical problems children have a wide range of strategies available to them, as opposed to progressing through specific developmental stages, and select an appropriate strategy depending upon the task demands.

Look at the following mathematical problems and see which principles or strategies you would use to solve the problems (e.g. counting on, counting all, retrieval, commutativity).

$1 + 1 = ?$
$42 + 37 = ?$
$13 \times 6 = ?$
$5 + 3 = 8: 8 - 5 = ?$

18.4.6 MATHEMATICAL CONCEPTS AND PROCEDURES

Children initially first understand arithmetic problems via the manipulation of objects and relying on very basic procedural strategies that require counting all objects presented in a problem (Resnick, 1992, 1994). Arithmetic becomes more complex when children begin to learn about the distinction between conceptual understanding and procedural knowledge (Canobi, 2004). The acquisition of mathematical knowledge in children generally progresses from laborious and error-prone procedural strategies towards the use of more advanced calculations. For example, young children will shift from using a 'counting all' strategy to a more advanced 'counting on' strategy. For example, they shift from answering a problem such as $3 + 2$ by counting 1, 2, 3, 4, 5 to counting on from the larger addend, 3, 4, 5 (Fuson, 1988; Garnett, 1992; Resnick, 1992; Siegler, 1988).

With more instruction, children's solutions to simple arithmetic problems become more covert and less reliant on the use of procedural strategies, and they do not rely solely on counting numbers on their fingers, but instead start to use more advanced calculations. Once children have become skilled at using procedural strategies they gain a better understanding of conceptual principles such as commutativity and are able to retrieve and utilise simple algorithms to solve problems, for example, if $a + b = c$, then $c + a = b$. Throughout a child's schooling in mathematics the child will utilise a broad range of strategies, with the composition of strategies and relative use of each strategy changing as they become more practised in using them (Siegler, 1996). As the child's conceptual knowledge increases, the child is able to utilise procedural skills more efficiently, calling on strategies that utilise principles such as order indifference, decomposition and non-procedural strategies, such as the direct retrieval of answers from memory (Canobi, Reeve, & Pattison, 1998, 2002, 2003).

18.5 CHANGING DYNAMICS IN A SOCIAL WORLD

Having considered the development of cognitive skills in the school years, the next stage is to consider some of the social issues that many children face as they progress through the school years. In this section we will consider the impact that different social situations may have on a child's later development, with specific emphasis on their school adjustment, the importance of peers and friends, and the role of bullying within the school context.

18.5.1 SCHOOL ADJUSTMENT AND SOCIAL DEVELOPMENT

As children enter school they are exposed to both changes in the physical and social environment and changes in the demands placed upon them. During this time, children must negotiate the complexity of new interpersonal relationships and learn how to behave in an appropriate and conventionally accepted manner (Wentzel, 1999). Therefore, the relationships that children develop with their peers and teachers are particularly important. Also, by developing positive relationships with teachers and peers, children are likely to benefit from the facilitative nature of these relationships during the transition to school (Johnson et al., 2000).

The early years of school are particularly important for fostering a sense of school adjustment, but 13–35% of children experience problems adjusting to school (Hughes, Pinkerton, & Plewis, 1979). The reason why children's initial school adjustment is so important is that the early years of school shape children's trajectories throughout their school career. Further, it is thought that early adjustment problems can lead to continued poor adjustment throughout children's school careers and also poorer academic performance. The reason for this, according to the cumulative deficit hypothesis, is that adjustment problems are perpetuated from one year to the next and cause the children to become more disadvantaged (Ackerman, Brown, & Izard, 2003). Alternative accounts, such as the developmental transaction systems perspective, suggest that children's school adjustment is influenced by the interaction between themselves and the hassles and uplifts in the environment (Santa Lucia et al., 2000). Finally, children's attributions towards their scholastic abilities may also influence their feelings towards, and behaviour in, school, and ultimately bear on their adjustment. Therefore, adjustment problems are not transient or trivial but are influential for later performance and adjustment (Dunn, 1988).

18.5.2 IMPORTANCE OF PEERS AND FRIENDS

One of the important aspects in children's social development concerns their relationship to peers and friends in the school environment. Children form two distinct types of relationship with their peers during the school years: companionship and intimate relationships (Buhrmester & Furman, 1987). Companionship represents the extent to which children are sociable with their peers and the extent to which they spend time sharing in common activities with others. Companionship has been regarded as the extent to which children are accepted by their peers. Peer acceptance is an indicator of how an individual child is regarded in terms of whether they are liked or disliked by a group of other children (Ladd, Birch, & Buhs, 1999). Intimate relationships, on the other hand, are regarded as much more exclusive and specific. Friendships are an example of an intimate relationship because they constitute a positive dyadic relationship which is characterised by an emotional connection between individuals (Ladd et al., 1999). Although both boys and

FIGURE 18.3 Harry and Daniel (age five and in their first year at primary school) are having fun playing lions and tigers and pulling faces in the school playground. The close friendship formed by the boys has helped them to successfully adjust to their new school environment

---

KEY STUDY

Kutnick, P., & Kington, A. (2005). Children's friendship and learning in school: cognitive enhancement through social interaction? *British Journal of Educational Psychology*, *75*, 521–538.

While there is a wealth of literature examining the importance of children's social relationships with their peers for their psychosocial adjustment, relatively few studies have examined the contribution of peers to performance on learning in school. Teachers often ask children to work together in pairs or small groups on tasks in school. Kutnick and Kington explored whether these pairs should comprise children who are friends.

Pairs of children were created based either on whether they were best friends or whether they were acquaintances. Children were asked to nominate their best friends in the class and then, based on these nominations, friendship pairs were created. Acquaintance pairs were created in consultation with the teachers and these had to comprise children who were not best friends but were of the same sex and ability and had previous experience of working together successfully. In total, 36 pairs were created to reflect high, middle and low ability, and the children were sampled from school years 1, 3 and 5 in the UK (approximately aged 5, 8 and 10, respectively). The pairs had to complete two science reasoning tasks. One task involved perspective-based drawing and predicting water levels in a jar that was sealed but tilted. The second task related to volume and weight. From the children's performance on the tasks, the researchers were able to determine the children's cognitive level based on predefined test score norms.

Kutnick and Kington found that girls' friendship pairs performed highest on the science reasoning task, whereas when boys worked in friendship pairs they performed at the lowest levels. When both boys and girls were in pairs of acquaintances they performed in the middle on the reasoning tasks. These findings were consistent across the year groups and also ability levels. Of course, pairing friends together to work on tasks needs to be done with caution. The results of the study suggest that boys do less well when paired with friends, and we're sure that you would agree that in some cases friendship pairs may spend more time solidifying their friendship than turning their attention to the school task in hand.

---

girls develop relationships characterised by intimacy and companionship, there are some differences. Girls tend to have a smaller group of close peers compared to boys, as well as having greater intimacy, companionship and prosocial support with their same-gender peers than boys (Hussong, 2000).

Research suggests that it is important for children to have friends while they are at school. Friendships facilitate children's adjustment to school because they provide academic and scholastic support. Also, children with a higher number of friends perform better academically than children with a lower number of friends. The reason why children's peers are so important for their performance at school is that peers can provide support networks and foster emotional and cognitive development (Hay et al., 2004). The importance of these support networks does not stop when children leave school because children who experience difficulties in establishing and maintaining peer relationships are more likely to experience maladjustment in later life. Having friends during adolescence has also been linked to higher levels of self-esteem and fewer mental health problems during adulthood (Bagwell, Newcomb, & Bukowski, 1998).

18.5.3 BULLYING AND SOCIALISATION

Recent figures suggest that almost half of all children report that they have experienced bullying at school, while teachers report that between 40% and 70% of pupils experience bullying (Bradshaw, Sawyer, & O'Brennan, 2007). 'Bullying' may cover a range of behaviours. Typically, it involves physical, verbal or relational aggression that is repeated and that involves a power difference between individuals. Children report that bullying occurs within the classroom, cafeteria, hallway and playground, with 70% of the children asked by Bradshaw and colleagues (2007) reporting that they had witnessed an instance of bullying within the last month while at school. Bullying is widespread and may adversely affect children's performance at school. Typically, those children who experience bullying tend to have lower academic performance and decreased self-efficacy, which can ultimately influence an individual's later socio-economic status (Schwartz et al., 2005). Given this association between experiencing bullying and adjustment, researchers have developed a number of interventions with the aim to reduce bullying. For example, interventions have been developed that directly target the individuals who experience bullying, whereas other interventions adopt a whole school, such as the KiVa programme developed in Finland (Kärnä et al., 2011). However, children's motives for engaging in bullying behaviours need to be considered when investigating bullying. For example, while some researchers have argued that bullying occurs because of some sorts of skill deficit, it has been suggested that some forms of bullying require high levels of cognitive ability (Juvonen & Graham, 2014).

18.5.4 MORAL DEVELOPMENT

Although developing a sense of morals is a complex process, children appear to be able to have an understanding of morality by the age of five (Helwig & Turiel, 2002). Similar to Piaget's stage theory, Kohlberg (1976) proposed a six-stage theory of moral development. Moral development was assessed through responses to a series of short stories. One of these was about Heinz, whose wife was near to death. A life-saving drug was available, but the drug was very expensive and Heinz could not afford it. Children were asked whether or not Heinz should steal the drug to save his wife.

Based on a series of studies, Kohlberg concluded that we progress through three levels of moral development, each of which has two stages. Stages 1 and 2 represent the pre-conventional level of moral reasoning. In the first stage, obedience to authority represents the right thing to do in a given situation, whereas disobedience is the wrong thing. In the second stage, right is regarded as doing what is in the individual's own interest and, as such, has been termed naive hedonism (Bee & Boyd, 2005). The conventional level (based on agreed rules) contains the third stage of right, in which people judge behaviour by what an individual is expected to do based on their current social role ('I was following orders'). Conversely, in the fourth stage, right is regarded as an action that supports the community and prevents the breakdown of society, so the societal norms are becoming more important in moral reasoning.

The fifth and sixth stages represent post-conventional reasoning (beyond socially agreed rules) where right is considered with regard to universal ethical principles and human rights. People using this level to make judgements will be looking beyond their own advantage, the advantage of their family and even their community when they make their judgements. If you think about the use of torture by the USA to obtain information from prisoners, then at a conventional level you might judge it to be acceptable because it might benefit the USA in their military campaigns; but at the post-conventional level you may judge it to be wrong because it infringes the human rights of the people being interrogated, regardless of who they are and what they have done. Later Kohlberg and Power (1981) argued that there was a seventh, more advanced, stage of moral development. Kohlberg's approach remains very controversial, not least because it seems to be culturally biased and to present people in the USA as more moral than people in most other countries. However, recent research does suggest that the stage descriptions are a useful way of looking at moral development (Boom, Wouter, & Keller, 2007).

Children typically give moral reasons for actions, which suggests that they have an understanding of moral behaviour equivalent to stage 1 in Kohlberg's model, with later stages becoming evident as children develop (Helwig & Turiel, 2002). However, there is debate over this notion of development, since some evidence suggests

KEY STUDY

Lillard, A.S. (2012). Preschool children's development in classic Montessori, supplemented Montessori, and conventional programs. *Journal of School Psychology*, *50*(3), 379–401.

Unlike conventional education programmes, the Montessori approach to education encourages children to have more choice in their learning activities from within the curriculum and places an emphasis on learning through action, with a focus on small-group or one-to-one teaching. Children are also placed in more flexible groupings and thus comprise mixed age groups. In classical Montessori education, the programme reflects the original programme outlined by Dr Montessori (1967), with a three-hour work block in the morning and, for children aged over four years, another three-hour block in the afternoon. Children are also educated within three-year groupings as opposed to the more traditional year-based cohorts. However, many of these approaches have been adapted to fit with cultural demands and more conventional educational outcomes, including the use of worksheets and set craft projects, where, as in a classical Montessori setup, the children have a free choice of tasks from low shelves that are organised into the Montessori curriculum areas. As a result, much of the literature on the effectiveness of these schools has been mixed.

Angeline Lillard (2012) set out to examine whether there was a difference between classic Montessori, supplemented Montessori or conventional schooling programmes on pre-schoolers' academic achievement and 'school readiness'. School readiness measured several outcomes, including theory of mind, executive functioning and social problem solving. In addition to these, reading, vocabulary and mathematic understanding provided the measures of academic achievement. In the study, Lillard sampled children aged between 33 months and 76 months, with 36 children coming from classical Montessori programmes, 95 from supplemented Montessori and 41 from conventional education programmes.

Taking into account the age and the demographics of the children, the classical Montessori setup showed greater end-of-year gains in executive functioning and social problem solving, although there was no significant difference between schooling programmes for gains in theory of mind. In addition, Lillard showed that a greater use of the classic Montessori materials within the classroom predicted greater gains in early reading and vocabulary. The key findings were that higher fidelity (classic) Montessori programmes were associated with significant gains in student achievement and social development compared with supplemented (non-classic) Montessori and conventional schooling. However, the author does acknowledge that parental influence may confound the findings as, ultimately, it is the parents who choose what school to send their child to. The participant demographics were also largely middle- to high-income children from well-educated backgrounds. Therefore, Lillard suggests that further follow-up studies are required to assess the impact of classical Montessori programmes on lower-income children and longitudinally across their schooling.

that individuals may on occasion regress to earlier stages (Gibbs et al., 2007). An adult example would be the expenses crisis in the UK Parliament in 2009. The Members of Parliament are used to making decisions based on the highest moral values, and some MPs chose to go against their colleagues and the Government to vote against the war on Iraq (stage 6). However, some of these same people used the much lower-level defence of 'it was in the rules' (stage 3) when it came to filling out their expenses and claiming for their moats to be cleaned or for houses for their parents to live in.

In addition, some researchers argue that the methods used to assess children's morals are very different from children's day-to-day experiences. More recently, researchers have used prosocial reasoning tasks (Eisenberg, 1986, 1992) and distributive justice tasks (Damon, 1977, 1980) to overcome the problems of asking the children to choose between two negative acts, as in the case of the original Heinz story. The prosocial reasoning tasks involve children being presented with scenarios where there is a choice between acting in a prosocial way that would benefit someone else or engaging in a behaviour that would serve their own self-interest. They then articulate to a researcher what they would do and why. The distributive justice task is an experimental task that allows researchers to examine children's understanding of social norms and their understanding of sharing with others. It measures children's knowledge of a range of different social norms while at the same time maximising rewards for themselves. This task has more recently been used to capture children's moral understanding.

EXERCISE: HOW MORAL ARE WE AS ADULTS?

Read the passage below (an adaptation of Kohlberg's passage), and then consider the five questions that follow. There are no right or wrong answers, but your attempt at answering the questions should provide a nice illustration with regard to some of the difficulties that many children face in developing moral understanding.

A woman is very ill, and the only drug that the doctors think might save her costs around £2,000. The drug was expensive to make, but the chemist is charging 10 times what the drug cost him to make – he paid £200 for the drug and charges £2,000 for a small dose to each customer. The sick woman's husband, Heinz, has been to everyone he knows to borrow the money, but he has only accumulated £1,000. He has been unable to raise the money to save his wife. So Heinz has become desperate and is considering breaking into the chemist's store to steal the drug for his wife.

1. Should Heinz steal the drug? Why or why not?
2. It is against the law for Heinz to steal. Does that make it morally wrong? Why or why not?
3. Should people do everything they can to avoid breaking the law?
4. How does this relate to Heinz's case?
5. Is there anything else that Heinz can do that is morally right?

18.6 CHAPTER SUMMARY

In this chapter we have looked at the concept of children's development during the school years, with a particular focus on cognitive, language and social skills. Specifically, we have examined what factors influence children's development as they enter school. We have discussed cognitive development during the school years and considered the implications of Piaget's and Vygotsky's theories for understanding children's learning. The chapter has focused on how children develop language, theory of mind and social reasoning during the school years, all of which are important skills for later development and social interactions. We have also discussed aspects of children's development within the context of school, including the importance of cultural tools and classroom-led instruction, and have focused particularly on early reading development and mathematical understanding. Finally, the chapter reviewed the changing dynamics of children's social world as they enter school by discussing school adjustment, socialisation and friendships, and the development of moral understanding. All of these topics emphasise the relative importance of the social context in explaining and understanding children's development in the school years and reinforce the argument that development can only occur through a child's interaction with their social environment.

(?) DISCUSSION QUESTIONS

How can the theories of cognitive development be applied to children's learning in school? How can the psychological literature inform teaching practices?

What are the key similarities and differences between Piaget's and Vygotsky's theories of development? How important are cultural tools in children's educational development?

What are the best ways to teach a child to read? Can you remember learning to read? Think about the strategies you used and how you would teach someone learning to read.

How do children develop a sense of moral understanding during the school years? How important are peer relationships to children's social development?

SUGGESTIONS FOR FURTHER READING

Crain, W.C. (2000). *Theories of development: concepts and applications*. Engelwood Cliffs, NJ: Prentice Hall. A good text that covers a range of different theories and perspectives predominant in developmental psychology and introduces students to varying perspectives in understanding child psychology.

Goswami, U., & Bryant, P. (1990). *Phonological skills and learning to read*. Hove: Erlbaum. A good text that clearly outlines the way in which children learn to read, with supporting evidence and clear psychological models of reading acquisition.

Pinker, S. (1995). *The language instinct: the new science of language and mind*. London: Penguin. This text is primarily aimed at addressing the development of language from an innate perspective, and allows students to understand the arguments in favour of nativist approaches to explaining early language development.

Smith, P., Cowie, H., & Blades, M. (2011). *Understanding children's development* (5th edn). West Sussex: Wiley-Blackwell. An introductory text that covers a range of approaches, including different social, emotional and cognitive aspects of children's development, in an easily accessible format.

Smith, P.K., & Hart, C.H. (2010). *Wiley-Blackwell handbook of childhood social development* (2nd edn). Oxford: Blackwell. A very detailed text that examines children's early social development across a range of different perspectives. This will provide a solid foundation for examining recent studies in social development.

Still want more? For links to online resources relevant to this chapter and a quiz to test your understanding, visit the companion website at edge.sagepub.com/banyard2e

19 ATYPICAL CHILD DEVELOPMENT

Lead authors: Gayle Dillon, Janine Coates, Andrew Grayson and Susannah Lamb

CHAPTER OUTLINE

19.1 Introduction	**332**
19.2 What is atypical development?	**332**
19.3 Within-child factors	**333**
19.3.1 Abnormalities, dysfunction or damage to the brain	333
19.3.2 Genetic factors	334
19.3.3 Developmental or maturational lag	336
19.3.4 Critical or sensitive periods	337
19.4 Outside influences on atypical development	**339**
19.4.1 'Outside-the-child' factors	339
19.4.2 Expectation and the self-fulfilling prophecy	339
19.4.3 Labelling	340
19.4.4 Providing appropriate opportunities	342
19.4.5 Providing appropriate learning contexts	343
19.4.6 Models of disability	344
19.5 Chapter summary	**345**
Discussion questions	**345**
Suggestions for further reading	**345**
Answers to exercise	**346**

19.1 INTRODUCTION

Every child is unique, possessing their own collection of abilities and talents which develop at their own pace. However, many children follow more or less predictable patterns of growth, and common features may be observed in the ways that cognitions, feelings and behaviours develop. This means we can build up a pattern of how most children develop (typical development) while being aware that not everyone follows this pattern (atypical development). Psychologists need to understand how typical development comes about and also what the implications of this are when dealing with children who develop atypically. The study of atypical development is essential for aiding our understanding of the diversity of paths that children can develop along and also for understanding their individual needs.

FRAMING QUESTIONS

- What is typical development?
- What is atypical development?
- How do factors (1) within the child and (2) external to the child contribute to atypical development?
- Are explanations of 'within' and 'external' factors of atypical development mutually exclusive?

19.2 WHAT IS ATYPICAL DEVELOPMENT?

Previous chapters have mainly been concerned with typical patterns of child development. However, not all children follow a typical developmental trajectory. Understanding why some children develop problems or difficulties that require specialist support or intervention is a key concern of developmental psychologists. Before we can begin to explore what is meant by the term 'atypical development', it is important to be clear about what typical development entails. Children who are classed as typically developing are those who follow a predictable developmental trajectory of physical and psychological development, achieving various milestones along the way. Such milestones relate to cognition (such as thinking, reasoning, problem solving, understanding), language, motor coordination (crawling, walking, jumping, hopping, throwing, catching), social interaction (initiating peer contact, group play) and adaptive development (dressing, eating, washing).

This developmental process may be disrupted, however, by biological and environmental factors which can result in a child developing in ways which do not follow an expected trajectory and which can be characterised as 'atypical child development'.

Many cultural, societal and personal values affect our classifications of typical and atypical development. For example, typical sleep patterns of young infants can vary dramatically across cultures. In their discussion about this kind of cross-cultural variation in development, Super and Harkness (1977) make a comparison between mothers in the USA and mothers of infants in rural western Kenya. Because of the different family practices framed by these different cultures, babies in the USA demonstrate much longer periods of sustained sleep compared with rural Kenyan babies. As well as recognising the role of culture in our description of what is typical and not typical, we need to acknowledge variation in development which can be attributed to individual differences. Just because one seven-year-old child demonstrates a particular ability and their friend of the same age does not, this is not necessarily an indication that either child's development is atypical. In any analysis of child development there is an acknowledgement that there can be a great deal of variation in the rates at which children 'typically' acquire certain skills.

The aim of this chapter is to discuss atypical child development from two key perspectives: explanations of atypical development that occurs as a result of factors described as arising from *within* the child, and explanations of atypical development that occurs as a result of factors that are *external* to the child. These factors are presented in separate sections only for the purposes of clarity. In reality, child development is a function of complex interactions between within-child factors and factors that are external to the child.

19.3 WITHIN-CHILD FACTORS

This section aims to highlight the role of several factors which psychologists might describe as being 'internal' to the child that might contribute to atypical development. In particular, it focuses on four explanations. These include abnormalities or damage to a child's brain, genetic factors, the concept of a developmental or maturational lag, and the notion of a critical or sensitive period of development.

19.3.1 ABNORMALITIES, DYSFUNCTION OR DAMAGE TO THE BRAIN

Our brains begin to develop around three weeks after conception, and at around seven months after conception the basic structure of the brain is complete (Nowakowski & Hayes, 2002). In the months following birth, the brain grows rapidly to end up forming a highly specialised mature brain with different psychological functions localised to particular regions, such as the ability to make and carry out plans. Of particular interest to developmental psychologists is what impact abnormalities or damage to the brain have on child development.

Numerous studies have investigated the impact of brain damage on development, in particular with respect to the timing of the damage relative to developmental stage. For example, Stiles et al. (2005) report that young children often recover skills after brain injury better than older children and adults. This is thought to be because certain functions are more easily reorganised in the young brain which may have greater **plasticity** (flexibility of organisation)

PLASTICITY The ability of the brain to adapt to deficits or injury.

AUTISM Another developmental disorder which represents a wide-ranging spectrum of behaviours. Diagnosis is usually made according to difficulties found in aspects of communication, social skills and repetitive behaviours.

ATTENTION DEFICIT HYPERACTIVITY DISORDER A behaviour disorder, usually first diagnosed in childhood, that is characterised by inattention, impulsivity and, in some cases, hyperactivity.

than older brains. Take, for example, a child who has been involved in a collision with a car in which some degree of brain damage occurred. If this damage leads to impaired language skills (because the left hemisphere of the brain took most of the impact from the collision) it would not be unusual for a young child's brain to be able to compensate for the damage and for full language skills to be restored several months later. This is because, in young children, the job of the damaged neural structures can be taken on by other structures which have not yet become specialised to other areas.

Brain damage does not just occur through traumatic injury, however. During development, the process of brain organisation can be interrupted or changed through other causal mechanisms, which are hypothesised to be the cause of several types of atypical development, such as **autism** or **attention deficit hyperactivity disorder** (ADHD). In the case of autism, Baird, Cass and Slonims (2003) argue that a variety of causes can underlie the atypical or disrupted development of the central nervous system that results in brain structures, such as the cerebellum, working differently in children and adults with autism (Allen & Courchesne, 2003; O'Halloran, Kinsella, & Storey, 2012).

Similarly, in the case of ADHD, one of the leading biological explanations suggests that hyperactivity is caused by brain abnormalities in three areas of the brain: the frontal lobes, the basal ganglia and the cerebellum (Casey, 2001; O'Halloran et al., 2012). Interestingly, other research suggests that ADHD is predominantly a genetic disorder, which underpins these differences found in the brains of individuals with ADHD (Campbell, 2000; Nadder et al., 2001). For example, twin studies show that identical twins are often both diagnosed with ADHD, whereas in fraternal twins (non-identical twins), this is uncommon (Pennington, Willcutt, & Rhee, 2005; Plomin, 1990). The exact primary cause of ADHD remains unclear, although many researchers would agree that it is the result of an interplay between genetics, brain abnormalities and the environment (Gelfand, Jensen, & Drew, 1997).

EXERCISE: LOOK INTO MY EYES

Terrified

Amused

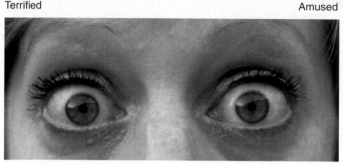

Regretful

Flirtatious

FIGURE 19.1 The eyes have it

Look at this picture of a pair of eyes. There are four emotion labels around the picture. The task is to select which one of the four emotions corresponds to the emotion that the eyes are showing.

This is one test that is used to explore social intelligence, specifically a person's ability to understand what another person might be feeling. The emotion displayed here is 'terrified'. The test presents 36 pictures of eyes, each with four mental state term descriptors. Only one of the descriptors is correct, the remaining three are distractors. Baron-Cohen et al. (2001) used this task to test the ability of individuals with autism to recognise emotion just from looking at the eyes. Individuals with autism typically find this task more difficult than individuals without autism and it is suggested this is related to atypical patterns of development with regard to social skills and understandings.

19.3.2 GENETIC FACTORS

CHROMOSOME A thread-like strand of DNA that carries the genes.

DNA Deoxyribonucleic acid, a chemical found primarily in the nucleus of cells. DNA carries the instructions or blueprint for making all the structures and materials that the body needs to function.

PHENYLKETONURIA An inherited, metabolic disorder that can result in learning difficulties and other neurological problems. People with this disease have difficulty breaking down and using the amino acid phenylalanine. PKU can be managed by a diet restricted in foods that contain this amino acid.

HUNTINGTON'S DISEASE A dominant genetic disorder in which a protein is produced abnormally, leading to the breakdown in the parts of the brain that control movement.

DOWN SYNDROME A congenital disorder, caused by the presence of an extra 21st chromosome. Also called trisomy 21.

The field of genetics looks at the way that traits and characteristics are passed down from one generation to another through a person's genes. The first stage of development begins at conception when each of us receives a unique combination of genes from our parents. At conception, 23 **chromosomes** from a father's sperm cell unite with 23 chromosomes from a mother's egg cell to form a new life. Contained within these chromosomes are our genes, which are the basic units of heredity. Our genes in turn are composed of a chemical called **deoxyribonucleic acid** (our **DNA**) (Kail, 2007).

In typical development, the newly fertilised egg proceeds through a process of rapid cell division and eventually, after around nine months of gestation, a baby is born. However, not all successful conceptions result in the birth of a child, with two out of every three being spontaneously aborted in the early months of pregnancy. In the majority of these cases the embryo has genetic or chromosomal abnormalities (Rosenblith, 1992) and the body's expulsion of the embryo is considered to be an example of natural selection. The more severe the abnormality, the less likely it is that the baby will survive to term or survive the trauma of birth.

Thousands of genetic disorders have been recognised so far. However, there are only a small number of these disorders for which we know what the contributing genes are and the ways in which these are thought to contribute. We do know that the genetic contribution to a disorder can occur in one of several ways. The first is through single-gene effects where an abnormality is due to the action of a recessive gene which both parents carry and which is passed on to the foetus at conception. **Phenylketonuria** (PKU) is an example of a

KEY RESEARCHER Simon Baron-Cohen

Simon Baron-Cohen is director of the Autism Research Centre (ARC) in Cambridge. He is also Professor of Developmental Psychopathology at the University of Cambridge. Baron-Cohen's first degree was in Human Sciences from New College, Oxford, followed by a PhD in Psychology from University College London, and an MPhil in Clinical Psychology from the Institute of Psychiatry.

Baron-Cohen's main research interests lie in seeking to identify the basic mental processes that are specific in autistic spectrum conditions. One of his key contributions to this area of research was the suggestion that children with autism find it difficult to read and understand other people's minds, which he termed 'mindblindness'. Whereas typically developing children and young people may find it relatively straightforward to work out what someone else is thinking or feeling, Baron-Cohen argues that those with autism find this difficult. This in turn, he suggests, impacts on an individual's ability to communicate and interact in the social world.

Some of Baron-Cohen's research focuses on testing the 'extreme male brain' theory of autism. This theory is based on the idea that babies who are exposed to high levels of male hormones in the womb (and thus who are more likely to develop what Baron-Cohen describes as an 'extreme male brain') are more likely to develop traits that are typical of autism.

FIGURE 19.2   Simon Baron-Cohen

recessive gene disorder which affects the metabolic system. The second is through dominant gene conditions. These are rarer than recessive single-gene conditions and can be passed down from one parent only (giving the child a 50% chance of inheriting the condition). The condition will usually show up in all carriers and so is relatively easy to identify. **Huntington's disease**, which affects the central nervous system to produce progressive dementia and involuntary movements, is an example of a dominant gene condition (Simpson & Harding, 1993).

Chromosomal disorders arise due to abnormalities in one or more pairs of chromosomes, which are present in every cell of the body. The most frequently used example of a chromosome disorder is **Down syndrome**, in which there is typically an extra chromosome 21 (so instead of having two copies of chromosome 21, individuals with Down syndrome have three). Down syndrome, which occurs in approximately one in 1,000 individuals, is thought to be caused by chance, one-off events in either the egg or the sperm cells. It is not, therefore, a hereditary disorder.

KEY STUDY

Wong, C., Meaburn, E., Ronald, A., Price, T.S., Jeffries, A., Schalkwyk, L., Plomin, R., & Mill, J. (2013). Methylomic analysis of monozygotic twins discordant for autism spectrum disorder and related behavioural traits. *Molecular Psychiatry*, *19*, 495–503.

Autism is a complex developmental disorder which occurs in approximately 1% of the population. It is commonly considered to be genetically determined. Researchers examining the causes of autism have found that it has strong

(Continued)

(Continued)

hereditability and, like many other developmental disorders, characteristics can often be present in several family members. Historically, this fact was used as evidence for the 'nature' side of the nature/nurture debate, which argues that atypical development has a strong genetic basis. However, over the last decade, a new area of genetic research called epigenetics (see Chapter 1) has started to question the deterministic claims of previous genetic research. Epigenetics refers to the way DNA is expressed and how it can be modified by external factors, turning certain characteristics or traits 'on' or 'off', much like a light switch.

Recent research has started to explore the reasons why some identical (also known as monozygotic) twins have very different autism characteristics despite having the same DNA. Typically, we would expect identical twins to have the same autism characteristics because they share the same DNA. This, however, is not the case because identical twins can be different in the ways that they behave and think. This new branch of epigenetic research has started to consider how we can use genetics to understand these differences in human development. Twin studies are a very good place to start. They allow researchers to understand how external environments interact with genes. Identical twins are important for this because while they share the same DNA, they might experience very different situations in their external environment and it is these 'transactions' between genes and their environment that are at the heart of epigenetics.

Epigeneticists study chemical reactions that occur at the genome site. The genome is the map of all genetic material found in our DNA. These chemical reactions are what modify sections of the genome which control certain behaviours depending on specific environmental factors.

Wong et al. put this to the test. A sample of 50 15-year-old identical twin pairs, all of whom were identified as being 'at risk' of autism on a standardised childhood autism scale, had their DNA tested for these chemical reactions. All of the twins involved had dissimilar autism characteristics compared to their identical twin (they were therefore said to be 'disconcordant').

DNA for each individual was extracted from a blood sample and tested at points of the genome which affect autism behaviours. Results showed significant differences in chemical reactions at these points for various autism characteristics which, the authors argue, explain the differences in characteristics between these twins.

These findings shed light on our understanding of genetics and autism. They show that genes are not static or unchanging and that there are environmental factors at play which might lead to these chemical differences – factors which determine when a genetic switch is turned on or off. In this study, the authors argue that it is the twins' non-shared environment which might have led to these changes. So, while two identical twins will have the same DNA, will be the same age, will have the same family and will probably go to the same school, there are other things that happen in their environment which are different. For example, they might have different friendship groups, eat different foods or be exposed to different chemicals in the environment. It is these environments which might lead to the changes in their gene expression, which result in their different characteristics.

These results help researchers to unravel complex developmental disorders such as autism, prompting a closer look at the environments in which children grow up. Although this area of study is in its infancy, there is still a lot to discover about the specific environmental factors that lead to these changes. Learning more about how genes work could, in the future, lead to new treatments for developmental disorders like autism. Nevertheless, research into epigenetic factors has started to bridge the gap between 'nature' and 'nurture'.

19.3.3 DEVELOPMENTAL OR MATURATIONAL LAG

Another key issue in the study of atypical development is the concept known as the developmental or **maturational lag**, which refers to delayed maturity in one or more areas of development. This explanation again mainly attributes the cause of atypical development to factors within the child. For example, children diagnosed with learning difficulties have been described as being characterised by a maturation lag which reflects delayed progress in certain aspects of neurological development. Since their rate of development is significantly slower than that of typically developing children, children with learning difficulties more frequently function at an immature stage for their age and consequently fail to attain the same final level of competence. This concept of immaturity suggests that the child continues to develop in the area of difficulty and may eventually reach a more typical level of competence in certain tasks. One of the main areas of research that has utilised the idea of the developmental lag is reading development, where researchers have investigated at what point parents and educators should be concerned about delays in a child's reading ability (Fletcher & Morris, 2011; Satz et al., 1978).

19.3.4 CRITICAL OR SENSITIVE PERIODS

A critical or sensitive period is a time during the lifespan in which an organism may be affected by a specific experience or event, more so than at any other time in development (Colombo, 1982). According to the critical period hypothesis, a child is more susceptible to environmental stimulation during a critical period than at other times during the lifespan. If specific experiences occur during this period, then development will continue on its typical course. If these specific experiences do not occur, there may be a significant disruption or difficulty in subsequent development.

The concept of a critical period is drawn predominantly from the work of ethologist Konrad Lorenz (1981), who noted that the young of some species, for example hens and ducks, learn to follow their mother soon after birth. Lorenz found that while the following behaviour was driven by instinct (also known as a 'canalised' process), there is some flexibility in learning what or whom to follow. Typically, young birds were found to learn the characteristics of a moving object during a period soon after hatching, which they then followed. This process of knowing which object to follow is known as *imprinting* and usually occurs in relation to the mother, since she is the main figure the offspring encounters during the critical or sensitive period after birth. Imprinting in which the young learn the characteristics of the parent is known as filial imprinting. However, Lorenz also found that imprinting to other objects can occur and he successfully imprinted ducklings on himself so that they then followed him.

Following on from this work on imprinting, Lorenz introduced the term **critical period** to describe the restricted period in which he believed imprinting took place. The critical period is defined by a window of opportunity which begins and ends abruptly and is a period beyond which the development of a specific behaviour or skill is unlikely to occur. This is contrasted with the notion of a **sensitive period** which is believed to begin and end more gradually than a critical period. The sensitive period refers to a time in which the organism is in a stage of maximum sensitivity to learning rather than a strict window of opportunity.

The idea of critical and sensitive periods has been shown to be valuable in studies of many aspects of development, including language acquisition, the development of attachment behaviours, and susceptibility to later psychopathology (Roth & Sweatt, 2011; Schaffer, 2000). In 1967, Eric Lenneberg first proposed the notion of a critical period for language acquisition which, he suggested, was the period between infancy and puberty (the beginning of adolescence). This period was thought to end at puberty because of important maturational changes in the brain that occur at this time. Evidence to support the notion of a critical period in language development comes from studies of children brought up in deprived circumstances.

MATURATIONAL LAG A delay in reaching developmental milestones. Generally, it suggests a non-linear rate of development.

GENERAL LEARNING DIFFICULTIES Global difficulties in learning which mean a child has different patterns of learning, or may learn more slowly, than same-age peers.

SPECIFIC LEARNING DIFFICULTIES Neurological-based difficulties that affect the way information is learned and processed. It is an umbrella term used to describe difficulties such as dyslexia, dyspraxia and dyscalculia. A child may have difficulties with one or two areas of learning, but other aspects of development are unaffected.

FIGURE 19.3 Konrad Lorenz taking his imprinted ducklings for a stroll

© Science Photo Library

CRITICAL PERIOD A limited period, usually early in life, in which a child is required to be exposed to a particular skill or experience in order for it to be learned.

SENSITIVE PERIOD A period of development, usually early in life, during which the individual is most sensitive to certain types of experience or learning. It refers to a period that is more extended than a critical period.

ATTACHMENT BEHAVIOUR Any behaviour that helps to form or establish an emotional bond between two individuals. Strong attachment bonds are usually formed between an infant and his or her caregiver.

Illustrative examples of the concept of a critical or sensitive period can also be found in the domain of social development. One particularly interesting example is the formation of the infant–parent attachment relationship. **Attachment** is defined as the strong emotional ties between an infant and a caregiver and is thought to develop over the first year of the child's life, in particular during the second six months of the first year (see also Chapter 17).

John Bowlby, a twentieth-century English psychiatrist, formulated and presented a comprehensive theory of attachment. Bowlby was the first to propose that there is a strong biological basis for the development of attachment behaviours. Accordingly. the infant–parent attachment relationship was suggested to develop because it is important to the survival of the infant. For example, a secure attachment provides a base from which the infant can feel safe exploring their environment.

KEY STUDY

Curtiss, S. (Ed.) (1977). *Genie: psycholinguistic study of a modern-day 'Wild Child'.* **New York: Academic Press.**

Genie was a girl discovered in 1970s America at the age of 13 after having been kept in virtual isolation for the majority of her life. After being told that Genie had possible learning difficulties at the age of two, her father kept her locked in her bedroom. She was tied to a potty chair for the majority of the day, and at night she was placed in a cot covered with a metal cover to keep her inside. Her mother and brother were forbidden to talk to her and she was growled at like a dog if she made a noise in order to keep her quiet.

Eventually, Genie's mother ran away, taking Genie to a welfare office in California. Genie's parents were initially charged with child abuse after welfare officers became concerned by Genie's poor development relative to her age. When she was discovered at around the age of 13, she had some understanding of language but did not speak. After a year of intensive training and instruction, she had a vocabulary of about 200 words and was speaking in two-word sentences. She walked awkwardly, had very little language and only ate baby food. After spending around a year in hospital, Genie went to live with one of her therapists. She was placed on an intensive programme of language and social development which allowed more insight into critical periods for language acquisition.

Although Genie made good progress in terms of her language development, she never became a proficient user of language and grammar. She also demonstrated some difficulties in forming attachments. After four years of living with her therapist, the funding that had been allocated to look after her was cut and she was returned to hospital, and eventually to her biological mother. Despite having made much progress, Genie still displayed some difficult behaviour, such as tantrums, and her mother found her difficult to cope with. Genie was subsequently placed in a series of foster homes where she was sometimes treated very badly, and she regressed dramatically.

What Genie's case shows us is that extreme deprivation and neglect have serious and long-lasting effects on both emotional and cognitive development. While the effects of such deprivation can be tempered by good support systems in later years, it appears to be very difficult to encourage development along a more typical developmental trajectory where severe deprivation has been prolonged and sustained.

Bowlby (1944, 1969) suggested that there was a sensitive period for the formation of the attachment relationship, by which he meant that strong attachment bonds were more likely to form within a constrained time frame. Bowlby's hypothesis was based in part on the findings from his work with juvenile thieves, the majority of whom he established had experienced early and prolonged separation from their mothers. Bowlby concluded from this that there is a significant relationship between maternal deprivation in infancy and subsequent emotional maladjustment.

It is now recognised, however, that even if an infant does not have access to a secure and loving relationship with a particular caregiver early in life, but does so later in life, it is still possible for an affectionate bond to be established. As a group, however, children who develop a bond later in life appear to be at increased risk for insecure or maladaptive attachment relationships with their adopted parents (DeKlyen & Speltz, 2001).

19.4 OUTSIDE INFLUENCES ON ATYPICAL DEVELOPMENT

Previous sections of this chapter have outlined some of psychology's contributions to understanding how and why development might not proceed as expected. These explanations have focused on factors which are considered to be 'internal' to the child, and generally arise from attempts to identify specific genetic, biological and cognitive differences. These differences can be related to a developmental trajectory that is considered to be atypical in domains such as social behaviour, communication and learning. Sometimes we observe unusual patterns of behaviours which we do not expect to see (e.g. in autism). In other cases, we observe behaviours that are more typical but occur later than we would expect (as we may see in children with learning difficulties). By understanding the internal causes of atypical development, we gain insight into the educational and social support that children might need, and at the same time we increase our theoretical understanding of typical development.

There are, however, other considerations when we are thinking about atypical development. Some of these require a shift in the way we think about the developmental trajectory, and we will return to these towards the end of the chapter. First, however, we will consider some aspects of psychological understanding that illustrate the significant contribution of factors which are external to the child, and which may play a part in the development of atypical behaviour. To do this we will first identify some environmental factors which have been demonstrated to relate quite clearly to children's development, particularly with respect to school performance and social and emotional development. The remainder of the discussion will then focus on a range of psychological constructs that contribute to our understanding of the causal effects (on typical and atypical development) of aspects of the child's environment.

19.4.1 'OUTSIDE-THE-CHILD' FACTORS

There are a range of factors 'external' to children that have an effect on children's behaviour and that may be thought to play some causal role in atypical development, such as the disadvantageous effects of different environments in which children may be brought up. For example, there has been much research into the effects of poverty on children's development. Duncan, Brooks-Gunn and Klebanov (1994) demonstrated that poor children usually do less well in school and score lower on standard IQ tests than wealthier children. Another aspect of the child's environment that has been of interest to researchers is that of family background, particularly with respect to the potential effects of divorce or separation. We use the word 'potential' here to highlight the fact that although there is evidence that has demonstrated the significant distress and consequent effect on children's behaviour when parents separate, this is not the only outcome for children of split families. Where the separation is managed carefully and the child's perspective is taken into account, the children might actually be at lower risk for the range of social, behavioural and academic problems that are sometimes associated with family discord (Hetherington & Stanley-Hagan, 1999). There are also, clearly, the effects of abusive relationships on children to consider (see the example of Genie, in the key study above).

19.4.2 EXPECTATION AND THE SELF-FULFILLING PROPHECY

In 1968, a study was undertaken by Rosenthal and Jacobson that has important implications for our understanding of children's development. These researchers demonstrated that, within a school situation, teachers' beliefs about children's abilities can affect how much children learn. More specifically, teachers in this study were told that some of the children in their classes had been identified through tests to be very likely to make great progress in the coming year. In actual fact, the children identified in this way had simply been selected at random from the school population.

What seemed to happen over a period of time was that those children who were expected by the teachers to do well actually *did* do better than those children for whom their teachers' expectations were lower, despite the real similarities of the groups. That is, the *expectations* of the teachers seemed to be exerting a causal effect on the

> **SELF-FULFILLING PROPHECY** A prediction that directly or indirectly causes itself to become true.

children's learning. Notwithstanding various methodological critiques of the study (Snow, 1969; Thorndike, 1968), this stands as an example of what has been termed a **self-fulfilling prophecy** (Merton, 1957). This refers to the suggestion that people tend to act in the way that others expect of them, or indeed in ways that they have come to expect of themselves.

The fact that our own and others' expectations influence behaviour is therefore a potentially significant factor for our understanding of the influences on development which lie outside the child. Rosenthal and Jacobson were specifically interested in the effect of teachers' expectations on children's performance in school tasks. However, given the many other studies that have investigated the powerfully causal role of expectations, it would seem reasonable to apply the same logic to other aspects of children's behaviour across other contexts. For example, if teachers' expectations can be demonstrated to affect children's learning, then maybe there are examples of adult expectations about other aspects of development (such as social behaviour or communication) that also have an effect on children's behaviour.

One question we can ask here, for example, concerns what happens when a parent learns that their newborn baby has a disability. Not surprisingly, a range of emotional reactions come with hearing this news, with feelings of anxiety and shock very often followed by elements of denial or disbelief. Of course, this very difficult situation is at times further exacerbated by the mothers having more limited contact with their babies in the period after birth than would normally be the case. Ludman, Lansdown and Spitz (1992) found that infants who underwent major surgery during their early days, and thus who were separated from their parents for lengthy periods, demonstrated an increased incidence of behavioural problems at age three, with higher rates of difficulties in the mother–child relationship compared with controls. The question here is whether these factors (maternal anxiety and the effects of early separation) alter the mother–child relationship in a way that will have consequences for the child in the long term. This is a good example of the potential 'external' influences on atypical behaviour.

Here, then, a range of evidence indicates that it is important to consider people's expectations when reflecting on possible 'outside' influences on behaviour. With respect to understanding atypical development, there would appear to be a continuum on which we might judge the significance of this effect. At one end of this continuum, it might be the case that expectations of others serve to increase aspects of the atypical behaviour; at the other end, there may be examples of expectations actually *causing* atypical development. For example, one of the key factors in adolescent drug abuse is known to be the availability of drugs and people to tempt such use (Herbert, 2008). Key characteristics of those using drugs are commonly cited as low self-esteem, a poor sense of psychological wellbeing and low academic aspirations (Herbert, 2008). Previous research has unequivocally demonstrated the links between societal expectations, the self-fulfilling prophecy and self-esteem (Krishna, 1971). We know that the expectations placed on an individual impact on their self-perception, in turn impacting on behavioural choices. Thus it is clear that there may be a causal link between expectation and atypical behaviour.

19.4.3 LABELLING

At this point it is important to refer to the process of 'labelling'. This creates a real tension within groups of people who are associated with children demonstrating atypical development, for example, parents, educationalists and clinicians. By labelling, we refer to the business of identifying a particular pattern of atypical behaviours and consequently attaching a label of diagnosis to the child demonstrating those behaviours. Many parents feel that having a label (a diagnosis) to describe their child's behaviours (e.g. dyslexia or autism) is an important step in ensuring that their child receives appropriate educational, social and financial support. It can also provide the child with a useful understanding about why they find some aspects of their work or their lives more difficult than their peers.

On the other hand, as we have just seen, a label might make other people expect a certain pattern of behaviour, which may indeed lead to an increase in that behaviour. A good example here is to consider the potential effects of the label of dyslexia on a school-aged child. It could be that being labelled dyslexic not only gives the child an 'excuse' for not doing well at school, but also means that the teacher may assume that the child is not going to succeed at the same level as their peers.

One of the ways in which a child is diagnosed with a condition, and therefore labelled, is through the use of diagnostic manuals (see Chapter 24). The **Diagnostic and Statistical Manual**, also known as the **DSM**, is one handbook available to clinicians to determine whether a child displays behaviours that are clinically important and which fit

DSM This stands for the Diagnostic and Statistical Manual that is published by the American Psychiatric Association. It is a diagnostic manual that it used by clinicians to diagnose a range of disorders in children and adults.

ICD This stands for the International Classification of Diseases which is a diagnostic tool that is used for defining and reporting diseases and health conditions. Whereas the DSM is produced by a single, national professional body, the ICD is produced by the World Health Organisation.

the description of a particular disorder. This can be very useful as it means that clinicians have a universal, standardised descriptor of a condition that they can use, alongside other measures, to determine whether a child needs additional support. In fact, the reason the DSM was created initially was as an attempt to standardise diagnostic practice so that an individual presenting with difficulties would stand a better chance of receiving the same diagnosis from different clinicians rather than a mix of opinions. The impact of this was to help to inform a clinician's intervention strategies to try to help that individual. An earlier version of DSM (DSM-III) provided consistency in labelling, but its validity (how well a diagnosis actually captured something that was real) was less convincing. Overtime, the DSM has been updated as research and knowledge about the behaviours associated with various conditions have progressed, though it remains a controversial tool for labelling people (Kutchins & Kirk, 2001).

Labelling according to standard criteria is one way of getting a consistent diagnosis across different parts of the country and between countries. However, there are difficulties in using labels. For example, one such difficulty in trying to assign a label to an individual is comorbidity, that is, the co-existence of other conditions. As more research is carried out, our understanding of the 'fuzziness' of boundaries between disorders has increased and a shared genetic underpinning of several disorders has now been established. One example of this is the finding that there is an overlap in the genetic component of autism, schizophrenia, ADHD, depression and bipolar disorder (Cross-Disorder Group of the Psychiatric Genomics Consortium, 2013). Acknowledging the existence of comorbidity means that it becomes very important to look at each individual and their unique set of strengths and challenges rather than trying to 'pigeonhole' them and apply a label that may not really capture individual needs.

Another challenge to applying labels relates to the changing nature of the way conditions are described and defined in the diagnostic manuals, and the subsequent impact on prevalence rates. A good example of this kind of change can be seen in relation to the autism spectrum. Autism was first described in 1943 by Leo Kanner, who reported on his work with eight boys and three girls, describing a set of behaviours that are subsumed under the umbrella label of 'autism spectrum disorder'. A year later, in 1943, Hans Asperger also published his work with four boys who appeared similar to those described by Kanner. Although there were similarities in the behaviours of the children described by each of these clinicians, differences in language ability between the groups led to two separate diagnoses being applied: classic autism (autistic disturbances of affective contact) for Kanner's group and autistic psychopathy in childhood for Asperger's group. Research into these conditions has grown immeasurably since these first descriptions, and the view of autism as a form of psychosis is no longer held.

EXERCISE: EMBEDDED FIGURES TEST

Look at the picture. Hidden within the scene is a face. Your task is to identify where the face is.

This type of task is called an embedded figures test and requires individuals to identify a concealed object or picture contained in a bigger picture. These sorts of tests have been designed to test perceptual skills and to help researchers to understand how people process complex visual information. Such tests have generally found that individuals with autism are better (faster) at completing these tasks than individuals who do not have autism.

FIGURE 19.4 An example of the embedded figures test (replicated courtesy of Jill Boucher, 2015)

ASIDE

Over-interpretation of evidence and understanding research agendas

In some areas of inquiry, researchers and consumers of research findings can be guilty of over-interpreting evidence and making claims that are not fully supported by evidence. One clear example of over-interpretation of empirical findings is in the autism research literature, where it is sometimes claimed that people with autism *lack* a theory of mind (the understanding of another person's thoughts and feelings). What actually appears to be the case is that people with autism may experience some challenges when it comes to engaging with the thoughts and feelings of others. This is quite different from 'lacking' a theory of mind.

It is also important to consider the significance of certain areas of research, relative to the amount that is published about them. For example, if we refer back to the issue of theory of mind in autism, a brief literature search using the term 'theory of mind' will result in the return of a large number of published papers in the area. While this is an important area of research, a similar search, for example investigating 'sensory issues in autism', results in the return of considerably fewer published articles. This does not mean that understanding sensory issues in autism is any less important than understanding theory of mind, although it might appear so based on the number of articles published in each area. The number of articles published in an area may have more to do with trends of thought and sources of funding than with the relative importance or otherwise of that area.

The first operational definition of autism was provided by DSM-III. As the literature in this area grows, changes to diagnostic criteria continue to be made. The latest version of DSM, DSM-5, has revised the way in which the range of disorders that are collectively known as 'autism' are defined by adopting the overarching term of autism spectrum disorder, removing all subtypes and reducing what used to be known as a triad of difficulties down to a dyad (difficulties in social communication and social interaction, and restricted and repetitive behaviour, interests or activities). Changing the way that a disorder is described, and thus diagnosed, has implications for how many individuals are subsequently given an official diagnosis or label, and it is important to note this when interpreting prevalence rates (Lai et al., 2013).

19.4.4 PROVIDING APPROPRIATE OPPORTUNITIES

So far, we have considered effects on development which have come about by, or are exacerbated by, the expectations and behaviours of others. At this point, we ought to acknowledge another – less direct but possibly more potent – way in which other people's expectations may exert an effect on development, and which is particularly pertinent when considering children who demonstrate patterns of atypical development. Patterns of behaviour which we find challenging, either because they are very different from what we expect or because we do not understand them, may lead us to make false assumptions about the abilities of the children demonstrating these behaviours. These assumptions may result in us failing to provide opportunities for children to develop in more typical ways, just because we believe that they cannot benefit from these opportunities.

For example, children with autism may live in a very unusual sensory world in which sights and sounds can be confusing, distracting, uncomfortable and even painful (Williams, 1996). A noisy, visually stimulating classroom might make it extremely difficult for a child with autism to participate with others, or to understand the words that are spoken to them which may not be 'sifted out' from the mass of information that is bombarding their senses. That child might employ behavioural strategies that are designed to help them cope with the situation, such as stereotypical hand flapping, or even behaviours that result in them being removed from the classroom. An outsider, looking in on that child's behaviour, might conclude (wrongly) that the child does not want to participate with others and that the child does not have a good understanding of spoken language. However, it can often be the case that if the sensory context can be adjusted to better suit a child with autism, the opportunities for that child increase dramatically (Gillingham, 2004).

19.4.5 PROVIDING APPROPRIATE LEARNING CONTEXTS

To examine a further way in which adults' expectations may come to influence development, we need to consider the ideas of the Soviet Belarusian psychologist Lev Vygotsky (1896–1934), whose work is also discussed in Chapter 18. Vygotsky's theoretical account of development was concerned with the relationship between language and communication and intellectual development. Vygotsky argued that higher-level cognitive processes are realised during interactions with others. When taking part in social interactions, children are observing, experimenting with and practising a range of behaviours which gradually become internalised and employed on an intra-individual level.

A central concept in Vygotsky's (1978) theory is the **zone of proximal development** (ZPD). The ZPD is located between what a child can achieve on his or her own and what that same child can achieve with the help of either an adult or a more capable peer. For learning to be most effective, teaching needs to be sensitive to the child's zone. Directing efforts below the level of the zone will result in no learning, because this is what the child can do already. Interactions directed above the zone will also result in little learning, as this will be at a level too difficult for the child to understand. Guiding the child within the ZPD, however, is likely to lead to the child learning (Chapter 18 outlines the ZPD in more detail).

You may now be wondering why we are spending time here considering a theoretical approach which was primarily developed through observations of interactions between typically developing children and their parents or peers. However, what we would like to suggest is that, within the framework of teacher expectations being proposed above, Vygotsky's thoughts about development generally, and about the ZPD specifically, may also have an important part to play in our understanding of atypical development. As has been established, learning through collaboration with others is most likely to occur when your partner (either an adult or a more capable peer) is able to provide a level of interaction that is within your ZPD. If a child's abilities are not clearly understood, it is likely that the level of interaction that is available to the child may not be appropriate for effective learning to take place.

A number of studies have explored aspects of teaching and learning for children demonstrating atypical developmental trajectories (see e.g. Cains, 2000; Dillon & Underwood, 2012; Hobsbaum, Peters, & Sylva, 1996; Lamb et al., 1998). Several of these studies draw attention to the fact that for many of these children, learning interactions have not been appropriately directed. When careful consideration is given to the nature of the interactions among children and between children and adults, significant changes in children's learning have been observed. This is also the case for children who have had a history of failure in school learning. For example, Ann Brown and her colleagues provide compelling evidence to demonstrate that children who have real difficulties with reading comprehension can make significant gains in reading achievement through a series of structured group reading events (Brown & Campione, 1990). This approach, which is known as 'reciprocal teaching', is informed quite explicitly by Vygotskian thinking about interaction and collaboration. In the reading groups, the teacher models appropriate reading behaviours and scaffolds the children in the use of a range of comprehension skills, for example questioning, clarifying, summarising and predicting. Through guided practice in applying these strategies, these comprehension-enhancing skills start to become an automatic part of the child's own reading process.

Researchers using integrated play groups (IPGs), whereby children with autism are introduced to groups with typically developing children as a means of promoting play, have also used Vygotskian principles to good effect. Such groups have been found to result in increases in social play and less isolated play by the children with autism (Bass & Mulick, 2007; Wolfberg & Schuler, 1993). What is important to recognise in these studies is that the children involved demonstrate 'atypical' development, and for many of them it had been assumed that progress in a range of different areas was unlikely. However, by providing an appropriate learning environment which is designed to take into account the specific nature of these children's abilities, progress in learning can be made.

The importance of learning environments for all children, not just those with additional support needs, is widely recognised in the literature (Fraser, 2012). However, it is not always the case that children with additional support needs are provided with an environment that is conducive to their learning. Sometimes this is because the additional needs are complex and schools may not always have the resources to be able to implement large-scale changes. Nonetheless, it is quite often the case that even very small changes to the environment in which a child is being taught can have a profound impact on school experience. Building strong links between parents and schools can be an effective way of ensuring that children are supported in the best way. Examples of small changes to a learning environment that can have a profound impact on the way that children with autism engage with lessons include changing the types of paper that a student writes on, providing a visual timetable of the day's activities, providing a sensory board with tactile stimuli that are comforting, or allowing a student discreetly to leave a classroom to go to a safe, designated place if they begin to feel overwhelmed by noise or other distractors (Dillon & Underwood, 2012).

19.4.6 MODELS OF DISABILITY

In the discussion that has been presented in this latter half of the chapter, we have suggested that it is necessary to look beyond the 'inside' of the individual child when considering the causes and developmental trajectory of children who are described as following an atypical developmental pathway. Specifically, we have drawn attention to the potential effect that the behaviours, knowledge and decisions of other people (in particular other adults) can have on a child's development.

We can take this argument one step further by considering the wider consequences and implications of some of the ideas presented here. One way of thinking about these issues is to refer to the distinction made between two different models of disability – the 'medical' model and the 'social' model – which present views about atypical development from two very different standpoints.

The medical model considers difficulties associated with atypical development as arising from within the individual, who needs to be supported by society or 'treated' to be 'made better'. This model describes atypical development in terms of diagnosis, labelling the problem and treating the child using interventions. For example, if we consider the behavioural disorder ADHD, we can see how this model works. First, a teacher or the child's parents will notice that the child behaves differently from their peers; they do not fit with the 'norm'. The child will then undergo clinical assessment, most likely by a child psychiatrist, and, once diagnosed with the disorder, will be offered treatments which might include medication or behavioural therapy. The assessment of atypical development using this model compares the individual against a set of norms, which results in individuals who do not meet those norms being labelled 'atypical'. These differences are believed to lie within the child. It tends to divert attention away from the influence of 'outside' factors, such as the child's social environment, on their difficulties. This is the model within which much of the research discussed in the first half of this chapter is framed.

In contrast, the social model regards disability as something located not within the individual, but within the attitudes, behaviours and assumptions of society that frame the transactions of each individual within that society. Using this framework, disability is the product of people within a society who build barriers that prevent people with disabilities from being fully included. These barriers may be organisational, physical or social and are found to exist in many settings. Social models challenge the view that disability should be defined using medical explanations and instead argue that disability needs to be understood in the transactions between the 'disabled' person and the 'disabling' society. From this point of view, for a disabled child to be successfully included in a school, it is the school that needs to adapt to the child, just as much as the child needs to adapt to the school.

The different perspectives have different implications when we come to think about things like schooling. The social model tends to be the model adopted by those who advocate inclusive education and who hold that a community's school should be for the children of that community – all of them, whatever their demographic. According to this view, a child with a disability would be expected to attend their local school, which should be resourced to enable children of varying abilities to attend and learn together.

So, while these two models present two very different perspectives, we can see them in practice in everyday life. Using the medical model allows us to understand the specific characteristics of different types of atypical development. This allows for specialised help for specific disorders. The social model, on the other hand, promotes inclusivity and encourages us as a society to change how we think and behave with regard to people with disabilities.

Additionally, these different models of disability may play a role in the process of changing children's views about disability. Such attitude shifts are, of course, related to increased inclusive practice in schools. For example, a study by Slininger, Sherril and Jankowski (2000) explored how attitudes towards a peer with a physical and/or learning disability might change with different levels of contact. They found that increased contact between children with and without disabilities resulted in increased enjoyment from the interactions for the non-disabled child, as well as improving general attitudes towards inclusion among the non-disabled children. Equally, research with children who have disabilities has shown that inclusion can have many benefits, such as helping children to feel supported and valued by peers and teachers, increasing social interaction with others and promoting feelings of equality among children (e.g. Coates & Vickerman, 2010; Goodwin & Watkinson, 2000). However, they also report times when inclusion might lead to bullying by others because of feeling different (Fitzgerald, 2005). A child from Coates and Vickerman's (2010) study illustrates this by saying, 'Everybody really picks on me. . . . Picking on me about like er my language cos I go to the speech therapy'. But these feelings can be more manageable when the child perceives the school as adapting and catering for their needs appropriately.

We raise this issue here to encourage you to think about the wider issues associated with an understanding of atypical development. Knowledge about the range of different courses that development may take as a consequence of a range of different genetic, biological and cognitive characteristics is important for a variety of reasons. Also important is an understanding of how society views these developmental differences and the potential effects of our assumptions about them, and equally how children perceive themselves and others. Through understanding these things, we are better able to make decisions about how to improve the ways we work with individuals who have different and diverse needs.

19.5 CHAPTER SUMMARY

This chapter has outlined some of the factors which we know contribute to development that can be described as following an atypical trajectory. We identified two key perspectives and considered the factors within two corresponding groups: those arising from *within* the child (such as brain damage, genetics and the importance of critical or sensitive periods of development), and those *external* to the child (such as societal expectation and the self-fulfilling prophecy, labelling and the provision of appropriate opportunities and learning contexts).

This discussion of 'within' and 'external' factors deliberately raises the issue of the interplay between these two perspectives. It is increasingly recognised that the way we think about atypical development needs to take account of these two perspectives and consider the implications for how we help children who are developing atypically. At the beginning and end of this chapter we discussed the question of how society views developmental differences and the role that individual differences play in determining whether development is considered to be atypical. As educators, parents and policy makers, when discussing atypical development and determining the nature of any subsequent help that is provided, we need to give consideration to the nature of societal expectations and the model of disability that we ascribe to.

(?) DISCUSSION QUESTIONS

William James is quoted as saying 'to study the abnormal is the best way of understanding the normal'. What does the study of atypical child development tell us about typical development? How much can we learn if we follow this principle? Should we follow this principle?

According to the Austrian psychologist Alfred Adler, 'the only normal people are the ones you don't know very well'. How would you apply this quotation to the arguments in this chapter? Consider your own definition of 'typical' and 'atypical'.

SUGGESTIONS FOR FURTHER READING

Fletcher, J.M., & Morris, R.D. (2011). Reading, laterality, and the brain: early contributions on reading disabilities by Sara S. Sparrow. *Journal of Autism and Developmental Disorders, 44,* 250–255. This paper discusses the work of Sara Sparrow and Paul Satz regarding developmental lags and reading difficulties.

Herbert, M. (2008). *Typical and atypical development: from conception to adolescence.* Malden, MA: Blackwell. This text describes the development a child undergoes while in the womb right through to adolescence. It is split into two: the first half of the book is dedicated to describing typical development; the second half provides an outline of atypical development, examining areas such as genetic disorders and emotional and behavioural difficulties.

Plomin, R., DeFries, J.C., McClearn, G.E., & McGuffin, P. (2005). *Behavioral genetics* (5th edn). New York: Worth. This is another key text that introduces findings from genetic studies of cognitive and developmental abilities, with a focus on the interplay between nature and nurture.

Regier, D.A., Kuhl, E.A., & Kupfer, D.J. (2013). The DSM-5: classification and criteria changes. *World Psychiatry*, *12*(2), 92–98. This is a clearly written journal article that discusses some of the most important and contentious changes made to the diagnostic criteria from DSM IV to DSM V.

Thomas, M.S., & Knowland, V. (2009). Sensitive periods in brain development: implications for education policy. *European Psychiatric Review*, *2*(1), 17–20. This paper reviews what is known about sensitive periods in development and discusses how knowledge about these periods may be used in education.

ANSWER TO EXERCISE

For those of you who were struggling to find the face, here she is!

 Still want more? For links to online resources relevant to this chapter and a quiz to test your understanding, visit the companion website at edge.sagepub.com/banyard2e

20 ADOLESCENCE, ADULTHOOD AND AGEING

Lead authors: Emily Coyne, Louise A. Brown and Claire Thompson

CHAPTER OUTLINE

20.1 Introduction	348
20.2 Adolescence	348
20.2.1 Traditional view of adolescence – 'storm and stress'	348
20.2.2 Cognitive development: the adolescent brain	349
20.2.3 Social development: identify formation	350
20.2.4 Emotional development: relationships and risky behaviours	351
20.2.5 Summary of adolescence	352
20.3 Adulthood	353
20.3.1 Levinson's stage model for adult development	353
20.3.2 Early adulthood: social and emotional wellbeing	354
20.3.3 Early adulthood: physical wellbeing	355
20.3.4 Early adulthood: cognitive wellbeing	355
20.3.5 Middle adulthood	355
20.3.6 Middle adulthood: social and emotional wellbeing	356
20.3.7 Middle adulthood: physical wellbeing	356
20.3.8 Middle adulthood: cognitive wellbeing	356
20.3.9 Summary of adulthood	357
20.4 Ageing	357
20.4.1 Cognitive ageing	357
20.4.2 Emotion and wellbeing in later life	359
20.4.3 Lifestyle factors	360
20.4.4 Summary of ageing	361
20.5 Chapter summary	362
Discussion questions	362
Suggestions for further reading	362

20.1 INTRODUCTION

This chapter will consider the key developmental trends that accompany adolescence, adulthood and ageing. When we think of development in psychology we tend to focus on development in childhood. However, this development continues throughout the lifespan and it is important to consider these stages as part of our understanding of human behaviour. Each section of the chapter will consider the cognitive, social and emotional aspects of development and will discover how lifestyle choices can impact on the experiences within each lifespan phase. First, we would like you to have a think about the framing questions and then attempt the stereotyping activity.

FRAMING QUESTIONS

- Is adolescence a period of 'storm and stress'?
- What impact do peers have on risky behaviour in adolescence?
- Does the concept of emerging adulthood have a place in the stage model of adulthood?
- What changes may somebody consciously make when they reach 'middle adulthood'?
- Does ageing impact all types of cognitive functioning equally?
- How does older age impact upon emotional wellbeing?

EXERCISE: STEREOTYPING

Before we start this chapter, we would like you to have a think about typical stereotypes for adolescents (aged 13–16), younger adults (aged 18–25) and older adults (aged 65+). What springs to mind? Make a few notes (or drawings!) and we will refer to this as we progress through our journey of the lifespan!

20.2 ADOLESCENCE

Adolescence is the period typically believed to be between childhood and adulthood. This encapsulates the teenage years and, biologically-speaking, begins with the onset of puberty. There are a lot of stereotypes that are associated with teenagers. What did you think of as a stereotyped adolescent? Moody, grumpy, arguing with parents or happy-go-lucky, party animal? These are a few of the stereotyped profiles that adolescents are often associated with. If you go to Google images and type in 'teenager' or 'adolescent', you primarily see pictures of happy groups of friends, so perhaps some of these stereotypes are out of date (try this out!). In this chapter, we will consider whether these traditional stereotypes are fair assessments of adolescence behaviour.

This section will consider the cognitive, social and emotional development during this stage as well as discussing the traditional view of adolescence as a period of 'storm and stress', and evaluate the evidence for this.

20.2.1 TRADITIONAL VIEW OF ADOLESCENCE – 'STORM AND STRESS'

The terminology 'storm and stress' in adolescence was originally proposed by Hall (1904) although ideas around this theme can be traced back to Aristotle and Socrates. Shakespeare also makes references to risky adolescent behaviour in

The Winter's Tale (Arnett, 1999). 'Storm and stress' was the idea that all of the biological changes lead to disruption in behaviour and conflict. This was believed to be a stressful time for all involved and Hall stated that this 'storm and stress' was experienced in a similar way by all, although he did identify that there were individual differences in the way this was encountered. The concept was further developed by key figures in psychoanalysis. Sigmund Freud discussed this period as an extension of psychosexual development with stages being revisited. Blos (1962) defined the period as a complete relearning of the world around us. He believed that the purpose of this stage was about gaining independence. As a result of all this change, Blos highlighted that there would be stressors associated with the dramatic change. However, it was Anna Freud (1958) who had the most extreme view of 'storm and stress' in adolescence. She felt that this was a universal stage in development and therefore everybody experienced this conflict and trauma. If there were no outward signs of this stage, then it was thought that it was being suppressed and 'bottled up', which Freud classified as pathological.

These views are extreme and are based on the assumption that this stage in life is difficult and full of stressors. More recently, attention has turned to evaluating the extent to which there is evidence for the 'storm and stress' account. Arnett (1999) examines the literature to see whether this period is really as terrible as it has been considered. Two of the areas that he identifies as being common stressors in adolescence are conflict with parents and mood disruption.

There is substantial evidence that conflict with parents exists during the adolescent period. Blos (1962) believed that conflict with parents during this developmental phase was healthy as it assisted with the necessary separation in order for the goal of independence to be gained. Galambos and Almeida (1992) examined the main source of these conflicts through a longitudinal study. They found that the main areas that caused conflicts were household chores, appearance, politeness (mood), finance, and substance use. Conflicts were most frequent in early adolescence and declined over time, although conflict about finance increased in intensity into older adolescence. Similarly, Laursen, Coy and Collins (1998) found through a meta-analysis that conflicts were most frequent in early adolescence, with a decline over time in frequency. While they found that the frequency of conflict declined over time, the impact of the conflict was greater in later adolescence. This data also suggested that the conflict was greater between the mothers and adolescents. More recently, Ehrlich, Dykas and Cassidy (2012) examined the link between parental conflict in adolescence and peer friendships. Using semi-structured discussions, they asked parents and teenagers to talk about conflict around topics, such as household chores. The teenagers were then asked to assess their behaviour and friendships via questionnaires. Results suggested that conflict with parents alone did not impact on social functioning, but if the adolescents reported conflict with peer groups as well, then they were likely to experience social issues.

Arnett (1999) also identified mood disruption as being a contributor to this idea of adolescence being a stressful period. Studies have found that mood disruptions during this developmental stage do exist. Buchanan, Eccles and Becker (1992) found that there was a link between hormones and moodiness. As a result of this, they also suggested that increased hormones could be linked to increased distance from parents. Larson and Richards (1994a) hypothesised that mood disruption was linked to cognitive changes, such as changes in abstract thought (being able to apply abstract concepts to situations) and environmental factors (such as peer groups) rather than simply about puberty and hormones. They found no evidence that mood disruption is linked to puberty. Larson and Richards (1994b) also highlighted that there are correlations between the emotions experienced by adolescents and those experienced by their parents. Therefore, this could illuminate the impact of the environment as the emotions experienced by parent–adolescent dyads are similar. Sleep has also been found to have an impact on mood disruption. Owens, Belon and Moss (2010) found that making the school day start 30 minutes later (resulting in an average of 45 minutes of additional sleep) left students feeling less depressed and more motivated to take part in activities.

As you can see, there is some evidence to support the 'storm and stress' hypothesis as there do appear to be accounts of conflict with parents and mood disruption. However, some of the traditional views may have been a bit extreme and many adolescents have a positive experience.

20.2.2 COGNITIVE DEVELOPMENT: THE ADOLESCENT BRAIN

During the adolescent period there are changes to the cognitive processing that happens in the developing brain. The cognitive skills that are developed during this period include hypothetical thinking, abstract thinking and decision-making.

In Chapter 18 we described how the final stage of Piaget's theory (the formal operational period) falls within adolescence. This stage of development represents a change in thought from what is 'concrete' and known about the world to be able to think hypothetically and therefore draw inferences. Inhelder and Piaget (1958) characterised this stage by using their pendulum task. In this task the adolescents were asked to adjust the length of the string and the weights to see what impacted on the swing. In order to do this the adolescents would have to generate hypotheses and test them using a more abstract type of thought processing. We know that there have been critiques of this stage, saying that some children do not achieve it until much later than Piaget claimed and that formal operational thinking develops in a more disorganised way (Martorano, 1977).

Decision making is another cognitive skill that is enhanced during adolescence. Older adolescents and young adults have been found to be significantly better at making decisions than children. As we get older we are better able to think through all of the options in order to choose the one that most closely matches our goals (Byrnes & McClenny, 1994) and we are more likely to think about the consequences of decisions (Halpern-Felsher & Cauffman, 2001). Adolescents and young adults develop the ability to learn from decisions that have been made and apply this knowledge to future decision making (Byrnes & McClenny, 1994). Giedd (2004) used MRI scanning to produce a longitudinal account of changes in the adolescent brain. One of the most interesting findings was that the dorsal lateral prefrontal cortex was the last area in the brain to show development and this was not until the participants were in their early 20s. This is interesting as this is a part of the brain that controls impulses and therefore plays a part in decision making, perhaps explaining why this develops later in adolescence (see the key study for more information on the impact of this area of the brain in adolescence).

20.2.3 SOCIAL DEVELOPMENT: IDENTIFY FORMATION

Identity is talked about as being an important psychological construct throughout the lifespan. However, as part of his theory of psychosocial development, Erikson (1968) developed a theory which explained development across the lifespan based on conflicts at each stage. In adolescence, he stated that identity crisis was the cause of a lot of turmoil. As puberty brings with it physical changes, it is to be expected that adolescents will think about their identities, whether it is expressed through fashion or their behaviour. Rosenblum and Lewis (1999) found that girls showed dissatisfaction with their bodies during this stage, often impacting on self-esteem. Teenagers in contemporary society not only have to think about their identity in real life, but also their online identity through social networking sites and online games (Manago et al., 2008).

During this stage, Erikson believed that adolescents were free to explore their identity and as a result they would try out different identities which could in turn impact on behaviour. This view was all based on Erikson's observations in clinical practice, and therefore needed empirical evidence to support this. Marcia (1966, 1980) developed this theory via interviews looking at religion, occupation, politics and attitudes towards sexual behaviours, and found that identity formation could be classified into four hierarchical key stages. The first stage was diffusion. This was where the adolescent had not really thought about their identity. This was believed to be the least mature status. The next level was foreclosure, where the beliefs of the family could be assisting in forming the adolescent's identity; for example if the family are all Catholic, then that may assist with their religious identity. The next stage reached simply from diffusion or via foreclosure (see Figure 20.1) was moratorium. This was the stage that Erikson was describing, the crisis in identity and the exploration of different identities. The final stage was 'achievement', where the identity was formalised, based on all of the stages, and the crisis was over.

Both Erikson and Marcia stood by the idea that identity was fully formed in adolescence and therefore all of the stages were achieved. However, there have been some critiques stating that identity development continues into adulthood and that these crises can still appear in adulthood. Waterman and Waterman (1975) looked at father–son dyads and found that the adolescent sons tended to be in diffusion or moratorium, but the fathers were categorised as being in foreclosure when asked about aspects of work. Furthermore, O'Connell (1976) suggested that the female's identity changes when she gets married, changes again when she has children, and that there is a further shift when the children go to school. As a result, it has been suggested that perhaps we should be talking about stability over time of identity rather than change in identity at certain stages of the lifespan (van Hoof, 1999). A five-year longitudinal study was used to examine this idea of change versus stability (Klimstra et al., 2010). Klimstra and colleagues found that adolescents' (both girls' and boys') identities were relatively stable over time, but that they showed small progressive changes over time. This seemed to give evidence for both approaches, suggesting that we need to take a more three-dimensional approach to identity formation in adolescence.

Overall, while identity formation is believed to be an important part of adolescence due to the impact on self-esteem and, potentially, peer groups, there is evidence that this formation is not only completed in this period, but rather that identity formation is a process that continues throughout the lifespan.

		Has the individual experienced a crisis?	
		No	Yes
Has the individual committed to an identity?	No	Diffusion	Moratorium
	Yes	Foreclosure	Achievement

FIGURE 20.1 Marcia's (1966) stages of identity formation

20.2.4 EMOTIONAL DEVELOPMENT: RELATIONSHIPS AND RISKY BEHAVIOURS

Friendships and relationships can have a big impact on how adolescence is experienced. In this period teenagers tend to spend a lot more time with friends than with parents. Peers/friends tend to come from school or from the local neighbourhood and they can have a large influence on behaviour. Coleman (1999) found that in early adolescence there is a lot of concern about rejection from friends and this is a constant source of worry. By 17 years old they feel more confident in their friendship groups. Interestingly, though, there have been a number of studies that find no link between the quality of friendships and self-esteem, which was an unexpected finding (see Keefe & Berndt, 1996).

Berndt (2002) highlights that healthy friendship should be about supporting one another and prosocial behaviour. However, there have been clear links found between peer groups and anti-social or delinquent behaviours. Adolescents in the seventh grade (12–13 years old) were asked to report the positive and negative features of their friendships. Those reporting that they were friends with disruptive pupils showed a significant increase in disruptive behaviour over an academic year, whereas those who had positive friendships showed increased involvement in activities at schools (Berndt & Keefe, 1995). It has also been found that negative behaviours can spread within a group. One study (Ennett & Bauman, 1994) found that non-smoking adolescents in peer groups where members smoked were more likely to start smoking, rather than the smokers to stop smoking. They suggested that behaviours were more likely to be initiated by peers, but there was little impact of cessation of behaviours. These negative behaviours, such as smoking, are often referred to in the literature as **risky behaviours** (see key study).

There have been studies examining the link between adolescents partaking in risky behaviours and family connections. The idea behind this was to see if there was any impact from divorced versus married families as well as looking at parental bonds. Arnett and Balle-Jensen (1993) completed a study in Denmark examining family influences on these risky behaviours. They found that risky behaviours (such as smoking, alcohol use, drug use and unprotected sex) increased throughout adolescence with illegal behaviours such as shoplifting and vandalism peaking at age 16–17. In this study they failed to show any influence of family background. However, Shulman and Scharf (2000) did find a correlation between parental **attachment** and emotional involvement with peers. This suggested that those with a close bond with parents were more emotionally involved in their friendship groups.

> **RISKY BEHAVIOUR** This may include behaviour that puts the person in danger physically or mentally. Common examples include use of alcohol and substances, unprotected sexual intercourse and illegal behaviours (such as shoplifting or vandalism).

> **ATTACHMENT** A close emotional bond with another person, for example a baby with a caregiver.

> **CONDUCT DISORDER** This is a disorder that shows long-lasting patterns of severe behaviour that may harm others/animals, damage property or cause emotional harm. This disorder impacts on the lives of both the person diagnosed and those around them.

> **DSM-5** *The Diagnostic Statistical Manual of Mental Disorders* (5th edition) (DSM-5; American Psychiatric Association, 2013) is a handbook which details criteria for diagnosing mental disorders. It is widely used by practitioners.

Extreme anti-social behaviours (such as vandalism, arson, theft, etc.) that are persistent in nature and disruptive to an adolescent's life could possibly be diagnosed as **conduct disorder**. Conduct disorder is classified as an emotional and behavioural disorder. For diagnosis, the behaviours have to be long-lasting and violate the rights of others as well as disregarding societal norms. Prevalence estimates of conduct disorder are around 2–10% with a higher occurrence in boys (**DSM-5**; American Psychiatric Association, 2013). Risk factors for conduct disorder are believed to be temperament, environmental factors such as delinquent peer groups, parental issues, substance use, and there have been some genetic links found (i.e. if the parent has conduct disorder, the adolescent is more likely to be diagnosed). For more information on this disorder, see the diagnostic criteria (see Aside) and complete the activity about Jane.

KEY STUDY

Pharo, H., Sim, C., Graham, M., Gross, J., & Hayne, H. (2011). Risky business: executive function, personality, and reckless behaviour during adolescence and emerging adulthood. *Behavioural Neuroscience, 125(6), 970–978.*

Researchers have long been trying to explain the individual differences that occur in the engagement of risky behaviours. The link between risky behaviours and hormones is not clear and therefore other explanations were sought. Pharo and colleagues wondered about the link between the developmental changes in the central executive (controls impulsivity) and partaking in risky behaviour. They took a sample of 136 adolescents between the ages of 13 and 17 years old. They completed personality questionnaires (that examined sensation seeking among other constructs), self-reports of risky behaviour as well as a battery of neuropsychological tasks that included memory, mathematical skill, stroop, card sorting and word association. They found that personality traits such as sensation seeking, impulsivity and sociability were linked with self-reported risky behaviour. Furthermore, they found that the scores on the neuropsychological tests were correlated with engagement in risky behaviour. This could be linked to the brain developments in the prefrontal cortex that control impulsivity. This study found that the neuropsychological tasks can tap into executive functioning, which can in turn explain individual differences in risk-taking behaviour.

ASIDE

Conduct disorder

Conduct disorder is diagnosed when disruptive behaviour is long-lasting and causing extensive issues for the adolescent. In order to get a diagnosis the behaviour has to be causing impairment in social, academic or occupational functioning with three of the diagnostic criteria being present in the last 12 months, and at least one behaviour in the last six months. The main criteria are aggression towards people or animals, destroying property, deceitfulness or theft, or serious violations of rules.

There are many behavioural interventions that are used to treat conduct disorder. One intervention that is showing good results is the 'Incredible Years Programme' (http://incredibleyears.com/), which works on strengthening parental skills and working together. Bywater et al. (2009) found short-term improvements in behaviours. However, when examined longitudinally they found that those gains remained and over time there was a decreased involvement of the authorities (such as social services or the police). This programme is widely used in the USA and the UK for disruptive behaviours.

20.2.5 SUMMARY OF ADOLESCENCE

Overall it is clear that during adolescence there is a lot of development still ongoing. The traditional view of 'storm and stress' may be a bit extreme, but researchers have found plenty of evidence that this is a stressful time, fraught with conflicts and mood disruption. However, we do acknowledge that there are huge individual differences in the experience of adolescence. This section has discussed the development of the cognitive system, developments in identity formation as well as the influence of peer groups and risky behaviour. Finally, reflect again on the stereotyping exercise that we started with. Have you changed your mind as a result of this section?

EXERCISE: CONDUCT DISORDER

Using the diagnostic criteria described in the Aside above, judge whether Jane fits the diagnostic criteria for conduct disorder or is simply behaving anti-socially. If you think it is conduct disorder, what behaviours lead you to that diagnosis?

Jane is 15 years old. She is the youngest of four siblings and her parents are divorced. She spends alternating weeks with each parent. Jane has been suspended from school three times in the last year for bullying and fighting in school. Out of school she often shoplifts make-up from the local chemists and the police have been called in the past. In the last month Jane has started hanging around with a new group and since then has been staying out late every night. Her parents do not know what to do about her behaviour.

20.3 ADULTHOOD

At what age do you become an adult? Is it when you reach a certain birthday, learn to drive a car, or do you have another marker? One of the problems with this question is that criteria for leaving adolescence and entering adulthood vary across and within societies. Other milestones, such as gaining financial independence, having children or buying your first home, are reached by different people at different times, if at all. If you never buy a house or have children, does that mean you stay a child? Of course not! In reality, no one single factor establishes an individual as an adult in all areas of their life. This is one of the main challenges of studying adulthood. Not only are the boundaries difficult to define, but people's experiences of adulthood vary greatly. Assuming we have a fairly normal lifespan in terms of duration, we spend most of our lives as adults; therefore it is just as important to look at what it means to be an adult as to study childhood or older age.

Traditionally, developmental psychologists have seen adulthood as an outcome to be achieved rather than a stand-alone phase worthy of independent research. Although changes that occur in adulthood are generally more gradual than those in childhood, adults have been shown to experience numerous transitions in various areas of their lives (Aldwin, Yancura, & Boeninger, 2010; Freund & Lamb, 2010; Holcomb, 2010).). As a consequence, there has been an increase in the number of studies exploring this phase of life. With adulthood being the longest phase of human development, one of the most logical ways of studying this period has been to split it into three wide-ranging stages: early adulthood (from approximately 18 up to 40 years of age), middle adulthood (41–65) and older adulthood (65+). Undoubtedly, there are changes within each phase and between individuals, but having such a framework allows for a more systematic look at the longest period of our lives. Ultimately, development is a lifelong affair that does not stop when we leave our teens.

20.3.1 LEVINSON'S STAGE MODEL FOR ADULT DEVELOPMENT

Investigations of personal development throughout adulthood have yielded a number of different arguments. One of the earliest researchers, Levinson (1978), drew on social psychological theory to explain the relationship between the developing individual and the varying demands of society by suggesting different developmental age-related stages. He emphasised the social role requirements at different life phases and the interaction between personal growth and relationships. Levinson maintained that all normally-developing adults progress through the same stages in the same sequence, and at roughly the same pace. Would you agree with him? The stages are shown in Figure 20.2.

A controversial development in the stage theories model of young adulthood has been Arnett's introduction of the 'emerging adulthood' concept (Arnett, 2007). Rather than seeing a clear distinction between adolescence and adulthood, he regards this period more as a transitional stage to be negotiated before becoming an adult (normally between the late teens and mid-twenties). Arnett emphasises that young people's lives have altered greatly even within the last decade. More young people are progressing into higher education, with marriage and parenthood often coming later in life for varying reasons. Consequentially, Arnett proposes that the move from adolescence to adulthood is now long enough to be a distinct and separate phase in itself, with the earlier stages (such as those suggested by Levinson) no longer relevant to today's society.

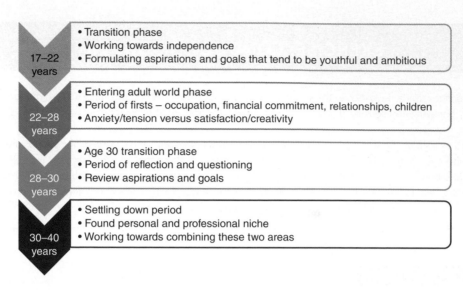

FIGURE 20.2 Levinson's stage model for adult development

The concept of emerging adulthood is not, however, without its critics. Hendry and Kloep (2010) challenged Arnett's notion of emerging adulthood by highlighting that young people may reach adult status in some areas before others. They also suggest an alternative concept to emerging adulthood, that of unending youth, wherein adults undertake plastic surgery, retain a youthful physique and mentality, and have children later, in essence never transitioning into adulthood. Hendry and Kloep also express concern over the uniformity of this group, highlighting subgroups of young people occupying a state of 'prevented adulthood' through lack of opportunities, and others who have had to develop early due to additional responsibilities (such as caring for ill parents). Ultimately, they endorse a shift from age-bound stage theories on the grounds that they are simply not diverse enough for today's society. But a move to what? That seems to be the current unanswered question.

20.3.2 EARLY ADULTHOOD: SOCIAL AND EMOTIONAL WELLBEING

Not many people would agree that they have the same social life at 18 as when they are 48 (despite how hard some may try!). Within early adulthood there are often major changes in only a few years. For many, their early 20s are often about establishing a career, which can involve further training or studying to gain vital qualifications.

It is often within this phase that young adults form their first serious relationship, and trying to understand the complex world of romance can lead to stress and confusion. Also thrown into the mix are changes in relationships with parents and other adult relatives and the increasing expectation that the young person is now responsible for their own life, including perhaps a shift to a new home. With all these changes occurring in a relatively short period of time it would not be unusual for the young adult to feel a range of emotions, including some they may not have experienced before. So while this period often brings about exciting changes, they can often be daunting, and a bit overwhelming too.

The adjustment problems of young adults are often distinct from those made in adolescence as they are more likely to be decisions of choice, such as getting married, having children, or career-related options. This is in contrast to problems concerning emotional conflict or insecurity that are often experienced in adolescence, but does not mean that young adults are fully secure in their identity. Often, making informed decisions (especially for the first time) may stir up insecurities remaining unresolved from previous years and so young adulthood is often still a period of ongoing development and change. Problematic behaviour often continues, especially if insecure attachment styles have developed during childhood. This would not have surprised John Bowlby (1988), who always maintained that there are strong similarities between how people develop early relationships with caregivers during infancy and intimate relationships in adult life (Holmes & Johnson, 2009).

20.3.3 EARLY ADULTHOOD: PHYSICAL WELLBEING

The first stage of adulthood for most men and women comprises the years of increased energy and productivity. This tends to peak during their late 20s and early 30s, being a period of the greatest physical fitness, strength and reaction time (Whitbourne, 2001). Manual dexterity, coordination and sensory abilities, such as hearing and vision, are also at their height. As individuals move into their 30s, their bodies and many of the physical factors attributed to them start to decline. Metabolism is a good example, and many people entering their 30s find it just a little bit harder to keep their waistline the same as when they were 18.

In general, however, people in early adulthood feel strong and energetic, although you may not agree first thing on a Monday morning! The bad news is that metabolism is not the only factor that begins to decline within this period. The ability to hear high-pitched noises, for example, can start to deteriorate as early as the late 20s (Whitbourne, 2001). Manual dexterity also declines in the mid 30s, so if you are left wondering why you cannot do the back flips, cartwheels and handstands of your youth, then you are usually right in blaming it on your age. Recent research, however, has shown that while declining physical development normally starts from the early 20s, we do not often notice a decline in sensory functions until well into our 40s (Drummond, 2011), or maybe this is just a good old case of denial. This is, perhaps, an unfair comment, as while decline within this phase is common, many of the changes can be subtle and have minimal impact on an individual's day-to-day functioning.

In relation to this period being one of genuine individual choice, in contrast to the more restricted choices of childhood, young adults now often start to organise their own eating habits and exercise regimes. Choices and decisions at this time regarding physical development often form the basis of health choices for the rest of an individual's life. This can have either a positive or negative impact on health dependent upon whether the additional freedom leads people to eat more fruit and vegetables or consume more takeaways!

20.3.4 EARLY ADULTHOOD: COGNITIVE WELLBEING

By the start of adulthood, most individuals have developed cognitive skills enabling them to function within society. While maturity is seen as a marker for the end of adolescence, the body continues to develop – as does the brain. There will always be vast differences in people's abilities. For example, your friend may be better at remembering telephone numbers while you may be better at solving problems. However, both of you have still developed sufficient cognitive skills to get on with your daily lives. Does this mean that cognitive development simply comes to a halt on your eighteenth birthday? Cognitive researchers think definitely not.

Riegel (1976) was one of the first to propose that experiences in adulthood expose us to a new level of cognitive challenges. With increased and more varied experiences, he stated, we start to learn that the world is often a contradictory and complicated place, and sometimes does not make sense at all! Riegel argued that achieving the intellectual ability to deal with contradictions that confront us entails achieving a more developed and detailed way of thinking, which he termed post-formal thought. Further research into postformal reasoning found that by being presented with more complex problems in adulthood, a more developed way of thinking occurs and certainly does not stop at a certain age.

More recent investigations into intellectual development in adulthood have been based more around the use of **psychometric** tests, with researchers seeking to ascertain whether there are age-related differences in IQ throughout adulthood.

> **PSYCHOMETRIC** Standardised psychological tests that are used to measure psychological constructs such as intelligence.

A pivotal longitudinal study examining intelligence throughout adulthood was carried out by Schaie (1996), who looked at a number of differing cognitive abilities over the course of an individual's life. Schaie studied five primary abilities: numeric ability, verbal recall, perceptual speed, inductive reasoning and spatial orientation. Schaie found that there are modest gains in most of the five areas during the 20s and 30s, suggesting that intelligence as a whole still generally increases well into adulthood and does not just stop when you reach 18. I'm sure you may be glad of that!

20.3.5 MIDDLE ADULTHOOD

Middle adulthood is probably the hardest phase to define. Does it start when you reach your mid-life crisis, or is it when you become a senior manager at work? Again, variance in individual lives results in each person reaching this point at different stages of development, although a rough measure of entry into middle age is around the age of 40. Referring back to Levinson's model, he went on to describe middle adulthood (40–65 years of age) as a stage in which biological functioning, although on the decline, is still sufficient for an active, personally fulfilling and socially rewarding life. So he certainly did not see it as a case of life going downhill after 40.

20.3.6 MIDDLE ADULTHOOD: SOCIAL AND EMOTIONAL WELLBEING

It is during this stage of middle adulthood that people usually reach more senior positions in varying aspects of their life. There is the expectation to take responsibility for their own work, that of others, and to be responsible for the development of younger adults. This too can be a period of self-satisfaction and peace of mind, but the added responsibility, emergent physical health problems, and anticipation of impending old age may also result in considerable stress and tension.

This period of middle adulthood is also associated with what is termed (especially in the media) as 'the mid-life crisis', often portraying individuals as comical and pitiful characters. However, Levinson (1978) argued that a 'mid-life crisis' is a process that happens to most of us. Building on Levinson's work, Erikson (1985) highlighted that an individual's perception of a 'crisis' would be highly subjective and could involve events such as children developing into adults and leaving the family home, physical signs of ageing, and boredom with a chosen career. Levinson's parting comment was that successful adult development beyond mid-life requires facing up to and resolving these crises. No pressure then!

20.3.7 MIDDLE ADULTHOOD: PHYSICAL WELLBEING

During middle adulthood, people experience a range of physical changes. It is often the time people start to notice (for example) the first sprouting of grey hairs, signs of baldness, or an increase in facial wrinkles. A tendency to put on weight around the waist or lower body ('middle-age spread') starts to reduce the efficiency of the cardiovascular, respiratory and nervous systems (Whitbourne, 2001).

One of the most notable changes within this period is to eyesight, with the changing shape of the eye lens resulting in difficulty reading small print. You may see people within this age range holding books and newspapers further away than a younger reader, with text often starting to appear blurry unless held at a distance. Ability to see in the dark and to recover from sudden glares of light also declines. Hearing too starts to weaken, with sensitivity to high frequency sounds declining during middle age (Cruickshanks et al., 1998).

> **MENOPAUSE** A series of changes in hormone functioning that occurs in women and results in an inability to have children.

For women, this period is often associated with the **menopause**, a time in their life when a series of hormonal changes eventually results in an inability to have children. This factor alone can result in some level of psychological distress, but a number of physical changes are also associated with it. Common early-stage symptoms are hot flushes, mood changes, loss of libido and insomnia.

The frequency and intensity of symptoms can vary dramatically between individuals, as can the age of onset and duration. Middle-age in general can be seen as a period of reflection and alteration, but the menopause (specifically the inability now to have children) in particular often results in women reviewing their lives and roles. The physical signs of ageing sometimes lead individuals to become dissatisfied with their bodies, or certainly more aware of issues related to physical health. New exercise regimes and healthy eating plans are often started, with people at this stage often having additional finances for a bit more TLC and more expensive wrinkle-busting moisturisers!

20.3.8 MIDDLE ADULTHOOD: COGNITIVE WELLBEING

Until recently, neuroscientists claimed that our brains start to shrink in middle adulthood, predominantly due to loss of active brain cells (Miller & O'Callaghan, 2005). More recent research has questioned this, with no substantial loss of neurons noticeable within this phase (Miller & O'Callaghan, 2005). On the contrary, new neurons have been shown to develop in certain parts of the brain throughout our life, including throughout adulthood (Gould, 2007; Leuner, Gould, & Shors, 2006). These neurons, thought to be potentially the result of new learning, are considered to play a significant role in future learning, or both (Leuner, Glasper, & Gould, 2010).

In terms of mental ability, middle-age is seen as a relatively stable period, with Schaie's data highlighting little variation throughout this time. While Schaie did find a decline in numerical ability, middle-aged people were seen to perform well in terms of overall intellectual functioning. As we move into our 50s, however, individuals do sometimes begin to see some intellectual shifts. Recovering information from long-term memory starts to take a little longer, as does learning new material. The first signs of having a declining memory are sometimes a trigger for an individual starting to 'feel their age'.

Each phase of adulthood brings its own challenges. By middle adulthood both personal and professional aspects of an individual's life have normally gone through different phases of difficulty and success. While this can encourage increased amounts of reflection and review, there are still everyday stressors (sometimes new) to be faced within this period. Some relate to domestic and family life, and others to the world of work. For many middle-aged individuals there are new parenting challenges as children reach adolescence, leave the family home and grandchildren start to appear. At a time when middle-aged adults are becoming ever more aware of their own physical decline, their children may be developing strength and attraction, bringing with it pride but also reflection on impending old age.

20.3.9 SUMMARY OF ADULTHOOD

Adulthood has historically been less extensively researched that its counterparts – childhood and older age. As mentioned earlier in the chapter, it was once seen as the goal of adolescence and not as a transitional stage in itself. However, this section has shown that the differing stages of adulthood provide varying developmental changes, not just physically, but also psychologically. It is a prolonged stage where roles and responsibilities can change dramatically, and with it people's views and aspirations. There will undoubtedly be further development of the models applied to this period, largely to reflect changes in expectations, for example the shifting average age of getting married. However, adulthood remains independent as a stand-alone phase that ultimately bridges the gap between childhood and older age.

20.4 AGEING

People are living longer and population ageing is a global phenomenon, which has profound implications for society. This trend poses a number of challenges, including limiting the potential for economic and social burden and maximising the positive contributions that older adults can make to society (UNFPA & HelpAge International, 2012). It is important to understand key concepts in the psychology of ageing, especially when taking into account the increasing importance of older age groups in society. If the effects of ageing are fully understood, healthy and successful ageing, and a better quality of life in older age, may be promoted. Fortunately, research into the psychological effects of ageing has seen an increase in recent years and therefore we are now beginning to understand the important psychological issues around ageing.

20.4.1 COGNITIVE AGEING

Cognitive functioning in older age is one of the most researched aspects of the psychology of ageing. Although some facets of cognition remain relatively stable or even continue to increase through the adult lifespan, some are very sensitive to the ageing process. In fact, cognitive decline is among the most feared aspects of growing older (Deary et al., 2009). Notably, unhealthy cognitive decline, which is often due to dementia, is a major age-related health concern that has

FLUID/CRYSTALLISED ABILITIES Fluid cognitive abilities, like short-term memory, require more processing resources than crystallised ones, such as long-term knowledge, and are more sensitive to age-related decline.

clear potential for economic and social burden, for example in the form of healthcare and care-home provision, and the requirement for support and care by family members. However, there are also many age-related changes in cognition that tend to accompany even the healthy ageing process, and this is our present focus.

A key distinction when considering cognitive ability in older age is whether one is considering a 'fluid' or 'crystallised' ability. In relation to the effects of ageing on cognition, one general finding is that **fluid abilities** tend to be more greatly affected than **crystallised** ones.

SPEED OF PROCESSING The rate at which information is taken in, processed and responded to is a strong predictor of cognitive ability in older age.

FRONTAL LOBE HYPOTHESIS The theory that decline in frontal lobe functioning underlies more general age-related cognitive decline.

NEGATIVE PRIMING When a participant is effectively inhibiting attention towards a distracting item. If that item is then deemed relevant in the next trial of the task, their response will typically be slowed.

LONGITUDINAL RESEARCH A piece of research that follows a set group of people over a prolonged period of time, usually over a number of years.

Park et al. (2002) showed that fluid abilities involving lots of cognitive resources, such as information processing speed and short- and long-term memory tasks, are susceptible to a linear, continuous decline, which starts in early adulthood. Abilities that require less processing resources, such as verbal knowledge, remain relatively stable and even continue to increase through older adulthood. In fact, one influential theory in the study of cognitive ageing is Salthouse's **speed of processing** theory (Salthouse, 1996). This theory suggests that a reduced speed of information processing, or cognitive slowing, underlies age-related cognitive decline.

So, the memory of older adults, for example, does not perform as well as that of younger adults because older adults are slower at taking in the information, at elaborating on the information, and rehearsing it. Across three studies, each involving over 200 adults aged between 20 and 84 years, Salthouse (1991) assessed a range of abilities, including speed of information processing, short-term (or 'working' memory) capacity and more complex cognitive functioning. Processing speed was measured using a paper-and-pencil task that required participants to compare pairs of letter strings or patterns and to report whether they were the same or different. Working memory capacity was determined by assessing the amount of information that could be simultaneously processed while also keeping in mind certain information. For example, one task required participants to solve a series of arithmetic problems while also retaining the answers to each one. Finally, a number of reasoning tasks, such as spatial reasoning, were used to create a general measure of 'cognition'. The results showed that speed of processing was shown to predict how people would perform in the higher-level cognitive tasks. Working memory predicted performance too, but age itself predicted only a very small amount of performance. Salthouse argued that speed of processing therefore underlies the age-related decline in cognitive performance.

Another prominent theory in cognitive ageing research is the **frontal lobe hypothesis**. The frontal lobes are believed to be involved in a range of skills important for moment-to-moment functioning, including controlled processing of information, inhibiting attention and focusing on the task at hand.

Reasoning skills and controlled access to long-term memory are also believed to draw upon the frontal lobes. Older adults, therefore, tend to exhibit less efficient attentional skills, particularly regarding the ability to inhibit the activation of items of information that are no longer relevant. Older adults have therefore been argued to be more susceptible to distraction than younger adults (Hasher & Zacks, 1988). Hasher et al. (1991) presented younger (average age 19 years) and older (average age 68 years) adults with pairs of letters for 200 milliseconds, one of which was to be named on the basis of having been presented in the target colour. On some trials, however, the target letter had appeared as the distracting item on the immediately previous trial. In these kinds of trials, while younger adults reliably exhibited a **negative priming** effect in which responses were slowed by about 8 ms on average, this was not evident in the older adults. Essentially, then, if older adults are less able than younger adults to suppress attention towards distracting items, then their working memory is more likely to become cluttered with information, thus reducing overall capacity to deal with the most relevant information. Indeed, other research in this area has suggested that, because of this reduced ability to suppress no-longer-relevant information, older adults, on average, are more likely than younger adults to be distractible, absent-minded and confused by competing ideas.

Although we are beginning to understand the effects of age on cognitive change across the adult lifespan, much more research is required. It is likely that a variety of research approaches will help us understand cognitive ageing more fully, including research that draws upon novel techniques and follows the same individuals over a long period of time (i.e. **longitudinal research**).

KEY RESEARCHER Ian Deary

FIGURE 20.3   Ian Deary

Ian Deary is Professor of Differential Psychology, and the director of the Centre for Cognitive Ageing and Cognitive Epidemiology (CCACE), at the University of Edinburgh. Generally, his research addresses how and why people's abilities and behaviours vary in factors like personality and intelligence. One of his particular interests is in cognitive ageing. The research carried out by Professor Deary and his team in CCACE has been very influential; it is multidisciplinary, so draws upon expertise from fields such as medicine and biology, but also employs a diverse range of methods. For example, CCACE research may use a correlational approach to try to determine the relationships among different measurements (psychological, social, health-oriented, etc.). Some of the research involves state-of-the-art neuroimaging techniques, to allow brain structure and functioning to be observed, and may also incorporate data about the genetic makeup of participants. Much of the research conducted within the Centre has involved special cohorts of older adult participants. For example, important data indexing mental ability in childhood exists for the participants in the Lothian Birth Cohorts (www.lothianbirthcohort.ed.ac.uk/), allowing prior mental ability to be taken into account in statistical analyses of characteristics in older age (Deary et al., 2009). Researchers at CCACE are therefore helping advance our understanding about age-related changes in cognition and how mental ability in youth affects future health and longevity. You are invited to view the CCACE website (www.ccace.ed.ac.uk/), which is a useful resource for anyone interested in cognitive ageing research. You could also follow the Centre's twitter feed (@CCACE)!

20.4.2 EMOTION AND WELLBEING IN LATER LIFE

Perhaps when you carried out the stereotyping exercise earlier in this chapter, one of the stereotypes you produced in relation to older age was the 'grumpy old man'. Some of you will not have done this because, thankfully, not all stereotypes are negative. Certainly, there are some positive ageing stereotypes: rather than focusing on the stereotype of declining function, some focus on increasing wisdom and life experience (e.g. the 'golden ager', and the 'perfect grandmother'). Unfortunately, research has shown that most ageing stereotypes are negative and, indeed, some of the most frequently produced ones are negative about emotional experience in older age (e.g. the 'shrew', 'despondent') (Hummert, 2011). On a more positive note, it is important to point out that stereotyping is reduced when more specific characteristics are available about individuals, for example if it is known that the individual is still in employment or in good health.

FIGURE 20.4   Research shows that with age comes wisdom, good sense and a lower level of risk taking

© iStock.com/sturti

Interestingly, despite the existence of negative stereotypes about older age, research has observed a 'paradox of ageing'. That is, contrary to the expectations of many individuals, older people report feeling happier than

KEY STUDY

Carstensen, L.L., Turan, B., Schiebe, S., Ram, N., Ersner-Hershfield, H., et al. (2011). Emotional experience improves with age: evidence based on over 10 years of experience sampling. *Psychology and Aging, 26*(1), 21–33.

Over a 10-year period, and in nearly 200 participants aged across the lifespan from early through to very late adulthood, Carstensen and colleagues examined emotion in everyday life using an experience sampling method. There were three waves of data collection – baseline (i.e. at the start), and at five and 10 years later. At each wave, over a one-week period, each participant was asked to report their emotional state at five randomly selected times every day. At each sampling episode, participants were asked to rate, on a scale from 1 (not at all) to 7 (extremely), the extent to which they were experiencing 19 different emotions, including, for example, happiness and joy (positive) and anger and sadness (negative). The researchers aimed to test a number of hypotheses based on socio-emotional selectivity theory, namely that, as people age, (1) positive emotions are experienced more frequently than negative ones, (2) emotional experience is more stable and (3) emotional experience is more complex, with a mixture of positive and negative emotions more likely to be reported within a given sampling episode. Results showed that positive experience increased through adulthood to a peak in the mid-60s, then levelled off. Although there is a drop in frequency again into very late adulthood, levels do not reach as low as in young adulthood. Of course, it is important to point out that the story is not quite straightforward as a number of other variables can affect one's emotional experience. For example, physical health and openness to new experiences were both related to more positive emotions. However, the researchers were careful to take these and lots of other potentially important variables, such as gender and personality, into account in their analyses, and the pattern of results regarding ageing remained significant after such adjustments. Strikingly, those who reported more frequent positive than negative emotional experiences at the initial wave of the study were more likely to have lived longer. Carstensen and colleagues also showed that (a) emotional stability increases linearly with ageing, so that there is less variability in the emotions that older adults report, and (b) emotional experience was more complex in older age. These latter findings in particular were argued to show that older adults are better at regulating their emotions and that, in the context of perceived time left, contrary to popular belief, one's happiest years may in fact be in the seventh decade of life, as opposed to earlier in the adult lifespan. You can view Professor Carstensen presenting her research at: www.ted.com/talks/laura_carstensen_older_people_are_happier.html

younger people. Laura Carstensen is the Director of the Stanford Center on Longevity. She has carried out lots of research to try to understand emotional experience in older age. Specifically, her research has shown that older adults report more positive emotional experiences, and are more emotionally stable than younger adults (see key study).

20.4.3 LIFESTYLE FACTORS

One key issue in the psychology of ageing is that there are, of course, individual differences in the extent of age-related decline that is observed. You may find yourself thinking that certain people 'look good for their age', and this is the observation that some individuals seem to age more successfully than others. Indeed, many older adults seem to reject the previously mentioned negative stereotypes of old age, appearing at least as active and healthy as younger adults. While we know that good genetic makeup contributes towards successful ageing, lifestyle factors also appear to be important, and researchers have been investigating the extent to which we may positively influence our chances of ageing more successfully.

Promisingly, keeping mentally and physically active have both been shown to exert protective effects upon ageing success. For example, intellectual stimulation and structured training on everyday memory techniques has been shown to offer good potential for increased cognitive performance in older age, but self-efficacy may play an important role. That is, the social support and encouragement offered by group activities as opposed to individual training may help to enhance one's perceived cognitive potential, and may therefore affect the extent to which training benefits are observed (Hastings & West, 2009).

Physical activity in later life also offers great potential for positively influencing cognitive ageing success. Specifically, aerobic activity has been shown to benefit cognitive functioning, particularly those functions that are sensitive to the ageing process, for example those that draw on the resources of the frontal lobes (Colcombe & Kramer, 2006). Furthermore, using neuroimaging techniques, researchers have been able to show that aerobic activity is beneficial at the neural level, resulting in improved brain structure over time, which may help to explain the mechanisms for the cognitive benefits observed in other studies (Colcombe et al., 2006).

Nutrition is another very important lifestyle factor that has been receiving increased research attention in relation to ageing, and a variety of nutritional substances have been implicated in more positive psychological outcomes. For example, omega-3 fatty acids offer great potential for benefiting cognitive function in later life; they are abundant in brain areas important for learning and memory, and have been implicated in preserving neuronal structure and functioning. Antioxidant vitamins and the polyphenols found in many fruits and vegetables (such as black grapes and blueberries) also offer potential, but many more experiments with humans are required (Brown, Riby, & Reay, 2010). For example, much of the research is correlational, and so the findings could be related to other, uncontrolled, factors. Ideally, more **randomised controlled trials** (RCTs) that follow individuals over a long period of time will be carried out in the future. However, it is important to point out that nutritional effects may operate synergistically, so that a variety of beneficial nutrients would deliver the best possible outcomes. Indeed, some scientists have been recommending the Mediterranean-style diet, as this is rich in oily fish, fruit and vegetables but, as yet, the findings are by no means conclusive.

> **RANDOMISED CONTROLLED TRIAL** To assess the effect of a treatment, the experiment should include appropriate control conditions (e.g. a 'no treatment' condition and a 'placebo' or 'dummy' treatment). Ideally, the participant and experimenter are 'blind' to the condition the participants belong to.

In the context of the beneficial effects of physical and mental activity on our psychological wellbeing in later life, it is interesting to consider the role of work in particular. Research has shown that the more intellectual stimulation and social interaction experienced in the workplace, the less risk of cognitive impairment later in life and, importantly, the associations are independent of the initial level of intelligence or education (Potter, Helms, & Plassman, 2008). Such findings, in relation to those highlighting roles for mental and physical activity within older age, bring into question the possible negative influence of retirement from work on wellbeing in older age, and this may be a particular concern where an individual does not engage in hobbies and interests that could offer opportunities to help preserve their levels of activity. Indeed, research has highlighted that engaging in voluntary work, or continuing paid work, even for as little as two hours per week, has a protective effect on health and wellbeing in older adults, to the extent that it is even related to a longer life (Luoh & Herzog, 2002). Of course, continuing to involve older adults in the workplace offers great potential for employer gains, too, due to the experience and mentoring opportunities that older workers can offer as well as increased attendance/reliability. It is important to highlight that continuing to work is related to a number of positive aspects of everyday life, such as gaining new experiences, maintaining a sense of purpose and keeping a regular schedule, in addition to mental and physical activity, and social engagement. It is therefore likely that a variety of factors are related to wellbeing in later life, and continuing to engage in an active, varied lifestyle may offer the best chance of successful ageing.

20.4.4 SUMMARY OF AGEING

At the start of this section it was stated that the study of the psychology of ageing has seen an increase in recent years. However, it is still a relatively young area of research. Hopefully, with a continued rise in the volume of research devoted to this topic, we will understand more fully such interesting issues as age-related changes in cognitive

> **POPULATION AGEING** The trend for the oldest age groups in society to grow faster than the younger age groups.

functioning and emotional experience, and the role of lifestyle factors in the ageing process. We have seen that ageing is not necessarily a story of decline and that, in fact, there are a number of areas of stability and improvement. Older adults should therefore be encouraged to continue or even increase their activities within society, thereby promoting more successful ageing and increased quality of life in individuals, benefits for younger people within society and, overall, helping to address some of the challenges we face as our **population ages**.

20.5 CHAPTER SUMMARY

In this chapter we have considered the key developmental trends that occur during adolescence, adulthood and ageing. Hopefully, as the chapter has progressed you have considered how well your stereotypes of a typical teenager or an older person fit with the theory and research about the particular stage in the lifespan. Finally, we would like you to think about the points for reflection below, and invite you to follow up with any of the additional reading.

DISCUSSION QUESTIONS

Is there a typical experience for each of these stages? Are the stereotypes for each group discussed here accurate, and can they be sustained by the research literature?

What impact can health have on each of these stages of life? What is the impact on psychological wellbeing for having either good or poor physical health?

What areas of ageing do you think need further research? Where are the gaps in knowledge and why might addressing these gaps be important for society?

SUGGESTIONS FOR FURTHER READING

Arnett, J.J. (1999). Adolescent storm and stress, reconsidered. *American Psychologist*, *54*, 317–326. This article examines this view of 'storm and stress' in detail, reconsidering this view.

Stuart-Hamilton, I. (2012). *The psychology of ageing: an introduction* (5th edn). London: Jessica Kingsley. This is an accessible introduction to the study of psychology and ageing, and covers a range of issues from cognitive ability to health and wellbeing.

Still want more? For links to online resources relevant to this chapter and a quiz to test your understanding, visit the companion website at edge.sagepub.com/banyard2e

SECTION F

THE PSYCHOLOGY OF INDIVIDUAL DIFFERENCES: HOW WE KNOW AND MEASURE OUR INDIVIDUALITY

Half of the people you know are below average.

Steven Wright

In our modern world, we categorise people on a whole range of abilities. 'He's very bright, you know', says the competitive (i.e. every) parent, as if it mattered, or as if they had actually tested their child and compared them to other children. In everyday conversation, we are always making comparisons between our expectations of individuals and how they actually behave. These differences between individuals have been one of the key concerns of psychology for over 100 years.

THE HISTORY OF INDIVIDUAL DIFFERENCES

Attempts to classify people into types are not new. The ancient Greek philosopher Hippocrates (460–*c*.370 BC), who is often credited with being the founder of Western medicine, proposed that disease was not a mystical thing but came instead from natural causes and in particular from four key humours. Later, Galen (AD 129–199) developed this idea and proposed that these humours give rise to four temperaments in people. We still use the labels of these temperaments today to describe people and their state of mind; melancholic, phlegmatic, choleric and sanguine. This is a basic typology of personality and it forms the basis for modern typologies (see Chapter 21).

The modern study of individual differences can be traced back to the work of Francis Galton, who invented and defined the field. In 1884, Galton created a mental testing laboratory – an anthropometric lab for testing data about people, such as visual acuity, strength of grip, colour vision, hearing acuity and hand preference (see Figure F.1). He hoped to use these measures to estimate people's hereditary intelligence. This is a key feature of much subsequent research, and the genetic explanation of individual differences has dominated the field. Galton's impressed inventory of new scientific ideas is described in Chapter 2.

FIGURE F.1   Galton's anthropometric laboratory that was set up at the International Health Exhibition in London in 1885

© Science Museum/Science & Society Picture Library

The field of individual differences seeks to categorise people by perceived differences in their personality and also by differences in their performance on cognitive tasks. This second area of interest was kick started by the work of French psychologist Binet at the turn of the twentieth century (see Chapter 22) to develop the first tests of intelligence. It is clear that we can measure differences in behaviour and performance between people, but what is not clear is where these differences come from, and this is a much more controversial issue than you might first think. The controversy develops because the cause of the differences will affect what we decide to do about them (see Chapter 22).

A different approach altogether that also comes under the heading of individual differences is the exploration of our unique individual differences (rather than a comparison to group norms). You might think of this as the 'Who am I?' question, and it concerns issues of identity. What are the things that define you and structure the relationships you have with other people? And where does your sense of self come from?

KEY ISSUES

One of the key issues in the field of individual differences concerns the usefulness of measuring and categorising people. The measured differences between us are usually very small but are used to rank people and to distinguish one person from another. This is fine, but another view of people could highlight how much we have in common. People are able to communicate, they are sociable, they have warm attachments to other people that endure over time, and they perceive and make sense of the world around them in very similar ways. However, at this point in our history we seem more bothered about what distinguishes one person from another than about what unites us. Hence the rise in importance of individual differences in psychology.

Another key issue for individual differences is the discussion over nature and nurture. This was first framed by Galton but has burned brightly ever since, as we try to explain why one group of people is better or worse than another group at a particular skill. The importance of this discussion is that the answer you come to guides you to certain solutions to social problems.

THIS SECTION

In this section, we have three chapters looking at the core areas of individual differences. Chapter 21 explores what psychologists have to say about personality: What is it? Is there such a thing as a normal or abnormal personality? How is personality measured? In Chapter 22 we look at differences in cognitive performance, and the most prominent concept here is intelligence. Is intelligence just the ability to learn, or is it problem-solving ability? Do we become 'more' intelligent as we grow older? Finally, in Chapter 23, we look at the self and ask 'Who am I?' 'How do I know who I am?'

21 PERSONALITY

Lead authors: David J. Wilde and Glenn A. Williams

CHAPTER OUTLINE

21.1 Introduction	368
21.2 What is personality?	368
21.3 Trait approaches to personality	369
21.3.1 Extraversion and neuroticism	370
21.3.2 The 16-factor model	370
21.3.3 The three-factor model	371
21.3.4 The five-factor model	372
21.3.5 HEXACO: the six-factor model	374
21.3.6 So how many factors are there?	375
21.4 The situationalist critique of trait psychology	375
21.4.1 Responding to the situationalist critique	376
21.5 An example of the application of personality theory and research to the real world: can your personality make you healthier than other people?	378
21.5.1 Type A and B personalities	378
21.5.2 Critique of the Type A/B personality theory	379
21.5.3 Type C personality and cancer	380
21.5.4 Type D personality: a 'distressed' personality	380
21.5.5 Personality and good health	380
21.6 Chapter summary	382
Discussion questions	382
Suggestions for further reading	383

21.1 INTRODUCTION

'Are you a *conscientious* type of person?' says the headline in the magazine, 'Take our personality test to find out how *conscientious* you are.' Obviously you can substitute *conscientious* with any personality characteristic of the moment, but you'll recognise this idea of a test of your personality that can be carried out with a few simple questions. In this chapter we focus on the attempt of psychologists to discover common traits and characteristics of our personalities and to then find ways of comparing individuals on these traits. We will look at the two main approaches in this tradition for studying and measuring personality. Measuring is the key here and this approach to personality emphasises the value of measurement. We go on to critique the use of traits in psychology and then apply the psychology of personality to the real-world situation of health, illness and wellbeing.

One of the recurrent themes in this text is the human quest to find out who and what we are. One of the ways we describe ourselves is in terms of our character or personality. This is the first of two chapters that look directly at these issues. We continue the discussion in Chapter 23 when we look at issues of self and identity.

FRAMING QUESTIONS

- What is this thing called 'personality'? What is it made up of?
- What kind of personality do you have? What influenced its development? Was it your genes or how you were brought up?
- Does your personality remain the same over time and in different situations, or does it change?

21.2 WHAT IS PERSONALITY?

Psychologists have had a range of theories as to what personality involves. The following two definitions should give you an insight into how much psychologists vary in their understanding of what it means to have a certain type of personality. One definition of personality has emphasised being able to *differentiate* between people by stating that it is:

… those internal stable factors that make people systematically and predictably different from one another. (Furnham & Heaven, 1999: 1)

Another definition has instead highlighted the *similarities* and common features people have, labelling personality as:

… a stable set of tendencies and characteristics that determine those commonalities and differences in people's psychological behavior. (Maddi, 1989: 8)

Although there is some variation in how personality is defined, psychologists seem to share some common ground. Furnham and Heaven (1999) have identified such agreement, with personality comprising:

- individual differences by stressing the uniqueness of individuals, but also the importance of being able to categorise, classify or describe this uniqueness along dimensions of personality;
- a combined system of cognitions, emotions and behaviours;
- stable, and sometimes predictable, behaviour;
- general dispositions, which are linked to specific needs or drives.

Therefore, a number of things need to be considered when examining personality. Each of us has our own unique personality, and this is evident in everyday life, in what we think about certain aspects of life, how we act around other people, what choices we make and how we work. For example, if you are reading this chapter, it may be that you are an extremely conscientious student who has decided that you would like to know more about personality and are preparing for an essay that you need to submit in a period that is due many weeks away. However, less conscientious (and organised) students may be reading this chapter after leaving revision for an exam until the last minute. Clearly, people differ along various spectrums of behaviours, feelings and thought processes. Personality traits (such as conscientiousness) may be one of the spectrums that we can use to differentiate between people. Traits are prevailing behaviour patterns within each of us that generally remain stable across time as well as across a variety of circumstances, and we shall examine the trait concept in the next section.

21.3 TRAIT APPROACHES TO PERSONALITY

One approach to personality is the **nomothetic** perspective, which investigates large numbers of people with a view to finding generalised laws governing behaviour that can be applied to everyone. This way of studying personality assumes that each person is a complex combination of universal behaviours and then assesses to what degree a person fits against a 'norm' for their sex and age group. With this nomothetic tradition to studying personality there are two major units of analysis – **traits** and **types**.

The type approach to personality groups individuals into a number of different categories, each of which is defined by a distinct collection of personality characteristics. One of the original type theorists was Carl Jung (1921/1971). Jung's work was later developed by Isabel Briggs Myers and her mother, Katharine Briggs, into the Myers-Briggs Type Indicator (MBTI) (Myers & Myers, 1980/1995). People answering this questionnaire are categorised according to type, for example, they can be either sensates or intuitives. Sensates focus on physical reality and base their judgements on sensory data. They are concerned by current, real-world situations. By contrast, intuitives pay more attention to their mental worlds by thinking in abstract terms, making decisions through gut feeling, and seek meaning from their inner worlds.

The **trait** approach views personality as comprising a number of durable characteristics along which individuals vary. This allows for a unique pattern of traits to be described that distinguishes a person's individuality. In the last half-century numerous trait personality models have emerged, each claiming to outline the structure of human personality. These are the 16-factor model (Cattell, Eber, & Tatsuoka, 1970), the three-factor model (Eysenck & Eysenck, 1991), the five-factor model (Costa & McCrae, 1992) and the six-factor (HEXACO) model (Ashton et al., 2004). The common term 'factor' refers to the use of the statistical technique of factor analysis to determine the underlying structure of the personality traits making up each model. In the following sections, we will look at the main personality traits in each of these four models.

FIGURE 21.1 The Seven Dwarfs from Snow White (here seen on holiday) show a 'type' approach to personality, with each character being defined by one feature, such as Grumpy or Dopey. This is a game for all the family to play as you try to define friends and family in just one characteristic. Expect arguments when you do this

© Bob Daemmrich/Corbis

NOMOTHETIC AND IDIOGRAPHIC Nomothetic approaches seek to establish the generalised laws of behaviour and are typified by observable, verifiable and quantifiable measurements. They are concerned with what we share with other people. By contrast, idiographic approaches concern themselves with what makes us unique and individual.

TRAIT A durable form of thinking, feeling or behaving in the world that is relatively stable and predictable over a variety of different situations.

FACTOR ANALYSIS A group of similar methods of statistical analysis that reduce complex numerical data into a smaller amount of dimensions or factors.

21.3.1 EXTRAVERSION AND NEUROTICISM

Two personality traits that have been consistently linked with several models of personality are extraversion and neuroticism. They are both common to the three-factor and five-factor models, with extraversion additionally included in the 16-factor model and also appearing as the 'X' in the six-factor 'HEXACO' model.

> **EXTRAVERSION** A general tendency towards outgoing, social behaviour.
>
> **NEUROTICISM** A personality trait characterised by feelings of anxiety, tension, anger and/or depression.

Those with high **extraversion** levels (often called 'extraverts') are socially outgoing and focused on the external world. They draw their energy from being around others and from exciting situations and environments. They tend to be impulsive and feel positively about themselves. On the other hand, those with low extraversion levels (often labelled as 'introverts') are more introspective, may feel uncomfortable if they are at the centre of social attention, and usually prefer the quieter life, engaging in pastimes such as reading and writing, rather than seeking excitement. They generally feel less energetic and less optimistic about themselves than do extraverts (Eysenck & Eysenck, 1991). This description of introversion may come across as portraying introverts as having negative qualities, but there is research (Cain, 2012) to show that the opposite may be the case. It has been argued that workplaces and educational settings tend to cater more to the extravert ideal, but it should be noted that creative and inspirational ways of working and learning may sometimes come from being more careful, methodical and solitary in one's approach, rather than assuming that the only way to excel is through working as a team player or as a leader.

Neuroticism is typified by emotional instability, feelings of anxiety, guilt, anger, envy and depression. Those with high levels of neuroticism are often emotionally volatile and are poor in responding effectively to stressful life events; they will often view events as very bleak, overwhelming and difficult, which many people might see as minor hindrances. As personality traits are seen as lying on a continuum, at the opposite end of the scale there are emotionally stable people, who have a good mastery of their emotional states and tend to act calmly and in a composed fashion even during stressful situations.

As noted above, extraversion and neuroticism are fundamental components of several models of personality. We will now examine these models in chronological order, beginning with the earliest – the 16-factor model.

21.3.2 THE 16-FACTOR MODEL

The 16-factor model was developed by Raymond Cattell in 1949 (Cattell & Mead, 2008). Cattell was committed to using the scientific method and was one of the first psychologists to utilise the statistical method of factor analysis to explore personality. One of his most influential results of this work was the discovery of 16 factors underlying personality structure. He termed these factors 'source traits' (Cattell, 1957) as he considered them to be the foundations of all human personality. He developed his theory into the 16 personality factor model and created an instrument, the 16 Personality Factor (PF) Questionnaire, to measure this.

According to Cattell, personality exists on a continuum of 16 traits. All humans are assumed to possess these traits to some extent, but they vary in prominence between individuals; some may be high in certain traits and lower in others. Cattell's 16 personality dimensions are listed in Table 21.1, along with descriptors of the high and low ranges for each dimension.

> **LEXICAL HYPOTHESIS** Sometimes also called 'the lexical approach', the lexical hypothesis involves making the assumption that the optimal way to understand and measure personality is through the analysis of language that the general population uses to portray people's personalities. With this assumption, there is also the hypothesis that personality can best be characterised through single words such as 'aggressive', 'sociable', 'punctual', 'irritating' (John, Angleitner, & Ostendorf, 1988).

Cattell's 16 personality factor model was a landmark in personality research and is still widely used today, but it has not been without its critics. The major criticism of the theory is that it has never been fully replicated, despite numerous attempts by a variety of researchers, many of whom were trained by Cattell and conversant with his methods (Eysenck, 1991). Cattell refuted this on the grounds that his exact methodology was not followed, but a study conducted by Kline and Barrett (1983), using an identical methodology to Cattell's, only verified four out of the 16 personality factors in Cattell's model. However, other researchers have replicated the

TABLE 21.1 The 16 primary factors developed by Cattell (adapted from Conn and Rieke, 1994)

DESCRIPTOR RANGE

PRIMARY FACTOR	HIGH		LOW
Abstractedness	Imaginative, creative	⟷	Practical, down to earth
Apprehension	Apprehensive, insecure	⟷	Complacent, carefree
Dominance	Aggressive, controlling	⟷	Passive, cooperative
Emotional stability	Calm, mature	⟷	Immature, highly strung
Liveliness	Enthusiastic, spontaneous	⟷	Serious, introspective
Openness to change	Liberal, adaptable	⟷	Traditional, restrained
Perfectionism	Compulsive, organised	⟷	Undemanding, undisciplined
Privateness	Pretentious, astute	⟷	Unpretentious, genuine
Reasoning	Abstract, fast learning	⟷	Concrete, low mental capacity
Rule-consciousness	Moralistic, sense of duty	⟷	Free-thinking, self-indulgent
Self-reliance	Leadership, self-sufficiency	⟷	Group-oriented, subordinate
Sensitivity	Sensitive, intuitive	⟷	Tough-minded, objective
Social boldness	Brave, adventurous	⟷	Cautious, timid
Tension	Driven, energetic	⟷	Relaxed, easy going
Vigilance	Suspicious, questioning	⟷	Accepting, trusting
Warmth	Open, warm-hearted	⟷	Detached, critical

primary 16-factor structure (e.g. Burdsal & Bolten, 1979). Notwithstanding the criticism that Cattell's model has received, it should be recognised that his pioneering research led to the development of the five- and six-factor models as they both used the lexical approach that Cattell had used, and all of these models have contributed greatly to our understanding of personality.

21.3.3 THE THREE-FACTOR MODEL

Eysenck's model of personality was originally described in 1947 as a two-factor model, which followed on from the work of Hippocrates (*c.* 460 BC) through to Galen (AD 129–199) and Kant (1907/2006). However, it is perhaps Galen's concept of the four humours or temperaments that is most pertinent to the development of Eysenck's theory. Galen postulated a four-fold descriptive typology of human character. There are the strongly emotional, unstable personalities: melancholic people tend to be moody, pessimistic, unsociable and anxiety-prone individuals (Eysenck's 'unstable introverts'), whereas choleric types are characterised as touchy, restless folk, who are aggressive and changeable ('unstable extraverts' in Eysenck's model). Then there are the more stable, less emotional characters: the sanguine person who is carefree, talkative, social and outgoing (equivalent to Eysenck's 'stable extraverts'), and the phlegmatic kind, who are generally peaceful, calm, controlled and thoughtful (corresponding to Eysenck's 'stable introverts') (Stelmack & Stalikas, 1991).

Figure 21.2 shows the inner circular portion depicting Galen's model of the temperaments, while the outer circular portion shows the twin bipolar dimensions of extraversion–introversion and neuroticism–emotional stability and how these relate to each other.

Eysenck (1967) proposed the idea that both extraversion and neuroticism could be explained by biological processes. For example, high

> **AUTONOMIC NERVOUS SYSTEM** A network of nerve fibres connecting the brain and spinal cord to the body. It regulates the major involuntary functions such as heart rate, digestion and respiration, and can prepare the body for action or rest.

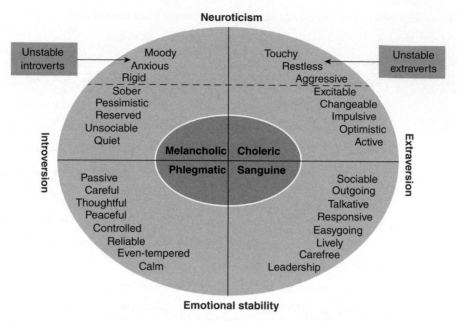

FIGURE 21.2   The Eysenck personality circle (adapted from Eysenck & Eysenck, 1991)

levels of arousal in a region of the brain called the **ascending reticular activating system (ARAS)** could account for why introverts seek stimulus-passive situations as they try to quell the level of stimulation in the ARAS. Conversely, extraverts are constantly seeking stimulation there as their levels of arousal in the ARAS are low. Higher levels of neuroticism are linked to the **autonomic nervous system (ANS)** and can be explained by an individual's tendency to react to stressful or threatening situations by invoking a 'fight-or-flight' response (Eysenck & Eysenck, 1985).

Eysenck, in collaboration with his wife, Sybil, added the third factor in the model, **psychoticism**, in the mid-1970s (Eysenck & Eysenck, 1976), although this trait is less well defined than extraversion and neuroticism. People who score highly on psychoticism are inclined to be non-conformists, risk takers, tough-minded, possibly engaging in anti-social behaviours, and unable to empathise with other people. The psychoticism scale bears some similarities with the trait of (low) conscientiousness and agreeableness (Eysenck, 1991).

Eysenck's model has enjoyed support from a number of studies that have confirmed its validity and structure, and has been widely used in a variety of clinical and other applied settings (Kline, 2000). We will now turn to arguably the most popular model of personality traits: the five-factor model.

21.3.4 THE FIVE-FACTOR MODEL

The **five-factor model** first appeared in 1985 and was developed by McCrae and Costa (1997). However, McCrae and Costa's model was not the first one to identify five personality factors, and its forerunners have been variously termed the 'Big Five' (Deary, 1996) or the 'Norman 5' (Norman, 1963). The McCrae and Costa model is often referred to by its acronyms, OCEAN or less commonly CANOE, which both stem from the initial letters of the model's five factors: Openness to experience, Conscientiousness, Extraversion, Agreeableness and Neuroticism (Matthews, Deary, & Whiteman, 2003).

Earlier we introduced you to two of this model's traits, extraversion and neuroticism. The three remaining traits can be described using the following characteristics:

People who score highly on openness to experience tend to have an appreciation for art, are intellectually curious and creative, full of unusual ideas and they display preferences for novelty and variety. At the opposite end of the scale, people scoring low on this trait are inclined to be cautious, like following routines, and prefer to have structure and predictability in their life.

Conscientiousness is characterised by a proclivity for self-discipline, acting dutifully and committed to hard work, diligence and thoroughness. People with high levels of conscientiousness have a need to accomplish goals and possess

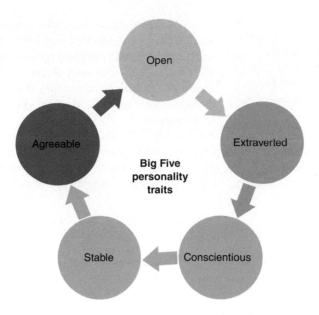

FIGURE 21.3   The Big Five personality traits

the right qualities needed to realise their objectives (Goldberg, 1992). Those low in conscientiousness may be unreliable, leave things to the last minute and can be prone to making impulsive or rash decisions.

Agreeableness involves characteristics such as trust, kindness and affection, and are able to 'get on' with other people. People who are less agreeable are generally not concerned about others' wellbeing, and are quite sceptical and suspicious about the motives of others, which leads them to be unfriendly and potentially manipulative.

KEY STUDY

Costa Jr, P.T., & McCrae, R.R. (1976). Age differences in personality structure: a cluster analytic approach. *Journal of Gerontology*, *31*(5), 564–570.

We introduced you to the researchers Costa and McCrae when we discussed the five-factor model earlier. Here we wish to focus on one of the first studies that they published together and one which reveals that they were already starting to view personality traits beyond the three-factor and 16-factor models.

In this study, Costa and McCrae (1976) administered the 16PF (Cattell et al., 1970) to a sample of 969 adult male volunteers and separated their participants into three major age groups (25–34 years, 35–54 years, 55+ years). The results of the study showed age group differences with regards to openness to experience, which was a relatively newly discovered trait at that time. Although Costa and McCrae had found no age differences on anxiety-adjustment (a trait comparable to the contemporary concept of neuroticism) or introversion-extraversion, the trait of openness to experience seemed to encompass three dimensions: openness to (1) feelings, (2) ideas and (3) feelings and ideas combined. The study showed that, of the three age groups, the 25–34 year olds reported a greater openness to feelings than the other two groups, whereas those aged 35–54 reported a greater openness to ideas. Participants in the 55 and over group were found to show more openness to both feelings and ideas.

Costa and McCrae's study proved to be a milestone in personality research as it shifted the focus from the notion of personality being mostly comprised of two core traits of neuroticism and extraversion, which we discussed earlier in this chapter, to the view that there were other just as important and valuable personality traits to be uncovered. Subsequent research has borne this out.

As we have seen earlier, Costa and McCrae began a fruitful research partnership as they continued to cultivate their ideas about how we might understand and measure personality traits, culminating in the development of the NEO-Personality Inventory (NEO-PI) (McCrae & Costa, 1983). Their seminal work has led to a wealth of research into personality traits and their five-factor model remains one of the most used in personality research to date.

MACHIAVELLIANISM Named after Renaissance Italian Niccolò Machiavelli (Google him), the term describes a duplicitous interpersonal style associated with cynical beliefs and pragmatic morality. It is sometimes referred to as one of the dark triad personalities.

The five-factor model has been tested and validated in numerous studies (e.g. Costa & McCrae, 1992; McCrae & Costa, 1997) and has been successfully applied cross-culturally (Thompson, 2008), but there are several criticisms of the model. Some psychologists disagree with the model because they think it disregards other personality domains, for example, **Machiavellianism**, religiosity and honesty (Paunonen et al., 2003; Paunonen & Jackson, 2000). A further criticism is that the model was derived mostly from the lexical approach, which Block (1995, 2001) suggests is inadequate when trying to uncover the central features of a dynamic system that is personality and its resulting behaviours. Despite these criticisms, the model remains popular and is widely used as a way of measuring personality in education, the workplace and in various health settings.

21.3.5 HEXACO: THE SIX-FACTOR MODEL

The most recent of the trait models to be developed is the **six-factor model** (Ashton et al., 2004). The six dimensions were derived from findings from lexical studies of personality structure conducted in a variety of European and Asian languages. The acronym HEXACO comes from the initial letters of five of the factors making up the model: Honesty-humility, Emotionality, Agreeableness, Conscientiousness and Openness to experience, with the 'X' derived from the second letter of the factor eXtraversion. The model builds upon the previously discussed five-factor model of Costa and McCrae (1992) and also from Goldberg's (1993) work.

Each of the six HEXACO dimensions is characterised by high and low levels of the traits making up each factor. We have already introduced you to the traits of extraversion, agreeableness, conscientiousness and openness to experience in previous sections. The remaining two personality traits in the HEXACO model are honesty-humility and emotionality.

The honesty-humility factor is arguably the HEXACO model's most unique addition to the trait approach. The main characteristics of this trait are sincerity, faithfulness, modesty, and low levels of slyness, pretentiousness and hypocrisy. Those scoring highly on this trait are people who do not wish to manipulate others for their own gain, tend to want to follow the rules of society, have a strong sense of fairness, and shy away from wealth and eminent social status. Conversely, people who score low on this trait are those inclined to try to control others and break rules for personal gain and material profit, and have a high sense of self-importance.

Although the emotionality scale may appear to resemble the neuroticism factor that is present in other personality trait models, it does differ in some respects. The main characteristics of the emotionality factor in the HEXACO model are sentimentality, oversensitivity, fearfulness, anxiety, toughness, independence and stability. A person scoring highly on the emotionality scale is someone who worries a lot, gets anxious in response to life stressors and would be similar to high neuroticism scorers in this respect. As opposed to high neuroticism scorers, high emotionality with the HEXACO model also entails having someone who is empathic and sentimental. Someone with low levels of emotionality would not feel afraid in physically dangerous situations, nor do they worry much in life, and respond robustly to life's stresses and threats. They can be emotionally detached from other people and have little or no need to share their emotions with others. Clearly the emotional detachment element of the emotionality scale would appear to be more akin to the tough-mindedness feature that is salient in the psychoticism scale of the three-factor model.

Being a trait-based taxonomy of human personality, the HEXACO model is susceptible to the same criticisms that have been aimed at similar factor analytically derived trait-based models, which we discussed in relation to the five-factor model. Factor analysis, although a widely used statistical method, does not always yield replicable results as it relies on the number of variables in the analysis (Goldberg, 1992), which are at the command of the researcher, and on the composition of how people respond to questions on surveys – for example, choosing between 'Yes' or 'No' (a dichotomous response), or perhaps rating responses on a five-point 'Likert' type scale, where 1 = 'strongly disagree' to 5 = 'strongly agree'. Replication is a particularly pertinent criticism of the honesty-humility factor, with some authors (e.g. Bashiri et al., 2011; Saucier, 2009; Thalmayer, Saucier, & Eigenhuis, 2011) questioning how different this factor is from the five-factor model factor of agreeableness (Maltby, Day, & Macaskill, 2013) due to the failure of honesty-humility to emerge as an independent factor in some studies. Nevertheless, the HEXACO model is now being used in a range of psychological research.

EXERCISE: TRAITS OF A ROLE MODEL?

Role models are people whom other people may admire, find inspirational, or try to emulate in some way. They can be forces for good in others, but some have a more negative effect, and are often called 'bad influences' by people other than the person who is influenced by these role models.

Now that we have covered the main trait models, try to recall someone who has influenced you in some way (it can be a teacher, friend, relative or someone in the public eye). List their key personality characteristics. Which ones resonate with you? Why do you think that is?

21.3.6 SO HOW MANY FACTORS ARE THERE?

The various models above have used similar techniques, commonly factor analysis, to find out what are the stable factors of personality that can be best used to describe us. They have all come to a different conclusion, which leaves the reader asking, so really how many factors are there? The fact that we can't give a clear answer to this question shows the limitations of this approach to personality and also the limitation of statistical techniques like factor analysis. Having said that, this approach to understanding human differences has been very popular and is commonly used in a range of areas, such as diagnosis and job selection. Clearly, many people find it a useful tool that can still be used while we edge our way to a better understanding of the processes behind personality.

From the above review we can see that the trait approach, while making a significant contribution to personality psychology, is not without its limitations and critics, which is something we explore further in the next section.

ASIDE

Reasons to be sceptical: How consistent are personality traits?

There is evidence to suggest that personality traits are relatively weak in predicting how people will behave in different scenarios. With the prediction of behaviour being one of the primary goals of the nomothetic approach, might we then question the power of the trait approach in predicting how a person will act, think and feel? One of the main assumptions of the trait approach is that traits are relatively stable and consistent over situations and time. You can test this assumption for yourself. Think about your own personality . . . Has it changed much or are you still the same person you were 10 years ago? If you were to attend a school reunion party, would your classmates recognise the 'old' you from your schooldays? Are you the same person acting the same way at every social event you attend? Or is there a core part of you that remains pretty much the same?

Now you have thought about this, what conclusions can you make about the consistency of personality traits?

21.4 THE SITUATIONALIST CRITIQUE OF TRAIT PSYCHOLOGY

Traits can offer us a useful vocabulary for comparing and contrasting between individuals within the limits of the nomothetic perspective to understanding personality. This vocabulary can be particularly promising as it helps us to understand that someone with high levels of extraversion is likely to have similar tendencies and is highly likely to resemble others who are equally extraverted. The problem arises when we start to look at variations *within* a person's everyday personality expression rather than when comparing *between* individuals. There are a number of problematic issues that trait approaches cannot seem to address adequately, particularly in helping us to comprehend why we might respond in ways that are uncharacteristic of our normal ways of thinking, feeling and acting. Certainly, there might be situations that force us to act in particular ways, but sometimes we just might want to act differently through purely arbitrary motives. An example of the effect of situation can be seen in Mischel's marshmallow experiment, which you can find in many versions on YouTube.

The nomothetic perspective and the language of traits, according to some theorists, are fundamentally flawed as they cannot tell us about what is happening when 'a person … is affable with peers, deferent to superiors, and nasty to individuals of lower rank' (Block, 1995: 196). Some psychologists, like Mischel (1968), have been called situationalists in their approach to personality and behaviour because they have argued that often the power of a situation may reign supreme and make us feel like we have to behave in a certain way. Although Mischel's work is now several decades old, it was seminal and controversial and led some psychologists to question whether personality actually existed (Roberts, 2009).

Mischel conducted a **meta-analysis** of many studies to see how strongly personality traits were correlated with specific behaviours. He found that, on average, **correlations** between traits and a given behaviour over time were rarely higher than 0.30. This 0.30 aggregate **correlation coefficient** was termed by Mischel as being a **personality coefficient**, and was then used as a method for examining the extent to which personality can explain a certain percentage of how variable people's behaviours can be. This percentage was calculated as being about 10% as the variance in behaviour was obtained by multiplying the correlation coefficient by itself ($0.30 \times 0.30 = 0.09$) and then multiplying that result by 100 to get a percentage. As this approximated to just under 10% Mischel saw personality as accounting for a small percentage of behavioural variation and argued that 90% of behavioural responses could be explained by other, more powerful influences. Overall, Mischel argued persuasively that personality traits cannot offer a complete explanation or means of predicting how people will act in a given situation, especially as the demands of a situation and needing to fulfil a certain social role are also highly influential.

> **META-ANALYSIS** A literature review that summarises and contrasts findings by calculating effect sizes.
>
> **CORRELATION COEFFICIENT** A number between −1 and +1 which expresses how strong a correlation is. If this number is close to 0, there is no real connection between the two. If it is close to +1, there is a positive correlation – in other words, if one variable is large, the other will also tend to be large. And if it is close to −1, there is a negative correlation – in other words, if one variable is large, the other will tend to be small.

21.4.1 RESPONDING TO THE SITUATIONALIST CRITIQUE

Some psychologists have refuted Mischel's criticisms of how influential personality is in determining how people will act. The first of these rebuttals was that Mischel's original analysis was based on an incomplete review of existing personality literature. Additionally, Mischel was criticised for selectively including studies, some with major methodological flaws, that mostly reported unimpressive results at the expense of studies that reported more impressive findings, and were conducted more robustly (Funder, 2010).

A second important criticism lies with the 'magical' 0.30 correlation coefficient that Mischel used to support his assertion that personality traits have little or no influence in determining behaviour. Some authors, such as Funder and Ozer (1983), have suggested that a correlation of 0.30 is not as small as some believe it to be, and can explain quite a bit of variance in itself. The counter-argument here is that this figure was derived from studies conducted within laboratory settings with little ecological validity to real-life behaviours. It may be that traits are generally poor behavioural predictors in laboratory situations, but they may be more stable at predicting behaviours that occur in the diverse range of naturally occurring situations beyond the laboratory (McAdams & Pals, 2006). In fact, Allport (1961) suggested that the influence of personality is likely to be greater in real-life situations that are personally important and meaningful. A further implication of this criticism is that with advances in research methods and better designed studies statistically better outcomes should follow.

Overall, the majority of personality researchers have reached a consensus that a person's behaviour is generally the product of both situational and personality factors. In specific scenarios, the role of situational factors is likely to compel certain behaviours, particularly in situations that are public, formal and novel (Buss, 1989). Traits, on the other hand, probably better account for patterns of behaviours occurring across situations (Fleeson, 2001), particularly if the situation is comparatively relaxed and private. Some researchers have suggested that personality traits can be developed and shaped through the aggregation of short-term goals, which are driven by meaningful situational factors, such as social roles (Heller, Perunovic, & Reichman, 2009).

The contemporary perspective psychology has on this debate is termed **interactionism**, which adopts the viewpoint that there is a reciprocal influence between personality, situations and environment. Situations and surroundings may play an important role in determining our goals and personalities, yet in many circumstances we take a dynamic role in shaping an environment to reflect our personalities (Buss, 1977). In the following sections, we shall investigate the personality–situation interaction as it occurs in the real-world setting of health, illness and wellbeing.

KEY STUDY

Cacioppo, J.T., Petty, R.E., & Kao, C.F. (1984). The efficient assessment of Need for Cognition. *Journal of Personality Assessment, 48*(3), 306–307.

Are you the kind of person who needs to be regularly solving problems or reading challenging books or doing anything else to keep you intellectually stimulated? Do you really enjoy engaging in thinking tasks and getting immersed in deep and meaningful discussions? If you are, then it is likely that you have a craving to fulfil a need known as Need for Cognition. This concept was originally examined by psychologists such as Maslow, who was looking at the role that various needs played in our lives. In the mid-1950s, Cohen and colleagues (Cohen et al., 1955) began to carry out empirical work into this need, but these studies were often small-scale (e.g. one published in 1955 involved an experiment with only 57 undergraduates; another looked at 35 undergraduates) and there wasn't a standardised, validated tool to measure Need for Cognition (see Cohen et al., 1955 for both studies). Cacioppo and Petty's (1982) work was the first of its kind to develop a psychometrically sound measure of need of cognition. It has been quoted and used in almost 3,000 studies in a range of areas such as: how Need for Cognition may (1) affect academic performance, (2) influence jury decision making and (3) be a crucial factor when advertising to certain target groups in the population.

The article that Cacioppo and Petty published showed, through four studies, how they developed the Need for Cognition scale through generating a pool of possible questionnaire items, such as 'I take pride in the products of my reasoning' and 'the notion of thinking abstractly is not appealing to me' (N.B. this item signified low levels of Need for Cognition). For generating these items, the researchers approached university students or those in a work environment where it was assumed that having a Need for Cognition was not the most important part of that job. For this purpose, the researchers studied assembly-line employees and then compared these workers on how they fared in relation to the students' responses to the survey items. Forty-five items had originally been generated, but only 34 of them successfully differentiated between the two groups of participants and these items were then used in a second study, which attempted to analyse the underlying structure to this 34-item Need for Cognition scale with a much larger sample.

Factor analysis was able to show that the scale was assessing just one psychological construct, rather than many different sub-elements. The third study was able to show that Need for Cognition was positively and significantly correlated with a measure of academic performance, and the fourth study was able to demonstrate that people with low Need for Cognition tended to enjoy more simple cognitive tasks and those with high Need for Cognition revelled in doing complex tasks.

Clearly, this research has helped set the agenda for future studies into a range of psychological phenomena, particularly in investigating how susceptible people may be to certain types of advertising. Studies have shown that consumers with a high Need for Cognition like to have advertising that has open-ended, comparative selections of brands to allow the consumer to make decisions about which brand is best. The concept of Need for Cognition has also been brought into the twenty-first century with a study (Martin, Sherrard, & Wentzel, 2005) into how people react to certain web page designs according to their degree of Need for Cognition, with high verbal complexity and low visual complexity being preferred by people with a high Need for Cognition. An 18-item version of the Need for Cognition scale is available in the literature, so why not see if you've got a high Need for Cognition and test yourself? The test can be found from accessing articles by Cacioppo et al. (1984) and Cacioppo et al. (1996).

21.5 AN EXAMPLE OF THE APPLICATION OF PERSONALITY THEORY AND RESEARCH TO THE REAL WORLD: CAN YOUR PERSONALITY MAKE YOU HEALTHIER THAN OTHER PEOPLE?

Understanding personality psychology can give us useful insight into the detrimental or protective influence our personalities have regarding our health, particularly when it comes to how susceptible we are to falling physically and mentally ill. Two main perspectives have been developed to explain the potential influence of personality on a person's health: (1) the **specificity approach** and (2) the **generality approach**. The specificity approach stipulates that our personalities have direct causal effects on our health and our proneness to disease and illnesses not, for example, hypertension, ulcerative colitis and rheumatoid arthritis (Alexander, 1950/2007). By contrast, the generality approach assumes that personality has an indirect effect by influencing how we feel and behave, which in turn will have an impact on our health (Ranchor & Sanderman, 1991).

SELF-EFFICACY The belief in one's own ability to plan and carry out a set of intended actions in order to accomplish tasks and reach one's goals.

LOCUS OF CONTROL This is a concept proposed by Rotter (1954) to explain a person's basic motivational orientations with reference to the degree of perceived control they have over daily activities and life in general. Those who have an internal locus of control believe they are able to control their lives; those who have an external locus of control believe what happens to them is down to forces beyond their control (e.g. fate or luck).

Take, for example, the concept of **self-efficacy** and how it can potentially govern behaviours related to dieting and weight control. Research has found that people with a high sense of self-efficacy, coupled with an internal **locus of control**, were more responsive to behavioural management for successful weight control than those with low self-efficacy (Chambliss & Murray, 1979).

Furthermore, the relationship between self-efficacy and addictive behaviour has been studied intensively. The successful quitting of cigarette smoking, for example, is more likely if the person trying to give up has an optimistic sense of self-belief (Baer & Lichtenstein, 1988; Carmody, 1992). These beliefs and motivations can be encouraged in various smoking cessation courses and, following successful completion of the programme, can be powerful factors in long-term resistance to smoking temptations (Kavanagh et al., 1993), with those displaying the greatest levels of self-efficacy also being the most steadfast quitters (Kok et al., 1991).

EXERCISE: WHAT DRIVES YOU?

Think of a situation (not necessarily a health one) in which you felt you were motivated to do something.

- What was your motivation?
- Was there any one element of that scenario you think inspired and/or supported your motivation?

In the rest of this section, we shall consider the generality approach in more depth by focusing on different 'types' of personality that have been related to health behaviours that may pose health risks (e.g. Type A, C and D) and also personality factors linked to good health (e.g. Type B, sense of coherence and hardiness).

21.5.1 TYPE A AND B PERSONALITIES

Type A personality has been associated with people's responses to stress and particularly their proneness to coronary heart disease (CHD). As a term, CHD covers a wide range of heart problems, such as angina and myocardial infarction (the medical term for a heart attack). The link between CHD and personality was made in 1910 by the Canadian physician William Osler, who described coronary-prone persons as:

> The robust, the vigorous in mind and body, the keen and ambitious man, the indicator of whose engine was always at full speed ahead. (Osler, 1910: 839)

This description contains what might be seen as the main features of the Type A personality (see Table 21.2). It wasn't until the mid-1970s that cardiologists Meyer Friedman and Ray Rosenman reported findings from a longitudinal study with 3,200 middle-aged male managers and executives that showed that a certain group of behaviours were associated with an increased risk of getting CHD (Rosenman & Friedman, 1977). They termed these behaviours the **Type A behaviour pattern**, or what is often called the **Type A personality**.

TABLE 21.2   Common Type A behaviours

- Highly competitive
- Very self-critical
- 'Hurry sickness'
  - Always seem to be 'up against the clock'
  - Restless, agitated, fast talking, always interrupting others
  - Impatient, easily wound up, quick to anger or become hostile with others
  - Often concurrently active (e.g. eating while working at the computer)
- Tendency to overreact
- Very goal-directed but unable to enjoy their achievements
- Significant life/work imbalance with emphasis on the latter
- Tend to have hypertension (high blood pressure)

Other research has supported the notion of a Type A personality. For example, in the Framingham Heart Study, Haynes and Feinleib (1980) investigated how employment status and employment-related behaviours were related to incidence of CHD. They found similar results to Rosenman and Friedman.

Rosenman and Friedman also found that Type B personalities were less prone to feel stress or suffer CHD then the Type As in their sample. The Type B personality is the opposite of Type A and characterises someone who lives a relatively low-stress lifestyle and who typically works at a steady pace. Type Bs find pleasure in their achievements but do not become stressed by lack of achievement; they enjoy competition but are not upset if they don't win. People with Type B personalities could be perceived and characterised as lazy, uninterested and detached by people who do not have such a personality type, particularly if those doing the judging have a Type A personality!

21.5.2 CRITIQUE OF THE TYPE A/B PERSONALITY THEORY

Although Friedman and Rosenman (1974) emphasised that the Type A behaviour pattern is not a fixed quality of a person's character, it has since become popularised as such (Pickering, 2009; Powell & Thoreson, 1987). Questionnaires that claim to measure Type A personality do have good internal reliability scores. However, there remains a lack of cultural research that limits the reliability and cultural validity of the theory. There are still questions to be answered regarding the relative contribution that the various Type A personality characteristics make to CHD proneness. For example, recent research findings suggest Type A characteristics like cynicism and hostility may contribute more to CHD than others (Tindle et al., 2009). Some researchers believe that the hostility characteristic is the main risk factor (Williams, 2001).

Most of the research on Type A personality is correlational, which does not imply a causal relationship. The correlations themselves are statistically significant but small, which could also mean reduced behavioural importance. Since Rosenman and Friedman's research was published, newer research has been carried out which suggests that there are other personality types that are also linked to illness and disease. These are Type C personality, which has been linked with cancer, and the Type D or 'distressed' personality. We shall now look at each of these in turn.

21.5.3 TYPE C PERSONALITY AND CANCER

Following heart disease, cancer is the major cause of death in most developed countries in the world. In 1990, Hans Eysenck described the 'cancer prone personality' (Eysenck, 1990). These were people who, when faced with stressful situations, responded with a sense of hopelessness, helplessness and had a tendency to repress their emotional reactions. This was not an entirely novel finding as Kissen (1966) had reported finding a link between personality factors and cancer in a study conducted with smokers suffering from lung cancer who demonstrated repressed emotions. In 1984, Temoshok and Fox published a paper in which they outlined the Type C or 'cancer prone' personality.

Type C persons are characterised as passive, conforming, compliant, appeasing, helpless, and react to stress with depression and hopelessness. On the other hand, some research suggests that certain personality characteristics can better one's chances of surviving cancer. Classen et al. (1996) found that patients who demonstrate a 'fighting spirit' tend to fare better than those patients who demonstrated the Type C characteristics of passive acceptance. However, Hansen et al. (2005) have been critical of many of the studies done on Type C personality and its proposed link to cancer, citing several major flaws in the design of studies that support such a link, for example, observation bias, interviewer bias, use of small populations, and failure to control for confounding or intermediate factors. When they conducted a large-scale prospective study of 29,595 individuals, they found no significant associations between neuroticism and extraversion, either independently or jointly, for any given cancer site. Thus the link remains tenuous and somewhat controversial.

21.5.4 TYPE D PERSONALITY: A 'DISTRESSED' PERSONALITY

The Type D personality is a medical psychology concept developed by Professor Johan Denollet. The concept emerged from a lack of consistency with Type A and illness and was based on clinical observations, empirically gathered evidence and personality theories existing at that time (Denollet, 1996). The Type D personality is characterised by a combination of negative affectivity (gloomy, anxious, irritable) across both time and different situations, and social inhibition (reticent, low sense of self-assurance, fear of rejection). Research has shown that Type D personality has been linked to CHD. Denollet and Brutsaert (1998) found that CHD patients who have Type D personalities had a poorer prognosis following a myocardial infarction (MI) than did non-Type D CHD patients. Furthermore, people exhibiting Type D personality characteristics are four times more likely to have another MI or fatal heart attack (Denollet, Vaes, & Brutsaert, 2000). On a more positive note, there are personality types and characteristics that have been associated with good health and wellbeing, which we will look at next.

21.5.5 PERSONALITY AND GOOD HEALTH

So far we have looked at personality and its relationship with illness and disease, but personality factors have also been associated with individual differences in good health and wellbeing. **Pathogenesis** (from Greek, *pathos* = suffering; Latin/Greek, *genesis* = origin) is the well-known concept of disease origin, as used in the biomedical sciences. In 1987, Aaron Antonovsky referred to the term **salutogenesis** (Latin, *salus, salutis* = health) to mean the science of studying wellbeing. The aims of salutogenesis are to uncover and explore factors underpinning the formation and maintenance of health. In this sense, salutogenesis and pathogenesis can be seen as opposite ends of a continuum of health. The word 'health' here is being used in its broadest context, as defined by the World Health Organisation (WHO):

> Health is a state of complete physical, mental and social well-being and not merely the absence of disease or infirmity. (WHO, 1946)

KEY RESEARCHER Shelley E. Taylor

FIGURE 21.4 Shelley E.Taylor

Shelley Elizabeth Taylor is a distinguished professor of psychology at the University of California in Los Angeles. One major contribution she has made to the field has been her work on positive illusions (Taylor & Brown, 1988), which is the process whereby people may possess idealistic attitudes about themselves or about those close to them. Essentially, positive illusions are an enhancing form of self-deception that makes a person feel good, preserves acceptable levels of self-esteem, and provides short-term protection against anxiety-provoking situations. Taylor and Brown's model suggested that these illusions are commonly experienced in everyday thought and are associated with measures of good mental health. Taylor and Brown's research identified three types of positive illusions: (1) an unrealistic positive evaluation of the self and one's abilities, (2) an illusory view of personal control and (3) an unrealistically optimistic assessment of the future. More recently, there has been some debate about how much people demonstrate positive illusions, and to what extent these illusions are of benefit to those having them (e.g. Kruger, Chan, & Roese, 2009; McKay & Dennett, 2009).

Another of Taylor's most significant contributions is the development of the Tend-and-Befriend theory (Taylor et al., 2000). Taylor and her colleagues put forward the Tend-and-Befriend theory and based it on evolutionary and psychobiological evidence that females tended to seek out the safety of their social group when a threat arises, particularly when there is a threat to one's offspring. By contrast, psychological theory and research had tended to espouse a dominant model of how people respond to stressful situations with the Fight-or-Flight model, in which a person would try to be aggressive or would wish to flee from a stressful situation. For many years, this model – developed by Walter Cannon in 1929 – had been the accepted wisdom of how both males and females respond to stress-inducing environments. Taylor and colleagues were able to show how this stress response would not be an adaptive response for females, when taking an evolutionary approach to the likely outcomes of such stress responses. The Tend-and-Befriend model was also able to demonstrate how the sexes may actually differ in the way in which they react to stress. It could also offer an effective understanding of individual differences that could exist between males and females when they adopt certain coping strategies in relation to stress and that the seeking of social support and provision of social support is often influenced by gendered roles. Taylor has continued her research into stress responses by investigating how psychobiological reactions to stress may pose particular problems in immunity from ill-health.

One aspect of this is an individual's quality of life. Antonovsky developed the concept of **sense of coherence** to explain how humans function in the face of stress to preserve their quality of life (Antonovsky, 1987). When someone experiences a sense of coherence to a high degree, the world is more comprehensible (life has cause and effect and is predictable), manageable (life can be personally controlled via a range of internal and external resources) and meaningful (life is worth living and is a source of satisfaction). This concept is supported by evidence; for example, patients with schizophrenia who had a high sense of coherence levels had greater subjective quality of life, overall health, global wellbeing and psychosocial functioning than did those who had a lower sense of coherence (Bengtsson-Tops & Hansson, 2001). Sense of coherence has also been found to be a factor involved in shielding against workers' stressful experiences of arduous working conditions (Söderfeldt et al., 2000).

Earlier in this section, we discussed how Type A individuals respond to stress and how that can lead to illness. Yet not everyone responds negatively to life stressors. Suzanne Kobasa (1979) reported findings from a study that outlined a set of personality characteristics that defined managing executives who seemed to maintain their health despite living stressful lives compared to those in similar positions who had developed health problems. Kobasa termed this pattern of characteristics hardiness (sometimes pre-fixed by 'psychological', 'personality' or 'cognitive').

The 'hardy' person is defined as someone who is able to demonstrate commitment or involvement in everyday activities, perceives they have control over daily life events, and views sudden changes or threats as challenges or opportunities for personal development as opposed to something to be avoided. By contrast, those who lack hardiness tend to be distant, sometimes hostile, have an external locus of control, prefer routine and try to avoid change in their lives (Maddi, 2004).

Even though there is a wealth of research showing how personality factors can make people disease- and illness-prone, there is an abundant source of research literature that highlights the positive roles that personality can play in maintaining good health. For example, Booth-Kewley and Vickers (1994) reviewed the literature on personality factors related to health behaviour. Different components of the five-factor model were shown to have associations with personality type and health. Both extraversion and conscientiousness have been linked to a person's inclination to live a healthier lifestyle. Openness to experience has been related to risky health-related behaviours, such as illegal drug use, as well as more health-promoting behaviours, such as mindfulness meditation (Baer et al., 2006). In summary, it seems that personality can play a significant role in affecting a person's risk of becoming ill or in protecting an individual from poor health.

21.6 CHAPTER SUMMARY

Throughout this chapter we have introduced you to some of the leading theories and theorists in the field of personality research. We have also given you some insights into how these theories can be applied in real-world situations. We began by examining personality in terms of the trait approach and outlined four different personality 'factor' models, and we discussed some of the similarities between them, for example, the common factors of extraversion and neuroticism. We noted how the trait approach has been criticised by some authors for being too general, and for its lack of power to discriminate how people behave over a diversity of situations and contexts. We also highlighted that people can sometimes behave in ways that differ from what the trait approach would suggest are their dominant traits, yet the trait approach is unable to account for this. Mischel (1968) offered an alternative explanation for these phenomena by suggesting that human beings are inconsistent in their behaviour and that it is the situations that the people find themselves in that are the best predictors of their behaviour. Counter-arguments to this claim have led contemporary personality psychologists to adopt an interactionist approach in which behaviour can be explained by a confluence of situational and personality factors. In the last section, we set out the ways in which psychologists have applied personality theories and research to a real-world setting, such as the field of health, illness and wellbeing.

 # DISCUSSION QUESTIONS

From the discussions in this chapter, it seems clear that both personality and situational factors have an important influence on how we behave. Now you are aware of this, think about how you would answer the following questions about personality:

- How many personality traits do we have? Are three too few and 16 too many? What does the empirical evidence mainly support?
- Think about situations that make it hard for people's personalities to shine through. Are there some people whose personality characteristics will still be highly present, even in the face of highly powerful and formal situations?
- Should health professionals screen their patients for certain personality traits that could pose a risk factor for ill-health?
- What could health professionals do to increase their patients' levels of self-efficacy, hardiness and sense of coherence? Are there any health-related behaviours that health professionals could promote for patients to have better levels of self-efficacy in a health context?

SUGGESTIONS FOR FURTHER READING

If you are interested in reading further in relation to some of the leading theories and theorists in the field of personality psychology, there are several very good introductory texts that we would recommend:

Carver, C.S., & Scheier, M.F. (2007). *Perspectives on personality*. Boston, MA: Allyn and Bacon.
Funder, D.C. (2010). *The personality puzzle* (5th edn). New York: W.W. Norton.
Maltby, J., Day, L., & Macaskill, A. (2013). *Personality, individual differences and intelligence* (3rd edn). Harlow: Pearson.

If you want to discover more about how personality traits are measured, and to use some trait-related scales in your own research, try the International Personality Item Pool, which can be accessed via: http://ipip.ori.org/ipip.

The Eysenck Personality Profiler is also available online and covers the three superfactors of the three-factor model and also the seven primary factors for each of these superfactors. In this way, the researcher can obtain a more nuanced assessment of respondents' personalities. It is available online through this web address: www.cymeon.com/epp_info.asp.

Still want more? For links to online resources relevant to this chapter and a quiz to test your understanding, visit the companion website at edge.sagepub.com/banyard2e

22 INTELLIGENCE: MEASURING THE MIND

Lead authors: Eva Sundin and Philip Banyard

CHAPTER OUTLINE

22.1 Introduction	**387**
22.2 Different views on intelligence	**387**
22.3 Early concepts of intelligence	**388**
22.3.1 Pioneers in psychometric theory of intelligence	389
22.3.2 Factor analysis and the structure of intelligence	392
22.3.3 Summary: the search for intelligence	393
22.4 Current concepts of intelligence	**393**
22.4.1 The one-factor model of intelligence revisited	393
22.4.2 The hierarchical models of intelligence revisited	394
22.4.3 Multiple intelligences	394
22.4.4 Successful intelligence	395
22.4.5 Summary: intelligence, one or many?	396
22.5 Controversies in intelligence	**396**
22.5.1 Differences between individuals	396
22.5.2 Differences between groups: gender	397
22.5.3 Differences between groups: race	397
22.5.4 The bell curve (1994)	398

22.6 Intelligence: knowns and unknowns   399

    22.6.1 The Flynn effect   399

    22.6.2 And now . . .   401

    22.6.3 Where does this leave us?   401

22.7 Chapter summary   402

Discussion questions   402

Suggestions for further reading   402

22.1 INTRODUCTION

This chapter will show how our thoughts about intelligence have changed from the end of the nineteenth century until today. We will start by looking at two early and very different approaches to the concept of intelligence. We will attempt to understand what is meant by intelligence, and also how the IQ tests we have today have developed. The chapter will then introduce you to some of the theoretical and methodological features of 'the psychometric approach' to intelligence, which uses factor analysis and other statistical techniques to understand intelligence. We will see how these theorists debate whether human intelligence is best understood as one general factor or as multiple dimensions of intellectual abilities.

The chapter will also explore why intelligence became such a controversial issue and to this day continues to generate a lot of heat. At the heart of this debate are questions about what makes us different from each other and what, if anything, we can do about these differences.

FRAMING QUESTIONS

- What is intelligence? Is there such a thing as general intelligence, or are there instead many different kinds of intelligence?
- Can we measure intelligence? If so, how?
- What accounts for differences in intelligence? What is the role of (1) hereditary and (2) environmental factors?
- What differences in intelligence exist, or appear to exist, between groups (e.g. between sexes or between races)? What are we to make of claims about such differences? Is there such a thing as a culturally unbiased intelligence test?
- Can we say anything sensible about differences in average IQ scores of people from different 'races'?

22.2 DIFFERENT VIEWS ON INTELLIGENCE

In research into intelligence, a number of questions recur. Just what does it mean to be intelligent? Is intelligence the ability to learn? Or how quickly we understand new information? Or is it the ability to learn from experience, to apply knowledge to solve problems and formulate new solutions to adapt in a new context? Is intelligence a single, general ability or is it many? Do we inherit intelligence from our parents or is intelligence developed as we go through life? Although researchers and scholars have struggled with these questions since the end of the nineteenth century, there is still no universal agreement on what the term 'intelligence' means.

Although a lot has been written about intelligence, and a lot of research carried out and a lot of tests devised, the actual definition of what we are talking about has been surprisingly difficult to tie down. There are many definitions and we've tried to capture the range in the quotations about intelligence below. As you read through them, try to identify similarities and differences between them.

It seems to us that there is a fundamental faculty in intelligence, any alteration or lack of which is of the utmost importance for practical life. This is judgement, otherwise known as common sense, practical sense, initiative, the ability to adapt oneself to circumstance. To judge well, to comprehend well, to reason well, these are the essential ingredients of intelligence. (Binet & Simon, 1905: 196–197)

EXERCISE: INTELLIGENCE-RELATED WORDS, PART 1: NAME THAT DUNCE

Intelligence is a very important concept for us. You can see this by thinking about the number of words you use to describe intelligence. (The point here is that the more important something is to us, the more words we have for it.)

Make two lists: one of words that describe intelligence in a positive way (e.g. 'brainy') and one that describes it in a negative way (e.g. 'moron'). Make each list as long as you can. It may help to involve members of your household as you do so. Take a few minutes to do this and you'll be surprised how many you come up with.

When prompted like this, many people can come up with dozens of words, although the majority are negative. Some of the words have a history of being used as a medical diagnosis, for example, 'cretin' and 'imbecile' were both used to categorise people who had what we call today severe learning difficulties. The term 'idiot' was used to described the severest conditions and the term 'moron' was invented by psychologists to describe people who had mild learning difficulties. These are all terms of abuse today. In fact, when you come to think about it, some of the terms that suggest high intelligence can also be used in a negative way, which shows what a complex relationship we have with this concept.

Retain these lists: we'll come back to them later in the chapter.

Intelligence is what is measured by intelligence tests. (Boring, 1923: 36)

A global concept that involves an individual's ability to act purposefully, think rationally, and deal effectively with the environment. (Wechsler, 1958: 7)

Intelligence is assimilation to the extent that it incorporates all the given data of experience within its framework. . . . There can be no doubt either, that mental life is also accommodation to the environment. Assimilation can never be pure because by incorporating new elements into its earlier schemata the intelligence constantly modifies the latter in order to adjust them to new elements. (Piaget, 1963: 6–7)

Intelligence is the ability to solve problems, or to create products, that are valued within one or more cultural settings. (Gardner, 1993a: x)

In a sense we have two brains, two minds – and two different kinds of intelligence: rational and emotional. How we do in life is determined by both – it is not just IQ, but *emotional* intelligence that matters . . . the abilities called here emotional intelligence, [which] include self-control, zeal and persistence, and the ability to motivate oneself. (Goleman, 1996: 28, xii)

The important point is not whether what we measure can appropriately be labelled 'intelligence', but whether we have discovered something worth measuring. (Miles, 1957: 159)

As you read through the above, you can see many different terms being employed to describe intelligence. There is talk of common sense, initiative, adaptability, comprehension, reason, purpose and problem solving. Keep this in mind as we go through the attempts to explain and measure intelligence.

22.3 EARLY CONCEPTS OF INTELLIGENCE

The word 'intelligence' has its root in Greek (like many English words) and the idea has a long history, though it has been thought of in different ways over time (Goodey, 2011). Our modern understanding of the term in the UK, however, is not much more than 100 years old and arrived with the introduction of mass schooling for children and a perceived need to rank them in order of their abilities. This attempt to rank people was controversial when it was introduced, and remains controversial today. Part of that controversy comes from a common understanding of the term – that intelligence is something we are born with. When we rank people by their intelligence, are we ranking their natural talent or their schooling and social environment? Whichever answer we choose has huge implications for how we should organise our education system and how we should treat children who do not do well on the tests of intelligence.

22.3.1 PIONEERS IN PSYCHOMETRIC THEORY OF INTELLIGENCE

One of the first to study individual differences in intelligence was Francis Galton (1822–1911). Galton believed that complex intellectual abilities are built on less complex abilities, such as capacity for labour (or energy), sensitivity to stimuli (e.g. touch, visual and auditory) and reaction time (for more information about Galton's research see the key researcher box in Chapter 2). Highly intelligent people supposedly had more capacity for labour and better abilities to process sensory information than less intelligent people. Galton also believed that we inherit intelligence from our parents. In his book *Hereditary genius* (1869/1892), he examined the family background of a group of 'eminent men' – judges, statesmen, commanders, scientists, poets, musicians, painters, divines, oarsmen and wrestlers. He found that an unexpectedly large proportion of these men had distinguished relatives. Based on this observation, he concluded that genius is passed down from generation to generation. Galton believed this link was genetic. There is, however, a plausible alternative explanation, namely that children from the homes of distinguished people had better education and better employment opportunities and hence more chance to develop their own skills. The link between heredity and intelligence, Galton hypothesised, was to be found in sensory discrimination, the reason for this being that genetic inheritance influences the system that processes sensory information – the nervous system.

Galton is considered a pioneer in the experimental study of intelligence. He concluded that his use of sensory tasks was a failure: he expected to find strong correlations between intellectual abilities and sensory discrimination and reaction time, but the correlations he obtained were in the moderate range. He concluded that his studies failed to support an association between psycho-physiological processes and intelligence. Although Galton discarded his

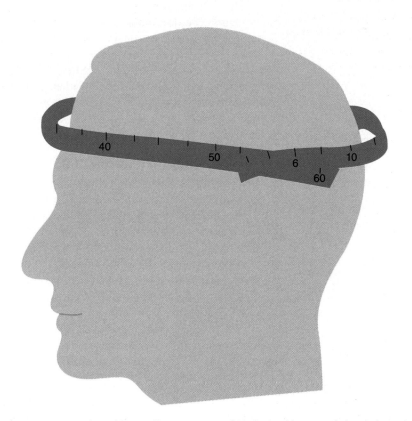

FIGURE 22.1 The Scoobymeasure. Look at this excellent measure of IQ devised by one of the authors. It involves using a calibrated IQ string (or tape measure) to estimate IQ. It is guaranteed to be 100% reliable. If you also think it is valid, please go to www.i'magullibleidiot.com and fill in your bank details to get your personal licence to use this

theoretical assumptions, his contributions inspired other, more recent researchers. It is noteworthy that the correlations that Galton reported were of the same magnitude as those observed by contemporary intelligence researchers. In contrast to Galton, these researchers interpret the correlations as indicators of a substantial association: reaction time is closely connected with intelligence (Hunt, 2005).

The first tests of intelligence were developed in France by Alfred Binet (1857–1911), who started his scientific studies by examining the relationship between head size and intelligence. Although you might expect that *big head = big brain = big intelligence*, Binet discovered that there is no relationship between these factors. Like Galton, Binet had a wide range of scientific interests and, like Galton, he had independent means so he wasn't forced to get a paid job. This allowed them both to follow their own varied interests, which they did very successfully. There is a big contrast here with modern science, where researchers commonly focus on a very narrow area of their subject and become experts in not very much.

Binet developed a scale that is known to us as the first intelligence test. The background of this initiative was that the French government had enacted a law that all children should be provided with public education. This implied that children who had learning difficulties should be given appropriate opportunities for education. In consequence, it became an issue to identify children who were in need of special education. The government asked Binet to develop an instrument that could be used to detect children with lesser intellectual resources so that they would be given an adequate education. Together with Theodore Simon, Binet developed a scale to determine whether a child ought to receive special education or conventional classroom instruction. In other words, the Binet–Simon scale was primarily developed as a rough guide for identifying children with learning difficulties, not as a device for rank ordering intelligence in children with normal cognitive functioning.

During the development of the scale, Binet and Simon also became aware of the need to consider the possible influence of interviewer bias. They paid attention to key principles in **psychometric** theory, especially various forms of validity. Specifically, they attended to questions of: internal validity (i.e. whether the test is a coherent measure of the trait it purports to measure); external validity (i.e. whether the test scores agree with 'real-world performance'); and inter-rater **reliability** (i.e. whether different raters who rate the same data agree with one another).

Not only was the Binet–Simon scale developed to meet the basic psychometric standards of validity and reliability, it was also standardised. Standardisation is the process of testing a pilot group who are similar to the people taking the test to see the scores that are attained. When using a standardised test, each child can compare their score with the standardisation group's score. The first version of the scale was introduced in 1905. Subsequently, Binet and Simon undertook several standardisations of the scale, using different samples of children from different age groups, representing children with different levels of cognitive functioning.

In 1911, German psychologist William Stern suggested the term *mental age* to describe the performance on the Binet–Simon tests compared to the average performance (Stern, 1914). So if an individual child obtained the same score as the average for a six-year-old, then they were said to have a mental age of six. Stern went further to suggest that this could be represented as a ratio with their chronological age, as shown below, and the concept of the **intelligence quotient** (IQ was born).

Intelligence quotient (IQ) = Mental age/Chronological age × 100

PSYCHOMETRIC TESTS Instruments which have been developed for measuring mental characteristics. Psychological tests have been developed to measure a wide range of things, including creativity, job attitudes and skills, brain damage and, of course, 'intelligence'.

RELIABILITY The reliability of a psychological measuring device (such as a test or a scale) is the extent to which it gives consistent measurements. The greater the consistency of measurement, the greater the tool's reliability.

INTELLIGENCE QUOTIENT (IQ) A numerical figure, believed by some to indicate the level of a person's intelligence, and by others to indicate how well that person performs on intelligence tests.

EUGENICS The political idea that the human race could be improved by eliminating 'undesirables' from the breeding stock, so that they cannot pass on their supposedly inferior genes. Some eugenicists advocate compulsory sterilisation, while others seem to prefer mass murder or genocide.

Using this formula, if an eight-year-old child has a mental age of eight (the average), their IQ will be $8/8 \times 100 = 100$. And if they have a mental age of 10 their IQ will be $10/8 \times 100 = 125$.

Binet did not approve of reducing intelligence to a single number, but it was Stern's view that prevailed and it is how we view the concept today. After Stern, the calculation of IQ has become more sophisticated. It is now based on *norm referencing* or, in other words, it depends on calculating the average performance for your peers then comparing you against the average.

The Binet–Simon test was translated into English by Henry Goddard and then amended by Lewis Terman, who named his version the *Stanford–Binet Test* (after the university where he was professor of psychology). Between them they developed and popularised the tests in the USA to the point that during the 1920s 4 million were sold each year (Schultz, 1996).

The revision resulted in the Stanford–Binet scale, which consisted of 90 items, and aimed to measure cognitive abilities of children and adults with inferior, normal or superior intelligence. The Stanford–Binet scale assesses four types of cognitive abilities: verbal reasoning, quantitative reasoning, abstract/visual reasoning and short-term memory. The Binet–Simon scale quickly became the standard of intelligence testing and was soon used throughout the USA in a variety of ways, including for the screening and placement of recruits (see the key study) during the First World War (1914–1919), school placements, admissions to university studies, and identifying children in need of learning difficulty

KEY STUDY

Gould, S.J. (1982). A nation of morons. *New Scientist*, May, 349–353.

In this article, Stephen Jay Gould describes the first mass testing of IQ by US psychologist Yerkes. The tests were in two forms (Alpha and Beta), one written and the other pictorial, so that men who couldn't read or write could still be tested. If a man failed the Alpha test he would be given the Beta test, and if he failed that he would be given an individual examination.

In reality the system didn't work like this. For example, there were long queues for the Beta tests, so men who should have done the Beta test had to do the Alpha test and ended up with zero scores.

Yerkes asserted that the tests measured 'native intellectual ability' (cited in Gould, 1981: 349), but the level of cultural and educational knowledge required is illustrated in the following examples:

'Washington is to Adams as first is to . . .'
'Crisco is a: patent medicine, disinfectant, toothpaste, food product.'
'Christy Mathewson is famous as a: writer, artist, baseball player, comedian.'
Gould reports that three 'facts' were created from the testing data:

1 The average mental age of white Americans was about 13. Unfortunately, this had been defined as the intellectual level of a moron, so the tests appeared to indicate that the average American was a moron. (Note: I advise readers to hold their ethnocentrism in check at this point.)
2 European immigrants could be graded by their country of origin.
3 The average score of black men was lower than the average score of white men.

These three 'facts' can be adequately explained by the administration difficulties of the testing and the level of literacy of the groups of people taking the tests. In fact, a reanalysis of the data showed that performance depended on the length of time a person had lived in America, suggesting that culture and language played a large part in test performance. However, a much more sinister explanation was given for the results. It was argued that white people were superior to black people, and that Americans were superior to many European peoples.

Once again, political beliefs triumphed over scientific analysis and the **eugenic** explanation took hold. One of the consequences of this was the passing of the Immigration Restriction Act in 1924 by the American Congress, which selectively stopped certain national groups from emigrating to the USA. The scientists who supported the eugenics argument lobbied the politicians and, according to Gould (1981: 352), 'won one of the greatest victories of scientific racism in American history'. Please note, this is *not* a good thing!

services. By the end of the war, the tests had been taken by more than 2 million men (McGuire, 1994). After the war, a new version of the military tests, the Scholastic Aptitude Test (SAT), was introduced. The SAT was soon used by colleges and universities throughout the USA as part of their admission criteria.

The widespread usage of intelligence testing in the USA provided researchers with large amounts of empirical data to examine differences in intelligence between individuals and groups. As you can can see from the key study by Gould, these data were interpreted in very controversial ways and we will return to this later in the chapter.

22.3.2 FACTOR ANALYSIS AND THE STRUCTURE OF INTELLIGENCE

Until the early 1900s, the approaches to intelligence had been pragmatic: tests of intellectual abilities were developed for particular needs. At that time, the British psychologist Charles Spearman (1863–1945) reported an observation that has impacted on later theories of intelligence. When he examined the data on many different cognitive abilities, using several different instruments, he found that all correlations between these tests were positive. Thus, if an individual obtains high scores on a test of verbal reasoning, s/he could be expected to obtain high scores on a second test, such as mathematical abilities. In the same way, individuals who had low scores on one test of cognitive abilities could be expected to score low on the other tests as well. Spearman argued that this overlap, or intercorrelation, indicated that these tests measure a general component of intelligence, in addition to measuring specific intellectual abilities.

To be able to examine the nature of the relationships between scores from several different tests, Spearman developed a mathematical method which in a refined version is known to us as **factor analysis**. As you will remember from Chapter 21, factor analysis is used for reducing a mass of information to a simple description. In this case, factor analysis involves exploring the underlying structure of many intelligence test scores. Spearman used factor analysis as a tool to examine whether intelligence had one big underlying factor or a range of many factors. He showed that one major factor was regularly being extracted in his analyses.

From this observation, Spearman formulated his assumption that a general intellectual ability, or g, underlies all human cognitive performance and could account for individual differences in scores on mental tests. Spearman believed that g should be considered as intelligence and he called the approach 'the two-factor theory of intelligence'. This approach indicates that the **general factor**, g, represents what all of the mental tests had in common. The second factor was identified as the **specific factor**, or s. The specific factor related to the unique ability that was measured by each test. The hierarchical model of intelligence is shown in Figure 22.2.

> **FACTOR ANALYSIS** A method of statistical analysis which examines intercorrelations between data in order to identify major clusters of groupings, which might be related to a single common factor.
>
> **GENERAL FACTOR (g)** The theoretical general factor of intelligence that some scientists believe underpins all cognitive activity.

Spearman did not seek to specify how many specific cognitive abilities exist: he was more interested in the general (g) factor. It is useful at this point to consider the relationship between Spearman's approach and that of Galton and Binet. Like Galton, Spearman assumed that individual differences in intellectual abilities are mainly hereditary. Spearman also agreed with Galton that sensory discrimination is positively correlated with intellectual ability. Not surprisingly, Spearman found it difficult to see benefits in Binet's intelligence scale. Binet was equally sceptical over Spearman's approach. In particular, Binet argued that it is not meaningful to measure someone's intelligence with a single score because two different individuals could obtain the same score although they had very different types of ability.

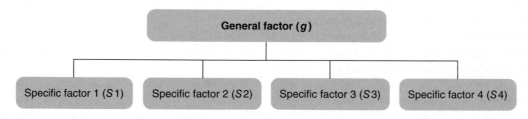

FIGURE 22.2 The hierarchical model of intelligence

Binet's criticism, and the fact that the research by Galton and others had failed to support the assumption that intelligence and acuity of perception are correlated, did not discourage Spearman. Instead, he suggested that the disappointing findings in previous research had resulted from not having taken account of uncertainties in the measurement. Spearman (1904) created a formula, *correction for attenuation*, which has been used since then to calculate the correlation between two variables as if they had been measured perfectly, without any measurement error. When he calculated the analysis using the new formula, the results of his study were in support of Galton's hypothesis.

Since Spearman presented his theory, other researchers have either expanded on his concept of *g* or challenged his approach. Many theorists, for example, have argued that people can be intelligent in many different ways. One of the first to do so was Louis Leon Thurstone, a US psychologist. His analysis suggested that, rather than there being one general factor, there is a small set of independent factors (mental abilities) of equal importance. His analysis suggested that there were seven unrelated components:

1   verbal comprehension (understanding of written words)
2   word fluency (speed of generating words)
3   arithmetic ability (solving mathematical problems)
4   memory (remembering lists of words and numbers)
5   perceptual speed (speed of recognising forms and symbols)
6   inductive reasoning (finding rules for solving problems)
7   spatial visualisation (imagining rotations of objects or pictures).

From this finding, Thurstone concluded that human intellectual ability should be presented as a profile of cognitive abilities rather than as a single IQ score.

22.3.3 SUMMARY: THE SEARCH FOR INTELLIGENCE

The ideas presented by Galton and Binet may appear to contradict one another. It has been suggested, however, that in fact they represent two different aspects of intelligence. Despite this, since Binet's days, one of the most persistent disputes in the field of intelligence has circled around the question: Is human intelligence best understood as one general factor (*g*) or as multiple dimensions of intellectual abilities? Although this might seem like a dry theoretical issue, it has an important implication. If you are proposing that the differences between people in their intelligence are largely due to inheritance, then there must be something that you can call intelligence and something you can inherit. If there are many intelligences and not one underlying factor, then the hereditary argument collapses. In the next section, we will see that this debate among theorists and researchers continues to flourish.

22.4 CURRENT CONCEPTS OF INTELLIGENCE

22.4.1 THE ONE-FACTOR MODEL OF INTELLIGENCE REVISITED

Most researchers acknowledge that intelligence involves several specific cognitive abilities. However, some emphasise the central importance of Spearman's *g*. Others suggest that neither Spearman's nor Thurstone's model gives a good account of intelligence because they emphasise different aspects of human intelligence rather than representing two complete models. These theorists have developed their own models by combining Spearman's and Thurstone's models in different ways. We will begin by examining the one-factor approach, and then the hierarchical approach to intelligence will be scrutinised.

Theorists who support the one-factor model maintain that *g* is a biological, hereditary component of intelligence that explains a large proportion of the variance in many measures of intelligence. These theorists have formulated a number of arguments, derived from psychometric research:

1   In his research, Hans Eysenck (1916–1997) showed that measures of reaction time were strongly related to total score on an *IQ test*, which supported the assumption that 'speed of information processing is the essential basis of *g*' (Jensen, 1993: 54).

2   The *g* factor is strongly related to all tests of cognitive abilities (Jensen, 1998). Jensen argued that the *g* factor, or the total score on a test battery, gives more information about individual differences in intelligence than the specific factors or the subscale scores.

3   *g* gives a better explanation of test performance on many cognitive ability tests than the specific factors do (Gottfredson, 1998).

4   *g* is a good predictor of educational achievement and work performance (Gottfredson, 1998).

In summary, the one-factor approach argues that it is necessary and sufficient to study one general underlying factor and essential if you want to maintain the hereditarian position on intelligence. Jensen, Eysenck and Gottfredson have all been strong supporters of that position.

22.4.2 THE HIERARCHICAL MODELS OF INTELLIGENCE REVISITED

Other theorists have attempted to combine Spearman's and Thurstone's approaches into a **hierarchical** approach. A hierarchical theory implies one or more higher-order factors and one or more lower levels with several factors. One of the first to develop a hierarchical theory was the British psychologist Philip Vernon (1905–1987). Vernon assumed that intelligence comprises abilities at four different levels of generality, where two new levels were inserted between Spearman's *g* and Thurstone's *s* factors.

A British psychologist, Raymond Cattell (1905–1998), suggested a model with two levels. On the highest level, there were two types of general intelligence: **fluid intelligence** (*gf*) and **crystallised intelligence** (*gc*). The general cognitive abilities are based on a large number of subordinate factors: *gf* includes reasoning and the cognitive ability to draw inferences; *gc* comprises the knowledge and skills that people gain throughout their lives (see below).

A North American psychologist, John Carroll (1916–2003), created a model with three levels or *strata*. In the first stratum, specific or 'narrow' abilities are included; in the second stratum, we find complex or 'broad' abilities; and finally, the third stratum comprises a single general ability.

There is a common basis to the models by Vernon, Cattell and Carroll: all of them are developed within the psychometric approach to intelligence. That is, they endorse the presumption that intelligence is a measurable phenomenon.

Other intelligence theorists are more critical of the psychometric approach and acknowledge that intelligence test scores are stable predictors of educational achievement. However, they believe that the attempt to 'base a concept of intelligence on test scores alone is to ignore many important aspects of mental ability' (Neisser et al., 1996: 78–79). Some of the aspects of mental ability that are ignored by the psychometric theory are emphasised in the approaches discussed below.

22.4.3 MULTIPLE INTELLIGENCES

A number of theorists have questioned the theoretical assumption that there is only one type of intelligence, which is measurable with intelligence tests. Instead, 'there are many different "intelligences" (systems of abilities), only a few of which can be captured by standard psychometric tests' (Neisser et al., 1996: 78). Thus, in addition to the cognitive abilities that we normally think of as intelligence, according to this school of thought there are several other types of intelligence. This theoretical approach is labelled cognitive-contextual: the focus is on the individual's abilities to adapt in different environmental contexts.

One influential theory about '**multiple intelligences**' was developed by an American psychologist, Howard Gardner. Gardner is critical of contemporary intelligence theorists' reliance on mental testing to assess intelligence while other ways of assessing cognitive abilities are devalued. If IQ tests are indispensable tools to assess intellectual abilities, how did people manage before the IQ test was invented? 'Were we incapable of making judgments about intellect before Alfred Binet and Francis Galton cobbled together the first set of psychometric items a century ago?' (Gardner, 1998: 18). Gardner pointed out that an abundant body of research has shown that the conventional method of intelligence assessment (that is, multiple choice tests) provides information about abilities in only one or two domains; that is, multiple choice tests may measure linguistic intelligence and logical-mathematical intelligence, but not the kinds of intelligence found in other domains.

Gardner defined intelligence as the capacity to solve problems and to create products that are valued in society (Gardner & Hatch, 1989). He developed the theory of multiple intelligences based on research findings which suggested that humans have a number of different intelligences that operate from different areas of the brain and thus the notion of a single intelligence is faulty. He also stated that different individuals have different combinations of the many intelligences.

Gardner initially defined seven different intelligences, although he suggested that there may be additional ones.

1 **Linguistic intelligence** is the capacity to use spoken and written words and languages.
2 **Logical-mathematical intelligence** is the capacity for logic reasoning and dealing with numbers.
3 **Musical intelligence** has to do with hearing and performing sounds, rhythm and music.
4 **Spatial intelligence** is the ability to perceive spatial information.
5 **Bodily-kinaesthetic intelligence** is the ability to use one's body in various movements and activities.
6 **Interpersonal intelligence** is the ability to understand others and interact based on that understanding.
7 **Intrapersonal intelligence** is the capacity to understand one's own behaviours, thoughts and emotions.

ASIDE

FIGURE 22.3   Wayne Rooney: an intelligent footballer

© Ben Radford/Corbis

The Rooney conundrum

One thing that doesn't seem to have changed in the UK is our view of what it means to be intelligent. For example, there is a common misconception about Wayne Rooney, the English footballer, that he is not very intelligent. However, a brief look at Gardner's intelligences show that Rooney is an exceptional performer on at least three of the dimensions. His spatial awareness allows him to create and respond to cognitive maps, and this allows him to pass to team mates and understand where to be at the best time to score a goal. His body control is clearly excellent, but so is his ability to read the behaviour of others. This allows him to anticipate and predict what other players will do, where they will be, and how they will respond. It also allows him to disguise his own intentions and bluff opponents. He is clearly exceptionally intelligent. So why is he not always given credit for this? Maybe that is more to do with issues of class (Rooney coming from working-class origins) and prejudice than clear thinking about intelligence.

22.4.4 SUCCESSFUL INTELLIGENCE

Building on Gardner's theory of multiple intelligences and cognitive psychology, American psychologist Robert Sternberg distinguished between different aspects of intelligence. Similar to Gardner, Sternberg saw conventional notions of intelligence as being too narrow. But he did not agree that the alternative theory of intelligence should encompass abilities such as musical and bodily-kinaesthetic ones. This was because, following his definition of intelligence as the individual's 'adaptation to, shaping of, and selection of real-world environments' (Sternberg, 1984: 271), these abilities do not match the criteria for intelligences. Instead, they should be thought of as talents.

Sternberg's triarchic (i.e. three-part) theory specifies three different aspects of intelligence: *analytic*, *creative* and *practical*. When someone has the ability to balance and use the three aspects of intelligence effectively, s/he has a **successful intelligence**.

The individual uses **analytical intelligence** when accomplishing tasks and overcoming obstacles to solve problems that s/he is familiar with. For example, when you think about how to get home from a night out, you might first consider the different modes of transport available – which are running, at what times and cost, how safe they are, etc. – in your analysis of how best to get home that night.

When the task is to function well in one's socio-cultural environment, **practical intelligence** is applied. The individual's thinking draws from previous, often tacit, experiences when adapting to a certain environment, reshaping that environment, or selecting a new environment. So, you have previously fixed your Playstation when it broke from overuse. You can use that experience to help you fix your Wii.

When people find themselves in a relatively new context, or are facing a new kind of problem, they are using **creative intelligence**. What would you do if an axe-wielding maniac suddenly appeared from nowhere and started running towards you screaming loudly? You would have to rely on your creative intelligence to come up with a way of dealing with this situation (which you probably haven't come across before).

EXERCISE: INTELLIGENCE-RELATED WORDS, PART 2: INTUITIVE MODELS OF INTELLIGENCE

Go back to the list of intelligence-related words we suggested you wrote in the exercise at the beginning of the chapter. Look at these words and think about when either you have used them yourself or someone has used them at you. What was happening to provoke the use of these words? For example, I forgot my phone the other day and immediately thought to myself, 'What a fool'. So, forgetting my phone made me think I had been stupid.

Make a long list of incidents and then look at what is behind each of these acts. That way you will get an idea of the things you think are intelligent and unintelligent. You might like to go one step further and look at an IQ test to see how many of the items you came up with are covered by the test. You will be surprised how few are there.

22.4.5 SUMMARY: INTELLIGENCE, ONE OR MANY?

Compared to the conventional view on intelligence, Gardner's and Sternberg's theories represent a completely different perspective. Both have questioned whether conventional tests really assess all abilities necessary to succeed in life and in school.

Gardner's theory of multiple intelligences has been well received, especially perhaps among practitioners. One example of how his work has been used is a report by Hoerr (2000) which seeks to show how Gardner's theory can be used in schools. Hoerr's idea is that the teacher who uses a teaching model based on Gardner's theory will recognise that not all people learn in the same way, nor do they prefer the same way of demonstrating their understanding. In Gardner's words, there 'is no reason why everyone has to learn … in the same way' (1993b: 21).

22.5 CONTROVERSIES IN INTELLIGENCE

Intelligence has been at the centre of political and scientific controversy since the development of the first tests. We will start this section by looking at the fallout from the mass testing of US serviceman in the First World War described in the key study above.

22.5.1 DIFFERENCES BETWEEN INDIVIDUALS

The results of the mass testing appeared to give a lot of support to the idea that differences in intelligence had a genetic basis. A closer look at the data, however, reveals that it doesn't really tell us anything about the reason for differences in groups' scores, only that the differences in IQ performance exist. But that is not how it was read at the time and so we will now have a look at the idea of heritability.

The issue here is often expressed in terms of whether intelligence is inherited or not. The real debate, though, is not about whether our genetic structure is an important component in our intelligence. It is clear that we need a body and a brain to act intelligently and these are formed from our genetic structure. The controversial issue is about whether the differences in intelligence *between individuals* and *between groups of people* can be explained by genetic or environmental causes. We are going to take a long look at this question to see where it comes from and why it is so controversial.

The Social Darwinists, like Galton, noticed that better healthcare and social conditions meant that not so many people were dying at a young age and they feared that the effect of natural selection was being blunted. In other words, if the weak survive, they will pass on their weak genes to the next generation. They proposed that instead of allowing the environment to selectively breed the better members of the species, this selection should be taken on by people. This selective breeding of a superior class of people could then be used to improve society and create a world where, for example, everyone will put the top back on a tube of toothpaste once they have used it.

These ideas were enthusiastically embraced in the USA where there were concerns about the possible decline of the genetic stock of the nation. Terman and Goddard, who brought IQ testing to the USA, were supporters of this view, as was Spearmen in the UK. These concerns were backed up by evidence from studies such as the mass testing by Yerkes and were used as justification for mass sterilisation programmes. The argument here, as mentioned above, was that if differences in intelligence are inherited, then we can improve the average intelligence of the nation by stopping people with low intelligence from having children.

Although this seems barely credible, in the USA between 1927 and 1957 it is estimated that approximately 60,000 people labelled either feeble-minded or insane underwent sterilisation at state institutions in the name of building a better society (Stubblefield, 2007). The aim of this programme was to eliminate the opportunities for these people to have children and therefore reduce and maybe eliminate learning disabilities from the population. These sterilisations were often carried out without the person knowing about it when they were in hospital for another reason, such as giving birth (Park & Radford, 1998). In Germany, by 1937 an estimated 225,000 people with mental illness or learning disability had been sterilised (Spann, 1975). Elsewhere the procedure continued to as late as 1976 in Sweden (Denekens, Nys, & Stuer, 1999).

22.5.2 DIFFERENCES BETWEEN GROUPS: GENDER

Most intelligence theorists agree that there is no difference in overall average intelligence scores between genders (Neisser et al., 1996). Over the years, this non-difference has been confirmed in many studies, yet there are some who claim that there are gender differences, with males having a higher average score than females. A strong advocate of this notion is Richard Lynn, a controversial UK psychologist.

Others have pointed out that research on gender differences in brain size has reported inconsistent findings (Witelson et al., 2006). Others again have suggested that the size of the brain is not that important. Instead, what matters is that the female brain has other advantages, such as a greater density of neurons, which results in more efficient processing (Jensen & Johnson, 1994).

North American psychologist Richard Haier and his co-workers are using brain imaging to study intelligence in men and women (Haier et al., 2004). They have concluded that there is no difference in general intelligence between men and women, and that men and women can achieve similar results on an intelligence test using different brain regions.

22.5.3 DIFFERENCES BETWEEN GROUPS: RACE

And so we come to one of the most toxic issues in psychology. As mentioned above, the results from Yerkes' IQ tests were used to suggest differences between different racial groups. This is an argument that has rumbled on for over 100 years without ever resolving itself. There are many problems with attempting any exploration of racial differences and none more so than the issue of intelligence. This is made particularly controversial because differences between one group and another are often presented as differences in ability rather than differences in performance.

Performance is what you actually do, and **ability** is what you are capable of. You might have heard a teacher say 'You have the ability, but you are not doing the work'. They mean that the reason you got a Grade E in your

HERITABILITY The proportion of variance in the phenotype (observable characteristics) that can be attributed to genetic variance. It is a widely misunderstood concept and is commonly misused in debates about nature and nurture. It is a measure that may vary with the range of genetic backgrounds and range of environments studied. It is therefore a mistake to argue that a high figure for heritability in a particular population in a particular environment means that the characteristic is genetically determined.

RACE Commonly used to refer to groups of people such as white people or black people. It implies a genetic component to the differences between these groups, but research shows that the term 'race' has no biological validity and is best described as a political construct.

RACISM The use of the pervasive power imbalance between races to oppress dominated peoples by devaluing their experience, behaviour and aspirations.

examinations was due to poor performance and not poor ability (and obviously not the teacher's fault either). Any test we give to someone can only measure their performance on that test, and not their ability. We can only infer their ability from that performance. So when we are measuring intelligence, we are, in fact, measuring *performance* on the particular test and not the underlying *intellectual ability*. In truth, the only evidence we have are performance scores, and we have to explain why groups perform differently.

There is also the matter of how the genetic effect is calculated, and the statistic that is commonly cited is **heritability**. This statistic estimates how much the variation within any given population is due to genetic factors. It does not, however, tell us about why two populations will differ, and so contributes nothing to our understanding of this issue (see Rose, Kamin, & Lewontin, 1984). It also fails to tell us anything about how much genetics affects the characteristics of an individual.

Added to the problems of defining and measuring heritability, there are also problems in designing research to look for differences between ethnic groups. One of the key problems concerns the political sensitivity of these issues, but there are many scientific problems as well. As Jones (1991) points out, these problems include:

- the difficulty in defining *race*;
- the history of social movement that has meant that many people have ancestors from many parts of the world;
- within-race variability is much greater than between-race variability;
- when comparative research is carried out, it has so far been impossible to obtain comparable samples of people from different races.

Problems like these make assertions about racial differences very difficult and, in fact, one of the UK's most influential psychometricians, Kline (1991) concluded that:

> . . . The only advantage in setting out the different scores on IQ tests of racial groups is to give ammunition to those who wish to decry them. It adds nothing to theoretical understanding or to the social or educational practice. (Kline, 1991: 96)

22.5.4 THE BELL CURVE (1994)

In 1994, the controversy about group differences in IQ was re-ignited by the publication of *The bell curve*, written by Richard Herrnstein and Charles Murray, which set out to explain the variations in intelligence in the USA. The basic argument of *The bell curve* is that intelligence is one of the most (if not THE most) important characteristic in a person's life and that it will predict their successes and failures much better than any other factor, including their socio-economic status. Herrnstein and Murray argue that the USA is becoming stratified not by class or money but by intelligence, and they go on to argue that low IQ is connected to social problems such as school drop-out, criminality and family breakdown. They go on to rank groups of people by ethnicity and finish with some suggestion for social change, including encouraging mothers with low IQ to put their children up for adoption, and also focusing resources on gifted rather than struggling children in schools. From what you have already read in this chapter you can see that the book was going to attract controversy from page one, and that was the case. If you want to find out quite how big the storm was (and is) then just Google it. We include a mention of the book here to illustrate how enduring the arguments are even in the face of overwhelming evidence against that position.

KEY STUDY

Sternberg, R.J., Grigorenko, E.L., Ngrosho, D., Tantufuye, E., Mbise, A., Nokes, C., Jukes, M., & Bundy, D.A. (2002). Assessing intellectual potential in rural Tanzanian school children. *Intelligence*, *30*, 141–162.

Some controversial researchers (Lynn & Vanhanen, 2002; Rushton & Jensen, 2005) have suggested that some populations with African heritage perform at lower mean levels on conventional IQ tests compared to populations with, for example, European heritage. This interpretation of the test results has been questioned by many other researchers, who have claimed that the IQ test measures intellectual abilities that are less relevant for black Africans who live in non-Westernised environmental contexts. In addition, these people may have no prior experience with the procedures of taking an IQ test.

To examine this claim, Sternberg and colleagues (2002) used an alternative to conventional testing to examine the performance of 358 children aged 11–13 from 10 schools in rural Tanzania. The alternative procedure used dynamic testing, which is based on Vygotsky's idea of the zone of proximal development (you will find more details about Vygotsky's theory in Chapter 18). Dynamic testing differs from conventional testing in three important ways: (1) it emphasises the psychological processes that are involved in learning and change rather than measuring pre-existing abilities; (2) the test taker receives feedback from the test administrator; and (3) the relationship between the test taker and the test administrator is an active, two-way interaction characterised by teaching and support.

The performance of the children in the experimental group was compared to the performance of a sample of 100 children who took the test administered using conventional procedures. A set of three tasks was administered to the children in the experimental group using the alternative procedures, and the same set of tasks was then administered to the control group, this time using conventional procedures. Each test given to the experimental group comprised (1) pre-test, (2) feedback and the teaching of skills and strategies that contributed to improve the test results and (3) post-test. Children in the control group received only the pre-test and the post-test. The results showed that children in the experimental group improved significantly more from pre-test to post-test compared to the children in the control group who did not receive feedback. Sternberg et al. concluded that the children in the experimental group had intellectual abilities not measured by conventional IQ tests.

22.6 INTELLIGENCE: KNOWNS AND UNKNOWNS

Following the publication of *The bell curve* (Herrnstein & Murray, 1994), the American Psychological Association (APA) came to the conclusion that there was a need for an authoritative report on intelligence and 'one that all sides could use as a basis for discussion' (Neisser et al., 1996: 77). A task force was created which was chaired by the highly esteemed Ulrich Neisser and included 10 other academics with a broad range of expertise and opinions.

The report was published by the APA in 1995 and an edited version appeared in the *American Psychologist* the following year (Neisser et al., 1996). The extensive and very detailed report was unanimously endorsed by all of the task force, and is a testament to the consensus-making skills of Neisser and also the professionalism of the task force members. As you can see from our earlier description of the controversies, consensus between the different camps is very hard to achieve.

The report gives a measured, detailed and dispassionate account of the evidence on intelligence. It does not fall into either of the entrenched political positions and provides support and challenge to both sets of arguments. As a contribution to scientific debate it is an excellent document, and if you are interested, then look it up on the internet.

22.6.1 THE FLYNN EFFECT

Over many years there has been a steady rise in IQ performance in most countries across the world. This has been noted by many researchers, but the first person to study this rise in a systematic way was James Flynn and so it is known as the *Flynn effect*. The average improvement is about three IQ points per decade and hence more than a full standard deviation (15 points) in the latter half of the twentieth century.

The Flynn effect is kept in check by recalibrating the tests every so often and resetting the average score to 100. So if you have just done an IQ test and scored 110, if you took a test from 30 years ago you would probably score about 120. Clearly, if you want to look good, make sure you choose old tests when you are testing your IQ online.

The Flynn effect is a puzzle, especially as performance on standard educational tests in the USA declined during a period when IQ tests were rising. This would appear to challenge the relationship between school performance and IQ. Another challenge that the Flynn effect creates is for the supporters of selective breeding (Terman and Galton, for example), who argued that the higher birthrate in women with lower IQ scores would lead to a decline in the average intelligence of the nation.

So how can we explain this effect? Well, not very easily, and the APA report (see above) concluded that the issue remains unresolved (Neisser et al., 1996). The most likely explanation is that modern life presents us all with problems of ever increasing complexity. Young children used to play in a sandpit (*you were lucky – we dreamed of a sandpit – Ed.*)

KEY RESEARCHER Pat Rabbitt

FIGURE 22.4 Patrick Rabbitt

Professor Patrick Rabbitt is an English psychologist working in the area of cognitive gerontology (http://psychology.wikia.com/wiki/Cognitive_gerontology). He worked at the Medical Research Council Applied Research Unit, Cambridge (1961–1968); the Department of Experimental Psychology and the Queen's College, University of Oxford (1968–1982); was Head of the Department of Psychology, University of Durham (1982–1983); and was Research Professor and Director of the Age and Cognitive Performance Research Centre, University of Manchester (1983–2004). He was made an Emeritus Professor of Psychology in 2004 (http://psychology.wikia.com/wiki/University_of_Manchester_Age_and_Cognitive_Performance_Research_Centre), and a Member of the European Academy in 2013.

Pat Rabbitt has made an incredible contribution to our understanding of the cognitive changes that occur with old age through his longitudinal studies of older people. His participants comprised a pool of over 6,500 elderly people who were invited back every two years to tackle a battery of intelligence tests and other measures of cognition. Some of the key results to emerge from this rolling research include the findings that support the notion that most of the cognitive declines in later life occur because of illnesses rather than simply age. Evidence from these remarkable volunteers is still accumulating. It shows that age-related changes in intelligence and information-processing speed and also memory reflect losses of brain volume and the accumulation of white matter lesions brought about by poorer brain blood circulation that can be remedied by more frequent exercise. While this might not seem so crucial for those of you reading this in their 20s, it is encouragement indeed for the team of editors writing this book!

Pat and his colleagues also tackled the issue of practice effects on intelligence tests. They found that their elderly research participants showed practice gains from a single 10-minute experience of an intelligence test when they returned eight years later to re-take the same intelligence test (this group has missed their previous appointment four years earlier, which allowed Pat and his team to explore whether practice effects still held true after an eight-year gap). This effect is interesting for two reasons. Not only does it show the incredible achievement of the ageing human brain, but it also offers an explanation for Jim Flynn's observation that, in many countries, intelligence test scores have increased over the years. Rabbitt and colleagues explained that growing exposure to, and awareness of, the types of problems found in intelligence tests was enough to account for the small increases observed in the 'Flynn effect'.

For more about Pat's research over the years, search for him in the British Psychological Society website (www.thepsychologist.org.uk/) or Google Scholar him to find an impressive array of research.

or with blocks. Now it is one of the wonders of the modern age to watch a two-year-old child successfully manipulating an iPad. Along with this complexity we are exposed to more information through various media and we stay in education longer. We also have more varied experiences, some of which can be quite challenging. Maybe these changes in the complexity of life have produced changes in the complexity of the way we organise information and ideas in our minds, and these changes have enhanced our performance on mental tests.

At the time that he first published his results, Flynn (1987) argued that the rise in IQ scores did not mean a rise in the general intelligence of the population. He suggested that the best way to explain the data was to say that IQ tests do not measure intelligence, but instead correlate with another factor that is related to intelligence, such as abstract problem solving. The debate about the Flynn effect is ongoing, but see the key researcher opposite (Pat Rabbitt) for another explanation.

22.6.2 AND NOW . . .

One of the developments in our view of intelligence that has gained more credibility over the years is the distinction between crystallised intelligence and fluid intelligence proposed by Raymond Cattell over 40 years ago (see above). A major scientific advance since the Neisser report is the development of brain scanning. One clear finding of this work has been to confirm that the front part of the brain (the prefrontal cortex) is associated with, among other things, fluid intelligence. By contrast, the abilities associated with crystallised intelligence appear to be unaffected by damage to this area (Waltz et al., 1999). The general picture, however, is less clear and although many brain areas have been identified as being important in intelligence by a few studies, very few areas of the brain have been agreed on by even 50% of the scanning studies (Colom, 2007).

Another big advance since the Neisser report has been our increased knowledge about genetics and the mapping of the human genome. This has led to the search for the genes that make us less or more intelligent. The bad news (or good news, depending on your point of view) is that this search has been relatively fruitless so far. Although nearly 300 genes have been found that contribute to learning difficulties (Inlow & Restifo, 2008), there has been very little success in finding genes that contribute to normal variation. One explanation for this lack of success is that there are many genes that are associated with IQ rather than a few, and hence they become very difficult to find. The difficulty of the work is illustrated by the search for genes associated with height. How tall we grow has been shown to be 90% heritable, but so far research has only found 20 genetics markers for height, which together explain only 3% of the variance (Weedon et al., 2008).

Evidence is hardening on the influence of the environment, as shown by the gains in IQ performance from children who are adopted into wealthier homes. The estimates for this advantage vary between 12 and 18 IQ points (Duyme, Dumaret, & Tomkiewicz, 1999; van IJzendoorn, Juffer, & Poelhuis, 2005). There is also more evidence to support the long-term benefits of preschool and primary school interventions designed to boost children from disadvantaged homes (Nisbett, 2009).

A further development, though not discussed in the report by Nisbett et al. (2012), is seen in the new understandings about *epigenetics*. The processes of inheritance have a further layer beyond the human genome and our knowledge is increasing about how the genetic code is expressed. Some genes can be switched on or switched off by changes in the environment. More remarkably, these alterations to the expression of genes can be passed on to the next generation. This complex and exciting new science has the potential to shine new light on intelligence and how it develops.

22.6.3 WHERE DOES THIS LEAVE US?

This chapter started with a look at our everyday understandings about intelligence and it seems right to return to that idea now. Perhaps one of the most striking observations is that evidence and the theories have little, if any, effect on these everyday understandings. What is clear, however, is that intelligence remains a very important ability for us and this is shown, for example, in the way we will buy products designed to boost intelligence.

One example of the public appetite for intelligence boosting is the Mozart effect. This effect allegedly shows the cognitive benefits of listening to the music of Mozart. Studies by Rauscher, Shaw and Ky (1993) examined the effect of listening to the first 10 minutes of the Mozart Sonata for Two Pianos in D Major. They reported a temporary improvement in visual-spatial reasoning on the Stanford–Binet test. Perhaps not surprisingly, replication of this finding has been very difficult outside their laboratory (Steele, Bass, & Crook, 1999). This lack of scientific support has not dented interest in this idea and an industry has developed around the Mozart effect. You can see it for yourself at their website (www.mozarteffect.com), where you can purchase all manner of products to boost the intelligence of your child. Before you sign up to purchase, though, you might like to know that much of Mozart's music is available on budget CDs and downloads and even appears as a regular feature in *Poundtime*.

The true description of the Mozart effect concerns not the impact of music on intelligence, but the enduring gullibility of people for snake oil remedies. When we want something very much, we are vulnerable to the false claims of pseudoscience. So the Mozart effect is best described as the willingness of otherwise intelligent people to spend money on worthless products in the mistaken belief that it will make their children more intelligent.

22.7 CHAPTER SUMMARY

The psychological study of intelligence has a long and controversial history. There is general agreement that it is possible to measure cognitive abilities and to put people in a rough rank order. There is also general agreement that we can use these scores to predict success at work and in education. Where the disagreements come is in the causes of these differences and what interventions we should make to respond to them. The answer you come to will depend less on your reading of the scientific evidence and more on your view of what it means to be a human being.

 ## DISCUSSION QUESTIONS

We have seen that there has long been a debate over whether there is one general kind of intelligence or several different kinds. Where do you stand on this question? What reasons can you give in support of your views?

There has also been lengthy debate over the role of (a) nature and (b) nurture in accounting for differences in intelligence. Which do you think is most important? What reasons can you give in support of your views?

What do you think IQ tests actually measure?

Consider the differences between the major theories of intelligence outlined in this chapter. What are the implications for (a) intelligence testing, (b) learning, (c) schooling?

SUGGESTIONS FOR FURTHER READING

You may wish to read about the development of intelligence, IQ testing or recent views on intelligence. The latter include the concept of 'emotional intelligence' put forward by Daniel Goleman. A good and interesting starting point for any student interested in intelligence is Mackintosh, N.J. (1998). *IQ and human intelligence.* Oxford: Oxford University Press.

On the history of intelligence, see Deary, I.J. (2000). *Looking down on human intelligence: from psychometrics to the brain.* Oxford: Oxford University Press; Richardson, K. (1991). *Understanding intelligence.* Milton Keynes: Open University Press; Sternberg, R.J. (Ed.) (2000). *Handbook of intelligence.* Cambridge: Cambridge University Press.

For information about IQ tests, see Gould, S.J. (1996). *The mismeasure of man.* New York: W.W. Norton; Mackintosh, N.J. (1998). *IQ and human intelligence.* Oxford: Oxford University Press.

For recent views on intelligence, see Khalfa, J. (Ed.) (1994). *What is intelligence?* Cambridge: Cambridge University Press; Sternberg, R.J., & Grigorenko, E. (2007). *Teaching for successful intelligence: to increase student learning and achievement* (2nd edn). Thousand Oaks, CA: Corwin.

If you are interested in an alternative view on intelligence, you may wish to look up literature on emotional intelligence, starting with a pop psychology book: Goleman, D. (1996). *Emotional intelligence.* London: Bloomsbury.

 Still want more? For links to online resources relevant to this chapter and a quiz to test your understanding, visit the companion website at edge.sagepub.com/banyard2e

23 SELF

Lead authors: Jill Arnold and Ben Oldfield

CHAPTER OUTLINE

23.1 Introduction	404
23.2 The question of self	404
23.2.1 Self and personality	405
23.2.2 The subjective experience of 'being me'	405
23.3 Constructing the self	407
23.3.1 Personal construct and social schemes	407
23.3.2 Social constructionism	407
23.3.3 Group membership and social identity	408
23.3.4 Social roles, the presentation of self and the dramaturgical analogy	409
23.4 Explaining identity	410
23.4.1 Discourse and identity	410
23.4.2 Personal histories	411
23.5 The cyborg self: material and virtual worlds	412
23.5.1 Embodied selves	412
23.5.2 The self in the digital age	413
23.5.3 Selves and social media	414
23.5.4 Online games and virtual self	416
23.5.5 The quantified self	418
23.6 Chapter summary	418
Discussion questions	418
Suggestions for further reading	419

23.1 INTRODUCTION

Who am I and how do I know who I am? When challenged to say who we are, we commonly reply with our name and a list of categories of things we do and places we go. Awareness of ourselves as individuals, the notion of a 'self', is something that most people believe differentiates us from other animals. Over the years, psychologists have proposed numerous explanations of what the self is and techniques to investigate and describe the self. This chapter introduces some of the most important discussions and methods.

FRAMING QUESTIONS

- Can you be whoever you want to be?
- Does what you own, eat or wear change who you are?
- What does it mean to 'perform' your 'gendered' self?
- How can we know ourselves when we change so much?
- How do you maintain a sense of identity when you play so many roles?
- How much are you 'yourself' when on Facebook or Instagram?

EXERCISE: WHO AM I? PART 1

Write down as many responses as you can (up to 20) as quickly as possible to the question 'Who am I?'. Keep these responses for analysis later on in the chapter.

23.2 THE QUESTION OF SELF

'Who are YOU?', said the Caterpillar.

Alice replied rather shyly, 'I hardly know sir, just at present – at least I know who I WAS when I got up this morning, but I think I must have changed several times since then'. 'What do you mean by that?,' said the Caterpillar sternly. 'Explain yourself!' 'I can't explain MYSELF, I'm afraid sir,' said Alice, 'because I'm not myself you see'. (Carroll, 1865/2003: Chapter 5)

IDENTITY Awareness of shared distinctive characteristics by members of a group. Identity may be considered in a number of ways, such as, for example, ethnic or religious identity, sexual orientation, or through something like shared music preference.

Psychologists trying to explain 'self' can fully appreciate the dilemma faced by Alice: 'Somehow psychological theory of the self must encompass both the stability and uniqueness; the variability and multiplicity' (Harré & Van Langenhove, 1999: 60). It seems so obvious that we are individual selves ('myself' or 'my self'), that we each have a *sense* of the self or know about it, can refer to ourselves and what we are like. It is also often taken for granted that we have many roles or **identities** that are recognisable by others. Even mere passers-by (like Alice's caterpillar) may assume we know what kind of person we are. If we are in doubt or are challenged about who or what we are, we can usually refer to our name, where we live or our school and perhaps offer ID, such as a driver's licence, to provide evidence for our claims. That we have an individual character, which is influenced by our families and biology and shaped by events and experiences, is familiar 'folk psychology'. There are, however, a number of questions for psychologists to consider concerning identity. On the one hand, each of us seems unique; on the other hand, we resemble other people in many ways, and while we all remain the same individual *bodily*, bodies change a good deal across the lifespan or with changing circumstances.

So a key issue faced by psychology (as the quote above suggests) concerns the complexity of self and identity: yes, people are always the same person, that is an *individual*, but at the same time they *appear* to be like some others (judging from the way they dress or talk or eat food or do certain jobs). Moreover, although we *are* just one person, at times we play our roles differently: when we are at home with our parents, we may not swear or get drunk, but when we are out with mates, we may do both those things, thereby revealing a different 'side' to us. We *also* have virtual or cyber selves, as we use the internet, social media, multi-user games and mobile phones to interact with others, and have multiple ways to present who we are to others. So, how do we understand and research these tensions concerning identity? This chapter will provide a tour of key psychological concepts which have been developed to address the complexities of being a person, including the virtual self.

23.2.1 SELF AND PERSONALITY

'Who in the world am I? Ah, that's the great puzzle'. (Carroll, 1865/2003: Chapter 2)

Mainstream psychology approached the 'puzzle' of self largely through the concept of **personality** and the idea that each individual possesses a set of attributes which are relatively fixed throughout life. In fact, the notion of personality is a very Western construct, reflecting the individualist ethos of nations like the USA and the UK (Rose, 1989). In other nations, such as Japan, India and Brazil (which are more *collectivist*), group memberships, social roles and obligations are emphasised rather than individual traits, preferences and achievements. The approaches outlined in *this* chapter rest on the belief that our personality is not as fixed as psychometricians would have us believe, but that it can be a dynamic creature, with multiple facets. Such a phenomenon is best captured through seeing it in action as it presents itself to others, communicates and interacts through dialogue and self-expression. Thus the methods most suited to understanding self are qualitative methods of research, such as those reported in Chapter 4, sections 4.3, 4.4 and 4.5 of this book.

> **PERSONALITY** The characteristic patterns of thoughts, feelings and behaviours that make a person unique.
>
> **PSYCHOMETRIC APPROACH** Any attempt to assess and express numerically the mental characteristics of behaviour in individuals, usually through specific tests for personality or intelligence or some kind of attitude measurement.

EXERCISE: WHO AM I? PART 2

Reflect on your responses to our opening 'Who am I?' exercise. Consider how many of your responses relate to personality traits (extraverted, intelligent, humorous, etc.). Then think how many relate to social categories, roles and group memberships (as, e.g. son, daughter, partner, student, Scottish, woman, man). Would you say those responses produced first are more important to your sense of self? How difficult do you find it to provide a satisfactory answer?

23.2.2 THE SUBJECTIVE EXPERIENCE OF 'BEING ME'

The concept of personality (and the assumptions made about its measurement) has been criticised for failing to recognise the complex, dynamic and socially embedded nature of subjective experience. Personality scales in **psychometric**

HUMANISTIC PSYCHOLOGY The humanistic approach explains the subjective experience of individuals in terms of the way they interpret past events. Humanistic psychology partly arose in reaction to the mechanical (stimulus response) models of behaviourism. Borrowing ideas from psychoanalysis, it sought to affirm the dignity and worth of all people (see Chapter 25 for therapeutic interventions based on humanistic psychology).

PHENOMENOLOGY Based on the idea that the ordinary world of lived experience is taken for granted and often unnoticed, phenomenology attempts to discover how people know and understand objects (and other people) from the way they perceive and construct ideas about the social world around them.

SELF-CONCEPT OR SELF-IDENTITY Self-knowledge and memory allow people to develop a life story and to understand how others perceive them. The self-concept is the product, therefore, of self-assessments – some relatively permanent, such as personality attributes and knowledge of skills and abilities, and others less so, such as occupation, interests and physical status.

INTERPRETIVE PHENOMENOLOGICAL ANALYSIS (IPA) An experiential qualitative approach to research in psychology and the social sciences. It was developed by Jonathan Smith and it offers insights into how a person makes sense of a particular experiential phenomenon – the 'insider's perspective'.

tests offer only a limited range of mutually exclusive options (e.g. yes/no, agree/disagree) and therefore do not allow individuals to elaborate on their responses. In contrast, psychologists who use qualitative research methods encourage individuals to talk about themselves and their experiences in their own terms.

Humanistic and **phenomenological** psychologists are interested in finding out about how people's **self-concept** is influenced by life events, typically involving a transition (e.g. falling ill, divorce, changing jobs) (see Stevens, 1996). All manner of experiences have been studied through compiling and analysing individuals' accounts, from being a victim of crime to enjoying 'peak' or 'flow' experiences, though the focus is often on 'lived experience', that is, those set in the context of their life-world. An assumption in such research is that individuals 'know' their own lives and can provide descriptions of their experiences. It is the job of the researcher to capture and identify the psychological aspects of these experiences. Another characteristic of this approach is that individuals' experiences are treated as unique (at least to some extent) and so everyone has a distinctive 'self', and whatever the experience being studied, the overarching aim of the analysis is to reveal some of a person's authentic sense of self. In the UK, the methodology known as **interpretive phenomenological analysis** (shortened to IPA: see Smith, 2004) is a popular qualitative approach for understanding individual experiences using in-depth, semi-structured interviews and systematic analysis of transcripts. IPA is notably used to investigate how individuals deal with life experiences (see Chapter 4, section 4.3 for a case study using IPA and Chapter 4, section 4.5 for an IPA study with convicted sex offenders).

Humanistic and *phenomenological* approaches have been criticised for neglecting the *wider* social and cultural contexts which influence individual experiences and identities. According to their critics, these approaches are preoccupied with the private and personal, and miss out the public and social. This is not to say that interpersonal relationships and environmental factors are not recognised by such approaches or that social influences are not reported by research participants. Rather, the emphasis tends to be on personal experiences and perceptions. In this way, humanistic and

KEY STUDY

Smith, J.A., & Osborn, M. (2007). Pain as an assault on the self: an interpretive phenomenological analysis. *Psychology and Health, 22*, 517–534.

Smith and Osborn's paper presents a study illustrating how chronic, benign, low back pain may have a serious debilitating impact on the sufferer's sense of self. Six patients were interviewed and transcripts were subjected to IPA. The analysis pointed to the powerful ways in which chronic pain has a negative impact on patients' self and identity, and some participants describe how the ensuing derogatory self-image seemed to lead to their directing negative emotions towards other people. The analysis gives a detailed account of these processes at work, which are considered in relation to the literature, including studies of illness and identity, shame and acceptance.

phenomenological approaches share a psychological emphasis with the psychometric focus on the individual, despite underlying methodological and theoretical differences. At the other end of the psychological spectrum, *social* psychologists have been concerned with studying those group and social identities to which individuals are drawn, and it is to these approaches which we now turn.

23.3 CONSTRUCTING THE SELF

23.3.1 PERSONAL CONSTRUCT AND SOCIAL SCHEMES

Many psychologists during the 1980s began to take a **social cognitive** approach to understanding 'who we are' and developed ideas about how we gain a sense of self through making sense of others in our social world. Social cognitive theories have been pioneered in various ways: from notions of **schemas** in Bartlett's book on *Remembering* (1932) to Kelly's (1955) theory of **personal constructs**. George Kelly (1955) maintained that the self is defined by relatively distinctive perceptions, or constructs, concerning our *personal* world, whereby individuals will see things in their various ways and use particular constructs to make sense of the [social] world around them. An individual will typically use only a few core constructs to explain the people and events around them, with further constructs used only occasionally. Kelly stressed the uniqueness of personal construct systems as a consequence of a person's life history, as well as the concept of **personal agency** as we actively try to make sense of our environment and anticipate future events, much like psychologists in fact!

How we categorise new information may not seem like a particularly important topic, and yet the constructs (or schemas) that we use to make sense of new information are important. They are the shortcuts that allow us to collect data from the endless incoming stream of information from the world around us, and then incorporate the data into our current views of the world, of others and (importantly) of our self. We need to assimilate such data if we are to become socialised and build on previous experiences (see Fiske & Taylor, 1991). Not only do schema organise our experiences into a coherent narrative, but they act as a guide to the maintenance of consistency about who we think we are (Markus, 1977).

Further ideas about how well we create and maintain a stable sense of self, with all its inherent contradictions, was also explored by Markus and Kunda (1986), who discussed the usefulness of the 'working self-concept'. The notion of a more dynamic self-concept (which may change according to the situation we are in) leads us to consider the development of a theory that offers further critical explanation of the functions of the self.

> **SOCIAL COGNITION** The way in which people perceive and process information to make sense of the social world. Ideas and concepts, developed in the 1980s by psychologists, that include stereotyping, memory, schemas, representation, social discourse and how we construct and organise social categories. Each has influenced the study of the self.
>
> **SCHEMAS** Ways of *organising* concepts or knowledge about the world (including the social world and ourselves) which then affect how we adopt *new* knowledge or use new knowledge to accommodate new experiences automatically, possibly stereotypically, especially when situations change rapidly.

23.3.2 SOCIAL CONSTRUCTIONISM

The **social constructionist** approach suggests an alternative to both traditional notions of personality and the self as a processor of information about social life. It views the self as a *product* of social encounters and relationships, rather than the source of personality (Gergen, 1997; Gergen & Gergen, 1988). Further, it suggests that people's *understanding* of self comes from communications and interactions with others (Burr, 2003), together with life story, memory (Neisser & Fivush, 1994; Neisser & Joplin, 1997) and our cultural narratives (Polkinghorne, 1996). Social constructionists have generated interest in the idea of diversity of experience rather than difference, and the importance of cultural, political, geographical and historical contexts in which interactions take place. So they study how people view themselves from multiple perspectives and in particular contexts, such as at work, at school, at the doctors. Some theorists think that the idea of a socially constructed self neglects bodily identity (Cromby, 2004, 2005), but feminist and critical psychologists have developed social constructionist approaches to understand, for example, **gendered identity** and sexuality, whereby the bodily identity (as male or female) is constructed, managed and performed

> **SOCIAL CONSTRUCTIONISM** An approach to psychology which focuses on *meaning* and *power*; it aims to account for the ways in which social phenomena and identity concepts develop agreed meanings adopted through prevailing social interactions.
>
> **GENDERED IDENTITY** The way that people *perform* their biological sexual identity. Just how or in what way gender is demonstrated will vary depending on social or cultural understanding, circumstances, expectations or requirements.

according to prevailing cultural notions of gender (Burman, 1998; Kitzinger & Wilkinson, 1996). A good example of this is presented by Seymour-Smith (2013) in Chapter 4, section 4.4 of this book, with the discursive analysis of how men deal with the loss of a testicle and its replacement with an implant.

One of the original puzzles of 'self' was the way we assume a 'consistent self' despite a changing body (perhaps not as dramatically as Alice experienced, but nevertheless as real), but social constructionist concepts explain how the sense of self results from active *processes* – constructing an *ongoing* sense of self as we age and change roles (Markus & Wurf, 1987).

As mentioned above, in order to be ourselves in whatever context – as man or woman, lover, patient or partner – we use the objects we carry in our bags (and indeed the bag itself), clothes and bodily adornment to communicate *something* (deliberately or inadvertently) about ourselves. We display our status or social class (e.g. police uniform, business suit), interests (badges, sports T-shirts), gender (style of clothes, jewellery, haircut), individuality and character (personal items), and we present ourselves as a certain *kind* of person (see Csikszentmihalyi & Rochberg-Halton, 1981; Finkelstein, 1991). Social constructionism proposes that our ideas about ourselves are both individual and social, with the narratives we create about ourselves (our life stories) used as a reference point for how we portray our *future* selves, that is what we might think or do in situations in the future (Crossley, 2000; Csikszentmihalyi, 1993; Polkinghorne, 2000). The culture in which we belong is not 'out there' to influence us, or as a 'container' to control us (Radley, 1991), but is there to provide us with stories or discourses from which we come to understand what to expect in our interactions with others. Social constructionism has enabled psychologists to develop ideas about self and how it relates to identity (social and performed) and personhood (the political and ideological). It has also enabled researchers to develop methodologies that allow the rigorous exploration of subjective experience as we engage in social or cultural discourse and interactions in real, virtual and cyborgian places.

23.3.3 GROUP MEMBERSHIP AND SOCIAL IDENTITY

> **SOCIAL IDENTITY THEORY** Tajfel and Turner's (1986) social identity theory examines intergroup and ingroup discrimination based on the idea that a person has several selves that function at different levels of social circles, such as personal, family, community, national.

One of the most important concepts in social psychology is the idea of the social or cultural group. A great deal of attention has been paid to research into the effects of intragroup (or within-group) and intergroup (between-group) dynamics (see Chapters 13 and 14). According to Henri Tajfel's (1981) **social identity theory (SIT)**, *identifying* (or, indeed, refusing to identify) as a member of a group, and whether membership is chosen (e.g. Manchester City Football Club fan) or designated (e.g. by sex, age, nationality, ethnicity), are important aspects of how we see and feel about ourselves: that is, they affect our sense of self. Tajfel's theory suggests that personal identity is linked to **social identity** and that group memberships help define who we are. He suggests that self-esteem may be boosted if our 'ingroups' are positively evaluated. For example, if our national identity is enhanced by, say, sporting success in international competitions (e.g. our team wins the World Cup), then it follows that we will feel good about ourselves.

Tajfel maintains that we are *motivated* to perceive our ingroups in positive ways, as this will lead to positive feelings about self. Conversely, we will also be motivated to perceive *outgroups* in negative ways to help ensure that our ingroups are viewed positively, relatively speaking. The theory has been influential as a way of explaining intergroup prejudice and conflict, whereby *assumed* distinctive characteristics of group behaviour arise from the psychological processes of categorisation and self-enhancement (see Chapter 13, section 13.4.3, for an account of how social identity theory explains group behaviour). These psychological characteristics include depersonalisation, ethnocentrism and a relative uniformity of action and attitude among group members (Abrams, 1992). There are many other aspects of social identity theory (SIT) that help us to appreciate how our self-image or identity is bound up with our identification with others in our group and the claims we make about who we are.

We can, however, criticise SIT on several grounds. One major problem is what counts as a group. Being male or female (or any other biological category, such as being old, diabetic, etc.) is not the same as a *social* group, such as following a football team or a religious system, although all such categories carry social meaning according to the culture as to what a person 'should' be like, or expectations about their behaviour, and we may often act in accordance with *perceived* group ideals. Alternatively, people may feel *ambivalent* about the groups they are associated with and have a complex, shifting perspective on group membership which may not entail hostility towards other groups. Indeed, individuals may find they have things in common with the 'outgroup', for example, someone may be a Catholic but disagree with edicts on contraception and women priests, and be sympathetic to Pagan spirituality. SIT therefore presents individuals as rather mechanistically 'contained' uniformly within a group and responding to group values and norms in predictable ways, almost as if we are cognitively wired to maximise intergroup difference in self-serving ways (see Billig, 1985; Radley, 1995). In real life this is clearly *not* the case, as we shall see in the next section.

23.3.4 SOCIAL ROLES, THE PRESENTATION OF SELF AND THE DRAMATURGICAL ANALOGY

In contrast to the group approaches outlined above (and in Chapters 13 and 14), social psychologists are also interested in how the self is presented in a range of social *roles*. One formerly popular perspective was **role theory** (see Dahrendorf, 1973), where individuals are characterised by roles played in different situations (e.g. at work, at home, with friends). The emphasis was not on a singular private self, but considered multiple *personas* across different social contexts. So, for example, a woman's behaviour as a mother would differ from her behaviour as a work colleague at Nottingham Trent University, or as the county's high jump champion. Each social role would carry different expectations, with motherhood *normatively* associated with being responsible and nurturing, while a work colleague will be expected to be hardworking and task-oriented (erm – and responsible and nurturing). Social roles will vary in importance for individuals, so being a parent might be central for some people, while being a lecturer at Nottingham Trent University might be the most important thing in their life for others. Trying to fulfil many (competing) demands of roles may result in **role conflict**. For example, trying to achieve good grades as a student while also being a paid worker to finance one's studies may create difficulties.

While traditional role theory considered the *actual* roles we play in everyday life (student, sister, customer), however, with the constraints and expectations people have about them, a contrasting theoretical approach to social self, called the **dramaturgical analogy**, offers a wider understanding of social roles and identity (Goffman, 1959). This approach looks at social life as if individuals are *performing* their everyday roles in ways thought acceptable or, sometimes strategically, to secure certain social outcomes. For example, a child may *present* as ill in order to receive sympathy from a parent and miss school, or an adolescent boy may present himself (his *self*) as 'cool' when interacting with a girl (or boy) he likes in front of his friends, and so on. Goffman invites us to think of self as *negotiated in the process of social interaction*, that is, as a set of 'performances' which evolve in the presence of others and which shift across time and place.

In order to be convincing in our various roles, avoiding embarrassment or conflict in the presentation of self, emphasis is placed on preparation for the performance of self (usually away from the public gaze, such as the routines involved in getting dressed to go out) and the need to choose the necessary 'props'. This perspective, according to which the *self as identity* is multiple and performed, has been developed in different ways by **ethnomethodologists** (see Garfinkel, 1967) and, more recently, by social psychologists interested in discourse practices (Edwards & Potter, 1992; Potter & Wetherell, 1987) and even the presentation of self in virtual spaces (Miller & Arnold, 2001).

ROLE THEORY A perspective in social psychology that considers how we manage everyday activity (rights, duties, expectations and norms of behaviour) by fulfilment of socially-defined social roles (e.g. mother, manager, teacher).

DRAMATURGICAL ANALOGY Erving Goffman proposed a theatrical metaphor as a way of understanding self in everyday life and seeing social interactions as though they were dramatic performances, considering the costumes, the props, etc. which go towards making up the 'scenes' played out by people.

ETHNOMETHODOLOGY Not a formal research method, but an approach to empirical study that aims to discover the things that people *do* in particular situations and how they create the patterns and orderliness of social life to gain a sense of social structure.

EXERCISE: SOCIAL ROLES

Goffman writes about how we manage the 'multiplicity' of social identities or selves. As you read the rest of the chapter, we invite you to consider the following questions and see how many different ways you can answer them:

- We may play different roles, but does this mean we have no 'true' self?
- How would other people describe you (e.g. parent, friend or colleague)? Do these descriptions differ and, if so, are you all of these selves? Are any of them how you see yourself? How do you 'manage' discrepancies?
- Are you ever aware of trying to fulfil too many or conflicting roles? How do you feel when this happens, and why?
- What happens when people challenge 'you', that is, when they are not convinced about your identity, authenticity or role? They may say things like 'You look too young', 'You're just a girl' or 'Who do you think you are?'.
- Can we be ourselves without an audience? How much do we rely on others (or virtual others) to help us be ourselves?
- How much can you be yourself without the appropriate 'props' and clothes, etc., or, for example, when only your voice, text messages, avatar or pictures are available to others?
- What exactly *do* you rely on to be you?

23.4 EXPLAINING IDENTITY

23.4.1 DISCOURSE AND IDENTITY

Role and social identity theorists have examined social identities by designing experiments involving group judgements or by observations of the way people manage performance of identity in social interactions. Another way of studying self and identity is to examine how people actually talk about themselves (and others) in practice. Social psychologists interested in **discourse** and social interaction have looked at the construction and negotiation of self and identity in various social contexts (Burman & Parker, 1993; Potter & Wetherell, 1987). In this body of work, *self* is regarded as a social construct and (as discussed previously) presented and negotiated during interactions with others. As such, self is not fixed, but an ongoing project that evolves and changes within diverse social contexts. Importantly. the presentation of self will be informed by culturally important discourses (which may vary depending upon the company you keep).

Discourse analysis of talk about race, gender or disability can be valuable in highlighting prejudice (and ways of 'doing' identity to distance yourself from accusations of prejudice). Research suggests that the use of *disclaimers* (Hewitt & Stokes, 1975) is common when people make potentially controversial claims about groups. In the context of race, the classic formulation runs 'I'm not racist but …'. Thus, a prefacing statement is used to manage possible accusations of racism before the speaker utters a statement which could be heard as prejudiced (see Billig, 1988). Such talk is also a way of doing what social psychologists call '*identity work*', that is, implicitly presenting one's own group as superior. Research by Gough (1998, 2002) examined heterosexual men's talk about women and gay men and highlighted similar disclaimers ('I've always tolerated it but …'). Gough argued that such patterns of talk are designed to inoculate the speaker against criticism while at the same time they may present their self, and (heterosexual) men in general, as 'masculine'. In this way, identity is relational, meaning that we describe ourselves implicitly or explicitly in relation to (or against) particular others (see also Gilligan, 1982).

Discourse analysts have also shown that talk about our selves is oriented to issues of **stake** and **accountability**. Thus, speakers are often concerned about attributing personal interest (stake) about an issue to self and others as well as attending to matters of blame and responsibility. For example, a house meeting arranged to discuss domestic chores might involve all sorts of claims from different parties about who is (un)interested in cleaning and who is (ir)responsible in matters of tidiness. Throughout this discussion, identities are being constructed, defended, negotiated, challenged and disavowed. For example, Sally's claim about being tidy might be disputed, while Dan's promise to clean the bathroom might be treated with incredulity. *Identity work* gets done in mundane situations like these all

KEY RESEARCHER Margaret Wetherell

In 1987, Margie Wetherell and Jonathan Potter wrote a ground-breaking book *Discourse and social psychology: beyond attitudes and behaviour* (Potter & Wetherell, 1987). It set out the principles of a psychological approach that challenged traditional ways of understanding social inter-actions and showed how discursive psychology, discourse analysis and the wider implications of patterns in people's talk was at the centre of the study of self and identity. These ideas have developed since then with increasingly diverse research (using ethnographic and other qualita-tive methods in social psychology) as part of postmodern, critical, social constructionist or feminist approaches to natural language use.

Margie Wetherell has played a key role in developing this research and our understanding of psychological states and subjectiv-ity (including emotion and memory), but also ideology and collective sense-making and the exploration of constructive and constructed language. Such developments (and in the findings from her work directing the Economic and Social Research Council, UK Identities and Social Action Programme) have also contributed to our understand-ing of self and identity in relation to such issues as racist discourse, healthcare decision making, gender identities (in particular, studies of masculinities), ethnic diversity, citizen participation and democratic decisions. Now retired as Professor of Social Sciences at the Open University, she continues her work as Emeritus Professor there and as Professor of Psychology at the University of Auckland, New Zealand. See *The SAGE handbook of identities* (Wetherell & Mohanty, 2010), and for other useful reading go to: www.psych.auckland.ac.nz/en/about/our-staff/academic-staff/margaret-wetherell.html.

FIGURE 23.1　Margaret Wetherell

the time, and in interactions with partners, colleagues, peers, children and parents. People are highly skilled and creative when discussing, arguing, joking, complaining and praising, all the while negotiating subject positions for themselves and others.

It is clear, however, that some subject positions are more diffi-cult to successfully claim than others because of prevailing normative assumptions or **hegemony**. For example, a man claiming an interest in cosmetics risks censure because of stereotypical notions of mas-culinity, while a woman professing an interest in weightlifting may also court controversy. Research by Wetherell and Edley (1999), based on group discussions with men, highlighted how many men are concerned to avoid claiming stereotypical 'macho' identities for themselves, while instead positioning themselves as 'ordinary' or 'rebellious'.

HEGEMONY A situation where the interests of the powerful can marginalise and counter the claims of other groups. Hegemonic masculinity is therefore one that subordinates women's activities and other (usually more effeminate) ways of being masculine. Wetherell and Edley (1999) provide a critical analysis of the concept of hegemonic masculinity. You could also consider how discourse around other aspects of gender perpetuates hegemony.

23.4.2 PERSONAL HISTORIES

Discourse analysts have produced rich, sophisticated accounts of identity work in a wide range of social contexts. However, the emphasis on social interaction perhaps glosses over questions of identity *within personal* contexts and it is to this aspect which we now turn. Some theorists, such as Wendy Hollway (Hollway & Jefferson, 2000) and Stephen Frosh (Frosh, Phoenix, & Pattman, 2001), point to the role of *early* experiences, especially within family contexts, on the performance of identities in the present. Their approach returns to *narrative* and *psychoanalytic* traditions in

DISCOURSE refers to way of organising knowledge, ideas or experience in written and spoken communications or conversations in social settings. They can be specific or specialised, such as medical or academic discourse, and are found across all media from tabloid newspapers to formal academic writing. The particular ways that concepts and categories are used in various discourses can actively influence social practices and purposes and so can be a means by which psychological ideas are interpreted and inform social action.

UNCONSCIOUS DEFENCE MECHANISMS (described by Sigmund Freud) The coping mechanisms that reduce anxiety generated by threats from negative impulses that we are not aware of.

psychology and the influence of life (his)stories on people's current self-presentations (see Chapter 24 if you are interested in the psychodynamic approach to psychopathology). Of course, researchers cannot access an individual's early experiences directly and so make use of the *life stories* provided during research interviews. Such interviews involve minimal intervention from the researcher and encourage the participant to provide as much detail as possible, in their own terms, on topics which they introduce as significant.

Evidence suggests that people who share similar backgrounds, or even the same family, may give very different accounts of their upbringing, placing emphasis on different features. Thus, the absence of a drunken father could be construed as a positive or negative factor depending on the perspective of the individual, and the perspective adopted could in turn help shape gender identities and attitudes to parenting. According to Hollway and Jefferson (2000), everyone experiences anxieties based on early life events which are difficult to tolerate, leading to **unconscious defence mechanisms**. Difficult encounters with the mother from the past may be idealised, and tensions and difficulties pushed away into the unconscious. They argue that a healthy adult sense of self may depend on how well early experiences are resolved, so when later stressful situations arise (e.g. becoming a parent) the need to confront conflict is diminished.

Considering childhood with a less traumatic base, Adam Phillips (Phillips 1993; Phillips & Taylor, 2009) provides accounts of how infants come to realise that they have separate selves and how they creatively (but often slowly) *invent* an identity, with repercussions that last throughout life. Psychoanalytically-informed research can yield rich, emotion-laden data relating to a person's biography and central values.

23.5 THE CYBORG SELF: MATERIAL AND VIRTUAL WORLDS

23.5.1 EMBODIED SELVES

'... Cassius has a lean and hungry look; ... such men are dangerous' (Shakespeare, *Julius Caesar*, Act 1, scene 2)

Until relatively recently, psychologists' emphasis on the social cognitive aspects of individuals has meant little attention was given to the psychological significance of people's bodies, and the connections between *social perceptions* of embodiment and character. However, the embodied self has emerged as a major theme, and it is clear that judging ourselves (or being judged) as fat, attractive, tall, cool, bald, etc. has implications for our *self-image* and **gendered identity.** Our feelings about ourselves change if we experience a bodily trauma, such as an injury, illness or disability, and many people spend time and effort on body care self-enhancing, whether by applying cosmetics, bodybuilding, dieting, purchasing fashionable clothes, or hair styling. The use of such products is no longer the preserve of younger women, since older people ('middle youth') and some men are investing in their appearance with cosmetics such as 'manscara' and 'guyliner'. Some social psychologists regard the body as a key *site* for self-identity and personal development, and exercising, hair transplants, tattoos etc. are regarded as attempts to define who we are and to differentiate ourselves from others. So our bodily practices are one way of being part of the culture we live in and are *performed* according to prevailing norms, particularly around gender, age and social class. Of course, body image or identity changes with age and life stage (teenage versus retired), bodily changes (e.g. pregnancy or illness), life events (accidents) and social class (e.g. fashion preferences for 'chav', 'preppy' or designer clothes). We attempt (and possibly fail: see Woodward, 2007) to represent 'who we are' through clothes and the *way* they are worn, and such body projects can be interpreted as a means of testing and *managing* our self-presentations (Goffman, 1959) so that we feel more confident, attractive and successful in the roles we play.

Our embodied identities are always social but are bound up with bodily extensions – the possessions and sundry desired items that are part of our cultural worlds. Indeed, such material objects (clothes, belongings, pets and everyday items that we keep in our homes, personal spaces, bedrooms or garden sheds) have been acknowledged as part of our self-identity since William James's *Principles of psychology* (1890). Everything, from treasured family photographs, coveted coffee mugs, DVDs, posters, letters, a skateboard, and even pieces of furniture (see Gosling, 2008, on snooping in personal spaces), can present different aspects of your sense of self that defines you. The contemporary trends for home (and self) makeovers highlight just how much we are inclined to invest in activities that provide opportunities for self-expression. You could check out the objects you have on you and what you are wearing: what items would make you less 'you' or without which you not be able to function as yourself?

FIGURE 23.2 Are adverts for 'guyliner' changing the way men think about their bodies?

(c) Ron Chapple Stock/Corbis

When we lose, break or change bits of the material world (objects that symbolise where we are from or show our interests, such as a team T-shirt, posters, concert tickets, etc.), we feel we are no longer ourselves. We can also ask what part mementos, like that old swimming trophy, or photos of yourself when younger etc., play in maintaining a narrative of ourselves, and continuity for who we claim to be. Sometimes, of course, we are restricted by social, monetary or cultural requirements, for example, wearing gender-, age- or work-appropriate clothes at school or a family wedding, but we do seem to live in a world where self and identity is (re)made in all manner of contexts.

Of all the many items we value, it is the tools for communication and connection to others, in both virtual and 'real' space, that emphasise both the importance of our *relational selves* (Gergen, 1994, 2009; Gilligan, 1982) and our ability to exploit technology to extend ourselves: from wearing glasses, driving cars, etc. to the use of mobile phones. Indeed, Haraway (1991) asserts that humans are 'natural-born cyborgs'. For many of us, the smartphone (or other such device) clearly functions as an *extension of self* (the cyborg self), through the personal information (numbers, images, texts, songs) and apps and connections it affords us. When lost, stolen or broken, we can feel lost, or threatened, and a period of disorientation may ensue before a functioning self can be re-established (Breakwell, 1986; Dittmar, 1992). Concern that our interactions with machines change us are possibly well founded (Clark, 2003; Ong, 1982), especially those that change our reading habits and sources of news and information, but these ideas are countered by psychologists who argue that our relationship with an increasingly sophisticated technology helps us to understand the psychology of self and identity (Gergen, 1996, 2000).

So far, the observations and theories we have discussed show that people have responded to the changing ways we interact with each other and our relationships to the 'things' that enable us to do so. However, a major question remains: How have people adapted their ideas about '*who they are*' and their sense of self, now that using social media and continuous connectedness of mobile devices has become a normal part of everyday life? The way people always carry the means to connect to others and check them constantly for new texts or 'updates' is a social phenomenon that psychologists are studying to discover what this means for the sense of self. In the next section, we explore how research into a selection of digital domains throws light on changes to how we manage our social selves in the digital age.

23.5.2 THE SELF IN THE DIGITAL AGE

One of the most significant challenges to traditional notions of the 'self' and identity has been the expansion of the internet, the rise of **digital domains** and the explosion of personal communication options that blur the boundaries of self in virtual worlds. Initially, these took the form of email, message boards, newsgroups and forums (Parks & Floyd, 1996), and were primarily text-based with **asynchronous conversations**. In early debates, researchers such

DIGITAL DOMAIN Digital domains enable people to access data (images, words, sounds, video, etc.) that have been converted into a digital format. Examples of digital domains include social media sites, such as Facebook and Instagram, and other internet sites or points of access, such as Twitter, email, Second Life, online games, etc.

ASYNCHRONOUS CONVERSATIONS Discussions that do not happen in real time; people contribute as and when they wish to, which may be five minutes, two days, or three months after the previous message was submitted.

as Turkle (1995) introduced important ideas about *online identities* and the concept of the *digital self*. She noted that her participants presented their online persona grounded in traits from the face-to-face (FtF) world, but that these changed over time, and many people used a *selection* of identities to represent themselves.

It soon became clear that the virtuality of the online self ('out-*there*') offered users the chance to remove some of the constraints of FtF interaction to present an *alternative* version of themselves, possibly more outgoing and less inhibited. Indeed, as the technology developed, playing *roles* as online presences did seem to offer opportunities to express aspects of self in different ways, for example, to change their role status (Miller & Arnold, 2000), or through *avatars* to escape physical disability or limitations in the embodied world (Joinson, 2003; Meadows, 2008). As discussed previously, people use their social and self-management skills to present themselves in acceptable ways that minimise risks to self-esteem, and so on. In this way, it did seem that online presence would enable people to *perform* who they *wanted* to be, free of the stereotypes or expected role performances associated with their 'real' characteristics, such as age, gender or status. Indeed, one of the assumed benefits of the removal of embodied 'boundaries' was that people could construct *any* version of the self (and nobody would know who you '*really*' were), and at first it *did* seem that people would abandon all restraint and play and experiment with alternative identities (especially gender).

Nevertheless, early research (see Parks & Floyd, 1996) focused on how computer-mediated communications (CMC) might affect psychological wellbeing (see Kraut et al., 1998, 2002; Oldfield, 2004). Indeed, with the loss of inhibition came 'flaming' or abusive communications on message boards or forums (Joinson, 2003), and then later what is known as 'trolling', with aggressive, threatening or offensive messages. Though at first this was not considered a major issue (see Niederhoffer & Pennebaker, 2002), with increased opportunities for unrestrained communication, online bullying now extends across all social media. In the past, people may well have spoken freely (and unwisely) in public, but they were immediately identified – they were *known*. Without immediate censure, people are prepared to go beyond social expansiveness to overtly break the law. So while idealised identities and the freedom of communication have been embraced wholeheartedly, it is as people in the embodied world, with all our well-practised social skills to manage, self-censor and minimise negative social judgements, that our humanity rests (Miller & Arnold, 2000).

23.5.3 SELVES AND SOCIAL MEDIA

When Facebook was founded in 2004, it rapidly changed people's social identities, as well as behaviour, and for 'native users', mobile phones and other 'i-platforms', multiple constant social media presences are now embedded into everyday life. Given what we have discussed so far, you will see that social media offer people even more ways to 'edit' identity, but also to display who they are through association with music, film, hobbies, pets, political events and commentaries, and to update and illustrate their experiences and social and cultural allegiances.

Instagram (IG) has become the perfect platform for people who share a common interest, such as their favourite dog breed. Indeed, some people take this even further and maintain an IG identity in the name of their beloved pet (well, we assume there is a human behind the account) and the dogs interact with each other on a daily basis, sympathising with each other when their humans are away, or revelling in the acquisition of treats. Below (Figure 23.3) are some of the Brussels Griffons found on IG who regularly exchange notes about their day. Other users become extremely attached to the dogs through 'following', them on IG – to the extent that these griffons may receive hundreds of messages of sympathy when they announce they are not feeling well (see Figure 23.3 opposite).

Another important aspect of social networks is that people may be more likely to reveal personal details, such as birthdays, family and private events, and daily activities to 'friends'. Notwithstanding the safeguards and privacy settings available to users, the information is still being shared in the *public sphere* (Gauntlett, 2000). However, we find that while online media offer people many opportunities to perform selves differently (Miller & Arnold, 2000), the need to manage identity continues (Miller & Arnold, 2003); a presence on Facebook, Instagram, web pages or blogs

@lucalovessausages

@count_von_chocula

@gilly_quincy

@Jumblegriffon

@blaine_griffon

@hubblegriffon

@graciegraygriffon

@penniethecurlycoatedgriff (aka @
penniethepoodle)

@dogsofdesire

FIGURE 23.3   Members of the thriving Brussels Griffon community on Instagram

means making decisions about what to reveal about ourselves (Miller & Arnold, 2001, 2003, 2009). People usually manage their online *narratives* and stories to maintain an ongoing identity (Gergen, 2009; Gergen & Gergen, 2003), portraying variations according to the version currently in play.

This is not, however, an individual, one-way line of communication, but an *interactive social process*. Walther et al. (2008) highlighted how 'attractiveness' of Facebook users can be influenced by photos, and Hong et al. (2012) demonstrated how social attractiveness and popularity can be positively influenced by factors, such as the comments on images posted by other users. Positive comments may then lead to more positive appraisals ('likes') by others. Thus, a person can maintain or even enhance their social image by the images and posts they make, and the comments they receive.

Even though people do tend to present a somewhat idealised version of themselves online (Back et al., 2010), Zhao, Grasmuck, and Martin (2008) describe Facebook as being 'nonymous' or providing only partial control over self images, as other users/friends can influence links to confirm or contradict what a user portrays. So, another user can reveal images we wish to keep private (Mazer, Murphy, & Simonds, 2007). Thus, a person may be a 'social smoker' but not want to identify as such; notwithstanding, a friend may post a picture of them smoking on a night out. After all, anyone carrying a smartphone has a camera and video recorder with them at all times, and social media can be aware of what you are doing even before you are!

Two studies highlight some of the ways we attempt to micro manage our cyber selves. Strano and Wattai-Queen (2012) found that in their initial study of 615 Facebook users, a total of 75% had removed a 'tag' from an image posted by another user. However, even though no longer linked to their identity, while still viewable to anyone accessing the account of the person who posted the image, it remains a potential threat to self identity. Another reason for 'untagging' a picture in Facebook is misidentification. Strano and Wattai-Queen (2012) found that 50% of respondents untagged such an image and, unsurprisingly (see Anderson et al., 2012; Strano & Wattai-Queen, 2012), 65% of respondents untagged an image because they felt it made them look unattractive, with significantly more women than men likely to untag for this reason. Furthermore, 54% of respondents untagged images to hide actions that might be disapproved by anyone (such as authority figures) viewing their account.

These discussions lead us to see how embracing social media as a way of living socially highlights the need to develop the skills to manage a sense of self *effectively*, because as in all social life, proactive and performed selves are vulnerable to negative interactions. The virtual spaces (as controlled technological spaces) we use do *not* always prevent harm. So researching safety issues for the cyborg self has become an ongoing project for cyberpsychologists who study how risks to a person's self can be understood and how we can help those potentially vulnerable to resist when negative incidents occur (Whitty & McLaughlin, 2007).

KEY STUDY

Strano, M.M., & Wattai-Queen, J. (2012). Covering your face on Facebook: suppression as identity management. *Journal of Media Psychology*, 24(4), 166–180.

Strano and Wattai-Queen present a paper that explores how identity is managed through social networking sites. Specifically, it focuses on Facebook and the control of a user's images, for example, untagging and privacy controls. A mixture of qualitative and quantitative research methods were employed in the study (see Chapter 4, section 4.5.1, for more about mixing qualitative and quantitative research methods). The results in this study showed that, while infrequent, participants did engage in suppression techniques, and that it was more common for someone to untag themselves and/or control who saw the image rather than request the removal of it. Participants also reported that they would simply not upload images of themselves they considered contrary to the impression they wanted to give of themselves. This online identity management is seen as an extension of how we actively engage with ways to manage social presentation of self whenever media affords us the opportunity to do so.

23.5.4 ONLINE GAMES AND VIRTUAL SELF

Our interest in the study of virtual selves is not limited to message boards, chat-rooms and social media. With increased use of computer and games consoles gaming, we find that people develop *parallel* identities. Online interaction through, for example, Second Life (see the Second Life web page) and gaming, offers unique and complex virtual characterisation through the use of *avatars*. These digital representations (Yee & Bailenson, 2009) are particularly highly developed in game consoles like the Nintendo Wii and the Microsoft Xbox franchises, with a range of options for individualising physical attributes of generic body shapes, implied gender, skin tones and facial features. Some offer details through clothing and extra accessories, such as toys and creatures, so a player can represent themselves in an extraordinary number of ways, depending on investment made or achievement of specific goals within the game. Games-playing like this is specialised but, as in offline sports or games, it is a familiar way of showing prowess as an expression of who they are. Given that an avatar can be changed and edited, striking differences arise. For example, Trepte and Reinecke (2010) found that avatars created in competitive games were *less* representative of a player's offline personality traits than avatars created for non-competitive games.

ASIDE

Avatars and you

FIGURE 23.4   Avatars and you

In games consoles like the Nintendo Wii, avatars are called the MII and highlight the bond between avatar and player, and the player's achievements as the game progresses. A social etiquette has quickly arisen: in the gamers' world, it is considered quite rude to use another player's avatar in a game, even to the point where people exclaim 'Hey that's my MII' when they see another person selecting their avatar to 'play'. What does this imply for our understanding of 'self'? People obviously make a claim on 'their' avatar, so when people can choose their identity they create a social/public representation of themselves as an extension of themselves.

Decisions made about how to represent yourself gives scope for fantasy, and in Second Life some people 'live' a parallel life, including relationships; 'marriage'; cultural (e.g. music events), social (bars, night clubs and dancing) and voluntary activities; work and shopping etc., all as a digital persona. If you already have representations of yourself in cyberspace (e.g. your photos on Facebook or the name or 'character' you adopt when you play computer games), think about how far you identify with this virtual 'you'. We would argue that a virtual self could hide or contradict aspects of your real-life personality, but consider how far the cyborg activities of texting and tweeting also demand identity creation and maintenance.

Not surprisingly, players in competitive games create avatar characters to maximise the requirements of the game and to be successful in ways they obviously cannot be in real life, such as performing spells to defeat mythical beasts or having gunfights with aliens! Klimmt, Hartmann and Frey (2007) found that non-competitive games offer a greater freedom of choice for players to create more self-representative avatars, with traits similar to their own, so players can identify with the avatar as themselves as a virtual being. In certain games, such as the World of Warcraft (WoW), players choose characters from a selection of 'clans' ('Night Elf', for example), but they can also create a 'history' or 'back story' for a more 'developed' character identity. Bessière, Seay and Kiesler (2007) found that players rated their avatars on having a personality that best met the requirements of the game (e.g. extroverted), irrespective of how they saw themselves.

There is, however, some suggestion that an avatar can influence the *player* (Yee & Bailenson, 2009), and psychologists of self are now studying how online experiences affect how we manage our embodied selves. Indeed, some people with particular disabilities take advantage of the possibilities afforded by these new social/cultural spaces to have new experiences and choices and gain confidence and skills that transfer to life on this side of the screen. You can read more about the issues raised when people create an avatar in Meadows (2008), and there is increasing cyberpsychology research into self and identity and computer-mediated communications and interactions of every kind: social networks, blogs, online dating and relationships (Ellison, Heino, & Gibs, 2006; Whitty, 2008), and many more.

23.5.5 THE QUANTIFIED SELF

SELF-SENSORS These collect data about any number of activities, including bodily functions, and can be embedded in our clothes and the things we use. As with smartphones, information can be recorded about where you are, for how long, or how often you go to places, and people you are in contact with, etc.

This chapter has explored the many ways by which psychologists have developed understandings of how people actively engage in being a person and acquire and maintain a sense of self. We conclude with a brief consideration of the developments and applications in technology that might have long-term effects on the concept of self. Einstein warned that 'not everything that counts can be counted, and not everything that can be counted, counts', but we can now acquire a great deal of *quantifiable* self knowledge or data about our bodies, actions, movements and so on using self-tracking tools called **self-sensors** and the statistics to analyse it all (see Wolf & Kelly, 2014, on the 'quantified self' or QS). With ever more apps available that can store and make sense of our personal data, people can gain detailed 'pictures' of themselves, possibly for self-knowledge but, increasingly, socially, as an extension to blogging or Facebook communications, to share thoughts and feelings with others too. We all collect and store information and data about ourselves anyway – everything from heart rates in a race or cycle ride, to diaries, blogs, photo collections, and our online shopping and internet use – and we do not know yet how much this kind of quantified self will contribute to our own, or indeed psychologists', understanding of self and identity, but we cannot ignore it as a phenomenon.

Undoubtedly, self-sensors have health applications, but some of the most exciting innovations in the cyberpsychology of self are linked to neuroscience, neurophysiology and medicine, in what is called **serious games research** (see Burke et al., 2009; Susi, Johannesson, & Backlund, 2007). Here, applications based on developments in brain–technology interaction have not only improved our understanding of our social selves in virtual worlds, but can be used to enhance people's lives. Thus they can help patients with neurological problems, children with learning difficulties and those with minimal physical movement to develop a sense of self from interactions in complex computer-generated worlds. These developments bring new challenges to theorists, technologists and users alike, but the study of our cyborg-selves (this side of the screen), and how we attempt to protect ourselves from increasing scrutiny and unwanted (and unwarranted) associations, is an important project. As long ago as 1991, Kenneth Gergen, in his book *The saturated self*, pointed the way to taking seriously the impact of information technology for the psychology of self and identity, so long as we remember that not everything that can be counted is necessarily important! Alice would understand that.

23.6 CHAPTER SUMMARY

In this chapter we have tried to address poor Alice's dilemma in answering the question – who are you? The earliest psychologists thought that it was a fundamental matter for psychology to investigate and devise theories that answered questions in their own terms and not those of the philosophers or playwrights (though Shakespeare did a good job). We have considered the main ways that, over the last 60 years or so, approaches have been successful, but have in turn raised further issues: of methodology, ontology, levels of explanation and real-world usefulness. We have also shown that recent studies have moved away from the traditional understanding of self as a fixed 'thing' that is 'real' or 'true', towards self as being produced through interactions that take place in specific cultural, political, social, temporal, geographic and, increasingly, virtual contexts or digital spaces. We see that psychological research can be interdisciplinary and provide useful understandings for people about ourselves in an increasingly technological world.

(?) DISCUSSION QUESTIONS

Why is it important to ask questions about identity that are not based on genetic or biological preconceptions about personality and character?

What aspects of your life illustrate that a *dynamic* (interactive, narrative, discursive, dramaturgical, cyborgian) approach to understanding the 'sense of self' has useful explanatory value?

In what ways could research on people's interactions with digital technology have beneficial applications?

After you have read Chapter 16 on *Critical Social Psychology*, consider what real-world benefits would arise from taking a critical approach to the study of self and identity constructs.

 # SUGGESTIONS FOR FURTHER READING

The following are some classic texts that cover a range of reading about ways of thinking about the self:

Csikszentmihalyi, M. (1993). *The evolving self: a psychology for the new millennium*. New York: HarperCollins. This author takes a long view, drawing on his long and wide experience of studying how people think about themselves and their experiences (check out his many books and articles, especially his discussion of the experience of 'flow') and how psychology can help us to understand ideas about self. In this book he argues how people evolve to meet new technological circumstances.

Goffman, E. (1959). *The presentation of self in everyday life*. New York: Doubleday Anchor. Although now over 50 years old, this is still an insightful read. It is the book that set out Goffman's original ideas about the 'performance' of self in our social interactions and relationships. His ideas about how we 'manage' and maintain continuity in our different roles and over life changes are brilliantly described.

Gosling, S. (2008). *Snoop: what your stuff says about you*. New York: Basic Books. This is an interesting discussion based on a series of inventive empirical studies of how people interpret others' characteristics from the things they have in their rooms. Again, it is an insightful, sometimes challenging, discussion of how 'what' we have and chose to display reflects 'who' we are.

Turkle, S. (1995). *Life on the screen: identity in the age of the internet*. New York: Simon & Schuster. Turkle's ground-breaking book, anticipating the impact of the 'cyberspace' of the internet, raised issues about how computers would enable alternative identities and affect the way we think and see ourselves. She also comments on gender differences in the use of technology and possible problems when children use the internet.

 Still want more? For links to online resources relevant to this chapter and a quiz to test your understanding, visit the companion website at edge.sagepub.com/banyard2e

SECTION G

APPLIED PSYCHOLOGY: HOW WE USE PSYCHOLOGY

So we have all this knowledge about people and how they think, feel and behave; what are we going to do with it? It is the application of psychology to real-life problems that draws many people to the subject. Sometimes this is a desire to know more about ourselves and our own behaviour and sometimes it is to marvel at the behaviour of others: the mad, bad and dangerous to know (*is that just the psychology staff? Ed.*).

When you think about it, many of the challenges for the world in the twenty-first century are to do with human behaviour. If we are to alleviate the problems caused by global warming, we have to find a way to change behaviour so that we use less energy, waste less water and create a sustainable food chain. The technical solutions to these issues can only go part of the way. It's down to us and our behaviour. The same is true in the field of health. There is currently a moral panic about obesity in Western countries, but the solutions will come from changing behaviour (mainly by eating less food – it's not rocket science) rather than creating new lines of food for Sainsbury's.

The issue with these behavioural problems is that we all know what the solution is, but actually doing it is much more tricky. We know what we need to do to have a balanced diet, but persuading ourselves to do this requires concentrated effort. It is this gap between intention and behaviour where psychology can contribute.

In this section, we are not aiming to capture the breadth of applied psychology, but just present three of the core areas. Those areas are clinical psychology, which focuses on mental disorders and difficulties in living, health psychology, which looks at how psychology can be used to improve the health of the nation, and finally forensic psychology, where techniques are used to reduce crime and to change or manage the behaviour of offenders.

All these areas have a long history of research and application by psychologists. For example, the involvement of psychologists in health education goes back to the First World War (1914–1918) when the American military were worried about the spread of venereal disease in its troops. They asked psychologists Karl Lashley and John Watson (1921) to investigate the effectiveness of filmed health education messages. Watson and Lashley made a number of observations that are relevant today, and remarkably do not seem to have been addressed throughout the 90 years since they were made. The observations they made about the relative ineffectiveness of health messages have relevance for the many flawed attempts to change behaviour that are made today.

ASIDE

Stay vigilant

During the Second World War it was noticed that the operators of the recently invented radar devices tended to miss rare and irregular events on the screens at the end of their shifts. British psychologist Norman Mackworth investigated this and initiated the systematic study of vigilance. After the war, Mackworth continued his work at the Applied Psychology Unit at Cambridge University (see Mackworth, 1950).

FIGURE G.1   A radar operator using an early version of this technology

© Bettmann/CORBIS

KEY ISSUES

Applying psychology to people in order to change their behaviour brings with it a new set of moral dilemmas. One of the early applied psychologists, J.B. Watson, suggested that the aim of psychology was to develop a technology that can control people. For example, in his 1924 book *Behaviorism* (reprinted in 1930) he wrote:

> The interest of the behaviorist in man's doings is more than the interest of the spectator – he wants to control man's reactions as physical scientists want to control and manipulate other natural phenomena. It is the business of behavioristic psychology to be able to predict and to control human activity. (Watson, 1930: 11)

The ability to be able to predict and control my own behaviour is very useful. I will be able to choose how to act rather than to react unthinkingly to changes in my environment. The ability to predict and control someone else's behaviour, on the other hand, raises a number of ethical and moral issues. So it is important to know how psychological information will be used and who will use it on whom. This is an ongoing dilemma for applied psychologists and you might like to consider this issue as you read through the various techniques that have been used to change behaviour.

THIS SECTION

In this section, we have four chapters looking at the work of applied psychologists. Chapters 24 and 25 look at what we understand about psychopathology (disorders of the mind) and what techniques have been developed to deal with these disorders. We also look at how we can evaluate the interventions that we use to bring about these changes in behaviour and experience. Chapter 26 looks at health psychology and focuses on issues such as stress as a way of showing how we can better understand the experience of illness. We finish with a chapter on forensic psychology which looks at issues such as the police and the courts (detecting deception, false confessions, eyewitness testimony), understanding why people commit crime (in particular, sexual and violent offences) and briefly looks at the imprisonment, rehabilitation and resettlement of offenders.

24 PSYCHOPATHOLOGY: THEORIES AND CAUSES

Lead authors: Claire Thompson, Karen Slade and Laura Hamilton

CHAPTER OUTLINE

24.1	Introduction	427
24.2	The concept of psychopathology	427
	24.2.1 The concept of abnormal	427
	24.2.2 The importance of culture in psychopathology	428
24.3	Defining psychological disorders	428
24.4	Classifying and diagnosing psychological disorder	429
	24.4.1 Problems with diagnosis	430
	24.4.2 Argument against diagnosis	431
	24.4.3 Argument for diagnosis	431
24.5	Assessing psychopathology	432
	24.5.1 Clinical interviews	432
	24.5.2 Clinical observation	432
	24.5.3 Clinical tests	433
24.6	Models of pathology	433
	24.6.1 The medical model	433
	24.6.2 The cognitive-behavioural model	433
	24.6.3 Humanistic and existential models	434
	24.6.4 The developmental model	434
	24.6.5 The psychodynamic model	435

24.7	**Disorders – symptoms and causes**	**435**
24.8	**Depressive disorders**	**437**
	24.8.1 Symptoms	437
	24.8.2 Course of the disorder	437
24.9	**Anxiety disorders**	**437**
	24.9.1 Anxiety symptoms	438
	24.9.2 Generalised anxiety disorder	438
	24.9.3 Phobias	438
24.10	**Schizophrenia spectrum**	**439**
	24.10.1 Symptoms	440
	24.10.2 Positive symptoms	440
	24.10.3 Negative symptoms	441
24.11	**Personality disorders**	**441**
24.12	**Chapter summary**	**442**
	Discussion questions	**443**
	Suggestions for further reading	**443**

24.1 INTRODUCTION

Have you ever spent time wondering whether you were *normal*? Or been *told* that you are 'not normal'? But then, what is normal? This is a question that has been puzzled over for many years. While many people believe they can recognise abnormal behaviour, psychopathology is a deceptively difficult concept to define. Ultimately, it comes back to answering the question: What is normal? This is not so easy in today's society, which has so much variety and freedom in how we behave.

Psychopathology is the study of psychological disorders: why they occur (aetiology), what they look or feel like (symptoms) and how they affect people's lives. Nobody is immune, with all ages, races and differing social groups being shown to be affected by some form of disorder. Alonso et al. (2004) proposed that, throughout our life-time, 25% of people experience a psychological disorder. This chapter will look at what we mean by psychopathology, the role of culture in its formation, how it is assessed, and take a more detailed look at some of the most prevalent types of the hundreds of psychological disorders detailed in the current diagnostic manuals. First, we would like you to consider the following framing questions before you go on to read about the concept of psychopathology.

PSYCHOPATHOLOGY The study of the origin, development and experience of psychological or behavioral disorders.

FRAMING QUESTIONS

- How does society define *normal* and what role does culture play in how we define *normal*?
- How do clinicians (as in psychiatrists and psychologists) define a psychological disorder? Is it possible for them to disagree?
- What is the difference between eccentric and disordered? How has this changed over time?
- How might a psychological disorder change throughout somebody's lifetime?

24.2 THE CONCEPT OF PSYCHOPATHOLOGY

The study of psychological disorders has historically been referred to as abnormal psychology. But over the last decade this has become increasingly referred to as psychopathology or psychological disorder, and both terms are used interchangeably throughout this chapter.

24.2.1 THE CONCEPT OF ABNORMAL

One of the hardest things about looking at psychopathology is trying to define abnormal. When asked to define 'abnormal', people may say it is behaviour that is happening infrequently, is dangerous or simply odd or bizarre. Although, these may all be reasonable answers for certain types of abnormal behaviour, none is sufficient in itself; plus, making all of these aspects compulsory in the definition makes it a very specific definition. An early way of defining 'abnormal' was through ascertaining whether the behaviour caused impairment in the person's life. The more the behaviour was seen as hindering daily functioning, the more likely the behaviour was to be classed as *abnormal*. When several such abnormal behaviours occurred, this was thought to constitute a disorder. More recently, however, there is an increasing view that using the term 'abnormal' is unhelpful (Cromby, Harper, & Reavey, 2013: 12) as psychopathology is common, and such terminology could be seen as increasing stigma and marginalising people who experience mental health difficulties.

24.2.2 THE IMPORTANCE OF CULTURE IN PSYCHOPATHOLOGY

Within a society there is often a diverse mix of moral, social, religious and political beliefs. One important question to consider is whether different societies draw the same line between wellbeing and distress or ultimately sanity and madness. The current diagnostic systems rely on agreement being reached about what disorders look like, what to call them and how best to manage and treat them, but what if different societies and cultures view these concepts and behaviours differently? If the variations are too great, does this make a universal model of psychopathology problematic?

> **DIAGNOSTIC AND STATISTICAL MANUAL (DSM)** Published by the American Psychiatric Association, the DSM offers a set of criteria for classifying mental disorders. The fifth edition was published in 2013.

An example of how culture can affect psychopathology is illustrated by recent development in China. In the late 1970s China brought in a system for classifying psychological disorders, based on the Western **Diagnostic and Statistical Manual (DSM)**. After it was introduced, the **prevalence** rates of clinical depression increased dramatically over the following 25 years (Kleinman, 1997). Does this mean the Chinese population were becoming increasingly depressed or was it due to the introduction of Western-influenced assessment and diagnosis systems?

Further evidence for the effects of culture can be seen in disorders that are more prevalent in or even unique to particular cultures. Staying with China, there are diagnoses that are seen much more commonly in China and other Asian cultures, such as Koro or genital reaction syndrome, where the person has an excessive fear of the genitals or of breasts shrinking or drawing back into the body. In the USA, there used to be a diagnosis of *drapetomania*, which described an irrepressible desire of a slave to escape slavery. Clearly, we would see this as a sign of bravery rather than insanity today. This is due to a shift in cultural attitudes regarding slavery, as opposed to changes in scientific or medical thinking. Culture can therefore also be seen to shape definitions of psychopathology.

Different cultures also make sense of mental illness in differing ways, this having implications for how they assess and treat conditions (Tseng, 2001). Spirit possession, for example, which is common in parts of Africa, Asia and the Middle East, is often associated with particular religious beliefs and in some communities revered as meaning the individual has higher powers. However, in more Western societies, the thoughts and behaviours which may be seen with 'spirit possession' may be perceived as a psychiatric or neurological disorder that requires medication. When considering the relationship between culture and psychopathology we must consider particular traditions and customs and how they may play a role in the development of the defining of specific mental health conditions.

KEY STUDY

Jenkins, R., Lewis, G., Bebbington, P., Brugha, T., Farrell, M., Gill, B., & Meltzer, H. (1997). The National Psychiatric Morbidity Surveys of Great Britain: initial findings from the Household Survey. *Psychological Medicine, 27*(4), 775–789.

While debate about the validity and reliability of psychopathology rolls on, there have been few large-scale studies which attempt to quantify its prevalence within the UK. One of the first was this study, which interviewed over 10,000 randomly selected members of the British public screening for a range of psychopathology. After the study, the authors proclaimed that for the first time data could be provided on the prevalence and correlates of psychiatric disorder nationwide.

24.3 DEFINING PSYCHOLOGICAL DISORDERS

Returning to the issue of 'abnormality', many definitions have developed over the years, though none is universally accepted (Pierre, 2010). However, there are key features that appear across the board, and these have become known as the *Four Ds*: deviance, distress, dysfunction and danger.

Deviance refers to emotions, thoughts and behaviours that are thought to be abnormal when they vary from a society's idea about appropriate functioning. A society in which competition and dominance is embraced would see an aggressive personality as normal, whereas a society that values compassion and cooperation may consider aggression not only unacceptable but abnormal.

Distress refers to a personal sense of suffering. For many people with a disorder, one of the most common reasons they access support services is that the disorder causes them distress. This does not have to be physical because psychological disorders primarily result in distressing emotions, thoughts or moods.

Dysfunction refers to the disordered behaviour that often brings with it some level of interference in **functioning**. To meet the criteria of a disorder, this interference has to be to the level that it affects somebody's daily life (though not necessarily every day). Disordered individuals will not normally be able to take care of themselves properly, interact appropriately with others or work effectively when unwell.

Danger refers to a potential for harm. Some people with psychological disorders become dangerous to themselves or others, though it is important to highlight that not everybody with a psychopathology presents with risky behaviours at all times. Danger is often cited, especially in the media, as a core feature of psychopathology. However, research indicates it is the exception rather than the rule (Hiday & Burns, 2009).

Using these four constructs, it is clear that the definition of abnormality relies heavily on social norms and values. However, societies still appear to have difficulty distinguishing between an individual who has a psychological disorder and someone who could be labelled eccentric: there is a fine line between madness and eccentricity. We may all know somebody who might be classed as odd or strange (*look no further than our staff corridor – Eds*), for example, the old woman who lives at the end of the street with two dozen cats yet talks to no one. While her lifestyle may not be your idea of normal, does this make her disordered? The behaviour of such an individual may be classed as different from the norm, but unless it leads to clear distress and dysfunction, most clinicians would judge it to be eccentric rather than abnormal.

EXERCISE: ECCENTRIC OR DISORDERED?

Table 24.1 details a number of real-life cases of people who have displayed eccentric behaviour. But, using the Four Ds model, would they be classed as disordered? It is your turn to play the psychiatrist and decide if you would diagnose them with a disorder or not.

24.4 CLASSIFYING AND DIAGNOSING PSYCHOLOGICAL DISORDER

A symptom is a physical, behavioural or mental feature presented by a person that helps indicate a condition, illness or disorder. So, for example, the symptoms of what is commonly known as hay fever would be itchy, watery eyes or a runny nose. For psychopathology, one of the problems with recognising symptoms is that they are not usually physical but rather in the mind, and are therefore not always obvious to the observer. For example, poor concentration may be a symptom of anxiety or if someone reports they are having visual hallucinations this might or might not indicate **schizophrenia**. These are both symptoms that, unless expressed by the sufferer, would not be obvious to the clinician. However, when certain symptoms regularly occur together and follow a particular course, clinicians may agree that the grouping makes up a specific disorder. The list of all the disorders that the clinicians might use to diagnose is called a classification system.

SCHIZOPHRENIA Schizophrenia is not a single condition but is best described as a syndrome. The typical symptoms include difficulties in organising behaviour (including speech) as well as detachment from reality which may involve delusion and/or hallucinations. Schizophrenia is often misrepresented in the popular media as a case of split or multiple personalities.

TABLE 24.1 Examples of eccentric and disordered behaviour

In the nineteenth century, **Hetty Green** was known in the city where she lived as the 'eccentric' miser as she was extremely wealthy yet went to great extremes to save money. When her son fell ill she disguised herself and took him to a charity hospital, but when she was recognised, she fled with her son, claiming she would treat him herself. Unfortunately, the son contracted gangrene, which resulted in him having his leg amputated. Hetty Green always wore the same dress and underwear, only purchasing new clothing when she had to throw the other out.

Simeon Ellerton was an eighteenth-century fitness fanatic who loved to walk long distances, often being employed to walk distances as a courier for the locals. On many occasions he would gather stones from the roadside and carry them on his head. His goal was to collect enough stones to enable him to build his own house. Eventually, he reached his goal and built his house, but after carrying the stones for so many years he felt strange without them and for the rest of his life could be seen carrying a large bag of stones upon his head.

Sir George Sitwell was a keen gardener and so annoyed by the wasps in his garden he spent many years devising a pistol to shoot them. Other eccentricities included trying to pay his son's school fees in carrots (even though he was very wealthy) and having all the cows on his estate stencilled in a blue and white Chinese willow pattern in order to make them 'more pleasing to the eye'. The sign that hung on the gate to his house stated 'I must ask anyone entering the house never to contradict me or differ from me in any way, as it interferes with the functioning of my gastric juices and prevents my sleeping at night'.

William Buckland became famous because of his love of animals and food. He claimed to have eaten every species of animal on the planet and would host dinner parties where he would only reveal to his guests what they had eaten after they had eaten it. For interest, he reported that a common garden mole and a bluebottle were the most disgusting things to eat.

David George was a gentleman who, by his own admission, was obsessed with Robin Hood, so much so that he legally adopted the name. He lived in Sherwood Forest, albeit in a semi-detached house, and wore every day a green jumper, trousers and hat and carried a makeshift cross-bow, just not when he was working as a telephone engineer!

The classification system for psychopathologies that is used by most countries throughout the world is the **International Classification of Diseases (ICD-10)**; it is published by the World Health Organisation. ICD is now in its tenth edition with an eleventh edition expected shortly. In the USA, the Diagnostic and Statistical Manual of Mental Disorders (DSM) is published by the American Psychiatric Association (and this is also widely used in the UK and the remainder of Europe). The most recent (fifth) version was published May 2013 and has introduced many changes to the categories, symptoms and criteria, which has caused a great deal of controversy.

When clinicians decide that a person's symptoms fit the criteria for a particular disorder, they are making a diagnosis. Most clinicians will use the DSM or ICD to help them with this process. Assigning a diagnosis suggests the client's pattern of dysfunction is the same as the patterns of symptoms displayed by others with the same disorder. Clinicians can then apply what is generally known from the research about the disorder to the individual.

24.4.1 PROBLEMS WITH DIAGNOSIS

DIAGNOSIS The process of categorising illness by examining signs and symptoms.

EXISTENTIAL CRISIS The realisation that you are alone in your experience of the world, and that the only meaning your life has is the meaning you choose to impose on it. Commonly experienced when you drop your choc ice.

Although mental health terms, such as anxiety, depression and schizophrenia, are common in the media, public discourse and daily conversations, accurate **diagnoses** of psychological disorders are sometimes quite elusive for clinicians. Even with effective assessment techniques and carefully researched classification categories clinicians sometimes arrive at the wrong conclusion (Fernbach, Darlow, & Sloman, 2011). Most famously, in the study by Rosenhan (1973), eight healthy people presented themselves at emergency psychiatric facilities in the USA saying that they were hearing a voice that said the words 'empty', 'hollow' and 'thud'.

This did not match any known criteria for a recognised mental disorder but bore a resemblance to an **existential crisis**. Despite this, they were all admitted with the diagnosis of schizophrenia. While in the hospitals all the pseudopatients behaved as they would in normal life, but many of their behaviours were interpreted as signs of their diagnosed mental disorder. They were released after between seven and 52 days and classified not as cured but as having schizophrenia in remission. It appeared that US psychiatrists were not able to distinguish the sane from the insane.

ASIDE

The myth of mental illness

The most common way of looking at psychological distress is to see it as an illness. This means we are assuming that it is a similar experience to a medical illness, such as measles, but is this helpful? In his critique of the medical model, Thomas Szasz (1960) argued that the medical model is unhelpful to our understanding of psychiatric conditions. The medical model suggests that all psychiatric problems will eventually be understood in terms of simple chemical reactions, and that 'mental illnesses' are basically no different from other diseases. Szasz argued that there are two errors in this view.

First, a disease of the brain is a neurological defect and not a problem of living. For example, a defect in a person's vision may be explained by correlating it with certain lesions in the nervous system. On the other hand, a person's belief, whether this is a belief in Christianity or Communism or that their genitals are retreating into their bodies, cannot be explained by a defect of the nervous system. Some beliefs are perfectly acceptable and some are thought to be a sign of mental disorder, but they are all beliefs.

Second, in medicine, when we speak of physical disturbances we mean either signs (e.g. fever) or symptoms (e.g. pain). When we speak about mental symptoms, however, we refer to how patients describe themself and the world around them. They might say that they are Napoleon or that they are being persecuted by aliens from another planet. These are symptoms only if the observer believes that the patient is not Napoleon, or not being persecuted by aliens. So to see a statement as a mental symptom we have to make a judgement that involves a comparison of the patient's ideas and beliefs with those of the observer and of the society in which they live.

Szasz suggests that the idea of mental illness is being used to obscure the difficulties we have in everyday living. In the Middle Ages it was demons and devils who were held responsible for the problems in social living. The belief in mental illness is no more sophisticated than a belief in demonology. Mental illness, according to Szasz, is 'real' in exactly the same way as demons were 'real'.

Subsequent studies have revealed occasional errors in assessment and diagnosis, particularly in psychiatric hospital (Mitchell & Coyne, 2010). In an often cited study, skilled clinicians were asked to re-evaluate the diagnoses of 131 patients at a mental health hospital (Lipton & Simon, 1985). Whereas 89 of the patients had originally received a diagnosis of schizophrenia, only 16 received it upon re-evaluation, and while 150 patients initially had been given a diagnosis of mood disorder, 50 received the same label on re-evaluation.

24.4.2 ARGUMENT AGAINST DIAGNOSIS

Simply classifying people can sometimes lead to unfortunate results, with diagnostic labels becoming self-fulfilling prophecies. Once a diagnosis has been made, others may react in ways that actually lead to those diagnosed behaving in more disordered ways, exacerbating the initial problem. Furthermore, our society often attaches a stigma or negative prejudice to mental disorders (Bell et al., 2011; Kavanagh & Banyard, 2014; Rosenberg, 2011). For example, people with such labels may find it hard to get jobs, particularly one with a high level of responsibility. Such a diagnosis would be recorded on medical records and therefore be potentially available to future employees and other interested parties. Some clinicians have argued for doing away with assessment and diagnosis altogether, believing it adds nothing to the process of recovery. If you'd like to read a lively and detailed demolition of the DSM, then pick up *Making us crazy* by Kutchins and Kirk (2001).

24.4.3 ARGUMENT FOR DIAGNOSIS

There are over 400 psychological disorders within the DSM and as you read through this chapter it will become apparent that there are a number of similarities and crossovers in symptoms. However, it should also become clear that each disorder generally needs a different form of treatment to successfully alleviate symptoms or cure the disorder altogether. Some people diagnosed with a disorder also state that they are grateful for the label as it helps them understand symptoms that have previously been unexplained, confusing and even scary. Some clinicians believe, therefore, that classification and diagnosis are essential to understanding and treating disorders and that we should continue to research psychological disorders to improve assessment and diagnostic techniques.

24.5 ASSESSING PSYCHOPATHOLOGY

In order to diagnose, clinicians must fully assess the individual. Clinical assessment is used to precisely identify both the disordered behaviour and the best treatment approach. The clinical assessment tools and techniques that have been developed broadly fall into three categories: clinical interviews, clinical observation and clinical tests. These are detailed below.

24.5.1 CLINICAL INTERVIEWS

Clinical interviews most often happen in a one-to-one setting and they are normally the starting point for most clinicians. They are most useful in eliciting detailed information and give clinicians the opportunity to interact and observe the interviewee fully. Interviews can either be structured (clinicians asking set questions in a certain order) or unstructured (where the clinician will often ask open-ended questions such as 'why you have come to see me today').

TABLE 24.2   Advantages and disadvantages of clinical interviews

STRUCTURED INTERVIEWING		UNSTRUCTURED INTERVIEWS	
Advantages	*Disadvantages*	*Advantages*	*Disadvantages*
Can elicit specific information	Requires more preparation	Allows interviewer to follow leads	Open more to interpretation
Consistency interviewing different individuals	Limits answers of client	Can be made client-centred	More open to cultural bias
Helps keep to time	Can sometimes feel controlling for client	Can encourage openness	Requires more skill on part of interviewer
Gives interview structure	Led by interviewer therefore can feel intrusive	Less threatening to client	Needs careful management in term of topics and timing
Can makes sure all areas of questioning are covered	Limited answers to questions	Needs less preparation	May not elicit required information

24.5.2 CLINICAL OBSERVATION

Another form of assessment of psychological disorders is the clinical observation of behaviour. Observation can be useful in allowing the clinician to observe the individual in their own environment, sometimes allowing for a more thorough understanding of the presenting problem.

This can either be in an artificial setting, such as a therapy office or hospital ward, or a naturalistic environment, where the client is observed in their own home, school or place of work. Observations are normally recorded and can be watched back to give the clinician a clearer picture of the symptoms or behaviours they are assessing. Clinical observations are not without their disadvantages as people may behave differently when they know they are being watched (or assessed) (Lane et al., 2011).

OBSESSIVE COMPULSIVE DISORDER (OCD) A condition associated with unwanted and unpleasant thoughts or images that repeatedly come to mind, causing anxiety. The thoughts are accompanied by a compulsion to make repetitive behaviours or mental acts to try to stop the obsession coming true.

Self-monitoring is a form of clinical observation, but it is where the individual monitors the problematic behaviour or feeling as they occur. In a case of somebody with **obsessive compulsive disorder (OCD)**, this could be recording how many times they wash their hands on a daily basis or how many cigarettes they smoke in a day. Again, self-report can be highly problematic in relation to changing behaviours. When your doctor asks you how much alcohol you drink or how many cigarettes you smoke a week, are you always honest?

24.5.3 CLINICAL TESTS

Clinical tests are tools that can be used to gather information about a person's mental functioning. This allows comparisons to be made and conclusions to be drawn about the relevance of a diagnosis or treatment. Such tools can be psychological questionnaires that assess specific domains, such as personality, intelligence or mood, but also encompass neuroimaging, which examines the different structures of the brain. They can be a time- and resource-effective way of gaining the required psychological information and be a more valid and reliable way of assessment than observation and interviews. However, for some tests you need to be a qualified practitioner to administer them, which therefore limits their availability.

24.6 MODELS OF PATHOLOGY

In this section we will look at the differing models used to explain psychopathology. They are used to understand an individual's disorder and will largely determine the form of treatment recommended. We will explore the medical model, which is more likely to propose medication as the main treatment, and contrast it to models such as **cognitive-behavioural** and **psychodynamic**, which advocate more talking therapy approaches. There is more information regarding the differing treatment approaches in Chapter 25.

24.6.1 THE MEDICAL MODEL

Medical practitioners generally view abnormal behaviour as an illness brought about by biochemical or structural malfunction in the brain, chemical imbalances or genetic predispositions (see the Aside above for a challenge to this view). The evidence has largely come from **correlational studies** which, while showing a relationship between the two areas, have not been clear on whether it is the deficit that causes the disorder or the other way round (Shah & Mountain, 2007). Advocates of this model also link mental disorder to either an excess or deficit of differing **neurotransmitters** or hormonal activity within the **endocrine system**, which consequentially inhibits brain functioning (Uher & McGuffin, 2008). Depression, for example, has been linked to insufficient levels of the neurotransmitters noradrenaline and serotonin as well as increased levels of the hormone cortisol (Fava, 2002).

CORRELATION A measure of how strongly two or more variables are related to each other.

NEUROTRANSMITTERS Chemical substances released from neurone terminals into the synaptic cleft that can affect the activation of another adjacent neurone.

ENDOCRINE SYSTEM A series of small organs responsible for producing hormones that regulate a variety of processes, including growth and development, metabolism and puberty.

HALLUCINATION A sensory perception experienced in the absence of an external stimulus.

The genetics of psychopathology also come under the medical model. Studies have found that the genes you inherit may play a part in schizophrenia, Alzheimer's disease, mood disorders, intellectual disability and other mental disorders. Oksenberg and Hauser (2010) state that there is no single gene that has been found to be responsible for a specific disorder, but instead that many genes combined may be attributable to a specific dysfunction.

Viral infection also adds weight to the medical model argument in relation to psychopathology. Research suggests that **hallucination** symptoms experienced in some individuals with schizophrenia may be related to exposure to certain viruses before, during or after childhood (Fox, 2010). Similar links have been made to anxiety and mood disorders (Fox, 2010).

24.6.2 THE COGNITIVE-BEHAVIOURAL MODEL

The cognitive-behavioural model proposes that psychological disorders result largely from a combination of problematic thinking patterns and learnt behaviours that mutually influence each other. According to this model, people's particular way

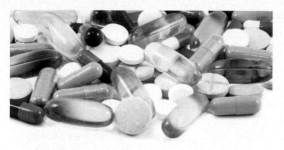

of thinking affects their behaviours, with the behaviours in turn reinforcing thinking, leading to a vicious circle in which people feel trapped. For example, an individual with anxiety may have some physical symptoms of anxiety, such as sweating, palpitations, tightness of chest. These could be related to a range of conditions but, for a student with anxiety and with imminent exams, the first thought (called 'automatic thoughts') may be that they are going to fail their exams and therefore they revise all night for a week. The student then falls asleep in the exam and fails, but feels this is down to their lack of revision and thinks that for their next exam s/he needs to revise harder! And so the cycle continues.

Cognitive-behavioural theorists also view emotions as integral to this cycle, with emotions interacting with both the thoughts and behaviours to produce dysfunction. The behaviours and the thinking patterns behind them (the cognitions) are focused on within cognitive behavioural therapy (CBT). Within this theory, thinking patterns are seen as a key factor in both normal and abnormal behaviours and disorders, with research showing that people with psychological disorders often display varying thinking errors and beliefs (Sharf, 2011).

24.6.3 HUMANISTIC AND EXISTENTIAL MODELS

Humanists believe that all of us are born with the potential for goodness and growth (Maslow, Frager & Cox, 1970). They feel that this can be achieved if an individual can accept their strengths and weaknesses and live by positive personal values. According to the humanist model, it is when people constantly deceive themselves and create a distorted view of the world that they are likely to experience some degree of psychological disorder.

One of the pioneering humanists was Carl Rogers (1951), who felt that it is when the basic need for unconditional positive regard from others (in particular, parents) isn't met that psychological disorder may occur. Rogers believed that children who felt they had to meet certain standards in order to gain love were stopped from meeting their full potential, thus creating a distorted view of themselves and others, and leading to differing levels of dysfunction.

Existentialists agree with humanists in that individuals have a good level of self-awareness and need to live purposeful lives in order to be well adjusted and ultimately not disordered. Existentialists believe that, from birth, individuals have the autonomy either to confront life and give meaning to it or to run away from responsibility, resulting in individuals who are empty, anxious, frustrated or depressed (Yalom & Josselson, 2011). The core of these models is human fulfilment, a concept that is fairly hard to define and research. It is only in recent years that controlled studies have been conducted by humanistic and existential researchers, which in turn have demonstrated the potential value of these models to the assessment and diagnosis of psychopathology. These models are referred to as non-empirical views as they currently lack the support or evidence for their use in assessing and diagnosing psychological disorders. They are grouped together here because of their emphasis on the wider dimensions of human life.

24.6.4 THE DEVELOPMENTAL MODEL

The developmental model is related to the study of how psychological disorders evolve in relation to a person's genes and early experiences and, importantly, the knock-on effect on later life (Sroufe & Rutter, 1984). Early problematic behaviours are thought to disrupt functioning as people develop into adult life (Cicchetti, 2010). Developmental psychologists believe that the cause of psychopathology can be a mix of genetics, early childhood experiences and environmental influences – so a bit of everything really!

Supporters of this model compare abnormal and normal behaviour and attempt to identify the differing developmental issues that have contributed to the negative behaviour. These are called risk factors. This allows the clinician to identify what is likely to be making the disorder worse and the risk factors that can be targeted in treatment. Also important within the developmental model is the concept of protective factors. These are factors that reduce the likelihood of disordered behaviour and help somebody build or maintain resilience to their disorder. Advocates of this model believe it is just as important to understand the strengths of an individual as well as their weaknesses.

24.6.5 THE PSYCHODYNAMIC MODEL

The psychodynamic model was initially developed from the theories of Sigmund Freud, who emphasised the importance of the early parent–child relationship. According to Freud, if a child does not successfully negotiate the different psychosexual stages, psychological disorder will develop. Freud proposed that a child's environment may prevent the development of these differing parts of the mind or hinder their interaction. He went further by suggesting that if this development does not occur, the child becomes fixated at a specific stage and disordered functioning becomes apparent.

Freud also believed a person's behaviour is determined by an underlying psychological force that they are not aware of, the **unconscious**. In relation to abnormal behaviour, Freud and the consequential psychodynamic theorists believe that when conflicts arise between the conscious and unconscious parts of the mind that psychological disorders occur. The psychodynamic model has some ardent supporters and critics, but generally research has failed to support the effectiveness of the model in relation to psychopathology diagnosis and treatment (Prochaska & Norcross, 2013). Like the existential and humanist models, it is therefore classed as a non-empirical approach.

> **UNCONSCIOUS MIND** The part of our mind that is beyond our conscious awareness.

24.7 DISORDERS – SYMPTOMS AND CAUSES

There are over 400 disorders in the DSM-5, and unfortunately not enough space to discuss most of them here. Table 24.3 lists the main psychological disorder subgroups and its equivalent using the ICD-10 framework. The

TABLE 24.3 Disorder classifications using DSM and ICD systems

DSM-5 GROUP	CHARACTERISTICS AND EXAMPLES OF DISORDER GROUP	ICD-10 EQUIVALENT
Neurodevelopmental disorders	Disorders seen to emerge before adulthood e.g. intellectual disability	Termed 'Disorders of psychological developmental', although mental retardation is in its own separate subgroup
Schizophrenia spectrum and other psychotic disorders	Marked by deterioration of functioning until state of psychosis is reached e.g. schizophrenia	Termed 'Schizophrenia, schizotypal and delusional disorders'
Bipolar and related disorders	Marked by severe disturbance in mood that includes depressed and manic mood states e.g. bipolar disorders	Mostly similar to DSM, although they continue to use the term 'affect', with depression also appearing under the category and not as a separate section
Depressive disorders	Marked by sad, empty or irritable mood that affects functioning e.g. major depressive disorder	Depression is mainly divided into a single episode or is recurrent. Classed alongside bipolar, not as distinct subsection
Anxiety disorders	Marked by excessive fear and anxiety e.g. phobias	Termed 'neurotic, stress-related and somatoform disorders' Also includes somatoform and dissociative disorders within this group
Obsessive compulsive and related disorders	Characterised by the presence of obsessions and/or compulsions. e.g. obsessive compulsive disorder	Classified under the group 'Neurotic, stress-related and somatoform disorders'
Trauma and stressor-related disorders	Marked by psychological distress following a traumatic event e.g. post-traumatic stress disorder	Classified under anxiety disorders with main remit of post-traumatic stress disorder

(Continued)

435

TABLE 24.3 (Continued)

DSM-5 GROUP	CHARACTERISTICS AND EXAMPLES OF DISORDER GROUP	ICD-10 EQUIVALENT
Dissociative disorders	Characterised by a disruption in consciousness, memory, identity, emotion, perception and behaviour that affects a person's functioning e.g. dissociative identity disorder	Similar versions to disorders listed in DSM-5 but classified under anxiety disorders
Feeding and eating disorders	Characterised by a persistent disturbance of eating or eating-related behaviours e.g. anorexia nervosa	Groups eating disorders under a wide category of 'Behavioural syndromes associated with physiological disturbances and physical factors'
Sexual dysfunctions	Characterised by a significant disturbance in a person's ability to respond to sexual stimulation e.g. erectile disorder	Classified under the heading 'Behavioural syndromes associated with physiological disturbances and physical factors'
Disruptive, impulse-control and conduct disorders	Characterised by violation of the rights of others, and brings a person into direct conflict with the society norms or authority figures e.g. pyromania	Same disorders as listed in the DSM but under a different heading: 'Disorders of adult personality and behaviour'
Substance-related and addictive disorders	Marked by a cluster of symptoms indicating that a person continues using the substance despite it impacting on their functioning e.g. alcohol use disorder	Similar disorders as termed in the DSM but classified under the heading 'Mental and behavioural disorders due to psychoactive substance use'
Neurocognitive disorders	Marked by a decline in cognitive functioning that has not been present since birth e.g. dementia	Similar listing as to the DSM but are referred to as 'Organic, including symptomatic mental disorders'
Personality disorders	10 different disorders that are characterised by an enduring pattern of behaviours that deviate markedly from the expectations of the individual's culture and environment e.g. borderline personality disorder	These have their own category in DSM but in ICD come under 'Disorders of adult personality and behaviour'. Obsessive-compulsive PD is referred to as Anankastic, antisocial PD as Dissocial, borderline PD as Emotionally unstable, and avoidant PD as Anxious. ICD does not have entries for schizotypal or narcissistic PD
Paraphilic disorders	Marked by an intense interest that is causing distress or impairment or causing potential harm to others	Paraphilias come under the heading 'Disorders of adult personality and behaviour'

FIGURE 24.2 Diagnoses. There are so many diagnoses possible that they are starting to affect the way we view everyday life

© Amir Ridhwan/Shutterstock.com

disorders which are considered to be the most prevalent will be looked at in more detail, exploring the symptoms, the differing views on causes and the usual course of the disorder.

This next section will discuss four of the most prevalent types of psychopathology in the UK (Singleton & Lewis, 2003): depressive disorders, anxiety disorders, schizophrenia spectrum and personality disorders.

24.8 DEPRESSIVE DISORDERS

Everybody's mood changes from one day to the next. We also react with different moods to different things throughout the day. If something were to happen, such as a bereavement, we would expect to feel sad for a short period of time – in fact, we may become worried if we weren't sad. However, for people with depressive disorders, the sadness can last a long time or seem to appear for no reason at all. Although depressive disorders have some symptoms in common, they are often different in terms of their prevalence and causes.

24.8.1 SYMPTOMS

One of the most serious in terms of symptoms is major depressive disorder. The primary symptom of this disorder is depressed or excessively low mood that goes further than simply feeling sad. Further symptoms may include the following:

- losing interest or pleasure in experiences that are usually enjoyed;
- changes in appetite that lead to significant weight loss or gain;
- changes in sleeping habit, either not getting enough or sleeping too much;
- low levels of energy, extreme fatigue and/or poor concentration, and little motivation to do activities that were done before;
- reduction in self-esteem, feeling worthless and blaming self for things that aren't necessarily their fault;
- feeling hopeless about the future.

We all may feel one of these symptoms at one time, but for it to become a disorder the symptoms need to be affecting the ability to function as well as causing distress. It is also important to ascertain whether the change is due to the depression. For example, somebody may already have a poor appetite, not necessarily because of a depressive disorder.

24.8.2 COURSE OF THE DISORDER

Although some people have isolated episodes of depression, most experience recurrent episodes where the disorder often becomes more severe over time (Taube-Schiff & Lau, 2008). Milder forms of depression, in which a few symptoms are experienced rather than more severe episodes, has historically been found to be one of the best predictors of a future, more serious, depressive episode (Pine et al., 2002).

24.9 ANXIETY DISORDERS

Anxiety is a set of symptoms, which may include:

- emotional symptoms, e.g. fear or worry;
- physical symptoms, e.g. fast-beating heart or sweating;
- cognitive symptoms, e.g. fear of dying or losing control.

When these symptoms are experienced together it is commonly called a panic attack. Like a depressed mood, anxiety is a common occurrence for most people with everybody having felt anxiety at some point in their lives, for example, when sitting exams or giving a presentation. In most situations, anxiety prepares the body to respond when it perceives

ASIDE

Is it mad to be happy?

Have you noticed how a new mental diagnosis seems to appear every week? Once upon a time some children were naughty, now they have conduct disorder, and some people just aren't very nice but now we diagnose them as having a personality disorder. Perhaps everything we do is odd.

In a gentle parody of psychiatric diagnosis, Richard Bentall (1992) proposed that happiness should be classed as a mental disorder and referred to under the new name of *major affective disorder, pleasant type.* In his article, he suggested that the relevant literature shows that happiness is statistically abnormal, is made up of a discrete cluster of symptoms, is associated with a range of cognitive abnormalities, and probably reflects the abnormal functioning of the central nervous system. He considered the possible objection that happiness is not thought badly of but he dismissed it as scientifically irrelevant. You would think that an article like this would contribute to the sum of human happiness, but sadly some people took it seriously and it made them sad. Humour is a serious business.

it is under threat. The anxiety prepares the body to either approach the threat or run in the opposite direction! Anxiety becomes a disorder when, in addition to the impairment in functioning, the fear reaction is caused by something that is not necessarily a threat. Feeling scared and anxious of poisonous snakes is understandable, having the same feelings brought on by fluffy teddy bears, not so much!

24.9.1 ANXIETY SYMPTOMS

In addition to the symptoms listed above, a diagnosis of an anxiety disorder generally has four things in common:

- There is a specific target that the person is afraid of (e.g. snakes or teddy bears).
- Heightened anxieties (or panic attacks) are experienced in response to the target.
- The target is avoided by the sufferer.
- Anxiety tends to be chronic, that is, it is persistent rather than experienced in episodes.

24.9.2 GENERALISED ANXIETY DISORDER

Generalised anxiety disorder is a disorder where people experience excessive anxiety that appears unrelated to any specific fear or trigger, appearing to worry instead about most things. Sufferers will typically appear restless, on edge or tense, find it hard to concentrate or sleep, and experience physical symptoms such as muscle tension, headaches and palpitations.

24.9.3 PHOBIAS

Phobias are the most common form of anxiety disorders and refer to a persistent and irrational fear of a particular object or situation. Kessler et al. (2010) suggested that 9% of society suffers from at least one phobia. While often caused by a specific anxiety, phobias often only occur in relation to the specific trigger, therefore they are not as generalised as most other anxiety disorders. While most people have a severe dislike of some things (e.g. spiders or flying), to be classed as a phobia there needs to be an extreme level of avoidance and dysfunction. For example, somebody with a fear of flying may lead a very productive life but simply isn't able to fly. This may affect their work, limiting the jobs they can take, or their family life by not being able to take holidays with relatives.

Cognitive behavioural models are seen to provide the best evidence for specific phobias (Gamble, Harvey, & Rapee, 2009). Although similar fears and phobias have been seen to run in families, this is not thought to be a case of genetics, rather a situation in which children are exposed to fears by their parents. For example, a mother who is afraid of dogs will inadvertently teach her child through her own avoidant behaviour that dogs are something to be scared of. Varying research has been indicated that fears can be acquired through this type of modelling (Wilson, 2011).

EXERCISE: MATCH THE OBJECT WITH THE PHOBIA

Table 24.4 lists a number of real-life phobias. Try to match them with their actual triggers!

TABLE 24.4   List of objects and corresponding phobias

OBJECT	PHOBIA
Beards	Bibliophobia
Books	Ommatophobia
Dolls	Pediophobia
Eyes	Pogophobia
Marriage	Phasmophobia
Ghosts	Eisoptrophobia
Wasps	Gamophobia
Snow	Siderodromophobia
Worms	Theophobia
Mirrors	Gephyrophobia
Railways	Chionophobia
God	Ombrophobia
Crossing a bridge	Spheksophobia
Shadows	Hedonophobia
Rain	Helminthophobia
Pleasure	Sciophobia

24.10 SCHIZOPHRENIA SPECTRUM

Schizophrenia is a mental disorder characterised by a range of symptoms that can be debilitating for those with the disorder. This is reflected in the higher rate of suicide in people with this disorder (Hawton et al., 2005). One of the earliest models applied to schizophrenia was the dopamine hypothesis. A medical theory, this model suggests that the disorder is due to an excess of the neurotransmitter dopamine. While this model is not without its critics, it is still today one of the dominant explanatory models of this disorder. The use of antipsychotic medication (which is discussed more in Chapter 25) provides some evidence for this theory. Research also shows additional neurotransmitters (glutamate and serotonin) may also play a part in schizophrenia (Bach, 2007).

Further research to support the medical model has led to it being generally accepted that people inherit a genetic predisposition to schizophrenia (Akbarian, 2006). Studies have frequently found schizophrenia to be more common among relations of people with the disorder (Conn et al., 2008). The more closely related the existing sufferer, the increased possibility of developing the disorder. However, one factor that needs to be considered is that a close relative will also have potentially experienced the same environment. Therefore, the role of environment cannot be ruled out altogether. Psychological and socio-cultural factors have been shown to have a precipitating factor and this is known as the diathesis stress model, where a biological predisposition may be triggered by psychological events, personal stress or societal factors. However, many believe that although there may be a biological underpinning for schizophrenia, it needs external stressors for the symptoms to be triggered (Holmes, 2010).

24.10.1 SYMPTOMS

People with schizophrenia can suffer what are called positive symptoms or negative symptoms, or a mixture of both. It can also be characterised by psychosis, which is when an individual behaves in a way that has little to do with reality. Impairments are often experienced in numerous areas of functioning – perception, thought, language, memory, behaviour and emotion.

24.10.2 POSITIVE SYMPTOMS

Positive symptoms are behaviours or thoughts that can appear as bizarre additions to a person's normal presentation. The most common are detailed below.

- **Delusions** are firmly held elaborate beliefs that do not appear factually correct, there often being evidence to the contrary. Delusions of persecution are the most common form of delusions experienced by people with schizophrenia (Langdon, Ward, & Coltheart, 2010). Sufferers with such beliefs would believe that they are being plotted against, victimised or spied on. For example, a schizophrenic may believe the government is plotting against them or **aliens** are plotting to kidnap them. **Delusions of grandeur** are also a common symptom of schizophrenia, with a sufferer believing, for example, that they are a member of the royal family or are religious figures.
- **Disorganised thinking and speech** is when somebody has rapid shifts in their thinking and their speech, the sufferer believing that what they are saying makes sense. Using bizarre or odd language may also be a symptom of schizophrenia, sufferers making up their own words (**neologisms**) that only they know and understand.
- **Hallucinations** are sounds, sights and other sensory events that are experienced in the absence of any external sensory stimulation. The most common form of hallucination is auditory, which is where the person hears sounds or voices from either inside or outside their head that are not audible to those around them. It is important to add that hearing voices is very common in people who do not have any form of mental disorder, for example, someone who is recently bereaved can often hear or sense their lost loved one (Dewi Rees, 1971).
- **Inappropriate affect** refers to emotions being displayed that aren't appropriate to either the situation or the environment. For example, laughing when being told some sad news or being upset in a happy situation. This can be accompanied by inappropriate shifts in mood.

24.10.3 NEGATIVE SYMPTOMS

Negative symptoms are the absence of characteristics or behaviours that effect a person's ability to function in society. The most common negative symptoms are as follows:

- **Poverty of speech** refers to a general reduction in speech. Some sufferers simply say very little, their interaction with others being minimal.
- **Flat affect** is when people with schizophrenia display little emotion, be it sadness, happiness, joy or any other feeling. This can often be accompanied by poor eye contact and a flat monotone voice.
- **Avolition** refers to a lack of energy or interest in goals or life in general, often serving to distance the sufferer even more from reality and increase isolation.
- **Withdrawal** involves the person moving their interests from issues around them to their own issues, which are often confused with ideas and fantasies.
- **Catatonia** is an extreme form of motionless state. Individuals may stop responding to their environments, remaining motionless and silent for prolonged periods.

KEY RESEARCHER Theodore Millon

Professor Theodore Millon was an American psychologist known for his influential work on personality disorders, becoming commonly known as the 'grandfather of personality'. He devised one of the most frequently used psychometric assessments of personality disorder, the Millon Clinical Multiaxial Inventory (MCMI), currently being used in its third revision. In his early career, Professor Millon worked as a mental health professional in a psychiatric hospital, rising through the ranks to the hospital's board of trustees. He gained notoriety for often allegedly pretending to be an inpatient to enable him to get better insight into his patients' problems. His clinical experience inspired Professor Millon to study and research the criteria that psychologists use to describe so-called disordered thinking, and the different personality traits that make up a diagnosis. By 1980, as part of a task force gathered by the American Psychiatric Association, he had arranged these traits into 11 standardised categories or 'subtypes' (later revised to 14), forming the basis for the third edition of the Diagnostic Statistical Manual of Mental Disorders (DSM-3). Before his death in January 2014, he had set up the Institute for Advanced Studies in Personology and Psychopathology, the website (http://millon.net) also serving as his official web page for his professional and scholarly activities.

FIGURE 24.3   Theodore Millon

24.11 PERSONALITY DISORDERS

The diagnoses of personality disorders are perhaps the most controversial area of psychopathology. For example, the 3:1 ratio of women to men receiving a diagnosis of borderline personality disorder might well reflect society's judgement on the behaviour of women rather than any underlying psychology disturbance. Despite these concerns, personality disorders are commonly diagnosed in Western countries. Most symptoms first become apparent in adolescence or early adulthood, with recent research predicting that between 9% and 13% of all adults have a diagnosable personality disorder (Paris, 2010).

So what exactly is a personality disorder? According to the DSM-5, a personality disorder is 'An enduring pattern of inner experience and behaviour that deviates markedly from the expectations of the individual's culture, is pervasive and inflexible, has an onset in adolescence or early adulthood, is stable over time, and leads to distress or impairment' (DSM-5 – American Psychiatric Association, 2013).

The DSM-5 lists 10 distinct personality disorders (ICD-10 has eight but includes other specifications).

Paranoid personality disorder is a pattern of distrust and suspiciousness such that others' motives are interpreted as malevolent.

Schizoid personality disorder is a pattern of detachment from social relationships and a restricted range of emotional expression.

Schizotypal personality disorder is a pattern of acute discomfort in close relationships, cognitive or perceptual distortions, and eccentricities of behaviour.

Anti-social personality disorder is a pattern of disregard for, and violation of, the rights of others.

Borderline personality disorder is a pattern of instability in interpersonal relationships, self-image and affects, and marked impulsivity.

Histrionic personality disorder is a pattern of excessive emotionality and attention seeking.

Narcissistic personality disorder is a pattern of grandiosity, need for admiration and lack of empathy.

Avoidant personality disorder is a pattern of social inhibition, feelings of inadequacy and hypersensitivity to negative evaluations.

Dependant personality disorder is a pattern of submissive and clinging behaviour related to an excessive need to be taken care of.

Obsessive compulsive personality disorder is a pattern of preoccupation with orderliness, perfectionism and control.

Did you recognise any personality traits? I'm sure as you read the list there may be symptoms you recognise in yourself! For example, many people have some obsessive-compulsive traits, whether it be needing to have all your baked beans pointing the right way in the cupboard or not stepping on cracks in the pavements. But does this mean you have a disorder? Absolutely not – revisit the Four Ds model if you want to be sure!

In terms of causes, only two personality disorders have been studied extensively. These are borderline personality disorder and anti-social personality disorder (in ICD-10 they are called emotionally unstable personality disorder and dissocial personality disorder respectively). For anti-social personality disorder, advocates of the behavioural models say the related anti-social behaviour is learnt through modelling (Gaynor & Baird, 2007). Evidence for this theory is the high rate of the disorder among parents and children (Archer & McDaniel, 1995). Advocates of the medical model refer to research which has shown that sufferers have been found to have lower serotonin activity than non-sufferers (Patrick, Fowles & Krueger, 2009). In addition, low serotonin levels have been linked to aggression and impulsivity, which are key characteristics of anti-social personality disorder.

In the case of borderline personality disorder, 2% of the general population are thought to suffer from this (Paris, 2010), with 75% of those diagnosed being women (Gunderson, 2011). There does not appear to be one dominant model of this disorder, although Linehan et al. (1994) developed the bio-social theory, incorporating varying theories for a more holistic approach.

24.12 CHAPTER SUMMARY

The aim of this chapter has been to provide an understanding of what disorders look like and how they progress, and common suggestions as to possible causes. You have read about some of the diagnosed psychological disorders – schizophrenia, mood disorders, anxiety and personality disorder. They by no means offer an exhaustive insight into all the disorders.

It should hopefully have become clear that there is still a lot to research about most, if not all, disorders. As more becomes known, it will bring with it changes to the assessment, diagnosis and treatment of psychological disorders. The expectation is that not only will current disorders become better understood, but that new ones may be unearthed and others may disappear completely.

DISCUSSION QUESTIONS

How does society measure abnormality? What implications does this have for individuality and cultural variation?

What should be the defining factors in future psychopathology research? Should the field be looking at expanding the range of diagnoses or reducing it?

How important is it to have a diagnosis for people with a reported psychopathology? What are both the positive and negative aspects for the individual?

SUGGESTIONS FOR FURTHER READING

Bentall, R.P. (2009). *Doctoring the mind: why psychiatric treatments fail*. Harmondsworth: Penguin. This book takes an in-depth look at mental healthcare in the West, claiming that it is too heavily reliant upon medication and profit. The author argues for a different approach to mental health, which would involve redefining the concept of mental illness and all consequential treatments.

Cromby, J., Harper, D., & Reavey, P. (2013). *Psychology, mental health and distress*. Basingstoke: Palgrave Macmillan. This book provides an overview of psychopathology, including detailed arguments both for and against the issue of diagnosis. There are useful and insightful sections on cultural variations and the experience of having psychopathology, written by service users worldwide.

Millon, T. (2011). *Disorders of personality: introducing a DSM/ICD spectrum from normal to abnormal* (3rd edn). Hoboken, NJ: John Wiley & Sons. Written by the 'grandfather of personality', this book provides extensive details of all the differing personality structures and how they relate to the differing personality disorders that are diagnosed by clinicians in today's society.

Still want more? For links to online resources relevant to this chapter and a quiz to test your understanding, visit the companion website at edge.sagepub.com/banyard2e

25 PSYCHOLOGICAL INTERVENTIONS

Lead authors: Karen Slade, Laura Hamilton and Claire Thompson

CHAPTER OUTLINE

25.1 Introduction	**447**
25.2 What is a psychological intervention?	**447**
25.2.1 Delivering psychological intervention	447
25.2.2 Outlining the treatment models	449
25.3 Psychodynamic therapy	**450**
25.3.1 Definition and goal	450
25.3.2 Assessing the unconscious world	451
25.3.3 Who is it for?	452
25.3.4 Practice applications and evaluation	452
25.4 Cognitive behavioural therapy	**452**
25.4.1 The cognitive model – what are you thinking?	453
25.4.2 Socratic questioning	454
25.4.3 Formulation	454
25.4.4 Cognitive techniques – changing your thinking	454
25.4.5 The ABCDE model	455
25.4.6 Behavioural therapy	456
25.4.7 Practice applications and evaluation	457

25.5 Humanistic/person-centred therapy   **458**

    25.5.1 Model and theory   458

    25.5.2 Core approach   459

    25.5.3 Practice applications and evaluation   459

25.6 Motivational interviewing   **460**

    25.6.1 Theory   460

    25.6.2 Methods   460

    25.6.3 The core skills of motivational interviewing   460

    25.6.4 When the client is not too sure he/she wants to change   461

    25.6.5 Practice applications and evaluation   461

25.7 Biological and pharmacological treatment   **462**

    25.7.1 Psychopharmacology (drug) treatments   462

    25.7.2 Practice applications and evaluation   463

    25.7.3 Electroconvulsive therapy (ECT)   463

    25.7.4 Practice applications and evaluation   463

25.8 Other issues   **464**

    25.8.1 Format of interventions   464

    25.8.2 What works? Evaluating treatment approaches   464

25.9 Chapter summary   **465**

Discussion questions   **465**

Suggestions for further reading   **466**

25.1 INTRODUCTION

The mind is complex and it can play tricks on us and things can go wrong, and we can think differently, feel bad or behave differently from other people. In the previous chapter, we introduced you to ideas of psychological abnormality and psychopathology. Now we will look at how we can change ourselves and introduce the most widely used psychological interventions available for the treatment of psychological abnormalities and difficulties. The interventions are drawn from a wide range of theories and all have different ways of doing things. We will look at how the interventions operate and how they work. All these interventions can be delivered by an applied psychologist or other trained professionals, although in some cases a psychiatrist or specialist doctor may also need to be involved. Psychological interventions have changed over time with different methods coming in and out of use, and so we will look at some of the history of psychological interventions. No one psychological intervention is suitable for everyone and this chapter will outline the different approaches and who they might be used with.

FRAMING QUESTIONS

- What are psychological interventions and how do they work? Which ones work best for which kind of issue?
- Are there different interventions for different issues, and how and why were they developed?
- What does an intervention look like? And what are the main aims and methods that they use?
- Do psychological interventions even work? And, if so, who do they work for best?

25.2 WHAT IS A PSYCHOLOGICAL INTERVENTION?

Psychological interventions have been present in our history probably since humans first realised that some people were a bit different. The definition of **psychopathology** has changed dramatically over the last 1000 years and so have interventions, which have ranged from the inspired to the bizarre. Some early explanations

> **PSYCHOPATHOLOGY** The study of the origin, development and experience of psychological or behavioral disorders.

of mental disorders focused on biological explanations, asserting that there was some sort of disease of the brain, and other explanations focused on the supernatural, such as demons or possession (see Figure 25.1).

The exact nature and purpose of psychological interventions has been continuously debated and interventions have fallen in and out of fashion. The approaches change depending on the underlying theoretical model, although all should be based on accepted psychological methods and are 'broadly based on the use of the interaction between therapist and service user to elicit changes in the service user's behaviour (for example, drug use), as well as other related factors, including cognition and emotion' (National Institute of Clinical Excellence (NICE), 2008). In the literature, the term 'psychosocial intervention' is also widely used. This is a broader term than psychological intervention and is defined as any intervention that emphasises psychological or social factors rather than biological factors (Ruddy & House, 2005). It therefore includes psychological interventions, but also includes educational programmes and social assistance, for example, parenting classes.

25.2.1 DELIVERING PSYCHOLOGICAL INTERVENTION

Psychological interventions are broad in scope and are used in a huge range of psychopathologies, difficulties and behaviours. There are many different types of clients of psychological interventions and they come from a range of

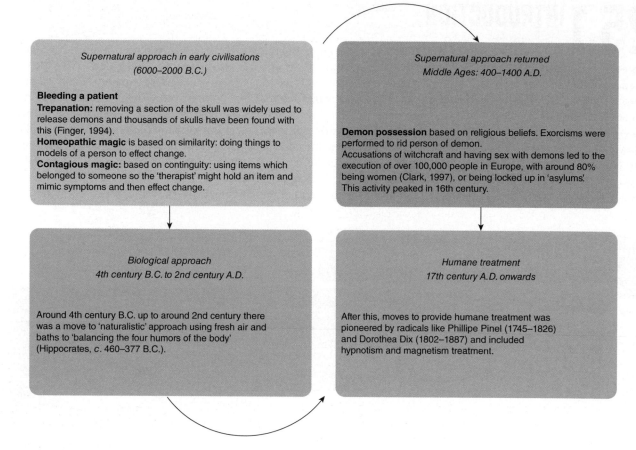

FIGURE 25.1   Early explanations of mental disorders

ASIDE

What is a 'therapy'?

'Therapies have been developed by physicians, priests, psychiatric and psychological specialists, interested layman, charlatans and quacks; the therapies vary accordingly' (Maher & Maher, 1985, p. 266).

SCHIZOPHRENIA Schizophrenia is not a single condition but is best described as a syndrome. The typical symptoms include difficulties in organising behaviour (including speech) as well as detachment from reality which may involve delusion and/or hallucinations. Schizophrenia is often misrepresented in the popular media as a case of split or multiple personalities.

sources. Some are diagnosed with a psychopathology (e.g. depression or **schizophrenia**) by a doctor who refers them to therapy. But psychologists also work with people who have decided to seek help for an issue with how they think or behave, or have been referred because their behaviour is harmful to themselves or others (e.g. deliberate self-harm and criminal behaviour). It has been suggested that up to 15% of people in the USA will access psychological interventions in the course of any one year (National Institute of Mental Health (NIMH), 2010).

Given the broad range of clients for psychological intervention, the interventions themselves take place in a wide range of locations, and with different methods. Serious, long-term disorders were often only treated in long-term institutions but this had other negative effects on the clients, so inpatient treatment is now used for only a few people (Craig & Power, 2010). Although inpatient treatment can be voluntary, it can also be involuntary (e.g. in the UK many of these inpatients will be sent to them by the courts in a process commonly called 'sectioning', which refers to the sections of the UK's Mental Health Act (1983 amended in 2007), under which they are detained). These decisions are reviewed regularly and people remain as an inpatient for as short a time as possible in the least restrictive conditions possible, therefore so the stay is now often weeks rather than months or years. The majority of interventions occur in an outpatient or community setting.

There are a broad range of professions who deliver psychological interventions, although the most common are applied psychologists, counsellors and psychotherapists. The training and qualifications for these practitioners have similarities and they are all trained and supervised in the delivery of one or more types of psychological intervention, depending on the therapy most suitable to their client group. Psychologists in the UK must meet the requirements of the Health and Care Professions Council (HCPC) in order to practise and most will also ensure they meet the competence standards of the British Psychological Society (BPS) to attain chartered psychologist status, and psychotherapists and counsellors generally meet the requirements of the British Association of Counselling and Psychotherapy (BACP).

25.2.2 OUTLINING THE TREATMENT MODELS

This chapter will focus on five approaches to psychological interventions that are widely used across the world:

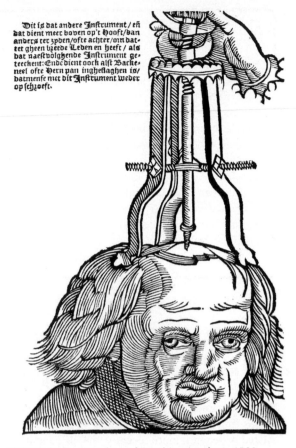

FIGURE 25.2 Woodcut of Trephination from 1593. Using an elevator to remove a piece of bone from the skull. Trephination as a therapeutic or magico-religious procedure dates back to Neolithic times, with trephines (or 'trepans') often used as a method of releasing evil spirits from the patient (Finger, 1994). Over the centuries, this surgical procedure continued to be used to treat a variety of symptoms, from migraine to mental illness

© Heritage Images/Corbis

1 psychodynamic therapy, drawn from the early work of Freud, but brought right up to date;
2 cognitive-behavioural therapy (changing what we think and what we do);
3 person-centred or humanistic therapy to help the client to find their own solution;
4 motivational interviewing to develop the client's motivation to change;
5 biological (including pharmacological) treatment.

For each of the interventions we will be:

- outlining the theory behind each intervention;
- exploring the purpose of treatment and the methods used;
- considering which psychological interventions are most effective for different psychopathologies or people.

To illustrate how each of the interventions might be used, we will follow the path of John as he undertakes each treatment to consider where and how it might be used. We will then explore some current controversies and ethical issues.

CASE STUDY: INTRODUCING JOHN

John is in his early 20s and has sought treatment for his drug addiction. He uses heroin every day and smokes cannabis most days. He has recently been in trouble with the law and the judge said that if he went for treatment he would not be sent to prison.

John tells the therapist about how his parents like to smoke cannabis and often ignored him. He says that when he tried to gain their attention, they disapproved of his loud behaviour and would often send him to his room. He felt unloved and became anxious to please them to get their love and support.

As he got older, he started to drink and smoke cannabis with his parents and felt accepted. He would get into trouble at school and most of his other friends and his teachers told him off about his behaviour so he stayed away from them and skipped school, spending more time with new drug-taking friends. However, he feels really lonely and unloved by his family and old friends. One day he was offered heroin and, once he took it, he felt great and without any worries. He then started to have panic attacks whenever he went into public places and he would take more drugs to feel better and calm again.

We will follow John as he goes through therapy . . .

25.3 PSYCHODYNAMIC THERAPY

25.3.1 DEFINITION AND GOAL

Psychodynamic therapy dates back to the nineteenth century and is one of the oldest therapies still available today. It was first suggested by Sigmund Freud, and since then has been developing with psychologists such as Carl Jung, Alfred Adler and, more recently, the influential British psychologist, Melanie Klein. The terms '**psychodynamic**' and '**psychoanalytic**' are often used to describe the therapy. However, this chapter will use the term 'psychodynamic' as it includes a broader range of treatment approaches.

PSYCHODYNAMIC Dealing with psychological forces that influence the mind and behaviour.

The underlying idea of psychodynamic theory is that people have an individual internal world which they are not always consciously aware of. The theory suggests that symptoms of distress and psychopathology (e.g. anxiety) are the external demonstration of a conflict between unconscious 'needs'. In addition, we have developed defences to defend these needs, but when these defences are inappropriately used or conflicts are strong, they come to the conscious 'surface'.

Freud's original model included three forces which interact and conflict. The first of these forces is the **id**, which is the force which generates all pleasure-seeking, selfish and hedonistic impulses, seeking immediate satisfaction and being oblivious of consequences. The second force is the **superego**, which establishes the rules and prohibitions, telling us what is the right thing to do and using guilt to override our id impulses. Essentially, Freud suggested that the superego is developed through childhood as we internalise the rules of authority figures, like our parents. The third force is the **ego**, which is the negotiator and makes compromises between the wishes of the id and the superego. Over time, the ego develops a range of approaches to manage these conflicts and these are called '**defence mechanisms**' (see Table 25.1).

DEFENCE MECHANISMS Protective strategies that the mind uses to defend itself against unwelcome or disturbing information.

The primary goal of psychodynamic therapy is to make the unconscious world conscious by helping clients to become aware of thoughts, feelings and other mental activities. This process has been termed 'insight', so psychodynamic therapy can also be called an 'insight-oriented' therapy. By bringing our thoughts, feelings, defences and the conflict fully into conscious awareness, we can make efforts to control them and develop more effective strategies to deal with them.

There are five key concepts which underlie psychodynamic therapy.

TABLE 25.1 Common defence mechanisms in psychodynamic therapy (adapted from Pomerantz, 2011)

Some common defence mechanisms which occur when the id has an impulse but this is rejected by the superego include when:
The ego represses the impulse of the id that is rejected by the superego. This means the ego sweeps the impulse 'under the rug' and pretends it's not there. This is called **Repression**.
The ego projects an id impulse onto other people, entitled **Projection** – trying to convince ourselves that the unacceptable thing belongs to someone else and not ourselves, e.g. wanting to smoke a cigarette and instead seeing everyone else who smokes as unacceptable.
The ego can form a reaction against the id impulse and do the exact opposite ('**Reaction Formation**'), e.g. when the id wants to do something for itself, the reaction is to do something for someone else.
The **Displacement** of the impulse by the ego towards a safer target can be used as a defence mechanism, e.g. kicking the dog rather than kicking your friend.
The ego redirects the impulse in such a way that the behaviour actually benefits others, e.g. stealing from the rich but giving it to the poor. This defence is called '**Sublimation**'.

A key pathway to change in psychodynamic therapy is the way in which painful feelings are dealt with through the *therapeutic relationship*. The key characteristics of this relationship are: (1) unconditional acceptance (implicit value as a human being); (2) neutrality (the therapist remains a blank slate/screen and does not provide any personal information); (3) containment (providing a safe environment where the client can express anything without rejection). *Boundaries* are also key to psychodynamic therapy, with the conditions or limits which are placed on the therapy providing consistency and predictability plus a safe place to share any feelings. They also provide points for discussion when boundaries are broken. These boundaries can be grouped into four aspects: Place (where sessions take place and positions within room); Time (timing and length of sessions); Conduct (conduct required within sessions); and Relationship (therapist maintains confidentiality and honesty but also their neutrality).

Transference and countertransference are terms related to the dynamic between the therapist and client. **Transference** broadly refers to the feelings that the client has about the therapist. Psychodynamic theory would suggest that (due to neutrality of the therapist) these feelings have been projected from other relationships and are often outside consciousness. This means that the person's relationships outside are mirrored in therapy, which allows an understanding of the client's internal world and interpersonal relationships. **Countertransference** broadly refers to the feelings felt by the therapist towards the client. However, these feelings originate with the client and can be seen as unconscious communication. So it may be that the therapist is feeling emotions which the client is really feeling – feelings the client is having difficulty in expressing or even feelings that others may have towards the client. These feelings can provide information on the true feelings in interpersonal relationships of the client.

Interpretations are the final key aspect in psychodynamic therapy. The interpretations of the therapist help the client to gain insight between their behaviour and their unconscious feelings. Interpretations are making the links between the unconscious and conscious world of the client.

25.3.2 ASSESSING THE UNCONSCIOUS WORLD

In order for the client to achieve insight and for the therapist to interpret, it is important to examine the unconscious. Psychodynamic therapists use a number of ways to infer an understanding of the client's unconscious world and hypothesise what is happening.

Free association is a strategy whereby therapists ask the clients to say whatever comes into their mind without stopping themselves. The therapist can gain an understanding of the unconscious world through the words which come to the surface.

Ever heard of Freudian slips? One of the most widely known methods in psychodynamic therapy is the exploration of these 'slips'. This method rests on the idea that no behaviour is random or accidental and if there is no conscious reason for the behaviour then it must be an indicator of our unconscious wishes coming to the surface. Most Freudian slips are verbal, but they can be behavioural as well. Freud also suggested that the raw thoughts and

EXERCISE: DREAMS

Think of a dream that you have had that you can remember vividly. What were the aspects of the dream that stood out? When you think about it, what do those aspects represent to you? That is, do they have other meanings or relevance?

feelings of the unconscious are developed into the specific content that we remember in our dreams and this unconscious world can be drawn out through Dream Analysis. The content of our dreams may be heavily disguised and distorted, but interpretation can be made through gaining insight from the perspective of the client (e.g. what does the dog represent in your dream?).

During therapy clients may indicate that 'they don't want to go there' either directly or indirectly (e.g. changing topic), and this suggests that certain unconscious thoughts or feelings have come to the surface too quickly or too strongly, creating anxiety. These topics are therefore indicative of a key area to be explored later in therapy, and identifying and exploring these topics is a method known as Interpreting Resistance.

Earlier on we explored the defence mechanisms for the unconscious world and so, in therapy, by Identifying the Defence Mechanisms, the client becomes more aware of them in their conscious world and can therefore begin to change them.

25.3.3 WHO IS IT FOR?

Psychodynamic therapy is often the longest type of therapy, with some clients being in treatment for years, although much shorter versions have been developed in more recent years. It is considered to be most beneficial for clients for whom interpersonal emotional issues are most prominent, where there are problems in the development of a sense of 'self' or where intrapsychic (in the mind) conflict is present.

Psychodynamic therapy has become less popular as a sole choice of therapy, but its concepts can be seen in other integrative approaches to treatment. In particular, the concepts of transference and countertransference are used in a range of treatment counselling situations.

25.3.4 PRACTICE APPLICATIONS AND EVALUATION

The nature of psychodynamic theory and its basic concepts makes evaluation difficult in an empirical manner so its critics suggest that it is not able to be fully tested. However, psychodynamic therapists would suggest that, given the powerful force of the unconscious, it is necessary to understand and control the unconscious to treat psychopathology. There have been a number of **outcome studies** completed for psychodynamic therapy, although the quality and volume of studies is considered to be somewhat less than therapies such as cognitive behavioural therapy (CBT) (Pomerantz, 2011). Large-scale reviews of psychodynamic therapy show that it can help clients improve significantly in conditions such as depression, bulimia, anxiety, anorexia and serious offending, although it is often inferior to other types of therapy (Galatzer-Levy et al., 2000; Leichsenring, 2009; Prochaska & Norcross, 2010).

OUTCOME STUDIES Research that is designed to measure responses to treatment and health status with the aim of supporting the development of guidelines for practice and improving quality of care.

25.4 COGNITIVE BEHAVIOURAL THERAPY

Cognitive behavioural therapy (CBT) is a model which integrates aspects from two models: largely, the cognitive model and, partially, the behavioural model. CBT is built around the concept that behaviour and feelings are both dependent on the way in which we interpret situations and the thoughts (cognitions) we have about

CASE STUDY CONTINUED: JOHN AND PSYCHOTHERAPY

John comes to therapy and the therapist asks John about his feelings towards his parents. John becomes a little unsettled and shifts around a bit in his chair.

John: I love my parents very much. They were not perfect but they were great.

Therapist: You seem a bit unsettled?

John: It's strange when I talk about my parents. One time I talked about them I felt a little uneasy so I tried to call my friend. He didn't answer his phone so I had an enormous argument with him because he didn't answer his phone and I thought he was ignoring me. But I love my parents very much.

What defence mechanisms might John be experiencing that you might want to explore further?

them. The underlying rationale is that our cognitions affect our behaviour. It is drawn from the cognitive model (Beck, 1963; Ellis, 1962), with the main aim of CBT being the development of rational thinking. With CBT, our behaviours are also important, and to change behaviour we need to develop and practise new behaviours. This aspect is drawn from the behavioural tradition (starting with Wolpe in 1958). The CBT model is one of the most widely used around the world for a range of psychological concerns, and it is increasing in popularity (Norcross, Karpiak, & Santoro, 2005).

Cognitive behavioural interventions begin by analysing the problem behaviour and understanding the thoughts and emotions behind it. The intervention is then tailored to the problematic behaviour, with a focus on the cognitions and emotions. Due to its direct approach, CBT is a much shorter intervention than psychodynamic approaches and can be just a few sessions long. To understand CBT we will start by exploring the theory and methods from the cognitive and the behavioural models which make up CBT.

25.4.1 THE COGNITIVE MODEL – WHAT ARE YOU THINKING?

The cognitive model came from the work of Aaron Beck and his Cognitive Therapy (Beck, 1963; Beck et al., 1979) and Albert Ellis and his Rational Emotive Behaviour Therapy (Ellis, 1962). The cognitive approach to therapy arose from a disillusionment with the psychoanalytic method and a desire to address clients' symptoms more directly. It therefore focuses on current behaviour, thoughts and emotions and not on unconscious or childhood experiences. It is drawn from the idea that the majority of emotional issues (including emotive behaviour) are due to irrational thinking. Ellis says these beliefs are illogical, damaging and self-sabotaging, and that irrational thinking does not lead to helpful emotions. For example, a man is made redundant from his job. To him it means that he was terrible at his job, his co-workers are much better and that no one will give him another job, and so he feels worthless and does not bother applying for any jobs. According to Ellis, people and things do not upset us, but we upset ourselves by believing that they can.

The cognitive model states that there are three different levels of beliefs which affect the way we interpret the world. These are:

Automatic thoughts: These are the first thing we think and are the thoughts we have every day (e.g. 'She's so rude!'). These thoughts directly influence our behaviour and mood, and represent how we think about the world. They are linked to deeper conditional or core beliefs.

Conditional beliefs: These are also called 'rules for living' and are the next level down. They are generally in our awareness. They involve assumptions (e.g. 'If she ignores me, it means she doesn't love me') or rules for life in the form of 'should, must or oughts' (e.g. others shouldn't push in the queue).

FIGURE 25.3   Cognitive triad example in cognitive behavioural therapy

Core beliefs: These are the deepest level beliefs and are sometimes called 'schema'. These beliefs are basic but extreme, developed early in life and are reinforced through experience. They can be functional, but some might cause us problems in some situations (e.g. 'I am worthless'). These are very resistant to change but are the basis of how we interpret everything.

Core beliefs are part of the '**cognitive triad**' (see Figure 25.3), which affects the more accessible conditional beliefs and automatic thoughts. This triad involves beliefs about self, others and the world, and it is theorised that when all three are negative, depression will result (Alford & Beck, 1997).

25.4.2 SOCRATIC QUESTIONING

Socratic questioning is a form of dialogue that helps a person to discover and attend to previously overlooked information, and to 'guide discovery' of the individual rather than interpretation from the therapist. It should draw the client's attention to information that is relevant but outside the client's current focus, and move the focus away from the concrete to the more abstract so the client can re-revaluate their conclusions or develop new ideas, for example, by asking 'What might you advise a friend who told you something similar?'. (For more detail, see Padesky, 1993.)

25.4.3 FORMULATION

CBT formulation is a way to understand the client's problem from all directions and how they link to each other. A formulation shows how dysfunctional thoughts and/or behaviours started, are maintained and made worse. It then can identify ways in which the situation might be changed through changing one part. One common way to do formulation is to use the 'five systems' model (Greenberger & Padesky, 1995), which outlines the Environment, Thoughts, Feelings/mood, Behaviour and Physical aspects/physiology of the client's issue (see Figure 25.4).

25.4.4 COGNITIVE TECHNIQUES – CHANGING YOUR THINKING

There are two longstanding methods from cognitive therapy which are used in CBT to understand and adapt thinking. These are (1) identifying **cognitive distortions** and (2) using the ABCDE model to understand and adapt them to make thinking more logical.

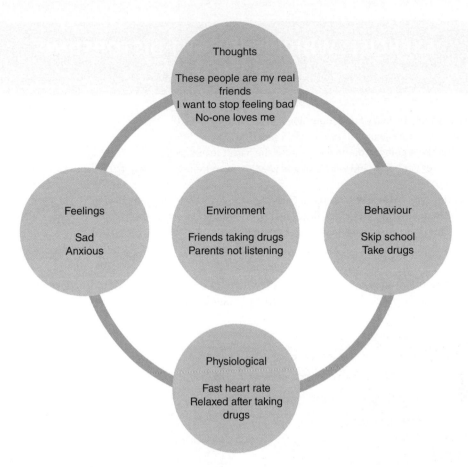

FIGURE 25.4   CBT formulation of John starting to take drugs

To help to identify dysfunctional thoughts or 'thinking errors', Beck and his colleagues developed a list of common thought distortions (e.g. Beck, 2002; Beck et al., 1979) that can be used to train clients to identify and monitor their own dysfunctional thoughts. Common thought distortions include:

All-or-nothing thinking: Only seeing the extremes and not seeing any of the 'grey' in a situation. Clients often use words such as 'always' or 'never', without seeing any of the middle ground or exceptions.

Catastrophising: Only seeing the worst in a situation or the future when, in fact, it is not that extreme. This is like all-or-nothing thinking but is focused on only seeing the extreme negative.

Magnification/minimisation: For events, either 'making a mountain out of a molehill' or playing down the importance, so giving more weight than is proportional to a particular aspect or exaggerating the importance of one incident.

Personalisation: Taking things too personally or assuming excessive personal responsibility for a situation.

Overgeneralisation: Applying rules too far where they don't really fit anymore.

Mental filtering: Only seeing some information and ignoring other contradictory information.

Mind reading: Thinking you know what others are thinking or feeling when in fact you do not.

25.4.5 THE ABCDE MODEL

The ABCDE model was developed by Albert Ellis (Ellis, 1962), although Beck also had a similar system known as the dysfunctional thought record. In Ellis's model, there are five stages to understanding and correcting unhelpful beliefs.

EXERCISE: WHICH THOUGHT DISTORTIONS ARE THESE?

1. That idiot should be locked up for pushing in front of me like that!
2. I must get As at college or else I won't get a good job.
3. I just know she is going to dump me because she hasn't texted today.
4. This will never get better and will always be like this, even though I do have good days now.

Think of the last time you became really angry. Which thought distortions were you having?

Answers: 1. Personalisation and magnification; 2. Catastrophising and all-or-nothing thinking; 3. Mind reading and overgeneralisation; 4. Catastrophising and overgeneralisation.

By identifying dysfunctional thoughts and then placing them in the ABCDE model, it is possible to re-train the mind so the client perceives their life and the world differently, changing emotion and behaviour.

TABLE 25.2 Description and example of ABCDE model in cognitive therapy

Activating event	The event which started unhelpful thoughts	Girlfriend said she can't come out this evening
Belief	Thoughts and the underlying conditional beliefs which are triggered	Automatic: She doesn't like me anymore Conditional: If she doesn't like me then I feel awful and I can't stand feeling like this Core: I am unlovable
Consequence (emotional)	Emotion felt as a result	Sad and anxious
Dispute	Challenges of the assumptions in the beliefs and thoughts	What other reasons might there be? Can I really not stand this feeling?
Effective new belief	New helpful beliefs and rules for the situation which reduce emotion	I can cope with one night on my own She still likes me and might be busy with homework

25.4.6 BEHAVIOURAL THERAPY

CLASSICAL CONDITIONING A form of learning which involves the pairing of a neutral stimulus with a reflex.

OPERANT CONDITIONING The process of learning, identified by B.F. Skinner, in which learning occurs as a result of positive or negative reinforcement of an animal or human being's action.

The founding of behaviourism by pioneers such as Watson and Skinner is outlined in Chapter 2. Watson and Skinner realised the importance of reinforcement and practice in behaviour change. The behavioural strategies used in CBT are about encouraging or reinforcing behaviour change, supporting cognitive change.

There are a number of behavioural techniques. These include Activity Monitoring, which highlights the triggers and patterns of behaviour that are helpful and unhelpful, and Activity Scheduling, which is used to target the client's key problems by scheduling the client to increase helpful activities and reduce unhelpful ones. Linked to activity scheduling is Behavioural Activation, whereby the client schedules in activities which they are avoiding in order to develop the chance to construct new 'rules' and cognitions.

Some of the most used techniques are linked to **classical conditioning**, They use Desensitisation and Exposure, where clients are gradually exposed to problematic situations in order to extinguish irrational fears. They are often used for anxiety and phobias, for example, having a fear of spiders. Treatment may start with a picture of a spider, gradually increasing exposure to handling a spider. Connected to conditioning, **operant conditioning** techniques use reinforcement and punishment to modify behaviour. This can be external (e.g. the therapist giving gold stars to a child for good behaviour) or internal (e.g. giving yourself praise when you have finished a task).

Other techniques include Modelling, which involves watching and learning from other people how you can act differently. The therapist may show the client a different way of behaving and encourages the client to do the same and to complete Skills Practice in order to develop new ways of behaving. Relapse Prevention can be the final stage of behaviourist approaches. It includes preparing plans for difficult situations and practising them in therapy before undertaking the new skills and behaviour in real life. Relapse prevention interventions often include skills practice where the client learns and practises new skills to develop new patterns of behaviour and links between thoughts and behaviour.

KEY STUDY

Young, K. (2007) Cognitive behavior therapy with internet addicts: treatment outcomes and implications. *Cyberpsychology & Behavior*, 10(5). DOI: 10.1089/cpb.2007.9971.

Are psychological interventions only for the common psychopathologies? No, far from it. They can work for all kinds of feelings and behaviours which can be disruptive to life and happiness. Kimberly Young showed that people who spend excessive time on the internet can be helped through CBT therapy. She showed that clients reported better motivation to reduce internet time, their online time management improved, they reduced their social isolation and even showed improvement for sexual dysfunction.

See how it is done

British Medical Journal video guide to CBT in obsessive compulsive disorder (OCD): www.youtube.com/watch?v=ds3wHk-wiuCo.

25.4.7 PRACTICE APPLICATIONS AND EVALUATION

CBT is used as a treatment in most emotional or behavioural psychological disorders and even in helping people adjust to situations. You can even use it if you are feeling a bit weird! Many applied psychologists will deliver CBT in some form and it is the first option of treatment for most disorders where psychological intervention is indicated. CBT has been shown to be as effective as pharmacological treatments for many disorders and it is often used in tandem with

KEY RESEARCHER Marsha Linehan

Marsha Linehan is a Professor of Psychology and of Psychiatry and Behavioral Sciences at the University of Washington and is Director of the Behavioral Research and Therapy Clinics. She is the developer of Dialectical Behavior Therapy (DBT), a skills-based treatment that is effective in reducing suicidal behaviour as well as other mental disorders. Currently, many consider it to be the gold-standard treatment for borderline personality disorder.

FIGURE 25.5   Marsha Linehan

POST-TRAUMATIC STRESS DISORDER An anxiety disorder resulting from experience with a catastrophic event beyond the normal range of human suffering, and characterised by (a) numbness to the world, (b) reliving the trauma in dreams and memories, and (c) symptoms of anxiety.

drug treatments to gain maximum long-term sustained improvement (Hollon, Haman, & Brown, 2002). This means that clients for whom medications may not be suitable may still benefit from CBT. In contrast to psychodynamic therapy, the concepts and methods making up CBT are easier to test, so CBT has a very large body of supporting research behind it, with hundreds of studies supporting its effectiveness with a large number of issues, including depression, anxiety disorders and **post-traumatic stress disorder** (PTSD) (Holman et al., 2002; Prochaska & Norcross, 2010). It has been suggested that CBT may not be as suitable for clients with poor memory or verbal skills since it relies on an analysis of thoughts and can be intellectually challenging (Whisman, 1993).

25.5 HUMANISTIC/PERSON-CENTRED THERAPY

Person-centred or humanistic therapy was initially developed by Carl Rogers in the 1940s. Carl Rogers believed that humans were inherently 'good' and that they would, if given the space to do so, do the best they could with the knowledge and skills they have. Person-centred therapy (PCT) assumes the client as the expert in their own situation and so the method is non-directive, meaning that the therapist does not guide the client to an answer, and only facilitates the client's thinking, trusting that the client will find their own understanding and the best solution.

25.5.1 MODEL AND THEORY

The aim of PCT is to increase the person's awareness of their deepest feelings, true thoughts and inner resources. The core principle is that humans are good and they drive towards being the best they can be. This drive towards becoming the best person they can be is called the 'self-actualising tendency'. This drive can be affected by negative influences and limitations on the resources available, so, for example, children who have suffered from neglect or abuse may have fewer resources to draw upon. However, PCT comes from the position that with the right support and circumstances the person can still flourish.

Within PCT there are a number of 'conditions' of therapy which interlink to create flourishing or non-flourishing people. These are (1) the organismic valuing processes, (2) the effects of others and the environment, (3) the conditions of worth, and (4) the locus of evaluation.

Organismic valuing processes: Everyone has an internal valuing system on which they rate everything. For example, you might rate skydiving as something highly likeable and exciting. Someone else may rate it is a low on likeable and high on fearful.

The effects of others and the environment: The surrounding conditions of a child will impact on the resources available to flourish and may support or inhibit their self-actualising tendency. The parental or caregiver response to the child will affect the view the child has of themselves and the child will begin to understand themselves through others' responses and develop a perception of themselves (**self-concept**).

Conditions of worth: For fully functioning adults, three factors must have been present from parents (Rogers, 1961):

- unconditional acceptance (accepted the way you are);
- unconditional positive regard (you are loved whatever you do);
- unconditional approval (you will always be supported).

The locus of evaluation: This is whether the person searches for the answers and guidance in themselves (internal) or from outside and from other people (external). PCT wants the reference point to be the client themselves and finding their own answers from their '*real self*'; not to have disturbance in their life, where trying to meet an '**ideal**

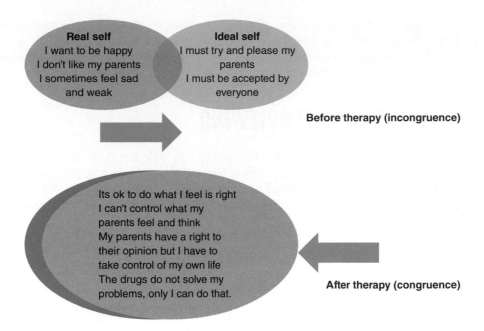

FIGURE 25.6   John's ideal and real self before and after PCT treatment

self', including gaining approval from others, means they deny their own real wishes (e.g. thinking 'I *ought* to behave this way').

PCT therapy aims to support people to become fully functioning adults who see the value in themselves and are able to flourish. It also seeks to help people to be able to experience without feeling threatened, to have confidence in making decisions which are congruent with their own values, and to lead the best life they can.

25.5.2 CORE APPROACH

The therapeutic relationship is the key factor in PCT. It aims to re-create aspects of the client's childhood to redefine their self-concept, as a lack of self-concept is a barrier to the self-actualising tendency. The therapist should therefore create an environment where unconditional acceptance, regard and approval are present. Core approaches of the PCT therapist are:

1   to be genuine and honest, but not an 'expert';
2   to offer unconditional positive regard and total acceptance;
3   to feel and communicate a deep empathic understanding.

By reflecting back to the client what the therapist hears and sees, it is possible to let the client 'hear themselves' and connect to their 'real self'. By reducing the incongruence between the real and ideal self, clients can find emotional congruence and their self-actualising tendency is supported – and able to find the best solution for them.

25.5.3 PRACTICE APPLICATIONS AND EVALUATION

PCT, by the nature of its aims, lends itself to problems of interpersonal discord and intrapersonal distress where there is a tension between the ideal and real self which needs to be resolved. Person-centred therapy has been part of the intervention tradition in the USA and Europe for many decades and although it is less widely used as a single approach than in earlier decades, some of its principles are still widely integrated in interventions. For example, the conditions for effective therapy have been integrated by most therapists. The role of the therapeutic relationship has been confirmed on many occasions as being the key factor in enhancing change and recovery in all forms of therapy (Martin, Garske,

& Davis, 2000). Thus, Rogers and PCT have made a valuable contribution to almost all psychological interventions. In evaluations of PCT, it has been shown to be effective in depression (Gibbard & Hanley, 2008). In random controlled trials on depression, PCT has also been shown to be able to hold its own against other psychological interventions with similar outcome results (e.g. Bower et al., 2000).

25.6 MOTIVATIONAL INTERVIEWING

Motivational interviewing (MI) is a client-centred therapy style that is directed at a particular outcome, that is, it develops internal motivation to change behaviour and lifestyle. It is often used for life-long health changes (e.g. eating habits) and substance misuse. MI was developed by Steve Rollnick and Bill Miller in 1983 and it is increasingly widely used across health services. They describe it as being about 'arranging conversations so that people talk themselves into change' (Miller & Rollnick, 2013).

25.6.1 THEORY

The MI model has links to Prochaska and DiClemente's Stages of Change model (Prochaska, DiClemente & Norcross, 1993), with the idea being that people may be ambivalent about change. The model suggests that by helping resolve this ambivalence towards making a change, the person is likely to make those changes. 'MI is a collaborative conversation style for strengthening a person's own motivation and commitment to change' (Miller & Rollnick, 2013). MI tries to encourage the client to develop an understanding of what is important to them, to weigh up the reasons for change against the reasons to stay the same to help make a firm decision, and also to develop confidence that they can make the change.

MI is underpinned by different skills and philosophies which together make up MI in practice. MI is not just about techniques. It embraces the idea of the relationship between therapist and client and that MI is a way of 'being' with the client which is as effective as the methods that might be used. MI focuses its therapy around an idea entitled the MI 'Spirit', which includes four key aspects:

1   **Partnership**: A collaborative relationship where client and therapist work together (Quote: MI is done 'for' and 'with' a person) (Miller & Rollnick, 2013, p. 15).
2   **Acceptance**: This does not mean approving a client's behaviour but accepting the person as having inherent worth, accepting that they can solve their own issues, being empathic to their situation and acknowledging the strengths of the person.
3   **Compassion**: The therapist actively promotes the client's welfare and gives priority to their needs.
4   **Evocation**: The therapist helps to call forth the answer from the client – the answers do not come from the therapist.

25.6.2 METHODS

There are four processes which form MI: *Engaging* (establishing the relationship); *Focusing* (directing the conversation on the key topic); *Evoking* (bringing out the client's reasons for change); and *Planning* (developing a plan for change). These steps can be seen as sequential, but also acknowledge that people will step backwards in their motivation. The therapist must therefore also be prepared to return to an earlier step.

25.6.3 THE CORE SKILLS OF MOTIVATIONAL INTERVIEWING

In order to move a client, MI uses a number of skills, many of which have been integrated into other forms of therapy. In order to gain the client's perspective and the full picture, it is important to ask *open questions* (e.g. 'What are some of the problems you are facing?') and not closed ones (e.g. 'Are you facing a debt problem?'). *Affirmation* is offering praise but without judging the person as good or bad. It emphasises the strengths of the client (e.g. 'You have shown you can pick yourself up when you need to'). A further fundamental skill in MI is *reflective listening*. The purpose of reflective listening is to let the client hear back what they are saying – sometimes with a twist! The therapist will therefore say back what they have heard (e.g. 'You say that things are bad for you right now, but that there is no problem with your drinking'), but this may include highlighting the discrepancies between what the client is saying or doing, thus 'developing discrepancy'. Finally, MI therapists will use *summarising* to bring together a collection of all the important things they have heard – to make sure they understand what the client is saying and also so the client can hear what they are saying.

CASE STUDY CONTINUED: JOHN AND MOTIVATIONAL INTERVIEWING

John is reluctant to consider giving up drugs but is aware that it is causing him difficulties. He sees an MI therapist for one session to think about what he wants to do about his drug use. MI was devised for substance use and he quickly finds himself thinking about his reasons for change and the reasons why he wants to stay the same. He realises that he is not really happy and that what he really wants is his old friends back – and that to do this he needs to give up the drugs. He decides that he will accept the therapist's offers of help to give up all the drugs.

25.6.4 WHEN THE CLIENT IS NOT TOO SURE HE/SHE WANTS TO CHANGE

MI makes certain assumptions about change. These assumptions may include the fact that not everyone is geared up and ready to change, and that even when someone starts thinking about change they may not be totally convinced. Although the purpose of MI is to develop change, it also includes techniques to help the client when they express lots of reasons to stay where they are (termed 'sustain talk') or when there is active resistance. MI is known for the phrase 'rolling with resistance', where the therapist does not need to challenge this natural process of being concerned about change, but 'rolls with it', using reflections to allow the client to find their own path.

25.6.5 PRACTICE APPLICATIONS AND EVALUATION

MI has been evaluated for use in many different settings with some of the best methods available, including random controlled trials, and has shown impressive results in meetings its aims. It is widely utilised and supported for use in substance-related disorders, smoking cessation, and a wide range of health issues where lifestyle changes are recommended (e.g. diabetes) (Burke, Arkowitz, & Mechola, 2003). MI is shown to be most effective when given in combination with other therapies. It can be a good precursor in developing motivation prior to more content-based therapies for change, such as CBT (McKee et al., 2007; Moyers & Houck, 2011).

KEY STUDY

Lösel, F., & Schmucker, M. (2005). The effectiveness of treatment for sexual offenders: a comprehensive meta-analysis. *Journal of Experimental Criminology, 1*(1), 117–146.

Did you know that psychological interventions have been used widely with people perpetrating all types of criminal behaviour? Knowing which interventions work is important because it impacts on whether people might hurt someone and end up on *Crimewatch*! Lösel and Schmucker also wanted to know what treatments worked to reduce offending. They completed a meta-analysis of 69 studies on sexual offenders, looking at a wide range of different interventions. They showed that biological treatments (e.g. drug treatment) and cognitive behavioural treatments are both effective in reducing the likelihood of crime, reducing sexual offending by up to 37% (compared to sexual offenders who did not receive any intervention). A massive improvement on the crime rate!

25.7 BIOLOGICAL AND PHARMACOLOGICAL TREATMENT

There is a broad range of biological psychological interventions with many different outcomes. They are largely defined as therapies which use biochemical and physical methods to help overcome psychological problems (Comer, 2013). Unlike the other interventions, biological treatments are often delivered by those with medical training, such as doctors, psychiatrists and nurse prescribers. We will look briefly at two types of biological intervention, *psychopharmacological (drug) therapy* and *electro-convulsive therapy*.

All biological interventions come from the tradition of the medical model of abnormality. This medical model suggests that abnormal psychology comes from a dysfunction in the brain and its connections. It sees patients as sick (as though they have an ear infection and need to be treated with antibiotics). Therefore, biological treatments suggest that they can be effective by addressing this dysfunction, either through medication or through other means which affect the person's physical body. The difficulties with defining people with the medical model were discussed in Chapter 24, but there are conditions which respond well to biological treatments and there is evidence that for some conditions biological treatments aid recovery and give symptom relief.

25.7.1 PSYCHOPHARMACOLOGY (DRUG) TREATMENTS

There are a range of psychotropic drugs (medications which work directly on the brain) available for many different conditions. Chapter 10, section 10.5.2, has examples of the biological mechanisms of some of these drugs. Broadly, these all fit into five categories (taken from Gelder, Mayou, & Geddes, 1999):

Anxiolytics drugs: These are also called antianxiety drugs and are used to help reduce anxiety or tension. One of best-known anxiolytic drugs is diazepam (commonly called Valium).

Antidepressant drugs: These medications are largely used to improve mood and depression, although they can also help anxiety. There are three sub-categories: (1) *monoamine oxidase inhibitors (MAOIs)*, which were widely used in the 1950s but are less used now; (2) *tricyclic medications*, which have three carbon rings and are widely used to block the reuptake of certain chemicals like dopamine, noradrenaline and serotonin. Amitriptyline is one the most widely used tricyclic drugs; (3) the next generation of antidepressants, *specific serotonin reuptake inhibitors (SSRIs)*, which selectively block the reuptake of serotonin into presynaptic neurons, making serotonin more available to the brain. Paroxetine and Fluoxetine (commonly known as Prozac) are two widely used SSRIs.

Mood-stabilising drugs: These are used to prevent affective (emotional) disorders. An example is lithium carbonate used to treat bipolar disorder.

Antipsychotics: These have been used since the 1950s and are also sometimes called 'major tranquilisers'. They help to reduce symptoms of psychotic disorders (such as schizophrenia). They manage the 'positive' (additional) symptoms, such as confusion, hallucinations and delusions, but do not work on 'negative' symptoms (e.g. emotional blunting, slow movement, social withdrawal). An example of an antipsychotic is Chlorpromazine (largactil). Newer antipsychotic drugs (e.g. Clozapine), which have less serious side-effects compared to earlier antipsychotic drugs, are now available, but these may impact upon the negative symptoms, as well as the positive symptoms, of schizophrenia. (There is an interesting key study in Chapter 10 on the discovery of antipsychotics.)

Detoxification: These are medications provided for people who are substance-dependent but who wish to reduce or stop taking substances. There are short- and long-term detoxification drugs, which initially support symptom relief, and long-term medications to prevent the return to drug use. Methadone is an example of a short- and long-term medication used for heroin withdrawal.

25.7.2 PRACTICE APPLICATIONS AND EVALUATION

Drug interventions are widely used and have been shown to have a modest effect on many conditions and symptoms. They are mainly used for treating psychopathology symptoms that are linked to a diagnosis (e.g. depression, schizophrenia, substance abuse) and a range of specialist drugs have been developed to target symptoms for these disorders.

The benefits of pharmacology on many disorders is relatively well established, and specific drugs have been developed and are widely used for specific disorders. Most drugs treatments have been found to be effective when compared to a placebo (dummy drugs) (e.g. Quitkin et al., 2000). There are concerns over the high relapse rate (return of symptoms) once drug treatment terminates and that to maintain effectiveness clients must continue to take drugs for long periods of time (Maj et al., 1992). For this reason, there is a growing trend to combine drugs treatments with other 'talking' psychological interventions to support the management of symptoms in the long term without drugs.

25.7.3 ELECTROCONVULSIVE THERAPY (ECT)

Electroconvulsive therapy (ECT) was first utilised in Italy in 1938 in an attempt to treat schizophrenia and was popular as a treatment in the USA in the 1940s; however, growing evidence suggests that it may be more effective for conditions other than schizophrenia. Although only evident in a handful of places in the UK and the USA, and rarely used outside these countries, it may be a useful treatment for patients who do not respond to conventional treatments.

In ECT, the patient is given an anaesthetic and muscle relaxant and electrodes are attached to the patient's forehead. Then they receive a short dose of electricity through the brain (commonly around 225 volts and 0.8 amps), which is enough to induce a seizure. This seizure or convulsion can last a few minutes, although it is often of a shorter duration. The procedure is repeated two to three times a week for an average of eight sessions. There have been concerns over its use, including that treatment can lead to memory disruption (Rami-Gonzalez, 2001), so ECT is often administered only to one side of the brain (the non-dominant hemisphere) to reduce this side-effect. You will not be surprised to hear that this is a very controversial treatment.

ASIDE

Hemingway and ECT

The great US author, Ernest Hemingway, underwent 20 gruelling sessions of ECT to treat him for depression. One of the side-effects of ECT is memory loss and he is reported to have said: 'Well, what is the sense of ruining my head and erasing my memory, which is my capital, and putting me out of business? It was a brilliant cure but we lost the patient.' Shortly after this he took his own life.

(*The Economist*, 2005)

25.7.4 PRACTICE APPLICATIONS AND EVALUATION

There is limited evidence of the global effectiveness of ECT, but there are some benefits. Many studies have concluded that there is a relapse of symptom rate of around 80% (Sackeim et al., 2001). However, in recent years, the National Institute of Clinical Excellence (2009) has considered evidence from over 119 randomised-controlled trials. NICE concluded that ECT may have some benefits for severe depression and schizophrenia, but that other treatments are better. According to NICE, ECT should only be used as a treatment of choice for resistant catatonia (a state of apparent unresponsiveness to external stimuli in a person who is apparently awake) and severe mania (abnormally excessive elevated mood disorder).

CASE STUDY CONTINUED: JOHN AND BIOLOGICAL TREATMENTS

John is ready to come off the drugs, but he is dependent on them and he doesn't like the sound of all the side-effects of 'cold turkey'. So, the doctor prescribes Methadone, which John will need to pick up from the pharmacy each day, but he must stay off the heroin! The doctor also prescribes an anxiolytic to help John with his anxiety, which sometimes leads him to take drugs.

25.8 OTHER ISSUES

25.8.1 FORMAT OF INTERVENTIONS

There are many different ways in which interventions can be undertaken and the approaches covered in this chapter have often been adapted to meet new demands for treatment which is more effective, reduces cost and allow for access by less accessible populations.

Individual therapy is the most commonly known format, where there is one client and one therapist – which takes us back to the image of the psychiatrist's couch. All of the psychological interventions in this chapter can be delivered in this individual format.

In *group therapy*, one or two therapists will facilitate a number of clients at once in a single room to deal with similar problems. This is a more cost-effective way of delivering interventions as it allows for one therapist to treat several clients at once, and it has been found that around one-third of clinical psychologists practise in group settings to some degree (Norcross et al., 2005). This is widely used for CBT forms of therapy and is utilised for a diverse range of disorders, from depression to violent and/or sexual offending.

Self-help groups are a common form of group therapy, where people with similar problems will meet and support each other. This approach differs from other forms of intervention as there is no leadership from a therapist. One of the best known examples of self-help groups is Alcoholics Anonymous, which operates a 12-step illness-model (alcoholism as an illness) approach to start and maintain abstinence from alcohol. Mentors from within the group support and guide other members.

A new and growing area for psychological intervention is *computerised and e-therapy*. The availability of the internet and computers in most homes allows people to access support and intervention at a time convenient for them. It allows treatment to be delivered with or without a therapist, where the client works through a computer-generated self-help 'workbook', or through online chats with trained therapists.

25.8.2 WHAT WORKS? EVALUATING TREATMENT APPROACHES

SO DOES IT MATTER WHICH THERAPY I GET?

Yes, it does, but only to a point. Some key meta-analysts in the 1970s considered the question as to whether psychological interventions were effective and which therapy was best. Singer and Luborsky (1975) and Smith and Glass (1977) completed a meta-analysis of the research and concluded that all the therapies were effective and generally equally effective! More recent studies (e.g. Elkin et al., 1989; Westen & Morrison, 2001) also found that therapies for depression fared evenly in outcome, but when followed up after two years, most of the clients had relapsed and only 26% of clients who entered treatment stayed well in the long term. However, in even more recent studies, there has been some differentiation in the outcome studies and now some therapies are seen to be better for certain conditions. Cognitive behavioural therapy, for instance, has been shown to be very helpful for depression, anxiety and panic disorders (Craske, 2010), and drug therapy is the single most helpful treatment for schizophrenia and bipolar disorder.

HOW CAN WE KNOW IF AN INTERVENTION WORKS?

Agreement on how to measure the effectiveness of different psychological interventions has been hard to develop. In 1952, Eysenck published an influential paper in which he stated that although it was difficult to use the scientific method to show that psychoanalysis was effective, it did not mean that it was ineffective. However, by 1960 he was arguing that behaviourism was the only therapy worth considering. Hmmm …

The difficulty in evaluating research is the number of questions that need to be answered. So, how do you decide what the outcome should be when clients are so different? How much improvement is enough? How do you measure the outcome? How do you prove that it was the therapy that made the difference?

Some psychological interventions lend themselves to the scientific method more easily, for example, behaviourist approaches, where the frequency of problem behaviour can be used as a measure of change. However, some psychological interventions involve more complex or less measureable changes, including emotional and cognitive aspects which must be less directly measured and may require self-reported assessment of change (e.g. feelings of depression or level of motivation to change).

There has been much debate over the best method of evaluation for interventions, with some authors suggesting that only those therapies that have been shown to be effective using high-quality random controlled trials (RCTs) should be available (e.g. Seligman, 1995). These are termed 'efficacy' studies. This approach is the one taken in medical trials where one group is given a drug and the other a placebo. Other authors have argued that RCTs have two major issues in applied practice. First, RCTs require clients to receive structured and identical treatment (sometimes from a strict manual) and so the therapy is not able to be flexible to the client, which is important to gain the full benefit. These authors argue that studies which evaluate whether the therapy was effective for the patient (with its flexibility) are also valid. These are called 'effectiveness' studies. Second, questions are raised regarding the ethics of RCTs as a group of clients would not receive the psychological intervention that another group does, and therefore one group may have to continue with the psychological issue which may be distressing or dangerous.

25.9 CHAPTER SUMMARY

A psychological intervention is an interaction between therapist and patient to elicit changes in the patient's behaviour, cognition or emotion. This chapter has explored some of the widely used psychological interventions, specifically psychodynamic, cognitive-behavioural, person-centred, motivational interviewing, and biological and pharmacological approaches. We spent time looking at the theory behind each intervention, what they aim to do and how they work. We have also looked at the methods used by each intervention and whether they are effective and with whom.

There is a broad selection of psychological interventions which come from different perspectives and use different methods. All of these psychological interventions have been shown to be effective in relieving issues and they are pretty similar in how effective they are. Some interventions have been shown to be better than others for specific issues, with CBT used for depression and anxiety disorders, motivational interviewing for substance misuse and biological (drug) treatments for schizophrenia. Many interventions now integrate aspects from other approaches to maximise their effectiveness, with therapeutic alliance (from person-centred therapy), transference and countertransference (from psychodynamic therapy) and 'rolling with resistance' (from motivational interviewing) often seen in counselling sessions.

(?) DISCUSSION QUESTIONS

How should you choose the best psychological intervention for a particular issue or person? The evidence is mixed for many of the issues that are taken to therapy, and which therapy is best depends a lot on the client and which therapy style they will respond to and which one meets their underlying issues. It has been argued that the best therapy is the one in which the client can develop a good therapeutic relationship with his/her therapist. So does this mean that we should leave the client to choose? What if the client chooses one and it doesn't work? Does this mean the client isn't trying hard enough, that the therapy doesn't work or that really it is not the best therapy for the presenting issue?

Some interventions are more easily evaluated and therefore lots of researchers study it because it is easy. Does this mean that only this intervention should be used? What does this mean for therapies that are tapping into unconscious thoughts or memories set down at a young age and are not conscious?

SUGGESTIONS FOR FURTHER READING

Feltham, C., & Horton, I. (2006). *The SAGE handbook of counselling and psychotherapy*. London: SAGE. Provides more in-depth information about the types of psychotherapy interventions.

Pomerantz, A. (2011). *Clinical psychology: science, practice and culture*. London: SAGE. Discusses the application of psychotherapy and how it might be used for different conditions.

Weatherhead, S., & Flaherty-Jones, G. (2012). *The pocket guide to therapy: a 'how to' of the core models*. London: SAGE. Provides brief information about most of the therapies and how they are used in practice.

Still want more? For links to online resources relevant to this chapter and a quiz to test your understanding, visit the companion website at edge.sagepub.com/banyard2e

26 HEALTH PSYCHOLOGY

Lead authors: Eva Zysk, Eva Sundin, Preethi Premkumar and Phil Banyard

CHAPTER OUTLINE

26.1 Introduction	468
26.2 What is health psychology?	468
26.2.1 Health psychologists	469
26.2.2 A brief history of health psychology	470
26.3 Models of health	470
26.3.1 The biomedical model	470
26.3.2 The biopsychosocial model	471
26.3.3 Psychology and health	471
26.4 Factors that influence health and ill-health	472
26.4.1 The role of biology and genetics	472
26.4.2 The role of individual characteristic and behaviours	473
26.4.3 The role of the physical environment	474
26.4.4 The role of social, socio-economic and socio-environmental influences	475
26.5 Stress and its effect on health	475
26.5.1 Defining and measuring stress	476
26.5.2 The role of appraisal in stress	476
26.5.3 Coping	478
26.6 Understanding health and illness	478
26.6.1 Obesity	479
26.6.2 Smoking	480
26.6.3 Pain	480
26.7 Chapter summary	481
Discussion questions	482
Suggestions for further reading	482

26.1 INTRODUCTION

Even if you have never studied health psychology before, you will have already had some experiences that relate to this discipline. For instance, you may have thought about how to improve your physical health (e.g. through exercise and healthy eating) and avoid illness and injury (e.g. through washing your hands during the flu season and wearing your seatbelt while driving). To achieve any of these, you will need to change your behaviour. Also, if you have attributed a headache to stress or an upset stomach to worry, you may already know that biology is not always the sole cause of illness and you are aware of the influence psychology can have on your health. You may also have made links between social influences and health behaviours, such as your peers urging you to drink alcohol or join the gym, and between your wellbeing and the availability of social support, such as having close friends or family to talk to when you need them. This chapter will look at some of the key ideas in health psychology and show how they have been applied to such conditions as stress and pain.

FRAMING QUESTIONS

- What is health and what is illness?
- What is health psychology?
- What is stress and how can we change our experience of it?
- How can psychology be used to improve health and reduce illness?

26.2 WHAT IS HEALTH PSYCHOLOGY?

Before we set out to look at health psychology, let's first try to define what we mean by health. This is not as easy as it sounds. Try the exercise below as a loosener before you read on.

EXERCISE: DEFINING HEALTH

How do you define health?

Make a list of the characteristics of yourself when you feel healthy. This will probably include some physical symptoms, some cognitive symptoms and some emotional symptoms. Now try to do the same for when you feel unhealthy.

When you look at your list, does it describe health as merely the absence of illness and injury, or did you consider other aspects that can be taken into account? The Constitution of the World Health Organisation (WHO, 1946) defines health as 'a state of complete physical, mental and social well-being and not merely the absence of disease or infirmity'. Often when thinking about health, we also think about quality of life. The WHO (1997) has defined quality of life as 'a broad-ranging concept affected in a complex way by the person's physical health, psychological state, level of independence, social relationships and their relationships to the salient features in their environment'.

It is difficult enough to be clear what we mean by good health, and if we start to introduce issues around quality of life then we further complicate the issue.

The questions in the exercise are addressed in health psychology, which is a field of psychology devoted to understanding the psychological and psychosocial aspects of human health and ill-health, understanding the relationship between psychological states and physical health, enhancement of health and prevention of disease, and improvement of healthcare systems.

Psychological aspects of health and ill-health include cognitions (such as beliefs and attitudes), emotions and behaviours that relate to health. Risk factors for ill-health have been identified that can be managed through changes to these cognitions, emotions and behaviours. For instance, health promotions can be set up to reduce unprotected sexual activity in adolescents.

Health psychology has been growing in importance and health psychologists are in increasing demand in health services. The number of people falling ill or becoming injured and the severity of the illnesses or injuries may have a direct impact on society, such as increased availability of medical care and support services, more funding for research being done on how to prevent or reduce the impact of health problems, and potential changes in policy (e.g. possible introduction of bicycle helmet laws). Therefore, health psychologists contribute to improving the healthcare system, placing a large focus on the prevention of ill-health and the promotion of good health. Health psychologists work with people to improve their health behaviours, help people deal with illness or injury, and improve people's quality of life. Health psychologists also carry out research. For instance, they may be interested in investigating factors that encourage or hinder people from using healthcare services. Health psychology research uses established psychological methods to gain an understanding of the role of beliefs and cognitions, attitudes and behaviours in health and illness. There are various types of health psychologists including clinical health psychologists, public health psychologists, community health psychologists, critical health psychologists and occupational health psychologists.

26.2.1 HEALTH PSYCHOLOGISTS

Clinical health psychologists help people affected by disability or acute or chronic illness to deal with their condition and the ways it has affected their lives. Clinical health psychologists may help people deal with difficult medical news and discuss various difficult treatment procedures (e.g. hysterectomy), overcome issues which may interfere with their treatment (e.g. needle phobia), cope with **chronic medical conditions**, such as chronic pain, and deal with anxiety or depression resulting from their condition or associated treatment.

CHRONIC MEDICAL CONDITION An illness or disease that develops gradually and which lasts for a long period of time or a lifetime, worsening over time (e.g. osteoporosis, chronic asthma, diabetes or cancer).

ACUTE MEDICAL CONDITION An illness, disease or affliction with a sudden onset and a rapid course (e.g. a cold, injury, heart attack or asthma attack). Acute conditions can sometimes become chronic.

Public health psychologists work to improve the overall health of populations at large or target specific populations (e.g. single mothers with chronic illness). Public health psychologists may be involved in developing public health programmes, strategies and education campaigns, and influencing government policy relating to public health.

Community health psychologists are similar to public health psychologists but rather than looking at larger populations they focus on communities, factors that are unique to those communities, and how these factors contribute to the health and ill-health of the community residents or specific groups within the community. For instance, some community health psychologists may be interested in the incidence of particular illnesses in specific communities and investigate the reasons for these rates. They may look for ways to help decrease the incidence of these illnesses through community education and identify other community-level interventions, such as disease prevention and promoting healthy behaviours.

Critical health psychologists ensure equality in the provision of health-related services across people of all races, social economic statuses, genders and ages. They aim to identify any power imbalances and promote public policy change to resolve these differences in order to ensure universal and fair access to healthcare services.

Occupational health psychologists are interested in investigating links between a type of job and/or workplace environment a person may have and that individual's health. People's mental or physical health may be affected by the mental or physical demands of their job, their relationships with employers and co-workers, and factors such as workplace stressors, job security, physical hazards, lighting and noise. Occupational health psychologists may assess and try to improve healthy workplace conditions, job satisfaction and employee morale, and reduce workplace risk. They may also carry out research in order to find out which jobs may be linked with negative effects on people's health, such as high blood pressure or depression, and help find ways to reduce these negative effects.

As you can see, each type of psychologist is concerned with different aspects of health and illness and their relevance to psychology. Health psychologists work on various levels in a range of different settings and with a variety of different people.

26.2.2 A BRIEF HISTORY OF HEALTH PSYCHOLOGY

Health psychology is a relatively new area within the discipline of psychology, having emerged within the 1970s. In ancient times, the body and mind were considered as a single entity. Over the course of time, different cultures developed various explanations for the causes of ill health. Early cultures believed illness resulted from evil spirits entering the body and that health could be restored through exorcising these spirits. The early Greeks developed a theory of illness which linked health and personality to four humours (body fluids): blood, phlegm, black bile and yellow bile. They believed that having an imbalance of any of these humours could result in disease, disability and abnormal behaviour. While the humoural theory is not accepted today, it is worthwhile noting that the early Greeks were one of the first groups to make the connection between the mind, body and health. In the religion-focused Middle Ages, disease was seen as punishment for sin. The Renaissance brought many medical advances. A scientific approach to health was adopted, and diagnosis and treatment came to be based on physical evidence. From this emerged modern psychology. In the late nineteenth century, Sigmund Freud, an influential early psychologist, theorised that physical disturbances characteristic of 'hysteria' were caused by repressed unconscious psychological conflicts, suggesting that the mind and body were inextricably linked. The 1930s gave rise to psychosomatic medicine, which associated particular diseases with personality types. In 1978 the American Psychological Association created a Division of Health Psychology and the field of health psychology was born.

Health psychology continues to develop and is now thought to be one of the most rapidly growing areas within psychology. Recently, there has been a rise in the popularity of health psychology, alongside an expansion of healthcare services in the UK, particularly with regard to the formulation of health belief models and the prevention and management of chronic illnesses.

26.3 MODELS OF HEALTH

Healthcare is associated with doing something physical to the patient, such as performing surgical operations or administering drugs. This is at the heart of the *biomedical model* of health.

26.3.1 THE BIOMEDICAL MODEL

The biomedical model has been the cornerstone of Western medicine for 300 years and, in some respects, bears a resemblance to mending a broken object. If something is going wrong, then it needs to be fixed in the same way we might fix a car or a machine. We make observations and diagnose the faulty bit, then we can repair it, if possible, or replace it if necessary. Sometimes we might benefit from a general overhaul and sometimes from some minor adjustments. This biomedical model has some appeal because we are clearly made up of biological bits, and also some biomedical treatments produce dramatic improvements in health.

One issue with the biomedical model is that it tends to look for a single cause of a disorder rather than looking for a range of contributory factors. For instance, there are numerous attempts to explain complex disorders in terms of a simple genetic effect. There is even a tendency to describe smoking as the cause of coronary heart disease, yet many smokers do not develop the disease and many non-smokers do. The process would seem to have more than one cause and more than one contributory factor. Another concern is the greater focus on illness rather than health. 'If it's broken, fix it' might be a suitable motto because the biomedical model deals with illness and the development of illness rather than the promotion of good health.

There are three main changes that have led to dissatisfaction with the biomedical model. First, throughout the twentieth century there was a decline in the incidence of infectious, single-cause diseases. In the UK at the beginning of the twentieth century, the three most common causes of death were:

1   influenza and pneumonia
2   tuberculosis
3   gastro-enteritis

These illnesses are all caused by micro-organisms, and can respond to better living conditions and relatively simple medical interventions, such as antibiotics.

On the other hand, by the end of the twentieth century the two illness that accounted for 64% of all deaths in the UK (Office for National Statistics, 2000) were:

1   heart disease
2   cancer

Neither of these has a known simple cause, and the medical interventions are often drastic and costly and have only limited success. The general picture is that large-scale infections (caused by simple micro-organisms such as bacteria) which were common in the early part of the twentieth century have been replaced by chronic diseases (such as cancer) which have multiple causes.

Second, there has been a dramatic increase in specialist technology and an equally dramatic increase in the cost of healthcare. The costs of treating someone who is ill are now prohibitively high, so there is a major incentive to prevent people getting ill in the first place. The third change is a growing emphasis on quality of life. People are developing an expectation that they should have a healthy, enjoyable and active life. These three factors have changed the general view of health from one where we deal with illness to one where we promote good health.

26.3.2 THE BIOPSYCHOSOCIAL MODEL

An alternative approach to the biomedical model is to look at all the biological, psychological and social factors that are associated with health and illness. This is referred to as the **biopsychosocial model** (see Figure 26.1). In contrast to the biomedical model, the biopsychosocial model looks at all levels of explanation from the micro-level (e.g. changes in body chemicals) to the macro-level (e.g. the culture that someone lives within). The biopsychosocial model does not look for single causes, but starts from the assumption that health and illness have many causes, and also many effects. The model does not make the distinction between mind and body, but instead looks at the connections between mental events and biological changes. Finally, the biopsychosocial model is concerned as much with health as it is with illness.

26.3.3 PSYCHOLOGY AND HEALTH

Psychology has two special features that it brings to the study of health. The first feature is the breadth of the subject. Within the same university department (our own) you might find one psychologist strapping magnets to a pigeon's head to see if it can navigate without information about the earth's magnetic fields, and another psychologist exploring the various behaviours associated with opening and closing doors. The study of health requires us to consider a broad range of issues and consider evidence from a wide range of sources.

The second important feature of psychology is its methodology (see Chapter 4). Psychology has 100 years of experience in trying to record and measure human behaviour and experience, and it has developed a wide range of useful methods that can be applied to health issues. In order to understand how we develop a wide range of illnesses we need to consider the following information: What do people do? Why do they do it? How do they explain their behaviour? And what would encourage them to change their behaviour? These are the types of questions that have led psychologists to become more involved in health.

The changing role of psychology in health was brought into sharper focus with the discovery of HIV/AIDS in the early 1980s which at the time had no medical treatments. The only solution was to change people's sexual behaviour

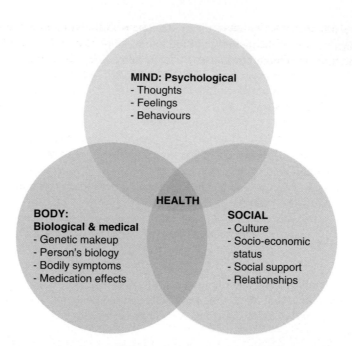

FIGURE 26.1 The biopsychosocial model: biological, psychological and social factors that interact to influence health

to reduce the spread of the disease. This disease posed a challenge for psychologists. Put bluntly, if you never have sex, and you never take intravenous drugs, and you never have blood transfusions, then, provided your mother was not infected when she carried you in utero, you will not get AIDS. Solved that one, then! Well, not quite, but the message is clear; you have to do something to get AIDS, and this is where psychologists come in. The disorder is transmitted behaviourally, and for many years once someone had contracted the infection there was no known cure. So, the only way to control the spread of HIV/AIDS was to change our behaviour and the behaviour of other people.

26.4 FACTORS THAT INFLUENCE HEALTH AND ILL-HEALTH

It is now recognised that individual and community health and ill-health is influenced by a combination of various states and circumstances which can broadly be explained by four factors: the person's biology, their personal characteristics and behaviours, their physical environment, and their social and economic environment.

26.4.1 THE ROLE OF BIOLOGY AND GENETICS

One of the factors involved in the development of ill-health is our genetics. Some illnesses run in families, suggesting that people who have a family member with a certain illness are more likely to develop the illness themselves. Susceptibility to an illness is passed on in families through genes. But for many illnesses, say diabetes, an individual who has inherited a predisposition for diabetes may not necessarily develop it because of the lifestyle choices that help to prevent developing the illness. However, the child of such a person may still inherit the predisposition.

Until relatively recently the main way of investigating genetic factors in human behaviour was to study family relationships. More recently, it is possible to carry out genetic analysis and look for differences in the genetic structure of people with and without certain symptoms or behaviours, such as addictions. In this case, the two methods tend to point to different answers. The family studies tend to emphasise the role of environmental factors in the development of addictive behaviours. A study of over 300 monozygotic (identical) twins and just under 200 same-sex dizygotic (fraternal) twins estimated different contributions of genetic factors and environmental factors to substance use in adolescence (Han et al., 1999). It concluded that the influences on the decision to use substances were largely environmental rather than genetic. Some family studies, however, suggest there is a link between addictive behaviour and personality traits. For example, Jang, Vernon and Lively (2000) looked at the relationship between alcohol use and personality in 300 monozygotic twins and over 300 dizygotic twins. They found a connection between genetics and anti-social personality characteristics (including attention seeking, not following social norms and violence), and between anti-social personality characteristics and alcoholism.

Studies that analyse the genetic structure of individuals tend to emphasise the role of genetics rather than the environment in addictive behaviours. Some genes have attracted particular attention and have been shown to appear more frequently in people with addictive behaviours than in people without. The problem is that these genes do not occur in all people with the addictive behaviour and they do appear in some people without it. For example, a gene referred to as DRD2 (no, it didn't appear in *Star Wars*) has been found in 42% of people with alcoholism. It has also been found in 45% of people with Tourette's syndrome and 55% of people with autism. It has also been found in 25% of the general population. This means that DRD2 appears more frequently in people with these behavioural syndromes, but it cannot be the sole explanation for the behaviour (Comings, 1998).

26.4.2 THE ROLE OF INDIVIDUAL CHARACTERISTIC AND BEHAVIOURS

Health psychology investigates how health and illness affect people's quality of life and wellbeing. But what factors are important for someone to maintain health and to cope well when ill? As is shown later in this chapter, these processes are influenced by health behaviours (e.g. smoking, exercise). Important factors also include social cognitions and health beliefs, as well as stress and coping reactions. Health psychology researchers have shown that personality traits are important predictors of health behaviours that influence long-term health outcomes (Ferguson, 2013). Individuals with higher levels of trait anxiety are more likely to suffer from asthma, ulcers, arthritis and headaches (Friedman & Booth-Kewley, 1987). Those who have high scores on neuroticism have a greater incidence of serious illness and shorter life spans (Suls & Bunde, 2006) and they are more likely to have a lifestyle that increases the risk for cancer, such as smoking tobacco (Munafo, Zetteler & Clark, 2007; Terracciano & Costa, 2004; van Loon et al., 2001).

Personality traits may directly influence susceptibility to illness and health behaviours as well as stress and coping reactions when faced with illness (Roberts et al., 2007). This is particularly important because being ill can create a whole new set of stressors, such as problems with finances, problems obtaining proper care, and problems with having to adjust your personal identity to involve being a sick person (Charmaz; Lively, & Smith, 2011). Personality can also influence intentions to seek treatment and care (Conner & Abraham, 2001) and how the individual communicates with health professionals (Ferguson, 2013).

Differences in health and health-related behaviours can also be down to gender. Men have a lower life expectancy than women: 78.9 years compared with 82.7 years (Office for National Statistics, 2014). Men are more likely to die from cancer, heart disease, HIV, accidents and suicide than women (Office for National Statistics, 2014). Men are more likely to take risks with their health than women. For example, on average they drink more alcohol, smoke more cigarettes and take more drugs (Office for National Statistics, 2000). They use less sun cream and they are involved in more accidents (Department of Health, 2001a). Men also have less contact with the health services than women. The consulting rate for women is 32% higher (Wang et al., 2013), with the greatest difference seen during the ages 16–60. Also, the gender difference is more pronounced in areas of economic deprivation. Interestingly, other issues of inequality are also more pronounced in men than women. In men, social class based on employment is the most important influence on early death. To put it brutally, the less you earn, the sooner you die. For women, however, although there is still an effect of income on early death, it is much weaker (Sacker et al., 2000). The puzzle for health workers is to understand why men have worse health and die younger, and why they make less use of the health services.

One of the issues for health workers is that men and women may have different symptoms when suffering from the same condition. While men usually experience crushing chest pain during a heart attack, women more often complain of pain just under the breastbone, abdominal pain, sensations of difficulty breathing, nausea or unexplained fatigue. Contrary to lay beliefs, women are about as likely to have a heart attack as men, but women suffering heart attack may often be misdiagnosed as having indigestion problems, gall bladder disease or an anxiety attack (WHO, 2013).

ASIDE

Magical beliefs about food and health

We might think we are rational people, but we commonly respond to superstitious ideas and folk beliefs. This thinking has an effect on our health behaviours.

Magical beliefs are a type of superstition which involve unscientific beliefs about causation or that things can influence one another at a distance through an unknown connection. Non-scientific health and food beliefs are often based on magical thinking, particularly following the law of contagion and the law of similarity (Lindeman et al., 2000).

The magical law of contagion holds that things that have been in contact with each other continue to act on each other at a distance through a magical link. This contagion can be either positive or negative. To take a positive example, have you ever rubbed a lucky charm for good luck before sitting an exam in hopes that the luck would act upon you as you write the exam? To take a negative example, if you were feeling a bit hungry and found a fresh apple on the floor of a dirty classroom, would you refuse to eat it even after it was given a thorough wash? If so, you probably have some magical beliefs.

The magical law of similarity holds that that superficial resemblances have a deeper link. For instance, we may have no problem cutting a pillow apart, but would hesitate to do the same to a stuffed animal (you can probably understand human beliefs in voodoo as well now). You may also love chocolate, but refuse it if it is in the shape of dog poo. Similarly, we may be suggestible to believe that heart-shaped leaves can treat heart disease, the lung of a fox can ameliorate respiratory difficulties (cf. Nisbett & Ross, 1980), and that consuming the penis bone of a tiger can treat erectile dysfunction. While there is no scientific evidence in support of these 'treatments', many of these continue to be endorsed around the world. Tiger poaching is a problem in Southeast Asia, and the black market trade of the tiger penis contributes to the tigers' endangerment.

FIGURE 26.2   You are able to cut up a cushion with ease, but can you cut the head off Binky the Bunny, even though it is just a shaped cushion (sorry if that spoils it for anyone)?

© Antonio Gravante/Shutterstock.com

26.4.3 THE ROLE OF THE PHYSICAL ENVIRONMENT

The physical environment is an important determinant of health. Examples of physical determinants include *air pollution*, which has been shown to be a leading cause of cancer in humans (Straif, Cohen & Samet, 2013), and ground water pollution, which can carry toxic substances that can cause cancer, birth defects and other illnesses. Currently, little is known about the specific effects of many toxic substances and hazardous wastes on health; studies are currently investigating how these exposures may impact human health.

The indoor environment has been gaining increased attention as most people in Western cultures spend the majority of their time indoors at home, work or school. Potential health threats in the indoor environment include indoor air pollution, inadequate heating and sanitation, electrical and fire hazards, and lead-based paint hazards and other toxic materials (e.g. asbestos).

Health psychology is also concerned with positive factors in both the indoor and outdoor environments. The availability of aesthetic elements, such as good lighting, parks and other communal areas, trees and benches, and the absence of trash are all important features of a good quality of life, which plays an important role for health and wellbeing. Environmental charities such as Trees for Cities (www.treesforcities.org) actively look to enhance the health and wellbeing benefits of their greening of urban landscapes.

It is also important to note that illness and injury can have a direct effect on our physical surroundings that in turn influence and are influenced by our personal beliefs and behaviours. If we are injured, we may not be able to keep up with our daily tasks, such as cleaning and tidying or picking up fresh groceries, potentially leading to us having a less healthy living environment. Falling ill can also change our beliefs about ourselves and our vulnerabilities.

26.4.4 THE ROLE OF SOCIAL, SOCIO-ECONOMIC AND SOCIO-ENVIRONMENTAL INFLUENCES

Throughout the Western world, the most consistent predictor of illness and early death is income. People who are unemployed, homeless or on low incomes have higher rates of all the major causes of premature death (Carroll, Davey Smith, & Bennett, 1994; Fitzpatrick & Dollamore, 1999). There is a plethora of reasons as to why this may be. Poorer people may be exposed to greater health risks in the environment, such as through holding more hazardous jobs and having poor quality living conditions. Physical inactivity, poor diet and smoking are just some of the risk factors that are more common in poorer people, which can lead to obesity, stroke, heart disease, premature or low birthweight infants, and some cancers (James et al., 1997). To take a specific example, people on low incomes usually buy cheaper foods which have a higher content of fat and sugar (which can increase risk for coronary heart disease, diabetes and obesity) and consume less fruit, vegetables and whole grains (which provide essential nutrients and have antioxidant properties). All this means that psychological interventions on behaviour can only have a limited effect since it is changes in economic circumstances that will do most to improve the health of the nation.

The effects of poverty are long-lasting and far-reaching. A remarkable study by Dorling et al. (2000) compared late twentieth-century death rates in London with modern patterns of poverty, and also with patterns of poverty from the late nineteenth century. The researchers used information from Charles Booth's survey of inner London, carried out in 1896, and matched it to modern local government records. When they looked at the *mortality* (death) rates from diseases that are commonly associated with poverty, such as stomach cancer, stroke and lung cancer, they found that the measures of deprivation from 1896 were even more strongly related to these diseases than the deprivation measures from the 1990s. They concluded that patterns of disease must have their roots in the past. It is remarkable, but true, that geographical patterns of social deprivation and disease are so strong that a century of change in inner London has not disrupted them.

Another study by Dorling et al. (2001) plotted the mortality ratio (rate of deaths compared to the national average) against voting patterns in the 1997 general election. They ordered the constituencies into 10 categories, from those that had the highest Labour vote to those that had the lowest. The analysis found that the constituencies with the highest Labour vote (72% on average) had the highest mortality ratio (127), and that this ratio decreased in line with the proportion of people voting Labour down to the lower Labour vote (22% on average) where there was a much lower mortality ratio (84). This means that early death, and presumably poor health, were more common in areas that chose to vote Labour. If we take Labour voting as still being influenced by class and social status, then this study gives us another measure of the effects of wealth on health.

The influence of poverty shows up in a number of ways in multiple disorders, such as glaucoma. Glaucoma is a damaging eye disease that can cause blindness if untreated. Fraser et al. (2001) looked at the differences between people who sought medical help early (early presenters) and those who sought help for the first time when the disease was already quite advanced (late presenters). The late presenters were more likely to be in lower occupational classes, more likely to have left full-time education at age 14 or younger, more likely to be tenants than owner occupiers, and less likely to have access to a car. It showed that someone's personal circumstances and the area where they lived had an effect on their decision to seek help with their vision. It also appeared that the disease developed quicker in people with low incomes.

We now go on to look at some examples of the application of health psychology, starting with the topic of stress.

26.5 STRESS AND ITS EFFECT ON HEALTH

Stress is a sensation we encounter regularly in our daily lives. It is a feeling of loss of control over a situation or being unable to keep up with often multiple competing events, such as completing a piece of coursework within a given deadline, keeping up

> **STRESS** A perception of conflict between desired goals and the actual outcome (Broome & Llewellyn, 1995).

with household chores, remembering to schedule a vet check-up for our pet, and keeping an appointment to meet with friends. We can feel stressed when we think we don't have enough time to meet these various demands. We often feel helpless when we are stressed if we don't know how to solve a practical problem, such as fixing a piece of computing software. These psychological states can exacerbate physiological sensations that range from acute responses, such as increased heart rate, breathlessness, sweaty palms and nervousness, to more chronic adaptations, such as high blood pressure or irritable bowel. In fact, it is thought that several physical disorders, such heart disease and autoimmune diseases, are affected by stress. Experiencing stress can maintain symptoms of otherwise easily treatable physical disorders. High stress levels have huge economic cost in terms of gross productivity. Understanding the causes and effects of stress and how to deal with stress at both the individual and wider community levels are a leading concern for health psychologists.

26.5.1 DEFINING AND MEASURING STRESS

> **ALLOSTASIS** The process of achieving stability, or homeostasis, through physiological or behavioural change.

Stress can be taken to be an absence of, or a deficiency in, the individual's ability to cope with the current environmental demands. Stress may be seen as **allostasis** (McEwen, 2007), which is the attempt to respond to events in a way that restores the body's homeostasis or normal way of being. The key processes in a person perceiving an event as stressful are (1) the presence of some sort of physical and/or psychological demand, which requires the person to (2) assess and (3) understand the situation, and (4) then respond to it. A commonly used self-report measure of stress is the Perceived Stress Scale (Cohen, Kamarck, & Mermelstein, 1983). It is a short 10-item inventory that asks about the person's thoughts and actions in the last month, such as 'In the last month, how often have you found that you could not cope with all the things that you had to do?'.

Early models of stress were based on evolutionary theory and physiological arousal, but more recently they have sought behavioural and cognitive explanations. The evolutionary theory (Cannon, 1932) posits that experiencing stress is a result of the fight-or-flight response. Here, external threats cause the individual to deal with the stressor or escape from it. In 1956, Hans Selye put forward the general adaptation syndrome model of stress. He identified three stages of the response to stress (Figure 26.3). The first stage, 'alarm', indicates an increase in resources used to constructively deal with the stressor. The second stage, 'resistance', indicates a threshold response where the person generates an optimal response to the stressor. In the third stage, 'exhaustion', the person's internal resources are depleted and the person perceives that he or she is no longer able to meet the demands of the stress.

There are many ways of classifying stress. Stress may be regarded as emotional and physical. Selye distinguished between *Eustress* and *Distress*. Eustress is a positive stress because it is associated with good emotions and physical health, such as exercise. Exercise is associated with an increased flow of endorphins, which are hormones that stimulate positive emotions. When people exercise they feel more energetic and alive, even though it is a result of the intense activity that includes increased heart rate, perspiration and breathlessness. Distress is associated with negative emotions and poor physical health. A frequent outcome of and closely-related concept to stress is anxiety. Anxiety occurs when there is a sense of fear arising from a repetitive evaluation of the perceived consequences of a stressor.

Both of these models regard stress as a state of physiological arousal and do not consider the cognitive appraisal and coping styles that allow people to modulate their response. Folkman and Lazarus (1984) were influential in understanding the ways of coping with stress. Lazarus (1993) described stress as a four-stage process: (1) a causal external or internal agent, (2) an evaluation that distinguishes what is threatening or noxious from what is benign, (3) a coping process used by the mind or body to deal with stressful demands, and (4) a complex pattern of effects on the mind and body.

26.5.2 THE ROLE OF APPRAISAL IN STRESS

In their description of stress, Lazarus and Folkman (1984) distinguished between primary and secondary appraisal (see Figure 26.4). In the primary appraisal we judge whether the event is *positive*, *negative* or *neutral*. So, developing a cold one evening might be positive (because you won't have to go to work tomorrow), it might be neutral (because you will be able to carry on with whatever you intended to do whether you have a cold or not), or it might be stressful (because you have an examination or interview tomorrow and you think you will not be able to do your best).

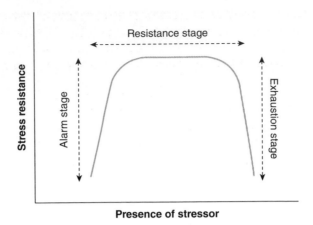

FIGURE 26.3   Selye's (1956) general adaptation syndrome

If we judge that the event is negative, we make further judgements on three issues. First, how much *harm* has already occurred ('oh no, its already a nightmare!'), second, what is the *threat* of further harm ('tomorrow will be a disaster!'), and third, what sort of *challenge* does this event offer ('I'll boldly go where no one has gone before!').

In the secondary appraisal we have to make judgements about our own abilities and our current state of mind and health. It doesn't necessarily follow on after the primary appraisal and it sometimes might even affect the primary appraisal, so if you make the assessment that you are in a poor state of mind (secondary appraisal of coping ability), this might lead you to see a normally safe event as being quite threatening (primary appraisal). For example, if you don't feel able to cope with people today, then a simple visit to the newsagent for your newspaper could appear quite taxing.

More recently, research has examined the role of cognitive reappraisal in emotion regulation in the context of stress (Troy, Shallcross, & Mauss, 2013). Understanding the psychological effects of cognitive reappraisal has informed psychological interventions, such as cognitive behavioural therapy for mental disorder. Cognitive reappraisal involves reframing one's thoughts about a stimulus in order to change its emotional impact of the stimulus (Gross, 1998). Importantly, Troy and colleagues (2013) recognise that being able to control the situation is a key factor in cognitive reappraisal and its effectiveness in regulating emotional behaviour. They argued that cognitive reappraisal may be more relevant in situations where it is not possible to exert control, whereas problem-focused coping may be more relevant where the person is able to control the situation.

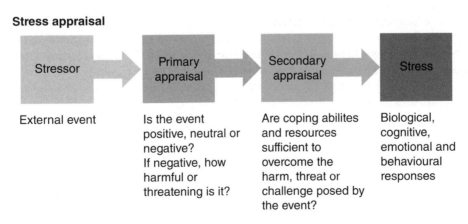

FIGURE 26.4   Folkman and Lazarus's (1984) model of appraisal

© mickythemartian

KEY STUDY

Troy, A.S., Shallcross, A.J., & Mauss, I.B. (2013). A person-by-situation approach to emotion regulation: cognitive reappraisal can either help or hurt, depending on the context. *Psychological Science*, 24(12), 2505–2514.

Troy, Shallcross and Mauss (2013) measured cognitive-reappraisal ability, people's perception of stressful life events as controllable and level of depression in 170 participants. The cognitive-reappraisal task involved participants watching three two-minute film clips of a sad scene. Participants were asked to think about the situation in a more positive light. If participants viewed their life events as causing uncontrollable stress, then being able to cognitive-reappraise the sad scenes positively was associated with lower depression. Furthermore, when participants viewed their life events as producing controllable stress, higher cognitive-reappraisal ability was associated with greater levels of depression. It seems that people who perceive their stressful life events as uncontrollable are more likely to use more cognitive-reappraisal styles to regulate their emotion. In turn, such individuals are more likely to have lower depression than those who view their stressful life events as controllable.

26.5.3 COPING

Lazarus and Folkman (1984) described coping as a person's ongoing effort in thought and action to manage specific demands appraised as taxing or overwhelming. They identified two ways of coping: problem-based coping and emotional coping. Problem-based coping involves a change in the person's relationship with the environment as a result of a direct action. Emotional coping is where the change is brought about only in the way one attends to or interprets the situation. Lazarus and Folkman devised the *Ways of Coping* questionnaire, which is a 67-item inventory about a person's thoughts and actions. Carver, Scheier and Weintraub (1989) revised the *Ways of Coping* scale in order to disentangle similarities between problem-based and emotion-based coping. The Coping Orientation to Problems Experience (COPE) scale (Carver et al., 1989) is a 60-item self-report questionnaire that consists of 15 subscales. This scale is now the industry standard for measuring coping.

EXERCISE: DEVISE YOUR OWN ILLNESS BELIEFS QUESTIONNAIRE

To understand how we can help people to best manage a severe illness, it is important to understand how they experience the illness and themselves as someone with an illness. How would you ask people about their beliefs concerning their own illness? Take a few minutes to think about what it might be important to know. What types of questions would you include? What questions would you leave out, and why? Draft four or five questions for your questionnaire. If you feel that a standard type questionnaire is not good enough, you can change it as you see fit. Perhaps you would like to add multiple choice questions or images to your survey.

26.6 UNDERSTANDING HEALTH AND ILLNESS

Some mental and physical disorders are life-long, and the patient must learn to endure and adjust to these. Such disorders include hypertension, stroke, obesity, metabolic syndrome, autoimmune diseases, and being grumpy, among many others. It then becomes a matter of key concern for patients to learn to recognise the symptoms of their illness early enough and how to manage them so that they are able to continue to go about their routine

KEY RESEARCHER Theresa Marteau

Professor Theresa Marteau is Director of the Behaviour and Health Research Unit at the University of Cambridge, the Department of Health-funded policy research unit in behaviour and health. She studied social psychology at the London School of Economics and Political Science and completed her training in Clinical Psychology at the University of Oxford. She gained a PhD in Health Psychology as an external student at the University of London while working as a Research Fellow at the University of Oxford. She is a Fellow of the Academy of Medical Sciences and of the Academy of Social Sciences.

Her research focuses on developing ways of changing behaviour at population levels, drawing on neuroscience, behavioural economics as well as psychology. Her research interests include: (1) risk perception and communication in particular of biomarker-derived risks, and their weak links with behaviour change (Marteau et al., 2010); and (2) the development and evaluation of interventions to change behaviour (principally diet, physical activity, tobacco and alcohol consumption) to improve population health and reduce health inequalities, with a particular focus on targeting non-conscious processes (Marteau et al. 2012).

FIGURE 26.5   Theresa Marteau

activities. Restoring equilibrium is central to coping with illness. This entails psychological, social and physical adjustment, and incorporates aspects such as reductions in distress, good illness management, minimising illness interference on life roles and relationships, and the ability to maintain positive affect (Moss-Morris, 2013). In the next few sections we will consider obesity, smoking, chronic illness and chronic pain as some disorders that have a known physical cause and effect, and consider what health psychology can contribute to our understanding of them.

26.6.1 OBESITY

The rising incidence of obesity in the general population has drawn much interest in understanding the internal (body) and external (environment) causes of obesity. There are several explanations for the cause of obesity. One explanation is genetic. The heritability rates of the body-mass index is between 40% and 70%. Adopted children resemble their biological parents in terms of their weights. This is because the *leptin gene* for producing leptin is mutated. Leptin is a key regulator of energy intake and eating behaviour, energy expenditure, neuroendocrine function and immunity (Ramachandrappa & Farooqi, 2011). Leptin deficiency is associated with a failure of normal pubertal development, but this deficiency can be corrected with Leptin supplements. Leptin supplements restore

normal pubertal development. Another explanation for the cause of obesity is altered metabolic rate (the body's conversion of food energy into physical energy). However, evidence is contradictory as to whether obese individuals have a lower or higher **metabolic rate** (Ogden, 1996). Behaviourally, the restraint theory suggests that obese individuals have greater difficulty in restraining their food intake.

METABOLIC RATE   The rate at which the body uses energy to perform various physical and biological activities, such as exercise, respiration and heartbeat.

The key to weight control, however, is defined by the first law of thermodynamics, which states that energy can neither be created or destroyed. With regard to diet control it means that the amount of energy someone takes in has to be matched by the amount of energy he or she uses in activity. So in very simple terms, if you want to lose weight, then follow a healthy diet and don't forget to exercise. Well, we say it can't fail, but it is obviously more difficult than it looks because it is difficult to control our own behaviour. This is where health psychology comes into practice, like encouraging us to engage in exercise and influencing our health behaviours.

KEY STUDY

White, B.A., Horwath, C.C., & Conner, T.S. (2013). Many apples a day keep the blues away: daily experiences of negative and positive affect and food consumption in young adults. *British Journal of Health Psychology, 18*(4), 782–798.

A recent study investigated the association between eating behaviours and mood in healthy young adults. Nearly 300 undergraduate students kept a daily diary of their mood states for three weeks. Levels of both positive (e.g. calm, cheerful and energetic) and negative (e.g. depressed, anxious, short-tempered) mood states and amounts of both healthy (fruits and vegetables) and unhealthy (e.g. crisps, chocolate or cakes) foods were assessed. The study did not find a significant relationship between consumption of particular foods and negative mood, but there was a relationship with positive mood. On the days when young adults reported eating more servings of vegetables and fruit they reported experiencing a more positive affect. It was also found that consumption of these healthy foods predicted increased positive mood the following day, and that mood was not predictive of the type of food intake (thereby allowing us to understand the direction of the relationship). The researchers suggest that eating seven to eight servings of fruits or vegetables daily may promote positive mood in young adults.

26.6.2 SMOKING

In England in 2010, 20% of adults (16 years and above) reported smoking, which is perhaps shockingly high but much lower than the 39% who reported smoking in 1980 (Health and Social Care Information Centre, 2013). Current smokers smoke an average of 12.7 cigarettes per day. Although the incidence of smoking is decreasing, the long-term effects of this behaviour are still being felt. In 2011–12 there were approximately 1.6 million hospital admissions in England of adults aged 35 and over with a primary diagnosis of a disease that has been linked to smoking. The annual number of admissions has been rising steadily since 1996–97 when the number of such admissions was 1.1 million.

There is now a wide choice of smoking cessation strategies, from nicotine patches, chewing gums and electronic cigarettes to behavioural counselling and group behaviour therapy. The National Institute of Health and Care Excellence (NICE) guidance on smoking cessation (NICE, 2008) has also recommended the use of bupropion hydrochloride, self-help material, telephone counselling and quitlines, and mass-media campaigns. However, bupropion hydrochloride is primarily an antidepressant and has many unwanted side-effects, such as agitation, insomnia and headaches.

Dijkstra and De Vries (2001) investigated the extent to which self-help interventions change specific cognitions and the extent to which changes in these cognitions are related to behaviour. They carried out a field experiment with follow-ups after two weeks and 12 weeks. Over 1,500 smokers were offered different types of self-help materials to aid giving up smoking. The research used two types of information: (1) information about the outcomes of smoking, such as shorter life expectancy and various unpleasant diseases, and (2) self-efficacy information telling people how to be successful at giving up.

About a quarter of the smokers attempted to quit, but most started smoking again. However, the rates of continuing to stay off the cigarettes were affected by the type of information they received. The main conclusion from the study was that self-efficacy information seems to be effective, and the outcome information had no measurable effect.

26.6.3 PAIN

Pain can be defined as 'an unpleasant sensory and emotional experience associated with actual or potential tissue damage, or described in terms of such damage' (Merskey & Bogduk, 1994). Although it seems obvious that pain is connected with injury, the story is not as straightforward as that. The study of pain presents a number of puzzles that challenge the link between tissue damage and feelings of pain. These puzzles include the experience of injury without pain, the experience of pain without injury, and the poor relationship between the size of the injury and the size of the pain.

An example of injury without pain is episodic analgesia (where people do not feel pain for some minutes or hours after an injury). The type of injury involved in episodic analgesia can range from minor abrasions to broken bones or even limb loss. Episodic analgesia is a puzzle for any theory of pain. The tissue damage is surely greatest at the time of the injury but the pain is delayed. This experience is quite common; Melzack et al. (1982) discovered that 37% of people arriving at the accident and emergency department of an urban American hospital with a range of injuries reported the experience of episodic analgesia.

There are also a number of examples of pain where there is no obvious physical cause, including *neuralgia*, *causalgia*, *headache* and *phantom limb pain*. Neuralgia is a sudden sharp pain along a nerve pathway. It occurs after a nerve-damaging disease (e.g. herpes) has ended. Causalgia is a burning pain that often develops as a consequence of a severe wound (e.g. from a knife). The remarkable thing about causalgia, like neuralgia, is that it develops after the wound has healed. Causalgia and neuralgia are not constant pains but they can be triggered by a simple stimulus in the environment, like a breeze or the vibration of an air conditioning unit.

To further confuse the issue, there are also several personal and psychological factors that influence the experience of pain. For example:

Learning: if migraine sufferers are shown words associated with pain, it increases their anxiety and their sense of pain (Jamner & Tursky, 1987).

Anxiety: in women with pelvic pain, there is a correlation between their anxiety and the strength of their pain (McGowan et al., 1998).

Gender: women have been shown to find post-surgical pain more intense than men, although men are more disturbed by low levels of pain that last several days (Morin et al., 2000).

Cognition: the way we think about the pain (e.g. whether we feel in control of it, or whether we feel able to do something about it) may well affect our sense of pain. This forms the basis for cognitive therapies that are used to help people with chronic (persistent) pain.

All the above observations tell us that pain does not have a clear relationship with tissue damage. It is clearly affected by a range of cognitive and emotional factors which means that health psychologists can contribute to the reduction and management of pain. For example, the fear-avoidance model of pain (Crombez et al., 2012) focuses on how patients interpret pain. If patients see pain as threatening and catastrophic, they may develop an excessive fear of pain and injury that gradually extends to a fear of physical movements. In this case, patients will avoid those physical activities that are presumed to worsen their problem. However, there is a danger with this approach that the pain that is being felt by the patients will be partially ignored by the therapist, who is focusing on what they think about the pain. It's a difficult call to make.

As with other disorders, there is a role for social support in minimising the perceived consequences of pain. Having a caregiver or close relative to share the burden of pain can help to reduce the disruption in performing daily activities. Practical social support in the form of seeking help from wider social services can help to address some of the motivational obstacles. Perceiving more social support is associated with lower pain (Jensen et al., 2011). However, if that well-meaning support goes too far, for example offering to carry out routine activities for the patient and providing encouragement to be less active, it can actually be associated with greater perceived pain in patients with physical disabilities, such as patients with amputations.

26.7 CHAPTER SUMMARY

In this chapter we have looked at what health psychologists do and how they can contribute to our understanding of health and illness. The traditional biomedical model of illness is becoming increasingly redundant because of its emphasis on medical causes, whereas the current big threats to health in the UK are cognitive and behavioural. Dealing with challenges such as widespread obesity and high levels of stress may not best be met through medical solutions such as medication. The best solutions are likely to be found by devising ways to change people's behaviour at a personal level, and also at a government level through the changing of social policy that influences our behaviour (e.g. banning smoking in public places).

DISCUSSION QUESTIONS

People sometimes use the phrase 'Nanny State' to refer to government institutions taking control of our lives and telling us what to do. Do you think there is a case for the Nanny State ensuring that we eat healthily and live longer, or can we make those decisions for ourselves?

In our National Health Service, do we, the patients, have responsibilities as well as rights? Do we have to try to be as healthy as possible or should we expect the NHS to treat us whatever we get up to?

As many of our current health problems are based on behavioural rather than medical factors, should we reduce the number of doctors and spend the NHS budget on encouraging behavioural change?

SUGGESTIONS FOR FURTHER READING

If you want a general text on UK health psychology, look no further than Jane Ogden's text: Ogden, J. (2012). *Health psychology: a textbook* (5th edn). Maidenhead: Open University Press.

If you want some details on specific issues, you could try a book of selected readings by the same author: Ogden, J. (2008). *Essential readings in health psychology*. Maidenhead: Open University Press.

If you want to check out the health of the nation, then browse through the data at the Office for National Statistics at www.ons.gov.uk/ons/index.html.

Still want more? For links to online resources relevant to this chapter and a quiz to test your understanding, visit the companion website at edge.sagepub.com/banyard2e

27 FORENSIC PSYCHOLOGY

Lead authors: Rebecca Lievesley and Helen Elliott

CHAPTER OUTLINE

27.1 Introduction	**484**
27.2 Psychology, police and the courts	**484**
27.2.1 Detecting deception	484
27.2.2 Techniques used to detect deception	485
27.2.3 False confessions	486
27.2.4 Eyewitness testimony	487
27.3 Offences and theories explored	**488**
27.3.1 Sexual offending	489
27.3.2 Violent offending	492
27.4 Imprisonment, rehabilitation and resettlement	**495**
27.4.1 Imprisonment	495
27.4.2 Risk assessments	496
27.4.3 Treatment in prison	496
27.4.4 Resettlement	496
27.5 Chapter summary	**498**
Discussion questions	**498**
Suggestions for further reading	**498**
Discussion of exercises	**499**

27.1 INTRODUCTION

Forensic psychology sits at the junction between psychology and the criminal justice system. It is concerned with the psychological aspects of legal processes, applying psychological theory to criminal investigations, understanding criminal behaviour and the treatment (and punishment) of offenders.

The work of forensic psychologists can vary greatly, but may involve the assessment and treatment of offenders, offender profiling, conducting applied research, developing policies or providing advice to parole boards and mental health tribunals. The largest employer of forensic psychologists within the UK is Her Majesty's Prison Service (HMPS), although forensic psychologists may also be employed in healthcare settings (such as rehabilitation units and secure hospitals), social services, universities or as private consultants.

This chapter explores some of the key areas in forensic psychology: psychology, police and the courts (detecting deception, false confessions, eyewitness testimony); understanding why people commit crime (in particular, sexual and violent offences); and briefly looks at the imprisonment, rehabilitation and resettlement of offenders. While each of these topics could fill a chapter in its own right, here we provide an introduction and overview of the fascinating field of forensic psychology.

FRAMING QUESTIONS

- How is forensic psychology relevant to the Criminal Justice System?
- What are the challenges in finding who is responsible for committing a crime?
- Why do people commit sexual crime? Or violent crime?
- How can we stop people from reoffending?
- What do forensic psychologists actually do in the prison service?

27.2 PSYCHOLOGY, POLICE AND THE COURTS

Forensic psychology has a growing place within the police and courts system in England and Wales. Psychological theories and practice are applicable to the **criminal justice system** (CJS) through, for example, helping police investigations and aiding court processes. Forensic psychologists may be called to court to act as expert witnesses in order to provide specialised knowledge to help a jury with their decision making, or they may be called in earlier in order to help police with their search for a particular offender. One well-known example of this is offender profiling, a tool that can help investigators predict the profile or characteristics of offenders (offender profiling is typically used in cases of serial murder or rape – see www.davidcanter.com/professional-services/offender-profiles/ if you are interested in reading more about this).

CRIMINAL JUSTICE SYSTEM Comprises all organisations that have a role in the detection, prosecution, sentencing and punishment/treatment of offenders in the UK. This includes the police, the Crown Prosecution Service, the courts, the Ministry of Justice and the National Offender Management Service.

Here, we have chosen to focus particularly on how psychology has influenced *lie detection*, a topic which has received increased attention over the last decade. We will also introduce *false confessions* (where a person admits guilt for a crime they did not commit) and, finally, we will examine how psychology has influenced the area of *eyewitness testimony*.

27.2.1 DETECTING DECEPTION

The process of detecting deception has been of longstanding interest to psychologists. Can we tell when someone is lying or not? Early research suggested that detecting lies was easy, but it has now been acknowledged that this is simply not true (it's a lie!). One of the difficulties is that there is no one single behaviour that can accurately 'demonstrate' truth. However, if psychologists could at least provide some insight into how to improve the ability of trained professionals to differentiate lies from the truth, this would help the police and courts considerably!

While there does not seem to be one single behaviour showing 'truth', some common features of liars have been identified. These include: (1) attempting to over-control behaviours that are associated with lying, such as fidgeting or looking away, leading to an unnatural, stiff position (Vrij, 2004); (2) appearing unpleasant or tense as a result of an individual knowing they are trying to deceive someone; (3) fewer body movements, longer pauses and averting eye contact due to the increased mental demand of lying (Vrij et al., 2008); and (4) sweating, heavy breathing and a high-pitched voice as a consequence of the stress and arousal associated with the fear of being judged as a liar (Ekman, 2001).

27.2.2 TECHNIQUES USED TO DETECT DECEPTION

Despite the difficulty in detecting deception, psychologists are able to use information like that described above to inform the process of detecting deception, producing devices such as the *polygraph*, improving interviewing techniques and using computer programs, such as *The Silent Talker*.

POLYGRAPH

The polygraph measures physiological responses such as blood pressure, breathing, skin conductivity and pulse rate. The idea is that if someone is lying, their physiological responses will be different from when they are telling the truth, that is, more arousal will be demonstrated. A number of different types of testing are used:

- *Control Question Test* – This is the earliest method. It uses one irrelevant question ('Is your name Simon?') and one relevant question ('Did you kill John?'). The approach assumes that a liar will be more physiologically aroused by relevant questions than irrelevant ones, whereas the innocent person (who did NOT kill John) will show no difference.
- *Comparison Question Test* – This uses three kinds of questions: irrelevant ('Is it Monday today?'), relevant ('Did you kill John?') and a comparison question. The comparison question is supposed to be a probable lie (e.g. 'have you *ever* stolen anything?'). The approach assumes liars will become more aroused by lying to relevant questions than to comparison questions, while those who are innocent of killing John will show higher levels of arousal to the comparison questions.
- *Directed Lie Test* – This uses similar questions to the comparison test, but the individual is instructed to lie to *all* comparison questions. This approach assumes a guilty person will show more arousal lying to relevant questions, while an innocent person will show most arousal lying to the comparison questions.
- *Concealed Information Test* – Rather than trying to detect arousal caused by lying, this approach attempts to detect arousal from recognition of 'guilty knowledge'.

The use of the polygraph has a long history dating back to the early 1920s in America, where it has been used in criminal investigations to induce confessions. However, despite claims of 80–90% accuracy by some advocates (see Grubin, 2008), there are downfalls to the polygraph that must be considered, namely: a lack of theory to establish a definitive relationship between deception and the physiological changes; a lack of standardisation across different polygraph tests (e.g. the presentation of the questions); as well as the measurement and quantification of the results. Moreover, some individuals may, unsurprisingly, attempt to fake the test in order to be found truthful through various techniques called **counter measures** (Ben-Shakhar, 2008).

Given the above, many might assert that the polygraph is not scientifically credible, arguing that it should not be used within criminal proceedings. Nevertheless, in England, legislation was passed in 2007 enabling a national trial of mandatory polygraph testing by the

> **COUNTER MEASURES** Techniques that may be used to invalidate a test assessing the 'truthfulness' of an individual. With the polygraph, this may be accomplished by actions such as lightly biting one's tongue or performing mental arithmetic when neutral (control) questions are asked. These actions would artificially elevate physiological arousal, making the distance between a 'lie' and a 'neutral' response too close to differentiate.

probation service (Grubin, 2008). The idea was that, used post-conviction, the polygraph does not have as many ethical implications (e.g. wrongfully convicting someone) and could be used for the supervision of sex offenders in the community, providing a more reliable and accurate sexual history and to ensure compliance. Following the success of this pilot (see Gannon et al., 2013), the Ministry of Justice (MoJ) announced in May 2014 that mandatory lie detector testing will be used by probation services across the UK on sex offenders. To read arguments for and against the use of this controversial tool, see Grubin (2008) and Ben-Shakhar (2008).

THE SILENT TALKER

Another method for detecting deception that has been developed is *The Silent Talker* (ST), a computer program created at Manchester Metropolitan University. It is a psychological profiling system that can apparently detect 93% of all human communication through detecting thousands of micro facial gestures which often go unnoticed to the naked eye. *The Silent Talker* claims to be the most accurate lie detection tool to date. It has been tested in laboratory settings and by a British police force (see Rothwell et al., 2006).

At present, no lie detection tool can adequately replace hard evidence, such as DNA at a crime scene. However, new tools are continually being created that claim high accuracy rates. What would this mean for police interviews, the courts, job interviews, airport security and much more? A world where people can no longer get away with lying would be a very different world from the one we are in now. Will the day come where we have a *Silent Talker* on our iPhones and we can point to someone's face to detect whether they are lying? Would that make life better or worse?

27.2.3 FALSE CONFESSIONS

A confession is when a suspect admits that they have committed a crime. This is one of the strongest forms of evidence presented in court. However, false confessions (when someone admits guilt for a crime they did not commit) also exist and this section will explore how and why this strange-sounding phenomenon occurs.

So why do people falsely confess? There are numerous factors that may lead someone to confess to a crime they did not commit. These can be split into two categories: (1) *situational factors* (e.g. police deception, intensity or length of the interrogation) and (2) *characteristics of the suspect* (such as age, intellectual functioning or mental health). Kassin and Wrightsman (1985) suggest three distinct types of false confession, each of which is outlined below. Consider for each type whether the false confession is likely to be mainly a result of situational factors or characteristics of the suspects.

1 *Voluntary false confessions* occur without any external pressure to confess. There are a variety of reasons why this is thought to occur, including a desire by individuals to achieve fame (or infamy), difficulty distinguishing between fact and fantasy, a feeling that they deserve punishment or to protect the real criminal. For example, in 1932, the toddler of the famous aviator Charles Lindbergh was kidnapped and later found murdered. During the investigation, more than 200 people falsely confessed to kidnapping the child. (See http://jimfisher.edinboro.edu/lindbergh/overview.html for more information.)

2 *Coerced (compliant) false confessions* occur when the suspect knows the confession is untrue but confesses in order to escape further questioning, to avoid an implied or explicit threat (such as 'if you don't confess now, we will have to beat the truth out of you') or to obtain a promised or implied reward (such as 'you can go home if you just say yes now'). A particularly famous example occurred in the 1989 case of a female jogger who was beaten, raped and left for dead in Central Park, New York, but survived the incident with no memory of it. Within two days, five teenagers, aged between 14 and 16, were arrested as suspects for the attack. During police interrogation, all five boys confessed to the crime. The confessions included descriptions of how they had committed the crime and even demonstrated remorse for the offence. Despite having no physical evidence of any of the suspects at the crime scene, the boys were arrested, convicted and imprisoned based on their confessions. Thirteen years later, while already imprisoned for murder and rape, Matias Reyes voluntarily confessed to the attack. DNA evidence corroborated his account of the offence and, in 2002, the original convictions were withdrawn and the five boys were released. The boys later explained that they had provided the confessions in the hope that they could then go home and stop the interrogation, but later withdrew their confessions once they realised this was not the case. In this case, one investigation resulted

in five false confessions. (See more about this case at www.falseconfessions.org/cases-the-exonerated/62-central-park-jogger-case.)

3 *Coerced (internalised) false confessions* occur when the suspect begins to question their own memory and wrongly believes that they actually committed the crime based on external information. This process is known as memory distrust syndrome. In 1998, 14-year-old Michael Crowe was arrested as a suspect for the murder of his sister, Stephanie. Initially, Michael completely denied any involvement in the murder but later stated that he was the killer. This followed three interrogation sessions in which Michael was told that he had failed a lie detector test, blood was found in his bedroom and his hair was at the crime scene, none of which was true. Unable to remember the stabbing, Michael was persuaded that he had blocked out the incident and therefore confessed, believing he had committed the offence. The charges against Michael were later dropped when a suspect was discovered and later convicted for the crime as a result of DNA evidence.

Coerced false confessions are typically the result of manipulative, suggestive or deceptive methods of interrogation. This is not surprising when, within the USA, a main objective of interrogation has been to obtain a confession, and police officers are still allowed to use deception to achieve this. For example, they may have informed their suspect that they have evidence (such as the suspect's DNA at the crime scene) when they do not. Within the UK, interrogation methods are less confrontational, police officers are not allowed to deceive suspects and all interviews are required to be video recorded.

27.2.4 EYEWITNESS TESTIMONY

Eyewitness testimony refers to an account given by someone of an event that they witnessed, which may be used as evidence in court. An eyewitness may also be asked to contribute to other aspects of the investigation, based on what they witnessed, for example, to identify the offender in a line-up. While it has an important role in investigations and may well be highly regarded evidence, it can also be unreliable. Refer to Chapter 5, section 5.3.1, for discussion of the influential research by Loftus et al. (1978) that first indicated just how unreliable eyewitness testimony can be and how it has influenced police procedures. The Innocence Project (DNA Exonerations Nationwide, n.d.; see www.innocenceproject.org/) reports that, of the 312 cases in which people were known to have been wrongfully convicted and later exonerated (due to DNA evidence) in the USA, 73% of these were due to incorrect identification by an eyewitness. Eyewitness testimony ultimately relies on the memory of the witness, which may be inaccurate for a number of reasons.

Numerous factors affect the accuracy of eyewitness testimony. Wells (1978) suggested these factors can be broadly categorised into two different types: *estimator variables* and *system variables*.

ESTIMATOR VARIABLES

Estimator variables occur at the time of the event and affect the encoding of the memory. They generally include both characteristics of the witness and characteristics of the event. Research has shown that witness characteristics affect eyewitness recall and identification (e.g. Wright & Stroud, 2002). The age of the witness has been consistently linked with identification performance, with young children and elderly people performing significantly worse than young adults (Pozzulo & Lindsay, 1998). Witnesses are better at recognising individuals of the same race, demonstrating an impairment in identification when the perpetrator is a different race from them. This is known as the cross-race effect (Michel et al., 2006). Another witness characteristic that affects recall is (perhaps not surprisingly) alcohol consumption (Yuille & Tollestrup, 1990). And no, recall does not get better the more one drinks!

Again, perhaps not surprisingly, research has demonstrated that distinctive, highly attractive (or highly unattractive) faces are more likely to be accurately recalled and therefore identified. Similarly, disguises, such as a mask, hat or sunglasses, reduce the chance of identification, while visual tattoos or body piercings increase the chance of identification (Wells & Olson, 2003). The presence of a weapon also reduces the accuracy of recall and identification (see key study below). Other characteristics that affect eyewitness memory and identification include fear and emotional stress, the amount of time the offender is in view, knowledge that the eyewitness is witnessing a crime, lighting conditions and the weather (Wells & Olson, 2003).

KEY STUDY

Loftus, E.F., Loftus, G.R., & Messo, J. (1987). Some facts about 'weapon focus'. *Law and Human Behavior, 11*(1), 55.

FIGURE 27.1 Weapon focus. If faced by someone with a gun, it is likely that you will focus on the gun and not notice key features of the person holding it

© gilotyna4/Shutterstock.com

Loftus, Loftus and Messo (1987) conducted two experiments examining the *weapon focus effect*, a phenomenon in which the presence of a weapon reduces the accuracy of recall and identification by witnesses (who tend to focus on the weapon instead of other vital identification aspects, such as the perpetrator's face!).

Experiment 1: Thirty-six university students were recruited and shown slides of customer interactions at a fast-food restaurant. Half the participants were shown the 'control' slides in which one of the customers hands over a cheque to the cashier, who then returns some money. The other half were shown the 'weapon' slides in which a customer pulls a gun on the cashier, who then hands over some money. Participant eye movements were recorded throughout the experiment and the results indicated that participants shown the 'weapon' slides looked more frequently and for longer periods of time at the gun (in comparison with the amount of time the other group viewed the cheque).

Experiment 2: Eighty university students were recruited, split into two groups and shown the same slides as in experiment 1. After viewing, participants were asked to complete a 12-item multiple choice test relating to the person with the gun/cheque and also asked to identify them in a 12-person line-up. Results indicated that the 'weapon' group were less accurate on both the test and line-up, demonstrating poorer memory than the 'control' group. These findings provided the first direct empirical support for the weapon focus effect.

SYSTEM VARIABLES

System variables are under the control of the CJS and occur during the retrieval of a memory within police investigations. They include line-up characteristics and instructions, and the behaviour of those running the line-up (Smith et al., 2001). For example, the individual administering the line-up (often an officer working on the case) can impact upon eyewitness identification by communicating knowledge regarding the suspect, or by making post-identification suggestions that will alter witness certainty. Pre-line-up instructions are also important for eyewitness identification. When witnesses are informed that the actual culprit 'might' or 'might not' be present in the line-up (as opposed to having no information as to whether the culprit is there or not), the misidentification rates are reduced (Steblay, 1997).

27.3 OFFENCES AND THEORIES EXPLORED

This section will examine as examples two major types of crime: sexual and violent offending. We will look at some facts and figures about each, and consider the victims and perpetrators of each of these broad categories of offences. We will then go on to explore the offences of adult rape, non-contact sex offences, robbery and murder in more depth, considering a number of psychological theories that can be applied to explain why people commit these crimes. We only have space in this chapter to briefly examine one theory relating to each offence, but Winder and Banyard (2012) comprehensively review the various theories for each offence (see suggested reading at the end of this chapter).

EXERCISE: JURY DECISION MAKING

Imagine you are a member of a jury for a murder case. On the first day the defendant arrives at court wearing a tracksuit and has tattoos. What would be your first impression of them? Do you think this would impact upon your decision making as a member of the jury? Would you feel any differently if they were smartly dressed? Would their gender or age make any difference to your judgements? Think about this and write down any factors that you think might affect your decision as a member of the jury. Try to explain the reasons you have written down.

27.3.1 SEXUAL OFFENDING

There are approximately 55,000 police-recorded sexual offences in England and Wales each year (Ministry of Justice, 2013a). The most frequent sexual offence was sexual assault (42%), followed by rape (31%) and then **exhibitionism** and **voyeurism** combined (12%). In 2013, there were 43,664 individuals registered as sexual offenders in the UK (Ministry of Justice, 2013a). The large majority of convicted sexual offenders are males, with women accounting for just under 1% of the sex offender population in prison (Ministry of Justice, 2013b). It is interesting to note that the psychiatric definitions of some of the sexual disorders that lead to offending are not necessarily exactly the same as the legal definitions.

EXHIBITIONISM The purposeful exposure of genitals with the intention that someone will see them and be alarmed or distressed. This is a sexual offence.

VOYEURISM The watching of others without their knowledge for the purpose of sexual gratification.

ADULT RAPE

The definition of rape, as provided by the Sexual Offences Act (Home Office, 2003), is the 'intentional penetration of the vagina, anus or mouth, without the person's consent and with no reasonable belief that the person consents'

EXERCISE: RAPE MYTHS

Read the following statements regarding rape and consider whether you believe them to be true or false:

1. Rape is sexually motivated
2. The majority of rapes are planned
3. Rapists are clinically unwell
4. A man cannot rape his wife
5. One in 20 women are rape victims
6. Male rape is homosexual
7. Women often make false claims
8. Prostitutes can be raped
9. Rapists are mostly strangers
10. Intoxicated people cannot consent

Refer to the end of the chapter for discussion of these.

(c. 42, p. 1). Over the years, the definition of rape has had to be expanded to expressly include the recognition of marital rape (in 1991) and male rape (in 1994), as well as the inclusion of oral penetration. Clarification of the term 'consent' has also been included in the Sexual Offences Act (2003).

FACTS AND FIGURES

Data released by the Ministry of Justice (2013b) indicate that 15,670 incidents of rape are recorded by the police on average per year. This equates to around 43 rapes being reported each day in England and Wales. However, we know that many sexual offences go unreported and, as such, it is estimated that the actual number of people raped on average per year are 60,000–90,000 (Office for National Statistics, 2013a).

THE VICTIMS

In the large majority of adult rape incidents, the victim is female, with only 8% of incidents reported to the police involving male victims (Ministry of Justice, 2013b). Myhill and Allen (2002) suggest that females aged 16–24 are most at risk.

THE OFFENDERS

Rapists are often separated into two broad categories: stranger (not known to the victim) and acquaintance (known to the victim for more than 24 hours). Research suggests that victims usually know the rapist. For example, Howitt (2012) found that 45% were a current partner, 16% were acquaintances, 11% were dates, 11% were ex-partners, 10% were other intimates and only 8% were strangers.

A number of typologies for understanding rapists have been suggested. Knight and Prentky (1990, as detailed in Langton & Marshall, 2001) reported a typology that categorised rapists into four main types according to their motivation: (1) *opportunistic*: looking for immediate sexual gratification, may use aggression, especially in the face of victim resistance, carried out by individuals with a history of anti-social behaviour; (2) *pervasively angry*: with a history of anti-social and aggressive behaviour; (3) *sexual*: includes both sadistic and non-sadistic forms – the individual has entrenched sexual preoccupation and motivation for rape, typically highly planned and rehearsed assaults, involving the playing out of deviant fantasies; (4) *vindictive*: the intention of the offence is to harm and/or humiliate victims rather than to live out paraphilic fantasies of rapist. The offence typically involves some form of aggression, from verbal threats to serious physical assault and potentially victim death.

While a number of typologies of rapists have been developed to help us understand why people commit the act of rape, the reality does not always provide such a perfect fit – individual rapists may differ on a number of personal characteristics, although anger and/or the desire for control and/or sexual preoccupation all feature highly in explanations of rape.

COGNITIVE DISTORTIONS AND RAPE

Cognitive distortions are 'articulated thoughts, attitudes and beliefs that seem to support sexual offending' (Fisher & Beech, 2007: 31), and almost all rapists will demonstrate cognitive distortions, such as claiming that the woman 'led them on' or 'wanted it' as a means of justifying their behaviour. These distortions can help us to understand the thought processes of a rapist. However, it is unclear whether they are present before the offence, playing a causative role, or whether they occur after the offence as a way of individuals excusing their behaviour or minimising blame.

More recent work considers the role of more entrenched cognitions (such as implicit theories) in providing motivations or explanations for sexual offending. Implicit theories develop in childhood and are used by individuals to explain their own and others' behaviour. They may also help us to understand people's future behaviours. Based on the original work with child abusers (Ward & Keenan, 1999), five implicit theories have been put forward as being typical or prominent in adult rapists, namely:

1 *Entitlement*: This proposes that men are entitled to have their needs, including sexual needs, met *on demand*. There is little, if any, consideration of the rights or needs of potential victims.
2 *Dangerous world*: Here the world is viewed as a dangerous place in which other people are likely to behave in an abusive or rejecting way. If women are perceived as rejecting to the individual, they may become selected as targets upon which the offender can retaliate and assert his dominance.

3   *Women as sex objects*: Women are perceived as constantly desiring sex, even if this is coerced or violent, with their main purpose being to meet the sexual needs of men, whenever such needs arise.

4   *Male sex drive is uncontrollable*: The male sex drive is viewed as difficult to manage, with women viewed as having a key part in this loss of control. Offending is attributed to external factors, such as the behaviour or apparel of the victim.

5   *Women are unknowable/dangerous*: This suggests that women are inherently different from men, a difference that men cannot understand. Women are seen as deceptive, and they do not communicate their beliefs and desires honestly to men. This last theory promotes negative views of women as dangerous and facilitates harm towards them (Fisher & Beech, 2007; Polaschek & Ward, 2002).

NON-CONTACT SEXUAL OFFENCES

As the name suggests, non-contact sex offences occur without any physical contact between the offender and the victim. The two most common non-contact sex offences (aside from internet sex offences) are voyeurism and exhibitionism.

> **DSM-5** The Diagnostic Statistical Manual of Mental Disorders (5th edition) (DSM-5, 2013) is a handbook which details criteria for diagnosing mental disorders. It is widely used by practitioners.

Voyeurism involves the offender watching others without their knowledge and gaining sexual gratification from this. A more common term used is 'peeping'. In psychiatric terms, voyeurism is defined as voyeuristic disorder (**DSM-5**; American Psychiatric Association, 2013): recurrent, intense sexual arousal from watching an unsuspecting person who is naked, while engaging in sexual activity. These urges or fantasies have to be present for a period of at least six months and the person must have acted on these urges, or the urges must be causing distress or impairment in the person's life. However, this is a narrow criterion for defining voyeurism as it states that victims should be in the process of undressing, be naked or involved in sexual activity. In reality, voyeurs may be sexually interested in watching a wide range of behaviours, such as defecating and urinating. Others enjoy looking at underwear or intimate parts of the body that the victim did not intend to show. The common themes in these behaviours are that the voyeur enjoys watching others engaging in behaviours that are private and/or not intended by the victim to be viewed by others. For the voyeur, it holds an element of secrecy that they are viewing others when they shouldn't be.

The legal definition of voyeurism is less restrictive and accounts for generally 'private' behaviours that were not intended to be seen by others. The Sexual Offences Act (2003) defines voyeurism as committing an offence to obtain sexual gratification through observing another person in private and knowing the person does not consent to this. This also includes recording other people or installing/altering equipment or structures for this purpose.

Exhibitionism involves the offender exposing themselves, usually their genitals, to victims, while sometimes also making suggestions or comments. The more common term used is 'flashing'. This usually occurs in public, but quiet, locations, with the aim of gaining sexual pleasure from exposing to unsuspecting strangers. The aim may be to cause shock or fear in the victims or the offender may hope that the victim will wish to engage in sexual contact.

> **PARAPHILIC DISORDER** When an atypical sexual interest causes significant distress to the individual or harm to others. Note that it is not considered a disorder to have an atypical sexual interest *per se*.

In psychiatric terms, exhibitionism is defined as exhibitionistic disorder (DSM-5; American Psychiatric Association, 2013): a **paraphilic disorder** in which the individual has 'recurrent intense sexually arousing fantasies, sexual urges or behaviours involving exposing one's genitals to an unsuspecting person over a period of at least six months and which cause distress or impairment in functioning for the individual'.

In legal terms, exhibitionism is known as exposure. It does not require the behaviour to be persistent, or for sexual gratification to be gained (as with 'real' exhibitionism), in order to be legally classed as an exhibitionist and to gain a conviction for this. The Sexual Offences Act (2003) defines exposure as the intentional exposure of genitals with the intention that someone will see them and be alarmed or distressed.

FACTS AND FIGURES

Official police statistics indicate that there are approximately 7,000 incidents of voyeurism or exhibitionism reported to the police in England and Wales each year (Ministry of Justice, 2013b). However, as with rape and all other sexual offences, non-contact sex offences are under-reported and difficult to detect. For instance, if a voyeur's victim is unaware they are being watched, how can they report the offence? Victim self-report research provides a better indicator of the prevalence of exhibitionism, with research suggesting that 33% of a university sample of students (Clark et al., 2014) and between 40% and 48% of community samples of women have been exposed to at some point in their lives (Murphy & Page, 2008).

THE VICTIMS

Non-contact sex offenders usually accrue a large number of victims in comparison to contact offenders, with extreme estimates asserting there are an average of 513 victims of exhibitionism per offender (Abel et al., 1987). Victims are typically young adult females. However, children and adolescents can also be the victim of such crimes, with research indicating that the reported age of first exposure for victims of exhibitionism is between 10 and 16 years (Clark et al., 2014).

THE OFFENDERS

The perpetrators of non-contact sex offences are usually strangers to their victims. There is a general consensus that such offences begin at an early age, although the offender may continue to offend in this way throughout their lives unless they are convicted and/or treated. Non-contact sex offences are committed by both males and females, but more commonly males, with women also less likely to be convicted (Hocken & Thorne, 2012).

COURTSHIP DISORDER

One theory that specifically attempts to explain voyeurism and exhibitionism, as well as other sexual offences, is courtship disorder (Freund, 1990). Within this, the courtship process is viewed as having four phases and it is assumed that individuals move through these. Relating this to sexual offending, offenders are viewed as trying to form a relationship through these same phases but are unable to achieve this and instead get stuck in one phase of the process. Disturbances in each of the four phases relates to particular sexual offences. Phase one involves looking for a partner (voyeurism). Phase two involves pre-tactile (non-contact) interaction, such as talking or non-verbal communication (exhibitionism, *telephone scatologia* (see Aside). Phase three involves tactile interactions (contact), such as kissing, embracing or holding hands (*frotteurism* (see Aside). Phase four involves sexual intercourse (rape).

While this theory is consistent and fits well with other research – for example, exhibitionists commonly report the desire for their victims to want sexual intercourse (Bader et al., 2008) – it is often criticised as it fails to explain how offenders get stuck in one phase of the process or why they do not progress and form relationships with non-victims (Morin & Levenson, 2008).

27.3.2 VIOLENT OFFENDING

Violent crime covers a wide range of offences, from assault (which may or may not result in physical harm), to serious incidents of domestic violence, wounding and murder. Police-recorded crime statistics report approximately 600,000

ASIDE

Telephone scatologia and frotteurism

Ever heard of people making rude phone calls to strangers? Or thought that someone was standing a little too close on a busy tram? These may be offences too. Telephone scatologia involves the offender making obscene phone calls to strangers in which they make inappropriate comments, threats or breathe heavily. Frotteurism involves the offender gaining sexual arousal from touching or pressing themselves against strangers, usually in busy places, such as public transport, where it will be less obvious. This is a contact offence whereas telephone scatologia is classed as non-contact.

violent offences against the person in England and Wales each year (Office for National Statistics, 2013b). However, the **Crime Survey for England and Wales** (CSEW), which is a measure of self-reported crime, indicates 1.9 million violent incidents in this time period, demonstrating that violent crime is grossly under-reported (Office for National Statistics, 2013b). According to the CSEW, after assault without injury, wounding accounted for 24% of all violence, followed by assault with minor injury (22%) and robbery (12%).

When considering violent offending, it is important to consider the definition of both violence and aggression: 'Human aggression is any behaviour directed toward another individual that is carried out with the proximate (immediate) intent to cause harm. In addition, the perpetrator must believe that the behavior will harm the target and that the target is motivated to avoid the behaviour' (Bushman & Anderson, 2001: 274). In comparison, 'violence is aggression that has extreme harm as its goal (e.g. death)' (Anderson & Bushman, 2002: 29). It is generally accepted across the literature that there can be aggression without violence, but not violence without aggression. Within the definition of violence (as with aggression), two distinct types are suggested, based on their motivation:

> **CRIME SURVEY FOR ENGLAND AND WALES** A questionnaire that measures the extent of crime through asking a representative sample of UK households if they have experienced crime in the last year. This differs from police-recorded crime figures that are limited to offences that are brought to the attention of the police and so are lower than those in the CSEW.

- *Instrumental violence*: To achieve a goal (e.g. attaining money)
- *Affective violence*: Emotionally motivated, impulsive, angry (i.e. reactive as opposed to considered) with an intention to hurt.

ROBBERY

'Robbery is an offence in which force or the threat of force is used either during or immediately prior to a theft or attempted theft' (Office for National Statistics, 2013b: 33). It can involve threats, violence and/or use of force and could involve weapons, for example, in armed robbery (Porter, 2010). There are various types of robbery, as outlined by the Crown Prosecution Service (2012): street robbery or mugging; robberies of small businesses; less sophisticated commercial robberies; violent personal robberies in the home; professionally planned commercial robberies.

FACTS AND FIGURES

In the year ending June 2013, 62,634 incidents of robbery were reported to the police (Office for National Statistics, 2013b). However, self-report indicates that 172,000 incidents were committed (Office for National Statistics, 2013b), suggesting that around 60% of robbery offences are not reported. Of those reported, around 90% were against personal property and the remainder were against business property. In addition, around 21% involved a knife/sharp instrument. Incidents of robbery are concentrated in specific geographical areas, with London recording over half of all robberies and the West Midlands, Greater Manchester and West Yorkshire reporting 18% combined.

THE VICTIMS

Smith's Home Office report (2003) indicates that robbery victims are predominantly young, with just over 50% being aged between 16 and 20. Victims are also predominantly male (76%).

THE OFFENDERS

Smith (2003) demonstrated that robbery offenders are also predominantly young, with just over 50% being aged between 16 and 20. The number of young robbery suspects has increased dramatically over the years: the proportion of suspects aged 11–15 was 15% in 1993 and increased to 36% in 2000, with males being the predominant suspects (94%). Female perpetrators of robbery are very rare, accounting for 6% of suspects. In addition, a large number of robberies occur in open public areas, normally the street, but also alleyways, parks, footpaths and subways. Those who commit personal robberies are more likely to commit them in groups of two or more, and at night time, with half occurring between 6 pm and 2 am, and half at the weekend. In addition, weapons are used in just over one in three personal robberies. Knives are the most commonly used weapon (21% of the time), whereas, in the UK, guns are only used 3% of the time.

FIGURE 27.2 Robbery. There's robbery and there's daylight robbery. Fred Goodwin led the Royal Bank of Scotland to the brink of insolvency in 2008 and it was only rescued by the injection of billions of pounds from UK taxpayers. If the bank had gone bust, Goodwin would have been entitled to a pension of £28,000 per year starting at age 65. As it was, because of the government rescue, he was able to resign on a pension of over £700,000 a year starting at age 50. Now that's daylight robbery

© Marco Secchi/Corbis

EXPLAINING ROBBERY THROUGH RATIONAL CHOICE THEORY

A dominant theory used to attempt to explain robbery is rational choice theory (RCT). RCT explains offending behaviour as arising from aiming to benefit oneself through criminal acts. Doing so involves making decisions and rational choices based upon the perceived risks and benefits of the act (Cornish & Clarke, 2013). The theory adopts a crime-specific focus, rather than focusing on the offender. For example, an offender may carefully select times when elderly people may be likely to collect their pensions from the Post Office, demonstrating a degree of planning. This active choice may also be due to the reduction of risk involved when targeting somebody who is vulnerable, thus reducing the potential cost of committing the act. In addition, RCT explains that an individual will offend when there are clear benefits – with robbery, there is clear financial or material gain. It has been argued that this theory focuses on economic gains, leading to criticism of its capacity to explain expressive crimes of hostility, anger and excitement (Hayward, 2007). However, RCT explicitly states that decisions may be rudimentary and constrained by time, leading to more impulsive actions, such as an offender assaulting the victim after being caught, but nonetheless, rational choices are still apparent.

MURDER

Murder is when a sane person unlawfully kills another person, and the act is neither done in self-defence, nor justified in any way, as defined by the Crown Prosecution Service. Homicide has a broader definition, which encapsulates all types of killing (including murder), regardless of motive. Definitions of several other types of homicide are as follows:

Manslaughter: (1) Killing with intent but where partial defence applies, (2) conduct that is grossly negligent, or (3) committing a dangerous and unlawful act that results in death.

Corporate manslaughter: An organisation causes a person's death and this is due to a breach of relevant duty of care of the organisation to the deceased.

Infanticide: Where a woman causes the death of her child (aged under 12 months).

(from Crown Prosecution Service, n.d.)

FACTS AND FIGURES

There are 500–600 police-recorded homicides in England and Wales each year (Office for National Statistics, 2013b), and there is a general trend of decline (in 2003, there were 1,047 police-recorded homicides). However, this downward trend should be treated with caution as in 2003, 172 of the homicides were attributed to Harold Shipman, and 52 homicides in 2006 were a result of the London bombings. Thus, data in any year can be skewed by multiple, mass or serial killings.

THE VICTIMS

Homicide statistics indicate that more adults have been victims of homicide than children (Office for National Statistics, 2013a), and that the majority of victims aged under 16 were killed by a parent or carer (60%), with more than two-thirds of victims being male. Female victims were more likely to be killed by someone they knew and, in most cases, the perpetrator was a current or ex-partner (51% of all female victims). In comparison, male victims were most likely to be killed by a friend or acquaintance (39%).

THE OFFENDERS

Statistics indicate that a sharp instrument is the most common method of killing (39%) (Office for National Statistics, 2013a); hitting or kicking without a weapon is the second most common, and this is much more common with male victims. In comparison, strangulation or asphyxiation is the second most common method with female victims. Over half of homicides (59%) result from a quarrel, an attack of revenge or a loss of temper, and these increase when the suspect was known to the victim (68%) (Office for National Statistics, 2013a). Due to the fact that almost three-fifths of homicides are centred around a close relationship (or at least the suspect is known to the victim), conviction rates for homicide are high in England and Wales.

UNDERSTANDING MURDER WITH SOCIAL LEARNING THEORY

There have been many psychological theories applied to violent acts such as murder in an attempt to explain them. One such theory is Bandura's social learning theory (1977), proposing that people learn how to act from others, through observation, imitation, reinforcement and modelling. In application to criminal behaviour, those who witness violent acts as a child or are a victim of abuse (or even watch numerous violent films) may be more likely to go on to commit similar violent acts, which may result in murder. Research supports this notion, asserting that exposure to some sort of violence during childhood appears to be a contributing factor in the background of those who go on to commit murder (see Allely et al., 2014).

27.4 IMPRISONMENT, REHABILITATION AND RESETTLEMENT

In this final section, we will discuss the aftermath of an offence, and the processes involved in imprisonment. The largest employer of forensic psychologists in England and Wales is the prison service, and this is where a large amount of forensic psychology's work is based. Forensic psychology's largest focus within prison is on the rehabilitation or treatment of offenders and these are the areas we will focus on in this chapter. Forensic psychology also impacts upon prison processes, for example, in the risk assessments of perpetrators, the area of resettlement, as well as analysing why people stop offending (desistance). We will start with the types of sentence that offenders may receive from the courts, and briefly cover some of the topics outlined above.

27.4.1 IMPRISONMENT

There are various sentencing avenues, dependent upon the type, seriousness and circumstances of a crime and the maximum penalty available by law:

- long prison sentence (for 'life', or with a long tariff of years to be spent in prison);
- short prison sentence (typically referring to sentences of 12 months or fewer);
- suspended sentence (offender does not go to prison unless they commit an additional offence while serving their 'suspended' sentence);
- community order (curfew, tagging, supervision, unpaid work, treatment);
- fine;
- discharge (no punishment is imposed and the offender is free to leave the court).

The Criminal Justice Act 2003 (s. 152(2); Home Office, 2003) states that imprisonment should occur only if the offence is 'so serious that neither a fine alone nor a community sentence can be justified'. Less serious crimes are sentenced in the Magistrates' Courts, where a maximum 12-month sentence can be given. More serious crimes are sent to the Crown Court, where they have increased sentencing powers. Certain crimes can only be tried in the Crown Court, on account of their seriousness (such as robbery, murder and rape).

> **RESTORATIVE JUSTICE (RJ)** Where the perpetrator of an offence is brought into communication with either the victim of their offence or someone harmed by their offence. RJ holds offenders to account for their crime and helps them to understand the impact of their actions, take responsibility for them and make amends.

The UK Criminal Justice Act (2003) outlines that the purpose of sentencing is to: (1) punish offenders; (2) reduce crime (including reduction by deterrence); (3) reform and rehabilitate offenders; (4) protect the public; and (5) make reparation by offenders to persons affected by their offences (e.g. **restorative justice** measures). When a judge or magistrate is giving a sentence, they must consider all of these aims.

27.4.2 RISK ASSESSMENTS

Risk assessment is concerned with the prediction of a person's risk of reoffending, and the subsequent management of this risk. Within a prison setting, this is a crucial part of a prisoner's sentence. A person's risk score will impact upon the type of psychological treatment they receive and may affect the result of their parole board review. There are different approaches to risk assessment within forensic psychology, and the main distinction is between actuarial and structured clinical risk assessments. *Actuarial risk assessments* involve answering a set number of specific questions, for example, the number of previous convictions, age at first offence, and so on. The answers to the questions are totalled and a risk score is produced that corresponds to a risk category (e.g. low, medium, high or very high). This type of risk tool is based on *static risk factors*, that is, factors that cannot change. An example of this is the Static-99, which is used with adult male sexual offenders (see www.static99.org/ for more information about this respected static risk measure).

> **CRIMINOGENIC NEEDS** Characteristics, traits and factors that are strongly correlated with reoffending. These needs are targeted in treatment so that they 'change', thereby reducing the likelihood of that individual reoffending.

We are also interested in *dynamic risk factors* which are aspects of risk that can be changed and so are of great interest to a forensic psychologist. These include personality characteristics that increase the risk of reoffending but which can be changed through treatment, as well as understanding the factors in an offender's immediate environment or in the offender's behaviour that may increase their risk of reoffending. *Structured (clinical) risk assessments* (again, based on evidence derived from research) are used to ascertain an individual's dynamic risk and, consequently, what their treatment (**criminogenic**) needs are. An example of a structured risk assessment used in the UK is the SARN (Structured Assessment of Risk and Need) (Webster et al., 2006). This is used to look at treatment needs for sexual offenders across four domains: sexual interests, self-management, distorted attitudes and the management of relationships. This leads us nicely onto the topic of treatments for offenders.

27.4.3 TREATMENT IN PRISON

The mainstream psychological treatments available within prisons are based upon the cognitive behavioural therapy model and are referred to as Offender Behaviour Programmes (OBPs). There are many different types of programme to address various aspects of offender behaviour. For example, the *Thinking Skills Programme* addresses thinking and behaviour associated with offending, such as problem solving and perspective taking. Another standard programme is the *Sex Offender Treatment Programme*, which targets specific risk areas related to sexual offending, such as attitudes that support sexual offending. OBPs usually form part of a prisoner's sentence plan. If you are interested in reading more about the treatments themselves, see Chapter 25 and, in particular, the section on cognitive-behavioural interventions.

27.4.4 RESETTLEMENT

Following a person's prison sentence, they are released back into the community. This process is called *resettlement* and refers to a prisoner's effective reintegration into the community. This is a vital area within forensic psychology, as resettlement needs are strongly related to criminogenic needs and, if unmet, can lead to reoffending.

KEY RESEARCHER Ruth Mann

FIGURE 27.3 Ruth Mann

Dr Ruth Mann is a chartered and registered forensic psychologist employed by the National Offender Management Service (NOMS) where she is the Head of Evidence for the NOMS Commissioning Strategies Group. In this role, Ruth monitors and translates research findings in the literature to inform the commissioning of research and practice so that it is evidence based. She also conducts and manages research projects designed to develop gaps in the evidence base. In this capacity, her current research interests concern the evaluation of prison-based rehabilitation initiatives, the measurement of prison culture, and the features of effective staff–prisoner relationships.

Ruth began her career as a prison psychologist working in a high security prison. She then worked as a Sex Offending Treatment Programme Treatment Manager and Head of Psychology in a large London prison, before moving to HM Prison Service Headquarters (now NOMS) where she managed the NOMS national strategy for the assessment and treatment of sexual offending, including the development, implementation, support and evaluation of sex offending treatment programmes in prison and probation. While working in this specific field, Ruth published numerous research and clinical articles and book chapters. She has published and lectured extensively on the rehabilitation of people convicted of crime. Ruth is highly influential in her current role, but is best known for her work on the assessment and treatment of sexual offenders. In 2010, Ruth received the BPS Division of Forensic Psychology senior award for her contribution to forensic psychology in the UK.

Historically, resettlement was aimed at meeting offenders' welfare needs and was often supported by volunteers and charities (Maguire & Raynor, 2006). However, since the 1960s, the probation service has been responsible for voluntary aftercare. Following this, there was a gradual decline in the number of offenders who received support, particularly those who had served a sentence of less than 12 months, and this is the most likely reason for the disproportionately high reconviction rates among this group (Boorman & Hopkins, 2012). In response, a refocus on resettlement began, and a number of reviews were produced to identify ways to tackle resettlement issues.

The Social Exclusion Unit (2002) was one of the earliest reports to spark a return to resettlement as a priority. The report highlighted nine areas of need: employment; education; drug and alcohol misuse; mental and physical health; attitudes and self control; institutionalisation and life skills; housing; financial support and debt; and family. In 2004 the 'Reducing Reoffending National Action Plan' was produced by the Home Office. It identified seven resettlement pathways to reduce reoffending: education training and employment; accommodation; physical and mental health; drugs and alcohol; family support; finance, benefits and debt; and thinking and behaviour (Maguire & Raynor, 2006). Many changes have come about in order to address these pathways, for example, **end-to-end offender management** and **throughcare**, multi-agency provisions for offenders dependent on need (e.g. **Multi Agency Public Protection Arrangements (MAPPA)** and Offending Behaviour

END-TO-END OFFENDER MANAGEMENT Taking care of offenders from their first contact with the correctional services right through to the very end of their sentence.

THROUGHCARE The provision of a range of social work and other services to prisoners and their families, from the point of sentence or remand, continuing throughout imprisonment, and following release into the community. The services are focused on helping ex-prisoners resettle into the community.

MULTI AGENCY PUBLIC PROTECTION ARRANGEMENTS (MAPPA) Comprise members of the National Probation Service, prison service and police who together oversee the management of high-risk sex offenders, violent offenders and other types of sexual offender who pose a serious risk of harm to the public.

KEY STUDY

Wilson, R.J., Picheca, J., & Prinzo, M. (2005). *Circles of support and accountability: an evaluation of the pilot project in South-Central Ontario.* **Ottawa: Correctional Service of Canada.**

Circles of Support and Accountability (CoSA) is a resettlement project aimed at promoting effective resettlement and reintegration into the community for sexual offenders. Circles comprise four volunteers and a 'core member' (sex offender), and they aim to meet once a week to provide the core member with emotional and practical support, as well as providing a form of supervision. Starting in Canada, one of the earliest models was evaluated by Wilson, Picheca and Prinzo (2005). They compared sex offenders who were taking part in CoSA to those who were not, matching them on relevant factors, including risk, previous treatment and time in the community. They followed the groups up for approximately 4.5 years and found that the overall reconviction rates of the CoSA group were half the rate of the comparison group (8.3% and 16.7%, respectively). In addition, the sexual reconviction rates of the CoSA group were just over a quarter of the expected rate, whereas the comparison groups' reconviction rates were well over half the expected rate. Even where there was a sexual reconviction in the CoSA group, these were 'less severe or invasive than the offence for which they had most recently served a sentence' (Wilson et al., 2005: 332). Thus, this resettlement initiative is seen to have had a great impact on improving sexual and violent reoffending rates, and the method is now utilised across the UK (see the Circles UK website: www.circles-uk.org.uk/).

Programmes in the community). One of the biggest recent changes is that individuals serving prison sentences of fewer than 12 months will also now receive community supervision.

27.5 CHAPTER SUMMARY

This chapter has touched upon some of the vital and growing areas within forensic psychology today. The field can impact upon many different processes within the police and courts, and the research and evidence base in this area is ever expanding as new discoveries are becoming crucial to criminal investigations. In addition, valuable research is being conducted into understanding why people offend (and thus what we can put in place to prevent them offending in the first place). Finally, we explored forensic psychology and treatment within the prison system. If you are interested in becoming a forensic psychologist, the chances are that you will find yourself working with prisoners in treatment. The work is rewarding and yet difficult, an epitaph that could apply to almost all areas of forensic psychology. In an introductory chapter such as this, we have only been able to skim the surface of what the world of forensic psychology can offer you; some suggested further reading is provided below.

? DISCUSSION QUESTIONS

What are the implications of some of the theories of offending discussed in this chapter on the treatment of offenders?
How do you think forensic psychology can impact upon crime prevention?
What are some of the implications of using the polygraph as a lie detection tool in criminal proceedings in the UK?
What factors account for the low levels of reporting in some violent and sexual offences?
What are the difficulties in assessing risk?

SUGGESTIONS FOR FURTHER READING

Kapardis, A. (2014). *Psychology and law: a critical introduction* (4th edn). Cambridge and New York: Cambridge University Press. This book provides a comprehensive guide to the psychological issues involved in different aspects of the law and the criminal justice system and provides more detail on those discussed within this chapter. Some of the topics covered include: witnesses, jury decision making, offender profiling and restorative justice.

Maruna, S. (2001). *Making good: how ex-convicts reform and rebuild their lives.* Washington, DC: American Psychological Association. This book explores the narratives of repeat offenders in order to consider the possibility of offender reform and rehabilitation, considering why some offenders are able to desist from or stop committing crime while others continue.

Winder, B., & Banyard, P. (2012). *A psychologist's casebook of crime: from arson to voyeurism.* London: Palgrave Macmillan. This readable book takes the unusual approach of exploring the world of forensic psychology on a crime-by-crime basis. It covers a range of crimes, including arson, paedophilia, murder, shoplifting, burglary, and takes the reader through various facts and figures about the offences as well as the psychological theories associated with each. The recommendation here is nothing to do with its two editors both being co-editors of this book, honest.

The Innocence Project www.innocenceproject.org/). This is an organisation devoted to justice, and dedicated to exonerating people who have been wrongfully convicted of crimes using 'hard' evidence (such as DNA testing). To really engage with the reality of wrongful conviction, listen to the album 'Black robes and lawyers' by William Dillon, and read his story at:

www.innocenceproject.org/Content/William_Dillon.php

The Safer Living Foundation (www.saferlivingfoundation.org).

FIGURE 27.4 SLF logo

The Safer Living Foundation is a joint venture between HMP Whatton, Nottingham Trent University, the National Probation Trust (East Midlands) and Nottinghamshire Police. It is a registered charity, whose aims are:

- to promote for the benefit of the public the protection of people from, and the prevention of, sexual crime;
- to promote for the public benefit the rehabilitation of persons who have committed or are likely to commit offences, particularly sexual offences against others.

Projects that the SLF is involved with include Whatton Circles of Support and Accountability (see key study above) and the Safer Living Foundation Prevention Project (inspired by the Dunkelfeld project: www.dont-offend.org/), which offers treatment to individuals who are sexually attracted to children and concerned that they may offend.

DISCUSSION OF EXERCISES

The term 'rape myths' surfaced in the 1970s to describe stereotypical, prejudiced and false beliefs or attitudes that shift the blame for rape from the perpetrator to the victim; for example, that a woman is asking to be raped by wearing a short skirt. Rape myths are still prevalent within the general public and the CJS, and still influence how victims and perpetrators are viewed.

1 Rape is sexually motivated ... myth!

Rapists often have stable sexual partners and so do not need to commit rape to achieve sexual gratification. Rape is an act of violence, and although sexual attraction can be an influential factor, it is not necessarily a primary motive.

2 The majority of rapes are planned ... fact!

A common myth is that victims (typically, women) incite men to rape, or that they are 'asking for it' by the way that they dress, etc. However, the victim has no control over this, as according to rape crisis centre data, the majority of rapes are premeditated.

3 Rapists are clinically unwell ... myth!

Research suggests that very few rapists are psychotic, mentally ill or referred for psychiatric treatment. The majority are sane and mentally well.

4 A man cannot rape his wife ... myth!

A common myth is that within a marriage a man has a right to engage in sex with his wife. However, since 1991, marital rape has been formally recognised as an offence and enshrined in the Sexual Offences Act 2003.

5 One in 20 women are rape victims ... fact!

British Crime Survey data indicates that approximately one in 20 women had been raped, and one in 10 women had experienced some form of sexual victimisation.

6 Male rape is homosexual ... myth!

Male rape victims often have concerns about reporting the offence to the police due to the embarrassment of having been sexually assaulted by another male. However, for the large majority of male rape cases, the rapist is heterosexual and often in a stable relationship with a woman.

7 Women often make false claims ... myth!

Rape, along with other sexual assaults, is grossly under-reported, with the reason for many being the fear of not being believed. Media focus on the very small number of cases of false allegations increases the perception that this is common. The Crown Prosecution Service (2013) confirmed false allegations of rape to be 'very rare' and suggest that they account for less than 1% of reports.

8 Prostitutes can be raped ... fact!

It is a common myth that prostitutes cannot be raped. However, prostitutes have the same rights to consent as anyone else, and the payment given by clients only applies to consensual activity.

9 Rapists are mostly strangers in dark alleys ... myth!

There is a common belief that most rapes occur at night, in dark alleys by a stranger. In reality, only around 8% of rapes are committed by a stranger, with the majority committed by someone known to the victim, and often in their homes or workplace.

10 Intoxicated people cannot consent … fact!

If a person is intoxicated, unconscious or their judgement is severely impaired by drugs or alcohol, legally they are incapable of giving consent. Any sexual activity under these circumstances (where the person does not have the capacity to give consent) may be sexual assault. Rapists cannot be excused due to intoxication. Of course, where both individuals are equally intoxicated, this would not be considered sexual assault by one person on the other – courts would look at where there was evidence that one person was substantially and substantively more impaired than the other through, for example, CCTV or witness evidence.

Still want more? For links to online resources relevant to this chapter and a quiz to test your understanding, visit the companion website at edge.sagepub.com/banyard2e

GLOSSARY

5-alpha reductase syndrome   Individuals who are genetically male but appear to be female at birth. During puberty, male genitalia then develop and the majority of such individuals develop a male gender identity.

Abnormal psychology   An interchangeable term with psychopathology which covers the scientific study of abnormal psychology.

Absolute refractory period   In a neurone, the period of time following an action potential during which another action potential cannot be generated.

Accentuation principle   Categorisation theory suggests that differences between members within the same category are underestimated and differences between members of different categories are accentuated.

Accommodation   The modification and expansion of pre-existing cognitive schemata in order to adapt to new experiences.

Acetylcholine (ACh)   Neurotransmitter abundant in the nervous system that acts as a fast excitatory neurotransmitter at the neuromuscular junction, although it can have inhibitory effects elsewhere.

Acetylcholineresterase (AChE)   Enzyme that inactivates acetylcholine.

Action potential   Mechanism of signalling information from one end of a neurone to the other achieved by the transitory change in membrane potential travelling down the neurone.

Action research   Tries to solve immediate problems by working as part of community practice. Such research leads to social action based on reflexive planning, action and fact-finding, either as participatory action in an organisation to change things as the research is being conducted or when an organisation is guided by professional researchers to improve practices, etc.

Activational hormones   Hormones that circulate in the bloodstream and can affect behaviour or physical characteristics when they bind to a receptor site.

Actor–observer effect   An extension of the fundamental attribution error. While attributing the actions of targets to their disposition, we are more likely to explain our own behaviour as influenced by the situation.

Acute medical condition   An illness, disease or affliction with a sudden onset and a rapid course (e.g. a cold, injury, heart attack or asthma attack). Acute conditions can sometimes become chronic.

Affordances   The notion that the function of objects can be directly perceived, with no prior experience being necessary.

Agonist   Drug that enhances effects of a neurotransmitter on the post-synaptic neurone.

Agreeableness   This personality trait mainly involves being motivated to help, serve and please others. A person with high levels of the agreeableness trait will often comply with requests for help and sometimes do things without worrying about their own interests. Agreeableness is a part of the five-factor model of personality.

Allocentric   The skill of memorising the position of an object in relation to other objects.

Allostasis   The process of achieving stability, or homeostasis, through physiological or behavioural change.

All-or-none law   The result of the threshold of excitation. An action potential is either triggered or not and so is always of the same strength.

Altruism   The act of helping someone, but without any expectation of getting something in return.

Amygdala   A structure of the limbic system located in the medial temporal lobe involved in emotional processes.

Analytical intelligence   The ability to evaluate ideas, solve problems and make decisions through analysing, evaluating and making inferences.

Androgen   A class of male sex hormones responsible for the maintenance and development of male characteristics.

Androgen insensitivity syndrome   A male with this condition is insensitive to the masculinising effects of androgens in the womb. Such individuals appear to be female, although they possess testes.

Animism   The attribution of life-like qualities to inanimate objects (for example, toys like Edmund Elephant).

Antagonist   Drug that inhibits the effects of a neurotransmitter on the post-synaptic neurone.

Anterograde axoplasmic transport   Forward conveyance of material such as neurotransmitter vesicles, along the axon of a neurone (from soma towards synaptic button).

Anthropocentrism or anthrocentrism   The belief that people (*anthro*) are the most important thing in the universe rather than the worthless pile of brown stuff that we really are!

Aphasia   Literally speaking, an absence of speech, but is commonly taken to mean an impairment of language, affecting the production or comprehension of speech and the ability to read or write.

Ascending auditory pathway   The pathway that runs from the ear to the brain.

Ascending reticular activating system (ARAS)   Sometimes known as the reticular activating system, this is a part of the

brain that affects, among other things, an individual's level of wakefulness and attentiveness. Hans Eysenck claimed that this part of the brain is what differentiates extraverts and introverts; extraverts seek out stimulation to the ARAS (i.e. being 'stimulus hungry'), whereas introverts avoid stimulation in the ARAS if they can help it (i.e. being 'stimulus aversive').

Assimilation   The incorporation of new experiences into pre-existing cognitive schemas.

Astrocytes   Glial cells shaped like stars that perform various functions for neurones within the CNS including physical support, producing the blood–brain barrier, isolation of synapses, providing nutrition and keeping the extracellular environment clean.

Attachment behaviour   Any behaviour that helps to form or establish an emotional bond between two individuals. Strong attachment bonds are usually formed between an infant and his or her caregiver.

Attention   Concentration of cognitive resources on some aspect or aspects of an environment while ignoring others.

Attention deficit hyperactivity disorder   A behaviour disorder, usually first diagnosed in childhood, that is characterised by inattention, impulsivity and, in some cases, hyperactivity.

Attenuate   The reduction of a signal or information.

Attitudes   The thoughts and opinions you have about any number of objects in the world.

Attribution   The act of making a decision as to why someone has acted in a particular way.

Auditory canal   The 'tube' running between the pinna and the tympanic membrane.

Authoritarianism   The theory that a person with this type of personality will be hostile to minority groups and has a predisposition to show prejudice.

Autism   A developmental disorder which represents a wide-ranging spectrum of behaviours. Diagnosis is usually made according to difficulties found in aspects of communication, social skills and repetitive behaviours.

Automatic thoughts   Specific upsetting thoughts that are felt to appear instantly and are generally negative in relation to psychpathology.

Autonomic nervous system   A network of nerve fibres connecting the brain and spinal cord to the body. It regulates the major involuntary functions such as heart rate, digestion and respiration, and can prepare the body for action or rest.

Autoreceptor   Pre-synaptic receptor that detects and signals levels of neurotransmitter in the synaptic cleft and so regulates release.

Axon   The long slender projection from a cell body to axonal branches or synaptic buttons. Its main purpose is to convey action potentials.

Axon hillock   Region of the axon that is adjacent to the soma (also known as the initial segment). It is here that post-synaptic potentials typically accumulate and determine whether an action potential is triggered or not.

Axonal branches   The division of the axon of the neurone into two or more sections. Occurs in certain types of neurone and only at the synaptic end.

Axoplasm   The fluid inside the axon of a neurone.

Babbling   A child appears to be experimenting with making the sounds of language, but is not yet producing any recognisable words. Also, what boys do when they are trying to ask someone out on a date.

Backwards saccade (regression)   Typically refers to a saccade in the opposite natural reading direction of a language.

Basal ganglia   A group of forebrain structures that integrates voluntary movement and consists of the caudate nucleus, globus pallidus and putamen.

Base rate fallacy   Ignoring the base rate of an event occurring when computing a probability.

Basilar membrane   A flexible membrane in the cochlea that moves in response to sound.

Bayes' theorem   A method of computing the probability of a hypothesis being true given some factual evidence related to the hypothesis.

Behavioural approach system (BAS)   BAS behaviour characterises a tendency to be attracted to appetitive stimuli.

Behavioural inhibition system (BIS)   BIS behaviour characterises a tendency to withdraw from aversive stimuli.

Behaviourism   A school of thought which holds that the observation and description of overt behaviour is all that is needed to comprehend the human being, and that manipulation of stimulus–response contingencies is all that is needed to change human behaviour.

Bipolar cells   A type of neurone which is specialised for dealing with sensory information.

Bipolar neurone   A type of neurone (usually a sensory neurone) named for its structure, having two processes arising from the cell body.

Blind spot   The point on the retina where there are no photoreceptor cells.

Blood–brain barrier   Protective barrier between the brain and blood vessels, providing a mechanism by which certain substances are prevented from entering the brain.

Bodily-kinaesthetic intelligence   The ability to use one's body in various movements and activities.

Bottom-up processing   A cognitive process that starts with simple (low-level) processes and builds up to the more complex higher levels. It doesn't depend on prior knowledge.

Brain   Large grey thing at the top of the neck.

Brain stem   The part of the brain that regulates vital reflexes such as heart rate and respiration; it consists of the midbrain, the pons and the medulla. It is activity or the lack of it in this region that is used by medics to establish whether a patient is 'brain dead'.

Bullying   This is a process involving exercise of power and control over a more vulnerable person. Bullying may take a verbal form (e.g. insults, threats and use of language to make the victim feel fearful). It might also be physical in nature such as when a group of bullies surrounds the victim (i.e. 'mobbing') in order to intimidate them.

Bystander effect   Lack of action in a given situation, based on the presence of other people. The higher the number of participants, the lower the probability that anyone will act.

Cardinality   The principle that a set of items has a cardinal value (a quantity), and this quantity is equal in value to another set of items with the same quantity. For example, although three horses might look visually different from three ducks, the principle of cardinality suggests that there are the same number, i.e. three.

Cardiovascular system   The system that consists of the heart and blood vessels responsible for circulating blood and the lymph glands and vessels responsible for circulating lymph through the body.

Cartesian dualism   The idea that we are made up of two parts, a mind and a body. The body is like all other material objects and can be examined using the material sciences, whereas the mind is not physical and cannot be measured.

Cartesian philosophy   Refers to the philosophy of René Descartes (1596–1650), who emphasised reason, thinking and logical analysis to ascertain the truth about the world. Descartes was uncertain about how we could 'know' the world (and his body) and the only certainty was that he knew he existed because as an *individual* he could think (cogito ergo sum). The problem of how the mind and the body are related was thereafter seen as a problem for philosophers and psychologists.

Catharsis   The release of built-up emotional energy. The term is generally used to typify a healthy and restorative outpouring of such energy.

Cell theory   Schwann's (1839) theory that all bodily tissues are composed of individual discrete cells.

Centration   The focusing of attention on one aspect of a situation while excluding the rest of the scenario.

Cerebellum   The lower part of the brain responsible for balance and coordination.

Cerebral cortex   The layer of neural tissue which covers the cerebral hemispheres and is involved in higher-order cognitive processes.

Cerebral hemispheres   The right and left halves of the most anterior part of the brain. They play a primary role in most of our mental abilities, such as language, attention and perception. This is another example of the nervous system being a system of twos.

Cerebrospinal fluid   The clear fluid that protects the central nervous system and fills the ventricular system, the subarachnoid space and the central canal.

c-fibres   Neurones that are found in the somatic sensory system and are unique because, unlike most other nerves in the nervous system, they are unmyelinated. They have a role in the transmission of pain.

Chemical synapses   Synapses that depend upon chemicals (transmitter substances), released by the pre-synaptic cell and recognised by the post-synaptic cell, for communication.

Chemically gated ion channels   Ion channels whose state (open or closed) is determined by the docking of an appropriate chemical onto a nearby receptor.

Child-directed speech (motherese)   The act of using a sing-song voice, speaking slowly, or using simple language when talking to an infant.

Chloride (Cl-)   Negatively charged ion that plays a role in producing and maintaining membrane potentials.

Chromosome   A thread-like strand of DNA that carries the genes.

Chronic medical condition   An illness or disease that develops gradually and which lasts for a long period of time or a lifetime, worsening over time (e.g. osteoporosis, chronic asthma, diabetes or cancer).

Chunk decomposition   The process of breaking down something that was initially perceived as a whole into its constituent parts – such as X being seen as two individual lines rather than as a letter of the alphabet.

Cisternae   Found in some synaptic buttons, cisternae repackage transmitter substances into vesicles.

Classical conditioning   Learning a new behaviour via the process of association between two stimuli.

Client   Someone receiving an intervention or treatment.

Clinical interview   An assessment technique used by clinicians that generally involves face-to-face interaction with the person they are assessing.

Clinical tests   A specific form of gathering information about a person's level of psychological functioning.

Cochlea   The spiral-shaped structure in the inner ear which generates electrical impulses in response to sound.

Cochlear duct   A fluid-filled chamber in the cochlea.

Cochlear implant   An electronic device which bypasses the damaged hair cells in the cochlea and directly stimulates the auditory nerve.

Cognition   Broadly, the activity of thinking.

Cognitive dissonance   The argument that if our own attitudes, thoughts or actions disagree with each other, a state of dissonance is created. This acts as a motivation to change one or more of these internal elements (Festinger, 1957).

Cognitive miser   In contrast to Heider's naive scientist perspective, the idea that we try to conserve mental energy and take shortcuts when making attributions (Fiske & Taylor, 1991).

Cognitive schemas   Mental representations and plans used to enact behaviours.

Cognitive schemata   Mental representations and plans used to enact behaviours.

Competitive binding   The situation where drugs and neurotransmitters are in competition for the same receptor sites.

Computerised (axial) tomography   A method of imaging that uses x-rays to form cross-sectional or three-dimensional images of structure.

Concrete vocabulary A precursor to abstract vocabulary, whereby children name objects at a subordinate level, e.g. chair and table, as opposed to an abstract superordinate level, e.g. furniture.

Conduct disorder This is a disorder that shows long-lasting patterns of severe behaviour that may harm others/animals, damage property or cause emotional harm. This disorder impacts on the lives of both the person diagnosed and those around them.

Cones The photoreceptor cells in the eye responsible for colour vision and visual acuity.

Conflict resolution When more than one rule (or production) is able to be used at any one time in a production system, it is said to be in conflict. Conflict resolution is the strategy used to resolve this conflict.

Congenital adrenal hyperplasia A female with this condition is exposed to an excess of androgens, produced by the adrenal glands, during prenatal development. As a consequence, a number of physical and personality characteristics are shifted in a male-typical direction.

Conscientiousness This personality trait is often demonstrated by an individual in a work or study setting, in which the individual is industrious and has an eye for detail in the work that is being done. People with high levels of conscientiousness are very practical and like to finish a project once they have started it. Conscientiousness is a part of the five-factor model of personality.

Consciousness Often used in everyday speech to describe being awake or aware in contrast to being asleep or in a coma. In psychology, the term has a more precise meaning concerning the way in which humans are mentally aware so that they distinguish clearly between themselves and all other things and events.

Conservation The understanding that certain properties of objects remain the same under transformation. These properties include quantity, weight and volume.

Consolidation theory The idea that memories are fragile and require time to consolidate before they can be stored in long-term memory.

Constraint relaxation The process of relaxing constraints that were unnecessarily imposed on a problem, such as believing coins could not be stacked on top of each other in the eight-coin problem.

Constructivist An approach which assumes that our perceptual experiences are constructed based on a combination of sensory input and what we know about the world.

Contact hypothesis The theory that bringing members of two different groups together within a cooperative, equal and supportive environment can reduce conflict between those two groups.

Content analysis A quantitative technique that involves the formal categorisation and the counting of frequencies of things in texts (particular words, phrases, ideas and so forth). It can be used with any medium that can be recorded and reviewed.

Context-dependent memory Where memory for an item improves when the original context in which it was presented is reinstated at test.

Core affect An overarching disposition present to some degree all the time manifesting in emotion or mood.

Cornea The transparent protective layer on the surface of the eye.

Corpus callosum The largest commissure in the brain that connects the two cerebral hemispheres.

Correlation A measure of how strongly two or more variables are related to each other.

Correlation coefficient A number between −1 and +1 which expresses how strong a correlation is. If this number is close to 0, there is no real connection between the two; if it is close to +1 there is a positive correlation – in other words, if one variable is large the other will also tend to be large; and if it is close to −1, there is a negative correlation – in other words, if one variable is large, the other will tend to be small.

Counter measures Techniques that may be used to invalidate a test assessing the 'truthfulness' of an individual. With the polygraph, this may be accomplished by actions such as lightly biting one's tongue, or performing mental arithmetic when neutral (control) questions are asked. These actions would artificially elevate physiological arousal, making the distance between a 'lie' and a 'neutral' response too close to differentiate.

Counter transference The feelings that the therapist has in reaction to the person, which may be transferred to the person and reflects what the person feels about the therapist.

Cranial nerves Part of the peripheral nervous system composed of a set of 12 pairs of nerves or pathways which transmit sensory and motor information to and from the brain.

Creative intelligence The ability to draw upon previous experience in order to come up with new solutions to both old and new problems.

Crime Survey for England and Wales A tool that measures the extent of crime through asking a representative sample if they have experienced crime in the last year. This differs from police recorded crime figures that are limited to offences that are brought to the attention of the police and so are lower than those in the CSEW.

Criminogenic needs Characteristics, traits and factors that are strongly correlated with reoffending. These needs are targeted in treatment so that they 'change', thereby reducing the likelihood of that individual reoffending.

Critical period A limited period, usually early in life, in which a child is required to be exposed to a particular skill or experience in order for it to be learned.

Crossed category membership The theory that encourages people to view others' membership in lots of different categories to reduce intergroup bias (this can include race, age, ethnicity, gender, university enrolment and economic status, to name just a few).

Cryptarithmetic A problem where an arithmetic sum is given using letters rather than numbers, with the goal of identifying which number from 0 to 9 corresponds to each of the letters.

Crystallised intelligence (*gc*) The ability to think and reason about abstract ideas, and to use knowledge and skills to solve problems.

Cued recall Where specific prompts or cues are used to direct recall (e.g. paired-associate learning).

Cultural tools Tools that help us to understand the world more fully by solving problems, measuring the environment, making calculations and storing information (e.g. books, number systems language, computers and calculators).

Cytoplasm Gel-like fluid, rich in salts, that is contained within the cell and surrounds organelles.

Danger Some people with psychological disorders become dangerous to themselves or others, though it is important to highlight that not everybody with some form of psychopathology presents with risky behaviours at all times. Danger is often cited, especially in the media, as a core feature of psychpathology, although research indicates that it is actually the exception rather than the rule (Hiday & Burns, 2009).

Decay An explanation of forgetting that suggests memories fade or deteriorate over time.

Declarative knowledge Factual information, such as that Paris is the capital of France.

Deductive reasoning A type of reasoning that uses a rule or a set of premises applied to specific instances to produce a conclusion.

Defence mechanisms Protective strategies that the mind uses to defend itself against unwelcome or disturbing information.

Deindividuation A process whereby the presence of others leads an individual to lose their sense of personal identity and to feel anonymous, becoming less socially responsible and guided by moral principles.

Demand characteristics Those aspects of a psychological study (or other artificial situation) which exert an implicit pressure on people to act in ways that are expected of them.

Dendrites The branching processes that emanate from the soma and receive inputs from other cells.

Dendritic arborisation The number and organisation of dendrites.

Deoxyribonucleic acid (DNA) Nucleic acid found in cells that contains the genetic instructions vital for the development and functioning of organisms.

Depolarisation Movement of the membrane potential towards zero. In the case of thc neurone, depolarising from the negative resting potential towards a positive value.

Depression A persistent sad state in which the sufferer can also feel that their life has no meaning; everyday processes often becoming overwhelming.

Desired state In problem solving, the ultimate state, i.e. when the problem is solved.

Determinism The idea that every event, including human thought and behaviour, is causally determined by an unbroken chain of prior events. According to this idea, there are no mysterious miracles and no random events.

Deviance Emotions, thoughts and behaviours are thought abnormal when they vary from a society's idea about appropriate functioning. A society in which competition and dominance is embraced would see an aggressive personality as normal, whereas a society that values compassion and cooperation may consider aggression not only unacceptable but abnormal. Moreover, a society's view over time may change, leading to new views on what is normal and abnormal.

Deviant sexual interest Sexual interests that encompass acts that are atypical in the general population. Generally, these are non-consensual, illegal and harmful. See also **paraphilia**.

Diagnosis The process of a clinician determining that a person's cluster of symptoms represents a certain disorder.

Diagnostic and Statistical Manual (DSM) Published by the American Psychiatric Association, the DSM offers a set of criteria for classifying mental disorders. The fifth edition was published in 2013.

Diencephalon The division of the forebrain that contains the thalamus and hypothalamus.

Diffusion Natural movement of molecules in solution from areas of high to low concentration.

Diffusion of responsibility The phenomenon of individuals taking less responsibility for events when there are other people present because they feel less personally responsible for what is happening.

Digital domain Digital domains enable people to access data (images, words, sounds, video, etc.) that have been converted into a digital format. Examples of digital domains include social media sites, such a Facebook, and other internet sites or points of access, such as Twitter, email, Second Life, online games, etc.

Dihydrotestosterone An androgen converted from testosterone by the actions of the enzyme 5-alpha reductase.

Discourse refers to way of *organising* knowledge, ideas or experience in written and spoken communications or conversations in social settings. They can be specific or specialised, such as medical or academic discourse, and are found across all media from tabloid newspapers to formal academic writing.

Discrimination The consideration or treatment of others based on general factors (e.g. their race, religion or some other grouping) rather than on individual merit.

Displacement Swapping negative feelings or aggression from one group or individual to another target.

Distress For many people with a disorder, one of the most common reasons they access services is that it causes them some level of distress. This does not necessarily have to be physical distress. Psychological disorders more often result in distressing emotions, thoughts or moods.

DNA (deoxyribonucleic acid) A chemical found primarily in the nucleus of cells. DNA carries the instructions or blueprint for making all the structures and materials that the body needs to function.

Dogmatism A rigid, inflexible approach which can cause prejudice through intolerance.

Dominant discourse This is a way of speaking or behaving on any given topic that appears most prevalent in a particular social group or society. Such speech and writing will reflect the ideologies of those who have the most power in the society or have authority to control, for example, the media or knowledge. A dominant discourse about a certain subject will affect how people adopt the beliefs and actions of those in power, which can eventually become the social norm. If it does this, then few people will challenge the ideas, or even if they want to, they may lack power to get their message across.

Double dissociation A term used in brain sciences to indicate that two cognitive processes are distinct, such that damage to a particular brain region affects one of those processes but not the other. For example, damage to Broca's area of the brain means a patient cannot speak but can still understand speech, whereas damage to Wernicke's area means a patient cannot understand speech but can still speak.

Double-blind control A form of experimental control which aims to avoid self-fulfilling prophecies, by ensuring that neither the subjects nor the experimenter who carries out the study are aware of the experimental hypothesis.

Down syndrome A congenital disorder, caused by the presence of an extra 21st chromosome. Also called trisomy 21.

Dramaturgical analogy Erving Goffman proposed a theatrical metaphor as a way of understanding self in everyday life and seeing social interactions as though they were dramatic performances, considering the costumes, the props etc. which go towards making up the 'scenes' played out by people.

Drugs Substances that produce observable changes to physiological processes and/or behaviour at relatively low doses.

DSM This stands for the Diagnostic and Statistical Manual that is published by the American Psychiatric Association. It is a diagnostic manual that it used by clinicians to diagnose a range of disorders in children and adults. The current edition is known as DSM-5.

DSM-V The Diagnostic Statistical Manual of Mental Disorders (5th edn); DSM 5, 2013) is a handbook which details criteria for diagnosing mental disorders. It is widely used by clinicians.

Dynamic equilibrium When two opposing processes operate at equivalent rates.

Dysfunction Disordered behaviour often brings with it some level of interference in functioning. To meet the criteria of a disorder this interference has to be to the level that it effects somebody's daily life (though not necessarily every day). Disordered individuals will not normally be able to take care of themselves properly, interact appropriately with others or work effectively.

DZ and MZ twins Fraternal or dizygotic (DZ) twins occur when two different eggs are fertilised by two different sperm. Identical or monozygotic (MZ) twins occur when a single fertilised egg divides into two identical copies.

Egocentric thinking When an individual has little regard for the views or interests of others, which may involve individuals memorising objects in relation to themselves.

Elaboration likelihood model Examines how attitudes are formed and changed by focusing on two routes to persuasion: the 'central route' and the 'peripheral route'.

Electrical synapses Synapses that depend upon electrical charge accumulated in the pre-synaptic cell passing to the post-synaptic cell for communication.

Electroencephalography (EEG) A temporally accurate brain imaging technique that is based on the electrical discharge to the surface of the brain due to neuronal firing.

Electrostatic pressure The force created because particles of opposite polarity (+ and −) are attracted towards each other and those of the same polarity are repelled.

Emotion A feeling deriving from a mood or an affective state.

Emotional intelligence An ability to identify, assess and manage the emotions of yourself, other individuals and groups.

Empathy The ability to feel or share another's experiences or emotions.

Encoding (in memory) The stage of memory involving interpreting and transforming incoming information in order to 'lay down' memories.

Encoding specificity principle This principle states that specific encoding operations performed at presentation determine what is stored, and therefore determine what retrieval cues are effective at test.

Endocrine system A series of small organs responsible for producing hormones that regulate a variety of processes, including growth and development, metabolism and puberty.

Endogenous Substances naturally found within the body (e.g. neurotransmitters).

End-to-end offender management Taking care of offenders from their first contact with the correctional services right through to the very end of their sentence.

Entitativity Refers to how coherent and connected a group is, i.e. how much the people in the group can be seen as being a part of the group rather than being a collection of individuals.

Enzymatic degradation Process by which certain neurotransmitters are broken down by enzymes.

Enzymes Typically, proteins that are catalysts important for biological reactions.

Epigenetics The study of heritable changes in gene expression that occur without changes to the genotype (DNA). So traits (these can physical and behavioural) that are inherited via epigenetics are not due to changes in the gene combinations, but due to changes in whether a gene is actively expressed or not.

Epistemology How we come to know things. If we question what knowledge is, we need to critically consider how it has been acquired. A theory of knowledge about social behaviour should also explore the extent to which bias and problems with methods change 'what we know' and if it makes a difference if knowledge is acquired in alternative ways. Also, we should ask if the language used to express that knowledge alters its meaning and who has control over that knowledge.

Equilibration This is when a child's set of schemas are balanced and not disturbed by conflict.

Equilibrium potential Each type of ion has its own equilibrium potential, which is the voltage at which the net effect of the passage of a given ion in and out of the cell is zero.

Estimator variables These influence the accuracy of eye-witness testimony and are not under the control of the criminal justice system. Examples are the age of the witness or the duration of the event.

Ethnocentrism A stance in which an individual believes that their own race or ethnic group (or aspects of it, e.g. its culture) is superior to other groups.

Ethnomethodology Not a formal research method, but an approach to empirical study that aims to discover the things that people do in particular situations and how they create the patterns and orderliness of social life to gain a sense of social structure.

Eugenics The political idea that the human race could be improved by eliminating 'undesirables' from the breeding stock, so that they cannot pass on their supposedly inferior genes. Some eugenicists advocate compulsory sterilisation, while others seem to prefer mass murder or genocide.

Eustachian tube A structure in the middle ear which helps regulate air pressure.

Event-related potentials (ERPs) Neuronal electrical activity related to a stimulus or response measured using EEG. An ERP is characterised by its positive or negative voltage and the latency of onset, e.g. a P300 is a positive waveform with an onset latency of 300 ms.

Excitatory post-synaptic potentials (EPSPs) Graded post-synaptic potentials that increase the likelihood that the post-synaptic cell will produce an action potential.

Exhibitionism The intentional exposure of genitals with the intention that someone will see them and be alarmed or distressed. This is a sexual offence (see also **exposure**).

Existential crisis The realisation that you are alone in your experience of the world and that the only meaning your life has is the meaning you choose to impose on it. Commonly experienced when you drop your choc ice.

Exocytosis Process by which substances are released from a cell.

Exogenous Substances originating outside the body (e.g. drugs).

Experiment A form of research in which variables are manipulated in order to discover cause and effect.

Experimenter effects Unwanted influences in a psychological study which are produced, consciously or unconsciously, by the person carrying out the study.

Explanatory pluralism Holds that different levels of description, like the psychological and the neurophysiological, can coevolve, and mutually influence each other, without the higher-level theory being replaced by, or reduced to, the lower-level one.

Explicit memory test Where the participant is told at test that the task involves memory for material presented earlier.

Exposure The intentional exhibiting of genitals with the intention that someone will see them and be alarmed or distressed (see also **exhibitionism**).

Expressed emotion Manifesting feelings in a vocal or physical emotional response.

External locus of control People with an external locus of control will usually see their lives as mainly subject to influence and control by other people (e.g. destiny affected by someone's family members, friends, boss, etc.).

Extraversion A general tendency towards outgoing, social behaviour.

Factor analysis A group of similar methods of statistical analysis that reduce correlational data down to a smaller amount of dimensions or factors.

False belief This is when an individual incorrectly believes a statement or scenario to be true when it is not. This is the basis of the false belief tasks used in the theory of mind experiments.

False consensus effect The effect seen when people overestimate the probability of other people thinking, feeling or acting the same way as they do.

False memories Where a person admits guilt for a crime they did not commit.

Filter In the context of attentional processing, a filter serves the purpose of allowing some sensations of stimuli through to be processed while screening out others. This is based on the theoretical approach that we can only cope with a limited amount of information and so select which stimuli to process.

Five-factor model This model of personality traits is sometimes called the Big 5 or the OCEAN model (after the initials for each of the five major traits: openness to experience, conscientiousness, extraversion, agreeableness and neuroticism). It is commonly used to assess personality in a range of settings, including the workplace. The model is highly popular in personality psychology and has been developed and promoted by Robert McCrae and Paul Costa Jr, both working at the National Institute of Aging, National Institutes of Health in the United States of America.

Fixation The maintaining of a visual gaze on a single location.

Fluid intelligence (*gf*) The ability to learn from previous experience.

Fluid/crystallised abilities Fluid cognitive abilities, like short-term memory, require more processing resources than crystallised ones, such as long-term knowledge, and are more sensitive to age-related decline.

Foetal alcohol syndrome Foetal abnormalities caused by alcohol consumption during pregnancy.

Folk psychology Ways of thinking about the mind that are implicit in how we make everyday attributions of mental states to ourselves and others.

Forebrain Most anterior division of the brain, containing the telencephalon and diencephalon.

Forgetting function The mathematical equation that determines the precise rate of forgetting as a function of time.

Fovea The part of the eye located in the centre of the macula which is responsible for high visual acuity.

Fraternal birth order effect The increased rates of homosexuality observed in males with a large number of older brothers.

Free recall Where the prompt for recall is quite general (e.g. 'remember as many words as you can from the first list').

Frontal lobe hypothesis The theory that decline in frontal lobe functioning underlies more general age-related cognitive decline.

Frustration-aggression hypothesis The theory that frustration leads to aggression; this can be used to explain prejudice.

Functional fixedness When one becomes fixated on the function of an object rather than considering other uses that the object could be applied to.

Functional magnetic resonance imaging (fMRI) A spatially accurate brain imaging technique that is based on the nuclear properties of protons (e.g. hydrogen) in the body tissue.

Functionalism In the philosophy of mind, functionalism refers to the idea that mental states can be defined by their causes and effects.

Fundamental attribution error The tendency to attribute the actions of a person we are observing to their disposition, rather than to situational variables.

g General factor of intelligence. Also a spot.

G protein Guanine nucleotide-binding proteins are coupled to metabotropic chemical receptors and are involved in cascade effects that result in the opening of ion channels.

Gendered identity The way that people perform their biological sexual identity. Just how or in what way gender is demonstrated will vary depending on social or cultural understanding, circumstances, expectations or requirements.

Gene The basic unit of heredity. It is a segment of DNA that occupies a specific place on a chromosome. Genes act by affecting the synthesis of proteins which in turn influence specific physical traits, such as the shape of a leaf, or the texture of a person's hair. Different forms of genes, called alleles, determine how these traits are expressed in a given individual.

General factor (g) The theoretical general factor of intelligence that some scientists believe underpins all cognitive activity.

General learning difficulties Global difficulties in learning which mean a child has different patterns of learning, or may learn more slowly, than same-age peers.

General problem solver (GPS) A computer program created in 1957 by Herbert Simon and Allen Newell to build a universal problem-solving machine.

Generality approach Researchers studying the link between personality and health may use the generality approach by analysing specific health-related behaviours that are influenced by personality. In essence, this approach assumes that health is affected by an indirect route from a personality trait or type contributing to a behaviour that is likely to impact upon health (e.g. smoking, alcohol use, taking fewer risks when driving, etc.).

Generate-recognise theory The theory that people use an initial prompt to generate a series of cues during recall until one of them matches an item shown at presentation and is recognised.

Genetic predisposition Any behaviour or physical characteristic that is present within an individual's genetic code. These characteristics may not always be activated, but there is a potential for them to be developed.

Genotype Genes that make up the genetic code for an individual are described as the genotype. In humans the genotype comprises approximately 25,000 genes. Genes mostly come in pairs. Each member of a pair of genes is referred to as an allele.

Genus A class, group or category that possesses common attributes. Our own species exists in the genus *Homo* alongside other species (all of which are now extinct).

Gestalt psychology A school of psychology that began in Germany in the first half of the twentieth century. It proposed that an experience or behaviour can only be understood as a whole, not by understanding the individual constituent parts.

Glial cells Non-neuronal cells performing a number of supporting roles in the nervous system.

Goal state In problem solving, a desired state for a subgoal of the problem-solving process.

Grammatical Relating to grammar, which is the structure of language.

Graphemes The graphical representation of a sound in written form.

Groupthink A style of thinking shown by group members who try to minimise conflict and reach a consensus without critically testing and evaluating ideas.

Habituation A method of measuring infant attention by habituating an infant to a particular stimulus until he or she becomes uninterested in the stimulus.

Hallucination A sensory perception experienced in the absence of an external stimulus.

Hawthorne studies and the Hawthorne effect Workers in the Hawthorne Works, having been found to work more productively as a result of someone showing an interest in them (rather than just being seen as an adjunct to production), led to the expression 'Hawthorne effect', which is taken to mean that people (whether in industry or in the psychological laboratory) always perform better when being observed – even if the only alteration of conditions is that they are observed.

Hegemony The situation where the interests of the powerful can marginalise and counter the claims of other groups. Where there is such dominance, some ideas will therefore be subordinated so, for example, the views of less powerful groups will be denigrated and thought to be of less value.

Helping behaviour The act of helping someone, but with the hope or expectation of getting something in return.

Heritability The proportion of variance in the phenotype that can be attributed to genetic variance. It is a widely misunderstood concept and is commonly misused in debates about nature and nurture. It is a measure that may vary with the range of genetic backgrounds and range of environments studied. It is therefore a mistake to argue that a high figure for heritability in a particular population in a particular environment means that the characteristic is genetically determined.

Hermaphrodite A term derived from Hermaphroditus, a Greek deity believed to possess both male and female attributes. Such individuals possess both testicular and ovarian tissue.

Heuristic A mental shortcut (or rule of thumb) that represents a 'best guess', allowing people to make solution attempts or make decisions quickly and efficiently (though not always correctly).

Heuristic systematic model A model that explains that, when making decisions, individuals either use heuristics and shortcuts or systematically process the merits and problems with a given argument.

Hierarchical models of intelligence These models imply one or more general, higher-order factor(s) of intelligences and one or more lower levels with several specific intelligence factors.

Hindbrain The most posterior division of the brain, containing the metencephalon and myelencephalon.

Hippocampus A structure of the limbic system located in the medial temporal lobe that plays an important role in memory.

Hormones From the Greek *horman*, 'to excite' or 'impetus'. Hormones are chemical messengers, released by the endocrine system, that are carried to other areas of the body through the bloodstream. Once they have reached a specific area of the body, they bind to certain receptor sites within tissues or organs and induce physiological change. Hormones have powerful effects on physiology and behaviour.

Humanistic psychology Humanistic psychology focuses on the potential of an individual and stresses the importance of personal growth and self-actualization. The basic belief of is that people are inherently good and that it is deviation from this natural state that brings about social and mental problems.

Humours These are the physical elements that ancient Greek and Roman doctors thought were flowing through a person's body. According to the Roman physician Galen, four main humours characterised a person's temperament, which were related to being sanguine, choleric, phlegmatic and melancholic. A person would tend to have a larger proportion of one or other of the humours and this would dictate how the person consistently reacted in a variety of situations.

Huntington's disease A dominant genetic disorder in which a protein is produced abnormally, leading to the breakdown in the parts of the brain that control movement.

Hypothalamus A part of the brain which controls the actions of the pituitary gland and, as such, controls hormone production in the human body. It is also involved in a variety of physiological processes, such as hunger, thirst, circadian rhythms and sexual behaviour.

Hysteria A condition in which physical symptoms appear in the absence of any obvious physical cause.

ICD This stands for the International Classification of Diseases, which is a diagnostic tool that is used for defining and reporting diseases and health conditions. Whereas the DSM is produced by a single, national professional body, the ICD is produced by the World Health Organisation.

ICD-10 The International Classification of Diseases which is the European based system used by clinicians to diagnoses psychological disorders. Published by the World Health Organisation and currently in its tenth edition.

Identity Awareness of shared distinctive characteristics by members of a group. Identity may be considered in a number of ways, e.g. in cultural terms as ethnic identity, or in terms of sexual orientation.

Identity theory Tajfel and Turner's (1979) social identity theory examines intergroup and ingroup discrimination based on the idea that a person has several selves that function at different levels of social circles, e.g. personal, family, community, national.

Ideology A set of ideas, beliefs and perspectives from which to interpret social and political realities and so inform actions. When used pejoratively it means how hidden aims and interests are achieved by distorting (or ignoring) social, political realities. For example, Karl Marx described how the ideology of the ruling class (in order to serve their class interests) promoted a 'false consciousness' in other classes that their ideas were universal truths.

Idiographic or idiothetic approach This perspective focuses on the uniqueness or idiosyncrasies of the person. It does not require trying to get a common language of personality traits or types to compare between people. Instead, it allows people to tell their stories of how they develop over time and attempts to understand their perceptions of why they say and do things. It recognises that a person evolves over time and that changing moods and perceptions can influence what that person may do in any given situation.

Illusion An error in perception.

Impasse When one becomes stuck during problem solving and cannot see a solution.

Implicit association test An indirect measure of psychological constructs which are typically sensitive or subject to social desirability.

Implicit memory test Where participants perform an activity at test that is apparently unrelated to the material that was originally presented.

Incentive An item or thing that motivates or encourages you.

Incidental learning Where participants in an experiment are not told at presentation that their memory for material will later be tested, assuming therefore that anything remembered was not deliberately learned.

Incongruence A lack of balanced overlap between the real self and the ideal self.

Inductive reasoning A type of reasoning that starts from specific instances or facts to produce general rules or theories.

Inferential statistics A way of using statistics to enable us to make inferences from data about relationships among variables, particularly with reference to cause and effect. This involves going beyond the data, hence the term 'inferential'. A contrast can be made with descriptive statistics.

Inferior colliculi Nuclei of the tectum in the midbrain that receives auditory information.

Informational influence Social influence due to others providing factual information and help with verifying or correcting such information.

Ingroup A group of which a person believes they are a member.

Inhibitory post-synaptic potentials (IPSPs) Graded post-synaptic potentials that decrease the likelihood that the post-synaptic cell will produce an action potential.

Innate Being present at birth (usually refers to a characteristic or behaviour that is deemed hereditary).

Inner ear The part of the ear which consists of the cochlea and the semicircular canals.

Inner hair cells The sensory receptors in the ear which are responsible for sending electrical signals to the brain.

Insight This is when we reach a dead end in problem solving, until suddenly – 'aha!' – we suddenly realise the solution. A rare phenomenon. Also refers to self-awareness or self-understanding.

Intelligence quotient (IQ) A numerical figure, believed by some to indicate the level of a person's intelligence, and by others to indicate how well that person performs on intelligence tests.

Intentional learning Where participants in an experiment are told at presentation that their memory for material will later be tested, assuming, therefore, that anything remembered was deliberately learned.

Interdependence The basic principle that the actual results of individuals' actions are dependent on other individuals' actions.

Interference An explanation of forgetting in which other learning (old or new) can disrupt or prevent retrieval.

Internal locus of control People with an internal locus of control see themselves as 'masters of their own destiny'. Locus of control relates to how individuals perceive the causes of events that occur to them. Internal locus of control is a personality type that categorises a person as seeing events that occur around them as being dependent on what they say or do. Someone with an internal locus of control is also said to have 'self-determination'

or 'personal control' or 'self-agency', which all refer to people seeing themselves as being integral to what happens to their lives.

Interneurone A neurone connecting two other neurones. Typically, for local connections confined to a specific region of the brain.

Interpersonal intelligence The ability to understand other people's thoughts, beliefs and intentions, and respond appropriately.

Interpretative Phenomenological Analysis (IPA) An experiential qualitative approach to research in psychology and the social sciences. It was developed by Jonathan Smith and it offers insights into how a person makes sense of a particular experiential phenomenon – the 'insider's perspective'.

Interrogation Accusatory questioning with suspects believed to be guilty in a somewhat forceful way to gain a confession.

Intersex An individual who has undergone atypical sexual differentiation, and has external genitalia that appear to be between those of a typical female and a typical male.

Intersubjectivity The process of psychological exchange or shared cognitions between people that affect our social behaviour. We may agree about the meaning of a particular social event but often agreement *is assumed* – psychologists included. Many 'common-sense' ideas are constructed by people from the same social background and used as an everyday way to interpret the meaning of social and cultural life. If people share 'common sense', then they share an intersubjective understanding of social situations.

Interviewing Non-accusatory, fact-gathering sessions.

Intrapersonal intelligence The ability to understand oneself and be aware of one's thoughts, beliefs and intentions, and use this understanding to guide one's behaviour.

Introversion This is the polar opposite of extraversion and lies at the other end of a continuum of how outwardly focused someone is. Introversion relates to a person being primarily focused on their own needs and drives. The concept is common to most theories relating to personality traits; it has been used in understanding and measuring personality types, as in the analytic psychology developed by Carl Jung and in assessing types through the use of the Myers–Briggs Type Indicator.

Investigative interviewing The interviewing process used by the police during the course of a criminal investigation (UK). The emphasis is on evidence gathering and less on obtaining confessions.

Ion channels Pores (formed by proteins) found in cell membranes that allow or restrict the passage of ions in and out of the cell.

Ionotropic receptors Chemical receptors that, when activated, act directly to open ion channels.

Ions Positively and negatively charged atoms that are vital to maintaining the membrane potential of cells.

Iris The coloured part of the eye which controls the amount of light that enters the pupil.

Job analysis   This is a process that entails unpacking the main tasks, roles and responsibilities that are undertaken by a person holding a specific job. Job analysis involves a lot of fact finding about the job role, but also the characteristics of the person who would be ideally suited to hold that role. Methods of job analysis include collecting data through interviews of current post-holders and observation of their behaviour.

Just-world hypothesis   The belief that people have a need to believe that we live in a world where people generally get what they deserve and deserve what they get.

Klinefelter's syndrome   A male who receives an additional X chromosome during conception (XXY sex chromosomes). Such individuals tend to have a more feminised appearance.

Laissez-faire capitalism   An economic system where transactions between private parties are free from government regulations (such as restrictions, tariffs and subsidies) except for rights to protect property.

Language acquisition device (LAD)   A system proposed by Chomsky that young infants have. It helps them navigate the grammar of language, which in turn helps language development.

Lateral geniculate nucleus   An area of the thalamus that processes visual information.

Lemma   An abstract concept that specifies the meaning of what is to be said but does not map directly onto any specific sounds.

Lens   The part of the eye that focuses incoming light onto the retina.

Levels of processing theory   The theory that deep, semantic processing leads to better retention than shallow, perceptual processing.

Lexeme   A basic unit of meaning regardless of the number of inflections or words.

Lexical   Relates to the words or vocabulary of a language.

Lexicon   A language's inventory of lexemes (a basic unit of meaning regardless of the number of inflections or words).

Ligand   Any substance (e.g. neurotransmitter or drug) with the capacity to bind to a receptor.

Likert scale   Developed by Rensis Likert (1932). A scale for measuring attitudes, typically using a score from 1 to 5 across a range of attitudes such as 'agree strongly' to 'disagree strongly'.

Limbic system   A group of interconnected forebrain structures that plays a role in memory and emotion.

Linguistic intelligence   The capacity to use spoken and written words and languages.

Lipids   Substances that are fat soluble.

Locus of control   The extent to which people believe they are in control of the events that affect them. People with an internal locus of control think that situations around them are the direct result of their own actions and can therefore influence them. In contrast, people with an external locus of control believe that the events are due to circumstantial factors that are completely outside their control.

Logical-mathematical intelligence   The capacity for logic reasoning and dealing with numbers.

Logogens   An array of specialised recognition units, each able to recognise one particular word.

Longitudinal design   A piece of research that follows a set group of people over a prolonged period of time, usually over a number of years.

Longitudinal studies   This is research that observes the same participants over a period of time. These observations can be over weeks, months or years, or perhaps even over someone's lifetime. These studies are important in areas such as developmental psychology, where researchers are interested in how people develop over a given period. The central feature of longitudinal research is that it tracks the same people. In personality psychology, this can be an important tool to see how people's personalities develop over time and in relation to positive and negative events.

Long-term memory   Memory for material that has left consciousness and has to be brought back into mind. This term also describes experiments with a long delay between presentation and test (presumed to measure long-term memory).

Long-term recency   Enhanced memory for the most recent of a sequence of items or events that are spread over a long period (e.g. for the last few films seen at the cinema).

Long-term store   A key component of the modal model of memory. Items held in the short-term store for an extended period are more likely to pass into the long-term store.

Machiavellianism   Named after Renaissance Italian Niccolò Machiavelli (Google him), the term describes a duplicitous interpersonal style associated with cynical beliefs and pragmatic morality. It is sometimes referred to as one of the dark triad personalities.

Macula   The area of the eye that falls in the centre of the retina.

Magnetic resonance imaging (MRI)   An imaging technique that measures the response of the protons in body tissues to high-frequency radio waves when placed in a strong magnetic field. It differs from fMRI in that it measures structure but not activity.

Material and immaterial   If something is material it is made up of the atoms and molecules that are building blocks of our world, whereas if it is immaterial it is not made up of these things. We cannot measure or see immaterial things, such as 'mind', which challenges their existence. The existence of immaterial things is a matter of belief rather than evidence.

Maturational lag   A delay in reaching developmental milestones. Generally, it suggests a non-linear rate of development.

Means–ends analysis   Setting a goal and then breaking it down to produce subgoals which need to be achieved, thus creating a 'means to an end'.

Medulla oblongata   Most caudal part of the brain stem that regulates breathing and heart rate.

Membrane potential   The voltage difference across the cell membrane, i.e. the differences in voltage between the interior and the exterior of the cell.

Memory distrust syndrome   When an individual begins to question their own memory and may, for example, wrongly believe that they actually committed a crime based on external information rather than relying on their own memories.

Meninges   The three protective membranes (dura mater, arachnoid and pia mater) that surround the brain and spinal cord.

Menopause   A series of changes in hormone functioning that occurs in women, that results in an inability to have children.

Mental illness   A psychological or behavioural abnormality of sufficient severity that psychological or psychiatric intervention is warranted.

Mental lexicon   The mental store of words that can be drawn upon in thought or speech.

Mental representations   An internal cognitive map of stimuli.

Mental states   In the philosophy of mind, a mental state is unique to thinking and feeling beings, and forms part of our cognitive processes. These processes include our beliefs and attitudes as well as our perceptions and sensations, such as the taste of wine or the pain of a headache.

Mere exposure   The finding that mere exposure to an item will increase positive feelings towards it (Zajonc, 1968).

Mesencephalon   Another name for midbrain.

Meshing   How an adult's and an infant's behaviours fit together.

Meta-analysis   A literature review that summarises and contrasts findings by calculating effect sizes.

Metabolic rate   The rate at which the body uses energy to perform various physical and biological activities, such as exercise, respiration and heartbeat.

Metabotropic receptors   A form of G protein coupled chemical receptor that when activated indirectly (via activation of a G protein) opens ion channels.

Metencephalon   The most anterior section of the hindbrain consisting of the cerebellum and the pons.

Microdialysis   A sampling technique that measures the concentration of extracellular substances in tissue. Used in neuroscience to measure the concentration of neurotransmitters in brain tissue.

Microglia   Small glial cells that constitute the major immune system of the CNS, 'swallowing' infectious agents (phagocytosis) and producing inflammatory responses.

Micrometre (μm)   Unit of measurement equal to 10^{-6} m.

Midbrain   The middle division of the brain that includes the tectum and the tegmentum.

Middle ear   The part of the ear that contains the ossicles and the Eustachian tube.

Millivolts (mV)   Unit of measurement equal to one-thousandth (10^{-3}) of a volt.

Mindfulness   Directing attention, on purpose, in the present and non-judgementally.

Minimal intergroup paradigm   An experimental technique used to form groups on an *ad hoc* basis to study social categorisation.

Minimal intergroup studies   A way of exploring the minimal conditions necessary for discrimination to occur.

Mitochondria   Organelles found within the neurone. They are important for producing chemical energy in the form of adenosine triphosphate, but also play a vital role in a number of other cellular processes.

Mnemonics   Strategies for helping people to remember information, usually involving cues such as rhyme or imagery.

Modal model   The model of short-term memory exemplified by Atkinson and Shiffrin (1968), which includes a limited capacity short-term store and an unlimited capacity long-term store.

Mood   A prevaling state of feeling in relation to a transient emotion.

Motherese   More recently termed 'child-directed speech', the act of using a sing-song voice, speaking slowly or using simple language when talking to an infant.

Motionese   The act of slowing down the pace of gestures, exaggerating and simplifying gestures when interacting with an infant.

Motivated tactician   As a midpoint between the naive scientist and the cognitive miser, the argument that we can use either of those strategies as the situation requires (Kruglanski, 1996).

Motivation   An internal state or desire that initiates or maintains behaviour.

Motor neurone   Type of neurone with its soma located in the CNS. Responsible for sending outgoing motor information along axons to sites outside the CNS (e.g. to muscles).

Multi Agency Public Protection Arrangements (MAPPA)   Comprise members of the National Probation Service, Prison Service and Police who together oversee the management of high-risk sex offenders, violent offenders and other types of sexual offender who pose a serious risk of harm to the public.

Multiple intelligences   The theory of multiple intelligences, proposed by Howard Gardner, holds that there are many kinds of human intelligence in addition to the intelligence that is measured with conventional IQ tests.

Multipolar neurone   The most common type of neurone in the CNS. Typically possesses a long axon and many dendrites.

Musical intelligence   Abilities that involve hearing and performing sounds, rhythm and music.

Myelin   Fatty insulating sheath deposited by glial cells that surrounds the axons of some neurones and nerve cells.

Naive scientist   The idea that when making attributions we try to understand other people's behaviour in a rational way, seeking to find stable causes, in a naive scientific manner (Heider, 1958).

Negative priming   When a participant is effectively inhibiting attention towards a distracting item, if that item is then deemed relevant in the next trial of the task, their response will typically be slowed.

Neurites Collective term for axons and dendrites (i.e. any projection from the soma).

Neurone doctrine The widely accepted theory, originally espoused by Cajal, that nerve cells are discrete units and are separate from one another.

Neurone membrane The 'skin' that bounds the neurone and which is composed of the phospholipid bilayer.

Neurones Specialised cells found in the CNS that are responsible for communication of information.

Neuroticism A personality trait characterised by feelings of anxiety, tension, anger and/or depression.

Neurotransmitters Chemical substances released from neurone terminals into the synaptic cleft that can affect the activation of another adjacent neurone.

Nodes of Ranvier Small gaps in the myelination of axons that are necessary for saltatory conduction of action potentials.

Nomothetic and idiographic measures Nomothetic approaches look for laws of behaviour and collect measures that can be observed and verified and quantified. They are concerned with averages and norms. By contrast, idiographic approaches look for unique and individual experiences. The term 'nomothetic fallacy' refers to the common belief that if you can name a problem, then you have solved it. For example, if you feel very upset and someone says you have post-traumatic stress, you still feel upset.

Normative influence The process by which the normal or ideal is defined and, by implication, set up as a standard which people should aim for. Also, the enhancement of happiness through having a lovely colleague called Christine Norman working with you.

Nucleus Organelle found within the soma of a cell that contains the genetic information necessary for cell form and function.

Object permanency This is the ability to understand that an object still exists even if it is no longer visible.

Obsessive compulsive disorder (OCD) A condition associated with unwanted and unpleasant thoughts or images that repeatedly come to mind, causing anxiety. The thoughts are accompanied by a compulsion to make repetitive behaviours or mental acts to try to stop the obsession coming true. Offers insights into how a person makes sense of a particular experiential phenomenon.

Old–new recognition A memory test in which one item is presented at a time and the participant indicates if it is a 'new' (unrecognised) or an 'old' (recognised) item.

Oligodendrocytes Glial cells responsible for myelination of neurone axons within the CNS.

Openness to experience One of the personality factors in the five-factor model. This factor refers to people who have high levels of creative tendencies, a thirst for knowledge and an active imagination. A high score on this factor may also indicate the drive to pursue an unconventional lifestyle.

Operant conditioning The process of learning identified by B.F. Skinner, in which learning occurs as a result of positive or negative reinforcement of an animal or human being's action.

Optic flow The apparent motion of objects in the visual scene caused by an observer moving through the scene.

Optic nerve An array of axons that carry information from the eye to the brain.

Orbitofrontal cortex Part of the prefrontal cortex of the brain located above the eye sockets. In humans, it is thought to be involved in decision making and in signalling the emotional value and expectation of reward punishments in a given situation.

Organ of Corti The sensory organ for hearing located in the cochlea.

Organelles Little 'organs' found within cells such as the nucleus, Golgi apparatus and endoplasmic reticulum. Organelles are membrane-bound and perform specialised roles within the cell.

Organisational hormones Hormones that a foetus is exposed to in the womb. Such hormones affect the structure of the developing foetal brain and their effects are set in place for life.

Ossicles The three small bones in the middle ear (stapes, hammer, anvil).

Outcome studies Research that is designed to measure responses to treatment and health status with the aim of supporting the development of guidelines for practice and improving quality of care.

Outer ear The external portion of the ear, consisting of the pinna, the auditory canal and the tympanic membrane.

Outer hair cells The sensory receptors in the ear which are responsible for injecting energy into the movement of the basilar membrane.

Outgroup Social group of which an individual believes they are not a member.

Over-regulation errors Children might overuse a rule that they have learnt in a particular context when it seems appropriate in a new context. In language, this might work for some invented words such as 'wug' and 'wugs' but not for irregular plurals such as 'sheep'.

Paraphilia An atypical sexual interest (see **paraphilic disorder**).

Paraphilic disorder When an atypical sexual interest causes significant distress to the individual or harm to others. Note that it is not considered a disorder or **deviant** to have an atypical sexual interest *per se*.

Paraplegia Paralysis characterised by failure to move and/or feel the lower part of the body due to damage in the thoracic, lumbar or sacral segments of the spinal cord.

Parasympathetic division Part of the autonomic nervous system that is mainly involved in restoring and preserving levels of energy in the body.

Parsimony The idea that 'less is better' and, in particular, that a complicated explanation is not needed when a simple one is sufficient.

Pavlov's log Conditioned reflex action causing bowels to relax as soon as you see the toilet door.

Perception The process of making sense of the world around us.

Perceptual constancies The way that perception of an object remains unchanged despite changes in lighting or viewing angle.

Perceptual processing Processing of material to extract superficial sensory characteristics, such as shape or colour.

Peripheral autonomic nervous system One of two divisions of the peripheral nervous system responsible for regulating the internal bodily environment by controlling organs, muscles and glands.

Peripheral nervous system The division of the nervous system outside the brain and spinal column consisting of the somatic and the autonomic systems.

Perseveration errors When a participant repeats items in a recall task.

Personality The characteristic patterns of thoughts, feelings and behaviours that make a person unique.

Personality coefficient Contrary to the belief that an individual's personality is consistent over time, Mischel (1968) suggested that humans are consistently inconsistent. By examining a range of studies into how personality traits are related to units of behaviour, Mischel found an average correlation coefficient of 0.30 (which represents a weak correlation at best) with regard to correlations between two single behaviours in two separate situations.

Phagocytes Cells which are able to 'swallow' and break down unwanted materials, such as pathogens and cell debris.

Phenomenology Based on the idea that the ordinary world of lived experience is taken for granted and often unnoticed, phenomenology attempts to discover how people know and understand objects (and other people) from the way they perceive and construct ideas about the social world around them.

Phenotype The characteristics of an organism resulting from the interaction between its genetic makeup and the environment. These characteristics can be biological or behavioural.

Phenylketonuria (PKU) An inherited, metabolic disorder that can result in learning difficulties and other neurological problems. People with this disease have difficulty breaking down and using the amino acid phenylalanine. PKU can be managed by a diet restricted in foods that contain this amino acid.

Phobia An unreasonable and persistent fear of a specific object, action or place.

Phoneme The smallest distinguishing unit in spoken language.

Phonemes The smallest unit of sound that is able to carry some meaning in language.

Photoreceptor cells The sensory receptors in the eye which are responsible for converting light energy into electrical signals.

Pidgin and creole A shared language developed when two communities with different languages join together.

Pinna The visible part of the ear, on the outside of our heads.

Pinocytosis The reverse process to exocytosis. The cell 'pinches up' the transmitter into vesicles and takes it back into the cell.

Pituitary gland Endocrine gland, also called hypophysis, that is ventral to the hypothalamus.

Placebo effect An inactive substance or fake treatment that produces a response in patients.

Plasticity The ability of the brain to adapt to deficits or injury.

Pons Metencephalic structure, ventral in the brain stem, that relays sensory information to the cerebellum and thalamus.

Population ageing The trend for the oldest age groups in society to grow faster than the younger age groups.

Positive manifold Charles Spearman's discovery that an individual's performance on any two tests of cognitive abilities is positively correlated.

Positive symptoms A set of symptoms experienced in Schizophrenia that appear to represent psychological excesses of behaviour. Includes delusions, disorganised thinking and speech, inappropriate affect and hallucinations.

Positron emission tomography (PET) A functional imaging technique that measures body tissue activity by detecting positrons that are emitted from radioactive substances that have been ingested, inhaled or injected.

Post-synaptic events Events that occur in the post-synaptic cell ('after' the synaptic cleft).

Post-synaptic membrane Synaptic element associated with the post-synaptic neurone. It is here that neurotransmitters bind to post-synaptic receptors.

Post-synaptic neurone Neurone that is 'after' the synaptic cleft (i.e. the receiving neurone).

Post-synaptic potentials Graded changes in membrane voltage in the post-synaptic cell (caused by input into that cell) that affects the likelihood that the post-synaptic cell will produce an action potential.

Post-traumatic stress disorder An anxiety disorder resulting from experience with a catastrophic event beyond the normal range of human suffering, and characterised by (a) numbness to the world, (b) reliving the trauma in dreams and memories, and (c) symptoms of anxiety.

Potassium (K^+) Positively charged ion that plays a role in producing and maintaining membrane potentials.

Practical intelligence The ability to solve problems in everyday life. This ability draws upon 'tacit knowledge' which is gained through experience and practice, and is difficult to explain with words.

Precursor In biochemistry, a substance from which more complex compounds are made.

Prefrontal cortex The anterior (front) most area of the frontal lobe of the brain thought to be responsible in humans for executive function, i.e. planning, problem solving, reasoning and working memory. It is divided into the orbitofrontal and dorsolateral regions.

Prejudice An unreasonable or unfair dislike of something or, more usually, of someone, typically because they belong to a specific race, religion or group.

Presentation The phase of a memory experiment in which the experimenter presents the to-be-remembered material to participants.

Pre-synaptic events Events that occur in the pre-synaptic neurone ('before' the synaptic cleft).

Pre-synaptic membrane Synaptic element associated with the pre-synaptic neurone. It is from here that neurotransmitters are released.

Pre-synaptic neurone Neurone that is 'before' the synaptic cleft (i.e. the transmitting neurone).

Primacy effect Good recall of the first few items of a set of stimuli (e.g. word list).

Primary auditory cortex The first cortical structure responsible for processing sound.

Primary dimensions of intellectual abilities Louis Leon Thurstone found that human intelligence comprises a number of independent cognitive abilities, all of which are of equal importance. Thurstone suggested that there are seven primary dimensions of intellectual abilities.

Primary memory James's (1890) term for the immediate contents of consciousness and a precursor to the more modern idea of a short-term store.

Proactive inhibition Prior learning makes it harder to learn new assocations (e.g. a prior dog–cat association makes it harder to learn dog–bone).

Probabilistic reasoning How we reason under varying degrees of uncertainty.

Procedural knowledge Knowledge that we have that is difficult to put into words, such as how to ride a bicycle.

Production system A system that uses facts and rules about those facts to govern its behaviour. The term arises because rules are also known as productions.

Progestin-induced pseudohermaphroditism A similar condition to congenital adrenal hyperplasia, whereby a foetus is exposed to an excess of androgen-like substances (progestin) in the womb.

Prosencephalon Another name for forebrain.

Prosocial behaviour The act of helping out another person, whether as a helping behaviour or as an act of altruism.

Protoconversations Early turn-taking behaviour between adults and infants whereby adults tend to vocalise when the infants are not vocalising.

Pseudohermaphrodites These individuals have gonads that are consistent with their sex chromosomes (ovaries in females and testes in males) but have ambiguous internal and external genitalia.

Psychodynamic Dealing with psychological forces that influence the mind and behaviour.

Psychological intervention A procedure that is designed to interrupt, interfere with or modify a pattern of thought, feeling, experience or behaviour.

Psychometric Standardised psychological tests that are used to measure psychological constructs such as intelligence.

Psychometric approach Any attempt to assess and express numerically the mental characteristics of behaviour in individuals, usually through specific tests for personality or intelligence or some kind of attitude measurement.

Psychometric tests Instruments which have been developed for measuring mental characteristics. Psychological tests have been developed to measure a wide range of things, including creativity, job attitudes and skills, brain damage and, of course, 'intelligence'.

Psychopathology The study of the origin, development and experience of psychological or behavioral disorders.

Psychopathy A personality type characterised by anti-social behaviour, callousness and the ability to charm and manipulate others.

Psychopharmacology The study of drugs with a focus on their psychological effects.

Psychoticism Hans Eysenck suggested a three-factor model of personality in which psychoticism represented individuals who are reckless, unable to empathise with others' situations and who are likely to commit anti-social acts. Psychoticism has also been termed 'tough-mindedness' (as opposed to 'tender-mindedness') and this is due to people with high psychoticism levels being likely to be ruthless in their dealings with others. Originally, Eysenck believed that high levels of psychoticism could predict an individual's vulnerability to experiencing psychotic symptoms, including schizophrenia.

Psychotropic drugs Medications which work directly on the brain.

Puberty The physiological process resulting in sexual maturity. This process is marked in males by the onset of sperm production and a liking for metal music (spermarche) while in females it triggers the onset of the menstrual cycle (menarche).

Pupil The opening in the iris through which light enters the eye.

Qualitative and quantitative methods These are different ways to research in psychology with different assumptions about what data can be obtained: **quantitative research** gathers data in forms which can be categorised, ranked or measured. Statistical analysis of the data enables hypotheses to be evaluated and interpretation made based on the probability that a significant effect has been measured, given that tests and sampling are valid; **qualitative research** gathers data from, for example, diary accounts, open-ended questionnaires, interviews and observations. It is useful for studies at the individual level and in-depth or case studies about people's experiences and accounts of social events. Data that is already 'out there', such as video or written accounts or conversations, can also be studied. Rigorous analyses can be undertaken at various levels to identify patterns or themes or ways of recognising ways of talking, as in discourse or conversation analysis.

Qualitative data Describe meaning and experience rather than providing numerical values for behaviour, such as frequency counts.

Quantitative data   Focus on numbers and frequencies rather than on meaning or experience.

Race   Commonly used to refer to groups of people such as white people or black people. It implies a genetic component to the differences between these groups, but research shows that the term 'race' has no biological validity and is best described as a political construct.

Racism   The use of the pervasive power imbalance between races to oppress dominated peoples by devaluing their experience, behaviour and aspirations.

Randomised controlled trial   To assess the effect of a treatment, the experiment should include appropriate control conditions (e.g. a 'no treatment' condition and a 'placebo', or 'dummy' treatment). Ideally, the participant and experimenter are 'blind' to the condition the participants belong to.

Rape acceptance myths   A person's, society's or culture's endorsement or subscription to rape myths. Rape myths are prejudicial, stereotyped or false beliefs about rape, rape victims and rapists which serve to justify and legitimise sexual aggression towards women and shift the blame onto rape victims.

Rate law   A law relating to the conduction of action potentials that the strength of an action potential is signalled by the frequency of firing as all action potentials are of the same size.

Reactivity   A term used to describe the way in which the behaviour of research subjects can be affected by some aspect of the research procedure. Most commonly, it is used to describe the way in which the behaviour of someone who is being observed is affected by the knowledge that they are being observed.

Realistic conflict theory   The theory that competition for resources between groups causes conflict.

Recall   Where participants are prompted to remember the material that was originally presented.

Recency effect   Good recall of the last few items of a set of stimuli (e.g. the last few items on a word list).

Receptors   Proteins embedded in cell membranes that respond to ligands (specific chemical substances, e.g. neurotransmitters).

Recessive gene   A gene which must be present on both chromosomes in a pair to show outward signs of a certain characteristic.

Reciprocity   Helping someone else, on the basis that they will voluntarily help you at some undefined point in the future.

Recognition   When the original material is re-presented and participants indicate whether they remember it or not.

Recognition failure   Recognition failure of recallable words occurs when participants recall items that they fail to recognise (a phenomenon impossible in generate-recognise theory).

Reductionism   The idea that a complex system is nothing more than the sum of its parts, and that a description of a system can be reduced to descriptions of the individual components.

Reductionist   See reductionism.

Reissner's membrane   A membrane in the cochlea.

Relative deprivation   An individual's perception that they are getting less than they deserve compared to other people or groups.

Reliability   The reliability of a psychological measuring device (such as a test or a scale) is the extent to which it gives consistent measurements. The greater the consistency, the more reliable the device.

Retention interval   The gap between presentation and test in a memory experiment.

Reticular formation   Network of neurones in the brain stem that regulates arousal and consciousness.

Reticular theory   The theory espoused by Golgi that nerve cells are continuous (actually join) to each other.

Retina   The sensory organ for sight that lines the back of the eye.

Retinal ganglion cells   Cells in the eye which receive information from the rods and cones.

Retrieval   The stage of memory where information is brought back into mind to be used or reported.

Retrieval cue   Any stimulus that helps us recall information, for example a picture, an odour or a sound.

Retroactive inhibition   Learning new material during the retention interval interferes with older learning (e.g. learning dog–bone would interfere with an earlier dog–cat association).

Retrograde axoplasmic transport   Backwards conveyance of material along the axon of a neurone (i.e. from synaptic button towards the soma).

Reuptake   Process by which certain neurotransmitters are taken back into the releasing cell.

Rhombencephalon   Another name for hindbrain.

Rhyme   This is where one word sounds the same as another word, for example 'stair' and 'pear'. They do not necessarily contain the same rime unit (consonants and vowel sequence).

Ribonucleic acid (RNA)   Nucleic acid that has a number of roles, including protein synthesis and gene regulation.

Rime   The vowel sound of a word followed by the subsequent consonants, for example, the rime of 'ham' is 'am'. When two words share the same rime unit, they can be said to rhyme.

Risk factor   Any factor that is felt to contribute to problematic behaviour or thought.

Risky behaviour   This may include behaviour that puts the person in danger physically or mentally. Common examples include use of alcohol and substances, unprotected sexual intercourse and illegal behaviours (such as shoplifting or vandalism).

Risky shift   When individual group members all favour a relatively risky course of action prior to group discussion, the decision made after group discussion is more risky than the average of individual positions would have predicted.

Rods   The photoreceptor cells in the eye which are extremely sensitive to movement and are responsible for our peripheral vision.

Role conflict   When an individual has two or more different and incompatible roles at the same time, resulting in anxiety and/or stress.

Role theory A perspective in social psychology that considers how we manage everyday activity (rights, duties, expectations and norms of behaviour) by fulfilment of socially defined social roles (e.g. mother, manager, teacher).

Saccades Fast movement of an eye between fixation points (measured by eye tracking).

Salutogenesis This concept focuses on the science of 'good health' and the factors that influence a person's physical and mental wellbeing.

Scaffolding This occurs when adults guide the learning of a child by simplifying the structure of the child's learning environment.

Scapegoat Someone who is (often unfairly) made to take the blame for something.

Schema A mental representation of some aspect of the world built from experience and into which new experiences are fitted.

Schizophrenia A psychological disorder marked by a range of positive and negative symptoms, predominantly disorganised thoughts, lack of contact with reality and sometimes hallucinations. Schizophrenia is not a single condition but is best described as a syndrome. The typical symptoms include difficulties in organising behaviour (including speech) as well as detachment from reality which may involve delusion and/or hallucinations. Schizophrenia is often misrepresented in the popular media as a case of split or multiple personalities.

Schizotypy The presence of certain stable features in the typical population that when high may suggest an increased risk for schizophrenia. These include a tendency for odd beliefs, such as belief in special, almost magical powers, or having the ability to read others' minds, unusual perceptions, lack of enjoyment from social sources and reckless behaviour.

Schwann cells Glial cells responsible for myelination of nerve axons within the PNS.

Scientific revolution In the sixteenth and seventeenth centuries there was a period of rapid change in the intellectual endeavour of making sense of the world in which people lived. Medieval philosophy was replaced by scientific principles of observation, measurement and experimentation. These developments are linked with Bacon (1561–1626), Galileo (1564–1642), Descartes (1596–1650) and Newton (1642–1727).

Search space The states that can be visited when trying to solve a problem.

Second messenger Substance released as part of a series of cascading effects in metabotropic receptors that result in the opening of ion channels.

Self-actualisation The full development of one's potential and realisation of one's potential.

Self-categorisation theory Building directly on social identity theory, Turner et al. (1987) focused on the social-cognitive effects that arise from putting oneself into a group, for example, the adoption of group norms derived from the concept of a prototypical group member.

Self-concept or self-identity 'The individual's belief about himself or herself, including the person's attributes and who and what the self is' Baumeister (1999).

Self-efficacy The belief in one's own ability to plan and carry out a set of intended actions in order to accomplish tasks and reach one's goals.

Self-fulfilling prophecy A prediction that directly or indirectly causes itself to become true.

Semantic Relating to the meaning of a word.

Semantic differential scales Developed by Osgood, Suci and Tannenbaum (1957), a set of diametrically opposite adjectives upon which the participant marks a score.

Semantic processing Processing of material that extracts meaning from it (e.g. deciding whether it completes a sentence).

Semi-permeable membrane A membrane that allows some ions or molecules to pass through it but not others.

Sensation The stimulation of our sensory systems which cause the nervous system to send electrical impulses to the brain.

Sense of coherence If a person has high levels of sense of coherence, this has been associated with having good mental health. With sense of coherence, a person's world is seen as controllable (i.e. she or he can influence what happens to them), sensible (i.e. the events that occur can be explained and understood) and meaningful (i.e. that person has a sense of purpose).

Sensitive period A period of development, usually early in life, during which the individual is most sensitive to certain types of experience or learning. It refers to a period that is more extended than a critical period.

Sensory neurone Type of neurone that has its cell body located in peripheral ganglia and receives sensory information from organs via (typically) long dendrites. In turn, this information is transmitted along axons to sites within the CNS.

Separation anxiety The resulting fear or apprehension of a child after the removal of a parent or other significant figure.

Serial position curve A plot of the percentage of correct responses as a function of order of presentation (e.g. the position of a word in a list).

Sexism A negative attitude towards a group on the basis of their sex/gender.

Sexual preoccupation An abnormally intense interest in sex; thinking about sex all the time and sexualising all one's encounters and interactions with others.

Short-term memory Memory for the immediate contents of consciousness (e.g. maintained by rehearsal or some other process that can act only in the short term). Also describes experiments that have an immediate test or only a brief interval between presentation and test (presumed to measure short-term memory).

Short-term store A key component of the modal model of short-term memory. Items enter the short-term store as a consequence of attention to environmental stimuli.

SIDE (social identity model of deindividuation effects) This model postulates that deindividuation involves a switch from personal to collective identity, rather than a loss of identity and the automatic adoption of negative behaviours.

Situationalism or situationalist critique   The viewpoint proposed by Walter Mischel (1968) and others that our behaviour is primarily determined by factors beyond our personalities. The overall emphasis of this approach is to demonstrate that personality traits or types are not the dominant factor influencing our actions; it is how we interpret situations, and our roles within the situations, that matter.

Snowball effect   The processes by which the opinions of the majority shift in order to agree with the position of the minority, which is then, strictly speaking, no longer a minority.

Social categorisation   The way in which we categorise people into social groups across society.

Social change   In social identity theory, the rejection of current relations between groups and the collective group effort to bring about a change in those relations.

Social comparison   The comparison of our own attitudes, beliefs and behaviours with other people's in order to establish whether they are acceptable.

Social constructionism   An approach to psychology which focuses on meaning and power; it aims to account for the ways in which phenomena are socially constructed.

Social constructivism   A theoretical approach that emphasises the role of culture and context in children's understanding and development.

Social facilitation   The effect that the presence of one or more people can have to boost our performance.

Social grooming or allogrooming   A behaviour seen in many social species, including our own. It involves an individual or individuals assisting others to keep clean and in good condition. In addition to the obvious health benefits, the behaviour has also taken on a significant social function.

Social hierarchies   Classic research describes a pecking order which determines the dominant and subordinate positions of individuals. This is a pyramid-like form of organisation that has at its head the most dominant individual, while others will be at various levels of dominance or influence.

Social identity   An individual's membership of a social group and their acceptance of the group's attitudes, beliefs and behaviours.

Social identity approach   First developed as social identity theory by H. Tajfel and J.C. Turner (1979), these approaches follow the notion that group memberships are central to our self-concept and self-evaluation, thus linking groups and individuals.

Social identity theory   The explanation of how group membership can influence behaviour. The theory suggests that as a member of a group it is our social self and not our personal self which guides our beliefs and attitudes and therefore our behaviours.

Social inhibition   Refers to how the presence of one or more people can have a detrimental effect on our performance.

Social loafing   The reduction in individual effort that can occur in tasks when only group performance is measured (not each person individually).

Social mobility   In social identity theory, when an individual moves from one group into another group with perceived higher status.

Social processes   The ways in which individuals or groups interact and how relationships and social understandings about what is happening affects decision making and behaviour.

Social responsibility   A social norm that says we should help those in trouble, particularly those who seem to be suffering unfairly.

Socio-technical systems   From identifying the social interactions between people in a work group or organisation (along with their needs), and identifying the more traditional cybernetic system of the work task, a socio-technical system is one which combines the two into a single larger and more complex system. Workers are not expected to contort themselves in order to serve inhuman and inflexible work demands. Rather, the technical requirements of the larger system are worked out in tandem with the social needs of the working group. The aim is improved sustainable working patterns resulting in better organisational output.

Sodium (NA+)   A positively charged ion that plays a role in producing and maintaining membrane potentials.

Soma   Cell body; contains the cell nucleus.

Somatic nervous system   The division of the peripheral nervous system that interrelates with the external world.

Somatotopical organisation   The arrangement of brain structures whereby regions of the brain represent particular parts of the body. For example, when the hand area in the primary motor cortex is activated, the hand moves.

Sound waves   Fluctuations in air pressure that result from physical vibrations in the environment.

Spatial intelligence   The ability to perceive spatial information.

Spatial resolution   In imaging, the precision with which minute adjacent points or details of an object can be distinguished.

Species   A group that exists within a genus. Members of a species in the same or different populations are able to interbreed under natural conditions to produce viable offspring. Species are defined by reproductive isolation. There is one hominid species to which we all belong called *Homo sapiens*.

Specific factors (s)   Spearman's intelligence theory suggested that each individual intelligence test measures a unique or specific factor s of intelligence, in addition to the general factor g which all of the intelligence tests have in common.

Specific learning difficulties   Neurological-based difficulties that affect the way information is learned and processed. It is an umbrella term used to describe difficulties such as dyslexia, dyspraxia and dyscalculia. A child may have difficulties with one or two areas of learning, but other aspects of development are unaffected.

Specificity approach   This is a way of seeing personality as influencing a person's tendency to experience disease or illness. Through this approach, personality is seen as directly contributing to the cause of a person's illness. For example, someone's personality can directly affect their physiology and make them experience a psychosomatic illness, such as having peptic ulcers or some kinds of skin disorders.

Speed of processing   The rate at which information is taken in, processed and responded to is a strong predictor of cognitive ability in older age.

Spinal cord   Part of the central nervous system located within the vertebral column.

Spinal nerve   A bundle of axons that transmits information to and from the spinal cord.

SRY gene   The 'sex determining region, Y chromosome' (Haqq et al., 1994). This is part of a group of genes referred to as testes determining factor (TDF).

Stereocilia   The stiff rods (or hairs) that protrude from the inner and outer hair cells in the ear.

Stereotype   An oversimplified, generalised impression of a group and its members.

Stereotype threat   The concern of an individual that they will be judged on the stereotypes of the social group to which they belong, and the concern that they will confirm this belief through their own actions (like the self-fulfilling prophecy).

Storage   The stage of memory between encoding and retrieval. Factors such as the length of the retention interval and exposure to interfering material may influence memory during this period.

Stress   'Stress is the psychological, physiological and behavioural response by an individual when they perceive a lack of equilibrium between the demands placed upon them and their ability to meet those demands, which, over a period of time, leads to ill-health' Palmer (1989).

Subarachnoid space   Space between the arachnoid layer and the pia mater that is filled with cerebrospinal fluid.

Successful intelligence   In Robert Sternberg's (2004) theory, intelligence is the individual's ability to select, shape and adapt to the environment. Someone with a high level of intelligence is successful in interacting with many different environments.

Superior colliculi   Nuclei of the tectum in the midbrain that receive visual information.

Superordinate goal   A goal desired by two or more groups which cannot be achieved by one group on its own, therefore necessitating cooperation between groups.

Syllogism   A form of deductive reasoning consisting of a major premise, a minor premise and a conclusion. For example, all Liverpool players are divers; Steven Gerrard is a Liverpool player; therefore Steven Gerrard is a diver.

Symbolic thought   The representation of reality through the use of abstract concepts such as words, gestures and numbers.

Sympathetic division   Part of the autonomic nervous system that is mainly involved in spending levels of energy in the body.

Synaethesia   Stimulation of one sense produces a sensory experience in a different sensory modality (e.g. hearing a sound produces experiences of a colour).

Synapse   Junction between cells across which information is transmitted in electrical or chemical form. Comprises a pre-synaptic and a post-synaptic membrane that are separated by the synaptic cleft.

Synaptic buttons   Terminal points of axonal branches from which the neurotransmitter is released and which form the pre-synaptic element of a synapse.

Synaptic cleft   Small (20 nanometre) gap that separates the pre- and post-synaptic membranes of a synapse.

Syntax   The rules that govern sentence structure.

System variables   These influence the accuracy of eyewitness testimony and are under the control of the criminal justice system. For example, police line-up procedures and interview techniques.

Tavistock Institute   A UK-based charitable group founded in 1947 to study and promote human relations in various social settings, including industry, commerce and healthcare. Their 'hallmark' is their use of psychoanalytic and open systems approaches to groups and organisations and, in the spirit of action-research, feeding back findings to that group or organisation as part of their intervention.

Tectorial membrane   A membrane in the cochlea.

Tectum   Dorsal division of the midbrain that consists of the superior and inferior colliculi and receives visual and auditory information.

Tegmentum   Ventral division of the midbrain that consists of the substantia nigra, red nucleus and part of the reticular formation.

Temperaments   In ancient times, a person's temperament was associated with the type of fluid (or 'humour') that was mainly flowing throughout that person's body. Nowadays, someone's temperament is mainly connected to how a person generally thinks, feels and acts; it is often associated with whether someone is prone to anxiety, anger or a range of other emotions.

Temporal resolution   The precision with which an event can be measured in time.

Teratogens   Substances or environmental influences that affect the development of the foetus, resulting in physical abnormalities.

Test   The phase of the task in which the experimenter attempts to measure memory for the material that was presented.

Testosterone   The primary type of androgen; involved in the development of male characteristics and sexual functioning.

Tetraplegia   Paralysis characterised by an inability to move and/or feel the lower part and most of the upper part of the body, secondary to damage in the cervical segments of the spinal cord.

Thalamus   Diencephalic structure that relays sensory and motor information to the cerebral cortex.

Theory of mind   The ability to attribute mental states such as beliefs, intentions and desires to yourself and others, and to understand that other people have beliefs, desires and intentions that are different from your own.

Therapist   A trained individual practising in the treatment of abnormal conditions.

Three-factor model   Also known as the PEN model after the initial letters of the three major personality traits that Hans Eysenck claimed were the core parts of people's personalities: psychoticism, extraversion and neuroticism.

Throughcare   The provision of a range of social work and other services to prisoners and their families, from the point of sentence or remand, continuing throughout imprisonment, and following release into the community. The services are focused on helping ex-prisoners resettle into the community.

Tonotopic   The spatial ordering (in the ear or brain) of the response to sound frequency, with low frequencies at one location and high frequencies at another.

Top-down processing   A way of explaining a cognitive process in which higher-level processes, such as prior knowledge, influence the processing of lower-level input, often involving voluntary control and regulation.

Tower of Hanoi   The Tower of Hanoi is a problem-solving puzzle consisting of three rods. On one of the rods are placed a number of disks of various sizes (placed in order of size from large to small). The aim is to move all disks onto another rod in the correct order of size. The constraints are that only one disk can be removed at a time and may not be placed on top of a smaller disk. The aim is to use the smallest possible number of moves to achieve the goal.

Trait   A durable form of thinking, feeling or behaving in the world that is relatively stable and predictable over a variety of different situations.

Transfer-appropriate processing   The idea that similar processing at encoding and retrieval enhances memory.

Transference   The feelings that the client has about the therapist, which are influenced by previous experiences of relationships.

Transporter molecules   Proteins integral to the cell membrane that are involved in the movement of substances (e.g. neurotransmitters) in and out of the cell.

Trial-and-error   Attempting to solve a problem by not applying any thought to it.

Turner's syndrome   A female with this condition inherits only a single X chromosome (XO sex chromosomes). Such females do not menstruate, are unable to become pregnant, do not develop breasts during puberty and are generally short in stature, but they do not differ from typical females in terms of their behaviour and interests.

Two-alternative forced-choice test   Recognition memory test in which the 'new' and 'old' items are presented simultaneously and the recognised option has to be selected.

Tympanic canal   A fluid-filled cavity in the cochlea.

Tympanic membrane   Also known as the ear drum. A thin membrane that vibrates in response to sound.

Type   A cluster of personality characteristics that consistently occur together.

Type A behaviour pattern or type A personality   This type of personality is normally linked to being at an increased risk of coronary heart disease. Two cardiologists, Friedman and Rosenman, found that the type A personality consists of a range of typical behaviour patterns ranging from irritability to competitiveness to restlessness. This type of personality is contrasted with people who have type B personality, which mainly involves a set of reactions such as being calm and relaxed and not overly competitive.

Types   Personality types are often categorisations that allow researchers to identify someone's most dominant way of thinking, feeling and acting. Whereas personality traits are assessed on many points on a continuum (i.e. ranging from high to moderate to low levels) on a given personality factor, personality types are often assessed by classifying into one category or another. For instance, if type psychology was being used and a person measured just over the average on an extraversion scale, that person would be labelled as an extravert.

Ultimate attribution error   The tendency to differentially explain similar actions by individuals of different social groups. With a member of an ingroup, if there is good behaviour or achievements, this is explained internally (within the individual, such as kindness), whereas if there is bad behaviour or failures, this is explained externally (societal or environmental factors, such as luck). The opposite applies to explanations of the behaviours of a member of another group (an 'outgroup').

Unconscious mind   The part of our mind that is beyond our conscious awareness.

Unconscious world   The part of the psyche that cannot be accessed by the conscious mind.

Unipolar neurone   Type of neurone (usually a sensory or autonomic nervous system neurone) named for its structure, having a single process arising from the cell body.

Validity   The question of whether a psychometric test or psychological measure is really measuring what it is supposed to.

Ventricle   Any of the four cavities in the brain filled with cerebrospinal fluid.

Vesicles   Membrane-bound packets of neurotransmitter found within the synaptic button.

Vestibular canal   A fluid-filled cavity in the cochlea.

Volition   The act of deciding to do something. It is also referred to as 'will'.

Voltage-gated channels   Ion channels that are sensitive to voltage and open to allow the passage of ions once a certain voltage is reached. For example, potassium channels are voltage-gated, only opening when the voltage inside the membrane becomes positive.

Voyeurism   The watching of others without their knowledge for the purpose of sexual gratification.

Withdrawal symptoms   Physiological, behavioural and/or psychological symptoms following the withdrawal of certain drugs.

Word pair   Stimulus used in a paired-associate learning-cued recall task, in which participants are presented with pairs of words to learn. At test, they are presented with one member of the pair as a cue to retrieve the other.

Working memory model   A model proposed by Baddeley and Hitch (1974) to account for many of the shortcomings of the modal model of short-term memory.

XXX syndrome   A female with this condition inherits an additional X chromosome (XXX sex chromosomes). XXX females do not have any distinguishing features and they are virtually impossible to tell apart from typical XX females.

XYY syndrome   A male with this condition inherits an additional Y chromosome (XYY sex chromosomes). Such individuals are virtually indistinguishable from typical males, though XYY males tend to be slightly taller in stature and have larger canine teeth.

Zombies and psychologists problem   Often referred to as the missionaries and cannibals problem, but we prefer our own version. Three psychologists and three zombies are on one bank of a river. They all need to cross the river but there are three constraints: (1) there is only one boat which holds a maximum of two people; (2) the number of psychologists on each river bank must at least equal the number of zombies, otherwise the zombies will eat the psychologists; (3) the boat must be occupied by at least one person whenever it crosses the river. Devise a sequence of river crossings that enable all six to cross the river while keeping within the constraints outlined.

Zone of proximal development (ZPD)   This is the gap between what a child can do by themselves and what they can achieve under adult guidance or collaboration.

α subunit   Portion of a G protein released as part of a series of cascading effects in metabotropic receptors resulting in the opening of ion channels.

REFERENCES

Abel, G.G., Becker, J., Mittelman, M., Cunningham-Rathner, J., Rouleau, J., & Murphy, W. (1987). Self-reported sex crimes of nonincarcerated paraphiliacs. *Journal of Interpersonal Violence, 2*, 3–25.

Abelson, R.P. (1972). Are attitudes necessary? In B.T. King & E. McGinnes (Eds), *Attitudes, conflict and social change.* New York: Academic Press.

Abrams, D. (1992). Processes of social identification. In G.M. Breakwell (Ed.), *Social psychology of identity and the self-concept* (pp. 57–99). London: Surrey University Press.

Ackerman, B.P., Brown, E., & Izard, C.E. (2003). Continuity and change in levels of externalizing behavior in school children from economically disadvantaged families. *Child Development, 74*, 694–709.

Adams, D. (1979). *The hitchhiker's guide to the galaxy.* London: Pan Macmillan.

Adorno, T.W., Brunswik, E.F., Levinson, D.J., & Sanford, R.N. (1950). *The authoritarian personality.* New York: Harper.

Aggleton, J.P. (1985). One-trial object recognition by rats. *Quarterly Journal of Experimental Psychology, 37*, 279–294.

Ahnert, L., Pinquart, M., & Lamb, M.E. (2006). Security of children's relationships with nonparental care providers: a meta-analysis. *Child Development, 74*, 664–679.

Ainsworth, M.D.S., Blehar, M.C., Waters, E., & Wall, S. (1978). *Patterns of attachment: a psychological study of the strange situation.* Hillsdale, NJ: Erlbaum.

Ajzen, I. (1991). Theory of planned behaviour. *Organisational Behavior and Human Decision Processes, 50*, 179–211.

Akbarian, S. (2010). Epigenetics of schizophrenia. *Current Topics in Behavioural Neuroscience, 4*, 611–628.

Akbarian, S., & Huang, H.S. (2006). Molecular and cellular mechanisms of altered expression in schizophrenia and related disorders. *Brain Research Reviews, 52*(2), 293–304.

Aldwin, C.M., Yancura, L.A., & Boeninger, D.K. (2010). Coping across the life span. In M.E. Lamb, A.M. Freund, & R.M. Lerner (Eds), *The handbook of lifespan development. Vol. 2: Social and emotional development* (pp. 298–340). Hoboken, NJ: John Wiley & Sons.

Alexander, F. (1950). *Psychosomatic medicine.* New York: W.W. Norton.

Alford, B., & Beck, A. (1997). *The integrative power of cognitive therapy.* New York: Guilford Press.

Allely, C.S., Minnis, H., Thompson, L., Wilson, P., & Gillberg, C. (2014). Neurodevelopmental and psychosocial risk factors in serial killers and mass murderers. *Aggression and Violent Behavior, 19*(3), 288–301.

Allen, G., & Courchesne, E. (2003). Differential effects of developmental cerebellar abnormality on cognitive and motor functions in the cerebellum: an fMRI study of autism. *American Journal of Psychiatry, 160*, 262–273.

Allen, L.S., & Gorski, R.A. (1990). Sex difference in the bed nucleus of the stria terminalis of the human brain. *The Journal of Comparative Neurology, 302*, 697–706.

Allen, L.S., & Gorski, R.A. (1992). Sexual orientation and the size of the anterior commissure in the human brain. *Proceedings of the National Academy of Sciences USA, 89*, 7191–7202.

Allen, L.S., Hines, M., Shryne, J.E., & Gorski, R.A. (1989). Two sexually dimorphic cell groups in the human brain. *Journal of Neuroscience, 9*, 497–506.

Allen, L.S., Richey, M.F., Chai, Y.M., & Gorski, R.A. (1991). Sex differences in the corpus callosum of the living human being. *Journal of Neuroscience, 119*, 933–942.

Allison, S.T., & Messick, D.M. (1985). The group attribution error. *Journal of Experimental Social Psychology, 21*(6), 563–579.

Allport, A. (1993). Attention and control: have we been asking the wrong questions? A critical review of twenty-five years. In D.E. Meyer and S. Kornblum (Eds), *Attention and performance XIV* (pp. 183–218). Cambridge, MA: MIT Press.

Allport, F.H. (1920). The influence of the group upon association and thought. *Journal of Experimental Psychology, 3*, 159–182.

Allport, F.H. (1924). *Social psychology.* Boston, MA: Houghton Mifflin.

Allport, G.W. (1935). Attitudes. In C. Murchison (Ed.), *Handbook of social psychology.* Worcester, MA: Clark University Press.

Allport, G.W. (1954). *The nature of prejudice.* Cambridge, MA: Addison-Wesley.

Allport, G.W. (1961). *Pattern and growth in personality.* New York: Holt, Rinehart.

Almers, W. (1990). Exocytosis. *Annual Review of Physiology, 52*, 607–624.

Alonso, J., Angermeyer, M.C., Bernert, S., Bruffaerts, R., Brugha, T.S., Bryson, H., & Vollebergh, W.A.M. (2004). Prevalence of mental disorders in Europe: results from the European Study of the Epidemiology of Mental Disorders (ESEMeD) project. *Acta Psychiatrica Scandinavica, 109*(s420), 21–27.

Altemeyer, B. (1998). The other 'authoritarian personality'. In M.P. Zanna (Ed.), *Advances in experimental social psychology* (pp. 47–92). San Diego, CA: Academic Press.

Amelang, M., & Ullwer, U. (1991). Correlations between psychometric measures and psychophysiological as well as experimental variables in studies on extraversion and neuroticism. In J. Strelau & A. Angleitner (Eds), *Explorations in temperament.* New York: Plenum.

American Psychiatric Association. (2013). *Diagnostic and statistical manual of mental disorders* (5th edn). Arlington, VA: American Psychiatric Publishing.

Amichai-Hamburger, Y., & McKenna, K.Y.A. (2006). The contact hypothesis reconsidered: interacting via the internet. *Journal of Computer-Mediated Communication*, *11*(3), 825–843.

Amir, Y. (1969). Contact hypothesis in ethnic relations. *Psychological Bulletin*, *71*, 319–342.

Anderson, B., Fagan, P., Woodnutt, T., & Chamorro-Premuzic, T. (2012). Facebook psychology: popular questions answered by research. *Psychology of Popular Media Culture*, *1*(1), 23–37.

Anderson, C.A., & Bushman, B.J. (2002). Human aggression. *Psychology*, *53*(1), 27.

Anderson, J.R. (1993). *Rules of the mind.* Hove: Erlbaum.

Anderson, J.R. (2000). *Cognitive psychology and its implications* (5th edn). New York: Worth.

Anderson, J.R. (2007). Using brain imaging to guide the development of a cognitive architecture. In Gray, W.D. (Ed.) *Integrated Models of Cognitive Systems* (pp. 49–62). Oxford: Oxford University Press.

Anderson, J.R., & Reder, L.M. (1979). An elaborative processing explanation of depth of processing. In L.S. Cermak & F.I.M. Craik (Eds), *Levels of processing in human memory* (pp. 385–403). Hillsdale, NJ: Erlbaum.

Anderson, J.R., & Schooler, L.J. (2000). The adaptive nature of memory. In E. Tulving & F.I.M. Craik (Eds), *Handbook of memory* (pp. 557–570). New York: Oxford University Press.

Anderson, R.C., & Pichert, J.W. (1978). Recall of previously unrecallable information following a shift in perspective. *Journal of Verbal Learning and Verbal Behavior*, *17*, 1–12.

Anderson, S., Dallal, G., & Must, A. (2003). Relative weight and race influence average age at menarche: results from two nationally representative surveys of U.S. girls studied 25 years apart. *Pediatrics*, *111*, 844–850.

Antonovsky, A. (1987). *Unraveling the mystery of health: how people manage stress and stay well.* San Francisco, CA: Jossey-Bass.

Archer, D., & McDaniel, P. (1995). Violence and gender: differences and similarities across societies. In R.B. Ruback & N.A. Weiner (Eds), *Interpersonal violent behaviors: social and cultural aspects* (pp. 63–87). New York: Springer.

Archer, J. (2004). Sex differences in aggression in real-world settings: a meta-analytic review. *General Review of Psychology*, *8*, 291–322.

Arminen, I. (2004). Second stories: the saliency of interpersonal communication for mutual help in Alcoholics Anonymous. *Journal of Pragmatics*, *36*, 319–347.

Arnett, J.J. (1999). Adolescent storm and stress, reconsidered. *American Psychologist*, *54*, 317–326.

Arnett, J.J. (2007). Emerging adulthood: what is it, and what is it good for? *Child Development Perspectives*, *1*(2), 68–73.

Arnett, J.J. (2008). The neglected 95%: why American psychology needs to become less American. *American Psychologist*, *63*(7), 602–614.

Arnett, J.J., & Balle-Jensen, L. (1993). Cultural bases of risk behavior: Danish adolescents. *Child Development*, *64*(6), 1842–1855.

Arnow, B.A., Desmond, J.E., Banner, L.L., Glover, G.H., Solomon, A., Polan, M.L., Lue, T.F., & Atlas, S.W. (2002). Brain activation and sexual arousal in healthy, heterosexual males. *Brain*, *125*, 1014–1023.

Aronson, E. (2008). *The social animal* (10th edn). New York: Worth.

Asch, S.E. (1951). Effects of group pressure upon the modification and distortion of judgments. In H. Guetzkow (Ed.), *Groups, leadership and men* (pp. 177–190). Pittsburgh, PA: Carnegie Press.

Asher, J.E., Lamb J.A., Brocklebank, D., Cazier, J.B., Maestrini, E., Addis, L., Sen, M., Baron-Cohen, S. & Monaco, A.P. (2009). A whole-Genome scan and fine mapping linkage study of auditory-visual synaesthesia reveals evidence of linkage to chromosomes 2q24, 5q33, 6p12, and 12p12. *American Journal of Human genetics*, *84*, 279–285.

Ashton, M.C., Lee, K., Perugini, M., Szarota, P., de Vries, R.E., Di Blas, L., Boies, K., & De Raad, B. (2004). A six-factor structure of personality-descriptive adjectives: solutions from psycholexical studies in seven languages. *Journal of Personality and Social Psychology*, *86*(2), 356–366.

Atchison, J. (1996). *The seeds of speech: language origin and evolution.* Cambridge: Cambridge University Press.

Atkinson, R.C., & Shiffrin, R.M. (1968). Human memory: a proposed system and its control processes. In K.W. Spence & J.T. Spence (Eds), *The psychology of learning and motivation: advances in research and theory* (vol. 2, pp. 742–775). New York: Academic Press.

Auer, M., & Griffiths, M.D. (2013). Limit setting and player choice in most intense online gamblers: an empirical study of online gambling behaviour. *Journal of Gambling Studies*, *29*, 647–660.

Auer, M., & Griffiths, M.D. (2014). An empirical investigation of theoretical loss and gambling intensity. *Journal of Gambling Studies*. DOI 10.1007/s10899-013-9376-7.

Awh, E., & Pashler, H. (2000). Evidence for split attentional foci. *Journal of Experimental Psychology: Human Perception and Performance*, *26*, 834–846.

Baars, B.J., Michael T.M., & Donald G.M. (1975). Output editing for lexical status in artificially elicited slips of the tongue. *Journal of Verbal Learning and Verbal Behavior*, *14*(4), 382–391.

Bach, P. (2007). Psychotic disorders. In D.W. Wood & I.W. Kanter (Eds), *Understanding behavior disorders: a contemporary behavioral perspective* (pp. 217–236). Reno, NV: Context Press.

Back, M., Stopfer, J., Vazire, S., Gaddis, S., Schmukle, S., Egloff, B., & Gosling, S. (2010). Facebook profiles reflect actual personality, not self-idealization. *Psychological Science*, *21*(3), 372–374.

Baddeley, A. (2000). The episodic buffer: a new component of working memory? *Trends in Cognitive Sciences*, *4*(11), 417–423.

Baddeley, A. (2012). Working memory: theories, models, and controversies. *Annual Review of Psychology*, *63*, 1–29.

Baddeley, A.D. (1978). The trouble with levels: a reexamination of Craik and Lockhart's framework for memory research. *Psychological Review*, *85*, 139–152.

Baddeley, A.D., & Hitch, G.J. (1974). Working memory. In G.H. Bower (Ed.), *The psychology of learning and motivation: advances in research and theory* (vol. 8, pp. 742–775). New York: Academic Press.

Baddeley, A.D., & Hitch, G.J. (1977). Recency reexamined. In S. Dornic (Ed.), *Attention and performance VI* (pp. 647–667). Hillsdale, NJ: Erlbaum.

Bader, S.M., Schoeneman-Morris, K.A., Scalora, M., & Cassidy, T.K. (2008). Exhibitionism: findings from a midwestern police contact sample. *International Journal of Offender Therapy and Comparative Criminology*, *52*, 270.

Baer, J.S., & Lichtenstein, E. (1988). Classification and prediction of smoking relapse episodes: an exploration of individual differences. *Journal of Consulting and Clinical Psychology*, *56*, 104–110.

Baer, R.A., Smith, G.T., Hopkins, J., Krietemeyer, J., & Toney, L. (2006). Using self-report assessment methods to explore facets of mindfulness. *Assessment*, *13*(1), 27–45.

Bagwell, C.L., Newcomb, A.F., & Bukowski, W.M. (1998). Preadolescent friendship and peer rejection as predictors of adult adjustment. *Child Development*, *69*, 140–153.

Bailey, D.H., & Geary, D.C. (2009). Hominid brain evolution. *Human Nature*, *20*(1), 67–79.

Bailey, J.M., Dunne, M.P., & Martin, N.G. (2000). Genetic and environmental influences on sexual orientation and its correlates in an Australian twin sample. *Journal of Personality and Social Psychology*, *78*, 524–536.

Bailey, J.M., & Pillard, R.C. (1991). A genetic study of male sexual orientation. *Archives of General Psychiatry*, *48*, 1089–1095.

Baird, G., Cass, H., & Slonims, V. (2003). Diagnosis of autism. *British Medical Journal*, *327*, 488–493.

Balbernie, R. (2013). The importance of secure attachment for infant mental health. *Journal of Health Visiting*, *1*, 210–217.

Baldwin, J. (1986). African (black) psychology: issues and synthesis. *Journal of Black Studies*, *16*(3), 235–249.

Ballard, P.B. (1913). Oblivescence and reminiscence. *British Journal of Psychology Monograph Supplements*, *1*, 1–82.

Bandura, A. (1977). *Social learning theory*. Englewood Cliffs, NJ: Prentice-Hall.

Banks, S.J., Eddy, K.T., Angstadt, M., Nathan, P.J., & Phan, K.L. (2007). Amygdala-frontal connectivity during emotion regulation. *Social, Cognitive, and Affective Neuroscience*, *2*(4), 303–212.

Banyard, P. (2010). Teaching the personal science: from impeccable trivia to the blooming buzzing confusion. *Psychology Teaching Review*, *16*, 38–44.

Banyard, V.L., Moynihan, M.M., & Plante, E.G. (2007). Sexual violence prevention through bystander education: an experimental evaluation. *Journal of Community Psychology*, *35*(4), 463–481.

Baptista, M. (2005). New directions in pidgin and creole studies. *Annual Review of Anthropology*, *34*, 33–42.

Bargh, J., McKenna, K., & Fitzimons, G. (2002). Can you see the real me? Activation and expression of the 'true self' on the internet. *Journal of Social Issues*, *58*(1), 33–48.

Baron, R.S. (1986). Distraction-conflict theory: progress and problems. In L. Berkowitz (Ed.), *Advances in experimental social psychology* (vol. 19, pp. 1–40). New York: Academic Press.

Baron-Cohen, S. (1995). *Mindblindness*. Cambridge, MA: MIT Press.

Baron-Cohen, S., Leslie, A.M., & Frith, U. (1985). Does the autistic child have a 'theory of mind'? *Cognition*, *21*, 37–46.

Baron-Cohen, S., Wheelwright, S., Hill, J., Raste, Y., & Plumb, I. (2001). The 'Reading the Mind in the Eyes' test revised version: A study with normal adults, and adults with Asperger syndrome or high-functioning autism. *Journal of Child Psychology and Psychiatry*, *42*(2), 241–251.

Baroody, A.J., & Gannon, K.E. (1984). The development of the commutativity principle and economical addition strategies. *Cognition and Instruction*, *1*, 321–339.

Bartlett, F.C. (1932). *Remembering: a study in experimental and social psychology*. Cambridge: Cambridge University Press.

Bashiri, H., Barahmand, U., Akabri, S.Z., Ghamari, H.G., & Vusugi, A. (2011). A study of the psychometric properties and the standardization of HEXACO personality inventory. *Procedia – Social and Behavioral Sciences*, *30*, 1173–1176.

Bass, J.D., & Mulick, J.A. (2007). Social play skill enhancement of children with autism using peers and siblings as therapists. *Psychology in the Schools*, *44*(7), 727–735.

Batson, C.D., Cochran, P.J., Biederman, M.F., Blosser, J.L., Ryan, M.J., & Vogt, B. (1978). Failure to help when in a hurry: callousness or conflict? *Personality and Social Psychology Bulletin*, *4*, 97–101.

Batson, C.D., & Coke, J.S. (1981). Empathy: a source of altruistic motivation for helping? In J.P. Rushton & R.M. Sorrentino (Eds), *Altruism and helping behavior: social, personality, and developmental perspectives*. Hillsdale, NJ: Erlbaum.

Batson, C.D., Sympson, S.C., Hindman, J.L., & Decruz, P. (1996). 'I've been there, too': effect on empathy of prior experience with a need. *Personality and Social Psychology Bulletin*, *22*(5), 474–482.

Batty M, & Taylor M.J. (2003). Early processing of the six basic facial emotional expressions. *Cognitive Brain Research*, *17*, 613–620.

Bauman, C.W., & Skitka, L.J. (2010). Making attributions for behaviors: The prevalence of correspondence bias in the general population. *Basic and Applied Social Psychology*, *32*(3), 269–277.

Baumeister, R.F. (Ed.) (1999). *The self in social psychology*. Philadelphia, PA: Psychology Press (Taylor & Francis).

Baumeister, R.F., Chesner, S.P., Senders, P.S., & Tice, D.M. (1988). Who's in charge here? Group leaders to lend help in emergencies. *Personality and Social Psychology Bulletin*, *14*, 17–22.

Bavelas, A. (1950). Communication patterns in task oriented groups. *Journal of the Acoustical Society of America*, *22*, 272–283.

Beauvois, J.-L., & Dubois, N. (1988). The norm of internality in the explanation of psychological events. *European Journal of Social Psychology*, *18*(4), 299–316.

Bebbington, P. & Kuipers, L. (1994). The predictive utility of expressed emotion in schizophrenia: an aggregate analysis. *Psychological Medicine*, *24*, 707–718.

Bechara, A. (2004). The role of emotion in decision-making: evidence from neurological patients with orbitofrontal damage. *Brain and Cognition*, *55*, 30–40.

Bechara, A. Damasio, H., & Damasio, A.R. (2000). Emotion, decision making and the orbitofrontal cortex. *Cerebral Cortex*, *10*, 295–307.

Bechara, A., Damasio, A.R., Damasio, H., & Anderson, S.W. (1994). Insensitivity to future consequences following damage to human prefrontal cortex. *Cognition*, *50*, 7–15.

Beck, A. (1963). Thinking and depression. *Archives of General Psychiatry*, *9*, 324–333.

Beck, A. (1987). Cognitive models of depression. *Journal of Cognitive Psychotherapy: An International Quarterly*, *1*, 5–37.

Beck, A. (1993). Cognitive therapy: past, present and future. *Journal of Consulting and Clinical Psychology*, *61*(2), 194–198.

Beck, A. (2002). Cognitive models of depression. In R.L. Leahy & E.T. Dowd (Eds), *Clinical advances in cognitive psychotherapy: theory and application* (pp. 29–61). New York: Springer.

Beck, A., Rush, A., Shaw, B., & Emery, G. (1979). *Cognitive therapy of depression*. New York: Guilford Press.

Beck, H.P., Levinson, S., & Irons, G. (2009). Finding little Albert: a journey to John Watson's infant laboratory. *American Psychologist*, *64*(7), 605–614.

Bee, H., & Boyd, D. (2005). *The developing child* (10th edn). Boston, MA: Pearson.

Beijersbergen, M.D., Juffer, F., Bakermans-Kranenburg, M.J., & van IJzendoorn, M.H. (2012). Remaining or becoming secure: parental sensitive support predicts attachment continuity from infancy to adolescence in a longitudinal adoption study. *Developmental Psychology*, *48*, 1277–1282.

Bell, L., Long, S., Garvan, C., & Bussing, R. (2011). The impact of teacher credentials on ADHD stigma perceptions. *Psychology in the Schools*, *48*(2), 184–197.

Bellezza, F.S., & Bower, G.H. (1981). Person stereotypes and memory for people. *Journal of Personality and Social Psychology*, *41*(5), 856–865.

Bem, D.J. (1965). An experimental analysis of self-persuasion. *Journal of Experimental Social Psychology*, *1*, 199–218.

Bem, S. (2001). The explanatory autonomy of psychology: why a mind is not a brain. *Theory and Psychology*, *11*(6), 785–795.

Bengtsson-Tops, A., & Hansson, L. (2001). The validity of Antonovsky's sense of coherence measure in a sample of schizophrenic patients living in the community. *Journal of Advanced Nursing*, *33*(4), 432–438.

Benjamin Jr, L.T., & Crouse, E.M. (2002). The American Psychological Association's response to Brown v. Board of Education: the case of Kenneth B. Clark. *American Psychologist*, *57*(1), 38–50.

Ben-Shakhar, G. (2008). The case against the use of polygraph examinations to monitor postconviction sex offenders. *Legal and Criminological Psychology*, *13*, 191–207.

Benson, P.L., Karabenick, S.A., & Lerner, R.M. (1976). Pretty pleases: the effects of physical attractiveness, race, and sex on receiving help. *Journal of Experimental Social Psychology*, *12*, 409–415.

Bentall, R. (1992). A proposal to classify happiness as a psychiatric disorder. *Journal of Medical Ethics*, *18*(2), 94–98, Copyright © 1992 by Institute of Medical Ethics

Bergman, E., & Roediger, H.L. (1999). Can Bartlett's repeated reproduction experiments be replicated? *Memory & Cognition*, *27*, 937–947.

Berkowitz, L. (1972). Social norms, feelings, and other factors affecting helping and altruism. In L. Berkowitz (Ed.), *Advances in experimental social psychology* (vol. 6, pp. 63–108). New York: Academic Press.

Berkowitz, L. (1993a). *Aggression: its causes, consequences, and control*. New York: McGraw-Hill.

Berkowitz, L. (1993b). Pain and aggression: some findings and implications. *Motivation and Emotion*, *17*, 277–293.

Berndt, T.J. (2002). Friendship quality and social development. *Current Directions in Psychological Science*, *11*(1), 7–10.

Berndt, T.J., & Keefe, K. (1995). Friends' influence on adolescents' adjustment to school. *Child Development*, *66*(5), 1312–1329.

Berntsen, D., & Thomsen, D.K. (2005). Personal memories for remote historical events: accuracy and clarity of flashbulb memories related to World War II. *Journal of Experimental Psychology: General*, *134*(2), 242.

Berridge, K.C., & Robinson, T.E. (1998). What is the role of dopamine in reward: hedonic impact, reward learning, or incentive salience? *Brain Research: Brain Research Reviews*, *28*(3), 309–369.

Berridge, K.C., Robinson, T.E., & Aldridge, J.W. (2009). Dissecting components of reward: 'liking', 'wanting', and learning. *Current Opinions in Pharmacology*, *9*(1), 65–73.

Bertenthal, B., & Fischer, K. (1978). Development of self-recognition in the infant. *Developmental Psychology*, *14*, 44–50.

Bessière, K., Seay, F., & Kiesler, S. (2007). The ideal elf: identity exploration in World of Warcraft. *CyberPsychology & Behavior*, *10*(4), 530–535.

Bickerton, D. (1984). The language bioprogram hypothesis. *Behavioral and Brain Sciences*, *7*(2), 173–221.

Bierhoff, H.W., Klein, R., & Kramp, P. (1991). Evidence for the altruistic personality from data on accident research. *Journal of Personality*, *59*(2), 263–280.

Biggerstaff, D. (2012). Qualitative research methods in psychology. In G. Rossi (Ed.), *Psychology: selected papers* (pp. 175–206). Rijeka, Croatia: InTech. Available at: www.intechopen.com/books/psychology-selected-papers/qualitative-research-methods-in-psychology (accessed 9 December 2013).

Bijeljac-Babic, R., Bertoncini, J., & Mehler, J. (1993). How do 4-day-old infants categorize multisyllabic utterances? *Developmental Psychology*, *29*, 711–721.

Billig, M. (1978). *Fascists: a social psychological view of the National Front*. London: Academic Press.

Billig, M. (1985). Prejudice, a categorization and particularization: from a perceptual to a rhetorical approach. *European Journal of Social Psychology*, *15*(1), 79–103.

Billig, M. (1988). The notion of prejudice: some rhetorical and ideological aspects. *Text*, *8*, 91–110.

Billig, M. (2001). Humour and hatred: the racist jokes of the Ku Klux Klan. *Discourse & Society*, *12*(3), 267–289.

Billig, M., & Tajfel, H. (1973). Social categorization and similarity in intergroup behaviour. *European Journal of Social Psychology*, *3*, 27–52.

Binder, J., Zagefka, H., Brown, R., Funke, F., Kessler, T., Mummendey, A., Maquil, A., Demoulin, S., & Leyens, J.P. (2009). Does contact reduce prejudice or does prejudice reduce contact? A longitudinal test of the contact hypothesis among majority and minority groups in three European countries. *Journal of Personality and Social Psychology*, *96*(4), 843–856.

Binet, A., & Simon, T. (1905). Méthodes nouvelles pour le diagnostic du niveau intellectuel des anormaux. *L'Anne Psychologique*, *11*, 191–244.

Bingham, W.V. (1937). *Aptitudes and aptitude testing*. New York: Harper.

Bion, W.R. (1955). Group dynamics: a review. In M. Klein, P. Heimann, & R. Money-Kyrle (Eds), *New directions in psycho-analysis*. London: Tavistock.

Bion, W.R. (1961). *Experiences in groups, and other papers*. London: Tavistock.

Birch, S.A.J., & Bloom, P. (2007). The curse of knowledge in reasoning about false beliefs. *Psychological Science*, *18*, 382–386.

Bittner, E. (1974). The concept of organization. In R. Turner (Ed.), *Ethnomethodology: selected readings*. Harmondsworth: Penguin.

Bjork, R.A., & Whitten, W.B. (1974). Recency-sensitive retrieval processes in long-term free recall. *Cognitive Psychology*, *6*, 173–189.

Blackless, M., Charuvastra, A., Derryck, A., Fausto-Sterling, A., Lauzanne, K., & Lee, E. (2000). How sexually dimorphic are we? Review and synthesis. *American Journal of Human Biology*, *12*, 151–166.

Blackmer, E.R., & Mitton, J.L. (1991). Theories of monitoring and the timing of repairs in spontaneous speech. *Cognition*, *39*, 173–194.

Blackmore, S. (1993). *Dying to live: science and the near death experience*. London: Grafton.

Blackmore, S. (1999). *The meme machine*. Oxford: Oxford University Press.

Blackmore, S. (2003). *Consciousness: an introduction*. London: Hodder & Stoughton.

Blackmore, S. (2005). *Conversations on consciousness*. Oxford: Oxford University Press.

Blackmore, S. (2009). *Ten Zen questions*. Oxford: OneWorld.

Blagden, N. (2012). *Policing and psychology*. Exeter: Learning Matters/SAGE.

Blagden, N., Winder, B., Gregson, M., & Thorne, K. (2014). Making sense of denial in sexual offenders: a qualitative phenomenological and repertory grid analysis. *Journal of Interpersonal Violence*, DOI: 0886260513511530.

Blagden, N., Winder, B., & Hames, C. (2014, in press). They treat us like human beings: experiencing a therapeutic sex offenders prison: impact on prisoners, staff and implications for treatment. *International Journal of Offender Therapy and Comparative Criminology*.

Blagden, N., Winder, B., Thorne, K., & Gregson, M. (2011). 'No-one in the world would ever wanna speak to me again': an interpretative phenomenological analysis into convicted sexual offenders' accounts and experiences of maintaining and leaving denial. *Psychology, Crime and Law*, *17*(7), 563–585.

Blair, R.J.R. (1995). A cognitive developmental approach to morality: investigating the psychopath. *Cognition*, *57*, 1–29.

Blair, R.J.R. (2001). Neurocognitive models of aggression, the antisocial personality disorder, and psychopathy. *Journal of Neurological and Neurosurgical Psychiatry*, *71*, 727–731.

Blair, R.J.R. (2003). Neurobiological basis of psychopathy. *British Journal of Psychiatry*, *182*(1), 5–7.

Blair, R.J.R. (2005). Applying a cognitive neuroscience perspective to the disorder of psychopathy. *Development and Psychopathology*, *17*, 865–891.

Blair, R.J.R. (2007). The amygdala and ventromedial prefrontal cortex in morality and psychopathy. *Trends in Cognitive Sciences*, *11*(9), 387–392.

Blair, R.J.R., Colledge, E., Murray, L., & Mitchell, D.G.V. (2001). A selective impairment in the processing of sad and fearful expressions in children with psychopathic tendencies. *Journal of Abnormal Child Psychology*, *29*(6), 491–498.

Blair, R.J.R., Morris, J.S., Frith, C.D., Perrett, D.I., & Dolan, R. (1999). Dissociable neural responses to facial expressions of sadness and anger. *Brain*, *122*, 883–893.

Blake, R.R., & Mouton, J.S. (1961). Reactions to intergroup competition under win–lose conditions. *Management Science*, *7*(4), 420–435.

Blake, R., & Sekular, R. (2006) *Perception*. Boston: McGraw Hill.

Blanchard, R. (1997). Birth order and sibling sex ratio in homosexual versus heterosexual males and females. *Annual Review of Sex Research*, *8*, 27–67.

Blanchard, R., & Bogaert, A.F. (1996) Homosexuality in men and number of older brothers. *American Journal of Psychiatry*, *153*, 27–31.

Blascovich, J., Mendes, W.B., Hunter, S.B., & Salomon, K. (1999). 'Social facilitation' as challenge and threat. *Journal of Personality and Social Psychology*, *77*, 68–77.

Block, J. (1995). A contrarian view of the five-factor approach to personality description. *Psychological Bulletin*, *117*, 187–215.

Block, J. (2001). Millennial contrarianism: the five-factor approach to personality description 5 years later. *Journal of Research in Personality*, *35*, 98–107.

Blos, P. (1962). *On adolescence: a psychoanalytic interpretation*. New York: Free Press.

Bluedor, A.C. (2002). *The human organization of time: temporal realities and experience*. Redwood City, CA: Stanford University Press.

Bock, J.K. (1996). Language production: methods and methodologies. *Psychonomic Bulletin & Review*, *3*, 395–442.

Bock, J.K., & Garnsey, S.M. (1998). Language processing. In W. Bechtel & G. Graham (Eds), *The Blackwell companion to cognitive science* (pp. 226–234). Oxford: Blackwell.

Bock, J.K., & Levelt, W.J.M. (1994). Language production: grammatical encoding. In M.A. Gernsbacher (Ed.), *Handbook of psycholinguistics* (pp. 945–984). London: Academic Press.

Boelens, H., Hofman, B., Tamaddoni, T., & Eenink, K. (2007). Specific effect of modeling on young children's word productions. *Psychological Record*, *57*, 145–166.

Bogaert, A.F. (2006). Biological versus nonbiological older brothers' and men's sexual orientation. *Proceedings of the National Academy of Sciences USA*, *103*, 10771–10774.

Bogaert, A.F., & Hershberger, S. (1999). The relation between sexual orientation and penile size. *Archives of Sexual Behavior*, *28*, 213–221.

Bogg, T., & Roberts, B.W. (2004). Conscientiousness and health behaviors: a meta-analysis of the leading behavioural contributors to mortality. *Psychological Bulletin*, *130*, 887–919.

Bolton, T. (1902). A biological view of perception. *Psychological Review*, *9*, 537–548.

Boom, J., Wouter, H., & Keller, M. (2007). A cross-cultural validation of stage development: a Rasch re-analysis of longitudinal socio-moral reasoning data. *Cognitive Development*, *22*, 213–229.

Boon, J.C., & Davis, G.M. (1987). Rumours greatly exaggerated: Allport and Postman's apocryphal study. *Canadian Journal of Behavioural Science*, *19*(4), 430–440.

Boorman, R., & Hopkins, K. (2012). Prisoners' criminal backgrounds and proven re-offending after release: results from the Surveying Prisoner Crime Reduction (SPCR) survey. Ministry of Justice Research Summary 8/12.

Booth, A.E., & Waxman, S. (2002). Word learning is 'smart' evidence that conceptual information affects preschoolers' extension of novel words. *Cognition*, *84*, B11–B22.

Booth-Kewley, S., & Friedman, H. (1987). Psychological predictors of heart disease: a quantitative review. *Psychological Bulletin*, *101*(3), 343–362.

Booth-Kewley, S., & Vickers, R.R. (1994). Associations between major domains of personality and health behaviour. *Journal of Personality*, *62*(3), 281–298.

Boring, E.G. (1923). Intelligence as the tests test it. *New Republic*, *35*, 35–37.

Bornstein, B.H., Deffenbacher, K.A., Penrod, S.D., & McGorty, E.K. (2012). Effects of exposure time and cognitive operations on facial identification accuracy: a meta-analysis of two variables associated with initial memory strength. *Psychology, Crime & Law*, *18*(5), 473–490.

Boroditsky, L., Schmidt, L., & Phillips, W. (2003). Sex, syntax, and semantics. In D. Gentner & S. Goldin-Meadow (Eds), *Language in mind: advances in the study of language and cognition*. Cambridge, MA: MIT Press.

Boucher, J. (2015). *The autistic spectrum: characteristics, causes and practical issues* (2nd edn). London: SAGE.

Bower, P., Byford, S., Sibbald, B., et al. (2000). Randomised controlled trial of non-directive counselling, cognitive-behaviour therapy, and usual general practitioner care for patients with depression. II: Cost-effectiveness. *British Medical Journal*, *321*, 1389–1392.

Bowlby, J. (1944). Forty-four juvenile thieves: their characters and their home life. *International Journal of Psycho-Analysis*, *25*, 107–127.

Bowlby, J. (1969). *Attachment and loss. Vol. 1: Attachment*. New York: Basic Books.

Bowlby, J. (1988). *A secure base: Parent–child attachment and healthy human development*. New York: Basic Books.

Boyd, R., & Richerson, P.J. (2005). Solving the puzzle of human cooperation. In S.Levinson (Ed.), *Evolution and Culture* (pp.105–132). Cambridge, MA: MIT Press.

Bradley, L., & Bryant, P. (1983). Categorising sounds and learning to read – a causal connection. *Nature*, *301*, 419–521.

Bradshaw, C.P., Sawyer, A.L., & O'Brennan, L.M. (2007). Bullying and peer victimization at school: perceptual differences between students and school staff. *School Psychology Review*, *36*, 361–382.

Bramel, D., & Friend, R. (2003). Hawthorne, the myth of the docile worker, and class bias in psychology. In M. Handel (Ed.), *The sociology of organisations* (pp. 97–107). London: SAGE.

Braverman, H. (1974). *Labor and monopoly capital*. New York: Monthly Review Press Trust.

Bray, R.M., & Noble, A.M. (1978). Authoritarianism and decisions of mock juries: evidence of jury bias and group polarization. *Journal of Personality and Social Psychology*, *36*, 1424–1430.

Breakwell, G.M. (1986). *Coping with threatened identities*. London: Methuen.

Brebner, J., & Cooper, C. (1985). A proposed unified model of extraversion. In J.T. Spence & C.E. Izard (Eds), *Motivation, emotion and personality*. Amsterdam: North-Holland.

Breckler, S.J. (1984). Empirical validation of affect, behavior, and cognition as distinct components of attitude. *Journal of Personality and Social Psychology*, *47*, 1191–1205.

Bretherton, I. (1991). The roots and growing points of attachment theory. In C.M. Parkes, J. Stevenson-Hinde, & P. Marris (Eds), *Attachment across the life cycle* (pp. 9–32). London: Routledge.

Brewer, M.B. (1999). The psychology of prejudice: ingroup love or outgroup hate? *Journal of Social Issues*, *55*(3), 429–444.

Brewer, M.B., & Brown, R.J. (1998). Intergroup relations. In D.T. Gilbert, S.T. Fiske, & G. Lindzey (Eds), *The handbook of social psychology* (pp. 554–594). New York: McGraw-Hill.

Bridges, L.J. (2003). Trust, attachment, and relatedness. In M.H. Bornstein, L. Davidson, C.L.M. Keyes, & K.A. Moore (Eds), *Well-being: positive development across the life course*. Mahwah, NJ: Erlbaum.

Brinkmann, S. (2005). Human kinds and looping effects in psychology. *Theory & Psychology*, *15*(6), 769–791. DOI:10.1177/0959354305059332.

Broadbent, D.E. (1958). *Perception and communication*. London: Pergamon.

Broadbent, D.E. (1975). The magic number seven after fifteen years. In A. Kennedy & A. Wilkes (Eds), *Studies in long-term memory* (pp. 3–18). New York: Wiley.

Broca, P. (1861). Nouvelle observation d'aphémie produite par une lésion de la troisième circonvolution frontale. *Bulletins de la Société d'Anatomie, 2*(6), 398–407.

Brody, G.H. (1998). Sibling relationship quality: its causes and consequences. *Annual Review of Psychology, 49*, 1–24.

Broks, P. (2004). *Into the silent lands: travels in neuropsychology*. London: Atlantic.

Broome, A., & Llewellyn, S. (1995). *Health psychology: Processes and applications*. London: Chapman and Hall.

Brown, A.L., & Campione, J.C. (1990). Communities of learning and thinking, or a context by any other name. In D. Kuhn (Ed.), *Developmental perspectives on teaching and learning thinking skills* (vol. 21, pp. 108–126). Basel: Karger.

Brown, G.D.A., Neath, I., & Chater, N. (2007). A temporal ratio model of memory. *Psychological Review, 114*, 539–576.

Brown, G.W., Birley, J.L.T., & Wing, J.K. (1972). Influence of family life on the course of schizophrenic disorders: a replication. *British Journal of Psychiatry, 121*, 241–258.

Brown, G.W., Monck, E.M., Carstairs, G.M., & Wing, J.K. (1962). The influence of family life on the course of schizophrenic illness. *British Journal of Preventive Social Medicine, 16*, 55.

Brown, G.W., & Rutter, M. (1966). The measurement of family activities and relationships. *Human Relations, 19*, 241–263.

Brown, L.A., Riby, L.M., & Reay, J.L. (2010). Supplementing cognitive aging: a selective review of the effects of ginkgo biloba and a number of everyday nutritional substances. *Experimental Aging Research, 36*, 105–122.

Brown, R. (1965). *Social psychology*. New York: Macmillan.

Brown, R. (1973). Development of the first language in the human species. *American Psychologist, 28*(2), 97–106.

Brown, R. (1995). *Prejudice: its social psychology*. Oxford: Blackwell.

Brown, R., & Kulik, J. (1977). Flashbulb memories. *Cognition, 5*(1), 73–99.

Bruner, J.S. (1975). From communication to language: a psychological perspective. *Cognition, 3*, 255–287.

Brunsden, V., & Goatcher, J. (2007). Reconfiguring photovoice for psychological research. *The Irish Journal of Psychology, 28*(1–2), 43–52.

Bryan, J.H., & Test, M.A. (1967). Models and helping: naturalistic studies in aiding behavior. *Journal of Personality and Social Psychology, 6*, 400–407.

Bryden, M.P., & MacRae, L. (1989). Dichotic laterality effects obtained with emotional words. *Neuropsychiatry, Neuropsychology, and Behavioral Neurology, 1*(3), 171–176.

Buchanan, C.M., Eccles, J., & Becker, J. (1992). Are adolescents the victims of raging hormones? Evidence for activation effects of hormones on moods and behavior at adolescence. *Psychological Bulletin, 111*, 62–107.

Bufkin, J.L., & Luttrell, V.R. (2005). Neuroimaging studies of aggressive and violent behavior: current findings and implications for criminology and criminal justice. *Trauma, Violence & Abuse, 6*(2), 176–191.

Buhrmester, D., & Furman, W. (1987). The development of companionship and intimacy. *Child Development, 58*, 1101–1113.

Burdsal, C.A., & Bolton, B. (1979). An item factoring of the 16PF-E: further evidence concerning Cattell's normal personality sphere. *Journal of General Psychology, 100*, 103–109.

Burke, B., Arkowitz, H., & Menchola, M. (2003). The efficacy of motivational interviewing: a meta-analysis of controlled clinical trials. *Journal of Consulting and Clinical Psychology, 71*(5), 843–861.

Burke, J.W., Charles, D.K., Morrow, P.J., Crosbie, J.H., & McDonough, S.M. (2009) Optimising engagement for stroke rehabilitation using serious games. *The Visual Computer, 25*(12), 1085–1099.

Burman, E. (Ed.) (1998). *Deconstructing feminist psychology*. London: SAGE.

Burman, E., & Parker, I. (Eds) (1993). *Discourse analytic research: repertoires and readings of texts in action*. London: Routledge.

Burnstein, E., Crandall, C., & Kitayama, S. (1994). Some neo-Darwinian decision rules for altruism: weighing cues for inclusive fitness as a function of the biological importance of the decision. *Journal of Personality and Social Psychology, 67*, 773 789.

Burnstein, E., & Vinokur, A. (1977). Persuasive argumentation and social comparison as determinants of attitude polarization. *Journal of Experimental Social Psychology, 13*, 315–332.

Burnyeat, M.F. (1997). Postscript on silent reading. *The Classical Quarterly (New Series), 47*, 74–76.

Burr, V. (2003). *Social constructionism* (2nd edn). London: Psychology Press.

Burt, C.L. (1957). *The causes and treatments of backwardness*. London: University of London Press.

Burt, M.R. (1980). Cultural myths and supports for rape. *Journal of Personality and Social Psychology, 38*(2), 217–230.

Burwood, S., Gilbert, G., & Lennon, K. (1999). *Philosophy of mind*. London: UCL Press.

Busemeyer, J.R., & Stout, J.C. (2002). A contribution of cognitive decision models to clinical assessment: decomposing performance on the Bechara gambling task. *Psychologica Assessment, 14*, 253–262.

Bushman, B.J., & Anderson, C.A. (2001). Is it time to pull the plug on hostile versus instrumental aggression dichotomy? *Psychological Review, 108*(1), 273.

Buss, A.H. (1989). Personality as traits. *American Psychologist, 44*, 1378–1388.

Buss, A.R. (1977). The trait-situation controversy and the concept of interaction. *Personality and Social Psychology Bulletin, 3*(2), 196–201.

Buss, D.M. (2009). *Handbook of evolutionary psychology*. Oxford: OUP.

Butterworth, G.E. (1977). Object disappearance and error in Piaget's stage IV task. *Journal of Experimental Child Psychology, 23*, 301–401.

Button, T.M.M., Maughan, B., & McGuffin, P. (2007). The relationship of maternal smoking to psychological problems in the offspring. *Early Human Development, 83*, 727–732.

Butzlaff, R.L., & Hooley J.L. (1998). Expressed emotion and psychiatric relapse: a meta-analysis. *Archives of General Psychiatry*, *55*, 547–552.

Byne, W., Lasco, M.S., Kemether, E., Shinwari, A., Edgar, M.A., Morgello, S., Jones, L.B., & Tobet, S. (2000). The interstitial nuclei of the human anterior hypothalamus: an investigation of sexual variation in volume and cell size, number and density. *Brain Research*, *856*, 254–258.

Byrnes, J.P., & McClenny, B. (1994). Decision-making in young adolescents and adults. *Journal of Experimental Child Psychology*, *58*, 359–388.

Byrnes, S. (2006). When it comes to facts, and explanations of facts, science is the only game in town. *New Statesman*, 10 April. Available at: www.newstatesman.com/node/152968 (accessed 9 December 2013).

Bywater, T., Hutchings, J., Daley, D., Whitaker, C., Yeo, S.T., Jones, K., & Edwards, R.T. (2009). Long-term effectiveness of a parenting intervention for children at risk of developing conduct disorder. *The British Journal of Psychiatry*, *195*(4), 318–324.

Cacioppo, J.T., & Petty, R.E. (1982). The need for cognition. *Journal of Personality and Social Psychology*, *42*(1), 116–131.

Cacioppo, J.T., Petty, R.E., Feinstein, J.A., & Jarvis, W.B.G. (1996). Dispositional differences in cognitive motivation: the life and times of individuals varying in need for cognition. *Psychological Bulletin*, *119*(2), 197–253.

Cacioppo, J.T., Petty, R.E., & Kao, C.F. (1984). The efficient assessment of need for cognition. *Journal of Personality Assessment*, *48*(3), 306–307.

Cain, S. (2012). *Quiet: the power of introverts in a world that can't stop talking*. London: Viking.

Cains, R.A. (2000). Children diagnosed ADHD: factors to guide intervention. *Educational Psychology in Practice*, *16*(2), 159–180.

Callaway, M., & Esser, J. (1984). Groupthink: effects of cohesiveness and problem-solving procedures on group decision making. *Social Behavior and Personality*, *12*, 157–164.

Calvete, E., Orue, I., Estévez, A., Villardón, L., & Padilla, P. (2010). Cyberbullying in adolescents: Modalities and aggressors' profile. *Computers in Human Behavior*, *26*(5), 1128–1135.

Calvin, W.H. (2002). *A brain for all seasons: human evolution and abrupt climate change*. Chicago, IL: University of Chicago Press.

Campbell, S.B. (2000). Developmental perspectives on attention deficit disorder. In A. Sameroff, M. Lewis, & S. Miller (Eds), *Handbook of child psychopathology* (2nd edn). New York: Plenum.

Cannon, W.B. (1929) *Bodily changes in pain, hunger, fear, and rage*. New York: Appleton-Century-Crofts.

Cannon, W.B. (1932). *The wisdom of the body*. New York: W.W. Norton.

Canobi, K.H. (2004). Individual differences in children's addition and subtraction knowledge. *Cognitive Development*, *19*(1), 81–93.

Canobi, K.H., Reeve, R.A., & Pattison, P.E. (1998). The role of conceptual understanding in children's addition problem-solving. *Developmental Psychology*, *34*, 882–891.

Canobi, K.H., Reeve, R.A., & Pattison, P.E. (2002). Young children's understanding of addition concepts. *Educational Psychology*, *22*, 513–532.

Canobi, K.H., Reeve, R.A., & Pattison, P.E. (2003). Patterns of knowledge in children's addition. *Developmental Psychology*, *39*, 521–534.

Cantor, J.M., Blanchard, R., Paterson, A.D., & Bogaert, A.F. (2002). How many gay men owe their sexual orientation to fraternal birth order? *Archives of Sexual Behavior*, *31*, 63–71.

Caplan, N., & Nelson, S. (1973). On being useful: the nature and consequences of psychological research on social problems. *American Psychologist*, *28*, 199–211.

Caputi, M., Lecce, S., Pagnin, A., & Banerjee, R. (2012). Longitudinal effects of theory of mind on later peer relations: the role of prosocial behavior. *Developmental Psychology*, *48*, 257–270.

Carlson, C.A., & Gronlund, S.D. (2011). Searching for the sequential line-up advantage: a distinctiveness explanation. *Memory*, *19*(8), 916–929.

Carmody, T.P. (1992). Preventing relapse in the treatment of nicotine addiction: current issues and future directions. *Journal of Psychoactive Drugs*, *24*(2), 131–158.

Carpenter, P.A., & Just, M.A. (1983). What your eyes do while your mind is reading. In K. Rayner (Ed.), *Eye movements in reading: perceptual and language processes*. New York: Academic Press.

Carpentier, M.Y., & Fortenberry, J.D. (2010). Romantic and sexual relationships, body image, and fertility in adolescent and young adult testicular cancer survivors: a review of the literature. *Journal of Adolescent Health*, *47*, 115–125.

Carraher, T.N., Carraber, D., & Schliemann, A.D. (1985). Mathematics in the streets and in schools. *British Journal of Developmental Psychology*, *3*, 21–29.

Carretié, L., Mercado, F., Tapia, M., & Hinojosa, J.A. (2001). Emotion, attention, and the 'negativity bias', studied through event-related potentials. *International Journal of Psychophysiology*, *41*, 75–85.

Carroll, D., Davey Smith, G., & Bennett, P. (1994). Health and socio-economic status. *The Psychologist*, *7*, 122–125.

Carroll, J., Snowling, M., Hulme, C., & Stevenson, J. (2003). The development of phonological awareness in pre-school children. *Developmental Psychology*, *39*, 913–923.

Carroll, L. (1865/2003). *Alice's adventures in Wonderland*. Harmondsworth: Penguin.

Carstensen, L.L., & Mikels, J.A. (2005). At the intersection of emotion and cognition: aging and the positivity effect. *Current Directions in Psychological Science*, *14*(3), 117–121.

Carstensen, L.L., Turan, B., Schiebe, S., Ram, N., Ersner-Hershfield, H., Samanez-Larkin, G.R., & Nesselroade, J.R. (2011). Emotional experience improves with age: evidence based on over 10 years of experience sampling. *Psychology and Aging*, *26*(1), 21–33.

Carter, C., & Steiner, L. (2003). *Critical readings: media and gender*. Maidenhead: Open University Press.

Carter, G.G., & Wilkinson, G.S. (2013). Food sharing in vampire bats: reciprocal help predicts donations more than relatedness or harassment. *Proceedings of the Royal Society B: Biological Sciences*, *280*(1753), 2012. 2573.

Carver, C.S., Scheier, M.F., & Weintraub, J.K. (1989). Assessing coping strategies: a theoretically based approach. *Journal of Personality and Social Psychology*, *56*, 267–283.

Casey, B.J. (2001). Disruption of inhibitory control in developmental disorders: a mechanistic model of implicated frontostriatal circuitry. In J. McClelland & R. Sieglar (Eds), *Mechanisms of cognitive development* (pp. 327–349). Mahwah, NJ: Erlbaum.

Castiello, U., & Umiltà, C. (1992). Splitting focal attention. *Journal of Experimental Psychology: Human Perception and Performance*, *18*, 837–848.

Castro, A., Díaz, F., & van Boxtel, G.J.M. (2007). How does a short history of spinal cord injury affect movement-related brain potentials? *European Journal of Neuroscience*, *25*, 2927–2934.

Cattell, H.E., & Mead, A.D. (2008). The sixteen personality factor questionnaire (16PF). In G.J. Boyle, G. Matthews & D.H. Saklofske (Eds), *The SAGE handbook of personality theory and assessment* (vol. 2, pp. 135–159). London: SAGE.

Cattell, R.B. (1957). *Personality and motivation structure and measurement*. New York: Harcourt, Brace and World.

Cattell, R.B. (1965). *The scientific analysis of personality*. Harmondsworth: Penguin.

Cattell, R.B., Eber, H.W., & Tatsuoka, M.M. (1970). *The 16-factor personality questionnaire*. Champaign, IL: IPAT.

Ceci, S.J., & Liker, J. (1986). A day at the races: a study of IQ, expertise, and cognitive complexity. *Journal of Experimental Psychology: General*, *115*, 255–266.

Cepeda, N.J., Pashler, H., Vul, E., Wixted, J.T., & Rohrer, D. (2006). Distributed practice in verbal recall tasks: a review and quantitative synthesis. *Psychological Bulletin*, *132*, 354–380.

Chai, H., Chen, W.Z., Zhu, J., Xu, Y., Lou, L., Yang, T., & Wang, W. (2012). Processing of facial expressions of emotions in healthy volunteers: an exploration with event-related potentials and personality traits. *Clinical Neurophysiology*, *42*(6), 369–375.

Chalmers, D. (1996). *The conscious mind*. New York: Oxford University Press.

Chamberlain, K. (2000). Methodolatry and qualitative health research. *Journal of Health Psychology*, *5*(3), 285–296.

Chambliss, C., & Murray, E.J. (1979). Cognitive procedures for smoking reduction: symptom attribution versus efficacy attribution. *Cognitive Therapy and Research*, *3*, 91–95.

Chávez-Bueno, S., & McCracken, G. (2005). Bacterial meningitis in children. *Pediatric Clinics of North America*, *52*, 795–810.

Chemers, M. (2002). Leadership effectiveness: an integrative review. In M. Hogg & R. Tinsdale (Eds), *Blackwell handbook of social psychology: group process*. London: Blackwell.

Cherry, E.C. (1953). Some experiments on the recognition of speech, with one and with two ears. *Journal of the Acoustical Society of America*, *25*, 975–979.

Choi, I., Nisbett, R.E., & Noenzayan, A. (1999). Causal attribution across cultures: Variation and universality. *Psychological Bulletin*, *125*, 47–63.

Christiansen, M.H., & Kirby, S. (2003a). Language evolution: consensus and controversies. *Trends in Cognitive Sciences*, *7*, 300–307.

Christiansen, M.H., & Kirby, S. (2003b). Language evolution: the hardest problem in science? In M.H. Christiansen & S. Kirby (Eds), *Language evolution*. Oxford: Oxford University Press.

Christopher, J.C., & Hickinbottom, S. (2008). Positive psychology, ethnocentrism, and the disguised ideology of individualism. *Theory & Psychology*, *18*(5), 563–589.

Churchland, P.M. (1981) Eliminative materialism and the propositional attitudes. *Journal of Philosophy*, *78*(2), 67–80.

Cialdini, R.B., Baumann, D.J., & Kenrick, D.T. (1981). Insights from sadness: A three-step model of the development of altruism as hedonism. *Developmental Review*, *1*(3), 207–223.

Cicchetti, D. (2010). Resilience under conditions of extreme stress: a multilevel perspective. *World Psychiatry*, *9*(3), 145–154.

Clark, A.J. (2003). *Natural-born cyborgs: minds, technologies and the future of human intelligence*. Oxford: Oxford University Press.

Clark, C.W. (1997) The witch craze in 17th century Europe. In W.G. Bringmann, H.E. Luck, R. Miller, & C.E. Early (Eds), *A pictorial history of psychology*. Carol Stream, IL: Quintessance Publishing.

Clark, S.K., Jeglic, E.L., Calkins, C., & Tatar, J.R. (2014). More than a nuisance: the prevalence and consequences of frotteurism and exhibitionism. *Sexual Abuse: A Journal of Research and Treatment*, DOI: 1079063214525643.

Clarke, S., Bellmann Thiran, A., Maeder, P., Adriani, M., Vernet, O., Regli, L., Cuisenaire, O., & Thiran, J.P. (2002). What and where in human audition: selective deficits following focal hemispheric lesions. *Experimental Brain Research*, *147*, 815.

Classen, C., Koopman, C., Angell, K., & Spiegel, D. (1996). Coping styles associated with psychological adjustment to advanced breast cancer. *Health Psychology*, *15*(6), 434.

Coates, J., & Vickerman, P. (2010). Empowering children with special educational needs to speak up: experiences of inclusive physical education. *Disability & Rehabilitation*, *32*(18), 1517–1526.

Coccaro, E.F., McCloskey, M.S., Fitzgerald, D.A., & Phan, K.L. (2007). Amygdala and orbitofrontal reactivity to social threat in individuals with impulsive aggression. *Biological Psychiatry*, *62*(2), 168–178.

Cohen, A.R. (1957). Need for cognition and order of communication as determinants of opinion change. In C.I. Hovland (Ed.), *The order of presentation in persuasion*. New Haven, CT: Yale University Press.

Cohen, A.R., Stotland, E., & Wolfe, D.M., (1955). An experimental investigation of need for cognition. *Journal of Abnormal and Social Psychology*, *51*(2), 291–294.

Cohen, S., Kamarck, T., & Mermelstein, R. (1983). A global measure of perceived stress. *Journal of Health and Social Behavior*, *24*, 385–396.

Colapinto, J. (2000). *As nature made him: the boy who was raised as a girl*. New York: HarperCollins.

Colcombe, S.J., Erickson, K.I., Scalf, P.E., Kim, J.S., Prakash, R., McAuley et al. (2006). Aerobic exercise training increases brain volume in aging humans. *Journal of Gerontology: Medical Sciences*, *61A*(11), 1166–1170.

Colcombe, S.J., & Kramer, A.F. (2006). Fitness effects on the cognitive function of older adults: a meta-analytic study. *Psychological Science*, *14*(2), 125–130.

Cole, J.D., & Kazarian, S.S. (1988) The Level of Expressed Emotion Scale: a new measure of expressed emotion. *Journal of Clinical Psychology*, *44*, 392–397.

Coleman, J.C. (1999). *The nature of adolescence*. London: Psychology Press

Colom, R. (2007). Intelligence? What intelligence? *Behavioural and Brain Sciences*, *30*, 155–156.

Colombo, J. (1982). The critical period concept: research, methodology, and theoretical issues. *Psychological Bulletin*, *91*(2), 260–275.

Comer, D.R. (1995). A model of social loafing in real work groups. *Human Relations*, *48*, 647–667.

Comer, R. (2013) *Fundamentals of abnormal psychology* (8th edn). New York: Macmillan.

Comings, D.E. (1998). The molecular genetics of pathological gambling. *CNS Spectrums*, *3*(6), 20–37.

Conn, P.J., Tamminga, C., Schoepp, D.D., & Lindsley, C. (2008). Schizophrenia. *Molecular Interventions*, *8*(2), 99.

Conn, S.R., & Rieke, M.L. (1994). *The 16PF fifth edition technical manual*. Champaign, IL: Institute for Personality and Ability Testing.

Conner, M., & Abraham, C. (2001). Conscientiousness and the theory of planned behavior: Toward a more complete model of the antecedents of intentions and behavior. *Personality and Social Psychological Bulletin*, *27*, 1547–1561.

Connolly, I., & O'Moore, M. (2003). Personality and family relations of children who bully. *Personality and Individual Differences*, *34*, 1–8.

Conway, M.A., Anderson, S.J., Larsen, S.F., Donnelly, C.M., McDaniel, M.A., McClelland, A.G.R., Rawles, R.E., & Logie, R.H. (1994). The formation of flashbulb memories. *Memory & Cognition*, *22*(3), 326–343.

Cook, S.W. (1978). Interpersonal and attitudinal outcomes in cooperating interracial groups: a context effect. *Journal of Personality and Social Psychology*, *49*, 1231–1245.

Cooper, R.P., & Aslin, R.N. (1990). Preference for infant-directed speech in the first month after birth. *Child Development*, *61*, 1584–1595.

Corneille, O., Klein, O., Lambert, S., & Judd, C.M. (2002). On the role of familiarity with units of measurement in categorical accentuation: Tajfel and Wilkes (1963) revisited and replicated. *Psychological Science*, *4*, 380–383.

Cornish, D.B., & Clarke, R.V. (Eds). (2013). *The reasoning criminal: rational choice perspectives on offending*. New Brunswick, NJ: Transaction.

Corr, P.J. (2004). Reinforcement sensitivity theory and personality. *Neuroscience and Biobehavioural Reviews*, *28*(3), 317–332.

Corr, P.J., & McNaughton, N. (2012). Neuroscience and approach/avoidance personality traits: a two-stage (valuation-motivation) approach. *Neuroscience and Biobehavioural Reviews*, *36*(10), 2339–2354.

Costa Jr, P.T., & McCrae, R.R. (1976). Age differences in personality structure: a cluster analytic approach. *Journal of Gerontology*, *31*(5), 564–570.

Costa Jr, P.T., & McCrae, R.R. (1992). *NEO PI–R professional manual*. Odessa, FL: Psychological Assessment Resources.

Cottrell, N.B., Wack, D.L., Sekerak, G.J., & Rittle, R.M. (1968). Social facilitation of dominant responses by the presence of an audience and the mere presence of others. *Journal of Personality and Social Psychology*, *9*, 245–250.

Cowan, N. (2001). The magical number 4 in short-term memory: a reconsideration of mental storage capacity. *Behavioral and Brain Sciences*, *24*, 87–185.

Cowan, N. (2005) *Working memory capacity: Essays in cognitive psychology*. New York: Psychology Press/Taylor & Francis.

Cowan, N. (2010). The magical mystery four: how is working memory capacity limited, and why? *Current Directions in Psychological Science*, *19*, 51–57.

Craig, T., & Power, P. (2010). Inpatient provision in early psychosis. In P. French, J. Smith, D. Shiers, M. Reed, & M. Rayne (Eds), *Promoting recovery in early psychosis: a practice manual* (pp. 17–26). Hoboken, NJ: Wiley-Blackwell.

Craik, F.I.M., & Lockhart, R.S. (1972). Levels of processing: a framework for memory research. *Journal of Verbal Learning and Verbal Behaviour*, *11*, 671–684.

Cramer, R.E., McMaster, M.R., Bartell, P.A., & Dragna, M. (1988). Subject competence and minimization of the bystander effect. *Journal of Applied Social Psychology*, *18*, 1133–1148.

Craske, M. (2010) *Cognitive behavioural therapy*. Washington, DC: American Psychological Association.

Creswell, J.W., & Plano Clark, V.L. (2007). *Mixed methods research*. London: SAGE.

Crick, F.H. (1994). *The astonishing hypothesis: the scientific search for the soul*. New York: Scribner.

Crisp, R.J. (2008). Recognising complexity in intergroup relations. *The Psychologist*, *21*(3), 206–209.

Crisp, R.J., Hewstone, M., & Rubin, M. (2001). Does multiple categorization reduce inter-group bias? *Personality and Social Psychology Bulletin*, *27*, 76–89.

Crisp, R.J., & Turner, R.T. (2007). *Essential social psychology*. London: SAGE.

Crombez, G., Eccleston, C., Van Damme, S., Vlaeyen, J.W., & Karoly, P. (2012). Fear-avoidance model of chronic pain: the next generation. *Clinical Journal of Pain*, *28*(6), 475–83.

Cromby, J. (2004). Between constructionism and neuroscience: the societal co-constitution of embodied subjectivity. *Theory & Psychology*, *14*(6), 797–821.

Cromby, J. (2005). Theorising embodied subjectivity. *International Journal of Critical Psychology, 15*, 133–150.

Cromby, J., Harper, D., & Reavey, P. (2013). *Psychology, mental health and distress*. Basingstoke: Palgrave Macmillan.

Cross-Disorder Group of the Psychiatric Genomics Consortium. (2013). Identification of risk loci with shared effects on five major psychiatric disorders: a genome-wide analysis. *The Lancet, 381*(9875), 1371.

Crossley, M. (2000). *Introducing narrative psychology: self, trauma and the construction of meaning*. Buckingham: Open University Press.

Crowder, R.G. (1993). Systems and principles in memory theory: another critique of pure memory. In A. Collins, M.A. Conway, S.E. Gathercole, & P.E. Morris (Eds), *Theories of memory* (pp. 139–161). Hillsdale, NJ: Erlbaum.

Crown Prosecution Service. (2012). *Robbery*. Retrieved from: www.cps.gov.uk/legal/s_to_u/sentencing_manual/robbery/ (accessed 15 August 2014).

Crown Prosecution Service. (n.d.). Retrieved 8 August, 2014, from http://www.cps.gov.uk/legal/h_to_k/homicide_murder_and_manslaughter/

Cruickshanks, K.J., Wiley, T.L., Tweed, T.S., Klein, B.E., Klein, R., Mares-Perlman, J.A., & Nondahl, D.M. (1998). Prevalence of hearing loss in older adults in Beaver Dam, Wisconsin: the epidemiology of hearing loss study. *American Journal of Epidemiology, 148*(9), 879–886.

Crundall, D., Crundall, E., Clarke, D., & Shahar, A. (2012). Why do car drivers fail to give way to motorcycles at t-junctions? *Accident Analysis and Prevention, 44*, 88–96.

Crundall, D., & Underwood, G. (2011). Visual attention while driving: measures of eye movements used in driving research. In B.E. Porter (Ed.), *Handbook of traffic psychology* (pp. 137–148). London: Elsevier.

Crundall, D., van Loon, E., & Underwood, G. (2006). Attraction and distraction of attention with outdoor media. *Accident Analysis and Prevention, 38*, 671–677.

Csikszentmihalyi, M. (1991). Design and order in everyday life. *Design Issues, 8*, 26–34.

Csikszentmihalyi, M. (1993). *The evolving self: a psychology for the new millennium*. New York: HarperCollins.

Csikszentmihalyi, M., & Rochberg-Halton, E. (1981). *The meaning of things: domestic symbols and the self*. Cambridge: Cambridge University Press.

Curt, B. (1994). *Textuality and tectonics: troubling social and psychological science*. Buckingham: Open University Press.

Curtiss, S. (Ed.) (1977). *Genie: psycholinguistic study of a modern-day 'wild child'*. New York: Academic Press.

Cushing, J.T. (1998). *Philosophical concepts in physics: the historical relation between philosophy and scientific theories*. Cambridge: Cambridge University Press.

Dąbrowska, E. (2004). *Language, mind and brain: some psychological and neurological constraints on theories of grammar*. Edinburgh and Washington, DC: Edinburgh University Press and Georgetown University Press.

Dahrendorf, R. (1973). *Homo sociologicus*. London: Routledge & Kegan Paul.

Daly, M., & Wilson, M. (1988). *Homicide*. New Brunswick, NJ: Transaction Publishers.

Damasio, H., Grabowski, T., Frank, R., Galaburda, A.M., & Damasio, A.R. (1994). The return of Phineas Gage: clues about the brain from the skull of a famous patient. *Science, 264*(5162), 1102–1105.

Damon, W. (1977). Measurement and social development. *Counseling Psychologist, 6*, 13–15.

Damon, W. (1980). Patterns of change in children's prosocial reasoning: a two year longitudinal study. *Child Development, 51*, 1010–1017.

Danziger, K. (1990). *Constructing the subject: historical origins of psychological research*. Cambridge: Cambridge University Press.

Darley, J.M., & Latané, B. (1970). Norms and normative behavior: Field studies of social interdependence. In J. Macaulay & L. Berkowitz (Eds), *Altruism and helping behavior*. NewYork: Academic Press.

Darwin, C. (1859). *On the origin of species by means of natural selection, or the preservation of favoured races in the struggle for life*. London: John Murray. Retrieved from http://en.wikisource.org/wiki/On_the_Origin_of_Species_ (1859). (accessed 21June 2014).

Darwin, C. (1871). *The descent of man, and selection in relation to sex*. London: John Murray.

Darwin, C. (1872). *The expression of the emotions in man and animals*. New York: Appleton & Co.

Davidson, R.J., Putnam, K.M., & Larson, C.L. (2000). Dysfunction in the neural circuitry of emotion regulation: a possible prelude to violence. *Science, 289*(5479), 591–594.

Davies, M.N.O., & Green, P.R. (1990). Optic flow-field variables trigger landing in hawk but not in pigeons. *Naturwissenschaften, 77*, 142–144.

Davies, M.N.O., & Green, P.R. (1994). *Perception and motor control in birds: an ecological approach*. Berlin: Springer.

Davis, K.L., Kahn, R.S., Ko, G., & Davidson, M. (1991). Dopamine in schizophrenia: a review and reconceptualization. *The American Journal of Psychiatry, 148*, 1474–1486.

Dawkins, R. (1976). *The selfish gene*. Oxford: Oxford University Press.

Dawkins, R. (1989). *The selfish gene* (3rd edn). Oxford: Oxford University Press.

De Dreu, C.K., & West, M.A. (2001). Minority dissent and team innovation: the importance of participation in decision making. *Journal of Applied Psychology, 86*, 1191–1201.

De Neys, W., Schaeken, W., & d'Ydewalle, G. (2005). Working memory and everyday conditional reasoning: retrieval and inhibition of stored counterexamples. *Thinking & Reasoning, 11*, 349–381.

de Spinoza, B. (1997). *The Ethics* (Part IV). Project Gutenberg. http://www.gutenberg.org/cache/epub/971/pg971.html

de Waal, F.B., & Suchak, M. (2010). Prosocial primates: selfish and unselfish motivations. *Philosophical Transactions of the Royal Society B: Biological Sciences, 365*(1553), 2711–2722.

Deacon, T.W. (1997). What makes the human brain different? *Annual Review of Anthropology, 26*, 337–357.

Deary, I. (1996). A (latent) Big Five personality model in 1915. *Journal of Personality and Social Psychology*, 6, 299–311.

Deary, I.J., Corley, J., Gow, A.J., Harris, S.E., Houlihan, L.M., Marioni, R.E., & Starr, J.M. (2009). Age-associated cognitive decline. *British Medical Bulletin*, 92, 135–152.

DeCasper, A.J., & Fifer, W.P. (1980). Of human bonding: newborns prefer their mothers' voices. *Science*, 208, 1174–1176.

DeCasper, A.J., Lecanuet, J.P., Busnel, M.C., Granier-Deferre, C., & Maugeais, R. (1994). Fetal reactions to recurrent maternal speech. *Infant Behavior and Development*, 17, 159–164.

DeKlyen, M., & Speltz, M.L. (2001). Attachment and conduct disorder. In J. Hill & B. Maughan (Eds), *Conduct disorders in childhood and adolescence* (pp. 320–345). Cambridge: Cambridge University Press.

Dell, G.S. (1986). A spreading activation theory of retrieval and sentence production. *Psychological Review*, 93, 283–321.

Denekens, J.P.M., Nys, H., & Stuer, H. (1999). Sterilisation of incompetent mentally handicapped persons: a model for decision making. *Journal of Medical Ethics*, 25, 237–241.

DeNicola, C.A., Holt, N.A., Lambert, A.J., & Cashon, C.H. (2013). Attention-orientating and attention-holding effects of faces on 4- to 8-month-old infants. *International Journal of Behavioural Development*, 37, 143–147.

Denollet, J., & Brutsaert, D.L. (1998). Personality, disease severity, and the risk of long-term cardiac events in patients with a decreased ejection fraction after myocardial infarction. *Circulation*, 97(2), 167–173.

Denollet, J., Sys, S.U., Stroobant, N., Rombouts, H., Gillebert, T.C., & Brutsaert, D.L. (1996). Personality as independent predictor of long-term mortality in patients with coronary heart disease. *Lancet*, 347(8999), 417–421.

Denollet, J., Vaes, J., & Brutsaert, D.L. (2000). Inadequate response to treatment in coronary heart disease: adverse effects of type D personality and younger age on 5-year prognosis and quality of life. *Circulation*, 102(6), 630–635.

DePalma, M.T., Madey, S.F., Tillman, T.C., & Wheeler, J. (1999). Perceived patient responsibility and belief in a just world affect helping. *Basic and Applied Social Psychology*, 21, 131–137.

Department of Health. (1998). *Inequalities in health*. London: HMSO.

Department of Health. (2001a). *Health Survey for England: The health of ethnic minority groups '99*. London: HMSO.

Department of Health. (2001b). *Health and Personal Social Services Statistics, Government Statistical Service* [2001, 02/08/01]. London: HMSO.

Deschamps, J.C., & Doise, W. (1978). Crossed category memberships in intergroup relations. In H. Tajfel (Ed.), *Differentiation between social groups*. Cambridge: Cambridge University Press.

Deutsch, J.A., & Deutsch, D. (1963). Attention: some theoretical considerations. *Psychological Review*, 70, 80–90.

Deutsch, M., & Gerard, H.B. (1955). A study of normative and informational social influences upon individual judgment. *The Journal of Abnormal and Social Psychology*, 51, 629–636.

Dewi Rees, W. (1971). The hallucinations of widowhood. *British Medical Journal*, 4(5778), 37–41.

Diamond, M. (1997). Sexual identity and sexual orientation in children with traumatised or ambiguous genitalia. *Journal of Sex Research*, 34, 199–211.

Diamond, M., & Sigmundson, H.K. (1997). Sex reassignment at birth: long-term review and clinical implications. *Archives of Pediatric and Adolescent Medicine*, 151, 298–304.

Dickstein, L.S. (1978). The effect of figure on syllogistic reasoning. *Memory and Cognition*, 6, 76–83.

Diehl, M., & Stroebe, W. (1991). Productivity loss in idea-generating groups: tracking down the blocking effect. *Journal of Personality and Social Psychology*, 61, 392–403.

Diener, E. (1977). Deindividuation: causes and consequences. *Social Behavior and Personality*, 5, 497–507.

Diener, E. (1980). Deindividuation: the absence of self-awareness and self-regulation in group members. In P.B. Paulus (Ed.), *Psychology of group influence* (pp. 209–242). Hillsdale, NJ: Erlbaum.

Diener, E., Fraser, S.C., Beaman, A.L., & Kelem, R.T. (1976). Effects of deindividuation variables on stealing among Halloween trick-or-treaters. *Journal of Personality and Social Psychology*, 33, 178–183.

Digman, J.M. (1990). Personality structure: emergence of the five-factor model. *Annual Review of Psychology*, 41, 417–440.

Dijkstra, A., & De Vries, H. (2001). Do self-help interventions in health education lead to cognitive changes, and do cognitive changes lead to behavioural changes? *British Journal of Health Psychology*, 6(2), 121–134.

Dillon, G. & Underwood, J. (2012). Parental perspectives of students with Autism Spectrum Disorders transitioning from primary to secondary school in the United Kingdom. *Focus on Autism and Other Developmental Disabilities*, 27(2), 111–121.

Dion, K.L. (2003). Prejudice, racism, and discrimination. In T. Millon & J. Lerner (Eds), *Handbook of psychology. Vol. 5: Personality and social psychology* (pp. 507–536). Hoboken, NJ: Wiley.

Dittman, M. (2002). Study ranks the top 20th century psychologists. *Monitor on Psychology*, 33, 28–29.

Dittmar, H. (1992). *The social psychology of material possessions: to have is to be*. Hemel Hempstead: Harvester Wheatsheaf.

DNA Exonerations Nationwide (n.d.). Innocence Project website, www.innocenceproject.org/Content/DNA_Exonerations_Nationwide.php (accessed 23 May 2014).

Docherty, N.M., St-Hilaire, A., Aakre, J.M., Seghers, J.P., McCleery, A., & Divilbiss, M. (2011). Anxiety interacts with expressed emotion: criticism in the prediction of psychotic symptom exacerbation. *Schizophrenia Bulletin*, 37, 611–618.

Dollard, J., Doob, L.W., Miller, N.E., Mowrer, O.H., & Sears, R.R. (1939). *Frustration and aggression*. New Haven, CT: Yale University Press.

Donaldson L. (2001). *The contingency theory of organizations*. Thousand Oaks, CA: SAGE

Dorling, D., Mitchell, R., Shaw, M., Orford, S., & Smith, G.D. (2000). The ghost of Christmas past: health effects of poverty in London in 1896 and 1991. *British Medical Journal*, *321*, 1547–1551.

Dorling, D., Smith, G.D., & Shaw, M. (2001). Analysis of trends in premature mortality by Labour voting in the 1997 general election. *British Medical Journal*, *322*, 1336–1337.

Doty, R.M., Peterson, B.E., & Winter, D.G. (1991). Threat and authoritarianism in the United States. *Journal of Personality and Social Psychology*, *61*, 629–640.

Douglas, M. (1992). *Risk and blame*. London: Routledge.

Dovidio, J.F., Gaertner, S.L., Validzic, A., Matoka, K., Johnson, B., & Frazier, S. (1997). Extending the benefits of recategorization: Evaluations, self-disclosure, and helping. *Journal of Experimental Social Psychology*, *33*(4), 401–420.

Dretske, F. (1988). *Explaining behavior: reasons in a world of causes*. Cambridge, MA: MIT Press.

Drummond, M. (2011). Men's bodies throughout the lifespan. In C. Blazina & D.S. Shen-Miller (Eds), *An international psychology of men: theoretical advances, case studies, and clinical innovations* (pp. 159–188). New York: Routledge/Taylor & Francis Group.

Drury, J., Cocking, C., & Reicher, S. (2009). The nature of collective resilience: survivor reactions to the 2005 London bombings. *International Journal of Mass Emergencies and Disasters*, *27*, 66–95.

Drury, J., & Reicher, S.D. (2000). Collective action and psychological change: the emergence of new social identities. *British Journal of Social Psychology*, *39*, 579–604.

Duckitt, J. (1992). Psychology and prejudice: a historical analysis and integrative framework. *American Psychologist*, *47*(10), 1182–1193.

Dunbar, R.I.M. (1995). Neocortex size and group size in primates: a test of the hypothesis. *Journal of Human Evolution*, *28*(3), 287–296.

Dunbar, R.I.M. (1996). *Grooming, gossip and the evolution of language*. Cambridge, MA: Harvard University Press.

Dunbar, R.I.M. (1998). The social brain hypothesis. *Evolutionary Anthropology*, *6*, 178–190.

Duncan, G.J., Brooks-Gunn, J., & Klebanov, P.K. (1994). Economic deprivation and early childhood development. *Child Development*, *65*, 296–318.

Duncan, L.G., Seymour, P.H.K., & Hill, S. (1997). How important are rhyme and analogy in beginning reading? *Cognition*, *63*, 171–208.

Dunifon, R. (2013). The influence of grandparents on the lives of children and adolescents. *Child Development Perspectives*, *7*, 55–60.

Dunn, J. (1988). Normative life events as risk factors in childhood. In M. Rutter (Ed.), *Studies of psychosocial risk: the power of longitudinal data*. Cambridge: Cambridge University Press.

Dunn, J. (2002). Sibling relationships. In P.K. Smith & C.H. Hart (Eds), *Blackwell handbook of childhood social development* (pp. 223–237). Malden, MA: Blackwell.

Dunst, C.J., Gorman, E., & Hamby, D.W. (2012). Child-directed motionese with infants and toddlers with and without hearing impairments. *CELL Reviews*, *5*, 1–11.

Duyme, M., Dumaret, A., & Tomkiewicz, S. (1999). How can we boost IQs of 'dull' children? A late adoption study. *Proceedings of the National Academy of Sciences, USA*, *96*, 8790–8794. DOI: 10.1073/pnas.96.15.8790.

Dweck, C.S. (2002). Beliefs that make smart people dumb. In R. Sternberg (Ed.), *Why smart people can be so stupid*. New Haven, CT: Yale University Press.

Dyson, B.J., & Ishfaq, F. (2008). Auditory memory can be object-based. *Psychonomic Bulletin and Review*, *15*, 409–412.

Eagly, A.H. (1995). The science and politics of comparing women and men. *American Psychologist*, *50*, 145–158.

Eagly, A.H., & Chaiken, S. (1993). *The psychology of attitudes*. Fort Worth, TX: Harcourt Brace Jovanovich.

Eagly, A.H., & Crowley, M. (1986). Gender and helping behavior: a meta-analytic review of the social psychological literature. *Psychological Bulletin*, *117*, 125–145.

Ebbesen, E.B., & Rienick, C.B. (1998). Retention interval and eyewitness memory for events and personal identifying attributes. *Journal of Applied Psychology*, *83*(5), 745.

Ebbinghaus, H. (1913). *Memory*. Trans. H.A. Rueger & C.E. Bussenius. New York: Teachers College (original work published 1885).

Edelman, G.M. (2006). *Second nature: brain science and human knowledge*. London and New Haven, CT: Yale University Press.

Edwards, D., & Potter, J. (1992). *Discursive psychology*. London: SAGE.

Edwards, D., & Potter, J. (2001). Introduction to discursive psychology. In A. McHoul & M. Rapley (Eds), *How to analyse talk in institutional settings: a casebook of methods* (pp. 12–24). London: Continuum International.

Ehrlich, K.B., Dykas, M.J., & Cassidy, J. (2012). Tipping points in adolescent adjustment: predicting social functioning from adolescents' conflict with parents and friends. *Journal of Family Psychology*, *10*, 776–783.

Eidelson, R., Pilisuk, M., & Soldz, S. (2011). The dark side of comprehensive soldier fitness. *American Psychologist*, *66*(7), 643–644.

Eimer, M. (2000). Effects of face inversion on the structural encoding and recognition of faces: evidence from event-related brain potentials. *Cognitive Brain Research*, *10*(1–2), 145–158.

Eisenberg, N. (1986). *Altruistic emotion, cognition and behaviour*. Hillsdale, NJ: Erlbaum.

Eisenberg, N. (1992). *The caring child*. Cambridge, MA: Harvard University Press.

Eisenberg, N., Fabes, R.A., & Spinrad, T. (2006). Prosocial development. In W. Damon, R.M. Lerner & N. Eisenberg (Eds), *Handbook of child psychology, Volume 3: Social emotional, and personality development* (6th edn). Hoboken, NJ: John Wiley & Sons.

Eisenberg, N., Guthrie, I.K., Murphy, B.C., Shepard, S.A., Cumberland, A., & Carlo, G. (1999). Consistency and development of prosocial dispositions: a longitudinal study. *Child Development*, *70*, 1360–1372.

Ekkekakis, P. (2013). *The measurement of affect, mood, and emotion: a guide for health-behavioral research*. New York: Cambridge University Press.

Ekman, P. (1993). Facial expression and emotion. *American Psychologist, 48*, 384–392.

Ekman, P. (1999). Facial expressions. In T. Dalgleish & M. Power (Eds), *Handbook of cognition and emotion* (Chapter 16). New York: John Wiley & Sons.

Ekman, P. (2001). *Telling lies: clues to deceit in the market-place, politics and marriage*. New York: W.W. Norton.

Elkin, I., Shea, M., Watkins, J., & Imber, S. (1989) National Institute of Mental Health Treatment of Depression collaborative research program: general effectiveness of treatments. *American Journal of Psychiatry, 46*, 971–982.

Ellis, A. (1962). *Reason and emotion in psychotherapy*. Secaucus, NJ: Lyle Stuart (Citadel Press).

Ellis, A. (2011). Rational emotive behaviour therapy. In R.J. Corsini & D. Wedding (Eds), *Current psychotherapies* (9th edn). Belmont, CA: Brooks/Cole.

Ellis, J., & Fox, P. (2001). The effect of self-identified sexual orientation on helping behavior in a British sample: are lesbians and gay men treated differently? *Journal of Applied Social Psychology, 31*, 1238–1247.

Ellis, L., & Ames, M.A. (1987). Neurohormonal functioning and sexual orientation: a theory of homosexuality–heterosexuality. *Psychological Bulletin, 101*, 233–258.

Ellison, N., Heino, R., & Gibs, J. (2006). Managing impressions online: self-presentation processes in the online dating environment. *Journal of Computer-Mediated Communication, 11*(2), article 2.

Elms, A.C. (1975). The crisis of confidence in social psychology. *American Psychologist, 30*(10), 967–976.

Else-Quest, N.M., Hyde, J.S., & Linn, M.C. (2010). Cross-national patterns of gender differences in mathematics: a meta-analysis. *Psychological Bulletin, 136*, 103–127.

Emswiller, T., Deaux, K., & Willits, J.E. (1971). Similarity, sex, and requests for small favors. *Journal of Applied Social Psychology, 1*, 284–291.

Ennett, S.T., & Bauman, K.E. (1994). The contribution of influence and selection to adolescent peer group homogeneity: the case of adolescent cigarette smoking. *Journal of Personality and Social Psychology, 67*(4), 653.

Eriksen, B.A., & Eriksen, C.W. (1974). Effects of noise-letters on identification of a target letter in a nonsearch task. *Perception & Psychophysics, 16*, 143–149.

Eriksen, C.W., & Yeh, Y. (1985). Allocation of attention in the visual field. *Journal of Experimental Psychology: Human Perception and Performance, 11*, 583–597.

Erikson, E. (1968). *Youth, identity and crisis*. New York: W.W. Norton.

Erikson, E.H. (1985). *The life cycle completed: a review*. New York: W.W. Norton.

Etkin, A., Egner, T., Peraza, D.M., Kandel, E.R., & Hirsch, J. (2006). Resolving emotional conflict: a role for the rostral anterior cingulate cortex in modulating activity in the amygdala. *Neuron, 51*, 871–882.

Evans, J.StB.T., Barston, J.L., & Pollard, P. (1983). On the conflict between logic and belief in syllogistic reasoning. *Memory and Cognition, 11*, 295–306.

Evans, J.StB.T., Newstead, S.E., & Byrne, R.M.J. (1993). *Human reasoning: the psychology of deduction*. Hove: Erlbaum.

Evardone, M., Alexander, G.M., & Morey, L.C. (2008). Hormones and borderline personality features. *Personality and Individual Differences, 44*, 278–287.

Everitt, B.J., & Robbins, T.W. (2005). Neural systems of reinforcement for drug addiction. *Nature Neuroscience, 8*(11), 1481–1489.

Eysenck, H. (1952). The effects of psychotherapy: an evaluation. *Journal of Consulting Psychology, 16*, 319–324.

Eysenck, H. (1953). *Uses and abuses of psychology*. Harmondsworth: Penguin.

Eysenck, H.J. (1967). *The biological basis of personality*. Springfield, IL: Thomas.

Eysenck, H.J. (1990). The prediction of death from cancer by means of personality/stress questionnaire: too good to be true? *Perceptual and Motor Skills, 71*, 216–218.

Eysenck, H.J. (1991). Dimensions of personality: 16, 5 or 3? Criteria for a taxonomic paradigm. *Personality and Individual Differences, 12*, 773–790.

Eysenck, H.J. (2004). *The decline and fall of the Freudian empire*. Edison, NJ: Transaction.

Eysenck, H.J., & Cookson, D. (1969). Personality in primary school children: ability and achievement. *British Journal of Educational Psychology, 39*, 109–122.

Eysenck, H.J., & Eysenck, M.W. (1985). *Personality and individual differences*. New York: Plenum.

Eysenck, H.J., & Eysenck, S.B.G. (1976). *Psychoticism as a dimension of personality*. London: Hodder & Stoughton.

Eysenck, H.J., & Eysenck, S.G. (1975). *Manual of the Eysenck Personality Questionnaire*. London: Hodder & Stoughton.

Eysenck, H.J., & Eysenck, S.G. (1991). *Manual of the Eysenck Personality Scales (EPS Adult): comprising the EPQ–Revised (EPQ–R), EPQ–R Short Scale, Impulsiveness (IVE) Questionnaire*. London: Hodder & Stoughton.

Eysenck, M.W. (1979). Depth, elaboration, and distinctiveness. In L.S. Cermack & F.I.M. Craik (Eds), *Levels of processing in human memory* (pp. 89–118). Hillsdale, NJ: Erlbaum.

Eysenck, M.W. (1982). *Attention and arousal: cognition and performance*. New York: Springer.

Eysenck, M.W., & Keane, M.T. (2005). *Cognitive psychology: a student's handbook,* (5th edn). London: Psychology Press.

Eysenk, M.W., & Keane, M.T. (2010). *Cognitive psychology: a student's handbook* (6th edn). London: Psychology Press.

Facebook. (2013). *Facebook factsheet*. https://newsroom.fb.com/Key-Facts (accessed 15 August 2014).

Fancher, R.E. (1996). *Pioneers of psychology* (3rd edn). New York: W.W. Norton.

Fantz, R. (1963). Pattern vision in newborn infants. *Science, 140*, 296–297.

Fausto-Sterling, A. (2000). *Sexing the body: gender politics and the construction of sexuality*. New York: Basic Books.

Fava, M. (2002). The role of the serotonergic and noradrenergic neurotransmitter systems in the treatment of psychological and physical symptoms of depression. *The Journal of Clinical Psychiatry*, *64*, 26–29.

Fazio, R.H., & Zanna, M.P. (1981). Direct experience and attitude-behavior consistency. *Advances in Experimental Social Psychology*, *14*, 161–202.

Fehr, F.S., & Stern, J.A. (1970). Peripheral physiological variables and emotion: the James–Lange theory revisited. *Psychological Bulletin*, *74*, 411–424.

Fenson, L., Dale, P.S., Reznick, J.S., Bates, E., Thal, D.J., Pethick, J., Tomasello, M., Mervis, C.B. & Stiles, J. (1994). Variability in early communicative development. *Monographs of the society for research in child development*, i–185.

Ferguson, C.K., & Kelley, H.H. (1964). Significant factors in overevaluation of own group's products. *Journal of Abnormal and Social Psychology*, *69*, 223–228.

Ferguson E. (2013). Personality is of central concern to understand health: towards a theoretical model for health psychology. *Health Psychology Review*, *7*(1), S32–S70.

Fernando, S. (2003). *Cultural diversity, mental health and psychiatry: the struggle against racism*. Hove: Brunner, Routledge.

Fernbach, P.M., Darlow, A., & Sloman, S.A. (2011). When good evidence goes bad: the weak evidence effect in judgment and decision-making. *Cognition*, *119*(3), 459–467.

Festinger, L. (1954). A theory of social comparison processes. *Human Relations*, *7*, 117–140.

Festinger, L. (1957). *A theory of cognitive dissonance*. Stanford, CA: Stanford University Press.

Festinger, L., Pepitone, A., & Newcomb, T. (1952). Some consequences of de-individuation in a group. *Journal of Abnormal and Social Psychology*, *47*, 382–389.

Fido, D., Gregson, M., Bloxsom, C.A., & Sumich, L.A. (in prep). Modulation of distress cue processing by psychopathic traits.

Fido, D., Santo, M.G.E., Bloxsom, C.A.J., Gregson, M., & Sumich, A. (In press). *Event Related Potential correlates of the Violence Inhibition Mechanism*.

Field, A. (2009). *Discover statistics using SPSS*. London: SAGE.

Finch, E., & Munro, V.E. (2005). Juror stereotypes and blame attribution in rape cases involving intoxicants: the findings of a pilot study. *British Journal of Criminology*, *45*(1), 25–38.

Finger, S. (1994). *Origins of neuroscience: a history of explorations into brain functions*. New York: Oxford University Press.

Finkelstein, J. (1991). *The fashioned self*. Cambridge: Polity Press.

Fischer, E. (1894). Einfluss der Configuration auf die Wirkung der Enzyme. *Berichte der deutschen chemischen Gesellschaft*, *27*(3), 2985–2993.

Fishbein, M., & Ajzen, I. (1975). *Belief, attitude, intention and behavior: an introduction to theory and research*. Reading, MA: Addison-Wesley.

Fisher, D., & Beech, A.R. (2007). The implicit theories of rapists and sexual murderers. In T.A. Gannon, T. Ward, A.R. Beech, & D. Fisher (Eds), *Aggressive offenders' cognition: theory, research, and practice* (pp. 31–52). Chichester: John Wiley & Sons.

Fisher, H. (1999). *The first sex: the natural talents of women and how they will change the world*. New York: Random House.

Fiske, S.T. (1993). Social cognition and perception. *Annual Review of Psychology*, *44*, 155–194.

Fiske, S.T. (1998). Stereotyping, prejudice, and discrimination. In D.T. Gilbert, S.T. Fiske, & G. Lindzey (Eds), *Handbook of social psychology* (pp. 357–411). New York: McGraw-Hill.

Fiske, S.T., & Taylor, S.E. (1991). *Social cognition* (2nd edn). New York: McGraw-Hill.

Fitzgerald, H. (2005). Still feeling like a spare piece of luggage? Embodied experiences of (dis)ability in physical education and school sport. *Physical Education & Sport Pedagogy*, *10*(1), 41–59.

Fitzpatrick, J., & Dollamore, G. (1999). Examining adult mortality rates using the National Statistics for Socio-Economic Classification. *Health Statistics Quarterly*, *2*, 33–40.

Fleeson, W. (2001). Toward a structure- and process-integrated view of personality: traits as density distribution of states. *Journal of Personality and Social Psychology*, *80*, 1011–1027.

Fletcher, J.M., & Morris, R.D. (2011). Reading, laterality, and the brain: early contributions on reading disabilities by Sara S. Sparrow. *Journal of Autism and Developmental Disorders*, *44*, 250–255.

Flower, L., & Hayes, J.R. (1981). A cognitive process theory of writing. *College Composition and Communication*, *32*(4), 365–387.

Flynn, J.R. (1987). Massive IQ gains in 14 nations: what IQ tests really measure. *Psychological Bulletin*, *101*, 171–191.

Foa, E.B., & Kozak, M.J. (1986). Emotional processing of fear: exposure to corrective information. *Psychological Bulletin*, *99*, 20–35.

Fodor, J.A. (1975). *The language of thought*. Cambridge, MA: Harvard University Press.

Ford, T.E., Boxer, C.F., Armstrong, J., & Edel, J.R. (2008). More than 'just a joke': the prejudice-releasing function of sexist humor. *Personality and Social Psychology Bulletin*, *34*(2), 159–170.

Forge, K.L., & Phemister, S. (1987). The effect of prosocial cartoons on preschool children. *Child Development Journal*, *17*, 83–88.

Fox, D. (2010). The insanity virus. *Discover Magazine*, *31*(5), 58–64.

Fox, D., & Prilleltensky, I. (Eds) (1997). *Critical psychology: an introduction*. London: SAGE.

Fraser, B.J. (2012). Classroom learning environments: Retrospect, context and prospect. In *Second international handbook of science education* (pp. 1191–1239). The Netherlands: Springer.

Fraser, S., Bunce, C., Wormald, R., & Brunner, E. (2001). Deprivation and late presentation of glaucoma: case control study. *British Medical Journal, 322* (7827), 639–643.

Freedman, J.L., Klevansky, S., & Ehrlich, P.R. (1971). The effect of crowding on human task performance. *Journal of Applied Social Psychology, 1*, 7–25.

Freeman, J.B., Ma, Y., Barth, M., Young, S.G., Han, S., & Ambady, N. (2013, in press). The neural basis of contextual influences on face categorization. *Cerebral Cortex*.

Freud, A. (1958). Psychological study of the child. *Adolescence, 13*, 255–278.

Freud, S. (1913). *The Interpretation of Dreams*, (3rd edn). Trans. by A.A. Brill. New York: The Macmillan Company; Bartleby.com, 2010. Retrieved from www.bartleby.com/285/. (accessed 21 June 2014).

Freud, S. (1920). *A general introduction to psychoanalysis*. New York: Boni & Liveright.

Freud, S. (1924). *Zur psychopathologie des alltaglebens*. (10th edn). Leipzig: Internationaler psychoanalytischer verlag (English version in *Basic Writings of Sigmund Freud* edited by A.A. Brill. New York Modern Library 1938).

Freud, S. (1938). *Basic writings of Sigmund Freud*. Ed. by A.A. Brill. New York: Modern Library.

Freund, A.M., & Lamb, M.E. (2010). Social and emotional development across the life span. In M.E. Lamb, A.M. Freund, & R.M. Lerner (Eds), *The handbook of life-span development. Vol. 2: Social and emotional development* (pp. 1–8). Hoboken, NJ: John Wiley & Sons.

Freund, K. (1990). Courtship disorder. In W.K. Marshall, D.R. Laws, & H.E. Barbaree (Eds), *Handbook of sexual assault* (pp. 195–207). New York: Plenum.

Friedman, M., & Rosenman, R.H. (1974). *Type A behaviour and your heart*. New York: Knopf.

Frith, C. (2007). *Making up the mind: how the brain creates our mental world*. Oxford: Blackwell.

Fritzsche, B.A., Finkelstein, M.A., & Penner, L.A. (2000). To help or not to help: capturing individuals' decision policies. *Social Behavior and Personality, 28*, 561–578.

Frohlich, N., & Oppenheimer, J. (1970). I get by with a little help from my friends. *World Politics, 23*, 104–120.

Frosh, S., Phoenix, A., & Pattman, R. (2001). *Young masculinities: understanding boys in contemporary society*. London: Palgrave Macmillan.

Funder, D.C. (1982). On the accuracy of dispositional versus situational attributions. *Social Cognition, 1*(3), 205–222.

Funder, D.C. (2010). *The personality puzzle* (5th edn). New York: W.W. Norton.

Funder, D.C., & Ozer, D.J. (1983). Behavior as a function of the situation. *Journal of Personality and Social Psychology, 44*(1), 107–112.

Furnham, A., & Allass, K. (1999). The influence of musical distraction of varying complexity on the cognitive performance of extraverts and introverts. *European Journal of Personality, 13*, 27–38.

Furnham, A., & Heaven, P. (1999). *Personality and social behaviour*. London: Arnold.

Furshpan, E.J., & Potter, D.D. (1959). Transmission at the giant motor synapse of the crayfish. *Journal of Physiology, 145*, 289–325.

Fuson, K.C. (1988). *Children's counting and concepts of number*. New York: Springer.

Gaertner, S.L., & Dovidio, J.F. (2000). Reducing intergroup bias: the benefits of recategorization. *Journal of Personality and Social Psychology, 57*, 239–249.

Galambos, N.L., & Almeida, D.M. (1992). Does parent–adolescent conflict increase in early adolescence? *Journal of Marriage and the Family, 54*, 737–747.

Galatzer-Levy, R., Bachrach, H., Skolnikoff, A., & Waldron, S. (2000) *Does psychotherapy work?* New Haven, CT: Yale University Press.

Galton, F. (1892). *Hereditary genius: an inquiry into its laws and consequences*. London: Macmillan. Retrieved from http://galton.org/books/hereditary-genius/text/pdf/galton-1869-genius-v3.pdf. (accessed 21 June 2014).

Gamble, A.L., Harvey, A.G., & Rapee, R.M. (2009). Specific phobia. In D.J.Stein, E.Hollande, & B. Rothbaum (Eds), *Textbook of anxiety disorders* (pp.525–543). Washington, DC: American Psychiatric Publishing.

Gannon, T., Wood, J., Pina, A., Tyler, N., Barnoux, M.F., & Vasquez, E.A. (2013). An evaluation of mandatory polygraph testing for sexual offenders in the United Kingdom. *Sexual Abuse: A Journal of Research and Treatment*. DOI: 1079063213486836.

Gardner, H. (1993a). *Frames of mind: theory of multiple intelligences*. London: Fontana.

Gardner, H. (1993b). Educating for understanding. *The American School Board Journal, 180*, 20–24.

Gardner, H. (1998). A multiplicity of intelligences. *Scientific American Presents: Exploring Intelligence, 9*, 18–23.

Gardner, H., & Hatch, T. (1989). Multiple intelligences go to school: educational implications of the theory of multiple intelligences. *Educational Researcher, 18*, 4–9.

Garfinkel, H. (1967). *Studies in ethnomethodology*. Englewood Cliffs, NJ: Prentice Hall.

Garnett, K. (1992). Developing fluency with basic number facts: intervention for students with learning disabilities. *Learning Disabilities Research & Practice, 7*, 210–216.

Gauld, A., & Stephenson, G.M. (1967). Some experiments related to Bartlett's theory of remembering. *British Journal of Psychology, 58*, 39–49.

Gauntlett, D. (Ed.) (2000). *Web studies: rewiring media studies for the digital age*. London: Arnold, pp. 43–51.

Gavrilov, A.K. (1997). Techniques of reading in classical antiquity. *The Classical Quarterly* (New Series), *47*, 56–73.

Gay, P. (Ed.) (1989). *The Freud reader*. New York: W.W. Norton.

Gaynor, S.T., & Baird, S.C. (2007). Personality disorders. In D.W. Woods & J.W. Kanter (Eds), *Understanding behaviour disorders: A contemporary behavioural perspective*. Reno, NV: Context Press.

Gazzaniga, M.S. (1970). *The bisected brain*. New York: Meredith.

Geer, J.H., & Jarmecky, L. (1973). Effect of being responsible for reducing another's pain on subjects' response and arousal. *Journal of Personality and Social Psychology, 26*(2), 232–237.

Geiselman, R.E., Fisher, R.P., MacKinnon, D.P., & Holland, H.L. (1986). Enhancement of eyewitness memory with the cognitive interview. *American Journal of Psychology*, *99*, 385–401.

Gelb, I.J. (1963). *A study of writing* (2nd edn). Chicago, IL: University of Chicago Press.

Gelder, M., Mayou, R., & Geddes, J. (1999). *Psychiatry* (2nd edn). Oxford: Oxford University Press.

Gelfand, D.M., Jensen, W.R., & Drew, C.J. (1997). *Understanding child behaviour disorders* (3rd edn). Fort Worth, TX: Harcourt Brace.

Gelman, A., & Hill, J. (2007). *Data analysis using regression and multilevel/hierarchical models*. Cambridge: Cambridge University Press.

Gelman, R., & Gallistel, C.R. (1978). *The child's understanding of number*. Cambridge, MA: Harvard University Press.

Gergen, K. (1973). Social psychology as history. *Journal of Personality and Social Psychology*, *26*, 309–320.

Gergen, K. (1991). *The saturated self: dilemmas of identity in contemporary life.* New York: Basic Books.

Gergen, K. (1994). *Realities and relationships: soundings in social construction*. Cambridge, MA: Harvard University Press.

Gergen, K. (1996). Technology and the self: from the essential to the sublime. In D. Grodin & T.R. Lindlof (Eds), *Constructing the self in a mediated world* (pp. 127–140). London: SAGE.

Gergen, K. (1997). *Realities and relationships: soundings in social construction*. Cambridge, MA: Harvard University Press.

Gergen, K. (2000). The self in the age of information. *The Washington Quarterly*, *23*(1), 201–214.

Gergen, K. (2009). *Relational being*. New York: Oxford University Press.

Gergen, K.J. (2001). *Social construction in context*. London: SAGE.

Gergen, K.J. (2011). *Relational being: beyond self and community* (2nd edn). Oxford: Oxford University Press (1st edn 2009).

Gergen, K.J., & Gergen, M. (1988). Narratives and the self as relationship. *Advances in Experimental Social Psychology*, *21*, 17–56.

Gergen, K.J., & Gergen, M. (2004). *Social construction: entering the dialogue*. Chagrin Falls, OH: Taos Institute Publications.

Gergen, K.J., Gulerce, A., Lock, A., & Misra, G. (1996). Psychological science in cultural context. *American Psychologist*, *51*(5), 496–503.

Gergen, M., & Gergen, K. (Eds) (2003). *Social construction: a reader*. London: SAGE.

Gerl, E.J., & Morris, M.R. (2008). The causes and consequences of color vision. *Evolution: Education and Outreach*, *1*(4), 476–486.

Ghashghaei, H.T., Hilgetag, C.C., & Barbas, H. (2007). Sequence of information processing for emotions based on the anatomic dialogue between prefrontal cortex and amygdala. *NeuroImage, 34*(3), 905–923.

Gibbard, I., & Hanley, T. (2008). A five-year evaluation of the effectiveness of person-centred counselling in routine clinical practice in primary care. *Counselling and Psychotherapy Research: Linking Research with Practice*, *8*(4), 215–222.

Gibbons, A. (1991). The brain as a 'sexual organ'. *Science*, *253*, 957–959.

Gibbs, J.C., Basinger, K.S., Grime, R.L., & Snarey, J.R. (2007). Moral judgement development across cultures: revisiting Kohlberg's universality claims. *Developmental Review*, *27*, 443–500.

Gibson, J.J. (1950). *The perceptions of the visual world*. Boston, MA: Houghton Mifflin.

Gibson, J.J. (1966). *The senses considered as perceptual systems*. Boston, MA: Houghton Mifflin.

Giedd, J.N. (2004). Structural magnetic resonance imaging of the adolescent brain. *Annals of the New York Academy of Sciences*, *1021*(1), 77–85.

Gilligan, C. (1982). *The relational self*. Boston, MA: Harvard University Press.

Gillingham, G. (2004). *Autism: handle with care!* Edmonton, Alberta: Tacit.

Giuliani, N.R., Drabant, E.M., & Gross, J.J. (2011). Anterior cingulate cortex volume and emotion regulation: is bigger better? *Biological Psychology*, *86*(3), 379–382.

Gladue, B.A. (1991). Aggressive behavioral characteristics, hormones, and sexual orientation in men and women. *Aggressive Behavior*, *17*, 313–326.

Gladue, B.A., & Bailey, J.M. (1995). Aggressiveness, competitiveness and human sexual orientation. *Psychoneuroendocrinology*, *20*, 475–485.

Glanzer, M., & Cunitz, A.R. (1966). Two storage mechanisms in free recall. *Journal of Verbal Learning & Verbal Behavior*, *5*(4), 351–360.

Glenberg, A.M., & Swanson, N.G. (1986). A temporal distinctiveness theory of recency and modality effects. *Journal of Experimental Psychology: Learning, Memory and Cognition*, *12*, 3–15.

Godden, D.R., & Baddeley, A.D. (1975). Context-dependent memory in two natural environments: on land and underwater. *British Journal of Psychology*, *66*, 325–331.

Goffee R. (1981). Incorporation and conflict: a case study of subcontracting in the coal industry, *Sociological Review*, *29*(3), 475–497.

Goffman, E. (1959). *The presentation of self in everyday life*. New York: Doubleday Anchor.

Goldberg, L.R. (1992). The development of markers of the Big-Five factor structure. *Psychological Assessment*, *4*, 2642.

Goldberg, L.R. (1993). The structure of phenotypic personality traits. *American Psychologist*, *48*(1), 26–34.

Goldberg, L.R., Johnson, J.A., Eber, H.W., Hogan, R., Ashton, M.C., Cloninger, C.R., & Gough, H.C. (2006). The International Personality Item Pool and the future of public-domain personality measures. *Journal of Research in Personality*, *40*, 84–96.

Goldin, P.R., & Gross, J.J. (2010). Effects of mindfulness-based stress reduction (MBSR) on emotion regulation in social anxiety disorder. *Emotion*, *10*(1), 83–91.

Goleman, D. (1996). *Emotional intelligence*. London: Bloomsbury.

Goodale, M.A., & Milner, A.D. (1992). Separate visual pathways for perception and action. *Trends in Neurosciences*, *15*, 20–24.

Gooden, R.J., & Winefield, H.R. (2007). Breast and prostate cancer online discussion boards: a thematic analysis of gender differences and similarities. *Journal of Health Psychology*, *12*, 103–114.

Goodey, C.F. (2011). *A history of intelligence and 'intellectual disabilit': the shaping of psychology in early modern Europe*. Farnham: Ashgate.

Goodhart, D. (2004a). Too diverse? *Prospect*, February, 30–37.

Goodhart, D. (2004b). Discomfort of strangers. *The GuardianI*, 24 February 2004. Available at http://www.theguardian.com/politics/2004/feb/24/race.eu

Goodwin, D., & Watkinson, J. (2000). Inclusive physical education from the perspectives of students with physical disabilities. *Adapted Physical Activity Quarterly*, *17*, 144–160.

Gopal, A., Clark, E., Allgair, A., D'Amato, C., Furman, M., Gansler, D.A., & Fulwiler, C.E. (2013). Dorsal/ventral parcellation of the amygdala: relevance to impulsivity and aggression. *Psychiatry Research*, *211*(1), 24–30.

Goren, C.C., Sarty, M., & Wu, P.Y.K. (1975). Visual following and pattern discrimination of face-like stimuli by newborn infants. *Pediatrics*, *56*, 544–549.

Gosling, S. (2008). *Snoop: what your stuff says about you*. New York: Basic Books.

Goswami, U. (1986). Children's use of analogy in learning to read: a developmental study. *Journal of Experimental Child Psychology*, *42*, 73–83.

Goswami, U. (1988). Orthographic analogies and reading development. *Quarterly Journal of Experimental Psychology: Human Experimental Psychology*, *40a*, 239–268.

Goswami, U., & Bryant, P. (1990). *Phonological skills and learning to read*. Hove: Erlbaum.

Goswami, U., Ziegler, J., Dalton, L., & Schneider, W. (2003). Nonword reading across orthographies: how flexible is the choice of reading units? *Applied Psycholinguistics*, *24*, 235–247.

Gottfredson, L.S. (1998). The general intelligence factor. *Scientific American Presents: Exploring Intelligence*, *9*, 24–29.

Gough, B. (1998). Men and the discursive reproduction of sexism: repertoires of difference and equality. *Feminism & Psychology*, *8*(1), 25–49.

Gough, B. (2002). 'I've always tolerated it but …': heterosexual masculinity and the discursive reproduction of homophobia. In A. Coyle & C. Kitzinger (Eds), *Lesbian and gay psychology*. Oxford: BPS/Blackwell.

Gould, E. (2007). How widespread is adult neurogenesis in mammals? *Nature Reviews Neuroscience*, *8*, 481–488.

Gould, S.J. (1981). *The mismeasure of man*. Harmondsworth: Penguin.

Gould, S.J., & Lewontin, R.C. (1979). The spandrels of San Marco and the Panglossian Paradigm: a critique of the adaptationist programme. *Proceedings of the Royal Society of London*, *B*, *205*(1161), 581–598.

Gouldner, A. (1954). *Patterns of industrial bureaucracy*, Glencoe, IL: Free Press.

Gouldner, A.W. (1960). The norm of reciprocity: a preliminary statement. *American Sociological Review*, *25*, 161–178.

Granhag, P.A., Strömwall, L.A., Willén, R.M., & Hartwig, M. (2013). Eliciting cues to deception by tactical disclosure of evidence: the first test of the Evidence Framing Matrix. *Legal and Criminological Psychology*. Available online. DOI: 10.1111/j.2044-8333.2012.02047.

Gravholt, C., Juul, S., Naeraa, R., & Hansen, J. (1998). Morbidity in Turner syndrome. *Journal of Clinical Epidemiology*, *51*, 147–158.

Gray, J.A. (1972). Learning theory, the conceptual nervous system and personality. In V.D. Nebylitsyn & J.A. Gray (Eds), *The biological bases of individual behaviour* (pp. 372–399). New York: Academic Press.

Gray, J.A., Joseph, M.H., Hemsley, D.R., Young, A.M., Clea Warburton, E., Boulenguez, P., ... & Feldon, J. (1995). The role of mesolimbic dopaminergic and retrohippocampal afferents to the nucleus accumbens in latent inhibition: implications for schizophrenia. *Behavioural brain research*, *71*(1), 19–31.

Gray, J.A., & McNaughton, N. (2000). *The neuropsychology of anxiety: an enquiry into the functions of the septo-hippocampal system*. Oxford: Oxford University Press.

Gray, J.A., & Wedderburn, A.A.I. (1960). Group strategies with simultaneous stimuli. *Quarterly Journal of Experimental Psychology*, *12*, 180–184.

Green, D.P., Glaser, J., & Rich, A. (1998). From lynching to gay bashing: the elusive connection between economic conditions and hate crime. *Journal of Personality and Social Psychology*, *75*(1), 82–92.

Greenberg, J., Pyszczynski, T., & Solomon, S. (1982). The self-serving attributional bias: beyond self-presentation. *Journal of Experimental Social Psychology*, *18*, 56–67.

Greenberger, D., & Padesky, C. (1995). *Mind over mood*. New York: Guilford Press.

Gregory, R.L. (1963). Distortion of visual space as inappropriate constancy scaling. *Nature*, *199*, 678–691.

Gregory, R.L. (1970). *The intelligent eye*. London: Weidenfeld & Nicolson.

Gregory, R.L. (1997). *Eye and brain: the psychology of seeing* (5th edn). Oxford: Oxford University Press.

Grieve, P., & Hogg, M.A. (1999). Subjective uncertainty and intergroup discrimination in the minimal group situation. *Personality and Social Psychology Bulletin*, *25*, 926–940.

Griffiths, M.D. (2003). Internet gambling: issues, concerns and recommendations. *CyberPsychology and Behavior*, *6*, 557–568.

Griffiths, M.D. (2010). The use of online methodologies in data collection for gambling and gaming addictions. *International Journal of Mental Health and Addiction*, *8*, 8–20.

Griffiths, M.D. (2011). Technological trends and the psychosocial impact on gambling. *Casino and Gaming International*, *7*(1), 77–80.

Griffiths, M.D. (2014). The use of behavioural tracking methodologies in the study of online gambling. *SAGE Research Methods Cases*. London: SAGE. Available at: http://dx.doi.org/10.4135/978144627305013517480.

Griffiths, M.D., & Auer, M. (2011). Approaches to understanding online versus offline gaming impacts. *Casino and Gaming International*, 7(3), 45–48.

Griffiths, M.D., & Barnes, A. (2008). Internet gambling: an online empirical study among student gamblers. *International Journal of Mental Health and Addiction*, 6, 194–204.

Griffiths, M.D., Davies, M.N.O., & Chappell, D. (2003). Breaking the stereotype: the case of online gaming. *Cyberpsychology and Behavior*, 6, 81–91.

Griffiths, M.D., & Whitty, M.W. (2010). Online behavioural tracking in internet gambling research: ethical and methodological issues. *International Journal of Internet Research Ethics*, 3, 104–117.

Griffiths, M.D., Wood, R.T.A., Parke, J., & Parke, A. (2007). Gaming research and best practice: gaming industry, social responsibility and academia. *Casino and Gaming International*, 3, 97–103.

Griffiths, M.D., Wood, R.T.A., & Parke, J. (2009). Social responsibility tools in online gambling: a survey of attitudes and behaviour among internet gamblers. *CyberPsychology and Behavior*, 12, 413–421.

Gross, J.J. (1998). Antecedent- and response-focused emotion regulation: Divergent consequences for experience, expression, and physiology. *Journal of Personality and Social Psychology*, 74, 224–237.

Gruber, H.E. (1995). Insight and affect in the history of science. In R.J. Sternberg & J.E. Davidson (Eds), *The nature of insight* (pp. 397–431). Cambridge, MA: MIT Press.

Grubin, D. (2008). The case for the polygraph testing of sex offenders. *Legal and Criminal Psychology*, 13, 177–189.

Guba, E.G., & Lincoln, Y.S. (1994). Competing paradigms in qualitative research. In N.K. Denzin & Y.S. Lincoln (Eds), *Handbook of qualitative research* (pp. 105–117). Thousand Oaks, CA: SAGE.

Guéguen, N., & Lamy, L. (2011). The effect of the word 'love' on compliance to a request for humanitarian aid: an evaluation in a field setting. *Social Influence*, 6(4), 249–258.

Gunderson, J.G. (2009). *Borderline personality disorder: a clinical guide*. Arlington, V.A.: American Psychiatric Publications.

Gupta, D. (2001). *Path to collective madness: a study in social order and political pathology*. Westport, CT: Greenwood Press.

Guzzo, R.A., & Dickson, M.W. (1996). Teams in organizations: recent research on performance and effectiveness. *Annual Review of Psychology*, 47, 307–338.

Hacking, I. (1995). The looping effects of human kinds. In D. Sperber, D. Premack & A. Premack (Eds), *Causal cognition: A multidisciplinary approach* (pp. 351–353). Oxford: Oxford University Press.

Hacking, I. (2006). Making up people. *London Review of Books*, 28(16), 23–26.

Hackney, C. (2002). From cochlea to cortex. In D. Roberts (Ed.), *Signals and perception: the fundamentals of human sensation*. London: Palgrave Macmillan.

Haggbloom, S.J., Warnick, R., Warnick, J.E., Jones, V.K., Yarbrough, G.L., Russell, T.M., et al. (2002). The 100 most eminent psychologists of the 20th century. *Review of General Psychology*, 6, 139–152.

Haier, R.J., Jung, R.E., Yeo, R.A., Head, K., & Alkire, M.T. (2004). Structural brain variation and general intelligence, *NeuroImage*, 23, 425–433.

Hall, G.S. (1904). *Adolescence: its psychology and its relation to physiology, anthropology, sociology, sex, crime, religion, and education* (Vols I & II). Englewood Cliffs, NJ: Prentice-Hall.

Hall, J.A.Y., & Kimura, D. (1995). Performance by homosexual males and females on sexually dimorphic motor tasks. *Archives of Sexual Behavior*, 24, 395–407.

Halpern, D.F., Benbow, C.P., Geary, D.C., Gur, R.C., Shibley Hyde, J., & Gernsbacher, M.A. (2007). The science of sex differences in science and mathematics. *Psychological Science in the Public Interest*, 8, 1–51.

Halpern-Felsher, B.L., & Cauffman, E. (2001). Costs and benefits of a decision: decision-making competence in adolescents and adults. *Journal of Applied Developmental Psychology*, 22, 257–273.

Hamer, D.H., Hu, S., Magnuson, V.L., Hu, N., & Pattatucci, A.M.L. (1993). A linkage between DNA markers on the X chromosome and male sexual orientation. *Science*, 261, 321–327.

Hamill, R., Wilson, T.D., & Nisbett, R.E. (1980). Insensitivity to sample bias: Generalizing from atypical cases. *Journal of Personality and Social Psychology*, 39(4), 578–589.

Hamilton, A., Plunkett, K., & Schafer, G. (2000). Infant vocabulary development assessed with a British communicative development inventory. *Journal of Child Language*, 27, 689–705.

Hamilton, D.L., & Crump, S.A. (2004). Stereotypes. In C. Spielberger (Ed.), *Encyclopedia of applied psychology* (pp. 479–484). New York: Elsevier.

Hamilton, W.D. (1964). The genetical evolution of social behaviour. I. *Journal of Theoretical Biology*, 7(1), 1–16.

Hampson, S. (1999). State of the art: personality. *The Psychologist*, 12(6), 284–288.

Han, C., McGue, M.K., & Iacono, W.G. (1999). Lifetime tobacco, alcohol and other substance use in adolescent Minnesota twins: univariate and multivariate behavioral genetic analyses. *Addiction*, 94(7), 981–993.

Handley, S.J., Capon, A., Copp, C., & Harper, C. (2002). Conditional reasoning and the Tower of Hanoi: the role of verbal and spatial working memory. *British Journal of Psychology*, 93, 501–518.

Hansen, P.E., Floderus, B., Frederiksen, K., & Johansen, C. (2005). Personality traits, health behavior, and risk for cancer: a prospective study of a Swedish twin cohort. *Cancer*, 103(5), 1082–1091.

Hanson, R.K., Harris, A.J.R., Scott, T.-L., & Helmus, L. (2007). *Assessing the risk of sexual offenders on community supervision: the Dynamic Supervision Project (Corrections Research User Report No. 2007–05)*. Ottawa, Ontario: Public Safety Canada.

Haqq, C.M., King, C.-Y., Ukiyama, E., Falsafi, S., Haqq, T.N., Donahoe, P.K., & Weiss, M.A. (1994). Molecular basis of mammalian sexual determination: activation of Müllerian inhibiting substance gene expression by SRY. *Science, 266,* 1494–1500.

Haraway, D. (1991). *Simians, cyborgs, and women: the reinvention of nature*. London: Free Association.

Hardyck, C.D., & Petrinovich, L.F. (1970). Subvocal speech and comprehension level as a function of the difficulty level of reading material. *Journal of Verbal Learning & Verbal Behavior, 9,* 647–65.

Harkins, S.G., & Szymanski, K. (1988). Social loafing and self-evaluation with an objective standard. *Journal of Experimental Social Psychology, 24,* 354–365.

Harley, T. (2001). *The psychology of language: from data to theory* (2nd edn). Hove: Psychology Press.

Harré, R. (1991). *Physical being*. Oxford: Blackwell.

Harré, R. (1998). *The singular self: an introduction to the psychology of personhood*. London: SAGE.

Harré, R. (1999). The rediscovery of the human mind: the discursive approach. *Asian Journal of Social Psychology, 2,* 43–62.

Harré, R. (2004a). Staking our claim for qualitative psychology as science. *Qualitative Research in Psychology, 4,* 3–14.

Harré, R. (2004b). Discursive psychology and the boundaries of sense. *Organization Studies, 25*(8), 1435–1453.

Harré, R. (2005). The relevance of the philosophy of psychology to a science of psychology. In C.E. Erneling & D.M. Johnson (Eds), *The mind as a scientific object: between brain and culture* (pp. 20–34). New York: Oxford University Press.

Harré, R. (2006). *Key thinkers in psychology.* London: SAGE.

Harré, R., & Van Langenhove, L. (Eds) (1999). *Positioning theory*. Oxford: Blackwell.

Harris, B. (1979). Whatever happened to Little Albert? *American Psychologist, 34,* 151–160.

Harris, M., & Coltheart, M., (1986). *Language and processing in children and adults: an introduction*. London: Routledge & Kegan Paul.

Harris, P.L. (1973). Perseverative errors in search by young children. *Child Development, 44,* 28–33.

Harrison, K. (2000). Television viewing, fat stereotyping, body shape standards, and eating disorder. *Communication Research, 27*(5), 617–640.

Harter, S. (1982). The perceived competence scale for children. *Child Development, 53,* 87–97.

Harter, S. (1987). The determinants and mediational role of global self-worth in children. In N. Eisenberg (Ed.), *Contemporary topics in developmental psychology* (pp. 219–242). New York: Wiley-Interscience.

Hasher, L., Stoltzfus, E.R., Zacks, R.T., & Rypma, B. (1991). Age and inhibition. *Journal of Experimental Psychology: Learning, Memory, and Cognition, 17*(1), 163–169.

Hasher, L., & Zacks, R.T. (1988). Working memory, comprehension, and aging: a review and a new view. In G.G. Bower (Ed.), *The psychology of learning and motivation* (vol. 22, pp. 193–225). San Diego, CA: Academic Press.

Haslam, S. A. (2001). Your wish is our command: the role of shared social identity in translating a leader's vision into followers' action. In M.A. Hogg & D.J. Terry (Eds), *Social Identity Processes in Organizational Contexts*. Hove: Psychology Press, pp. 213–228.

Hastings, E.C., & West, R.L. (2009). The relative success of a self-help and a group-based memory training program for older adults. *Psychology and Aging, 24*(3), 586.

Hastings, M.E., Tangney, J.P., & Stuewig, J. (2008). Psychopathy and identification of facial expressions of emotions. *Personality and Individual Differences, 44*(7), 1474–1483.

Hatcher, P.J., Hulme, C., & Snowling, M.J. (2004). Explicit phoneme training combined with phonic reading instructions helps young children at risk of reading failure. *Journal of Child Psychology & Psychiatry, 45,* 338–358.

Havard, C., & Memon, A. (2013). The mystery man can help reduce false identification for child witnesses: evidence from video line-ups. *Applied Cognitive Psychology, 27*(1), 50–59.

Hawton, K., Sutton, L., Haw, C., Sinclair, J., & Deeks, J.J. (2005). Schizophrenia and suicide: systematic review of risk factors. *The British Journal of Psychiatry, 187*(1), 9–20.

Hay, D.F., Nash, A., & Pedersen, J. (1981). Response of six-month-olds to the distress of their peers. *Child Development, 52,* 1071–1075.

Hay, D.F., Nash, A., & Pedersen, J. (1983). Interaction between six-month-old peers. *Child Development, 54,* 577–562.

Hay, D.F., Payne, A., & Chadwick, A. (2004). Peer relations in childhood. *Journal of Child Psychology and Psychiatry, 45,* 84–108.

Haynes, S.G., & Feinleib, M. (1980). Women, work and coronary heart disease: prospective findings from the Framingham Heart Study. *American Journal of Public Health, 79,* 133–141.

Hayward, K. (2007). Situational crime prevention and its discontents: rational choice theory versus the 'culture of now'. *Social Policy and Administration, 41*(3), 232–250.

Hazlett, H.C., Poe, M., Gerig, G., Smith, R.G., Provenzale, J., Ross, A., Gilmore, J., & Piven, J. (2005). Magnetic resonance imaging and head circumference study of brain size in autism: birth through age 2 years. *Archives of General Psychiatry, 62*(12), 1366–1376.

Health and Social Care Information Center (2013) *Statistics on Smoking, England – 2013*. Available at http://www.hscic.gov.uk/catalogue/PUB11454

Heider, F. (1958). *The psychology of interpersonal relations*. New York: Wiley.

Heider, F., & Simmel, M. (1944). An experimental study of apparent behavior. *The American Journal of Psychology, 57,* 243–259.

Heller, D., Perunovic, W.Q.E., & Reichman, D. (2009). The future of person–situation integration in the interface between traits and goals: a bottom-up framework. *Journal of Research in Personality, 43*(2), 171–178.

Helwig, C.C., & Turiel, E. (2002). Children's social and moral reasoning. In P.K. Smith & C.H. Hart (Eds), *Blackwell handbook of childhood social development*. Oxford: Blackwell.

Hendry, L.B., & Kloep, M. (2010). How universal is emerging adulthood? An empirical example. *Journal of Youth Studies*, *13*(2), 169–179.

Henrich, J., Heine, S.J., & Norenzayan, A. (2010). The weirdest people in the world? *Behavioral and Brain Sciences*, *33*(2–3), 61–83.

Henrich, J., & McElreath, R. (2009). Dual-inheritance theory: the evolution of human cultural capacities and cultural evolution. In R. Dunbar & L. Barrett (Eds), *Oxford Handbook of Evolutionary Psychology* (pp. 555–570). Oxford: Oxford University Press.

Henwood, K., & Pidgeon, N. (1992) Qualitative research and psychological theorising. *British Journal of Psychology*, *83*, 97–111.

Herbert, M. (2008). *Typical and atypical development: from conception to adolescence*. Malden, MA: Blackwell.

Hergenhahn, B.R. (2005). *An introduction to the history of psychology*. Belmont, CA: Wadsworth.

Herrnstein, R.J., & Murray, C. (1994). *The bell curve*. New York: Free Press.

Hertel, G., Kerr, N.L., & Messé, L.A. (2000). Motivation gains in performance groups: paradigmatic and theoretical developments on the Köhler effect. *Journal of Personality and Social Psychology*, *79*, 580–601.

Hetherington, E.M., & Stanley-Hagan, M. (1999). Adjustment of children with divorced parents: a risk and resiliency perspective. *Journal of Child Psychology and Psychiatry*, *40*, 120–140.

Heuser, J.E., & Reese, T.S. (1973). Evidence for recycling of synaptic vesicle membrane during transmitter release at the frog neuromuscular function. *Journal of Cell Biology*, *57*, 315–344.

Hewitt, J.P., & Stokes, R. (1975). Disclaimers. *American Sociological Review*, *40*(1), 1–11.

Hewstone, M. (1990). The 'ultimate attribution error'? A review of the literature on intergroup causal attribution. *European Journal of Social Psychology*, *20*(4), 311–335.

Hewstone, M., Islam, M.R., & Judd, C.M. (1993). Models of crossed categorization and intergroup relations. *Journal of Personality and Social Psychology*, *65*(5), 779–793.

Hewstone, M., & Swart, H. (2011). Fifty-odd years of intergroup contact: from hypothesis to integrated theory. *British Journal of Social Psychology*, *50*(3), 374–386.

Hiday, V.A., & Burns, P.J. (2009). *Mental illness and the criminal justice system: a handbook for the study of mental health*. New York: Cambridge University Press, pp. 478–498.

Hinsz, V., & Davis, J. (1984). Persuasive arguments theory, group polarization, and choice shifts. *Personality and Social Psychology Bulletin*, *10*(2), 260–268.

Hintzman, D.L. (1986). 'Schema abstraction' in a multiple trace memory model. *Psychological Review*, *93*, 411–428.

Hobsbaum, A., Peters, S., & Sylva, K. (1996). Scaffolding in reading recovery. *Oxford Review of Education*, *22*, 17–35.

Hocken, K., & Thorne, K. (2012). Voyeurism, exhibitionism and other non-contact sexual offences. In B. Winder & P. Banyard (Eds), *A psychologist's casebook of crime: from arson to voyeurism* (pp. 243–263). London: Palgrave Macmillan.

Hoerr, T.R. (2000). *Becoming a multiple intelligence school*. Alexandria, VA: Association for Supervision and Curriculum Development.

Hofstadter, R.D., & Dennett, D.C. (1981). *The mind's I: fantasies and reflections on self and soul*. Brighton: Harvester.

Hogg, M.A. (1996). Group polarisation. In A. Manstead & M. Hewstone (Eds), *The Blackwell encyclopaedia of social psychology*. London: Blackwell.

Hogg, M.A. (2006). Social identity theory. In P.J. Burke (Ed.), *Contemporary social psychological theories* (pp. 111–136). Palo Alto, CA: Stanford University Press.

Hogg, M.A., & Vaughan, G.M. (2008). *Social psychology* (5th edn). Harlow: Prentice Hall.

Hogg, M.A., & Vaughan, G.M. (2013). *Social psychology* (7th edn). Harlow: Prentice Hall

Holcomb, T.F. (2010). Transitioning into retirement as a stressful life event. In T.W. Miller (Ed.), *Handbook of stressful transitions across the lifespan* (pp. 131–146). New York: Springer Science & Business Media.

Hollon, S., Haman, K., & Brown, L. (2002). Cognitive-behavioural treatment of depression. In I.H. Gotlieb & C.L. Hammen (Eds), *Handbook of depression* (pp. 383–403). New York: Guilford Press.

Hollway, W., & Jefferson, T. (2000). *Doing qualitative research differently: free association, narrative and the interview method*. London: SAGE.

Hollway, W., and Jefferson, T. (2005). Panic and perjury: a psychosocial exploration of agency. *British Journal of Social Psychology*, *44*, 147–163.

Holmes, B.M., & Johnson, K.R. (2009). Adult attachment and romantic partner preference: a review. *Journal of Social and Personal Relationships*, *26*(6–7), 833–852.

Holmes, D.A. (2010). *Abnormal, clinical and forensic psychology*. Harlow: Pearson.

Holmes, E.A., Mathews, A., Mackintosh, B., & Dalgleish, T. (2008). The causal effect of mental imagery on emotion assessed using picture-word cues. *Emotion*, *8*(3), 395–409.

Home Office (2003a). *Criminal Justice Act 2003*. London: HMSO.

Home Office (2003b). *Sexual Offences Act 2003*. London: HMSO.

Hong, S., Tandoc, E., Kim, E.A., Kim, B., & Wise, K. (2012). The real you? The role of visual cues and comment congruence in perceptions of social attractiveness from Facebook profiles. *Cyberpsychology, Behavior, and Social Networking*, *15*(7), 339–344.

Hooley, J.M., & Teasdale, J.D. (1989). Predictors of relapse in unipolar depressives: expressed emotion, marital distress, and perceived criticism. *Journal of Abnormal Psychology*, *98*, 229–235.

Hope, L., Gabbert, F., & Fisher, R.P. (2011). From laboratory to the street: capturing witness memory using the self-administered interview. *Legal and Criminological Psychology*, *16*(2), 211–226.

Horton-Salway, M. (2001). Narrative identities and the management of personal accountability in talk about ME: a discursive approach to illness narrative. *Journal of Health Psychology*, 6(2), 261–273.

Hosken, D.J., & Ward, P.I. (2001). Experimental evidence for testis size evolution via sperm competition. *Ecology Letters*, 4(1), 10–13.

Hovland, C., & Sears, R.R. (1940). Minor studies in aggression VI: correlation of lynchings with economic indices. *Journal of Psychology*, 9, 301–310.

Howard, G. (1985). The role of values in the science of psychology. *American Psychologist*, 40, 255–265.

Howe, N., Aquan-Assee, J., Bukowski, W.M., Lehoux, P., & Rinaldi, C.M. (2001). Siblings as confidants: emotional understanding, relationship warmth, and sibling self-disclosure. *Social Development*, 10, 439–454.

Howes, O.D., & Kapur, S. (2009). The dopamine hypothesis of schizophrenia: version III – the final common pathway. *Schizophrenia Bulletin*, 35(3), 549–562.

Howitt, D. (2012). *Introduction to forensic and criminal psychology* (4th edn). Harlow: Pearson Education.

Huchting, K., Lac, A., & LaBrie, J.W. (2008). An application of the theory of planned behavior to sorority alcohol consumption. *Addictive Behaviours*, 33(4), 538–551.

Hughes, C., Jaffee, S., Happ, F., Taylor, A., Caspi, A., & Moffitt, T. (2005). Origins of individual differences in theory of mind: from nature to nurture? *Child Development*, 76, 356–370.

Hughes, M., Pinkerton, G., & Plewis, I. (1979). Children's difficulties on starting infant school. *Journal of Child Psychology and Psychiatry*, 20, 187–196.

Hugh-Jones, S., Gough, B., & Littlewood, A. (2005). Sexual exhibitionism can be good for you: a critique of psycho-medical discourse from the perspectives of women who exhibit. *Sexualities*, 8(3), 259–281.

Hull, D.L., & Van Regenmortel, M.H.V. (2002). Introduction. In M.H.V. Van Regenmortel & D.L. Hull (Eds), *Promises and limits of reductionism in the biomedical sciences* (pp. 1–13). Chichester: Wiley.

Hulme, C., Hatcher, P.J., Nation, K., Brown, A., Adams, J., & Stuart, G. (2002). Phoneme awareness is a better predictor of early reading skill than onset-rhyme awareness. *Journal of Experimental Child Psychology*, 82, 2–28.

Hummert, M.L. (2011). Age stereotypes and aging. In K.W. Schaie & S.L. Willis (Eds), *Handbook of the psychology of aging* (7th edn, pp. 249–262). London: Academic Press.

Hunt, E. (2005). Information processing and intelligence: where we are and where we are going. In R.J. Sternberg & J.E. Pretz (Eds), *Cognition and intelligence* (pp. 1–25). Cambridge: Cambridge University Press.

Hussong, A.M. (2000). Distinguishing mean and structural differences in adolescent friendship quality. *Journal of Social and Personal Relationships*, 17, 223–243.

Hyde, J.S. (2005). The gender-similarities hypothesis. *American Psychologist*, 60, 581–592.

Hyde, T.S., & Jenkins, J.J. (1969). Differential effects of incidental tasks on the organization of recall of a list of highly associated words. *Journal of Experimental Psychology*, 82, 472–481.

Hylton, P.L., & Miller, H.W. (2004) Now that we've found love what are we gonna do with it? A narrative understanding of black identity. *Theory & Psychology*, 14(3), 373–408.

Imperato-McGinley, J., Peterson, R.E., Gautier, T., & Sturla, E. (1979). Androgen and the evolution of male-gender identity among male pseudohermaphrodites with 5a-reductase deficiency. *New England Journal of Medicine*, 300, 1233–1237.

Ingalhalikar, M., Smith, A., Parker, D., Satterthwaite, T.D., Elliott, M.A., Ruparel, K., Hakonarson, H., Gur, R.E., Gur, R.C., & Verma, R. (2014). Sex differences in the structural connectome of the human brain. *Proceedings of the National Academy of Sciences*, 111, 823–828.

Ingham, A.G., Levinger, G., Graves, J., & Peckham, V. (1974). The Ringelmann effect: studies of group size and group performance. *Journal of Experimental Social Psychology*, 10, 371–384.

Inhelder, B., & Piaget, J. (1958). *The growth of logical thinking from childhood to adolescence*. New York: Basic Books.

Inlow, J.K., & Restifo, L.L. (2004). Molecular and comparative genetics of mental retardation. *Genetics*, 166, 835–881.

Isenberg, D.J. (1986). Group polarization: a critical review and meta-analysis. *Journal of Personality and Social Psychology*, 50(6), 1141–1151.

Itier, R.J., & Taylor, M.J. (2004). Source analysis of the N170 to faces and objects. *Neuroreport*, 15(8), 1261–1265.

Izquierdo, A., Suda, R.K., & Murray, E.A. (2005). Comparison of the effects of bilateral orbitofrontal cortex lesions and amygdala lesions on emotional responses in rhesus monkeys. *Journal of Neuroscience*, 25, 8534–8542.

Izzard, C. (2007). Basic emotions, natural kinds, emotion schemas, and a new paradigm. *Perspectives on Psychological Science*, 2(3), 260–280.

Jackson, J., & Harkins, S.G. (1985). Equity in effort: an explanation of the social loafing effect. *Journal of Personality and Social Psychology*, 49, 1199–1206.

Jackson, J.M., & Latané, B. (1981). All alone in front of all those people: stage fright as a function of number and type of co-performers and audience. *Journal of Personality and Social Psychology*, 40, 73–85.

Jackson, J.W. (1993). Realistic group conflict theory: a review and evaluation of the theoretical and empirical literature. *Psychological Record*, 43(3), 395.

James, W. (1884). What is emotion? *Mind*, ix, 189.

James, W. (1890). *Principles of psychology*. Cambridge, MA: Harvard University Press.

James, W. (1894). The physical basis of emotion. *Psychological Review*, 7, 516–529.

James, W. P., Nelson, M., Ralph, A., & Leather, S. (1997). Socioeconomic determinants of health. The contribution of nutrition to inequalities in health. *British Medical Journal*, 314(7093), 1545–1549.

Jamner, L.D., & Tursky, B. (1987). Syndrome-specific descriptor profiling: A psychophysiological and psychophysical approach. *Health Psychology*, 6, 417–430.

Jang, K.L., Vernon, P.A., & Livesley, W.J. (2000). Personality disorder traits, family environment and alcohol misuse: a multivariate behavioural genetic analysis. *Addiction*, *95*(6), 873–888.

Jang, S.M. (2013). Framing responsibility in climate change discourse: Ethnocentric attribution bias, perceived causes, and policy attitudes. *Journal of Environmental Psychology*, *36*, 27–36.

Janis, I.L. (1972). *Victims of groupthink*. Boston, MA: Houghton Mifflin.

Janis, I.L. (1982). *Groupthink: psychological studies of policy decisions and fiascos*. Boston, MA: Houghton Mifflin.

Janis, I.L. (1983). *Groupthink*. Boston, MA: Houghton Mifflin.

Janis, I.L., & Mann, L. (1977). *Decision making: a psychological analysis of conflict, choice, and commitment*. New York: Free Press.

Javal, L.É. (1879). Essai sur la physiologie de la lecture. *Annales d'Oculistique*, *82*, 242–253.

Jenkins, J.G., & Dallenbach, K.M. (1924). Obliviscence during sleep and waking. *American Journal of Psychology*, *35*, 605–612.

Jenkins, J.J., Strange, W., & Edman, T.R. (1983). Identification of vowels in 'vowelless' syllables. *Perception and Psychophysics*, *34*, 441–450.

Jensen, A.R. (1993). Why is reaction time correlated with psychometric g? *Current Directions in Psychological Science*, *2*, 53–56.

Jensen, A.R. (1998). *The g factor: the science of mental ability*. Westport, CT: Praeger.

Jensen, A.R., & Johnson, F.W. (1994). Race and sex differences in head size and IQ. *Intelligence*, *18*, 309–333.

Jensen, M.P., Moore, M.R., Bockow, T.B., Ehde, D.M., & Engel, J.M. (2011) Psychosocial factors and adjustment to chronic pain in persons with physical disabilities: a systematic review. *Archives of Physical Medicine and Rehabilitation*, *92*(1), 146–60.

Jetten, J., Haslam, C., & Haslam, S.A. (Eds). (2012). *The social cure: identity, health and well-being*. Hove: Psychology Press.

John, O.P., Angleitner, A., & Ostendorf, F. (1988). The lexical approach to personality: a historical review of trait taxonomic research. *European Journal of Personality*, *2*, 171–203.

Johnson, C., Ironsmith, M., Snow, C.W., & Poteat, G.M. (2000). Peer acceptance and social adjustment in preschool and kindergarten. *Early Childhood Education Journal*, *27*, 207–212.

Johnson, F., & Johnson, D.W. (1987). *Joining together: group theory and group skills* (3rd edn). London: Prentice Hall.

Johnson, M.H., & Morton, J. (1991). *Biology and cognitive development: the case of face recognition*. Oxford. Blackwell.

Johnson, R., & Downing, L.L. (1979). Deindividuation and valence of cues: effects on prosocial and antisocial behaviour. *Journal of Personality and Social Psychology*, *37*, 1532–1538.

Johnson, W.A. (2000). Toward a sociology of reading in classical antiquity. *The American Journal of Philology*, *121*, 593–627.

Johnson-Laird, P.N. (1983). *Mental models*. Cambridge: Cambridge University Press.

Johnson-Laird, P.N. (1999). Deductive reasoning. *Annual Review of Psychology*, *50*, 109–135.

Johnson-Laird, P.N. (2004). The history of mental models. In K. Manktelow & M.C. Chung (Eds), *Psychology of Reasoning: Theoretical and Historical Perspectives* (pp. 179–212). New York: Psychology Press.

Johnson-Laird, P.N., & Byrne, R.M.J. (1991). *Deduction*. Hove: Erlbaum.

Johnson-Laird, P.N., Gibbs, G., & de Mowbray, J. (1978). Meaning, amount of processing, and memory for words. *Memory & Cognition*, *6*, 372–375.

Johnson-Laird, P.N., & Oatley, K. (2008). The language of emotions: an analysis of a semantic field. *Cognition & Emotion*, *3*, 81–123.

Johnston, R.S., & Watson, J. (2004). Accelerating the development of reading, spelling and phonemic awareness. *Reading and Writing*, *17*, 327–357.

Joinson, A. (2003). *Understanding the psychology of internet behaviour: virtual worlds, real lives*. Basingstoke: Palgrave Macmillan.

Jonas, E., Schimel, J., Greenberg, J., & Pyszczynski, T. (2002). The Scrooge effect: evidence that mortality salience increases prosocial attitudes and behavior. *Personality and Social Psychology Bulletin*, *28*, 1342–1353.

Jones, A.P., Laurens, K.R., Herba, C.M., Barker, G.J., & Viding, E. (2009). Amygdala hypoactivity to fearful faces in boys with conduct problems and callous-unemotional traits. *American Journal of Psychiatry*, *166*, 95–102.

Jones, E.E. (1979). The rocky road from acts to dispositions. *American Psychologist*, *34*, 107–117.

Jones, E.E., & Davis, K.E. (1965). From acts to dispositions: the attribution process in person perception. In L. Berkowitz (Ed.), *Advances in experimental social psychology* (vol. 2, pp. 219–266). New York: Academic Press.

Jones, E.E., & Harris, V.A. (1967). The attribution of attitudes. *Journal of Experimental Social Psychology*, *3*, 1–24.

Jones, E.E., & Nisbett, R.E. (1972). The actor and the observer: divergent perceptions of the causes of behaviour. In E.E. Jones, D.E. Kanouse, H.H. Kelley, R.E. Nisbett, S. Valins, & B. Weiner (Eds), *Attribution: perceiving the causes of behaviour* (pp. 79–94). Morristown, NJ: General Learning Press.

Jones, G. (2003). Testing two cognitive theories of insight. *Journal of Experimental Psychology: Learning, Memory, and Cognition*, *29*, 1017–1027.

Jones, J.M. (1991). Psychological models of race: what have they been and what should they be? In J.D. Goodchilds (Ed.), *Psychological perspectives on human diversity in America* (pp. 3–45). Washington, DC.: American Psychological Association.

Jones, P.E., & Roelofsma, P.H.M.P. (2000). The potential for social contextual and group biases in team decision-making: biases, conditions and psychological mechanisms. *Ergonomics*, *43*(8), 1129–1152.

Jones, R. (1991). *Black psychology* (3rd edn). Berkeley, CA: Cobb & Henry.

Jost, A. (1897). Die Assoziations festigkeit in ihrer Abahängigkeit von der Verteilung der Wiederholungen [The strength of associations in their dependence on the distribution of repitions]. *Zeitschrift fur Psychologie und Psysiologie der Sinnesorgane*, *14*, 436–472.

Judge, T., Piccolo, R., & Ilies, R. (2004). The forgotten ones? The validity of consideration and initiating structure in leadership research. *Journal of Applied Psychology*, *89*(1), 36–51.

Jung, C.G. (1921/1971). *Psychological types: collected works* (vol. 6). Princeton, NJ: Princeton University Press.

Just, M.A., & Carpenter, P.A. (1980). A theory of reading: from eye fixations to comprehension. *Psychological Review*, *87*(4), 329–354.

Juvonen, J., & Graham, S. (2014). Bullying in schools: the power of bullies and the plight of victims. *Annual Review of Psychology*, *65*, 159–185.

Kagan, C., Burton, M., Duckett, P., Lawthom, R., & Siddiquee, A. (2011). *Critical community psychology*. Chichester: Wiley.

Kagan-Krieger, S. (1998). Women with Turner syndrome: a maturational and developmental perspective. *Journal of Adult Development*, *5*, 125–135.

Kahneman, D., & Tversky, A. (1972). Subjective probability: a judgment of representativeness. *Cognitive Psychology*, *3*, 430–454.

Kail, R.V. (2007). *Children and their development* (4th edn). Upper Saddle River, NJ: Pearson.

Kam, C.L.H., & Newport, E.L. (2005). Regularizing unpredictable variation: the roles of adult and child learners in language formation and change. *Language Learning and Development*, *1*(2), 151–195.

Kamin, L.J. (1977). *The science and politics of IQ*. Harmondsworth: Penguin.

Kamoche, K., & Maguire, K. (2011). Pit sense: appropriation of practice-based knowledge in a UK coalmine. *Human Relations*, *64*(5), 725–744.

Kant, I. (1907/1978). *Anthropology from a pragmatic point of view*. Trans. V.L. Dowdell. Carbondale, IL: Southern Illinois University Press. (*Anthropologie in pragmatischer Hindsicht*. Berlin: Reimer.)

Kant, I. (2006). *Kant: anthropology from a pragmatic point of view*. Trans. and Ed. R.B. Louden. Cambridge: Cambridge University Press.

Karau, S.J., & Williams, K.D. (1993). Social loafing: a meta-analytic review and theoretical integration. *Journal of Personality and Social Psychology*, *65*, 681–706.

Kärnä, A., Voeten, M., Little, T.D., Poskiparta, E., Kaljonen, A., & Salmivalli, C. (2011). A large-scale evaluation of the KiVa Antibullying Program: grades 4–6. *Child Development*, *82*(1), 311–333.

Kassin, S.M., Fein, S., & Markus, H.R. (2008). *Social psychology* (7th edn). Boston, MA: Houghton Mifflin.

Kassin, S.M., & Wrightsman, L.S. (1985). Confession evidence. In S.M. Kassin & L.S. Wrightsman (Eds), *The psychology of evidence and trial procedure* (pp. 67–94). Beverley Hills: SAGE.

Kavanagh, D.J., Pierce, J., Lo, S.K., & Shelley, J. (1993). Self-efficacy and social support as predictors of smoking after a quit attempt. *Psychology and Health*, *8*, 231–242.

Kavanagh, M., & Banyard, P. (2014). The effect of an alternative term for schizophrenia in reducing discriminatory attitudes of the English-speaking lay public. *International Journal of Mental Health*, *42*(4), 3–33.

Kaye, K., & Brazelton, T.B. (1971). Mother–infant interaction in the organization of sucking. Paper presented to the Society for Research in Child Development, Minneapolis, March.

Kaye, K., & Fogel, A. (1980). The temporal structure of face-to-face communication between mother and infants. *Developmental Psychology*, *16*, 454–464.

Kaye, K., & Marcus, J. (1981). Infant imitation: the sensorimotor agenda. *Developmental Psychology*, *17*, 258–265.

Keefe, K., & Berndt, T.J. (1996). Relations of friendship quality to self-esteem in early adolescence. *The Journal of Early Adolescence*, *16*(1), 110–129.

Kelley, H., Holmes, J., Kerr, N., Reis, H., Rusbult, C., & Van Lange, P. (2001). *An atlas of interpersonal situations*. Cambridge: Cambridge University Press.

Kelley, H.H. (1967). Attribution theory in social psychology. Paper presented at the Nebraska Symposium on Motivation, Nebraska.

Kelley, H.H. (1973). The processes of causal attribution. *American Psychologist*, *28*(2), 107–128.

Kellogg, R.T. (1994). *The psychology of writing*. New York: Oxford University Press.

Kellogg, T.R. (2003). *Cognitive psychology* (2nd edn). Thousand Oaks, CA: SAGE.

Kelly, G.A. (1955). *The psychology of personal constructs* (vol. l). New York: W.W. Norton.

Kendler, K.S., Thornton, L.M., Gilman, S.E., & Kessler, R.C. (2000). Sexual orientation in a US national sample of twin and non-twin sibling pairs. *The American Journal of Psychiatry*, *157*, 1843–1846.

Keppel, G. (1968). Retroactive and proactive inhibition. In T.R. Dixon & D.L. Horton (Eds), *Verbal behavior and general behavior theory* (pp. 172–213). Englewood Cliffs, NJ: Prentice Hall.

Kerr, N.L., & Bruun, S.E. (1983). Dispensability of member effort and group motivation losses: free-rider effects. *Journal of Personality and Social Psychology*, *44*(1), 78–94.

Kessler, R.C., Ruscio, A.M., Shear, K., & Wittchen, H.U. (2010). Epidemiology of anxiety disorders. In *Behavioral neurobiology of anxiety and its treatment* (pp. 21–35). Berlin/Heidelberg: Springer.

Kilby, L., Horowitz, A.D., & Hylton, P.L. (2013). Diversity as victim to 'realistic liberalism': analysis of an elite discourse of immigration, ethnicity and society. *Critical Discourse Studies*, *10*(1), 47–60.

Kissen, D.M. (1966). The significance of personality in lung cancer in men. *Annals of the New York Academy of Sciences*, *125*, 820–826.

Kitzinger, C., & Wilkinson, S. (1996). *Representing the other: a feminism & psychology reader*. London: SAGE.

Klauer, K.C., Musch, J., & Naumer, B. (2000). On belief bias in syllogistic reasoning. *Psychological Review, 107*, 852–884.

Klein, M. (1948). *Contributions to psycho-analysis 1921–1945*. London: The Hogarth Press.

Kleinman, A. (1997). Triumph or pyrrhic victory? The inclusion of culture in DSM-IV. *Harvard Review of Psychiatry, 4*(6), 343–344.

Klimmt, C., Hartmann, T., & Frey, A. (2007). Effectance and control as determinants of video game enjoyment. *CyberPsychology & Behavior, 10*, 845–847.

Klimstra, T.A., Hale, W.W., III, Raaijmakers, Q.A., Branje, S.J., & Meeus, W.H. (2010). Identity formation in adolescence: change or stability? *Journal of Youth and Adolescence, 39*(2), 150–162.

Kline, P. (1991). *Intelligence: the psychometric view*. London: Routledge.

Kline, P. (1993). *The handbook of psychological testing*. London: Routledge.

Kline, P. (2000). *The handbook of psychological testing* (2nd edn). London: Routledge.

Kline, P., & Barrett, P. (1983). The factors in personality questionnaires among normal subjects. *Advances in Behaviour Research and Therapy, 5*(3), 141–202.

Knight, R.A., & Prentky, R.A. (1990). Classifying sexual offenders. In W.L. Marshall, D.R. Laws, & H.E. Barbaree (Eds), *Handbook of sexual assault* (pp. 23–52). New York: Plenum.

Knoblich, G., Ohlsson, S., Haider, H., & Rhenius, D. (1999). Constraint relaxation and chunk decomposition in insight problem solving. *Journal of Experimental Psychology: Learning, Memory, and Cognition, 25*, 1534–1555.

Knoblich, G., Ohlsson, S., & Raney, G.E. (2001). An eye movement study of insight problem solving. *Memory and Cognition, 29*, 1000–1009.

Knowles, M., & Gardner, W. (2008). Benefits of membership: the activation and amplification of group identities in response to social rejection. *Personality and Social Psychology Bulletin, 34*(9), 1200–1213.

Kobasa, S.C. (1979). Stressful life events, personality, and health: inquiry into hardiness. *Journal of Personality and Social Psychology, 37*(1), 1–11. DOI: 10.1037/0022-3514.37.1.1.

Kodituwakku, P.W. (2007). Defining the behavioral phenotype in children with fetal alcohol spectrum disorders: a review. *Neuroscience and Biobehavioral Reviews, 31*, 192–201.

Koelega, H.S. (1992). Extraversion and vigilance performance: thirty years of inconsistencies. *Psychological Bulletin, 112*, 239–258.

Kogut, T. (2011). Someone to blame: when identifying a victim decreases helping. *Journal of Experimental Social Psychology, 47*(4), 748–755.

Kohlberg, L. (1976). Moral stage and moralization: the cognitive-developmental approach. In T. Lickona (Ed.), *Moral development and behaviour: theory, research and social issues* (pp. 84–107). New York: Holt, Rinehart & Winston.

Kohlberg, L., & Power, C. (1981). Moral development, religious thinking and the question of the seventh stage. *Journal of Religion and Science, 16*, 203.

Köhler, O. (1927). Uber den Gruppenwirkungsgrad der menschlichen Körperarbeit und die Bedingung optimaler Kollektivkraftreaktion [On group efficiency of physical labour and the conditions of optimal collective performance]. *Industrielle Psychotechnik, 4*, 209–226.

Köhler, W. (1925). *The mentality of apes*. New York: Harcourt Brace & World.

Kok, G., de Vries, H., Mudde, A.N., & Strecher, V.J. (1991). Planned health education and the role of self-efficacy: Dutch research. *Health Education Research, 6*(2), 231–238.

Konczak, J., & Timmann, D. (2007). The effect of damage to the cerebellum on sensorimotor and cognitive function in children and adolescents. *Neuroscience and Biobehavioral Reviews, 31*, 1101–1113.

Korte, C. (1971). Effects of individual responsibility and group communication on help-giving in an emergency. *Human Relations, 24*(2), 149–159.

Kozlowski, L.T., & Cutting, J.E. (1977). Recognizing the sex of a walk from a dynamic point-light display. *Perception and Psychophysics, 21*, 575–580.

Kraut, R., Kiesler, S., Boneva, B., Cummings, J., Helgeson, V., & Crawford, A. (2002). Internet paradox revisited. *Journal of Social Issues, 58*(1), 49–74.

Kraut, R., Patterson, M., Lundmark, V., Kiesler, S., Mukopadhyay, T., & Scherlis, W. (1998). Internet paradox: a social technology that reduces social involvement and psychological well-being? *American Psychologist, 53*(9), 1017–1031.

Kravitz, D.A., & Martin, B. (1986). Ringelmann rediscovered: the original article. *Journal of Personality and Social Psychology, 50*, 936–941.

Krishna, D. (1971). The self-fulfilling prophecy and the nature of society. *American Sociological Review, 36*(6), 1104–1107.

Krueger, J. (2011) Shock without awe. *American Psychologist 66*(7), 642–643.

Kruger, J., Chan, S., & Roese, N. (2009). (Not so) positive illusions. *Behavioral and Brain Sciences, 32*(6), 526–527.

Kruglanski, A.W. (1996). Motivated social cognition: principles of the interface. In E.T. Higgins & A.W. Kruglanski (Eds), *Social psychology: handbook of basic principles* (pp. 493–520). New York: Guilford Press.

Krull, D.S. (1993). Does the grist change the mill? The effect of the perceiver's inferential goal on the process of social inference. *Personality and Social Psychology Bulletin, 19*, 340–348.

Krull, D.S., Hui-Min Loy, M., Lin, J., Wang, C., Chen, S., & Zhao, X. (1999). The fundamental fundamental attribution error: Correspondence bias in individualist and collectivist cultures. *Personality and social Psychology Bulletin, 25*(10), 1208–1219.

Kuhl, P.K., & Padden, D.M. (1982). Enhanced determinability at the phonetic boundaries for the voicing feature in macaques. *Perception & Psychophysics, 32*, 542–550.

Kutchins, H., & Kirk, S.A. (2001). *Making US crazy: DSM – the psychiatric bible and the creation of mental disorders*. London: Constable.

Kutnick, P., & Kington, A. (2005). Children's friendship and learning in school: cognitive enhancement through social interaction? *British Journal of Educational Psychology*, *75*, 521–538.

Ladd, G.W., Birch, S.H., & Buhs, E.S. (1999). Children's social and scholastic lives in kindergarten: related spheres of influence? *Child Development*, *70*, 1373–1400.

Lai, M.C., Lombardo, M.V., Chakrabarti, B., & Baron-Cohen, S. (2013). Subgrouping the Autism "Spectrum. *PLoS biology*, *11*(4), e1001544.

Lamb, S.J., Bibby, P.A., Wood, D.J., & Leyden, G. (1998). An intervention programme for children with moderate learning difficulties. *British Journal of Educational Psychology*, *68*(4), 493–504.

Lamme, V.A.F. (2003). Why visual attention and awareness are different. *Trends in Cognitive Sciences*, *7*, 12–18.

Lane, K.L., Menzies, H.M., Bruhn, A.L., & Crnobori, M. (2011). *Managing challenging behaviours in schools: research-based strategies that work.* New York: Guilford Press.

Lang, P.J. (1994). The varieties of emotional experience: a meditation on James–Lange theory. *Psychological Review*, *101*, 211–221.

Langdon, R., Ward, P.B., & Coltheart, M. (2010). Reasoning anomalies associated with delusions in schizophrenia. *Schizophrenia Bulletin*, *36*(2), 321–330.

Lange, C., & James, W. (1922). *The emotions.* Trans. I.A. Haupt. Baltimore, MD: Williams & Wilkins.

Langens, T.A., & Schuler, J. (2005). Written emotional expression and emotional well-being: the moderating role of fear of rejection. *Personality and Social Psychology Bulletin*, *31*(6), 818–830.

Langton, C.M., & Marshall, W.L. (2001). Cognition in rapists: theoretical patterns by typological breakdown. *Aggression and Violent Behavior*, *6*(5), 499–518.

Lansdale, M.W. (2005). When nothing is 'off the record': exploring the theoretical implications of the continuous recording of cognitive process in memory. *Memory*, *13*, 31–50.

Lansdale, M.W., & Baguley, T. (2008). Dilution as a model of long-term forgetting. *Psychological Review*, *115*(4), 864–892.

LaPierre, R.T. (1934). Attitudes vs. actions. *Social Forces*, *13*, 230–237.

Larkin, J. (1983). The role of problem representation in physics. In D. Gentner & A.L. Gentner (Eds), *Mental models* (pp. 75–98). Hillsdale, NJ: Erlbaum.

Larsen, R.J., & Buss, D.M. (2008). *Personality psychology: domains of knowledge about human nature.* New York: McGraw-Hill.

Larson, R., & Richards, M.H. (1994a). *Divergent realities: the emotional lives of mothers, fathers, and adolescents.* New York: Basic Books.

Larson, R., & Richards, M.H. (1994b). Family emotions: do young adolescents and their parents experience the same states? *Journal of Research on Adolescence*, *4*(4), 567–583.

Lasco, M.S., Jordan, T.J., Edgar, M.A., Petito, C.K., & Byne, W. (2002). A lack of dimorphism of sex or sexual orientation in the human anterior commissure. *Brain Research*, *936*, 95–98.

Lashley, K., & Watson, J.B. (1921) A psychological study of motion pictures in relation to venereal disease. *Social Hygiene*, *7*, 181–219.

Latané, B., & Darley, J. (1969). Bystander apathy. *American Scientist*, *57*(2), 244–268.

Latané, B., Williams, K.D., & Harkins, S.G. (1979). Many hands make light the work: the causes and consequences of social loafing. *Journal of Personality and Social Psychology*, *37*, 822–832.

Latané, B., & Wolf, S. (1981). The social impact of majorities and minorities. *Psychological Review*, *88*(5), 438–453.

Laursen, B. (1993). Conflict management among close peers. In B. Laursen (Ed.), *Close friendships in adolescence: new directions for child development* (pp. 39–54). San Francisco, CA: Jossey-Bass.

Laursen, B., Coy, K.C., & Collins, W.A. (1998). Reconsidering changes in parent–child conflict across adolescence: a meta-analysis. *Child Development*, *69*, 817–832.

Lavie, N. (1995). Perceptual load as a necessary condition for selective attention. *Journal of Experimental Psychology: Human Perception and Performance*, *21*, 451–468.

Lavie, N., & Driver, J. (1996). On the spatial extent of attention in object-based visual selection. *Perception & Psychophysics*, *58*, 1238–1251.

Lazarus, R.S. (1993). From psychological stress to the emotions: A history of changing outlooks. *Annual Review of Psychology*, *44*, 1–21.

Lazarus, R.S., & Folkman, S., (1984). *Stress, Appraisal and Coping.* New York: Springer.

Lea, M., & Spears, R. (1991). Computer-mediated communication, de-individuation and group decision-making. *International Journal of Man Machine Studies*, *34*, 283–301.

Leahey, T.H. (2004). *A history of psychology: main currents in psychological thought* (6th edn). Englewood Cliffs, NJ: Prenticem Hall.

Leana, C.R. (1985). A partial test of Janis's groupthink model: effects of group cohesiveness and leader behaviour on defective decision making. *Journal of Management*, *11*, 5–17.

Le Bon, G. (1895). *The crowd: a study of the popular mind.* London: Ernest Benn.

Lecanuet, J.-P. (1998). Foetal responses to auditory and speech stimuli. In A. Slater (Ed.), *Perceptual development: visual, auditory and speech perception in infancy.* Hove: Psychology Press.

Lederman, R., & Weis, K. (2009). Psychosocial adaptation in pregnancy: assessment of seven dimensions of maternal development. In *Psychosocial adaptation to pregnancy* (pp. 1–38). New York: Springer.

Lee, D.N. (1976). A theory of visual control of braking based on information about time-to-collision. *Perception*, *5*, 437–459.

Lee, D.N., Lishman, J.R., & Thomson, J.A. (1982). Regulation of gait in long jumping. *Journal of Experimental Psychology: Human Perception and Performance*, *8*, 448–459.

Lee, J.D. (2008). Fifty years of driving safety research. *Human Factors*, *50*, 521–528.

Leichsenring, F. (2009). Psychodynamic psychotherapy: a review of efficacy and effectiveness studies. In R.A. Levy & S. Ablon (Eds), *Handbook of evidence-based psychodynamic psychotherapy: bridging the gap between science and practice* (pp. 3–27). New York: Humana.

Leifer, A.D., Leiderman, P.H., Barnett, C.R., & Williams, J.A. (1972). Effects of mother–infant separation on maternal attachment behavior. *Child Development*, *43*(4), 1203–1218.

Leis, J.A., Heron, J., Stuart, E.A., & Mendelson, T. (2014). Associations between maternal mental health and child emotional and behavioral problems. *Journal of Abnormal Child Psychology*, *42*(1), 161–171. DOI: 10.1007/s10802-013-9766-4.

Lemay, E.P., & Clark, M.S. (2008). 'Walking on eggshells': how expressing relationship insecurities perpetuates them. *Journal of Personality and Social Psychology*, *95*(2), 420–441.

Lenneberg, E.H. (1967). *Biological foundations of language*. New York: Wiley.

LePine, J.A., & Van Dyne, L. (2001). Voice and cooperative behaviour as contrasting forms of contextual performance: evidence of differential relationships with Big Five personality characteristics and cognitive ability. *Journal of Applied Psychology*, *86*, 326–336.

Lerner, M. (1965). Evaluation of performance as a function of performer's reward and attractiveness. *Journal of Personality and Social Psychology*, *1*, 355–360.

Lerner, M.J., & Miller, D.T. (1978). Just world research and the attribution process: looking back and ahead. *Psychological Bulletin*, *85*, 1030–1051.

Leuner, B., Glasper, E.R., & Gould, E. (2010). Parenting and plasticity. *Trends in Neurosciences*, *3*(10), 465–473.

Leuner, B., Gould, E., & Shors, T.J. (2006). Is there a link between adult neurogenesis and learning? *Hippocampus*, *16*(3), 216–224.

LeVay, S. (1991). A difference in hypothalamic structure between heterosexual and homosexual men. *Science*, *253*, 1034–1037.

Levine, J.M. (1989). Reaction to opinion deviance in small groups. In P. Paulus (Ed.), *Psychology of group influence* (2nd edn). Hillsdale, NJ: Laurence Erlbaum Associates.

Levine, M., Prosser, A., Evans, D., & Reicher, A. (2005). Identity and emergency intervention: how social group membership and inclusiveness of group boundaries shape helping behavior. *Personality and Social Psychology Bulletin*, *31*(4), 443–453.

Levine, M., & Thompson, K. (2004). Identity, place, and bystander intervention: social categories and helping after natural disasters. *Journal of Social Psychology*, *144*(3), 229–245.

Levinson, D.J. (1978). *The seasons of a man's life*. New York: Random House.

Levitt, S., & List, J. (2011). Was there really a Hawthorne Effect at the Hawthorne Plant? An analysis of the original illumination experiments. *American Economic Journal: Applied Economics*, *3*, 224–238.

Lewis, D. (1966). An argument for the identity theory. *Journal of Philosophy*, *63*, 17–25.

Lewis, M. (2005). The child and its family: the social network model. *Human Development*, *48*, 8–27.

Lewis, M., & Brooks-Gunn, J. (1979). *Social cognition and the acquisition of self*. New York: Plenum.

Lichtenstein, S., Slovic, P., Fischhoff, B., Layman, M., & Combs, B. (1978). Judged frequency of lethal events. *Journal of Experimental Psychology: Human Learning and Memory*, *4*, 551–578.

Lieberman, M.A. (2008). Gender and online cancer support groups: issues facing male cancer patients. *Journal of Cancer Education*, *23*(2), 167–171.

Lievesley, R., Elliott, H., Winder, B., & Norman, C. (2014, in press). Understanding service user and therapists' experiences of incarcerated sex offenders receiving pharmacological treatment for sexual preoccupation and/or hypersexuality. *Journal of Forensic Psychiatry and Psychology*.

Lievesley, R., Winder, B., Elliott, H., Kaul, A., Thorne, J., & Hocken, K. (2013). The use of medication to treat sexual preoccupation and hypersexuality in sexual offenders. *Prison Service Journal*, 208.

Likert, R. (1932). A technique for the measurement of attitudes. *Archives of Psychology*, *140*, 1–55.

Lillard, A.S. (2012). Preschool children's development in classic Montessori, supplemented Montessori, and conventional programs. *Journal of School Psychology*, *50*(3), 379–401.

Lindeman, M., Keskivaara, P., & Roschier, M. (2000). Assessment of magical beliefs about food and health. *Journal of Health Psychology*, *5*(2), 195–209.

Linehan, M.M., Tutek, D.A., Heard, H.L., & Armstrong, H.E. (1994). Interpersonal outcome of cognitive behavioral treatment for chronically suicidal borderline patients. *American Journal of Psychiatry*, *151*(12), 1771–1775.

Lippmann, W. (1922). *Public opinion*. London: Allen & Unwin.

Lipton, A.A., & Simon, F.S. (1985). Psychiatric diagnosis in a state hospital: Manhattan State revisited. *Psychiatric Services*, *36*(4), 368–373.

Liu, Y., Perfetti, C.A., & Hart, L. (2003). ERP evidence for the time course of graphic, phonological, and semantic information in Chinese meaning and pronunciation decisions. *Journal of Experimental Psychology: Learning, Memory, and Cognition*, *29*(6), 1231–1247.

Lively, K.J., & Smith, C.L. (2011). Identity and Illness. In B.A. Pescosolido, J. Martin, J. McLeod, & A. Rogers. *Handbook of the Sociology of Health, Illness, and Healing* (pp. 505–525). New York: Springer Publishers.

Loftus, E.F. (1996). *Eyewitness testimony*. Cambridge, MA: Harvard University Press.

Loftus, E.F., Loftus, G.R., & Messo, J. (1987). Some facts about 'weapon focus'. *Law and Human Behavior*, *11*(1), 55.

Loftus, E.F., Miller, D.G., & Burns, H.J. (1978). Semantic integration of verbal information into a visual memory. *Journal of Experimental Psychology: Human Learning and Memory*, *4*, 19–31.

Loftus, E.F., & Pickrell, J. (1995). The formation of false memories. *Psychiatric Annals*, *25*, 720–725.

Lohmann, H., Carpenter, M., & Call, J. (2005). Guessing versus choosing – and seeing versus believing – in false belief tasks. *British Journal of Developmental Psychology*, *23*, 451–469.

Looren de Jong, H. (2001). Introduction: a symposium on explanatory pluralism. *Theory and Psychology*, *11*(6), 731–735.

Lorenz, K. (1981). *The foundation of ethology*. New York: Springer.

Luborsky, L., Singer, J., & Luborsky, L. (1975). Comparative studies of psychotherapy. *Archives of General Psychiatry*, *32*, 995–1008.

Ludman, L., Lansdown, R., & Spitz, L. (1992). Effects of early hospitalization and surgery on the emotional development of 3 year olds: an exploratory study. *European Child and Adolescent Psychiatry*, *1*(3), 186–195.

Lumby, C., & Albury, K. (2010). Too much too young? The sexualisation of children debate in Australia. *Media International Australia*, *135*, 141–152.

Luna, K., & Migueles, M. (2009). Acceptance and confidence of central and peripheral misinformation. *The Spanish Journal of Psychology*, *12*(2), 405–413.

Luoh, M., & Herzog, A.R. (2008). Individual consequences of volunteer and paid work in old age: health and mortality. *Journal of Health and Social Behavior*, *43*(4), 490–509.

Lynn, R., & Vanhanen, T. (2002). *IQ and the wealth of nations*. Westport, CT: Praeger.

Lyons, A., & Kashima, Y. (2001). The reproduction of culture: communication processes tend to maintain cultural stereotypes. *Social Cognition*, *19*(3), 372–394.

Lyons, A., & Kashima, Y. (2003). How are stereotypes maintained through communication? The influence of stereotype sharedness. *Journal of Personality and Social Psychology*, *85*(6), 989–1005.

Lyoo, I.K., Han, M.H., & Cho, D.Y. (1998). A brain MRI study in subjects with borderline personality disorder. *Journal of Affect Disorders*, *50*, 235–243.

Maass, A., & Clark, R.D. (1983). Internalization versus compliance: differential processes underlying minority influence and conformity. *European Journal of Social Psychology*, *13*, 197–215.

Maass, A., & Clark, R.D. (1984). Hidden impact of minorities: fifteen years of minority influence research. *Psychological Bulletin*, *95*, 233–243.

Maccoby, E.E. (1988). Gender as a social category. *Developmental Psychology*, *24*, 755–765.

Maccoby, E.E. (1990). Gender and relationships: a developmental account. *American Psychologist*, *45*, 513–520.

Maccoby, E.E., & Jacklin, C.N. (1974). *The psychology of sex differences*. Stanford, CA: Stanford University Press.

MacCoun, R.J., & Kerr, N.L. (1988). Asymmetric influence in mock jury deliberation: jurors' bias for leniency. *Journal of Personality and Social Psychology*, *54*, 21–33.

MacGregor, J.N., Ormerod, T.C., & Chronicle, E.P. (2001). Information processing and insight: a process model of performance on the nine-dot and related problems. *Journal of Experimental Psychology: Learning, Memory, and Cognition*, *27*, 176–201.

Mackworth, N.H. (1950) Researches on the measurement of human performance. *Medical Research Council Special Report 268*. London: HMSO.

Maddi, S.R. (1989). *Personality theories: a comparative analysis*. Chicago, IL: Dorsey.

Maddi, S.R. (2004). Hardiness: an operationalization of existential courage. *Journal of Humanistic Psychology*, *44*(3), 279–298. DOI: 10.1177/0022167804266101.

Magana, A.B., Goldstein, M.J., Karno, M., Miklowitz, D.J., Jenkins, J., & Falloon, I.R. (1986). A brief method for assessing expressed emotion in relatives of psychiatric patients. *Psychiatry Research*, *17*, 203–212.

Maguire, E.A., Gadian, D.G., Johnsrude, I.S., Good, C.D., Ashburner, J., Frackowiak, R.S.J., & Frith, C. (2000). Navigation-related structural change in the hippocampi of taxi drivers. *Proceedings of the National Academy of Science*, *97*, 4398–4403.

Maguire, M., & Raynor, P. (2006). How the resettlement of prisoners promotes desistance from crime, or does it? *Criminology and Criminal Justice*, *6*(1), 19–38.

Maher, W.B., & Maher, B.A. (1985). Psychopathology II: from eighteenth century to modern times. In G.A. Kimble & K. Schlesinger (Eds), *Topics in the history of psychology* (vol. 2). Hillsdale, NJ: Erlbaum.

Maier, N.R.F. (1931). Reasoning in humans. II: the solution of a problem and its appearance in consciousness. *Journal of Comparative Psychology*, *12*, 181–194.

Main, M., & Solomon, J. (1990). Procedures for identifying infants as disorganised/disoriented during the Ainsworth Strange Situation. In M. Greenberg, D. Cicchetti, & E. Cummings (Eds), *Attachment in the preschool years* (pp. 121–160). Chicago, IL: University of Chicago Press.

Maj, M., Veltro, F., Pirozzi, R., Lobrace, S., & Magliano, L. (1992). Pattern of recurrence of illness after recovery from an episode of major depression: a prospective study. *American Journal of Psychiatry*, *149*, 795–800.

Malcolm, N (1958). *Ludwig Wittgenstein: A Memoir*. Oxford: Oxford University Press.

Malle, B.F. (2006). The actor-observer asymmetry in attribution: a (surprising) meta-analysis. *Psychological Bulletin*, *132*(6), 895–919.

Malle, B.F. (2011). Time to give up the dogmas of attribution: an alternative theory of behavior explanation. *Advances in Experimental Social Psychology*, *44*(1), 297–311.

Malpass, R.S., & Devine, P.G. (1981). Guided memory in eyewitness identification. *Journal of Applied Psychology*, *66*(3), 343.

Maltby, J., Day, L., & Macaskill, A. (2013). *Personality, individual differences and intelligence* (3rd edn). Harlow: Pearson.

Manago, A.M., Graham, M.B., Greenfield, P.M., & Salimkhan, G. (2008). Self-presentation and gender on MySpace. *Journal of Applied Developmental Psychology*, *29*(6), 446–458.

Mancillas, A. (2006). Challenging the stereotypes about only children: a review of the literature and implications for practice. *Journal of Counseling & Development*, *84*, 258–275.

Mandler, G. (1967). Organization and memory. In K.W. Spence & J.T. Spence (Eds), *The psychology of learning and motivation* (vol. 1, pp. 327–372). New York: Academic Press.

Maner, J.K., & Gailliot, M.T. (2007). Altruism and egoism: prosocial motivations for helping depend on relationship context. *European Journal of Social Psychology*, *37*(2), 347–358.

Mani, A., Mullainathan, S., Shafir, E., & Zhao, J. (2013). Poverty impedes cognitive function. *Science*, *341*, 976–980.

Mann, R.E., Hanson, R.K., & Thornton, D. (2010). Assessing risk for sexual recidivism: some proposals on the nature of psychologically meaningful risk factors. *Sexual Abuse: A Journal of Research and Treatment*, *22*(2), 191–217.

Manning, R., Levine, M., & Collins, A. (2007). The Kitty Genovese murder and the social psychology of helping: the parable of the 38 witnesses. *American Psychologist*, *62*(6), 555–562.

Manstead, A., & Hewstone, M. (1996). *The Blackwell encyclopaedia of social psychology*. London: Blackwell.

Marcia, J.E. (1966). Development and validation of ego-identity status. *Journal of Personality and Social Psychology*, *3*(5), 551.

Marcia, J.E. (1980). Identity in adolescence. *Handbook of Adolescent Psychology*, *9*, 159–187.

Markus, H. (1977). Self-schemata and processing information about the self. *Journal of Personality and Social Psychology*, *35*, 63–78.

Markus, H., & Kunda, Z. (1986). Stability and malleability of the self-concept. *Journal of personality and social psychology*, *51*(4), 858.

Markus, H., & Nurius, P. (1986). Possible selves. *American Psychologist*, *41*, 954–969.

Markus, H., & Wurf, E. (1987). The dynamic self concept: a social psychological perspective. *Annual Review of Psychology*, *38*, 299–333.

Marom, S., Munitz, H., Jones, P.B., Weizman, A., & Hermesh, H. (2005). Expressed emotion: relevance to rehospitalization in schizophrenia over seven years. *Schizophrenia Bulletin*, *31*, 751–758.

Marschark, M., & Surian, L. (1989). Why does imagery improve memory? *European Journal of Cognitive Psychology*, *1*, 251–263.

Marsh, A.A., & Blair, R.J.R. (2008). Deficits in facial affect recognition among antisocial populations: a meta-analysis. *Neuroscience of Biobehavior Reviews*, *32*, 454–465.

Marslen-Wilson, W. (1987). Functional parallelism in spoken word recognition. *Cognition*, *25*, 71–102.

Marslen-Wilson, W.D., & Welsh, A. (1978). Processing interactions during word-recognition in continuous speech. *Cognitive Psychology*, *10*, 29–63.

Marteau, T.M., French, D.P., Griffin, S.J., Prevost, A.T., Sutton, S., Watkinson, C., Attwood, S., & Hollands, G.J. (2010) Effects of communicating DNA-based disease risk estimates on risk-reducing behaviours. *Cochrane Database of Systematic Reviews*, *6*(10), CD007275.

Marteau, T.M., Hollands, G.J., & Fletcher, P.C. (2012). Changing human behavior to prevent disease: the importance of targeting automatic processes. *Science*, *337*(6101), 1492–1495.

Martin, B., Sherrard, M., & Wentzel, D. (2005). The role of sensation seeking and need for cognition on website evaluations: a resource matching perspective. *Psychology and Marketing*, *22*(2), 109–126.

Martin, D., Garske, J., & Davis, M. (2000). Relation of the therapeutic alliance with outcome and other variables: a meta-analytic review. *Journal of Consulting and Clinical Psychology*, *68*(3), 438–450.

Martin, J.T., & Nguyen, D.H. (2004). Anthropometric analysis of homosexuals and heterosexuals: implications for early hormone exposure. *Hormones and Behavior*, *45*, 31–39.

Martorano, S.C. (1977). A developmental analysis of performance on Piaget's formal operations tasks. *Developmental Psychology*, *13*, 666–672.

Maslow, A.H., Frager, R., & Cox, R. (1970). *Motivation and personality* (vol. 2). Ed. J. Fadiman & C. McReynolds. New York: Harper & Row.

Massaro, D.W. (1987). Categorical partition: a fuzzy logical model of categorization behavior. In S. Harnad (Ed.), *Categorical perception: the groundwork of cognition* (pp. 254–283). Cambridge, MA: Harvard University Press.

Matlin, M.W., & Foley, H.J. (1992). *Sensation and perception* (3rd edn). Boston, MA: Allyn & Bacon.

Matthews, G., Deary, I.J., & Whiteman, M.C. (2003). *Personality traits*. Cambridge: Cambridge University Press.

Matthews, G., Jones, D.M., & Chamberlain, A.G. (1989). Interactive effects of extraversion and arousal on attentional task performance: multiple resources or encoding processes? *Journal of Personality and Social Psychology*, *56*, 629–639.

Maynard-Smith, J. (1964). Group selection and kin selection. *Nature*, *201*, 1145–1147.

Mazer, J., Murphy, R., & Simonds, C. (2007). 'I'll see you on Facebook': the effects of computer-mediated teacher self-disclosure on student motivation, affective learning, and classroom climate. *Communication Education*, *56*(1), 1–17.

Mbiti, J. (1970). *African Religions & Philosophy*. New York: Anchor Books. Doubleday.

McAdams, D.P., & Pals, J.L. (2006). A new Big Five: fundamental principles for an integrative science of personality. *American Psychologist*, *61*(3), 204–217.

McCauley, C. (1989). The nature of social influence in groupthink: compliance and internalization. *Journal of Personality and Social Psychology*, *57*, 250–260.

McClelland, J.L., & Rumelhart, D.E. (1986). Parallel distributed processing. In *Explorations in the microstructure of cognition. Vol. 2: Psychological and biological models*. Cambridge, MA: MIT Press.

McCormick, C.M., & Witelson, S.F. (1991). A cognitive profile of homosexual men compared to heterosexual men and women. *Psychoneuroendocrinology*, *15*, 459–473.

McCrae, R.R., & Costa, P.T. (1997). Personality trait structure as a human universal. *American Psychologist*, *52*(5), 509–516.

McCrae, R.R., & Costa, P.T. (1983). Joint factors in self-reports and ratings: neuroticism, extraversion and openness to experience. *Personality and Individual Differences*, *4*, 245–255.

McEwen, B.S. (2007) Physiology and neurobiology of stress and adaptation: Central role of the brain. *Physiological Reviews*, *87*, 873–904.

McGeoch, J.A. (1932). Forgetting and the law of disuse. *Psychological Review*, *39*, 352–370.

McGeoch, J.A. (1942). *The psychology of human learning: an introduction*. New York: Longmans.

McGowan, L.P.A., Clarke-Carter, D.D., & Pitts, M.K. (1998). Chronic pelvic pain: a meta-analytic review. *Psychology and Health*, *13*, 937–951.

McGuire, F. (1994). Army alpha and beta tests of intelligence. In R.J. Sternberg (Ed.), *Encyclopedia of intelligence* (vol. 1, pp. 125–129). New York: Macmillan.

McGurk, H., & MacDonald, J. (1976). Hearing lips and seeing voices. *Nature*, *264*, 746–748.

McKay, R.T., & Dennett, D.C. (2009). The evolution of misbelief. *Behavioral and Brain Sciences*, *32*(6), 493–561.

McKee, S.A., McKee, K.M., Carroll, R., Sinha, J.E., Robinson, C., Nich, D., Cavallo, S., & O'Malley, S. (2007). Enhancing brief cognitive-behavioral therapy with motivational enhancement techniques in cocaine users. *Drug and Alcohol Dependence*, *91*, 91–101.

McNemar, Q. (1946). Opinion-attitude methodology. *Psychological Bulletin*, *43*(4), 289–374.

McRae, C.N., Hewstone, M., & Griffiths, R.J. (1993). Processing load and memory for stereotype-based information. *European Journal of Social Psychology*, *23*(1), 77–87.

McSmith, A. (2010). First Obama, now Cameron embraces 'nudge theory'. *The Independent*, 12 August. Available at: www.independent.co.uk/news/uk/politics/first-obama-now-cameron-embraces-nudge-theory-2050127.html (accessed 9 December 2013).

Meadows, M. (2008). *I, avatar*. Berkeley, CA: New Riders.

Mearns, D., & Thorne, B. (1998). *Person-centred counselling in action*. London: SAGE.

Mehrabian, A., & Ksionzky, S. (1970). Models for affiliative and conformity behaviour. *Psychological Bulletin*, *74*, 110–126.

Meltzoff, A.N., & Moore, M.K. (1977). Imitation of facial and manual gestures by human neonates. *Science*, *198*, 74–78.

Meltzoff, A.N., & Moore, M.K. (1983). Newborn infants imitate adult facial gestures. *Child Development*, *54*, 702–709.

Melzack, R. (1992). Phantom limbs. *Scientific American*, April, 90–96.

Melzack, R., & Wall, P. (1988). *The Challenge of Pain*. London: Penguin.

Melzack, R., Wall, P.D., & Ty, T.C. (1982). Acute pain in an emergency clinic: latency of onset and descriptor patterns. *Pain*, *14*, 33–43.

Memon, A., Hope, L., & Bull, R.H.C. (2003). Exposure duration: effects on eyewitness accuracy and confidence. *British Journal of Psychology*, *94*, 339–354.

Mental Health Act (2007). London: The Stationery Office.

Menzies, I.E.P. (1960). A case-study in the functioning of social systems as a defence against anxiety: a report on a study of the nursing service in a general hospital. *Human Relations*, *13*, 95–121.

Merskey, H., & Bogduk, N. (1994). *Classification of chronic pain* (210). Seattle, USA: International Association for the Study of Pain Press.

Merton, K. (1957). *Social theory and social structure* (rev. edn). New York: Free Press.

Mesoudi, A. (2011). *Cultural evolution: how Darwinian theory can explain human culture and synthesize the social sciences*. Chicago: University of Chicago Press.

Meyer-Bahlburg, H.F.L., Dolezal, C., Baker, S.W., & New, M.I. (2008). Sexual orientation in women with classical or non-classical congenital adrenal hyperplasia as a function of degree of prenatal androgen excess. *Archives of Sexual Behavior*, *37*, 85–99.

Meyer-Lindenberg, A., & Weinberger, D.R. (2006). Intermediate phenotypes and genetic mechanisms of psychiatric disorders. *Nature Reviews Neuroscience*, *7*, 818–827.

Michel, C., Rossion, B., Han, J., Chung, C., & Caldara, R. (2006). Holistic processing is finely tuned for faces of one's own race. *Psychological Science*, *17*(7), 608–615.

Miklowitz, D.J., Goldstein, M.J., Doane, J.A., Nuechterlein, K.H., et al. (1989). Is expressed emotion an index of a transactional process? I. Parents' affective style. *Family Process*, *28*, 153–167.

Miles, T.R. (1957). Contributions to intelligence testing and the theory of intelligence. I: On defining intelligence. *British Journal of Educational Psychology*, *27*, 153–165.

Milgram, S. (1974). *Obedience to authority: an experimental view*. London: Tavistock.

Miller, D.B., & O'Callaghan, J.P. (2005). Aging, stress and the hippocampus. *Ageing Research Review*, *23*, 123–140.

Miller, D.T., & Ross, M. (1975). Self-serving biases in the attribution of causality: fact or fiction? *Psychological Bulletin*, *82*(2), 213–225.

Miller, G.A. (1956). The magical number seven, plus or minus two: some limits on our capacity for processing information. *Psychological Review*, *63*(2), 81–97.

Miller, G.A. (1969). Psychology as a means of promoting human welfare. *American Psychologist*, *24*(12), 1063–1075.

Miller, H., & Arnold, J. (2000). Gender and web home pages. *Computers and Education*, *34*, 335–339.

Miller, H., & Arnold, J. (2001). Breaking away from grounded identity? Women academics on the web. *Cyberpsychology and Behaviour*, *4*(1), 95–108.

Miller, H., & Arnold, J. (2003). Self in web home pages: gender, identity and power in cyberspace. In G. Riva & C. Galimberti (Eds), *Towards cyberpsychology: mind, cognition and society in the internet age* (pp. 74–93). Amsterdam: IOS.

Miller, H., & Arnold, J. (2009). Identity in cyberspace. In S. Wheeler (Ed.), *Connected minds, emerging cultures: cybercultures in online learning* (pp. 53–64). Charlotte, NC: Information Age.

Miller, J.G. (1984). Culture and the development of everyday social explanation. *Journal of Personality and Social Psychology*, *46*(5), 961–978.

Miller, W., & Rollnick, S. (2013). *Motivational interviewing: helping people change* (3rd edn). New York: Guilford Press.

Miller, W.R. (1983). Motivational interviewing with problem drinkers. *Behavioural Psychotherapy*, *11*(2), 147–172.

Millon, T., Millon, C., Davis, R., & Grossman, S. (2006). *MCMI-III Manual* (3rd edn). Minneapolis, MN: Pearson Education.

Milner, A.D., & Goodale, M.A. (1995). *The visual brain in action*. Oxford: Oxford University Press.

Milner, P. (1970). *Physiological psychology*. New York: Holt, Rinehart & Winston.

Ministry of Justice. (2013a). Multi-agency public protection arrangements annual report 2012/13. Retrieved from: www.gov.uk/government/publications/multi-agency-public-protection-arrangements-mappa-annual-report-2012-13 (accessed 29th August 2014).

Ministry of Justice. (2013b). An overview of sexual offending in England and Wales. Retrieved from: www.justice.gov.uk/statistics/criminal-justice/sexual-offending-statistics (accessed 29th August 2014).

Mischel, W. (1968). *Personality and assessment*. New York: Wiley.

Mitchell, A.J., & Coyne, J.C. (2009). *Screening for depression in clinical practice: an evidence-based guide*. Oxford: Oxford University Press.

Moffitt, T.E. (1993). Adolescence-limited and life-course persistent antisocial behavior: a developmental taxonomy. *Psychological Review, 100*, 674–701.

Moghaddam, F.M., & Harré, R. (1992). Rethinking the laboratory experiment. *American Behavioural Scientist, 36*(1), 22–38.

Mohler, E., Parzer, P., Brunner, R., Wiebel, A., & Resch, F. (2006). Emotional stress in pregnancy predicts human infant reactivity. *Early Human Development, 82*, 731–737.

Molden, D.C., & Higgins, E.T. (2012). Motivated thinking. In K.J. Holyoak & R.G. Morrison (Eds), *The Oxford Handbook of Thinking and Reasoning*, (pp. 390–409).

Money, J. (1975). Ablatio penis: normal male infant sex-assigned as a girl. *Archives of Sexual Behavior, 4*, 65–71.

Montessori, M. (1967). *The Absorbent Mind*. New York: Henry Holt and Company.

Moon, C., Pannenton-Cooper, R.P., & Fifer, W.P. (1993). Two-day-olds prefer their native language. *Infant Behaviour and Development, 16*, 495–500.

Moore, B.C.J. (2003). *An introduction to the psychology of hearing* (5th edn). San Diego, CA: Elsevier.

Moore, B.C.J., & Glasberg, B.R. (1986). The role of frequency selectivity in the perception of loudness, pitch and time. In B.C.J. Moore (Ed.), *Frequency selectivity in hearing*. London: Academic Press.

Moorhead, G. (1982). Groupthink: hypothesis in need of testing. *Group and Organizational Studies, 7*, 429–444.

Moorhead, G., Ference, R., & Neck, C.P. (1991). Group decision fiascoes continue: space shuttle Challenger and a revised groupthink framework. *Human Relations, 44*, 539–550.

Moorhead, G., & Montanari, J. (1986). An empirical investigation of the groupthink phenomenon. *Human Relations, 39*, 399–410.

Moray, N. (1959). Attention in dichotic listening: affective cues and the influence of instructions. *Quarterly Journal of Experimental Psychology, 11*, 56–60.

Moreland, R.L., & Levine, J.M. (1982). Socialization in small groups: temporal changes in individual–group relations. *Advances in Experimental Social Psychology, 15*, 137–192.

Morgan, M.J., & Casco, C. (1990). Spatial filtering and spatial primitives in early vision: an explanation of the Zöllner–Judd class of geometrical illusion. *Proceedings of the Royal Society of London Series B, 242*, 1–10.

Morin, C., Lund, J.P., Clokie, C.M., & Feine, J.S. (2000). Differences between the sexes in post-surgical pain. *Pain*, 85.

Morin, J.W., & Levenson, J.S. (2008). Exhibitionism assessment and treatment. In D.R. Laws & W.T. O'Donohue (Eds), *Sexual deviance: theory, assessment, and treatment* (2nd edn, pp. 76–107). New York: Guilford Press.

Morra, S., Gobba, C., Marini, Z., & Sheese, R. (2007). *Cognitive development: a neo-Piagetian perspective*. Mahwah, NJ: Erlbaum.

Morris, C.D., Bransford, J.D., & Franks, J.J. (1977). Levels of processing versus transfer appropriate processing. *Journal of Verbal Learning and Verbal Behaviour, 16*, 519–533.

Morris, J.A., Jordan, C.L., & Breedlove, S.M. (2004). Sexual differentiation of the vertebrate nervous system. *Nature Neuroscience, 7*, 1034–1039.

Morris, M.W., & Peng, K. (1994). Culture and cause: American and Chinese attributions for social and physical events. *Journal of Personality and Social Psychology, 67*, 949–971.

Morse, J.M. (1991). Approaches to qualitative-quantitative methodological triangulation. *Nursing Research, 40*(2), 120–123.

Morton, J. (1970). A functional model for memory. In D.A. Norman (Ed.), *Models of human memory*. New York: Academic Press.

Morton, N., & Browne, K.D. (1998). Theory and observation of attachment and its relation to child maltreatment: a review. *Child Abuse & Neglect, 22*, 1093–1104.

Moscovici, S. (1980). Toward a theory of conversion behavior. *Advances in Experimental Social Psychology, 13*, 209–239.

Moscovici, S., & Nemeth, C. (1974). Social influence. II: Minority influence. In C. Nemeth (Ed.), *Social psychology: classic and contemporary readings*. Oxford: Rand-McNally.

Moscovici, S., & Zavalloni, M. (1969). The group as a polarizer of attitudes. *Journal of Personality and Social Psychology, 12*, 125–135.

Moss-Morris, R. (2013) Adjusting to chronic illness: Time for a unified theory. *British Journal of Health Psychology, 18*(4), 681–686.

Moyers, T.B., & Houck, J. (2011). Combining motivational interviewing with cognitive-behavioral treatments for substance abuse: lessons from the COMBINE Research Project. *Cognitive and Behavioral Practice, 18*(1), 38–45.

Muczyk, J., & Reimann, B. (1987). The case for directive leadership. *Academy of Management Review, 16*, 637–647.

Mullen, B., Atkins, J.L., Champion, D.S., Edwards, C., Hardy, D., Story, J.E., & Vanderklok, M. (1985). The false consensus effect: A meta-analysis of 115 hypothesis tests. *Journal of Experimental Social Psychology, 21*(3), 262–283.

Mullen, B., & Hu, L.T. (1988). Social projection as a function of cognitive mechanisms: Two meta-analytic integrations. *British Journal of Social Psychology*, *27*(4), 333–356.

Mullen, B., Johnson, C., & Salas, E. (1991). Effects of communication network structure: components of positional centrality. *Social Networks*, *13*, 169–186.

Munafo, M., Zetteler, J., & Clark, T. (2007). Personality and smoking status: a meta-analysis. *Nicotine & Tobacco Research*, *9*, 405–413.

Murphy, W., & Page, I. (2008). Exhibitionism: psychopathology and theory. In D.R. Laws & W.T. O'Donohue (Eds), *Sexual deviance: theory, assessment, and treatment* (2nd edn, pp. 61–75). New York: Guilford Press.

Mustanski, B.S., DuPree, M.G., Nievergelt, C.M., Bocklandt, S., Schork, N.J., & Hamer, D. (2005). A genomewide scan of male sexual orientation. *Human Genetics*, *116*, 272–278.

Myers, I., & Myers, P.B. (1980/1995). *Gifts differing: understanding personality type*. Mountain View, CA: Davies-Black.

Myhill, A., & Allen, J. (2002). Rape and sexual assault of women: the extent and nature of. *Home Office Research, Development and Statistics Directorate*. London: Home Office.

Mynatt, C.R., Doherty, M.E., & Tweney, R.D. (1977). Confirmation bias in a simulated research environment. *Quarterly Journal of Experimental Psychology*, *29*, 85–95.

Nadder, T.S., Silberg, J.L., Rutter, M., Maes, H., & Eaves, J. (2001). Comparison of multiple measures of ADHD symptomatology: a multivariate of genetic analysis. *Journal of Child Psychology and Psychiatry and Allied Disciplines*, *42*, 475–486.

Nakamura, M., Nestor, P.G., Levitt, J.J., Cohen, A.S., Kawashima, T., Shenton, M.E., & McCarley, R.W. (2008). Orbitofrontal volume deficit in schizophrenia and thought disorder. *Brain*, *131*, 180–195.

National Institute of Clinical Excellence (NICE). (2008). *Drug misuse–psychosocialinterventions*.CG51.London:National Institute for Health and Clinical Excellence. Retrieved from: http://publications.nice.org.uk/drug-misuse-psycho social-interventions-cg51 (accessed 1 March 2014).

National Institute of Health and Care Excellence (NICE) (2008). *NICE guidelines PH10 Smoking cessation services*. Retrieved from http://www.nice.org.uk/guidance/PH10. (accessed 21.06.14).

National Institute of Clinical Excellence. (2009). *NICE technology appraisal guidance* (issued: April 2003; last modified: October 2009). TA59 Guidance on the use of electroconvulsive therapy. London: National Institute for Health and Clinical Excellence.

National Institute of Clinical Excellence. (2014). *Psychosis and schizophrenia in adults* (update). CG178. London: National Institute for Health and Clinical Excellence.

National Institute of Mental Health (NIMH) (2010). *Use of mental health services and treatment among adults*. London: NIMH. Retrieved from: www.nimh.nih.gov/statistics/ 3USE_MT_ADULT.shtml (accessed 1 March 2014).

Neath, I., & Suprenant, A.M. (2003). *Human memory: an introduction to research, data, and theory* (2nd edn). Belmont, CA: Wadsworth.

Neck, C.P., & Moorhead, G. (1995). Groupthink remodelled: the importance of leadership, time pressure, and methodical decision-making procedures. *Human Relations*, *48*(5), 537–557.

Neisser, U., Boodoo, G., Bouchard, T.J., Jr, Boykin, A.W., Brody, N., Ceci, S.J., Halpern, D.F., Loehlin, J.C., Perloff, R., Sternberg, R.J., & Urbina, S. (1996). Intelligence: knowns and unknowns. *American Psychologist*, *51*, 77–101.

Neisser, U., & Fivush, R. (1994). *The remembering self*. Cambridge: Cambridge University Press.

Neisser, U., & Joplin, D. (Eds) (1997). *The conceptual self in context: culture, experience, self understanding*. New York: Cambridge University Press.

Nemeth, C.J. (1986). Differential contributions of majority and minority influence. *Psychological Review*, *93*, 23–32.

Nemeth, C.J., Swedlund, M., & Kanki, B. (1974). Patterning of the minority's responses and their influence on the majority. *European Journal of Social Psychology*, *4*(1), 54–64.

Nettle, D., & Clegg, H. (2006). Schizotypy, creativity and mating success in humans. *Proceedings of the Royal Society Series B*, *273*, 611–615.

Newell, A., Shaw, J.C., & Simon, H.A. (1958). Elements of a theory of human problem solving. *Psychological Review*, *65*, 151–166.

Newell, A., & Simon, H. (1972). *Human problem solving*. Englewood Cliffs, NJ: Prentice Hall.

Newstead, S.E., Pollard, P., Evans, J.StB.T., & Allen, J.L. (1992). The source of belief bias effects in syllogistic reasoning. *Cognition*, *45*, 257–284.

Neylan, T.C. (1999). Frontal lobe function: Mr Phineas Gage's famous injury. *Journal of Neuropsychiatry and Clinical Neuroscience*, *11*, 280–281.

Niccols, A. (2007). Fetal alcohol syndrome and the developing socio-emotional brain. *Brain and Cognition*, *65*, 135–142.

Niederhoffer, K., & Pennebaker, J. (2002). Linguistic synchrony in social interactions. *Journal of Language and Social Psychology*, *21*, 337–360.

Nightingale, D.J., & Cromby, J. (2001). Critical psychology and the ideology of individualism. *Journal of Critical Psychology, Counselling and Psychotherapy*, *1*(2), 117–128. http:// homepages.lboro.ac.uk/~hujc4/critical%20psychology%20 individualism.pdf (accessed 9 December 2013).

Nijboer, F., Sellers, E.W., Mellinger, J., Jordan, M.A., Matuz, T., Furdea A., Halder, S., Mochty, U., Krusienski, D.J., Vaughan, T.M., Wolpaw, J.R., Birbaumer, N., & Kübler, A. (2008). A P300-based brain–computer interface for people with amyotrophic lateral sclerosis. *Clinical Neurophysiology*, *119*(8), 1909–1916.

Nisbett, R.E. (2009). *Intelligence and how to get it: why schools and cultures count*. New York: Norton.

Nisbett, R.E., Aronson, J., Blair, C., Dickens, W., Flynn, J., Halpern, D.F., & Turkheimer, E. (2012). Intelligence: new findings and theoretical developments. *American Psychologist*, *67*(2), 130–159.

Nisbett, R.E., & Ross, L. (1980). *Human inference*. Englewood Cliffs, NJ: Prentice Hall.

Niza, C., Tung, B., & Marteau, T.M. (2013). Incentivizing blood donation: systematic review and meta-analysis to test Titmuss' hypotheses. *Health Psychology, 32*(9), 941–949.

Nobles, W. (1976). The extended self: rethinking the so-called negro self-concept. *Journal of Black Psychology, 2*(2), 15–24.

Nobles, W. (1991) African Philosophy: foundations of Black psychology. In R.L Jones (Ed.), *Black Psychology* (3rd edn) (pp. 47–65). Berkley, CA: Cobb & Henry.

Norcross, J., Karpiak, C., & Santoro, S. (2005). Clinical psychologists across the years: the division of clinical psychology from 1960 to 2003. *Journal of Clinical Psychology, 61*, 1467–1483.

Norenzayan, A., & Nisbett, R.E. (2000). Culture and causal cognition. *Current Directions in Psychological Science, 9*, 132–135.

Norman, W.T. (1963). Toward an adequate taxonomy of personality attributes: replicated factor structure in peer nomination ratings. *Journal of Abnormal and Social Psychology, 66*, 574–583.

Nosek, B.A., Greenwald, A.G., & Banaji, M.R. (2007). The implicit association test at age 7: a methodological and conceptual review. In J.A. Bargh (Ed.), *Automatic processes in social thinking and behavior* (pp. 265–292). Hove: Psychology Press.

Nowakowski, R.S., & Hayes, N.L. (2002). General principles of CNS development. In M.H. Johnson, Y. Munakata, & R.O. Gilmore (Eds), *Brain development and cognition: a reader*. Oxford: Blackwell.

Oakes, P.J., Haslam, S.A., & Turner, J.C. (1994). *Stereotyping and social reality*. Oxford: Blackwell.

Oates, J. (2005). First relationships. In J. Oates, C. Wood, & A. Grayson (Eds), *Psychological development and early childhood*. Oxford: Wiley-Blackwell.

Oberauer, K. (2002). Access to information in working memory: Exploring the focus of attention. *Journal of Experimental Psychology: Learning, Memory, and Cognition, 28*(3), 411–421.

O'Brien, M. (1992). Gender identity and sex roles. In V.B. van Hasslet & M. Hersen (Eds), *Handbook of social development: a lifespan perspective* (pp. 325–345). New York: Plenum.

O'Connell, A.N. (1976). The relationship between lifestyle and identity synthesis and resynthesis in traditional, neo-traditional, and non-traditional women. *Journal of Personality, 44*(4), 675–687.

Office for National Statistics. (1998). *General Household Survey for 1996*. London: HMSO.

Office for National Statistics. (2000). *Social Trends 30*. London: HMSO. Retrieved from http://www.ons.gov.uk/ons/rel/social-trends-rd/social-trends/no--30--2000-edition/index.html (accessed 21 June 2014).

Office for National Statistics. (2013a). Focus on: violent crime and sexual offences, 2011/12. *Statistical Bulletin*. London: Office for National Statistics.

Office for National Statistics. (2013b). Crime in England and Wales, year ending June 2013. *Statistical Bulletin*. London: Office for National Statistics.

Office for National Statistics. (2013c). *Opinions and Lifestyle Survey, Smoking Habits Amongst Adults*, 2012. Accessed from http://www.ons.gov.uk/ons/publications/re-reference-tables.html?edition=tcm%3A77-315987.

Ogden, J. (1996). *Health psychology: A textbook*. Buckingham: Open University Press.

O'Halloran, C.J., Kinsella, G.J., & Storey, E. (2012). The cerebellum and neuropsychological functioning: a critical review. *Journal of Clinical & Experimental Neuropsychology, 34*(1), 35–56.

Ohlsson, S. (1992). Information-processing explanations of insight and related phenomena. In M. Keane & K. Gilhooly (Eds), *Advances in the psychology of thinking* (pp. 1–44). London: Harvester-Wheatsheaf.

Oksenberg, J.R., & Hauser, S.L. (2010). Mapping the human genome with new found precision. *Annals of Neurology, 67*(6), A8–10.

Oldfield, B. (2004). Internet use and loneliness in adolescents. Paper presented to the Association of Internet Researchers (AOIR) annual conference, Brighton University, UK.

Öllinger, M., Jones, G., Faber, A.H., & Knoblich, G. (2012). Cognitive mechanisms of insight: the role of heuristics and representational change in solving the eight-coin problem. *Journal of Experimental Psychology: Learning, Memory, and Cognition, 39*(3), 931.

Öllinger, M., Jones, G., & Knoblich G. (2014). The dynamics of search, impasse and representational change provide a coherent explanation of difficulty in the nine dot problem. *Psychological Research, 78*, 226–275.

Ong, W.J. (1982). *Orality and literacy*. London: Methuen.

Onwumere, J., Kuipers, E., Bebbington, P., Dunn, G., Freeman, D., Fowler, D., & Garety, P. (2009). Patient perceptions of caregiver criticism in psychosis: links with patient and caregiver functioning. *Journal of Nervous and Mental Disease, 197*, 85–91.

Ormerod, T.C., MacGregor, J.N., & Chronicle, E.P. (2002). Dynamics and constraints in insight problem solving. *Journal of Experimental Psychology: Learning, Memory, and Cognition, 28*, 791–799.

Orne, M.T. (1962). On the social psychology of the psychological experiment: with particular reference to demand characteristics and their implications. *American Psychologist, 17*(11), 776–783. DOI: 10.1037/h0043424.

Ornstein, R.E. (1975). *On the experience of time*. Oxford: Penguin.

Osborn, A.F. (1957). *Applied imagination* (rev. edn). New York: Scribner.

Osgood, C.E., Suci, G.J., & Tannenbaum, P.H. (1957). *The measurement of meaning*. Urbana, IL: University of Illinois Press.

Osler, W. (1910). The Lumleian lectures on angina pectoris. *The Lancet, 175*(4517), 839–844.

Otten, C.A., Penner, L.A., & Waugh, G. (1988). What are friends for: the determinants of psychological helping. *Journal of Social and Clinical Psychology, 7*, 34–41.

Owens, J.A., Belon, K., & Moss, P. (2010). The impact of delaying school start time on adolescent sleep, mood, and behaviour. *Archives of Pediatrics & Adolescent Medicine*, *164*, 608–614.

Padesky, C. (1993). Socratic questioning: changing minds or guiding discovery? A keynote address delivered at the European Congress of Behavioural and Cognitive Therapies, London, 24 September.

Palmer, S. (1989). Occupational stress. *The Health and Safety Practitioner*, *7*(8), 16–18.

Pantin, H.M., & Carver, C.S. (1982). Induced competence and the bystander effect. *Journal of Applied Social Psychology*, *12*(2), 100–111.

Papadopoulos, L. (2010). *Sexualisation of young people review*. London: UK Home Office. Retrieved from: http://dera.ioe.ac.uk/10738/1/sexualisation-young-people.pdf (accessed 14 August 2014).

Papez, J.W. (1937). A proposed mechanism of emotion. *Journal of Neuropsychiatry and Clinical Neuroscience*, *7*(1), 103–112.

Pardini, D.A., & Phillips, M. (2010). Neural responses to emotional and neutral facial expressions in chronically violent men. *Journal of Psychiatry Neuroscience*, *35*(8), 390–398.

Paris, J. (2010). Estimating the prevalence of personality disorders in the community. *Journal of Personality Disorders*, *24*(4), 405–411.

Park, D.C., Lautenschlager, G., Hedden, T., Davidson, N.S., Smith, A.D., & Smith, P.K. (2002). Models of visuospatial and verbal memory across the adult lifespan. *Psychology and Aging*, *17*, 299–320.

Park, D.C., & Radford, J.P. (1998). Reconstructing a history of involuntary sterilisation. *Disability and Society*, *13*, 317–342.

Parker, I. (1992) *Discourse dynamics: critical analysis for social and individual psychology*. Florence, KY: Taylor & Frances/Routledge.

Parks, M., & Floyd, K. (1996). Making friends in cyberspace. *Journal of Communication*, *6*, 80–97.

Parks, M.J., Osgood, D.W., Felson, R.B., Wells, S., & Graham, K. (2013). Third party involvement in barroom conflicts. *Aggressive Behavior*, *39*(4), 257–268.

Parsons, T. (1954). *The social system*. Chicago, IL: Chicago University Press.

Patrick, C.J. (2007). Antisocial personality disorder and psychopathy. In W. O'Donohue, K.A. Fowler, & S.O. Lilienfeld (Eds), *Personality disorders: Toward the DSM-V* (pp. 109–166). Thousand Oaks, CA: SAGE.

Patrick, C.J., Fowles, D.C., & Krueger, R.F. (2009). Triarchic conceptualization of psychopathy: Developmental origins of disinhibition, boldness, and meanness. *Development and psychopathology*, *21*(3), 913–938.

Patten, C.J., Kircher, A., Ostlund, J., & Nilsson, L. (2004). Using mobile telephones: cognitive workload and attention resource allocation. *Accident Annalysis and Prevention*, *36*(3), 341–350.

Paulmann, S., Bleichner, M., & Kotz, S.A. (2013). Valence, arousal, and task effects in emotional prosody processing. *Frontiers in Psychology*, *4*, article 345.

Paunonen, S.V., Haddock, G., Forsterling, F., & Keinonen, M. (2003). Broad versus narrow personality measures and the prediction of behaviour across cultures. *European Journal of Personality*, *17*(6), 413–433.

Paunonen, S.V., & Jackson, D.N. (2000). What is beyond the Big Five? Plenty! *Journal of Personality*, *68*(5), 821–835.

Pawlby, S. (1977). Imitative interaction. In H.R. Schaffer (Ed.), *Studies in mother–infant interaction*. London: Academic Press.

Payne, G.D., & Wenger, M.J. (1998). *Cognitive psychology*. Boston, MA: Houghton Mifflin.

Payne, S.J., & Baguley, T. (2006). Memory for the process of constructing an integrated mental model. *Memory & Cognition*, *34*, 817–825.

Pena Trevino, R. (1955). Introduction of Dr Henri Laborit from France at the meeting of the Academy on 8 March 1955. *Cirugia y Cirujanos*, *23*(4), 181–182.

Penfield, W. (1958). *The excitable cortex in conscious man*. Liverpool: Liverpool University Press.

Penfield, W. (1975). *The mystery of the mind: a critical study of consciousness and the human brain*. Princeton, NJ: Princeton University Press.

Penfield, W., & Jasper, H.H. (1954). *Epilepsy and the functional anatomy of the human brain*. Boston, MA: Little, Brown.

Pennington, B.F., Willcutt, E., & Rhee, S.H. (2005). Analyzing comorbidity. In R.V. Kail (Ed.), *Advances in child development and behaviour*. San Diego, CA: Elsevier.

Perkins, J.M., Perkins, H.W., & Craig, D.W. (2010). Peer weight norm misperception as a risk factor for being over and underweight among UK secondary school students. *European Journal of Clinical Nutrition*, *64*(9), 965–971.

Perkins, J.M., Perkins, H.W., & Craig, D.W. (2014). Misperception of peer weight norms and its association with overweight and underweight status among adolescents. *Prevention Science*. DOI: 10.1007/s11121-014-0458-2.

Perner, J., Leekam, S.R., & Wimmer, H. (1987). Three-year-olds' difficulty with false belief: the case for a conceptual deficit. *British Journal of Developmental Psychology*, *5*, 125–137.

Perrin, A.J. (2005). National threat and political culture: authoritarianism, antiauthoritarianism, and the September 11 attacks. *Political Psychology*, *26*(2), 167–194.

Perrow, C. (1970). *Organisational analysis*. London: Tavistock.

Perrow, C. (1972). *Complex organisations*. Glenview, IL: Scott Foresman and Co.

Petersen, M.B., Sell, A., Tooby, J., & Cosmides, L. (2010) Evolutionary psychology and criminal justice: a recalibrational theory of punishment and reconciliation. In H. Høgh-Olesen (Ed.), *Human morality and sociality: evolutionary and comparative perspectives* (pp. 72–131). Basingstoke: Palgrave Macmillan.

Petitto, L.A., Holowka, S., Sergio, L.E., Levy, B., & Ostry, D.J. (2004). Baby hands that move to the rhythm of language: hearing babies acquiring sign languages babble silently on the hands. *Cognition*, *93*, 43–73.

Pettigrew, T.F. (1958). Personality and sociocultural factors in intergroup attitudes: a cross-national comparison. *Conflict Resolution*, *2*, 29–42.

Pettigrew, T.F. (1979). The ultimate attribution error: extending Allport's cognitive analysis of prejudice. *Personality and Social Psychology Bulletin, 5,* 461–476.

Pettigrew, T.F. (1997). Generalised intergroup contact effects on prejudice. *Personality and Social Psychology Bulletin, 23,* 173–185.

Pettigrew, T.F., & Tropp, L.R. (2006). A meta-analytic test of intergroup contact theory. *Journal of Personality and Social Psychology, 90*(5), 751–783.

Pfabigan, D.M., Alexopoulos, J., & Sailer, U. (2012). Exploring the effects of antisocial personality traits on brain potentials during face processing. *PLoS One,* 7, e50283.

Pharo, H., Sim, C., Graham, M., Gross, J., & Hayne, H. (2011). Risky business: executive function, personality, and reckless behaviour during adolescence and emerging adulthood. *Behavioural Neuroscience, 125*(6), 970–978.

Phillips, A. (1993). *On kissing, tickling and being bored: psychoanalytic essays on the unexamined life.* Cambridge, MA: Harvard University Press.

Phillips, A., & Taylor, B. (2009). *On kindness.* London: Penguin.

Phipps, S. (2011). Positive psychology and war: An oxymoron. *American Psychologist, 66*(7), 641–642.

Phoenix, C.H., Goy, R.W., Gerall, A.A., & Young, W.C. (1959). Organizing action of prenatally administered testosterone propionate on the tissues mediating mating behavior in the female guinea pig. *Endocrinology,* 65, 369–382.

Piaget, J. (1952). *The origins of intelligence in children.* New York: International University Press.

Piaget, J. (1953). How children develop mathematical concepts. *Scientific American, 189,* 74–79.

Piaget, J. (1963). *The psychology of intelligence.* New York: Routledge.

Pickering, D. (2009). The role of perceived social support and stress in the type A cognition–symptom relationship. *Journal of Rational-Emotive & Cognitive Behavior Therapy, 27*(1), 1–22.

Pierre, J.M. (2010). The borders of mental disorder in psychiatry and the DSM: past, present, and future. *Journal of Psychiatric Practice, 16*(6), 375–386.

Piliavin, J.A., Piliavin, I.M., Dovidio, J.F., Gaertner, S.L., & Clark, R.D.I. (1981). *Emergency intervention.* New York: Academic Press.

Pillsbury, W.B. (1911). *Essentials of psychology.* New York: Macmillan.

Pine, D.S., Cohen, P., Johnson, J.G., & Brook, J.S. (2002). Adolescent life events as predictors of adult depression. *Journal of Affective Disorders, 68*(1), 49–57.

Pinker, S. (1995). *The language instinct: the new science of language and mind.* London: Penguin.

Pinker, S. (2002). *The blank slate: the modern denial of human nature.* London: Penguin.

Pinker, S., & Prince, A. (1988). On language and connectionism: analysis of a parallel distributed processing model of language acquisition. *Cognition, 28*(1), 73–193.

Place, U.T. (1956). Is consciousness a brain process? *British Journal of Psychology, 47,* 44–50.

Plomin, R. (1990). The role of inheritance in behaviour. *Science, 248,* 183–188.

Plomin, R., DeFries, J.C., McClearn, G.E., & McGuffin, P. (2005). *Behavioral genetics* (5th edn). New York: Worth.

Polaschek, D.L., & Ward, T. (2002). The implicit theories of potential rapists: what our questionnaires tell us. *Aggression and Violent Behavior, 7*(4), 385–406.

Polkinghorne, D.E. (1996). Explorations of narrative identity. *Psychological Inquiry, 7*(4), 363–367.

Polkinghorne, D.E. (2000). The unconstructed self. *Culture & Psychology,* 6, 265.

Pomerantz, A. (2011). *Clinical psychology: science, practice and culture.* London: SAGE.

Popper, K.R. (1968). *The logic of scientific discovery.* London: Hutchinson.

Porter, L.E. (2010). Robbery. In J. Brown & E.A. Campbell (Eds), *The Cambridge handbook of forensic psychology* (pp. 535–542). New York and Cambridge: Cambridge University Press.

Posner, M.I. (1980). Orienting of attention. *Quarterly Journal of Experimental Psychology, 32,* 3–25.

Postman, L., & Phillips, L.W. (1965). Short-term temporal changes in free recall. *Quarterly Journal of Experimental Psychology, 17,* 132–138.

Postmes, T., & Spears, R. (1998). Deindividuation and antinormative behavior: a meta-analysis. *Psychological Bulletin, 123*(3), 238–259.

Potter, G.G., Helms, M.J., & Plassman, B.L. (2008). Associations of job demands and intelligence with cognitive performance among men in late life. *Neurology, 70*(19), 1803–1808.

Potter, J. (1996). *Representing reality: discourse rhetoric and social construction.* London: SAGE.

Potter, J., & Wetherell, M. (1987). *Discourse and social psychology: beyond attitudes and behaviour.* London: SAGE.

Powell, L.H., & Thoreson, C.E. (1987). Modifying the type A behavior pattern: a small group treatment approach. In P.D. Blumenthal & D.C. McKee (Eds), *Applications in behavioral medicine and health psychology: a clinician's guide* (pp. 98–106). Sarasota, FL: Professional Exchange.

Pozzulo, J.D., & Lindsay, R.C.L. (1998). Identification accuracy of children versus adults: a meta-analysis. *Law and Human Behavior, 22*(5), 549.

Pozzulo, J.D., & Lindsay, R.C.L. (1999). Elimination lineups: an improved identification procedure for child eyewitnesses. *Journal of Applied Psychology, 84*(2), 167.

Premack, D., & Woodruff, G. (1978). Does the chimpanzee have a theory of mind? *Behavioral and Brain Sciences, 1*(4), 515–526.

Premkumar, P., Cooke, M.A., Fannon, D., Peters, E., Michel, T.M., Murray, R.M., Kuipers, E., & Kumari, V. (2008). Misattribution bias of threat-related facial expressions is related to a longer duration of illness and poor executive function in schizophrenia and schizoaffective disorder. *European Psychiatry, 23,* 14–19.

Premkumar, P., Ettinger, U., Inchley-Mort, S., Sumich, A., Williams, S.C.R., Kuipers, E., & Kumari, V. (2012). Neural processing of social rejection: the role of schizotypal personality traits. *Human Brain Mapping, 33,* 695–706.

Premkumar, P., Fannon, D., Kuipers, E., Simmons, A., Frangou, S., & Kumari, V. (2008). Emotional decision-making and its dissociable components in schizophrenia and schizoaffective disorder: a behavioural and MRI investigation. *Neuropsychologia, 46,* 2002–2012.

Premkumar, P., Williams, S.C.R., Lythgoe, D., Andrew, C., Kuipers, E., & Kumari, V. (2013). Neural processing of criticism and positive comments from relatives in individuals with schizotypal personality traits. *World Journal of Biological Psychiatry, 14,* 57–70.

Prentice-Dunn, S., & Rogers, R.W. (1982). Effects of public and private self-awareness of deindividuation and aggression. *Journal of Personality and Social Psychology, 43,* 503–513.

Prigogine, I., & Stengers, I. (1984). *Order out of chaos: man's new dialogue with nature.* London: Heinemann.

Prilleltensky, I. (1994). *The morals and politics of psychology: psychological discourse and the status quo.* New York. SUNY Press.

Prochaska, J., & DiClemente, C. (1983). Stages and processes of self-change in smoking: toward an integrative model of change. *Journal of Consulting and Clinical Psychology, 5,* 390–395.

Prochaska, J., DiClemente, C., & Norcross, J. (1993). In search of how people change: applications to addictive behaviors. *Journal of Addictions Nursing, 5*(1), 2–16 (DOI: 10.3109/10884609309149692).

Prochaska, J., & Norcross, J. (2010). *Systems of psychotherapy: a transactional analysis* (7th edn). Belmont, CA: Brooks Cole.

Pruden, S., Hirsh-Pasek, K., Golinkoff, R., & Hennon, E. (2006). The birth of words: ten-month-olds learn words through perceptual salience. *Child Development, 77*(2), 266–280.

Pudlinski, C. (2005). Doing empathy and sympathy: caring responses to troubles tellings on a peer support line. *Discourse Studies, 7*(3), 267–288.

Pulvermuller, F. (2002). *The neuroscience of language: on brain circuits of words and serial order.* Cambridge: Cambridge University Press.

Pye, C. (1986). Quiche Mayan speech to children. *Journal of Child Language, 13,* 85–100.

Quinlan, P.T., & Wilton, R.N. (1998). Grouping by proximity or similarity? Competition between the Gestalt principles in vision. *Perception, 27,* 417–430.

Quinn, P.C., Westerlund, A., & Nelson, C.A. (2006). Neural markers of categorisation in 6-month-old infants. *Psychological Research, 17,* 59–66.

Quitkin, F., Rabkin, J., Gerald, J., Davis, J., & Klein, D. (2000). Validity of clinical trials of antidepressants. *American Journal of Psychiatry, 157,* 327–337.

Raby, K.L., Cicchetti, D., Carlson, E.A., Cutili, J.J., Englund, M.M., & Egeland, B. (2012). Genetic and caregiving-based contribution to infant attachment: unique associations with distress reactivity and attachment security. *Psychological Science, 23,* 1016–1023.

Radley, A. (1991). *In social relationships.* Milton Keynes: Open University Press.

Radley, A. (1995). The elusory body and social constructionist theory. *Body & Society, 1*(2), 3–23.

Rahman, Q., Abrahams, S., & Wilson, G.D. (2003). Sexual orientation related differences in verbal fluency. *Neuropsychology, 17,* 240–246.

Rahman, Q., Andersson, D., & Govier, E. (2005). A specific sexual orientation-related difference in navigation strategy. *Behavioral Neuroscience, 119,* 311–316.

Rahman, Q., & Wilson, G.D. (2003). Born gay? The psychobiology of human sexual orientation. *Personality and Individual Differences, 34,* 1337–1382.

Rahman, Q., Wilson, G.D., & Abrahams, S. (2003). Sexual orientation related differences in spatial memory. *Journal of the International Neuropsychological Society, 9,* 376–383.

Raine, A., Lencz, T., Bihrle, S., LaCasse, L., & Colletti, P. (2000). Reduced prefrontal gray matter volume and reduced autonomic activity in antisocial personality disorder. *Archives of General Psychiatry, 57,* 119–127.

Raine, A., Melroy, J.R., Bihrle, S., Stoddard, J., LaCasse, L., & Buchsbaum, M.S. (1998). Reduced prefrontal and increased subcortical brain functioning assessed using positron emission tomography in predatory and affective murderers. *Behavioral Sciences & the Law, 16,* 319–332.

Ramachandran, V.S., & Blakeslee, S. (1998). *Phantoms in the brain: probing the mysteries of the human mind.* New York: Morrow.

Ramachandran, V.S., & Hubbard, E.M. (2001). Synaesthesia: a window into perception, thought and language. *Journal of Consciousness Studies, 8*(12), 3–34.

Ramachandrappa, S., & Farooqi, I.S. (2011). Genetic approaches to understanding human obesity. *Journal of Clinical Investigation, 121*(6), 2080–2086.

Rami-Gonzalez, L., Bernardo, M., Boget, T., Salamero, M., Gil-Verona, J., & Junque, C. (2001) Subtypes of memory dysfunction associated with ECT: Characteristics and neurobiological bases , *Journal of ECT, 17*(2), 129–135.

Ramus, F., Hauser, M.D., Miller, C., Morris, D., & Mehler, J. (2000). Language discrimination by human newborns and by cotton-top Tamarin monkeys. *Science, 288*(5464), 349–351.

Ranchor, A.V., & Sanderman, R. (1991). The role of personality and socio-economic status in the stress–illness relation: a longitudinal study. *European Journal of Personality, 5*(2), 93–108.

Rauschecker, J.P., & Tian, B. (2000). Mechanisms and streams for processing of 'what' and 'where' in auditory cortex. *Proceedings of the National Academy of Sciences, 97,* 11800–11806.

Rauscher, F.H., Shaw, G.L., & Ky, K.N. (1993) Music and spatial task performance. *Nature, 365,* 611.

Rayner, K., & Duffy, S.A. (1986). Lexical complexity and fixation times in reading: effects of word frequency, verb complexity, and lexical ambiguity. *Memory & Cognition, 14,* 191–201.

Rayner, K., Foorman, B.R., Perfetti, C.A., Pesetsky, D., & Seidenberg, M.S. (2001). How psychological science informs the teaching of reading. *Psychological Science in the Public Interest, 2,* 31–74.

Rayner, K., & Pollatsek, A. (1989). *The psychology of reading.* Englewood Cliffs, NJ: Prentice Hall.

Rayner, K., & Well, A.D. (1996). Effects of contextual constraint on eye movements in reading: a further examination. *Psychonomic Bulletin & Review, 3,* 504–509.

Reicher, S. (2001). The psychology of crowd dynamics. In M.A. Hogg & S. Tindale (Eds), *Blackwell handbook of social psychology: Group processes.* Oxford: Blackwell.

Reicher, S. (2004). The context of social identity: domination, resistance and change. *Political Psychology, 25*(6), 921–945.

Reicher, S., & Haslam, S.A. (2006). Rethinking the psychology of tyranny: the BBC prison study. *British Journal of Social Psychology, 45,* 1–40.

Reicher, S., & Haslam,S.A. (2009). FORUM: the real world. *The Psychologist, 22*(6), 469.

Reicher, S., & Hopkins, N. (2001). Psychology and the end of history: a critique and a proposal for the psychology of social categorization. *Political Psychology, 22*(2), 383–407.

Reicher, S., & Stott, C. (2012). *Mad mobs and Englishmen? Myths and realities of the 2011 riots.* London: Constable and Robinson.

Reicher, S.D. (1982). The determination of collective behaviour. In H. Tajfel (Ed.), *Social identity and intergroup relations.* New York: Cambridge University Press..

Reicher, S.D. (1984). The St Pauls' riot: an explanation of the limits of crowd action in terms of a social identity model. *European Journal of Social Psychology, 14,* 1–21.

Reicher, S.D. (1987). Crowd behaviour as social action. In J.C. Turner, M. Hogg, P. Oakes, S. Reicher, & M. Wetherell (Eds), *Rediscovering the social group: a self-categorization theory.* Oxford: Blackwell.

Reicher, S.D., Spears, R., & Postmes, T. (1995). A social identity model of deindividuation phenomena. *European Review of Social Psychology, 6,* 161–198.

Rensink, R.A. (2002). Change detection. *Annual Review of Psychology, 53,* 245–477.

Resnick, L.B. (1992). From protoquantities to operators: building mathematical competence on a foundation of everyday knowledge. In G. Leinhardt, R. Putnam, & R.A. HatCrup (Eds), *Analysis of arithmetic for mathematics teaching* (vol. 19, pp. 275–323). Hillsdale, NJ: Erlbaum.

Resnick, L.B. (1994). Situated rationalism: biological and social preparation for learning. In L.A. Hirschfeld & S.A. Gelman (Eds), *Mapping the mind: domain specificity in cognition and culture* (pp. 474–493). Cambridge: Cambridge University Press.

Rice, G., Anderson, C., Risch, N., & Ebers, G. (1999). Male homosexuality: absence of linkage to microsatellite markers at Xq28. *Science, 284,* 665–667.

Richards, G. (1996). *Putting psychology in its place: an introduction from a critical historical perspective.* London: Routledge.

Riegel, K.F. (1976). The dialectics of human development. *American Psychologist, 31*(10), 689.

Ringelmann, M. (1913). Recherches sur les moteurs animés: travail de l'homme [Research on animate sources of power: the work of man]. *Annales de I'lnstitut National Agronomique,* 2e série, XII, 1–40.

Roberts, B.W. (2009). Back to the future: personality and assessment and personality development. *Journal of Research in Personality, 43,* 137–145.

Roberts, B. W., Kuncel, N.R., Shiner, R., Caspi, A., & Goldberg, L.R. (2007). The power of personality: The comparative validity of personality traits, socioeconomic status, and cognitive ability for predicting important life outcomes. *Perspectives on Psychological Science, 2,* 313–345.

Robinson, T.E., & Berridge, K.C. (1993). The neural basis of drug craving: an incentive-sensitization theory of addiction. *Brain Research Reviews, 18,* 247–291.

Robinson, T.E., & Berridge, K.C. (2003). Addiction. *Annual Reviews in Psychology, 54,* 25–53.

Robinson, T.E., & Berridge, K.C. (2008). The incentive sensitisation theory of addiction: some current issues. *Philosophical Transactions of The Royal Society of London B, 363,* 3137–3146.

Rock, I., & Gutman, D. (1981). Effect of inattention on form perception. *Journal of Experimental Psychology: Human Perception and Performance, 7,* 275–285.

Roediger, H.L., III, & Karpicke, J.D. (2006). Test-enhanced learning: taking memory tests improves long-term retention. *Psychological Science, 17,* 249–255.

Rogers, C. (1961) *On becoming a person: a therapist's view of psychotherapy.* London: Constable.

Rogers, C.R. (1951). *Client-centered therapy: its current practice, implications and theory.* Boston, MA: Houghton Mifflin.

Rogoff, B. (1990). *Apprenticeship in thinking: cognitive development in social context.* New York: Oxford University Press.

Rose, S., Kamin, L.J., & Lewontin, R.C. (1984). *Not in our genes.* Harmondsworth: Penguin.

Rosenberg, L. (2011). Mental health first aid: a 'radical efficiency' in health promotion. *The Journal of Behavioral Health Services and Research, 38*(2), 143–145.

Rosenblith, J. (1992). *In the beginning: development from conception to age two* (2nd edn). Newbury Park, CA: SAGE.

Rosenblum, G.D., & Lewis, M. (1999). The relations among body image, physical attractiveness, and body mass in adolescence. *Child Development, 70*(1), 50–64.

Rosenhan, D.L. (1973). On being sane in insane places. *Science, 179,* 250–258.

Rosenman, R.H., & Friedman, M. (1977). Modifying type A behavior patterns. *Journal of Psychosomatic Research, 21,* 323–331.

Rosenthal, R., & Jacobson, L. (1968). Pygmalion in the classroom. *The Urban Review, 3*(1), 16–20.

Ross, L. (1977). The intuitive psychologist and his shortcomings. In L. Berkowitz (Ed.), *Advances in experimental social psychology* (vol. 10, pp. 173–220). San Diego, CA: Academic Press.

Ross, L., Greene, D., & House, P. (1977). The 'false consensus effect': an egocentric bias in social perception and attribution processes. *Journal of Personality and Social Psychology, 35,* 485–494.

Rossion, B., Joyce, C.A., Cottrell, G.W., & Tarr, M.J. (2003). Early lateralization and orientation turning for face, word, and object processing in the visual cortex. *Neuroimage*, *20*(3), 1609–1624.

Roth, T.L., & Sweatt, J.D. (2011). Annual research review: epigenetic mechanisms and environmental shaping of the brain during sensitive periods of development. *Journal of Child Psychology & Psychiatry*, *52*(4), 398–408.

Rothwell, J., Bandar, Z., O'Shea, J., & McLean, D. (2006). Silent talker: a new computer-based system for the analysis of facial cues to deception. *Applied Cognitive Psychology*, *20*, 757–777.

Rotter, J.B. (1954). *Social learning and clinical psychology.* New York: Prentice Hall.

Rubie-Davies, C., Hattie, J., & Hamilton, R. (2006). Expecting the best for students: teacher expectations and academic outcomes. *The British Journal of Educational Psychology*, *76*, 429–444. DOI: 10.1348/000709905X53589.

Rubin, M., & Hewstone, M. (2004). Social identity, system justification, and social dominance: commentary on Reicher, Jost et al., and Sidanius et al. *Political Psychology*, *25*(6), 823–844.

Ruble, D.N., & Martin, C.L. (1998). Gender development. In W. Damon (Ed.), *Handbook of child psychology. Vol. 3: Social, emotional, and personality development* (5th edn, pp. 933–1016). New York: Wiley.

Ruble, T.L. (1983). Sex stereotypes: issues of change in the 1970s. *Sex Roles*, *9*, 397–402.

Ruddy, R., & House, A. (2005). Psychosocial interventions for conversion disorder. *Cochrane Database of Systematic Reviews*, *4*. Article No.: CD005331.

Ruffman, T., Slade, L., Rowlandson, K., Rumsey, C., & Garnham, A. (2003). How language relates to belief, desire, and emotion understanding. *Cognitive Development*, *18*, 139–158.

Rundus, D. (1971). Analysis of rehearsal processes in free recall. *Journal of Experimental Psychology*, *89*, 63–77.

Rusch, N., Tebartz van Elst, L., Ludaescher, P., Wilke, M., Huppertz, H.J., Thiel, T., … Ebert, D. (2003). A voxel-based morphometric MRI study in female patients with borderline personality disorder. *NeuroImage*, *20*, 385–392.

Rushton, J.P., & Campbell, A. (1977). Modeling, vicarious reinforcement and extraversion on blood donating in adults: immediate and long term effects. *European Journal of Social Psychology*, *7*, 297–306.

Rushton, J.P., & Jensen, A.R. (2005). Thirty years of research on race differences in cognitive ability. *Psychology, Public Policy, and Law*, *11*, 235–294.

Rushton, J.P., Russell, R.J., & Wells, P.A. (1984). Genetic similarity theory: beyond kin selection. *Behavior Genetics*, *14*, 179–193.

Rylands, A.J., McKie, S., Elliott, R., Deakin, J.F., & Tarrier, N. (2011). A functional magnetic resonance imaging paradigm of expressed emotion in schizophrenia. *Journal of Nervous and Mental Disease*, *199*, 25–29.

Sackeim, H.A., Haskett, R.F., Mulsant, B., et al. (2001) Continuation pharmacotherapy in the prevention of relapse following electroconvulsive therapy: a randomized controlled trial. *The Journal of the American Medical Association*, *285*, 1299–1307.

Sacker, A., Firth, D., Fitzpatrick, R., Lynch, K., & Bartley, M. (2000). Comparing health inequality in men and women: prospective studies of mortality 1986–96. *British Medical Journal*, *320*, 1303–1307.

Sacks, O. (1973). *Awakenings*. New York: Vintage.

Saddoris, M.P., Gallagher, M., & Schoenbaum, G. (2005). Rapid associative encoding in basolateral amygdala depends on connections with orbitofrontal cortex. *Neuron*, *46*, 321–331.

Salter, A.C. (2001). *Predators: pedophiles, rapists and other sex offenders*. New York: Basic Books.

Salthouse, T.A. (1991). Mediation of adult age differences in cognition by reductions in working memory and speed of processing. *Psychological Science*, *2*(3), 179–183.

Salthouse, T.A. (1996). The processing-speed theory of adult age differences in cognition. *Psychological Review*, *103*(3), 403–428.

Sameroff, A.J., & Chandler, M.J. (1975). Reproductive risk and the continuum of caretaking casualty. In F.D. Horowitz, M. Hetherington, S. Scarr-Salapatek, & G. Siegel (Eds), *Review of child development research* (vol. 4). Chicago, IL: University of Chicago Press.

Sampson, E.E. (1977) Psychology and the American ideal. *Journal of Personality and Social Psychology*, *35*, 767–782.

Sanders, G., & Wright, M. (1997). Sexual orientation differences in cerebral asymmetry and in the performance of sexually dimorphic cognitive and motor tasks. *Archives of Sexual Behavior*, *26*, 463–480.

Sanders, G.S., & Baron, R.S. (1977). Is social comparison irrelevant for producing choice shifts? *Journal of Experimental Social Psychology*, *13*, 303–314.

Santa Lucia, R.C., Gesten, E., Redina-Gobioff, G., Epstein, M., Kaufmann, D., Salcedo, O., et al. (2000). Children's school adjustment: a developmental transactional systems perspective. *Journal of Applied Developmental Psychology*, *24*, 429–446.

Satz, P., Taylor, H.G., Friel, J., & Fletcher, J.M. (1978). Some developmental and predictive precursors of reading disability. In A.L. Benton & D. Pearl (Eds), *Dyslexia: an appraisal of current knowledge* (pp. 457–501). New York and Oxford: Oxford University Press.

Saucier, G. (2009). Recurrent personality dimensions in inclusive lexical studies: indications for a Big Six structure. *Journal of Personality*, *77*, 1577–1614.

Saudino, K.J., Carter, A.S., Purper-Ouakil, D., & Gorwood, P. (2008). The etiology of behavioral problems and competencies in very young twins. *Journal of Abnormal Psychology*, *117*, 48–62.

Schaffer, H.R. (2000). The early experience assumption: past, present, and future. *International Journal of Behavioral Development*, *24*(1), 5–14.

Schaie, K.W. (1996). *Intellectual development in adulthood: the Seattle longitudinal study*. Cambridge: Cambridge University Press.

Scheerer, M. (1963). Problem solving. *Scientific American, 208*, 118–128.

Schlenker, B.R., Phillips, S.T., Boniecki, K.A., & Schlenker, D.R. (1995). Championship pressures: choking or triumphing in one's territory? *Journal of Personality and Social Psychology, 68*, 632–643.

Schmalhofer, F., & Glavanov, D. (1986). Three components of understanding a programmer's manual: verbatim, propositional and situational representations. *Journal of Memory and Language, 25*, 279–294.

Schmolck, H., Buffalo, E.A., & Squire, L.R. (2000). Memory distortions develop over time: recollections of the OJ Simpson trial verdict after 15 and 32 months. *Psychological Science, 11*(1), 39–45.

Schoppe-Sullivan, S., Kotila, L.E., Jia, R., Lang, S.N., & Bower, D.J. (2013). Comparisons of levels and predictors of mothers' and fathers' engagement with their preschool-aged children. *Early Child Development and Care, 183*, 498–514.

Schultz, D.P. (1996) *A history of modern psychology* (6th edn). Orlando, FL: Harcourt Brace.

Schulz-Hardt, S., Brodbeck, F.C., Mojzisch, A., Kerschreiter, R., & Frey, D. (2006). Group decision making in hidden profile situations: dissent as a facilitator for decision quality. *Journal of Personality and Social Psychology, 91*, 1080–1093.

Schwann, T. (1839). *Mikroskopische Untersuchungen über die Uebereinstimmung in der Struker und dem Wachsthum der Thiere und Pflanzen*. Berlin: Reimer. English trans. H. Smith 1845, reprinted New York: Kraus, 1969.

Schwartz, D., Gorman, A.H., Nakamoto, J., & Toblin, R.L. (2005). Victimization in the peer group and children's academic functioning. *Journal of Educational Psychology, 97*, 425–435.

Schwarze, C.E., Mobascher, A., Pallasch, B., Hoppe, G., Kurz, M., Hellhammer, D.H., & Lieb, K. (2013). Prenatal adversity: a risk factor in borderline personality disorder?. *Psychological medicine, 43*(6), 1279–1291.

Schweiger, D.M., Sandberg, W.R., & Rechner, P.L. (1989). Experiential effects of dialectical inquiry, devil's advocacy and consensus approaches to strategic decision making. *Academy of Management Journal, 32*, 745–772.

Seale, C., Zeibland, S., & Charteris-Black, J. (2006). Gender, cancer experience and internet use: a comparative keyword analysis of interviews and online cancer support groups. *Social Science & Medicine, 62*, 2577–2590.

Sear, R., Mace, R., & McGregor, I. A. (2000). Maternal grandmothers improve nutritional status and survival of children in rural Gambia. *Proceedings of the Royal Society of London, Series B: Biological Sciences, 267*(1453), 1641–1647.

Searcy, J.H., Bartlett, J.C., & Memon, A. (1999). Age differences in accuracy and choosing in eyewitness identification and face recognition. *Memory & Cognition, 27*(3), 538–552.

Searle, J. (1980). Minds, Brains and Programs, *Behavioral and Brain Sciences, 3*, 417–457.

Sebastian, C.L., Tan, G.C., Roiser, J.P., Viding, E., Dumontheil, I., & Blakemore, S.J. (2011). Developmental influences on the neural bases of responses to social rejection: implications of social neuroscience for education. *NeuroImage, 57*(3), 686–694.

Second Life (2009). http://secondlife.com/whatis/avatar.php (accessed 2014).

Seligman, M. (1995). The effectiveness of psychotherapy: the Consumer Reports survey. *American Psychologist, 50*, 965–974.

Scligman, M. (1998). The President's address. *American Psychologist, 54*, 559–562.

Seligman, M. (2002). *Authentic happiness* London: Nicholas Brealey.

Seligman, M. (2011). Helping American soldiers in time of war: Reply to comments on the comprehensive soldier fitness special issue. *American Psychologist, 66*(7), 646–647.

Seligman, M., & Csikszentmihalyi, M. (2000). Positive psychology: an introduction. *American Psychologist, 55*, 5–14.

Selye, H. (1956). *The stress of life*. New York: McGraw-Hill.

Sereno, S.C., & Rayner, K. (2003). Measuring word recognition in reading: eye movements and event-related potentials. *Trends in Cognitive Sciences, 7*, 489–493.

Sergeant, M.J.T., Dickins, T.E., Davies, M.N.O., & Griffiths, M.D. (2006). Aggression, empathy and sexual orientation among males. *Personality and Individual Differences, 40*, 475–486.

Servaas, M.N., Riese, H., Renken, R.J., Marsman, J.B., Lambregs, J., Ormel, J., & Aleman, A. (2013). The effect of criticism on functional brain connectivity and associations with neuroticism. *PloS One, 8*(7), e69606.

Seyfarth, R., & Cheney, D. (1990). The assessment by vervet monkeys of their own and another species' alarm calls. *Animal Behaviour, 40*(4), 754–764.

Seymour-Smith, S. (2013). A reconsideration of the gendered mechanisms of support in online interactions about testicular implants: a discursive approach. *Health Psychology* (Special Series: Men's Health), *32*(1), 91–99.

Shah, P., & Mountain, D. (2007). The medical model is dead – long live the medical model. *The British Journal of Psychiatry, 191*(5), 375–377.

Shallice, T. (1982). Specific impairments of planning. *Philosophical Transactions of the Royal Society of London, 298*, 199–209.

Shallice, T., & Warrington, E.K. (1970). Independent functioning of verbal memory stores: a neuropsychological study. *Quarterly Journal of Experimental Psychology, 22*, 261–273.

Sharf, R. (2011). *Theories of psychotherapy and counseling: concepts and cases*. Belmont, CA: Cengage Learning.

Shaw, M.E. (1964). Communication networks. In L. Berkowitz (Ed.), *Advances in experimental social psychology* (vol. 6). New York: Academic Press.

Sherif, M. (1936). *The psychology of social norms*. Oxford: Harper.

Sherif, M. (1966). *Group conflict and cooperation: their social psychology*. London: Routledge & Kegan Paul.

Sherrington, C. (1897). The central nervous system. . In M.A. Foster & C.S. Sherrington (Eds), *Textbook of physiology* (Vol. 3). London: Macmillan.

Shevlin, M., Walker, S., Davies, M.N.O., Banyard, P., & Lewis, C. (2003). Can you judge a book by its cover? Evidence of self–stranger agreement on personality at zero acquaintance. *Personality and Individual Differences, 35*, 1373–1383.

Shotter, J. (1989). Social accountability and the social construction of 'you'. In J. Shotter & K.J. Gergen (Eds), *Texts of identity* (pp. 133–151). London: SAGE. Available at: www.johnshotter.com/papers/Shotter%20You.pdf (accessed 9 December 2013).

Shotter, J. (1990). Social individuality versus possessive individualism: the sounds of silence. In I. Parker & J. Shotter (Eds), *Deconstructing social psychology* (pp. 155–169). London: Routledge.

Shulman, S., & Scharf, M. (2000). Adolescent romantic behaviors and perceptions: age- and gender-related differences, and links with family and peer relationships. *Journal of Research on Adolescence, 10*(1), 99–118.

Siegel, A., & Victoroff, J. (2009). Understanding human aggression: new insights from neuroscience. *International Journal of Law and Psychiatry, 32*(4), 209–215.

Siegler, R.S. (1988). Strategy choice procedures and the development of multiplication skills. *Journal of Experimental Psychology, General, 117*, 258–275.

Siegler, R.S. (1996). *Emerging minds: the process of change in children's thinking.* New York: Oxford University Press.

Siever, L.J. (2008). Neurobiology of aggression and violence. *American Journal of Psychiatry, 165*, 429–442.

Simon, H.A. (1971). Designing organizations for an information-rich world. In M. Greenberger (Ed.), *Computers, communication, and the public interest* (pp. 37–72). Baltimore, MD: The Johns Hopkins Press.

Simons, D.J., & Chabris, C.F. (1999). Gorillas in our midst: sustained inattentional blindness for dynamic events. *Perception, 28*, 1059–1074.

Simons, D.J., & Levin, D.T. (1998). Failure to detect changes to people during a real-world interaction. *Psychonomic Bulletin and Review, 5*, 644–649.

Simpson, B., & Willer, R. (2008). Altruism and indirect reciprocity: The interaction of person and situation in prosocial behavior. *Social Psychology Quarterly, 71*(1), 37–52.

Simpson, S.A., & Harding, A.E. (1993). Predictive testing for Huntington's disease: after the gene. The United Kingdom Huntington's Disease Prediction Consortium. *Journal of Medical Genetics, 30*, 1036–1038.

Sinclair, H.C., Ladny, R.T., & Lyndon, A.E. (2011). Adding insult to injury: effects of interpersonal rejection types, rejection sensitivity, and self-regulation on obsessive relational intrusion. *Aggressive Behavior, 37*(6), 503–520.

Singer, J.E., Brush, C.E., & Lublin, S.C. (1965). Some aspects of deindividuation: identification and conformity. *Journal of Experimental Social Psychology, 1*, 356–378.

Singh, I.L. (1989). Personality correlates and perceptual detectability of locomotive drivers. *Personality and Individual Differences, 10*, 1049–1054.

Singleton, N., & Lewis, G. (2003). *Better or worse: a longitudinal study of adults living in private households in Great Britain.* London: The Stationery Office.

Skinner, B.F. (1948). *Walden two.* Oxford: Macmillan.

Skinner, B.F. (1957). *Verbal behaviour.* New York: Appleton-Century-Crofts.

Skinner, B.F. (1971). *Beyond freedom and dignity.* New York: Knopf/Random House.

Skinner-Buzan, D. (2004). I was not a lab rat. *The Guardian.* Retrieved from http://www.theguardian.com/education/2004/mar/12/highereducation.uk. (accessed 21 June 2014).

Slater, R. (2007). Attachment: theoretical development and critique. *Educational Psychology in Practice, 23*, 205–219.

Slee, P.T., & Rigby, K. (1993). The relationship of Eysenck's personality factors and self-esteem to bully–victim behaviour in Australian schoolboys. *Personality and Individual Differences, 14*, 371–373.

Slininger, D., Sherril, C., & Jankowski, C. (2000). Children's attitudes towards peers with severe disabilities: revisiting contact theory. *Adapted Physical Activity Quarterly, 17*, 176–198.

Smart, J.J.C. (1959). Sensations and brain processes. *Philosophical Review, 68*, 141–156.

Smith, C.A., & Farrington, D.P. (2004). Continuities in antisocial behaviour and parenting across three generations. *Journal of Child Psychology and Psychiatry, 45*(2), 230–247.

Smith, J. (2003). *The nature of personal robbery.* Home Office Research Study 254. London: Home Office.

Smith, J.A. (1999). Identity development during the transition to motherhood: an interpretative phenomenological analysis. *Journal of Reproductive and Infant Psychology, 17*, 281–299.

Smith, J.A. (2004). Reflecting on the development of interpretative phenomenological analysis and its contribution to qualitative research in psychology. *Qualitative Research in Psychology, 1*, 39–54.

Smith, J.A., & Osborn, M. (2003). Interpretative phenomenological analysis. In J. Smith (Ed.), *Qualitative psychology: a practical guide to methods* (pp. 51–80). London: SAGE.

Smith, J.A., & Osborn, M. (2007). Pain as an assault on the self: an interpretative phenomenological analysis. *Psychology and Health, 22*, 517–534.

Smith, M., & Glass, G. (1977). *Meta-analysis of psychotherapy outcome studies.* Baltimore, MD: Johns Hopkins University Press.

Smith, P.K. (2005). Grandparents and grandchildren. *The Psychologist, 18*, 684–687.

Smith, P.K., Cowie, H., & Blades, M. (2011). *Understanding children's development* (5th edn). West Sussex: Wiley-Blackwell.

Smith, S.M., Brown, H.O., Toman, J.E., & Goodman, L.S. (1947). The lack of cerebral effects of d-tubercurarine. *Anesthesiology, 8*, 1–14.

Smith, S.M., Lindsay, R.C.L., Pryke, S., & Dysart, J.E. (2001). Postdictors of eyewitness errors: can false identifications be diagnosed in the cross-race situation? *Psychology, Public Policy, and Law, 7*, 153–169.

Snow, C.E. (1999). Social perspectives on the emergence of language. In B. Macwhinney (Ed.), *The emergence of language* (pp. 257–276). London: Erlbaum.

Snow, R.E. (1969). Unfinished Pygmalion. *Contemporary Psychology*, *14*, 197–199.

Snowden, R., Thompson, P., & Troscianko, T. (2006). *Basic vision: an introduction to visual perception*. Oxford: Oxford University Press.

Snyder, J., & Miene, P.K. (1994). On the functions of stereotypes and prejudice. In M.P. Zanna & J.M. Olson (Eds), *The psychology of prejudice: the Ontario symposium* (pp. 33–54). Hove: Erlbaum.

Social Exclusion Unit (2002). *Reducing re-offending by ex-prisoners*. London: Social Exclusion Unit.

Söderfeldt, M., Söderfeldt, B., Ohlson, C.-G., Theorell, T., & Jones, I. (2000). The impact of sense of coherence and high-demand/low-control job environment on self-reported health, burnout and psychophysiological stress indicators. *Work & Stress*, *14*(1), 1–15.

Soderstrom, H., Tullberg, M., Wikkelso, C., Ekholm, S., & Forsman, A. (2000). Reduced regional cerebral blood flow in non-psychotic violent offenders. *Psychiatry Research*, *98*, 29–41.

Soloff, P.H., Nutche, J., Goradia, D., & Diwadkar, V.A. (2008). Structural brain abnormalities in borderline personality disorder: a voxel-based morphometry study. *Psychiatry Research*, *164*(3), 223–236.

Spann, W. (1975). Rechtsgrundlagen der operativen Sterilisation beim Mann und beider Frau in der Bundesrepublik Deutschland. *Geburtshilfe Frauenheilkunde*, *35*, 501–503.

Spearman, C. (1904). General intelligence objectively determined and measured. *American Journal of Psychology*, *15*, 201–293.

Sperling, J.M., Prvulovic, D., Linden, D.E.J., Singer, W., & Stiml, A. (2006). Neuronal correlates of colour-graphemic synaesthesia: a fMRI study. *Cortex*, *42*(6), 295–303.

Sperry, R. (1968). Hemisphere deconnection and unity in consciousness. *American Psychologist*, *23*, 723–733.

Sperry, R.W. (1964). Problems outstanding in the evolution of brain function. James Arthur Lecture. New York: American Museum of Natural History. Reprinted 1977 in R. Duncan & M. Weston-Smith (Eds), *Encyclopedia of ignorance* (pp. 423–433). Oxford: Pergamon.

Spies, R.A., & Plake, B.S. (2005). *The sixteenth mental measurement yearbook*. Lincoln, NE: Buros Institute of Mental Measurements.

Sroufe, L.A., & Rutter, M. (1984). The domain of developmental psychopathology. *Child Development*, *55*(1), 17–29.

Stangor, C., & Schaller, M. (1996). Stereotypes as individual and collective representations. In C.N. Macrae, M. Hewstone, & C. Stangor (Eds), *Foundations of stereotypes and stereotyping* (pp. 3–37). New York: Guilford Press.

Staske, S. (1998). The normalization of problematic emotion in conversations between close relational partners: interpersonal partner work. *Symbolic Interaction*, *21*, 59–86.

Stasser, G., & Titus, W. (1985). Pooling of unshared information in group decision making: biased information sampling during discussion. *Journal of Personality and Social Psychology*, *48*, 1467–1478.

Stasser, G., & Titus, W. (2003). Hidden profiles: a brief history. *Psychological Inquiry*, *14*, 304–313.

Staub, E. (2000). Genocide and mass-killing: origins, prevention, healing and reconciliation. *Political Psychology*, *21*(2), 367–382.

Steblay, N.M. (1997). Social influence in eyewitness recall: a meta-analytic review of lineup instruction effects. *Law and Human Behavior*, *21*(3), 283.

Steele, C.M. (1997). A threat in the air: how stereotypes shape intellectual identity and performance. *American Psychologist*, *52*(6), 613–629.

Steele, C.M., & Aronson, J. (1995). Stereotype threat and the intellectual test performance of African Americans. *Journal of Personality and Social Psychology*, *69*(5), 797–811.

Steele, C.M., Spencer, S.J., & Aronson, J. (2002). Contending with bias: the psychology of stereotype and social identity threat. In M.P. Zanna (Ed.), *Advances in experimental social psychology* (vol. 34, pp. 277–341). San Diego, CA: Academic Press.

Steele, K.M., Bass, K.E., & Crook, M.D. (1999). The mystery of the Mozart effect: failure to replicate. *Psychological Science*, *10*, 366–369.

Steiner, I.D. (1972). *Group process and productivity*. New York: Academic Press.

Stelmack, R.M., & Stalikas, A. (1991). Galen and the humour theory of temperament. *Personality and Individual Differences*, *12*(3), 255–263.

Stern, W. (1914). *The psychological methods of intelligence testing*. Baltimore MD: Warwick & York, Inc. Retrieved from http://archive.org/stream/psychologicalmet00ster/ psychologicalmet00ster_djvu.txt. (accessed 21 June 2014).

Sternberg, R.J. (1984). Toward a triarchic theory of human intelligence. *Behavioral and Brain Sciences*, *7*, 269–315.

Sternberg, R.J. (2004). The concept of intelligence. In R. Sternberg (Ed.), *Handbook of intelligence* (pp. 3–15). Cambridge: Cambridge University Press.

Sternberg, R.J., Grigorenko, E.L., Ngrosho, D., Tantufuye, E., Mbise, A., Nokes, C., Jukes, M., & Bundy, D.A. (2002). Assessing intellectual potential in rural Tanzanian school children. *Intelligence*, *30*, 141–162.

Stevens, D., Charman, T., & Blair, R.J.R. (2001). Recognition of emotion in facial expressions and vocal tones in children with psychopathic tendencies. *Journal of Genetic Psychology*, *162*(2), 201–211.

Stevens, J.R., Cushman, F.A., & Hauser, M.D. (2005). Evolving the psychological mechanisms for cooperation. *Annual Review of Ecology, Evolution and Systematics*, *36*, 499–518.

Stevens, R. (1996). *Understanding the self*. Milton Keynes: Open University Press/SAGE.

Stevens, R.J., & Slavin, R.E. (1995). The cooperative elementary school: effects on students' achievement, attitudes, and social relations. *American Educational Research Journal*, *32*, 321–351.

Stiles, J., Reilly, J., Paul, B., & Moses, P. (2005). Cognitive development following early brain injury: evidence for neural adaptation. *Trends in Cognitive Sciences*, *9*, 136–143.

Stinson, M., Liu, Y., Saur, R., & Long, G. (1996). Deaf college students' perceptions of communication in mainstream classes. *Journal of Deaf Studies and Deaf Education*, *1*(1), 40–51.

Stitch, S.P., & Ravenscroft, I. (1994). What is folk psychology? *Cognition*, *50*(1–3), 447–468.

Storms, M.D., & Thomas, G.C. (1977). Reactions to physical closeness. *Journal of Personality and Social Psychology*, *35*, 412–418.

Stormshak, E.A., Bellanti, C.J., & Bierman, K.L. (1996). The quality of sibling relationships and the development of social competence and behavioral control in aggressive children. *Developmental Psychology*, *32*, 79–89.

Stott, C., Hutchison, P., & Drury, J. (2001). 'Hooligans' abroad? Inter-group dynamics, social identity and participation in collective 'disorder' at the 1998 World Cup Finals. *British Journal of Social Psychology*, *40*(3), 359–384.

Stott, C., & Reicher, S.D. (1998a). How conflict escalates: the inter-group dynamics of collective football crowd violence. *Sociology*, *32*, 353–377.

Stott, C., & Reicher, S.D. (1998b). Crowd action as intergroup process: introducing the police perspective. *European Journal of Social Psychology*, *28*, 509–529.

Strack, F., Martin, L.L., & Stepper, S. (1988). Inhibiting and facilitating conditions of facial expressions: a non-obtrusive test of the facial feedback hypothesis. *Journal of Personality and Social Psychology*, *54*, 768–777.

Straif, K., Cohen, A., & Samet, J., (Eds) (2013). Air Polution and Cancer. *International Agency for Research on Cancer Scientific Publication No. 161*. Retrieved from http://www.iarc.fr/en/publications/books/sp161/index.php. (accessed 21 June 2014).

Strano, M.M., & Wattai-Queen, J. (2012). Covering your face on Facebook: suppression as identity management. *Journal of Media Psychology*, *24*(4), 166–180.

Strayer, D.L., & Johnston, W.A. (2001). Driven to distraction: dual-task studies of simulated driving and conversing on a cellular phone. *Psychological Science*, *12*, 462–466.

Strickland, B. (1989). Internal–external control expectancies: from contingency to creativity. *American Psychologist*, *44*, 1–12.

Stuart, M. (1999). Getting ready for reading: early phoneme awareness and phonics teaching improves reading and spelling in inner-city second language learners. *British Journal of Educational Psychology*, *69*, 587–605.

Stubblefield, A. (2007). 'Beyond the pale': tainted whiteness, cognitive disability, and eugenic sterilization. *Hypatia: A Journal of Feminist Philosophy*, *22*(2), 162–181. DOI: 10.1111/j.1527-2001.2007.tb00987.

Sulloway, F.J. (2001). Birth order, sibling competition, and human behavior: conceptual challenges in everyday evolutionary psychology. *Studies in Cognitive Systems*, *27*, 39–83.

Sulmont-Rosse, C., Chabanet, C., Issanchou, S., & Koster, E.P. (2008). Impact of the arousal potential of uncommon drinks on the repeated exposure effect. *Food Quality and Preference*, *19*(4), 412–420.

Suls, J., & Bunde, J. (2005). Anger, anxiety and depression as risk factors for cardiovascular disease: the problems and implications of overlapping affective dispositions. *Psychological Bulletin*, *131*(2), 260–300.

Sumner, W. (1906). *Folkways*. New York: Ginn.

Super, C.M., & Harkness, S. (1977). The infants niche in rural Kenya and metropolitan America. In L.L. Adler (Ed.), *Issues in cross-cultural research* (pp. 326–331). New York: Academic Press.

Susi, T., Johannesson, M., & Backlund, P. (2007). *Serious games – An overview*. Skovde: University of Skovde (technical report HS-IKI-TR-07-001).

Swaab, D.F., & Hoffman, M.A. (1990). An enlarged suprachiasmatic nucleus in homosexual men. *Brain Research*, *24*, 141–148.

Swaab, D.F., Gooren, L.J.G., & Hoffman, M.A. (1995). Brain research, gender and sexual orientation. *Journal of Homosexuality*, *28*, 283–301.

Szasz, T.S. (1960). The myth of mental illness. *American Psychologist*, *15*, 113–118.

Taft, M., & Hambly, G. (1986). Exploring the cohort model of spoken word recognition. *Cognition*, *22*, 259–282.

Tajfel, H. (1978). *Differentiation between social groups: studies in the social psychology of intergroup relations*. London: Academic Press.

Tajfel, H. (1979). Individuals and groups in social psychology. *British Journal of Social and Clinical Psychology*, *18*(2), 183–190.

Tajfel, H. (1981). *Human groups and social categories*. Cambridge: Cambridge University Press.

Tajfel, H. (Ed.) (1982). *Social identity and intergroup relations*. Cambridge: Cambridge University Press.

Tajfel, H., Billig, M.G., Bundy, R.P., & Flament, C. (1971). Social categorization and intergroup behaviour. *European Journal of Social Psychology*, *1*, 149–177.

Tajfel, H., & Turner, J.C. (1979). An integrative theory of intergroup conflict. In W.G. Austin & S. Worchel (Eds), *The social psychology of intergroup relations* (pp. 33–47). Monterey, CA: Brooks/Cole.

Tajfel, H., & Wilkes, A. (1963). Classification and quantitative judgement. *British Journal of Social Psychology*, *54*, 101–114.

Talarico, J.M., & Rubin, D.C. (2003). Confidence, not consistency, characterizes flashbulb memories. *Psychological Science*, *14*(5), 455–461.

Talati, A., Bao, Y., Kaufman, J., Shen, L., Schaefer, C.A., & Brown, A.S. (2013). Maternal smoking during pregnancy and bipolar disorder in offspring. *American Journal of Psychiatry*, *170*, 1178–1185.

Taube-Schiff, M., & Lau, M.A. (2008). Major depressive disorder. In M. Hersen & J. Rosqvist (Eds), *Handbook of psychological assessment, case conceptualization, and treatment* (pp. 319–351). New Jersey: John Wiley and Sons.

Taylor, D.W., Berry, P.C., & Block, C.H. (1958). Does group participation when using brainstorming facilitate or inhibit creative thinking? *Administrative Science Quarterly*, *3*(1), 23–47.

Taylor, S.E. (1981). A categorization approach to stereotyping. In D.L. Hamilton (Ed.), *Cognitive processes in stereotyping and intergroup behavior*, (pp. 83–114). Hillsdole, NJ: Erlbaum.

Taylor, S.E., & Brown, J.D. (1988). Illusion and well-being: a social psychological perspective on mental health. *Psychological Bulletin*, 103(2), 193–210.

Taylor, S.E., Klein, L.C., Lewis, B.P., Gruenewald, T.L., Gurung, R.A.R., & Updegraff, J.A. (2000). Biobehavioral responses to stress in females: tend-and-befriend, not fight-or-flight. *Psychological Review*, 107, 411–429.

Temoshok, L., & Fox, B.H. (1984). Coping styles and other psychosocial factors related to medical status and to prognosis in patients with cutaneous malignant melanoma. In B.H. Fox and B.H. Newberry (Eds), *Impact of psychoendocrine systems in cancer and immunity* (pp. 86–146). New York: C.J. Hogrefe.

Terracciano, A., & Costa, P.T., Jr. (2004). Smoking and the Five-Factor Model of personality. *Addiction*, 99, 472–481.

Tesser, A., Gatewood, R., & Driver, M. (1968). Some determinants of gratitude. *Journal of Personality and Social Psychology*, 9, 233–236.

Tetlock, P.E. (1979). Identifying victims of groupthink from public statements of decision makers. *Journal of Personality and Social Psychology*, 37, 1314–1324.

Thaler, R., & Sunstein, C. (2008). *Nudge: The gentle power of choice architecture*. New Haven, CT: Yale.

Thalmayer, A.G., Saucier, G., & Eigenhuis, A. (2011). Comparative validity of brief to medium-length Big Five and Big Six Personality Questionnaires. *Psychological Assessment*, 23(4), 995–1009.

The Economist (2005) Shocking treatment. *The Economist*, www.economist.com/node/4400883 (accessed 16 August 2014).

Thomas, T. (2005). *Sex crime: sex offender and society*. Cullompton, Devon: Willan.

Thomas, W.I., & Znaniecki, F. (1918). *The Polish peasant in Europe and America*. Chicago IL: The University of Chicago Press.

Thompson, E.R. (2008). Development and validation of an international English Big-Five mini-markers. *Personality and Individual Differences*, 45(6), 542–548.

Thompson, M.M., Zanna, M.P., & Griffin, D.W. (1995). Let's not be indifferent about (attitudinal) ambivalence. In R.E. Petty & J.A. Krosnick (Eds), *Attitude strength: antecedents and consequences* (pp. 361–386). Mahwah, NJ: Erlbaum.

Thompson, P. (1980). Margaret Thatcher: a new illusion. *Perception*, 9, 483–484.

Thompson, P. (1982). Perceived rate of movement depends on contrast. *Vision Research*, 22, 377–380.

Thompson, R.A. (2000). The legacy of early attachments. *Child Development*, 71, 145–152.

Thompson, R.H., Cotnoir-Bichelman, N.M., McKerchar, P.M., Tate, T.L., & Dancho, K.A. (2007). Enhancing early communication through infant sign training. *Journal of Applied Behavior Analysis*, 40, 15–23.

Thorndike, R.L. (1968). Review of the book *Pygmalion in the classroom*. *American Educational Research Journal*, 5, 708–711.

Thornton, S. (2008). *Understanding children's development*. London: Palgrave Macmillan.

Tindle, H.A., Chang, Y.F., Kuller, L.H., Manson, J.E., Robinson, J.G., Rosal, M.C., Siegle, G.J., & Matthews, K.A. (2009). Optimism, cynical hostility, and incident coronary heart disease and mortality in the Women's Health Initiative. *Circulation*, 120(8), 656–662.

Tomasello, M. (2000). Do young children have adult syntactic competence? *Cognition*, 74(3), 209–253.

Trask, R.L. (1999). *Language: the basics* (2nd edn). London and New York: Routledge.

Traxler, M.J, & Gernsbacher, M.A. (Eds) (1992). *Handbook of psycholinguistics*. Amsterdam: Elsevier.

Treisman, A.M. (1960). Contextual cues in selective listening. *Quarterly Journal of Experimental Psychology*, 12, 242–244.

Treisman, A.M. (1964). The effect of irrelevant material on the efficiency of selective listening. *American Journal of Psychology*, 77, 533–546.

Treisman, A.M., & Gelade, G. (1980). A feature-integration theory of attention. *Cognitive Psychology*, 12(1), 97–136.

Trepte, S., & Reinecke, L. (2010). Avatar creation and video game enjoyment. *Journal of Media Psychology*, 22(4), 171–184.

Trepte, S., Reinecke, L., & Behr, K.-M. (2009). Creating virtual alter egos or superheroines? Gamers' strategies of avatar creation in terms of gender and sex. *International Journal of Gaming and Computer-Mediated Simulations*, 1(2), 52–76.

Triplett, N. (1898). The dynamogenic factors in pacemaking and competition. *American Journal of Psychology*, 9, 507–533.

Trist, E.L., Susman G.I., & Brown, G.R. (1977). An experiment in autonomous working in an American underground coal mine. *Human Relations*, 30(3), 201–236.

Tropp, L.R., & Pettigrew, T.F. (2005). Relationships between intergroup contact and prejudice among minority and majority status groups. *Psychological Science*, 16(12), 951–957.

Troy, A.S., Shallcross, A.J., & Mauss, I.B. (2013). A person-by-situation approach to emotion regulation: cognitive reappraisal can either help or hurt, depending on the context. *Psychological Science*, 24(12), 2505–2514.

Tseng, W.S. (2001). *Handbook of cultural psychiatry*. San Diego, CA: Academic Press.

Tuckman, B.W. (1965). Developmental sequence in small groups. *Psychological Bulletin*, 63, 384–399.

Tulving, E., & Pearlstone, Z. (1966). Availability versus accessibility of information in memory for words. *Journal of Verbal Learning and Verbal Behavior*, 5, 381–391.

Tulving, E., & Thomson, D.M. (1973). Encoding specificity and retrieval processes in episodic memory. *Psychological Review*, 80, 352–373.

Turkle, S. (1995). *Life on the screen: identity in the age of the internet*. New York: Simon & Schuster.

Turner, J.C. (1975). Social comparison and social identity: some prospects for intergroup behaviour. *European Journal of Social Psychology*, 5, 5–34.

Turner, J.C. (1991). *Social influence*. Belmont, CA: Thomson Brooks/Cole; Buckingham: Open University Press.

Turner, J.C. (1996). Henri Tajfel: an introduction. In W.P. Robinson (Ed.), *Social groups and identities: developing the legacy of Henri Tajfel* (p. 1). London: Routledge.

Turner, J.C., Hogg, M.A., Oakes, P.J., Reicher, S.D., & Wetherell, M.S. (1987). *Rediscovering the social group: a self-categorization theory*. Oxford: Blackwell.

Turner, R.H., & Killian, L.M. (1972). *Collective behaviour* (2nd edn). Englewood Cliffs, NJ: Prentice Hall.

Turner, R.N., & Crisp, R.J. (2010). Imagining intergroup contact reduces implicit prejudice. *British Journal of Social Psychology*, 49, 129–142.

Turner, R.N., Crisp, R.J., & Lambert, E. (2007). Imagining intergroup contact can improve intergroup attitudes. *Group Processes & Intergroup Relations*, 10, 427–441.

Tversky, A., & Kahneman, D. (1974). Judgment under uncertainty: heuristics and biases. *Science*, 185, 1124–1131.

Tversky, A., & Kahneman, D. (1980). Causal schemata in judgments under uncertainty. In M. Fishbein (Ed.), *Progress in social psychology* (vol. 1, pp. 49–72). Hillsdale, NJ: Erlbaum.

Tversky, A., & Kahneman, D. (1983). Extensional versus intuitive reasoning: the conjunction fallacy in probability judgment. *Psychological Review*, 90, 293–315.

Tweney, R.D., Doherty, M.E., Worner, W.J., Pliske, D.B., Mynatt, C.R., Gross, K.A., et al. (1980). Strategies for rule discovery in an inference task. *Quarterly Journal of Experimental Psychology*, 32, 109–123.

Tzeng, O.J.L. (1973). Positive recency effect in a delayed free recall. *Journal of Verbal Learning and Verbal Behavior*, 12, 436–439.

Uher, R., & McGuffin, P. (2008). The moderation by the serotonin transporter gene of environmental adversity in the aetiology of mental illness: review and methodological analysis. *Molecular Psychiatry*, 13(2), 131–146.

UK ECT Review Group (2003). Efficacy and safety of electroconvulsive therapy in depressive disorders: a systematic review and meta-analysis. *The Lancet*, 361, 799–808.

Umiltà, C. (2001). Mechanisms of attention. In B. Rapp (Ed.), *The handbook of cognitive neuropsychology* (pp.135–158). Hove: Psychology Press.

Underwood, B.J. (1957). Interference and forgetting. *Psychological Review*, 64, 49–60.

Underwood, B.J., & Ekstrand, B.R. (1967). Effect of distributed practice on paired-associate learning. *Journal of Experimental Psychology*, Monograph Supplement 1, 73, 1–21.

Underwood, G. (2007). Visual attention and the transition from novice to advanced driver. *Ergonomics*, 50, 1235–1249.

Underwood, J., Baguley, T.S., Banyard, P., Coyne, E., Farrington-Flint, L., & Selwood, I. (2007). *Impact 2007: personalising learning with technology*. Final report. Coventry: British Educational Communication and Technology Agency (BECTA).

Underwood, J., Banyard, P., Betts, L., Farrington-Flint, L., Stiller, J., & Yeomans, S. (2009). *Narrowing the gap: literature review*. Coventry: British Educational Communication and Technology Agency (BECTA).

Underwood, J., Banyard, P., & Davies, M.N.O. (2007). Students in digital worlds: lost in Sin City or reaching Treasure Island? British Learning Through Digital Technologies. *British Journal of Educational Psychology Monograph Series*, 5, 83–99.

UNFPA & HelpAge International (2012). *Ageing in the twenty-first century: a celebration and a challenge*. New York and London: United Nations Population Fund & HelpAge International.

Vaillancourt, T. (2013). Do human females use indirect aggression as an intrasexual competition strategy? *Philosophical Transactions of the Royal Society*, 368, 1–7.

Vainio, S., Heikkilä, M., Kispert, A., Chin, N., & McMahon, A.P. (1999). Female development in mammals is regulated by Wnt–4 signalling. *Nature*, 397, 405–409.

Valenza, E., Simion, F., Macchi Cassia, V., & Umiltà, C. (1996). Face preference at birth. *Journal of Experimental Psychology: Human Perception and Performance*, 22, 892–903.

Van der Kolk, B.A., & Fisler, R. (1995). The psychological processing of traumatic memories: review and experimental confirmation. *Journal of Traumatic Stress*, 8, 505–525.

Van Gompel, R.P.G., Fischer, M.H., Murray, W.S., & Hill, R.L. (2007). Eye-movement research: an overview of current and past developments. In R.P.G. van Gompel, M.H. Fischer, W.S. Murray, & R.L. Hill (Eds), *Eye movements: a window on mind and brain* (pp. 1–28). Oxford: Elsevier.

van Hoof, A. (1999). The identity status field re-reviewed: an update of unresolved and neglected issues with a view on some alternative approaches. *Developmental Review*, 19(4), 497–556.

van IJzendoorn, M.H., Juffer, F., & Poelhuis, C.W.K. (2005). Adoption and cognitive development: a meta-analytic comparison of adopted and nonadopted children's IQ and school performance. *Psychological Bulletin*, 131, 301–316. DOI: 10.1037/0033-2909.131.2.301.

Van Langenhove, L. (1995). The theoretical foundations of experimental psychology and its alternatives. In J.A. Smith, R. Harré, & L. Van Langenhove (Eds), *Rethinking methods in psychology* (pp. 10–24). London: SAGE.

Van Loon, A.J., Tijhuis, M., Surtees, P.G., & Ormel, J. (2001). Personality and coping: their relationship with lifestyle risk factors for cancer. *Personality and Individual Differences*, 31, 541–553.

Van Rossum, J.M. (1966). The significance of dopamine receptor blockade for the mechanism of action of neuroleptic drugs. *Archives Internationales Pharmacodynamie et de Thérapie*, 160, 492–494.

Vaughn, C.E., & Leff, J.P. (1976). The measurement of expressed emotion in the families of psychiatric patients. *British Journal of Social and Clinical Psychology*, 15, 157–165.

Voland, E., Siegelkow, E., & Engel, C. (1991). Cost/benefit oriented parental investment by high status families: The Krummhörn case. *Ethology and Sociobiology*, *12*(2), 105–118.

Volkow, N.D., Ding, Y.-S., Fowler, J.S., Wang, G.J., Logan, J., Gatley, S.J., … Wolf, A.P. (1995). Is methylphenidate like cocaine? Studies on their pharmacokinetics and distribution in human brain. *Archives of General Psychiatry*, *52*, 456–463.

Vrij, A. (2004). Why professionals fail to catch liars and how they can improve. *Legal and Criminological Psychology*, *9*, 159–181.

Vrij, A., Granhag, P.A., & Porter, S. (2010). Pitfalls and opportunities in nonverbal and verbal lie detection. *Psychological Science in the Public Interest*, *11*, 89–121.

Vrij, A., Mann, S., Fisher, R.P., Leal, S., Milne, R., & Bull, R. (2008). Increasing cognitive load to facilitate lie detection: the benefit of recalling an event in reverse order. *Law and Human Behaviour*, *32*, 253–265.

Vygotsky, L.S. (1978). *Mind and society: the development of higher mental processes*. Cambridge, MA: Harvard University Press.

Walk, R.D., & Gibson, E.J. (1961). A comparative and analytical study of visual depth perception. *Psychological Monographs*, *75*, 15.

Walker, F. (2007). Huntington's disease. *The Lancet*, 369, 219–228.

Walkerdine, V. (2002). *Challenging subjects: critical psychology for a new millennium*. Basingstoke: Palgrave.

Wallace, A.R. (1858). *On the tendency of varieties to depart indefinitely from the original type*. Available at: http://people.wku.edu/charles.smith/wallace/S043.htm (accessed 16 August, 2014).

Wallace, D. (2004). *Random acts of kindness: 365 ways to make the world a nicer place*. London: Ebury.

Walther, J., Van De Heide, B., Kim, S.-Y., Westerman, D., & Tong, S. (2008). The role of friends' appearance and behavior on evaluations of individuals on Facebook: are we known by the company we keep? *Human Communication Research*, *34*, 28–49.

Waltz, J.A., Knowlton, B.J., Holyoak, K.J., Boone, K.B., Mishkin, F.S., & de Menezes Santos, M. (1999). A system for relational reasoning in human prefrontal cortex. *Psychological Science*, *10*(2), 119–125. DOI: 10.1111/1467-9280.00118.

Wang, C., & Burris, M. (1997). Photovoice: concept, methodology and use for participatory needs assessment. *Health Education and Behaviour*, *24*, 369–387.

Wang, C.C., & Wang, C.H. (2008). Helping others in online games: prosocial behavior in cyberspace. *CyberPsychology & Behavior*, *11*(3), 344–346.

Wang, Y., Hunt, K., Nazareth, I., Freemantle, N., & Petersen, I. (2013). Do men consult less than women? An analysis of routinely collected UK general practice data. *BMJ Open* 2013;3:e003320 doi:10.1136/bmjopen-2013-003320.

Wansink, B., & Sobal, J. (2007). Mindless eating: The 200 daily food decisions we overlook. *Environment and Behavior*, *39*(1), 106–123.

Ward, T., & Keenan, T. (1999). Child molesters' implicit theories. *Journal of Interpersonal Violence*, *14*(8), 821–838.

Warneken, F., & Tomasello, M. (2009). The roots of human altruism. *British Journal of Psychology*, *100*(3), 455–471.

Wason, P.C. (1960). On the failure to eliminate hypotheses in a conceptual task. *Quarterly Journal of Experimental Psychology*, *12*, 129–140.

Waterman, C.K., & Waterman, A.S. (1975). Fathers and sons: a study of ego identity across two generations. *Journal of Youth and Adolescence*, *4*(4), 331–338.

Watson, D., Clark, L.A., Weber, K., & Assenheimer, J.S. (1995). Testing a tripartite model. 2. Exploring the symptom structure of anxiety and depression in student, adult, and patient samples. *Journal of Abnormal Psychology*, *104*, 15–25.

Watson, D., Clark, L.A., Weber, K., Assenheimer, J.S., Strauss, M.E., & Mccormick, R.A. (1995). Testing a tripartite model .1. Evaluating the convergent and discriminant validity of Anxiety and Depression Symptom Scales. *Journal of Abnormal Psychology*, *104*, 3–14.

Watson, J.B. (1913). Psychology as the behaviorist views it. *Psychological Review*, *20*, 158–177.

Watson, J.B. (1924). *Behaviorism*. New York: People's Institute Publishing Co.

Watson, J.B. (1930). *Behaviorism* (2nd edn). New York: W.W. Norton.

Watson, J.B. & Rayner, R. (1920). Conditioned emotional reactions. *Journal of Experimental Psychology*, *3*, 1–14.

Watson, S.E., & Kramer, A.F. (1999). Object-based visual selective attention and perceptual organization. *Perception & Psychophysics*, *61*, 31–49.

Waugh, N.C. (1970). Primary and secondary memory in short-term retention. In K.H. Pribram & D.E. Broadbent (Eds), *The biology of memory*. New York: Academic Press.

Waugh, N.C., & Norman, D.A. (1965). Primary memory. *Psychological Review*, *72*, 89–104.

Webster, S.D., Mann, R.E., Carter, A.C., Long, J., Milner, R.J., O'Brien, M.D., Wakeling, H.J., & Ray, N.L. (2006). Inter-rater reliability of dynamic risk assessment with sexual offenders. *Psychology, Crime and Law*, *12*(4), 439–452.

Wechsler, D. (1958). *The measurement and appraisal of adult intelligence* (4th edn). Baltimore, MD: Williams & Wilkins.

Weedon, M.N., Lango, H., Lindgren, C.M., Wallace, C., Evans, D.M., Mangino, M., et al. (2008). Genome-wide association analysis identifies 20 loci that influence adult height. *Nature Genetics*, *40*, 575–583.

Weiskrantz, L., Warrington, E.K., Sanders, M.D., & Marshall, J. (1974). Visual capacity in the hemianopic field following a restricted occipital ablation. *Brain*, *97*, 709–728.

Weissenberg, P., & Kavanaugh, M. (1972). The independence of initiating structure and consideration: a review of the evidence. *Personnel Psychology*, *25*, 119–130.

Wellman, H.M., Cross, D., & Watson, J. (2001). Meta-analysis of theory-of-mind development: the truth about false belief. *Child Development*, *72*, 655–684.

Wells, G.L. (1978). Applied eyewitness-testimony research: system variables and estimator variables. *Journal of Personality and Social Psychology*, *36*(12), 1546.

Wells, G.L. (1984). The psychology of lineup identifications. *Journal of Applied Social Psychology*, *14*(2), 89–103.

Wells, G.L., & Olson, E.A. (2003). Eyewitness testimony. *Annual Review of Psychology*, *54*(1), 277–295.

Wentzel, K.R. (1999). Social influences on school adjustment: commentary. *Educational Psychologist*, *34*, 59–69.

Wernicke, C. (1874). *Der aphasische Symptomencomplex. Eine psychologische Studie auf anatomischer Basis.* Breslau: Cohn and Weigert.

Westen, D., & Morrison, K. (2001). A multidimensional meta-analysis of treatments for depression, panic, and generalized anxiety disorder: an empirical examination of the status of empirically supported therapies. *Journal of Consulting and Clinical Psychology*, *69*(6), 875–899.

Wetherell, M., & Edley, N. (1999). Negotiating hegemonic masculinity: imaginary positions and psycho-discursive practices. *Feminism & Psychology*, *9*(3), 335–356.

Wetherell, M., & Potter, J. (1992). *Mapping the language of racism: discourse and the legitimation of racism.* Hemel Hempsted: Harvester Wheatsheaf.

Whisman, M. (1993). Mediators and moderators of change in cognitive therapy of depression. *Psychological Bulletin*, *114*(2), 248–265.

Whitbourne, S.K. (2001). Stability and change in adult personality: contributions of process-oriented perspectives. *Psychological Inquiry*, *12*(2), 101–103.

White, B.A., Horwath, C.C., & Conner, T.S. (2013). Many apples a day keep the blues away: daily experiences of negative and positive affect and food consumption in young adults. *British Journal of Health Psychology*, *18*(4), 782–798.

Whitney, P. (1993). *The psychology of language.* Pacific Grove, CA: Wadsworth.

Whittlesea, B.W.A., & Dorken, M.D. (1993). Incidentally, things in general are particularly determined: an episodic account of implicit learning. *Journal of Experimental Psychology, General*, *122*, 227–248.

Whitty, M.T. (2008). Revealing the 'real' me; searching for the 'actual' you: presentations of self on an internet dating site. *Computers in Human Behaviour*, *24*, 1707–1723.

Whitty, M.T., & McLaughlin, D. (2007) Online recreation: The relationship between loneliness, Internet self-efficacy and the use of the Internet for entertainment purposes. *Computers in Human Behavior*, *23*(3), 1435–1446.

Wicklund, R.A. (1975). *Objective self-awareness.* New York: Academic Press.

Wiener, N. (1948). *Cybernetics, or control and communication in the animal and the machine.* Cambridge, MA: Technology Press.

Wilke, H., & Lanzetta, J.T. (1970). The obligation to help: The effects of amount of prior help on subsequent helping behavior. *Journal of Experimental Social Psychology*, *6*(4), 488–493.

Wilke, H., & Lanzetta, J.T. (1982). The obligation to help: Factors affecting response to help received. *European Journal of Social Psychology*, *12*(3), 315–319.

Wilkinson, S., & Kitzinger, C. (1993). *Heterosexuality.* London: SAGE.

Williams, D. (1996). *Autism: an inside-out approach. An innovative look at the 'mechanics' of 'autism', and its developmental 'cousin'.* London: Jessica Kingsley.

Williams, G.A. (2003). Intrapersonal and extrapersonal factors in stressor perceptions, coping and strain among NHS staff. Unpublished PhD thesis. London South Bank University.

Williams, J. (2013). Financial analysts and the false consensus effect. *Journal of Accounting Research*, *51*(4), 855–907.

Williams, J.E., Paton, C.C., Siegler, I.C., Eigenbrodt, M.L., Nieto, F.J., & Tyroler, H.A. (2000). Anger proneness predicts coronary heart disease risk: prospective analysis from the Artherosclerosis Risk in Communities (ARIC) Study. *Circulation*, *101*, 2034–2039.

Williams, K.D., & Karau, S.J. (1991). Social loafing and social compensation: the effects of expectations of co-worker performance. *Journal of Personality and Social Psychology*, *61*, 570–581.

Williams, R.B. (2001). Hostility: effects on health and the potential for successful behavioral approaches to prevention and treatment. In A. Baum, T.A. Revenson, & J.E. Singer (Eds) *Handbook of health psychology*. Mahwah, NJ: Erlbaum.

Willig, C., & Stainton Rogers, W. (Eds) (2007). *SAGE handbook of qualitative research in psychology.* London: SAGE.

Willig, C., & Stainton Rogers, W. (Eds) (2008). *The SAGE handbook of qualitative research in psychology.* London: SAGE.

Wilson, D. (2009). *A history of British serial killing: the shocking account of Jack the Ripper, Harold Shipman and beyond.* London: Hatchette Digital.

Wilson, G., & Rahman, Q. (2005). *Born gay: the psychobiology of sexual orientation.* London: Owen.

Wilson, G., & Rahman, Q. (2008). *Born gay: the psychobiology of sex orientation* (2nd edn). London: Peter Owens.

Wilson, G.T. (2011). Behavior therapy. In R. Corsini & D. Wedding (Eds), *Current psychotherapies* (9th edn). Florence, KY: Cengage Learning.

Wilson, R.J., Picheca, J., & Prinzo, M. (2005). *Circles of support and accountability: an evaluation of the pilot project in South-Central Ontario.* Ottawa: Correctional Service of Canada.

Wilson, T.D. (2005). The message is the method: celebrating and exporting the experimental approach. *Psychological Inquiry*, *16*(4), 185–193.

Wimmer, H., & Perner, J. (1983). Beliefs about beliefs: representation and constraining function of wrong beliefs in young children's understanding of deception. *Cognition*, *13*, 103–128.

Winch, A. (2013) Want to explore women's relationships? Forget the science. *The Guardian*, 18 November, www.theguardian.com/commentisfree/2013/nov/18/womens-relationships-science-research-indirectly-competitive (accessed 9 December 2013).

Windelband, W. (1894/1998). History and natural science (trans. J.T. Lamiell). *Theory & Psychology*, *8*(1), 6–22.

Winder, B., & Banyard, P. (2012). *A psychologist's casebook of crime: from arson to voyeurism.* London: Palgrave Macmillan.

Winder, B.C., & Gough, B. (2010). 'I never touched anybody – that's my defence': understanding the world of internet sex offenders using interpretative phenomenological analysis. *Journal of Sexual Aggression, 16*(2), 125–141.

Winder, B., Gough, B., & Seymour-Smith, S. (2014, in press). Stumbling into sexual crime: the passive perpetrator in accounts by male internet sex offenders. *Archives of Sexual Behavior.*

Winder, B., Lievesley, R., Elliott, H.J., Norman, C., & Kaul, A. (2014). Understanding the journeys of high risk male sex offenders voluntarily receiving medication to reduce their sexual preoccupation and/or hypersexuality. In D.T. Wilcox, T. Garrett, & L. Harkin, (Eds), *Sex offender treatment: a case study approach to issues and interventions.* Chichester: Wiley & Sons.

Winder, B., Lievesley, R., Kaul, A., Elliott, H.J., Thorne, K., & Hocken, K. (2014). Preliminary evaluation of the use of pharmacological treatment with convicted sexual offenders experiencing high levels of sexual preoccupation, hypersexuality and sexual compulsivity. *Journal of Forensic Psychiatry and Psychology, 25*(2), 176–194.

Winnicott, D.W. (1964). *The child, the family, and the outside world.* Harmondsworth: Penguin.

Winston, A.S., & Blais, D.J. (1996). What counts as an experiment? A transdisciplinary analysis of textbooks, 1930–1970. *American Journal of Psychology, 109*(4), 599–616.

Winter, J.S.D., & Couch, R.M. (1995). Sexual differentiation. In P. Felig, J.D. Baxter, & L.A. Frohman (Eds), *Endocrinology and metabolism* (3rd edn, pp. 1053–1104). New York: McGraw-Hill.

Wise, R.A. (2004). Dopamine, learning and motivation. *Nature Reviews Neuroscience, 5*, 483–494.

Wisman, M. (1993). Mediators and moderators of change in cognitive therapy of depression. *Psychological Bulletin, 114*, 248–265.

Witelson, S.F., Beresh, H., & Kigar, D.L. (2006). Intelligence and brain size in 100 postmortem brains: sex, lateralization and age factors. *Brain, 129*, 386–398.

Witelson, S.F., Kigar, D.L., Scamvougeras, A., Kideckel, D.M., Buck, B., Stanchev, P.L., Bronskill, M., & Black, S. (2008). Corpus callosum anatomy in right-handed homosexual and heterosexual men. *Archives of Sexual Behavior, 37*(6), 857–863.

Wixted, J.T. (2004a). The psychology and neuroscience of forgetting. *Annual Review of Psychology, 55*, 235–269.

Wixted, J.T. (2004b). On common ground: Jost's (1897) law of forgetting and Ribot's (1881) law of retrograde amnesia. *Psychological Review, 111*, 864–879.

Wixted, J.T. (2005) A theory about why we forget what we once knew. *Current Directions in Psychological Science, 14*, 6–9.

Wojcieszak, M.E. (2011). Computer-mediated false consensus: Radical online groups, social networks and news media. *Mass Communication and Society, 14*(4), 527–546.

Woldorff, M.G., Gallen, C.C., Hampson, S.R., Hillyard, S.A., Pantev, C., Sobel, D., & Bloom, F.E. (1993). Modulation of early sensory processing in human auditory cortex during auditory selective attention. *Proceedings of the National Academy of Sciences, 90*, 8722–8726.

Wolf, G., & Kelly, K. (2014). *Quantified Self. Knowledge through numbers.* https/quantifiedself.com (accessed 16 August 2014).

Wolfberg, P.J., & Schuler, A.L. (1993). Integrated play groups: a model for promoting the social and cognitive dimensions of play in children with autism. *Journal of Autism and Developmental Disorders, 23*(3), 467–489.

Wolpe, J. (1958). *Psychotherapy by reciprocal inhibition.* Stanford, CA: Stanford University Press.

Wood, D., Bruner, J., & Ross, G. (1976). The role of tutoring in problem solving. *Journal of Child Psychology and Psychiatry and Allied Disciplines, 17*(2), 89–100.

Wood, R.T.A., & Griffiths, M.D. (2007). Online data collection from gamblers: Methodological issues. *International Journal of Mental Health and Addiction, 5*, 151–163.

Woodward, J. (1958). *Management and technology* (vol. 3). London: The Stationery Office.

Woodward, S. (2007). *Why women wear what they wear.* Oxford: Berg.

Woolfenden, G.E. (1984). *The Florida scrub jay: Demography of a cooperative-breeding bird.* Princeton NJ: Princeton University Press.

Worchel, S. (1979). Co-operation and the reduction of intergroup conflict: some determining factors. In W.G. Austin & S. Worchel (Eds), *The social psychology of intergroup relations* (pp. 262–273). Monterey, CA: Brooks/Cole.

World Health Organisation. (1946). Preamble to the constitution of the World Health Organisation as adopted by the International Health Conference, New York, 19–22 June 1946, and entered into force on 7th April 1948.

World Health Organisation. (1992). *The ICD-10 classification of mental and behavioural disorders: clinical descriptions and diagnostic guidelines* (vol. 1). New York: World Health Organisation.

World Health Organisation (1997). *WHOQOL: Measuring the quality of life.* World Health Organisation. Retrieved from http://www.who.int/mental_health/media/en/68.pdf. (accessed 21 June 2014).

World Health Organisation (2013). *Gender, Health and Ageing.* WHO. Retrieved from http://www.who.int/gender/documents/en/Gender_Ageing.pdf. (accessed 21 June 2014).

Wright, D.B., & Loftus, E.F. (2008). Eyewitness memory. In G. Cohen & M.A. Conway (Eds), *Memory in the real world* (3rd edn, pp. 91–106). Hove: Psychology Press.

Wright, D.B., & Stroud, J.N. (2002). Age differences in lineup identification accuracy: people are better with their own age. *Law and Human Behavior, 26*(6), 641–654.

Wright, M.F., & Li, Y. (2011). The associations between young adults' face-to-face prosocial behaviors and their online prosocial behaviors. *Computers in Human Behavior, 27*(5), 1959–1962.

Wright, S.C., Aron, A., McLaughlin-Volpe, T., & Ropp, S.A. (1977). The extended contact effect: knowledge of cross-group friendships and prejudice. *Journal of Personality and Social Psychology, 73*, 73–90.

Wundt, W. (1862). *Beiträge zur Theorie der Sinneswahrnehmung* [*Contributions to the theory of sensory perception*]. Leipzig und Heidelberg: C.F. Winter.

Wundt, W. (1873). *Principles of physiological psychology*. Leipzig: Engelmann.

Wynn, K. (1990). Children's understanding of counting. *Cognition*, *36*(2), 155–193.

Wyvell, C.L., & Berridge, K.C. (2000). Intra-accumbens amphetamine increases the conditioned incentive salience of sucrose reward: enhancement of reward 'wanting' without enhanced 'liking' or response reinforcement. *Journal of Neuroscience*, *20*(21), 8122–8130.

Yalom, I., & Josselson, R. (2011). Existential psychotherapy. In R.J. Corsini & D. Wedding (Eds), *Current psychotherapies* (9th edn, pp. 310–341). Florence, KY: Cengage Learning.

Yang, Y., Raine, A., Narr, K.L., Colletti, P., & Toga, A.W. (2009). Localization of deformations within the amygdala in individuals with psychopathy. *Archives of General Psychiatry*, *66*(9), 986–994.

Yechiam, E., Veinott, E.S., Busemeyer, J.R., & Stout, J.C. (2007). Cognitive models for evaluating basic decision processes in clinical populations. In R. Neufeld (Ed.), *Advances in clinical cognitive science: formal modeling and assessment of processes and symptoms*. Washington, DC: APA Publications.

Yee, N., & Bailenson, J. (2009). The difference between being and seeing: the relative contribution of self-perception and priming to behavioral changes via digital self-representation. *Media Psychology*, *12*(2), 195–209.

Yeung, N.C.J., & von Hippel, C. (2008). Stereotype threat increases the likelihood that female drivers in a simulator run over jaywalkers. *Accident Analysis & Prevention*, *40*(2), 667–674.

Yuille, J.C., & Tollestrup, P.A. (1990). Some effects of alcohol on eyewitness memory. *Journal of Applied Psychology*, *75*(3), 268.

Zaccaro, S.J. (1984). Social loafing: the role of task attractiveness. *Personality and Social Psychology Bulletin*, *10*, 99–106.

Zajonc, R.B. (1965). Social facilitation. *Science*, *149*, 269–274.

Zajonc, R.B. (1968). Attitudinal effects of mere exposure. *Journal of Personality and Social Psychology*, Monograph Supplement 2, Part 2, *9*, 1–27.

Zarkadi, T., Wade, K.A., & Stewart, N. (2009) Creating fair line-ups for suspects with distinctive features. *Psychological Science*, *20*, 1448–1453.

Zetzsche, T., Frodl, T., Preuss, U.W., Schmitt, G., Seifert, D., Leinsinger, G., … Meisenzahl, E.M. (2006). Amygdala volume and depressive symptoms in patients with borderline personality disorder. *Biological Psychiatry*, *60*, 302–310.

Zhao, S., Grasmuck, S., & Martin, J. (2008). Identity construction on Facebook: digital empowerment in anchored relationships. *Computers in Human Behavior*, *24*, 1816–1836.

Zimbardo, P.G. (1969). The human choice: individuation, reason, and order vs. deindividuation, impulse and chaos. In W.J. Arnold & D. Levine (Eds), *Nebraska Symposium on Motivation* (pp. 237–307). Lincoln, NB: University of Nebraska Press.

Zuberbühler, K. (2002). A syntactic rule in forest monkey communication. *Animal Behaviour*, *63*(2), 293–299.

INDEX

Tables and Figures are indicated by page numbers in bold print.

abnormal, concept of 30, 427, 428–9
abnormal psychology *see* psychopathology
action research 282, 283
Adams, Douglas 3
adaptive character of thought-rational (ACT-R) 117
addictive behaviour 218, 219, 378, 472–3
Adey, Christian 150, 318
adolescence 348–52
    cognitive development 349–50
    conduct disorder 351–2, 353
    conflict with parents 349
    decision making 350
    drug abuse 340
    emotional development 351–2
    fear of rejection 216
    friendships 351
    identity formation 350–**1**
    mood disruption 349
    risky behaviour 351, 352
    stereotypes 348
    'storm and stress' 348–9
Adorno, T.W. et al 250
adulthood:
    stage model 353–**4**
    early adulthood 354–5
        cognitive wellbeing 355
        health 355
        identity 354
        relationships 354
        sensory decline 355
    middle adulthood 355–7
        memory 357
        menopause 356
        mid-life crisis 356
    ageing:
        cognitive ageing 357–8, 400
        continuing to work 361
        dementia 357
        fluid/crystalised abilities 357–8
        frontal lobe hypothesis 358
        mental stimulation 361
        nutrition 361
        physical activity 360, 361
        speed of processing 358
        stereotypes 359
        wellbeing 359, 360
aggression 214, 220–1
    and bystanders 264–5, 272–4
    catharsis 249
    crowds and deindividuation 235
    cyberaggression 272
    definition 493
    frustration-aggression hypothesis 249–50

aggression *cont.*
    low empathetic response 221
    reactive 222
    see also violent offending
Ainsworth, Mary 308
Ainsworth, Mary et al 307, 308
Ajzen, I. 269
alcoholism 473
allostasis 476
Allport, G.W. 235, 255, 256
Altemeyer, B. 250
altruism and cooperation 10–12
    charity donations research 274
    evolutionary models 270–1
    online prosocial behaviour 272
    theories of prosocial behaviour 271–2
American Psychological Association 19, 66, 399, 470
American Psychologist 285, 399
amphetamine 189
Anderson, R.C. and Pichert, J.W. 85
animal studies 32–3, 34
ant-social personality disorder 442
anthropocentrism 22
anthropological methods 10
anthropomorphism 14
anti-Semitism 250
antidepressants 434, 462
antipsychotics 462
Antonovsky, A. 381
anxiety 215, 435, 437, 438, 476
    and pain 481
anxiolytics drugs 462
applied psychology 30, 31, 422–3
Archimedes 118
Arnett, J.J. 291, 349, 353–4
Arnett, J.J. and Balle-Jensen, L. 351
artificial intelligence (AI) 70
Asperger, Hans 341
Atkinson, R.C. and Shiffrin, R.M. 78
attachment 268–70, 307–9, **308**, 338
attention 93–4, 104–8
    auditory 104–7
    and awareness 108–9
    negative priming 358
    in older adults 358
    perceptual load 107
    types 104
    visual 107–8
attention deficit hyperactivity disorder (ADHD) 333, 344
attitudes 268–70
    and behaviour 269
    research 268–9
    theory of planned behaviour (TPB) 269–70
attributions 261–8
    applications 267, 268
    correspondent inference theory (CIT) 262

attributions *cont.*
  covariation model 263
  errors:
    actor-observer effect 265–6
    false consensus effect (FCE) 266
    fundamental attribution error (FAE) **263**–4
    group attribution error (GAE) 264, 266
    self-serving bias (SBB) 266–7
    ultimate attribution error (UAE) 265
atypical development:
  attention deficit hyperactivity disorder (ADHD) 333, 344
  autism 333, 334, 335–6, 341, 342, 343
  barriers to inclusion 344
  brain abnormalities 333
  critical/sensitive periods 337–8
  developmental lag 336–7
  Down syndrome 334, 335
  dyslexia 340
  external factors 339–44
  factors 332–3
  genetic factors 334, 335
  Huntington's disease 334, 335
  labelling 340–1, 342
    changes in descriptions 341
    comorbidity 341
    Diagnostic and Statistical Manual (DSM) 340–1, 342
    International Classification of Diseases (ICD) 340
  learning:
    appropriate interactions 343
    and expectations 339–40, 342
    integrated play groups (IPGs) 343
    learning environment 343–4
    with others 342, 343
    zone of proximal development 319, 320, 343, 399
  learning difficulties 336–7
  medical and social models of disability 344–5
  phenylketonuria (PKU) 334, 335
  school inclusion 344–5
audition 96–8
auditory attention 104–7
  attenuating filter model **106**
  cocktail party effect 104–5
  dichotic listening task **105**
  late selection model **106**–7
  selective filter model 105, **106**
Auer, M. and Griffiths, M.D. 62
Augustine, St 134
authoritarianism 250–1
autism 333, 334, 335–6
  'extreme male brain' 335
  studies with twins (Wong, C. et al) 335–6
  and theory of mind 342
automatic thoughts 453
avatars 416–**17**
avoidant personality disorder 442
awareness 108–9
  visual neglect 109

Baars, B.J. et al 139
Baddeley, A.D. and Hitch, G.J. 79, 80
Bandura, A. 250, 271, 495
Baron-Cohen, Simon **335**
Baron-Cohen, Simon et al 334

Bartlett, Frederic 34, 70, 84–5, 407
Beck, A. 453
Beck, A. et al 33
Behavioural Insights Team 291
behaviourism 32–4, 423
beliefs and desires 44, 47
Bell-Magendie law 166–7
Benson, P.L. et al 272
Bentall, Richard 438
Berndt, T.J. 351
Berntsen, D. and Thomsen, D.K. 88
Berserkers 12
Binder, J. et al 256
Binet, Alfred 27, 364, 390–1, 392–3
Bjork, R.A. and Whitten, W.B. 79
'black identity' 291
Blackmer, E.R. and Mitton, J.L. 137
Blackmore, Susan 16
Blair, R.J.R. 222
Blair, Tony **233**
blank slate theory 32
Blos, P. 349
Bock, J.K. and Levelt, W.J.M. 136–8, 147
borderline personality disorder 299, 442
Boroditsky, L. et al 134
botox 187, 188
Bowlby, J. 307, 338, 354
Boyd, R. and Richerson, P.J. 17
Bradshaw, C.P. et al 327
brain:
  activity and power 176
  in adolescence 350
  and atypical development 333
  as biological machine 151
  in Cartesian dualism 41
  communicating with computers 165
  and computer programs 116
  development 159, 333
  disrupted development 333
  double dissociation 97
  and emotions 212–16
  evolution 13, 14, 15
  hearing 97, 150
  history of research 150
  and intelligence 397, 401
  and language 150, 161
  and memory 150, 162
  in middle adulthood 356
  and movement 166
  and pathology 433
  and perception 70, 100
  personality change 161, 162
  and psychopathy 221–2
  reward pathways 218–19
  scanning 38–9, 43, 189, 190, 212, 221
  sex differences 200
  sexual orientation 204–5
  social brain hypothesis 13–14, 15, 16
  speech production 150
  synaesthesia 103
  and thinking 24, 25
  and vision **95**–6
  see also mind-body problem

brain structure:
  amygdala 162, 214, 221
  anterior cingulate cortex 222
  basal ganglia 163
  brain stem 166
  cerebellum 165–6
  cerebral cortex **160**–2
  cerebral hemispheres **158**, 160
  colliculi 165
  corpus callosum 160
  cyngulate gyrus 162
  dorsal lateral prefrontal cortex 350
  endocrine system 164, 165, 433
  frontal lobe 358
  glial cells 178
  grey and white matter 167
  hippocampus 157, 162, 221
  hypothalamus 156, 157, 164–5, 200, 204, 205
  limbic system 162, 222
  lobes **160**, 161, 221
  medulla oblngata 166
  memes 17
  metencephalon 165–6
  midbrain (mesencephalon) 165
  motor cortex 160, 160–1
  myelencephalon 166
  neocortex 15
  neurones 155, 176–8, **177**, 178–84
  neurotransmitters 184–90
  pituitary gland 165
  planes **158**
  plasticity 333
  pons 165, 166
  protection 167
  reticular formation 165
  and structure of nervous system 155, **156**
  tectum 165
  tegmentum 165
  terminology 156, **157**
  thalamus 164
  see also nervous system
Brazil 405
Bristol, St Paul's riots 237
British Journal of Psychology 52
British Psychological Society (BPS) 55
Broadbent, Donald 77, 105, 106
Broca, Paul 150
Broks, Paul 191
Brown, Ann et al 343
Brown, G.D.A. et al 84
Bryden, M.P. and MacRae, L. 161
Buchanan, C.M. et al 349
Burt, M.R. 247
Burwood, S. et al 46
Butterworth, G.E. 302
Buzan-Skinner, Deborah 33
Byne, W. et al 204
bystander behaviour 264–5, 272–4

Cacioppo, J.T. et al 377
Cannon, W.B. 211
Caplan, N. and Neslon, S. 289
Carlsson, Arvid 186

Carroll, John 394
Carstensen, L.L. 360
catharsis 249
Cattell, Raymond 370–1, 394
Centre for Cognitive Ageing and Cognitive Epidemiology (CCACE) 359
change:
  motivation to change 460
  readiness to change 461
change blindness (CB) 108–9
Cherry, E.C. 104–5
children:
  bullying 327, 344–5
  child soldiers **309**
  cognitive development 34, 39, 316–20
    assimilation 317
    cultural tools 316, 319
    and environment 319
    scaffolding 319, 320
    and social development 319–20
    stages (Piaget) 316–19, **317**, **318**
    zone of proximal development 319, 320, 343, 399
  early years *see* infant development
  family background 339
  language development:
    critical period in 337
    grammatical awareness 320–1
    language acquisition device (LAD) 320
  mathematics 323–5
    concepts and procedures 324–5
    counting principles 323–4
    cultural differences 323
  Montessori learning 328
  moral development 327, 328
    distributive justice task 328
    prosocial reasoning tasks 328
    stages (Kohlberg) 327
  peers and friends 325–7, **326**
    in emotional development 326–7
    and learning 326
    sex differences 325, 326
  poverty 339
  reading skills 321–2
    phonics teaching 322
    phonological awareness 321–2
    reading instruction 322
    reciprocal teaching 343
  school readiness 328
  school-led development 321–2, 323–5
  severe deprivation 338
  sexualisation of 65–6
  social development and school 325
  social learning 271
  see also adolescence; atypical development; infant development; learning
China 428
Chomsky, Noam 70, 133, 320
Christiansen, M.H. and Kirby, S. 132
Christopher, J.C. and Hickinbottom, S. 286, 287
chromosomes 334
Cialdini, R.B. et al 271
citations 54
Clarke, Kenneth and Mamie 283

Coates, J. and Vickerman, P. 344–5
cognitive behavioural therapy (CBT) 433–4, 452–8
    ABCDE model 455, **456**
    applications 457, 458
    behavioural therapy 456–7
    cognitive model 453–4
    cognitive techniques 454
    cognitive triad **454**
    formulation 454, **455**
    for pain 481
    socratic questioning 454
    thinking errors 455
cognitive development:
    in adolescence 349–50
    of children 34, 39, 316–20
    and cognitive ageing 357–8, 400
cognitive neuroscience 35
cognitive psychology:
    computers/robots and people **70**
    development 34, 70
    key issues 70–1
Coleman, J.C. 351
collective consciousness 235
communication online 58
comparative methods of study 10
complexity of human behaviour 10–11
computerised therapy 464
conditional beliefs 453
conditioning 32–4, 456
conditions of worth 458
conduct disorder 351–2, 353
confidentiality 55
consciousness 15, 16, 155
    and behaviourism 32
    biological adaption 31
consent 55
contingencies of reinforcement 33
conversation 14–15, 307
Copernicus 6
Coping Orientation to Problems Experience (COPE) scale 478
core beliefs 454
core effect 210
Corneille, O. et al 245–6
corporate manslaughter 494
Costa Jr, P.T. and McCrae, R.R. 373
Cowan, N. 77
Craik, F.I.M. and Lockhart, R.S. 80
creative intelligence 396
Crick, Francis 43
crime *see* forensic psychology
Crime Survey for England and Wales 493
Criminal Justice Act (2003) 495
critical psychology (CP) 278–9, 280
    criticality 279
critical social psychology (CSP):
    experimental methods 281
    feminist approaches 284
    ideologies 285–7
    individualism and collectivism 287–9
    methodology 281–2
    power 283–5
    psychology and everyday life 289–91

crowd behaviour 226, 234–7
    deindividuation 235–6, 236–7
    group mind 235
    social identity accounts 237
    see also prejudice and discrimination
Crowe, Michael 487
Crundall, David 62
culture:
    as adaptive trait 17
    conformist and prestige biases 17, 18
    definitions 16
    dual-inheritance model 17
    and evolution 16, 17
    and memes 16–17
    and mental illness 428
Curtiss, S. 338

dangerous disorders 429
Danziger, K. 290–1
Darwin, Charles 6–7, 22, 23, 45, 212
Dawkins, R. 7, 16, 17
Deary, Ian **359**
DeCasper, A.J. et al 304
DeCasper, A.J. and Fifer, W.P. 303
defence mechanisms 450, 452
deindividuation 235–6, 236–7
Dell, G.S. 138–9, 140
delusions 440
demand characteristics 279
dementia 357
deoxyribonucleic acid (DNA) 176, 334
dependant personality disorder 442
depression 433, 437
    antidepressants 434, 462
    prevalence 428
    symptoms 437
    therapies 464
Descartes, René 39–41, 288
descriptive statistics 52
desensitisation 456
determinism 22–3
    and free will 31
detoxification 462
Deutsch, J.A. and Deutsch, D. 106–7
developmental psychology: scope and key issues 294
deviance 429
diabetes 472
Diagnostic and Statistical Manual (DSM) 340–1, 342, 428, 441
Dialectical Behavior Therapy (DBT) 457
Diamond, Milton 199
digital domains 413, 414
digital selves 414
Dijkstra, A. and De Vries, H. 480
Dilthey, Wilhelm 24, 25
discourse analysis 410, 411
discursive psychology 52
disorders and normality 429, 430
distress 429, 431, 476
Dollard, J. et al 249
dominant discourses 284
Donaldson, Margaret 318
Donders, F.C. 27

INDEX

dopamine (DA) 184, 185, 186, 187, 188, 218–19, 439
Dorling et al 475
DRD2 gene 473
dreams 30, 452
drugs:
   aberrant salience 190
   abuse 340
   addiction 218
   antipsychotics 188, 189–90, 191
   psychotropic 462–3
   for schizophrenia 188, 189–90, 191
   smart drugs 188
   used with CBT 457, 458
Drury, J. et al 236, 238
Duckitt, J. 254
Dunbar, Robin **12**, 15, 16
dysfunction 429

ears:
   cochlear implants 97–**8**
   pathway to brain 97
   structure **96**–7
Ebbinghaus, Hermann 29, 82
ego 450
Ehrlich, K.B. et al 349
Ekman, P. 211
electroconvulsive therapy (ECT) 463
electroencephalography (EEG) **172**, 212, 213
Ellis, Albert 453
Ellis, L. and Ames, M.A. 203–4
Elms, A.C. 279
emotional development:
   in adolescence 351–2
   children 326–7
emotions 210–16
   biases in processing **215**–16
   classification 211–12
   conditioning 33
   definition 210
   early theories 211
   emotional health through adulthood (Carstensen, L.L. et al) 360
   emotionality on HEXACO model 374
   event-related potentials 213, 214
   in facial expressions 210, 211, 213, 221, 301
   fight-or-flight response 212, 381, 476
   and mindfulness 217
   neural pathways 212–**13**
   and psychiatric disorder 219–20
   recognition of 214
   top-down processing 214
   verbal expressions 211–12
empathy 58, 221, 222, 442
environment and health 474–5
epigenetics 17–18, 401
episodic analgesia 481
epistemology 39, 281
Erikson, E. 350, 356
ethnocentrism 248–9, 250, 251, 286
ethnomethodology 409
eugenics 390, 391, 397
Euler and Weitzel 12
Euripides 134

eustress 476
event-related potentials 213, 214, 302
Everitt, Barry **219**
evolution:
   concept of fitness 7, 8
   and cooperation 270–1
   human evolution 7–8, 9–10, 15, **23**
      see also brain; genes; kin selection
   natural selection 7
   primates **8**–9, 13, **14**
   relationship to culture 17
exam revision 88–9
exhibitionism 489, 491, 492
existentialism 434
expectations and behaviour 339–40
experimental methodology 34–5, 62–4, 281
experimenter effects 279
explanatory pluralism 47
eye gaze 63
eyes:
   primary visual pathway **95**–6
   structure **94**
eyewitness memory 85–8, 487–8
   line-ups 87, 488
   misidentification 87, 487
   reconstructive processes 86
Eysenck, Hans 371–2, 393, 465

Facebook 414, 416
factor analysis 369, 392–3
families, studies of 472–3
Fantz, R. 301
Fechner, Gustav 27
feminist perspectives 284
fight-or-flight 212, 381, 476
Flower, L. and Hayes, J.R. 146–7
Flynn, James 399–400, 401
folk psychology 44–5, 47, 405
Folkman, S. and Lazarus, R.S. 476, 477
forensic psychology 484–98
   criminal justice system 484
   detecting deception 484–6
      counter measures 485
      polygraph 485–6
      Silent Talker 486
   end-to-end management 497
   eyewitness testimony 484, 487–8
      estimator variables 487
      system variables 488
      weapon focus **488**
   false confessions 484, 486–7
   imprisonment 495–6, 497, 498
      resettlement 496, 497–8
      risk assessment 496
      treatment in prison 496
   lie detection 485–6
   multi agency public protection arrangements (MAPPA) 497–8
   offender profiling 484
   restorative justice 496
   sex offenders 486
   sexual offending 489–92
   Social Exclusion Unit 497

577

forensic psychology *cont.*
  thoroughcare 497
  violent offending 492, 493–5
Fraser et al 475
free association 451
free will 30, 31
Freud, Anna 349
Freud, Sigmund 23, 29–30, 135, 249, 349, 435, 470
  psychodynamic therapy 450, 451, 452
Friedman, Meyer and Rosenman, Ray 379
functional magnetic resonance imaging (fMRI) 39, 189, 212
functionalism 31, 32
Funder, D.C. and Ozer, D.J. 376
Fyodor 133

Gage, Phineas 161, 162
Galambos, N.L. and Almeida, D.M. 349
Galen 364, 371
Gall, Franz Josef 140
Galton, Francis 27, **28**, 389–90, 392
  anthropometric laboratory **364**
  Hereditary genius 389
Gambia 13
gambling online 61–2
Gardner, Howard 394–5
Gavrilov, A.K. 134
Geiselman, R.E. et al 86
Geistenwissenschaft 24, 27
Gelman, R. and Gallistel, C.R. 323–4
gender and discourse analysis 284
gender identity 194, 407, 412
gender roles 194, 312
gender stereotyping 312, 411
gendered communication 58
genes/genetics 7–8, 334
  and altruism 11
  definition 7
  epigenetics 17–18, 401
  gay genes 202–3
  and health 472–3
  and intelligence 401
  methylation 18
  and obesity 479
  and personality 473
genetic disorders 334–6, 472–3
Genie (modern day 'Wild Child') 338
genius 389
genotypes 7
genus 10
Gergen, K.J. 279, **280**, 290, 418
Gergen, K.J. and Gergen, M. 284
Germany 197, 254, 397
Gestalt psychology 34
  and insight 118–19
Gibson, J.J. 99
Giedd, J.N. 350
Glanzer, M. and Cunitz, A.R. 79
Goffman, Erving 409, 410
Goldin, P.R. and Gross, J.J. 217
Gonçalves, B. et al 15
Goodhart, D. 287
Goodwin, Fred **494**
Goswami, Usha 322, **323**

grandmothers, role of 13
Gray, J.A. and Wedderburn, A.A.I. 105
Great War 31
Gregory, Richard 100
Griffiths, Mark 61–2
grounded theory 52
group therapy 464
groups:
  ambivalent membership 409
  categorisation 245–6, 252–4
  close-mindedness 232
  concepts of **230**–1
  crossed category membership 257
  crowd behaviour 226, 234–7
  decision making 232–3
  definitions 244, 245
  ethnocentrism 248–9
  group attribution error (GAE) 264, 266
  interdependence 231
  intergroup contact 255, 256–7
  intergroup and interpersonal behaviour 244–5
  and language 14–15
  minimal intergroup studies 252
  motivation 233, 234
  norms 231–2
  prejudice and discrimination 249–55
  process losses 233
  production blocking 233
  radicalisation 231
  self-categorisation theory 234
  stereotyping 245–8
  superordinate goals 257
  work performance 233
Guéguen, N. and Lamy, L. 274

Hacking, I. 290
Haldane, J.S. 11
Hall, R.J. 349
hallucinations 433, 440
Hamill, R. et al 264
Hamilton, W.D. 11
happiness 33, 46, 438
Harcourt, A.H. 8
Harcourt, A.H. and Stewart, K.H. 8
Hardyck, C.D. and Petrinovich, L.F. 142
Harré, R. 34, 282, 289
Harris, B. 33
Haynes and Feinleib 379
health psychology 468–82
  acute medical conditions 469
  chronic medical conditions 469
  clinical health psychologists 469
  community health psychologists 469
  critical health psychologists 469
  definition of health 469
  factors in health and ill-health:
    biology and genetics 472–3
    individiual characteristics and behaviours 473
    physical environment 474–5
    socio-economic conditions 475
  glaucoma 475
  health and gender 473
  health and personality 378, 380, 381–2, 473

health psychology *cont.*
  health and poverty 475
  historical views of health 470
  history of health psychology 470
  magic and superstition in health 474
  models of health:
    biomedical model 470–1
    biopsychosocial model 471, **472**
  obesity 479–80
  occupational health psychologists 469–70
  pain 480–1
  public health psychologists 469
  role of health psychologists 468, 469–70
  smoking 480
  stress 475–8
hearing 96–8
hegemony 283, 411
Heider, Fritz 261–2
Helmotz, Hermann von 26
Hemingway, Ernest 463
Hendry, L.B. and Kloep, M. 354
Henrich, J. and McElreath, R. 17
Henwood, K. and Pidgeon, N. 52
heritability 398
Herrnstein, Richard and Murray, Charles 398
Hertel, G. et al 234
heuristics 122, 262
Hippocrates 364, 371
histrionic personality disorder 442
HIV/AIDS 204, 471, 472
Hofstadter, R.D. and Dennett, D.C. 42
Holmes, E.A. et al 212
homicide 494–5
homosexuality:
  genes 202–3
  role of organisational hormones 203–4
hormones and risky behaviour 352
Hosken, D.J. and Ward, P.I. 10
Hovland, C. and Sears, R.R. 249–50
Howes, O.D. 189, 190
Hull, Clark Leonard 34
human beings as animals 32
human genome 401
human universals 9
humanism 35, 406, 434
humanistic psychology 406
humanistic/person-centred therapy (PCT) 458–60
  applications 459–60
  core approach 459
  theory 458
Huntingdon's disease 163
Hylton, P.L. and Miller, H.W. 291
hypotheses 53
hysteria 30, 470

id 450
identical states 40
identity *see* self-identity
identity formation 350–**1**
identity work 410, 411
ideologies 280
idiographic approaches 25
implicit association tests 254

imprinting 337
incentive sensitization theory 218–19
India 405
individual differences 364–5
individual therapy 464
individualism 281, 285, 287–9
  blame of individuals 288–9
  and intersubjectivity 288
infant development 299–312
  animism 317, 318
  centration 318
  conservation **318**
  cultural differnces 332
  egocentric stage 302
  face perception **301**
  foetal alcohol syndrome 300
  gender roles 312
  genetic influences 299
  instrumental conditioning (Skinner) 33
  language development 303–6
    child-directed speech 305
    grammar and syntax 306
    language production 304–5
    pidgin and creole 305–6
    prenatal 304
    sound discrimination 303–4
    speech clarity 303
    symbolic thought 317
  mental representations 302
  methods of study 300–1
  object and category perception 301–2, 317
  object permanency 317
  Piaget's stages 317
  policy changes 308
  prenatal development 299, 304, 334
  prenatal environmental factors 299–300
  relationships 306–10
    attachment 307–9, **308**, 338
    day care 309
    disabled children 340
    grandparents 309
    imitation of infants' behaviours 307
    meshing 306–7
    protoconversations 306–7
    role of father 308–9
    siblings 309
    turn-taking in conversation 307
  self-awareness **310**
  sensorimotor stage 302
  social learning 271
  theory of mind 310–12
    false belief tests 310, 311, 312
  variation 332
  see also adolescence; atypical development; children
infanticide 494
Ingalhalikar, M. et al 200
Inhelder, B. and Piaget, J. 349–50
insight 117–21
  chunk decomposition 118, 119
  constraint relaxation 118–**19**
  constraint for satisfactory progress theory 119
  eight-coin problem **119**–20
  functional fixedness 118

insight *cont.*
    and Gestalt psychology 118–19
    Maier's two-string problem **118**
    nine-dot problem 120
    representational change theory 118–19
    as restructuring 118
Instagram (IG) 414, **415**
instinct 32
intelligence 387–402
    and ageing 400
    analytic 395–6
    artificial intelligence (AI) 70
    and brain 200, 397, 401
    components 393
    creative 396
    definitions and terms for 387–8
    and environment 401
    factor analysis 392–3
    fluid and crystalised 394, 401
    Flynn effect 399–400, 401
    gender differences 200, 397
    general factor (g) **392**
    hierarchical models 394
    individual differences 396–7
    inherited 389, 396–7, 398, 401
    intelligence quotient (IQ) 390–1, 398, 399–400, 401
    Mozart effect 401–2
    multiple intelligences 394–**5**
    one-factor models 393–4
    practical 396
    and psycho-physilogical processes 389
    and race 391, 398, 399
    selective breeding 397
    Stanford-Binet scale 391, 392
    testing 27, 28, 53, 390–3, 394, 397–8
intention and behaviour 282, 422
International Classification of Diseases (ICD-10) 430
interpretive phenomenological analysis 406
intersubjectivity 288
introspective method 28–9
Izzard, C. 211

James, William 30, 31, 93, 211, 345, 413
Jang et al 473
Japan 405
Jenkins, J.G. and Dallenbach, K.M. 83
Jenkins, R. et al 428
Jetten, J. et al 238
Johnson-Laird, P.N. and Oatley, K. 211–12
Jones, E.E. and Davis, K.E. 262
Jones, E.E. and Harris, V.A. 263
Journal of Experimental Psychology 33
journals 54
Jung, Carl 369, 450
just noticeable difference (JND) 27
just-world hypothesis 271

Kanner, Leo 341
Kant, Immanuel 26, 371
Kapur, Shitij et al 189–90
Kassin, S.M. and Wrightsman, L.S. 486
Kelley, Harold 263
Kelly, George 407

Kenya 332
Keppel, G. 83
Kerslake, K. 111
Kilby, L. et al 287
killing-murder distinction 46
kin selection 11, 12, 13
Klein, Melanie 450
Klimstra, T.A. et al 350
Kline, P. and Barrett, B. 370
Knight and Prentky 490
Knoblich, G. et al 119
Kobasa, Suzanne 381
Koffka, Kurt 102
Kohlberg, L. 327
Köhler, Wolfgang 102, 118, 234
Koyré, Alexandre 23
Kozlowski, L.T. and Cutting, J.E. 101–2
Külpe, Oswald 29
Kutnick, P. and Kington, A. 326

L-DOPA 185, 186, 187, 189
Laborit, Henri 188
Lange, Carl 211
language:
    aphasia 134
    and brain structure 161
    as cultural tool 319
    development in children 303–6, 320–1
    language acquisition device (LAD) 320
    origins 131–3, **132**
        assigning symbols (Bouba-Kiki effect) **132**, 133
        big brain theory 131
        gesture development theory 131–3
        primates 14
        social bonding 13, 14–15
    speech perception:
        auditory comprehension 140
        direction perception theory 141
        fuzzy logic theory (FLT) 141
        in infants 303–4
        motor theory 141
    speech production:
        Dell's connectionist model **138–9**, 140
        errors 135–6, **137**, **138–9**
        lemmas 137
        lexemes 137
        mental lexicon 135
        serial and parallel models 139–40
        speech processing (Bock and Levelt) 136–8, **137**, 139, 140
    and thought 133–5, 150
        general resource hypothesis 134
        identity hypothesis 133
        interactive processes 134, 135
        linguistic relativity (Sapir-Whorf) hypothesis 134
        modularity hypthesis 133
    word identification:
        cohort model **145**–6
        interactive activation model 144
        logogens 144, 145
    writing **146**–7
Lansdale, M.W. and Baguley, T. 83–4
LaPierre, R.T. 268–9
Larkin, J. 116

Larson, R. and Richards, M.H. 349
Lashley, Karl 150
Lashley, Karl and Watson, John 422
Latané, B. and Darley, J. 273
Laursen, B. et al 349
Lazar, M.M. 284
Lazarus, R.S. and Folkman, S. 476, 478
Le Bon, Gustave 226, 235
Leahey, T.H. 25, 30
learning
    conditioning 32–3
    cultural differences 323
    emotional responses 33
    and exam revision 88–9
    in friendship pairs 326
    influence of expectations 339
    language acquisition 303–6, 320–1
    learning difficulties 336–7
    and levels of interaction 343
    mathematics 323–5
    Montessori schools 328
    and multiple intelligences 396
    and pain 481
    by reading aloud 143
    reading skills 321–2, 343
    school readiness 328
    social learning theory 495
    social norms 271
    spaced learning 89
    see also adolescence; atypical development; children; infant
        development
Leibniz, G.W. von 40
Lenneberg, Eric 320, 337
leptin 479
LeVay, S. 204
Levine, Mark **264**–5
Levine, Mark et al 272
Levinson, D.J. 353, 354, 356
life expectancy 473
Lillard, A.S. 328
Linehan, Marsha **457**
Lippmann, W. 245
locus of control 271, 378
Loftus, E.F. et al (1978) 86, 487
Loftus, E.F. et al (1987) 488
Loftus, Elizabeth **86**
Lohmann, H. et al 311
London, 7 July bombings (2005) 236
longitudinal research 358
Lorenz, Konrad **337**
Lösel, F. and Schucker, M. 461
Ludman, L. et al 340
Lynn, Richard 397
Lyons, A. and Kashima, Y. 246

McClelland, J.L. and Rumelhart, D.E. 144
McGeoch, J.A. 83
MacGregor, J.N. et al 119
McGurk, H. and MacDonald, J. 103
Machiavellianism 374
Mackworth, Norman 422
Maguire, E.A. et al 162
Malle, B.F. 265–6

Mani, A. et al 289
Mann, Ruth **497**
manslaughter 494
Marcia, J.E. 350, 351
Markus, H. and Kunda, Z. 407
Marslen-Wilson, William 144, 145
Marteau, Theresa **479**
Maslow, Abraham 35
Massaro, D.W. 141
material and intentional properties 282
materialism 26
mathematics learning 323–5
Matlin, M.W. and Foley, H.J. 104
meaningfulness of behaviour 48
Meltzoff, A.N. and Moore, M.K. 301
memes 16–17
memory 74–90
    and brain 150, 162
    context-dependent memory 81
    depth of processing 81
    encoding 75, 80
        and retrieval 75, 80–1
    encoding specificity principle 81
    exam revision 88–9
    exercise: memory for films 76, 80
    exercise: Royal Wedding 75, 84, 87
    explicit and implicit tests 76
    eyewitness memory 85–8, 487–8
    flashbulb memories 88
    forgetting 82–4, 90
        consolidation theory 83
        cue-dependent forgetting 82
        decay 82–3
        fogetting function **82**
        interference 83
        Jost's law 83–**4**
        population dilution model 83
        proactive inhibition (PI) 83
        retroactive inhibition (RI) 83
    incidental and intentional 75, 85
    in infants 302
    levels of processing theory 80–1, 89
    memory distrust syndrome 487
    memory experiments 74–6
    in middle adulthood 357
    mnemonics 89
    in older adults 357, 358
    and perception 100
    perceptual processing 80, 81
    and problem solving 112
    recall 76, 77, 86–7
    recognition 76, 87, 88
    as reconstructive process 84–5, 90
    retention intervals 74
    retrieval cues 81
    schema theory 85
    semantic processing 80, 81
    short and long-term memory 76–80, 89
        modal model **78**–9
        recency effects 79
        serial position curves **78**
        short term capacity 77
        stores 77–8

memory *cont.*
    temporal distinctiveness 80
    working memory model 79–80
  spatial 162
  and stereotyping 246, 247
  storage 75, 77–8
  transfer-appropriate processing 81
  unconscious memory system 76
  and writing **146**–7
Mendel, Gregor 7
meningitis 167
mental chronometry 27
mental illness 431
mentor 61
metabolic rate 479
Metropolis by Fritz Lang **41**
Miller, George 66–7, 70, 77
Millon, Theodore **441**
Milner, Peter 151
mind-body problem 38–45, 470
  Cartesian dualism 39–41, 42, 46
    and mind-body closeness 40
  folk psychology 44–5
  identity theory 42, 43–4
    brain scans 43, 44
  interaction 40–1
  knowledge of body and mind 40
  material and immaterial 39, 40
  mental states 39
    access to 38, 39
    and brain states 38, 39
    privacy of 38, 39
  volition 39
  see also brain; reductionism
mindfulness 217
Mischel, W. 376
mob psychology 226
modelling 457
Money, J. 199
mood 210
  and healthy eating 480
mood-stabilising drugs 462
Morris, C.D. et al 81
motivation
  definition 217
  in groups 233, 234
  incentive sensitization theory 218–19
  Iowa Gambling Task **218**
  orbitofrontal cortex abnormality 218
  reward sensitivity theory 217–18
motivational interviewing (MI) 460–1
  applications 461
  core skills 460–1
  methods 460
  theory 460
movement and action 46–7
  and dopamine 185, 186
MRI (magnetic resonance imaging) scans 43
Müller-Lyer illusion **101**
murder:
  and kin selection 12, 13
  and social learning theory 495
Myers-Briggs Type Indicator (MBTI) 369

narcissistic personality disorder 442
National Institute of Clinical Excellence (NICE) 447, 463, 480
National Offender Management Service (NOMS) 497
natural sciences, success of 26
natural and social science models 24, 25
need for cognition 377
Neisser, U. et al 399
NEO-Personality Inventory (NEO-PI) 373
neocortex 15
nervous system:
  afferent and efferent nerves 156–7
  central nervous system:
    astrocytes 178
    blood-brain barrier 167, 168, 178
    cerebrospinal fluid 167
    glial cells 178
    lateral preferences 168
    meninges 167
    mycroglia 178
    protection 167–8
    spinal cord 156, 166–7
    structure **156**
    subarachnoid space 167
    ventricular system 167
  directions and planes 156, 157–**8**
  evolution 155
  neuroanatomical and neurofunctional methods:
    computerised (axial) tomography (CAT) 169–70
    electroencephalography **172**, 212
    functional magnetic resonance imaging (fMRI) **171**–2
    magnetic resonance imaging (MRI) **170**
    positron emission tomography (PET) 170–1, 189
    spatial resolution 170
    temporal resolution 171
  peripheral nervous system 155, 156
    autonomic nervous system 169, 371, 372
      parasympathetic nervous system 169
      sympathetic nervous system 169
    somatic nervous system:
      cranial nerves 168
      spinal nerves 168, 169
  structure 155–**6**
  terminology 156, **157**
  terms **157**
neurones 155, 176–8, **177**, 178–84
  basic components 176–**7**
    axons 177–8, 180
    dendrites 176–7, 176–**7**
    nucleus 176
    soma 176, 180
    synaptic buttons 177, 178, 180, 182, 183
  basic functions 190
  communication between 182–4
    chemical synapses and pre-synaptic events 183
    receptor activation and post-synaptic events 183–4
    termination of signal 184
  communication within 178–82
    action potentials 180–2, **181**
    axon hillock 180
    depolarisation 181
    dynamic equilibrium 179
    equilibrium potential 180, 181
    excitatory post-synaptic potentials (EPSPs) 182

neurones *cont.*
    inhibitory post-synaptic potentials (IPSPs) 182
    ion channels 179, 180
    membrane 179
    membrane potentials 179–**80**
    post-synaptic potentials 182
    saltatory conduction 182
    voltage-gated channels 180
  cytoplasm 176
  deoxyribonucleic acid (DNA) 176, 334
  myelin 177–8, 181
  nodes of Ranvier **177**, 178, 181, 182
  oligodendrocytes 177–8
  organelles 176
  and response to change 191
  Schwann cells 177
neurotransmitters 183, 184–5, 186
  agonist and antagonist effects 187, 188
  classes 184, **187**
  dopamine (DA) 184, 185, 186, 187, 188, 218–19
  and drugs 186–90
    antipsychotics 188, 191
    botox 187, 188
    termination of the signal 188, 189
  ligands 187
  measuring 189
  and mental disorder 433
  microdialysis 189
  nigro-striatal system **185**
  precursors 185
  serotonin (5-HT) 184, 185, 187
  soluble gases 186
Newell, A. and Simon, H.A. 70, 112, 114–16
  Human Problem Solving 116
Newton, Sir Isaac 22, 24, 45
Nijboer, F. et al 165
Nintendo Wii 416, 417
Nisbett et al 401
nomothetic approaches 25, 376
  and idiographic approaches 369
nomothetic fallacy 25
normative influence 279

Obama, Barack 244
obesity 422, 479–80
  and genes 479
Observer 61
obsessive compulsive disorder (OCD) 432, 442
O'Connell, A.N. 350
Öllinger, M. 120
online bullying 414
online prosocial behaviour 272
operant conditioning 456–7
organic and inorganic material 45
organismic valuing processes 458
Orne, M.T. 279
Osler, William 379
Owens, J.A. et al 349

pain 480–1
paired-associate learning (PAL) 76
paranoid personality disorder 442
paraphilic disorder 491

paraplegia 167
parental investment 12, 13
Park, D.C. et al 358
Park, Nick **45**
Parkinson's disease 185, 186, 187
Parks, M.J. et al 274
paternity uncertainty 12, 13
patholgy *see* psychopathology
Pavlov, Ivan 32
Penfield, W. 39
Penfield, W. and Jasper, H.H. 161
Perception 103
perception:
  affordances 99
  bottom-up approaches 98, 99
  and brain 70
  change blindness 108–9
  constancy scaling **100–1**
  constructivist theories 100–1
  direct perception **99**
  faces 104
  Gestalt psychology **102**
  information from biological motion 101–2
  McGurk effect 103
  and memory 100
  optic flow 99
  perceived intensity 27
  perceptual constancies **100**
  and senses 70, 93
  synaesthesia 103
  top-down approaches 98, 99, 100–1
  and vision 99, 100
  visual illusions 100–**1**
perceptual skills tests 341
Perkins, J.M. et al 267
Perner, J. et al 311
personal agency 407
personal constructs 407
personality 368–82
  age differences 373
  behavioural activation/inhibition system (BAS/BIS) 217
  and cancer 380
  definitions 368
  extraversion and neuroticism 370, 371–**2**
  five-factor model 372–4, **373**
  and health 378, 380, 381–2, 473
  HEXACO six-factor model 370, 374
  introversion 370, **372**
  lexical hypothesis 370
  need for cognition 377
  personality coefficient 376
  sixteen-factor model 370–**1**
  three-factor model 371–**2**
  traits 369–75
    and behaviour over time 376
    situationalist critique 375–7
  Type A/B personality 378–80, **379**
  Type C (cancer prone personality) 380
  Type D personality (distressed personality) 380
  types **369**
  as Western construct 405
  see also self-identity
personality disorders 210, 441–2

Pettigrew, T.F. 246, 265
phantom limbs 163
Pharo, H. et al 352
phenomenology 406
phenotypes 7
phobias 438–**9**
physiological psychology 28–9, 286
Piaget, Jean 34, 39, 51, 70, 302, 349
    stage account of learning 316–19
Plato 237
PlayScan 61–2
population ageing 361
positive illusions 381
positive psychology 285, 286–7
post-traumatic stress disorder (PTSD) 215, 458
Postman, L. and Phillips, L.W. 77, 78
postron emission tomography (PET) 38
poverty 339, 475
practical intelligence 396
precursors 185
prejudice and discrimination:
    disclaimers 410
    and economic hardship 149–50
    frustration: 'taking out' on someone 249
    frustration-aggression hypothesis (FAH) 249–50
    ingroups and outgroups 248–9, **252**–3, 265, 272
    intergroup contact 255
    and personality 250–1
    and psychological research 254–5
    realistic conflict theory 251–2, 257
    scapegoats 249
    social identity theory 234, 252–4
    see also attributions; racism
primates **8**–9, 13, **14**
    and language 14, 303
    social bonding 13, **14**
problem solving 112–21
    adaptive character of thought-rational (ACT-R) 117
    conflict resolution 117
    cryparithmetic **115**
    desired states and goal states 115
    factual and procedural knowledge 117
    general problem solver (GPS) 115–16
    goals and subgoals 114–15
    insight 117–21
    means-ends analysis 114–15
    Newell and Simon theory 114–16
    operators 115
    production systems 116
    search space **113**–14
    Tower of Hanoi problem 117
    Tower of London problem **113**, 115
    trial-and-error 113
    Zombies and Psychologists (missionaries and cannibals) problem 116
    see also reasoning
Prochaska, J. et al 460
proximate and ultimate explanations 10
psychodynamic therapy 30, 450–2
    applications 452
    key concepts **451**
    outcome studies 452

psychological interventions 447–65
    case study 450, 453, 455, 459, 461, 464
    effectiveness 465
    evaluations 465
    format of interventions 464
    nature and purpose 447
    with offenders 461
    random controlled trials (RCTs) 465
    treatment models 449–64
        biological and pharmacological 462–4
        cognitive behavioural therapy 452–8
        humanistic/person-centred therapy 458–60
        motivational interviewing 460–1
        psychodynamic therapy 450–2
    trephination **449**
psychology:
    breadth of 471
    as moral science 289, 291
    privileged position 290–1
    as science 24–9, 47, 289
    and social life: 'looping effect' **288**
psychometric tests 390, 405
psychopathology:
    abnormal, concept of 427, 428–9
    classifying disorders 429, 430
    clinical interviews **432**
    clinical observation 432–3
    clinical tests 433
    cultural differences 428
    definition 447
    diagnosis 430, 431–2
    disorders:
        early explanations **448**
        and eccentricity 429, 430
        most prevalent 437–**41**
        symptoms and causes **435–6**, 448
        models of pathology:
            cognitive-behavioural model 433–4
            developmental model 434
            humnistic and existential model 434
            medical model 433
            psychodynamic model 435
    see also psychological interventions
psychopathy 210
    and brain anatomy 221
    and brain functional changes 221–2
psychosis and trauma 440
psychosomatic medicine 470
psychoticism 372
puberty 350
punishment and welfare trade-off ratio 11–12
pychopathy, definition of 221

quantification 26–8
quantitative and qualitative research 24, 25, 35, 51–3, 65, 281–2
Quinn, P.C. et al 301

Rabbit, Patrick **400**
race and intelligence 398
racism 249–50, 254, 283, 286
    and intelligence testing 391
    racial lynching **250**

Rahman, Qazi **205**
Ramachandran, Vilyanur S. 163
randomised controlled trials 361
rape 489–91
  definition 90, 489
  myths and rape acceptance 247, 489
  offenders 490
  victims 490
rape myth acceptance (RMA) scale 247
rational relations 44–5, 47
Rayner, R. 33
reaction time 393
Read, J. et al 440
reading:
  dyslexia 340
  eye movement **142**–3
  lag in development 337
  phonics teaching 322
  phonological awareness 321–2
  reading aloud and learning 143
  reading instruction 322
  silent reading 134
  skills 321–2
  subvocal speech 142
real self 459
reasoning:
  and cognitive ageing 357–8
  deductive **123**–4
  inductive 124–5
  probablilistic 121–3
    base rate fallacy 122
    Bayes theorem 122
    fallacies 122–3
    uncertainty 121
  syllogisms 123–4
reductionism 26, 42, **45**
  in psychology 46–7
reflective listening 460
Reicher, Steve 236, 237
Reimer, David **199**
rejection sensitivity 216, 217
relapse prevention 457
research in psychology:
  applied research examples
    behavioural tracking 61–2
    content analysis 58
    controls 65
    digital technologies in educational performances 65
    discursive methods 57–9
    double-blind control 55, 65
    Driving Behaviour 62–4, 65
      bus shelter and pole-mounted advertisements, attention to **64**
      eye gaze locations **63**
    experimental methods 62–4
    eye-tracking methods 62–4
    focus on groups or individuals 65
    Foster Care 55–7, 65
      superordinate and subordinate themes **57**
    generalisability 65
    mixed methods 59–61
    Online Gambling 61–2, 65
    photo-elicitation 56, **57**

research in psychology *cont.*
    placebo effects 65
    Sexual Offenders 59–61, 65–6
    Testicular Implants 57–9, 65
      extracts **59**
  choosing a method 52, 282
  confidentiality 55
  data and analysis 51–3
  demand characteristics 55
  ethics 55
  experimenter effects 55, 281
  experiments 53, 281
  inferential statistics 53
  Interpretative Phenomenological Analysis (IPA) 52, 53, 56
  observational studies 53
  psychometric tests 53
  quantitative and qualitative research 51–3, 65, 281–2
  reactivity 55
  reliability 54, 390
  replication 54
  sampling 54, 55
  validity 54
  values and goals 66–7
researcher-researched relationship 281
Review of General Psychology 86
reward and punishment 217–18, 271
'riddle of our selves' 23, 47, 288
  and riddle of the universe **24**
  see also self-identity
Right Wing Authoritarianism (RWA) scale 250
Robinson, T.E. and Berridge, K.C. 219
Rogers, Carl 35, 434, 458, 460
role conflict 409
role models 375
role playing 414
role theory 409
Rollnick, Steve and Miller, Bill 460
Rooney, Wayne **395**
Rosenthal, R. and Jacobson, L. 279, 339, 340
Ross, L. et al 266
Rotter, J.B. 378
Rundus, D. 79

Sachs, Oliver 186
Safer Living Foundation (SLF) 499
Salthouse, T.A. 358
schizoid personality disorder 442
schizophrenia 210, 216, 439–41
  dopamine hypothesis 189–90, 439
  drugs 188, 189–90, 191
  family adjustment to 220
  neuroimaging research 220
  symptoms 429, 440–1
schizotpy 216
schizotypal personality disorder 442
Schmolock, H. et al 88
Scholastic Aptitude Test (SAT) 392
Science 204
science as by-product of Western culture 281
scientific method 22, 23
  in the emergence of psychology 24–9
scientific revolution 6

scientism 48
Searle, J. 70, 116
Sebastian, C.L. et al 216
Second Life 417
self-actualising tendency 458
self-efficacy 378
self-help groups 464
self-identity 35, 288, 364, 404–5, 458
  bodily 407–8, 412–**13**
  discourse analysis 410, 411
  embodied self 412–13
  extensions of self throgh technology 413
  gendered 194, 407, 412
  and life-events 406, 411–12
  online selves 413–14, 414–15, 416
  and pain 406
  personal constructs 407
  personal histories 411–12, 414, 415
  relational selves 413
  and self-value 459
  social 408–9
  social constructionism 407–8, 410
  social media 414–16
  and social roles 409–10
  virtual selves 416–**17**
self-image 412, 415–16
self-monitoring 432–3
self-sensors 418
Seligman, Martin 285
Selye, Hans 476, 477
Semenya, Casta 207
sensations 93
  transformed into perceptions 26, 27, 93
sense of coherence 381
senses 94–8
  and perceptions 70, 103
sensory receptors 166–7
sex differences:
  and behaviour 201
  in the brain 200
  cognitive differences 202
  and feminism 201
  and health 473
  intelligence 200
  pain 481
  and personality disorders 441, 442
  puberty 201, 206
  sex typing at sports events 206–7
  and sexism 207
  and socialisation 201
sex and gender 194
sex offenders 489–92
  Circles of Support and Accountability (CoSA) 498
  cognitive distortions 490–1
  courtship disorder 492
  non-contact offences 491–2
  police statistics 489, 490, 491–2
  psychological interventions 461
  rape 489–91
  stereotypes of 246
  telephone scatologia 492
  typologies 490

sexual abuse and hysteria 30
sexual differentiation 195–200
  atypicality:
    5-alpha reductase syndrome 199
    androgen insensitivity syndrome 198–9
    congenital adrenal hyperplasia 199–200
    indeterminate sex 197, 199
    intersex conditions (hermaphrodites) 197
    Klinefelter's syndrome 198
    pseudohermaphrodites 197
    Turner's syndrome 198
    XXX syndrome 198
    XYY syndrome 198
  dihydrotestosterone 197
  hormones 197
  pre-natal development 195–7, **196**
  reproductive organs 195, **196**, 197
  sex chromosomes 195
  testosterone 195, 197
sexual orientation 202–6
  and behaviour 205, 206
  bisexuality 207
  and the brain 204–5
  gay genes 202–3
  heterosexuality as 'normal' 287
  hypothalmmic structure 204
  motor behaviours 206
  and organisational hormones 203–4, 206
sexual preoccupation 60
Sherif, M. et al 244, 251, 257
Sherrington, Charles 182
Shulman, S. and Scharf, M. 351
sight see vision
Simon, Herbert Alexander **114**
Simons, D.J. and Chabris, C.F. 108
Simons, D.J. and Levin, D.T. 109
Sistine Chapel, Rome **23**
Skinner, B.F. 33–4, 305, 456
  human Skinner box **33**
skull 167
Slininger, D. et al 344
Smith, J.A and Osborn, M. 406
Smith, S.M. et al 133
smoking 480
social anxiety disorder (SAD) 217
social constructionism 280, 407–8
social Darwinists 397
social groups and language 14–15
social identity theory (SIT) 408–9
social media 272
  and privacy 414
  social attractiveness 415–16
social processes 279
social psychology 226, 279, 407
  'crisis' in 279, 280
social responsibility 271
social roles 409–10
  dramaturgical analogy 409
social science model of psychology 24
sound **282**
Spearman, Charles 392–3
species 10

Specific Language Impairment (SLI) 133
Sperry, Roger 150
spirit possession 428
Stages of Change 460
Steele, C.M. 247
Stephens, Helen 206
Sterberg, R.J. et al 399
stereotyping 245–8, **246**
    of adolescents 348
    effects 246, 247
    gender 312, 411
    gender and rape myth acceptance 247
    older people 359
    and stereotype threat 247
    'ultimate attribution error' 246
Stern, William 27, 390
Sternberg, Robert 395
Stevens, J.R. et al 270–1
Stiles et al 333
Stott et al 237
Strano, M.M. and Wattai-Queen, J. 416
stress 475–8
    appraisal 476–**7**
    coping 478
    definition 475, 476
    evolutionary theory 476
    general adaptation syndrome **477**
    stages of response 476
substance monism 46
Super and Harkness 332
superego 450
Sweden 397
Szasz, Thomas 431

Taft, M. and Hambly, G. 145
Tajfel, H. 245, 408
Tajfel, H. et al 252–3
Tanzania 399
Taylor, Shelley E. **381**
Tend-and-Befriend theory 381
Terman and Goddard 397
tetraplegia 167
theory of mind 310–12
    and autism 342
    false belief tests 310, 311, 312
therapeutic relationship 451, 460
thinking:
    in cognitive behavioural therapy (CBT) 454, **455**
    logical and intuitive 70–1
    see also cognitive development; problem solving; reasoning
Thompson, Peter 103–4
Thompson (Thatcher) illusion 104
Thorndike, Edward 32
Thurstone, Louis Leon 393
Titchener, Edward 29, 31
Tolman, Edward Chace 34
touch 166
transference and countertransference 451
transsexuals 194
Treisman, A.M. 106, 107
Treisman, A.M. and Gelade, G. 108
Triplett, Norman 226

Tropp, L.R. and Pettigrew, T.F. 255, 256
Troy, A.S. et al 477, 478
Tulving, E. and Pearlstone, Z. 82
Tulving, E. and Thomson, D.M. 81
Turing, Alan 70
Turkle 413–14
Turner, J.C. et al 234
Turner, R.H. and Killian, L.M. 236
Turner, Rhiannon **256**
Tversky, A. and Kahnemann, D. 122
Twitter 15
Tzeng, O.J.L. 79

unconscious defence mechanisms 412
unconscious mind 30, 435, 450
unconscious needs 450
Underwood, Jean 65, 66
universality of psychological principles 286
USA:
    climate change 267
    dapretomania 428
    eugenics 391, 397
    false confessions 487
    infant care 332
    racism 244, 249–**50**, 254, 268–9
    rape myths 247

Vaillancourt, T. 390
'value-neutral' psychology 290
Vernon, Philip 394
victim blaming 246, 289
violent offending 221, 492, 493–5
    definition of violence 493
    homicide 494–5
    offenders 493
    rational choice theory (RCT) 494
    robbery 493, 494
    and social learning 495
    statistics 493, 494
    victims 493
viral infection 433
virtual selves 416–17
vision 94–6
visual attention 107–8
    feature-integration theory **108**
    object-based 107–8
    space-based 107
    spotlight theory 107
    zoom lens theory 107
visual illusions 100–1
visual neglect (VN) 109
Voland, E. et al 10
volition 39
Völkerpsychologie 29
voyeurism 489, 491
Vygotsky, Lev 288, 319–20, 321, 343

Wallace and Grommitt **45**
Wang, C.C. and Wang, C.H. 272
Waterman and Waterman 350
Watson, John B. 32, 133, 423, 456
welfare trade-off ratio (WTR) 11

Wertheimer, Max 102
Wetherell, M. and Potter, J. 283, **411**
White, B.A. et al 480
Wilkinson, S. and Kitzinger, C. 287
Wilson, David 65
Wilson, R.J. et al 498
Winch, W. 390
Wittgenstein, Ludwig 133
Wixted, J.T. 83
Wong, C. et al 335–6

World Health Organisation (WHO) 469
Wright, M.F. and Li, Y. 272
Wundt, Wilhelm 22, 25, 28–9, 31, 70, 211

Yerkes 391
Yeung, N.C.J. and von Hippel, C. 247
Young, K. 457

zone of proximal development (ZPD) 319, 320,
    343, 399